CHRISTM

To P.A.,

HAVE YOU LOOKED

AT "SALLY BUSHER"?

YOUR PAL,

DICKY

The ABCs of
THOROUGHBRED
HANDICAPPING

ALSO BY JAMES QUINN

The Best of Thoroughbred Handicapping
High-Tech Handicapping in the Information Age
The Handicapper's Condition Book
Class of the Field

The ABCs of THOROUGHBRED HANDICAPPING

JAMES QUINN

WILLIAM MORROW AND COMPANY, INC.
New York

Library of Congress Cataloging-in-Publication Data

Quinn, James, 1943–
    The ABCs of thoroughbred handicapping / James Quinn.
      p.   cm.
    Bibliography: p.
    ISBN 0-688-06550-3
    1. Horse race betting—Examinations, questions, etc.
2. Competency based educational tests.   3. Thoroughbred horse.
I. Title.
SF331.Q543   1988   88-10025
798.4'01—dc19   CIP

Printed in the United States of America

First Edition

1 2 3 4 5 6 7 8 9 10

BOOK DESIGN BY BERNARD SCHLEIFER

Contents

The ABCs of
THOROUGHBRED
HANDICAPPING

Prologue: X, Y, & Z

ON THE SUPPOSEDLY arcane matter of instruction in thoroughbred handicapping, there is so much that might be entered in preface to this special project. I shall resist the temptations, allowing, if you will, of three vital exceptions.

X. The first, and by far the greatest, regards the much-cherished myth, passed down among the generations by unsuspecting horsemen, jockeys, turf writers, and other assorted insiders and virtually institutionalized by the very racetrack managers who promote the pari-mutuel wagering games, that you can't beat the races. All should understand up front that the 30 percent handicapper who gets 5–2 odds on winners has a 5 percent edge on the game. That customer can be a winner.

The enormous paradox of the racetrack is exactly that so many customers should lose so regularly at a game so deceptively beatable. The requisite degree of proficiency, moreover, is surely attainable by anyone who cares.

To pursue the reality, the 35 percent handicapper who gets the same 5–2 odds on winners enjoys a 22.5 percent edge. If that handicapper persisted in betting prudent proportions of capital for an investment period extending three to five seasons, he or she could absolutely clobber the races. Those goals, not readily accomplished, but for reasons in the main disassociated with an accumulation of competency in handicapping, remain nonetheless attainable.

Yet the much-cherished myth endures—is propagated, in fact, by the very economic interests that would be served better by a public perception that skillful players can beat this game, and for not unimportant money.

9

The myth does, of course, satisfy certain purposes. If you can't beat the races, it makes no sense to try. This relieves the racetrack customer of the burdens that normally attach to the activities of systematic thought, study, and practice. Idle recreation substitutes for the goal-directed behavior of handicapping. Gambling substitutes for managing money intelligently.

The myth serves as well a far more circumspect purpose. It encourages the industry to discount for itself and its best customers the kind of rigorous regulation and supervision that would elevate the image of the sport as professional, and deserving of professional respect. It relieves the racing associations of the pressing responsibility of coming firmly to grips at last with a number of daily practices that cannot square with the customer's right to a truly run race. The daily customer's laments are readily understandable;

with medication rules insanely inconsistent from state to state, and information about permissible drugs distributed or not to racing's customers just as irrationally;

with racing secretaries relentlessly pressing trainers to fill small fields with unintended or unready horses, but without advising the public;

with horses running off from the post parades or breaking through the starting gates without being scratched and tickets refunded;

with unpardonable late program scratches, still later jockey changes, and gate scratches that should have occurred in the morning so reflexively permitted;

with the almost astonishingly incompetent, unaware, and inconsistent judgments handed down from the stewards' stands so reflexively ignored, the bettors expected to suffer the consequences silently and repeatedly;

in all of this the tracks and their executives share a deep responsibility, leading thousands of disabused customers to conclude that rather than initiate meaningful change, the tracks prefer to hold the bettors in contempt.

But too many racetrack operators merely shrug and assume a familiar pose. If you can't beat the races, what does it matter anyway? Well, you *can* beat the races and it *does* matter—a lot. By affirming the impossibility of beating the game by rational means, the much-cherished myth allows that the abdication of responsibility toward the bettors—gamblers—can be complete.

Finally, the much-cherished myth serves as a convenient, socially accepted excuse among the massive majorities of racegoers, horsemen, and bettors who, despite best efforts to combat the tendency, continue to lose too much money at the races;

for the racetrack hardboot who arrives at the track at last with a homemade system or hot tip for beating the races;

for the trainer who has brought his horse to the peak of performance and can't see how it can fail against this pitiful field;

for the self-styled expert handicapper who has sized up today's situation perfectly and expects to make a killing.

When the horses lose after all, how convenient to remark over a warm dinner and dry wine that everyone knows you just can't beat the races. No excuse could be more impenetrable.

Y. The second proposition, itself a logical consequence of the much-cherished myth, regards the lamentable state of customer education in this specialized field.

Racetrack fans remain the most poorly educated on their sport in America. Not one percent knows what a par time represents. Not 10 percent can define an overlay. Of the millions that flock to racetracks annually, relatively few have been exposed to a thoughtful presentation on the fundamentals of handicapping or money management at the races. Fewer still can implement systematic methods that make sense or have been demonstrably effective in tossing profits.

Intellectually, psychologically, and emotionally—by any human standard that counts—playing the races is a difficult, challenging game. Uninformed or inexperienced play results in financial losses. The losses add up. The customers need help. They deserve that help.

What factors have been shown to affect the outcomes of races significantly? What principles of handicapping have been confirmed as effective? How do the fundamental ideas relate to one another? Which are relatively important, unimportant? Under what conditions do the basic principles become more or less important?

What methods of handicapping are known to be demonstrably effective? What procedures are associated with each method? What are the attainable results? What books and periodicals should be consulted by the interested customers?

What are the basic facts and principles of pari-mutuel wagering? How might the customers judge whether the odds on horses represent bets that are potentially positive or negative? Under what circumstances do the various types of wagers make sense, nonsense?

What methods of money management make sense? Which are foolish? What betting procedures are associated with each?

What are the realistic expectations as to how much profit skillful handicappers can anticipate? How much might authentic experts earn in a season? How might handicappers who want to improve their play evaluate themselves? What are the best sources of instruction on money management and pari-mutuel wagering?

As matters stand, unless new and potentially loyal customers manage first to discount the much-cherished myth, and second, to locate reliable sources of instruction by their own devices, the probability they will become steady customers and loyal fans remains unacceptably low.

The healthy news is that since the late 1960s the knowledge base of handicapping and pari-mutuel wagering has grown dramatically in substance and coherence and has been distributed to the local bookstores by major publishing houses, a break from the almost-barren past.

The real breakthrough, however, basic education for the recreational handicapper, awaits a slumbering industry still. As custodians of racing's customers, only the local tracks have the power to transform casual, occasional racegoers into loyal fans, the kind of proficient, enthusiastic handicappers who return and wager repeatedly. A marketing policy emphasizing customer education and information services, long past due, could reverse an unfortunate legacy of decades of benign neglect within five years.

As the tracks' economic incentives to do so are enormous, it's curious why they so instinctively retreat and resist. Once, paranoia that the tracks were promoting betting—gambling— dictated that the sport be marketed solely as spectacle, eschewing the participative motives of the customers. But that position has long since worn thin. Attendance continues to be down and dwindling. Social betting has achieved social acceptance. Lotteries proliferate. Casinos prosper. Racing in the past twelve years has lost more than 50 percent of its market share of the gaming-industry financial pie, a felonious indictment of the status quo.

In the not-too-distant future sports betting will be legalized in this country, instantly attracting millions of recreational bettors who enjoy wagering on uncertain games about which they have formulated a knowledgeable opinion. Racetrack executives who thought they had met the enemy lottery and survived, have not seen the enemy yet. If racing has not mobilized to educate its customers before sports betting rears its ugly head, the entire infrastructure of the contemporary sport could collapse.

Of the rational explanations racing executives put forth to justify the neglect of customer education, two merit consideration: (1) not enough customers are sufficiently serious about handicapping for profit to warrant the educational costs and (2) the tracks are not staffed to provide the education—or to separate the wheat from the chaff among those who might.

Of point one, nobody should expect to convert casual customers into handicapping experts capable of thrashing the game. That's not the idea. The idea instead is to convert casual racegoers into competent handicappers, a far less ambitious objective.

The motivation required to play the races expertly or professionally is abnormal, and not widely distributed. The costs of time and energy are too great. But the motivation to play the races competently is altogether normal and universal. Everyone prefers to win, and almost everyone will take reasonable steps to learn how to win.

The contents of this book, for example, promote both "minimum competency" and a mid-level "mastery" of handicapping and pari-mutuel wagering. The book intends a level of knowledge and skill sufficient to certify its consumers possess a coping measure of proficiency. Racetracks should intend no less.

Of point two, in every major U.S. racing market adequately credentialed consultants—several of them academics—are now available to refer track executives to a number of mature, authentic experts on handicapping and pari-mutuel betting. The references would be provided free. The men and women so hired could prepare basic programs of instruction at nominal fees or perhaps for free for interested customers. If the tracks endorsed the courses, and perhaps conducted them on site, enrollments might be surprisingly large. Word of mouth would follow. A cultural change to informed participation would be under way. Young adults especially would be more strongly attracted to the sport.

The specialists might also develop instructional materials for distribution on race days, provide information services to regulars, contribute to racetrack newsletters, arrange track-sponsored seminars consisting of genuinely skillful and articulate practitioners, identify books and articles of merit, analyze the daily programs in new ways which would actually assist the customers in refining their own handicapping and betting, and elaborate morning lines that estimate horses' chances as a function of state-of-the-art handicapping.

Advances of this kind would literally alter the character of a day at the races. In imaginative hands, the educational prospects become exciting. Consumer interest should soar. Low-cost high-tech information systems, as one provocative alternative, could send meaningful handicapping and wagering information from the racetrack directly into the dens of customers daily. The same systems could send a variety of timely handicapping reports to on-track information centers, to intertrack wagering sites, and to off-site teletheaters. Would information services like that stimulate interest, attendance, and betting? The possibilities are virtually endless.

I would like to tell progressive racetrack managers everywhere that the cost-effectiveness of customer-education programs and information services, especially in the high-tech context, will be tremendous. They are the future, if there will be a future.

Z. A third proposition on instruction in handicapping is far more sanguine and reassuring. It concerns the pleasures that accrue to the individual on becoming a competent handicapper and the delights to be derived from a day at the races that proceeds from an informed, well-educated point of view.

Playing the races is a game of knowledge and skill, of percentages and probabilities. On every criterion worth citing— recreation, leisure, active participation, meeting a challenge, learning a new skill, taking a calculated risk, reaping a just reward, finding success, accomplishing a personal goal, even facing disappointment and failure—the customer's day at the races improves in a measure calibrated almost exactly to the know-how he or she brings to the experience. The game itself is so richly complex and diverse, the individual's development and improvement can become continuous.

Last season at Santa Anita long-time turf club patron Marty Townsend approached me animatedly on arrival.

"I had two dollars on that $200 winner yesterday," he exclaimed. A lively, detailed rationale for the killing followed.

Townsend for years had supplemented his arithmetical handicapping ratings with a keen appreciation of equine body language. He had caught the $200 horse using an observation skill he had lacked a week earlier. But Townsend had just purchased a newly released video on the body language of horses, produced by Greg Lawlor and featuring Bonnie Ledbetter, the leading authority. Townsend had learned something new, bet on it, won, and could not possibly contain his enthusiasm.

During the current season, 1988, another handicapping colleague, to remain anonymous, began to purchase daily the professional speed figures of a legitimate national service. The figures worked well enough. My colleague was practically transformed from a tabby into a tiger. After numerous forgetful seasons of scrambling, for the first time he ended the year a certified winner.

A substantive point on instruction in handicapping is germane to this prologue.

The timeless notion that experience is the greatest teacher remains true of thoroughbred handicapping as well, but with a prerequisite rarely mentioned. Experience without a knowledge base that informs it amounts to inexperience of a tragic kind.

The veterans at racetracks who have depended from the outset on experience alone, or worse, on the misguided disorganized experiences of others—the famous insiders—are among the biggest, sorriest losers of all. They comprehend a fraction of what they purport to know, and the ignorance has cost them dearly, the decades notwithstanding.

Imagine novices playing dozens or even hundreds of games of chess or bridge without taking lessons or consulting a substantial text. Given that raw experience, what have the callow fellows learned? How many mistakes have been detected, let alone corrected? To be sure, grade-school children exiting a basic course of instruction can humiliate these "experienced" adults in head-to-head chess or bridge. Untutored handicappers can anticipate a fate even worse.

In 1984 I had occasion to examine the evidence from cognitive psychology evidence on experts and how they get that way. The researchers studied how experts solved problems and made decisions, in comparison with novices and journeymen. They observed waiters, doctors, taxi drivers, teachers, chess players, dentists, veterinarians, baseball players, and accountants, but not, regrettably, racetrack handicappers, a particularly fascinating population that performs in a natural laboratory and supports its decisions with money.

In the experiments, however unrelated to their specialties, the experts solved problems faster and made decisions better than did novices and journeymen. They even took the measure of a third comparison group not expected to capitulate—computers.

How do the experts do it?

A consistent finding is that they do not do it with intelligence or aptitude. That bears repeating. Experts do not rely on superior intelligence to perform. The implication is clear and greatly reassuring. Individuals of ordinary intelligence, of below-average aptitude even, can become the real experts.

What factors make the difference?

There are three: knowledge, information resources, experience.

Of the trio, knowledge supersedes all else. The other two factors will be influenced by the presence or absence of knowledge; in fact, are predicated upon it.

The implication of this is just as plain. Extensive skill in handicapping depends upon a comprehensive knowledge base. The knowledge is reinforced and amplified by information resources. The application of knowledge and information becomes refined through repeated experience.

This book deals exclusively with the knowledge base of handicapping and pari-mutuel wagering, presumptively in innovative ways. Its raw material has been siphoned from forty information sources, books mainly. Handicappers unacquainted with the books will stumble about repeatedly, not really understanding why. The hope is that many will be provoked to set sails on new courses of study.

I shall make an extravagant assertion with complete confidence: Anyone who engages the chapters of the instructional sources to be recommended here will have developed a knowledge base unsurpassed by the most devoted denizens of the nation's racetracks.

They will be prepared to accumulate the information resources and varied experiences that transform knowledge into expertise.

In another five to seven years, maybe less, they will have evolved into fully accredited members of an open-ended but highly discriminating club. The exclusive club of racetrack experts.

PART A

Test Preparation

Introduction:
A Competency-Based
Approach to Achievement
in Handicapping

UNTIL NOW, my exposition on thoroughbred handicapping has been aimed exclusively at serious hobbyists and professionals.

Recreational handicappers, those casual hobbyists and occasional racegoers who represent the massive majorities at racetracks and go to the races equally motivated by fun and profits, have been unattended. They have been unattended as well by the best treatments of the pastime across the past fifteen years.

This book seeks to remedy those omissions. Its target audience includes the most occasional to the most experienced of handicappers. To the dilettante the book intends a fundamental kind of education. To the expert it intends an interesting challenge of advanced knowledge and skill. In between those extremes journeymen handicappers should discover where they stand.

The book represents, too, an exciting opportunity to its author. For years I have desired to transfer to handicapping the expertise I have gathered as a management consultant in competency-based education and program evaluation. The disciplines can be intermingled imaginatively and, I believe, usefully. You are about to entertain the outcome.

Competency-based education can be viewed as an approach to learning that emphasizes testing as the means of instruction.

This book is crammed with tests and test items. There are minimum competency tests, mastery tests, performance tests, and almost 900 test items. I feel safe in asserting that the contents represent the most unconventional program of instruction ever extended to racing's customers. I am equally optimistic that the approach works.

In the conventional educational setting, the schools, the competency-based approach embraces five integral steps:

1. Identify the intended outcomes of instruction in terms of the knowledge and skills the learners (handicappers) should be expected to demonstrate.
2. Set proficiency standards, or decide how well the learners should know the subject matter or perform the skills.
3. Target the means of instruction toward the intended outcomes.
4. Construct competency tests, or highly specific measures of the knowledge and skills the learners are expected to demonstrate.
5. Evaluate the results and re-direct instruction to identified areas of weakness until the proficiency standards have been met.

The adaptation here is to use the competency tests as the principal means of instruction, a wrinkle perfectly acceptable but uncommon in the classroom. Additional sources of instruction, book chapters mainly, will be cited for the competencies associated with each subject area.

In a competency-based program, if learners do not pass the tests, the assumption is held that something is wrong with the program, presumably faulty instruction, perhaps the standards of evaluation, but not the learners. The instruction is repeated, in various formats perhaps, until the competency tests have been mastered by all the learners or at least a high proportion of them. That at least is the theoretical ideal. It rarely happens as designed, of course, in the actual schools.

COMPETENCY TESTS AND ACHIEVEMENT TESTS

Handicappers must understand that competency tests of knowledge and skill are vastly dissimilar from conventional achievement tests. Achievement tests are designed to distinguish high achievers from average achievers and low achievers. The test items are constructed, therefore, by means that accomplish the desired discrimination; that is, that rank a group of learners from high achievers to low achievers.

Competency tests are designed to assess whether the learners have mastered a subject matter adequately or can display a skill satisfactorily, perhaps know the standards of positive form or calculate speed figures. The test items are constructed to obtain a representative sample of the learner's proficiency on a set of specific tasks.

Achievement tests are characterized as *norm-referenced* because the test scores are interpreted in relation to the scores of others who have previously taken the tests. The earlier test scores are called norms, or subjective standards against which new test scores are compared.

In achievement testing it's crucial that the norm group (the people who first took the test) represent the new testing groups well, or else the comparisons of scores will be meaningless or misleading.

Suppose a test of handicapping skill were designed to identify the best handicappers in the nation. Test items would be included or not to the extent high achievers answered them and low achievers missed them. If casual racegoers took the test, the scores they obtained would be necessarily low. Yet many of the casual racegoers would be competent handicappers, to be sure.

Competency tests are characterized as *criterion-referenced* because the test scores are interpreted in relation to an objective standard, not the scores of others. Competency tests are not concerned with comparing the scores obtained by various individuals or groups or with ranking the testing group from high to low. They are concerned with assessing proficiency on tasks against a predetermined objective standard of performance.

For example, if ten athletes competed in a mile run, the norm-referenced test (achievement) of success would be the ability to finish first, or at least in the top portion of the group. The criterion-referenced test (competency) of the same skill would be the ability to complete the mile run against an objective time standard, say within eight minutes.

It should be obvious that in achievement testing only some learners can succeed. Others must fall behind or fail. In competency testing, all the participants can succeed. All they must do is satisfy the proficiency standard; run the mile within eight minutes.

Whenever we want to determine whether explicit increments of learning have occurred, competency tests are appropriate.

Whenever we want to compare learners with one another, achievement tests are appropriate.

Both types of tests appear in this book. Thus handicappers can perform well on the competency tests and not so well on the achievement tests. We can anticipate a certain measure of correlation—that is, high scores on the competency tests should contribute to high scores on the achievement tests—but a strong positive correlation is not guaranteed.

Achievement depends in part on factors other than satisfactory competence, such as intelligence, motivation, doggedness, and fortunate circumstances. Success at the racetrack depends in part on factors other than satisfactory proficiency in handicapping and wagering. No one of any trackside worldliness can express surprise at this.

More importantly for recreational handicappers, the obverse of the point is undeniable. High achievement—success at the racetrack—cannot result from low competence.

We proceed here, in fact, from a conviction that successful racetrack achievement depends in part on a level of knowledge and skill in handicapping that exceeds minimum competency and approaches mastery, and handicappers can expect the tests to prove difficult, the standards of proficiency strict.

The "minimum competency" tests will be pedestrian and elementary for experienced handicappers, but not altogether easy. They provide an excellent grounding for novices and a back-to-basics refresher for journeymen.

The "mastery" tests are rugged, and deliberately intended to be. I predict without hesitation that numerous handicappers will score below standard on several of them.

That is because journeymen handicappers notoriously can be classified as method players. They comprehend pet methods well, the remaining intricacies of handicapping not nearly so well. If advancement from novice to journeyman depends upon mastery of a methodology, the evolution from journeyman to expert depends upon mastery of the handicapping process as a whole. That is a fact, not an opinion, as suggested in the prologue. Experts know roughly all there is to know, not just a thick slice of the whole.

On the other hand, handicapping hobbyists might choose to conquer the mastery tests only of subject matter of special interest and discount the others. This is fair play, by all means. Not everyone cares to be the expert, and this book promotes levels of knowledge and skill intended to enhance one's pleasure and profit at the racetrack, not extract a living from it.

I shall return to the types of tests in the book again.

THE CONTENT VALIDITY OF TEST ITEMS

An aspect of this book will be highly controversial, no doubt. Competency tests are valid (accurate) measures only to the extent they possess the attribute known as *content validity*. This means:

- test items assess the competencies they are intended to assess, and
- the test in its entirety elicits a representative sample of the handicapper's performance in the *competency domain* (the array of factual knowledge or skills to be assessed).

The index of content validity is the judgment of subject-matter experts.

Does this test item measure what it is supposed to measure?

Does the test assess the *competency domain* adequately?

Multiple expert opinions of a test item's content validity are preferable to one. Thus I consulted authentic experts on the items assessing special topics—Steve Roman on pedigree, Tom Brohamer on pace, and Dick Mitchell on probability, for example—but in the main relied upon my interpretation of other authors' treatments of the subjects in books or, to less extent, on personal experience and expertise.

Another "expert" would certainly judge several items invalid or best eliminated. Many readers as test-takers will just as surely argue the same, notably regarding items they have answered incorrectly when supremely confident of being correct. Regardless, the sticky issues of test validity are less important than the utility of the general approach and of numerous items as sources of instruction in handicapping. As a consulting colleague likes to say, this is not a testing program. It's an exercise in education. Intemperate discussions of reality provoked by controversial measures of handicapping can only help to clear the air.

Users can be assured the items and tests have been carefully constructed and reviewed. I present the material as a fair evaluation of proficiency in handicapping. Racegoers who aspire to become competent handicappers should insist they perform well. Low scores amount to bad news. Far more than test revision, they beg the handicapper's personal improvement.

As the book's title intimates, and certain terminology until now has certified, an academic tone and ambiance hover about these contents.

I trust not many handicappers will be unduly upset or put off by that. Instruction and evaluation of results, after all, are rooted in academics.

I admit not many handicappers master the subjects of handicapping sequentially, as organized here, and I do not pretend that handicapping competency, as reflected by paper tests, can be taken to predict success at the racetrack. It cannot. But to dismiss the book's approach on those grounds is to dismiss its more narrow purpose out of hand.

And the academic tone and terms persist only throughout Part A. Relief is on the way. The next section is probably the worst, but it must be said.

CHAPTER 1

A Back-to-Basics Curriculum for Handicappers

IT'S IMPORTANT TO BECOME clear as to the desired competencies of handicapping. In academe this is the province of curriculum development, the notion of specifying the intended outcomes of instruction.

What factual knowledge should handicappers comprehend?

What skills should they be able to demonstrate?

The answers are really value judgments and they vary widely, even as do speed handicappers, class handicappers, pace handicappers, trip handicappers, form analysts, trainer specialists, pedigree specialists, body language experts, and the rest.

Few practitioners would suggest that the array of knowledge and skills influencing the chances of winning at the races has not increased dramatically in recent seasons. My personal training and experience has been substantial but I am repeatedly impressed at the overlays spotted by bias experts, body language experts, even pace experts, that I have inadvertently overlooked. The pertinent factors are many, the interrelationships numerous, and the liberally educated handicapper, in my judgment, displays a working knowledge of all of them. Missing a few, the practitioner misses as well a number of winners and overlays potentially within his grasp.

From the great variety and diversity, a core curriculum can be elaborated. Deep intimate acquaintance with the general practice and its literature indicates the competencies the well-equipped handicapper applies. The competencies can be grouped under the subject-matter headings they define. These include:

- Past performance tables and results charts
- Early speed
- Class appraisal
- Speed handicapping
- Pace analysis
- Form analysis
- The distance factor
- Trips and track bias
- Trainer, jockey, weight, and post position
- Pedigree, imports, and grass racing
- Body language
- Probability, odds, money management, and pari-mutuel wagering

The subjects form no hierarchy of utility or value, although the first precurses and facilitates all else and the last applies to every race. All can be relatively influential or decisive, though some will be decisive more frequently than others. Certain topics have been clustered because they regularly must be juxtaposed in analyzing races.

For each subject, a list of four to eight essential competencies can be identified. These represent the knowledge and skills a "competent" handicapper should demonstrate. I call them *competency domains*. This book addresses the twelve competency domains above. It promotes sixty-six handicapping competencies the author considers essential. Here's an illustration:

Past Performance Tables and Results Charts

Competencies

1. Know the meanings of symbols and data items.
2. Identify the points of call at various distances.
3. Calculate fractional times and lengths gained or lost between calls.
4. Interpret past performance and chart data according to the handicapping values they represent.

Each competency domain has a corresponding *item domain*. The item domain consists of the universe of test items that assess the competencies accurately, another theoretical position. In practice, the practical imperative recommends relatively large pools of test items that can assess the complete range of difficulty of the competencies.

The four competencies listed under "past performance tables and results charts," for example, might be assessed by hundreds of test items. But a few dozen items can yield a reliable estimate of competency. The idea is to construct a pool of items having a range of difficulty corresponding to the complexity of the competency. In that way a test of the competency domain can be considered representative. That procedure has been followed here.

To assess handicappers' proficiency with "past performance tables and results charts," a competency test of forty items has been constructed. The test design confers the added benefit that slack performance on a subset of items assessing a specific competency, such as Number 2 above, indicates where the brushing up might begin.

Another step is crucial.

How well should competent handicappers know a subject matter or demonstrate a skill? Absolutely? With 80 percent proficiency? Seventy-five percent? Sixty percent? Less than 50 percent proficiency? This introduces the tricky problem of setting proficiency standards.

To a degree, proficiency standards are subjective. They depend upon the opinions and values of all interested parties. Suppose, for example, a group of handicapping practitioners agreed that the skill of interpreting past performance and result-chart symbols and data were so fundamental to higher-order learning in handicapping that "competent" handicappers should demonstrate 100 percent proficiency in the item domain. By this standard the passing score on a competency test of the subject matter would be 100 percent correctness. Miss an item, fail the competency test.

A second group of handicappers could disagree. Far from being fundamental, they might argue, the skills of interpreting past performance and chart symbols are superfluous to effective handicapping. Only the symbols and data items actually used in one's play are meaningful. Such arguments would intensify when discussing the proficiency standards appropriate to many other skills of handicapping.

How well should competent handicappers be able to calculate pace ratings?

How well must competent handicappers understand the class demands of eligibility conditions?

How well should competent handicappers recognize the

positive and negative signs of equine body language?

How well should competent handicappers estimate horses' winning chances and convert the probabilities to legitimate odds lines?

Opinions and values on these matters tend to fly in each other's face, and the debates rage on furiously. Final solutions reflect compromises that not only pacify no one, but also subvert the underlying educational issues.

The practical remedy evades the thornier problem of setting standards by identifying the competencies considered "essential," those competencies required either for higher-order learning or fundamental proficiency in the competency domain. A dichotomous decision—essential or not essential—replaces an acrimonious debate and majority rules. Everyone quickly agrees the "essential" competencies merit strict standards of proficiency. In practice, this means a minimum of 75 to 80 percent of the items on a competency test should be answered correctly by "competent" learners (handicappers).

The sixty-six handicapping competencies that appear in this book have been deemed essential by me, an author's prerogative, and proficiency standards will be high. A simple procedure allows readers to disagree. Test items are identified by the competencies they assess. Handicappers should bypass the competencies and corresponding test items they judge superfluous, extraneous, or disagreeable. This caveat does not extend to novices or to journeyman handicappers of less than five years experience.

Regrettably, a flaw hounds this approach to setting standards, as even essential competencies promote a range of knowledge and skill having various degrees of complexity. The tests will have a corresponding range of item difficulty. Some test items will be easy, some difficult. Too often users can pass the test, that is, "master the competencies," without answering enough of the more difficult test items accurately. This defeats the purpose.

A pragmatic solution divides the *item domain* for a *competency domain* into "minimum competency" tests and "mastery" tests. The minimum competency tests consist of test items having a relatively low level of difficulty. The mastery tests consist of test items having moderate to high levels of difficulty. Proficiency standards on mastery tests are lowered in relation to the standards characteristic of minimum competency tests.

To demonstrate "competency," both tests must be passed. Scoring below standard on the minimum competency portion indicates additional study and practice should precede taking the mastery portion. That procedure is strongly recommended here.

To assign items to the two types of tests, I took the item pool to Mark Cramer's class on probabilities in handicapping at Los Angeles City College and posed a rhetorical question of each item: What percentage of reasonably competent handicappers should be able to answer this test item correctly?

Any test item the students indicated should be answered correctly by 80 percent of the "competent" handicappers, I assigned to the minimum competency tests. Passing scores on these tests are 80 percent item correctness, 90 percent on the test of "past performance tables and results charts."

The remaining test items were assigned to the mastery tests. Proficiency standards will be lower.

So a competency-based approach to instruction and evaluation in handicapping attends to three complementary tasks:

- Identifying the essential competencies handicappers should be prepared to demonstrate.
- Constructing the competency tests.
- Setting proficiency standards and passing scores.

The achievement tests of Part C, as mentioned, are different in design. So are the standards for evaluating results. Here we best rely on norms. Certain evidence is well-known. The public picks 33 percent winners, gets 8–5 odds on average. These norms can help us establish realistic proficiency standards.

By multiplying the win percentage and average odds on winners, we can establish a numerical index of handicapping effectiveness that anticipates success. The public earns a 53. This is not good enough. The public loses nine cents a dollar on its favorites.

If we replace the 8–5 odds on the public's winners with 5–2 odds and lower the expected win percentage to 30, the index of desired performance on each performance test is 75. Such performance, handicappers should appreciate, amounts to a 5 percent profit on the invested dollar. This amounts to satisfactory competency, but not an adequate profit.

Much preferred is 33 percent winners at 5–2 odds, or 30 percent at 3–1 odds. The seemingly small improvement amounts to mastery and upwards of 15 percent on the invested dollar.

Handicappers should expect to do at least as well, should they not?

CHAPTER 2

Competency Testing and Racetrack Performance

ANY ACADEMIC DISCOURSE on a topic as complicated in practice as handicapping for profit incurs the wrath of the practitioner. In reaction to this book's ambitions, a chorus will cry out that scores on competency tests bear no resemblance to performance at the racetrack. The din becomes louder, angrier, and scornful to the extent that members of the chorus have been inveterate losers.

The charge is despairingly false. It amounts to an assertion that knowledge bears no relationship to the implementation of knowledge. Yet the educational issues implicit in the charges are real and intriguing, and I prefer to deal with them pointedly before the testing begins.

Let's concede that handicappers might answer 900 test items on handicapping correctly and perform pitiably at the track. Among the explanations as to why implementation so often fails instruction, two are themselves academic and germane:

- The knowledge and skills promoted during instruction are not sufficiently related to the skills and experience required during implementation.
- The lower-order knowledge and skills (fundamentals) prerequisite to the higher-order competencies (mastery) required for effective implementation have not been adequately mastered during instruction. Thus, effective implementation is compromised.

The first problem normally is corrected by experience, and normally the correction takes years. Many professionals can testify to the point. CPAs, MBAs, physical scientists, lawyers—all require years of experience before they can implement their academic training expertly. Book-versed handicappers are not only not alone in their incompetency, they stand in solidly credentialed company.

The second problem is significantly worse. The solution requires corrective instruction. Experience, in fact, normally worsens the problem, as faulty implementation becomes a way of life.

To appreciate the subtleties of instruction and implementation in handicapping, practitioners are implored to have patience with the discussion below. Educators have developed means of classifying the types of cognitive skills promoted in any discipline, including, if you will, the discipline of handicapping.

In the best-known classification scheme, the prominent university educator Benjamin Bloom has identified six intellectual skills inherent in the teaching-learning process. From the simple to the complex, they are:

1. Knowledge — The ability *to recognize* familiar events.
   The ability *to recall* familiar events.

2. Comprehension — The ability *to understand* or *interpret the meaning of* events. Includes three sub-skills:
   - *to translate,* or the ability to change events from one form to another
   - *to discriminate,* or the ability to distinguish classes of events based on given criteria
   - *To extrapolate,* or the ability to infer events from events that have a logical extension.

3. Application — The ability *to solve problems* that are *new* or *unfamiliar.*

4. Analysis — The ability *to divide a whole into its constituent parts* such that the relations between the parts are identified.

5. Synthesis — The ability *to form new wholes* from a *combination of parts* or *events.*

6. Evaluation — The ability *to judge the worth* of events according to specified criteria.

The mental skills of handicapping can be classified according to Bloom's taxonomy. A few examples should be strikingly familiar.

Knowledge
By examining a horse's lifetime record of wins and losses, a handicapper knows whether its win percentage this season and last characterizes the horse as a consistent contender (recognition).

A handicapper remembers a horse raced five wide on the clubhouse turn and three wide on the far turn last out (recall), clarifying an unexpectedly dull performance.

Comprehension
A handicapper notes a horse earned a *Form* speed rating of 86 on a day the *Form* variant was 20, meaning the horse ran approximately six lengths faster than the average winner on that day (understanding).

A speed handicapper converts the fractional times, final times, and beaten lengths in a horse's past performances to speed and pace figures (translation).

A class handicapper determines that a claiming horse has invariably won, run second, or finished close at $25,000 or below, but has not won and usually performs poorly at $32,000 or higher (discrimination).

A form analyst notices that in a short series of races following a lengthy layoff, a sprinter has run closer at the second call two races back, closer still at the stretch call last out. He expects the horse to give its best effort today (extrapolation).

Application
A local handicapper analyzes a shipper's past performances using subtle variations of the same speed, pace, and class methods he invokes every day (solving problems that are new or unfamiliar).

Analysis
After identifying the entrants in a twelve-horse field well suited to the class demands of today's eligibility conditions, a well-rounded handicapper determines which of the contenders has the best early speed, which runs the fastest figures, which has handled the swiftest early pace, which look in peaking or improving form, which will be comfortable at the distance, and which should benefit from today's trip circumstances and biases (dividing a whole into its constituent parts).

Synthesis
After analyzing the speed, class, and probable pace, a handicapper visualizes how today's race will be run at each point of call and concludes that one of the horses has a decisive pace advantage, making it the probable winner (form new wholes from a combination of parts).

Evaluation
A handicapper ponders three horses he realizes have relatively even chances to win. Horse A is 2–1, Horse B is 5–2, and Horse C is 8–1. The handicapper decides to bet on Horse C (judging the worth of an event).

All disciplines and most courses of instruction can be organized in ways that develop from the simple to the complex. Although humans do not necessarily learn in the simple-to-complex pattern, the simple-to-complex organization of instruction supports a basic tenet of learning theory. Mastery of lower-order skills facilitates the learning of higher-order skills. Abundant knowledge, in-depth comprehension, extensive application—these conditions soften the handicapper's tasks of analysis, synthesis, and evaluation.

Disciplines can be characterized also as relatively abstract to relatively concrete.

Mathematics, philosophy, physics, logic—these disciplines are abstract. Early during instruction the fundamental facts, concepts, and principles are presented and absorbed. Factual knowledge and a low comprehension can be gained quickly enough. Soon arrive the complexities of problem solving, however, and the skills of analysis, synthesis, and evaluation must be demonstrated by an intellectual process that is far more logical than factual.

Reading, history, the social sciences, business administration—these disciplines are concrete. Numerous facts, concepts, and principles must be presented and absorbed. Instruction remains in the knowledge and comprehension phases for lengthy periods. So long, in fact, that applications presented during instruction tend to be narrow, trivial, and familiar. Post-instructional, real-world applications tend to be truly new and unfamiliar, delaying effective implementation until experience complements the classroom.

From a teaching-learning perspective, the most complicated and time-consuming of disciplines are characterized by polar extremes, an abundance of factual knowledge whose effective implementation depends upon the higher-order thinking skills. The law leaps to mind. Advanced accounting. Psychology qualifies well, one reason it remains the dark science today.

In the world of games and recreation, handicapping qualifies as well, even as chess does not. The former is information-driven, the latter an exercise in logical thinking.

All of this is meant to suggest that the ability to handicap well depends first on the accumulation and comprehension of factual knowledge. That is not sufficient, but it is necessary. To repeat a sad theme, one need only consider that many of the worst of handicappers have been practicing the skill for years. They have been analyzing racehorses and their racetrack experiences throughout an adult lifetime, but with grains of success that slip through their fingers like the sand. Perhaps the poor performances can be traced to repetitive applications of faulty learning experiences horrendously low on factual knowledge and its comprehension.

Sadly, too, the conventional instruction in handicapping provided to racegoers by a reluctant industry suffers the opposite shortcoming. The instruction in its entirety consists of factual knowledge and of factors incidental to the substance of effective handicapping.

Denotative explanations of the *Daily Racing Form*'s symbols and data items; trainer and jockey standings; official track conditions; overweights; horses on lasix or other medications; frequencies of winning post positions: all of this and more reduces assistance in handicapping obtainable at the racetracks to the recognition of trivial facts, the lowest form of knowledge, without regard to comprehension. The customers who have absorbed all of it have understood nothing. The explanation why so many casual occasional racegoers do not purchase the *Daily Racing Form* is not because they cannot read the past performance tables. It's because they don't know what they mean.

Other forms of handicapping instruction have proliferated at racetracks lately, with greater hope of broadening comprehension.

Trackside seminars at which reputed authorities supply the customers with daily selections and opinions impart abundant knowledge of handicapping, but usually attach little meaning to it. When the authorities make factual or descriptive comments, they impart knowledge, not so much of handicapping as of particular horses.

"This horse has fine early speed and should go to the front

here. He had a bad trip last out and gets seven pounds off today. The trainer and jockey are both among the leaders. I think he'll be right there."

When the authorities offer interpretive comments instead, they promote comprehension.

"This horse's early speed should count for more than meets the eye here. Even when frontrunners are contested, one of them frequently wins, especially when the pace figures to be average or slow for the class, as it does here.

"He raced wide most of the way last out but was still digging in at mid-stretch, suggesting he might have finished closer. The trainer wins with this kind of horse more frequently than with others; it's one of his main strengths."

The second commentary not only supplies the details of a horse's performance but gives meaning and context to the factors of early speed, trips, and trainer data.

To the extent the principals can provide meaning, context, and evaluation of relevant factors, trackside seminars promote a greater understanding of handicapping knowledge and its application. To the extent the experts provide isolated facts, personal selections, and preoccupy the discussion with defending or justifying their opinions, they become useless.

An unfortunate aspect of trackside seminars as a group is the commentators' repetitive references to a subset of factors that are continually present and therefore overly identifiable even to members of the casual audience—early speed, jockey changes, successful and unsuccessful trainers, inside and outside posts, troubled trips. The experts share a tendency to attribute to a few highly visible factors a kind of significance they often do not deserve. Too many customers get a misleading impression.

And a disservice the seminars promote unthinkingly finds the experts making selections to win, without advising the audience of the fair-value odds the horses' chances reflect.

The point cannot be brushed aside. Making selections is only a part of the customer's problem. What are the contending horses' relative chances of winning? What are the acceptable win odds on each? Which horses should be conspicuous underlays? Which might become attractive overlays? A rule of thumb encouraging dissemination of that information would be a giant step ahead.

As a source of instruction, needless to say, the professional selection cards brandished to racing's customers outside the gates of racetracks are pointless. They provide no intellectual nourishment to anyone who cares to understand handicapping.

This is not to intimate the cards are not redeemable. As now legislated, attempting to pick every race, the services can be guaranteed to lose. This reinforces the much-cherished myth. A regulatory change, permitting the pros to handicap only the races they understand, would result in the better services actually winning. The tracks would be forced to monitor the cards' performance records and post results, an inconvenience. But the sight of occasional winners would debunk the much-cherished myth and encourage the art of handicapping. In a twinkling, at no overhead, the racetracks would now be supporting professional services capable of demonstrating to the multitudes that you can beat the races.

A few observations on the hierarchy of cognitive skills are also pertinent.

Notice that the skill of application refers to situations that are *new* or *unfamiliar*.

In the classroom, application refers to the ability to solve problems other than the kind used to illustrate ideas during the regular course of instruction.

At the racetrack, application refers to analyzing races that feature new or unfamiliar horses, trainers, jockeys, and track surfaces. These changes, of course, occur almost daily. The dramatic difference, however, regards the difference between applying factual knowledge and transferring comprehension.

Many experienced handicappers admit they become lost, for example, when visiting new or unfamiliar tracks. If the problem is so serious as to be paralyzing, it suggests the afflicted handicappers are getting by at home through extensive knowledge of the local scene—familiarity with the local horses, trainers, jockeys, and surfaces—and not enough by a deeper understanding of handicapping principles and methods. The principles and methods are transportable. Accomplished speed, class, pace, and trip handicappers who have a firm grasp of the fundamentals besides, may not do as well when playing at unfamiliar tracks, but they do not fall apart.

Finally, the most advanced cognitive skill, of evaluation, is almost completely ignored in the conventional discourse on handicapping as an intellectual challenge game.

Somehow the thought has been practically immortalized that the objective of handicapping is making selections that figure to win. Not so. The art of handicapping is not limited to the art of picking winners. Handicapping is the art of appraising the relative chances of the horses in a field. The distinction is vital. The evaluative definition opens handicappers to the possibility of identifying underlays and overlays. Underlays should be ignored, even when having the strongest probability of winning. Overlays can be supported, even when they are not the likeliest to win.

A fair number of the test items here assess the handicappers' skill of evaluation. They honor the proposition that handicapping does not end following the race analysis or the synthesis that occurs when a probable winner has been found. The thinking ends, as it should, with a final evaluation of all that has gone before.

MINIMUM COMPETENCY TESTS

The minimum competency tests are intended to assess either (a) basic knowledge and skill prerequisite to higher-order learning, or (b) the essential competencies of handicapping at low levels of complexity. Proficiency standards must be rigorous.

To assess minimum competency reliably, ten to fifteen test items usually suffice. Passing scores will be a minimum of 75 to 80 percent item correctness. The entire forty-item test of the past performance tables and results charts is considered a minimum competency test. Only knowledge and low-level comprehension are required. I'm tempted to demand 100 percent proficiency on these prerequisites, but shall retreat kindly to a 90 percent position. The passing score is 36.

Minimum competency standards on the tests of speed handicapping, class handicapping, pace handicapping, and other subjects fall to 80 percent proficiency. For a few subjects the standards become 75 percent proficiency. None fall below that.

Many handicappers not as finely versed in the basics as they might have imagined will prefer to trivialize the results of minimum competency tests. Who cares? What does it matter? The dismissives should not obscure a serious proposition. In any risk-management game, mental as well as physical, fundamental faults contribute to self-defeating mistakes, notably when the pressure mounts.

In any goal-directed endeavor it's healthy procedure to correct fundamental faults before pressing on. The principle applies here. Handicappers who fall below standard on the minimum competency tests should consult the recommended sources of instruction on the incorrect items prior to proceeding. The items are carefully constructed, clear, and not difficult.

Experienced handicappers, notably those enjoying consistent success, can disregard the minimum competency tests that do not interest them. Success earns it rewards.

Novices, recreational handicappers who attend the races infrequently, relatively inexperienced handicappers, and inveterate punters should not skip the minimum competency tests. Method players discontented with the returns on their specialty should attend to the tests outside their customary pursuits. All of the above, furthermore, might insist on getting perfect scores on these preliminary tests.

MASTERY TESTS

The centerpieces of any competency-based program are its mastery tests. The emphases of instruction and objectives of learning are reflected here.

In between the untutored inexperience of the novice and the successful experience of the professional lies a vast knowledge wilderness. No one should doubt that expertise accumulates by crisscrossing these intellectual landscapes successively and determinedly. Mastery tests assess the entire scope of a subject's competencies at several levels of complexity. The tests embody the entire range of cognitive skills from knowledge to comprehension, application, analysis, synthesis, and evaluation. Emphases will be on comprehension and application.

Proficiency standards are not as rigorous, but far from loose. Competent handicappers should expect to attain 70 percent proficiency or better in each competency domain, from early speed, to speed and class handicapping, to pace analysis, to body language and the rest. Specific proficiency standards and passing scores have been set for each mastery test. The test length varies from 32 items to 80. Where specialties are engaged, such as speed handicapping, method players should substitute proficiency standards of 90 percent item accuracy. Specialists do not get that way as a result of ordinary performance.

Proficiency standards and passing scores arouse the impression that the purpose of mastery testing is to evaluate respondents who attempt the tests. This is partially untrue. The purpose instead is to help the respondents master the material by clarifying their status in relation to the learning objectives. The desired learning can be facilitated once several test items assessing specific competencies have been missed. If a test assesses a half-dozen competencies, and the items for a specific one are missed repeatedly, obviously new instruction should be targeted there. If handicappers apply the same proficiency standards for the test as a whole to particular competencies embedded in the test, then in effect, numerous diagnostic tests have been administered and any additional instruction can be more carefully targeted.

If mastery tests have been failed miserably, the results should be considered seriously. The shortcomings no doubt reveal themselves as well at the track. Consult the book chapters and articles cited as sources of instruction, checking the contents in relation to the content of the mistaken items.

Following a review and any discussion with other handicappers, retake the mastery tests. On second attempts pay closer attention to the item stems and response alternatives than to the correct responses only. Determine why the item was missed initially. On second testings, also, do not answer any item if you are uncertain about the correct response. Go back to these individual items later, again consulting the instructional resources. Repeat the instruction and assessment cycles until all the items have been answered correctly.

If handicappers satisfy the proficiency standards of mastery tests, they can discount the incorrect responses on the items missed, unless several of the items missed assess the same competency. Item ambiguity does exist, but tends to reveal itself most noticeably by examining—statistically—the incorrect items of respondents who did best on the test as a whole. If mastery tests are passed, but particular competencies within the test failed, by all means pursue additional instruction on the weaknesses. If mastery tests are passed, and several items were missed haphazardly in the bargain, go on to the next subject.

THE TEST ITEMS

The majority of the test items present the multiple-choice format. The remainder have the true-false format.

Item formats eliciting short selected responses invariably invoke a spate of emotional criticism. Much of the criticism is ill-advised. Of the six test-item formats, many will be surprised to learn, the multiple-choice format is the most valuable and by a convincing margin. It's overwhelmingly best for the present purposes.

The assertion is worth documenting. After studying the question empirically, the Center for the Study of Evaluation at UCLA ranked the six-item formats on eight testing criteria. A rating of 1 is low, 6 is high. The results appear in Table 1.

Examine the three criteria, bottom left of table 1, denoting

**Table 1. General relative advantages and disadvantages
of the six major kinds of item formats**

	Selected Response			Constructed Response		
	True-False	Multiple Choice	Matching	Completion	Short Answer	Essay
Time it takes to construct and key one good item.	6	5	2.5	4	2.5	1
Time it takes an examinee to answer one item.	6	5	4	3	2	1
Time it takes to score one item.	6	5	4	3	2	1
Objectivity of the scoring procedures, i.e., "scorer reliability."	5	5	5	3	2	1
Item reliability, i.e., consistency of the measurement.	5	6	3	3	3	1
Item validity, i.e., accuracy of the measurement.	3	6	3	3	5	1
Number and range of objectives for which the format can be used effectively.	4	6	2	4	4	1
Overall efficiency and effectiveness.	4	6	2	3	5	1

The six formats have been ranked on each dimension in terms of their *relative* efficiency and effectiveness. *The higher the rank, the better the item format.* The essay test, for example, has a rank of "1" on the third dimension because it takes the longest to score properly. In some cases, it has been necessary to assign tied ranks.

item validity (critical), number and range of objectives for which the format can be used effectively, and overall efficiency and effectiveness. The multiple-choice item ranked highest on all three. No other item format was rated 6 on any of the three. On the eight criteria, the multiple-choice item was never rated below 5.

The essay item ranked lowest on all eight criteria, a cruel blow, to be sure, to the masses who for some reason have come to believe only the essay format can assess higher-order learning effectively. To be fair, essay tests do evaluate the cognitive skills of synthesis and evaluation particularly well, skills that handicappers ultimately rely upon. We confront the assessment of these skills in the performance tests near the end.

Table 2 summarizes the advantages and disadvantages of the multiple-choice format.

Table 2. Multiple-choice items advantages and disadvantages

Advantages

1. *Efficient* in terms of the time it takes to construct, administer, and score relative to their reliability and validity. All things considered, it is probably the *most efficient* and *effective* of all test formats.
2. Easily understood format.
3. *Are less subject to biases* due to guessing than other selected response formats.
4. Allow for *control of item difficulty* through adjusting the homogeneity of the alternatives.
5. The *most sensitive to actual student knowledge,* since the more the student knows, the better his score.
6. The *most versatile and widely applicable* of all test forms. They can be used to measure almost every kind of cognitive ability, skill, or knowledge.

Disadvantages

1. Sometimes *difficult to construct,* particularly in developing an adequate number of truly effective distractors.
2. Require *more reading time per item* than several other item formats, although only the true-false and matching formats are more economical in terms of the total time it takes to answer each item.
3. Often *subject to many different kinds of construction errors,* such as distractors containing irrelevant clues to the correct answer or an undue emphasis on isolated pieces of information.

Item ambiguity cannot be ruled out until a few thousand people have completed the tests and the items are examined statistically. Certain terminology can be confusing, and practitioners who have not digested a decent book on handicapping in a long time will encounter numerous new terms here. Item ambiguity should not be confused with item difficulty. As a practical assist, a definition of formal and unusual handicapping terms can be found following the brief introductory remarks to each subject's tests. If handicappers judge an item's stem confusing, they should omit the item. If they judge two response alternatives appropriate, select the best. The minimum competency tests and mastery tests have a single "correct" answer to each item. There are no "trick" items.

As a rule, test items are grouped by the competencies they assess, but dozens of exceptions will be noted. Competencies and test items are numbered consecutively. Answer keys are provided. Handicappers can readily track item scores, competency scores, and mastery scores for a subject area.

A final brief section of Part A advises handicappers on procedures for taking and scoring the book's competency tests. First a few additional, highly academic comments on a sobering topic.

WHY COMPETENT HANDICAPPERS LOSE: THE AFFECTIVE DOMAIN

Incompetent handicappers have scarcely a chance to win at the races, but competent handicappers have a splendid chance to lose nonetheless. Racetrack success traces in part to a number of nonintellectual traits and skills. The traits include motives, values, interests, and beliefs. The skills include emotional control and performance under pressure.

Since the emphases here are instruction and evaluation, let's examine the problem from an educational perspective. The educator Bloom did not classify only the cognitive skills of the teaching-learning process. He concerned himself, too, with the affective and motor skills on which learning depends.

Consider the hierarchy of affective skills that have an impact on learning:

1. Attending   The capacity to become aware of events in the environment.

2. Responding	The capacity to react to events in a purposeful or goal-directed manner.
3. Valuing	The degree to which events are perceived or judged as important or worthwhile.
4. Value organization	The arrangement by which a set of values is organized in a hierarchy.
5. Character	The capacity to demonstrate values consistently in accord with the way they have been organized in the personality.

As academic as they sound, the skills of Bloom's affective domain apply with tremendous practical force to the development of handicapping proficiency.

For example, almost all racegoers *attend* (become aware of) to the skills of handicapping when actually playing the races, but only a minority *respond* (act with purpose or in a goal-directed manner) to that awareness off-track by deliberately striving to improve their skills.

Why?

For one reason, the majority of racegoers *value* the recreational aspects of a day at the races. Integral to the recreation is the easy thinking that accompanies the sizing up of horses' competitive chances, picking contenders, and deciding what and how to bet.

This majority does not value as much the art of handicapping to win, not realizing that the integration of the two values (recreation and competent handicapping) amounts to a pleasure greater than either value alone provides.

Of the minority who *organize* their recreational *values* in a hierarchy that places competent handicapping at or near the top, fewer still have the *character* to apply the principles of handicapping persistently, especially in the face of the emotional duress and imbalance that often results.

The racing game is characterized by a huge error factor. The errors provoke strong emotional reactions. The emotional responses conflict with the preparation for success. Human character is tested severely. Often it does not survive.

So to become successful, racegoers must not only develop a challenging array of intellectual skills, but also endure an erratic run through a gauntlet of motives, values, and emotional reactions not adequately anticipated. The reason few racegoers win is thus a matter of both intellectual and nonintellectual competence; of developing the fantastic array of skills that must be mastered.

What of competent handicappers? Why do they lose? It's a matter again of character. Hundreds of competent handicappers possess the character to win at the races season after season, and they do. Thousands more do not. Thus they lose.

THE ACHIEVEMENT TESTS

Two forms of an achievement test in Part C will be familiar to handicappers everywhere. Past performances are presented and three tasks must be performed.

When handicappers break a race down into its component parts, identifying the class of the field, the high-figure horse, the early speed, the horses favored or disadvantaged by the probable pace, horses showing improving or deteriorating form, and the rest, the skill of analysis must be displayed at a high order of complexity.

When handicappers stitch a severely dissected race together anew, now forming mental versions of the probable outcome, this is synthesis, a high-order form of composition.

When handicappers judge the probabilities that certain horses will win in relation to the odds offered by bettors, and decide on the types and sizes of bets affording best values, this is evaluation, the highest-order skill, not only of the cognitive domain, but of handicappers besides.

In fact, thoroughbred handicapping serves as a kind of quintessential testing ground for the higher-order thinking skills of analysis, synthesis, and evaluation, a dubious thought for educators.

The test items of the achievement tests ask handicappers to do nothing they do not inevitably do. Three tasks are promoted:

- Analyze the past performances according to which horse(s) figure best on a specific factor or combination of factors.
- Select the most probable winner of a race or among given contenders.
- Decide which horse(s) offer positive or negative value at the odds.

Each of the two forms of the test contains 60 items. A few items require multiple answers to be judged correct. Handicappers should expect to perform as well as the racetrack crowd—33 percent item accuracy.

Since the purpose of achievement testing is to compare handicappers with one another, the test scoring differs. We can multiply the percent of winners by the average odds on winners and rank handicappers by the final totals.

It's possible also to norm a form of the achievement test (Form B) on large samples of handicappers who complete the test. The process of norming would tell handicappers what percentage of test respondents their individual score exceeded. That is, raw scores can be converted to percentile scores.

The test can be normed or standardized according to the scores obtained by two groups: professionals, and journeymen handicappers having at least five years of experience. The test feedback would compare the individual with both groups, an interesting experiment.

To norm the test, the reader's cooperation will be necessary. See the instructions on page 526. A computer will score the answer forms, norm the test, and report the results. Individuals will receive the report in six to eight weeks.

HOW TO TAKE THE TESTS

Following a few trusty guideposts can maximize the instructional value inherent in competency testing. Novices especially are urged to adhere to these procedures.

1. Note the proficiency standards, number of items, and passing scores for each subject area; review the introductory remarks and definitions of terms preceding each test. The definitions of terms, in fact, will represent the correct answers to a few items.
2. Without consulting the sources of instruction listed for each subject, take the minimum competency test. Score it. If your score falls below standard, consult the sources of instruction fully and retake the failed items. Do not proceed to the mastery tests until the minimum competency tests have been completed satisfactorily.
3. Each mastery test should be completed at a single session.
4. Each mastery test should be scored upon completion in two ways. First, obtain total test scores. Second, obtain subscores on the specific competencies under each subject. Each subscore should satisfy the proficiency standard for the test as a whole. Items will be referenced to the competencies they assess.

5. If mastery scores or competency scores fall below standard, pursue the sources of instruction at your convenience. Retake the failed items. Repeat this cycle until passing scores have been obtained. In the meantime, go on to the next tests.
6. An item not answered represents an incorrect response. Exceptions are items you judge ambiguous, not merely difficult or unfamiliar. Mark ambiguous items (X) without answering them.
7. Mark your answers on separate answer forms, which are not provided in the book. Or use color-coded ink to circle responses in the book. Use a different ink each time you retake mistaken items.
8. Competency tests are not timed. They can be taken in any order—minimum competency tests in conjunction with mastery tests—as handicappers prefer.

When the twelve mastery tests have been completed satisfactorily, handicappers who had trouble exceeding the standards are urged to take the tests again consecutively, all 557 items, at a double or triple marathon session or on consecutive days for long periods. Proficiency standards on the retesting is 80 percent mastery, or 445 items correct. The repetition is for emphasis, a tactic of competency-based instruction.

Interested handicappers can conduct a pretest-posttest experiment with the pair of achievement tests.

Take Performance Test A before attempting any of the competency tests.

When all twelve mastery tests have been finished satisfactorily, take Performance Test A again. Look for a significantly higher percentage-correct score, perhaps 20 percent improvement, or for a raw score of 20 items correct (33 percent proficiency).

A variation of this procedure has handicappers complete the odd items (30) of form A prior to completing the competency tests, and the even items (30) of form A following the competency tests. This reduces the testing time, without overly distorting results. Expect the same positive changes. If this variation is followed, retake the odd items as well after completing the even items on the posttest, and obtain a total test score. Use the scoring procedure outlined.

Finally, as soon as possible after completing form A, take Performance Test B. This should enhance the second score, at least some. Record your form B answers on the answer key provided. Score form B for your own information.

Afterward, submit Performance Test B's answer form to be evaluated in relation to other handicappers' scores—without changing any of the original responses, of course. I implore any suddenly weak-kneed test-takers to appreciate that changing incorrect answers to correct after looking is not only cheating oneself, but will distort the norming procedure and resulting percentile ranks.

On the matter of percentile scores, a low raw score does not necessarily equal a low precentile rank. Depending on the raw scores of others, low raw scores often will be converted to unexpectedly high percentile scores. It happens all the time. Do not despair too soon. You may be looking better than you think!

The academic presentation ends here. Now the fun begins.

PART B
Competency Tests

Past Performance Tables and Results Charts

Competencies

1. Know the meanings of symbols and data items.
2. Identify the points of call at various distances.
3. Calculate fractional times and lengths gained or lost.
4. Interpret past performances and chart data in terms of the handicapping information they represent.

	Minimum Competency Test	Mastery Test
Proficiency standards	90%	X
Number of items	40	X
Passing scores	36	X

Sources of Instruction

- *Ainslie's Complete Guide to Thoroughbred Racing*, Chapter 20
- *Betting Thoroughbreds*, Chapter 3
- *The Winning Horseplayer*, Appendix 1
- *Daily Racing Form*, "How to Read the Past Performances," a regular feature.

Comments

The regional editions of the *Daily Racing Form* differ from one another slightly. Readers of the Eastern edition can be excused from item #3 and item #40 below. No other excuses should be plausible to handicappers for missing the items here.

No new terms beg for definition. The numerals in parentheses beside each item refer to the competencies each item assesses.

On this subject only, no mastery test follows the minimum competency test.

MINIMUM COMPETENCY TEST

1. Which horse has performed best in the mud?

A. Broad Brush X **(1)**
B. Danzig Connection *
C. *Muralto
D. *Erimo's Lady *

2. Which workout was best at the distance that morning?

A. 34⅕ b **(1)**
B. *47 h
C. 59 hg
D. 1:00 b(d)

3. Which horse wears blinkers?

A. **(1)**

Earthland B. f. 4, by Northern Baby—Joy Land, by Bold Ruler
Br.—Hancock & Bowen (Ky) 1987 1 M 0 1 $3,750
MCHARGUE D G 124 Tr.—Nor Fabio 1986 3 M 0 0
Own.—Nor Joanne H Lifetime 4 0 0 1 $3,750 Turf 3 0 0 0
19Mar87-6SA 1 :47^{1} 1:13 1:39 ft 14 120 6$^{6\frac{1}{2}}$ 4$^{2\frac{1}{2}}$ 3^{4} 3$^{6\frac{1}{4}}$ DelahoussyeE^{3} [F]Mdn 67-21 FabulousTrick,LaurenLeigh,Erthlnd 9
19Aug86◆3Wexford(Eng) a1$\frac{7}{16}$ 2:52^{3}gd 7 118 [T] 12^{39} MnnKJ Eniscrthy Plt(Mdn) Excellency, Rapazola, Lindbergh 12
21May86◆4Navan(Ire) 1¼ 2:35^{4}sf 5 123 [T] 8^{20} GillspD Klmssn Plt(Mdn) IdleTale,GallantGold,FestivalTown 25
31Mar86◆6Mallow(Ire) 1⅛ 2:10^{1}sf *4-5 123 [T] 5^{12} GillespiD City Plt(Mdn) WorldCourt,Euripus,CllysKingdom 14
Apr 28 Hol 5f ft 1:00^{4} h Apr 22 Hol 5f ft 1:00^{1} h Apr 18 Hol 3f ft :37^{3} h Mar 15 Hol 4f ft :48^{4} hg

B.

Hilo Baba B. f. 3, by Raja Baba—Hilo Hop, by T V Lark
Br.—Bettersworth J R (Ky) 1987 2 M 0 1 $3,875
VALENZUELA P A 115 Tr.—Jones Gary 1986 2 M 2 0 $7,400
Own.—Paulson A E Lifetime 4 0 2 1 $11,275
5Apr87-4SA 6½f :22^{2} :46^{1} 1:17^{4}ft *8-5e 117 3$^{1\frac{1}{2}}$ 6^{5} 5$^{7\frac{1}{2}}$ 5$^{6\frac{3}{4}}$ Toro F^{8} [F]Mdn 74-16 CreamSauce,NoRomance,PrivteArt 8
5Apr87—Bumped start; lugged in backstretch
15Mar87-4SA 6f :22^{1} :45^{2} 1:10^{2}ft *6-5e 117 3^{2} 4^{5} 3$^{5\frac{1}{2}}$ 3$^{5\frac{3}{4}}$ Valenzuela PA^{3} [F]Mdn 80-20 Fleet Road, Charmed One,HiloBaba 9
20Dec86-6Hol 7f :22^{1} :45^{4} 1:24 ft *6-5 118 3$^{2\frac{1}{2}}$ 3$^{2\frac{1}{2}}$ 2$^{2\frac{1}{2}}$ 2$^{2\frac{3}{4}}$ Valenzuela PA^{6} [F]Mdn 81-15 Chic Shirine, Hilo Baba, Cee'sVigor 8
15Nov86-6Hol 6f :22 :46^{2} 1:11^{4}ft 8-5e 118 4$^{1\frac{1}{4}}$ 3$^{1\frac{1}{2}}$ 3$^{2\frac{1}{2}}$ 2^{5} Valenzuela PA^{8} [F]Mdn 79-14 TimelyAssertion,HiloBb,LivlyMiss 11
15Nov86—Wide 3/8; lugged in stretch
Apr 24 Hol 4f ft :47 h Apr 18 Hol 3f ft :36^{3} h Apr 2 Hol 4f ft :52^{3} b ●Mar 28 Hol 4f ft :47^{3} h

C.

Ninepaytheline Ch. f. 3, by Golden Eagle II—Only a Rose, by Groton
Br.—Auerbach E A (Cal) 1987 3 M 0 2 $6,875
MEZA R Q 115 Tr.—Tinsley J E Jr 1986 4 M 1 0 $7,550
Own.—Hirmez & Sittu Lifetime 7 0 1 2 $14,425
25Apr87-4Hol 6f :22 :45^{3} 1:10^{3}ft 21 110^{5} 8$^{6\frac{1}{2}}$ 8^{9} 5$^{8\frac{1}{2}}$ 3^{6} Patton D B^{9} [F]Mdn 84-13 Raise You, Flood, Ninepaytheline 9
25Apr87—Wide
18Apr87-6SA 6½f :22^{1} :45^{2} 1:17^{4}ft 12 117 5^{3} 5$^{3\frac{1}{2}}$ 5^{7} 3$^{10\frac{1}{2}}$ Sibille R^{4} [F][S]Mdn 70-18 Pirte'sKernel,NoRomnc,Ninpythlin 8
18Apr87—Wide final 3/8
4Apr87-3SA 6f :21^{2} :44^{1} 1:10^{1}ft 9¾ 117 5$^{3\frac{3}{4}}$ 4$^{4\frac{1}{2}}$ 5^{9} 5$^{9\frac{1}{4}}$ CastanonAL^{7} [F][S]Mdn 78-17 MissSprinklt,Pirt'sKrnl,JklinAndHd 8
18Aug86-8Dmr 7f :22 :44^{3} 1:22^{3}ft 27 115 7$^{4\frac{1}{4}}$ 8^{7} 8^{11} 9^{16} BazeRA^{2} [F]Sorrento 76-14 Brave Raj, Breech, Footy 10
18Aug86—Grade III
9Aug86-6Dmr 6f :22^{1} :45^{3} 1:11^{4}ft 2¾ 117 6$^{2\frac{3}{4}}$ 8$^{4\frac{1}{4}}$ 6$^{3\frac{1}{2}}$ 5^{4} ShoemkerW^{5} [F][S]Mdn 75-14 WildManor,Kavalla,HeavyWeather 10
9Aug86—Bumped start; steadied at 3 1/2, again at 1/8
25Jly86-8Dmr 6f :22 :45^{2} 1:11 ft 13 114 5$^{3\frac{1}{2}}$ 5$^{2\frac{3}{4}}$ 5$^{3\frac{1}{4}}$ 4$^{2\frac{1}{4}}$ BlackCA^{2} [F][S]C T B A 81-18 SrosBrig,JoeyTheTrip,WindyTripIK. 8
25Jly86—Wide late
11Jly86-6Hol 5½f :22^{2} :45^{4} 1:04^{2}ft 15 113^{5} 8$^{7\frac{1}{2}}$ 8$^{8\frac{3}{4}}$ 5$^{8\frac{1}{2}}$ 2^{9} Black C A^{8} [F]Mdn 83-14 Schuist,Ninepythlin,AlwysAWomn 11
Apr 15 SA 4f ft :48^{3} h Mar 29 SA 5f ft 1:00^{2} h Mar 23 SA 5f ft 1:02^{1} h Mar 17 SA 6f ft 1:14^{1} hg

D.

Emerald Eve — B. f. 3, by Green Dancer—Sparkling Spear, by Raise a Native
Br.—North Ridge Farm (Ky) — 1987 4 M 0 1 $7,150
SIBILLE R 115 — Tr.—Moreno Henry — 1986 0 M 0 0
Own.—Wichita Equine Inc (Lessee) — Lifetime 4 0 0 1 $7,150

5Apr87-4SA	6½f :22^2	:46^1	1:17^{4}ft	7¾	117	$5^{2\frac{1}{2}}$	$4^{3\frac{1}{2}}$	$4^{6\frac{1}{2}}$	$4^{5\frac{3}{4}}$	Sibille R 7	ⒻMdn	75-16	CreamSauce,NoRomance,PrivteArt	8
5Apr87—Bumped start														
22Mar87-6SA	6½f :21^4	:45^2	1:19^{1}gd	3¼	118	$6^{3\frac{1}{2}}$	5^4	5^4	4^4	Pincay L Jr 7	ⒻMdn	70-23	HlloSwtThng,MndstMnk,VvSllyAnn	8
7Mar87-6SA	7f :22^4	:45^4	1:23^{4}gd	*2¼	117	$2^{\frac{1}{2}}$	2^1	$5^{7\frac{1}{2}}$	$5^{11\frac{3}{4}}$	Pincay L Jr 5	ⒻMdn	69-19	Rose's Record,Reiterate,WhiteFury	8
7Mar87—Broke in, bumped														
15Feb87-3SA	6½f :22^3	:45^3	1:17^{2}m	4¼	117	2^{hd}	$2^{\frac{1}{2}}$	3^4	3^5	McHargue DG 2	ⒻMdn	78-17	GentleSpirit,Rose'sRecord,EmrldEv	6

Apr 29 Hol 4f ft :49^4 h — Apr 23 Hol 5f ft 1:02^1 h — Apr 11 SA 4f ft :49^2 h — Apr 3 SA 3f rt :36 h

4. A speed rating of 82 in the *Daily Racing Form* means

A. The track surface was 18 lengths slow **(1)**
B. The horse ran 3⅗ seconds slower than the track record for the distance
C. The winner ran 18 lengths slower than the track record for the distance
D. The final time was 3⅗ seconds below par for the class

5. A daily variant of 22 published by the *Daily Racing Form* means

A. The winners that day finished 22 lengths behind the track records for the distances on average **(1)**
B. The horse ran 4⅖ seconds slower than the track's distance record
C. The track surface was 22 lengths slow that day
D. The final time for the race was roughly four seconds slower than usual

6. If the *Form* speed rating and daily variant are added and the sum equals 102, that means

A. It was not a particularly fast race **(4)**
B. The horse ran two lengths faster than the typical winner that day
C. The winner ran faster than the track record for the distance
D. The track surface was relatively even that day

7. The pre-stretch call at 1¼ mile occurs at

A. ¾M **(2)**
B. 1M
C. 1⅛M
D. ½M

8. The first call of routes from 1M to 1¾M occurs after the horses have run ½M.

   A. True   **(2)**
   B. False

9. The second call of a 1¹⁄₁₆M route is how far from the finish line?

   A. ⅞M   **(2)**
   B. ½M
   C. ⁵⁄₁₆M
   D. ¼M

10. At 1¼M, the second call occurs after the horses have run

   A. 6F   **(2)**
   B. 1M
   C. 1¹⁄₁₆M
   D. 1⅛M

11. At 1½M, the first call occurs after the horses have run

   A. ¼M   **(2)**
   B. ½M
   C. ¾M
   D. 1M

12. In races of 1¹⁄₁₆M, the first call is always after ·

   A. ¼M   **(2)**
   B. ½M
   C. 6F
   D. 1M

13. Regardless of distance, the stretch call always occurs at the ⅛th pole.

   A. True   **(2)**
   B. False

14. Which are the first and second calls of a 5-furlong dash for 2-year-olds?

   A. ¼M and ½M   **(2)**
   B. ¹⁄₁₆M and ⅜M

C. ⅛M and ¼M
D. 3⁄16M and ⅜M

15. At 1½M, the second call occurs after the horses have run

A. ½M (2)
B. ¾M
C. 1M
D. 1¼M

16. How fast did the place horse run in the stretch?

A. 13⅖ (3)
B. 30⅖
C. 13⅕
D. 30⅕

FIRST RACE
Aqueduct
OCTOBER 29, 1986

1 ⅛ MILES.(Turf). (1.47) CLAIMING. Purse $20,000. Fillies and mares. 3-years-old and upward. Weight, 3-year-olds 119 lbs.; older, 122 lbs. Non-winners of two races at a mile or over since October 1 allowed 3 lbs.; of such a race since then 5 lbs. Claiming price $35,000. (Races when entered to be claimed for $25,000 or less not considered.) (7th Day. WEATHER CLEAR. TEMPERATURE 66 DEGREES)

Value of race $20,000; value to winner $12,000; second $4,400; third $2,400; fourth $1,200. Mutuel pool $42,832, OTB pool $108,914. Exacta Pool $42,174. OTB Exacta Pool $87,396.

Last Raced	Horse	Eqt.	A.	Wt	PP	St	¼	½	¾	Str	Fin	Jockey	Cl'g Pr	Odds $1
22Oct86 ^{5}Aqu^{5}	Deauville Love		4	112	4	7	7	7	1^{hd}	1^{5}	$1^{4\frac{1}{2}}$	Baird E T^{5}	35000	16.50
18Oct86 ^{3}Bel^{6}	Diplomat's Needle	b	5	117	6	5	6^{2}	$6^{1\frac{1}{2}}$	3^{hd}	$2^{1\frac{1}{2}}$	$2^{\frac{1}{2}}$	Martens G	35000	6.60
23Oct86 ^{6}Aqu^{6}	Colloquium		3	114	1	1	5^{1}	5^{hd}	6^{3}	4^{hd}	$3^{\frac{1}{2}}$	Migliore R	35000	1.90
18Oct86 ^{3}Bel^{4}	Lady Dictator	b	5	117	3	6	4^{2}	$4^{1\frac{1}{2}}$	5^{hd}	5^{4}	$4^{\frac{1}{2}}$	Cruguet J	35000	1.90
17Oct86 ^{5}Med^{6}	Tricky Tune	b	5	110	7	4	3^{hd}	3^{hd}	4^{2}	$3^{\frac{1}{2}}$	$5^{13\frac{1}{2}}$	Ortiz E^{7}	35000	16.90
18Oct86 ^{3}Bel^{10}	Her Mink		4	107	2	3	2^{hd}	2^{1}	7	7	$6^{5\frac{3}{4}}$	Nuesch D^{10}	35000	7.10
29Sep86 ^{5}Bel^{4}	Sweet Renee	b	4	117	5	2	1^{6}	1^{6}	2^{1}	6^{2}	7	Ward W A	35000	5.00

OFF AT 12:30 Start good, Won handily. Time, :24⅖, :48⅕, 1:14⅖, 1:41⅕, 1:54⅗ Course good.

17. If the August 31 stretch call were timed as 58⅗ seconds, how fast did *Noholme Gold* run in the stretch?

A. 19⅘ (3)
B. 33⅕
C. 32⅕
D. 18⅘

Noholme Gold — **Dk. b. or br. g. 2, by Noholme Way—Little Gyro, by Mr Mustard**
BAZE R A **114** — **Br.—Hoctor C & Cynthia (Wash)** — **1986 6 1 0 0 $4,345**
Tr.—Klokstad Bud **$25,000**
Own.—Kays & Klokstad — **Lifetime 6 1 0 0 $4,345**

31Aug66-8Lga	6½f :22	:45^{1}	1:18^{2}ft	8	121	$5^{1\frac{1}{4}}$	$4^{3\frac{1}{4}}$	5^{8}	$5^{3\frac{1}{4}}$	Aragon V A^{9}	Aw11100	74-22	OhShckyDrn,‡SrGhrrdll,BnchryFy	10
23Aug86-9Lga	6f :21^{3}	:44^{2}	1:10^{1}ft	29	116	11^{13}	10^{11}	9^{16}	$7^{7\frac{1}{2}}$	HnsnRD^{6}	[R]Wash Brds	77-15	A'laNatural,Runagte,OhShuckyDrn	13
2Aug86-9Lga	6f :21^{3}	:45	1:10 ft	*7-5e	120	3^{3}	$4^{5\frac{1}{2}}$	13^{22}	$13^{17\frac{1}{4}}$	Loseth C^{12}	Strplng	69-16	O. K. Yet, Hear The Band, Utewin	14
19Jly86-6Lga	5½f :22^{1}	:45^{3}	1:05 ft	9	120	1^{hd}	2^{hd}	$1^{1\frac{1}{2}}$	$1^{1\frac{1}{2}}$	Hansen R D^{6}	M40000	87-17	NoholmeGold,Sm'sDerby,BldeRejct	9
11Jly86-6Lga	5½f :22^{1}	:46^{1}	1:06^{2}gd	3½	120	$5^{2\frac{3}{4}}$	$5^{8\frac{1}{2}}$	$6^{8\frac{1}{2}}$	$6^{10\frac{1}{2}}$	Hansen R D^{6}	[S]M25000	69-22	Stogie, Apple Market, Regal Tide	7
27Jun86-3Lga	5f :22^{1}	:45^{4}	:57^{4}ft	7½	120	—	—	—	—	DominguzRE^{10}	M25000	— —	SarajevoMerit,Utewin,AppleMrket	10

27Jun86—Lost rider
Oct 25 BM 5f ft 1:01^{2} h **Oct 19 BM 5f ft 1:01^{4} h** **Oct 12 BM 4f ft :48^{3} b**

18. Which race represents the fastest come-home time in *Spark of Love's* record?

A. Oct. 5 (3)
B. July 3

C. June 22
D. June 4

Spark of Love — B. g. 3, by Foolish Pleasure—Spark of Life, by Key to the Mint
Br.—Mellon P (Va) — 1986 9 2 0 1 $35,880
Own.—Rokeby Stable — 115 — Tr.—Miller Mack — Turf 2 0 0 0
Lifetime 9 2 0 1 $35,880

5Oct86-5Bel 1 :47 1:11^4 1:36^{3}ft 5 114 53¼ 5^4 5^6 46¾ Romero R P^8 Aw26000 75-18 BetterBeSingle,GrenKnight,FstStp 8
14Aug86-5Sar 1$\frac{1}{16}$ Ⓣ:45^{4}1:09^{4}1:41 fm 15 114 8^{11} 78½ 7^{10} 611¼ Bailey J D^5 Aw26000 81-15 El Jefe, Deity Dash, Dancin OnPins 9
4Aug86-6Sar 1$\frac{3}{16}$ Ⓣ:49^{1}1:13 1:57^{4}gd 14 114 116½109¾ 87¾ 86½ Bailey J D^7 Aw26000 70-21 ‡AgnTomorrow,NggtPnt,UpprBnd 11
3Jly86-7Bel 1$\frac{1}{16}$:47^4 1:12 1:42^{3}ft 3 113 4^3 31½ 1^{hd} 1½ Bailey J D^3 Aw25000 89-16 SprkofLove,NovembrBns,JohnMuir 6
22Jun86-5Bel 1 :47^3 1:11^3 1:36^{1}ft 5¾ 114 3^2 31½ 3^4 43¾ Bailey J D^5 Aw25000 80-19 DecortdEmpror,GoldAlrt,JohnMuir 7
4Jun86-3Bel 1$\frac{1}{16}$:46^2 1:11^2 1:44^{3}ft *1 122 31½ 1^{hd} 11½ 11¾ Santos J A^7 Mdn 79-22 SparkofLove,MnosDePiedr,Dimtion 7
25May86-1Bel 1 :46^1 1:10^2 1:35^{1}ft 4¾e113 96½ 76½ 56½ 59¾ Bailey J D^8 Mdn 79-12 ‡Macbest,StageWhisper,GallicWar 12
25May86—Placed fourth through disqualification
14May86-4Bel 7f :22^2 :45 1:22^{3}ft 8e122 6^8 6^9 57½ 55½ Santos J A^6 Mdn 83-15 Michel'sDncr,ClssicMov,Convntionr 6
Oct 26 Bel 6f ft 1:14 h Oct 21 Bel 4f ft :47^3 h Oct 17 Bel 5f ft 1:01 h Oct 11 Bel 4f ft :49^4 b

19. In the past performances above for *Spark of Love*, how fast did the winner run the final quarter-mile on Oct. 5?

A. $24\frac{4}{5}$ **(3)**
B. 25
C. $25\frac{2}{5}$
D. data not available

20. Which horse below ran the fastest second fraction in its last race?

A. *Affirmed Native* **(3)**
B. *Count the House*
C. *Golden Groom*
D. *Sand and Sea*

Affirmed Native — B. g. 4, by Affirmed—Asbury Mary, by Seven Corners
BAZE R A [redacted] 120 — Br.—Tillman I C (Md) — 1986 9 2 1 1 $12,025
Tr.—Hollendorfer Jerry $6,250 — 1985 6 0 1 1 $6,415
Own.—Halo Farms — Lifetime 25 3 2 4 $32,200 — Turf 1 0 0 0

11Oct86-3BM 6f :22^2 :45^3 1:10^{2}ft *6-5 120 64¾ 41¼ 1^4 1^6 Baze R A^4 6250 87-18 AffirmdNtv,NturlShow,HustlADnc 10
26Sep86-7Pom 6f :22^3 :47^3 1:14^{1}sl 3½ 116 5^3 3^2 2^{hd} 1^{nk} Castanon A L^9 6250 80-29 AffirmedNtive,Mr.BrAbl,Jov'sSilor 10
26Sep86—Wide 1st turn
22Sep86-13Pom 1$\frac{1}{16}$:46^1 1:11^2 1:44^{3}ft 9 116 43½ 32½ 66¾ 69¾ Castanon A L^8 8500 78-19 ScheerBob,Orn'sBllrd,VisibleAsset 10

Count The House — B. g. 5, by Nostalgia—First Census, by Best Turn
SCHVANEVELDT C P [redacted] 114 — Br.—Mabee Mr-Mrs J C (Cal) — 1986 10 3 0 1 $12,880
Tr.—Clements John $6,250 — 1985 19 1 2 2 $18,120
Own.—Cope R — Lifetime 39 6 3 4 $64,500 — Turf 2 0 0 0 $1,650

17Oct86-2BM 6f :22^1 :45^3 1:10^{3}ft 3½ 114 42½ 2^1 42½ 4^5 SchvaneveldtCP^6 6250 81-16 PicO'Morn,SpouseTroubl,EmrldCut 7
4Oct86-3BM 6f :22^2 :45^3 1:10^{4}ft 5 115 75½ 7^8 66¾ 64¾ Hummel C R^{11} 6250 80-16 StreetsmartNative,StrRoute,Roots 11
13Sep86-7Bmf 6f :23 :46^3 1:12^{1}ft 11 115 52½ 62½ 4^2 3^{nk} SchvnevldtCP^9 Ⓢ 6250 78-31 FleetWver,ClLLuIh,CountThHous 12

Golden Groom — Ch. g. 7, by Wheres Goldie—Summer Bride, by Summer Tan
TOHILL K S [redacted] 114 — Br.—McGhan Farms (Cal) — 1986 14 0 1 2 $3,073
Tr.—Orr Ike $6,250 — 1984 10 0 0 1 $767
Own.—Sherry Ann Stable — Lifetime 39 6 3 3 $35,910 — Turf 1 0 0 0

24Oct86-5BM 6f :22^3 :45^4 1:11^{4}ft 27 114 9^8 56¼ 56¼ 6^4 Tohill K S^2 Ⓢ 6250 76-25 HoldTheDic,PromisMRb,IrishGurd 12
11Oct86-7BM 6f :22 :45 1:10^{3}ft 52 114 108¾ 9^{10} 98¼ 76¼ Ochoa A^{12} 10000 80-18 UntdVctory,ShdwWtch,WstsdGrg 12
26Jly86-8SR 5½f :22 :45^4 1:03^{4}ft 24 114 4^4 32½ 4^6 74¾ Ochoa A^6 Ⓢ 6250 87-08 PetesInnate,Pat'sLnding,MjorBill 10

Sand And Sea — Ch. g. 6, by Windy Sea—Rowisa, by Windy Sands
HANSEN R D [redacted] 114 — Br.—Tradewind Thrghbd Fm (Cal) — 1986 2 0 1 0 $1,170
Tr.—Dutton Jerry $6,250 — 1985 4 1 2 0 $12,900
Own.—Volkman R — Lifetime 21 3 7 1 $56,795

11Oct86-7BM 6f :22 :45 1:10^{3}ft *2½ 114 2^{hd} 1^{hd} 41¾ 86½ Chapman T M^8 10000 79-18 UntdVctory,ShdwWtch,WstsdGrg 12
28Sep86-5BM 6f :22^3 :46 1:11^{1}ft *2¼ 114 2^{hd} 11½ 1^3 2^2 Chapman T M^{10} c6250 81-18 KuKanaka,SandAndSea,GreyZnthe 12
10Nov85-7BM 6f :22^1 :45^2 1:10^{4}m 3½ 117 1^{hd} 2^{hd} 3^2 911½ Wilburn J^1 10000 74-28 BeOnGuard,NuestroSol,Contequos 11
10Nov85—Lugged out backstretch

21. Which horse above ran the fastest final fraction in its last race?

A. *Affirmed Native* **(3)**
B. *Count the House*
C. *Golden Groom*
D. *Sand and Sea*

22. How fast did the lead horse complete the second fraction on Oct. 24?

A. 23 **(3)**
B. 24⅗
C. 24
D. 47

Commonwealth Club — Ch. c. 3, by Key To The Mint—Virginiana, by Sir Ivor

Own.—Rokeby Stables **120** — Br.—Mellon P (Va) — Tr.—Miller Mack

1986 3 M 0 0 — 1985 0 M 0 0

Lifetime 3 0 0 0

24Oct86-6Aqu	6f	:23	:47	$1:11^{3}$ft	*6-5e	119	$1^{\frac12}$	$1^{\frac12}$	$3^{3\frac12}$	5^{6}	Guerra W A^{1}	Mdn	77-20	GlttrngDwn,NorthrnGod,BllyWlbr		13
15Jun86-3Bel	$1\frac{1}{16}$	:46	$1:10^{2}$	$1:43^{4}$ft	4e	114	6^{7}	5^{12}	5^{15}	$7^{23\frac12}$	Santos J A^{5}	Mdn	59-21	JackOfClubs,MnosDePiedr,Royume		8
21May86-3Bel	6f	:22	$:44^{4}$	1:10 gd	37	122	9^{13}	8^{12}	8^{15}	$9^{22\frac12}$	Bailey J D^{9}	Mdn	69-16	Dashing Groom, Ormonte, Litany		11

Oct 30 Bel 4f ft $:47^{3}$ h — Oct 20 Bel 4f ft :49 hg — Oct 15 Bel 4f sy $:46^{2}$ h — Oct 11 Bel 3f ft $:36^{1}$ b

23. How many lengths did *The Savage* gain in the stretch of its last winning race?

A. 4¼ **(3)**
B. 6
C. 7¾
D. 2½

The Savage — Gr. c. 3, by I'ma Hell Raiser—Millie and Me, by Wise Exchange

Own.—Schwartz B K **115** — Br.—Stonewall Farm (NY) — Tr.—Levine Bruce

1986 12 2 1 2 $50,102 — Turf 1 0 0 0

Lifetime 12 2 1 2 $50,102

9Oct86-7Bel	$1\frac{1}{16}$Ⓣ	$:47^{3}$	1:12	$1:44^{2}$fm	$8\frac14$	114	$10^{9\frac34}$	11^{12}	11^{11}	$11^{12\frac14}$	$MiglioreR^{11}$	[S]Aw29500	62-26	VtzMtter,ExpditionMoon,RcPoint		12
27Sep86-4Bel	7f	$:22^{1}$	$:45^{2}$	$1:23^{4}$sy	5	113	$7^{8\frac12}$	7^{10}	$5^{8\frac12}$	$5^{11\frac34}$	Santos J A^{1}	70000	71-17	Golden Olden, Shear, B. C. Sal		8
9Aug86-1Sar	$1\frac18$	$:47^{4}$	$1:11^{4}$	$1:51^{1}$ft	$2\frac12$	113	4^{7}	$4^{5\frac12}$	$4^{3\frac12}$	3^{2}	Murphy D J^{6}	70000	77-17	TheLoneRnger,ForTheGippr,ThSvg		7
26Jly86-5Bel	6f	$:22^{4}$	:47	$1:11^{4}$ft	$3\frac34$	111	7^{9}	7^{10}	6^{6}	$5^{2\frac14}$	$GuerraWA^{5}$	[S]Aw28000	81-28	Exmoon, Flag King, What A Philip		8
26Apr86-8Aqu	1	$:45^{3}$	$1:10^{1}$	$1:36^{1}$ft	4e	112	$9^{8\frac34}$	$9^{9\frac12}$	$6^{8\frac14}$	5^{10}	$MrpDJ^{6}$	[S]Big Apple H	75-16	LndngPlot,I'mYorBy,NstyAndTgh		11
6Apr86-8Aqu	7f	:23	$:46^{1}$	$1:23^{1}$m	$6\frac12$e	114·	$9^{5\frac34}$	$9^{5\frac34}$	$7^{5\frac34}$	$4^{7\frac34}$	$MrpDJ^{3}$	[S]D Clinton H	77-20	Tnchn'sPrnc,NstyAndTogh,MdSyn		10
29Mar86-4Aqu	6f	:23	$:46^{4}$	$1:11^{3}$ft	$6\frac34$	112	$10^{5\frac34}$	$8^{4\frac14}$	5^{2}	$4^{3\frac12}$	$MurphyDJ^{3}$	[S]Aw28000	75-21	RstlssSson,H.T.Willis,Tuckr'sCbin		10
29Mar86—Bmpd start																
9Mar86-1Aqu	1^{70}[•]	$:49^{2}$	1:15	$1:46^{3}$ft	*2	117	6^{5}	7^{6}	$3^{2\frac12}$	$1^{1\frac34}$	$MurphyDJ^{4}$	[S]Aw29500	67-27	The Savage,MasterDamon,MediSyn		8

Oct 30 Aqu 6f ft $1:16^{2}$ b — Sep 25 Aqu 3f ft $:36^{1}$ h — Sep 16 Aqu 5f ft $1:02^{1}$ h — ●Sep 11 Aqu 6f ft $1:13^{2}$ h

24. How fast did *Mistress Montague* run between the first and second calls on Oct. 18?

A. 31 **(3)**
B. 25⅖
C. 24⅘
D. data not available

Mistress Montague — Ch. f. 4, by Gallant Romeo—Regent Gal, by Vice Regent
Own.—Morgans-Ford Farm — **115** — Br.—Kasper A A (Ky) — Tr.—Wright William W

1986	10	1	3	1	$30,640
1985	7	3	0	0	$38,283
Lifetime	17	4	3	1	$68,923
Turf	1	0	0	0	

18Oct86-6Med	170	:461	1:11	1:42	ft	5	113	31	43½	67	1010¼	SntsJA1	ⒻSisterhood	76-15	FrostyVlentine,IMenIt,BriefRmrks	[illegible]
12Oct86-7Bel	7f	:22	:434	1:23	ft	28	115	59	415	37½	21½	Day P6	ⒻAw36000	85-13	ReelEsy,MistressMontgue,Argntrio	[illegible]
30Jly86-6Sar	6½f	:221	:451	1:16	ft	35	115	46	66½	813	812½	Cruguet J9	ⒻAw36000	79-13	Clemann'sRose,Verblity,Gene'sLdy	[illegible]
18Jly86-8Bel	1 1/16	:461	1:104	1:421	ft	13	114	2hd	52½	512	518½	Cruguet J6	ⒻHcp0	72-12	CoupDeFusil,PtriciJ.K.,KeyWitness	7
30Jun86-8Bel	1	:461	1:103	1:361	ft	6	117	31½	22½	23	22¾	Cruguet J2	ⒻAw40000	81-21	BrownCrown,MistressMontgu,LSlw	5
22May86-7Bel	7f	:223	:453	1:232	sy	3	119	2hd	21	512	613¾	Cruguet J7	ⒻAw36000	71-15	SlntAccount,BrownCrown,KyWtnss	7
19Apr86-10Hia	1 1/16 Ⓣ			1:413	fm	14e	113	42	42½	1015	1210¼	DrtJC15	ⒻColumbinH	80-14	SoSheSleeps,LakeCountry,Bilrullh	16
19Apr86—Grade III																
29Mar86-8Hia	1 1/16	:454	1:094	1:421	gd	2½	117	12	12½	11½	12½	Cruguet J1	ⒻAw14000	92-06	MstrssMontgu,MdmoslIJol,DrbyLdy	7

Oct 29 Bel tr.t 6f gd 1:151 b   Oct 11 Bel 3f ft :364 b   Oct 6 Bel 5f ft 1:00 h   Sep 30 Bel 5f ft :593 h

25. How many lengths was *Waynette* beaten at the second call?

A. 5 **(3)**
B. 1½
C. 1
D. 4

FIRST RACE
Ak-Sar-Ben
JULY 20, 1986

6 FURLONGS. (1.07⅗) CLAIMING. Purse $5,500 (plus $800 from NTBDF). Fillies. 3-year-olds. Weight, 122 lbs. Non-winners of two races since June 20 allowed 2 lbs.; a race since then, 4 lbs.; a race since May 20, 6 lbs. Claiming price $11,000; for each $500 to $9,000 allowed 1 lb. (Races where entered for $8,500 or less not considered in allowances). 61st DAY. WEATHER CLEAR. TEMPERATURE 81 DEGREES.

Total purse $6,300. Value of race $5,500; value to winner $3,300; second $1,100; third $605; fourth $330; fifth $165. ($800 reverts to NTBDF). Mutuel pool $47,933.

Last Raced	Horse	Eqt.	A.	Wt	PP	St	¼	½	Str	Fin	Jockey	Cl'g Pr	Odds $1
12Jly86 1Aks7	Bets Lass	b	3	118	8	1	2½	1½	1hd	1¾	Pettinger D R	11000	2.80
6Jly86 4Aks6	Rammerillo	b	3	112	9	4	32	2½	21	2no	Cordova D W	9000	17.70
25Jun86 2Aks2	Waynette		3	116	3	2	41	54	43	32	Williams R D	11000	6.20
3Jly86 4Aks1	Melissa's Phantom		3	120	6	6	51	4hd	3hd	4½	Doocy T T	11000	.90
25Jun86 2Aks9	Kel Jo's Princess		3	114	4	8	85	6½	5½	5½	Walker B J Jr	10000	48.30
12Jly86 1Aks6	Spotlight Gal	b	3	116	2	7	7½	73	6½	61½	Guerra V J	11000	9.80
12Jly86 1Aks9	My Mom's Easy	b	3	120	7	9	9	81	7½	72	McGurn C	11000	20.50
6Jly86 4Aks5	Miss Princess Bank	b	3	116	5	3	1½	3½	87	89	Patterson G	11000	18.10
15Jun86 5Ato6	Kelsey Lea		3	115	1	5	6hd	9	9	9	Anderson W	9000	64.40

OFF AT 2:01. Start good. Won driving. Time, :22⅘, :45⅘, :58⅖, 1:12 Track fast.

26. Using the chart below, which is true of *Barbitoo* at the stretch call?

A. She was 1½ lengths behind the winner **(3)**
B. She had gained 3½ lengths on the winner
C. She was 1½ lengths ahead of the 4th horse
D. She had gained 3½ lengths on *Fare*

SEVENTH RACE
Ak-Sar-Ben
JULY 20, 1986

1 1/16 MILES. (1.40⅗) CLAIMING. Purse $6,000 (plus $1,000 from NTBDF). Fillies and mares. 4-year-olds and upward. Weight, 122 lbs. Non-winners of two races at one mile or over since June 20 allowed 2 lbs.; one such race, 4 lbs.; such a race since May 30, 6 lbs. Claiming price $10,000; for each $500 to $8,000 allowed 1 lb. (Races where entered for $7,500 or less not considered in allowances.)

Total purse $7,000. Value of race $6,000; value to winner $3,600; second $1,200; third $660; fourth $360; fifth $180. ($1,000 reverts to NTBDF.) Mutuel pool $100,970.

Last Raced	Horse	Eqt.	A.	Wt	PP	St	¼	½	¾	Str	Fin	Jockey	Cl'g Pr	Odds $1
26Jun86 4Aks2	Steel Josie		5	116	5	7	8	7hd	6hd	22	1nk	Guerra V J	10000	6.00
11Jly86 9Aks1	Fare		6	116	6	4	4hd	3½	2hd	12	24	Cordova D W	10000	1.20
6Jly86 6Aks2	Barbitoo		4	116	8	3	64	63	75	31½	32	Doocy T T	10000	6.30
10Jly86 5Aks4	ⒹSarpy County Gang	b	4	116	2	2	22	2hd	3½	4½	41	Masters T A	10000	14.90
3Jly86 7Aks5	Sweet Murr		5	118	4	6	3hd	41	51	56	55	Maple S	10000	12.20
6Jly86 6Aks8	Infinite Sidney		5	116	1	8	72	8	8	62	63½	Cordova B J	10000	44.00

3Jly86 ^{7}Aks^{4}	Fire Jumper	4 111	3	1	5^{4}	5^{4}	4½	7½	7½	Brown T L^{5}	10000	3.40
4Jly86 ^{3}Aks^{4}	Gentle Hold	4 116	7	5	1^{2}	1^{4}	1^{1}	8	8	Walker B J Jr	10000	13.20

D–Sarpy County Gang Disqualified and placed eighth.

OFF AT 4:32. Start good. Won driving. Time, :23⅘, :48, 1:13⅖, 1:40, 1:46⅗ Track fast.

$2 Mutuel Prices:			
5–STEEL JOSIE	**14.00**	**5.00**	**3.60**
6–FARE		**3.00**	**2.60**
8–BARBITOO			**3.20**

Dk. b. or br. m, by Steel Nucleus—Little Jo Mel, by Truly Royal. Trainer Eikleberry Kevin S. Bred by De Mara J (Colo).

STEEL JOSIE was well back in the early running, came on well to gain the lead in the stretch then held off FARE at the wire. The latter was never far back while racing on the outside. BARBITOO moved up on the outside. SARPY COUNTY GANG drifted out just after entering the stretch to bother FIRE JUMPER and was disqualified and placed last. SWEET MURR faltered in the drive. INFINITE SIDNEY passed tired horses. FIRE JUMPER was moving up along the inside on the final turn when she was forced to settle then hit the heels of SAPRY COUNTY GANG just after entering the stretch and stumbled badly. GENTLE HOLD tired after setting the pace.

Owners— 1, Norton J T; 2, Bowline Steve J & Mike R; 3, Cowan Claude; 4, Little Papio Stable; 5, Christensen & Inman; 6, Sundberg Edward; 7, Hillcrest Farm; 8, Pfeiffer Harry L & Conforti J.

Trainers— 1, Eikleberry Kevin S; 2, Goodridge Ronald O; 3, Morse Willard R; 4, White Warren; 5, Inman Hoss; 6, Lee Robert Enos; 7, Klein Francis J; 8, Michalek Mark.

Corrected weight: Sweet Murr 118 pounds; Fire Jumper 111.

27. Using the chart above, how fast did *Steel Josie* run the final ¹⁄₁₆ of a mile?

A. 6⅗ **(3)**
B. 7⅖ seconds
C. 6 seconds
D. 6⅕ seconds

28. If the Sept. 19 stretch call were timed in :56^{1}, how fast did *Holy Rascal* run in the stretch?

A. 12⅕ **(3)**
B. 23⅖
C. 11⅗
D. 24⅕

Holy Rascal — **Dk. b. or br. c. 4, by Holy War—Rosie's Rascal, by Amber Moon**

BAZE R A — **115** — **Br.—Cottingham Farm (Wash)** — **1986 4 1 1 0 $7,630**

Tr.—Klokstad Bud — **1985 9 6 1 0 $102,810**

Own.—Klokstad B — **Lifetime 23 10 4 1 $135,480** — **Turf 1 0 0 0**

19Sep86-9Lga	6f	:21^{4}	:44^{1}	1:08^{2}ft	*4-5	113	6^{4}½	5^{4}	2^{2}½	1½	Aragon V A^{1}	Aw10100	94-18	HolyRscl,BigBdBombr,MjsticEffort	6
19Sep86—Bumped 5/16															
5Sep86-9Lga	6f	:21^{4}	:45	1:09^{1}ft	*1	122	4^{5}	4^{1}¾	3^{2}½	2¾	Delgadillo C^{3}	Aw9400	89-22	MjstcEffort,HolyRscl,UnclBrrydwn	7
5Sep86—Blocked 1/4															
10Aug86-8Lga	6½f	:21^{2}	:43^{3}	1:14 ft	3	115	3^{6}	3^{4}½	3^{4}	5^{6}	Hansen R D^{4}	Aw11600	93-13	ZuluWhiz,Rueful'sNightOut,Shrpnel	6
6Apr86-9Lga	5½f	:22^{1}	:45	1:03^{1}ft	9-5	120	8^{5}¼	8^{6}¼	6^{9}	6^{6}	Baze G^{6}	S Lws Clrk H	90-19	MongoDrums,ZuluWhz,RunRonRun	8
22Dec85-8BM	6f	:22^{2}	:45	1:09^{1}ft	2½	115	7^{5}½	6^{4}	2½	1^{2}½	Baze R A^{4}	Lind Stnfrd	93-20	HolyRscl,RoylBlueEyes,DysSurpssd	7

29. The running lines of results charts are often a critical clue to

A. class within a class **(4)**
B. improving and deteriorating form
C. which qualities of class the contenders exhibited
D. track biases

30. If the *Form*'s speed rating and track variant are combined, which rating below is best?

A. 90   **(4)**
B. 100
C. 102
D. 95

31. Which workout is most impressive?

A. *47h   **(4)**
B. 1:00b
C. *1:13b
D. 1:36h

32. Which workout is most impressive?

A. 47h   **(4)**
B. *48hg
C. 48b
D. 48h (trt)

33. Which workout is most impressive?

A. 1:01hg   **(4)**
B. 59h
C. 1:00bg
D. 59⅖b

34. Which is the most important piece of chart information that does not appear in the past performances?

A. lengths behind the leader at each call   **(4)**
B. identities of trainers
C. overweights
D. blinker changes

35. What is the most important piece of chart information that does not appear in the past performances?

A. the size of the purse   **(4)**
B. the identities of claimed horses
C. horses' positions at the start
D. the internal fractional times

36. How should handicappers use the track variant published by the *Daily Racing Form*?

A. to judge the relative speed of the track surface on   **(4)**
   various racing days

B. to adjust final times up or down
C. add it to the speed rating
D. compare it to the variants of other contenders

37. A *Form* variant of 09 probably should be interpreted to mean

A. Better horses were running that day **(4)**
B. The speed ratings should be lower than usual
C. The track surface was relatively fast that day
D. The card was loaded with sprints

38. Which is the most important fact about *Bets Lass's* win revealed only in the chart (see Item 25)?

A. the trip description in the running line **(4)**
B. it was able to defeat older horses
C. it barely beat a 3-year-old entered for $9000
D. the name of the winning trainer

39. Using the chart of Item 26, if *Fare, Barbitoo,* and *Sweet Murr* all win their next start, what is probably true of *Steel Josie*?

A. She can move ahead in class and win again **(4)**
B. She probably benefited from a rapid early pace
C. She will be a good claim if started within thirty days
D. She will be an overlay next time out

40. What do handicappers know about *Charmed One* from the information shown?

Charmed One
DELAHOUSSAYE E   **115**
Own.—Wild Plum Farm

B. f. 3, by Dewan—Charming Little, by Personality
Br.—Wild Plum Farm (Colo)
Tr.—Tuck Mary Lou
Lifetime   4 0 2 1 $12,000

1987   2 M   2 0 $3,000
1986   2 M   0 1 $3,000

29Mar87-4SA	6f :21⁴ :45 1:10¹ft	3 118	1ʰᵈ 2ʰᵈ 2² 2⁴	DelahoussyeE 7 ⓔMdn 83-18	SkyShot,ChrmedOne,FleurDeLune 11	
29Mar87—Lugged out late						
15Mar87-4SA	6f :22¹ :45² 1:10²ft	29 117	2ʰᵈ 21¼ 2³ 2⁴	DelahoussyeE 5 ⓔMdn 82-20	Fleet Road, Charmed One,HiloBaba 9	
15Mar87—Broke in, checked						
30Nov86-6Hol	6f :21³ :45² 1:10⁴ft	49 118	109¾10¹² 9¹² 9¹³¼	Ortega L E⁷	ⓔMdn 76-16	Dvl'sBrd,SmmrSonds,DncAllSmmr 12
30Nov86—Lugged out turn						
2Nov86-4SA	6½f :21³ :44¹ 1:16 ft	46 117	89¼ 5¹¹ 4¹³ 3¹¹¼	Ortega L E⁸	ⓔMdn 78-10	Young Flyer, Afloat, CharmedOne 10
2Nov86—Lugged out 3/8						

Apr 28 SA 4f ft :49 h   Apr 22 SA 3f ft :35¹ h   Apr 14 SA 7f ft 1:31² h   Apr 8 SA 4f ft :48³ h

A. An inside post should result in a better clocking **(4)**
B. The filly has run faster each time
C. This is a lightly raced improving 3YO
D. The maiden improved dramatically with blinkers on

Answer key: Past performances and
results charts

Minimum Competency Test

1. A	11. B	21. A	31. D
2. B	12. B	22. C	32. B
3. D	13. A	23. D	33. C
4. B	14. D	24. B	34. B
5. A	15. D	25. B	35. A
6. B	16. C	26. C	36. C
7. B	17. D	27. D	37. C
8. A	18. B	28. C	38. C
9. C	19. D	29. D	39. A
10. B	20. A	30. C	40. D

CHAPTER 4

Early Speed

Competencies

5. Know the basic facts and probabilities underlying the importance of early speed.
6. Know the reliable indicators of early speed.
7. Understand early speed in relation to the factors of distance, class, pace, form, and track surface.
8. Calculate the "speed points" various horses have earned in sprints and routes.
9. Interpret early advantages and disadvantages in familiar race situations.

	Minimum Competency Test	Mastery Test
Proficiency standards	90%	75%
Number of Items	10	50
Passing Scores	9	38

Sources of Instruction

- *Winning at the Races*, chapters 1 & 2
- *Percentages and Probabilities*, Chapter 5

Comments

The best statistical studies ever conducted on this sport have revealed the importance of early speed. Those data are reflected in several of the items here. Handicappers who cannot handle the minimum competency test will be embarrassed on the mastery test, unless they consult the two sources of instruction first.

The general preoccupation with early speed contributes to a number of amazingly false impressions. In analyzing the 1987

Kentucky Derby for a television audience, a leading, respected Los Angeles handicapper noted that *Capote* had every right to steal the classic on a solitary lead. Not only had the 1986 juvenile champ been in awful form in its New York Derby preps, no horse "steals" the Kentucky Derby. Early speed is important, but it is far from everything.

Definition of Terms

• *Speed points.* A technique for rating early speed numerically, based upon position and beaten lengths at the first calls of three ratable races. A lucid, nicely illustrated explanation of the concept and method is provided by the technique's inventor, William L. Quirin, in Chapter 2 of *Winning at the Races* (Morrow 1979). The technique is easy to understand and apply. It is strongly recommended.

• *Probability.* As used here, the term refers to the impact value of a handicapping characteristic, that is, early speed. The impact value is expressed numerically. A value of 1.00 means the handicapping factor wins its fair share of the races. Above 1.00 means it wins more races than expected. Below 1.00 means the factor wins fewer races than expected.

When the term *probability* appears on any of the competency tests through "Body Language," it is being used to describe the impact value of a handicapping factor.

EARLY SPEED: MINIMUM COMPETENCY TEST

41. In major racing, horses that run 1st, 2nd, or 3rd at the first-call position win roughly what proportion of all races?

A. 40%   (5)
B. 50%
C. 60%
D. 70%

42. A clear early lead means in front at the first call by

A. ½ length   (6)
B. a length
C. 2 lengths
D. any margin more than a length

43. As a general rule, the closer a horse runs to the lead at the first-call position, the closer it will be at the finish.

A. True (9)
B. False

44. Early speed duels tend to be deadlier in routes than in sprints.

A. True (7)
B. False

45. Which is the most reliable indicator of early speed?

A. first-call fractional time (6)
B. beaten-lengths at the first call
C. running position at the first call
D. first-call velocity rating

46. Horses that run 3rd at the first-call position in routes generally win their fair share of the races.

A. True (5)
B. False

47. Favorites that lack acceptable early speed are among the leading candidates to be upset by early speed horses.

A. True (7)
B. False

48. Early speed horses are generally overbet.

A. True (5)
B. False

49. Dramatically improved speed to the first call can be accepted as a sign of

A. improved form (7)
B. a positive speed bias
C. a more suitable class level
D. trainer maneuver

50. How many speed points does *Parlapiano* get for today's race at a mile?

A. 0 **(8)**
B. 1
C. 2
D. 3

Parlapiano — Ch. h. 5, by Out of the East—Sister Mel, by Pellinore
DOUGLAS R R — **116** — Br.—Dante T C (Cal) — Tr.—King Hal — $10,000
Own.—Hanna B

1986	22	2	4	2	$30,695
1985	12	2	2	3	$24,570
Turf	3	1	1	0	$8,780
Lifetime	59	10	10	8	$104,638

3Nov86-1SA	6f	:21^3	:44^4	1:11 ft	8¾	116	9^{13}	8^{14}	8^{9½}	7^{4½}	Guerra W A^2	Ⓢ 12500	78-14	HachalaTachl,Melchip,ShuttleOne	10
12Oct86-1SA	6½f	:22	:45^2	1:17^{4}ft	13	116	11^{6¾}	11^{9¼}	11^{10}	10^{9½}	Hawley S^3	16000	71-21	Unagloshi,Menswear,StrOfAmeric	12
12Oct86—Bumped start															
1Oct86-9SA	1$\frac{1}{16}$	:46^1	1:11	1:44^{3}ft	6	116	5^{8½}	7^{8¼}	7^9	7^{8¾}	Ortega L E^4	16000	69-18	PintyConscous,CptnDoubl,ARghtId	8
16Sep86-8Pom	6½f	:22	:45	1:15^{3}ft	9½	116	9^{9¾}	9^{12}	8^{11}	2^9	Ortega L E^{10}	16000	93-05	CoursingEgl,Pripno,PrcousBmbno	10
15Aug86-1Dmr	6f	:22	:45^1	1:10 ft	9½	116	6^{7¾}	7^{8¾}	6^6	4^{3¾}	DelahoussayeE^1	20000	84-12	Philosopher,Reinbow'sCup,DeltTrc	7
31Jly86-3Dmr	6f	:22	:45^2	1:09^{4}ft	8¼	118	8^{5¼}	8^{4¾}	6^{7½}	4^{5¼}	Ortega L E^8	Ⓢ c16000	83-12	Rodney, Grenoble, Go Go Debonair	8
31Jly86—Bumped hard start; wide final 3/8															
11Jly86-9Hol	7f	:22^3	:46	1:23^{3}ft	9½	119	6^{8½}	6^{7½}	5^4	2^{2½}	Ortega L E^7	16000	83-14	One EyedRomeo,Parlapiano,Eterno	7
28Jun86-4Hol	1	:45^3	1:10^3	1:36^{1}ft	6	116	9^{5¼}	10^{9¼}	8^9	8^{10¾}	Kaenel J L^5	16000	71-12	MsterCwston,OneEydRomo,Etrno	10
18Jun86-7Hol	7f	:22^2	:45^4	1:23^{4}ft	19	116	9^{12}	8^{5½}	4^4	1^{1¾}	Ortega L E^5	16000	85-15	Parlapiano,ColdNose,SirEdgarAllan	9
1Jun86-4Hol	1	:45^2	1:10^3	1:36^{2}ft	31	116	11^9	10^8	5^9	5^{9¼}	Higuera A R^5	16000	72-14	TnksBrigd,DoublDfct,FlthorpMrnr	11
1Jun86—Pinched at start															

This is the end of the minimum competency test. Check your answers. If your score falls below standard, do not proceed to the mastery test until you have reviewed the sources of instruction.

EARLY SPEED: MASTERY TEST

51. Early speed refers to

A. the lead horse at the first call **(6)**
B. position or beaten lengths at the first call
C. cumulative fractional time at the second call
D. par or faster fractional time to the first call

52. Which is a fair generalization about early speed as a factor in handicapping?

A. It is negatively related to distance **(7)**
B. It is interchangeable with early pace
C. It is severely compromised when contested by horses of comparable class
D. It is positively related to a drop in class

53. The probability that any random early speed leader will win is approximately

A. 1.25 **(5)**
B. 1.40
C. 1.70
D. 2.20

54. Early speed in routes refers to running position after four furlongs.

A. True   **(7)**
B. False

55. Any nonfavorite, regardless of odds, capable of getting a clear early lead is worth the bettor's consideration.

A. True   **(5)**
B. False

56. Probability studies indicate the *best* speed advantage on the turf is

A. less than a length in slow fractions   **(5)**
B. running directly behind two or more frontrunners
C. a one-length lead at the first call
D. 2 lengths in par or better at each of the first two calls

57. Under what conditions are the general advantages of having early speed likeliest to disappear?

A. on the turf   **(5)**
B. at 1½M or farther
C. in the mud
D. in a stakes race

58. Which indicates acceptable early speed in a 6F sprint?

A. position among the first four at the first call   **(6)**
B. 23 seconds or less first fractional time
C. beating at least half the field to the first call
D. a first-call position within 2 lengths of the leader

59. Which factor is most likely to nullify a clear early lead?

A. superior class   **(7)**
B. an overly fast early pace
C. a track bias favoring closers
D. mud

60. In calculating speed points in 7F races, in order to earn a point for position at the first call a horse must be running

A. 1st   **(8)**
B. 1st or 2nd

C. 1st, 2nd, or 3rd
D. in the top half of the field

61. Calculate *Siraluovat's* speed points for a route.

A. 1 **(8)**
B. 3
C. 5
D. 7

Siraluovat — B. g. 6, by Somethingfabulous—June's Memory, by Snow Sporting
WARREN R J JR — 116 — Br.—Old English Rancho (Cal) — 1985 3 0 0 1 $3,120
Own.—Jhnstn-Jhnstn-Tvtrs et al — Tr.—Warren Donald — $10,000 — 1984 2 1 0 0 $11,550
Lifetime 16 2 1 4 $42,945 — Turf 4 0 1 1 $7,700

23Sep85-13Pom	$1\frac{1}{16}$:47^1 1:12^1 1:43^{2}ft	$7\frac{1}{2}$	114	$7^{4\frac{3}{4}}$	5^3	3^4	$3^{7\frac{3}{4}}$	Solis A^6	14000 — —	Pet's Best, Rapid Ember,Siraluovat	7
15Sep85-12Pom	$1\frac{1}{16}$:46^3 1:12^2 1:45^{4}ft	$4\frac{1}{4}$	116	$3^{2\frac{1}{2}}$	$6^{4\frac{1}{4}}$	5^6	$5^{7\frac{1}{2}}$	Mena F^2	16000 — —	GllntSpcil,OnYourOwn,Third'sWtch	9
31Aug85-9Dmr	$1\frac{1}{16}$:46^1 1:11 1:43^{1}ft	12	115	$3^{2\frac{1}{2}}$	4^2	3^7	5^{10}	Mena F^6	20000 74-11	Muft,BouncngButtons,LVrn'sBgMc	9
30Aug84-7Dmr	1 :45^4 1:09^4 1:34^{2}ft	19	117	$8^{8\frac{3}{4}}$	$8^{8\frac{1}{2}}$	6^{14}	$7^{16\frac{3}{4}}$	Hawley S^5	Aw20000 79-16	LrdAtWr,AmrcnStndrd,TMchFrT.V.	8
2Jan84-9SA	$1\frac{1}{16}$:47^4 1:12^1 1:43^{4}ft	$7\frac{1}{2}$	114	7^7	$4^{3\frac{1}{2}}$	2^{hd}	1^{nk}	ValenzuelPA^7	Aw21000 82-15	Siraluovat, Procurer, Tres Don	8
2Jan84—Broke slowly, steadied at 6 1/2											
19Dec83-8Hol	$1\frac{1}{8}$ Ⓣ:47^3 1:12^3 1:50^{2}fm	$*3\frac{1}{2}$	115	$6^{5\frac{3}{4}}$	$5^{1\frac{3}{4}}$	$7^{5\frac{1}{4}}$	6^3	ValenzuelPA^1	Aw25000 75-20	Red Don, North Of Lake, Rajaba	10
19Dec83—Lacked racing room 3/8 turn											
24Nov83-8Hol	$1\frac{1}{16}$:46^2 1:10^3 1:42^{1}ft	20	113	$6^{6\frac{1}{2}}$	5^6	$6^{6\frac{3}{4}}$	$6^{6\frac{1}{2}}$	Hawley S^5	ⓈG S Sires 77-18	SuprDimond,GlcilStrm,ChfCornstlk	6
30Oct83-9SA	$1\frac{1}{16}$:46^1 1:11^1 1:44 ft	$5\frac{3}{4}$	114	$8^{8\frac{3}{4}}$	$7^{7\frac{3}{4}}$	$4^{3\frac{1}{2}}$	$4^{3\frac{1}{2}}$	ShoemkerW^3	Aw22000 77-18	ExplosiveTwist,R.J.'sOrphan,Agitto	8
30Oct83—Lugged in stretch											
10Jly83-3Hol	1 :45^4 1:10^4 1:37^{1}ft	$3\frac{1}{2}$	107^5	$6^{9\frac{1}{2}}$	$5^{5\frac{1}{2}}$	$3^{2\frac{1}{2}}$	$3^{1\frac{3}{4}}$	Fuentes F P^4	Aw22000 78-21	KhalDave,NatomsExchange,Sirluvrt	8
10Jly83—Bumped at start											
25Jun83-7Hol	$1\frac{1}{16}$ Ⓣ:46^4 1:11^1 1:41^{4}fm	*6-5	115	5^{14}	5^6	4^3	$2^{3\frac{1}{2}}$	ValenzuelPA^1	Aw22000 86-10	Subsidize, Siraluovat, R. J's Orphan	7

Nov 6 Hol 4f ft :47^4 h — Oct 30 SA 1 ft 1:41^4 h — Oct 26 SA 4f ft :48 h — Oct 21 SA 7f ft 1:29^2 h

62. Calculate the speed points for *It's Never Dull* in a route.

A. 3 **(8)**
B. 4
C. 5
D. 6

It's Never Dull — Dk. b. or br. g. 6, by What Luck—Sharp Pencil, by Olden Times
SOTO S B — 116 — Br.—Forrester Geri (Md) — 1986 7 1 0 0 $8,175
Own.—Mancini & Timphony — Tr.—Timphony Vincent — $10,000 — 1985 14 1 3 3 $33,730
Lifetime 42 4 6 7 $75,720 — Turf 7 1 3 1 $26,705

10May86-7GG	$1\frac{1}{16}$:47^2 1:12^3 1:44^{4}ft	6	115	1^{hd}	$3^{1\frac{1}{2}}$	9^{19}	$12^{27\frac{1}{2}}$	Patterson A^8	12500 51-22	InnocentAge,Lee'sFmily,Stbilized	12
10Apr86-5SA	$1\frac{1}{16}$:46^4 1:11^2 1:43^{4}ft	20	113^5	4^4	$4^{5\frac{1}{4}}$	$6^{8\frac{1}{4}}$	$6^{11\frac{1}{2}}$	Crowder S J^1	20000 70-21	MostDetrmind,RightOnRd,WhidbyT	8
23Mar86-5SA	a$6\frac{1}{2}$f Ⓣ:21^3 :44^2 1:15^{1}fm	122	114	4^2	$4^{1\frac{3}{4}}$	$10^{6\frac{1}{4}}$	$10^{9\frac{1}{4}}$	Castanon A L^7	70000 74-19	AmrcnLgn,EmprdrAlNrt,FrnchsLc	12
8Mar86-9GG	$1\frac{1}{16}$:47 1:11^4 1:45^{1}m	$3\frac{3}{4}$	114	1^2	$1^{1\frac{1}{2}}$	1^2	1^3	Castaneda M^2	16000 77-20	It's NeverDull,OurNordic,NativeAct	5
15Feb86-2SA	$6\frac{1}{2}$f :21^3 :44^2 1:16^{1}gd	43	117	10^{10}	10^{15}	11^{18}	$10^{14\frac{1}{2}}$	Caraballo R^{12}	25000 74-14	Yield To Call, Shuttle Trip, Jovial	12
15Feb86—Wide final 3/8											
18Jan86-9SA	$1\frac{1}{16}$:46^1 1:11 1:43^{2}ft	$3\frac{1}{4}$	116	$2^{3\frac{1}{2}}$	$2^{\frac{1}{2}}$	$8^{7\frac{3}{4}}$	$8^{13\frac{3}{4}}$	Olivares F^5	c20000 70-12	ShuttleOne,DarkSuce,ByTheRiver	12
18Jan86—Eased in stretch											
5Jan86-9SA	$1\frac{1}{16}$:46^4 1:11^3 1:43^{4}ft	14	111^5	2^{hd}	2^{hd}	2^1	$4^{3\frac{3}{4}}$	Black C A^2	32000 78-14	SpruceHrbor,Espontno,Impulsivly	11
5Jan86—Bobbled start											
30Nov85-9Hol	$1\frac{1}{8}$:46^1 1:10^3 1:48^{3}m	$8\frac{3}{4}$	114	$2^{3\frac{1}{2}}$	$2^{3\frac{1}{2}}$	$3^{5\frac{1}{2}}$	$3^{9\frac{1}{2}}$	Olivares F^2	45000 84-09	AmorousII,VgorosVgors,It'sNvrDll	7
9Nov85-3SA	7f :22^3 :45^1 1:22 ft	20	114	9^{11}	$8^{6\frac{3}{4}}$	5^7	$6^{6\frac{1}{4}}$	Olivares F^{10}	45000 84-13	Mark The Lark, Good Finish,Viron	10
9Nov85—Broke in a tangle											
11Sep85-7Dmr	1 Ⓣ:47 1:10^4 1:34^{4}fm	*9-5	118	$2^{\frac{1}{2}}$	2^1	$4^{4\frac{1}{2}}$	5^8	Olivares F^1	62500 90-05	Dncbl,EmprdorAlNort,AtlnticSlmon	7
11Sep85—Rank into backstretch											

Oct 31 SA 4f ft :48^4 h — Oct 19 SA 5f ft 1:03 h — Oct 13 SA 5f ft 1:03^3 h — Oct 7 SA 5f ft 1:04^3 b

63. Acceptable early speed is indicated by how many speed points?

A. 3 **(8)**
B. 4
C. 5
D. 6

64. What is *Landseer II's* speed point total for today's route?

A. 2 **(8)**
B. 3
C. 4
D. 5

***Landseer II** — Dk. b. or br. g. 6, by Lochnager—Parlais, by Pardao
STEVENS S A 116 — Br.—Gordon-Spriggs J (Eng) — 1986 9 0 0 0 $3,875
Own.—Cunningham-Kerly-Redding — Tr.—Redding Anthony $10,000 — 1985 11 0 0 2 $1,141
Lifetime 47 2 2 2 $13,079 — Turf 38 2 2 2 $9,204

25Oct86-1SA	6½f	:22^{1}	:45^{1}	1:17^{1}ft	32	116	6$^{4\frac14}$	5^{6}	5^{5}	5^{8}	Pedroza M A^{8}	10000	76-17	Oh Dad, Melchip, Crimaurie	8
8Oct86-1SA	1 1/16	:46^{1}	1:11^{4}	1:44^{3}ft	37	116	5$^{3\frac12}$	4^{4}	6^{7}	6^{11}	Ortega L E^{3}	10000	67-20	I'll Smoke, Oh Dad, Hachi	12
19Sep86-12Pom	1 1/16	:45^{4}	1:11^{1}	1:46 ft	6¾	116	3^{5}	2^{2}	2^{1}	5^{2}	Pedroza M A^{4}	12500	79-09	A. J.Ruler,InNaturalForm,RedDusty	9
11Sep86-12Pom	a1⅛	:47	1:11^{4}	1:51^{2}ft	13	114	2^{1}	2^{1}	3^{1}	4$^{7\frac34}$	Pedroza M A^{4}	A12500	82-08	Son Of Raja, Morse, Her Threat	9
30Aug86-1Dmr	6f	:21^{4}	:45	1:09^{2}ft	14	116	9$^{7\frac12}$	7^{8}	8^{10}	8$^{10\frac12}$	Pedroza M A^{10}	12500	80-10	ExclusivKing,CoursngEgl,Unglosh	10
30Aug86—Wide final 3/8															
13Aug86-9Dmr	1 1/16	:45^{1}	1:10^{2}	1:43^{1}ft	92	116	2^{4}	2^{2}	8$^{8\frac12}$	8$^{10\frac14}$	Ortega L E^{4}	20000	74-15	Revolutionary, Tom, Our Nordic	11
26Jly86-1Dmr	6½f	:22^{1}	:45^{3}	1:17 ft	17	116	6$^{2\frac34}$	5$^{5\frac14}$	4$^{4\frac12}$	5$^{6\frac14}$	Olivares F^{2}	20000	81-13	Fall Flyer, Vinegarone, Slugfest	9
4Jly86-3Hol	6f	:22	:45^{1}	1:10 ft	25	116	5$^{4\frac14}$	5^{6}	5$^{8\frac12}$	5$^{10\frac12}$	Pedroza M A^{5}	25000	83-09	FlyngLssons,ToughEnvoy,NutrlPlyr	7
22Jun86-1Hol	6f	:22	:45^{1}	1:10 ft	15	116	5^{6}	5$^{4\frac12}$	4^{5}	4^{5}	Pedroza M A^{1}	25000	89-08	SndDiggr,FlyingLssons,SwordPrinc	7
24Oct85♦6Redcar(Eng)	6f			1:12 fm	14	113	Ⓣ	8$^{3\frac12}$			EddrPA			RedcarAutumnH PowderBlue,CowlShore,Moninsky	24

Nov 7 SA 5f ft 1:01 h

65. How many speed points does *By Four Thirty* get for today's route?

A. 1 **(8)**
B. 3
C. 5
D. 7

By Four Thirty — Dk. b. or br. f. 4, by Proudest Roman—Scotch Castle, by Traffic Judge
Br.—Cabin Branch Farms (NC) — 1986 23 5 3 4 $64,040
Own.—Ospam Stable 112^{5} — Tr.—Hernandez Sandino $17,500 — 1985 8 M 4 2 $7,669
Lifetime 31 5 7 6 $71,709 — Turf 2 0 0 0 $219

30Oct86-2Aqu	6f	:22^{3}	:46^{2}	1:11^{4}ft	11	115	2½	1^{hd}	4$^{2\frac12}$	7$^{11\frac12}$	Graell A^{6}	Ⓕ 22500	70-21	DwnBrk,PltinumPostr,BlckMdllion	9
24Oct86-1Aqu	1⅛	:48^{4}	1:14	1:52^{1}ft	6¾	115	5^{2}	5$^{2\frac34}$	8^{22}	8$^{37\frac14}$	Graell A^{6}	Ⓕ 22500	37-20	SoloEnergy,Karabr,FriskyAndRisky	9
1Oct86-8Bel	6f	:22^{2}	:45^{2}	1:10 ft	17	115	5$^{3\frac14}$	3^{2}	4^{6}	4$^{8\frac34}$	Graell A^{2}	ⒻAw36000	83-17	T.V.Snow,Ruthi'sMov,JckiO'Lntrnn	6
18Sep86-2Bel	7f	:23^{2}	:46^{4}	1:25^{1}ft	3¾	117	1½	1½	1^{hd}	1½	Graell A^{8}	Ⓕ 22500	76-17	ByFourThirty,HiddenFntsy,Mjnniqu	9
6Sep86-2Bel	6f	:22^{1}	:45^{2}	1:10^{4}gd	7	113	2$^{2\frac12}$	2$^{2\frac12}$	2$^{1\frac12}$	1^{hd}	Graell A^{2}	Ⓕ 20000	88-10	ByFourThirty,SoloEnergy,SweetRn	6
24Aug86-1Sar	6½f	:22^{1}	:45^{3}	1:18^{4}m	2½	113	2^{hd}	2½	1½	5^{9}	Migliore R^{5}	Ⓕ 20000	69-13	GunsilII,Bonnie'sPoker,ProvnRcord	7
14Aug86-9Sar	7f	:22^{3}	:45^{3}	1:25 ft	3¾	113	1^{1}	1^{hd}	1^{hd}	3$^{3\frac14}$	Migliore R^{2}	Ⓕ 20000	74-20	FigurNvidn,MgicMist,ByFourThirty	9
21Jun86-3Bel	6f	:22^{3}	:45^{1}	1:10^{1}ft	11	113	3$^{1\frac12}$	2^{2}	2^{4}	6$^{7\frac14}$	Guerra W A^{10}	Ⓕ 20000	84-10	ScondStoryGrl,Dddy'sSlggr,Mjnnq	10

Sep 15 Aqu 3f ft :37^{4} b   Sep 3 Aqu 4f ft :50^{1} b

66. Early speed is *not* as powerful as usual in one-turn routes.

A. True **(9)**
B. False

67. Regardless of the likely competition for the early lead, an early speed horse has an especially good chance to win if it

A. is the speed of the speed **(9)**
B. exits an inside post in a middle distance route
C. can be rated behind the early pace
D. is dropping significantly in class

68. What are the chances—roughly—that horses engaged in early speed duels will win nonetheless?

A. 0.40   **(5)**
B. 0.85
C. 1.20
D. 1.80

69. The rear half of the field wins approximately what percentage of the races they should be expected to win?

A. 20%   **(5)**
B. 40%
C. 50%
D. 70%

70. Horses that run 2nd at the first call in sprints win significantly more races than expected.

A. True   **(6)**
B. False

71. At what distance is the early speed horse at greatest risk of being passed?

A. 6F   **(7)**
B. 7F
C. 1M
D. 1¼M

72. Acceptable early speed in a route can be defined as first-call position within how many lengths of the leader?

A. 1   **(6)**
B. 2
C. 3
D. 4

73. When all types of races and racetracks are considered, the typical odds on winners that controlled the early speed are

A. 8–5   **(5)**
B. 5–2
C. 7–2
D. 9–2

74. Regardless of racetrack or distance, horses that have a clear lead at the first call win roughly how many times their fair share of the races?

A. 2.5 **(5)**
B. 1.25
C. 1.75
D. 4

75. Horses that run 4th at the first-call position in sprints generally will win their fair share of the races.

A. True **(5)**
B. False

76. Speed duels in sprints normally reduce the likelihood that either frontrunner will win.

A. True **(9)**
B. False

77. Which is the best-documented method for predicting the early speed of any race?

A. Quirin's speed points **(5)**
B. Beyer's projected times
C. The Sartin Methodology
D. Class-Distance Fractional Pars

78. Early speed in sprints refers to running position at the first call; in routes, it refers to running position at the second call.

A. True **(6)**
B. False

79. Early speed at less than 6F is best determined by first-call fractional time.

A. True **(7)**
B. False

80. In which common situations are early speed advantages not as meaningful as usual?

A. stakes races **(9)**
B. 2-year-old routes
C. at classic distances
D. one-turn routes

81. Which advantage in speed points is most likely to win?

    A. 8 to 6   **(9)**
    B. 6 to 4
    C. 4 to 1
    D. 7 to 5

82. In general, a speed point advantage of how many points significantly improves a frontrunner's chances?

    A. 1   **(5)**
    B. 2
    C. 3
    D. 4

83. Which speed point "advantage" is most likely to cause the frontrunner serious problems?

    A. 8 to 7   **(9)**
    B. 6 to 5
    C. 5 to 5
    D. 3 to 2

84. Early speed and a drop in class in combination tends to be most dangerous

    A. in classified allowance races   **(9)**
    B. in one-turn routes
    C. on the grass
    D. in claiming races

85. Early speed and early pace can be considered interchangeable.

    A. True   **(7)**
    B. False

86. What percentage of the speed points for an entire field must one horse have before its advantage becomes statistically significant?

    A. 20%   **(5)**
    B. 30%
    C. 40%
    D. 50%

87. If *Tommow Miss* will be routing today, what is the filly's speed point total?

A. 0 **(8)**
B. 1
C. 2
D. 4

Tommow Miss — B. f. 3, by Hurricane Ed—Yesterday's Dream, by Mid Arc
Br.—Hild Sharon L (Ark) — 1986 24 2 4 3 $33,57.
Own.—Tresvant Stable — 101^{10} Tr.—Sedlacek Sue — $15,500 — 1985 3 1 0 0 $5,790
Lifetime 27 3 4 3 $39,365 — Turf 3 0 1 0 $3,050

16Oct86-3Bel	1$\frac{1}{16}$	:47^4	1:13^1	1:46 ft	*1	109^7	4^4	5^7	4$^{6\frac{1}{2}}$	3$^{7\frac{1}{2}}$	Belmonte JF^2	Ⓕ 17500	64-19	Strongbck,KimsIndin,TommowMiss	6
1Oct86-5Med	6f	:22^3	:45^4	1:11 ft	10	110^5	6$^{3\frac{1}{2}}$	5$^{5\frac{1}{2}}$	4^3	2^2	Bielby J A^5	Ⓕ 20000	85-14	HollyHagley,TommowMiss,IrishMar	7
23Sep86-6Med	6f	:22^2	:45^4	1:12 ft	15	106^7	9$^{8\frac{1}{4}}$	8$^{6\frac{3}{4}}$	6$^{4\frac{3}{4}}$	4^4	Belmonte JF^2	Ⓕ 22500	78-23	Joannin,HennGirl,BiddinOnABeuty	10
10Sep86-4Med	1$\frac{1}{16}$ [T]	:48	1:12^3	1:44^{3}fm	15	109^5	2$^{\frac{1}{2}}$	2$^{\frac{1}{2}}$	3^2	4^6	Bielby J A^2	Ⓕ 25000	74-12	MildyConsents,MullOverM,GrtTril	10
3Sep86-8Med	1$\frac{1}{16}$ [T]	:47^2	1:11^2	1:44^{2}fm	8$\frac{1}{4}$	106^7	5^7	8^{13}	8^{12}	7$^{14\frac{1}{2}}$	Belmonte JF^7	Ⓕ 28000	66-19	MyElnor,SwtstMomm,DolcDolcDlc	9
21Aug86-6Mth	1$\frac{1}{16}$	:47^3	1:13^4	1:48^{3}sy	*8-5	114	4$^{5\frac{1}{2}}$	4^4	2$^{\frac{1}{2}}$	3$^{6\frac{1}{2}}$	Antley C W^3	Ⓕ 25000	55-27	FlyingBirdi,MullOvrM,TommowMss	6
13Aug86-4Mth	1 Ⓣ	:47^4	1:12^2	1:38^{4}fm	*3$\frac{1}{4}$	114	5^5	3$^{1\frac{1}{2}}$	2^1	2$\frac{1}{2}$	Antley C W^6	Ⓕ 20000	80-16	TunThDic,TommowMiss,FlyingBrd	10
4Aug86-8Mth	1$\frac{1}{16}$	:48^4	1:12^4	1:45^{3}ft	7$\frac{1}{4}$	112	4$^{2\frac{1}{2}}$	5$^{1\frac{1}{2}}$	3^1	2$^{1\frac{1}{2}}$	Antley C W^5	Ⓕ 20000	75-20	Explodom,TommowMiss,TraflgrLss	7

88. Calculate *Lady Boom Boom's* speed points for a 6F race.

A. 4 **(8)**
B. 5
C. 6
D. 7

Lady Boom Boom — Dk. b. or br. f. 3, by Family Doctor—Boomies Girl E, by Figonero
Br.—Burke W J (Fla) — 1986 17 4 3 1 $50,002
Own.—Klein Ladonna — 106^7 Tr.—Tufariello Frank — $15,500 — 1985 4 2 0 1 $13,860
Lifetime 21 6 3 2 $63,862

23Oct86-1Aqu	7f	:22^4	:45^4	1:24 ft	6	114	2^{hd}	1^{hd}	11^{16}	12$^{19\frac{1}{2}}$	Venezia M^{10}	Ⓕ 15500	61-17	Berry'sChpter,ChrokChill,TimlyRis	13
6Oct86-9Bel	6f	:23	:46^4	1:12^{3}ft	3$\frac{3}{4}$	114	2^{hd}	1$^{\frac{1}{2}}$	1^2	1$^{\frac{3}{4}}$	Venezia M^6	Ⓕ 15500	79-24	LdyBoomBom,SwtAtlnts,NtrlAppl	11
29Sep86-1Bel	6f	:22^4	:46^3	1:11^{3}gd	*1	118	1^1	1$^{\frac{1}{2}}$	2^{hd}	2$^{2\frac{1}{4}}$	Venezia M^2	Ⓕ 17500	82-14	FrscoDlght,LdyBoomBoom,SclGstr	7
13Sep86-2Bel	6f	:23	:46^3	1:11^{2}ft	*2$\frac{1}{2}$	112	2$^{\frac{1}{2}}$	2$^{\frac{1}{2}}$	2^{hd}	1$^{2\frac{1}{2}}$	Venezia M^6	Ⓕ 15500	85-11	LdyBoomBoom,SocilGstur,TimlyRs	7
4Sep86-9Bel	6f	:22^2	:45^3	1:11^{4}ft	4$\frac{3}{4}$	112	8^8	5^6	5$^{5\frac{1}{2}}$	11^7	Venezia M^4	Ⓕ 20000	76-18	HelluvRise,TurnpikPrincss,VgsElli	11
19Jly86-4Bel	6f	:22^4	:45^4	1:10^{2}ft	3	118	5$^{4\frac{1}{2}}$	6^5	8$^{8\frac{1}{4}}$	6^9	Venezia M^6	Ⓕ 25000	81-15	TurnpikePrincess,VegsEllie,ElitStrt	9
2Jly86-9Bel	1	:46	1:11^2	1:37^{4}sy	6	116	2$^{1\frac{1}{2}}$	2^2	2$^{2\frac{1}{2}}$	4$^{4\frac{3}{4}}$	Venezia M^5	Ⓕ 25000	71-14	Triomph'sGlory,AskDrctons,TmlyRs	9
21Jun86-9Bel	7f	:22^4	:46	1:24^{1}ft	*1	118	6^4	5$^{3\frac{1}{2}}$	5$^{4\frac{1}{2}}$	7$^{7\frac{1}{2}}$	Venezia M^3	Ⓕ 25000	73-10	RoylTntrum,Whirlybird,TorridZone	9

21Jun86—Broke in air

89. At what distance should a "definite" early speed horse be most strongly expected to be on the early lead?

A. 6F **(7)**
B. 7F
C. 1M
D. 1⅛M

90. How many speed points does *Invalid* earn for today's 6F sprint?

A. 0 **(8)**
B. 1
C. 2
D. 4

Invalid B. f. 3, by Valid Appeal—Miz Mazie, by Amazing
Br.—Norton E (Fla) 1986 7 1 1 0 $6,820
Own.—Nagle K 111 Tr.—Ferriola Peter $15,500 1985 8 1 3 1 $18,580
Lifetime 15 2 4 1 $25,400

13Oct86-8Det 170:49 1:151 1:46 gd 5¾ 112 1½ 51¾ 610 723¾ Lopez R D4 ⒻAw8200 43-28 OnebyBandy,BabRebob,Gee'sTrder 8
2Oct86-5Det 6f :224 :464 1:124sy *1 112 58 54 32 13½ Lopez R D1 Ⓕ 10000 76-22 Invalid, Little Alpo, Deer Lake 6
9Jly86-3Bel 6f :23 :464 1:122ft 5½ 116 52½ 97½ 1013 1110 Santagata N6 Ⓕ 17500 70-23 TmmwMss,FrscDlght,TrnpkPrncss 11
28Jun86-2Bel 6f :224 :461 1:113ft 3½ 1115 74½ 74¾ 88 65 Decarlo C P9 Ⓕ 17500 79-15 MdvlMlody,FrscoDlght,SlvrPltdCd 10
11Jun86-1Bel 6f :224 :462 1:114ft 5½ 1115 45½ 57½ 48 58¾ Decarlo C P10 Ⓕ 25000 74-19 LdyBoomBm,RylTntrm,SlvrPltdCd 12
31May86-1Bel 6f :23 :462 1:11 ft 6 1115 1hd 11½ 11½ 21¼ Decarlo C P9 Ⓕ 25000 86-18 LdyBoomBoom,Invlid,SilvrPltdCd 10
9May86-10Det 6f :214 :453 1:12 ft 19 109 24 23 33 55 Guerra L R8 ⒻAw8000 75-22 SweetSaush,MissLd,Shnnon'sBeuty 9
2Nov85-7Med 6f :224 :463 1:114ft 8¾ 113 55 44½ 54½ 811¾ SantagatN9 ⒻAw14000 71-18 Trcy'sEspoir,TurnndDnc,DrstRuby 10
Oct 24 Aqu 3f ft :372 b Sep 26 Det 3f gd :363 h Sep 17 Det 5f ft 1:013 h Sep 14 Det 5f ft 1:00 hg

91. The total speed points for the six horses entered in the 9th at Aqueduct below is

A. 13 **(8)**
B. 18
C. 22
D. 25

9th Aqueduct

6 FURLONGS. (1.08⅘) CLAIMING. Purse $13,000. Fillies and Mares, 3-year-olds and upward. Weight, 3-year-olds 120 lbs. Older 122 lbs. Non-winners of two races since October 1 allowed 3 lbs. Of a race since then 5 lbs. Claiming Price $17,500; for each $1,000 to $15,500 2 lbs. (Races when entered to be claimed for $14,000 or less not considered.)

Coupled—Tell Aunt Susan and By Four Thirty.

Star's Estrelita Ch. f. 4, by Harvard Man—Star's Baby, by Hard Rock Man
Br.—Giacoppo Monika (NY) 1986 8 1 1 1 $21,220
Own.—Giacoppo Monika 113 Tr.—Pratt Michael $15,500 1985 10 M 1 3 $14,260
Lifetime 18 1 2 4 $35,480 Turf 1 0 0 0

26Oct86-4Aqu 6f :224 :461 1:112m 15 117 75 79¼ 1117 1118¼ MrtnsG10 ⒻⓈAw26500 66-18 Xenon,PassTheCandy,Anchorgram 11
17Oct86-9Bel 6f :23 :464 1:11 ft 26 117 21½ 65 1023 1120¾ Graell A1 Ⓕ 17500 66-14 Oaxaca, Solo Energy, Our Trisha 11
1Apr86-7Aqu 6f :224 :464 1:131ft 18 119 73¼ 52 64½ 94¾ Graell A9 ⒻⓈAw26500 70-27 HppyAplch,HngArond,LvIsInThAr 13
22Mar86-4Aqu 6f :233 :481 1:133ft 4¾ 119 1hd 1½ 21½ 35 Graell A3 ⒻⓈAw26500 68-25 MonChoCho,WmbornBll,Str'sEstrlt 8
1Mar86-9Aqu 6f ⊡:233 :4831:15 ft 7½ 122 41½ 54½ 715 88½ Graell A4 ⒻⓈAw26500 60-25 Silhonette,WimborneBelle,EverTn 10
21Feb86-6Aqu 6f ⊡:223 :47 1:13 sy 27 122 22 2½ 13 12½ Graell A3 ⒻMdn 79-21 Str'sEstrlit,RossGlor,PrincssIvory 12
12Feb86-3Aqu 6f. ⊡:231 :4731:133ft 3½ 122 42½ 54 56 53¾ Graell A4 ⒻMdn 72-16 ByRumTlc,PrincssIvory,ThThrMris 7
23Jan86-4Aqu 6f ⊡:231 :4741:123ft 8 122 52¾ 31½ 25 28½ Graell A3 ⒻMdn 72-21 Evrbright,Str'sEstrlit,PrincssIvory 10
Oct 24 Bel tr.t 3f ft :361 h Oct 9 Aqu Ⓣ 5f fm 1:034 h (d) Sep 14 Aqu 5f ft 1:033 b Sep 8 Aqu 4f ft :494 b

Romeo's Mistress Dk. b. or br. m. 5, by Romeo—Prime Mistress, by Young Emperor
Br.—Fairview Farm (Ky) 1986 21 2 4 1 $40,740
Own.—Adler M 113 Tr.—Martello Gene $15,500 1985 21 3 2 0 $34,600
Lifetime 72 11 8 2 $127,895 Turf 3 0 0 0

10Oct86-7Bel 6½f :23 :463 1:181ft 4¾ 1125 42½ 35½ 612 616 Murray D8 Ⓕ 25000 68-20 SoloEnergy,DwnBrek,ImbicPntmtr 8
29Sep86-5Bel 6f :22 :453 1:104ft 10 1105 33 3½ 22 21½ Murray K C1 Ⓕ 22500 86-14 Mjnniqu,Romo'sMistrss,ByRumTlc 7
25Sep86-2Bel 6f :23 :461 1:11 ft 5½ 115 54 44 56 56¼ RydowskSR6 Ⓕ c16500 81-19 Mjnniqu,TllAuntSusn,PltinumPostr 9
27Jly86-2Bel 7f :231 :464 1:261sy *4 113 3½ 32 2hd 13¾ Rydowski SR4 Ⓕ 15500 71-25 Rm'sMstrss,TmmwMss,TllAntSsn 11
4Jly86-2Bel 6f :223 :462 1:121ft *3½ 117 73¾ 42½ 32 21¼ Attanasio R5 Ⓕ 14000 80-11 MyPrncss,Romo'sMstrss,ColrflMss 9
4Jly86—Off slow
19Jun86-3Bel 7f :23 :464 1:25 ft 8¼ 117 12 1½ 2½ 44 Attanasio R12 Ⓕ 14000 73-19 MrryWidowWltz,MmCb,ByThStrm 14
24May86-2Bel 6½f :224 :463 1:174ft 11 117 2hd 1hd 2hd 75¾ Venezia M3 Ⓕ 17500 81-12 Mjennique,TheBkr'sWif,SoloEnrgy 9
11May86-9Bel 7f :223 :454 1:251ft 24 113 75¼ 65¾ 33 34¼ Venezia M2 Ⓕ 20000 72-15 RondRvw,ByThStrm,Rom'sMstrss 12
Oct 16 Aqu 6f ft 1:143 h Sep 19 Bel tr.t 5f ft 1:03 b Sep 13 Bel tr.t 5f ft 1:06 b Sep 7 Bel tr.t 5f ft 1:053 b

Sheri's Knockoff B. f. 3, by Batonnier—Angel Aid, by Gentle Art
Br.—Koones R (Ky) 1986 10 1 0 1 $10,785
Own.—Koones R 111 Tr.—Sofia J $15,500 1985 4 1 2 0 $13,420
Lifetime 14 2 2 1 $24,205

4Jly86-4Mth 6f :214 :453 1:132ft 15 115 54½ 54¾ 43½ 52¾ MrquezCHJr1 Ⓕ 16000 70-20 Mm'sOnAndOnl,KlssAttch,HthrRs 11
24Jun86-10Mth 6f :234 :472 1:131ft 23 115 51¾ 64½ 66½ 47 MrquezCHJr7 Ⓕ 20000 67-20 Kolctoo'sCntss,DrJnn,Wndy'sThm 11
11Jun86-1Bel 6f :224 :462 1:114ft 61 116 77½ 69 611 1011½ Guerra W A6 Ⓕ 25000 71-19 LdyBoomBm,RylTntrm,SlvrPltdCd 12
19May86-2Bel 7f :224 :461 1:251ft 22 112 62½ 96½ 88½ 78½ Velasquez J2 Ⓕ 20000 67-23 ScyN'Clssy,LdyBoomBom,TrrdZn 12
30Apr86-2Aqu 6f :23 :473 1:131ft 4¾ 116 43 32 32 1¾ Davis R G4 Ⓕ 17500 75-24 Shr'sKnockoff,BrvShdow,RskyFrnd 9
12Apr86-2Aqu 6f :232 :48 1:131ft 5 116 53½ 67 1016 1018½ Davis R G11 Ⓕ 17500 56-25 OutofthStorm,OurPggyLou,Shirbll 13
12Apr86—Stumbled start
27Mar86-2Aqu 6f :231 :472 1:14 ft 3¼ 116 31½ 2½ 21½ 84 Davis R G10 Ⓕ 25000 67-29 Girlish Glee, Tina's Robin, RioTrip 10
5Feb86-1Aqu 6f ⊡:222 :4611:123sy 5½ 116 2½ 35½ 512 712½ Velasquez J2 Ⓕ 35000 68-17 Our Peggy Lou,ForeverSpecial,Flip 9
Oct 22 Bel tr.t 5f ft 1:02 h Oct 17 Bel tr.t 5f ft 1:021 b

Pretty Member *
Own.—Agati B
Ch. f. 3, by Red Wing Bold—Pretty Annie, by Beau Busher
Br.—Murray W H (Fla) 1986 10 2 1 1 $23,520
10510 Tr.—Agati James $17,500 1985 9 3 1 2 $14,345
Lifetime 19 5 2 3 $37,865
23Oct86-1Aqu 7f :224 :454 1:24 ft 53 10610 1hd 5¾ 1216 1322½ Lee W3 Ⓕ 17500 58-17 Berry'sChpter,ChrokChill,TimlyRis 13
23Oct86—Lacked room
18Sep86-9Bel 7f :23 :463 1:24 ft 24 116 32 1219 1235 1239¾ Graell A2 Ⓕ 25000 42-17 UthPine,TimelyRise,AskDirections 12
18Apr86-2Aqu 6f :222 :454 1:11 gd 8 1085 2½ 21½ 914 1015¼ VasquezMM10 Ⓕ 30000 71-20 Sally's Heroine, Flip, Aquebogue 10
29Mar86-2Aqu 6f :221 :461 1:112ft 8¼ 114 31½ 42½ 56½ 819 Estrada J C8 Ⓕ 32500 65-21 ForvrSpcl,BddnOnAButy,Drcy'sSstr 9
9Mar86-4Aqu 6f ⊡:224 :47 1:13 ft *6-5 1117 21½ 2½ 2½ 33¾ Rolon E M3 Ⓕ c25000 75-27 ForeverSpcil,GirlishGl,PrttyMmbr 12
1Mar86-6Aqu 6f ⊡:224 :4641:113ft 6½ 1097 1½ 3½ 36 714 Rolon E M2 ⒻAw24000 72-25 RoseRoug,ForvrRoving,ChrokChill 10
20Feb86-5Aqu 6f ⊡:223 :4541:11 m 9¼ 1077 1½ 13 14 13¼ Rolon E M5 Ⓕ 45000 89-10 PrettyMembr,WlcomOn,Drcy'sSistr 8
5Feb86-7Aqu 6f ⊡:214 :4531:113sy 28 1097 54¼ 64½ 76¾ 48¼ Rolon E M7 ⒻAw24000 78-17 RllyForJustice,LtinLook,CllMHony 8
Oct 18 Aqu 4f ft :482 h Sep 7 Aqu 6f ft 1:164 h

Wild Triumph
Own.—Demola Dorothy
Gr. f. 4, by Triumphant—Pen Drift, by Wild Drift
Br.—Sabiston J T (Ont-C) 1986 9 0 0 0 $960
1067 Tr.—Demola R $15,500 1985 8 1 0 1 $9,360
Lifetime 18 1 0 1 $10,320
30Oct86-2Bel 6f :224 :461 1:113ft 42 1107 31 43 78 711½ Ortiz E6 Ⓕ 14000 72-17 PltnumPostr,TllAuntSusn,LovlyNrs 8
25Sep86-2Bel 6f :23 :461 1:11 ft 74 1087 78½ 711 915 915½ Clayton C2 Ⓕ 16500 71-19 Mjnniqu,TllAuntSusn,PltinumPostr 9
25Sep86—Slow start
6Aug86-6Mth 6f :222 :451 1:114ft 33 112 2hd 67½ 79¾ 716¼ Messina R4 Ⓕ 14000 65-22 WildlyWondrful,ShrryB.,SquirrlRun 8
3May86-1Aqu 6f :232 :482 1:133ft 27 117 2½ 31½ 67 718 MrquezCHJr6 Ⓕ 14000 55-28 SonPlaisir,LadyNizon,Sham'sBeuty 7
10Apr86-3Aqu 6f :224 :47 1:124ft 29 117 52 52½ 710 814¾ Santagata N4 Ⓕ 17500 62-28 KidsN'Kts,RoundRvw,AHotNumbr 10
22Mar86-9Aqu 6f :224 :472 1:134ft 17 117 2hd 2hd 75½ 912¼ Santagata N1 Ⓕ 17500 60-25 Bonnie'sPoker,RiseAndTost,Ms.Bry 9
2Mar86-3Aqu 6f ⊡:224 :4731:13 ft 64 113 62¼ 62¼ 95¾ 1013½ Thibeau R J7 Ⓕ 20000 65-26 TeriykiStk,OurTrish,ByFourThirty 12
19Feb86-3Aqu 6f ⊡:221 :4541:11 gd 20 1107 43½ 55½ 66½ 8n¼ Paneto W R1 Ⓕ 25000 81-13 MoodyMondy,Rom'sMstrss,OrTrsh 12
Oct 12 Aqu 4f ft :52 b Sep 15 Aqu 5f ft 1:012 h

Loyal Diplomat
Own.—Krohn Deborah
Ch. m. 7, by Diplomat Way—Loyal Subject, by Roman Patrol
Br.—Giglio S (Fla) 1986 8 1 2 0 $13,200
1067 Tr.—Krohn Nat $15,500 1985 17 1 1 1 $15,170
Lifetime 59 8 8 4 $106,615
23Apr86-2Aqu 7f :234 :481 1:262sy *3-2e 117 11½ 11½ 1½ 22 Martens G7 Ⓕ 14000 67-30 SonPlsr,LoylDplomt,GoodwllMsson 9
13Apr86-2Aqu 6f :223 :463 1:122ft 8½ 115 11½ 2½ 44½ 69 Martens G9 Ⓕ 13000 78-19 Sly Iron, Anselma, Blinker Baby 11
25Mar86-1Aqu 6f :224 :47 1:124ft 5¾ 1107 2½ 21 44½ 910 Rolon E M6 Ⓕ 14000 67-26 ColorfulMiss,GoodwillMisson,Crot 13
27Feb86-5Aqu 6f ⊡:23 :4731:134ft 6 1087 2hd 2½ 42½ 74¾ Rolon E M6 Ⓕ 16500 78-24 PrOfQuns,AHotNumbr,TllAuntSsn 11
22Feb86-2Aqu 6f ⊡:231 :4631:114m 4 1087 14 15 15 14 Rolon E M8 Ⓕ 13000 85-17 LoylDplomt,AHotNmbr,GdwllMssn 8
3Feb86-1Aqu 6f ⊡:224 :4711:123gd 8½ 1107 1½ 1hd 32 45¾ Rolon E M8 Ⓕ 14000 75-16 Pondero,ColorfulMiss,JungleSecrt 10
24Jan86-1Aqu 6f ⊡:232 :48 1:131ft 4 1107 1hd 42 810 911¼ Rolon E M9 Ⓕ 14000 67-25 DuckyDuchesse,Pondro,RiltoRippl 12
5Jan86-1Aqu 6f ⊡:224 :4641:12 gd 20 1087 2½ 2½ 2½ 21½ Rolon E M5 Ⓕ 13000 83-16 MoodyMndy,LylDplmt,ScyChllng 10
Oct 9 Bel tr.t 4f ft :471 h Oct 1 Bel tr.t 4f ft :494 h ●Sep 21 Bel tr.t 3f ft :361 h

92. How many horses in the Aqueduct race have acceptable early speed?

A. 1 **(9)**
B. 2
C. 3
D. 4

93. What percentage of the early speed is accounted for by *Loyal Diplomat*?

A. 20% **(8)**
B. 28%
C. 37%
D. roughly half

94. *Loyal Diplomat* in the 9th Aqueduct appears to enjoy a decisive early speed advantage.

A. True **(9)**
B. False

95. Which horse in the Hollywood Park field below has not earned a single speed point?

A. *Count Eric* **(8)**
B. *Time Share*
C. *Sebucan*
D. *Fracoza*

5th Hollywood

6 FURLONGS. (1.08⅗) CLAIMING. Purse $15,000. 3-year-olds. Weight, 122 lbs. Non-winners of two races since September 1 allowed 3 lbs.; a race since then, 6 lbs. Claiming price $40,000; if for $35,000 allowed 2 lbs. (Races when entered for $32,000 or less not considered.)

Pialor
CASTANON A L 117
Own.—Gherardi Mr-Mrs R
B. c. 3, by Zoot Alors—Pia Mater, by Pia Star
Br.—Dollase & Duffel (Cal) 1986 9 2 1 1 $13,775
Tr.—Magana Roberto $35,000 1985 0 M 0 0
Lifetime 9 2 1 1 $13,775

18Oct86-7AC 6f :222 :442 1:09 ft 4¾ 1115 31 1hd 11½ 11 Delgadillo A2 Aw5000 94-13 Pialor, Quantus, Silver Ticket 9
11Oct86-5AC 6f :222 :45 1:094gd 9-5 114 2hd 21 33½ 36 Delgadillo BD6 Aw5000 84-19 Ramses, Leopold, Pialor 6
14Sep86-10Pom 6½f :213 :45 1:162ft 61 112 66¼ — — — Patterson A2 Aw25000 — — Tuono, Growler Sandue, BoldDecree 9
14Sep86—Pulled up; Lugged out, wide first turn
31Aug86-9Dmr 1 :452 1:102 1:363ft 41 116 1hd 42½ 917 — Castanon A L9 40000 — — Joab, Arbitrate, Gaelic Knight 9
31Aug86—Eased; Took up 1/4
20Aug86-6Dmr 6f :221 :46 1:111ft 5¼ 116 41½ 41½ 11 12 CastnonAL10 Ⓢ M32000 82-11 Pialor,DowdCanyon,JumpingJklin 12
20Aug86—Wide 3/8, into stretch
27Jly86-4Dmr 6f :22 :452 1:10 ft 56 116 41¾ 53¾ 97¾ 98¾ Castanon A L9 Mdn 79-10 Lud, Danielli, Prince O' Fire 9
9Jly86-7Hol 6f :221 :46 1:112ft 30 115 31½ 55 1125 — Castanon A L5 Ⓢ Mdn — — TmForSkrto,PrncO'Fr,DowdCnyon 11
9Jly86—Eased
20Jun86-5Hol 6f :222 :454 1:102ft 2 115 52 42 44 49¾ Castanon A L6 Ⓢ Mdn 82-11 RepeatImage,ZambeziPass,ChiliHill 8
6Jun86-3Hol 6f :222 :461 1:121ft 38 115 31 1hd 2hd 21¾ Castanon A L7 Ⓢ Mdn 82-15 Kimridge Road, Pialor, Due Up 8
Nov 3 AC 6f ft 1:13 h Oct 6 AC 6f ft 1:12 h Sep 29 AC 6f ft 1:15 h

Count Eric
SOLIS A 116
Own.—Park Place Thoroughbreds
B. c. 3, by Riverman—Miss Carmie, by T V Lark
Br.—Carmie Partners (Ky) 1986 12 0 0 1 $6,200
Tr.—Cerin Vladimir $40,000 1985 4 1 1 1 $17,800
Lifetime 16 1 1 2 $24,000 Turf 3 0 0 1 $3,450

31Oct86-6SA 6f :212 :443 1:093ft 56 116 87 76½ 56½ 57¾ Solis A9 50000 82-16 MischievousMtt,Jimed,RosesArRb 11
4Oct86-1SA 6½f :214 :45 1:17 ft 43 116 56 44½ 79 85½ Doocy T T2 50000 79-18 Inherent Kal, EastTulip,Bruli'sAnte 9
8Sep86-3Dmr 6f :214 :45 1:09 ft 16 117 44½ 45½ 48½ 47½ Pincay L Jr9 62500 85-14 Notoriety,UrbnCowboy,BolgerMgic 9
1Aug86-5Dmr 1$\frac{1}{16}$ Ⓣ:47 1:114 1:432fm 38 1115 11½ 2hd 56 710 Patton G D7 Aw20000 79-11 Cro'sHollywood,Grgson,TmFrSkrt 10
1Aug86—Lugged out 7/8 turn, down backstretch
17Jly86-6Hol 1 Ⓣ:454 1:101 1:36 fm 10 1115 22½ 22½ 23½ 35 Black C A6 62500 — — Dmon'sGme,DoubleQust,CountEric 6
4Jly86-9Hol 1$\frac{1}{16}$ Ⓣ:454 1:10 1:413fm 96 116 21 21½ 43 87¾ Pedroza MA8 Aw23000 88 — Full Charm, Gaelic Knight, Jota 12
4May86-6Hol 1 :444 1:103 1:371ft 26 1115 34 48 612 716¾ Black C A7 Aw22000 60-18 Tourismo,SouthernHalo,CutByGlss 8
4May86—Lugged out backstretch
3Apr86-7SA 6f :213 :442 1:093ft 17 117 77 89½ 713 712¼ Pincay L Jr3 Aw24000 78-22 Beu'sLeder,TimeToSmok,IronEys 11
21Mar86-6SA 6½f :211 :434 1:164ft 11 117 67 79½ 68 54 Pincay L Jr3 Aw28000 82-15 RoylTresure,Beu'sLedr,TripoliShors 9
21Mar86—Veered in start
9Mar86-1SA 1 :451 1:103 1:381sy 16 115 512 617 619 620¾ Hernandez R4 Aw31000 56-19 LightningTouch,AckAckHr,ClrChoc 6
9Mar86—Rank at 7 1/2
Oct 22 SA 4f ft :49 h Sep 30 SA 5f ft 1:001 h Sep 22 SA 4f ft :50 h

Roses Are Reb
STEVENS G L 116
Own.—Thompson L E Jr
B. g. 3, by Reb's Policy—Personality Rose, by Personality
Br.—Licht R (Cal) 1986 8 3 0 2 $34,950
Tr.—Canani Julio C $40,000 1985 0 M 0 0
Lifetime 8 3 0 2 $34,950

31Oct86-6SA 6f :212 :443 1:093ft 5¾ 114 21½ 31 31½ 34½ Stevens G L3 45000 85-16 MischievousMtt,Jimed,RosesArRb 11
21Sep86-9Pom 6f :214 :45 1:111ft *1 1125 62¾ 43 43½ 54¼ Black C A3 57500 91-07 TimShr,Hrpr'sRidg,WhipUpThTmpo 8
21Sep86—Bumped at break, wide into lane
11Sep86-11Pom 6½f :22 :454 1:164ft 2¼ 117 1½ 1hd 46 410½ Stevens G L1 Foothill 85-08 J.R.Johnson,ElCorzon,LghtnngToch 8
31Aug86-3Dmr 6f :22 :45 1:092ft *8-5 1115 2hd 31½ 41½ 33¾ Black C A7 Aw24000 87-12 SureToFir,AmzingCourg,RossArRb 7
11Aug86-7Dmr 6f :213 :443 1:092ft 5½ 1085 21 21½ 1hd 1¾ Black C A3 Aw19000 91-13 RosesArRb,Mr.Mdi,WhipUpThTmpo 7
11Aug86—Broke in, bumped

4Aug86-5Dmr 6f :21^4 :45 1:09^{2}ft 12 113^5 2^{hd} 1^{hd} 1^1 1^{1}¾ Black C A^6 c32000 91-13 Roses Are Reb,Notoriety,Arbitrate 12
11Jly86-4Hol 6f :22^2 :46^2 1:11^{3}ft 3½ 109^5 5^2 3^{nk} 1^3 1^{3}½ Black C A^8 M32000 86-14 RossArRb,BoldBrvoII,‡GntlmnDon 11
7Jun86-4Hol 6f :22^1 :45^4 1:11^{1}ft 6¼ 108^5 5^{3}½ 4^{3}½ 4^{7}½ 4^{10}½ Black C A^5 M45000 77-17 Eighty Below Zero, Blue Ice,Felino 8
7Jun86—Broke slowly
Oct 23 SA 6f ft 1:14^3 h Oct 17 SA 6f ft 1:14^4 h Oct 11 SA 5f ft 1:00^3 h Oct 5 SA 5f ft 1:02^1 h

Time Share

Ch. c. 3, by Be a Native—Flower Key, by T V Lark
PEDROZA M A 119
Br.—Pascoe W T III (Cal) 1986 10 3 0 0 $38,375
Tr.—Aguilera Humberto $40,000 1985 4 1 0 1 $3,460
Own.—Aguilera H
Lifetime 14 4 0 1 $39,835

23Oct86-7SA 1 :45 1:10^4 1:38 ft 30 116 4^{6}½ 4^{2}½ 5^{1}¼ 6^{8}½ Douglas R R^4 50000 63-20 BoldDecree,TrojnTrick,Bruli'sAnte 10
5Oct86-7SA 1 :45 1:10^1 1:36^{1}ft 30 111^5 6^{6}¼ 7^{5}¾ 8^{10} 8^{15}¼ Black C A^3 Aw30000 72-15 Full Charm, Scrapbook, Lud 8
21Sep86-9Pom 6f :21^4 :45 1:11^{1}ft 8¼ 116 8^{4}¾ 7^{7}½ 5^{5}½ 1^1 Douglas R R^7 62500 95-07 TimShr,Hrpr'sRidg,WhipUpThTmpo 8
8Sep86-3Dmr 6f :21^4 :45 1:09 ft 30 118 8^{9}¼ 8^{9}¼ 6^{11} 6^{9}¾ Douglas R R^2 62500 84-14 Notoriety,UrbnCowboy,BolgerMgic 9
31Aug86-9Dmr 1 :45^2 1:10^2 1:36^{3}ft 5½ 116 8^{6}½ 6^3 5^3 4^{3}¾ Hernandez R^1 40000 81-12 Joab, Arbitrate, Gaelic Knight 9
3Aug86-2Dmr 6f :21^4 :45 1:09^{3}ft 19 119 10^{7}¾ 9^{5}¾ 4^{5}½ 5^5 Hernandez R^3 50000 85-10 UrbnCowby,EghtyBlwZr,TmthyDy 10
3Aug86—Crowded early; lugged out, steadied 5 1/2
17Jly86-9LA 6½f :22 :45^2 1:17 ft 7½ 109 6^{3}¼ 5^{2}¾ 3^2 1^{1}½ Douglas R R^3 Aw13500 92-11 Time Share,PowerfulEyes,FallFlyer 6
9Jly86-1Hol 6f :22^1 :45^4 1:11 ft 11 116 6^5 6^4 5^{4}½ 5^{5}¼ Hernandez R^7 50000 84-18 Exuberat'sImge,FleetAlbert,EndPly 7
14Jun86-2Hol 6f :22 :45^2 1:10^{4}ft 104 116 4^4 4^{3}½ 3½ 1^{hd} Hernandez R^{10} 32000 90-14 Time Share, East Tulip, New Doc 12
15May86-5Hol 1 :45^3 1:10^3 1:37 ft 32 117 6^{4}¼ 6^{6}¾ 7^{11} 6^{11}¾ Pincay L Jr^2 40000 66-13 Gaelic Knight, Saros Chick, Joab 9
15May86—Bumped; steadied
Oct 31 Hol 4f ft :48^1 h Oct 19 SA 5f ft 1:00^4 h Sep 16 Pom 6f ft 1:15^1 h

Sebucan

B. c. 3, by Exuberant—Exacting Lady, by Disciplinarian
DELAHOUSSAYE E 116
Br.—Saiden A (Fla) 1986 6 2 2 0 $21,675
Tr.—Barrera Lazaro S $40,000 1985 5 M 0 0 $2,125
Own.—Saiden A
Lifetime 11 2 2 0 $23,800

26Oct86-1SA 6f :21^3 :45 1:11 ft 5 116 9^7 7^{4}½ 4^{2}½ 1no DelahoussayeE^1 32000 83-16 Sebucan, End Play, Fleet Albert 12
26Oct86—Veered out, bumped break; steadied, bumped entering stretch
9Jly86-1Hol 6f :22^1 :45^4 1:11 ft 3¾ 116 7^{5}½ 5^{3}½ 4^3 4^{1}¾ Stevens G L^4 50000 87-18 Exubernt'sImge,FleetAlbert,EndPly 7
9Jly86—Bumped start
25Jun86-4Hol 1 :45^2 1:10^4 1:37^{1}ft 2¾ 116 2½ 2½ 3^1 6^4 Stevens G L^5 50000 73-13 Trojan Trick, Joab, Inherent Kal 7
5Jun86-2Hol 6f :22^3 :46^3 1:11 ft *1 115 3^{1}½ 1^{hd} 1^4 1^{10} Stevens G L^6 M32000 89-16 Sbcn,JohnsTomorrow,PlntyOfPlsr 12
26May86-2Hol 6f :22^2 :46 1:11^{4}ft *2 115 8^{4}¾ 5^3 3^{1}½ 2^{hd} Stevens G L^2 M32000 85-17 Fracoza, Sebucan, Watch'n Win 12
10May86-2Hol 6f :22^2 :46 1:11 ft 12 113 6^{5}¾ 3^5 3^{4}½ 2^2 Stevens G L^2 M35000 87-12 Cutting Line, Sebucan, T. H. Lark 8
10May86—Impeded at 5/16
12Dec85-3Hol 1 :45^4 1:11^4 1:38^{1}ft 11 118 2^1 2^{hd} 5^4 7^{7}½ Pedroza M A^9 M40000 64-22 Manzanero,MiamiDrem,Dodo'sLnd 12
22Nov85-4Hol 7f :22 :45^1 1:23 ft 64 118 6^{3}¾ 5^{2}½ 6^{8}½ 4^{11}¼ Pedroza M A^1 M40000 78-10 Air Pirate, Sarotimes, Notoriety 11
22Nov85—Steadied at 5/16
15Nov85-4Hol 1 :46 1:12 1:39^{3}ft 12 118 8^{5}¼ 5^{6}½ 4^8 4^{7}¼ Hernandez R^5 M32000 58-22 ForevrBluJns,MskdChrgr,Thocrtic 11
15Nov85—Pinched back start
25Oct85-4SA 1 1/16 :47^3 1:13^1 1:46^{1}ft 54 118 8^{10} 9^{12} 7^{15} 5^{12}½ Hernandez R^8 M40000 57-23 WhtShowrs,ComtsFlr,ForvrBluJns 11
25Oct85—Bumped 3 1/2
●Nov 3 SA 5f ft :59^1 h Oct 22 SA 5f ft 1:00^2 h ●Oct 14 SA 4f ft :46^4 h Oct 5 SA 3f ft :35^4 h

Another Bloom

B. c. 3, by Beau's Eagle—In the Bloom, by Ruken
PINCAY L JR 116
Br.—Relatively Stable (Cal) 1986 6 1 1 0 $17,425
Tr.—Rose Larry $40,000 1985 1 1 0 0 $10,450
Own.—Relatively Stb & Magnin
Lifetime 7 2 1 0 $27,875

4Oct86-1SA 6½f :21^4 :45 1:17 ft 2¼ 118 2^{1}½ 2^{hd} 1½ 4^2 Pincay L Jr^4 50000 83-18 Inherent Kal, EastTulip,Bruli'sAnte 9
31Aug86-3Dmr 6f :22 :45 1:09^{2}ft 9¼ 116 5^{2}¼ 5^{3}¼ 5^5 6^{8}¾ Sibille R^6 Aw24000 82-12 SureToFir,AmzingCourg,RossArRb 7
15Aug86-7Dmr 7f :22^1 :45 1:22^{3}ft 4 115 1½ 2^{hd} 2^2 5^6 ValenzuelPA^8 Aw21000 86-12 J. R. Johnson, East Tulip,GoSwiftly 8
15Aug86—Lugged in late
23Jly86-7Dmr 6f :21^4 :45^2 1:09^{3}ft 3¾ 115 2½ 2½ 2^{hd} 1^{hd} McCrrnCJ^9 Ⓢ Aw19000 90-12 AnothrBloom,Bugrin,FlyingLssons 10
26Jan86-7SA 6f :21^2 :44^1 1:09^{4}ft *8-5 120 2^{hd} 1^{hd} 5^2 7^{6}¼ Solis A^8 Ⓢ Aw24000 83-12 Air Pirate, Frisco Dennis, Witching 8
9Jan86-5SA 6f :21^3 :44^2 1:09^{2}ft *2½ 120 1^{1}½ 1^1 1^1 2no Solis A^2 Aw24000 91-20 KeenKnight,AnotherBloom,PrssOn 9
28Dec85-3SA 6f :21^2 :44^2 1:09^{3}ft 3 117 2½ 2½ 2½ 1¾ Solis A^2 Ⓢ Mdn 90-14 AnotherBloom,KidShlln,Scrpbook 11
28Dec85—Lost whip 1/8
Nov 4 SA 4f ft :48 h Oct 27 SA 5f ft 1:02^2 h Oct 20 SA 5f ft 1:00^4 h Sep 21 SA 5f ft 1:02^1 h

Lans Manus

Ch. g. 3, by Canadian Gil—Six Pillows, by Golden Eagle II
VALENZUELA P A 116
Br.—Wood Mrs S (Cal) 1986 11 2 2 1 $22,325
Tr.—Stepp William T $40,000 1985 4 1 1 0 $10,625
Own.—Greenberg–Lanni–Stepp
Lifetime 15 3 3 1 $32,950

29Oct86-1SA 6½f :21^4 :44^3 1:17 ft 2½ 116 1^{hd} 1½ 1½ 1^{2}¾ Solis A^6 20000 85-17 LansManus,KeniDncer,PecefulImge 8
16Oct86-5SA 6½f :21^3 :44^4 1:17^{1}ft 8½ 116 2½ 2^{hd} 1^{hd} 1^{1}¾ Solis A^9 16000 84-19 Lans Manus, Blue Ice, BlackCross 11
9Oct86-7BM 6f :22 :45^1 1:10^{2}ft 7 115 3^1 4^{1}¼ 1½ 2¾ Maple S^7 16000 86-19 SecrtArch,LnsMnus,BoldrWhnOldr 9
27Sep86-8Pom 6½f :21^2 :44^4 1:18^{2}ft 5½ 116 1^{hd} 2^1 2^{1}½ 8^{9}¾ Mena F^5 32000 78-10 ‡Trinity Hall, Premiere, Noon Sun 9
20Sep86-8Pom 6½f :21^2 :45 1:17 ft 11 116 5^{5}¼ 4^6 4^{3}½ 3^{4}¾ Douglas R R^3 22500 90-09 New Doc, Sea And Sew,LansManus 8
11Sep86-10Pom 6½f :22 :46 1:17^{2}ft 10 112 4^{1}½ 4^3 4^4 2^{2}½ Stevens S A^{10} 22500 90-08 NtvForcst,LnsMnus,RnnngRmpnt 10
31Aug86-2Dmr 6f :21^4 :44^4 1:08^{4}ft 7½ 116 2^1 2^{2}½ 2^4 5^{11}¾ Fernandez AL^{12} 25000 82-12 GrowlrSnd,HndflOfDmnd,Prcntstr 12
31Aug86—Rough start
21Jly86-5LA 6½f :22 :45^4 1:17^{2}ft 4¼ 114 1^{1}½ 2^{hd} 2^{1}½ 5^9 Fernandez A L^1 25000 81-12 JohnsTomorrow,ActvRmn,Prcntstr 5
9Jly86-1Hol 6f :22^1 :45^4 1:11 ft 14 115 1^1 4^{3}½ 7^{12} — Valenzuela P A^1 45000 — — Exubernt'sImge,FleetAlbert,EndPly 7
9Jly86—Eased
7Mar86-2SA 6f :21 :44^1 1:10 ft 18 114 5^7 8^{9}¾ 8^{10} 6^{13}½ Hernandez R^3 40000 74-14 HovringPrsnc,GrnPirr,BckStrtBlus 8
7Mar86—Eased in stretch
Oct 8 BM 3f ft :38^4 h

```
Fleet Albert                       Gr. c. 3, by First Albert—Grey Sister, by Iron Ruler
                                   Br.—Hughes Stable (Fla)                1986 14 0 1 2     $18,065
  FERNANDEZ A L            116     Tr.—Cerin Vladimir           $40,000   1985  6 1 2 0      $7,725
Own.—Landsburg A                   Lifetime   20 1 3 2   $25,790
26Oct86-1SA   6f :21^3 :45 1:11 ft       19 116  10^9½ 10^6¾ 5^2½ 3^1¼  Solis A^9          32000 82-16 Sebucan, End Play, Fleet Albert 12
    26Oct86—Steadied start
13Oct86-3SA   6f :22 :45^3 1:11 ft       5¾ 116  6^2¾ 5^2 3^5 4^5¾      Soto S B^6         40000 77-19 Wtch'nWin,EndPly,MischievousMtt 6
    13Oct86—Wide final 3/8
5Oct86-3SA    6f :21^2 :44^1 1:10^2 ft   13 116  5^2½ 4^1½ 4^2¾ 4^4½    Soto S B^9         32000 81-15 SprbMomnt,HmngAngl,EghtyBlwZr 9
    5Oct86—Drifted out, wide into stretch
14Sep86-10Pom 6½f :21^3 :45 1:16^2 ft    19 112  8^6¾ 6^11 6^8½ 5^5½    Castanon A L^1 Aw25000 92-08 Tuono, Growler Sandue,BoldDecree 9
15Aug86-3Dmr  6f :21^4 :45^2 1:09^3 ft   7½ 116  11^7¾ 10^3¾ 6^4½ 5^5½  Ortega L E^7       40000 84-12 Frcoz,SprbMomnt,Mybrry'sMdnss 12
3Aug86-2Dmr   6f :21^4 :45 1:09^3 ft     *2 117  5^5½ 6^5 6^8 7^10¼     Pincay L Jr^4      50000 80-10 UrbnCowby,EghtyBlwZr,TmthyDy 10
    3Aug86—Bumped, steadied at 5 1/2
9Jly86-1Hol   6f :22^1 :45^4 1:11 ft     9¼ 116  5^4 3^2 3^1½ 2^no      Soto S B^6         50000 89-18 Exubernt'sImge,FleetAlbert,EndPly 7
26Jun86-1Hol  6f :22 :45 1:09^4 ft       18 114  8^6¾ 7^7¼ 6^7¼ 5^7¼    Castanon A L^7     57500 88-12 J. R. Johnson, Totality, Rinnegato 8
    26Jun86—Bumped start
15Jun86-3Hol  6f :22^1 :45^3 1:11^1 ft   14 116  6^4½ 5^3¾ 3^3½ 4¾      Castanon A L^9     50000 87-13 J.R.Johnson,AnglArc,EghtyBlowZro 9
21May86-7Hol  6f :22^3 :46^3 1:11^1 ft   42 116  4^1½ 3½ 3^1½ 4^4       ValenzuelPA^6  Aw20000 84-13 Mrvn'sPolcy,TommyThHwk,SmrtLf 9
  Oct 23 SA 3f ft :36^2 h        Sep 27 SA 5f ft 1:01 h
```

```
Fracoza                            Ch. g. 3, by Messenger of Song—Long Issue, by Long Position
                                   Br.—Cozza F (Cal)                      1986 8 2 1 1      $21,175
  OLIVARES F               116     Tr.—Dorfman Leonard          $40,000   1985 0 M 0 0
Own.—Blalunt Mr–Mrs D              Lifetime    8 2 1 1   $21,175
31Oct86-6SA   6f :21^2 :44^3 1:09^3 ft   8¼ 116  6^3½ 5^4 4^5½ 4^7½     Olivares F^11      50000 82-16 MischievousMtt,Jimed,RosesArRb 11
8Sep86-3Dmr   6f :21^4 :45 1:09 ft       3¾ 116  5^4¾ 6^8¼ 8^13 7^9½    Olivares F^5       62500 83-14 Notoriety,UrbnCowboy,BolgerMgic 9
    8Sep86—Lugged out badly; took up at 3/16, wide into stretch
15Aug86-3Dmr  6f :21^4 :45^2 1:09^3 ft   *5 116  9^2¼ 3½ 2½ 1^2½        Olivares F^12      40000 90-12 Frcoz,SprbMomnt,Mybrry'sMdnss 12
    15Aug86—Wide 3/8 turn
3Aug86-2Dmr   6f :21^4 :45 1:09^3 ft     12 115  8^6¼ 8^5¼ 7^7¼ 6^8     Olivares F^8       45000 82-10 UrbnCowby,EghtyBlwZr,TmthyDy 10
    3Aug86—Broke slowly, bumped steadied start; lugged out 3/8 turn
12Jly86-7Hol  6f :22^1 :45^2 1:10^4 ft   18 119  5^2½ 3^2 2^3½ 2^3½     Olivares F^10      32000 86-14 New Doc, Fracoza,NativeForecast 11
26May86-2Hol  6f :22^2 :46 1:11^4 ft     6¾ 115  3½ 1^hd 1^hd 1^hd      Olivares F^4      M32000 85-17 Fracoza, Sebucan, Watch'n Win 12
27Apr86-2Hol  6f :22^2 :46^2 1:12^1 ft   4½ 115  6^5½ 6^6¼ 4^5½ 3^3     Olivares F^11     M32000 80-15 Ego Buck, Native Reality, Fracoza 12
10Apr86-3SA   6f :21^4 :45 1:11^3 ft     3¾ 118  6^4 7^7 5^3½ 4^2       DelhoussyE^8  [S]M32000 78-21 SrosChick,CuttingLin,SplshOfWtr 12
  Oct 27 SA 5f ft 1:02^2 h    Oct 20 SA 5f ft :59[illegible] h    Oct 13 SA 5f ft 1:04 h    ●Sep 19 SA tr.t 5f ft 1:00^3 h
```

96. One horse in the Hollywood sprint has a clear early speed advantage. Which is it?

A. *Pialor* **(9)**
B. *Roses Are Reb*
C. *Another Bloom*
D. *Lans Manus*

97. How many horses in the Hollywood field have acceptable early speed?

A. 4 **(9)**
B. 5
C. 6
D. 3

98. The highest percentage of speed points accumulated by any horse in the Hollywood race is

A. 22% **(9)**
B. 25%
C. 28%
D. 33%

99. The most useful guideline regarding the relationship between early speed and class is

A. In routes among nonclaiming horses, class laughs **(7)**
at early speed
B. The horses most likely to rise in class successfully
have high early speed
C. High early speed is the hallmark of superior class
D. The class horse on the lead alone is the likeliest
winner at any track

100. Which factor most frequently provides the explanation when an uncontested frontrunner collapses?

A. pedigree **(7)**
B. class
C. weight
D. form

Answer key: Early speed

Minimum Competency Test

41. C	46. A
42. B	47. A
43. A	48. B
44. A	49. A
45. C	50. A

Mastery Test

51. B	61. C	71. B	81. D	91. D
52. D	62. B	72. C	82. B	92. C
53. C	63. B	73. D	83. A	93. C
54. A	64. D	74. A	84. D	94. B
55. A	65. C	75. B	85. B	95. D
56. C	66. A	76. B	86. B	96. D
57. A	67. C	77. A	87. D	97. A
58. D	68. D	78. B	88. C	98. B
59. C	69. C	79. B	89. B	99. D
60. A	70. A	80. D	90. B	100. D

CHAPTER 5

Class Appraisal

Competencies

10. Know the basic facts, probabilities, and conventional methods of class appraisal.
11. Identify past performance patterns well-suited and not suitable to specific conditions of eligibility that are standard in U.S. racing.
12. Understand the relationships between class and speed.
13. Relate the class factor to the basic principles of form, pace, sex, age, et al.
14. Interpret familiar class drops and class rises.
15. Interpret horses' records in terms of demonstrated class and potential class.
16. Presented the records of two or more horses, select the best horse.

	Minimum Competency Test	Mastery Test
Proficiency standards	80%	70%
Number of items	25	80
Passing scores	20	56

Sources of Instruction

- *The Handicapper's Condition Book*, chapters 2–8, 10–11
- *Betting Thoroughbreds*, chapters 9 & 10
- *Class of the Field*, chapters 1–3, 6 & 8

Comments

Class handicapping as method has been out of fashion since the mid-seventies, as numerical speed rating methods that emphasized data not trapped in the past performance tables of the *Daily Racing Form* began to find the overlays. But nobody can beat this game for important money if they are not equipped to make accurate class distinctions.

The rub is precisely that. Too many expert method players fall apart embarrassingly on the class factor. Speed and pace fanciers, the numbers merchants, seem peculiarly susceptible to the tendency. No doubt too many of them have fallen under the spell of their figures. But the numbers are intended to reflect reality, not substitute for it. When the figures are wrong, misleading, or inconclusive, as happens often, it's clever to recognize the situation for what it is and recognize which horse "figures" to reign as class of the field.

A huge slice of the practitioner's problem can be traced to the conventional wisdom on class, not excluding the definitions and methods distributed in books. Much of it is nonsense. Incomplete definition, inaccurate definition, and global definition have led to methods of class handicapping similarly encompassing, incomplete, and faulty.

I have never believed the class factor the most important in handicapping, but long, thoughtful experience has convinced me that for most practitioners it is the most difficult. The tests that follow are intended to help set the record straight. If experience proves instructive, they should also be the most troublesome for most readers of this book.

Definitions of Terms

- *Good race.* A finish in the money or within two lengths in sprints; within three lengths in routes.

- *Listed stakes.* A stakes race of sufficient prestige or value to be "listed" on the pages of international sales catalogs; has no eligibility restrictions and a minimum purse of $50,000 added.

- *NW2XMC.* A notation that means "nonwinners two times other than maiden or claiming (races)." This is a shorthand for notating the eligibility conditions of the nonwinners allowance races. The numerals change from 1 to 4.

CLASS APPRAISAL: MINIMUM COMPETENCY TEST

101. The fastest horses are also the classiest.

A. True   (12)
B. False

102. Horses dropping in class win twice as many races as probabilities would expect.

    A. True   **(10)**
    B. False

103. The most reliable method of modern class appraisal emphasizes

    A. the average purse values of a horse's good perfor-   **(10)**
       mances
    B. the typical class demands of eligibility condi-
       tions
    C. consistency against a specific level of opposition
    D. pace ratings at both fractional and final points of
       call

104. The classiest colt of any generation is likely to be a brilliant horse (high speed) that can win in above-average time at classic distances.

    A. True   **(12)**
    B. False

105. Which is usually the toughest step-up in claiming class?

    A. $2500 to $5000   **(14)**
    B. $5000 to $10,000
    C. $10,000 to $20,000
    D. $20,000 to $40,000

106. Class tends to become more decisive as distances lengthen.

    A. True   **(13)**
    B. False

107. Which factor is most likely to nullify a decisive edge in class?

    A. lack of recency   **(13)**
    B. high weight
    C. track bias
    D. a troubled trip

108. In what kind of races open to older horses do the 3-year-olds of June hold a decisive advantage?

A. maiden **(13)**
B. nonwinners allowance
C. restricted stakes
D. claiming

109. In Grade 1 races 3up at classic distances, class laughs at pace.

A. True **(13)**
B. False

110. A class drop of what percentage is the most powerful known impact value in handicapping?

A. 20% **(10)**
B. 25%
C. 30%
D. 40%

111. Which horses are most likely to move ahead in class dramatically?

A. lightly raced nonclaiming 3YOs **(14)**
B. first-time stakes winners
C. 4up claiming horses that have back class
D. bred for grass, poor dirt form, switching from dirt to turf today

112. Which statement best summarizes *Gentleman Don's* first race against winners?

Gentleman Don	Ch. g. 3, by Crimson Star—Gentleman's Fancy, by Gallant Heritage	
MENA F	Br.—Vanston E (Ark)	1986 8 1 1 0 $6,680
	114	Tr.—Sherman Art $16,000	1985 0 M 0 0
Own.—Marelich or Marelich	Lifetime 8 1 1 0 $6,680	

260ct86-5BM   6f :222 :454 1:113ft *3-2 114   42 41¾ 75½ 62½   Baze R A5   c12500 79-20 TmpstDTmpo,NvrSyDn,GdOlBddy 12
  260ct86—Crowded 3/16
160ct86-3BM   6f :22   :45 1:09 ft *3-5 117   1hd 11 11½ 12½   Baze R A4   M12500 94-18 GntlmnDon,Erin'sGlory,Wdsworth 12
18Sep86-4Pom 6¼f:22   :454 1:184ft *6-5 114   1hd 12 12½ 2¾   Pedroza M A4 M25000 85-12 GrampyJck,GentlemnDon,Mfunzio 10
28Aug86-2Dmr 6f :214 :452 1:112ft *2 117   12½ 13½ 13 54½   Douglas R R10 M32000 77-18 FstFling,PrincelyPretense,Sobrity 11
  28Aug86—Broke in, bumped
13Aug86-2Dmr 6f :214 :452 1:104ft   11 116   2hd 11 11½ 42½   Douglas R R3 M32000 82-15 Brand Image, Blue Ice, Shucinto 12
  13Aug86—Green backstretch, 3/8 turn
23Jly86-4Dmr 6⅜f:224 :453 1:161ft   4¾ 116   — — — —   DelahoussyeE1 M32000 — — TahoeTngo,SirDmon,SlipperySilver 9
  23Jly86—Lost rider; Veered in sharply break
11Jly86-4Hol 6f :222 :462 1:113ft   11 116   2nd 1hd 23 34¾ † DelahoussyeE9 M32000 81-14 RossArRb,BoldBrvoII,‡GntlmnDon 11
  11Jly86—Drifted out, bumped late; †Disqualified and placed fourth
Oct 12 BM 4f ft :481 h   Oct 5 BM 3f ft :362 h

A. The gelding was a distinct underlay **(15)**
B. The bad trip discounts the loss, and the horse is acceptable today versus $16,000 winners

C. The class rise following the claim is perfectly acceptable

D. As an obviously improving 3YO, the gelding is not really rising in class at all

113. The 3YO below is acceptable on class at the $16,000 claiming level.

A. True **(15)**

B. False

Good Ol Buddy — Ch. g. 3, by Buddy Larosa—Table Prize, by Tilt Top
DOOCY T T — 114 — Br.—Morris Boyd G Mr (Okla) — 1986 6 1 2 1 $10,531
Tr.—Green Mike — $16,000 — 1985 0 M 0 0
Own.—Foster-Green-Halcomb — Lifetime 6 1 2 1 $10,531

26Oct86-5BM	6f	$:22^2$	$:45^4$	$1:11^3$ft	23	114	2½	1^{hd}	1^1	3^1	Lamance C^{11}	12500	80-20	TmpstDTmpo,NvrSyDn,GdOlBddy	12
9Oct86-7BM	6f	:22	$:45^1$	$1:10^2$ft	21	114	1^1	1^{hd}	2½	$7^{5¼}$	SchvneveldtCP^1	16000	82-19	SecrtArch,LnsMnus,BoldrWhnOldr	9
29Aug86-7Cby	6f	$:22^3$	$:45^1$	1:11 ft	*2-3e	112	4^{4½}	3^{4½}	2^{4½}	2^2	Smith M E^8	Ⓡ Aw15930	90-11	Fast Catch, Good Ol Buddy, Waseca	8
23Aug86-1Cby	6f	$:23^1$	:47	$1:14^1$ft	*2-3	118	1½	1½	1^{1½}	1^{1½}	Kutz D^5	Ⓡ M25000	76-13	Good Ol Buddy, Sarah C., Lanade	11
17Aug86-2Cby	6f	:23	$:46^3$	$1:13^1$ft	4¼	118	1^3	2^{hd}	2^{1½}	2^{1½}	Kutz D^6	Ⓡ Mdn	79-14	RoylExbrnc,GodOlBddy,SnppyVctry	6
18Jly86-1BRD	5½f	:22	:46	$1:05^3$ft	5	115^5	7^{4½}	7^{9½}	5^{12}	5^{16¼}	Deaver K P^3	Mdn	73-13	IronSpud,MssBoldPrncss,RskyCty	10

Nov 7 BM 3f ft $:35^3$ h — Oct 19 BM 5f ft $1:03^2$ h — Oct 5 BM 4f ft :50 h — Sep 30 BM 5f ft $1:03^1$ h

114. At what class level should *Little Lou* be expected to run its next good race?

A. Alw, NW1XMC **(15)**

B. $50,000

C. $25,000

D. $12,500

Little Lou — Dk. b. or br. f. 2, by Regal Bearing—Scimitara, by Drum Fire
HANSEN R D — 113 — Br.—Rick-Hard Stables (Wash) — 1986 3 1 1 0 $5,310
Tr.—Wright Richard
Own.—Reiniger R — Lifetime 3 1 1 0 $5,310

29Oct86-6Lga	6½f	$:21^4$	$:45^2$	$1:18^1$sy	3½	113^5	3^6	2^2	1½	1^4	Gibson R G^1	Ⓕ M25000	78-26	LittleLou,BonnieMusic,Dosewallips	9
11Oct86-4Lga	6½f	$:21^3$	$:44^3$	$1:17^4$ft	9	113^5	8^{6¼}	7^{8¼}	4^{8½}	2½	$GbsnRG^{10}$	Ⓕ Ⓢ M25000	79-16	ShdowMker,LittleLou,SntimntlWy	12
26Sep86-4Lga	6½f	$:21^4$	$:46^4$	$1:22^2$m	13	118	5^{11}	3^{4½}	4^{10}	4^{9½}	$WardWA^{10}$	Ⓕ Ⓢ M25000	47-45	MssSllong,ShdowMkr,WndyTALrk	10

Nov 7 BM 3f ft $:36^3$ h — Oct 24 Lga 4f ft $:49^4$ b — Oct 5 Lga 4f ft $:50^4$ b — Sep 21 Lga 4f ft :49 b

115. Which is the most impressive performance in *Ocean View's* record?

A. San Matean H. **(15)**

B. All-American

C. Oakland H.

D. Breeders' Cup H.

Ocean View

Ch. h. 5, by Nodouble—Summertide, by Crewman

CASTANEDA M	**119**	Br.—Elmendorf Farm (Ky)	1986 10 3 1 3	$198,850
Own.—Cardiff Stud Farm		Tr.—McAnally Ronald	1985 7 2 2 0	$47,350
		Lifetime 34 8 8 4 $408,575	Turf 15 3 4 2	$252,575

17Oct86-8BM	1$\frac{1}{16}$:461 1:093 1:402ft	8$\frac{1}{2}$ 116	78$\frac{1}{2}$ 77$\frac{3}{4}$ 69$\frac{1}{2}$ 59$\frac{1}{2}$	CstndM8 B M Br Cp H 80-16	Hopeful Word, Armin, Bozina 8
4Oct86-8BM	1$\frac{1}{8}$①:4841:13 1:483fm	11 116	21$\frac{1}{2}$ 2$\frac{1}{2}$ 56 68$\frac{1}{2}$	CstndM8 Tanforan H 88-03	TruceMker,CleverSong,HonorMedl 8
4Oct86—Grade III					
13Sep86-11Bmf	1$\frac{1}{16}$:4821:12 1:422fm	2$\frac{1}{2}$ 120	2$\frac{1}{2}$ 1hd 2nd 3$\frac{1}{2}$	CstndM4 Sn Matean H 90-09	Quintillon, El Mansour, OceanView 7
7Jun86-8GG	1$\frac{1}{16}$:471 1:103 1:423ft	*6-5 122	3^2 52$\frac{1}{2}$ 54$\frac{1}{2}$ 46	CstdM2 ㊫Dmg CtIlvH 84-15	PrinceDonB.,RpidRogu,LordNorman 6
7Jun86—Steadied 1st turn; lugged out drive					
25May86-8GG	7$\frac{1}{2}$f①:22 :452 1:28 fm	4$\frac{1}{2}$ 117	45$\frac{1}{2}$ 57 43 34	CstndM5 All Amrcn H 96-09	CleverSong,TruceMaker,OceanView 7
25May86—Grade III; Crowded backstretch					
10May86-8GG	1$\frac{1}{16}$:461 1:103 1:424ft	3$\frac{1}{2}$ 120	2^1 21$\frac{1}{2}$ 2nd 1$\frac{3}{4}$	CastndM6 Oakland H 89-22	OcenView,Ascension,CelticVenture 7
19Apr86-6GG	1$\frac{1}{16}$①:4631:1031:42 fm	4$\frac{1}{2}$ 113	46$\frac{1}{2}$ 34$\frac{1}{2}$ 23 1nk	CstndM3 Brdrs' Cup H 92-09	OceanView,Introspective,Alphbtim 7
12Apr86-8GG	1$\frac{1}{16}$①:4621:1111:42 fm	5 118	57 3$\frac{1}{2}$ 1hd 1nk	CstdM4 ㊫Tly Pp Iv H 92-09	OcenView,Introspective,DrkAccnt 11
5Apr86-4GG	7$\frac{1}{2}$f①:223 :4541:282fm	4$\frac{1}{2}$ 115	42 44 33$\frac{1}{2}$ 29	CastanedaM1 Aw22000 89-08	Clever Song, Ocean View, Ablantin 9
19Jan86-8BM	1 :463 1:112 1:364gd	10 116	6$\frac{4}{2}$ 63$\frac{3}{4}$ 33 33	CstndM5 W P Kyne H 81-29	PrinceDonB.,BedsidPromis,OcnViw 7
Nov 6 BM 4f ft :483 h		Oct 31 BM 5f ft 1:00 h		Oct 12 BM 5f ft :592 h	Sep 27 BM 5f m 1:023 h

116. The most reliable means of evaluating a 2-year-old's ability is

    A. speed figures   **(13)**
    B. dosage indexes
    C. early speed
    D. average purse values

117. *Reel Easy* is well-suited to the conditions.

    A. True   **(11)**
    B. False

8th Aqueduct

1 $\frac{1}{8}$ MILES. (1.47) 9th Running THE BUSHER HANDICAP. $60,000 Added. Fillies. 3-year-olds. By subscription of $100 each, which should accompany the nomination; $1,000 to pass the entry box, with $60,000 added. The added money and all fees to be divided 60% to the winner, 22% to second, 12% to third and 6% to fourth. Weights Tuesday, November 4. Starters to be named at the closing time of entries. A trophy will be presented to the winning owner. Closed Wednesday, October 22, 1986, with 21 nominations.

Reel Easy

B. f. 3, by Northern Baby—Kushka, by First Landing

	114	Br.—Jones Brereton C (Ky)	1986 9 3 2 0	$70,083
Own.—Peskoff S D		Tr.—Preger Mitchell C	1985 3 2 0 0	$28,800
		Lifetime 12 5 2 0 $98,883	Turf 1 0 0 0	

23Oct86-8Aqu	1 :454 1:103 1:36 ft	*3-2 112	1hd 2hd 22$\frac{1}{2}$ 22	Migliore R5 ㊫HcpO 84-17	Crrie'sDrem,ReelEsy,CherryJubilee 6
12Oct86-7Bel	7f :22 :434 1:23 ft	19 112	37 213 25 11$\frac{1}{2}$	Migliore R7 ㊫Aw36000 87-13	ReelEsy,MistressMontgue,Argntrio 8
22Jun86-9Aks	1$\frac{1}{16}$:482 1:124 1:444ft	*6-5 120	11$\frac{1}{2}$ 11 11$\frac{1}{2}$ 13$\frac{1}{2}$	Lively J4 ㊫Princess 79-25	ReelEsy,TrustAQun,SndnillDimond 6
31May86-8Aks	170:482 1:141 1:461ft	2$\frac{3}{4}$ 110	21 2hd 1hd 1nk	Lively J4 ㊫Aw16700 66-32	Reel Easy, Pet Bird, Stan's Lady 8
18May86-6Aks	170:51 1:183 1:53 sl	3$\frac{3}{4}$ 108	56$\frac{1}{2}$ 714 716 716$\frac{3}{4}$	CordovDW1 ㊫Aw20000 — —	BellStt,RiseUpAndOnce,BbyBupers 7
12Mar86-7SA	1 :462 1:12 1:37 sy	8-5e 114	23 23 37$\frac{1}{2}$ 416$\frac{3}{4}$	Solis A3 ㊫Aw35000 66-25	Nture'sWy,SilntArrivl,TropiclHolidy 5
20Feb86-8SA	6$\frac{1}{2}$f :22 :453 1:174m	15 117	32 33$\frac{1}{2}$ 47 48$\frac{1}{2}$	Solis A4 ㊫Aw31000 73-27	NervousBb,SilentArrivl,AnEmpress 7
12Jan86-8Aqu	170⊡:4741:1241:434ft	2$\frac{3}{4}$ 116	55 46$\frac{1}{2}$ 413 4:7	CordroAJr8 ㊫Busanda 64-20	PatriciJ.K.,Trcy'sEspoir,DynmicStr 8
Nov 1 Bel 4f ft :48 b		Oct 9 Bel 5f ft :593 h		● Sep 30 Bel 6f ft 1:13 h	Sep 22 Bel 5f ft 1:00 h

118. When in form, to what claiming level should *Exuberant Devil* be expected to rise?

    A. $8000   **(14)**
    B. $10,000
    C. $12,500
    D. $16,000

```
Exuberant Devil               Dk. b. or br. h. 5, by Exuberant—Demi Devil, by Herbager
  SOTO S                      Br.—Opstein K (Fla)                       1986 11  1  3  2     $16,635
                        114   Tr.—Greenman Walter            $6,250     1985 12  1  0  1     $11,825
Own.—Avina & Perez          Lifetime   43  4  8  4   $65,704
     Entered 22Nov86- 3 BM
 8Nov86-10BM    1 1/16:463 1:12  1:451ft  *2½ 114  34  11  41¾ 57½  Gonzalez R M8    6250 58-25 Longpo Free, Malta, Accu Back   11
25Oct86-10BM    1 1/16:462 1:111 1:44 ft   7¼ 114  13  13  2½  22¼  Gonzalez R M1    8000 69-21 BrgnStndrd,ExbrntDvl,TostYorHst  9
16Oct86-1SA     1    :461 1:113 1:381ft    8¾ 118  33½ 55  812 914¼ Soto S B7       10000 63-19 VisibleAsset,BombyBrtndr,Bstl.dr 10
24Sep86-10Poma  1⅛   :473 1:132 1:544sy    5½ 117  811 1020 —  —    Sibille R3       9000 — — Nostradamus, PrideOfTroy,OhDad  10
     24Sep86—Eased; Steadied at break
 4Sep86-3Dmr   7f    :224  :46 1:232ft   *4-5 122  1hd 5½  76½ 810½ Valenzuela P A7 10000 77-14 Nostrdmus,AffirmedNtiv,AccuBck  10
     4Sep86—Wide 3/8 turn
25Aug86-9Dmr    1    :454 1:112 1:372ft   *2½ 118  1½  11  12½ 21¼  Valenzuela P A2 10000 80-16 Morse, ExuberantDevil,SurgingOn 10
17Aug86-1Dmr    1    :461 1:113 1:372ft    *1 116  11½ 11½ 11½ 1½   Valenzuela P A2 10000 81-16 ExubrntDvil,GrnBrb,ClsscEndvour  10
30Jly86-1Dmr    1⅛   :451 1:101 1:484ft     6 116  33  1hd 1hd 31   Soto S B2       12500 85-11 Vorlaufer,VictoryLe,ExuberntDevil 8
     30Jly86—Very wide late
23Jly86-1Dmr    1 1/16:45 1:094 1:422ft    7½ 114  44  34  34  46¼  Soto S B2       14000 82-12 OnEydRomo,FlthorpMrinr,Susumu   11
     23Jly86—Checked, altered course at 7/8
 4Jly86-1Hol   6f    :221  :453 1:102ft     8 116  53¼ 43  34  22¼  Soto S B2       12500 90-09 ExclusivKing,ExubrntDvil,Inquisitiv 6
  Nov 5 BM 3f ft :364 h          Oct 11 Hol 5f ft 1:022 h          Oct 5 Hol 3f ft :353 h
```

119. *Pair of Aces* would be clearly outclassed in a listed stakes.

A. True **(11)**
B. False

```
Pair Of Aces                  Ch. g. 6, by Beau Buck—Spring Pear, by Poleax
  BAZE R A                    Br.—Hawn W R (Ky)                         1986 17  5  2  3     $81,655
                        115   Tr.—Roberts Tom                           1985 15  2  2  4     $59,650
Own.—Love & Tulving Jr      Lifetime   59 13  7 13  $301,945            Turf 29  8  2  8    $174,750
26Oct86-6BM    7½f Ⓣ:231 :4641:294fm*7-5 114  610 53  2hd 1½   Baze R A3        Aw22000 95-05 PairOfAces,NewAtraction,ReglBrek 6
     26Oct86—Drifted in 1/8
18Oct86-5BM    1 1/16Ⓣ:48 1:1231:432fm*6-5 114 86½ 63¼ 11  1no  Baze R A7          65000 86-16 PirOfAces,LittleLook,Position'sBst 9
27Sep86-6BM    1 1/16Ⓣ:4821:1221:43 yl  2¾ 114  43  31½ 1½  13   Tohill K S3       c50000 88-12 PirOfAces,Sidersell,Position'sBest 10
13Sep86-11Bmf  1 1/16Ⓣ:4821:12 1:422fm  8½ 113  42  3½  3nk 41   ThllKS5 Sn Matean H 90-09 Quintillon, El Mansour, OceanView 7
     13Sep86—Wide far turn, drive
31Aug86-9Bmf   7½f Ⓣ:224 :4541:291fm    3 115  59  58  12  1½   Tohill K S5         65000 98-02 PirOfAcs,DiplomtRulr,NwAtrction 10
17Aug86-10Stk  1 1/16:483 1:123 1:43 ft *2-3 116  32  31  1hd 2hd  CstnedM2 Sweepida H 88-07 GrndExchnge,PirOfAcs,LordNormn 5
 3Aug86-11SR   1 1/16:45 1:09  1:394ft   4¼ 112  56  55  32½ 31½  Tohill KS3 J T Grce H 103-03 Castle Tweed, Armin, Pair Of Aces 7
20Jly86-11Sol  1 1/16:463 1:103 1:42 ft   5 112  33  32  24  27   Tohill K S5 Val Dy H 82-14 Armin, Pair Of Aces, Lord Norman 9
     20Jly86—Bumped 1/8
 6Jly86-11Pln  1⅛ :48  1:121 1:494ft    11 112  21  1hd 612 613¾ Castro J M1 Almdn H 72-18 HonorMedal,Ascension,Impulsively 7
15Jun86-4GG    1 1/16Ⓣ:4841:2411:434fm 3½ 116  1½  1hd 1hd 1¾   Baze R A1           65000 83-14 PairOfAces,ElMansour,RosaCarnin 6
  Nov 5 BM Ⓣ4f fm :504 h (d)   Oct 15 BM Ⓣ4f fm :492 h (d)   Oct 18 BM 4f ft :472 h   Sep 12 BM 3f ft :373 h
```

120. What kind of horse is *Foligno*?

A. classified allowance **(15)**
B. open and listed stakes
C. high-priced claiming
D. nonwinners allowance

```
Foligno                       Gr. rig. 4, by Foolish Pleasure—Zerelda, by In Reality
                              Br.—Miller & West Mr-Mrs R S (Ky)         1986 14  5  2  2    $115,077
Own.—Augustin Stablees  115   Tr.—Sheppard Jonathan E                   1985 15  3  2  5     $83,583
                            Lifetime   36 11  4 10  $236,304            Turf  8  1  1  1     $32,033
 1Nov86-6Aqu   7f   :23   :454 1:223ft    4½ 117  83½ 63¼ 31½ 1nk  Antley C W3   Aw36000 88-19 Foligno,‡Mr.T.AndM,BoltingHolm  10
18Oct86-3Med   170 :472 1:113 1:411ft     2 122  41½ 2hd 12  1¾   Santos J A3   Aw25000 90-15 Foligno, Misty Mac, Plairoh      6
 9Oct86-9Med   1 1/16:473 1:123 1:431ft   2½ 122  45  42½ 3½  47   Santos J A3   Aw25000 80-20 Skip Trial, Just A Miner, Old Main 6
27Sep86-8Med   170 :471 1:113 1:411sy     4¼ 122  21½ 21  2½  11   Santos J A5   Aw25000 90-18 Foligno, Fuzzy, Lutz II          5
19Sep86-8Med   170 :471 1:12  1:412ft   *7-5 115  42½ 41½ 3nk 1¾   Santos J A5   Aw25000 89-17 Foligno,KingOfBridlewood,IronFce 9
 1Sep86-6Pha   1   :48  1:121 1:371ft    *2¼ 122  42¼ 2½  1hd 21¼  Dufton E2     Aw17000 87-18 Flight of Time, Foligno, Fuddy Dud 6
16Aug86-6Pim   6f  :231  :461 1:111ft    *2¼ 119  79¾ 77¼ 77½ 52   BraccialeVJr6 Aw18000 88-19 Bryantown,DoverRidge,Sparrowvon 7
26Jly86-8Pha   6f  :212  :441 1:09 ft     12 115  69¾ 76¾ 56  44½  WlfrdJ5 Gallnt Bob H 91-12 Berngoo, Embi's Drone, Jyp      7
  ●Sep 15 Med 5f ft :583 h
```

121. What claiming class would be most hospitable to *Vatza Matter*?

A. $50,000 **(11)**
B. $40,000
C. $30,000
D. $60,000

Vatza Matter B. c. 3, by Vatza—Hollow Creek Miss, by Restless Native
Br.—Buckingham Farm &Freeman (NY) 1986 9 3 1 2 $57,280
Own.—Buckingham Farm 117 Tr.—Freeman Willard C $50,000 1985 2 M 0 0
Lifetime 11 3 1 2 $57,280 Turf 9 3 1 2 $57,280

9Oct86-7Bel	$1\frac{1}{16}$Ⓣ:$47^3$1:12 1:44^2fm	16	114	$7^{4\frac{3}{4}}$	$6^{4\frac{1}{4}}$	3^1	$1^{\frac{1}{2}}$	Davis R G^5	[S]Aw29500	74-26	VtzMtter,ExpditionMoon,RcPoint	12
21Sep86-4Bel	$1\frac{1}{4}$[T]:$50^1$1:$38^2$2:03^1hd	8-5	113	$4^{2\frac{1}{2}}$	1^{hd}	2^{hd}	$2^{2\frac{3}{4}}$	Davis R G^6	[S]Aw28000	75-20	SingWithMe,VtzMtter,FestYourEys	8
1Sep86-6Bel	$1\frac{1}{16}$Ⓣ:$47^1$1:$11^1$1:43^2fm	$5\frac{3}{4}$	117	5^4	$6^{2\frac{3}{4}}$	$2^{1\frac{1}{2}}$	$1^{2\frac{1}{4}}$	Davis R G^1	35000	79-18	VatzaMtter,GlintChmp,CowboyUp	11
15Aug86-4Sar	$1\frac{1}{16}$Ⓣ:$46^4$1:10 1:42^1fm	$8\frac{3}{4}$	117	$5^{5\frac{3}{4}}$	5^{10}	5^{13}	$5^{13\frac{3}{4}}$	Davis R G^5	Aw25000	72-18	SirCorbin,Loose,FrenchChampagne	5
30Jly86-5Sar	$1\frac{1}{16}$[T]:$48^2$1:13 1:45^2fm	*3-2	116	$4^{3\frac{1}{2}}$	4^3	$4^{2\frac{1}{2}}$	$3^{5\frac{3}{4}}$	Cruguet J^4	[S]Aw28000	72-21	Talc Buster, RioBelle,VatzaMatter	10
17Jly86-5Bel	$1\frac{3}{8}$[T]:48 1:38 2:16^4fm	$4\frac{1}{4}$	116	$4^{3\frac{1}{2}}$	2^{hd}	$1^{\frac{1}{2}}$	$1^{\frac{3}{4}}$	Cruguet J^7	[S]Mdn	73-21	VtzMtlr,CtchThMoon,PlcInThSun	13
14Jun86-4Bel	1 Ⓣ:$46^1$1:$11^2$1:37^1gd	$7\frac{1}{2}$	114	8^6	11^{12}	9^{11}	$9^{15\frac{1}{4}}$	Cruguet J^1	Mdn	64-24	SirCorbin,One'sCstl,TwicChrming	12
28May86-6Bel	$1\frac{1}{16}$Ⓣ:47 1:$11^1$1:43^1fm	$4\frac{1}{2}$	113	9^6	$6^{7\frac{1}{2}}$	$7^{5\frac{1}{2}}$	$3^{3\frac{1}{4}}$	Davis R G^{12}	Mdn	77-15	Flash Force, Lathom,VatzaMatter	12

Nov 16 Bel 6f ft 1:17 h   Nov 11 Bel tr.t 4f ft :50^4 b   Nov 4 Bel tr.t 5f ft 1:03 b   Oct 30 Bel 4f ft :49^3 b

122. A perfectly acceptable principle on the relationship between class and speed is that better horses will generally run as fast and hard as they can when matched against horses of comparable ability and spirit. This explains why classy horses sometimes beat cheaper horses in slower time than the cheaper horses have already run.

A. True **(12)**
B. False

123. Most operational definitions of class are

A. too vague **(10)**
B. overly focused on running time
C. trivial
D. incomplete

124. Which horse below gets the nod for class?

A. **(16)**

Certain Treat * Ch. h. 6, by Affirmed—Berta's Dandy, by Grey Dawn II
Br.—Crook J B (Ky) 1987 4 3 0 0 $30,025
BAZE R A 119 Tr.—Hollendorfer Jerry $32,000 1986 22 6 3 5 $67,150
Own.—Hollendorfr-Morony-Morony Lifetime 58 15 6 8 $187,285 Turf 7 0 0 1 $9,795

4Apr87-10GG	$1\frac{1}{16}$Ⓣ 1:43 fm	$4\frac{1}{4}$	122	9^{14}	$10^{7\frac{3}{4}}$	7^7	$4^{5\frac{1}{2}}$	Baze R A 3	50000	81-11	MinutesAwy,SetPoint,FlyingSnow	12
7Mar87-4GG	$1\frac{1}{16}$:46^4 1:11^1 1:43^1ft	*6-5	119	3^3	$3^{2\frac{1}{2}}$	1^{hd}	$1^{\frac{3}{4}}$	Baze R A 2	50000	87-16	CertainTreat,SnsRivl,SensitiveCopy	6
11Feb87-8GG	1 :46^4 1:10^4 1:36^1ft	$2\frac{3}{4}$	116	$3^{\frac{1}{2}}$	1^1	$1^{\frac{1}{2}}$	1^3	Baze R A 1	Aw20000	87-21	CertinTret,StudiousOn,SnsitivCopy	7
3Jan87-7BM	$1\frac{1}{16}$:47^3 1:12^3 1:45 sy	*1	118	5^5	$3^{\frac{1}{2}}$	1^{hd}	$1^{\frac{1}{2}}$	Baze R A 8	25000	67-23	CertainTreat,NickelBack,BeuDuncn	8
22Nov86-7BM	$1\frac{1}{16}$:47 1:11^3 1:43^4ft	*4-5	120	$6^{2\frac{1}{4}}$	$5^{2\frac{3}{4}}$	$4^{\frac{3}{4}}$	$1^{\frac{3}{4}}$	Baze R A 6	25000	73-24	CertinTret,Telrhyme,DimondGeorg	8
25Oct86-9BM	$1\frac{1}{16}$:46^2 1:11 1:43^1ft	*6-5	117	$2^{\frac{1}{2}}$	$1^{\frac{1}{2}}$	$1^{\frac{1}{2}}$	$1^{2\frac{1}{2}}$	Baze R A 1	25000	76-21	Certain Treat, Big Dan Ryan, Clear	7
11Oct86-9BM	$1\frac{1}{16}$:46^4 1:11^1 1:43 ft	*4-5	114	3^2	$3^{1\frac{1}{2}}$	$3^{1\frac{1}{2}}$	$1^{\frac{3}{4}}$	Baze R A 5	25000	77-18	CertainTreat,Dve'sRelity,BigDnRyn	6
27Sep86-7BM	$1\frac{1}{16}$:47^4 1:13^1 1:45^2sl	*$2\frac{1}{4}$	114	6^7	$6^{4\frac{3}{4}}$	3^2	2^1	Diaz A L 1	25000	64-27	Olimpic Bingo, Certain Treat, Clear	9
30Aug86-10Bmf	1 :45^4 1:09^4 1:35^1ft	$3\frac{1}{4}$	115	4^5	3^4	3^3	$2^{\frac{3}{4}}$	Baze R A 2	25000	91-12	LoadedDeck,CertinTret,Lrk'sLegcy	8
3Aug86-10SR	$1\frac{1}{16}$:45^3 1:10^3 1:41^4ft	$4\frac{1}{2}$	119	7^9	5^3	2^1	$3^{\frac{1}{2}}$	Hummel C R 8	25000	94-03	Petrone'sKismet,MloKing,CrtinTrt	9

Apr 19 GG 4f ft :48 h   Apr 13 GG 4f ft :51^2 h   Apr 1 GG Ⓣ 4f fm :50^4 h (d)   Mar 26 GG 4f ft :47^4 h

B.

Inherent Kal ✻ B. c. 4, by Inherent Star—Kalliste, by Crocation
Br.—Svihla A (Cal) 1987 5 0 0 1 $3,350
JUDICE J C 116 Tr.—Christiansen Albert $32,000 1986 19 4 2 5 $68,250
Own.—Svihla A Lifetime 27 5 2 6 $78,050 Turf 4 0 0 0 $1,650
17Apr87-6GG 6f :214 :442 1:093ft 5½ 119 56½ 67½ 77½ 74¼ Judice J C 6 Aw17000 87-16 DrbyBoss,StretchItOut,TredOnWilli 7
17Apr87—Bumped start
21Mar87-7GG 1 :46 1:102 1:364gd 13 119 56 55 33 32 Judice J C 5 Aw18000 82-19 SuperChrge,BrginStndrd,InherntKl 8
1Mar87-1SA 6½f :214 :442 1:162ft 20 116 1218 1214 1011 89½ Shoemaker W 3 32000 78-15 SprbMomnt,DshonorblGst,Dnsprt 12
1Mar87—Poor start
7Feb87-3SA 1 1/16 :463 1:101 1:432ft 5 116 45 512 512 513¾ DelahoussayeE 2 40000 70-14 AlibiIke,TooMuchForT.V.,PiprJohn 5
7Feb87—Bumped start
30Jan87-5SA 1¼Ⓣ:47 1:363 2:021fm 11 116 55½ 97½ 1010 1012¾ DelhoussyeE 5 Aw28000 63-24 Atreak, ‡Agitate's Pride, Chili Hill 10
28Dec86-5SA 1 1/16 :462 1:104 1:431ft 11 116 56 23 25 35¾ ValenzuelPA 3 Aw28000 79-14 ReEnter,Card'sPlease,InherentKal 10
28Dec86—Bumped start
10Dec86-3Hol 1 :454 1:104 1:371ft 2½ 116 77½ 74¾ 54 55 Stevens G L 6 50000 72-20 Sebucan, Agitate's Pride, Alibi Ike 7
26Nov86-5Hol 1 :454 1:102 1:353ft 5¾ 116 87½ 68½ 57¼ 34¼ DelahoussayeE 5 62500 81-20 BrightTom,MischivousMtt,InhrntKl 8
4Oct86-1SA 6½f :214 :45 1:17 ft 10 118 912 88½ 55½ 1¾ DelahoussayeE 6 50000 85-18 Inherent Kal, EastTulip,Bruli'sAnte 9
20Sep86-11Pom 1 1/16 :451 1:103 1:44 ft 15 114 510 413 711 79¼ HrnndzR 3 ⓇDerby Trl 82-09 BoldBrvoII,Rfl'sDncr,J.R.Johnson 10
Apr 9 GG 5f ft 1:044 h

C.

Impulsively B. g. 7, by Decidedly—Hill Flag, by Hillary
Br.—Pope Mrs G A Jr (Cal) 1987 7 1 1 1 $22,025
CASTANEDA M 116 Tr.—Hilling J M $32,000 1986 22 2 3 7 $59,780
Own.—Todd R & A Lifetime 64 9 9 13 $196,810 Turf 7 0 1 2 $11,550
18Apr87-11GG 1⅜Ⓣ:48 1:39 2:164fm 11 116 510 64½ 45½ 34¼ Castaneda M8 50000 77-16 ShdowsFII,MinutesAwy,Impulsively 8
28Mar87-9GG 1 1/16 Ⓣ:482 1:121 1:433fm 17 117 78 89½ 78½ 47½ CastanedaM6 Aw20000 76-20 Shanaar, Sensitive Copy,FleetForm 8
8Feb87-9SA 1 1/16 :464 1:104 1:431ft 22 118 66 57 46 23 Solis A 8 c25000 82-14 VideoKid,Impulsively,ILoveRacing 12
1Feb87-9SA 1 1/16 :464 1:112 1:434ft 38 116 116¾ 106¼ 107¾ 108¾ Black C A 10 32000 73-16 GumFleet,ShowerDecree,Dcontrol 12
1Feb87—Broke slowly;wide
17Jan87-9SA 1 1/16 :462 1:112 1:434ft 10 116 1013 1011 1111 119¾ Black C A 10 32000 72-18 PiperJohn,ForHimself,ShowerDcr 12
17Jan87—Lugged in final 3/8
11Jan87-9SA 1 1/16 :473 1:113 1:443ft 4¼ 117 78 55 33 1½ Pincay L Jr 3 25000 78-21 Impulsively, Pegus, Bedouin 9
3Jan87-9SA 1 1/16 :47 1:113 1:433ft 9¾ 116 79 77¼ 55½ 44¼ DelahoussayeE 7 32000 79-16 NorthrnProvdr,Rnbw'sCp,FrgnLgn 10
7Dec86-6Hol 1⅛ :472 1:121 1:514gd 6 116 814 812 89¾ 815½ Stevens G L 2 32000 62-18 VlintGeorge,GumFleet,ForignLgion 9
7Dec86—Broke slowly
20Nov86-5Hol 1⅛ :464 1:114 1:512ft 7½ 116 913 911 73¾ 52¾ Stevens G L8 32000 77-16 Oak TreeII.Bedouin,ValiantGeorge 11
20Nov86—Steadied 3/16
5Nov86-7Hol 1⅛Ⓣ:473 1:113 1:483fm 22 116 78¾ 76¾ 56¾ 54¾ Valenzuela P A5 50000 80-14 Too Much For T. V.,Massera,Tarver 8
Apr 29 GG 4f ft :481 h   Apr 16 GG 3f ft :372 h   Apr 9 GG 6f ft 1:163 h   Mar 25 GG 3f ft :372 h

D.

Easy Mover ✻ Ch. g. 7, by Advisedly—Cloo Tie, by Poona II
Br.—Lee & Ripley (Cal) 1987 7 0 3 1 $19,510
SCHVANEVELDT C P 116 Tr.—Offield Duane $32,000 1986 12 3 6 1 $52,800
Own.—Lee & Ripley Lifetime 52 11 14 5 $158,370 Turf 3 0 0 0
16Apr87-6GG 1 :462 1:101 1:35 ft *8-5 116 21 21 21½ 22 Baze R A 4 40000 91-14 Tobin's Wish, EasyMover,Reckoner 6
18Mar87-9SA 1 1/16 :47 1:111 1:43 ft 4¾ 116 2½ 2hd 1hd 32½ Meza R Q 6 50000 83-17 Poley, Video Kid, Easy Mover 8
27Feb87-6GG 1 :46 1:094 1:35 ft 5¾ 117 31 1½ 1½ 2hd Baze R A 2 Aw20000 93-14 Olajuwon, Easy Mover, Innerspace 7
11Feb87-8GG 1 :464 1:104 1:361ft *2¼ 116 2hd 21 31 46¾ Doocy T T 4 Aw20000 80-21 CertinTret,StudiousOn,SnsitivCopy 7
1Feb87-9BM 1 1/16 :474 1:13 1:444ft 2½ 115 31½ 3½ 2hd 4½ Gonzalez R M 6 40000 67-25 AckLikeMe,Witin'ForBever,Libnon 6
1Feb87—Lost whip 1/16
9Jan87-8BM 1 :472 1:131 1:382sl 7¼ 114 32½ 2hd 2hd 22½ GonzalezRM 2 Aw18000 73-34 Spacecpit,EsyMover,AudciousRullh 6
1Jan87-8BM 1 1/16 :461 1:104 1:441gd 4½ 113 43¼ 42½ 66¼ 610 GnlRM 3 ⓇNw Yr Iv H 61 — CalvaryCharge,OnRetiner,Dormello 8
7Dec86-7BM 1 1/16 :464 1:12 1:461sl 5 117 1hd 1½ 1½ 1no Gonzalez R M 4 40000 61-38 EsyMovr,Witin'ForBvr,OrindOrgnl 10
23Nov86-6BM a1⅛Ⓣ 1:483fm 9½ 114 64½ 64¼ 89¼ 814 GonzalezRM 3 Aw19000 78-08 SoldatBieu,DiplomatRuler,JaySwift 9
23Nov86—Steadied repeatedly early to avoid loose horse
2Nov86-4BM 1 1/16 :463 1:11 1:43 ft *6-5 114 2½ 1hd 1½ 11½ Baze R A 4 40000 77-21 Easy Mover, Big Jesse, E. J. Junior 7
Apr 14 GG 3f ft :374 h

125. In the sense that it is most frequently decisive, class is probably the most important handicapping factor of all.

A. True **(10)**
B. False

This is the end of the minimum competency test. If your score falls below the desired standard, do not proceed to the mastery test until you have consulted the recommended sources of instruction and retaken the failed items.

CLASS APPRAISAL: MASTERY TEST

126. Which is not necessarily an attribute of high class?

A. brilliance   **(10)**
B. consistency
C. determination
D. endurance

127. The essential attribute of class is

A. brilliance   **(10)**
B. courage
C. willingness
D. endurance

128. Which conditions of eligibility are likely to attract the best field of $2500 claiming horses?

A. nonwinners of 2 races this season   **(11)**
B. nonwinners of 3 races lifetime
C. nonwinners of a race at a mile or over
D. nonwinners of 2 races since a specified date

129. Which is likely to be the best allowance race?

A. NW2   **(11)**
B. NW1XMC
C. NW$30001XMC
D. starter allowance $25k or less

130. Which conditions of eligibility are more likely to attract stakes quality horses?

A. Alw, NW3XMC, 3YO   **(11)**
B. $75,000 claiming, 4up
C. Clf Alw, highly restricted, 4up
D. starter handicap, 3 up, 1¼M

131. Which is usually the toughest step-up in class?

A. Alw, NW1XMC to NW2XMC   **(14)**
B. Alw, NW2XMC to NW3XMC
C. stakes, Grade 3 to Grade 2
D. stakes, Grade 2 to Grade 1

132. Which is the toughest step-up in the stakes ranks?

A. restricted to open unlisted   **(14)**
B. open unlisted to listed
C. listed to Grade 3
D. purse of $75,000-added to purse of $150,000-added

133. Which winner is likely to earn the class handicapper's highest rating

A. fast at every call in wire-to-wire romp   **(15)**
B. slow time, but competitive at every call
C. average pace all the way, typical competitive
    challenge and response patterns
D. fast competitive race to the pre-stretch call, slow
    finish by pace survivor

134. Class ratings are likely to supersede speed figures most frequently in

A. high-priced claiming routes   **(12)**
B. classified allowance sprints
C. the nonwinners allowance series
D. turf routes

135. In general, a thoroughbred's innate ability begins to deteriorate from stress and strain at age

A. 4   **(13)**
B. 5
C. 6
D. 7

136. Which statement characterizes better 3YOs fairly in a seemingly contradictory way?

A. They can be consistently inconsistent   **(13)**
B. They tend to run faster when pressed, slower when
    uncontested
C. The more racing experiences they accumulate, the
    "greener" they run
D. They cannot be reliably classified until they chal-
    lenge older horses

137. Which horse is most likely to prosper in a Grade 2 stakes?

A. a recent Grade 3 winner   **(11)**
B. the lightly raced improving 3YO that has won re-
   peatedly at lower levels
C. a close finisher in a Grade 1 event
D. an impressive winner of a listed stakes having a
   purse of $100,000 or more

138. In which race are 3YOs most likely to beat older horses?

A. a classified allowance sprint   **(13)**
B. a restricted stakes that bars winners of a specified
   amount since a specified date
C. $20,000 claiming
D. Alw, NW2XMC

139. In which race during October do older horses hold a decisive advantage versus 3YOs?

A. Grade 1 stakes   **(13)**
B. classified allowance, highly restricted
C. restricted stakes
D. $50,000 claiming

140. Graded stakes are best distinguished by

A. track class   **(11)**
B. adjusted final times
C. purse size
D. the class of the winner

141. Of nonwinners allowance races, which statement makes the most sense?

A. Manner of victory is more important than final   **(11)**
   time
B. Final time is more important than manner of victory
C. Manner of victory, final time, and margin of victory can be equally important
D. Quality of opposition is the critical clue to the
   relative class of the winner

142. Which is the best race?

A. Alw, NW2XMC, 4up   **(11)**
B. Alw, NW3XMC, 3YO

    C. $50,000 claiming, 3 up
    D. $80,000 claiming, 3YO

143. At which class level are final times most reliable?

    A. maiden-claiming $32,000   **(12)**
    B. $10,000 claiming
    C. maiden special weight
    D. Alw, nonwinners of two races

144. Claiming class can be estimated most reliably by

    A. speed figures   **(10)**
    B. average earnings
    C. consistency rates
    D. average purse values

145. Horses closely matched on relative class are best separated by

    A. form analysis   **(13)**
    B. early speed
    C. speed figures
    D. pace ratings

146. A huge inexplicable class drop in a claiming race can be accepted when accompanied by (a) acceptable form, (b) one of the two top class ratings or speed figures in the field, and (c)

    A. a leading claiming trainer   **(14)**
    B. an acceptable price
    C. a favorable pace
    D. a leading jockey

147. When judging class rises in claiming races, which claiming-price guideline makes the most sense?

    A. 25% to 30%   **(14)**
    B. 50% for 3YOs, 25% for 4up
    C. within customary price brackets or one bracket higher
    D. up to and including "back class" levels

148. Class is most difficult to evaluate among

    A. older claiming horses   **(10)**
    B. fillies and mares

C. stakes horses

D. 3-year-olds

149. Which represents a sensible formula for evaluating class numerically?

A. par ± (final time ± daily track variant) **(10)**

B. (wins/.60) + (places/.20) + (thirds/.15) / money won

C. speed X competitiveness / level of opposition

D. this season's + last season's wins / number of starts

150. Class rises are most dramatic among

A. 2-year-olds **(14)**

B. 3-year-olds

C. fillies

D. geldings

151. Class and speed as factors in handicapping have a perfect positive correlation.

A. True **(12)**

B. False

152. The most reliable measure of juvenile class is adjusted final time.

A. True **(13)**

B. False

153. Which statement best reflects the relationship between class and weight as factors in handicapping?

A. The correlation between the two factors approaches zero **(13)**

B. Weight shifts are more instrumental in nullifying class advantages than are high weights

C. In separating horses closely matched on class, weight should be used negatively, that is, if you do not like the weight, do not bet the horse

D. If handicappers had no other information about the true relative abilities of horses, they should favor the high-weighted horses

154. After a developing 3YO wins its second allowance race, many stables will conclude they've got a good one. At that point, which step-up in class is most likely to prove too aggressive and result in a shellacking and a temporary setback?

A. Alw, NW4XMC   (14)
B. open stakes limited to 3YOs
C. restricted stakes open to older horses
D. listed stakes, 3up

155. Which is the most difficult simultaneous class-distance move by a nonclaiming 3-year-old?

A. Mdn to Alw, sprint to route   (13)
B. lower grade to Grade 1 stakes, middle distance to
   classic distance
C. NW2XMC to open stakes, 7F to 1M
D. NW3XMC to Grade 3 stakes, 6F to 1⅛M

156. Three-year-olds stretching out from sprints to middle distances are most likely to succeed when moving from

A. maiden to allowance conditions   (13)
B. Alw, NW1XMC to Alw, NW2XMC
C. maiden-claiming to a claiming race open to win-
   ners at $20,000 or below
D. Alw, NW2X to a listed stakes

157. Which horses should be preferred in a starter handi-cap?

A. finished 2nd in a similar race last out   (11)
B. the high weights
C. any horse particularly well-suited to the dis-
   tance, track surface, and probable pace
D. won a previous starter race this season at the same
   starting price

158. Class is reflected best in races that demand

A. speed and competitiveness in combination   (10)
B. unusually high speed
C. unusually strong determination
D. high weight be carried over long distance

159. Determination is best observed as

A. acceleration between calls **(10)**
B. overcoming mishaps caused by traffic or trouble
C. a sustained response to challenge
D. final quarter time

160. The likeliest winner of any starter race is the horse that has won at the highest open claiming price this season.

A. True **(11)**
B. False

161. Which statement best reflects the contemporary relationship between class and form?

A. Superior class overcompensates for a shortfall of form **(13)**
B. Class is more a function of form than ever
C. Form advantages become more significant as class levels rise
D. Recency is indispensable in low-priced claiming races

162. What class level would be most appropriate for *Coaraze Nay's* next start?

A. Alw, NW3XMC **(15)**
B. Grade 3 stakes
C. classified allowance, highly restricted
D. Grade 2 stakes

```
*Coaraze Nay                      Ch. c. 4, by Tip Moss—Tainova, by Novara
                                  Br.—Pelat N (Fra)                        1986  3 2 1 0   $39,200
 PINCAY L                   116   Tr.—Gosden John H M                      1985  6 1 2 2   $19,214
Own.—Davis & Spelling             Lifetime   9 3 3 2   $58,414             Turf  9 3 3 2   $58,414
26Oct86-7SA    1⅛Ⓣ:461 1:11 1:48 fm *2 117  33 31½ 12 14½  Pincay L Jr1 Aw45000 87-13 Coaraze Nay, Pudahuel, Montecito 6
12Oct86-6BM    1 1/16Ⓣ:473 1:122 1:431fm 2 114  42½ 32 1½ 11½  Baze R A4  Aw19000 87-13 Coaraze Nay, Jack Tar, JustInCase 7
17Aug86-5Dmr   1 Ⓣ:461 1:103 1:351fm 3¼ 117  42 2hd 1hd 2no  Pincay L Jr9 Aw20000 96-05 Rai Den, Coaraze Nay, Lud 10
 8Sep85♦2Longchamp(Fra) a1¼ 2:103gd  4 119  Ⓣ 31½  LquuxA   Px dBord d l'Eau  Melun, Aboudy, Coaraze Nay 6
18Aug85♦5Deauville(Fra) a1¼ 2:122sf  7¾ 123  Ⓣ 32¼  GibertA   Px d Hras dFrny  Soir deNoces, Antheus,CoarazeNay 9
21Jly85♦6MLaffitte(Fra) a1⅜ 2:154gd *4-5 123  Ⓣ 18  Gibert A   Px Bnstr  CoarazeNay,Bandinelli,DearThomas 7
12Jly85♦7Evry(Fra) a1¼ 2:123gd  3 123  Ⓣ 2¾  LwniczkD   Px d Vilarche  Pylades, Coaraze Nay, Belly 10
22May85♦7Evry(Fra) a1 5/16 2:154gd 3¼ 120  Ⓣ 2nk  Wahl P   Px Ls Cssnt  Aboudy, Coaraze Nay, Montesano 13
 5May85♦2Longchamp(Fra) a1¼ 2:101gd 26 123  Ⓣ 41  LnckD   Px desGblns(Mdn)  Melun,Meitred'Arms,WindsorKnot 11
   Nov 3 SA Ⓣ6f fm 1:143 h (d)   ●Oct 23 SA Ⓣ5f fm 1:004 h (d)  Oct 6 SA Ⓣ7f fm 1:291 h (d)   Sep 29 SA 6f ft 1:16 h
```

163. The best contemporary definition of consistency is

A. won 2 of last 6 **(10)**
B. won 1 of 4 this season and last
C. won 1 of 5 lifetime
D. won 3 of last 10

164. As class levels rise, which attribute of class becomes correspondingly more decisive?

A. brilliance **(10)**
B. stamina
C. determination
D. consistency

165. What is the lowest class level at which *Skip Out Front* would be clearly outgunned?

A. open stakes **(10)**
B. listed stakes
C. Grade 3 stakes
D. Grade 2 stakes

Skip Out Front **B. c. 4, by Bynoderm—She's Out Front, by Highbinder**
SOLIS A **113** **Br.—Dewries Dorothy (Fla)** **1986 12 2 3 0 $49,694**
Own.—Peak-n-Valley Stable **Tr.—Harmatuck Michael** **1985 17 7 1 3 $51,902**
Lifetime 32 10 4 3 $105,796 **Turf 20 5 3 2 $77,529**

22Oct86-7SA 1⅛Ⓣ:4541:1021:4711fm 6½ 115 65 41¾ 63½ 43 Solis A4 Aw35000 88-12 Nugget Point, Catane, Schiller 10
22Oct86—Crowded entering stretch; checked, altered path 1/8
11Oct86-7SA 1⅛Ⓣ:4631:1031:4811fm 23 115 57 45½ 23 21¾ Solis A7 Aw45000 84-21 Nasib, Skip Out Front, Pudahuel 8
13Sep86-9Suf a1 1/16 Ⓣ 1:463fm 5¾ 120 51¾ 41¼ 12 1nk † ThsDB9 Old Irnsds H 99-06 ‡SkpOtFront,Ronbr,LondnExchng 10
†13Sep86—Disqualified and placed second
6Sep86-3Bel 1 1/16 [T]:49 1:1321:45 gd 10 118 62½ 84¾ 84¾ 63½ Samyn J L3 90000 72-27 NewTerms,MjesticRoberto,Brddells 8
16Aug86-4Sar 1 1/16 [T]:4911:1331:444yl 8½ 117 63½ 54½ 66 67¼ Samyn J L6 Aw29000 74-26 GoldMeridin,ReglFlier,NuggetPoint 6
21Jly86-5Bel 1 Ⓣ:4521:10 1:342fm 5½ 112 78¾ 64 2½ 12¾ Samyn J L3 75000 93-10 Skip Out Front, Braddells, Attune 8
4Jly86-9Atl 5½f :212 :443 1:023ft 14 116 410 47½ 46½ 48½ OcsoLJr4 [R]Long Port 92-12 Aeronotic,MoonProspctor,KingBbr 4
26May86-9Hia 1 1/16 Ⓣ 1:423fm 2½ 113 42 32½ 34 54¾ PezuaJM6 Mem Day H 80-24 NordicKing,ElScrmento,DonEdurdo 6
4May86-10Hia 1⅛Ⓣ 1:51 gd 2¾ 114 52½ 53¾ 46 52¼ Lester R N6 [S]Ocala H 75-26 NordicKing,SnglSolo,ShllowDplomt 8
27Apr86-8Hia a1 1/16 Ⓣ 1:422fm*8-5 1125 2hd 11½ 15 13½ Lester R N9 Aw13900 86-17 SkipOutFront,DoubleHelix,Dcndin 10
Nov 2 SA 5f ft 1:011 h **Oct 8 SA 5f ft :594 h**

166. The filly *Flight Above* can be accepted as a contender in an allowance race for 3up, nonwinners of a race other than maiden or claiming.

A. True **(15)**
B. False

Flight Above **Dk. b. or br. f. 3, by Crow—Shouting Distance, by Within Hail**
BLACK C A **113** **Br.—Pillar Stud Inc (Ky)** **1986 10 2 0 0 $22,575**
Own.—Silver Star Stable **Tr.—Bunn Thomas M Jr** **Turf 5 0 0 0 $1,050**
Lifetime 10 2 0 0 $22,575

19Oct86-1SA 6½f :212 :443 1:172ft 28 1095 816 89½ 44 1¾ Black C A7 Ⓕ 45000 83-18 FlightAbove,DuchessZnth,LdingLss 8
19Oct86—Stumbled badly break
8Sep86-5Dmr 1 Ⓣ:47 1:1141:362fm 10 116 11 65 107¼ 109¼ DelhoussyeE1 Ⓕ 62500 81-10 Sweetest,DrmticElgnc,DwnOfHop 10
28Aug86-5Dmr 1 Ⓣ:4711:1141:362fm 40 117 109¼ 89 79½ 55¾ McHrgDG7 ⒻAw22000 84-05 TotllyHonst,IrishKristn,T'dAndTru 10
15Aug86-5Dmr 1 1/16 Ⓣ:48 1:1231:434fm 36 117 52½ 31½ 32 53¼ Baze R A7 ⒻAw20000 84-13 Danish Dancer, FineKudos,Gayliole 9
15Aug86—Fanned wide onto main course, into 7/8 turn
31Jly86-5Dmr 1 1/16 Ⓣ:4711:1131:423fm 15 115 46 53½ 65 64¾ Baze R A7 ⒻAw20000 88-04 ArlibraLdy,Melv'sPride,DnishDncer 9
31Jly86—Veered in, bumped start
17Jly86-4Hol 6f :214 :451 1:102ft 11 116 610 612 57½ 46 DelhoussyeE2 Ⓕ 80000 86-17 MillersSttionry,Witchery,Mlv'sPrid 6
3Jly86-4Hol 1 :453 1:111 1:363ft 17 112 1hd 3nk 44½ 48½ Ortega LE4 ⒻAw23000 71-16 MissRoyalMonte,St.Moritz,Tntlized 6
20Jun86-7Hol 1 Ⓣ:4541:1031:352fm 12 108 2hd 2hd 1010 1013 ShomkrW10 ⒻAw21000 — — MediGirl,Jclyn'sChoice,DwnOfHop 10
6Jun86-2Hol 6f :222 :464 1:114ft 3¼ 116 51¼ 11 14 18 DelhoussyE7 ⒻM32000 85-15 Flight Above, IrishVal,FreakAZoid 12
Nov 5 Hol 4f ft :492 h **Oct 29 SA 5f ft 1:022 h** **Oct 9 SA 5f ft 1:011 h** **Oct 2 SA 5f ft 1:011 h**

167. What is the highest U.S. class level at which this Argentine import should be accepted?

A. restricted stakes **(15)**
B. open stakes
C. Grade 2 stakes
D. Grade 3 stakes

```
*Salvate Tel                          Ch. h. 5, by Telefonico—Salmah, by Merchant Venturer
                                      Br.—Haras Rincon del Pino (Arg)          1986  1  1  0  0     $74,904
 TORO F                     118       Tr.—McAnally Ronald                      1985  9  4  4  1     $46,691
Own.—Paulson A E                    Lifetime   13  6  4  1  $124,649           Turf 10  5  3  0     $89,345
 1Feb86♦7SanIsidro(Arg)  a1½   2:25^4gd  7½  132  Ⓣ 1^3   MacielJ   GP CrlsPllgrni(Gr1) Salvate Tel, Bonsoir, Categorico        20
19Nov85♦7LaPlata(Arg)  a1½    2:36^1hy  3½  132    1^5   McielJ    G P Drd Rcha(Gr1)   SalvateTel, Magiar, Zafarrancho         19
27Oct85♦10Hipodromo(Arg) a1¼  2:01 ft   3¾  132    2^3   McielJ    Cl MrnoMrno(Gr2)    MisterMarco,SlvteTel,SweetCherry         7
 7Oct85♦6Hipodromo(Arg)  a1¼  2:01^3ft  4¼  132    3^5   Maciel J  Cl Italia(Gr3)      Strong Wood, Oversea, Salvate Tel        6
 8Sep85♦9SanIsidro(Arg)  a1⅛   1:48^1fm  3¾  132  Ⓣ 2½   Maciel J  Cl Prgrso(Gr2)      Ataviado, SalvateTel, MisterMarco        6
21Aug85♦9SanIsidro(Arg)  a1    1:38^1fm*6-5 124  Ⓣ 1^nk  Maciel J  Pr Ppntas H         SalvateTel, Maspicante, Legacy           9
23Jly85♦2SanIsidro(Arg)  a1⅜   2:14 fm*6-5 126  Ⓣ 2^1½  Maciel J  Pr Orcjstra(Alw)    Fray Airoso,SalvateTel,Encaminado        4
26Jun85♦9SanIsidro(Arg)  a1    1:34^1fm*8-5 123  Ⓣ 2¾   MciJJ  Pr Csa D Teatro(Alw)   Naranjo enFlor, Salvate Tel,Morito       7
  ●Nov 3 SA 1 ft 1:40^4 h     Oct 27 SA Ⓣ 1 fm 1:42^2 h (d)     Oct 20 SA Ⓣ 7f fm 1:29^2 h (d)     Oct 12 SA 1 ft 1:40^2 h
```

168. This 6YO is plunging $50,000 in claiming class and switching from jockey Pincay to Solis. Which statement best describes the situation for handicappers?

```
*Mount Bidder                         Gr. h. 6, by Mount Hagen—Sheana, by Silver Shark
                                      Br.—Collins J & Phyllis (Ire)                1986  2  0  0  0
 PINCAY L JR                116       Tr.—Vienna Darrell             $50,000      1985  6  2  1  0      $23,477
Own.—O'Neill R J                    Lifetime   32 12  8  2  $192,900              Turf 32 12  8  2     $192,900
 5Feb86-5SA   1⅛Ⓣ:46^2 1:11^1 1:49^3fm   4 116   1½  1½  74¾ 710¾  Solis A^4     100000 68-21 DonnyK.,Gourmi,BoomTownChrlie 10
     5Feb86—Bumped after start
16Jan86-8SA   1⅛Ⓣ:46 1:10^1 1:47^3fm    10 115   3^2 3^2 76½ 910½  McHrgueDG^3  Aw45000 78-11 Truculnt,DoublQckTm,TppngWood  9
     16Jan86—Bumped at start
13Oct85-7SA   a6½f Ⓣ:21^2 :44 1:14^4fm  18 115   76¼ 75¾ 88¼ 87¼  Toro F^4      Aw45000 78-15 Silveyville, DefectingDancer,Tights 8
     13Oct85—Broke slowly
 2Jun85♦5Milan(Italy)  a1     1:40^1sf     5 129  Ⓣ 6^8   DplmsM     Pr Eml Trti(Gr1)   King ofClubs,WillDancer,CapoNord      7
26May85♦6Rome(Italy)   a1¼    2:05^4sf     4 132  Ⓣ 4^7   DplsM      Pr Prs d'Rep(Gr1)  Bob Back, Reco, Dreyer                8
14Apr85♦4Rome(Italy)   a1     1:40^4sf *4-5 124  Ⓣ 2½    DplsM      Pr Ntl d Roma(Gr3) My Jewellery,MountBidder,Malevic      6
24Mar85♦5Rome(Italy)   a1     1:45^2sf *2-5 130  Ⓣ 1^no  DeplmsM    Pr Signorino       Mount Bidder, Astrea, MyJewellery     5
15Feb85♦5Rome(Italy)   a1       :    gd*1-2 129  Ⓣ 1¾    DplsM      Pr Crco Mssmo      MountBiddr,MyJwllry,AgnstThWnd        6
     15Feb85—No time taken
15Dec84♦6Naples(Italy) a1⅜    2:21 gd    4¾ 132  Ⓣ 1^1   DplsM      Pr UNIRE (Gr3)     MountBidder,MircoUmbro,Atitlan       14
18Nov84♦5Rome(Italy)   a1     1:44 sf     8 123  Ⓣ 2^1   CarsonW    Pr Ribot(Gr2)      KngoofClubs,MountBddr,LrKnght        13
  Nov 3 SA tr.t 5f ft 1:05 h    Oct 29 SA tr.t 5f ft 1:02^2 b    Oct 24 SA tr.t 5f ft 1:04^4 h    Oct 19 SA tr.t 3f ft :39 h
```

A. It is probably outclassed today **(15)**
B. The horse could easily have a decisive class edge
C. The horse looks acceptable on class
D. There is no basis for making a reliable class evaluation

169. Review this 3YO's entire record, top down first, bottom up next. At what class level will it most likely settle?

Earl's Valentine

VALENZUELA P A   113

Own.—Green Thumb Farm Stable

B. f. 3, by Saros—Izsa Valentine, by Bicker
Br.—Green Thumb Farm Stb (Cal)   1986 4 0 0 2 $3,475
Tr.—Manzi Joseph   1985 3 1 1 0   ;14,450
Lifetime 7 1 1 2 $22,925

26Oct86-3SA	6f :21³ :45 1:10³ft	4½ 116	4² 41½ 41½ 33	VlenzulPA⁶ ⒻAw25000 82-16 Sown,HairlessHeiress,Erl'sVlentine 9
10Oct86-5SA	6f :21⁴ :44⁴ 1:10²ft	9-5 117	43½ 45 69½ 69½	PincyLJr⁷ ⒻⒼAw25000 76-18 SeriousGal,Luck'sFantsy,TrumTime 7
10Oct86—Broke slowly,wide
7Sep86-3Dmr	6f :21³ :45¹ 1:10³ft	*1 117	45½ 66⅔ 52½ 33½	Pincay LJr² ⒻAw21000 81-13 Ssh'sJoi,QueenMrlene,Erl'sVlentine 7
7Sep86—Broke slowly
30Aug86-7Dmr	6½f :21⁴ :45 1:16⁴ft	*3-2 117	4⅔ 41½ 51½ 45½	Pincay LJr⁶ ⒻAw21000 83-18 Fshionlity,HerRegency,LuckySilvr 1(
30Aug86—Wide 3/8 turn, into stretch
22Nov85-8Hol	6f :22 :45¹ 1:09²ft	*4-5 118	1hd 12 1hd 2½	VlenzulPA⁵ ⒻAw20000 96-18 T.V.Residul,Erl'sVlentine,TopCorsg 8
22Nov85—Broke slowly
2Nov85-2Aqu	1 :45² 1:10⁴ 1:35⁴ft	22 119	31½ 43½ 81410¹8½	McCrrCJ⁴ ⒻBrCpJuvF 68-10 TwilightRidge,FmilyStyle,StlAKiss 1:
2Nov85—Grade I; Slow start
13Oct85-6SA	6f :22 :45 1:10⁴ft	*1-2 117	1hd 13½ 14 15	ValenzuelPA⁵ ⒻⒼMdn 84-17 Erl'sVlentine,FlyingHill,StephN'Srn 8
13Oct85—Broke slowly

Oct 20 SA 5f ft 1:02¹h   Oct 14 SA 4f ft :51²h   Oct 8 SA 3f ft :34⁴hg

A. nonwinners allowance   (15)
B. classified allowance
C. $40,000 claiming
D. open stakes

170. If *Cold Pearl* is next entered in an allowance sprint, NW1XMC, how should handicappers best determine whether the 2YO filly is an authentic contender?

A. Examine the adjusted final time in relation to to-   (15)
day's par
B. Relate the manner of victory at one lower step to the horse's pedigree and stable
C. Rely on the statistics that tell how well maiden winners move up and win
D. Emphasize today's probable early pace and deter-mine whether the filly will have the same pace advantage as in its maiden race

Cold Pearl

DIAZ A L

Own.—Lukas D W   120

B. f. 2, by Icecapade—Single Pearl, by Top Command
Br.—Weber F X (Fla)   1986 1 1 0 0 $7,150
Tr.—Lukas D Wayne
Lifetime 1 1 0 0 $7,150

26Oct86-18M	6f :22³ :46 1:12 ft	*7-5 117	1hd 11½ 12 14	Diaz A L⁶ ⒻMdn 79-20 CldPrl,PingThrgh,MsshghAndmght 7

Oct 22 BM 4f ft :51⁴h   Oct 15 BM 5f ft 1:00 hg   Oct 8 BM 4f ft :49²hg

171. A reliable means or method of identifying races of rel-atively high class at any specific class level focuses on the re-sults charts. Handicappers should look for races where

A. The first four finishers were closely matched in   (10)
rapid time
B. The winner won not only easily but with obvious reserves of speed and power

C. Several graduates won their next starts
D. Three-year-olds beat older horses

172. An automatic contender in a starter race is any horse that has

A. recently demonstrated dramatically improved form   **(11)**
B. won at a higher open claiming price anytime this season
C. dropped in class inexplicably to today's starting price last out
D. been claimed this season by a leading claiming stable

173. In what class of race are adjusted final times and speed figures usually most meaningful?

A. claiming   **(12)**
B. nonwinners allowance
C. classified allowance
D. stakes

174. If class ratings and speed figures are contradictory, the speed figures should always take precedence when trying to predict

A. 2-year-olds at the route   **(12)**
B. 3YOs stretching out
C. claiming horses on the rise
D. classified allowance sprinters

175. A trio of 3YOs moving ahead from a nonwinners two times (other than maiden or claiming) allowance race to a non-winners three times allowance race have earned the speed figures below in their two allowance victories.
Which horse is best today?

Horse A	88	91
Horse B	92	92
Horse C	86	101

A. Horse A   **(12)**
B. Horse B
C. Horse C
D. Not known

176. At what claiming level should *Big Eric* be expected to register its next win?

A. $50,000 **(15)**
B. $40,000
C. $25,000
D. $20,000

Big Eric
GONZALEZ R M **114**
Own.—Derby Daze Farm & Parker

Dk. b. or br. c. 4, by Steve's Friend—Dougs Choice, by Stage Director
Br.—Crescent S Farms (Fla)
Tr.—Couto Mark **$50,000**
Lifetime 36 4 5 7 $83,025

1986	10	1	2	4	$27,225
1985	17	1	3	1	$24,970
Turf	5	0	0	0	$3,575

26Oct86-9BM	6f	:221 :45 1:101ft	17	114	43½	45	57½	65	Gonzalez R M4	50000	83-20	Donnaskra,Lrk'sLegcy,Tobin'sWish	7
14Jun86-7GG	1	:452 1:093 1:353ft	9	116	2½	21	33½	46¾	GonzalezRM7	Aw18000	83-09	Reckoner,QulityJet,NightDetectiv	10
22May86-8GG	6f	:22 :441 1:081ft	6¾	113	22	23	23	33¾	CampbellBC1	Aw20000	94-13	Stan's Bower, Reckoner, Big Eric	5
10May86-9GG	1 1/16	Ⓣ:4741:1141:43 fm	22	114	11½	3½	68	69½	CampbellBC4	Aw20000	77-15	VirginiPrivtr,CorrdorKy,NwAtrcton	7
26Apr86-10Fno	6f	:22 :45 1:09 ft	7¾	116	83	33	25	34½	Munoz E6	Bulldog	90-15	Macho Comacho,QualityJet,BigEric	9
26Mar86-8GG	6f	:221 :444 1:084ft	2¾	114	42½	42	33	33½	GonzalezRM4	Aw22000	91-18	Barbex, Royal Blue Eyes, Big Eric	6
26Mar86—Lugged in down backside													
28Feb86-8GG	6f	:221 :444 1:084ft	10	114	53	33	34½	35	GonzalezRM9	Aw22000	90-22	SirMacamillion,Mr.Brilliant,BigEric	9
11Feb86-8GG	1	:463 1:104 1:36 ft	4½	114	21	2hd	1hd	2½	GonzalezRM7	Aw17000	87-18	Pacific Mail, BigEric,MerlinOfYork	8
25Jan86-4BM	6f	:222 :45 1:093ft	11	114	12	11½	13	11	Gonzalez R M3	40000	91-19	Big Eric, Marketal, Auntie Rose	6
1Jan86-7BM	6f	:223 :453 1:113gd	5½	114	11	1½	21½	21	Archuleta S7	25000	80-34	Macho Comacho,BigEric,K.L'sPapa	9

●Nov 5 BM 3f ft :342 hg Oct 19 BM 5f ft 1:003 hg Oct 15 BM 6f ft 1:134 h Oct 9 BM 5f ft 1:02 h

177. Which horse is most likely to win under today's conditions?

7th BayMeadows

6 FURLONGS. (1.07⅘) CLAIMING. Purse $18,000. 3–year–olds and upward. Weights, 3–year–olds and upward, 118 lbs.; older, 120 lbs. Non–winners of two races since October 1 allowed 3 lbs.; a race since then, 6 lbs. Claiming price $50,000. (Maiden, starter and claiming races for $40,000 or less not considered.)

A. **(11)**

Verboten
CAMPBELL B C **112**
Own.—Two Rivers Farm & Klinger

Dk. b. or br. g. 3, by Verbatim—Be Kama Star, by Pia Star
Br.—Kama Farms Inc (Ky)
Tr.—Mason Lloyd C **$50,000**
Lifetime 17 4 2 1 $48,115

1986	7	2	1	0	$24,635
1985	10	2	1	1	$23,480
Turf	3	0	0	0	$1,710

29Oct86-8BM	1	Ⓣ:4641:12 1:373fm	8½	114	1hd	2hd	41½	89¼	ChapmanTM1	Aw20000	83-08	CalvaryCharge,ArtOfDwn,ElCorzon	9
17Oct86-6BM	6f	:22 :441 1:084ft	16	114	21	31½	33	64¼	ChapmanTM1	Aw20000	91-16	Stn'sBowr,SngrChif,ImpriousSpirit	7
4Oct86-7BM	6f	:222 :451 1:094ft	3½	113	2½	2hd	11	11	Chapman T M6	40000	90-16	Verboten,BuenJefe,RelaunchATune	9
21Sep86-6BM	1	Ⓣ:46 1:1011:361fm	7	114	11	2hd	2½	41¾	ChapmanTM3	Aw19000	97-01	Menevazzle, Jay Swift,BolgerMagic	8
28Aug86-11Sac	5½f	:211 :434 1:023ft	2	117	35	32½	22½	2nk	Lozoya D A3	Aw11000	95-13	MchoComcho,Vrbotn,LuckyMsddo	5
5Jun86-8GG	6f	:214 :443 1:09 ft	7½	113	11	1½	11½	12	Lozoya D A4	Aw19000	94-14	Verboten, RoyalAlloy,BlondeNative	6
16May86-7GG	5½f	:214 :453 1:033ft	11	113	11	12	12	4¾	Lozoya D A2	Aw17000	92-18	MacarthurFce,RoylAlloy,BrodJump	7
3Nov85-9BM	1	:462 1:104 1:37 ft	8¾	117	812	67¼	44	43	Baze R A8	Aw16000	80-17	CountryModl,CriJillHjj,VgorousDg	10
3Nov85—Fractious at gate; broke slowly													
20Oct85-8BM	1	Ⓣ:4641:1041:36 fm	13	116	42½	76	66¼	79¼	Long B8	Sn Mateo	91 —	LdyMxineD.,CountryModel,Python	10
20Oct85—Wide in drive													
4Oct85-8BM	1	:452 1:102 1:37 ft	7½	114	32	32	54¼	58½	Hummel C R4	Fall Juv	74-19	AuBonMrche,CriJillHjji,AllThBucks	8
4Oct85—Ducked in start													

Sep 16 BM 5f gd 1:013 h

B.

Buen Jefe
CASTANEDA M **114**
Own.—Howard Mymy

Ch. h. 5, by Delaware Chief—Asterisca, by No Prevue
Br.—Howard Mymy (Cal)
Tr.—Utley C L **$50,000**
Lifetime 40 8 4 11 $132,115

1986	4	2	1	1	$23,240
1985	16	3	1	5	$56,060
Turf	2	0	0	0	$450

18Oct86-6BM	6f	:223 :462 1:092ft	*6-5	117	32	31½	2hd	12	Castaneda M5	40000	92-16	BuenJefe,E.J.Junior,RelunchATune	6
4Oct86-7BM	6f	:222 :451 1:094ft	*2½	117	76	74¾	32	21	Castaneda M9	40000	89-16	Verboten,BuenJefe,RelaunchATune	9
21Sep86-9BM	6f	:222 :452 1:093ft	2	115	44½	33	41½	11	Castaneda M2	35000	91-18	BuenJefe,TheAysHvIt,Don'tFightIt	8
12Jan86-4BM	1	:461 1:094 1:35 ft	2¾	115	52¼	42½	41½	32	ChapmanTM3	Aw18000	91-15	BennettPeak,SonnyBrich,BuenJefe	7

22Dec85-6BM 1 1/16 :46 1:093 1:421ft 3¾ 117 33 33 32½ 3¾ ChapmanTM4 Aw18000 80-20 BrghtAndRght,Json'sDrummr,BnJf 9
7Dec85-6BM 1 :47 1:122 1:391m 6½ 117 56½ 47 47 34 ChapmanTM5 Aw19000 68-37 ComeAwyClen,ExcessProfit,BuenJf 8
17Nov85-9BM 1 :464 1:11 1:353ft 6½ 1105 43 33 33½ 33 Aragon V A5 50000 87-20 FreeForce,DimondGeorge,BuenJefe 7
7Nov85-8BM 1 :47 1:11 1:361ft 4 117 53 63¾ 53¾ 43 ChapmanTM1 Aw22000 84-21 KngTobn,LordNormn,SomthngGrgs 6
26Oct85-6BM 1 :47 1:111 1:363ft 6¾ 114 53 52¾ 2½ 1¾ ChapmanTM1 Aw20000 85-16 Buen Jefe, LordNorman,MeloKing 10
12Oct85-6BM 6f :221 :442 1:09 ft 4 114 88¾ 76¼ 64¾ 41¼ Diaz A L5 40000 93-16 CooleenJack,EsyCsh,BlueRimRock 8
●Nov 5 BM 5f ft :593 h Oct 26 BM 5f ft 1:00 h Oct 16 BM 3f ft :353 h ●Oct 11 BM 5f ft :593 h

178. Under what conditions is *El Corazon* most likely to win next?

A. listed stakes **(15)**
B. Alw, NW4XMC
C. open stakes
D. $50,000 claiming

El Corazon — **B. c. 3, by Raja Baba—Dan's Dream, by Your Host**
TOHILL K S **109** **Br.—Jones Jr & Farish III (Ky)** **1986 14 4 2 2 $113,605**
Tr.—Fanning Jerry **1985 4 M 3 0 $10,040**
Own.—Singer C B **Lifetime 18 4 5 2 $123,645** **Turf 1 0 0 1 $2,800**

29Oct86-8BM 1 Ⓣ:464 1:12 1:373fm 9½ 115 3½ 3nk 2½ 34½ Maple S7 Aw20000 87-08 CalvaryCharge,ArtOfDwn,ElCorzon 9
17Oct86-6BM 6f :22 :441 1:084ft 17 115 67½ 69 67 76¾ Hansen R D5 Aw20000 88-16 Stn'sBowr,SngrChif,ImpriousSpirit 7
27Sep86-9Pom a1⅛ :462 1:12 1:503ft 9¾ 122 32 42 44 710¼ Toro F9 Pom Dby 84-10 LghtnngToch,Rfl'sDncr,BoldBrvII 10
27Sep86—Run in divisions
11Sep86-11Pom 6½f :22 :454 1:164ft 3 122 3½ 2hd 21½ 25 Toro F6 Foothill 91-08 J.R.Johnson,ElCorzon,LghtnngToch 8
5Jly86-8Hol 1 :443 1:08 1:324ft 282 116 117 1012 1018 1021¾ LiphamT5 Slvr Scrn H 77-08 Melair, Southern Halo, SnowChief 12
5Jly86—Grade II; Wide 3/8 turn
26May86-9Spt 1⅛ :461 1:112 1:521sy 2¾ 124 43 45 615 730 Meier R4 Ill Dby 54-18 BolshoBoy,SpdyShnnon,BluBckroo 8
26May86—Grade III
17May86-7Spt 1 :474 1:131 1:402sy 3¾ 121 1hd 11½ 12 14 Meier R1 Nash Mem 78-23 ElCorzon,Jy'sTiger,ExclusiveDndy 10
5May86-9Spt 6f :233 :464 1:124ft *1 119 44 42½ 2hd 1¾ Meier R1 Aw20500 86-21 ElCorazon,Serenius,ExclusiveDndy 9
5May86—Bore out first turn
19Apr86-9Spt 6f :232 :463 1:131ft 7¼e 113 76 55½ 31 13 Meier R8 Maxwell G H 84-29 ElCorzon,VinnietheVipr,CroupirLdy 9
30Mar86-6SA 7f :222 :454 1:234ft 3 117 2½ 2hd 12½ 13 Lipham T6 Mdn 81-24 El Corazon, Cheapskate, Atreak 12
Nov 7 BM 4f ft :491 h Oct 25 BM 5f ft :593 h Oct 14 BM tr.t 5f ft 1:011 h Oct 6 SA 4f ft :48 h

179. It's Sunday, Nov. 9. Which horse is best suited to the class of today's eligibility conditions?

7th Aqueduct

1 MILE. (1.33⅕) ALLOWANCE. Purse $40,000. 3-year-olds and Upward which have not won two races of $17,500 at a mile or over in 1985–86. Weights, 3-year-olds 120 lbs., Older 122 lbs., Non-winners of a race of $17,500 at a mile or over since October 1, 3 lbs. Of such a race since August 15, 5 lbs. Of such a race since July 1, 7 lbs. (Maiden, Claiming, Starter and restricted races not considered.)

A. **(11)**

Cognizant — **B. h. 5, by Explodent—I Understand, by Dr Fager**
Br.—Happy Valley Farm &Peskoff (Fla) **1986 12 3 0 1 $99,630**
Own.—Happy Valley Farm **1127** **Tr.—Dutrow Richard E** **1985 15 5 0 1 $70,130**
Lifetime 32 8 0 2 $171,980 **Turf 8 1 0 1 $31,620**

30Oct86-8Aqu 1 1/16 Ⓣ:481 1:121 1:444fm 11 122 13 11 2hd 55½ Migliore R6 Aw40000 75-26 Wollaston, Equalize, My Man John 8
16Oct86-8Bel 1 Ⓣ:47 1:124 1:381sf 4 116 54¼ 613 619 625 Migliore R4 HcpO 49-28 ExclusivePrtnr,FlingGllnt,Wollston 7
29Sep86-8Bel 1 1/16 Ⓣ:48 1:12 1:444gd 6 115 15 12½ 12 11¼ Migliore R2 Aw40000 77-30 Cognizant,FieryCelt,WatchForDwn 8
17Sep86-8Bel 6f Ⓣ:214 :443 1:092fm 3 119 22 43½ 44 42¾ Santos J A3 HcpO 90-17 Basket Weave,Alev,RedWingDream 7
31Aug86-8Bel 6f :22 :444 1:092ft 19 129 11½ 1½ 42 53 SamynJL1 Fall Hiwt H 92-11 Funistrada,Raja'sShark,LoveThtMc 6
31Aug86—Grade II
22Aug86-8Sar 6f :22 :452 1:103ft 4½ 117 35 42½ 56½ 44¾ MapleE4 Crnsh Prince 82-17 Shdowmr,CostConscious,Cullendle 6
17Aug86-8Sar 7f :214 :441 1:211m 31 117 22 35½ 713 815 BaileyJD3 Forego H 81-11 Groovy, Turkoman, Innamorato 8
17Aug86—Grade II
2Aug86-5Sar 6f :213 :442 1:091ft 3½ 117 11½ 11½ 12 1nk DayP1 A Phenomenon 94-10 Cognizant,RoyalPennant,Cullendale 7
●Oct 9 Aqu Ⓣ 6f fm 1:154 h (d) ●Sep 25 Aqu 5f ft 1:004 h ●Sep 16 Aqu 3f ft :342 h Sep 11 Aqu 5f ft 1:011 b

B.

Fobby Forbes *
Own.—Brennan R 113
B. c. 3, by Bold Forbes—Plum Happy, by Round Table
Br.—Due Process Stable (Fla) 1986 10 2 4 0 $314,690
Tr.—Garcia Carlos A 1985 2 2 6 0 $14,400
Lifetime 12 4 4 0 $329,090

21Jun86-8Lrl 1⅛:483 1:131 1:502ft *4-5 117 55½ 54½ 47 47½ BrcclVJr3 Gov's CupH 86-19 PrdeMrshl,MircleWood,BorduxBob 9
7Jun86-8Bel 1½:474 2:04 2:294sy 22 126 79½ 63¾ 57½ 59 BrccilVJr1 Belmont 62-16 DnzgConncton,JohnsTrsur,Frdnnd 10
7Jun86—Grade I
26May86-9GS 1¼:47 1:372 2:03 ft 7½ 126 77½ 33½ 45½ 44¾ BrccilVJr7 Jersey Dby 84-20 Snow Chief, Mogambo, Tasso 10
26May86—Grade II
3May86-8CD 1¼:451 1:37 2:024ft 16f 126 1217106½ 77¾ 710¾ RomrRP16 Ky Derby 73-18 Frdinnd,BoldArrngmnt,BrodBrush 16
3May86—Grade I; Very wide
19Apr86-9GS 1⅛:462 1:113 1:51 ft 2½ 115 611 43 3½ 1½ RrRP10 Garden State 74-21 FobbyForbes,Zabalet,MircleWood 10
5Apr86-9GS 1 :462 1:114 1:384ft *8-5 116 44½ 52½ 3½ 2½ RomrRP9 Chrry Hill H 80-22 BordxBob,FobbyForbs,MrclWood 12
19Mar86-6GS 1 :47 1:123 1:392ft *2-5 115 55 21 12 14½ Romero R P2 Aw12500 78-28 FobbyForbs,Dnny'sKys,NorthForst 7
1Mar86-8Pim 1$\frac{1}{16}$:464 1:112 1:441ft 5½ 116 64¾ 53½ 23½ 2no Hunter MT5 Fed Tesio 83-20 BrodBrush,FobbyForbes,DoublFint 7
Nov 3 Lrl 6f gd 1:152 b Oct 28 Lrl 5f m 1:022 bg ●Oct 22 Lrl 3f ft :36 b Oct 17 Lrl 5f ft 1:022 b

C.

Island Sun *
Own.—Live Oak Plantation 115
Dk. b. or br. c. 4, by Noble Dancer—Guadalupe, by Sigebert
Br.—Stock Green Farm (NY) 1986 14 5 2 2 $203,592
Tr.—Kelly Patrick J 1985 3 2 0 1 $33,600
Lifetime 17 7 2 3 $237,192 Turf 8 3 1 1 $155,462

25Oct86-9Lrl 1¼Ⓣ:4611:35 1:592fm 2¼ 113 21 21½ 54 57¼ MigliorR2 Turf Cup H 103 — StormOnTheLoose,I'mABnkr,Ronbr 7
25Oct86—Grade III
11Oct86-8Bel 1⅜[T]:4821:3622:142fm 18 126 21 21½ 69 613 MiglorR2 Man O' War 72-17 Dance of Life, Duty Dance,Pillaster 7
11Oct86—Grade I
20Aug86-8Sar 1$\frac{1}{16}$Ⓣ:4541:10 1:412fm *1 125 42 1hd 1hd 11 MlrR2 [S]West Point H 90-11 Island Sun, Judge Costa, Mugatea 14
10Aug86-8Sar 1⅛Ⓣ:4841:1241:504gd 6½ 116 63½ 66¼ 52 73 MiglorR5 B Baruch H 70-25 ExclusivPrtnr,I'mABnkr,CrmFrich 12
10Aug86—Grade II
30Jly86-7Sar 1$\frac{1}{16}$Ⓣ:47 1:11 1:424fm 2¾ 117 11 11½ 1½ 21¾ MigliorеR1 Daryl's Joy 81-21 Mourjane, Island Sun, Little Look 6
31May86-6Bel 1¼[T]:4731:3541:59 fm *2¼ 118 12 2hd 23½ 34½ MiglorR9 Red Smith H 94-15 Divulge, Tri For Size, Island Sun 9
31May86—Grade II; Run in two divisions
1May86-8Bel 1¼[T]:50 1:3832:022fm 4½ 119 11 11 12½ 13½ Migliore R6 Poker 82-18 Island Sun, Divulge, Equalize 10
6May86-8Aqu 1$\frac{1}{16}$Ⓣ:4811:1211:423fm 8¾ 119 2½ 11½ 16 18¾ MigliorR10 [S]Kingston 92-12 IslndSun,NoisyWhenHot,JudgCost 11
Nov 5 Bel 4f ft :494 b Oct 23 Bel [T] 3f fm :38 b ●Oct 7 Bel Ⓣ 6f gd 1:152 b Oct 2 Bel [T] 4f sf :501 b (d)

180. What kind of stakes quality has *Steal A Kiss* demonstrated? **(15)**

A. Grade 1
B. Grade 2
C. Grade 3
D. listed stakes

Steal A Kiss
Own.—Galbreath D M 116
B. f. 3, by Graustark—Queen's Paradise, by Summer Tan
Br.—Galbreath Mrs J W (Ky) 1986 6 2 2 0 $128,878
Tr.—Veitch John M 1985 8 1 3 3 $234,560
Lifetime 14 3 5 3 $363,438

11Oct86-7Kee 1⅛:46 1:104 1:481ft 7¾ 119 89½ 66½ 54½ 54½ BileyJD2 ⒻSpinster 92-12 Top Corsage, Endear,LifeAtTheTop 8
11Oct86—Grade I
21Sep86-8Bel 1⅛:454 1:093 1:464ft 16 109 67 58 36 28 BileyJD1 ⒻRuffian H 85-12 Lady's Secret, Steal A Kiss,Endear 6
21Sep86—Grade I
6Sep86-8Bel 1 :454 1:094 1:332ft 9½ 109 63¾ 44½ 45 27 BilyJD4 ⒻMaskette 91-10 Lady's Secret, Steal A Kiss,Endear 6
6Sep86—Grade I
27Aug86-6Bel 1 :474 1:122 1:362ft *7-5 112 52¼ 32 1hd 12¾ Maple E3 ⒻAw29000 83-16 StelAKiss,DesertView,SocilBusinss 8
11Aug86-5Sar 7f :221 :452 1:243ft *4-5 112 31½ 1hd 12 16 Maple E3 ⒻAw25000 79-17 Steal A Kiss, Reactress, Day Off 7
22Feb86-6GP 7f :224 :46 1:224ft 2½ 115 86½ 86¼ 710 515 VlsqzJ2 ⒻRegal Quillo 75-18 Lotka,MadameTreasurer,ClssyCthy 8
24Nov85-8Aqu 1⅛:491 1:133 1:501ft 5¾ 112 65 63¾ 3½ 3½ CrdrAJr8 ⒻDemoiselle 83-15 I'm Sweets,FamilyStyle,StealAKiss 8
24Nov85—Grade I
2Nov85-2Aqu 1 :452 1:104 1:354ft 20 119 107½ 87¾ 37½ 38¼ CrdrAJr10 ⒻBrCpJuvF 79-10 TwilightRidge,FmilyStyle,StlAKiss 12
2Nov85—Grade I
Nov 1 Bel 6f ft 1:16 b Oct 25 Bel 3f ft :38 b ●Oct 10 Kee 3f ft :362 b ●Oct 5 Kee 6f ft 1:113 h

181. At what class level is *Happy Cherokee* most likely to win next?

```
Happy Cherokee                          Dk. b. or br. f. 3, by Cherokee Fellow—Happy Hawaii, by Hawaii
                                        Br.—Mangurian H T Jr (Fla)              1986 10 0 1 5     $27,800
Own.—Mangurian H T Jr             107   Tr.—Root Thomas F                       1985 12 2 5 4     $54,530
                                     Lifetime  22 2 6 9  $82,330                Turf 1 0 0 0
18Oct86-1Bel  1⅛ :462 1:11 1:494ft  6½ 114  2½ 2hd 1hd 2nk  ThibeauRJ6 ⒻAw26000 78-17 OrientlSilk,HppyCheroke,Mrs.Bton 6
9Oct86-8Bel   1 1/16 :462 1:11 1:432ft  15 114  21 2½ 24 34½  ThibeauRJ5 ⒻAw29000 80-18 LPolonise,BllOfWstviw,HppyChrok 6
26Sep86-5Bel  6f :222 :453 1:093m  11 113  33 44 54¾ 46½  ThibeauRJ1 ⒻAw25000 87-19 LeftCourt,Bishop'sDelight,DerlyBrd 6
15Sep86-7Bel  1 :461 1:111 1:364ft  26 113  34½ 22½ 22½ 32¼  ThibeauRJ5 ⒻAw26000 79-15 ClaraBow,Flantasia,HappyCherokee 8
3Sep86-5Bel   7f :221 :45 1:23 ft  9½ 113  47½ 66½ 64½ 45½  ThibeauRJ4 ⒻAw25000 81-15 In Full Swing, Flantasia, Clara Bow 7
9Aug86-8Mth   1 1/16 Ⓣ:4641:1131:434+fm17 113  63¾104¾101010 1017¼  VrME3 ⒻAm Capable 65-17 SprucFr,GrnBoundry,TruChompon 11
20Jly86-5Bel  6f :22 :452 1:094ft  14 114  56½ 55 36 37¼  ThbRJ3 ⒻBatontwirler 86-14 SilntAccount,SucyMssy,HppyChrok 5
29Jun86-1Bel  1 :471 1:121 1:361ft  8 112  2hd 1hd 22 38½  VelsquezJ1 ⒻAw26000 75-14 ClbberGirl,PilgrimEr,HppyCheroke 7
   Nov 3 Bel tr.t 5f ft 1:034 b    Oct 5 Bel tr.t 4f ft :483 h    Sep 24 Bel tr.t 3f ft :362 h    Sep 11 Bel tr.t 3f ft :372 b
```

A. Alw, NW2XMC **(15)**
B. $62,500 claiming
C. classified allowance, highly restricted
D. $40,000 claiming

182. What claiming level is likely to be most suitable to 3YOs such as *Round The State*?

A. $62,500 **(11)**
B. $50,000
C. $40,000
D. $25,000

```
Round The State                         Dk. b. or br. c. 3, by State Dinner—Roundabend, by Never Bend
                                        Br.—Regal Oak Farm (Fla)                1986 15 2 1 3     $39,360
Own.—Listort P E                 1087   Tr.—Aquilino Joseph          $45,000    1985 4 M 1 1      $5,320
                                     Lifetime  19 2 2 4  $44,680                Turf 2 0 0 0
15Nov86-5Aqu  1 :453 1:112 1:373ft  15f 1087  66½ 52 1hd 1nk  Nuesch D10 Aw25000 78-22 RoundTheStte,ClssicMove,Dlmtin 13
6Nov86-7Aqu   1⅜ :484 1:393 2:183gd  12 115  2hd 1hd 3½ 35¼  Messina R8 Aw25000 83-24 FbulousMov,CndnWntr,RondThStt 9
27Oct86-3Aqu  6f :222 :454 1:112sy  6¼e 115  88¼ 811 78 34¼  Messina R1 20000 80-20 Aquhero,Crig'sPower,RoundThStt 10
3Oct86-6Bel   1 1/16 :47 1:114 1:441ft  15f 115  85½ 811 89½ 86¾  Rydowski S R8 32500 74-17 SlyCindy,GllntChief,RoylPotentte 12
19Sep86-7Bel  1 1/16 :462 1:102 1:403ft  50 113  45 48½ 514 413¾  RydowskiSR1 Aw25000 85-12 Macbest, I'm Ahead, Life Guard 7
7Sep86-3Bel   1⅛ :462 1:103 1:50 ft  45 113  811 811 58½ 45  RydowskiSR4 Aw25000 72-14 Godbey, Carnivore, Fabulous Move 8
21Aug86-9Sar  7f :221 :452 1:24 ft  51 115  76 97¼ 68 57¾  Rydowski S R8 32500 74-23 Macho, Col. Yoni, Better BeSingle 10
4Aug86-1Sar   1⅜ Ⓣ:51 1:4122:183gd  30 113  815 817 817 817¼  Skinner K7 45000 56-21 Anbaal, Dark Flood, Beat It Kid 8
   Oct 22 Aqu 4f ft :493 b    Oct 13 Aqu 5f ft 1:023 b    Sep 29 Aqu 4f ft :503 b
```

183. The 2YO below was entered in the Grade 1 Demoiselle Stakes at Aqueduct following its maiden win. Under what circumstances is this class maneuver acceptable to handicappers?

```
Graceful Darby                          B. f. 2, by Darby Creek Road—Graceful Touch, by His Majesty
                                        Br.—Phillips Mr–Mrs J W (Ky)            1986 3 1 1 1      $21,280
Own.—Phillips J W                 112   Tr.—Veitch John M
                                     Lifetime  3 1 1 1  $21,280
16Oct86-7Bel  1 :462 1:121 1:374ft  *2-3 117  41½ 1½ 15 15¾  Bailey J D7 ⒻMdn 76-19 GrcfulDrby,TurnSwift,MssUnnmbl 10
28Sep86-6Bel  7f :231 :463 1:224m  3¾ 117  32½ 21½ 27 212¾  Bailey J D2 ⒻMdn 75-15 PersonlEnsign,GrcefulDrby,Nstique 7
11Sep86-4Bel  6f :224 :461 1:112ft  13 117  42½ 47 48 39¼  Bailey J D8 ⒻMdn 76-21 VlidLine,RullhRunner,GrcefulDrby 12
   Nov 16 Bel 1 ft 1:442 b    Nov 11 Bel tr.t 5f ft 1:033 b    Oct 31 Bel 4f ft :491 h    Oct 24 Bel 3f ft :364 b
```

A. rarely **(11)**
B. whenever adjusted times and manner of victory indicate clearly superior stakes class
C. only when the field is devoid of previous Grade 1 stakes winners
D. in 2-year-old sprint stakes only

184. It's Nov. 23 in New York. Which horse is better suited to the conditions of eligibility?

6th Aqueduct

7 FURLONGS. (1.20⅗) ALLOWANCE. Purse $36,000. Fillies and Mares, 3-year-olds and upward which have never won a race of $17,500 since January 1. Weight, 3-year-olds, 120 lbs. Older, 122 lbs. Non-winners of two races of $16,500 since August 1 allowed 3 lbs. Of two such races since June 1, 5 lbs. Of such a race since October 1, 7 lbs. (Maiden, claiming, starter and restricted races not considered.)

A. **(11)**

Barbicue Sauce — **B. f. 3, by Sauce Boat—Lady Barbizon, by Barbizon**
Own.—Reynolds D P **113** **Br.—Reynolds D P (Ky)** **1986 11 3 5 0 $51,790**
Tr.—Kelly Thomas J **1985 2 1 0 0 $13,200**
Lifetime 13 4 5 0 $64,990

Entered 22Nov86- 8 MED

3Nov86-8Aqu	7f	:223	:452	1:22 ft	5¼	113	53	54	28	213	Antley CW2	[F]Aw36000	78-22	Argentario,BarbicueSuce,TopIssue	6
24Oct86-8Med	6f	:222	:453	1:102ft	17	116	75¼	54	33½	21¼	AtlCW5	[F]Convenienc	89-21	Noranc,BarbicueSuce,NeedlesLdy	10
6Oct86-5Med	6f	:23	:464	1:112ft	*2	113	41¾	41½	1½	1¾	Antley CW3	[F]Aw17000	85-26	Barbicue Sauce,Rajiste,CrownSable	5
5Sep86-7Med	6f	:221	:453	1:113sy	4	112	42	52	52¼	42	Antley CW6	[F]Aw25000	82-21	Crr'sDrm,BoldlyDrd,Kolctoo'sPowr	9
20Aug86-9Mth	6f	:224	:452	1:103ft	9-5	115	42½	43	32½	2½	Antley CW6	[F]Aw17000	86-21	DncngDmscus,BrbcuSuc,DnzgDrlng	6
25Jly86-9Mth	6f	:22	:442	1:11 ft	*2-3	114	34	25	21	13½	Antley CW4	[F]Aw14000	85-16	BrbicueSuce,Merebot,SwtstMomm	7
17Jly86-7Mth	6f	:223	:451	1:111ft	3	114	41¾	35	32½	2¾	Antley CW6	[F]Aw14000	83-22	Rajiste, Barbicue Sauce, SpruceFir	9
17Jly86—Stmbld st railied															
3Jly86-7Mth	6f	:224	:463	1:12 ft	*2-3	112	3nk	21	1hd	11½	Antley CW8	[F]Aw13000	80-24	BarbicueSauce,DarkTzarin,GiniDoll	8

Nov 1 Bel tr.t 4f ft :502 b   Oct 21 Bel tr.t 4f ft :482 h   Oct 16 Bel tr.t 4f ft :49 b

B.

Dame Gris — **Gr. f. 4, by Grey Dawn II—Bessie's Mother, by Olden Times**
Own.—Centennial Farm **115** **Br.—Bright View Farm Inc (NJ)** **1986 9 0 3 1 $31,341**
Tr.—Jerkens H Allen **1985 16 4 2 1 $65,988**
Lifetime 28 4 5 3 $101,102 **Turf 4 0 2 0 $16,480**

29Jun86-5Bel	1¼[T]:493	1:394	2:03	fm	4	117	52	54	42½	42¼	Santos J A7	[F]Aw40000	77-13	TriArgo,CourgeousKrn,SmokthQun	7
19Jun86-7Bel	1 [T]:454	1:103	1:36	fm	3½	117	63¾	41	1½	31¼	Santos J A6	[F]Aw32000	84-18	‡SmoketheQueen,Bailrullh,DmeGris	8
19Jun86—Placed second through disqualification															
7Jun86-9Mth	1 :48	1:13	1:381	sy	5	112	32	43	59	514¾	MdrdAJr4	[F]RumsonH	67-22	FlyingHeat,QuietPansy,Rolfe'sRuby	5
7Jun86—Run in Divisions															
15May86-8Bel	1 1/16 [T]:474	1:122	1:431	fm	12	119	42	41½	21	21½	Santos J A2	[F]Aw32000	78-22	CapoDiMonte,DameGris,MrkedLdy	7
15May86—Checked															
21Apr86-8Aqu	1 :454	1:102	1:353	sy	18	119	21	11½	21½	26¾	Santos J A5	[F]Aw40000	81-21	Flying Heat, DameGris,TizzieTazzle	5
5Apr86-8GS	170 :47	1:122	1:433	ft	5¼	119	55	48	715	816¾	RomeroRP5	[F]Aw17000	64-22	FrostyVlentine,OneDouble,DoublOn	9
22Mar86-9GS	6f :223	:462	1:121	ft	8½	112	68¼	57	55½	34½	MdrdAJr2	[S]Tosmah H	76-24	Ruthie's Move,TwoOnery,DameGris	7
6Mar86-8Aqu	1 1/16 [•]:48	1:133	1:483	ft	19	1105	47	66	96½	99¾	MrqzCHJr5	[F]Aw40000	57-31	Leecoo, Stay Home, Truly Best	9

Nov 20 Bel tr.t 4f ft :50 b   Nov 15 Bel 4f ft :481 b   Nov 11 Bel 4f gd :49 b   Nov 8 Bel 4f sy :523 b

185. What claiming class is likely to be most suitable for *Lord Pacal*?

A. $50,000 **(11)**
B. $40,000
C. $25,000
D. No basis for saying

```
Lord Pacal                                   Ch. g. 3, by Czaravich—Rosy Tinted, by Drone
                                             Br.—LaBrot Barbara (Ky)                        1986  9 1 0 3     $15,000
Own.—LaBrot Barbara W                  113   Tr.—Turner William H Jr          $45,000       1985  4 M 0 1      $3,960
                                           Lifetime  13 1 0 4   $18,960                     Turf  2 0 0 1      $3,000
16Nov86-2Aqu  7f :224 :46 1:24 ft        31 113  131413129119 10   Murphy D J7     45000 71-23 BulletBlde,ForTneGippr,PlcidWtrs 13
27Oct86-6Aqu  1⅛:482 1:13 1:501sy        14 1095 85¾ 69½ 513 516½  Baird E T8    Aw25000 67-20 FutureFble,CndinWintr,Cory'sComt 9
5Oct86-1Bel   1 1/16:454 1:103 1:423ft   4¾ 117  68½ 64¾ 57 58¾   Maple E2        50000 80-18 Michael'sDancer,BoldMruder,Aside 7
7Sep86-9Bel   1 :46 1:111 1:371ft        21 113  912 85¼ 63¾ 3nk   Samyn J L3      45000 79-14 Macho, For The Gipper,LordPacal 10
     7Sep86—Off poorly
1Sep86-6Bel   1 1/16(T):4711:1111:432fm   5 117  88 95¼ 97 98      Bailey J D8     35000 71-18 VatzaMtter,GllntChmp,CowboyUp 11
     1Sep86—Off slowly
30May86-5Bel  1 (T):4521:0911:343hd      19 117  75½ 64¼ 55½ 310   Bailey J D5   Aw25000 82-13 DanceCardFilled,Dr.Siegal,LordPacl 9
     30May86—Hesitated st.
16May86-9Bel  6f :224 :464 1:123ft        3 113  97½ 74½ 32 11¼    Bailey J D4    M50000 79-17 LordPcl,MtAuburnExprss,GlddNtv 12
     16May86—Hesitated st.
25Apr86-9Aqu  1 :472 1:123 1:381ft     *9-5 112  1½ 2½ 3½ 33       Bailey J D4    M35000 72-28 JohnMuir,MaskofRoses,LordPacal 12
   Nov 11 Bel tr.t 4f ft :49 b     ●Nov 3 Bel 3f gd :35 h     Oct 24 Bel 5f ft 1:03 b     Oct 19 Bel 4f ft :49 h
```

186. How would class handicappers evaluate *Lovelier's* chances in today's Grade 1 stakes?

A. Excellent (15)
B. Good
C. Fair
D. Poor

```
Lovelier                                     Dk. b. or br. f. 2, by Affirmed—La Mesa, by Round Table
                                             Br.—Harbor View Farm (Ky)                      1986  8 3 0 2     $91,022
Own.—Harbor View Farm                  119   Tr.—Lukas D Wayne
                                           Lifetime  8 3 0 2   $91,022
8Nov86-8Aqu   1⅛:484 1:122 1:521sy     *3-2 116  — — — 12½          CrdrAJr1 (F)Miss Grillo 74-22 Lovelier, Nastique, SpectacularBev 8
     8Nov86—Grade III; Running positions omitted because of weather conditions
24Oct86-9Med  1 1/16:47 1:114 1:451ft    11 118  64¼ 66 55¾ 56¼    RmrRP7    (F)Gardenia   71-21 Collins, Silent Turn, Dr. Myrtle 12
     24Oct86—Grade II
3Oct86-8Med   1 :48 1:123 1:384sy         3 120  1hd 13 15 16      RomeroRP6 (F)Aw15000    81-20 Lovelier,SpartnFbles,WoodlndMnor 8
12Sep86-5Bel  6½f :232 :47 1:191ft        5 118  1½ 21 2½ 3¾       CordroAJr1 (F)Aw24000   78-20 Sweetbreads, Karan Ann, Lovelier 6
31Aug86-8Pha  6f :22 :45 1:103ft         11 117  25 37 411 49¾     McNilFA7 (F)Signature   78-19 CgeyExuberncCougrSu,FlyingKtun 8
7Aug86-4Sar   7f :221 :461 1:28 sy     *8-5 117  1½ 15 17 1hd      Cordero A Jr8 (F)Mdn    62-38 Lovelier, Lotus Lane,MissSwooning 8
28Jly86-5Bel  6f :221 :453 1:113gd        9 117  31½ 44½ 44½ 34¼   Cordero A Jr6 (F)Mdn    80-12 RoomfortheSuc,MissilMgic,Lovlir 13
     28Jly86—Steadied
25Jun86-4Bel  5½f :224 :46 1:05 ft       8½ 117  98¾ 89¼ 812 79¾   Bailey J D3   (F)Mdn    80-12 OurLittleMargie,Nijinov,FlyingKtun 9
     25Jun86—In tight early
   ●Nov 3 Bel 5f gd 1:002 h     Oct 18 Bel 6f ft 1:133 h     Oct 13 Bel 5f ft 1:033 b     Sen 26 Bel 5f ft 1:011 b
```

187. What is the most advanced class at which *Soaring Princess* would be acceptable next out?

```
Soaring Princess                             B. f. 2, by Sensitive Prince—Soar Aloft, by Avatar
                                             Br.—Babcock Shirley N (Ky)                     1986  3 2 0 0     $27,600
Own.—Babcock Shirley N                 112   Tr.—Burch William E
                                           Lifetime  3 2 0 0   $27,600
29Oct86-7Aqu  7f :223 :444 1:221ft       36 116  31½ 41¼ 21 11½    Migliore R6 (F)Aw24000  90-15 SoaringPrincess,LostPeace,MyPerl 8
17Aug86-1Sar  6f :22 :454 1:103m         5¼ 121  54 36 58½ 717     CordroAJr5 (F)Aw24008   70-11 Bound, Found a Jewel, Karan Ann 7
3Aug86-4Sar   6f :221 :454 1:12 sy        5 117  44 45 2hd 12½     Cordero A Jr4 (F)Mdn    88-16 SoringPrincess,PelicnBy,DotsPlsur 9
   Nov 16 Bel 6f ft 1:161 b     Nov 11 Bel 4f gd :502 b     Oct 25 Bel 5f ft 1:02 b     ●Oct 19 Bel 6f ft 1:153 h
```

A. Alw, NW2XMC (15)
B. Alw, NW3XMC
C. Grade 3 stakes
D. open unlisted stakes

188. Can *Truly Best* stand the $10,000 class rise?

A. Yes **(14)**
B. No

Truly Best — Dk. b. or br. m. 5, by Turn And Count—Sulayma, by True Knight
Own.—Rory Green Stables **117**
Br.—Whiting Mr–Mrs P J (Cal) — 1986 11 2 2 3 $45,600
Tr.—Sedlacek Michael C $35,000 — 1985 17 6 2 2 $56,665
Lifetime 48 11 7 7 $131,420 — Turf 5 0 0 0 $390

4Nov86-2Aqu	1	:452	1:11	1:38 ft	6	117	89	77¼	45	1nk	Murphy D J8	Ⓕ 25000	76-22	TrulyBest,SoloEnrgy,K.'sSolution	13
12Oct86-3Bel	7f	:224	:452	1:211ft	26	117	69½	618	624	623¾	RomeroRP6	ⒻAw27000	72-13	Wisla, Hedonic, Clabber Girl	6
1Sep86-1Bel	1 1/16 Ⓣ	:463	1:114	1:421fm	2½e	113	86½	86¾	89	712½	Velasquez J2	Ⓕ 70000	77-18	MusicOfLov,DoublSucy,LotusDlght	8
10Aug86-1Sar	7f	:23	:461	1:233ft	17	112	52½	42½	69	67¾	Migliore R6	Ⓕ 175000	76-14	TeriykiStke,LdyD.,ImpetuousPunch	7
9Jly86-8Mth	170	:464	1:112	1:421ft	8¾	117	54	45½	46	34	ThomasDB8	ⒻAw16000	81-19	Rosemont Risk,Floating,TrulyBest	10
24Apr86-8Aqu	1⅛	:49	1:133	1:52 ft	3¼	119	32	77½	67	66¼	RomeroRP1	ⒻAw29000	69-25	Beths Song,ViaSistina,PrettyTricky	7
4Apr86-8Aqu	1⅛	:484	1:141	1:523ft	*3-2	119	1hd	3½	34	34¼	Davis R G1	ⒻAw29000	68-26	Catatonic, Stoke TheFire,TrulyBest	7
14Mar86-5Aqu	1⅛	:471	1:122	1:523sy	5½	117	35½	33½	21	21	MacBethD3	ⒻAw29000	71-26	Marked Lady, Truly Best, Skÿjak	11

Nov 16 Aqu 4f ft :494 b — Oct 30 Aqu 5f ft 1:012 h — Oct 25 Aqu 5f ft 1:04 b — Oct 7 Aqu 5f ft 1:013 h

189. Which is the most probable selection on class when analyzing an $8000 claiming race?

A. a runner-up for $8000 last out where the winner was dropping from a par race at $12,500 **(11)**
B. a big winner at $6250 seven days ago
C. a multiple $8000 winner this season
D. a horse that finished 3rd, beaten a nose last out, versus $10,000 horses

190. What kind of races are class handicappers most frequently likely to avoid?

A. closely matched stakes **(10)**
B. claiming races for 3YOs
C. preliminary nonwinners allowances
D. starter races

191. Which horse below is more likely to win a $25,000 claiming race?

A. **(11)**

Sun Vest — Ch. g. 3, by Sunday Guest—Miss Raedine, by Vested Power
JUDICE J C **114**
Own.—Vatne R
Br.—Wood Prairie Farm (Wash) — 1986 16 2 3 2 $18,780
Tr.—Leonard Jack R $25,000 — 1985 4 2 0 1 $2,720
Lifetime 20 4 3 3 $21,500
Entered 21Nov86-10 BM

30Oct86-9BM	1 1/16	:451	1:101	1:433ft	19	114	23	22	1hd	41½	Judice J C3	20000	72-24	CptnO'Dsy,SnstvCopy,RtnlApp'ch	11
18Sep86-7Lga	6f	:214	:444	1:092ft	5	120	42	33	34½	25	Moore D1	16000	84-23	Timothy Pat, SunVest,HijoElToro	10
7Sep86-4Lga	6½f	:213	:44	1:151ft	9	118	2hd	2½	25	48	Moore D4	20000	85-14	NrthrnPlcy,PlckyEmprr,BlzngThng	7
30Aug86-7Lga	6½f	:221	:45	1:18 gd	6¼	120	2½	1[illegible]	11	2hd	Moore D2	16000	79-22	Joe'sMmoris,SunVst,TmpstDTmpo	10
23Aug86-7Lga	6½f	:212	:432	1:143ft	11	116	22½	22½	45	47	Moore D7	20000	89-15	AgntTodd,PlckyEmpror,NrthrnPlcy	9
16Aug86-4Lga	6f	:22	:451	1:101ft	6	120	1hd	1½	2hd	1½	Moore D7	16000	85-14	Sun Vest, Merry Yanky, Tar War	8
2Aug86-5Lga	1 1/16	:463	1:122	1:44 ft	4	120	11½	11½	22½	34½	Cooper B5	16000	74-16	Bold Habit, Macadon, Sun Vest	8
26Jly86-5Lga	6f	:22	:443	1:094ft	32	120	12½	11	11½	2¾	Cooper B9	16000	86-15	TempestDTmpo,SunVst,MrryYnky	11
9Jly86-7Lga	6f	:213	:442	1:092ft	28	120	54½	31½	35½	46½	Barnese V J8	16000	82-16	PluckyEmpror,P.J.'sNtiv,ShilsholBy	9
13Jun86-5Lga	6½f	:214	:442	1:154ft	7	120	64	63¾	613	76¾	Barnese V J10	16000	83-12	Joe'sMemories,Sndigr,Hsmybuddy	10

Nov 10 BM 1 ft 1:442 h — Oct 26 BM 1 ft 1:454 h — Oct 19 BM 7f ft 1:311 h — Oct 3 Lga 3f sl :383 b

B.

Zacbee — B. g. 3, by Gallant Best—Repeatable, by Irepeat

TOHILL K S **114** — Br.—Leckbee M & Roberta (Wash) — 1986 12 0 2 1 $6,47

Tr.—Cummings William R $25,000 — 1985 11 1 1 3 $10,48

Own.—Smith P W — Lifetime 23 1 3 4 $16,955

14Nov86-7BM	1 1/16 :464 1:111 1:43 ft	65	114	42½	53¾	813	814¾	Tohill K S6	40000	62-20	Arbitrate,DoctorDakota,GreekNtive
17Oct86-9Lga	6½f :214 :441 1:144ft	9½	116	33½	33	33	33¾	Hanna M A2	40000	91-18	Northern Policy, Mr. Spade,Zacbee
8Oct86-9Lga	1 1/16 :462 1:112 1:434ft	16	117	98¼	94½	513	57¼	Hanna M A6	Aw9300	73-19	ImATrooper,SenorSpanish,BigDuk
20Sep86-9Lga	1⅛ :464 1:104 1:49 ft	41	115	79¾	97½	820	812¼	HMA3	[S]B Mrcs Prt H	76-18	Sssy'sHllr,GllntSlor,CrrncyControl
12Sep86-9Lga	1 :461 1:103 1:353ft	20e	115	77	87¼	816	77¼	Hanna M A7	Aw10000	84-19	CrrncyControl,Sssy'sHllr,SnrSpnsh
22Aug86-9Lga	1 :453 1:101 1:351ft	37	114	66	76¼	917	810¾	Hanna M A7	Aw10000	82-17	Sssy'sHllr,CrrncyContrl,BrndyRsrv
16Jly86-9Lga	1 1/16 :474 1:134 1:483m	27	117	78	51¾	22½	21½	Hanna M A6	Aw11100	54-39	Darby Gray, Zacbee, Jim Joe
28Jun86-9Lga	1 :472 1:11 1:354ft	17	117	84¾	77½	813	810	Hanna M A3	Aw10000	80-14	CurrncyControl,BlckBllmy,SirLyor
11Jun86-9Lga	6½f :214 :442 1:151ft	5	120	811	87¾	74¾	57¼	Drexler H2	Aw9300	86-15	LdingHour,HousSpcilty,CougrDivi
4Jun86-9Lga	6f :213 :442 1:102ft	11	117	58½	49	45½	21½	Hanna M A6	Aw10100	82-24	Krupa, Zacbee, Docaly

Nov 8 BM 4f ft :49 h

192. What kind of horse best fits the conditions below?

8th BayMeadows

1 MILE. (1.33⅗) 5th Running of The WOODSIDE HANDICAP. $50,000 added. Fillies and mares. 3-year-olds and upward. By subscription of $50 each, which shall accompany the nomination, $200 to pass the entry box, and $250 additional to start, with $50,000 added, of which $9,000 to second, $6,500 to third, $4,000 to fourth, $1,750 to fifth and $1,250 to sixth. Weights Sunday, November 16. Starters to be named through the entry box Friday, November 21, by the usual time of closing. A trophy will be presented to the owner of the winner. Closed Thursday, November 13, 1986 with 27 nominations. High weight preferred.

A. a previous Grade 1 winner **(11)**
B. a 4YO that has won a listed stakes
C. a 3YO that has won two allowance races impressively before running 2nd in a Grade 3 stakes limited to 3YOs
D. a multiple open stakes winner, 4up

193. What is the most suitable class level for *Sweet Drop*?

A. $50,000 Clm **(15)**
B. Alw, NW2XMC
C. Alw, NW3XMC
D. Clf Alw

Sweet Drop — B. f. 4, by Sir Jason—Sovereign Way, by Mr Leader

SOTO S **114** — Br.—Degwitz F (Fla) — 1986 12 1 0 2

Tr.—Azpurua Eduardo Jr — 1985 11 3 1 2

Own.—Degwitz F — Lifetime 23 4 1 4 $66,057 — Turf 15 3 0 2

12Nov86-8Hol	1 1/16 (T):482 1:12 1:413fm	15	115	31½	31½	34½	46	Solis A6	(F)Aw40000	80-14	Solva, Miss Clipper, D
10Oct86-8SA	1⅛ (T):464 1:104 1:481fm	6	114	12½	1½	32	48	Solis A4	(F)Aw45000	78-14	Bonne Ile, Miss Clipp
10Oct86—Bobbled start											
10Sep86-7Dmr	1 (T):463 1:102 1:352fm	13	115	58	58	54	51½	Solis A1	(F)Aw40000	93-07	Infinidad, Adalia, Reg
10Sep86—Broke slowly											
14Aug86-8Dmr	1 (T):472 1:114 1:351fm	53	115	62¾	72¾	53½	65¾	CstnonAL5	(F)Aw35000	90-04	Auspiciante,RoyalRe
9Jly86-8Hol	1 (T):462 1:101 1:342fm	33	115	55	53	54	65¾	Solis A2	(F)Aw40000	— —	BlushingAllOver,Folk
13Jun86-8Hol	1 1/16 (T):462 1:102 1:41 fm	5¼	117	41½	43	31	1½	Solis A5	(F)Aw25000	99-01	Sweet Drop, Jigalore
1Jun86-5Hol	1 1/16 (T):481 1:12 1:412fm	11	116	44	43½	44	47½	McHrDG5	(F)[R]CntryQn	89-07	Park Appeal, Zaide,
14May86-8Hol	1⅛ (T):463 1:103 1:464fm	33	117	67½	52	41½	34¾	McHrgDG3	(F)Aw32000	93-02	Tremulous, Only, Sw
1May86-8Hol	1 1/16 (T):47 1:102 1:412fm	5	117	25	23½	21½	56¾	McHrgDG1	(F)Aw32000	90-03	Cenyak'sStar,Luckyl
1May86—Rank 7/8 turn											
13Apr86-7SA	1⅛ (T):463 1:12 1:482fm	25	116	65½	74½	63¾	32¼	DlhoussyE8	(F)Aw35000	83-17	Affirmance, Balladr
13Apr86—Bumped at start, 6-wide into stretch											

Nov 7 Hol 5f ft :594 h **Oct 31 Hol 4f ft :473 h** **●Oct 25 Hol 5f ft 1:00 h** **Oct 5 Hol 5f ft 1:002 h**

194. Which horse is well-suited to the conditions specified?

6th BayMeadows

BAY MEADOWS
1⅛ MI. TURF

ABOUT 1 ⅛ MILES. (Turf). (1.47) ALLOWANCE. Purse $19,000. 3-year-olds and upward. Non-winners of $3,000 three times other than maiden, starter or claiming. Weights, 3-year-olds, 117 lbs.; older, 120 lbs. Non-winners of two such races at one mile or over since October 1 allowed 3 lbs.; two such races at one mile or over since September 1, 5 lbs.; one such race at one mile or over since August 1, 7 lbs.

A. **(11)**

Kentucky Laurel
TOHILL K S 115
Own.—Smithers R
Ch. g. 4, by Sassafras—Gentle Feather, by Sensitivo
Br.—Shadowlawn Fm (Ky) 1986 10 1 1 0 $15,755
Tr.—Conner Kay 1985 10 2 1 1 $22,625
Lifetime 20 3 2 1 $38,380 Turf 5 0 1 0 $5,505

2Nov86-6BM 1 Ⓣ:473 1:11 1:363fm 7¼ 117 53¾ 46½ 57½ 46 Tohill K S4 Aw20000 91-03 Spellbound,AudaciousRuliah,Swllge 8
15Oct86-8BM 1 Ⓣ:46 1:104 1:364fm 21 115 43 43¾ 33½ 21 Tohill K S1 Aw19000 95-04 Marcel,KentuckyLaurel,SafetyBank 6
28Sep86-6BM 1 Ⓣ:464 1:111 1:372gd 24 117 52¼ 63 714 715½ Tohill K S6 Aw19000 77-08 WellRelated,SoldtBleu,OrindOriginl 8
28Sep86—Bumped, steadied 3/16
13Sep86-10Bmf 1 :454 1:11 1:371ft 27 115 57 41¾ 31½ 1nk Tohill K S7 Aw17000 82-31 KntuckyLurl,H'sSpiritd,PorchLight 7
1Aug86-10SR 1 :471 1:111 1:364ft 48 1105 77 1014 1016 97¾ McGrath M8 Aw13000 80-12 CrystalTas,IHeardAVoice,FaliPlaz 10
1Aug86—Wide 7/8
18Jly86-3Sol 1 :462 1:112 1:36 ft 9¾ 115 56¼ 69 713 721½ Caballero R4 Aw13000 72-12 BuckRoyl,LondonExprss,BigDrRyn 7
18Jly86—Bumped start
1Jly86-11Pln 1 1/16 :464 1:112 1:434ft 9¼ 115 21 32 45 53¾ Tohill K S6 Aw16000 81-18 Frivolissimo,BigJess,LondonExprss 7
3May86-4GG 1 1/16 :463 1:103 1:433ft 29 114 38 411 516 516 CampbellBC6 Aw20000 69-21 Buckohoy,PririeBreker,Impulsively 6
19Apr86-4GG 1 :461 1:101 1:353ft 50 111 35½ 37½ 511 613¾ Campbell BC4 ⓇHcp0 76-12 Dunant, Prince Don B., GreyMissile 6
28Mar86-7GG 6f :22 :442 1:093ft 21 115 68½ 68½ 814 812¾ Hummel C R7 Aw18000 78-20 BonanzaBar,Overhold,AndrewNMe 8
28Mar86—Bobbled start
●Nov 18 GG 5f ft :594 h ●Oct 28 GG 5f ft :592 h ●Oct 7 GG 5f ft 1:002 h

B.

Orinda Original ✻
MAPLE S 115
Own.—Duffel J A
B. rig. 4, by Beau's Eagle—Bold Louise, by Bold Hour
Br.—Duffel J A (Ky) 1986 6 1 0 2 $15,530
Tr.—Weaver Joey 1985 5 2 0 0 $9,991
Lifetime 13 3 0 2 $25,521 Turf 8 1 0 2 $6,371

26Oct86-6BM 7½f Ⓣ:231 :464 1:294fm 19 113 23 21 45 510 Lamance C4 Aw22000 85-05 PairOfAces,NewAtraction,ReglBrek 6
10Oct86-8BM 1 1/16 :474 1:112 1:44 ft 9½ 115 1½ 11½ 11½ 1¾ Maple S1 Aw17000 72-18 OrindaOriginl,AirDevil,U.LuckyShot 8
28Sep86-6BM 1 Ⓣ:464 1:111 1:372gd 19 115 1hd 1hd 2½ 32½ Maple S7 Aw19000 90-08 WellRelated,SoldtBleu,OrindOriginl 8
17Feb86-6GG 1 1/16 :483 1:122 1:452sy 6 1122 46½ 45½ 55 52¼ YammotoTJ4 Aw18000 74-26 Julie'sMark,DiplomtRuler,Pgmento 6
8Feb86-7GG 1 1/16 :461 1:10 1:414ft 15 1095 65¼ 69½ 810 78 Yamamoto T J6 40000 86-11 Melo King, Easy Mover, Big Jesse 9
19Jan86-6BM 7½f Ⓣ:233 :48 1:314yl 3¼ 120 45 54 46½ 36 Baze R A6 Aw18000 85-09 SonnyBrich,WlkAndDnc,OrindOrgnl 8
30Dec85-7BM 1 1/16 :46 1:11 1:443m 23 1095 46 41 22 1½ YammotoTJ9 Aw17000 69-21 OrindaOriginal,MotorBoat,NtiveAct 9
22Dec85-6BM 1 1/16 :46 1:093 1:421ft 52 1095 44½ 68½ 811 86½ YammotoTJ1 Aw18000 74-20 BrghtAndRght,Json'sDrummr,BnJf 9
3Oct85♦6Newmarket(Eng) 1¼ 2:063gd 33 109 Ⓣ 11 Carter G Exning H HenrytheLion,Tracing,RitualMusic 14
8Apr85♦4Nottingham(Eng) 1¼ 2:323sf *7-5 128 Ⓣ 522 Carter G Clumber SanCrlos,Stymn'sTop,Tolly'sTonic 15
●Nov 14 GG 6f ft 1:13 h Nov 8 GG 4f ft :52 h Oct 7 BM 4f ft :481 h ●Sep 25 BM 6f m 1:153 h

C.

Soldat Bleu
CASTANEDA M 113
Own.—SheikManaBnRshdAlMktoum
B. c. 4, by Lyphard—Summer Mark, by Summer Tan
Br.—Gainesway Fm & CrescentFm (Ky) 1986 5 1 1 0 $23,530
Tr.—Drysdale Neil 1985 3 0 1 1 $2,706
Lifetime 12 2 3 1 $33,234 Turf 12 2 3 1 $33,234

22Oct86-7SA 1⅛ Ⓣ:454 1:102 1:471fm *3 117 43½ 51¾ 85 77¾ Pincay L Jr3 Aw35000 83-12 Nugget Point, Catane, Schiller 10
22Oct86—Steadied 1/8
11Oct86-7SA 1⅛ Ⓣ:463 1:103 1:481fm 4½ 115 46 35½ 44 53¾ Stevens G L6 Aw45000 82-21 Nasib, Skip Out Front, Pudahuel 8
28Sep86-6BM 1 Ⓣ:464 1:111 1:372gd *2¼ 115 812 87 45 21 CastanedaM5 Aw19000 92-08 WellRelated,SoldtBleu,OrindOriginl 8
28Sep86—Stumbled at start
12Apr86-5SA 1⅛ Ⓣ:471 1:113 1:473fm 5¼ 119 31 3½ 32 64 Pincay L Jr5 Aw35000 85-14 Rich Earth, Snowcreek, Rivlia 8
23Feb86-7SA 1⅛ Ⓣ:471 1:12 1:504fm 8½ 117 97¼ 85½ 21½ 1hd Pincay L Jr2 Aw34000 73-24 Soldat Bleu, Kala Dancer, Solstein 9
23Feb86—Wide into stretch
27Jly85♦1Ascot(Eng) 1 1:433fm 5¼ 129 Ⓣ 21½ JusterM Hope Diamnd Field Hand, SoldatBleu,SheerCliff 24
9May85♦4Chester(Eng) a1¼ 2:131gd 3½ 124 Ⓣ 634 Piggott L Dee(Gr3) Infantry, Trucidator, Vertige 7
1May85♦4Ascot(Eng) 1¼ 2:093gd *2¼ 126 Ⓣ 34 SnbrnWR White Rose Vertige, Trojan Prince, Soldat Bleu 7
1Sep84♦3Sandown(Eng) 7f 1:291gd 10 123 Ⓣ 55¼ SwnbrnWR Solario OhSoSharp,YoungRunwy,StHilrion 9
Nov 21 Hol 3f ft :354 h Nov 16 Hol 6f ft 1:132 h Nov 11 Hol 5f ft 1:014 h Oct 18 SA 5f ft 1:003 b

D. None of the above

For items 195 through 205 examine the past performances provided and identify the best horse.

195.

A. **(16)**

```
Jet Royale                          B. c. 4, by Tri Jet—Royal Togs, by Prince Royal II
  GRABLE T C                        Br.—El Conquistador Farm (Fla)           1986 10  1  2  2    $10,525
                              114   Tr.—Webb Bryan               $6,250      1985 13  1  2  2    $18,900
Own.—Volkman R                     Lifetime  28  3  4  4   $37,775
25Sep86-12Poma1⅛:49  1:16  1:563m  *7-5 1095  53¾ 1hd 1hd 15½  Black C A1     5000 64-30 Jet Royale, Old Pet,Caesar'sDancer 7
19Sep86-5Pom  7f :22   :452 1:25 ft   2 1115  10121015 911 2hd  Black C A10    6250 94-09 Burgundy,JetRoyale,GallantSpecil 10
11Sep86-9Pom  6½f:22   :46  1:172ft   6¾ 1115  109½ 813 77½ 44¼  Black C A1     8000 89-08 ‡Cody'sChnce,Nostrdmus,Bu'sHop 10
     11Sep86—Awarded third purse money; Wide 1st turn
21Mar86-9GG   1⅛:472 1:121 1:504ft  10 114   811 85½ 32  32½  Mena F3        6250 76-22 Polliniferous, Excell'em,JetRoyale 11
16Mar86-2SA   1  :47  1:121 1:383sy  9½ 115   58½ 47  58  414¼ Castanon A L4 10000 61-24 PyrmidZotts,ClssicEndvour,BlzFlm 5
6Mar86-9SA    1⅛:463 1:11  1:502ft  13 116   86½ 89¾ 712 815¾ Kaenel J L8   10000 61-15 VictoryLea,Cheers,ClssicEndevour 11
19Feb86-9SA   1⅛:483 1:131 1:521sy  11 1115  76¼ 78½ 612 613  Black C A6    12500 55-24 Dr.Coercion,Bcklog,LVerne'sBigMc 8
29Jan86-9SA   1 1/16:463 1:113 1:441ft  8¼ 1135  99¾ 88  88¾ 79½  Alvarez A8   c10000 70-15 PolcPurst,Lghthwyholm,Hrdtohndl 9
17Jan86-2SA   1 1/16:47  1:121 1:443ft  16 1125  87¼ 41½ 31  2¾   Alvarez A2   10000 77-15 Bedouin, Jet Royale, County Seat 12
11Jan86-1SA   1  :463 1:112 1:363ft  18 1085   73  53½ 55  66½  Alvarez A6   18000 78-11 BolgerBoy,BigDanRyn,BoldInititive 9
  Oct 15 BM 5f ft 1:01 hg     Sep 9 Pom 4f ft :494 h     ●Sep 1 GD tr.t 7f ft 1:283 h     Aug 27 GD tr.t 6f ft 1:15 h
```

B. **(16)**

```
Hail The Judge *                    Dk. b. or br. g. 6, by Advocator—Hail Mary, by Amber Morn
  SCHVANEVELDT C P                  Br.—Conway Marietta (Ky)                 1986  9  2  1  2     $9,632
                              114   Tr.—Benedict Jim             $6,250      1985 20  9  3  1    $29,836
Own.—Great Western Stable          Lifetime  54 15  8  6   $56,679           Turf  9  0  1  2       $859
13Oct86-2BM   6f :223  :46  1:104ft   7 114   67  65¾ 55¼ 33   SchvaneveldtCP2 6250 82-21 TossThCon,BrnngBthEnds,HlThJdg 7
21Sep86-3BM   1 1/16:453 1:10  1:442ft *9-5 114  715 716 513 47½  Baze R A1      6250 62-18 DnceOnDown,Dino'sBy,ThJndyMn 12
6Sep86-12Bmf  1  :462 1:111 1:373ft   5¾ 113   53½ 43  41½ 42   Caballero R8   6250 78-18 MoonKmp,Don'tRjctM,ShstClown 10
24Aug86-10Sac 1 1/16:461 1:101 1:423ft   3 114   1hd 1hd 1hd 22   Caballero R1   6250 88-12 ShstClown,HilThJudg,Don'tRjctM 10
10Aug86-8Stk  1  :464 1:114 1:372ft  *2½ 118   32  3½  11  11   Caballero R6   5000 91-13 Hail The Judge, Jubal Jack,KyOtee 8
26Jly86-12SR  1 1/16:453 1:10  1:421ft   3½ 1085  57  44½ 33  33½  Barton J6      5000 89-08 ShastClown,Procurer,HilTheJudge 10
6Jly86-10Pln  1 1/16:47  1:112 1:45 ft  *2½ 1105  44½ 66  68  69¾  Barton J4      8000 69-18 Addend,ALovelyTerrc,GnrlAgrmnt 10
21Jun86-3GG   1 1/16:47  1:113 1:44 ft   5¼ 1095  4¾  12  1½  11   Barton J3      6250 83-15 HilThJudg,SprtnConqust,Imnough 12
     21Jun86—Bumped break
1Jun86-3GG    6f :222  :442 1:10 ft  44 1095   98  813 710 54½  Barton J4      8000 84-11 Plastic Avenue, Safarian,IrishCast 11
8Dec85-5BM    1 1/16:483 1:144 1:493sl   6½ 1095  69  813 822 920¾ Aragon V A9    6250 — — Addend, Pat Moran, Malta 11
```

196.

A. **(16)**

```
Andtheniwokeup                      B. f. 3, by Val Del'Orne—Grise Petite, by Dancer's Image
                                    Br.—Fuller P (Md)                        1986  9  1  1  2    $12,019
Own.—Fuller P                 112   Tr.—Lake Robert P            $45,000     Turf  1  0  0  0       $408
                                   Lifetime   9  1  1  2   $12,019
9Oct86-5Bel   6f :223  :46  1:113ft  13 112   46½ 45  43  42¾  Maple E1      Ⓕ 45000 81-18 Spiriting, Grotona, Exotic Power 7
25May86-6Suf  a170Ⓣ          1:471yl   7 114   41¾ 43  53½ 67½  VrsJL8 ⒻⓇApril Prom 72-17 Mrgret'sChrm,MoreBlloons,Mrzipp 8
12May86-4Suf  6f :231  :474 1:133ft   3 1085  21  2½  2hd 2no  CmpbllTM1 ⒻAw10000 73-30 SnstvStph,Andthnwkp,DrwsACrwd 7
28Apr86-9Suf  6f :23   :464 1:121gd  3¾ 1075  21  2½  24½ 37   CmpbllTM3 ⒻAw10500 73-29 SprLoopr,DrwsACrowd,Andthnwkp 6
20Apr86-8Rkm  6f :213  :444 1:114ft  21 113   68  511 512 419¾ MooreDN5 ⒻRockette 65-22 RoylTsh,OurCutMombo,Soni'sScmp 6
6Apr86-6Suf   1  :492 1:153 1:433ft  2¾e 1105  32  41½ 42  65   CmpbllTM1 ⒻAw12500 54-32 FightOnJerthe,LdyFrncs,FlorinFrkl 8
28Mar86-7Suf  6f :231  :482 1:154ft  *2 1155   44  3nk 11  14   Campbell T M7 ⒻMdn 62-39 Andtheniwokeup,BitBbe,ClevrGlmn 9
21Mar86-6Suf  6f :231  :481 1:161ft   5½ 1155  2hd 2hd 2½  35¾  Campbell T M3 ⒻMdn 54-39 SensitiveStph,BilFst,Andthniwokup 7
  Oct 17 Aqu 4f ft :484 h     Oct 6 Aqu 4f ft :48 h     Sep 30 Aqu 6f ft 1:154 h     Sep 22 Aqu 7f ft 1:302 bg
```

B.

Ziad Tribette

Own.—Nagle K **112**

B. f. 3, by Ziad—High Tribette, by High Tribute
Br.—Buckram Oak Farm (Fla)
Tr.—Ferriola Peter $45,000
Lifetime 31 11 6 2 $99,830

1986	14	2	6	1	$46,510
1985	17	9	0	1	$53,320
Turf	3	0	0	1	$4,350

17Oct86-1Bel	7f	:23	:46^{2}	1:24^{1}ft	4¼	116	2^{hd}	11½	1½	2^{2}	Migliore R^{5}	Ⓕ 35000	79-14	ForeverSpecial,ZidTribette,Smores	9
21Sep86-3Bel	1$\frac{1}{16}$	:46^{4}	1:12	1:44^{1}ft	*2¼	112	2^{1}	43½	3^{6}	2^{5}	Migliore R^{7}	Ⓕ 45000	76-12	TorridZone,ZiadTribette,BoldPrima	8
5Sep86-2Bel	1$\frac{1}{16}$	:47	1:12^{1}	1:45^{1}ft	6	114	21½	21½	1^{2}	15¼	Migliore R^{1}	Ⓕ 22500	76-18	ZidTribtt,AncintGold,AskDirctions	11
25Aug86-4Sar	7f	:22^{1}	:45^{2}	1:25^{2}ft	7½	116	7^{8}	7^{10}	7^{6}	63¾	Migliore R^{4}	Ⓕ 25000	71-19	AncintGold,TurnpikPrincss,VgsEll	10
7Aug86-1Sar	1⅛	:47^{4}	1:13^{3}	1:55^{2}sy	7½	118	7^{12}	9^{21}	9^{22}	829¾	Vasquez J^{5}	Ⓕ 25000	28-38	Tromph'sGlry,AlbnyClny,CllMHny	10
24Jly86-5Mth	1	:47^{3}	1:12	1:38^{1}ft	10	114	3^{1}	3½	3½	1^{1}	Messina R^{2}	Ⓕ 35000	82-21	ZdTrbtt,FrostCov,Kolctoo'sContss	7
12Jly86-5Bel	1$\frac{1}{16}$	:46^{1}	1:11^{4}	1:44 m	8½	112	4^{4}	8^{11}	9^{21}	926½	Vasquez J^{2}	Ⓕ 45000	55-15	Tromph'sGlory,JustGorgos,Frothy	11
29Jun86-1Bel	1	:47^{1}	1:12^{1}	1:36^{1}ft	22	112	74¼	7^{7}	6^{18}	5^{22}	Migliore R^{6}	ⒻAw26000	62-14	ClbberGirl,PilgrimEr,HppyCheroke	7

Sep 19 Aqu 6f ft 1:16^{4} b

197.

A. **(16)**

Big Dan Ryan *

SCHVANEVELDT C P **114**
Own.—Turman E

B. g. 4, by Universal—Miss Bold Allison, by Bold Hitter
Br.—Allison D (Cal)
Tr.—Martin R L $25,000
Lifetime 34 4 5 4 $59,740

1986	15	3	3	3	$39,040
1985	15	1	2	1	$20,175
Turf	1	0	0	0	

11Oct86-9BM	1$\frac{1}{16}$	:46^{4}	1:11^{1}	1:43 ft	4	114	2½	1^{hd}	1^{1}	3¾	SchvneveldtCP^{3}	25000	76-18	CertainTreat,Dve'sRelity,BigDnRyn	6
24Sep86-9BM	1	:47^{1}	1:13	1:39^{3}sl	*2½	114	21½	21½	11½	1^{1}	SchvneveldtCP^{5}	16000	70-31	BigDanRyn,Frivolissimo,NewStorm	7
6Sep86-7Bmf	1	:45^{3}	1:10	1:35^{2}ft	2½	115	42½	3^{2}	2^{2}	2^{5}	SchvneveldtCP^{2}.	16000	86-18	Sidersell, Big DanRyan,NewStorm	10
30Aug86-8Bmf	6f	:22^{2}	:45	1:09^{2}ft	5¼	117	44¼	4^{3}	4^{2}	2^{1}	SchvneveldtCP^{6}	16000	91-12	Volamo, Big Dan Ryan,Lee'sFamily	7
1Aug86-10SR	1	:47^{1}	1:11^{1}	1:36^{4}ft	5¼	122	87½	7^{11}	8^{14}	10^{8}	Tohill K S^{1}	Aw13000	80-12	CrystalTas,IHeardAVoice,FaliPlaz	10
18Jly86-3Sol	1	:46^{2}	1:11^{2}	1:36 ft	9½	122	2^{hd}	2^{hd}	2^{1}	32½	Tohill K S^{6}	Aw13000	91-12	BuckRoyl,LondonExprss,BigDnRyn	7
28Jun86-9Pln	1^{70}	:46^{4}	1:11	1:40^{4}ft	16	115	52½	51¼	3½	1^{1}	Tohill K S^{8}	Aw15000	90-11	Big DanRyan,EverBrilliant,Tamoure	8
15Jun86-7GG	1$\frac{1}{16}$	:46^{1}	1:10^{4}	1:43^{4}ft	6¼	115	55¼	53½	43½	4^{8}	McCarron C J^{7}	c16000	76-14	Frivolissimo,OurNordic,GllntMick	11
24May86-9Hol	1	:45^{4}	1:11^{1}	1:37 ft	4¼	116	31½	63½	63¾	57¾	Valenzuela P A^{2}	16000	70-16	Lithan, One Eyed Romeo, ValDeRoi	8
17May86-3Hol	6f	:22^{3}	:45^{4}	1:11 ft	18	116	76¾	7^{8}	76¾	66½	Valenzuela P A^{3}	20000	82-14	PowerfulEyes,Grenobl,SwordPrinc	11

17May86—Bumped break, took up

Oct 22 BM Ⓣ 4f fm :53^{4} h (d) Oct 4 BM 5f ft 1:01 h Sep 17 BM 4f gd :50^{2} h ● Aug 28 BM 3f ft :35^{1} h

B.

*Pas Plus

GONZALEZ R M **114**
Own.—Kyees O W

Dk. b. or br. g. 5, by Bartender's Pride—Plus Ultra, by Climber
Br.—Haras Los Sauces (Arg)
Tr.—Mastrangelo William $25,000
Lifetime 24 2 1 3 $13,216

1986	10	0	0	1	$3,780
1985	10	2	1	1	$9,018
Turf	17	2	1	1	$11,118

9Sep86-10Bmf	1	:45^{3}	1:10^{3}	1:37^{1}ft	41	110^{5}	78¾	10^{11}	10^{15}	9^{13}	Barton J^{6}	Aw17000	69-21	PassPassPssed,ClvryChrge,Plnter	10
14Aug86-10Stk	1	:46^{2}	1:11^{2}	1:36^{2}ft	2½	115	3^{5}	46½	47½	6^{16}	CampbellBC^{1}	Aw11000	80-06	SnowSkimmr,ThAysHvIt,HghChrmr	8
24Jly86-11SR	1	:46^{2}	1:10^{3}	1:37 ft	8¼	115	55½	54½	3^{4}	33¾	CampbellBC^{4}	Aw12000	83-15	SingleThread,EverBrilliant,PasPlus	7
22Jun86-4GG	1$\frac{1}{16}$ Ⓣ	:47^{1}	1:11^{2}	1:42^{2}fm	10	115	1½	3½	7^{15}	720¼	GonzalezRM^{1}	Aw18000	70-14	CastlemartinKing,Daniyr,Kingsbury	7
31May86-9Hol	1$\frac{1}{16}$ Ⓣ	:46^{3}	1:11^{3}	1:42^{2}fm	4¾	111^{5}	3^{2}	72¾	6^{10}	614½	Black C A^{5}	Aw22000	77-06	Baroncello, Garrion, Shanaar	8
4Apr86-5SA	1⅛ Ⓣ	:46^{2}	1:11^{1}	1:49 fm	21	109^{5}	1^{hd}	1^{hd}	4^{5}	88½	Black C A^{6}	Aw26000	73-16	Super Lucent, SpiceTrade,Garrion	12

4Apr86—Veered in start

20Mar86-5SA	1⅛ Ⓣ	:46^{1}	1:11^{1}	1:49^{3}gd	18	111^{5}	45½	6^{4}	42½	77½	Black C A^{9}	Aw29000	71-20	Caro's Lad, Andor, Bemidgi	10
8Feb86-5SA	1¼ Ⓣ	:46^{4}	1:38^{2}	2:03^{4}fm	22	112^{5}	3^{4}	2^{hd}	21½	46¼	Black C A^{8}	Aw28000	62-28	Gallant Archer, Decieboy,HelloBill	10

8Feb86—Bumped start

16Jan86-7SA	1$\frac{1}{16}$	:46^{4}	1:10^{2}	1:42^{1}ft	65	118	66½	6^{11}	6^{11}	612½	Sibille R^{5}	Aw26000	77-15	Koshare, Hydrostatic, Rodrigue	7

16Jan86—Fanned wide 7/8

1Jan86-5SA	1¼ Ⓣ	:47	1:37^{1}	2:02^{3}fm	13	117	5^{5}	6^{5}	76½	812½	Stevens G L^{2}	Aw26000	61-23	Loverue, Star Formation, Witan	12

Oct 21 BM 5f ft 1:02^{4} h Oct 16 BM 5f ft 1:01^{4} h Oct 10 BM 6f ft 1:15 h Oct 3 BM 3f ft :36^{3} h

C.

Dave's Reality ✻ Dk. b. or br. h. 6, by In Reality—Pleasant Girl, by Knightly Manner

Br.—Bright View Farm Inc (NJ) 1986 14 2 4 2 $31,010

HANSEN R D 114 Tr.—Roberts Tom $25,000 1985 13 1 0 4 $21,870

Own.—Love J B Lifetime 50 10 5 6 $191,904 Turf 8 0 0 1 $9,625

110ct86-9BM 1 1/16 :464 1:111 1:43 ft 4½ 114 1½ 2hd 21 2¾ Hansen R D1 25000 76-18 CertainTreat,Dve'sRelity,BigDnRyn 6
27Sep86-7BM 1 1/16 :474 1:131 1:452sl 2¼ 115 11 2hd 55 510½ Hansen R D6 25000 54-27 Olimpic Bingo, Certain Treat, Clear 9
13Sep86-8Bmf 1 1/16 :461 1:113 1:44 ft 4½ 115 12 11½ 13 2no Castaneda M7 25000 72-31 Melo King,Dave'sReality,OurNordic 7
16Aug86-6Lga 1 1/16 :454 1:104 1:424ft *3-2 117 21 2½ 21½ 34½ Hansen R D3 20000 80-14 Ruful'sRondr,StrghtAdhm,Dv'sRlty 7
5Jly86-6Lga 1 1/16 :46 1:102 1:422ft 5¼ 117 1½ 1hd 12 11½ Hansen R D5 20000 87-16 Dave's Reality, Town,DeeDeeDaddy 7
1Jun86-7GG 1 1/16 :471 1:111 1:432ft 4¾ 115 77¾ 88 911 911 Hummel C R1 c16000 75-11 Veronica'sMrk,Frivolissimo,Plnter 12
17May86-7GG 1 1/16 :46 1:103 1:43 ft 5¼ 115 21½ 22 54 66¼ Hummel C R5 25000 82-13 EverBrillint,John'sRuffi,Andrw'NM 7
12Apr86-6GG 1 1/16 :463 1:111 1:43 ft 5¼ 115 24 22 22 22½ Hummel C R8 25000 85-17 FlyingBob,Dave'sReality,WhtAPly 10
12Apr86—Bobbled start
29Mar86-9GG 1 1/16 :462 1:102 1:421ft 4¼ 115 31 31½ 24 27 Hummel C R6 25000 85-12 HollywoodPrty,Dve'sRelity,NtivMrd 7
22Mar86-7GG 6f :222 :451 1:10 ft 7½ 114 55 65 65½ 63½ Castaneda M9 25000 85-16 CooleenJck,NustroSol,Don'sDstinv 9

Oct 22 BM 3f ft :361 h Sep 24 BM 4f m :513 h (d) Sep 10 BM 4f ft :484 h Aug 29 BM 4f ft :492 h

198.

A. (16)

G'Day Mate B. c. 3, by Darby Creek Road—Hagley's World, by Hagley

Br.—Chancellor Farm (NY) 1986 6 2 1 1 $43,690

Own.—Chernick Carolyn 114 Tr.—Miles Thomas M Turf 2 1 1 0 $23,290

Lifetime 6 2 1 1 $43,690

130ct86-5Bel 6f :224 :46 1:103ft 3¾ 114 915 78 58½ 45¼ Santos J A7 ⓈAw28000 84-16 CollegeCheer,TropiclFront,RootCnl 9
6Jly86-9Bel 1 1/16 Ⓣ:462 1:102 1:42 fm*8-5 112 79½ 77¼ 47½ 23 Santos J A6 ⓈAw29500 83-18 Wanderkin,G'DayMte,Chestertown 10
6Jly86—Steadied
26May86-6Bel 1 1/16 Ⓣ:463 1:104 1:423fm 6¼ 108 63¼ 85½ 44 12¼ Day P7 ⓈAw28000 83-15 G'DyMte,FestYourEyes,Chstrtown 12
22May86-9Bel 6f :222 :46 1:111sy 2½ 113 77½ 54½ 43½ 11 Santos J A5 ⓈMdn 86-15 G'DyMte,TllRomn,M.SensitiveStn 10
22May86—Altered course,dr
30Apr86-6Aqu 6f :23 :471 1:121ft 3½ 112 31½ 42 33 33 Santagata N3 ⓈMdn 77-24 Wanderkin, Go Renor, G'DayMate 10
9Apr86-6Aqu 6f :23 :473 1:132ft 13 112 95¾ 88 44 43 Santagata N9 ⓈMdn 71-31 Balia, Extended Forecast, Va Bien 12
9Apr86—Slow start

Oct 20 Bel tr.t 6f ft 1:174 b Oct 8 Bel tr.t 5f ft 1:03 b Oct 5 Bel tr.t 5f ft 1:06 b Sep 30 Bel tr.t 5f ft 1:06 b

B.

Chubby Babe Gr. c. 4, by Jacques Who—Miss Jitters, by Scottsdale

Br.—Grondin J A (NY) 1986 8 0 1 0 $3,770

Own.—Grondin J A 117 Tr.—Rich David 1985 9 2 2 1 $13,865

Lifetime 17 2 3 1 $17,635 Turf 2 0 0 0

28Sep86-9Bel 7f :223 :453 1:232m 20 117 76 54½ 37 58½ Maple E6 ⓈAw28000 76-15 Melstrom,CollegeChr,TropiclFront 10
29Aug86-6Bel 1 1/16 Ⓣ:49 1:134 1:461gd 14 117 43½ 52½ 66 68½ Maple E4 ⓈAw29500 56-31 Romanizer,RootCanal,GroundShker 7
22Aug86-5Sar 1 1/16 Ⓣ:47 1:104 1:42 fm 18 117 32½ 42½ 41¼ 53¼ Maple E2 ⓈAw29500 84-13 Rio Belle, Chestertown,TalcBuster 10
10Aug86-2Sar 7f :222 :452 1:241ft 14 117 63 51¾ 71½ 65½ Maple E6 ⓈAw28000 75-14 Section Three, FlagKing,Romanizer 9
24Mar86-6GS 1 1/16 :471 1:123 1:471ft 11 115 21 22½ 25 43¾ Lopez C8 Aw12500 68-25 Seagry, Mr. Realtor, Cherokee D'Or 8
12Mar86-9GS 6f :222 :454 1:114ft 9½ 115 79½ 610 55½ 53¾ Madrid A Jr5 Aw11500 79-29 Hiccups,MajesticHalo,MysticBadge 7
21Feb86-6GS 6f :23 :464 1:124m 6½ 115 46½ 33 32½ 23½ Vigliotti M J4 Aw11500 74-29 CentennialLne,ChubbyBbe,Hiccups 5
4Jan86-7Pha 170 :474 1:123 1:432m 10 114 41¾ 35 516 527½ FiorntinoCT6 Aw12500 55-29 HurdyGurdyMn,ChfNchols,Mr.Rltor 7

●Sep 20 Sar tr.t 4f ft :492 h

C.

Race Point Dk. b. or br. g. 3, by Talc—Drylook, by Sky High II

Br.—Mulholland M (NY) 1986 6 2 1 1 $39,750

Own.—Offbroadway Stable 119 Tr.—Figueroa Carlos Jr 1985 1 M 0 0 —

Lifetime 7 2 1 1 $39,750 Turf 5 2 1 1 $39,750

120ct86-1Bel 1 Ⓣ:48 1:114 1:37 fm*6-5 119 1½ 1½ 11 12 Santos J A4 ⓈAw28000 80-15 RcePoint,CtchTheMoon,SummerTl 7
90ct86-7Bel 1 1/16 Ⓣ:473 1:12 1:442fm *2 114 1½ 1hd 1½ 31 GuerraWA1 ⓈAw29500 73-26 VtzMtter,ExpditionMoon,RcPoint 12
19Sep86-4Bel 1 Ⓣ:454 1:101 1:354fm 8 118 21 12 15 12¾ Guerra W A6 Mdn 86-15 RacePoint,CatchTheMoon,Mr.Fife 12
25Aug86-2Sar 1⅛ Ⓣ:472 1:12 1:502fm 13 117 2½ 1hd 2½ 21¾ Santos J A7 ⓈMdn 73-15 Lyphrd'sFthrs,RcPont,RuffldGros 12
30Jly86-5Sar 1 1/16 Ⓣ:482 1:13 1:452fm 45 111 86½ 87¾ 66 69½ GuerraWA5 ⓈAw28000 68-21 Talc Buster, RioBelle,VatzaMatter 10
18Jun86-6Bel 6f :224 :461 1:111ft 84 114 109¼ 1113 913 910 Guerra W A9 ⓈMdn 76-15 Tall Roman, Crobosity, Mokos 14
29Nov85-9Aqu 6f :231 :464 1:113sy 44 118 88¼ 1112 1115 1017½ Gomez E R8 ⓈMdn 66-22 NstyAndTogh,Tckr'sCbn,TllRomn 11

Oct 2 Aqu Ⓣ 4f gd :51 h (d) ●Sep 15 Sar tr.t 5f ft 1:033 h Sep 8 Sar tr.t 4f ft :514 b

D.

Expedition Moon *

B. c. 3, by Exceller—Moonscape, by Tom Fool
Br.—Clermont Farms Ltd (NY) 1986 16 1 7 3 $58,964
Own.—Vanier Nancy **114** **Tr.—Becker E Wayne** 1985 2 1 0 0 $6,354
Lifetime 18 2 7 3 $65,318 Turf 6 1 5 0 $33,680

9Oct86-7Bel 1$\frac{1}{16}$Ⓣ:47^{3}1:12 1:44^{2}fm 3 114 5$^{2\frac{1}{4}}$ 3$^{1\frac{1}{2}}$ 4^{1} 2½ RomeroRP^{4} [S]Aw29500 73-26 VtzMtter,ExpditionMoon,RcPoint 12
22Sep86-7Bel 1$\frac{1}{16}$Ⓣ:48^{1}1:12^{1}1:42^{4}fm*6-5 113 4$^{2\frac{1}{2}}$ 4$^{2\frac{1}{2}}$ 3$^{3\frac{1}{2}}$ 2$^{2\frac{3}{4}}$ RomeroRP^{6} [S]Aw29500 79-21 Chstrtown,ExpdtonMoon,TrpclFrnt 7
16Aug86-8Pha 1⅛Ⓣ:49^{2}1:13^{2}1:50^{2}fm*3-2 110 2½ 3^{nk} 1½ 2^{nk} Lloyd J S^{9} Aw13000 — — PrincOfDstiny,ExpditionMoon,Sizbl 9
4Aug86-8Sar 1⅛:47 1:11^{2} 1:51^{3}ft 6 114 6$^{2\frac{1}{2}}$ 5$^{2\frac{1}{4}}$ 3$^{2\frac{1}{2}}$ 3$^{4\frac{1}{4}}$ Romero RP^{6} [S]Albany 73-18 Chpskt,Tinchn'sPrnc,ExpdtonMoon 7
20Jly86-8Pha 1$\frac{1}{16}$:47^{2} 1:12^{2} 1:43^{4}ft 8 115 2^{hd} 1^{hd} 1½ 2no Lloyd J S^{2} HcpO 85-16 Prt'sSkff,ExpdtonMoon,NorthForst 7
3Jly86-7Pha 1$\frac{1}{16}$:47^{1} 1:12^{1} 1:44^{4}ft *2½ 113 6$^{2\frac{3}{4}}$ 4$^{2\frac{1}{4}}$ 2^{3} 3$^{5\frac{1}{4}}$ Lloyd J S^{7} Aw13000 75-23 BuckieBoy,Sizeble,ExpeditionMoon 8
8Jun86-9RD 1 Ⓣ:46^{3}1:12 1:37^{1}gd 9e 121 7$^{8\frac{1}{2}}$ 5$^{5\frac{1}{2}}$ 1½ 2$^{1\frac{1}{2}}$ ♦ Lloyd J S^{11} Spartacus 89-09 NdstColny,ExpdtnMn,SnOfThDsrt 12
♦ 8Jun86—Dead heat; Breeders' Cup Award to Nudist Colony
11May86-7CD 1 :45^{1} 1:10^{3} 1:36^{2}ft 4¼ 118 7$^{9\frac{1}{2}}$ 5^{6} 3$^{3\frac{1}{2}}$ 3^{6} Espinoza JC^{1} Aw17020 81-15 ArilDsply,DnctothWr,ExpdtonMoon 8
Oct 21 Bel 5f ft 1:02^{4} h **Sep 20 Pha 5f ft 1:01^{3} h** **Sep 15 Pha 4f ft :48 b** **Sep 9 Pha 5f ft 1:02^{2} h**

199.

A. **(16)**

What A Flip

Ro. f. 4, by Flip Sal—Molly's Pleasure, by What a Pleasure
Br.—DiMauro & Tufano (NY) 1986 9 1 0 0 $55,080
Own.—DiMauro S **115** **Tr.—DiMauro Stephen L** 1985 17 6 1 2 $141,823
Lifetime 31 7 3 3 $212,783 Turf 1 0 0 0

14Sep86-1Bel 7f :22 :44^{1} 1:22 ft 20 115 3^{5} 3^{10} 6^{12} 7$^{15\frac{3}{4}}$ Martens G^{1} ⒻAw36000 76-11 PineTreeLane,Lotka,Clemnn'sRose 7
8Sep86-8Bel 6f :22^{3} :45 1:08^{4}ft 21 115 5$^{5\frac{3}{4}}$ 4^{6} 4$^{6\frac{1}{2}}$ 4$^{7\frac{3}{4}}$ Davis R G^{4} ⒻAw36000 90-11 PineTreeLne,Verblity,Donut'sPride 6
31Aug86-9FL 1^{70}:47^{2} 1:12^{4} 1:44^{1}ft 2 123 3$^{3\frac{1}{2}}$ 3^{3} 3$^{3\frac{1}{2}}$ 4$^{6\frac{1}{2}}$ WtlK^{3} Ⓕ[S]SBAnthnyh 73-17 StrikeUsRich,Clsszone,JcquesPride 6
15Aug86-6Sar 7f :22^{4} :45^{4} 1:22^{4}ft 8¾ 115 4^{4} 3^{5} 4$^{3\frac{1}{2}}$ 4$^{7\frac{1}{2}}$ Davis R G^{3} ⒻAw36000 80-16 FindHppiness,Verblity,Crrie'sDrem 6
30Jly86-6Sar 6½f :22^{1} :45^{1} 1:16 ft 24 115 5^{6} 5$^{6\frac{1}{2}}$ 5^{5} 5$^{7\frac{1}{4}}$ Davis R G^{5} ⒻAw36000 85-13 Clemann'sRose,Verblity,Gene'sLdy 9
15Feb86-7Aqu 1^{70}[•]:46^{3}1:11^{4}1:42^{4}ft 5½ 115 4^{3} 4$^{3\frac{1}{2}}$ 6$^{5\frac{1}{4}}$ 7^{9} SantagatN^{1} ⒻAw40000 77-16 CherryJubile,SwtInnocnc,MdmClld 8
3Feb86-8Aqu 1$\frac{1}{16}$[•]:48^{1}1:13 1:45^{3}gd 2 115 3^{1} 2½ 4¾ 4$^{2\frac{1}{2}}$ SantagatN^{7} ⒻAw40000 79-16 SuceSuprm,ChrryJubil,SwtInnocnc 8
19Jan86-8Aqu 1^{70}[•]:47^{4}1:13 1:43^{2}gd 6½ 120 2½ 1^{hd} 1½ 1^{nk} SttN^{8} Ⓕ[S]Broadway H 83-22 WhatAFlip,StokeTheFire,BzookBbe 9
Oct 22 Bel tr.t 4f ft :48^{3} h **Oct 17 Bel tr.t 4f ft :48^{2} h** **Oct 10 Bel 5f ft 1:02 b** **Oct 5 Bel 5f ft 1:04^{3} b**

B.

Luminosity

Dk. b. or br. f. 4, by Angle Light—Yeroque, by El Centauro
Br.—Tanzi J (KY) 1986 1 0 0 0 $960
Own.—Tall Oaks Farm **115** **Tr.—Trovato Joseph A** 1985 9 4 1 1 $74,338
Lifetime 10 4 1 1 $75,298

21Jun86-6Mth 6f :22^{2} :45^{4} 1:10^{3}ft 2¾ 115 4$^{2\frac{3}{4}}$ 4$^{2\frac{1}{2}}$ 4^{8} 4$^{12\frac{1}{4}}$ Krone J A^{8} ⒻAw16000 75-16 RllyFrJstc,JckO'Lntrnn,CnfrmdAffr 9
21Jun86—Ran out
1Nov85-3Aqu 7f :23 :46 1:22^{3}ft *1-2 115 1^{3} 1^{4} 1^{6} 1$^{6\frac{1}{4}}$ VelsquezJ^{2} ⒻAw27000 88-15 Luminosity,GrndCrton,ElnHmmngs 6
24Oct85-6Med 1$\frac{1}{16}$:47^{3} 1:11^{4} 1:44^{1}ft *7-5 117 1^{1} 2^{hd} 3^{1} 4$^{4\frac{1}{2}}$ VlsquzJ^{3} ⒻLady Dean 77-21 PremierPrincss,DnvrExprss,Tbyour 6
24Oct85—Stumbled st.
18Oct85-8Bel 1$\frac{1}{16}$:46^{1} 1:11 1:45 ft 9¼ 116 5^{5} 4$^{4\frac{1}{2}}$ 3^{1} 2^{hd} Santos J A^{8} ⒻAw40000 77-27 Robin's Rob, Luminosity, Le Slew 8
5Oct85-5Bel 1 :46 1:10^{3} 1:36 sy 16 112 3^{3} 5$^{7\frac{1}{2}}$ 5^{13} 5$^{20\frac{1}{4}}$ StsJA^{3} ⒻRare Perfum 65-19 KamikzeRick,WisingUp,Videogenic 5
5Oct85—Grade III
13Sep85-5Bel 1 :47 1:11^{1} 1:36^{3}ft 3¼ 113 1^{hd} 1^{hd} 1½ 1^{nk} VelsquezJ^{4} ⒻAw26000 82-17 Luminosity,BrownCrown,Spryberry 6
11Aug85-5Sar 1⅛:46^{4} 1:11^{3} 1:51^{3}ft 2¾ 112 2^{1} 1^{1} 2^{4} 3$^{10\frac{3}{4}}$ CordroAJr^{7} ⒻAw26000 66-18 KeyWitness,MgicCircle,Luminosity 7
11Aug85—Unruly pre-st.
10Jly85-5Bel 7f :23 :46^{1} 1:24^{3}ft 3½ 121 2^{2} 2^{2} 2$^{1\frac{1}{2}}$ 2^{hd} VelsquezJ^{2} ⒻAw24000 79-23 ‡Sherry B.,Luminosity,BrownCrown 7
10Jly85—Placed first through disqualification; Impeded
Oct 13 Aqu 3f ft :35^{4} h **Oct 9 Aqu Ⓣ 5f fm 1:02^{2} h (d)** **Oct 2 Aqu Ⓣ 5f gd 1:05^{1} b (d)** **● Sep 4 Aqu Ⓣ 5f sf 1:04 b (d)**

200.

A. (16)

```
Loa                                      B. f. 3, by Hawaii—Tiy, by Nalees Man
                                         Br.—Labrot Barbara (Ky)                     1986 11 4 1 0    $66,721
Own.—LaBrot Barbara W               110  Tr.—Turner William H Jr                     1985  2 M 0 0
                                       Lifetime  13  4  1  0   $66,721               Turf  8 3 1 0    $60,121
20ct86-8Bel   1 1/16[T]:482 1:12 1:442gd 8¼ 116   31½ 77½ 67 49½   Bailey J D1 ⒻAw40000 69-28 Festivity,DesertView,WendyWalker 8
12Sep86-6Bel  7f Ⓣ:231 :46 1:224fm 25 112        2hd 1hd 21½ 42¼   Bailey J D9 ⒻManta 88-08 Duckweed, Top Issue, Tarifa 9
     12Sep86—Run in Divisions
29Aug86-7Med  1 1/16[T]:464 1:103 1:413fm 10 117  810 69½ 813 812½  BilyJD1 ⒻBoil'g Sp H 82-03 SmllVirtu,SwtVlocity,CountryRcitl 11
     29Aug86—Grade III; Run in division
19Aug86-9Mth  1 1/16Ⓣ:482 1:134 1:464sf 3 119    97¾ 98 79½ 812¾   BileyJD1 ⒻL. Silver H 58-29 SprucFr,MyMomGnny,GrnBondry 10
     19Aug86—Grade III
17Jun86-9Mth  1 Ⓣ:463 1:112 1:364fm *9-5 118      56 21½ 1hd 1½     Bailey J D6 ⒻRevidere 91-13 Loa, She's A Mystery, Small Virtue 9
1Jun86-7Bel   1 Ⓣ:46 1:104 1:361gd 7½ 114         31½ 2½ 1hd 1hd    Bailey JD11 ⒻAw26000 84-21 Loa, Clabber Girl, Lake Cecebe 12
16May86-5Bel  1 Ⓣ:461 1:103 1:363fm *3-5 111      1hd 1hd 1½ 1nk    Bailey J D4 ⒻAw25000 82-18 Loa, Chehana, Legacy of Strength 6
12May86-2Bel  1 1/16[T]:481 1:121 1:422fm 10 111  11 1hd 1½ 22½     Bailey J D8 ⒻAw25000 86-16 Hofuf, Loa, Roberto's Social 8
  ●Oct 20 Bel tr.t 4f ft :471 h    Oct 13 Bel tr.t 4f ft :47 h    Sep 29 Bel tr.t 4f ft :49 b    Sep 21 Bel tr.t 5f ft 1:01 b
```

B.

```
Reel Easy                                B. f. 3, by Northern Baby—Kushka, by First Landing
                                         Br.—Jones Brereton C (Ky)                   1986  8 3 1 0    $61,283
Own.—Peskoff S D                    112  Tr.—Preger Mitchell C                       1985  3 2 0 0    $28,800
                                       Lifetime  11  5  1  0   $90,083               Turf  1 0 0 0
12Oct86-7Bel  7f :22 :434 1:23 ft 19 112          37 213 25 11½     Migliore R7 ⒻAw36000 87-13 ReelEsy,MistressMontgue,Argntrio 8
22Jun86-9Aks  1 1/16:482 1:124 1:444ft *6-5 120   11½ 11 11½ 13½    Lively J4 ⒻPrincess 79-25 ReelEsy,TrustAQun,SndhillDimond 6
31May86-8Aks  170:482 1:141 1:461ft 2¾ 110        21 2hd 1hd 1nk    Lively J4 ⒻAw16700 66-32 Reel Easy, Pet Bird, Stan's Lady 8
18May86-6Aks  170:51 1:183 1:53 sl 3¾ 108         56½ 714 716 716¾  CordovDW1 ⒻAw20000 — — BellStt,RiseUpAndDnce,BbyBupers 7
12Mar86-7SA   1 :462 1:12 1:37 sy 8-5e 114        23 23 37½ 416¾    Solis A3 ⒻAw35000 66-25 Nture'sWy,SilntArrivl,TropiclHolidy 5
20Feb86-8SA   6½f :22 :453 1:174m 15 117          32 33½ 47 48¼     Solis A4 ⒻAw31000 73-27 NervousBb,SilentArrivl,AnEmpress 7
12Jan86-8Aqu  170[•]:474 1:124 1:434ft 2¾ 116     55 46½ 413 417    CordroAJr8 ⒻBusanda 64-20 PatriciJ.K.,Trcy'sEspoir,DynmicStr 8
3Jan86-8Aqu   170[•]:491 1:134 1:432sy *4-5 116   33 34 32½ 23¼     CordroAJr6 ⒻAw26000 80-23 Patricia J. K., ReelEasy,TwiceRegal 5
  ●Sep 30 Bel 6f ft 1:13 h
```

C.

```
Key Witness *                            B. f. 4, by Key To The Mint—Summer Guest, by Native Charger
                                         Br.—Mellon P (Va)                           1986  4 1 0 3    $50,199
Own.—Rokeby Stables                 116  Tr.—Miller Mack                             1985 11 4 1 3   $103,369
                                       Lifetime  16  5  1  6   $153,568              Turf  5 0 1 2    $24,716
18Jly86-8Bel  1 1/16:461 1:104 1:421ft *2¼ 115    3½ 1hd 35½ 311    Bailey J D4 ⒻHcp0 80-12 CoupDeFusil,PtriciJ.K.,KeyWitness 7
5Jly86-9Mth   1 1/16:46 1:091 1:411ft 6¾ 112      32 35½ 37 38½     BilyJD8 ⒻM Pitcher H 90-13 Lady's Secret, Chaldea,KeyWitness 8
     5Jly86—Grade II
12Jun86-8Bel  1 1/16:462 1:103 1:431m *2-3 117    13 15 16 18¾      Bailey J D2 ⒻAw40000 86-20 KyWtnss,AwsomAccont,SmokthQn 5
22May86-7Bel  7f :223 :453 1:232sy 5¼ 119         33 31 39 34       Bailey J D3 ⒻAw36000 81-15 SlntAccount,BrownCrown,KyWtnss 7
3Nov85-8Aqu   1½Ⓣ:501 2:044 2:291fm 8¾ 107        11½ 1½ 2hd 66     GrrWA3 ⒻL Island H 89-01 Videogenic, Duty Dance, Mariella 9
     3Nov85—Grade II; Run in Divisions
19Oct85-7Bel  1⅜[T]:49 1:384 2:152fm 14 108       41½ 3½ 1hd 31½    GrrWA12 ⒻAthenia H 78-20 Videogenic,PersianTir,KeyWitness 13
     19Oct85—Grade III
5Oct85-8Med   1¼:483 1:403 2:08 sy 3¼ 109         53 2½ 2hd 31      GrrWA2 ⒻQn Chrlte H 61-30 Cato Double, Isayso, Key Witness 12
     5Oct85—Grade II
21Sep85-9Bel  1¼[T]:481 1:361 2:003fm 8¼ 116      33½ 2hd 31½ 33½   Santos J A6 ⒻFriliery 87-07 Videogenic,DutyDnce,KeyWitness 10
  Oct 9 Bel 6f ft 1:142 h    Oct 3 Bel 4f ft :471 h    Sep 26 Bel 6f ft 1:14 h    Sep 19 Bel 4f ft :472 h
```

201.

A. **(16)**

He's Spirited

HANSEN R D **114**

Own.—Jimac Stable & Volkman

Dk. b. or br. g. 4, by Hold Your Peace—Turbulent Miss, by Petare
Br.—Meadowbrook Farms Inc (Fla) 1986 10 1 3 2 $26,690
Tr.—Dutton Jerry 1985 11 3 5 0 $26,015
Lifetime 26 4 8 2 $53,055

10Oct86-8BM	$1\frac{1}{16}$	:47^{4}	1:11^{2}	1:44 ft	*3	114	$4^{2\frac{1}{2}}$	$5^{2\frac{1}{2}}$	$3^{1\frac{1}{2}}$	$4^{1\frac{1}{4}}$	Baze R A^{7}	Aw17000	71-18	OrindaOriginl,AirDevil,U.LuckyShot	8
25Sep86-8BM	$1\frac{1}{16}$	:48^{2}	1:13^{2}	1:47^{2}sl	4	114	2^{hd}	2^{hd}	2^{1}	$2^{\frac{3}{4}}$	Grable T C^{3}	Aw17000	54-35	Fair Go, He's Spirited, Porch Light	5
13Sep86-10Bmf	1	:45^{4}	1:11	1:37^{1}ft	*2	115	3^{3}	2^{hd}	$1^{1\frac{1}{2}}$	2^{nk}	Grable T C^{6}	Aw17000	82-31	KntuckyLurl,H'sSpiritd,PorchLight	7
13Sep86—Drifted out badly late															
5Sep86-11Bmf	6f	:22^{1}	:44^{4}	1:09^{2}ft	17	117	7^{11}	$7^{7\frac{1}{2}}$	$4^{5\frac{1}{2}}$	$3^{4\frac{1}{2}}$	Grable T C^{7}	Aw17000	87-30	OurLordship,SfetyBnk,He'sSpirited	8
3Aug86-7Dmr	6f	:21^{3}	:44^{4}	1:09^{1}ft	22	119	$12^{9\frac{1}{2}}$	11^{8}	$9^{8\frac{1}{2}}$	$9^{9\frac{3}{4}}$	Baze R A^{7}	Aw21000	82-10	Ondarty, High Hook, J. R.Johnson	12
24Jun86-11Pln	$5\frac{1}{2}$f	:21^{4}	:44^{3}	1:03 ft	$3\frac{3}{4}$	122	$6^{6\frac{1}{2}}$	$6^{9\frac{1}{2}}$	5^{6}	3^{3}	Baze R A^{1}	Aw16000	92-11	BlondeNtive,Contrbnd,He'sSpiritd	10
24Jun86—Bumped start; steadied 1/2, lugged out 3/8															
11Jun86-6GG	6f	:21^{3}	:44^{4}	1:09^{1}ft	*8-5	115	8^{11}	$7^{8\frac{1}{2}}$	$5^{2\frac{3}{4}}$	1^{hd}	Baze R A^{2}	Aw17000	93-10	He'sSpirited,Vannastar,BobCourtny	8
31May86-7GG	6f	:22	:44^{4}	1:09^{2}ft	$4\frac{3}{4}$	116	$8^{8\frac{1}{4}}$	$7^{6\frac{1}{2}}$	4^{5}	2no	Kaenel J L^{7}	25000	92-13	Andrw'NM,H'sSprtd,EsyComEsyG	11
17May86-4GG	6f	:22^{2}	:45	1:09^{3}ft	$6\frac{1}{2}$	114	6^{7}	$5^{6\frac{1}{2}}$	$5^{5\frac{1}{2}}$	$4^{\frac{3}{4}}$	Chapman T M^{5}	25000	90-13	GrayPinstripe,Calbong,CommerceII	7
19Apr86-7GG	6f	:22^{2}	:45^{1}	1:10 ft	$6\frac{1}{2}$	116	$7^{8\frac{1}{4}}$	$7^{6\frac{1}{2}}$	$5^{5\frac{1}{2}}$	$5^{3\frac{3}{4}}$	DelahoussayeE^{6}	25000	85-12	InugurlStr,BOnGurd,DistinctvlyDon	8

Oct 8 BM Ⓣ 4f fm :50^{4} h (d) **Sep 20 BM 3f ft :35 h** **Aug 24 BM 7f ft 1:29 h**

B.

Pass Pass Passed

DIAZ A L **117**

Own.—Greenman D

Ch. g. 4, by Pass the Glass—Frecklestone, by Prince John
Br.—Landon'sThoroughbredHorses (Cl) 1986 17 4 4 2 $35,374
Tr.—Greenman Walter 1985 7 0 1 0 $4,075
Lifetime 28 5 5 2 $42,008

10Oct86-9SA	$1\frac{1}{8}$	:46^{3}	1:12	1:51^{4}ft	*$2\frac{1}{4}$	118	$6^{7\frac{1}{2}}$	$5^{2\frac{1}{2}}$	4^{2}	$1^{1\frac{1}{4}}$	Pincay L Jr^{2}	12500	70-24	PassPssPssed,RinShelter,SonOfRj	11
27Sep86-8BM	$1\frac{1}{8}$	:47^{2}	1:12	1:51 sl	13	114	6^{12}	6^{10}	$6^{8\frac{1}{2}}$	6^{10}	Diaz AL^{4}	ⓇS Jqn Iv H	66-27	Ascension,SomthingGorgous,Armin	6
9Sep86-10Bmf	1	:45^{3}	1:10^{3}	1:37^{1}ft	16	115	9^{13}	$7^{5\frac{3}{4}}$	$4^{4\frac{1}{2}}$	1no	Diaz A L^{5}	Aw17000	82-21	PassPassPssed,ClvryChrge,Plnter	10
28Jun86-6Pln	$1\frac{1}{8}$	:46^{4}	1:12^{3}	1:49^{1}ft	*6-5	119	$2^{1\frac{1}{2}}$	$2^{1\frac{1}{2}}$	2^{hd}	$2^{\frac{1}{2}}$	Baze R A^{1}	A5000	88-11	A.J.Ruler,PssPssPssed,Cesr'sDncer	7
20Jun86-9GG	$1\frac{3}{16}$	:49^{3}	1:14^{1}	1:57^{2}ft	$2\frac{1}{2}$	117	5^{3}	1^{hd}	$3^{\frac{1}{2}}$	$4^{3\frac{1}{4}}$	Baze R A^{2}	A5000	73-17	Pow, A. J. Ruler, Snow Sioux	8
6Jun86-7GG	$1\frac{1}{2}$	:48^{1}	2:04^{2}	2:31^{3}ft	*$2\frac{1}{4}$	120	$4^{1\frac{1}{2}}$	2^{2}	2^{1}	2^{1}	Baze R A^{8}	A5000	88-13	NobleDuc,PssPssPssd,SnowSioux	12
23May86-6GG	$1\frac{1}{4}$	:48^{4}	1:37^{4}	2:02^{3}ft	*8-5	115	3^{3}	1^{hd}	$1^{\frac{1}{2}}$	$1^{2\frac{1}{2}}$	Baze R A^{7}	A5000	78-18	PassPssPssed,SnowSioux,A.J.Ruler	7
9May86-6GG	$1\frac{1}{4}$	:47^{4}	1:38^{1}	2:06^{3}ft	*$2\frac{1}{4}$	110^{5}	$4^{1\frac{1}{2}}$	2^{hd}	$1^{1\frac{1}{2}}$	2no	Yamamoto T J^{9}	A5000	58-27	SnowSioux,PassPassPassed,Durant	9
9May86—Drifted out drive, bumped															
25Apr86-9GG	$1\frac{1}{4}$	:47^{1}	1:36^{4}	2:02^{3}ft	$6\frac{1}{4}$	109^{5}	$6^{5\frac{1}{4}}$	$5^{3\frac{1}{2}}$	3^{1}	$1^{2\frac{1}{2}}$	Yamamoto T J^{5}	A5000	78-20	PssPssPssd,AlrtRspons,SnowSioux	9
11Apr86-7GG	$1\frac{1}{4}$	:47^{3}	1:37^{2}	2:03^{3}ft	15	109^{5}	5^{4}	$5^{2\frac{3}{4}}$	4^{2}	2^{2}	Yamamoto T J^{6}	A5000	71-20	SnowSioux,PssPssPssed,Mewinnr	10

Sep 25 BM 3f sl :38^{4} h **Sep 19 BM 3f ft :37^{2} h** **Sep 5 BM 5f ft 1:04^{4} h** **Aug 30 BM 5f ft 1:02^{1} h**

C.

Touchy Avie

MAPLE S **110**

Own.—Frank & Polan

Dk. b. or br. c. 3, by Lord Avie—Cirenes Touch, by Count Amber
Br.—Badgett B (Ky) 1986 17 3 3 2 $40,969
Tr.—Twardy James E Turf 5 1 1 1 $17,450
Lifetime 17 3 3 2 $40,969

13Oct86-6BM	6f	:22^{1}	:45^{1}	1:09^{1}ft	19	115	$6^{2\frac{1}{4}}$	4^{3}	$6^{9\frac{1}{2}}$	$6^{11\frac{1}{2}}$	Castaneda M^{6}	40000	81-21	DoctorDkot,RlrOfFlts,HlHollywood	8
8Sep86-8Haw	1	Ⓣ:47^{2}	1:11^{4}	1:37 hd	*9-5e	116	5^{5}	$4^{2\frac{1}{2}}$	2^{4}	3^{7}	Fires E^{4}	Aw15000	— —	Tabuk,HngingPunches,TouchyAvie	7
23Aug86-8AP	$1\frac{1}{8}$	Ⓣ:48^{3}	1:13	1:49^{1}fm	51	112	$7^{3\frac{1}{4}}$	7^{7}	8^{14}	8^{21}	Lindsay R^{8}	R Table	70-06	Mrvin'sPolicy,Autobot,BlndfordPrk	8
23Aug86—Grade II															
3Aug86-7Haw	7f	Ⓣ:23^{1}	:47	1:25 hd	*$2\frac{1}{2}$e	112	8^{13}	$6^{6\frac{1}{4}}$	$3^{\frac{1}{2}}$	1^{nk}	Lindsay R^{2}	Aw18000	— —	TouchyAvi,HolyMoldy,HighFrquncy	8
28Jly86-8Haw	$6\frac{1}{2}$f	:23	:46^{3}	1:18 ft	5	112	2^{hd}	$2^{\frac{1}{2}}$	5^{7}	$7^{10\frac{1}{4}}$	Silva C H^{8}	Aw16000	73-23	Rogue Star, Log Creek, LuckyTrick	8
12Jly86-8Haw	$1\frac{3}{16}$	Ⓣ:49	1:15	2:00^{2}sf	37	115	$3^{2\frac{1}{2}}$	$3^{1\frac{1}{2}}$	7^{13}	$8^{18\frac{1}{4}}$	Silva CH^{2}	Haw Dby	— —	Autobot,Spellbound,SonOfThDsrt	11
12Jly86—Grade III															
9Jun86-8Haw	a7f	Ⓣ:23	:46^{4}	1:27^{2}gd	14	114	5^{9}	5^{11}	5^{9}	$2^{8\frac{1}{2}}$	Gallitano G^{4}	Aw28750	— —	Dusty Axe, Touchy Avie,FlyingSisu	7
27May86-8Haw	$6\frac{1}{2}$f	:23	:46^{1}	1:19^{2}gd	7	114	3^{2}	$2^{3\frac{1}{2}}$	$3^{6\frac{1}{2}}$	$5^{9\frac{3}{4}}$	GllitnoG^{6}	Al Hattab H	66-28	Serenius, Dr. Fisher,TulsaHurricane	8
20May86-7Spt	$6\frac{1}{2}$f	:23^{2}	:47^{4}	1:20^{2}ft	*$2\frac{1}{4}$	114	1^{2}	1^{2}	1^{3}	1^{5}	Gallitano G^{5}	Aw15400	75-29	TouchyAvie,Rullah'sExchange,MxB.	8
15May86-7Spt	6f	:24	:48	1:13 sy	*2	117	$2^{1\frac{1}{2}}$	2^{1}	2^{4}	$3^{4\frac{3}{4}}$	Silva C H^{4}	Aw16400	80-23	ClssiclRule,Chd'sHonor.TouchyAvie	7

Oct 7 BM 5f ft 1:01^{2} h

D.

Parramon
B. c. 4, by Lyphard—Misgivings, by Cyane

CASTANEDA M **114** **Br.—Hanes Mrs J W (Ky)** 1986 2 0 1 0 $4,560

Tr.—McAnally Ronald 1985 6 1 1 2 $4,303

Own.—Cardiff Stud Farm **Lifetime 8 1 2 2 $8,863** Turf 6 1 1 2 $4,303

Entered 18Oct86- 7 BM

9Oct86-8BM 6f :22 :44 1:08^{3}ft 4¼ 115 4^2 21½ 2^4 2^6 CastanedaM^7 Aw16000 90-19 Chaka, Parramon, Ghaza 7

24Sep86-6BM 6f :23^1 :46^3 1:12^{3}sl 6½ 115 74¾ 6^4 66½ 44½ CastanedaM^5 Aw16000 71-31 WildPursuit,Arbitrte,BlzingSunshin 7

21Oct85♦6Leicester(Eng) 1 1:36^{1}fm 7 123 Ⓣ 46½ Quinn T Badger Siyah Halem,Askrano,FreshBreeze 10

15Oct85♦5Warwick(Eng) 1 1:39^{3}gd 4 126 Ⓣ 55¾ Quinn T Queen Bess Smoky'sScrt,FrdomsChoic,Axiom 17

7Oct85♦3Bath(Eng) a1 1:46^{4}sf 6 132 Ⓣ 3^4 Quinn T Morris Dancer H Pictograph, Single, Parramon 11

9Sep85♦4Nottingnam(Eng) 1^{50} 1:43^{1}gd 3½ 127 Ⓣ 2^3 Quinn T Sterope H ItsMyTurn, Parramon, PowerPlan 13

24Aug85♦3N'wcastle(Eng) 1 1:46^{2}gd 4½ 116 Ⓣ 43½ Quinn T HnlysNcstlFrdH ‡BoldAndButiful,SmChifny,Shllmn 10

24Aug85—Placed third through disqualification

26Jun85♦7Salisbury(Eng) 1 1:48 gd*8-5 126 Ⓣ 1^{nk} Quinn T Pembroke Parramon,SentimentlRoses,Dronjic 9

●Oct 19 BM 4f ft :47 h ●Oct 3 BM 4f ft :45^3 h Sep 17 BM 5f gd 1:01 h ●Sep 10 BM 6f ft 1:12^3 h

202.

A. **(16)**

Stage Native
Dk. b. or br. f. 3, by Gold Stage—Aggressive Native, by In Reality

Br.—Hofmann Georgia E (Fla) 1986 3 1 1 1 $11,580

Own.—Hofmann Mrs P B **116** **Tr.—Curtis William Jr** 1985 0 M 0 0

Lifetime 3 1 1 1 $11,580

28Sep86-3Bel 7f :22^4 :46^1 1:24^{2}m 4 118 33½ 33½ 34½ 3^5 Cruguet J^1 ⒻAw24000 75-15 Grotona,UnattendedDate,StgeNtive 7

19Sep86-6Med 6f :23 :46^4 1:11^{3}ft *3 118 1^{hd} 1^5 1^6 16½ Edwards J W^3 ⒻMdn 84-17 StgeNtive,LeSireneuse,CoolQueen 12

25Aug86-10Mth 6f :22^4 :46^2 1:12^{2}ft 11 115 11^{13} 97¾ 54½ 2^{nk} EdwardsJW^3 ⒻM18000 78-18 HapiCley,StageNative,RunShnRun 11

25Aug86—Slow st.

Oct 15 Mth 4f m :49^3 b (d) ●Sep 18 Mth 3f ft :36 b ●Sep 13 Mth 6f ft 1:14^3 h Sep 7 Mth 3f gd :38^4 b

B.

Rep's Retton
Dk. b. or br. f. 3, by J O Tobin—Repetitious, by Northfields

Br.—ChmpnshpBrdgPrtI-TrmblAnn (K) 1985 1 1 0 0 $13,200

Own.—Ramos Jackie **114** **Tr.—Preger Mitchell C**

Lifetime 1 1 0 0 $13,200

7Nov85-6Aqu 7f :22 :44^3 1:24^{1}ft 9½ 117 5^5 68½ 2½ 1^{nk} Lovato F Jr^7 ⒻMdn 80-14 Rp'sRttn,LdKndlyLght,RttngTrck 13

Oct 17 Bel 4f ft :47^2 h ●Oct 12 Bel 5f ft :59 h ●Oct 6 Bel 7f ft 1:27 b Sep 29 Bel 6f gd 1:15 h

C.

Miss Scandal
Ch. f. 3, by Inverness Drive—Lady Corniche, by Cornish Prince

Br.—Rutherford M G (Ky) 1986 1 1 0 0 $13,200

Own.—Sabarese T M **119** **Tr.—Parisella John** 1985 0 M 0 0

Lifetime 1 1 0 0 $13,200

20Oct86-3Bel 6f :22^2 :45^2 1:09^{4}ft *6-5 119 2^1 1½ 1^6 19½ Davis R G^5 ⒻMdn 93-09 Miss Scandal, Bribed, Our Millie 8

Oct 12 Bel tr.t 7f ft 1:34 b Sep 30 Bel tr.t 4f ft :51^1 b Sep 26 Bel tr.t 4f ft :51^4 b Sep 23 Bel tr.t 4f ft :50 b

D.

Poelish Hills
B. f. 3, by Danzig—Virginia Hills, by Tom Rolfe

Br.—Caper Hill Farm (Ky) 1986 2 1 1 0 $18,700

Own.—Caper Hill Farm **114** **Tr.—Penna Angel Jr** 1985 0 M 0 0

Lifetime 2 1 1 0 $18,700

3Jly86-9Bel $1\frac{1}{16}$:46^3 1:11 1:43 ft *7-5 113 1^{hd} 1½ 1^{hd} 2^7 Vasquez J^2 ⒻAw25000 80-16 Ananas, Poelish Hills, Flantasia 7

2Jun86-6Bel 7f :23 :47 1:24^{1}ft 3½ 121 21½ 11½ 13½ 1^3 Vasquez J^5 ⒻMdn 81-13 PoelishHills,BoldPrim,BrightOmen 10

Oct 15 Bel 5f sy 1:02^4 b Oct 8 Bel 6f ft 1:15^3 b Oct 2 Bel 5f ft 1:02^3 b Sep 21 Bel 4f ft :48^1 h

203.

A. **(16)**

Sports Medicine

Dk. b. or br. g. 4, by Hard Work—Bow My Dear, by Knightly Manner

Br.—Oakland Farm Partnership (Ky) 1986 9 2 1 1 $29,780

Own.—Bauer R J 113 Tr.—Dutrow Richard E $30,000 1985 13 4 3 1 $44,109

Lifetime 25 8 4 2 $85,493 Turf 1 0 0 0

16Nov86-1Aqu 6f $:22^4$ $:46^4$ $1:11^3$ft 10 117 $7^{3\frac{1}{4}}$ $8^{2\frac{1}{2}}$ 1^{hd} 1^4 Cordero A Jr^2 25000 83-23 SportsMdicin,NorthGld,DrngGroom 8

26Sep86-2Bel 6f $:22^3$ $:45^4$ 1:10 m $5\frac{1}{2}$e113 $6^{6\frac{1}{2}}$ 6^4 10^{11} $10^{11\frac{1}{4}}$ Samyn J L^6 c30000 81-19 FlyingSkipper,Charismo,UpperStr 10

11Apr86-2Aqu 1 $:45^3$ $1:10^3$ $1:35^4$ft $3\frac{1}{2}$e117 $6^{5\frac{1}{2}}$ $6^{8\frac{1}{2}}$ 6^{14} $7^{17\frac{1}{4}}$ Davis R G^5 50000 70-27 Boutinierr,GoldnImmigrnt,CpBdgtt 9

6Apr86-6Aqu 7f $:22^4$ $:45^3$ $1:22^2$m 11 113 10^8 9^{11} $10^{6\frac{3}{4}}$ $10^{8\frac{1}{4}}$ Vasquez J^5 70000 81-20 Sidi Bou Said, IrishOre,TalcPower 10

29Mar86-3Aqu 7f $:22^3$:46 $1:24^1$ft $2\frac{1}{4}$ 119 4^6 $4^{4\frac{1}{2}}$ 4^2 3^4 Davis R G^1 50000 76-21 FngrsInthTll,AsYoLkIt,SportsMdcn 7

17Mar86-5Aqu 6f $:22^1$:45 1:10 ft 4 113 $6^{5\frac{1}{4}}$ $6^{4\frac{1}{2}}$ $4^{3\frac{1}{4}}$ $4^{2\frac{3}{4}}$ Davis R G^9 70000 88-21 Atom Smasher, IrishOre,TalcPower 9

10Mar86-6Aqu 6f ⊡:22 :46 1:12 ft *7-5e117 $7^{5\frac{3}{4}}$ $8^{4\frac{1}{2}}$ 3^1 1^{nk} Davis R G^7 50000 84-27 SportsMdcn,SpcMontn,AtomSmshr 9

3Mar86-7Aqu 6f ⊡$:22^3$:46 $1:11^3$ft 10 116 7^4 7^4 $6^{3\frac{3}{4}}$ 5^6 Cordero AJr^7 Aw36000 80-29 MightyCourgeous,AswnHigh,Hmlet 9

3Mar86—Blocked 8th pl

Oct 21 Aqu 5f ft 1:03 b **Oct 16 Aqu 4f ft :49 b**

B.

*Quiet Royalty

Dk. b. or br. g. 5, by Quiet Fling—Spice Berry, by Tutankhamen

Br.—Sugden C M (Eng) 1986 10 2 3 0 $22,968

Own.—Scherr N 113 Tr.—Lenzini John J Jr $30,000 1985 15 1 0 2 $10,500

Lifetime 51 9 6 5 $92,392 Turf 3 0 0 0

16Jun86-7Lrl 1 $:47^4$ 1:13 $1:38^2$ft $5\frac{1}{2}$ 109^5 6^4 6^5 5^4 $4^{4\frac{3}{4}}$ ♦ Stacy A T^1 25000 75-22 Ramten, Corsican Lt., Benny Q. 8

♦16Jun86—Dead heat

15May86-8GS 1 $:47^3$ 1:12 1:38 ft $5\frac{3}{4}$ 113 $7^{6\frac{3}{4}}$ 6^5 $7^{8\frac{1}{4}}$ 6^7 Fox W I Jr^6 35000 78-24 Msssoit,SovereignSong,ScrdMotion 7

1May86-8Pim $1\frac{1}{16}$ $:47^2$ 1:12 $1:44^4$ft 7 119 $6^{9\frac{1}{2}}$ 6^{10} 6^8 $5^{5\frac{1}{4}}$ Delgado A^4 35000 75-25 HailToNauset,Sportive,BoulderTalk 7

15Apr86-3GS $1\frac{1}{16}$ $:48^1$ $1:13^1$ $1:45^3$gd *$2\frac{1}{4}$ 116 $4^{3\frac{1}{2}}$ $4^{2\frac{1}{2}}$ $2^{\frac{1}{2}}$ 1^1 Fox W I Jr^1 32000 80-22 QuitRoylty,UpPopsThDvil,PrmJohn 6

31Mar86-6GS $1\frac{1}{16}$ $:47^4$ $1:12^4$ $1:45^4$ft $3\frac{1}{4}$ 116 $5^{6\frac{1}{2}}$ $5^{3\frac{3}{4}}$ 4^2 2no Fox W I Jr^1 32000 79-25 OxfordStar,QuietRoyalty,Abdenago 5

31Mar86—Checked

16Mar86-7Pen $1\frac{1}{16}$ $:48^1$ $1:12^3$ $1:44^2$ft $4\frac{1}{2}$ 113 $4^{5\frac{1}{2}}$ $4^{4\frac{1}{2}}$ 2^6 $2^{5\frac{1}{4}}$ Colton R E^1 Aw10400 79-25 LndofBelieve,QuitRoylty,DiscoDom 5

3Mar86-3GS $1\frac{1}{16}$ $:46^4$ $1:11^2$ $1:44^3$ft $5\frac{1}{2}$ 116 4^{13} 5^{14} 6^{13} 4^5 Fox W I Jr^2 40000 80-22 Flight of Time, Double No, Acolyte 6

22Feb86-3GS 1^{70} $:47^1$ $1:12^3$ $1:43^2$m 12 116 6^{10} $3^{4\frac{1}{2}}$ $2^{1\frac{1}{2}}$ 2^1 Fox W I Jr^2 32000 81-24 Bucky, Quiet Royalty, Ron Rivers 8

Nov 26 Aqu 4f m $:50^3$ b **Nov 18 Aqu 5f ft $1:02^3$ b** **Nov 11 Aqu 5f ft $1:01^3$ h** **Nov 4 Aqu 5f ft $1:02^2$ b**

C.

Flunky Home

Dk. b. or br. g. 4, by Circle Home—Flying Flunky, by Olden Times

Br.—Joselson S I (Ky) 1986 17 5 2 5 $83,685

Own.—Warfield T R 119 Tr.—Zito Nicholas P $35,000 1985 15 1 6 2 $29,268

Lifetime 37 8 8 8 $131,028 Turf 1 0 0 0

9Nov86-1Aqu 6f $:22^2$ $:45^4$ $1:10^4$sy $4\frac{1}{2}$ 115 1^2 $1^{3\frac{1}{2}}$ $1^{2\frac{1}{2}}$ $1^{3\frac{3}{4}}$ Antley C W^1 32500 87-22 Flunky Home, Exmoon, McMichael 7

23Oct86-7Aqu 6f :22 :45 1:10 ft $8\frac{1}{2}$ 113 $1^{\frac{1}{2}}$ $5^{5\frac{1}{2}}$ 10^{14} $10^{17\frac{1}{4}}$ Guerra W A^1 45000 74-17 GreenShekl,FlyingSkippr,StrkScrt 10

11Oct86-1Bel 7f $:22^3$ $:45^3$ $1:23^2$ft 12 110^7 1^{hd} $2^{1\frac{1}{2}}$ 7^{13} $7^{27\frac{3}{4}}$ Clayton C^8 50000 57-19 Frontier Justice,StarkSecret,Semaj 7

21Sep86-2Bel 7f $:22^4$:46 $1:22^3$ft $5\frac{1}{4}$ 117 $1^{1\frac{1}{2}}$ 1^1 $2^{1\frac{1}{2}}$ $3^{4\frac{1}{2}}$ Guerra W A^3 50000 84-12 Semaj,FrontierJustice,FlunkyHome 6

20Aug86-1Sar 6f :22 :45 $1:09^3$ft $2\frac{1}{4}$ 117 1^2 $2^{\frac{1}{2}}$ $2^{1\frac{1}{2}}$ $3^{6\frac{3}{4}}$ Santos J A^2 c50000 85-12 Best By Test, Semaj, Flunky Home 6

31Jly86-1Sar 6f :22 $:45^1$ 1:11 ft $2\frac{1}{4}$ 117 2^{hd} 1^{hd} 1^{hd} $3^{2\frac{3}{4}}$ Santos J A^8 50000 82-19 Bowladrome, In Law, Flunky Home 8

13Jly86-3Bel 7f $:22^3$ $:45^2$ $1:21^4$m $2\frac{3}{4}$ 108^5 $5^{2\frac{1}{2}}$ $5^{3\frac{1}{4}}$ 6^{15} $6^{22\frac{1}{4}}$ Vasquez M M^3 70000 71-15 First OneUp,Sagittarian,FeuD'enfer 6

13Jly86—Broke poorly

16Jun86-5Bel 6f $:22^4$ $:46^2$ $1:10^3$ft *1 119 2^{hd} 2^{hd} 1^2 3^{nk} Migliore R^1 c50000 89-20 TalcPower,McMichael,FlunkyHome 9

16Jun86—Brk in air

Nov 25 Bel 4f sy :51 b **Nov 16 Bel 4f ft $:50^2$ b** **Nov 5 Bel 4f ft $:47^4$ h** **Nov 1 Bel 4f ft $:47^4$ h**

204.

A. **(16)**

Pair Of Aces

BAZE R A **114**

Ch. g. 6, by Beau Buck—Spring Pear, by Poleax
Br.—Hawn W R (Ky) **1986 15 3 2 3 $59,555**
Tr.—Roberts Tom $65,000 **1985 15 2 2 4 $59,650**
Own.—Love & Tulving Jr **Lifetime 57 11 7 13 $279,845** **Turf 27 6 2 8 $151,650**

27Sep86-6BM 1 1/16 Ⓣ:48^2 1:12^2 1:43 yl 2 3/4 114 4^3 3$^{1\frac12}$ 1$^{\frac12}$ 1^3 Tohill K S^3 c50000 88-12 PirOfAces,Sidersell,Position'sBest 10
13Sep86-11Bmf 1 1/16 Ⓣ:48^2 1:12 1:42^{2}fm 8 1/2 113 4^2 3$^{\frac12}$ 3^{nk} 4^1 ThllKS^5 Sn Matcan H 90-09 Quintillon, El Mansour, OceanView 7
13Sep86—Wide far turn, drive
31Aug86-9Bmf 7 1/2f Ⓣ:22^4 :45^4 1:29^{1}fm 3 115 5^9 5^8 1^2 1$^{\frac12}$ Tohill K S^5 65000 98-02 PirOfAcs,DiplomtRulr,NwAtrction 10
17Aug86-10Stk 1 1/16 :48^3 1:12^3 1:43 ft *2-3 116 3^2 3^1 1^{hd} 2^{hd} CstnedM^2 Sweepida H 88-07 GrndExchnge,PirOfAcs,LordNormn 5
3Aug86-11SR 1 1/16 :45 1:09 1:39^{4}ft 4 1/4 112 5^6 5^5 3$^{2\frac12}$ 3$^{1\frac12}$ Tohill KS^3 J T Grce H 103-03 Castle Tweed, Armin, Pair Of Aces 7
20Jly86-11Sol 1 1/16 :46^3 1:10^3 1:42 ft 5 112 3^3 3^2 2^4 2^7 Tohill K S^5 Val Dy H 82-14 Armin, Pair Of Aces, Lord Norman 9
20Jly86—Bumped 1/8
6Jly86-11Pln 1 1/8 :48 1:12^1 1:49^{4}ft 11 112 2^1 1^{hd} 6^{12} 6$^{13\frac34}$ Castro J M^1 Almdn H 72-18 HonorMedal,Ascension,Impulsively 7
15Jun86-4GG 1 1/16 Ⓣ:48^4 1:12^4 1:43^{4}fm 3 1/2 116 1$^{\frac12}$ 1^{hd} 1^{hd} 1$^{\frac34}$ Baze R A^1 65000 83-14 PairOfAces,ElMansour,RosaCarnin 6
7Jun86-6GG 7 1/2f Ⓣ:22^3 :46^1 1:29^{1}fm 6 3/4 114 9$^{8\frac14}$ 7^8 3$^{\frac12}$ 3^1 Castro J M^1 65000 93-10 NturlsGrnd,Witin'ForBvr,PirOfAcs 10
19Apr86-9GG 1 Ⓣ:46^4 1:11^1 1:35^{3}fm 7 1/2 114 7$^{7\frac34}$ 5$^{6\frac12}$ 4$^{2\frac14}$ 3$^{1\frac14}$ Castro J M^1 65000 88-09 HollywoodPrty,NtrlsGrnd,PrOfAcs 12
19Apr86—Drifted out 1/4
Oct 15 BM Ⓣ4f fm :49^2 h (d) **Oct 10 BM 4f ft :47^2 h** **Sep 12 BM 3f ft :37^3 h** **Aug 30 BM 3f ft :38^1 h**

B.

Iron Leader

OLIVARES F **114**

B. g. 6, by Mr Leader—Iron Hinge, by Iron Ruler
Br.—Morgan Nancy P (Ky) **1986 7 1 1 2 $27,165**
Tr.—Gosden John H M $65,000 **1985 7 2 0 1 $63,240**
Own.—Sangster R E **Lifetime 31 7 2 5 $152,969** **Turf 25 6 2 3 $103,529**

5Oct86-6BM 1 1/8 Ⓣ:47 1:12 1:49^{3}fm *3-2 114 4^{10} 5^5 5$^{3\frac34}$ 2^1 Baze R A^5 50000 91-08 Flying Snow, Iron Leader, Daniyar 9
5Oct86—Bumped 3/16
21Sep86-10Pom 1 1/16 :46^1 1:10^2 1:43 ft 4 1/4 117 6^{13} 5$^{6\frac12}$ 5^8 3$^{8\frac34}$ OlivresF^2 Ⓡ C B Aflrbh 87-07 Emperdori, Estate, Iron Leader 7
23Jly86-5Dmr 1 1/16 Ⓣ:46^2 1:11^3 1:41^{3}fm 5 3/4 118 7$^{5\frac14}$ 5$^{2\frac34}$ 4$^{2\frac12}$ 7^6 McCarron C J^1 62500 92-04 El Mansour, Massera, Piper John 10
6Jly86-10Hol 1 1/8 Ⓣ:47^3 1:11^4 1:48^{2}fm *2 3/4e 119 8$^{7\frac14}$ 5$^{2\frac34}$ 3^2 3^3 Toro F^6 50000 87-07 TooMuchForT.V.,Rajhn,IronLeder 10
15Jun86-9Hol 1 1/4 Ⓣ:47^2 1:35^1 2:00^{1}fm 4 1/2 119 3$^{3\frac12}$ 4$^{2\frac12}$ 9$^{5\frac14}$ 10^{10} DelahoussayeE^6 62500 96 — Crony, Le Fur, Nonno 11
1Jun86-7Hol 1 1/8 Ⓣ:47^3 1:12^1 1:48^{4}fm 8 1/4 116 6$^{6\frac12}$ 6$^{2\frac12}$ 2^{hd} 1^{hd} Toro F^3 62500 88-07 IronLeder,Nonno,SuccessfulBidder 8
11May86-9Hol 1 :46 1:10^2 1:35^{1}ft 14 116 7$^{6\frac12}$ 7$^{7\frac34}$ 7^{13} 7$^{16\frac14}$ Toro F^4 80000 71-15 AmericanLegion,RisingChum,Kilue 7
16Nov85-9Hol a1 1/8 Ⓣ 1:45^{4}fm 10 118 6^9 9^6 5$^{3\frac12}$ 4$^{3\frac34}$ Pincay L Jr^6 115000 — — Caballo, Steepbank, Cutting Wind 9
16Nov85—Crowded, checked into far turn; Error in placement of starting gate
2Nov85-10LA 1 1/8 :45^4 1:10^3 1:47^{3}ft 3 1/4 116 6^8 5$^{5\frac12}$ 6^7 6$^{8\frac14}$ OlivresF^3 Ornge Cty H 90-12 Restge,BeldleLer,Rueful'sNightOut 6
29Sep85-11Poma1 1/8 :47^2 1:11^4 1:49^{2}ft 2 3/4 118 5^4 5$^{3\frac12}$ 4$^{3\frac12}$ 5^4 Olivares F^1 Pom Inv H — — Artichok,LstCommnd,PtrickMcFig 7
Oct 14 BM 5f ft 1:04^4 h **Oct 1 BM Ⓣ4f fm :52 h (d)** **Sep 15 Hol 6f ft 1:16^4 b** **Sep 5 Hol 7f ft 1:24^1 h**

C.

Position's Best *

GONZALEZ R M **114**

B. g. 6, by Long Position—Our Baby Doll, by Fleet Nasrullah
Br.—Westerly Stud Farms (Cal) **1986 10 0 2 2 $20,065**
Tr.—Utley Doug $65,000 **1985 19 6 2 1 $130,075**
Own.—Delaney & Utley **Lifetime 61 17 9 3 $257,790** **Turf 26 10 5 3 $186,155**

11Oct86-8BM 7 1/2f Ⓣ:22^3 :45^3 1:30^{1}fm 6 3/4e 113 1$^{1\frac12}$ 1^2 2^1 3^3 GnzlzRM^4 Mark's P H 90-07 PerfcTrvl,NwAtrction,Position'sBst 9
27Sep86-6BM 1 1/16 Ⓣ:48^2 1:12^2 1:43 yl *2 3/4 114 1^2 1$^{\frac12}$ 3^1 3^5 Gonzalez R M^6 50000 83-12 PirOfAces,Sidersell,Position'sBest 10
20Sep86-5BM 1 Ⓣ:46^1 1:10 1:35^{1}fm 4 1/4 114 1^2 1$^{1\frac12}$ 2$^{\frac12}$ 2$^{2\frac12}$ Gonzalez R M^8 65000 101 — JackTr,Position'sBest,OnoGummo 10
19Apr86-9GG 1 Ⓣ:46^4 1:11^1 1:35^{3}fm 9 1/4 114 1^2 1$^{1\frac12}$ 2^{hd} 4$^{1\frac14}$ Gonzalez R M^8 65000 88-09 HollywoodPrty,NtrlsGrnd,PrOfAcs 12
12Apr86-8GG 1 1/16 Ⓣ:46^2 1:11^1 1:42 fm 6e 119 1^{hd} 4^1 11^{13} 11^{18} GnlRM^6 Ⓡ Tly Pp Iv H 74-09 OcenView,Introspective,DrkAccnt 11
5Apr86-4GG 7 1/2f Ⓣ:22^3 :45^4 1:28^{2}fm 4 114 1^1 1^2 5$^{8\frac12}$ 6$^{17\frac12}$ GonzalezRM^2 Aw22000 80-08 Clever Song, Ocean View, Ablantin 9
22Mar86-8GG 1 Ⓣ:45^4 1:11^1 1:36^{2}fm 18 114 1^2 1^1 4$^{1\frac12}$ 7$^{9\frac12}$ GnzlzRM^3 S F Mile H 75-15 HilBoldKing,RightCon,LuckyNGrn 12
8Mar86-6GG 1 :47^2 1:11^4 1:37^{3}m 3e 114 1^1 2^1 6$^{8\frac34}$ 7^{17} GonzalezRM^6 Aw22000 63-20 ScurII,BrightAndRight,NwAtrction 7
25Jan86-6BM 1 1/16 Ⓣ:47^4 1:12^2 1:44^{3}fm 3 122 1$^{1\frac12}$ 1^2 1^{hd} 2^{hd} GonzalezRM^5 Aw22000 85-15 ChlcotonBlz,Poston'sBst,CttngWnd 8
5Jan86-8BM 1 :46^3 1:11^4 1:38^{1}m 3 3/4e 117 6$^{9\frac12}$ — — — Gonzalez R M^5 Bart H — — BrMnmm,Frnch'sLc,BrghtAndRght 6
5Jan86—Eased
Oct 8 BM 5f ft 1:00^3 h **Sep 16 BM 7f gd 1:29^2 h** **Sep 11 BM Ⓣ6f fm 1:14^3 h (d)** **●Sep 5 BM 6f ft 1:12^3 h**

D.

Little Look — Ro. h. 5, by Little Current—Come Hither Look, by Turn-to
CASTANEDA M — **114** — Br.—Mereworth Farm (Ky) — 1986 9 1 0 2 $53,917
Tr.—Vollstedt Jack F — $65,000 — 1985 5 2 0 2 $46,017
Own.—Vollstedt J F — Lifetime 26 5 4 7 $109,202 — Turf 26 5 4 7 $109,202
5Sep86-9Med 1⅜Ⓣ:4841:4012:184yl 39 126 65½ 41 511 619¼ Bailey J D6 Ballantine 52-29 Manila, I'm A Banker, Fiery Celt 9
5Sep86—Grade III
23Aug86-7Sar 1 1/16Ⓣ:4611:0931:404fm 25 110 98½ 98¾ 107½ 94½ SmnJL5 Bud Brdrs Cp 89-08 Dnger'sHour,‡SilverVoice,SlmDriv 10
10Aug86-8Sar 1⅛Ⓣ:4841:1241:504gd 8f 112 43 31½ 41¾ 62¾ SmnJL11 B Baruch H 70-25 ExclusivPrtnr,I'mABnkr,CrmFrich 12
10Aug86—Grade II
30Jly86-7Sar 1 1/16Ⓣ:47 1:11 1:424fm 8½ 115 57 43½ 2½ 32 McCrrCJ4 Daryl's Joy 81-21 Mourjane, Island Sun, Little Look 6
15Jun86-8Bel 1⅜[T]:4931:3742:144fm 49 111 86½ 97 1211 119½ MrtsG12 Bwl Green H 73-19 UptownSwell,PalcePnther,Equlize 13
15Jun86—Grade I; Off slowly
31May86-6Bel 1¼[T]:4731:3541:59 fm 8¾ 115 79¼ 56 58 68½ Toro F1 Red Smith H 90-15 Divulge, Tri For Size, Island Sun 9
31May86—Grade II; Run in two divisions
4May86-8Hol 1⅛Ⓣ:4941:1411:484fm 15 116 2hd 2hd 3½ 32¾ DlhossyE3 Jn Hnry H 85-13 PalceMusic,CleverSong,LittleLook 5
4May86—Grade I
25Apr86-8Hol 1 1/16Ⓣ:46 1:0941:401fm 6¾ 117 78½ 75¼ 1hd 12 Toro F3 Aw35000 103 — LittleLook,BolderThnBold,PineBelt 7
25Apr86—Fanned wide in stretch; bumped break
12Apr86-5SA 1⅛Ⓣ:4711:1131:473fm 14 116 53 74 64½ 52½ DelhoussyeE6 Aw35000 86-14 Rich Earth, Snowcreek, Rivlia 8
12Apr86—Wide, lugged in stretch
Oct 6 SA 1 ft 1:423 h — Oct 1 SA 4f ft :50 h — Sep 27 SA 5f ft 1:021 h — Sep 23 SA 5f ft 1:022 h

205.

A. **(16)**

Special Victory — Gr. f. 3, by Hawkin's Special—Vicki's Choice, by Beau Busher
MAPLE S — **114** — Br.—Van Berg Jack (Ky) — 1986 12 3 3 4 $46,884
Tr.—Van Berg Jack C — 1985 7 1 1 2 $10,340
Own.—Franks John — Lifetime 19 4 4 6 $57,224 — Turf 6 3 0 2 $34,089
11Nov86-8Hol 1 Ⓣ:4531:1021:351fm 34 113 33½ 41¾ 2hd 32¼ Meza R Q4 ⒻHcp0 89-09 AnEmpress,MissAlto,SpcilVictory 10
21Sep86-10LaD 1⅛:48 1:123 1:504ft 12 112 33 34 55½ 59½ SnyderL1 ⒻLa D Oaks 81-23 TopCorsg,HppyHllwMss,SclBsnss 11
17Aug86-10LaD 1 1/16Ⓣ:47 1:1041:413fm 4 116 22 22 52¾ 55 TrsclrAJ1 ⒻLyrique H 88-08 Dusty Fare, Miss Alto, Lead Pak 9
3Aug86-10LaD 1 Ⓣ:4731:1131:364fm 3 111 11 1hd 2hd 11 TrosclirAJ6 ⒻAw15500 87-12 SpecilVictory,MinnesotBbe,Sondor 8
28Jun86-5Cby 7½f Ⓣ:234 :47 1:293fm *9-5 119 42 31 22 31¾ BaileyJD1 ⒻSvana Slw — — NymphOfThNght,WnGrl,SpclVctory 6
30May86-10LaD a1 Ⓣ 1:354fm 2½ 112 11 11½ 1½ 13 Snyder L3 ⒻAw12500 88-12 Special Victory, Stir, Racy Suzy 10
30May86—Hand timed
4Apr86-6OP 6f :214 :451 1:11 ft 13 120 2hd 2hd 33 36 MelnconL2 ⒻAw15500 79-20 DvonGold,RunMrisRun,SpcilVictory 7
15Mar86-8FG a7½f Ⓣ:244 :4841:353fm *4-5 119 45½ 46½ 2hd 12 Day P1 ⒻAw9500 71-30 SpclVctr,ClbrtdSkrts,WdnDtchkWn 8
5Mar86-9FG 140:48 1:143 1:44 ft *1 120 43 32 21½ 3½ Faul J H3 ⒻAw9500 72-25 BoldPrincs,ClbrtdSkirts,SpclVctory 8
20Feb86-8FG 140:472 1:133 1:433ft *2 119 45½ 31½ 32½ 22¼ Faul J H5 ⒻAw9500 72-20 DwnOfHop,SpcilVctory,ClbrtdSkrts 9

B.

Stemware — B. m. 5, by Pass the Glass—Susan Subtle, by Hillary
HANSEN R D — **114** — Br.—Jefferson Mrs J M (Cal) — 1986 5 3 0 1 $59,475
Tr.—Headley Bruce — 1985 3 0 0 1 $4,650
Own.—Qvale K H — Lifetime 20 6 3 4 $123,725 — Turf 4 0 0 0
3Nov86-7SA 1 :452 1:101 1:36 ft *6-5e 114 98½ 85 64¼ 33½ MezaRQ9 ⒻPrncs Rny 84-14 Infinidad, Fairly Old, Stemware 9
23Oct86-3SA 1 :46 1:11 1:37 ft 9-5 119 58½ 43 1½ 14 Meza R Q1 Ⓕ 80000 83-20 Stmwr,LotusDlight,AffctionAffrmd 6
23Oct86—Wide into stretch
18Aug86-7Dmr 1 :452 1:10 1:35 ft 6 116 69½ 65 43½ 1hd McCrrnCJ6 ⒻAw27000 93-14 Stemware, Infinidad, Silent Arrival 7
18Aug86—Wide into stretch
21Feb86-8SA 1 :453 1:104 1:364gd 3½e 115 611 54½ 54½ 52¾ Meza R Q2 ⒻAw39000 81-22 Kinda Beau, Balladry, Emmaline 8
17Jan86-9SA 1 :454 1:103 1:362ft 3¼ 116 68½ 76½ 1½ 11¼ Meza R Q7 Ⓕ 62500 86-15 Stemware,PetBird,KarandebsBigKt 8
17Jan86—Wide into stretch
8Mar85-7SA 1⅛Ⓣ:4611:1111:50 fm 7¼ 114 617 613 611 67¼ ShoemakerW1 Ⓕ 70000 70-18 Sheera,Nan'sTurnToStar,FrrNviden 7
8Mar85—Wide into stretch
15Feb85-9SA 1 1/16:462 1:113 1:443ft 2½ 115 68¼ 66¼ 55½ 3½ McCarron CJ2 Ⓕ 62500 77-17 StrightStory,GoldenBnner,Stemwre 8
19Jan85-5SA a6½f Ⓣ:213 :4431:151fm 9½ 115 88 88¼ 89 68¼ ValenzuelPA5 Ⓕ 85000 75-15 Early Quest, Positioned, Sheera 8
19Jan85—Bumped start, wide into stretch
9Nov84-5Hol 1 :46 1:112 1:371ft 17 115 117½ 99¼ 77¼ 56 VllPA9 ⒻAsk Me Now — — Dancing, How Ya Doon,DearCarrie 11
26Oct84-7SA 1⅛Ⓣ:4831:1231:491fm 6½ 115 52¼ 73¾ 67 68½ VlenzulPA3 ⒻAw33000 72-19 Hot Princess, Dacertina, RedEmber 7
Oct 16 SA 5f ft 1:00 h — Oct 11 SA 7f ft 1:271 h — Oct 5 SA 5f ft 1:003 h — Sep 30 SA 5f ft :593 h

C.

Goldspell — Gr. f. 4, by Caro—Lucky Spell, by Lucky Mel

CHAPMAN T M 115 — Br.—Wilder & Burris (Ky) — Tr.—Moreno Henry

Own.—Burris & Wilder

1986	2	0	0	0	$2,000
1985	10	4	1	2	$124,385
Turf	2	0	0	0	$6,250

Lifetime 12 4 1 2 $126,385

1Feb86-8SA 1 1/16 :453 1:12 1:443m 37 114 715 76 611 616 1/4 HrndR7 ⒻSta Mria H 62-24 Love Smitten, Johnica, North Sider 9
1Feb86—Grade II
15Jan86-8SA 7f :221 :44 1:213ft 31 116 89 79 1/2 57 55 1/4 HrndR8 ⒻSt Mnca H 87-14 HerRoylty,NorthSider,TkeMyPictur 8
15Jan86—Grade III
3Nov85-8SA 1 1/16 :45 1:103 1:422ft 6 118 55 42 1/2 32 31 1/4 HrndR8 ⒻLnda Vsta H 88-15 Savannah Slew,Waterside,Goldspell 8
3Nov85—Grade III
19Oct85-8SA 1 1/8 Ⓣ:453 1:094 1:471fm 38 113 54 54 1/2 34 56 1/2 HrndR6 ⒻLs Plms H 84-12 Estrapade, L'Attrayante, Johnica 11
19Oct85—Grade II
22Sep85-10LaD 1 1/8 :48 1:114 1:512ft *8-5 120 2 1/2 2 1/2 2 1/2 2hd HrnndzR2 ⒻLad Oaks 88-20 JustAnythng,Goldspll,CrmsonOrchd 7
6Sep85-8Dmr 1 1/16 :463 1:111 1:412ft 6 1/2 117 2 1/2 2hd 13 11 3/4 Meza RQ2 ⒻⓇTry Pns 93-14 Goldspell, Folk Art, Lucky Roberta 7
17Aug85-8Dmr 1 1/16 Ⓣ:473 1:12 1:423fm 12 117 33 1/2 22 42 1/2 45 3/4 MezRQ4 ⒻⓇSn Clmnt 89-03 MintLef,QuenOfBronz,StksToWin 10
29Jly85-7Dmr 7f :223 :452 1:23 ft 3 1/2 117 64 1/2 66 1/4 38 35 1/2 Pincay LJr8 ⒻAw23000 87-17 BronessDirect,CostlyArry,Goldspll 10
22Jun85-8Hol 1 :441 1:084 1:341ft 3 1/2 117 53 1/4 510 612 713 3/4 PncyLJr7 ⒻPrncs 88-03 Frn'sVlntn,RgnngCntss,ChrmngSsn 7
22Jun85—Grade III
30May85-8Hol 6f :221 :45 1:102ft *4-5 117 31 22 1/2 11 1/2 12 1/4 Pincay LJr4 ⒻAw34000 95-10 Goldspell, Alyanna, Elegant Falcon 5
Nov 20 Hol 4f ft :472 h ●Nov 15 Hol 1 ft 1:374 h Nov 9 Hol 6f ft 1:133 h Nov 5 Hol 3f ft :361 h

D.

Wine Taster — Ch. m. 5, by Nodouble—Regal Wine, by Finnegan

SCHACHT R 114 — Br.—Meyer & Winchell (Ky) — Tr.—Gilchrist Greg

Own.—V H W Stable (Lessee)

1986	11	4	3	0	$62,140
1985	8	1	0	0	$21,375
Turf	13	4	2	0	$70,480

Lifetime 33 9 4 0 $139,213

12Oct86-11Fno 1 1/16 :451 1:101 1:411ft *1-2 122 36 1/2 1hd 1 1/2 14 1/2 Schacht R1 ⒻTulare 93-07 Wine Taster, Cathy's Fun,SpurLark 6
4Oct86-6BM 1 :47 1:112 1:362ft 4 114 42 32 31 1/2 2no ScctR7 ⒻⓇB Bsh Iv H 86-16 NorthSider,WineTaster,BarbieKren 8
22Aug86-7Dmr 1 Ⓣ:463 1:111 1:361fm 9 3/4 120 31 1/2 41 1/4 2hd 12 Baze R A4 Ⓕ 62500 91-09 WineTaster,Tantalized,Beaulahland 8
22Aug86—Checked 1st turn, again into stretch
11Aug86-5Dmr 1 :452 1:104 1:37 ft 8 1/2 120 45 32 1/2 31 1/2 11 1/4 Baze R A8 Ⓕ 40000 83-13 WineTster,RdFrnchy,Dlt'sGoldCoin 9
11Aug86—Took up start
27Jly86-1Dmr 1 :454 1:104 1:363ft 11 119 65 54 44 45 Toro F3 Ⓕ 50000 80-10 BroadStreet,Plumpetra,LuckySilver 7
27Jly86—Broke slowly
9Jly86-11Sol 1 :472 1:113 1:374ft *9-5 114 2hd 1hd 1hd 1nk Schacht R5 ⒻAw15000 85-17 WnTstr,MssApplBlossom,Cthy'sFn 5
22Jun86-6GG 1 1/16 Ⓣ:474 1:121 1:441fm 6 1/4 114 74 1/2 79 65 1/2 45 3/4 Schacht R6 ⒻⓇHcp0 75-14 BannerRose,PurpleBbe,NorthMist 10
8Jun86-6GG 1 :46 1:101 1:361ft 17 114 67 1/4 65 64 1/2 52 1/4 Schacht R2 ⒻⓇHcp0 85-11 Computadora,HetSpell,StedyPenny 8
8Jun86—Jumped shadow at 4 1/2, stumbled 1st turn; steadied 1/16
1Jun86-10GG 1 1/16 Ⓣ:471 1:123 1:444fm 2 3/4 114 33 31 42 1/2 21 Schacht R2 Ⓕ 50000 77-16 Girl InBlue,WineTaster,BrunedeMai 8
1Jun86—Crowded 3/16
18May86-6GG 7 1/2f Ⓣ:233 :471 1:31 fm 4 1/4 117 43 1/4 44 1/2 43 1/2 44 1/2 SchnldtCP3 ⒻAw22000 80-19 Amand'sAffir,BnnerRose,BrbieKren 6
Nov 16 BM 7f ft 1:26 h ●Nov 6 BM 6f ft 1:12 h ●Oct 29 BM Ⓣ5f fm 1:032 h (d) ●Sep 29 BM 6f ft 1:133 h

E.

Petillante — Dk. b. or br. f. 4, by Riverman—Ball Gate, by Snow Ball

CASTANEDA M 114 — Br.—Ring G (Va) — Tr.—Drysdale Neil

Own.—Meynet Madame Paulette

1986	9	1	2	4	$40,920
1985	7	1	2	1	$24,180
Turf	4	0	1	1	$9,925

Lifetime 16 2 4 5 $65,100

26Oct86-5SA 1 1/16 :463 1:111 1:433ft 9 1/4 117 33 1/2 42 1/2 33 33 Pincay LJr3 ⒻAw30000 80-16 Fairly Old, Python, Petillante 9
26Oct86—Lugged in stretch
12Oct86-8BM 1 1/16 :473 1:122 1:433ft 2 1/2 115 21 1/2 2 1/2 3nk 31 CastanedM3 ⒻTizna H 73-19 Good Zar, North Sider, Petillante 4
26Sep86-8BM 1 1/16 :472 1:12 1:444gd *9-5 114 77 64 32 3 3/4 Baze R A2 ⒻAw18000 67-29 Heartlifter, Golden Take, Petillante 8
8Aug86-7Dmr 1 :454 1:103 1:352ft *2 1/2 117 95 1/2 63 1/4 44 34 3/4 Pincay LJr3 ⒻAw23000 86-13 MissBevrlyHills,PollyLFmm,Ptillnt 9
8Aug86—Checked off heels 1st turn; lugged in stretch
13Jly86-7Hol 7f :222 :452 1:223ft *2 1/2 122 65 1/2 79 713 714 1/2 Pincay LJr2 ⒻAw23000 76-15 OurSweetShm,LBellWilson,LDivrtid 8
16May86-7Hol 1 :452 1:102 1:353ft 9-5 117 31 3nk 11 1/2 15 1/4 Pincay LJr4 ⒻAw22000 85-19 Petillante,GloriousAmazon,GoodZr 9
27Feb86-5SA 1 :463 1:111 1:363ft 3 1/2 117 64 1/2 52 1/4 33 21 3/4 Pincay LJr5 ⒻAw30000 83-18 AffctonAffrmd,Ptllnt,NPlmsTnght 10
17Jan86-7SA 1 1/16 :464 1:111 1:43 ft 4 1/2 117 62 3/4 31 1/2 21 1/2 21 1/2 Pincay LJr2 ⒻAw26000 85-15 Sir'sNewHope,Petillnt,Vronic'sQust 8
17Jan86—Off slowly, shuffled back start
4Jan86-6SA 1 1/16 :47 1:11 1:424ft 7 117 52 1/2 54 46 1/2 58 Pincay LJr2 ⒻAw26000 79-13 MyVirgnRl,Sr'sNwHop,Vronc'sQust 7
4Jan86—Stumbled start
22Nov85-7Hol 1 1/16 Ⓣ:47 1:113 1:432fm *3-2 119 33 1/2 22 31 1/2 64 1/2 DlhoussyE5 ⒻAw22000 — — Kr-Dgh,Lock'sDrem,Veronic'sQust 10
Nov 17 Hol 6f ft 1:132 h Nov 11 Hol 6f ft 1:134 h Nov 6 Hol 4f ft :482 h Oct 23 SA 4f ft :483 h

F.

Missadoon
JUDICE J C
Own.—La Barca Syndicate

Dk. b. or br. f. 4, by Matsadoon—Statue, by Exclusive Native
Br.—Mulholland Brothers (Ky)
Tr.—Hess R B

113

									1986 12 4 1 2	$58,635
1985 12 1 4 3	$29,865
Lifetime 25 6 5 5 $95,100	Turf 2 0 0 0

14Nov86-8BM 6f :224 :452 1:10 ft *8-5 115 1hd 22 24 35½ Judice J C¹ ⓕAw22000 83-20 AbstractEnergy,CndinJill,Missdoon 7
1Nov86-12BM 6f :23 :46 1:103ft 9½ 114 2½ 1½ 1½ 12 Judice J C⁴ ⓕAw20000 86-21 Missadoon, Gal0RoseA,PirateAnnie 6
8Jun86-6GG 1 :46 1:101 1:361ft 7½ 115 32½ 31 3² 75½ Judice J C⁵ ⓕⒷHcpO 82-11 Computadora,HetSpell,StedyPenny 8
22May86-6GG 1 :443 1:093 1:353ft 8 116 44 34 1hd 1nk Judice J C⁴ ⓕAw20000 90-13 Missadoon, Steady Penny, Tamure 5
11May86-8GG 6f :214 :443 1:093ft 4½e114 45½ 44 46 56 JudicJC¹ ⓕRchmnd H 85-18 MuiLyphrJ,ApplngToYou,LL'Argnt 7
4May86-9GG 1 :47 1:112 1:372ft 14 114 1½ 1hd 21½ 22½ Judice J C⁷ ⓕⓇInv H 78-19 RealEger,Missdoon,Veronic'sQuest 8
10Apr86-6GG 6f :22 :443 1:10 ft 14 115 3² 3½ 22 42½ CaballeroR⁷ ⓕAw22000 87-19 AppelingToYou,StedyPenny,TvyBlu 7
29Mar86-4GG 7½f ⓣ:233 :4711:294fm 22 117 2½ 2½ 813 911¾ CaballeroR⁵ ⓕAw22000 79-11 CblesComet,Greenstone,BnnerRos 10
7Mar86-8GG 6f :223 :454 1:104sy 7 115 2³ 2² 2½ 12 CaballeroR⁷ ⓕAw20000 85-21 Missadoon,LteNightWomn,Chrysili 8
21Feb86-8GG 6f :222 :452 1:102m 5 115 1hd 3nk 2½ 32½ CaballeroR⁵ ⓕAw20000 84-18 SteadyPenny,PirateAnnie,Missdoon 6
Nov 12 BM 3f ft :361 h   Oct 29 BM 4f ft :481 h   Oct 23 BM 5f ft 1:002 hg   Oct 16 BM 5f ft 1:01 h

Answer key: Class appraisal

Minimum Competency Test

101. B	106. A	111. A	116. A	121. B
102. A	107. C	112. A	117. B	122. A
103. B	108. A	113. A	118. C	123. D
104. A	109. A	114. D	119. A	124. D
105. A	110. C	115. B	120. A	125. B

Mastery Test

126. B	142. B	158. A	174. C	190. C
127. A	143. B	159. C	175. C	191. A
128. D	144. A	160. A	176. B	192. B
129. C	145. D	161. A	177. B	193. A
130. A	146. B	162. B	178. D	194. D
131. B	147. C	163. A	179. C	195. B
132. B	148. D	164. C	180. B	196. A
133. C	149. C	165. D	181. D	197. C
134. D	150. B	166. B	182. C	198. D
135. B	151. A	167. B	183. B	199. B
136. A	152. A	168. C	184. A	200. B
137. C	153. D	169. C	185. C	201. A
138. D	154. D	170. A	186. D	202. C
139. D	155. B	171. C	187. D	203. A
140. C	156. B	172. C	188. B	204. D
141. C	157. D	173. A	189. A	205. C

CHAPTER 6

Speed Handicapping

Competencies

17. Know the basic facts and conventional methods of modern speed handicapping.
18. Understand class-distance pars and the standard adjustments for class, sex, and age.
19. Calculate daily track variants and adjusted final times.
20. Use a speed-figure chart to convert adjusted final times to speed figures and to compare performances at various distances.
21. Interpret speed figures and adjusted times in the context of familiar racing situations.
22. Understand the speed factor in relation to other factors of handicapping, especially class and pace.

	Minimum Competency Tests	Mastery Test
Proficiency standards	80%	70%
Number of items	20	60
Passing Scores	16	42

Sources of Instruction

- *Picking Winners*, chapters 7–9
- *Thoroughbred Handicapping: State of the Art*, chapters 9 & 10
- *Betting Thoroughbreds*, chapters 11 & 12
- *My $50,000 Year at the Races*, Chapter 6

Comments

No source of instruction or expertise has advanced the practice of handicapping in this country as the developments of modern speed handicapping. The case cannot be overstated. Anyone who

121

aspires to competency in this field should understand the following points:

- The raw times recorded by racehorses do *not* indicate how fast or slow races have actually been run; that is, they do not reflect the true speed of racehorses.
- The speed ratings and daily track variants published by the *Daily Racing Form* do *not* achieve the purpose they are intended to achieve; that is, they do not adjust final times to reflect the speed of the track surface on a given day.
- Neither the actual times nor speed ratings of the *Daily Racing From* can be used to compare the true speed of horses competing at various distances or different racetracks.
- Prior to 1975, most attempts to estimate the true speed of racehorses by adjustments to actual times and by procedures to render adjusted times comparable among horses and racetracks provided *poor estimates* of reality which were far more misleading than helpful. Until recently, that is, speed handicapping was bad handicapping.

Modern speed handicapping has corrected the intricate problems of its predecessors. It has been no small achievement. The concepts and skills reflected by these test items are nothing less than basic weapons for up-to-date handicappers everywhere. They are intended for everyone, regardless of persuasion.

Modern speed handicapping also has its limitations. It is not all things for all seasons. It's convenient to understand the applications that serve us well and others not so well.

Definitions of Terms

- *Pars.* The typical (average) final times recorded for a specific class of horse at the regularly run distances at a particular racetrack, such as $20,000 claiming horses 4up at 6F, 6½F, 7F, 1M, 1¹⁄₁₆M, and 1⅛M at Santa Anita.

- *Daily track variant.* A measure of the relative speed of the racing surface on a given day.

- *Adjusted final times.* Actual final times adjusted for the combined influences of class and track surface speed.

- *Speed figures.* A systematic chart of numbers (arbitrary in origin) intended to reflect (a) the values of different adjusted times at the same distance, (b) the relative value of the same adjusted times at related and new distances, and (c) the relative value of adjusted times recorded at different racetracks.

• *Projected times.* The expected final times of specific horses based upon (a) the consistency of prior speed figures and/or (b) the circumstances of today's race.

SPEED HANDICAPPING: MINIMUM COMPETENCY TEST

206. Modern speed handicapping relies on final times adjusted for class and what other factor simultaneously?

A. weight   **(17)**
B. post position
C. track surface speed
D. trips

207. One reason better horses can defeat cheaper horses in slower time than the cheaper horses have previously run is because cheaper horses often give up the fight earlier when they sense they're overmatched. Another reason is more strongly related to speed handicapping than class handicapping.

A. Pace makes the race   **(22)**
B. The apparently slower times are actually faster when adjusted for track surface speed
C. Class is more important than speed
D. Speed is a function of form, and form cycles vary tremendously, affecting final times in kind

208. A thoroughbred can be expected to reveal its true speed when

A. allowed to run alone on the front   **(17)**
B. it approaches the midpoint of its 4-year-old season
C. matched against horses of relative equal ability
D. in the peak of health and conditioning

209. Modern speed handicappers can compare horses' final times at different distances effectively by utilizing speed charts that emphasize the concept of parallel time.

A. True   **(17)**
B. False

210. If handicappers know the par times for $10,000 males 4up at the local track, they can construct an accurate speed chart for all classes of claiming horses.

A. True   **(18)**
B. False

211. If par for $20,000 older males at a mile is 1:37⅖, what is the mile par for the same class of older fillies and mares?

A. 1:38   **(18)**
B. 1:38⅖
C. 1:37⅖
D. 1:37⅗

212. Maiden-claiming horses in sprints are normally how much slower than winning claiming horses of the same selling prices?

A. ⅗ second   **(18)**
B. one second
C. 1⅗ seconds
D. 2 seconds

213. Par-time differences between classes can be considered standard and predictable in both sprints and routes.

A. True   **(18)**
B. False

214. The pars for maiden special weights and classified allowance races allow handicappers to compare the caliber of racing at different tracks.

A. True   **(18)**
B. False

215. It is practically impossible to make a valid statement about how fast a 2-year-old can be expected to run at a route distance.

A. True   **(18)**
B. False

216. The evidence about par times and class levels at all distances suggests a perfect positive correlation between class and speed.

A. True   (22)
B. False

217. Speed and class are interlocking; therefore it's fair to assert, the better the horse, the faster it can run.

A. True   (22)
B. False

218. How many races for a specific class at a specific distance are advisable to construct an accurate class-distance par chart?

A. 5.   (18)
B. 15
C. 20
D. 30

219. What does the daily track variant reveal to all handicappers?

A. the best and worst races on a program   (17)
B. how fast a typical race should have been run
C. how fast or slow the track surface was on a given day
D. a basis for comparing the surface speeds of different racetracks

220. Which factor does *not* introduce a bias of one kind or another to a speed handicapper's figures?

A. a wire-to-wire easy win   (22)
B. a program consisting entirely of better races for better horses
C. an unusually fast or slow early pace
D. a track condition favoring the inside paths

221. Handicappers should distrust unusually high speed figures earned in the slop.

A. True   (21)
B. False

222. What is the best estimate of the daily variant?

Race	Variant
1.	+1
2.	−1
3.	Even
4.	−6
5.	+2
6.	Even
7.	+1
8.	−1
9.	−2

A. Even   **(19)**
B. −2
C. +1
D. −6

223. If the final time for the 2nd race is 1:44 ⅕ and the day's route variant Slow 2, what is the adjusted final time?

A. 1:44⅗   **(19)**
B. 1:43⅘
C. slower than par
D. faster than par

224. Which statement about the day's track variant makes the most sense?

Race	Variant
1.	+2
2.	0
3.	+1
4.	+2
5.	+3
6.	−2
7.	−4

Race	Variant
8.	-3
9.	-3

A. The track was Slow 4 (-4) **(19)**
B. The track surface changed in mid-card
C. The day's routes were slower than the sprints
D. The track was Slow 1 (-1)

225. When does a final time of 1:11⅖ become faster than a final time of 1:10⅖?

A. When the early pace of the 1:11⅖ race has been **(21)**
at least a second faster than the 1:10⅖ race
B. When a relatively classy horse records the 1:11⅖ and a cheaper horse the 1:10⅖
C. When the daily track variants have been applied to both raw times
D. Infrequently; final time differences of a full second or more can rarely be adjusted to favor the seemingly slower horse

This is the end of the minimum competency test on speed handicapping. Check your answers. If your score falls below standard, do not proceed to the mastery test until you consult the recommended sources of instruction.

SPEED HANDICAPPING: MASTERY TEST

226. The fundamental principle upon which modern speed handicapping depends holds that

A. Speed and class are essentially interchangeable **(17)**
B. Adjusted times are far better estimates of true speed than are actual times
C. The only quality of the thoroughbred than can be measured accurately is its speed
D. No matter what has happened earlier, the best horse is the horse that has run the fastest final time

227. A stakes sprinter runs 1:09⅘ to win by a nose, and two weeks later loses by a nose in 1:11 flat. A speed handicapper

demonstrates the two final times make perfect sense. What did he show?

A. Better horses competed in the 1st race   **(19)**
B. The track surface was Fast 3 for the 1st race, Slow 3 for the 2nd race
C. Weight shifts adding to 15 pounds made the difference
D. The early pace of the 2nd race was significantly faster than the early pace of the 1st race

228. Par-time differences among classes and distances can be fairly characterized as

A. one to two points faster per class level in sprints   **(18)** but unpredictable in routes
B. *widely* varied from track to track
C. likely to change from season to season at many tracks
D. one or two points up or down with every class drop or class rise

229. The speed handicapper's main problem with reliance on class-distance pars is

A. daily changes in track surface speed   **(18)**
B. comparing final times at different distances
C. distinguishing class within a class
D. evaluating shippers

230. A $10,000 horse is a $10,000 horse is a $10,000 horse— just about anywhere.

A. True   **(18)**
B. False

231. The final times of allowance races, for nonwinners two times other than maiden or claiming races, will generally be as fast as what level of claiming horses?

A. $20,000   **(18)**
B. $25,000
C. $35,000
D. $45,000

232. If 4up $10,000 claiming sprinters run 1:12 on average at 6F at Local Downs, $50,000 claiming sprinters at the same track will average roughly

A. 1:10 **(18)**
B. 1:10⅖
C. 1:10⅘
D. 1:11⅕

233. The par times for what class of horses are the bases for constructing the speed charts for all nonclaiming horses at each track?

A. maiden, 3up **(18)**
B. Alw, NW2XMC, 3up
C. $10,000 claiming, 4up
D. open stakes, 4up

234. The adjustment to the 4up par for 3YO sprints of March is

A. Slow 1 **(18)**
B. Slow 3
C. Slow 5
D. Slow 7

235. The adjustment to the 3up par for the 3YO miles of June is

A. Slow 1 **(18)**
B. Slow 2
C. Slow 3
D. Slow 4

236. The adjustment to the 3up par for 3YO races at 1⅛M in July is

A. Slow 1 **(18)**
B. Slow 2
C. Slow 3
D. Slow 4

237. The adjustment to the 3up par for the 3YO sprints of July–Aug.–Sept.–Oct. is

A. 0 **(18)**
B. Slow 1

C. Slow 2
D. Slow 3

238. The adjustment of the 3up par for 3YO races at 1¹⁄₁₆M in April is

A. Slow 2   (18)
B. Slow 3
C. Slow 4
D. Slow 5

239. If par for $7500 males 3up at 6F is 1:11²⁄₅, what is the par for the same class of fillies and mares?

A. 1:11³⁄₅   (18)
B. 1:11⁴⁄₅
C. 1:12²⁄₅
D. 1:12⁴⁄₅

240. If the 6F par for 2-year-olds of June is 1:11²⁄₅, what is the 6F par for 2-year-olds of October?

A. 1:11   (18)
B. 1:10⁴⁄₅
C. 1:10³⁄₅
D. 1:10²⁄₅

241. The main problem modern speed handicappers experience with the Daily Racing Form's speed rating and daily variant is

A. The ratings become obsolete whenever a new track   (17)
   time record is set
B. They cannot be used to compare horses compet-
   ing on different days
C. They are not sensitive to the influences of class
D. They cannot be used to evaluate shippers

242. How much slower on average are 2YO maiden-claimers at 6F during fall than their maiden-special counterparts?

A. 5 lengths   (18)
B. 7 lengths
C. 9 lengths
D. 12 lengths

243. Given: par for $32,000 males, 4up, 6F, is 1:10²⁄₅.
What is par for the winner of a $32,000 maiden-claiming race for 3YO fillies at 6F on March 15?

A. 1:11   **(18)**
B. 1:11⅖
C. 1:12
D. 1:12⅖

244. Given: par for Alw, NW3XMC, 3up, 7F is 1:22⅘.
What is par for 3YO fillies at the same class and distance in
May?

A. 1:23⅕   **(18)**
B. 1:23⅖
C. 1:23⅘
D. 1:24

245. Maiden-claiming horses at the route are normally how
much slower than claiming horses of the same selling prices?

A. ⅘ lengths   **(18)**
B. 1⅖ lengths
C. 2 seconds
D. 2⅖ seconds

246. If par is 1:10⅘ and the daily variant is Fast 3, what is
the adjusted final time of the day's fastest sprint?

A. 1:10⅕   **(19)**
B. 1:11⅖
C. something slower than 1:10⅘
D. cannot be determined from the facts provided

247. Reliance on projected times to calculate variants and
make figures is most reliable when

A. par times are not well known   **(19)**
B. evaluating sprints
C. highly consistent horses are entered
D. comparing horses at related distances

248. What is the daily route variant below?

Race Conditions	Variant
1. 6F, 4up, $25 Clm	− 3
2. 1M, 3YO, Alw	+ 1
3. 1M, 3YO(f), Alw	+ 2
4. 6½F, Mdn-Clm, 3up	− 2
5. 1¹⁄₁₆M, $20 Clm, 3up	0
6. 6F, Mdn, 3YO	− 1

Race Conditions	*Variant*
7. 1$\frac{1}{16}$M(t), 3up, \$62,500 Clm	no variant
8. 1$\frac{1}{8}$M(f), Grade 3, 3up	+3
9. 1$\frac{1}{16}$M, 3up, \$40 Clm	+2

A. 0 **(19)**
B. +1$\frac{3}{5}$
C. +2
D. −2

249. If only a single dirt route has been carded, how should speed handicappers estimate the day's route variant?

A. use the sprint variant **(19)**
B. accept a route variant of plus or minus three
C. modify the sprint variant up or down by ½
D. use projected times to get the route variant

250. Speed charts based on the concept of proportional time allot one length or one-fifth of a second greater value in a route.

A. True **(17)**
B. False

251. If all the race variants for a card cluster around par, the daily variant can be estimated reliably by adding the race variants and dividing by the number of races.

A. True **(19)**
B. False

252. Using proportional times to make speed figures, what is the value of one length in a 6F sprint timed in 1:10 flat?

A. 1.4 points **(20)**
B. 2.8 points
C. 4.2 points
D. 5.6 points

253. If the actual final time is 1:35$\frac{2}{5}$ and the daily variant is Fast 5, how fast did the winner actually run?

A. 1:36$\frac{2}{5}$ **(19)**
B. 1:34$\frac{2}{5}$
C. 1:35$\frac{7}{5}$
D. cannot be determined from the facts provided

254. Which is the fastest race?

A. final time 1:35⅘, variant Fast 4 **(19)**
B. final time 1:37⅖, variant Slow 6
C. final time 1:36⅖, variant Even
D. final time 1:34⅗, variant Fast 9

255. Which daily variant below best brings together the following two final times:

Oct. 15	6F	1:11⅗
Oct. 21	6F	1:09⅘

A. Oct. 15 Fast 4 **(19)**
B. Oct. 21 Fast 6
C. Oct. 21 Slow 4
D. Oct. 15 Slow 8

256. The track is fast. What do the race variants below suggest about the day's program?

Race Conditions	*Pace Variant*	*Final Time Variant*
1. Clm $10, 6F, 4up	−2	−3
2. Mdn-Clm $32, 6F, 3YO	−2	−6
3. Clm $25(f), 1M, 3YO	−5	−4
4. Mdn-Clm $32(f), 6F, 3YO	0	0
5. Alw, NW1XMC(f), 6F, 4up	0	+1
6. Mdn-Clm $32(f), 1M, 3YO	+5	+4
7. Alw, NW2XMC, 6F, 4up	−1	+6
8. Alw, NW3XMC, 9F(t), 4up	no variants	
9. Clm $16, 1¹⁄₁₆M, 4up	−1	−2

A. the track surface was abnormally slow **(19)**
B. the surface speed changed in mid-card
C. the early races were composed of weak fields
D. the sprints were slower than the routes

257. If final time is 1:11⅖, and the daily variant Fast 2, what is the adjusted final time of a horse beaten 4¾ lengths?

A. 1:12⅘ **(19)**
B. 1:10⅖
C. 1:11⅘
D. 1:12

258. If the final time is 1:45⅗ and the daily variant Slow 6, what is the adjusted final time of a horse beaten 3¼ lengths?

A. 1:43⅘   (19)
B. 1:45
C. 1:45⅕
D. 1:46⅖

259. The easiest, most effective way for recreational handicappers to convert adjusted final times to speed figures is

A. Buy a speed chart for the local track   (20)
B. Set the 3up $10,000 pars equal to 100 and add/subtract a point for each one-fifth of a second the other pars are higher or lower
C. Set all the 6F sprint pars equal to 100 and construct a parallel time chart using the average time it takes 3up $10,000 claiming horses to run the intervals for each regularly run distance
D. Use the projected times of consistent horses at every class-distance category as pars, set these times equal to any arbitrary number, such as 80, and add/subtract a point for each adjusted time faster or slower than the projected times

260. An excellent use of speed figures is to evaluate 3YOs and 4YOs at new or unfamiliar distances.

A. True   (22)
B. False

261. Using the concept of proportional times to construct a speed-figure chart, many modern speed handicappers proceed by

A. determining the value of one length or one-fifth   (20)
of a second at each of the regularly run distances
B. setting the various par times for the regularly run distances equal to 100
C. determining how many seconds on average it takes a common class of horses to run the intervals between the regularly run distances
D. calculating the 6F and 1M pars for the various classes at the local track and setting those times equal to an arbitrary figure, that is, 88 for sprint pars and route pars, respectively

262. If a horse earns a speed figure of 88 at 6F by running 1:10⅖, how would speed handicappers use a local speed chart to predict the horse's final time at 1¹⁄₁₆M?

A. Check a class-distance par chart and note the   **(20)**
   1¹⁄₁₆M final time associated with the 1:10⅖ fractional par
B. Find the 1:10⅖ final time in the 6F column. Move
   to the right across the row of times from 1:10⅖
   until you reach the 1¹⁄₁₆M column. Use that final
   time.
C. Find the average time it takes the same class of
   horses to run from 6F to 1¹⁄₁₆M at the local track
   and add that number to 1:10⅖.
D. Find the 88 rating in the 1¹⁄₁₆M column of figures
   and note the corresponding final time.

263. High speed figures are often unreliable when

A. evaluating maidens   **(21)**
B. horses are moving ahead in class
C. horses have gone wire to wire uncontested
D. distances change by more than one-sixteenth of a
   mile

264. A nicely developing 3YO that has never routed has earned figures of 92–94–96 in three consecutive sprints. What figure would speed handicappers expect the same horse to earn when first switched to 1¹⁄₁₆M?

A. lower   **(21)**
B. 94
C. 96
D. higher

265. Speed handicappers can get overlays from their figures most consistently when

A. maidens graduate to nonwinners allowance sprints   **(21)**
B. the pace is unusually fast or slow
C. 3YOs that have never won a stakes are entered in
   a restricted or open unlisted stakes
D. claiming horses move up in class

266. The figure horse is at its greatest advantage when

A. running on a speed-biased track   **(21)**
B. either of its top two figures is higher than any
   one figure of the other contenders
C. its latest figure is its highest by five points or more
   and the high figure in the field today
D. it is not outclassed

267. Speed figures can be especially useful for indicating whether last season's stakes horses are performing as well again this year.

A. True   **(21)**
B. False

268. When a horse gets a speed figure that is inexplicably high in relation to its past figures, speed handicappers will often

A. discount the high figure in favor of past figures   **(21)**
B. prepare to support the horse seriously next out
C. rely on pace ratings instead
D. wait to see another race before evaluating the horse
   one way or the other

269. Frontrunners will usually earn their best figures as a result of what kind of pace?

A. fast early, fast late   **(22)**
B. slow early, fast late
C. fast early, average late
D. average early, fast late

270. If a closer has earned the highest speed figures in the field, handicappers should insist

A. the horse is also the class of the field   **(21)**
B. the early pace will be favorable
C. the track bias will favor closers
D. the horse has raced within the past 21 days

271. If the 6F $10,000 3up claiming par is adjusted to 1:11⅕ after the variant has been added and the adjusted time is set equal to a speed figure of 100, what is the speed figure of another 6F sprint winner that day whose final time is 1:09⅗?

A. 92   **(20)**
B. 104

C. 108
D. 111

272. Speed figures are just as reliable on the grass as on the dirt.

A. True **(22)**
B. False

273. A useful description of the relationship between speed and form is

A. High speed is a function of peaking form **(22)**
B. Speed figures can reflect the ups and downs of form cycles
C. Horses away for more than thirty days do not often repeat their top figures
D. Horses that retain winning form for long periods earn the same figures consistently

274. Modern speed charts assume that horses that have run 6F in 1:10 flat will complete the extra quarter-mile of a mile race correspondingly faster than horses that have run 6F in 1:11 flat.

A. True **(17)**
B. False

275. Use the variants below and the speed chart on page 139 to identify *Sacahuista's* speed figure in the 1986 Breeders' Cup fillies stakes.

Sacahuista — B. f. 2, by Raja Baba—Nalees Flying Flag, by Hoist the Flag
PINCAY L JR — 120 — Br.—Humphrey Jr & Farish (Ky) — 1986 8 4 2 0 $467,865
Own.—Beal & French Jr — Tr.—Lukas D Wayne
Lifetime 8 4 2 0 $467,865

1Nov86-2SA $1\frac{1}{16}$:45^3 1:10^1 1:43^{1}ft *9-5 119 5^7 7^9 7^{13} 4$^{10\frac{3}{4}}$ PcLJr^8 ⒻBr Cp Juv F 74-13 Brave Raj, Tappiano, Saros Br'g 12
1Nov86—Grade I
5Oct86-8SA $1\frac{1}{16}$:45^3 1:10^2 1:44^{3}ft 9-5 115 2$^{1\frac{1}{2}}$ 2$^{\frac{1}{2}}$ 1$^{\frac{1}{2}}$ 1$^{2\frac{1}{4}}$ McCrrCJ^5 ⒻOak Leaf 78-15 Sacahuista, Silk'sLady,DelicateVine 7
5Oct86—Grade I
10Sep86-8Dmr 1 :45^2 1:10^1 1:35^{3}ft 5 117 1^{hd} 2$^{\frac{1}{2}}$ 1^{hd} 2no Day P^1 Dmr Fut 90-11 Qualify, Sacahuista, Brevito 9
10Sep86—Grade I
29Aug86-6AP 7f :22^1 :45 1:23^{2}ft $3\frac{1}{4}$ 122 2$^{\frac{1}{2}}$ 2^{hd} 2^{hd} 2$^{1\frac{1}{4}}$ McCrrCJ^6 ⒻArlWasLs 84-19 DelicateVine,Sacahuist,RulingAngel 6
29Aug86—Grade I
14Aug86-8Sar 6f :22 :45^2 1:11 ft *1-3 119 2$^{\frac{1}{2}}$ 2^{hd} 1^{hd} 1^1 McCrrCJ^6 ⒻAdrondck 85-20 Sacahuista, Collins, Release theLyd 7
14Aug86—Grade II
30Jly86-8Sar 6f :22 :45^2 1:10^{3}ft *$2\frac{1}{4}$ 114 2^1 1^{hd} 1$^{2\frac{1}{2}}$ 1$^{3\frac{1}{2}}$ McCrrCJ^5 ⒻSchuylrvll 87-13 Sacahuista, OurLittleMargie,Collins 9
30Jly86—Grade III
11Jly86-6Hol $5\frac{1}{2}$f :22^2 :45^4 1:04^{2}ft $9\frac{1}{4}$ 118 1^1 1^{hd} 1^4 1^9 McCarron CJ^{10} ⒻMdn 92-14 Schuist,Ninepythlin,AlwysAWcmn 11
5Jun86-5Hol 5f :22^2 :46^2 :59^{3}ft 15 118 8$^{8\frac{1}{2}}$ 8^{10} 6^7 5$^{6\frac{1}{4}}$ Valenzuela PA^3 ⒻMdn 82-16 PrchncToDrm,RomnGm,QckMssngr 9
5Jun86—Green 3/8 turn
Nov 23 Hol 5f ft 1:00^2 h **Nov 15 Hol 5f ft 1:00 b** **Oct 24 SA 6f ft 1:13^1 h** **Oct 15 SA 6f ft 1:12^3 h**

Oak Tree at Santa Anita Daily Variants

Dates	Sprints	Routes
Nov. 1	+2	+2
Oct. 5	+2	−1

A. 104   **(20)**
B. 95
C. 112
D. 87

276. Examine the past performances and variants for *Saca-huista* again. If par for the Oct. 5 Oak Leaf Stakes is 1:43⅗, how many speed-figure points faster or slower did *Sacahuista* run its Oak Leaf win than its Breeders' Cup loss?

A. Slow 6   **(20)**
B. Fast 10
C. Fast 4
D. Slow 2

277. Review *Sacahuista's* past performances again. Use the speed chart and variants again to determine how many lengths faster winner *Brave Raj* (Nov. 1) ran in the Breeders' Cup Fillies than *Sacahuista* ran in winning the Oak Leaf Stakes.

A. 17   **(20)**
B. 11
C. 7
D. 4

278. If the daily variant is Fast 3, use the speed chart to find *Lively Miss's* speed figure in its first start.

Lively Miss
OLIVARES F
Own.—Tabello R G

B. f. 2, by To the Quick—Miss Ivor, by Sir Ivor
Br.—Neuman Dr—Mrs E A (Ky)   1986 1 M 0 1 $2,700
118   Tr.—Klitou George
Lifetime 1 0 0 1 $2,700

15Nov86-6Hol   6f :22   :46² 1:11⁴ft   34 118   1ʰᵈ 1ʰᵈ 21½ 35¾   Olivares F⁴   ⓜMdn 78-14 TimelyAssertion.HiloBb,LiviyMiss 11
Nov 28 Hol 4f ft :48⁴ h   Nov 23 Hol 5f ft :59⁴ h   Nov 13 Hol 4f ft :48² h   Nov 9 Hol 6f ft 1:15⁴ h

A. 59   **(20)**
B. 75
C. 66
D. 79

Santa Anita Speed Figures

6f		6½f		7f		1m		1¹⁄₁₆		1⅛	
1:08	135	1:15	124	1:21	127	1:34	136	1:40	140	1:46	144
1	132	1	121	1	125	1	134	1	138	1	142
2	129	2	119	2	122	2	132	2	136	2	140
3	126	3	116	3	120	3	129	3	134	3	138
4	123	4	113	4	117	4	127	4	132	4	136
1:09	121	1:16	111	1:22	115	1:35	125	1:41	130	1:47	134
1	118	1	108	1	113	1	123	1	128	1	132
2	115	2	106	2	110	2	121	2	126	2	130
3	112	3	103	3	108	3	119	3	124	3	128
4	109	4	100	4	105	4	117	4	122	4	127
1:10	106	1:17	98	1:23	103	1:36	115	1:42	120	1:48	125
1	103	1	95	1	101	1	113	1	118	1	123
2	100	2	93	2	98	2	111	2	116	2	121
3	98	3	90	3	95	3	108	3	114	3	119
4	95	4	87	4	93	4	106	4	112	4	117
1:11	92	1:18	85	1:24	91	1:37	104	1:43	110	1:49	116
1	89	1	82	1	89	1	102	1	108	1	114
2	86	2	80	2	85	2	100	2	106	2	112
3	84	3	77	3	84	3	98	3	104	3	110
4	81	4	74	4	81	4	96	4	103	4	108
1:12	78	1:19	72	1:25	79	1:38	94	1:44	101	1:50	107
1	75	1	69	1	77	1	92	1	99	1	105
2	72	2	67	2	74	2	90	2	97	2	103
3	70	3	64	3	72	3	88	3	95	3	101
4	67	4	62	4	70	4	86	4	93	4	99
1:13	64	1:20	59	1:26	68	1:39	84	1:45	91	1:51	98
1	61	1	57	1	65	1	82	1	89	1	96
2	59	2	54	2	63	2	80	2	87	2	94
3	56	3	52	3	61	3	78	3	85	3	92
4	53	4	49	4	58	4	76	4	84	4	90
1:14	51	1:21	47	1:27	56	1:40	74	1:46	82	1:52	89
						1	72	1	80	1	87
						2	70	2	78	2	85
						3	68	3	76	3	83
						4	66	4	74	4	81
						1:41	64	1:47	72	1:53	80

Beaten-Lengths Adjustment Chart

Margin	5f.	6f.	7f.	Mile	1¹⁄₁₆	1⅛	1½
neck	1	1	1	0	0	0	0
½	1	1	1	1	1	1	1
¾	2	2	2	1	1	1	1
1	3	2	2	2	2	2	1
1¼	4	3	3	2	2	2	1
1½	4	4	3	3	3	2	2
1¾	5	4	4	3	3	3	2
2	6	5	4	4	3	3	2
2¼	7	6	5	4	4	4	3
2½	7	6	5	4	4	4	3
2¾	8	7	6	5	5	5	3
3	9	7	6	5	5	5	3
3¼	9	8	7	6	5	5	4
3½	10	9	7	6	6	6	4
3¾	11	9	8	7	6	6	4
4	12	10	8	7	7	6	5
4¼	12	10	9	8	7	7	5
4½	13	11	9	8	8	7	5
4¾	14	11	10	9	8	8	5
5	15	12	10	9	8	8	6
5½	16	13	11	10	9	9	6
6	18	15	12	11	10	9	7
6½	19	16	13	12	11	10	8
7	20	17	14	13	12	11	8
7½	22	18	15	13	13	12	9
8	23	20	17	14	13	13	10
8½	25	21	18	15	14	13	10
9	26	22	19	16	15	14	11
9½	28	23	19	17	16	16	11
10	29	24	20	18	17	17	12
11	32	27	23	20	18	18	13
12	35	29	25	21	20	20	14
13	38	32	27	23	22	22	15
14	41	34	29	25	23	23	16
15	44	37	31	27	25	25	17

279. Use the variants below and speed chart on page 139 to identify *Up The Pole's* highest speed figure in its past four races.

Variants

0
−2
−7
+2

A. 88 **(20)**
B. 77
C. 83
D. 96

Up The Pole — B. g. 4, by Crystal Water—Why Four, by Coursing
PINCAY L JR — **117** — Br.—Rowan L R (Cal) — 1986 8 1 3 0 $12,175
Own.—Rowan L R (Lessee) — Tr.—Canney William T — $10,000 — 1985 2 M 0 0
Lifetime 14 1 4 1 $18,075

3Nov86-1SA 6f :21^3 :44^4 1:11 ft 3¾ 117 4 5½ 5^5 6^6 6 3½ Pincay L Jr^{10} [S] 12500 79-14 HachalaTachl,Melchip,ShuttleOne 10
3Nov86—Lugged in
17Oct86-1SA 6½f :21^3 :44^2 1:17^{1}ft 9 115 4 3¾ 3 4½ 3^5 2^5 Castanon A L^2 12500 79-21 Jacart, Up The Pole, Inquisitive 9
17Oct86—Drifted out late
26Sep86-10Pom 1$\frac{1}{16}$:48 1:14^1 1:47^{3}sl 10 116 3^2 3 1½ 3 3½ 2 6¾ Castanon A L^9 12500 66-29 InNaturlForm,UpThePole,SonOfRj 10
21Sep86-8Pom 6f :22^1 :45^2 1:10^{3}ft 14 116 3^1 4 3½ 4 4½ 5 6¼ Mena F^{10} 12500 92-07 Jacart, Inquisitive, Philip Nolan 10
8Sep86-2Dmr 6f :21^4 :45^4 1:10 ft 2 119 3 1½ 4 1½ 4 3½ 4 3½ Lipham T^2 [S] 12500 84-14 StrOfAmeric,BeThnkful,DollrTrppr 7
8Sep86—Checked 5/16
18Aug86-2Dmr 6f :22 :45^2 1:10^{2}ft 16 120 3^{nk} 2^{hd} 2½ 2½ Lipham T^2 12500 85-14 DoublDficit,UpThPol,CoursingEgl 11
18Aug86—Lugged in backstretch
31Jly86-3Dmr 6f :22 :45^2 1:09^{4}ft 25 116 5^2 7 4½ 7 8½ 6^8 Lipham T^3 [S] 16000 81-12 Rodney, Grenoble, Go Go Debonair 8
31Jly86—Bumped start; very rank to backstretch; wide into stretch
14Jly86-3LA 6½f :22 :46^1 1:17 ft 4 122 1 1½ 1^{nk} 1 1½ 1 3¼ Lipham T^9 M12500 92-15 Up The Pole, Morse, Little Tyrant 9
22Apr85-3SA 6f :22 :45^3 1:11^{3}ft 3 113^5 3^2 3 3½ 4 5½ 6^{12} Lozoya D A^4 [S]M32000 68-21 ToldYouTwice,NobleDuc,HdTurnr 10
11Apr85-6SA 6½f :21^4 :45 1:17^{2}ft 6 118 2½ 4 1½ 9^{14} 9 22½ Pincay L Jr^9 [S]Mdn 60-18 FlshyNorthStr,Prt'sCop,RnnngDbnr 9
11Apr85—Lugged in; bumped
Oct 16 SA tr.t 5f ft 1:03 h

280. If the variant is Fast 2, what is *Pensar's* speed figure for its Nov. 1 win? Use the speed chart.

A. 109 **(20)**
B. 98
C. 103
D. 101

Pensar — Dk. b. or br. h. 7, by Private Thoughts—Realize, by In Reality
CHAPMAN T M — **117** — Br.—Sandera Farm (Mich) — 1986 12 1 4 0 $14,866
Own.—Goldstein S — Tr.—Jenda Charles J — $8,000 — 1985 21 5 2 4 $39,608
Lifetime 71 18 9 10 $181,131 — Turf 5 1 1 0 $11,622

16Nov86-9BM 6f :23 :45^4 1:10^{3}ft *2 114 2 1½ 2^2 5 6½ 7 13½ Chapman T M^1 16000 72-21 BOnGurd,RdwoodBoy,Accptr'sPrnc 7
1Nov86-9BM 6f :22^3 :45^3 1:10^{1}ft *2½ 114 4^1 1½ 1^2 1^3 Chapman T M^8 12500 88-21 Pensr,UnitedVictory,PlentyBrcwn 12
18Oct86-2BM 6f :22^4 :45^4 1:10^{1}ft 8¼ 114 3 1½ 3 1½ 2^{hd} 2^{hd} Chapman T M^2 12500 88-16 HesStorminNormn,Pensr,DowrRng 7
27Sep86-2BM 6f :23 :46^2 1:11^{1}sl 4½ 114 5^8 3 4½ 2^4 2 4½ Grable T C^4 c10000 78-27 Jolly And Brave, Pensar, Irish Cast 7
20Sep86-10BM 6f :22^3 :46 1:11^{1}ft 5¼ 114 4 1½ 2^{hd} 1^1 2½ Razo E^3 c8000 82-19 AvengingWarrior,Pensr,PetesInnte 9
20Sep86—Lugged in 1/4
27Aug86-7Cby 6f :22^1 :45 1:10^{2}ft 11 114 7^{10} 7^{12} 7 9½ 5 5¾ Razo E Jr^6 20000 89-14 Muralto, Bertie Boy, Record 7
7Aug86-2Cby 6½f :22^3 :45^2 1:17^{4}ft *3 116 4^2 2½ 2^2 5 7¼ Hawley S^4 c16000 85-19 SmothShn,ShmrckMcGrdr,FrlthFlg 7
13Jly86-6Cby 6f :22^1 :45^1 1:11^{1}gd 13 115 2^{hd} 1^{hd} 2½ 4 3¼ Montoya D^3 20000 88-09 Bertie Boy, Sa Got, Cherokee Gold 9
5Jly86-4Cby 5½f :22^3 :45^3 1:05^{2}ft 7¼ 115 3 1½ 2^{hd} 1 1½ 2^2 Hawley S^3 16000 91-17 Cherokee Gold,Pensar,Gloversville 10
6Feb86-8FG 6f :22^3 :47 1:12^{3}ft 5 117 3 1½ 3 1½ 7^6 8 9½ Ketner R^4 12500 72-26 Cherry Rum, Hillson, Rose Blanket 9
Nov 25 BM 3f ft :35^2 h — Nov 9 BM 3f ft :38^1 h — Oct 27 BM 4f ft :53 h — Oct 14 BM 4f ft :47^3 h

281. Use the speed chart on page 139 to answer the following.

If the final time is 1:18⅕, the sprint variant Slow 5, and Horse A was beaten a neck, how fast would Horse A be expected to run a mile?

A. 1:38⅕   **(20)**
B. 1:36⅖
C. 1:37⅘
D. 1:38

282. The relationship between speed and class indicated by the par figures for the class levels listed below suggests that

Class	Par Figure
$10–12,000	85
$14–16,000	88
$18–20,000	91
$20–25,000	94
$30–35,000	96
$40–50,000	100
Maiden special weight	90
Nonwinners of $2500 . . .	98
Nonwinners of $2500 twice . . .	101
Nonwinners of $2500 three times . . .	105
Other allowances	107
Stakes	114

A. Stakes horses almost always run much faster than   **(22)**
   allowance horses
B. High-priced claimers can generally hold their own
   in preliminary nonwinners allowance races
C. Maiden winners that go directly into claiming
   races should be expected to win next near the
   $20,000 level
D. Their speed figures are too close to distinguish
   among nonclaiming horses reliably

283. Use the par figures of the item above and the speed chart of page 139 to answer the following.

Which par time below is *not* representative of a $10,000 claiming horse?

A. 1:45⅗   **(20)**
B. 1:11⅗

C. 1:18⅗
D. 1:39

284. Use the par figures of Item 282 to answer the following.
The par figures for the various class levels suggest what kind
of class change will be most difficult at Local Downs?

A. $20,000 claiming to $50,000 claiming   **(22)**
B. nonwinners allowance to classified allowances
C. classified allowances to stakes
D. maiden to $40,000 claiming

285. Today's pace figures to be fast early and average late, a
very common scenario. Here are the four contenders, their speed
figures, and running styles. Which horse is likeliest to win?

Horse A	97	Closer
Horse B	99	Frontrunner
Horse C	99	Frontrunner
Horse D	96	Off-pace tactical speed type

A. Horse A   **(22)**
B. Horse B
C. Horse C
D. Horse D

Answer key: Speed handicapping

Minimum Competency Test

206. C	211. A	216. A	221. A
207. B	212. B	217. A	222. A
208. C	213. A	218. B	223. B
209. B	214. A	219. C	224. B
210. A	215. A	220. B	225. C

Mastery Test

226. D	241. C	256. C	271. C
227. B	242. C	257. A	272. B
228. D	243. D	258. B	273. B
229. C	244. A	259. B	274. A
230. A	245. B	260. A	275. D
231. C	246. D	261. A	276. B
232. C	247. C	262. D	277. C
233. A	248. C	263. C	278. A
234. B	249. C	264. C	279. A
235. C	250. B	265. D	280. B
236. D	251. A	266. B	281. D
237. B	252. B	267. A	282. C
238. D	253. A	268. A	283. C
239. B	254. B	269. A	284. D
240. A	255. D	270. B	285. A

CHAPTER 7

Pace Analysis

Competencies

23. Know the basic facts and conventional practices of pace analysis.
24. Understand pace as the interrelations among rates of speed, points of call, running styles, racing shapes, and final times.
25. Identify pace lines that represent horses' current abilities reliably.
26. Calculate conventional pace ratings accurately.
27. Interpret pace ratings in the context of other factors of handicapping and familiar racing situations.

	Minimum Competency Test	Mastery Test
Proficiency standards	80%	70%
Number of items	16	50
Passing scores	13	35

Sources of Instruction

- *Ainslie's Complete Guide to Thoroughbred Racing,* Chapter 13
- *Thoroughbred Handicapping: State of the Art,* Chapter 10
- *The Follow Up,* a quarterly newsletter/periodical of the Sartin Methodology handicapping group, Volume 1 to the present, from winter of 1987 to the present. Includes treatments of energy distribution and velocity ratings as measures of pace capacity, identifying representative pace lines, software programs for ranking contenders on various intervals of pace, and various relations among pace, class, and other selected factors of handicapping.

Comments

The role of pace analysis in classical handicapping has been as a separation factor. Among horses already considered suited to the class, distance, and other circumstances of the race and in positive form—the contenders—pace analysis might determine whether one horse possesses a rate of speed or style of running that might benefit best from today's probable pace's.

The traditional methods proposed to accomplish this objective have varied greatly. Some focus on race segments, others on the relations among race segments, and still others on the relations between fractional times and final times. None have been put forth with persuasive evidence of their effectiveness, leading many handicappers—myself included—to conclude that pace analysis supersedes pace ratings.

In practice, procedures for obtaining pace ratings have taken a back seat to modern methods of speed handicapping since the mid-seventies. In recent seasons, however, pace handicapping has been born again.

Modern methods of pace analysis continue the tradition of separating horses already classified as contenders. New procedures for obtaining pace ratings, notably the Sartin Methodology and Quirin's power ratings—both requiring high-tech support, by the way—offer a far greater promise than their predecessors fulfilled. We should all be very grateful.

Definition of Terms

- *Velocity ratings.* A rate of speed equal to distance divided by time. Expressed as feet-per-second.

- *Sustained pace.* The capacity to extend an early rate of speed to the finish. A measure of late pace *as a function of* early pace; calculated as early pace plus late pace, divided by half.

- *Off-pace type.* A horse that usually runs behind the early pace but no farther back than the middle of the field.

PACE ANALYSIS: MINIMUM COMPETENCY TEST

286. The classic definition of pace is the

A. rate of speed at each point of call   (23)
B. relationship between fractional time and final time
C. relationship between running style and track sur-
   face conditions
D. rates of speed during specific race segments

287. Pace analysis is generally more important in routes than sprints.

A. True (23)
B. False

288. In picking representative pace lines, handicappers need to be most concerned with what factor?

A. track bias (25)
B. form
C. distance
D. class

289. Pace ratings supersede pace analysis.

A. True (23)
B. False

290. Which horse has covered 6F the fastest?

	¼	½	¾	Finish
Horse A	22	45⅕	1:11	Won
Horse B	22⅕	45⅗	1:10⅖	Lost by 2
Horse C	22⅖	45⅖	1:10⅗	Lost by nk

A. Horse A (26)
B. Horse B
C. Horse C

291. In Grade 1 races at classic distances, which statement below makes the most sense regarding the relations between class and pace?

A. class supersedes pace (27)
B. pace makes the race
C. weight brings them together regardless
D. pedigree becomes more important than either

292. Pace analysis suggests the likeliest winner in any race is the class horse on a clear lead.

A. True (23)
B. False

293. Other factors being relatively equal, at what standard distance is pace analysis likely to be most decisive?

A. 6F **(27)**
B. 7F
C. $1\frac{1}{16}$M
D. $1\frac{1}{8}$M

294. Which horse has run the fastest mile?

	4F	*6F*	*1M*	*Finish*
Horse A	$45\frac{4}{5}$	$1{:}11\frac{3}{5}$	$1{:}38\frac{1}{5}$	Lost by 1
Horse B	$46\frac{1}{5}$	$1{:}11\frac{4}{5}$	$1{:}36\frac{4}{5}$	Lost by 2
Horse C	46	1:11	$1{:}37\frac{2}{5}$	Lost by ns

A. Horse A **(26)**
B. Horse B
C. Horse C

295. Normally, early pace at middle distances is best assessed after the horses have run

A. 2F **(23)**
B. 4F
C. 5F
D. 6F

296. The likeliest reason the most recent race would *not* offer handicappers a representative pace line for rating a claiming horse is

A. The distance was not correct **(25)**
B. The horse showed no early speed
C. Form has been obviously deteriorating
D. The horse was obviously outclassed

297. Under what conditions is the most recent race almost always preferred as the most representative pace line?

A. open to 4up or 3up **(25)**
B. claiming races
C. following a lengthy layoff
D. the last race was a win

298. As a general rule, which makes the most sense when picking pace lines for horses 4up?

A. Use the best recent race versus the most ad- **(25)**
   vanced competition
B. Any of the most recent six races that is "good"
   can be selected to rate
C. One of the most recent two races should be used
   whenever possible
D. Do not use races where the distance, trip, class,
   or footing is not the same as (related to) today's
   conditions

299. A fast early, slow late race shape favors

A. frontrunners **(24)**
B. off-pace types
C. closers
D. no particular running style

300. Pace ratings will generally be most effective when

A. one horse earns a rating significantly higher than **(23)**
   the others
B. used to separate contenders well-suited to the basic class demands of the race
C. the track surface is unbiased
D. the early pace and late pace both will be completed today in average time

301. Early speed and early pace are essentially interchangeable.

A. True **(23)**
B. False

This is the end of the minimum competency test of pace analysis. Check your answers. If your score falls below the desired
standard, consult the sources of instruction before proceeding
to the mastery test.

PACE ANALYSIS: MASTERY TEST

302. What is pace analysis?

A. calculating rates of speed at each point of call **(23)**
B. understanding the early speed and late speed re-
   quirements of today's race

    C. clarifying the relationships between fractional
       times and final times
    D. evaluating running styles in a context of today's
       track conditions

303. If a horse can attend and sustain a fast early pace, it
has a decisive pace advantage against a horse that can track and
overtake a similar early pace.

    A. True   **(23)**
    B. False

304. Why are pace ratings as calculated by recreational
handicappers frequently misleading?

    A. The measures are too imprecise   **(23)**
    B. The ratings have been too insensitive to real dif-
       ferences in class
    C. The early pace proves too unpredictable much of
       the time
    D. They equate one length with one-fifth of a second

305. Early pace is measured best as

    A. rate of speed to the first call   **(23)**
    B. rate of speed from start to second call
    C. the leader's time at the pre-stretch call
    D. the average beaten lengths of winners at the sec-
       ond call of today's distance

306. The best measure of sustained pace is

    A. rate of speed for the entire race   **(23)**
    B. the second quarter time plus the final quarter time
    C. early pace plus late pace, divided by two
    D. the rate of speed from the pre-stretch call to the
       finish

307. In which race segments of routes do the winners also
most often display the fastest rates of speed?

    A. first ½M   **(23)**
    B. first 6 furlongs
    C. third and fourth calls combined
    D. final ¼M

308. Studies of pace in sprints show the lowest proportion of winners is associated with the fastest rates of speed during the

A. first ¼M (23)
B. first ½M
C. final ¼M
D. race in its entirety

309. Velocity ratings are equal to distance divided by time.

A. True (23)
B. False

310. When using velocity ratings to obtain pace ratings, a beaten length is equal to roughly how many feet?

A. 5 (26)
B. 10
C. 15
D. 20

311. Pace analysis supersedes pace ratings primarily because

A. The small numerical differences characteristic of (23)
   pace ratings cannot separate closely matched
   contenders reliably
B. Pace ratings do not reflect class differences
C. Pace ratings too often do not reflect the advantages and disadvantages of running styles in relation to today's probable race shape
D. The methods of obtaining pace ratings are so various, they emphasize relationships that may or may not be important today

312. Pace ratings can be particularly susceptible to subtle changes in

A. class (27)
B. early speed
C. form
D. track bias

313. Which running style is favored by an average-fast race shape?

A. frontrunner   (24)
B. closer
C. off-pace type
D. none

314. Which race shape is most unlikely to be won by a closer?

A. fast-fast   (24)
B. average-fast
C. fast-slow
D. slow-slow

315. Which race shape favors no particular running style?

A. fast-fast   (24)
B. average-average
C. slow-slow
D. average-fast

316. Which race shape is particularly convincing if won by a frontrunner?

A. fast-slow   (24)
B. slow-average
C. fast-fast
D. fast-average

317. Which running style is most impressive as the winner of a fast-slow race shape?

A. frontrunner   (24)
B. off-pace type
C. closer
D. none in particular

318. An off-pace type is most likely to win what kind of race?

A. fast-slow   (24)
B. fast-fast
C. average-fast
D. average-slow

319. A closer is most impressive by winning what kind of race?

A. fast-fast   (24)
B. average-slow

C. fast-average
D. slow-fast

320. A fast-average race is more impressive if won by a frontrunner than a closer.

    A. True   **(24)**
    B. False

321. A slow-slow race is usually won by what kind of horse?

    A. frontrunner   **(24)**
    B. off-pace type
    C. closer
    D. no particular advantage

322. A horse exiting a fast-fast race is likeliest to repeat if it is the only horse of its kind in a

    A. nonwinners allowance race   **(27)**
    B. claiming race
    C. graded stakes
    D. any kind of race

323. When does late pace become significantly more important than usual?

    A. the early pace figures to be both fast and hotly   **(27)**
       contested between two frontrunners
    B. the fastest late-pace horse is also the class of the
       field
    C. when late-running sprinters switch from 6F to 7F
    D. the track surface is characterized by a negative
       speed bias

324. How should daily track variants be applied to fractional times to produce useful pace ratings?

    A. Apply one-half the variant to the second fraction   **(26)**
       in sprints, the full variant to the second call in
       routes.
    B. Apply one-half the variant to the second fraction
       in sprints, one-third to the second fraction in
       routes
    C. In sprints and routes alike apply one-quarter of
       the variant to the first fraction and one-half to the
       second fraction

D. Instead of dividing the variant at all, calculate the adjusted final time and use the fractional par associated with it

325. Studies of pace in sprints show the highest proportion of winners also record the fastest rate of speed during the

A. first ¼M   **(23)**
B. first ½M
C. final ¼M
D. race in its entirety

326. The most precise, accurate measures of rates of speed are

A. fractional times   **(23)**
B. the sum of a horse's actual fractional times divided by 3
C. velocity ratings
D. final times plus beaten lengths

327. Maiden winners graduating to their first allowance sprint can often be distinguished best on pace by

A. final-quarter fractions   **(27)**
B. rate of speed to the second call
C. second-quarter fractions
D. first-quarter fraction plus final-quarter fraction

328. In picking pace lines to obtain pace ratings, which guideline makes the most practical sense?

A. Do not use races at unrelated distances   **(25)**
B. Never go back beyond the second most recent race
C. In unclear cases, select multiple pace lines and use the best rating
D. Limit pace ratings to the authentic contenders

329. Using the best race this season against the most advanced competition is a useful guideline for selecting pace lines to evaluate

A. claiming horses 4up   **(25)**
B. grass horses
C. nonclaiming 3YOs
D. stakes horses in overnight races

330. If the race is a Grade 1 or Grade 2 stakes for 3up, which kind of pace lines are acceptable?

A. the most recent graded or listed stakes win or close finish **(25)**
B. only other Grade 1 and Grade 2 races
C. the most impressive nonclaiming win within the previous sixty days
D. the most recent good stakes race open to older horses

331. Under nonclaiming conditions for 3YOs, the more recent the race the more likely it will offer handicappers a horse's most representative pace line.

A. True **(25)**
B. False

332. It's Jan. 10, 1987. It's a 7F allowance race, for nonwinners three times other than maiden or claiming (f), purse of $33,000.

Which is the most representative pace line in *Twilight Ridge*'s record?

A. Dec. 27, 1986 **(25)**
B. Oct. 11, 1986
C. Mar. 23, 1986
D. Nov. 2, 1985

```
Twilight Ridge                    B. f. 4, by Cox's Ridge—Waving Sky, by Quibu
 VALENZUELA P A             114   Br.—Burrow T E (Fla)                       1986  7 0 3 0
                                  Tr.—Lukas D Wayne                          1985  5 3 1 1
Own.—Klein Mr-Mrs E V            Lifetime   12  3  4  1   $726,613           Turf  1 0 0 0
27Dec86-3SA  6½f:224 :454 1:162ft   *2½ 113   72¾ 62 54½ 43    StevensGL7 ⒻAw33000   85-19 MllrsSttonry,GoodZr,O
     27Dec86—Wide final 3/8
16Nov86-8BM  1 1/16:454 1:11 1:432ft *4-5 123 2hd 52¾ 69 615½  CstdM1 ⒻSan Jose H   59-21 NovelSprite,Chnngo'sA
 1Nov86-5SA  1¼:461 1:344 2:011ft  *1-2e119   46 46½ 613 616¾  RmrRP3 ⒻBr Cp Dstff  66-13 Ldy'sScrt,Frn'sVlntin,O
     1Nov86—Grade I; Checked 1st turn
25Oct86-5SA  1⅛Ⓣ:4711:1141:484fm   2¾ 112    3½ 2hd 64 89¾     Meza R Q5 ⒻAw35000    73-17 PerfectMtchII,Rekindli
     25Oct86—Steadied at 1/8
11Oct86-3SA  1 :46 1:102 1:363ft    *1 113    22 21 21½ 24½    StevensGL1 ⒻAw35000   80-17 Wterside,TwilightRidge
     11Oct86—Lugged in, checked at 3/16
23Mar86-8SA  1 1/16:463 1:112 1:422ft 3-2e117 21½ 2½ 21 21½    McCrrCJ6 ⒻS A Oaks    87-17 HiddnLight,TwilightRid
     23Mar86—Grade I; Lugged in stretch
 1Mar86-8SA  1 :46 1:102 1:361ft   *1e121     43½ 42¼ 21½ 2¾   McCrrCJ7 ⒻLs Vrgnes   86-16 LifAtThTop,TwilightRd
     1Mar86—Grade III; Lugged in, bumped 1/8, again late
 1Dec85-8Hol 1 :451 1:102 1:36 gd  *2-3 120   63¼ 32 31½ 34¾   PncyLJr8 ⒻHol Strlt   78-16 I'mSplndid,TrimColony,
     1Dec85—Grade I; Lugged in stretch
 2Nov85-2Aqu 1 :452 1:104 1:354ft  *3-5e119   52¾ 2hd 12½ 11   VlszJ11 ⒻBr Cp Juv F  87-10 TwilightRidge,FmilySty
     2Nov85—Grade I
19Oct85-8Pha 6½f:22 :45 1:161ft    *2-3 121   2hd 21 33 22½    McNlFA3 ⒻCriticlMis   89-20 Brt'sDrm,TwlghtRdg,Tr
  Dec 19 Hol 4f ft :474 b        Dec 12 Hol 5f ft 1:004 h        Dec 5 Hol 4f ft :484 h
```

333. Even when the track surface is even and unbiased, a clear early pace advantage on turf is generally not as significant as on the dirt.

A. True **(23)**
B. False

334. If the daily track variant has been Slow 6 for Horse A, Fast 4 for Horse B, which horse ran the fastest pace?

	½	¾	*Finish*
Horse A	45⅗	1:11⅘	Lost by 1
Horse B	44	1:09⅕	Lost by 7

A. Horse A **(26)**
B. Horse B

335. When two or more frontrunners engage in an early pace duel, the most probable result is

A. The frontrunners will weaken one another and another horse will come on late and win **(23)**
B. One of the frontrunners will win anyhow
C. The fastest closer will win
D. The early pace horse will win in sprints and the sustained pace horse will win in routes

336. Which race in *T.V. Residual's* record offers the best pace line for evaluating its chances under the conditions below?

7 FURLONGS. (1.20) ALLOWANCE. Purse $33,000. Fillies and mares. 4-year-olds and upward which are non-winners of $3,000 three times other than maiden, claiming or starter. Weights, 4-year-olds, 121 lbs.; older, 122 lbs. Non-winners of two such races since November 3 allowed 3 lbs.; of such a race of $13,000 since then, 5 lbs.; of such a race of $15,000 since October 1. 7 lbs.

A. Oct. 31 **(25)**
B. Oct. 4
C. Sept. 4
D. Dec. 28

T. V. Residual — **B. f. 4, by Pirate's Bounty—T V Caper, by T V Lark**

TORO F — **116** — **Br.—Wygod M J (Cal)** — **Tr.—Cross Richard J**

Own.—Wygod M J

Lifetime 14 3 6 2 $87,075

1986	**8**	**1**	**5**	**1**	**$58,075**
1985	**6**	**2**	**1**	**1**	**$29,000**
Turf	**4**	**0**	**3**	**1**	**$21,700**

31Oct86-8SA	1 1/16	$:46^3$	$1:11^2$	$1:43^1$ft	9¼	114	5^3	4^2	$6^{7½}$	$5^{9½}$	StsGL5	ⒻLnda Vst H	75-16	Mrinn'sGirl,WinterTresur,FinKudos	9
31Oct86—Grade III															
4Oct86-7SA	1	$:46^1$	$1:11^4$	$1:37^2$ft	*2	113	$5^{2¾}$	$4^{1¼}$	$3^{1½}$	2^{hd}	StevensGL5	ⒻAw30000	81-18	Mille Et Une, T.V.Residual,GoodZar	9
4Oct86—Awarded first purse money; Crowded 3/8 turn															
4Sep86-8Dmr	1 1/16	$:45^3$	$1:10^1$	$1:42^1$ft	4	114	$4^{1¼}$	2^{hd}	1^1	$2^{½}$	StvnsGL6	Ⓕ[R]Try Pns	88-14	MrgrtBooth,T.V.Rsidul,SportngAck	7
14Aug86-5Dmr	1 1/16 Ⓣ	$:47^1$	$1:11^2$	1:42 fm	2½	116	$5^{4½}$	$3^{1½}$	$2^{1½}$	2^4	Toro F8	ⒻAw23000	92-04	Kremer,T.V.Rsidul,ShotgurWdding	8
2Aug86-8Dmr	1 1/16 Ⓣ	:49	$1:13^1$	$1:43^1$fm	2¾	115	5^2	$5^{1¾}$	4^5	$3^{4¾}$	Toro F2	Ⓕ[R]Sn Clmnt	85-10	OurSweetShm,MillEtUn,T.V.Rsidul	10
2Jly86-7Hol	1 1/16 Ⓣ	$:47^3$	$1:11^1$	$1:41^3$fm	19	111	3^1	3^1	3^1	2^{nk}	Solis A9	ⒻAw25000	96-07	Rekindling, T. V. Residual,Kraemer	9
5Jun86-8Hol	1 1/16 Ⓣ	$:47^1$	$1:11^2$	$1:42^1$fm	4¼	115	2^{hd}	$1^{½}$	$1^{½}$	$2^{1½}$	StevensGL7	ⒻAw23000	91-07	PuzzlBook,T.V.Rsdul,ShotgnWddng	7
5Jun86—Wide 7/8 turn															
21May86-8Hol	6f	$:22^2$	$:45^4$	$1:10^4$ft	5½	115	2^{hd}	$1^{½}$	$2^{1½}$	$2^{5½}$	McCrrCJ1	ⒻDrmaCrtc	84-13	WintrTrsur,T.V.Rsidul,ChickOrTwo	9
28Dec85-8SA	7f	$:22^1$	$:44^4$	$1:23^4$ft	*2¾e	116	$5^{3¼}$	2^3	$2^{2½}$	$6^{2¾}$	McCrrCJ1	Ⓕ[S]ClBrdrs	78-14	BlconyPss,Egle'sMusic,SilntArrivl	12

337. Which pace line best represents *Fashion Book's* chances under the race conditions provided?

6 ½ FURLONGS. (1.14) ALLOWANCE. Purse $26,000. Fillies and mares 4-year-olds and upward which have never won two races. Weights, 4-year-olds, 119 lbs.; older, 120 lbs. Non-winners of a race other than claiming since November 3 allowed 3 lbs.

A. June 14 **(25)**
B. May 18
C. Apr. 30
D. Mar. 21

Fashion Book — B. f. 4, by Flying Paster—General Store, by To Market
CASTANON A L — 116 — Br.—The Hat Ranch West (Cal) — 1986 8 0 2 0 $35,800
Own.—The Hat Ranch — Tr.—Stute Melvin F — 1985 6 1 1 0 $15,925
Lifetime 14 1 3 0 $51,725 — Turf 5 0 0 0 $8,800

14Jun86-8GG 1 1/16 (T):463 1:112 1:434fm *3-2 115 38 56 69½ 57 CstAL10 (F)[S]Imprs Stl 76-18 JoysOfSprng,LdyPstr,Crys'lShwrs 10
18May86-7Hol 1 1/16 (T):47 1:111 1:414fm 64 114 2½ 2½ 96 99 CstAL3 (F)Hymn H 86-03 AnEmpress,TopCorsage,Mircuious 10
18May86—Grade III; Bumped start; steadied midstretch
30Apr86-8Hol 1 1/16 (T):473 1:121 1:423fm 9¼ 114 11 11 4¾ 53 CstnonAL1 (F)Senorita 88-09 Nature'sWay,AnEmpress,Mirculous 7
9Apr86-8SA 1⅛ (T):464 1:112 1:474fm 11 114 31½ 41½ 41¾ 42½ CstnnAL5 (F)[R]Prvdnca 85-17 Mirculous,TopCorsge,Roberto'sKey 8
9Apr86—Checked 3/16
21Mar86-5SA a6½f (T):213 :44 1:16 fm 26 114 53½ 95¼ 75¼ 54½ CstAL8 (F)[R]Swt Diane 74-21 Nature'sWy,TopCorsge,SilentArrivl 9
7Mar86-6SA 1 :452 1:093 1:361ft 9-5 119 56½ 613 720 721¼ CstnonAL7 (F)Aw31000 66-14 LovrsNtv,WondrfulFrnd,ArctcMoon 7
7Mar86—Fanned wide 7/8
19Feb86-8SA 1 1/16 :473 1:13 1:444sy 3 115 11 1hd 12½ 2hd CstnAL2 (F)[R]Sta Ysbl 77-24 TrimColony,FshionBook,TopCorsge 5
8Jan86-8SA 1 :464 1:112 1:373ft 17 114 11 11½ 11½ 21½ CstAL7 (F)[R]La Cntnla 78-16 ShotgnWddng,FshonBok,SlntArrvl 7
28Dec85-4SA 1 :47 1:121 1:373ft 11 117 1½ 11 13 12 Castanon A L1 (F)Mdn 80-14 FshionBook,Beulhlnd,LeftHerMrk 10
24Nov85-4Hol 1 :45 1:102 1:362ft 7¾ 118 1hd 65 912 916½ Castanon AL10 (F)Mdn 64-08 PrivteSorrow,BrTime,LeftHerMrk 10
24Nov85—Steadied 1/4
Jan 5 SA 5f sy :592 h Dec 30 SA 5f ft 1:003 h Dec 24 SA 1 ft 1:40 h Dec 19 Hol 7f ft 1:294 h

338. If today's race is a Jan. 11 route at 1 1/16M on dirt for $16,000 claiming horses 4up, which is *Slugfest's* most representative pace line?

A. Jan. 3 **(25)**
B. Nov. 16
C. Nov. 3
D. Sept. 13

Slugfest — Ch. g. 6, by Dimaggio—Good Personality, by Personality
STEVENS G L — 116 — Br.—Valpredo D (Cal) — 1987 1 0 0 0
Own.—Runion L T — Tr.—Lewis Craig A — $16,000 — 1986 8 1 3 2 $28,565
Lifetime 34 4 7 2 $88,445 — Turf 3 0 0 0

3Jan87-1SA 6f :214 :444 1:111ft 5 116 52¾ 64¾ 76¼ 65½ Pedroza M A8 [S] 20000 76-16 KidShelleen,JustTheFcts,Dd'sQust 10
3Jan87—Lugged out backstretch; wide 3/8 turn
16Nov86-1Hol 1 :443 1:103 1:372ft 3½ 116 1hd 11 2hd 21 Solis A5 25000 75-18 Billy's Special, Slugfest, Paskanell 7
16Nov86—Lugged out stretch
3Nov86-9SA 1 1/16 :462 1:11 1:43 ft 5¾ 117 33 22½ 21½ 31¼ Pincay L Jr3 25000 85-14 Bemidgi, Restage, Slugfest 9
3Nov86—Lugged out
18Oct86-5SA 6f :214 :444 1:11 ft 5½ 118 53½ 68½ 89½ 46½ Pincay L Jr2 25000 76-20 Grenoble, Bizeboy, Calabonga 9
20Sep86-9Pom 6½f :214 :45 1:163ft *7-5 119 63¾ 65¼ 3nk 21¼ Solis A5 25000 96-09 Yukon's Star, Slugfest, Calabonga 8
20Sep86—Bumped at start
13Sep86-8Pom 6½f :221 :453 1:162ft 7¾ 114 1hd 11 11 11¾ Solis A1 22500 98-10 Slugfst,Mummy'sPlsur,BoldTopsidr 9
1Sep86-1Dmr 6f :22 :45 1:092ft 4½ 116 42½ 32½ 22½ 22 Pedroza M A7 20000 89-13 NorthernDiscovery,Slugfest,FllFlyr 8
13Aug86-9Dmr 1 1/16 :451 1:102 1:431ft 12 116 46½ 44 34½ 74¼ Pedroza M A5 20000 80-15 Revolutionary, Tom, Our Nordic 11
13Aug86—Bumped start
26Jly86-1Dmr 6½f :221 :453 1:17 ft 9 116 21 21½ 22½ 32½ Pedroza M A9 20000 84-13 Fall Flyer, Vinegarone, Slugfest 9
21Sep85-8Pom 6½f :22 :453 1:171ft 4 116 53¼ 45 42½ 1nk Pedroza M A7 25000 — — Slugfest, Reinbow's Cup,FiveNorth 8
Dec 19 Hol 5f ft 1:03 h Dec 1 Hol 5f ft 1:013 h

For items 339 through 345, use the conditions provided to select the most representative pace line for each horse presented.

Today is Jan. 11. The race is 1¹⁄₁₆M for $50,000-45,000 claimers 4up. Select the most appropriate pace line for rating each horse.

339.

A. Dec. 17 **(25)**
B. Dec. 4
C. Oct. 23
D. July 10

Lotus Delight Ch. m. 6, by Mongo—Dot In Spot, by Alternative
Br.—Schosberg Jane M (NY) 1986 13 4 1 2 $64,790
STEVENS G L 121 Tr.—Mitchell Mike $50,000 1985 14 1 2 3 $49,574
Own.—Lane G E Lifetime 52 9 7 7 $222,792 Turf 21 4 2 4 $89,908

17Dec86-9Hol 1 Ⓣ:471 1:112 1:363fm *8-5 119 52½ 41¾ 41 1nk Stevens G L2 Ⓕ 50000 84-13 Lotus Delight,Volanda,BroadStreet 9

4Dec86-9Hol 1 :452 1:102 1:364ft 3½ 116 32½ 32 1½ 1¾ ValenzuelPA2 Ⓕ 50000 79-25 LotusDelight,Beaulahland,LdyShmn 7

19Nov86-3Hol 1 :454 1:104 1:371ft 3¼ 116 2½ 53¼ 58½ 614½ ValenzuelPA2 Ⓕ 62500 62-21 StrightStory,Volnd,AffctionAffrmd 6

19Nov86—Steadied 1/2

23Oct86-3SA 1 :46 1:11 1:37 ft 11 117 11½ 12 2½ 24 ValenzuelPA2 Ⓕ 70000 79-20 Stmwr,LotusDlight,AffctionAffrmd 6

23Oct86—Broke slowly

14Sep86-2Bel 7f Ⓣ:23 :46 1:231fm 3 113 53½ 54½ 41¾ 1¾ Migliore R7 Ⓕ 70000 88-13 LotusDlght,MoodyMondy,DoublScy 8

1Sep86-1Bel 1¹⁄₁₆ Ⓣ:463 1:114 1:421fm 2½e 113 1½ 1hd 31½ 37¼ Migliore R1 Ⓕ 70000 83-18 MusicOfLov,DoublSucy,LotusDlght 8

20Aug86-5Sar 1 Ⓣ:471 1:131 1:37 fm 7½ 1085 38 42½ 43½ 51 Paneto W R3 Ⓕ 70000 90-11 SrhSils,DoubleSucy,WyetteCoghlin 8

20Aug86—Steadied

8Aug86-4Sar 1⅛ :47 1:12 1:511m 5½ 119 2½ 42½ 714 722¼ Migliore R7 Ⓕ 50000 57-17 Mingledle,BllOfWstviw,MissFlming 7

23Jly86-8Bel 1¼ Ⓣ:49 1:372 2:014fm 13 115 21 76½ 65¾ 66¾ SntosJA8 ⒻⓈMt Vrnn 78-17 WendyWlker,LkeCecb,SmokthQun 10

10Jly86-5Bel 1¹⁄₁₆ Ⓣ:474 1:121 1:433fm *6-5 1105 31½ 32 32 31 Paneto W R5 Ⓕ 70000 77-14 KntuckyQnII,I'mABllRsr,LotsDlght 8

Jan 7 SA 4f sy :521 h (d) Dec 29 SA 3f ft :364 h Nov 30 Hol 5f ft 1:004 h Nov 17 Hol 4f ft :48 h

340.

A. Oct. 26
B. Aug. 31
C. Mar. 13
D. Feb. 16

Jell Ch. m. 6, by Gummo—Interact, by Verbatim
Br.—Elmendorf Farm (Cal) 1986 6 1 1 1 $31,900
COX D W 1115 Tr.—Borick Robert $50,000 1985 12 2 1 4 $48,350
Own.—Four Four Forty Farms Lifetime 40 5 6 8 $136,825 Turf 5 0 0 1 $4,000

26Oct86-5SA 1¹⁄₁₆ :463 1:111 1:433ft 28 1115 911 87¾ 67½ 66 Black C A9 ⒻAw30000 77-16 Fairly Old, Python, Petillante 9

26Oct86—Wide into stretch

31Aug86-7Dmr 6½f :222 :453 1:162ft 29 118 87¾ 87¼ 76¾ 76½ HernndezR4 ⒻAw24000 83-12 Miss O. B.E.,BalconyPass,AllInTune 8

31Aug86—Broke slowly; wide into stretch

13Mar86-5SA 1 :474 1:134 1:402sy *8-5 1145 55½ 53 33 21¼ Black C A2 Ⓕ 62500 65-30 Emacia, Jell, Blade Of Luck 9

6Mar86-7SA 1 :462 1:11 1:363ft 10 1105 74¼ 62½ 54 32 Black C A3 ⒻAw35000 83-15 Rea, Affection Affirmed, Jell 7

6Mar86—Altered path 1/8

16Feb86-3SA 1 :471 1:124 1:382gd *2¼ 1085 64½ 31 11 12¾ Black C A5 Ⓕ 55000 76-14 Jell, Emacia, Count On Lyn 6

17Jan86-9SA 1 :454 1:103 1:362ft 10 1095 810 65½ 85¼ 57¾ Alvarez A8 Ⓕ 57500 78-15 Stemware,PetBird,KarandebsBigKt 8

17Jan86—Placed fourth through disqualification; Hit rail,steadied

28Dec85-1SA 1¹⁄₁₆ :474 1:121 1:433ft 11 1085 53 42¼ 31½ 1¾ Alvarez A2 Ⓕ 45000 83-14 Jell, Prospector's Queen, Pet Bird 9

28Dec85—Steadied on turn

6Nov85-9SA 1 :461 1:111 1:372ft 14 115 76¾ 54½ 66 54¼ Meza R Q1 Ⓕ 50000 77-17 Straight Story,Tamure,RedHillGirl 10

11Oct85-9SA 1 :454 1:11 1:372ft 9½ 116 810 76¾ 64¼ 45 DelhoussyeE4 Ⓕ 50000 76-17 SoloTmbl,StrghtStory,AwsomPrms 9

9Aug85-9Dmr 1¹⁄₁₆ :462 1:111 1:433ft 7 116 912 65½ 25 32½ DelhoussyeE6 Ⓕ 50000 79-15 Solo Tumble, B. Elite, Jell 9

Jan 3 SA 1 ft 1:434 h Dec 27 SA 7f ft 1:302 h Dec 21 SA 6f ft 1:161 h Dec 15 SA 5f ft 1:03 h

341.

A. Dec. 30
B. Dec. 17
C. Nov. 16
D. Aug. 24

***Skimbleshanks** — Ch. m. 6, by Bold Lad—Thimblerigger, by Sharpen Up
BAZE G — **114** — Br.—Moyns Park Stud (Eng) — Tr.—Roberts Craig — $45,000
Own.—Roberts Connie

1986	11	1 0 1		$7,918
1985	9	1 3 0		$8,619
Lifetime	42	4 7 4	$45,117	
Turf	14	1 3 2		$20,690

30Dec86-5SA 1⅛Ⓣ:47 1:112 1:484fm 32 115 62¾ 52 66 612¾ Baze G8 Ⓕ 70000 70-17 Benzina, Mangez Les, Kinda Beau 10
17Dec86-9Hol 1 Ⓣ:471 1:112 1:363fm 23 116 65 73¾ 63 51¾ Meza R Q9 Ⓕ 50000 82-13 Lotus Delight,Volanda,BroadStreet 9
17Dec86—Wide 7 1/2, stretch
16Nov86-4BM 1 1/16Ⓣ:491 1:14 1:464fm 39 114 66½ 55 42 41½ Johnson B G3 Ⓕ 50000 67-31 One Drum, Girl In Blue, Real Eager 7
11Oct86-8StP 6f :223 :454 1:112ft 6½e 117 56¾ 46½ 34 47¾ MalgriniTM7 ⒻAw7875 82-19 RegalCage,LittlePrincess,IvoryMist 7
24Aug86-7NP 1 1/16 :463 1:114 1:442ft 59 116 85½ 75¾ 104¾ 1011¼ MlrnTM2 ⒻEdmntn H 80-16 BrghtBouqut,ExpoPrncss,PlnumB 11
3Aug86-9NP 1 :47 1:121 1:384ft 34 117 22 31½ 52¼ 713¾ MlrnTM1 ⒻMdmsle H 71-22 PlenumB,BrightBouqut,HstyMort 10
23Jly86-8AsD 1 :48 1:131 1:392ft 4¾ 115 24 21½ 22 45½ Shaw K4 ⒻAw7820 76-14 ShrpDuchss,ElctrcFvr,TouchyTrsur 7
11Jly86-6AsD a7f :26 :503 1:28 m 2¼e 114 11½ 1nk 12½ 15 Shaw K7 ⒻAw6420 81-26 Skmblshnks,TouchyTrsur,SolrAwrd 7
1Jly86-10AsD 1 :462 1:102 1:38 ft 9¾ 115 511 411 411 58¼ HdrcsK6 ⒻCanadaDyH 81-18 OnMorLdy,ShrpDuchss,ElctricFvr 12
5Jun86-8NP 6f :223 :46 1:12 ft 6¾ 116 43½ 32¾ 31¾ 65½ Niblett G3 ⒻAw8475 83-19 BrghtBoqt,TmforWords,BckbordSx 7
Dec 26 SA 4f ft :481 h Dec 3 GG 6f ft 1:154 h Nov 22 GG 3f ft :363 h Nov 11 BM 5f ft 1:00 h

342.

A. Dec. 14
B. Dec. 5
C. Sept. 26
D. Aug. 14

Keep Dating * — Ch. m. 5, by Try Sheep—Keep It Low, by Mandate
PINCAY L JR — **116** — Br.—Middle Ranch (Cal) — Tr.—Velasquez Danny — $50,000
Own.—Seven Star Stable

1986	21	2 2 4		$69,370
1985	15	1 2 1		$20,225
Lifetime	42	3 4 6	$86,760	
Turf	12	0 2 2		$22,725

14Dec86-1Hol 1 :461 1:112 1:372ft 9 116 66 69 78 79½ Olivares F5 ⒻAw25000 66-18 Mrs.V.,Melva'sPride,Veronic'sQuest 7
14Dec86—Wide final 3/8
5Dec86-8Hol 1⅛ :472 1:121 1:503ft 4½ 116 54 42 35 37¼ Olivares F3 ⒻAw25000 77-17 CseMoney,Veronic'sQuest,KpDting 6
28Nov86-9Hol 1 1/16Ⓣ:462 1:104 1:411fm 8½ 116 47½ 43½ 78½ 79 DelhoussyeE9 Ⓕ 80000 79-11 AffectionAffirmed,Benzin,KindBu 10
28Nov86—Lugged in
17Oct86-7SA 1 1/16 :463 1:112 1:434ft 7½ 116 713 67½ 55½ 44¼ Olivares F5 ⒻAw27000 78-21 Annpurn,LCodorniz,Veronic'sQuest 8
17Oct86—Wide backstretch
26Sep86-11Pom 1 1/16 :473 1:134 1:464sl 6 114 711 75¾ 32 33¼ OlivaresF5 ⒻLs Mds H 74-29 OurSweetShm,LeL'Argent,KpDting 7
3Sep86-5Dmr 1 1/16Ⓣ:474 1:123 1:443fm 3½ 117 31½ 51¾ 33½ 43½ Ortega LE5 ⒻAw23000 79-12 NatalieKnows,Corbella,Ohslewsnn 11
14Aug86-7Dmr 1 1/16 :454 1:104 1:432ft 7 118 99¼ 74¾ 54 41¼ Ortega LE9 ⒻAw20000 82-17 MargretBooth,Plumpetr,DonATop 10
14Aug86—Wide 3/8 turn, into stretch
26Jly86-5Dmr 1 1/16Ⓣ:474 1:12 1:423fm 19 112 87 84¾ 55 66¼ OrtegLE1 ⒻⓇOsnts H 87-05 Loucoum,Felliniana,SeasonlPickup 8
26Jly86—Run in divisions
25Jun86-9Hol 1 1/16Ⓣ:462 1:103 1:412fm 7½ 116 78½ 52¼ 2hd 32¼ Olivares F1 Ⓕ 80000 95-03 Jigalores, Bullion, Keep Dating 7
11Jun86-7Hol 1 1/16Ⓣ:47 1:111 1:413fm 14 116 105½ 96¼ 74¼ 52¾ Olivares F2 ⒻAw21000 93-04 Rekindling,LovedFromAfr,Grmticl 10
11Jun86—Wide into stretch
Jan 6 SA tr.t 5f gd 1:024 h Dec 29 SA 5f ft 1:02 h Dec 24 SA 4f ft :474 h Nov 23 Hol 6f ft 1:142 h

343.

A. Dec. 30
B. Dec. 17
C. Dec. 4
D. July 27

Broad Street * — Dk. b. or br. m. 5, by Austin Mittler—Clemency, by George Lewis

SIBILLE R — 116 — Br.—Magerman A P (Cal) — 1986 17 5 1 3 [illegible] $77,675

Tr.—Harper David B — $50,000 — 1985 9 3 0 1 $32,775

Own.—Tuscany Farms (Lessee) — Lifetime 34 10 1 5 $126,862 — Turf 3 0 0 1 $3,000

30Dec86-9SA 1 1/16 :47^1 1:12^1 1:44^{4}ft 6¼ 116 2^{hd} 12½ 13½ 11¼ Sibille R^7 Ⓕ 40000 77-18 Broad Street, Soonermoon,Gayliole 8

17Dec86-9Hol 1 Ⓣ:47^{1}1:11^{2}1:36^{3}fm 29 116 3½ 3^{nk} 2^{hd} 31½ Sibille R^1 Ⓕ 50000 82-13 Lotus Delight,Volanda,BroadStreet 9

4Dec86-9Hol 1 :45^2 1:10^2 1:36^{4}ft 14 116 6^5 67½ 67½ 611½ Sibille R^3 Ⓕ 50000 67-25 LotusDelight,Beaulahland,LdyShmn 7

6Nov86-9Hol 1 :45^3 1:10^1 1:36^{1}ft 14 116 52¾ 35½ 36½ 410¼ Sibille R^3 Ⓕ 50000 72-17 Straight Story, Volanda, Fleet Rain 8

26Oct86-5SA 1 1/16 :46^3 1:11^1 1:43^{3}ft 26 116 7^6 99¾ 9^{18} — Hawley S^6 ⒻAw30000 — — Fairly Old, Python, Petillante 9

26Oct86—Eased; Wide

5Sep86-9Dmr 1 :46 1:11^2 1:36^{4}ft *2½ 118 7^{11} 76¼ 6^9 6^{14} Stevens G L^1 Ⓕ c40000 70-16 Emacia,BrunedeMai,Reput:ionMiss 7

5Sep86—Reared at start

24Aug86-3Dmr 1 :45^2 1:10^3 1:36^{2}ft 7½ 116 3½ 3^{nk} 53¼ 68¼ Kaenel J L^1 ⒻAw25000 78-12 LaDivertida,GoodZar,Polly'LFemme 6

27Jly86-1Dmr 1 :45^4 1:10^4 1:36^{3}ft *6-5 113 2^{hd} 1½ 1^{hd} 12½ Stevens G L^2 Ⓕ 45000 85-10 BroadStreet,Plumpetra,Lu:kySilver 7

19Jun86-9Hol 1 :45^4 1:11 1:36^{1}ft *2¾ 116 3½ 1^1 2½ 21¼ Stevens G L^5 Ⓕ 50000 81-14 AllInTune,BrodStreet,BmsGoldnEgl 7

30May86-7Hol 1 :45^4 1:11^1 1:37^{3}ft 8 114 4^2 51¾ 65½ 6^7 Stevens G L^6 Ⓕ 57500 68-24 Straight Story, Bullion, Fleet Rain 11

30May86—Checked 3/16

Jan 9 SA 3f sl :38^1 h Dec 26 SA 4f ft :50^1 h Dec 11 SA 3f ft :35^3 h Dec 2 SA 4f ft :48^1 h

344.

A. Dec. 11
B. Nov. 26
C. Nov. 7
D. Oct. 24

Eastern Glamour — Dk. b. or br. f. 4, by Summer Time Guy—July Song, by T V Lark

MEZA R Q — 113 — Br.—Hawn W R (Cal) — 1986 10 3 2 1 $34,750

Tr.—Palma Hector O — $45,000 — 1985 1 M 0 0 $475

Own.—Longo I S — Lifetime 11 3 2 1 $35,225

11Dec86-1Hol 1 :46^1 1:12 1:37^{4}ft *3-2 118 7^4 21½ 2^2 21¼ Stevens G L^4 Ⓕ 32000 73-21 Dncer'sRegrds,EsternGlmour,Vlvtn 8

11Dec86—Wide 3/8 turn

26Nov86-6Hol 1 :46 1:11^1 1:37^{2}ft *2½ 118 4^{nk} 31½ 2^2 21¼ ShoemakerW^4 Ⓕ 32000 75-20 RochellsGirl,EsternGlmour,Velvetn 9

7Nov86-9Hol 1 :45^1 1:09^4 1:35^{2}ft 3¾ 116 51½ 6^4 67½ 611½ ValenzuelPA^6 Ⓕ 50000 74-18 Leading Lass, Beaulahland, Mrs. V. 7

7Nov86—Wide into stretch

24Oct86-5SA 1 1/16 :47 1:12 1:44^{2}ft *2½ 117 42½ 3½ 2½ 3^{nk} ValenzuelPA^8 Ⓕ 40000 79-20 Gayliole,Melv'sPride,EsternGlmour 9

24Oct86—Lugged out late

9Oct86-1SA 1 :46^2 1:11^4 1:38^{2}ft 10 115 5^3 21½ 21½ 1^2 McCarron CJ^6 Ⓕ 35000 76-21 EstrnGlmor,Mlv'sPrd,RbrtsRglGrl 10

19Sep86-11Pom 1 1/16 :46^1 1:10^4 1:43^{2}ft 24 115 66½ 8^{16} 8^{18} 825¼ CstAL^8 Ⓕ[S]C T BAMn 69-09 ProperMry,Symboliclly,SilentArrivl 8

4Sep86-9Dmr 1 :45^2 1:11^3 1:37 ft 4¾ 115 76¼ 1^{hd} 12½ 12½ McCrronCJ^{10} Ⓕ 20000 83-14 EstrnGlmour,ArForcBby,BrooksPl 10

20Aug86-2Dmr 6f :22 :45^2 1:10^{3}ft 3½ 118 105½ 9^8 88½ 65½ Hernandez R^5 Ⓕ 25000 79-11 TBImprssv,Sh'sSBld,DstntCmmnd 11

1Aug86-7Dmr 6f :21^3 :44^2 1:09^{2}ft 20 116 6^6 6^7 67¾ 67¼ ValenzuelPA^8 Ⓕ 50000 84-13 Witchery,DremPolicy,DuchssZnth 10

17Jly86-5Hol 6f :22^2 :46^3 1:11^{4}ft 8-5 115 65¾ 3^3 22½ 11¼ VlnzulPA^3 Ⓕ[S]M32000 85-17 EstrnGlmr,FlyMTThMn,DymDrlng 9

17Jly86—Bumped at start

Jan 8 SA 5f m 1:01^1 h Jan 1 SA 5f ft 1:01^1 h Dec 26 SA 5f ft :59^4 h Dec 19 Hol 5f ft 1:01^3 h

345.

A. Dec. 28
B. Dec. 4
C. Nov. 7
D. July 26

Beaulahland — B. f. 4, by Drum Fire—Phil's Chapeau, by Philately

DELAHOUSSAYE E — 115 — Br.—CulpepperTb&NrthwstFms (Wash) — 1986 12 2 4 1 $40,365

Tr.—Dollase Wallace — $50,000 — 1985 9 M 2 5 $20,850

Own.—Dollase-Lucian-McNamee — Lifetime 21 2 6 6 $61,215 — Turf 2 0 0 1 $4,125

28Dec86-2SA 6f :22 :45^2 1:11 ft 4 109^5 5^3 65¾ 6^7 64¾ Patton D B^2 Ⓕ 50000 78-14 Cresta Lady, My Tara, TraumaTime 7

28Dec86—Bumped at 1/2

4Dec86-9Hol 1 :45^2 1:10^2 1:36^{4}ft *2 108^5 21½ 21½ 3^1 2¾ Patton D B^7 Ⓕ 50000 78-25 LotusDelight,Beaulahland,LdyShmn 7

7Nov86-9Hol 1 :45^1 1:09^4 1:35^{2}ft 6¼ 108^5 6^3 5^3 3^2 2^2 Patton D B^1 Ⓕ 45000 84-18 Leading Lass, Beaulahland, Mrs. V. 7

9Oct86-1SA 1 :46^2 1:11^4 1:38^{2}ft *2¾ 118 96¾ 108¾ 10^{15} 9^{17} McHargueDG^8 Ⓕ 40000 59-21 EstrnGlmor,Mlv'sPrd,RbrtsRglGrl 10

9Oct86—Stumbled start

8Sep86-5Dmr 1 Ⓣ:47 1:1141:362fm *2½ 118 75½ 76 52½ 54¾ McHargueDG8 Ⓕ 62500 85-10 Sweetest,DrmticElgnc,DwnOfHop 10

22Aug86-7Dmr 1 Ⓣ:4631:1111:361fm 6¾ 116 2½ 1hd 1hd 32 McHargueDG8 Ⓕ 62500 89-09 WineTaster,Tantalized,Beaulahland 8

26Jly86-7Dmr 1 :452 1:11 1:371ft 5¾ 116 22 1½ 11½ 1½ McHrgDG1 ⒻAw20000 82-13 Beulhlnd,Bggr'sWllt,RoylD-by'sLov 8

9Jly86-3Hol 6f :223 :462 1:112ft 12 116 63 42½ 42 2nk McHargueDG8 Ⓕ 40000 87-18 CoffeeRoll,Beaulahlnd,MriSupreme 8

23Mar86-10TuP 1 :471 1:114 1:372ft 3-2 118 53½ 43 1hd 13½ StMrtinE6 ⒻLndlce H 82-18 Beaulahland,FrnniePooper,ReilDrin 7

1Mar86-4SA 1 1/16 :454 1:104 1:443ft 6 117 47 44½ 43 67 Stevens G L4 ⒻMdn 71-16 PuzzleBook,MybAKiss,WddingDncr 9

Jan 9 SA 3f sl :371 h   Dec 21 Hol 5f ft 1:03 h   Dec 14 Hol 4f ft :491 h   ●Dec 1 Hol 4f ft :474 h

For items 346 through 349, using whatever methods you prefer, find the horse with the highest pace rating. Use the most recent race. Ignore variants. Rate the race as a whole, not a race segment or combination of segments.

346.

A. (26)

Double Song   Ch. c. 2, by Messenger of Song—Mazda's Double, by Nodouble

PEDROZA M A 114   Br.—Mamakos J L (Cal)   1986 6 1 1 1 $15,600

Own.—Berlin & Loewy   Tr.—Gerber Greg D $40,000

Lifetime 6 1 1 1 $15,600

20Nov86-3Hol 6f :22 :454 1:121ft *8-5 115 13 12½ 11 34 Pedroza M A1 32000 78-16 TheQuipper,Rakaposhi,DoubleSong 8

25Oct86-8SA 1 :444 1:101 1:383ft 19 114 46 37 69½ 711½ PdrozMA2 [S]B J Rddr 63-17 ‡PsDGurr,FlyngLtnnt,BrodwyPont 11

12Oct86-7SA 6f :214 :444 1:111ft 53 116 43 44¼ 35 54¼ Pedroza MA6 Aw25000 78-21 SpecilTrick,FleetingJt,StylishWinnr 9

12Oct86—Bumped start

1Oct86-3SA 7f :22 :444 1:234ft 15 115 21 2hd 44 46¾ Kaenel J L4 Aw25000 74-18 GoldOnGren,SpcilTrick,SuprmStnd 6

1Oct86—Rough start

18Sep86-11Pom 6½f :213 :45 1:172ft 2 115 32½ 21½ 21 22¾ Kaenel JL4 Beau Brml 90-12 CctusClipper,DoublSong,HighRgrds 6

18Sep86—Bumped start

5Sep86-2Dmr 6f :22 :454 1:11 ft *1 118 4nk 14 17 19 ValenzuelPA8 Mc32000 83-16 DoubleSong,UnivrslMn,LuckyLoky 12

Oct 23 SA 4f ft :47 hg   Sep 29 SA 3f ft :37 h

B.

Greenspin   Ch. c. 2, by Shecky Greene—Spindrift, by Al Hattab

STEVENS G L 117   Br.—Kidder C L (Ky)   1986 4 1 1 0 $9,050

Own.—Malorrus F   Tr.—Sadler John W $40,000

Lifetime 4 1 1 0 $9,050

5Nov86-4Hol 6f :224 :462 1:123ft *4-5 118 2hd 1hd 12½ 14 Patterson A8 Mc32000 80-17 Greenspin,OurDpperDn,EsternSpirit 9

5Nov86—Bumped far turn

24Oct86-2SA 6f :22 :453 1:111ft 9¾ 118 31 2hd 21½ 2¾ Patterson A2 M40000 81-20 P.T.Hustlr,Grnspn,HotAndSmoggy 12

24Oct86—Crowded 1/2; lugged in, checked stretch

3Oct86-6SA 6f :214 :443 1:092ft 174 118 22½ 35½ 613 720 Patterson A12 Mdn 71-17 Cpot,WndwoodLn,BooBoo'sBckro 12

7Sep86-6Dmr 6f :221 :453 1:101ft 9¼ 117 1112 1120 1123 1119¾ Patterson A4 Mdn 67-13 Agn'sBolgr,Crbonro,WindwoodLn 11

Nov 21 Hol 5f ft 1:021 h   Nov 15 Hol 4f ft :494 h   Oct 20 SA 4f ft :48 h   Oct 11 SA 4f ft :494 h

C.

Beaucoup Jet   B. c. 2, by Tri Jet—Arcadia Kid, by Jeff's Uh Oh

CORDERO A JR 117   Br.—Bussman Mr–Mrs R F (Fla)   1986 5 1 1 0 $8,745

Own.—Turley D B   Tr.—Van Berg Jack C $40,000

Lifetime 5 1 1 0 $8,745

21Nov86-5Hol 6f :222 :451 1:093ft 19 117 42½ 46½ 59½ 510¾ Sibille R1 Aw23000 84-20 BrodwyPont,HostonBrgg,AdmBmb 6

4Oct86-8LaD 7f :23 :452 1:25 sy 39 121 87¼ 811 1021 1029¾ PttnrD13 Spt O Kings 53-29 Brevito,Perdition'sSon,JubileeTril 13

21Sep86-1LaD 7f :233 :47 1:254ft *1 118 11 12 16 18 Pettinger D4 Mdn 79-23 BeaucoupJet,Pyrophoric,OcalDove 11

10Sep86-1LaD 6f :223 :46 1:124ft *8-5 118 2½ 1½ 2½ 21 Trosclair A J9 Mdn 77-24 Sortble,BeucoupJet,SuperiorTribe 11

15Aug86-1LaD 6f :224 :47 1:131ft 2½ 118 3½ 3½ 32 44 Trosclair A J7 Mdn 72-21 SquirePercivl,JubileeTril,RodGrdr 12

Nov 16 SA 7f ft 1:272 h   Nov 4 SA 5f ft 1:001 h   Oct 29 SA 4f ft :472 h   Oct 23 SA 5f ft 1:004 h

D.

Glamorous Al   B. g. 2, by O Big Al—Glamorous Nora, by Glamor Kid

MEZA R Q 115   Br.—Ross A & Mildred (Cal)   1986 1 1 0 0 $6,050

Own.—Ross A & Mildred   Tr.—Jones Gary $35,000

Lifetime 1 1 0 0 $6,050

14Nov86-6Hol 6f :22 :461 1:131ft 11 118 1½ 1hd 1½ 1nk Baze G7 M32000 77-16 GlamorousAl,Nourished,Vlidictorin 8

Nov 26 Hol 4f ft :504 h   Nov 21 Hol 3f ft :361 h   Nov 7 Hol 6f ft 1:172 hg   Nov 2 SA 6f ft 1:154 h

347.

A.

```
Jerell's Guy                        Dk. b. or br. g. 5, by Search for Gold—Mail Box, by Francis S
  TORO F                            Br.—Frankel J (Cal)                    1987  8  5  0  1     $23,728
                          119       Tr.—French Neil            $20,000     1986 20  6  3  6     $20,536
Own.—Walker Bonnie J              Lifetime   29 11  3  7   $44,256         Turf  6  3  0  1     $16,160
24Apr87-5Hol  1 1/16:463 1:113 1:441ft  8¼ 119  76½ 74½ 74¾ 63½  Stevens G L3  40000 84-12 Genuine John, Le Cid, Tarver 7
 4Apr87-9TuP  1  :452 1:094 1:344ft  6¼ 120  34½ 43 45 37  Licata F2  Aw9000 88-18 FoolTheExperts,MinTop,Jerll'sGuy 6
22Mar87-9TuP  1  (T):4711:1141:37 fm  3 112  24 2½ 1hd 1¾  Licata F2  Aw9000 97-03 Jerell'sGuy,StndingGood,Unbetble 10
15Mar87-10TuP 1  (T):4641:1021:361fm  6½ 114  811 89¼ 67½ 55¾  Licata F7  Gvnrs H 95 — ChuckNLuck,Shanaar,SonoitaBlue 12
18Feb87-8TuP  1  (T):4731:12 1:372fm  *2¼ 114  52¼ 42 42½ 1½  Dahl S M2  c25000 95-05 Jerell's Guy,SenatorMcGuire,Kayus 8
 6Feb87-10TuP 7f (T):224 :4621:232fm  *3¾ 114  59 56 54 1hd  Dahl S M5  Aw8000 102 — Jerell's Guy, Native Fella,Calixtus 10
18Jan87-8TuP  6½f:214 :442 1:16 ft  3½ 118  78¼ 74¼ 31½ 1no  Noda R H7  18000 91-20 Jerell's Guy, Chork, Big Attraction 8
10Jan87-7TuP  1  :453 1:102 1:362ft  3½ 115  75½ 51½ 22 1½  Noda R H9  16000 87-14 Jerell's Guy, Hatamoto, Chork 9
13Dec86-8TuP  6f :214 :444 1:102ft  2 115  74¾ 53 45½ 33½  Noda R H3  16000 80-23 Radial, Makero, Jerell's Guy 7
30Nov86-8TuP  6½f:223 :443 1:151ft  7¼ 115  42 41¾ 21 2hd  Noda R H8  16000 95-15 ArtisticVntur,Jrll'sGuy,DoublDficit 8
    Apr 22 Hol 3f ft :37 h      Apr 12 TuP 5f ft 1:01 h      Mar 30 TuP 4f ft :523 h      Mar 14 TuP 3f ft :394 h
```

B.

```
Chagrining                          Ch. g. 5, by Blushing Groom—Takebackyourmink, by Raise a Native
  MEZA R Q                          Br.—Mandell R K (Ky)                   1987  6  1  3  0     $21,725
                          116       Tr.—Cleveland Gene         $20,000     1986  6  0  0  2      $3,600
Own.—Malmuth-Malmuth-Mandell      Lifetime   18  2  3  2   $29,205         Turf  1  0  0  0
12Apr87-9SA   1 1/16:471 1:114 1:44 ft  8 115  2hd 1hd 1½ 2hd  Meza R Q 3  20000 81-18 Trento, Chagrining, Item Two 12
 1Apr87-9SA   1 1/16:462 1:114 1:45 ft  4¼ 115  42½ 21 21 12  Meza R Q 5  16000 76-23 Chagrining,Camilla'sBoy,Navegante 7
17Mar87-2SA   1 1/16:463 1:112 1:434ft  30 116  64 3nk 1hd 22¾  Meza R Q 8  16000 79-16 Trento, Chagrining,Bigbadandmean 8
 4Mar87-9SA   1 1/16:463 1:112 1:441ft  13 116  64¾ 64¼ 68½ 511¼  Valenzuela P A 5  16000 69-16 Idol, Oak Tree II, Cojak Man 8
      4Mar87—Bumped start
21Jan87-1SA   6½f:221 :453 1:18 ft  6 116  96¾ 74½ 84½ 54½  Meza R Q 8  12500 75-19 Melchip,M.J.'sDelight,NeutrlPlyer 11
      21Jan87—Awarded fourth purse money; Stumbled at start, wide into stretch
 9Jan87-9SA   6f :214 :453 1:124sl  8 116  88¾ 77¼ 52½ 21  Meza R Q 1  12500 73-26 West Boy II, Chagrining, Melchip 11
      9Jan87—Broke slowly
30Dec86-3SA   6f :212 :442 1:112ft  15 116  48 47 47 3hd  Meza R Q 6  12500 81-18 LuckyMasadado,VlDeRoi,Chgrining 7
      30Dec86—Broke slowly
 6Dec86-2Hol  6f :221 :46 1:114gd  27 117  32½ 31½ 32 32¾  Meza R Q 8  10000 81-16 John's Jove, Cordon, Chagrining 8
      6Dec86—Wide backstretch; lugged in stretch
19Nov86-6Hol  7f :224 :46 1:241ft  6 116  64½ 65 68 713  Meza R Q 3  10000 70-21 Comets Flare,Gulfstreamer,Pulsate 9
      19Nov86—Broke slowly
 2Nov86-1SA   6½f:213 :442 1:16 ft  23 1115  34 34¾ 68 711¾  Valenzuela F Z 8  16000 78-10 Rinbow'sCup,WstBoyII,LordPncho 9
    Apr 29 SA 4f ft :494 h      Apr 23 SA 4f ft :492 h      Mar 26 SA 4f ft :493 h      Mar 14 SA 3f ft :362 h
```

C.

```
Bedouin *                           Ro. g. 6, by Al Hattab—Lady in Red, by Prince John
/ VALENZUELA P A                    Br.—Elmendorf Farm (Ky)                1987  7  2  1  1     $27,700
                          116       Tr.—Canani Julio C         $20,000     1986 26  6  1  0     $88,075
Own.—Gleason L                    Lifetime   58 11  5  2  $262,244         Turf 12  1  1  0     $29,915
19Apr87-7SA   1 1/16:46 1:104 1:432ft  3½ 117  815 78 45 52  Pincay L Jr 8  32000 82-17 Foreign Legion, Cold,SwordPrince 10
29Mar87-9SA   1 1/16:462 1:12 1:44 ft  3¼ 117  78½ 41¾ 2hd 21  Pincay L Jr 6  32000 80-18 ValiantGeorge,Bedouin,NordicLight 9
      29Mar87—Wide final 3/8
14Mar87-9SA   1 1/16:47 1:121 1:44 ft  4½ 117  106¾ 62¾ 32½ 11¼  Pincay L Jr 3  20000 81-16 Bedouin, Video Sid, Night Swope 11
      14Mar87—Bumped break; wide into stretch
 7Mar87-9GG   1 1/16:462 1:11 1:431ft  *2¾ 116  89¾ 64 1½ 1nk  Diaz A L 5  16000 87-16 Bedouin, Fulger, Ever Brilliant 9
24Jan87-9SA   1 1/16:471 1:113 1:434ft  4½ 116  1010 813 812 511  Shoemaker W6  c25000 71-18 Dcontrol,ForgtThRng,DckAndHgh 12
11Jan87-9SA   1 1/16:473 1:113 1:443ft  6½ 1115  89½ 67 44 3½  Patton D B5  25000 77-21 Impulsively, Pegus, Bedouin 9
      11Jan87—Broke slowly
 3Jan87-9SA   1 1/16:47 1:113 1:433ft  5½ 1115  68 67 66½ 56  Patton D B3  32000 77-16 NorthrnProvdr,Rnbw'sCp,FrgnLgn 10
      3Jan87—Broke slowly
17Dec86-3Hol  1 1/16:47 1:122 1:442ft  4¼ 1115  510 57½ 47 45½  Patton D B4  40000 81-22 LeCid,ForeignLegion,ValintGeorge 6
20Nov86-5Hol  1 1/8:464 1:114 1:512ft  8¾ 1115  65½ 56½ 1hd 2hd  Patton D B3  32000 80-16 Oak TreeII,Bedouin,ValiantGeorge 11
 3Nov86-9SA   1 1/16:462 1:11 1:43 ft  7½ 1115  713 78½ 57 54¾  Patton D B9  c25000 81-14 Bemidgi, Restage, Slugfest 9
      3Nov86—Bumped break
    Apr 13 SA 4f ft :462 h      Apr 7 SA 4f ft :484 h      Mar 25 SA 4f ft :473 h
```

D.

New Storm
SOLIS A **116**
Own.—Depietro-Jordan-Msnvchetal

B. g. 5, by Petrone—Sands Affair, by Tumble Wind
Br.—McCollum Pattrica (Cal) 1987 7 2 1 1 $24,675
Tr.—Jordan James $20,000 1986 16 2 1 7 $26,105
Lifetime 45 7 5 9 $78,493 Turf 3 0 0 0 $2,340

23Apr87-9Hol	1 1/16	:46^{2}	1:11^{2}	1:43 ft	*3¾	119	1 1½	2^{hd}	1½	1½	Pincay L Jr 3	c16000	94-09	New Storm, Navegante,Bruli'sAnte	8
15Apr87-3SA	1 1/16	:46^{4}	1:11^{4}	1:45^{1}ft	*1	118	2½	2½	3^{nk}	1no	Pincay L Jr 1	16000	75-21	NewStorm,Bruli'sAnte,Halo'sSword	5
15Apr87—Bumped at 3/16															
5Apr87-1SA	7f	:22^{1}	:44^{4}	1:24 ft	4	115	7^{4}½	7^{7}½	6^{4}¾	3^{1}¼	Stevens G L^{10} [S]	16000	79-16	Like Shantin, AirPirate,NewStorm	16
5Apr87—Bumped 1/8															
27Feb87-5SA	6f	:21^{3}	:44^{3}	1:09 ft	6¼	116	7^{6}¾	8^{8}	7^{9}	5^{9}	Stevens G L^{3} [S]	20000	84-16	Pialor, Melchip, Detector	11
18Feb87-9SA	1 1/16	:46^{2}	1:11^{2}	1:43^{2}ft	*2½	116	2^{hd}	3½	7^{7}	7^{12}½	DelahoussyeE^{9}	c16000	71-19	Navegante, Robersky, GreyMissile	11
18Feb87—Broke slowly															
13Feb87-4GG	1 1/16	:46^{2}	1:10^{2}	1:43^{3}gd	*9-5	118	3^{1}	4^{nk}	4^{2}	5^{6}	Doocy T T 1	Aw16000	79-23	IvnPhllps,Ptron'sKsmt,Ed'sExclusv	6
4Jan87-9SA	1⅛	:47^{3}	1:12^{2}	1:51^{4}sy	3	116	3^{nk}	2½	2^{4}	2^{4}	Stevens G L 2	20000	66-22	HurricneHec,NewStorm,ShuttleOne	7
13Dec86-9BM	1 1/16	:46^{2}	1:11^{2}	1:43^{1}ft	3	113	3^{2}	3^{1}½	2½	2^{1}½	Doocy T T 7	Aw17000	74-19	CllThGurd,NwStorm,It'sNotMyJob	8
13Dec86—Drifted in late															
29Nov86-7BM	1 1/16	:45^{4}	1:10^{1}	1:42 ft	6¾	113	3^{2}	3^{1}½	3^{1}½	3^{1}½	Doocy T T 2	Aw16000	81-17	Arbitrte,Petrone'sKismet,NwStorm	9
15Nov86-9BM	1 1/16	:46^{1}	1:11	1:44 ft	7½	113	8^{7}¾	5^{3}¾	2^{1}	3^{3}	Doocy T T 7	Aw17000	69-21	Planter, Midnight Ice, New Storm	12
15Nov86—Hopped in air															

Apr 22 SA 3f ft :39^{1} h   Apr 13 SA 4f ft :48^{3} hg   Apr 1 SA 5f ft 1:01^{3} h   Mar 25 SA 5f ft 1:01^{2} h

348.

A.

Blue Frosting
MAPLE S **118**
Own.—Deloux Farm

Dk. b. or br. f. 4, by Blue Eyed Davy—Djebel Dunit, by Djebel Al
Br.—Deloux E (Cal) 1987 1 0 0 0 $550
Tr.—Hirsch Arthur 1986 2 1 1 0 $10,625
Lifetime 3 1 1 0 $11,175

22Apr87-3Hol	6f	:22^{1}	:45^{4}	1:10^{3}ft	10	115	2^{hd}	2^{hd}	3^{2}	5^{8}	Sibille R^{3}	ⒻAw22000	82-18	SuchASplash,TraumaTime,BoldDyn	5
15Jun86-5GG	6f	:22^{2}	:45	1:10^{4}ft	*6-5	113	2^{hd}	1½	1½	1no	Lamance C^{5}	ⒻMdn	85-14	BlFrostng,ByAnyOthrNm,SoftlySd	12
1Jun86-4GG	6f	:22^{3}	:44^{2}	1:10^{1}ft	7½	113	3^{nk}	2^{hd}	1½	2½	Lamance C^{8}	ⒻMdn	87-11	TopFlsh,BlueFrosting,WhirlingToo	11

● Apr 17 GG 4f ft :46 h   Apr 9 SA 6f ft 1:14^{2} hg   Apr 3 SA 5f ft 1:01^{2} h   Mar 28 SA 6f ft 1:16^{1} hg

B.

Kina Coulee
SCHVANEVELDT C P **118**
Own.—Alldredge R & Claudia

B. f. 4, by Coulee Man—Kinabalu, by Zip Pocket
Br.—Hawkins Barbara (Cal) 1987 3 0 2 0 $6,600
Tr.—Offield Duane 1986 10 1 3 0 $17,810
Lifetime 14 1 5 1 $26,370

24Apr87-5GG	6f	:21^{1}	:44	1:10^{4}ft	9	116	2½	2^{hd}	1^{hd}	2^{nk}	SchvnvldtCP^{6}	Ⓕ 40000	85-16	LaTurquita,KinaCoulee,Blke'sDncer	8
27Mar87-8GG	6f	:22^{1}	:45	1:09^{4}ft	6½	118	1½	1^{1}½	1^{1}	2^{3}½	SchnldtCP^{3}	ⒻAw17000	86-16	Sharpest,KinCoulee,DetermineCne	10
14Mar87-9GG	6f	:22^{4}	:46^{4}	1:12^{1}m	21	118	7^{5}	6^{4}	6^{4}	6^{6}	Judice J C^{4}	ⒻAw17000	72-23	E'Mirage,GranEmotion,RoyalZona	10
14Mar87—Wide															
16Nov86-6BM	1 1/16	:46^{3}	1:11^{4}	1:44^{3}ft	42	110	2^{2}	3^{4}	—	—	Aragon VA^{2}	ⒻAw17000	— —	RiseAnAlydr,BrmbleDwn,Meritros	10
16Nov86—Eased; Lugged out 3/8															
24Oct86-8BM	6f	:22^{2}	:45^{2}	1:11 ft	30	114	2½	2^{hd}	3½	6^{7}	LamanceC^{9}	ⒻAw17000	77-25	DelEmStright,MyLdiesTiger,PggyD	9
3Oct86-7BM	6f	:21^{4}	:44^{3}	1:11 ft	20	113	3^{4}½	3^{3}	4^{3}½	7^{5}¾	LamanceC^{7}	ⒻAw16000	78-21	Perriddle, Sobranie, Lady Tascha	8
19Sep86-8BM	6f	:22	:45^{1}	1:11^{4}ft	5¾	113	5^{5}¼	4^{4}	8^{8}	10^{18}¼	LamanceC^{7}	ⒻAw16000	62-26	ByAnyOtherName,EdnaN.,Sobrnie	10
19Sep86—Bore out backside															
6Jun86-6GG	5½f	:21^{1}	:44^{4}	1:03^{3}ft	8½	115	5^{5}	4^{2}½	2^{hd}	4^{2}¾	Judice J C^{8}	ⒻAw17000	90-13	MnhttnQun,GoodFrndShp,Drmscll	12
15May86-8GG	6f	:22^{3}	:45^{3}	1:10 ft	7	115	2^{hd}	2^{hd}	2^{hd}	2^{2}	Judice J C^{6}	ⒻAw17000	87-15	OlympicClssic,KinCoulee,LdyPstor	6
13Apr86-8GG	6f	:22^{2}	:45^{4}	1:11^{2}gd	38	112	11^{10}	10^{10}	11^{16}	10^{9}¼	YmtTJ^{6}	Ⓕ[S]Miss Cal	73-25	SiientArrivl,LdyMxineD.,Witchery	12

Apr 14 GG 3f ft :36 h   ● Mar 25 GG 3f ft :34^{3} h   ● Mar 9 GG 6f ft 1:13^{2} h   ● Mar 2 GG 4f ft :45^{1} h

C.

Vikki's Secret
GONZALEZ R M **118**
Own.—Bonde-Padilla & Yorn

Dk. b. or br. f. 4, by What Luck—Ms Native Hostess, by Native Host
Br.—Austin Cherie M (Ky) 1986 3 1 1 0 $10,475
Tr.—Bonde Jeff 1985 0 M 0 0
Lifetime 3 1 1 0 $10,475

12Oct86-7BM	6f	:22	:44^{3}	1:09^{2}ft	7	114	1^{hd}	3^{1}½	4^{6}	5^{9}½	Judice J C^{4}	ⒻAw16000	82-19	Balimonday,DelEmStright,L'Athen	10
11Feb86-6GG	6f	:22^{1}	:44^{4}	1:11^{1}ft	3	120	1^{hd}	2^{hd}	1^{1}	2½	Munoz E^{6}	ⒻAw15000	82-18	PttiPrkins,Vkk'sScrt,QunOfWstbnk	6
25Jan86-2BM	6f	:22^{3}	:46^{1}	1:10^{4}ft	8	117	1½	1^{1}	1^{1}	1^{hd}	Munoz E^{8}	ⒻMdn	85-19	Vikki'sSecret,BrambleDwn,Fndrel	11

Apr 26 GG 5f ft 1:00^{3} hg   ● Apr 20 GG 5f ft :58^{3} h   ● Apr 14 GG 3f ft :35 h   ● Apr 7 GG 5f ft :59 hg

D.

Mythical Mood
BAZE R A — 121
Own.—Jones A U
B. f. 4, by Bold Forbes—Miss Musket, by Gunflint
Br.—Jones A U (Ky) — 1987 3 1 0 0 $8,870
Tr.—Fierce Fordell — 1986 0 M 0 0
Lifetime 3 1 0 0 $8,870

27Mar87-8GG	6f	$:22^1$	:45	$1:09^4$ft	*2½	121	2½	$2^{1½}$	$4^{3½}$	6^6	Maple S^{10}	ⒻAw17000	84-16	Sharpest,KinCoulee,DetermineCne	10
13Mar87-1GG	6f	:22	$:45^3$	$1:11^3$gd	*4-5	120	1^{hd}	1^1	1^1	1^2	Baze R A^1	ⒻMdn	81-22	MythclMd,Ktty'sEvrywhr,LftHrMrk	8
10Jan87-6BM	6f	:23	:47	$1:12^2$sl	*2¼	119	$5^{3½}$	$5^{5½}$	4^4	$4^{5½}$	Castaneda M^2	ⒻMdn	71-34	Sweepy,MissClassyAna,BalletBlnc	12

10Jan87—Bumped start, rank down backside, around turn
●Apr 28 GG 4f ft :47 h   Apr 22 GG 6f ft $1:14^3$ h   ●Apr 12 GG 4f ft $:45^2$ h   ●Mar 4 GG 4f ft $:45^4$ h

349.

A.

Eastern Jo
LOZOYA D A — 117
Own.—Penrod & Vella Mmes
Dk. b. or br. g. 6, by Out of the East—Little Bigjo, by War Emperor
Br.—Dante T C (Cal) — 1987 7 0 0 1 $2,262
Tr.—Walker Lloyd A — $6,250 — 1986 15 0 2 1 $3,673
Lifetime 70 6 10 11 $67,085 — Turf 2 0 1 1 $3,880

15Apr87-7GG	6f	$:21^4$	$:44^2$	$1:10^1$ft	16	117	11^{15}	11^{17}	11^{15}	$6^{6½}$	Rond D^5	Ⓢ 6250	81-19	PetsInnt,UndrcovrEgl,C.HowitFitz	11
25Mar87-2GG	6f	$:22^1$	:45	$1:10^2$ft	15	115	$7^{8¾}$	$6^{7½}$	$7^{7½}$	$5^{4¾}$	Rond D^2	7500	82-18	WestsideGeorge,Tabular,FleetWver	8
3Mar87-6GG	1 1/16	:46	1:10	$1:42^4$ft	9	116	6^{13}	8^{16}	7^{13}	$6^{11½}$	Chapman T M^5	6250	77-10	ShstClown,LndMine,RitchieExprss	10
21Feb87-2GG	6f	$:22^3$	:46	1:11 ft	5¾	117	8^{11}	8^{10}	$6^{6¾}$	4^3	Chapman T M^8	Ⓢ 6250	81-14	LuckyJohnD.,ArthrFy,AvngngWrror	9
14Feb87-4GG	1 1/16	$:46^2$	$1:11^1$	$1:45^3$gd	15	116	$5^{7½}$	5^7	5^3	$5^{7¼}$	Lozoya D A^6	8000	68-21	MissABid,NickelNssu,BorregoSun	11
7Feb87-1BM	6f	:22	$:45^2$	$1:10^4$ft	18	115	6^{11}	6^9	$5^{8½}$	$3^{5½}$	Lozoya D A^6	12500	79-19	Che, Move Free, Eastern Jo	6
1Feb87-5BM	6f	$:23^1$	$:46^4$	1:12 ft	21	115	8^{11}	8^{11}	8^{11}	$8^{7¼}$	Loseth C^3	8000	72-25	RunCougrRun,Zd'sSovnr,SposTrobl	8
2Nov86-3BM	6f	$:22^3$	$:45^4$	$1:10^2$ft	14	114	$10^{9¼}$	$8^{8½}$	9^8	$8^{8¼}$	Tohill K S^3	6250	79-21	JustTurnLeft,StrRoute,ImTrckStr	11
17Oct86-7BM	6f	$:22^2$	:45	1:10 ft	10	114	6^{11}	6^{10}	$5^{9½}$	3^4	Tohill K S^3	6250	85-16	StrRoute,StreetsmrtNtive,EsternJo	8
5Oct86-5BM	1	$:46^3$	$1:11^4$	1:38 ft	8½	114	$8^{6¾}$	$6^{5½}$	6^6	$6^{4½}$	Ochoa A^9	Ⓢ 6250	73-21	KissNCasey,Galawac,HoldTheDice	10

●Apr 26 Sac 1 ft 1:41 h

B.

Imasonofagunn
MUNOZ O R — 112^5
Own.—Gunn C & Charlene
Dk. b. or br. g. 6, by Fleet Velvet—Gunnagetit, by Promulgation
Br.—Gunn Charlene (Cal) — 1985 5 1 0 2 $6,957
Tr.—Steele Eileen — $6,250 — 1984 14 M 4 2 $10,160
Lifetime 19 1 4 4 $17,117

1Aug85-10SR	6f	$:22^1$	:45	$1:10^2$ft	*1	114	$10^{9¼}$	9^{11}	7^{10}	$5^{2½}$	Sanchez R A^9	8500	87-11	Cachesce, Gold To Go, Exciting V.	10
1Jly85-9Pln	6f	$:22^2$	:45	$1:09^4$ft	6¼	115	$9^{3¼}$	$8^{8¼}$	$5^{6½}$	$3^{6½}$	Delgadillo C^3	Ⓢ 12500	86-14	ThAysHvIt,ShdyHost,Imsonofgnn	10

1Jly85—Off slowly

1Jun85-7GG	6f	$:22^2$	$:45^3$	$1:10^3$ft	12	115	$9^{9¼}$	8^{12}	5^5	$3^{2½}$	Delgadillo C^6	10000	83-15	BeABend,EltedDuke,Imsonofgunn	10
11May85-5GG	6f	$:22^2$	:45	$1:11^1$ft	*2½	122	$9^{7¾}$	7^7	4^2	1^{nk}	Delgadillo C^{10}	M16000	83-16	Imsonofgunn,I'mnektoo,ShdyHost	12

11May85—Ducked in start

4Jan85-5BM	6f	$:22^3$	:46	$1:12^4$ft	*2¼	119	$8^{6¼}$	$6^{4¾}$	5^3	$4^{2¾}$	Archuleta S^6	M10000	72-24	Vronic'sFrst,BoldPrvldg,StylshEgl	11
21Dec84-2BM	6f	$:22^4$	$:45^4$	$1:10^3$ft	3¼	118	$8^{6¼}$	7^8	$5^{5½}$	$2^{1½}$	Chapman TM^3	M10000	84-13	JustASmile,Imsonofgun,Jov'sSilor	12
30Nov84-1BM	1 1/16	$:46^1$	1:11	$1:44^3$ft	3	117	6^7	$5^{4½}$	$6^{6¾}$	6^{10}	Baze R A^8	M12500	59-24	SoloOrbit,MidnightSnacker,Darlnge	8
25Nov84-3BM	6f	:23	:47	$1:13^2$m	*2¾	118	$7^{6¾}$	$6^{8¾}$	$5^{7½}$	$3^{2¼}$	Baze R A^8	M16000	70-27	ClodyNorth,LonlyHntr,Imsonofgn	10
11Nov84-2BM	6f	$:22^4$	:46	$1:11^4$sy	4	118	7^6	5^8	3^5	2^6	$SchvnldtCP^2$	ⓈM20000	74-30	BennettPek,Imsonofgun,H'sADriftr	7

11Nov84—Bumped break

14Oct84-2BM	6f	$:23^1$	$:46^2$	$1:11^1$ft	*2¼	117	$5^{2½}$	$4^{3¼}$	$3^{2½}$	$4^{2¾}$	$SchvneveldtCP^2$	M20000	80-14	KissNCsey,BuckRodgers,Jov'sSilor	9

14Oct84—Broke in a tangle
Apr 21 GG 5f ft $1:03^2$ h   Apr 12 Sac 4f ft :47 h   Mar 22 Sac 6f gd $1:15^2$ h   ●Mar 14 Sac 6f sy $1:17^1$ h

C.

Barouti
DAVIDSON J R — 117
Own.—Jennings B
B. h. 7, by Queen's Knight—The Poona Look, by Poona II
Br.—Blue Seal Stable (Cal) — 1987 6 1 1 1 $3,504
Tr.—Jennings Bobby — $6,250 — 1986 3 0 0 0
Lifetime 39 6 8 3 $68,449 — Turf 2 0 0 0 $1,530

4Apr87-5GG	6f	$:21^4$	$:44^2$	$1:10^3$ft	10	118	3^1	2^{hd}	$1^{1½}$	$2^{¾}$	Davidson J R^3	6250	85-12	NoblePsser,Brouti,WhipsN'Jingles	12
25Mar87-7GG	1 1/16	:46	$1:10^1$	1:44 ft	10	116	2^{hd}	2^1	3^6	$6^{8½}$	Lambert J^5	6250	74-18	StrRout,HighChrmr,SprtnConqust	12
13Mar87-9GG	6f	:22	$:45^2$	$1:11^4$gd	14	119	1½	1^{hd}	$2^{½}$	3^5	Judice J C^8	6250	75-22	WestsideGeorge,DenvrGold,Brouti	11
28Feb87-3GG	6f	$:21^4$	$:44^3$	$1:09^2$ft	9	119	$3^{1½}$	$5^{3½}$	7^7	$11^{13½}$	$SchvneveldtCP^{12}$	6250	78-10	ClLeLuIh,HesGs,HsStorminNormn	12
1Feb87-6PM	6f	$:22^2$	$:45^3$	$1:11^3$gd	4¾	121	1^{hd}	1^3	1^5	$1^{1¾}$	Reyes R J^6	6250	89-17	Brouti,Sierr'sPlesure,EglesFlyHigh	8
23Jan87-7PM	6f	$:22^1$	$:45^4$	$1:11^4$sy	10	113^5	1½	1^{hd}	2^{hd}	5^2	Luark R^7	5000	86-19	EglsFlyHigh,LookMstrLook,SkpTht	7
15Nov86-3BM	6f	$:22^2$	:46	1:11 ft	53	114	6^4	$7^{4¾}$	9^{10}	$9^{13¼}$	Caballero R^{12}	6250	71-21	TossTheCoin,StarRoute,Cracovyk	12
1Nov86-8BM	6f	$:22^4$	$:46^2$	$1:11^2$ft	12	114	5^4	5^3	$5^{7½}$	$7^{15½}$	Judice J C^3	Ⓢ 8000	66-21	FleetWver,HustleADnce,DustyTrder	8
25Oct86-2BM	6f	$:22^3$	$:45^4$	$1:10^2$ft	10	114	$8^{9¼}$	8^{14}	8^{14}	$9^{13¼}$	Judice J C^3	10000	74-21	ShdowWtch,QuitFrnd,AvngngWrror	9
28Sep85-9BM	1 1/16	$:45^4$	$1:10^1$	$1:42^3$ft	15	110^5	1^{hd}	2^{hd}	3^3	$6^{6½}$	Shaw K^8	12500	72-19	LimestoneLouie,HardJohn,AlleyFox	9

Apr 27 Pln 5f ft $1:02^3$ h

D.

*Ayaabi			B. g. 6, by Habitat—Demare, by Pardao			1987	9	0	1	1	$3,470
CAMPBELL B C		117	Br.—Spann G (Eng)		$6,250	1986	10	0	1	0	$1,880
Own.—Two Rivers Farm			Tr.—Mason Lloyd C			Turf	25	4	3	0	$49,998
			Lifetime	43	4	4	1	$55,843			

```
16Apr87-7GG   6f :22  :444 1:092ft    8½ 117   62½ 53½ 65½ 33    Campbell B C 9   6250 89-14 Cal Le Lu Iah,AlwaysQuick,Ayaabi 11
28Mar87-2GG   6f :222 :45  1:101ft   11 117   107¾ 89½ 77½ 43½   Tohill K S 2     6250 84-14 Intrigdor,TexolticTom,NoblePsser 12
  28Mar87—Crowded 1/2
13Mar87-2GG   6f :22  :451 1:112gd    6 112⁵ 1011 8⁸ 6⁷ 5⁷      Munoz O R 6      6250 75-22 Galawc,EconomicGrowth,Crcovyk 11
  13Mar87—Pinched at break
4Mar87-4GG   1¹⁄₁₆:461 1:102 1:44 ft   7 116   713 813 818 822½  SchvneveldtCP 10 8000 60-12 Delta Raider, Miss A Bid, Otrebor 10
20Feb87-2GG   6f :221 :452 1:103ft   11 117   810 76½ 63½ 41½   Cooper B 1       8000 84-18 SpousTroubl,StrRout,Lght ngSprt 12
10Feb87-2GG   6f :221 :444 1:094ft    6½ 117   41½ 64½ 56½ 24    Cooper B 4       6250 86-11 DetermindWillow,Ayaabi,SubSinker 9
1Feb87-5BM   6f :231 :464 1:12 ft    11 115   22  21½ 43  53½   Lozoya D A 5     8000 76-25 RunCougrRun,Zd'sSovnr,SposTrobl 8
18Jan87-10BM  1¹⁄₁₆:47 1:113 1:443ft  34 115   76 1112121912163 Campbell B C 7   8000 52-26 Fulger, Imaenough, Borrego Sun 12
  18Jan87—Ducked in start
3Jan87-5BM   6f :222 :454 1:111sy    16 115   44½ 44½ 77½ 79    Campbell B C 2   10000 74-23 BchRomo,BlzingZulu,Acciptr'sPrnc 8
14Jly86-10Sol  1 :462 1:11 1:382ft    5 115   11½ 2ʰᵈ 42  55   6 Lozoya D A 1     16000 77-19 FeltyCould,GallntMick,ShcowWtch 7
  14Jly86—Bumped hard start, 3/8; 6Dead heat
Apr 6 GG 4f ft :481 h          Mar 24 GG 4f gd :492 h
```

350. If the pace of a race is fast early and fast late and Horse Z has a running style best described as average early and fast late, when is Horse Z most likely to win?

A. The early pace is actually slower than expected   (27)
B. Its late pace ability is combined with an edge in class
C. The fast early pace collapses
D. It gets a ground-saving trip into the stretch

351. Using figures instead of times, if the race pars are 95 to the fractional time and 95 final time and today's race shape figures to be fast-average, which horse below has a pace advantage?

	Pace figure	Final figure
Horse A	98	92
Horse B	97	96
Horse C	95	99
Horse D	93	97

A. Horse A   (27)
B. Horse B
C. Horse C
D. Horse D

Answer key: Pace analysis

Minimum Competency Test

286. B	294. C
287. A	295. D
288. D	296. D
289. B	297. B
290. C	298. C
291. A	299. A
292. A	300. B
293. C	301. B

Mastery Test

302. C	315. B	328. D	340. A
303. A	316. C	329. C	341. B
304. B	317. D	330. B	342. A
305. B	318. C	331. B	343. A
306. C	319. D	332. A	344. A
307. A	320. A	333. A	345. A
308. C	321. D	334. B	346. C
309. A	322. B	335. B	347. D
310. B	323. D	336. B	348. B
311. C	324. A	337. D	349. D
312. D	325. D	338. A	350. C
313. A	326. C	339. B	351. C
314. B	327. C		

CHAPTER 8

Form Analysis

Competencies

28. Know the basic facts and probabilities of thoroughbred form.
29. Know the classical standards of positive and negative form.
30. Know the indicators of form defects and form advantages.
31. Relate current form to other factors of handicapping, especially class, age, and trainer.
32. Make reliable form eliminations.
33. Interpret changes of form in terms of their most probable effects.

	Minimum Competency Test	Mastery Test
Proficiency standards	75%	67%
Number of Items	12	67
Passing scores	9	45

Sources of Instruction

- *How Will Your Horse Run Today?*, chapters 1–7
- *Ainslie's Complete Guide to Thoroughbred Handicapping*, Chapter 9
- *Winning at the Races*, chapters 6–11
- *Fast Tracks to Thoroughbred Profits*, chapters 6, 8, & 10

Comments

In the past twenty years two substantial changes have guided the handicapper's application of the form factor. In the late sixties came the most comprehensive guidelines on form ever, specifying strict concrete standards for form eliminations and for awarding extra credit on the factor.

Since then, as the game has changed, so have the standards of form analysis. A steady liberalization of the standards of acceptable form has been the modern trend. The probability data here has been enormously helpful. It has destroyed several myths. The tests that follow have been well grounded in known facts.

The most difficult trick in handicapping is to eliminate as many horses as possible on form, without eliminating many winners. Performing that trick has become increasingly problematic, as more horses now qualify on form. A practical remedy postpones form analysis until the later stages of the handicapping process, as a means of making final eliminations or distinguishing contenders on fine points. Form eliminations can be determined a priori as well, but the horses had better look sorry enough that they practically eliminate themselves.

Price represents another salient factor when evaluating form. The crowd notoriously overbets good form. Smart modern handicappers remain sufficiently flexible and lenient on form that they can take advantage of the overlays.

Definition of Terms

- *Lengthy layoff.* Sixty days or longer.

- *Up close.* Within striking position of the leader at any point of call, especially the stretch call; expressed as a specific number of beaten lengths that varies by distance.

FORM ANALYSES: MINIMUM COMPETENCY TEST

352. The classical standards of positive and negative form include recent races and

A. key races   (29)
B. speed ratings
C. workouts
D. trainer maneuvers

353. Claiming horses generally need recent racing more than nonclaiming horses in order to win.

A. True   (29)
B. False

354. Standards of acceptable form are more liberal today than ever.

A. True **(28)**
B. False

355. The bulk of the available evidence suggests current form becomes significantly less predictable when the number of days away exceeds

A. 14 **(28)**
B. 21
C. 28
D. 60

356. "Hidden form" involves racing an unready horse into defeat as part of the conditioning process.

A. True **(28)**
B. False

357. "Up close" at 7F means within two lengths at the stretch call.

A. True **(30)**
B. False

358. Horses returning to the same class level following a win are likelier to repeat the winning form if

A. they have worked out between races **(30)**
B. it's a sprint and they have good early speed
C. they do not have to carry as many as seven additional pounds
D. they won the last race by three lengths or more

359. 59⅖ hg is comparable to

A. 59b **(28)**
B. 1:00⅖ bg
C. 1:00 h
D. 58⅖ h

360. Which claiming horse is best eliminated on form?

A. has not run within the past 28 days **(32)**
B. has not run in 21 days and has not worked out since
C. has not won in its previous 13 starts
D. lost more than two lengths in the stretch after being up close at the first three calls against the same class as today's

361. The main problem with emphasizing good recent form in handicapping and decision-making is

A. The horses have no real advantage statistically **(28)**
B. The tactic does not separate contenders reliably
C. Too many extraneous factors obscure a horse's true form
D. The horses almost invariably are overbet

362. Which statement corresponds well with *Double Smooth's* current form cycle?

Double Smooth — B. m. 5, by Overskate—So Smooth, by Third Martini
Own.—S K S Stable — **117** — Br.—Farish W S III (NY) — Tr.—Seewald Alan — $50,000

1986	13	2	2	2	$31,145
1985	18	2	0	3	$41,916
Turf	22	2	1	4	$62,717
Lifetime	41	5	4	7	$105,992

25Nov86-9Med	170 :462 1:122 1:432ft	*2½	117	45½	2hd	1hd	1½	SantagatN 5	Ⓕ Aw19000	79-22	DoubleSmooth,Athbsc,PnnntWinnr	7
19Nov86-5Med	1 1/16 :473 1:123 1:45 ft	2	115	53½	3½	11	15½	Santagata N 6	Ⓕ 35000	78-25	DoubleSmooth,Spir'sImg,OnForBss	6
12Nov86-9Med	1 1/16 :474 1:121 1:443gd	3	117	47½	37½	27	28	SantagatN 1	Ⓕ Aw18000	72-21	Dave'sKate,DoubleSmooth,CdbrAbr	5
4Nov86-8Med	1 :482 1:134 1:394ft	21	117	63¾	63½	44½	3¾	SantagatN 5	Ⓕ Aw18000	75-24	SheSkates,Athabasc,DoubleSmooth	6
26Oct86-3Pha	1 :464 1:13 1:402sy	4¾	116	49	49	57½	310½	Thomas D B 2	Ⓕ 32000	61-21	DiscoMgic,DoubleOn,DoublSmooth	7
13Oct86-9Pha	6f :213 :442 1:102gd	16	115	98½	912	713	66¼	Lopez C C 4	Ⓕ Aw15000	83-15	BoxofBirds,SnappyRuler,DremPuss	9
19Sep86-7Med	1 1/16 Ⓣ:47 1:1131:431fm	11	114	42	31½	34	87	Jimenez I J 6	Ⓕ 37500	79-11	SarahSails,Athabasca,Rolfe'sRuby	12
29Aug86-6Mth	1 1/16 :48 1:122 1:443ft	3½	115	2hd	2hd	24	26	McCuleyWH 6	Ⓕ 32000	76-18	WvrngLght,DoblSmooth,SmlAngln	6

Feb 18 Bel tr.t 3f ft :353 hg — Feb 12 Bel tr.t 6f ft 1:18 b — Feb 3 Bel tr.t 5f sy 1:023 b — Jan 25 Bel tr.t 5f ft 1:04 b

A. The Nov. 25 allowance win was predictable following the big win for $35,000 Clm on Nov. 19 **(33)**
B. Form remains a plus factor as the horse returns to face $50,000 Clm horses
C. The horse is likely to show declining form in its next start
D. The Nov. 19 win was foreshadowed by the improved 2nd-place finish Nov. 12

363. Which horse(s) can be eliminated on form? It's Oct. 31.

6th Aqueduct

1 ⅛ MILES. (Turf). (1.47) ALLOWANCE. Purse $26,000. 3-year-olds and upward.

A. **(32)**

Faraway Island — Ch. c. 3, by Banquet Table—Tuvalu, by Our Native
Own.—Kimmel C P — **114** — Br.—Kimmel & Thomas (Ky) — Tr.—TONER JAMES J

1986	13	0	3	3	$32,642
1985	5	2	1	0	$41,210
Turf	10	0	3	3	$32,512
Lifetime	18	2	4	3	$73,852

19Oct86-7Bel	1 Ⓣ:47 1:1121:363fm	6¾	115	11½	1hd	32	35¾	Samyn J L5	Envoy	76-23	RealCourage,Trubulare,FarwyIslnd	7
3Oct86-7Bel	1 1/16 Ⓣ:4611:1111:443gd	10	114	2hd	67½	615	417½	Romero R P2	Aw26000	55-27	IcyGroom,ChristianHundred,Ioskeh	8
13Sep86-3Bel	1 1/16 [T]:4721:11 1:413fm	25	113	15	11½	12½	2no	Romero R P8	Aw26000	93-09	JackOfClubs,FarwyIslnd,Torquemd	8
7Sep86-5Bel	1 1/16 Ⓣ:4721:1141:434gd	12	118	11½	1½	2hd	2¾	Davis R G4	90000	76-23	Trubulare,FrwyIslnd,TheLoneRnger	9
27Aug86-7Bel	1 Ⓣ:4711:11 1:36 fm	33	112	106¼	79	89½	79½	Migliore R2	Aw26000	75-18	FrdAstir,Torqumd,ChristinHundrd	10
27Jun86-7Bel	1 Ⓣ:4731:12 1:361fm	3½	112	1hd	42½	813	918¾	Migliore R7	Aw26000	65-20	RockCrystl,RecordTurnout,Kruckel	9
14Jun86-7Bel	1 1/16 Ⓣ:4521:0941:44 gd	4¼	109	36½	27	34½	33	Samyn J L4	Aw26000	73-24	RightValue,MadGuard,FarwyIslnd	10
29May86-7Bel	1 Ⓣ:4441:09 1:341fm	12	109	21½	2hd	2½	34¾	Samyn J L8	Aw26000	89-08	ShrpGinistrelli,LserLne,FrwyIslnd	12

●Oct 16 Aqu 4f ft :472 h — Sep 28 Aqu 4f sy :50 b — Sep 22 Aqu 4f ft :48 h — ●Sep 3 Aqu 3f ft :36 h

B.

Corey's Comet

B. c. 3, by Stalwart—Flaxen, by Graustark
Br.—Gentry T (Ky) 1986 8 1 0 3 $25,140
Own.—Shanus S 114 **Tr.—LEVINE BRUCE** 1985 1 M 0 0
Lifetime 9 1 0 3 $25,140 **Turf 3 0 0 2 $6,000**

27Oct86-6Aqu 1⅛ :482 1:13 1:501sy 2¾ 114 3½ 21 24 38¼ Maple E4 Aw25000 76-20 FutureFble,CndinWintr,Cory'sComt 9
6Oct86-7Bel 1¼[T]:50 1:4022:07 gd 12 114 43 34 31½ 31 Migliore R5 Aw25000 58-39 Dwno'TheDnce,Esternr,Cory'sComt 6
31Aug86-6Bel 1¼[T]:4911:39 2:032fm 26 112 21½ 21½ 33 33¾ Lovato F Jr3 Aw25000 73-20 ConsulGenerl,Mcbest,Corey'sComt 7
25Aug86-7Sar 1 1/16 (T):47 1:1131:42 fm 34 112 96¾ 88¾ 911 813½ Velasquez J12 Aw25000 73-15 Jack Of Clubs, Godbey, Loose 12
6Aug86-7Sar 6f :214 :451 1:11 sy 9 112 914 814 715 515¼ Velasquez J2 Aw24000 70-26 AlDavis,ClassicMove,Michel'sDncer 9
11May86-5Bel 1 1/16 :454 1:10 1:414ft 5 112 31½ 42 34 410 Santos J A4 Aw25000 83-15 PersonalFlag,Carnivore,FlyMeAgin 7
28Apr86-7Aqu 7f :223 :452 1:224ft 9¼ 119 42½ 52½ 55 47¾ Santos J A9 Aw24000 79-25 Forty Kings,FastPhillip,Danotable 10
31Mar86-4Aqu 6f :23 :464 1:113ft 3 122 11½ 12 13 15¾ Maple E12 Mdn 83-20 Corey'sComet,Prsrving,PlsurKick 12
Oct 23 Aqu (T) 7f fm 1:283 h (d)   Oct 16 Aqu (T) 5f yl 1:043 h (d)   Sep 25 Aqu (T) 5f fm 1:044 b (d)   ●Sep 11 Aqu (T) 4f fm :493 h (d)

C.

The Lone Ranger

B. g. 3, by Shelter Half—Anti Social, by Pretense
Br.—Four Bros Stable (Ky) 1986 16 3 4 7 $137,552
Own.—Rory Green Stables 119 **Tr.—SEDLACEK MICHAEL C** 1985 5 1 0 1 $8,760
Lifetime 21 4 4 8 $146,312 **Turf 8 1 2 4 $95,760**

4Oct86-7Bel 1½(T):48 2:0942:372sf 7¾ 114 58 1hd 1hd 1hd McCrrCJ4 Lawce Real 37-63 TheLoneRanger,Southjet,DrkFlood 7
4Oct86—Grade II; Brushed, drvg
17Sep86-7Bel 1¼[T]:5021:3712:014fm 3½ 113 56 59½ 59 36 Romero R P3 Aw25000 79-17 Ioskeh,ExclusivProvinc,ThLonRngr 8
7Sep86-5Bel 1 1/16 (T):4721:1141:434gd 5½ 116 44 43 33 3¾ Romero R P3 85000 76-23 Trubulare,FrwyIslnd,TheLoneRnger 9
7Sep86—Forced out
17Aug86-3Sar 1⅝(T):5212:07 2:452sf 9-5 112 68 35 35½ 33¾ Davis R G5 Aw25000 54-42 DarkFlood,Macbest,TheLoneRnger 6
9Aug86-1Sar 1⅛ :474 1:114 1:511ft 5¼ 113 611 57 22 1hd Davis R G5 70000 79-17 TheLoneRnger,ForTheGippr,ThSvg 7
25Jly86-8Bel 1¼[T]:50 1:3912:032fm 4½ 1065 66 76½ 47½ 36¼ Paneto W R7 Aw25000 71-19 I'mHopeful,Unnswered,ThLonRngr 8
7Jly86-7Bel 1⅜[T]:4831:3832:141fm 4¾ 111 65¾ 64½ 56 26½ Davis R G7 Aw25000 79-14 StgeWhispr,ThLonRngr,ConsulGnrl 9
7Jly86—Steadied
30Jun86-2Bel 1 1/16 (T):4621:11 1:432fm 3¾ 113 913 713 47½ 2nk Davis R G3 45000 79-21 MnInMoton,ThLonRngr,LstyGrsty 11
●Oct 1 Aqu 3f ft :351 h   Sep 2 Aqu 4f ft :482 h

D.

Flow Technology

B. c. 3, by Super Concorde—Spiranthes, by Vaguely Noble
Br.—Moyglare Stud Farm Ltd (Ky) 1986 3 1 1 0 $1,900
Own.—Haefner W 114 **Tr.—NICKERSON VICTOR J** Turf 3 1 1 0 $1,900
Lifetime 3 1 1 0 $1,900

23Aug86♦4PhoenixPk(Ire) 1½ 1:57 yl 4 123 (T) 47½ PrnellD Persian Bold Stakes Dochas, StopTheFighting,Forlaway 6
10Jly86♦6GowranPark(Ire) 1¼ 2:093gd *2-5 126 (T) 12 KnMJ Dunbell Plate (Mdn) FlowTchnology,Ambivlnt,MrryWtt 14
29Mar86♦4Leopardst'n(Ire) 1 1:572sf *3-2 126 (T) 23 KMJ Westminster Plate (Mdn) MroSvr,FlowTchnology,ThFordrgh 11
Oct 23 Aqu (T) 4f fm :50 b (d)   Oct 9 Aqu 5f ft 1:011 h   ●Oct 4 Aqu 5f m 1:033 b (d)   Sep 29 Aqu 4f ft :50 b

E.

Sir Corbin

B. c. 3, by King Pellinore—Demoniac, by First Landing
Br.—Humphrey Louise & Sally (Ky) 1986 9 2 1 2 $44,144
Own.—Camgi Stables 114 **Tr.—VIOLETTE RICHARD JR** 1985 3 M 0 2 $5,400
Lifetime 12 2 1 4 $49,544 **Turf 8 2 1 2 $42,764**

4Oct86-7Bel 1½(T):48 2:0942:372sf 9½ 114 34 516 520 527½ MrtensG5 Lawce Real — — TheLoneRanger,Southjet,DrkFlood 7
4Oct86—Grade II
6Sep86-7Bel 1⅜[T]:4941:39 2:164gd 22 112 11 1hd 22 42½ Martens G3 [R]Sten 70-27 IfIHdAHmmer,UpperBend,SkiFleet 7
15Aug86-4Sar 1 1/16 (T):4641:10 1:421fm *3-2 112 3nk 1hd 2hd 1no Martens G3 Aw25000 86-18 SirCorbin,Loose,FrenchChampagne 5
31Jly86-2Sar 1 1/16 (T):4841:1321:434fm 8 111 41½ 51¾ 43½ 34½ Martens G3 Aw25000 73-23 NewTerms,PrinceDaniel,SirCorbin 11
12Jly86-8Bel 1¼[T]:4941:39 2:031yl 39 114 31 44½ 68 68½ VasquezJ2 Lexington 69-22 Manila, Glow, Dance Card Filled 10
12Jly86—Grade II
28Jun86-4Bel 1 1/16 (T):47 1:12 1:434fm *8-5 114 42 31 32 33¾ Vasquez J2 Aw25000 73-19 DancinOnPins,Mr.VnDell,SirCorbin 7
14Jun86-4Bel 1 (T):4611:1121:371gd 5½ 114 64½ 44½ 12 12¼ Vasquez J9 Mdn 79-24 SirCorbin,One'sCstl,TwicChrming 12
7May86-4Aqu 1⅛(T):4811:1341:522fm 7½ 113 12 11 2hd 22 Vasquez J12 Mdn 71-29 PrinceDaniel,SirCorbin,IndinRiver 12
Sep 15 Bel tr.t 6f ft 1:18 b   Sep 5 Bel tr.t 3f ft :37 b   Sep 1 Bel [T] 6f fm 1:143 h

F.

I'm Hopeful
Own.—Brookfield Farms **114**

Ro. c. 3, by Cormorant—Invision, by Grey Dawn II
Br.—Isaacs H S (Ky) **1986 6 2 1 0 $33,860**
Tr.—KELLY EDWARD I **Turf 4 1 0 0 $15,000**
Lifetime 6 2 1 0 $33,860

20Oct86-9Bel	1	Ⓣ:46^3 1:11^3 1:36^{3}fm	10	114	7^5	9^{11}	10^{13}	$10^{12\frac{3}{4}}$	Vasquez J^6	Aw26000	69-19	Dwno'ThDnc,ChrstnHndrd,Torqmd	11
13Sep86-3Bel	$1\frac{1}{16}$	[T]:47^2 1:11 1:41^{3}fm	$3\frac{1}{4}$	113	4^6	7^5	7^{10}	$7^{9\frac{1}{2}}$	Davis R G^5	Aw26000	83-09	JackOfClubs,FarwyIslnd.Torquemd	8
16Aug86-7Sar	$1\frac{1}{8}$	Ⓣ:50^2 1:14^2 1:52^{1}yl	2	115	$1^{\frac{1}{2}}$	3^2	5^5	$5^{4\frac{3}{4}}$	VsquezJ^5	Gallant Man	61-26	DnceofLife,Southjet,DnceCrdFilled	6
25Jly86-8Bel	$1\frac{1}{4}$	[T]:50 1:39^1 2:03^{2}fm	*8-5	116	$1^{\frac{1}{2}}$	1^1	1^6	$1^{6\frac{1}{4}}$	Vasquez J^4	Aw25000	77-19	I'mHopeful,Unnswered,ThLonRngr	8
12Jly86-6Bel	$1\frac{3}{8}$	:47^2 1:38 2:17^{2}m	*8-5	116	$2^{\frac{1}{2}}$	$2^{\frac{1}{2}}$	1^6	$1^{6\frac{1}{2}}$	Vasquez J^9	Mdn	93-15	I'mHopful,TwicChrming,TruVigor	11
2Jly86-2Bel	$1\frac{1}{16}$	:46^1 1:10^1 1:42^{2}sy	$6\frac{1}{2}$	116	5^{10}	5^{15}	5^{11}	2^7	Davis R G^4	Mdn	83-14	HarveyPack,I'mHopeful,One'sCstle	6

Oct 17 Bel 5f ft 1:02 b   Oct 7 Bel 5f ft 1:03^4 b   Oct 3 Bel 4f ft :48^4 b   Sep 11 Bel 3f ft :36 b

This is the end of the minimum competency test. Check your answers. If your score falls below standard, consult the recommended sources of instruction before proceeding to the mastery test.

FORM ANALYSIS: MASTERY TEST

364. Which is the strongest sign of positive form?

A. a gate blowout the day before a race **(29)**
B. an impressive stretch gain last out
C. unusual early speed
D. a return to the races in five days

365. Lack of recent activity becomes less alarming the farther a horse must run.

A. True **(28)**
B. False

366. Which workout is most impressive?

A. 46 hg **(29)**
B. 1:00 b
C. 59 hg
D. 1:13 h

367. "Up close" at the stretch call of a 1¹⁄₁₆M race means within how many lengths of the leader?

A. 1¾ **(30)**
B. 2¾
C. 3¾
D. 4¾

368. Horses away as long as ninety days can be acceptable on form if they show a 5F workout in the past 12 days.

A. True (28)
B. False

369. The stretch loss and stretch gain are equally significant as indicators of improving and declining form.

A. True (28)
B. False

370. When 3YO speed horses switch from sprints to routes, the most critical conditioning factor becomes

A. responsiveness to the rider (31)
B. changing leads into and out of the turns
C. developing stamina
D. a relaxed stride

371. Which is not an indicator of positive form?

A. recent action (29)
B. regular workouts
C. early speed carried to the top of the stretch
D. an all-out driving finish in a losing effort

372. The "bid and hung" move between the pre-stretch and stretch calls is a sign of improving form.

A. True (30)
B. False

373. Any horse dropping in class can be accepted on form if it raced up close in the classier race at

A. the stretch call (30)
B. the pre-stretch call
C. any two consecutive calls
D. any call

374. A flash of early speed following a number of dull efforts is one of the best signs of impending victory, usually at a good price.

A. True (33)
B. False

375. Recent form is most likely to be misleading when evaluating

A. fillies and mares   **(31)**
B. stakes horses returning from layoffs
C. 2-year-olds
D. 3-year-olds

376. Which is generally a plus factor in form analysis?

A. a stretch gain of three lengths or more   **(30)**
B. an up close position at each point of call in the
   latest running line
C. a favorable jockey switch
D. the last race was an improved performance within
   the past twelve days

377. Which kind of horses have the most difficulty repeating a recent win?

A. horses rising in class   **(31)**
B. stakes winners
C. 4up exiting an all-out driving finish
D. maiden graduates

378. Back class is a significant positive sign that a claiming
horse can repeat a recent win.

A. True   **(33)**
B. False

379. A small drop in class that quickly follows a win usually reflects

A. a trainer maneuver to keep a sharp horse active   **(31)**
B. physical problems that will show up soon
C. a declining form cycle
D. peaking form today

380. What factors in combination contribute best to repeat
victories among claiming horses?

A. raced within 2 lengths of the pre-stretch call and   **(30)**
   won by 5 or more lenghts
B. an easy win wire to wire and an improved workout since
C. won by at least 3 lengths and has another plus
   factor for form
D. a drop in class and a reduction in weight simultaneously

381. A bullet workout is most impressive

A. in company   **(30)**
B. at 5 furlongs
C. out of the gate
D. at 3 furlongs the day before a race

382. The assertion that 85 percent of all winners have raced within two weeks is much less meaningful than it sounds because

A. too many contenders normally qualify on the point   **(28)**
B. the public usually overbets those kind
C. 85 percent of all starters have raced within two weeks
D. recency is less decisive than ever in handicapping

383. An impressive 5F workout would be more frequently meaningful at

A. Santa Anita   **(31)**
B. Oaklawn Park
C. Canterbury Downs
D. Saratoga

384. When evaluating current form, which is the most telltale sign of a winning performance next out?

A. a 2nd place finish last out   **(28)**
B. improving early speed carried to the stretch call
C. a big win last race
D. ran the final quarter-mile in 24 seconds or less

385. The most misleading kind of recent "good race" results from

A. an all-out drive throughout the stretch   **(33)**
B. an up close performance at every call of a route race
C. overextension following a lengthy layoff
D. an inordinately slow early pace

386. For handicappers wanting a good price, finding knocks on recent good races is more fruitful than finding excuses for bad races.

A. True   (33)
B. False

387. Older horses are less likely than their younger counterparts to bounce back from poor efforts.

A. True   (29)
B. False

388. Younger horses are more difficult to train into shape
without actual races than their older rivals.

A. True   (29)
B. False

389. Maidens that have won their first starts are the likeliest
horses to win following long layoffs.

A. True   (31)
B. False

390. Horses away thirty days or longer win what proportion
of their fair share of their starts?

A. 30%   (28)
B. 50%
C. 70%
D. 90%

391. A recent sharp race is especially impressive on a tiring
surface.

A. True   (31)
B. False

392. "Good" form horses can be bet to win profitably at what
stage of the season?

A. early   (28)
B. middle
C. late
D. none

393. Layoffs of 45 days or so are least worrisome among the
2-year-olds.

A. True   (29)
B. False

394. The strongest known improvement factor among relatively fresh horses is

A. bid and hung   (28)
B. surprise speed
C. stretch rally
D. up close at every call

395. When analyzing relatively fresh horses, which factor most reliably predicts sharp form next out?

A. two moves at different points of call   (29)
B. raced closer to the lead at each call
C. big win last out
D. surprise early speed

396. The most overrated improvement factor in handicapping is

A. bid and hung   (28)
B. fast workouts
C. surprise early speed
D. the stretch gain

397. The most powerful form cycle bets can be saved for

A. horses that win fresh after a long layoff   (29)
B. sprinters making their third or fourth starts after
   a layoff, provided the last race was a sharp performance
C. routers returning to middle distances following a
   layoff and a single sprint
D. 3-year-olds dropping in claiming class

398. Repeated all-out stretch drives are too taxing for all but the best horses in each division.

A. True   (30)
B. False

399. The best conditioning pattern for routers following a layoff is

A. a single sprint   (28)
B. a pair of sprints
C. a sprint and a route
D. a pair of routes

400. An unusually positive sign of form that handicappers have traditionally misinterpreted is

A. the surprise early speed of horses that normally show no speed **(29)**
B. an all-out win following a layoff
C. an easy win after running up close to the stretch call
D. the taxing stretch drive

401. Statistics indicate how many bad races in the recent record can be excused?

A. 0 **(28)**
B. 1
C. 2
D. 3

402. Studies show clearly that horses wearing front bandages win far fewer than their rightful share of races.

A. True **(28)**
B. False

403. Statistics indicate horses having form excuses due to bad trips win significantly more than their fair share of their next starts.

A. True **(28)**
B. False

404. Which horse is most likely to repeat its recent win?

A. **(30)**

Videogenic × — B. m. 5, by Caucasus—Video Babe, by T V Commercial
Own.—Davis A — 121 — Br.—Singer J B (Ky) — 1987 3 1 1 0 $62,490
Tr.—Davis Barbara — 1986 20 5 0 2 $308,762
Lifetime 51 18 2 5 $827,247 — Turf 21 8 1 3 $478,383

31Jan87-7Aqu 1$\frac{1}{8}$ ⊡ :48^{2}1:14^{3}1:55^{1}sy 6$\frac{1}{2}$ 119 4^3 2^{hd} 1^1 1^3 GraellA^8 ⒻRare Tr't H 66-34 Videogenic, SquanSong,BethsSong 8
31Jan87—Grade III
17Jan87-8Aqu 1$\frac{1}{16}$ ⊡ :48^{2}1:13^{2}1:46^{1}ft 11 122 11^{14}11$^{9\frac{3}{4}}$ 9$^{7\frac{3}{4}}$ 9$^{8\frac{1}{4}}$ DvisRG^2 ⒻAffectnly H 71-20 SqunSong,Clemnn'sRose,Ms.Elois 11
17Jan87—Grade III; Dull effort
2Jan87-8Aqu 1$\frac{1}{4}$ ⊡ :48^{4}1:40 2:06^{1}sy *7-5 122 2$^{1\frac{1}{2}}$ 3$^{3\frac{1}{2}}$ 2$^{1\frac{1}{2}}$ 2$^{1\frac{3}{4}}$ Davis R G^4 ⒻHcp0 82-21 Beths Song, Videogenic,FlyingHeat 5
20Dec86-8Aqu 1$\frac{5}{8}$ ⊡ :50^{3}2:07^{3}2:44^{1}ft 3$\frac{1}{2}$e 111 1$^{1\frac{1}{2}}$ 1$^{1\frac{1}{2}}$ 1^{hd} 5^5 SamynJL^6 Gllnt Fox H 86-09 BuckleyBoy,FlyMeAgin,FelingGllnt 7
20Dec86—Grade II

B.

Tricky Squaw — B. f. 4, by Clever Trick—Black Apache, by Gainsworth
Own.—Klein E V — 110 — Br.—Hess John (Ill) — 1987 2 2 0 0 $38,200
Tr.—Lukas D Wayne — 1986 9 1 2 3 $24,365
Lifetime 18 5 5 4 $95,807

25Jan87-8BM 1$\frac{1}{8}$:46^2 1:10^3 1:49^{4}gd 6$\frac{1}{4}$ 116 1$^{1\frac{1}{2}}$ 1^1 1$^{1\frac{1}{2}}$ 1^2 DcyTT^2 ⒻⓇSpr Bwl H 82-25 TrickySquw,Missdoon,SpcilVictory 8
15Jan87-8BM 1 :46^2 1:12^1 1:38 ft 3 120 1^3 1^2 1^2 1$^{1\frac{1}{4}}$ Doocy T T^5 ⒻAw18000 78-30 Tricky Squaw, Gray Tab, Bubali 6
31Dec86-8BM 1 :46^2 1:12 1:38^{3}gd 4$\frac{1}{2}$ 113 1^4 1^1 1^1 1$^{2\frac{1}{2}}$ Doocy T T^6 ⒻAw17000 75-32 TrickySquaw,CanadianJill,Saillante 7
18Dec86-8BM 1 :46^2 1:13 1:40^{2}m 21 113 1^4 1^2 1^{hd} 3$^{4\frac{1}{2}}$ Doocy T T^1 ⒻAw17000 61-41 Gray Tab, Saillante, Tricky Squaw 8

5Dec86-8BM 6f :222 :453 1:111sl 16 112 3½ 42¼ 57½ 312 ♦ Doocy T T3 ⒻAw19000 71-26 Luisant, Chrysilia, Izabelle's Quillo 5
♦ 5Dec86—Dead heat
20Nov86-8BM 6f :223 :452 1:10 ft 17 112 43 44½ 57½ 510¾ Doocy T T3 ⒻAw19000 78-22 Admat, Luisant, Balimonday 7
30Oct86-8BM 5½f :214 :444 1:031ft 3½e115 11½ 11 51½ 77¼ CastnedM4 ⒻAw19000 89-24 Canadian Jill, Admat, Coffee Roll 7
31May86-9Aks 6f :23 :462 1:13 ft *2-5e120 1hd 21 21½ 22½ Doocy T T1 ⒻGd Life 69-32 MiniDocN'Me,TrickySquw.Life'sBst 7
●Feb 18 Aqu ⊡ 4f ft :47 h ●Jan 9 BM 5f gd 1:01 h

C.

Alyosha
B. c. 3, by Big Spruce—Ivy Road, by Dr Fager
Br.—Nerud J A Revocable Trust (Fla) 1987 3 1 0 0 $9,000
Own.—Nerud J A 117 Tr.—Nerud Jan H 1986 3 M 0 1 $2,760
Lifetime 6 1 0 1 $11,760
7Feb87-3Aqu 1⅛ ⊡ :4741:1331:542ft *1 122 33 2hd 1½ 11¾ Davis R G7 M50000 70-21 Alyosha,TimeForUs,GreatContract 12
14Jan87-6Aqu 1⅛ ⊡ :4941:1411:524ft 7½e122 52½ 32 45 58 Bailey J D5 Mdn 70-16 Pi Phi Prince,Endorse,Hoistn'Hail 10
3Jan87-6Aqu 6f ⊡ :23 :4621:113m 7½ 122 76¾ 616 519 516 Davis R G7 Mdn 70-16 Pop John, Township, Quick Debut 8
27Nov86-4Aqu 7f :234 :473 1:254gd 4¼ 1135 31 64¼ 612 615 Baird E T5 Mdn 57-29 MajorBerd,InAllRespects,SirBemis 9
17Nov86-4Aqu 1 :47 1:12 1:372ft 14 1135 2hd 2hd 34 310½ Baird E T9 Mdn 68-20 FastForward,FoolishPirate,Alyosha 9
27Sep86-9Bel 6f :221 :454 1:114sy 13 118 813 821 821 715½ Davis R G8 Mdn 67-17 Into The Sun,Tangazo,ItsAcedemic 8
Jan 12 Bel tr.t 5f ft 1:04 b Dec 27 Bel tr.t 4f ft :504 b

D.

Forest Fair
B. c. 3, by Naskra—Fairest Forest, by Big Spruce
Br.—Meadowhill (Ky) 1987 1 1 0 0 $16,200
Own.—Marano G 119 Tr.—Lenzini John J Jr 1986 2 1 0 1 $16,440
Lifetime 3 2 0 1 $32,640
21Jan87-6Aqu 1 1/16 ⊡ :4721:1211:444sy *6-5 117 1½ 1½ 14 18¾ Santos J A1 Aw27000 86-17 Forest Fair, Coco'sDouble,TargetX. 6
29Dec86-4Aqu 6f ⊡ :221 :4531:111ft *6-5 118 2hd 1½ 11½ 1½ Antley C W1 Mdn 88-18 ForstFir,Gnom'sPlsur,I'mExubrnt 12
17Aug86-6Sar 6f :22 :453 1:103m *6-5 118 31 32 24 38 Cordero A Jr3 Mdn 79-11 Peaceable,ChariotofWar,ForestFir 11
●Feb 20 Aqu ⊡ 3f ft :36 h Feb 13 Aqu ⊡ 7f ft 1:294 b Feb 6 Aqu ⊡ 5f ft 1:014 h ●Jan 14 Aqu ⊡ 1 ft 1:423 b

405. On form analysis, which maiden is most likely to win its next start?

A. **(30)**

Fast Lead
B. c. 3, by Romantic Lead—Swift Accipiter, by Accipiter
Br.—DiMauro Stephen A (NY) 1987 2 M 0 1 $4,200
Own.—DiMauro Mrs S 122 Tr.—DiMauro Stephen L 1986 0 M 0 0
Lifetime 2 0 0 1 $4,200
4Feb87-6Aqu 6f ⊡ :23 :4641:114gd 8 122 31½ 2½ 34 34¼ Migliore R2 Mdn 81-14 Gnome'sPleasure,Briskeen,FstLed 12
18Jan87-4Aqu 6f ⊡ :23 :4641:121ft 13e122 62¼ 42 52½ 42½ Belmonte J F2 [S]Mdn 80-20 HotAmber,AcadianLuck,PttiesBoy 12
Jan 30 Bel tr.t 4f ft :483 h Jan 25 Bel tr.t 4f ft :49 b Jan 14 Bel tr.t 4f ft :491 b Jan 9 Bel tr.t 5f ft 1:021 hg

B.

I'm Exuberant
Ch. c. 3, by Exuberant—I'm Absolute, by Mr Leader
Br.—Isaacs Harry Z (Ky) 1987 1 M 1 0 $5,060
Own.—Brookfield Farms 122 Tr.—Kelly Michael J 1986 3 M 0 1 $2,760
Lifetime 4 0 1 1 $7,820
10Jan87-4Aqu 6f ⊡ :223 :4621:111gd 12 122 41¼ 11½ 11 2¾ Davis R G10 Mdn 87-10 PocktBook,I'mExbrnt,Gnom'sPlsr 10
29Dec86-4Aqu 6f ⊡ :221 :4531:111ft 17 118 85¾ 65½ 56½ 34 Samyn J L5 Mdn 84-18 ForstFir,Gnom'sPlsur,I'mExubrnt 12
22Dec86-4Aqu 6f ⊡ :223 :4631:112ft 18 118 31 32 34½ 55½ Samyn J L2 Mdn 81-17 WrongDoctor,StarRacer,Unlevened 9
12Dec86-6Aqu 6f ⊡ :222 :4611:11 m 9¼ 118 68 55 56½ 611½ Davis R G2 Mdn 77-16 MstrS.M.,Wrd'sPrd,ChrstphrsPppy 9
Feb 20 Bel tr.t 3f ft :36 h ●Feb 8 Bel tr.t 5f ft 1:003 h

C.

Front Linesman
B. c. 3, by Princelet—Stormy Shower, by Moving Target
Br.—John P. Campo (Ky) 1987 1 M 0 0
Own.—Campo J P 122 Tr.—Campo John P 1986 0 M 0 0
Lifetime 1 0 0 0
12Feb87-5Aqu 6f ⊡ :23 :4711:13 gd 2½ 122 84¼ 56 56 66¾ Privitera R3 Mdn 72-23 ProdlyConfdnt,LgnD'Hnr,MkYrPc 10
12Feb87—Slow start
●Feb 7 Bel tr.t 5f ft :583 hg Jan 31 Bel tr.t 5f sy 1:024 h Jan 28 Bel tr.t 4f ft :482 hg Jan 18 Bel tr.t 6f ft 1:174 b

D.

Wasichus
Ch. c. 3, by Nodouble—Explorare, by Dr Fager
Br.—Tartan Stable (Fla) 1987 0 M 0 0
Own.—Tartan Stable 122 Tr.—Nerud Jan H 1986 0 M 0 0
Lifetime 0 0 0 0
Feb 18 Bel tr.t 3f ft :353 bg Feb 13 Bel tr.t 4f ft :482 b

406. The maiden below does not show the kind of 2nd-place finish that often predicts a win next out. Why?

Affluenza

Dk. b. or br. f. 4, by Honest Pleasure—Blithe Spirit, by Raise A Native

	Br.—Meyerhoff R E (Md)	1987 1 M 1 0 $2,750
Own.—Meyerhoff R E	**122** Tr.—Small Richard W	1985 6 M 4 1 $11,610
	Lifetime 7 0 5 1 $14,360	

2Feb87-2Lrl	6½f :231 :481 1:214m	*4-5 122	2nd 1½	2½	2nd	Bracciale V Jr3	ⓕMdn	72-29 Frances P., Affluenza,MorningHour 6
21Nov85-3Lrl	1¹⁄₁₆:473 1:14 1:462ft	*1-2e 119	2nd 1½	3¹¹⁄₂ 47		Wright D R7	ⓕMdn	74-20 Hum a Tune,PotOfAntics,BeatItKid 9
9Nov85-5Lrl	1 :464 1:12 1:381ft	3½ 119	3½ 2nd	2nd 2nk		Bracciale V Jr4	ⓕMdn	81-14 SrchForShltr,Afflunz,PotOfAntics 10
9Nov85—Bore in								
31Oct85-6Lrl	6½f :231 :472 1:194ft	*7-5 119	1hd 2nd	2nd 2¾		Wright D R10	ⓕMdn	81-18 NancyMassie,Affluenza,Quadorian 11
10Oct85-2Lrl	7f :224 :464 1:254ft	4½ 119	1¹¹⁄ 11	2nd 2½		Wright D R3	ⓕMdn	80-18 ThrowAwyThKy,Afflunz,NncyMssi 10
28Sep85-1Lrl	6½f :222 :462 1:19 ft	3½ 119	54½ 66	46 39		Wright D R5	ⓕMdn	77-14 Gala De Oro, HumaTune,Affiuenza 11
18Sep85-5Pim	6f :233 :47 1:123ft	*9-5 119	2¹ 44	35 27½		Bracciale V Jr1	ⓕMdn	75-21 Toes Knows,Affluenza,AutumnPlaᵥ
18Sep85—Steadied								

Jan 18 Pim 6f sy 1:16 b ● Jan 13 Pim 4f ft :483 b Dec 28 Pim 5f ft 1:03 b

A. the horse is a 4-year-old (30)
B. the race Feb. 2 was in the mud
C. it has finished 2nd too often
D. eight is too many starts without winning

407. The current form of 3YO claiming horses often looks much worse than it actually is because

A. Stables have not yet discovered their horses' dis- (33) tance and pace preferences
B. Cheaper 3YOs tend to need more seasoning before they are ready to show their best
C. Form cycles of developing horses are just too uneven and unpredictable
D. The horses have been seriously outclassed while running with unrealistically high selling tags

408. "Acceptable form" in a race of a higher class than today's would include

A. an even effort versus today's class some 7 to 10 (30) lengths behind the leaders
B. no early speed but a finish that beats half the field
C. racing up close at any point of call
D. passing tiring horses in the stretch

409. A stakes horse that races about once a month gives an unusually dull effort. It returns in seven days in a classified allowance race. This is a positive sign.

A. True (33)
B. False

410. When evaluating nonclaiming 3YOs on form, handicappers must be primarily concerned with

A. recency   **(31)**
B. soundness
C. readiness
D. consistency

411. Assuming it were not plainly outclassed, a horse approaching winning form should have been up close at the stretch call of its previous race unless

A. it has a come-from-behind running style   **(30)**
B. the distance was longer by a furlong or more
C. it was up close at each of the first two calls
D. all of the above

412. Any horse not dropping in class, which was up close at the stretch call of its last race but lost two lengths or more in the stretch, deserves a form defect unless

A. It showed high early speed   **(30)**
B. It has a come-from-behind running style
C. It finished in-the-money regardless
D. It was the first race following a layoff

413. A subtle aspect of form analysis that defeats many talented younger horses in allowance and stakes races they would have won handily six months later is

A. unresponsiveness to the rider's signals   **(31)**
B. the proper blend of speed and stamina in their
    training pattern
C. a pattern of workouts that are just too fast
D. seasoning in challenging competition

414. A demonstrably effective way that trainers manipulate form and get good mutuels to boot is

A. a three-to-four week layoff, no workouts, long, hard   **(31)**
    gallops
B. dull race, drop in class, switch to a more favor-
    able jockey
C. one dull sprint following a long layoff, switch to
    a route
D. a series of dull races at unrealistically high class
    levels, followed by a huge, suspicious class drop

415. Class is a function of form.

A. True   (31)
B. False

416. The most dramatic improvement factor not obvious in the past performances or results charts is

A. a successful trainer maneuver   (28)
B. first time on lasix
C. a positive change in body language
D. changing leads correctly at last

417. The best trainers of younger developing horses, notably nonclaiming 3YOs, reveal a skillful combination of

A. patience and aggressiveness   (31)
B. alternating sprints and routes
C. speed workouts and longer workouts
D. running styles and jockeys

418. A perfectly acceptable form guideline urges handicappers to bet on no horse beyond age seven.

A. True   (31)
B. False

419. Which statement best characterizes the form of 2-year-olds?

A. Form cycles are frequently uneven and unpre-   (31)
   dictable
B. Lengthy layoffs following a good race are definite
   negative signs
C. Workouts should be frequent, fast, and easily accomplished, even after racing has begun
D. Two-year-olds tend either to improve rapidly or
   to deteriorate dramatically

420. Which is most likely to disrupt the improving form of an impressive 3-year-old?

A. competing with small, nagging physical ailments   (33)
B. premature or unrealistic entry in a Grade 1 or
   Grade 2 stakes
C. repeated all-out stretch drives while moving ahead
   in class
D. inability to relax or to respond to the jockey's rat-
   ing when trying to route

421. Modern form eliminations are best identified

A. in the initial phase of handicapping, so that the crucial work of speed, class, and pace handicapping can be concentrated on the authentic contenders **(32)**
B. by conservative standards of recent action but liberal standards of recent performance
C. in the later phases of handicapping, so that too many eventual winners will not be eliminated prematurely
D. by forsaking the obviously dull horses, but letting the odds dictate on the relatively large number of horses having questionable or dubious condition

422. It's Nov. 3. Which horse(s) below can be eliminated reliably on form?

5th Aqueduct

7 FURLONGS. (1.20⅕) CLAIMING. Purse $20,000. 3-year-olds and upward. Weights, 3-year-olds, 120 lbs. Older, 122 lbs. Non-winners of two races since October 15 allowed 3 lbs. Of a race since then, 5 lbs. Claiming Price $50,000; for each $2,500 to $45,000, 2 lbs. (Races when entered to be claimed for $40,000 or less not considered.)

Coupled—Flying Skipper and Stark Secret.

(32)

A.

College Cheer — **Own.—Woodcliff Stable** — 117

Ch. g. 4, by Harvard Man—Little Outcry, by Rash Prince
Br.—Elmendorf Farm (NY)
Tr.—Baeza Braulio $50,000
Lifetime 37 3 8 4 $123,360

1986	21	2	7	2	$91,540
1985	16	1	1	2	$31,820
Turf	5	0	0	0	$3,420

13Oct86-5Bel	6f	:224	:46	1:103ft	6	117	11	1½	14	11¼	Graell A9	ⓈAw28000	89-16	CollegeCheer,TropiclFront,RootCnl	9
28Sep86-9Bel	7f	:223	:453	1:232m	6¾	117	2½	21	24	25¼	Graell A8	ⓈAw28000	80-15	Melstrom,CollegeChr,TropiclFront	10
7Sep86-1Bel	6f	:222	:454	1:094ft	5½	117	34½	45	56½	58¾	RomeroRP1	ⓈAw28000	84-14	Zonter, Flag King, Be A Tyrant	7
22Aug86-5Sar	1 1/16 Ⓣ	:47	1:104	1:42 fm	26	117	21½	53	107¼	1010¼	RomeroRP8	ⓈAw29500	77-13	Rio Belle, Chestertown,TalcBuster	10
10Aug86-2Sar	7f	:222	:452	1:241ft	4¼	117	31	2hd	1hd	42	RomeroRP7	ⓈAw28000	79-14	Section Three, FlagKing,Romanizer	9
26Jly86-5Bel	6f	:224	:47	1:114ft	*7-5	117	31½	32	31	41¾	Venezia M8	ⓈAw28000	81-28	Exmoon, Flag King, What A Philip	8
13Jly86-2Bel	7f	:223	:454	1:231m	5	117	31	32½	23	23¼	VelsquezJ6	ⓈAw28000	83-15	I'mYourBoy,CollegeCheer,Romnizr	8
6Jly86-9Bel	1 1/16 Ⓣ	:462	1:102	1:42 fm	16	117	22	23	36½	48¼	RomroRP10	ⓈAw29500	78-18	Wanderkin,G'DayM:r,Chestertown	10

Nov 1 Bel tr.t 3f ft :37 b   Oct 21 Bel tr.t 5f ft 1:051 b   Oct 8 Bel tr.t 4f ft :482 h   Sep 26 Bel tr.t 3f ft :36 h

B.

Askrano — **Own.—Judd Monte Farms** — 1085

B. c. 4, by Naskra—Noble Lady, by Vaguely Noble
Br.—Grousemont Farm (Ky)
Tr.—Johnson Philip G $45,000
Lifetime 19 3 3 0 $36,683

1986	12	1	1	0	$16,210
1985	7	2	2	0	$20,473
Turf	5	1	2	0	$3,973

23Oct86-7Aqu	6f	:22	:45	1:10 ft	25	1085	85½	97	68½	74¼	Baird E T2	45000	87-17	GreenShekl,FlyingSkippr,StrkScrt	10
5Sep86-6Bel	1	:444	1:093	1:353ft	11	117	69½	510	69½	68½	Samyn J L1	75000	78-18	Best ByTest,Bienestar,SidiBouSaid	8
18Aug86-3Sar	7f	:222	:453	1:234gd	7e	117	44	42½	65¼	65¾	Samyn J L8	Aw27000	77-21	CutlssRelity,Thundercrckr,SunnyFt	8
18Jly86-5Mth	170	:462	1:104	1:41 ft	8¼	119	35½	33	44½	55¼	Sint-MrtinE4	Aw16000	86-18	WiseTimes,Mykawa,StacySumTime	6
1Jly86-8Pha	170	:453	1:103	1:412ft	*8-5	118	45	42	53½	53	Sint-MrtinE3	Aw14000	90-13	ClockTowr,GrndHorzon's,JmpoffJo	7
14Jun86-6Mth	170	:473	1:121	1:423ft	2¾	118	31	3½	1hd	12	Sint-MrtinE5	Aw15000	83-21	Askrno,ComeHomeBoy,DnctothWir	5
28May86-7Bel	1 1/16	:473	1:121	1:424ft	20	119	62¾	84¼	811	819¼	Samyn J L5	Aw26000	69-20	PersonalFlag,Kamakura,Hberdsher	8
28May86—Veered in st.															
17May86-4Bel	1	:47	1:113	1:371ft	18	119	53½	2½	2½	2nk	Samyn J L6	Aw26000	79-15	CharmedRook,Askrano,Haberdsher	8

Oct 31 Bel tr.t 4f ft :501 b   Oct 22 Bel tr.t 3f ft :361 h   Oct 17 Bel tr.t 5f ft 1:011 h   Oct 7 Bel 3f ft :374 b

C.

Silent Hour
Own.—Jennings L W **113**

B. h. 5, by Bold Hour—Cabin's Squaw, by Cabin
Br.—Marriott P M (Fla)
Tr.—Jennings Lawrence W **$45,000**
Lifetime 23 5 7 2 $80,331

1986	4	0	2	0	$7,440
1985	8	2	3	1	$43,281
Turf	2	0	0	0	$1,275

25Oct86-3Med	6f	$:22^2$	$:45^2$	1:11 ft	*2¼	116	5^6	4^6	5^3	2^{nk}	McCauley W H^8	35000	87-18	YoungJedi,SilentHour,SmartFalcon	8
22Aug86-5Mth	6f	$:22^4$	$:45^4$	$1:10^3$ft	*1	116	4^3	4^2	$3^{1/2}$	2^{hd}	Sousonis S^6	32000	87-18	Fast Caz, Silent Hour, Super Count	6
13Aug86-8Mth	6f	$:22^4$	$:45^3$	$1:10^1$ft	*4-5	116	4^3	4^2	$4^{3 1/2}$	$4^{3 1/4}$	Rocco J^3	35000	86-19	LordBlcony,ScrdMotion,SmrtFlcon	6
2Aug86-5Mth	6f	:22	$:44^1$	$1:09^3$ft	7½	115	$5^{4 1/4}$	5^5	$5^{2 1/4}$	$4^{3 3/4}$	Rocco J^5	Aw20000	88-12	Habitoni,Thundercrcker,AerilDisply	7
2Sep85-6Med	6f	$:22^2$	:45	$1:09^2$ft	4¼	115	$4^{3 1/2}$	$4^{4 1/2}$	3^3	2^1	Rocco J^1	Rise Jim H	94-10	MjesticVenture,SilntHour,KingBbr	4
17Aug85-8Mth	6f	$:22^3$	$:44^4$	1:09 ft	9	115	$4^{4 1/4}$	3^3	$4^{3 1/4}$	2^5	Rocco J^2	Aloma's Rlr	90-10	Aeronotic, Silent Hour, For Halo	8
5Aug85-9Mth	6f	$:22^4$	:45	$1:09^4$ft	6½	115	3^{nk}	2^{hd}	2^2	1no	Rocco J^3	Aw25000	91-18	SilentHour,RmblerRed,Jesse'sHope	8
22Jly85-9Mth	6f	$:23^2$	$:46^1$	1:10 ft	2¾	117	$4^{1 1/4}$	$3^{1 1/2}$	$2^{2 1/2}$	2^3	Rocco J^4	Aw16000	87-21	Now'sTheTime,SilentHour,SportJet	5

Oct 21 Mth 5f ft $1:01^1$ b   Oct 16 Mth 4f ft $:49^2$ b (d)   Oct 12 Mth 4f ft $:49^1$ b

D.

Up Pops Awinner
Own.—Hobeau Farm **117**

Gr. h. 5, by Sawbones—Not Many Pops, by Beau Gar
Br.—Hobeau Farm Inc (Fla)
Tr.—Jerkens H Allen **$50,000**
Lifetime 37 6 8 6 $164,999

1986	10	0	3	2	$36,896
1985	6	0	2	0	$17,893
Turf	6	0	0	1	$9,000

26Oct86-6Lrl	6f	$:22^3$	$:46^3$	$1:11^1$sy	3¼	117	5^6	$6^{8 1/4}$	$5^{9 1/2}$	$5^{9 3/4}$	BraccialeVJr^2	Aw20000	77-25	WillrdScott,MidnghtCll,SfOnScond	6
12Oct86-6Bel	7f	$:22^3$	$:45^2$	1:22 ft	12	115	$4^{4 1/2}$	5^5	$5^{8 1/2}$	$4^{8 3/4}$	DeCarlo C P^2	Aw36000	83-13	BestByTest,SentorBrdy,CutlssRlity	5
2Oct86-7Bel	6f	$:22^1$	$:44^4$	1:08 ft	4¼	115	8^{10}	$8^{7 3/4}$	8^{11}	$5^{11 1/2}$	DeCarlo C P^2	Aw36000	90-09	BestByTest,TonkaPss,Mr.T.AndMe	8
19Sep86-5Bel	6f	$:22^1$	$:45^1$	$1:09^3$ft	*2¼	116	$5^{3 1/2}$	$2^{1 1/2}$	$3^{1/2}$	$2^{1/2}$	DeCarlo C P^8	85000	93-12	AtomSmshr,UpPopsAwnnr,BldMrdr	8
1Sep86-13Rkm	1⅛	$:46^2$	$1:10^2$	1:50 ft	13	114	4^4	$5^{5 1/2}$	10^{14}	$12^{14 1/2}$	VrsJL^{10}	N H'mpshr H	76-16	DoItAginDn,SunMster,‡EntitledTo	14

1Sep86—Grade III

13Aug86-5Sar	7f	$:22^3$	$:45^1$	1:23 ft	3½	115	$3^{6 1/2}$	3^7	3^2	$3^{3/4}$	Santos J A^3	Aw36000	86-17	Shdowmr,E.K.Sptz,UpPopsAwinner	7
6Jly86-7Bel	7f	$:22^4$	$:45^1$	$1:23^1$ft	23	115	7^9	8^{14}	7^6	$2^{1 1/2}$	Decarlo C P^3	Duc D'or	84-16	Cogniznt,UpPopsAwinner,Cullendle	8
5Jun86-8Bel	7f	$:22^4$	$:46^1$	$1:23^3$ft	6¾	117	4^3	$5^{5 1/2}$	5^5	$4^{3 1/4}$	Santagata N^4	Aw36000	81-17	H.T.Wills,AnothrSummr,DoItAgnDn	7

●Sep 17 Bel 3f ft $:32^4$ h   Sep 13 Bel 5f ft $1:00^2$ h

E.

Tumbler
Own.—Harry Hatch Stable **113**

B. h. 5, by Key To The Mint—Call The Queen, by Hail To Reason
Br.—North Ridge Farm (Ky)
Tr.—Ferriola Peter **$45,000**
Lifetime 48 6 9 7 $157,660

1986	8	0	1	0	$6,980
1985	8	1	0	2	$16,848
Turf	1	0	0	0	$160

11Oct86-1Bel	7f	$:22^3$	$:45^3$	$1:23^2$ft	4½	117	$7^{8 3/4}$	$7^{6 1/2}$	$6^{4 3/4}$	$4^{2 3/4}$	Migliore R^1	50000	82-19	Frontier Justice,StarkSecret,Semaj	7
19Sep86-5Bel	6f	$:22^1$	$:45^1$	$1:09^3$ft	3¾e	113	8^{13}	8^{12}	$8^{5 1/2}$	5^2	Lovato F Jr^2	75000	92-12	AtomSmshr,UpPopsAwnnr.BldMrdr	8
1Sep86-5Bel	7f	$:22^4$	$:45^4$	1:22 ft	7	117	$6^{5 1/2}$	$7^{6 1/2}$	7^{11}	$6^{11 3/4}$	Davis R G^4	c50000	80-14	Bowladrome, Habitonia, Revelrout	8
25Jly86-1Bel	6f	$:22^2$	:46	1:10 ft	14	113	$6^{9 1/2}$	$6^{5 1/2}$	5^6	$4^{6 1/4}$	Maple E^2	70000	86-20	Cmptr'sChc,MtthT.Prkr,AtmSmshr	6
17Jly86-9Bel	7f	$:23^1$	:46	$1:23^2$ft	14	117	$2^{1/2}$	1^{hd}	1^1	2no	Santos J A^5	50000	85-11	Lucky Belief, Tumbler,SilverStark	11
4Jly86-1Bel	1$\frac{1}{16}$	$:46^1$	$1:10^4$	$1:41^4$ft	16	117	3^2	5^5	6^{13}	$6^{17 1/2}$	Samyn J L^6	75000	75-11	Carjack,FirstOneUp,RmblingRector	6
23Jun86-8Bel	7f	:23	$:46^1$	$1:22^2$ft	55	117	6^4	$8^{6 1/2}$	$7^{7 3/4}$	5^{12}	Samyn J L^4	Aw36000	78-13	DoItAgnDn,AnothrSmmr,CtlssRlty	10
31May86-4Bel	7f	$:22^3$	$:45^4$	$1:23^1$ft	40	122	$6^{5 1/2}$	$5^{6 1/2}$	5^7	6^5	Samyn J L^7	100000	81-18	Computr'sChoic,Pttngl,NtonlEnrgy	7

Oct 31 Aqu 3f ft :39 b   Sep 15 Aqu 3f ft $:37^3$ b   Sep 12 Aqu 5f ft $1:02^3$ b

F.

Lucky Belief
Own.—Davis A **113**

B. c. 4, by Believe It—Lucky Return, by Bagdad
Br.—Stephens Lucille E (Ky)
Tr.—Moschera Gasper S **$45,000**
Lifetime 17 3 4 2 $61,850

1986	9	1	2	1	$23,400
1985	8	2	2	1	$38,450
Turf	1	0	0	0	

8Oct86-9Bel	7f	$:22^4$	$:46^1$	$1:23^1$ft	20	107^{10}	$3^{1 1/2}$	$3^{1/2}$	3^2	$4^{6 3/4}$	Correa C J^{10}	35000	79-19	FingersIntheTill,Revirout,TlcPowr	12
17Jly86-9Bel	7f	$:23^1$	:46	$1:23^2$ft	2½	117	$4^{2 1/2}$	4^2	$3^{1 1/2}$	1no	Maple E^2	c50000	85-11	Lucky Belief, Tumbler,SilverStark	11

17Jly86—Jst up, ret. lame

22Jun86-1Bel	1⅛	:47	$1:11^1$	1:49 ft	4¾	113	$6^{4 1/2}$	6^4	$4^{4 1/2}$	$5^{3 1/2}$	Bailey J D^3	70000	76-19	Carjck,FirstOneUp,FingersIntheTill	7
14Jun86-2Bel	1$\frac{1}{16}$	$:46^4$	$1:11^2$	$1:43^4$ft	*2¾	117	6^4	4^4	3^4	2^2	Maple E^4	50000	81-20	Carjck,LuckyBelief,Nijinsky'sRuler	7
19May86-5Bel	1$\frac{1}{16}$ Ⓣ	:46	$1:10^2$	$1:41^1$fm	24	119	6^5	$10^{8 1/2}$	11^{14}	$11^{21 1/4}$	Bailey J D^7	Aw26000	69-16	DoubleFeint,FarawayIsland,Srppel	12
11May86-4Bel	7f	$:22^4$	$:45^4$	$1:23^1$ft	3	117	4^2	4^2	5^3	$3^{2 1/4}$	Maple E^6	50000	84-15	NtionlEnergy,TlcPower,LuckyBelif	7
29Mar86-12Hia	1$\frac{1}{16}$	$:46^4$	$1:10^3$	$1:42^4$ft	*2¾	116	2^1	2^6	2^5	2^2	Maple E^2	50000	87-06	Jumpoff Joe,LuckyBelief,AlwaysUp	8
22Mar86-10Hia	6f	$:22^1$	:45	$1:09^2$ft	4½	114	8^8	$8^{8 3/4}$	$9^{9 3/4}$	$7^{8 3/4}$	St Leon G^5	70000	84-15	Alaskan Jim, My Mac, Hi Ideal	10

Oct 24 Bel tr.t 4f ft $:49^1$ b   Sep 20 Bel tr.t 5f ft $1:02^3$ b   Sep 15 Bel tr.t 4f ft $:50^1$ b   Sep 8 Bel 4f ft :49 h

423. It's Oct. 31. Which horse(s) can be eliminated on form?

6th BayMeadows

6 FURLONGS. (1.07⅘) CLAIMING. Purse $13,000. 2-year-olds. Weight, 120 lbs. Non-winners of two races since September 15, 3 lbs.; a race since then 6 lbs. Claiming price $25,000; for each $2,500 to $20,000, 1 lb. (Maiden and claiming races for $16,000 or less not considered.)

A. **(32)**

Rule The Night

Dk. b. or br. c. 2, by Codex—Reporting Act, by Roberto

MAPLE S **114** **Br.—Mel Hatley Racing Stables (Okla)** **1986 7 1 3 0 $10,004**

Tr.—Lukas D Wayne $25,000

Own.—Lukas & Hatley **Lifetime 7 1 3 0 $10,004**

16Oct86-6BM 6f :22 :45^1 1:10^{2}ft 6 115 5^{3½} 4^{1½} 2^{hd} 2^1 Maple S^4 25000 86-18 FlyngCommndr,RlThNght,Vntr'sStr 6

26Sep86-2BM 1 :47^3 1:13 1:40 gd *8-5 118 2^{hd} 1^{hd} 1^{hd} 1^{1½} Maple S^4 M16000 68-29 RuleTheNight,FinllyProved,GrtZoot 9

11Aug86-2Dmr 6f :22 :45^4 1:11^{4}ft 6¼ 118 8^{3¾} 8^{7¾} 9^{6¼} 8^{8¼} McCarron C J^6 M32000 71-13 DelVolante,ScoreHigh,Bwn'sFields 12

11Aug86—Wide into stretch; eased late

28Jly86-4Dmr 6f :22^1 :46 1:11^{3}ft *8-5 117 6^{2¾} 8^{11} 8^{16} 8^{18¾} McCarron C J^8 M32000 61-16 BoldBrgin,DrbyChck,EghtIsEnough 8

28Jly86—Veered out start; erratic backstretch

9Jly86-4Hol 5½f :23 :47^1 1:06^{1}ft *8-5 118 5^{2¾} 5^{2¼} 5^{4½} 6^{7¾} McCarron C J^8 M50000 75-18 StrdustFolly,Rkposh,You'rGlorous 11

26Jun86-1CD 5f :23 :47^1 1:00^{1}ft 2½ 119 5^4 5^{6½} 4^3 2^{1½} Bass S H^3 M35000 86-17 LserLike,RulethNight,SplndidRtort 9

12Jun86-4CD 5f :23^1 :47^2 1:00^{2}ft *8-5 118 2^{1½} 2^1 2^{1½} 2^{nk} Day P^4 M35000 87-15 Cdillc'sKing,RulethNight,StlwrtFlg 8

Oct 8 BM 4f ft :48^3 h Sep 18 BM 5f ft 1:02 h

B.

Super Adios

Dk. b. or br. g. 2, by Adios—Flit to Sunrise, by Flit-to

BONILLA R **114** **Br.—Resnick R (Cal)** **1986 9 1 0 1 $8,875**

Tr.—Byrd Adolph $25,000

Own.—Bryant J **Lifetime 9 1 0 1 $8,875**

9Oct86-3SA 6f :22 :45^2 1:11^{3}ft 30 116 10^{12} 10^{12} 10^{16} 10^{18¾} DelahoussayeE^8 40000 61-21 SundnceSqure,Rkposhi,Terrefying 10

9Oct86—Reared at start; wide into stretch

25Sep86-11Pom a1⅛ :48^4 1:15^3 1:56^{4}m 63 114 2^{hd} 4^{8½} 10^{26} — StvnsSA^5 Gtwy To Gly — — SvonTower,OkWin,WildrnssBound 10

25Sep86—Eased

18Sep86-11Pom 6½f :21^3 :45 1:17^{2}ft 42 114 4^4 4^{11} 5^{8½} 6^{13¼} StevnsSA^5 Beau Brml 80-12 CctusClipper,DoublSong,HighRgrds 6

18Sep86—Bumped start

12Sep86-7Pom 6f :21^4 :45^1 1:10^{4}ft 55 114 6^6 6^{12} 7^{14} 6^{11¾} Scott J M^8 Aw20000 85-11 SavonaTower,Robert'sLd,Rkposhi 10

24Jly86-4Dmr 6f :22^3 :47 1:12 ft *2½ 117 1^1 1^{½} 1^3 1^{5½} DelhoussyE^4 [S]M32000 78-15 SprAdos,FrstShootr,SoldGoldSnd 12

12Jly86-3Hol 5½f :22^2 :46 1:05 ft 67 118 4^{4½} 4^8 6^{11} 6^{16} Castanon A L^6 Mdn 73-14 Bold Jade, Soy Amigo, Candi'sGold 8

2Jly86-3Hol 5½f :22^2 :45^4 1:04^{2}ft 34 118 5^{2½} 6^{3¾} 6^{8¼} 5^{11¾} Castanon A L^5 [S]Mdn 80-09 FleetTito,SoyAmigo,GoldOnGreen 10

2Jly86—Checked on turn

25Jun86-5Hol 5f :22^3 :46^1 :58^{4}ft 16 118 5^4 4^{3½} 3^5 3^5 Castanon A L^2 M50000 87-13 ChocoltBlls,DrbyChick,SuprAdios 10

13Jun86-5Hol 5f :22^2 :46^1 :59 ft 12 118 4^{3½} 5^6 7^8 7^{9¾} Pedroza M A^1 [S]Mdn 81-17 Cuneo,NeverSmoke,FleetingTntoul 9

Oct 26 Hol 5f ft 1:01^2 h Oct 16 SA 5f ft 1:04^4 h Oct 5 SA 4f ft :48^1 h Sep 6 Pom 5f ft 1:01^4 hg

C.

Bold Bargain

Dk. b. or br. g. 2, by Bargain Day—Royally Rewarded, by Bold Forbes

CASTANEDA M **114** **Br.—Goldman & Coleman (Cal)** **1986 5 2 0 0 $11,550**

Tr.—Chew Matthew $25,000

Own.—Perez & McKinley **Lifetime 5 2 0 0 $11,550**

9Oct86-4BM 6f :22^3 :46 1:11^{2}ft *6-5 115 1^{hd} 1^1 1^{½} 1^{nk} Castaneda M^6 16000 82-19 BoldBargain,Honey'sCbret,HighStll 8

12Sep86-7Pom 6f :21^4 :45^1 1:10^{4}ft 7¼ 114 5^5 5^{7½} 5^{12} 8^{14¼} Mena F^2 Aw20000 83-11 SavonaTower,Robert'sLd,Rkposhi 10

27Aug86-8Dmr 7f :22^1 :45^2 1:23 ft 80 115 1^{hd} 2^{hd} 6^{7¼} 7^{13½} Soto S B^5 Balboa 76-14 TemperateSil,PolrJet,GoldOnGreen 8

27Aug86—Grade III; Veered in start; lugged in badly

28Jly86-4Dmr 6f :22^1 :46 1:11^{3}ft 3¼ 115 2^{hd} 1^{2½} 1^{3½} 1^{5½} Soto S B^4 M28000 80-16 BoldBrgin,DrbyChck,EghtIsEnough 8

16Jly86-3Hol 5½f :22^3 :46^1 1:06 ft 9¾ 116 4^3 3^2 3^{2½} 5^{6¼} Soto S B^5 M45000 78-15 Blue Allied,CoolTalker,NaturalDad 11

Oct 18 BM 5f ft 1:02^2 h Oct 7 BM 3f ft :36^2 h Sep 6 Dmr 3f ft :34^4 h Sep 3 Dmr 6f ft 1:16 h

D.

Native Free

Ch. g. 2, by Drouilly—Grateful Native, by Native Born

HANSEN R D **114** **Br.—Northwest Farms (Wash)** **1986 1 1 0 0 $3,300**

Tr.—Dutton Jerry $25,000

Own.—Dutton J **Lifetime 1 1 0 0 $3,300**

9Oct86-3BM 6f :23^1 :47 1:12^{3}ft *2½ 118 2^1 2^{hd} 1^1 1^{nk} Hansen R D^1 M12500 76-19 NtiveFree,DeepKnowledg,KniKing 11

9Oct86—Broke slowly

Oct 29 BM 4f ft :47 h Oct 22 BM 5f ft 1:00^4 h Oct 7 BM 4f ft :48^3 h Oct 1 BM 6f ft 1:15 hg

E.

Quite A Reminder — Ch. g. 2, by Nostalgia—Only the Finest, by Fleet Mel
JUDICE J C — 114 — Br.—Hountalas Mary G (Cal) — 1986 6 1 3 1 $12,775
Own.—Campiotti G — Tr.—Campiotti George $25,000
Lifetime 6 1 3 1 $12,775

```
19Oct86-5BM   6f :224 :454 1:104ft  32 118  2½ 2hd 1hd 1no  Judice J C2   Mdn    85-17 QtARmndr,ProprToff,FlyngBonty 10
4Oct86-1BM    6f :221 :454 1:113ft   2 118  4¼ 22 23 23½    Judice J C5   M25000 77-16 Aezp,QuiteAReminder,DdictdScholr 7
20Sep86-4BM   1  :472 1:131 1:384ft  8½ 1185 1½ 2hd 55 512½ Barton J1     Mdn    61-19 FlyingLieutnnt,PicchoPss,SntinlStr 9
4Sep86-6Bmf   6f :224 :463 1:121ft   4 1135 32 32 1hd 2nk   Barton J10    M20000 78-19 CmlDrivr,QutARmndr,CountyGrov 11
23Aug86-6Sac  5½f:221 :454 1:04 ft  4¾ 1125 31½ 42½ 32 24   Barton J3     Mdn    84-12 Big Boi, Quite AReminder,Tonopah 7
16Jly86-7Sol  5½f:221 :454 1:042ft  16 118  32 32 34 37½    Sanchez RAJr3 M16000 81-13 MgicDoor,CptinPreil,QuiteARmindr 9
```

F.

Paddy Muldoon — B. g. 2, by Matsadoon—Irish Wedding, by Advocator
LOZOYA D A — 114 — Br.—Mulholland N W (Ky) — 1986 1 1 0 0 $4,125
Own.—Two Rivers Farm — Tr.—Mason Lloyd C $25,000
Lifetime 1 1 0 0 $4,125

```
15Oct86-1BM   6f :223 :454 1:113ft  46 118  54¾ 32 1½ 12     Lozoya D A9   M16000 81-17 PaddyMuldoon,Huigar,SndyPririe 12
  Oct 27 BM 4f ft :482 h   Oct 12 BM Tr.5f ft 1:02 hg   Oct 5 BM Tr.5f ft 1:02 hg   Sep 30 BM 5f ft 1:022 h
```

G.

Princeps — Ch. c. 2, by Cajun Prince—Daragaya, by Capacitator
LAMANCE C — 114 — Br.—Stein D M (Cal) — 1986 3 1 0 0 $4,425
Own.—Stein D M — Tr.—Offield Duane $25,000
Lifetime 3 1 0 0 $4,425

```
2Oct86-6BM    6f :223 :453 1:103ft  14 113  56 68 67 610¾     Lamance C3  Aw15000   75-19 Stn'sBck,CondctonChrgr,MostGlint 6
17Sep86-1BM   5½f:224 :464 1:064gd *2¼ 118  22 2hd 1½ 12      Lamance C4  [S]M16000 78-31 Princeps, Kid Zuni, I'm Notorious 8
3Sep86-8Bmf   6f :224 :461 1:12 ft   4¼ 118  68½ 68½ 58½ 58  Lamance C4  [S]Mdn    71-21 DizzieBrgin,J.D.Commish,GmeBrekr 6
  3Sep86—Lugged in stretch
  Oct 24 BM 5f ft 1:032 h   Oct 17 BM 7f ft 1:302 h   Oct 12 BM 4f ft :483 h   Sep 13 BM 4f ft :474 h
```

424. It's Oct. 31. Which horse(s) can be eliminated on form?

7th BayMeadows

1 1/16 MILES. (1.38⅘) CLAIMING. Purse $13,000. Fillies. 3-year-olds. Weight, 120 lbs. Non-winners of two races at one mile or over since September 15, 3 lbs.; one such race since then, 6 lbs. Claiming price $25,000; for each $2,500 to $20,000, 1 lb. (Maiden and claiming races for $16,000 or less not considered.)

A. (32)

Now Now Nicole * — Dk. b. or br. f. 3, by Kris S—Hepatica, by Tibaldo
RINNE C E — 114 — Br.—Meadowbrook Farms Inc (Fla) — 1986 5 3 0 0 $12,375
Own.—R L Shipp Trust — Tr.—Retherford N J $25,000 — 1985 3 M 1 1 $3,540
Lifetime 8 3 1 1 $15,915

```
25Sep86-9BM   1 1/16:481 1:142 1:493sl  4¼ 114  11 1½ 13 12½        Rinne C E3      (F) 16000  44-35 NowNowNcl,DblDcrtd,Chrs'sGlmr 10
10Sep86-12Bmf 1 1/16:47 1:113 1:45 ft    7 113  23 11 13 15          Rinne C E2      (F) 10000  67-22 NowNowNicole,OutOfMind,TnteBlu 7
29Jly86-4SR   6f :221 :452 1:11 ft      12 116  31 21½ 12 16         Rinne C E1      (F)M12500  87-17 NowNowNcol,PshyFoot,ShkItLos 10
11Jun86-4GG   6f :22 :45 1:094ft        28 114  1215 1219 1223 1225  Mena F9         (F)M20000  65-10 HollyAnn,VentureGained,IllicitJoy 12
  11Jun86—Lugged out
26May86-4GG   6f :221 :452 1:114ft      11 114  109¾ 912 816 89¾     Mena F6         (F)Mc16000 70-18 Glass Devil, Holly Ann, Scurley 12
  26May86—Ducked in start
2Nov85-8LA    6½f:22 :472 1:184ft       3¾ 118  41½ 53 76¾ 39¼       DominguezRE3    (F)Mdn     74-12 FryGodmthr,RchlTnnss,NwNwNcl 10
17Oct85-4SA   6f :212 :444 1:114ft      19 118  1013 914 714 812¼    DelhoussyE6     (F)M40000  67-19 Michel'sSpcil,Witchry,OurSwtShm 12
  17Oct85—Veered in start; wide into stretch
12Sep85-4Pom  6f :234 :474 1:124ft      11 116  32½ 52¾ 31 22¼       Ortega L E2     (F)Mdn     — — DesrtTon,NowNowNicol,FrnchTrt 10
  Oct 30 BM 3f ft :374 h   Oct 18 BM 6f ft 1:154 h   Oct 7 BM 5f ft 1:003 h   Sep 7 BM 4f ft :49 h
```

B.

Stopping Time — B. f. 3, by Stop the Music—Beauty Hour, by Bold Hour
SCHVANEVELDER C P — 114 — Br.—Elmendorf Farm (Ky) — 1986 7 1 0 1 $14,145
Own.—Bassett G — Tr.—Utley Doug $25,000 — 1985 2 M 0 0
Lifetime 9 1 0 1 $14,145

```
15Oct86-6BM   6f :221 :452 1:102ft  5½ 114  69 59 57 45¼        YamamotoTJ7 (F) 25000 82-17 OneDrum,NturlBlonde,Blke'sDncer 7
19Jly86-7Hol  1  :452 1:103 1:37 ft  10 115  88 812 816 821½    Soto S B1   (F) 32000 56-15 CuriousPrincess,Velveten,SundyMil 8
  19Jly86—Broke slowly
```

13Jun86-9Hol 1 :461 1:111 1:363ft 2¾ 1105 65½ 54 68 611½ Black C A1 Ⓕ 40000 68-17 DwnOfHope,Velveteen,RufflesNBus 7
22May86-4Hol 1 :454 1:104 1:362ft 13 1085 69 46 45½ 36½ Black C A4 Ⓕ 45000 74-15 OurSwtShm,VolnMlody,StoppngTm 7
25Apr86-7Hol 1 :463 1:12 1:373ft 9½ 1105 52½ 21 33 44¾ Black C A3 Ⓕ 50000 71-16 HopefulGl,RufflsNBus,OurSwtShm 7
14Feb86-4SA 1 1/16 :472 1:121 1:451gd 7½ 1125 63¾ 1hd 12 12½ Black C A8 ⒻM40000 75-16 StoppingTim,Comps,DrmticElgnc 12
19Jan86-1SA 1 1/16 :452 1:101 1:441ft 91 1125 46½ 34½ 48½ 510½ Barton J4 ⒻMdn 69-12 Beggr'sWllet,BrTime,WeddingDncr 8
28Dec85-4SA 1 :47 1:121 1:373ft 70 1125 62½ 53½ 67½ 610½ Barton J2 ⒻMdn 69-14 FshionBook,Beulhlnd,LeftHerMrk 10
16Nov85-6Hol 6f :221 :454 1:103ft 79 1135 1011 1012 912 812¾ Barton J10 ⒻMdn 78-14 ChickOrTwo,Alquizer,SeldomSnSu 11
Oct 29 BM 4f ft :504 h ●Oct 6 BM 6f ft 1:124 h ●Sep 29 BM 4f ft :463 h ●Sep 23 GD tr.t 5f ft 1:00 h

C.

Forumstar

Ch. f. 3, by Inherent Star—Distinguished Gal, by Forum

HANSEN R D 112 Br.—Keshishian & McCone (Cal) 1986 13 2 2 2 $23,645

Tr.—Dutton Jerry $20,000 1985 3 1 0 0 $3,525

Own.—Keshishian & McCone Lifetime 16 3 2 2 $27,170 Turf 1 0 0 1 $3,500

16Oct86-1BM 1 :464 1:111 1:37 ft 3 114 11½ 1½ 1hd 2hd Hansen R D3 Ⓕ 16000 83-18 Haida Star,Forumstar,SpecialEagle 6
16Oct86—Lugged out
12Sep86-10Bmf 6f :221 :453 1:12 ft 13 1095 85¾ 109¾ 95 31½ Pfau R K6 Ⓕ 16000 77-29 Blke'sDncr,Chris'sGlmor,Forumstr 11
12Sep86—Wide into stretch
16Jly86-9Sol 6f :22 :444 1:10 ft 7½ 1095 31½ 45 34 67½ Pfau R K5 Ⓕ 25000 85-13 OlympicBell,MysteryMaid,IllicitJoy 9
16Jly86—Lugged out
2Jly86-11Pln 5½f :221 :461 1:05 ft 18 114 108¾ 87¼ 86½ 75 CpbllBC10 ⒻAw16000 80-18 EstrggLbth,MrnngstrLn,NrthrnIsl 10
2Jly86—Lugged out 3/8
5Jun86-6GG 6f :22 :444 1:093ft 24 124 31 42½ 66½ 67½ CmpbllBC2 ⒻAw19000 84-14 BargainFun,Chrysilia,SpiritedMadm 9
15May86-8GG 6f :223 :453 1:10 ft 9½ 120 53½ 42 53½ 57½ Diaz A L3 ⒻAw17000 81-15 OlympicClssic,KinCoulee,LdyPstor 6
23Apr86-8GG 1 Ⓣ:4821:1331:382fm 14 114 21½ 21½ 33½ 39 Diaz A L2 ⒻAw25000 66-25 NovelSprit,JoysOfSpring,Forumstr 7
2Apr86-8GG 6f :223 :453 1:112ft 13 114 32 21 1hd 11 ‡Diaz A L3 ⒻAw16000 82-21 JoysOfSpring,Forumstar,FoolishIce 6
‡2Apr86—Dead heat
20Mar86-7GG 6f :223 :462 1:114ft 6¼ 114 75¾ 64½ 53 52½ Diaz A L7 Ⓕ 25000 77-24 OhHowRight,MysteryMaid,Ptriotic 7
20Mar86—Broke in air
6Mar86-6GG 6f :221 :453 1:112ft 5¼ 114 31 3½ 53 810½ Baze R A8 Ⓕ 25000 71-24 JoysOfSpring,DanceNorth,L'Indin 10
Oct 10 BM 4f ft :484 h Oct 1 BM 4f ft :473 h Sep 21 BM 3f ft :371 h

D.

Cuchi Love

Ch. f. 3, by Cuchillo—Love Abounding, by Run for Nurse

DIAZ A L 114 Br.—Caldwell T M (Ore) 1986 11 3 0 1 $20,525

Tr.—Utley Doug $25,000 1985 0 M 0 0

Own.—Bloodhorse Syndicate Lifetime 11 3 0 1 $20,525

3Oct86-9BM 1 1/16 :47 1:114 1:441ft 3¾ 114 14 14 2hd 44 Gonzalez RM4 Ⓕ 25000 67-21 Saillnte,SpecilReserve,Blke'sDncer 7
17Sep86-6BM 1 :472 1:13 1:404gd *7-5 114 11 11 2½ 34½ Gonzalez RM7 Ⓕ 25000 59-31 RobrtsRglGirl,AllDckdOut,CuchLov 7
5Sep86-10Bmf 6f :222 :451 1:112ft 3 114 2½ 22 23 43½ Gonzalez RM8 Ⓕ 25000 78-30 MysteryMaid,HollyAnn,LovableFlirt 8
23Jly86-9SR 5½f :22 :452 1:034ft 8 114 44½ 2½ 11 11½ Gonzalez RM5 Ⓕ 16000 92-14 Cuchi Love, HotCache,MissUragold 8
23Jly86—Veered out, bumped hard start
11Jly86-9Sol 6f :214 :444 1:103ft 5 114 3nk 23 56½ 59½ † Lamance C6 Ⓕ 16000 80-15 Crist'sIc,BrginBsmnt,Michl'sSpcil 10
†11Jly86—Disqualified and placed tenth
12Jun86-6GG 6f :22 :444 1:093ft 4½ 114 52 41½ 76½ 710 Gonzalez RM5 Ⓕ 25000 81-14 Glass Devil,AirForceBaby,Drumcliff 8
12Jun86—Hopped at start
5Jun86-9GG 6f :22 :444 1:103ft *2½ 115 32 33½ 44½ 54½ Baze R A6 Ⓕ c20000 82-14 AbovThRst,ChmpgnBby,MystryMid 8
15May86-6GG 6f :213 :45 1:104ft 3½ 115 52¾ 41¾ 46 46 Judice J C4 Ⓕ 25000 79-15 Lady Shaman, Lecci, I Walk Alone 6
24Apr86-1GG 6f :222 :451 1:103ft *1 115 31 2hd 1hd 1nk Baze R A7 Ⓕ 16000 86-16 Cuchi Love,MoveAway,CreativeFun 8
2Apr86-8GG 6f :223 :453 1:112ft 7 115 53 42 52½ 41½ Baze R A4 ⒻAw16000 81-21 JoysOfSpring,Forumstar,FoolishIce 6
Oct 29 BM 3f ft :36 h Oct 19 BM 5f ft 1:02 h Sep 29 BM 5f ft 1:003 h Sep 14 BM 3f ft :364 h

E.

Foxy Glass

Ch. f. 3, by Pass the Glass—Foxy Terri, by Bicker

BAZE R A 114 Br.—Roberts G C (Wash) 1986 3 0 0 0 $1,750

Tr.—Benedict Jim $25,000 1985 3 1 2 0 $11,545

Own.—Eidson D Lifetime 6 1 2 0 $13,295

15Oct86-7BM 6f :22 :45 1:093ft *3½ 115 66 78 712 610 SchvnvldtCP7 Ⓕ 25000 81-17 MyLdiesTiger,Drumscell,PttiPrkins 8
31Jan86-6BM 6f :222 :454 1:113sy 5¾ 114 65½ 56 66 41¾ Judice J C8 ⒻAw15000 79-27 Naski, PattiPerkins,NightimeDerby 9
20Jan86-8BM 1 :47 1:121 1:38 gd *1 113 2hd 31 57½ 59½ ChpmnTM4 ⒻAw16000 69-20 Rchel'sExclibur,Cdor,SpecilReserve 6
29Dec85-6BM 1 :462 1:113 1:382sy 7½ 1085 32½ 1½ 2hd 2no Aragon VA5 ⒻAw17000 76-24 CrystlShowers,FoxyGlss,Life'sBest 7
2Dec85-4BM 6f :23 :463 1:13 m 8 115 2½ 22 45½ 23½ Baze R A4 Ⓕ 25000 70-34 Waltz Around, Foxy Glass,E'Mirage 7
2Dec85—Bumped at 1/16
18Oct85-4BM 6f :222 :46 1:123ft *2½ 117 66 67 33 1¾ Winick D5 ⒻM25000 76-24 FoxyGlass,TanteBleue,PttiPerkins 10
18Oct85—Broke in a tangle
Oct 23 BM 6f ft 1:151 h Oct 11 BM 4f ft :471 hg Oct 4 BM 6f ft 1:131 h Sep 27 BM 5f m 1:02 h

425. It's Nov. 8. Which horse(s) can be eliminated on form?

6th Aqueduct

1 ⅛ MILES. (1.47) CLAIMING. Purse $20,000. 3-year-olds and upward. Weights, 3-year-olds, 120 lbs. Older, 122 lbs. Non-winners of two races at a mile or over since October 15, allowed 3 lbs. Of such a race since then, 5 lbs. Cliaming price $35,000 for each $2,500 to $30,000 2 lbs. (Races when entered to be claimed for $25,000 or less not considered).

A. **(32)**

Attune
Own.—Barrera O S 108 7
B. h. 5, by Raja Baba—Piper's Tune, by Princequillo
Br.—North Ridge Farm (Ky) 1986 16 1 2 2 $38,860
Tr.—Barrera Oscar S $32,500 1985 10 3 2 0 $51,740
Lifetime 36 5 4 3 $101,910 Turf 10 1 1 2 $28,090

3Nov86-7Aqu 1⅛ Ⓣ:484 1:133 1:50 fm 19 1107 35 65¼ 511 715 Ortiz E Jr7 Aw29000 70-22 Ioskeha,CaptainArthur,‡G'DayMate 9
3Nov86—Placed sixth through disqualification
12Oct86-2Bel 1⅛ :462 1:111 1:50 ft *7-5e 1087 74½ 66¾ 58½ 411 Belmonte J F3 22500 66-13 Our Triumph, Roomie, Stop Light 8
31Aug86-3Bel 1¼ [T]:502 1:40 2:031 fm 4¼ 117 1010 1114 1115 1116¾ Cordero A Jr9 35000 61-20 Temujin, Terson, Sarappeal 11
20Aug86-1Sar 6f :22 :45 1:093 ft 5 113 613 59 47½ 47¼ Cordero A Jr1 45000 85-12 Best By Test, Semaj, Flunky Home 6
11Aug86-7Sar 1 1/16 Ⓣ:48 1:113 1:431 gd 10 115 64¾ 77½ 77 77 Samyn J L4 Aw40000 74-23 EL Mansour, Mascot, WhateverFor 8
30Jly86-3Sar 1⅛ :463 1:111 1:491 ft 5½ 117 410 53½ 36 42¾ Cordero AJr7 Aw29000 86-13 WaikikiStar,BoyishChrm,Scrimshw 7
24Jly86-8Bel 1 1/16 :473 1:114 1:423 ft 4½ 115 44 44½ 31½ 42¾ Cordero AJr6 Aw40000 86-15 DoItAginDn,GoldCrst,FingrsInthTill 6
21Jly86-5Bel 1 Ⓣ:452 1:10 1:342 fm 2½e 112 68½ 53 42 34½ Santos J A7 75000 88-10 Skip Out Front, Braddells, Attune 8
Oct 10 Bel tr.t 3f ft :372 b

B.

***Oversea**
Own.—Brazil Stable 117
Dk. b. or br. h. 5, by Salt Marsh—Odalisca, by Mount Athos
Br.—Haras La Quebrada (Arg) 1986 7 0 0 1 $2,760
Tr.—Fernandez Floreano $35,000 1985 12 1 3 1 $12,215
Lifetime 31 3 7 4 $25,850 Turf 11 0 2 0 $5,655

18Sep86-3Bel 1⅛ :463 1:104 1:482 ft 7¼ 113 712 611 714 717¼ Santos J A5 45000 68-17 RmblngRctor,FngrsInthTll,StrkScrt 8
4Sep86-1Bel 1⅛ :474 1:113 1:491 ft 14 113 611 68 43½ 33¾ Santos J A6 45000 77-18 Fly Me Again,Mr.Murtaugh,Oversea 6
23Aug86-4Sar 1⅛ [T]:482 1:11 1:48 fm 34 113 44 712 713 710¾ Santos J A2 70000 89-08 QuickDip,DomintngDooly,SlntSlndr 9
6Aug86-3Sar 1⅜ [T]:52 1:414 2:202 sf 20 113 42½ 75½ 66½ 59¼ Santagata N4 45000 57-29 RocmdourII,Cloutier,WesternChmp 8
25Jly86-7Bel 1⅜ Ⓣ:481 1:361 2:14 fm 8¼ 113 31½ 47 612 516¼ Cruguet J1 70000 76-19 If I HadAHammer,Sarappeal,ATitle 6
13Apr86♦8Hipodromo(Arg) a1⅞ 3:101 hy 21 134 1026 GllsR GrPremioRpublicArg(Gr1) Fain, Newmarket, Cabileno 13
6Jan86♦5Maronas(Uru) a1½ 2:293 ft *2½ 132 57¾ SttV GrPrJoseP.Ramirez(Gr1) Vivaz, Smart, Ta Ta Tan 11
19Nov85♦7LaPlata(Arg) a1½ 2:361 hy 3½ 132 46½ LtRE GrnPremioDrdoRoch(Gr1) SalvateTel, Magiar, Zafarrancho 19
Oct 13 Bel tr.t 5f ft 1:033 b

C.

Spicey Bones
Own.—L'ilusion Stable 113
Ro. g. 4, by Sawbones—Cinnamon Cake, by Peace Corps
Br.—Hobeau Farm Inc (Fla) 1986 18 2 2 2 $35,640
Tr.—Barrera Guillermo S $30,000 1985 14 1 4 1 $29,040
Lifetime 39 3 6 4 $68,940 Turf 2 0 0 0

1Nov86-9Aqu 1⅛ :493 1:133 1:511 ft 4 113 32½ 33 32 2¾ Marquez C HJr3 20000 78-19 OurTriumph,SpiceyBones,IronSway 7
9Oct86-1Bel 1⅛ :471 1:114 1:502 ft 3½ 113 31½ 11 16 15 Romero R P6 15500 75-18 SpcyBons,BtWhoKnows,StrghtSht 8
28Sep86-2Bel 7f :23 :463 1:24 m 4¼ 117 79½ 75¾ 46½ 33¾ Cordero A Jr3 14000 78-15 PledgeCp,ArcticSong,SpiceyBones 7
18Sep86-1Bel 6f :222 :454 1:10 ft 5 117 714 811 69¼ 46½ Santos J A4 14000 85-17 Scott'sNative,PledgeCp,ArcticSong 8
8Aug86-5Sar 7f :221 :45 1:22 m 15 117 1012 1017 817 619¾ Guerra W A6 25000 72-17 BestandBold,HarryL.,BigJimTylor 10
26Jly86-9Bel 7f :224 :46 1:24 sy 5 113 68 55½ 35½ 36 Cordero A Jr1 15500 76-18 Startop, Koffkoff, Spicey Bones 10
16Jly86-3Bel 7f :234 :464 1:232 ft 11 1105 75¾ 79¾ 67¼ 65¼ Vasquez M M6 22500 80-17 FlyingSkippr,SixthofMy,ArcticSong 7
6Jly86-5Bel 6½f :223 :452 1:162 ft 34 1105 89 89½ 79½ 54¼ Vasquez M M8 22500 90-16 UpperStar,AsYouLikeIt,SixthofMay 9
Oct 22 Bel tr.t 4f ft :493 h **Sep 12 Bel tr.t 4f ft :483 h**

D.

Roomie
Own.—Sommer Viola 115
Ch. c. 4, by Naskra—Elopement, by Gallant Romeo
Br.—Green R L (Ky) 1986 13 1 4 2 $28,908
Tr.—Martin Frank $32,500 1985 14 1 1 1 $19,940
Lifetime 34 2 5 3 $49,928 Turf 9 0 1 1 $7,420

30Oct86-9Aqu 7f :222 :461 1:234 ft 9¾ 117 1115 108¼ 106¾ 85¼ Davis R G1 35000 77-21 EqulTerms,TlcPower,Vinny'sPride 11
22Oct86-4Aqu 1 3/16 :48 1:113 1:564 ft 6 117 52½ 46 49 37¼ Davis R G6 35000 71-16 Harry L., Our Triumph, Roomie 7
12Oct86-2Bel 1⅛ :462 1:111 1:50 ft 2 1127 2½ 2hd 21 23 Ortiz E Jr5 c25000 74-13 Our Triumph, Roomie, Stop Light 8
2Oct86-1Bel 1 1/16 :481 1:122 1:43 ft 4¾ 1125 2hd 31 2½ 1nk Brown T L6 25000 87-09 Roomie,AccountReceivble,HotDebt 7
2Sep86-7Pim 1 1/16 :463 1:12 1:46 sy *3 117 57 45 34 23¼ Delgado A9 Aw13700 71-21 Taras Bulba, Roomie, Space Out 9
22Aug86-7Pim 1 1/16 :471 1:124 1:46 gd 6½ 117 711 78 46 2¾ Delgado A2 Aw13700 73-23 VirgininRebel,Roomie,DeckeledEdg 7
2Aug86-4Pim 1 1/16 Ⓣ:483 1:13 1:444 fm 7¼ 117 85½ 78½ 711 715 Delgado A4 Aw13700 64-20 Mdow'sDr.Brtt,ChspkBch,Volgogrd 8
13Jly86-3Pha 1 1/16 :473 1:122 1:45 m *2½ 118 43½ 34 32 35 Black A S3 Aw12030 74-21 Royal Rickie, King Size, Roomie 6
Sep 20 Pim 3f ft :383 b

E.

***Arctic Song** — B. h. 5, by Arctic Tern—Bell Song, by Tudor Melody
Br.—SocCivileAgricoledelaPerrigne (Fr) — 1986 30 7 7 7 $138,170
Own.—Barrera O S — 1067 — Tr.—Barrera Oscar S — $30,000 — 1985 18 2 6 3 $45,990
Lifetime 56 9 14 10 $188,828 — Turf 14 1 1 1 $15,618

30Oct86-1Aqu	1⅛	:481	1:13	1:511ft	*1	1067	73	41½	1½	13	Belmonte J F8	15500	79-21	ArctcSong,LondonMrkt,DbosHnds	10
25Oct86-1Aqu	1⅛	:49	1:133	1:514ft	*6-5	1067	55½	42½	11½	12	Belmonte J F4	12000	76-18	ArctcSong,BtWhoKnows,NwAdvntr	9
19Oct86-1Bel	7f	:23	:461	1:241ft	2¾e	1067	66½	54¾	32	2nk	Belmonte J F8	12000	81-14	PledgeCp,ArcticSong,JustAnyTime	9
13Oct86-3Bel	7f	:232	:463	1:231ft	6½	1067	85¼	66	47½	34¾	Belmonte J F7	15500	81-16	KingBabr,FlshyDimond,ArcticSong	9
8Oct86-1Bel	6f	:22	:453	1:114ft	*9-5e	1067	614	59½	38	21	Belmonte J F1	12000	82-19	RivrDmon,ArcticSong,IrshIsCtchng	9
28Sep86-2Bel	7f	:23	:463	1:24 m	*3-5e	1067	66½	43	24	22¼	Belmonte J F7	12000	80-15	PledgeCp,ArcticSong,SpiceyBones	7
18Sep86-1Bel	6f	:222	:454	1:10 ft	3e	113	639	58½	37	35½	Romero R P6	12000	86-17	Scott'sNative,PledgeCp,ArcticSong	8
1Aug86-1Sar	1⅛	:473	1:123	1:513ft	7	113	99	77	79½	512¾	Rydowski S R6	20000	64-17	FbulousMove,GoldenChif,BLughing	9

426. Which would be a mistaken form elimination among maidens?

A. has never finished in-the-money in five attempts **(32)**
B. had one race, beaten badly at every call
C. much-improved form when dropped from straight maiden to high-priced maiden-claiming race, returned to straight maiden competition today
D. has finished 2nd or 3rd repeatedly

427. No horse should be permitted to move up in class following an all-out stretch drive in which it lost ground, even if winning.

A. True **(32)**
B. False

428. It's Nov. 15. Which horse(s) are best eliminated on form?

2nd Aqueduct

6 FURLONGS. (1.08⅘) CLAIMING. Purse $13,000. 3-year-olds, weights, 122 lbs. Non-winners of two races since October 15, allowed 3 lbs. Of a race since then, 5 lbs. Claiming price $17,500; for each $1,000 to $15,500 2 lbs. (Races when entered to be claimed for $14,000 or less not considered).

A. **(32)**

Stay Gold — Ch. c. 3, by Governor's Pardon—Chris a Bell, by Villamor
Br.—Lewis Penny (Fla) — 1986 18 2 1 1 $18,155
Own.—Rena-Kim Stable — 1067 — Tr.—Jacobs Robert E — $15,500 — 1985 2 2 0 0 $7,080
Lifetime 20 4 1 1 $25,235 — Turf 1 0 0 0 $225

29Oct86-8Med	6f	:221	:451	1:11 ft	53	1067	66¼	69½	66½	76	Belmonte J F4	30000	81-21	EverAStar,Lumumba,BoogieTheBer	9
9Oct86-8Med	6f	:23	:46	1:103ft	15	1085	53¼	811	811	712½	Bielby J A6	Aw16000	76-20	LordOfThNght,HyNowHrry,WtrCnn	8
23Sep86-8Med	6f	:223	:453	1:113ft	18	1075	3½	53½	2hd	12½	Bielby J A2	16000	84-23	Stay Gold,TestofLoyalty,Onnagata	10
23Aug86-9Atl	6f	:214	:451	1:111ft	*9-5	112	23	22½	1no	11¾	Parisi E6	5000	86-16	Stay Gold, Yojo, Dumpty Favor	8
12Aug86-8Atl	5½f Ⓣ	:22	:451	1:034fm	38	110	66	66½	61¾	53¼	Parisi E4	19000	91-17	AnothrRippl,PocktBndit,DndyDnny	6
7Aug86-8Atl	5½f	:222	:46	1:044ft	6	111	44	45	46	43¾	Parisi E6	A11000	86-22	AwesomeRebl,RvnDlight,RngdWild	6
14Jly86-5Atl	6f	:223	:461	1:113ft	*9-5	116	32	31	35	37½	Parisi E5	10000	76-24	VguelyAlert,BrefootGreen,StyGold	6
14Jly86—Lugged in															
2Jun86-9Bel	6f	:224	:46	1:111ft	33	113	1115	1216	1213	1113¼	Lovato F Jr5	20000	73-13	Crig'sPowr,GllntChif,John'sEvnng	12

Nov 6 Med 4f m :493 b — Oct 23 Med 4f ft :481 b — ●Oct 15 Med 4f ft :48 b — Oct 4 Med 4f m :502 b

B.

Quarter Time
Own.—Iron Lance Stables **113**
B. c. 3, by Timeless Moment—Iesi, by Bold Lad
Br.—Stilz R C (Ky) 1986 12 1 0 0 $6,600
Tr.—Fernandez Floreano $15,500 1985 0 M 0 0
Lifetime 12 1 0 0 $6,600

24Oct86-9Aqu	7f	$:22^3$	:46	$1:23^3$ft	39	108^5	9^{10}	11^{13}	12^{22}	11^{20}	Brown T L^7	15500	63-20	SwitchInTime,BrillintCsting,AlVet	12
3Oct86-5Bel	6f	:23	$:46^1$	1:11 ft	48	113	$8^{9\frac34}$	$8^{9\frac14}$	$7^{7\frac14}$	$7^{8\frac14}$	Graell A^5	15500	79-17	SnsiblHour,Crig'sPowr,BrillntCstng	8
28Sep86-2Bel	7f	:23	$:46^3$	1:24 m	16	113	$1^{1\frac12}$	1^{hd}	7^{14}	$7^{23\frac12}$	Martens G^2	14000	58-15	PledgeCp,ArcticSong,SpiceyBones	7
8Sep86-9Bel	7f	:23	$:46^2$	$1:23^4$ft	34	113	$3^{1\frac12}$	$3^{1\frac12}$	9^{11}	$9^{15\frac12}$	Graell A^9	14000	67-11	ShyHughes,LondonMarket,Justawy	9
29Aug86-2Bel	6f	$:22^3$	:46	$1:10^2$gd	29	112	$1^{\frac12}$	$2^{\frac12}$	$3^{3\frac12}$	$9^{12\frac12}$	Graell A^4	14000	77-19	Pledge Cap, AnvilMan,ShyHughes	10
19Jly86-2Bel	$1\frac{1}{16}$	$:46^2$	$1:11^1$	$1:42^2$gd	43	106^5	2^{hd}	$9^{8\frac14}$	9^{22}	$9^{28\frac14}$	Decarlo C P^8	17500	62-15	ExclusiveJ.S.,GoldnChif,CnnonRoyl	9
15Jun86-1Bel	7f	$:23^1$	:47	$1:24^2$ft	66	113	4^2	$3^{1\frac12}$	6^{15}	$7^{18\frac12}$	Rojas R I^9	20000	61-21	SensibleHour,VagbondGeorge,Revy	9
28Apr86-3Aqu	1	$:47^3$	$1:12^2$	$1:37^4$ft	10	117	$6^{2\frac14}$	9^8	8^{11}	$8^{16\frac14}$	Cruguet J^7	c17500	61-25	MnofAction,RdChlk,TurnToThRoss	9

C.

Great Tendancies
Own.—Jal Stable **110^7**
B. c. 3, by Lyphard's Wish—Rough Cat, by Roman Line
Br.—Dickey M (Ky) 1986 22 2 3 2 $56,908
Tr.—Aquilino Joseph $17,500 Turf 8 1 0 1 $23,988
Lifetime 22 2 3 2 $56,908

3Nov86-1Aqu	1	$:46^4$	$1:11^3$	$1:38^1$ft	34	110^7	1^{hd}	2^{hd}	13^{13}	$13^{13\frac12}$	Nuesch D^4	25000	61-22	BrillintCsting,RoylPotntl,TllRomn	14
9Oct86-2Bel	$6\frac12$f	$:22^1$	$:45^3$	$1:17^1$ft	27	117	5^4	$7^{6\frac14}$	9^{11}	$8^{11\frac14}$	Messina R^2	35000	78-18	Macho, Lord's Wish, McNaz	10
26Sep86-6Bel	$1\frac{1}{16}$ [T]	:47	1:12	1:46 gd	34	113	$2^{\frac12}$	8^5	8^{12}	$8^{13\frac34}$	Messina R^2	Aw25000	57-28	Trubulare, Easterner, Dr. Danzig	8
7Sep86-9Bel	1	:46	$1:11^1$	$1:37^1$ft	25	117	$7^{5\frac12}$	$9^{9\frac14}$	9^{16}	$9^{12\frac14}$	Maple E^7	50000	67-14	Macho, For The Gipper,LordPacal	10
25Aug86-6Sar	7f	:22	:45	$1:23^4$ft	29	113	6^6	4^5	$4^{5\frac12}$	$5^{6\frac12}$	Maple E^2	70000	76-19	HeyNowHrry,ForTheGippr,BoldMin	8
9Aug86-1Sar	$1\frac18$	$:47^4$	$1:11^4$	$1:51^1$ft	12	113	2^{hd}	$3^{\frac12}$	5^5	$5^{10\frac12}$	Maple E^1	70000	68-17	TheLoneRnger,ForTheGippr,ThSvg	7
6Aug86-7Sar	6f	$:21^4$	$:45^1$	1:11 sy	30	112	7^{13}	9^{14}	8^{17}	$6^{17\frac12}$	Bailey J D^6	Aw24000	67-26	AlDavis,ClassicMove,Michel'sDncer	9
25Jly86-5Bel	$1\frac14$ [T]	$:48^2$	1:38	$2:04^1$fm	$*2\frac12$	117	$3^{3\frac12}$	3^3	3^6	$7^{10\frac14}$	Migliore R^5	c50000	63-19	Anbaal, J. Z.'s Pleasure,DarkFlood	11

Oct 27 Aqu 4f sy $:50^3$ b (d) Sep 22 Aqu 4f ft $:46^3$ hg

D.

Jugglebucks
Own.—Walutch N **112^5**
B. g. 3, by Buckpoint—Jongleuse, by African Sky
Br.—Walutch N (NY) 1986 11 1 0 0 $15,980
Tr.—Morguelan Steven L $17,500 Turf 2 0 0 0
Lifetime 11 1 0 0 $15,980

3Nov86-1Aqu	1	$:46^4$	$1:11^3$	$1:38^1$ft	7f	117	14^{14}	12^9	$12^{9\frac34}$	10^8	Cruguet J^5	25000	67-22	BrillintCsting,RoylPotntl,TllRomn	14
21Sep86-4Bel	$1\frac14$ [T]	$:50^1$	$1:38^2$	$2:03^1$hd	12	113	1^1	$3^{\frac12}$	$7^{8\frac12}$	$8^{18\frac14}$	Cruguet J^2	[S]Aw28000	60-20	SingWithMe,VtzMtter,FestYourEys	8
14Sep86-9Bel	7f	$:23^1$	:46	$1:23^4$ft	$8\frac14$	113	$8^{8\frac12}$	7^{11}	$7^{6\frac12}$	6^6	Cruguet J^9	[S]Aw26500	77-11	FifthFlight,BeATyrant,StrApprent	10
11Aug86-9Sar	7f	$:22^1$	:45	1:24 ft	20	114	11^{17}	8^{12}	$5^{6\frac12}$	$5^{6\frac34}$	Cruguet J^9	[S]Aw20000	75-17	Zonter, Zactay, Fast Step	11
23Jly86-9Bel	6f	$:22^2$	:46	$1:11^1$ft	19	116	9^{11}	8^{11}	5^{11}	6^{10}	Cruguet J^{12}	[S]Aw26500	76-11	WhatAPhilip,BeATyrnt,FifthFlight	12
12Jly86-9Bel	7f	:23	$:46^3$	1:25 m	16	116	$6^{8\frac12}$	$2^{1\frac12}$	1^4	$1^{3\frac12}$	Cruguet J^7	[S]Mdn	77-15	Jugglbcks,IrrsstblBr,SymphonySd	10
29Jun86-4Bel	$1\frac{1}{16}$ (T)	:49	$1:14^2$	$1:45^4$fm	7	114	$2^{1\frac12}$	3^1	2^5	$5^{12\frac12}$	Romero R P^1	[S]Mdn	54-13	SingWithM,SktNorth,RuffldGrous	10
5Jun86-4Bel	7f	$:23^1$	$:46^4$	1:26 ft	13	114	12^{11}	9^{13}	10^{12}	$6^{10\frac14}$	Cruguet J^6	[S]Mdn	62-17	VenturOn,IrrsistiblBr,ScottishRow	14

5Jun86—Off slowly

Oct 29 Bel tr.t 5f gd 1:01 h Oct 22 Bel 4f ft $:52^2$ b Oct 16 Bel 5f ft 1:03 b Oct 9 Bel 5f ft $1:03^3$ b

E.

Effervescive
Own.—Martin M T **110^7**
Ch. c. 3, by Effervescing—Golden Jolie, by Royal Serenade
Br.—Sunset Hill Breeding Assoc (Md) 1986 9 1 2 0 $14,520
Tr.—DeStasio Richard T $17,500 1985 2 M 0 0
Lifetime 11 1 2 0 $14,520 Turf 1 0 0 0

27Oct86-3Aqu	6f	$:22^2$	$:45^4$	$1:11^2$sy	15	109^{10}	7^8	7^{11}	5^7	$5^{6\frac34}$	Nuesch D^2	22500	77-20	Aquhero,Crig'sPower,RoundThStt	10
27Oct86—Checked															
13Oct86-9Bel	6f	$:22^2$	$:46^1$	$1:11^1$ft	$4\frac14$	109^{10}	3^2	$3^{\frac12}$	1^{hd}	$1^{\frac34}$	Nuesch D^6	M35000	86-16	Effervescive,GoldenChnce,DelrJff	10
8Oct86-2Bel	1 (T)	$:45^4$	1:12	$1:38^2$fm	19e	109^{10}	1^{hd}	2^{hd}	4^6	$10^{11\frac12}$	Nuesch D^{11}	Mdn	61-29	FleetingSnow,I'mNoYnke,Snd-Up	12
15Sep86-9Bel	6f	$:22^4$	$:46^1$	$1:11^2$ft	12	108^{10}	$6^{6\frac12}$	$7^{8\frac14}$	5^7	$4^{4\frac12}$	Nuesch D^8	M35000	80-15	Big Coda, Aptitude, Jeannies Boy	11
20Jly86-9Bel	1	:46	$1:11^2$	1:38 ft	$5\frac34$	116	3^3	4^{11}	6^{18}	$7^{21\frac14}$	Bailey J D^7	M50000	54-14	Easterner, Majestic Cast, Bye Dad	11
6Jly86-2Bel	6f	:23	$:46^3$	1:12 ft	*8-5	112	3^1	$5^{7\frac12}$	5^9	$7^{9\frac12}$	Lovato F Jr^8	M70000	72-15	LeveTheKeys,ClridgDriv,StormSsh	10
11Jun86-3Bel	6f	$:23^1$	$:46^4$	$1:11^4$ft	11	122	$4^{1\frac12}$	4^3	$3^{1\frac12}$	$4^{6\frac12}$	Lovato F Jr^8	Mdn	76-19	MomntofHop,NorthrnClssc,Cultvt	14
1Jun86-9Bel	6f	$:22^2$	$:45^2$	1:11 ft	$6\frac12$	114	3^4	3^7	$4^{3\frac12}$	2^{nk}	Lovato F Jr^{10}	M75000	87-10	Mr. Quartz, Effervescive, Ioskeha	11

Nov 5 Bel tr.t 4f ft :50 b Oct 22 Bel 6f ft $1:16^2$ b Sep 30 Bel tr.t 4f ft $:48^4$ b Sep 23 Bel 4f ft :51 b

429. It's Oct. 31. Which horse(s) can be eliminated on form?

8th Aqueduct

1 ⅛ FURLONG. (Turf). ALLOWANCE. Purse $40,000. Fillies and mares. 3-year-olds and upward.

A. **(32)**

***Philyra**
B. m. 5, by Fabulous Dancer—Tadjikie, by Prince Taj
Br.—Benilleouche S (Fra) 1986 6 1 1 0 $49,576
Own.—Silver Creek Farm 1127 Tr.—Wachs Michael 1985 13 4 3 1 $64,663
Lifetime 33 11 5 3 $198,202 Turf 29 10 4 3 $148,626
18Oct86-7Bel 1⅜[T]:48 1:38 2:16 gd 90 108 86 96¾ 69½ 610½ LopezV2 (F)Athenia H 66-29 Dwn'sCurtsey,Festivity,PrfctPoint 10
18Oct86—Grade III
3Oct86-9Med 1¼:471 1:363 2:033sy 15 112 49½ 517 520 524 Rini W3 (F)Q Chrltte H 60-20 AprilAgain,CopeOfFlowers,Devalois 5
3Oct86—Grade II; Run in divisions
20Sep86-7Bel 1 1/16[T]:4621:0941:41 hd 11 119 713 716 718 723¾ Migliore R6 (F)Leixable 72-10 Fama, Tax Dodge, Anka Germania 7
20Sep86—Run In Divisions
16Aug86-10Tdn 1⅛:464 1:111 1:494ft 7¾ 110 54½ 77½ 55¾ 55¼ Rini W4 Bud Brd Cup 83-16 ZanyTctics,BigCrown,Forkintherod 9
12Jly86-9Det 1 1/16:481 1:131 1:454ft 3 112 69 63¾ 11 11 Rini W1 (F)Bud Brd 74-18 Philyra, MyGarage,ThePrivateOne 10
29Jun86-7Tdn 6f :223 :462 1:122ft *2 113 98¼ 812 57½ 23½ Rini W3 (F)Aw13000 78-26 Dance On Over, Philyra, Replevin 9
Oct 1 Aqu 4f ft :481 h Sep 15 Tdn (T) 1 fm 1:42 b

B.

***Tarifa**
Gr. m. 6, by Pitskelly—Slap Up, by Gala Performance
Br.—Vigors T C (Eng) 1986 4 0 0 1 $11,499
Own.—Dileo P 117 Tr.—O'BRIEN LEO 1985 13 3 2 1 $100,931
Lifetime 39 8 3 5 $166,541 Turf 37 8 3 5 $166,541
13Oct86-9Lrl 1 1/16(T):4711:1211:423fm 6 115 1011 910 813 710 BrcclVJr9 (F)QIsabellH 80-10 KittyTatch,Carlyph,MeddlinMggie 11
20Sep86-8Pha 1⅛(T):4811:1221:49 fm *3 115 58½ 55 44½ 58¾ ThrbrB2 (F)Susquehana 77-17 PerfectPoint,SpruceLuck,AprilAgin 9
20Sep86—Run in Divisions; Lacked room
12Sep86-6Bel 7f (T):231 :46 1:224fm 21 115 97¼ 83¾ 42½ 32 Davis R G5 (F)Manta 88-08 Duckweed, Top Issue, Tarifa 9
12Sep86—Run in Divisions
1Sep86-9Med 1 1/16(T):4711:1021:411fm 23 114 79½ 87¾ 66¼ 55½ VergME2 (F)Violet H 90-07 LakeCountry,Duckweed,AnkGermni 8
1Sep86—Grade III
9Nov85-6Lrl 1⅛(T):5121:1641:56 yl 2¼ 116 75¾ 65½ 54¼ 66¼ BrcclVJr4 (F)Chrysm H 51-42 Wlksfr,DncingSlippers,Chinguetti 11
9Nov85—Grade III; Run in divisions
1Nov85-8Aqu 1 (T):47 1:1041:343fm 34 116 77½ 78½ 77¼ 89¼ MglrR1 (F)Ryl Heroine 94 — PossibleMte,Agcerie,CoupDeFolie 11
1Nov85—Run in Divisions
14Oct85-6Lrl 1 1/16(T):4711:1221:441fm *1 115 54 31 15 17½ BrcclVJr7 (F)QIsabellH 82-14 Tarif,NothingSweeter,BirthdyFling 8
14Oct85—Run in Divisions
Oct 9 Bel (T) 4f gd :474 h (d)

C.

Courageous Karen
Ch. m. 5, by Caucasus—Dream Date, by Rough 'N Tumble
Br.—Fuller P (Ky) 1986 12 1 1 2 $32,320
Own.—Nirth Hills Stable 10810 Tr.—FERRARO JAMES W JR 1985 17 1 5 3 $61,722
Lifetime 49 4 10 9 $141,237 Turf 28 2 4 6 $80,072
17Oct86-6Bel 1⅜[T]:4931:41 2:191gd 9¼ 1087 11½ 11 33½ 79½ Ortiz E Jr6 (F)Aw40000 51-36 SmoketheQun,KshiLgoon,Chingutti 7
20Sep86-1Bel 1¼[T]:49 1:3712:011hd 5½ 1125 1½ 67½ 511 513¾ Brown T L1 (F)Aw29000 74-10 Festivity, Keep TheFaithII,Guadery 8
14Sep86-7Bel 1¼[T]:5021:38 2:012fm 18 1095 2½ 65½ 69½ 69¾ Brown T L3 Aw29000 77-13 FredAstaire,Akabir,MjesticRoberto 6
11Aug86-8Sar 1⅛(T):4741:12 1:494gd 35 102 74½ 63½ 99½ 913¼ PrvtrR10 (F)Diana H 65-23 DutyDnce,Dismsted,KpluButterfly 11
11Aug86—Grade III
28Jly86-8Bel 1 1/16:46 1:102 1:432gd 2 109 33½ 32 33½ 33¾ Samyn J L1 (F)HcpO 81-12 TriykiStk,SurprisSpcl,CourgousKrn 4
15Jly86-7Mth 1 1/16(T):4831:1211:431+fm8½ 113 33½ 41 87¼ 89¼ MplE3 (F)Eatontown H 76-18 Mazatleca,CopeOfFlowers,Drbrielle 8
15Jly86—Run in divisions
29Jun86-5Bel 1¼[T]:4931:3942:03 fm 3½ 117 31 32 32 2no Davis R G1 (F)Aw40000 79-21 TriArgo,CourgeousKrn,SmokthQun 7
12Jun86-6Bel 1 1/16:462 1:113 1:451m 2½ 117 32½ 2½ 14 110¾ Samyn J L4 (F)Aw26000 76-20 CourgousKrn,NmbusStr,C'stMoMm 7
Sep 11 Aqu 4f ft :541 b Sep 1 Aqu 1 ft 1:44 b

D.

Loa B. f. 3, by Hawaii—Tiy, by Nalees Man
Br.—LaBrot Barbara W (Ky) 1986 12 4 1 0 $66,721
Own.—LaBrot Barbara W 116 Tr.—TURNER WILLIAM H JR 1985 2 M 0 0
Lifetime 14 4 1 0 $66,721 Turf 8 3 1 0 $60,121
23Oct86-8Aqu 1 :454 1:103 1:36 ft 18 110 43¼ 41 55½ 58¾ Samyn J L4 ⒻHcp0 77-17 Crrie'sDrem,ReelEsy,CherryJubilee 6
20ct86-8Bel 1 1/16 [T]:4821:12 1:442gd 8¼ 116 31½ 77½ 67 49½ Bailey J D1 ⒻAw40000 69-28 Festivity,DesertView,WendyWalker 8
12Sep86-6Bel 7f Ⓣ:231 :46 1:224fm 25 112 2hd 1hd 21½ 42¼ Bailey J D9 ⒻManta 88-08 Duckweed, Top Issue, Tarifa 9
12Sep86—Run in Divisions
29Aug86-7Med 1 1/16 [T]:4641:1031:413fm 10 117 810 69½ 813 812½ BilyJD1 ⒻBolng Sp H 82-03 SmllVirtu,SwtVlocity,CountryRcitl 11
29Aug86—Grade III; Run in division
19Aug86-9Mth 1 1/16 Ⓣ:4821:1341:464sf 3 119 97¾ 98 79½ 812¾ BileyJD1 ⒻL. Silver H 58-29 SprucFr,MyMomGnny,GrnBondry 10
19Aug86—Grade III
17Jun86-9Mth 1 Ⓣ:4631:1121:364fm*9-5 118 56 21½ 1hd 1½ Bailey J D6 ⒻRevidere 91-13 Loa, She's A Mystery, Small Virtue 9
1Jun86-7Bel 1 Ⓣ:46 1:1041:361gd 7½ 114 31½ 2½ 1hd 1hd Bailey JD11 ⒻAw26000 84-21 Loa, Clabber Girl, Lake Cecebe 12
16May86-5Bel 1 Ⓣ:4611:1031:363fm*3-5 111 1hd 1hd 1½ 1nk Bailey J D4 ⒻAw25000 82-18 Loa, Chehana, Legacy of Strength 6
●Oct 20 Bel tr.t 4f ft :471 h Oct 13 Bel tr.t 4f ft :47 h Sep 29 Bel tr.t 4f ft :49 b Sep 21 Bel tr.t 5f ft 1:01 b

E.

Spruce Luck Dk. b. or br. m. 5, by Big Spruce—Beshore, by Lucky Mel
Br.—Cowan Ruth (Ill) 1986 6 2 1 1 $39,560
Own.—Kenimer W E 115 Tr.—TRIBERT C DOUGLAS 1985 8 2 0 5 $31,571
Lifetime 16 5 1 6 $78,919 Turf 15 5 1 6 $78,919
18Oct86-7Bel 1⅜ [T]:48 1:38 2:16 gd 33 113 109½ 63¾ 58 59¾ VscuzJ5 ⒻAthenia H 67-29 Dwn'sCurtsey,Festivity,PrfctPoint 10
18Oct86—Grade III
20Sep86-8Pha 1⅛ Ⓣ:4811:1221:49 fm 4½ 114 916 97¼ 66¼ 27 McCrrG3 ⒻSusquehan 79-17 PerfectPoint,SpruceLuck,AprilAgin 9
20Sep86—Run in Divisions
5Jly86-8Lrl 1⅛ Ⓣ:4631:1031:473fm*6-5 114 716 712 66¾ 34½ MllrDAJr3 ⒻLdyBltreh 94-07 NothingSweetr,Subjctiv,SprucLuck 8
5Jly86—Run in divisions
16Jun86-9Lrl 1 1/16 Ⓣ:4611:11 1:42 fm 2¾ 121 712 65½ 2hd 11 MillerDAJr5 ⒻAw20000 93-06 Spruce Luck, LisaLeigh,EtaCarinae 7
10May86-8Pim 1½ Ⓣ:4912:0232:272fm 17 112 911 1010 1118 1217¼ HttonGW2 Dixie H 83-05 UptownSwell,SouthrnSultn,Crlyph 13
10May86—Grade II; Taken up; Breeders' Cup Fund Awards to: Uptown Swell, Carylpha
16Apr86-8Kee 1⅛ Ⓣ:4921:15 1:543fm 3½ 114 54 42 13 14¼ BrumfildD7 ⒻAw20300 84-16 Spruce Luck, My Garage, Mahalia 10
18Dec85-9Crc a1⅛ Ⓣ 1:484fm 33 112 33 85 56½ 35¼ PnD1 ⒻMy Charmer H 74-18 ShockerT.,Erin'sDunlo,SprucLuck 12
18Dec85—Run in divisions
9Nov85-8Lrl 1⅛ Ⓣ:4941:16 1:554yl 12 115 1112 108 43½ 34¼ MllrDAJr11 ⒻChrsmH 54-42 BrindyBrindy,VrsLCiss,SprucLuck 12
9Nov85—Grade III
Oct 18 Bel 5f ft 1:02 b ●Aug 31 Tim 3f ft :382 b

430. Which horse below should benefit most from "first time on lasix"?

A. **(33)**

Real Eager B. m. 5, by Eager Eagle—Real Sangre, by Knight in Armor
Br.—Carver J (Cal) 1986 11 2 1 1 $31,495
TOHILL K S 114 Tr.—Orr Ike $50,000 1985 10 1 0 3 $40,050
Own.—Carver & McVeigh Lifetime 41 10 2 6 $142,445 Turf 11 1 0 1 $15,175
30Oct86-8BM 6f :222 :45 1:103ft 25 115 43½ 44 43½ 61¼ Tohill K S6 ⒻAw20000 85-21 AbstractEnergy,FagersChrm,Erliest 6
22Jun86-6GG 1 1/16 Ⓣ:4741:1211:441fm 24 114 32 44 76 911¼ LamanceC10 Ⓕ[R]Hcp0 70-14 BannerRose,PurpleBbe,NorthMist 10
26May86-8GG 1 1/16 Ⓣ:4721:1221:43 fm 19 114 42½ 43 54¾ 79½ LncC3 Ⓕ[R]M Dt Iv H 77-17 Zaide, Banner Rose, Barbie Karen 9
26May86—Steadied 1st turn
4May86-9GG 1 :47 1:112 1:372ft 10 113 33½ 2hd 11½ 12½ Lamance C8 Ⓕ[R]Inv H 81-19 RealEger,Missdoon,Veronic'sQuest 8
24Apr86-8GG 1 1/16 Ⓣ:4631:1111:432fm 11 114 42½ 42 31½ 51¾ LamanceC7 ⒻAw25000 83-15 Normira, North Mist, Silk Chiffon 9
8Apr86-8GG 1 Ⓣ:4631:1211:372gd 9 114 68 76 53½ 63 LamanceC5 ⒻAw20000 77-20 Poshy, Running Luck, La Burlona 10
27Mar86-6GG 1 :473 1:114 1:374ft 9-5 114 2hd 1hd 11 13 Lamance C1 Ⓕ 40000 79-20 RelEger,MissAppleBlossom,StrPirt 5
21Mar86-8GG 1 1/16 :48 1:12 1:451ft 7 113 51¾ 32 33½ 37 LamanceC4 ⒻAw22000 70-22 Steady Penny,BerthaFay,RealEager 6
27Feb86-6GG 1 :49 1:123 1:382ft 4¾ 1095 31½ 2½ 21½ 2¾ Aragon VA5 ⒻAw22000 75-20 BerthaFay,RealEger,KrndebsBigKt 6
12Feb86-6GG 6f :221 :45 1:103sy 16 117 68½ 711 79½ 68 SchvnvldtCP3 Ⓕ 40000 78-20 StedyPenny,SupremeMignon,Dnish 8
Oct 10 BM 5f ft 1:01 h Sep 26 BM 5f gd 1:023 h Sep 20 BM 5f ft 1:034 h Sep 14 BM 5f ft 1:03 h

B.

Pirate Annie ✻
Ch. f. 4, by Pirateer—Go Lately, by Philately
Br.—Lang J A (Wash) 1986 15 3 4 1 $45,535
CHAPMAN T M 114 Tr.—Leonard Jack R $50,000 1985 21 7 3 3 $61,485
Own.—Adams J E Lifetime 44 11 8 7 $114,280
17Aug86-8Lga 6½f :214 :442 1:152ft 2¾ 114 35 45½ 46½ 42½ Steiner J J1 Ⓕ 60000 89-13 TributeToDanny,Blimondy,TvyBlue 5
3Aug86-8Lga 6½f :22 :451 1:161ft 6½ 120 33 43 63½ 45¼ Cooper B4 ⒻAw10100 83-15 Silk Chiffon, GalORoseA,BerthaFay 6
20Jly86-9Lga 1 1/16 :462 1:11 1:422ft *8-5e 114 52½ 52 54¾ 45 GnslsFA4 ⒻLuella G H 82-16 NorthrnNms,GlORosA,BromptnMst 9
20Jun86-9Lga 6f :222 :452 1:091ft 5 120 41¾ 41¼ 55 57¼ Steiner J J5 ⒻAw11600 83-19 NorthernNums,GlORoseA,Blimondy 7
1Jun86-9Lga 6½f :221 :452 1:17 ft 24 115 52½ 43¼ 56½ 63½ SteinrJJ4 ⒻEverett H 80-21 ShootingPitch,Bix'sBet,CountryJwl 7
21May86-9Lga 6½f :221 :45 1:17 ft *2-3 117 21½ 2½ 2½ 1½ Baze G4 Ⓕ c40000 84-34 PirateAnnie,SaberLind,MissMonco 5
11May86-8Lga 6f :212 :441 1:10 ft 2¾ 116 34 33½ 47½ 31½ Baze G1 Ⓕ 50000 84-18 Mrlu'sFirst,NorthernNums,PirtAnni 6
1May86-8Lga 6½f :214 :444 1:17 sy 2½ 118 53¼ 21 21½ 2no Baze M B5 Ⓕ 40000 84-22 Blimondy,PirteAnni,NorthrnSwing 10
18Apr86-9Lga 6f :22 :451 1:10 ft *1 120 41½ 31½ 22½ 22½ Long B7 ⒻAw10700 83-19 Mrlu'sFirst,PirteAnnie,CountryJewl 7
27Mar86-8GG 6f :222 :452 1:104ft 2¼ 115 42 42¼ 21 2½ Baze R A4 Ⓕ 50000 84-20 FrnnieMeret,PirtAnni,StockMrktII 6
Oct 14 BM 5f ft 1:012 h Oct 7 BM 1 ft 1:453 h Sep 30 BM 5f ft 1:022 h

C.

Olympic Classic
Dk. b. or br. f. 3, by Olympiad King—Classic Kitten, by Cougar II
Br.—Rancho Felicia (Cal) 1986 9 3 1 0 $29,195
CASTANEDA M 111 Tr.—Hollendorfer Jerry $50,000 1985 7 2 0 0 $12,975
Own.—Hollendorfer & Lewis Lifetime 16 5 1 0 $42,170 Turf 1 0 0 0
17Aug86-2Dmr 6f :214 :451 1:101ft 4¼ 116 86½ 89¾ 812 817½ Olivares F3 Ⓕ 40000 69-16 HirlessHeiress,LcyLinn,ForvrABlurr 8
1Aug86-7Dmr 6f :213 :442 1:092ft 5¾ 116 911 78 77¾ 57 Baze R A4 Ⓕ 50000 84-13 Witchery,DremPolicy,DuchssZnth 10
1Aug86—4 wide into stretch
8Jly86-11Sol 6f :221 :45 1:102ft 3½ 118 33½ 32 4¾ 21 CstndM5 Ⓕ[R]Fairfield 90-22 Chnngo'sAlb,OlympcClssc,BrgnFun 7
4Jun86-6GG 1 1/16 Ⓣ:4711:1211:442fm 11 114 55 33½ 711 89¼ GonzlzRM2 ⒻAw20000 71-20 VllyVictory,JoysOfSpring,Trnsgogo 9
4Jun86—Rank 1st turn
15May86-8GG 6f :223 :453 1:10 ft *1 117 1hd 1hd 1hd 12 CastnedM2 ⒻAw17000 89-15 OlympicClssic,KinCoulee,LdyPstor 6
15Apr86-8GG 6f :222 :454 1:112gd 4½e 115 33 55 57 75¼ CstndM2 Ⓕ[S]Miss Cal 77-25 SilentArrivl,LdyMxineD.,Witchery 12
20Mar86-8GG 6f :221 :453 1:102ft *6-5 114 24 21 1½ 15 CastnedM2 ⒻAw17000 87-24 OlympicClssic,IWlkAlone,Trnsgogo 6
5Mar86-1GG 6f :222 :452 1:104ft 3 115 22 21 14 17 Castaneda M4 Ⓕ 16000 85-19 OlympicClssc,FoolshIc,WltzAround 6
20Feb86-4GG 6f :222 :453 1:114m 3½ 115 43½ 32 21½ 44½ Castaneda M3 Ⓕ 20000 75-20 OhHowRght,Bold'NFshon,BrnnMrn 8
20Feb86—Jumped in air
12Dec85-1BM 1 :471 1:124 1:401ft *8-5 115 511 46 54½ 52¾ Baze R A7 Ⓕ c16000 64-24 TllMTomorrow,DncNorth,ClsscQlty 8
Oct 12 BM 5f ft 1:011 h Sep 24 BM 5f m 1:033 h (d) Sep 18 BM 6f ft 1:161 h Sep 12 BM 5f ft 1:024 h

D.

***Girl In Blue**
Dk. b. or br. m. 7, by Garda's Revenge—Regal Star, by Dark Star
Br.—Mullins Mrs P (Ire) 1986 11 4 2 1 $50,850
DIAZ A L 120 Tr.—Greenman Walter $50,000 1985 9 2 1 2 $25,980
Own.—Greenman Jean Lifetime 54 11 4 6 $99,283 Turf 51 11 4 6 $97,933
28Sep86-9BM 7½f Ⓣ:231 :4641:303gd 3¾ 114 67 64½ 53 1no Chapman TM8 Ⓕ 50000 91-08 Girl InBlue,BrownBess,J.D.Canyon 10
11Sep86-11Bmf 7½f Ⓣ:222 :46 1:30 fm*3-2 114 611 63½ 51¾ 1¾ ChpmnTM8 ⒻAw19000 94-06 GirlInBlue,GlORoseA,CrystlShowrs 8
22Aug86-7Dmr 1 Ⓣ:4631:1111:361fm 8¾ 116 74½ 63¼ 74¼ 75½ ValenzuelPA5 Ⓕ 62500 85-09 WineTaster,Tantalized,Beaulahland 8
11Aug86-5Dmr 1 :452 1:104 1:37 ft 5¼ 116 88¾ 99¼ 912 911¼ Pincay L Jr6 Ⓕ 40000 72-13 WineTster,RdFrnchy,Dlt'sGoldCoin 9
11Aug86—Lugged out
9Jly86-11Sol 1 :472 1:113 1:374ft 3 114 33 33 33 44¾ CastnedM4 ⒻAw15000 80-17 WnTstr,MssApplBlossom,Cthy'sFn 5
1Jun86-10GG 1 1/16 Ⓣ:4711:1231:444fm *2½ 117 43¼ 41¼ 12 11 Castaneda M3 Ⓕ 50000 78-16 Girl InBlue,WineTaster,BrunedeMai 8
17May86-9GG 1 1/16 Ⓣ:47 1:1211:45 fm 2¼ 114 65 22 11½ 14½ Castaneda M4 Ⓕ 50000 77-17 GirlInBlu,ShipToShor,StockMrktII 9
17May86—Rank 1st turn
30Apr86-8GG 1 1/16 Ⓣ:4831:13 1:45 fm 7-5 114 44½ 31½ 22 22 Judice J C3 Ⓕ 50000 75-23 BmsGoldnEgl,GrlInBlu,HowrdSttn 6
11Apr86-8GG 1 1/16 Ⓣ:4831:1231:434fm 3 115 32 43½ 53¾ 53 HummlCR1 ⒻAw20000 80-17 I'llTryII,FrnnieMerete,BeImpressiv 8
11Apr86—Lacked room 5/16
28Mar86-8GG 1 1/16 Ⓣ:4721:1211:434fm *2¼ 114 77 65¾ 52¾ 34 CastnedM5 ⒻAw20000 79-17 Heat Spell, La Burlona, Girl InBlue 7
Oct 12 BM 5f ft 1:02 h Sep 24 BM 3f m :383 h (d) Sep 4 BM Ⓣ 3f fm :393 h (d)

Answer key: Form analysis

Minimum Competency Test

352. C	356. A	360. B
353. A	357. B	361. D
354. A	358. D	362. A
355. C	359. D	363. D & F

Mastery Test

364. D	378. A	392. A	405. B	418. A
365. A	379. A	393. A	406. C	419. D
366. C	380. C	394. A	407. D	420. B
367. D	381. B	395. C	408. C	421. C
368. A	382. C	396. D	409. B	422. B & D
369. B	383. C	397. B	410. C	423. B & G
370. D	384. A	398. B	411. B	424. D & E
371. A	385. C	399. B	412. D	425. A & B
372. A	386. A	400. D	413. D	426. B
373. D	387. A	401. B	414. B	427. B
374. A	388. B	402. A	415. A	428. B & E
375. D	389. B	403. B	416. B	429. A & B
376. B	390. C	404. D	417. A	430. C
377. A	391. A			

CHAPTER 9

The Distance Factor

Competencies

34. Know the basic facts and probabilities associated with the distance factor.
35. Understand changes of distance in relation to running styles, early speed, pace, track bias, and form.
36. Understand changes of distance in relation to class, age, and eligibility conditions.
37. Interpret performances at various distances.

	Minimum Competency Test	Mastery Test
Proficiency standards	80%	70%
Number of items	12	38
Passing Scores	10	27

Sources of Instruction

- *Ainslie's Complete Guide to Thoroughbred Racing*, Chapter 8
- *Winning at the Races*, Chapter 6
- *Thoroughbred Handicapping: State of the Art*, Chapter 2

Comments

Like several fundamental factors of handicapping, distance has long been a subject sadly misapprehended in the general discourse and therefore happily submitted to a revisionist treatment resulting from the best probability data we have.

The classical position holds that horses can be accepted as contenders only when entered at distances the past performances have indicated as suitable or comfortable. Horses 4up by this view should have won at exact distances (as today's).

Any exceptions should have won at closely related distances, within one-sixteenth of a mile perhaps.

The new-wave authors of the seventies and eighties have issued a massive dissent, taking a flexible approach to distance. The figure charts of modern speed and pace handicappers presuppose a logic by which running times are fully transportable among all regularly run distances. If a 3YO colt has finished 6F in 1:10⅕, that means he can be expected to finish 1¹⁄₁₆M in 1:42⅘. No one quibbles on the point. The topic is not even discussed. An 80 is an 80 is an 80 is an 80, distance notwithstanding.

Horsemen vary in kind on the matter. No less a spokesman than Charles Whittingham has, throughout an illustrious career, been painstakingly precise about his horses' suitability to exact distances. Whittingham dearly prizes an animal that's at its best beyond 1¼M—an anomaly in American racing—because he knows few horses do their best when going that far. But Whittingham specializes as no one else has—John Gosden possibly excepted—in blueblooded stakes horses 4up, and mainly distance specialists. The trainer's posture on distance surely reflects a highly specialized practice.

Most trainers experiment freely with horses and distances. The common practice just as surely reflects an attitude that racehorses generally do well enough at related distances, and many of them in fact can shine at several unrelated distances.

Probability data have shed much light on the arguments. The data generally support the common practice—versatility—but with several interesting adaptations handicappers need to know.

Definitions of Terms

- *Related distances.* Sprints up to 7F, and one-turn miles. Middle distances, including two-turn miles and routes to 1³⁄₁₆ miles. Classic distances, or races at 1¼M or farther.

DISTANCE: MINIMUM COMPETENCY TEST

431. In what races is the distance factor likely to be most decisive?

    A. 7F   (34)
    B. 1M
    C. 1¹⁄₁₆M
    D. 1½M

432. Probability studies reveal that inexperience at the distance is only a serious disadvantage in routes.

A. True (34)
B. False

433. Which is *not* a related distance?

A. 1M (34)
B. 7F
C. 1³⁄₁₆M
D. 1⅛M (t)

434. At distances shorter than 6 furlongs, the most significant factor of handicapping is

A. class (34)
B. final time
C. early speed
D. pedigree

435. Horses having no experience in routes are often attractive overlays in their first try around two turns.

A. True (34)
B. False

436. Horses unable to keep up in the early stages of routes have little chance of winning sprints.

A. True (35)
B. False

437. At mile tracks, which distance is most susceptible to a post position bias?

A. 6F (35)
B. 7F
C. 1¹⁄₁₆M
D. 1⅛M

438. Of the horses depicted below, which can usually handle 7 furlongs most effectively?

A. a router having early speed (35)
B. a closer at 6F
C. frontrunners in the shorter sprints

D. sprinters that win from slightly behind the early pace

439. As distance increases, which factor below intensifies in importance?

A. class **(36)**
B. speed
C. form
D. weight

440. Champions, division leaders, and Grade 1 stakes horses are best distinguished at what distance?

A. 1⅛M **(36)**
B. 1¼M
C. 1½M
D. 1¾M

441. A reasonable standard of "respectable time" for $10,000 4up claiming horses at the route is a *Form* speed rating of

A. 67 **(34)**
B. 73
C. 78
D. 82

442. Which is *Stark Secret*'s best distance?

A. 6F **(37)**
B. 7F
C. 1$\frac{1}{16}$M
D. 1⅛M

Stark Secret *
Own.—Kinsman Stable **117**
B. c. 4, by Graustark—Secretarial Queen, by Secretariat
Br.—Gentry Tom (Ky)
Tr.—Lenzini John J Jr **$50,000**
Lifetime 14 3 2 2 $60,120
1986 10 1 1 2 $27,080
1985 4 2 1 0 $33,040
Turf 1 0 0 0

23Oct86-7Aqu	6f	:22	:45	1:10	ft	*2¼e	117	$9^{5\frac{1}{2}}$	7^{6}	$5^{6\frac{1}{2}}$	$3^{1\frac{1}{2}}$	Vasquez J^{7}	50000	89-17	GreenShekl,FlyingSkippr,StrkScrt	10
23Oct86—Steadied																
11Oct86-1Bel	7f	$:22^{3}$	$:45^{3}$	$1:23^{2}$	ft	*7-5e	117	$6^{8\frac{3}{4}}$	6^{6}	$4^{2\frac{1}{2}}$	$2^{\frac{3}{4}}$	Vasquez J^{4}	50000	84-19	Frontier Justice,StarkSecret,Semaj	7
28Sep86-1Bel	$1\frac{1}{16}$	$:46^{3}$	$1:11^{1}$	$1:42^{3}$	m	3½	117	$3^{3\frac{1}{2}}$	$3^{1\frac{1}{2}}$	3^{1}	$4^{2\frac{1}{2}}$	Cordero A Jr^{4}	50000	66-15	Mr.Murtugh,BrbdinRf,RmblngRctor	7
18Sep86-3Bel	1⅛	$:46^{3}$	$1:10^{4}$	$1:48^{2}$	ft	8½	117	2^{1}	1^{1}	$2^{2\frac{1}{2}}$	$3^{6\frac{1}{2}}$	Romero R P^{7}	50000	78-17	RmblngRctor,FngrsInthTll,StrkScrt	8
4Sep86-1Bel	1⅛	$:47^{4}$	$1:11^{3}$	$1:49^{1}$	ft	9-5	117	1^{1}	$1^{1\frac{1}{2}}$	$2^{1\frac{1}{2}}$	$4^{4\frac{1}{4}}$	Cordero A Jr^{5}	50000	77-18	Fly Me Again,Mr.Murtaugh,Oversea	6
27Aug86-7Bel	1 Ⓣ	$:47^{1}$	1:11	1:36	fm	37	117	8^{6}	$8^{9\frac{1}{2}}$	$9^{9\frac{1}{2}}$	$8^{9\frac{3}{4}}$	Lovato F Jr^{4}	Aw26000	75-18	FrdAstir,Torqumd,ChristinHundrd	10
17Aug86-2Sar	7f	$:23^{1}$	$:46^{2}$	$1:23^{1}$	m	4½	117	$5^{2\frac{1}{2}}$	3^{2}	$3^{2\frac{1}{2}}$	1^{4}	Velasquez J^{5}	50000	86-11	StarkSecret,IceColdGold,DnceMsk	6
30Jly86-9Mth	$1\frac{1}{16}$	$:46^{1}$	$1:10^{2}$	1:42	ft	4¾	117	2^{3}	$4^{5\frac{1}{2}}$	4^{10}	$4^{18\frac{3}{4}}$	Verge M E^{1}	Aw16000	76-15	SovrignSong,BsLnding,DnctothWir	4

Sep 14 Aqu 5f ft 1:03 h

This is the end of the minimum competency test. Check your answers. If your score falls below standard, consult the recommended sources of instruction before proceeding to the mastery test.

DISTANCE: MASTERY TEST

443. No previous experience at the distance is most disadvantageous in races of

    A. 6F   **(34)**
    B. 1M
    C. $1\frac{1}{16}$M
    D. $1\frac{1}{4}$M

444. Probability studies show that lack of experience at the distance is a serious disadvantage only in sprints.

    A. True   **(34)**
    B. False

445. In evaluating sprinters attempting to route, handicappers typically will overemphasize

    A. early speed   **(35)**
    B. the trainer's ability when switching distances
    C. probable effects of early pace
    D. the impressive stretch gain

446. The most difficult distance switch of all is

    A. 6F to 7F   **(34)**
    B. 6F to $1\frac{1}{16}$M
    C. 1M to 6F
    D. $1\frac{1}{8}$M to 1M

447. What kind of sprinter is often the best bet in a middle distance claiming route?

    A. runs evenly all the way   **(35)**
    B. shows early speed to the pre-stretch call
    C. presses the pace before moving up into the stretch
    D. closes strongly from far behind

448. A router with sharp early speed can be most effective in sprints of

    A. 6F   **(35)**
    B. $6\frac{1}{2}$F
    C. 7F
    D. $5\frac{1}{2}$F

449. Frontrunners that quit in sprints sometimes can win middle distance routes because

    A. They can outrun the early route speed and con-   **(35)**
       trol the early pace
    B. The early pace is slower and they can relax
    C. The stamina in their pedigree finally has a chance
       to operate
    D. The conditions bar the recent multiple route win-
       ners

450. As a group, 2YO winners at 6F have dosage indexes of roughly

    A. 5.50   **(35)**
    B. 6.50
    C. 7.50
    D. 8.50

451. Under what claiming conditions would sprinters be most likely to win route races?

    A. nonwinners of a race since a specified date   **(36)**
    B. nonwinners of three races lifetime
    C. nonwinners at a mile or over this season
    D. a starter handicap at $5000 or less

452. It is a statistically verifiable fact that frontrunners do better in two-turn routes than they do in one-turn routes.

    A. True   **(34)**
    B. False

453. A reasonable standard of "respectable time" for non-claiming routers is a *Form* speed rating of

    A. 75   **(34)**
    B. 80
    C. 84
    D. 87

454. Which is the most difficult change in class and distance to accomplish at the same time?

    A. Mdn to Alw / 6F to 1M
    B. Clm $16k to Clm $25k / 1M to 1¼M   **(36)**
    C. open stakes to graded stakes / 7F to 1¹⁄₁₆M
    D. Alw, NW1XMC to Clf Alw / 6F to 1⅛M

455. What kind of horse is most likely to change distances effectively?

A. fully mature horses and mares, regardless of class **(36)**
B. nonclaiming 3YOs
C. claiming horses, 4up
D. 2-year-olds bred to route

456. At tracks having a circumference greater than a mile, which distance is most susceptible to a post position bias?

A. 7F **(35)**
B. 1M
C. 1⅛M
D. 1¼M

457. What kind of 3YO is least likely to change from sprints to routes successfully at first try?

A. has demonstrated unmistakable brilliance **(36)**
B. unable to break its maiden in six tries
C. has a dosage index above 4.00
D. has returned from a lengthy layoff and is stretch-
   ing out following a single sprint

458. Which is the most difficult class and distance switch in combination?

A. Minor stakes to graded stakes, middle distance to **(36)**
   classic distance
B. Alw, NW2XMC to Alw, NW3XMC; 1M to 6F
C. Clf to open stakes, sprint to middle distance
D. Mdn to Alw, 1 to 1⅛M

459. Horses returning from lengthy layoffs are more likely to succeed in sprints than routes.

A. True **(35)**
B. False

460. Which horse is most likely to switch from 6F to 1¹⁄₁₆M successfully?

A. a lightly raced, improving 3YO **(36)**
B. a stakes-winning sprinter dropping in class
C. a leading 2YO
D. a consistent, versatile $10,000 5YO claiming horse

461. Frontrunning 3-year-olds switching to turf routes are more likely to succeed if they

    A. have already won an allowance race   **(36)**
    B. have worked out on the grass
    C. run relaxed on the lead
    D. have performed satisfactorily in an open stakes

462. Turf routes are more hospitable to horses having

    A. outside posts   **(35)**
    B. inside posts
    C. early speed
    D. late speed

463. Pace handicappers rating a router off a route race but running 6F today will typically adjust the first-fraction time of the routes by

    A. minus ⅘ seconds   **(35)**
    B. one-half the daily variant
    C. 2 seconds or more
    D. minus ⅖ seconds

464. For pace ratings, the key internal fraction at middle distances is

    A. 2F   **(35)**
    B. 4F
    C. 6F
    D. 7F

465. What kind of router is most likely to drop back to a sprint and win?

    A. runs evenly all the way   **(34)**
    B. shows early speed to first two calls
    C. shows "bid and hung" improvement factor
    D. closes strongly from behind

466. The best dosage index for 2YOs entered in 5-furlong dashes is

    A. 4.00   **(35)**
    B. 6.50
    C. 10.00
    D. 21.00

467. Horses 4up are acceptable on distance if they have

A. won at today's exact distance **(36)**
B. finished within 2 to 3 lengths at related distances
C. won at a related distance and have finished in-the-money at today's exact distance
D. won at distances both shorter and longer than today's

468. In practice, the notion of related distances means that sprinters that have won at 6F can be accepted on distance at all other sprint distances.

A. True **(37)**
B. False

469. Following a lengthy layoff, which is the best-known pattern of stretching out from sprint to route?

A. one sprint **(35)**
B. two sprints
C. one sprint and one route
D. a pair of routes

470. Which two distances are most strongly related?

A. 6F and 7F **(34)**
B. 1M and 1$\frac{1}{16}$M
C. 1¼M and 1½M
D. 5F and 5½F

471. Is this gelding acceptable at today's new distance?

A. Yes **(37)**
B. No

7th Aqueduct

1 MILE. (1.33⅕) ALLOWANCE. Purse $25,000. 3-year-olds and upward which have never won a race other than Maiden, Claiming or Starter. Weights, 3-year-olds 119 lbs. Older 122 lbs. Non-winners of a race other than claiming at a mile or over since October 15 allowed 3 lbs. Of such a race since October 1 5 lbs.

***Switch In Time** — Ch. g. 3, by Kris—Match Bend, by Never Bend
Br.—Moyglare Stud Farm inc (Ire) — 1986 16 3 4 2 $56,760
Own.—Vee Pee Jay Stable **114** Tr.—Ferriola Peter — Turf 1 0 0 0
Lifetime 16 3 4 2 $56,760

24Oct86-9Aqu	7f	:22^3	:46	1:23^{3}ft	6¾	117	1^2	1^2	1^6	1^7	Santagata N^{12}	17500	83-20	SwitchInTime,BrillintCsting,AlVet	12
29Sep86-3Bel	6f	:22^2	:46	1:10^{3}gd	15	117	$8^{7\frac{1}{4}}$	$9^{9\frac{1}{4}}$	9^{12}	9^{11}	Santagata N^3	25000	78-14	MistyAqu,EvryPlsur,NorthrnRustc	10
27Aug86-9Bel	7f	:23	:46^1	1:24^{2}ft	*2½	117	$4^{2\frac{1}{2}}$	$6^{2\frac{1}{2}}$	$9^{8\frac{1}{2}}$	$10^{9\frac{3}{4}}$	Migliore R^6	25000	70-16	VgbondGeorg,FlyGryFly,GllntChif	12
6Aug86-7Sar	6f	:21^4	:45^1	1:11 sy	14	112	$5^{8\frac{1}{2}}$	6^{10}	9^{20}	$9^{23\frac{3}{4}}$	Santagata N^7	Aw24000	61-26	AlDavis,ClassicMove,Michel'sDncer	9
26Jly86-3Bel	7f	:23	:46^1	1:25 ft	2¾	112	6^5	$7^{8\frac{1}{2}}$	6^8	$5^{8\frac{1}{2}}$	Migliore R^3	Aw24000	68-28	Ormonte, Carnivore, Little Tuggy	7
29Jun86-3Bel	6f	:22^4	:46^1	1:11 ft	4½	117	7^6	5^5	$3^{2\frac{1}{2}}$	$2^{\frac{3}{4}}$	Migliore R^2	Aw24000	86-14	ClerHorizon,SwitchInTime,Col.Yoni	7
20Jun86-9Bel	6½f	:22^3	:45^2	1:16^{1}ft	6¾	113	$4^{2\frac{1}{2}}$	$3^{\frac{1}{2}}$	2^{hd}	$3^{2\frac{1}{2}}$	Migliore R^{11}	70000	92-10	GldnOldn,GrndExchng,SwtchInTm	11
11Jun86-9Bel	7f	:23^1	:47	1:25^{1}ft	*2	117	2^1	2^1	$1^{\frac{1}{2}}$	1^4	Velasquez J^{10}	c35000	76-19	SwitchInTime,McNz,DistinctEdge	12

Oct 17 Aqu 4f ft :49^1 h   Sep 15 Aqu 5f ft 1:04^4 h   Sep 12 Aqu 4f ft :53 h

472. What is this 3YO's best distance?

A. 6F **(37)**
B. 1M
C. 1 1/16M
D. not well-suited for any specific distance

Stock N Trade Ch. g. 3, by Rising Market—Mrs Stengel, by Fleet Allied
Br.—Russell Mr–Mrs J B (Cal) 1986 10 0 1 1 $4,840
TOHILL K S 114 Tr.—Lyons Val Tohill $20,000 1985 3 2 0 0 $18,400
Own.—Tohill Kathleen D Lifetime 13 2 1 1 $23,240
30ct86-5BM 1 1/16 :463 1:11 1:441ft 15 114 57 55½ 54¼ 74¾ Tohill K S7 25000 66-21 NightSwope,YehMeDo,CochConwy 8
19Sep86-9BM 1 1/16 :472 1:121 1:454ft 8¼ 114 52¼ 31½ 53½ 65¼ Tohill K S7 25000 58-28 BonVvntDottor,CchCnwy,LrryRlnd 7
30Aug86-9Sac 6f :224 :451 1:092ft 4½ 114 2hd 2hd 31½ 24½ Stallings W E2 25000 87-12 NeverSayDino,StockNTrade,Sagitte 5
27Jun86-8Pln 170 :462 1:112 1:411ft 9 113 32½ 31½ 33 32¾ Tohill K S2 16000 85-11 WildPursuit,Mostccioli,StockNTrde 9
27Jun86—Lugged out
7May86-1GG 1 1/16 :471 1:12 1:442ft 4½ 114 2½ 1hd 32 56¾ Diaz A L4 c16000 74-20 SensitiveCopy,FrostyEgl,CutHimFr 6
7May86—Broke slowly
1May86-7GG 6f :221 :45 1:10 ft 14 114 87¼ 69 68½ 67¼ Diaz A L10 25000 82-16 DarkMenace,FlagOfTruce,NoBker 11
17Apr86-6GG 6f :231 :464 1:122sl 7¾ 114 53½ 66 56½ 58 Tohill K S4 25000 69-40 Willie's Power,LaRisque,Jettisoned 7
17Apr86—Lacked room
14Mar86-8GG 1 :464 1:112 1:364gd 81 117 811 813 817 723½ ScldtCP5 [R]Bly Bl IvH 60-23 ToAirIsEquin,SpdyShnnon,SngrChf 8
14Mar86—Ducked out start
4Mar86-8GG 1 :463 1:104 1:38 ft 19 116 35 38 314 516¾ SchvnvldtCP3 Aw19000 61-23 SngerChief,TimothyDy,RulerOfFlts 5
25Jan86-8BM 1 1/16 :471 1:111 1:431ft 8 115 710 79¾ 713 715¾ Tohill K S2 Atherton 60-19 AudcosRllh,LdyMxnD.,LordBlodgtt 7
25Jan86—Bumped hard start
●Oct 20 BM 7f ft 1:253 h Oct 16 BM 6f ft 1:183 h Sep 28 BM 5f ft 1:044 h Sep 13 BM 6f ft 1:163 h

473. The best indication that horses that have never competed at a flat mile can win at that distance is

A. a come-from-behind powerful win in a sprint **(37)**
B. brilliant early speed in sprints
C. a win at any middle distance
D. wins at distances both shorter and longer

474. What can handicappers conclude about *Mine Tonight* and distance?

Mine Tonight Ch. f. 3, by Upper Nile—Mardi Gras Maid, by King of the Tudors
Br.—McFadden D & Judy (Wash) 1986 9 2 0 3 $31,920
Own.—N.Y. Edition Form 116 Tr.—Daggett Michael H $50,000 Turf 3 1 0 0 $13,800
Lifetime 9 2 0 3 $31,920
26Sep86-7Bel 1 (T):4631:12 1:382gd 14 113 64 44 59 59½ Maple E1 (F)Aw25000 63-28 ‡MssSrhJoy,Lvphrd'sFthr,Lomhoil 12
4Sep86-4Bel 1 1/16 [T]:4641:11 1:432fm 20 116 32 22 1½ 1¾ Maple E2 (F) 50000 84-22 Mine Tonight, Bourse Grise,Frothy 8
16Aug86-1Sar 6f :222 :454 1:111sy 9¾ 116 57½ 514 516 412¾ Maple E2 (F) 50000 71-22 SkiBunny,SocilEnggmnt,ChrokChill 5
24Jly86-5Bel 1 1/16 (T):47 1:1111:423fm 18 112 31½ 3½ 89 817¾ Migliore R8 (F)Aw25000 65-16 Ruiensk,LegcyofStrngth,OnForBss 10
4Jly86-3Bel 6f :222 :462 1:112ft 2¾ 114 11½ 1½ 11½ 11 Migliore R4 (F)M72500 85-11 MinTonght,SnoozYouLoos,CoolQun 9
22Jun86-4Bel 7f :224 :454 1:252ft *2½ 121 1½ 1hd 44 65 Migliore R4 (F)Mdn 70-19 Bold Prima,SaltInMyStew,Festivity 9
25May86-3Bel 1 :464 1:112 1:364ft 3¾ 121 21½ 21 2½ 33¼ Migliore R9 (F)Mdn 78-12 ChristmsCov,Tht'sFin,MinTonight 10
15May86-3Bel 7f :224 :461 1:242ft 7¾ 121 1½ 1hd 1hd 32¼ Migliore R4 (F)Mdn 78-16 StrkABinc,SnoozYoLoos,MnTonght 7
Oct 29 Bel 3f m :36 h Oct 23 Bel 5f ft 1:04 b Oct 17 Bel 5f ft 1:012 h Oct 3 Bel tr.t 4f ft :524 b

A. The filly's best distance is probably a flat mile **(37)**
B. The filly is a sprinter
C. The filly is a router
D. The filly has looked equally impressive in sprints and routes

475. Which statement is supported by *Hot Debate*'s record?

```
Hot Debate                     B. c. 4, by Overskate—Hot Rumer, by Swift Ruler
                               Br.—Farish W S III & Somoza (NY)          1986  8 0 1 1    $8,960
Own.—Barrera O S        110^7  Tr.—Barrera Oscar S                       1985  8 0 0 0    $4,890
                               Lifetime  22 3 4 1  $221,656              Turf  4 0 0 0
   Entered 1Nov86- 9 AQU
19Oct86-6Bel  1      :45^4 1:10    1:34^2ft  5½e110^7 79½ 7^16 7^17 6^20  Belmonte JF^2 Aw29000 73-14 Clear Choice, I Rejoice,BalthazarB. 7
8Oct86-8Bel   1 1/16 :46^2 1:10^4  1:41^3ft  9½ 108^7 2½ 54¾ 6^17 6^20  Ortiz E Jr^1  Aw40000 74-19 CostConscious,WikikStr,MrclWood 6
2Oct86-1Bel   1 1/16 :48^1 1:12^2  1:43 ft   5½ 117   3½ 1^hd 1½ 3½     Davis R G^2   c25000  86-09 Roomie,AccountReceivble,HotDebt 7
12Sep86-2Bel  7f     :23^1 :46^3   1:23^1ft  5¾ 117   74¼ 54½ 66½ 6^9   Martens G^5   35000   77-20 Timperature,UpperStr,AsYouLikeIt 9
28Aug86-1Bel  1      :46^1 1:11^1  1:37 m    11 117   4^4 4^3 2^1 2^4   Martens G^6   35000   76-16 Harry L., Hot Debate, Powell'sCove 9
20Aug86-8Sar  1 1/16 [T]:45^4 1:10 1:41^2fm  14 111   128¾ 11^11 88¾ 88¼ VlszJ^6 [S]West Point H 82-11 Island Sun, Judge Costa, Mugatea 14
4Aug86-7Sar   1      [T]:48^1 1:12^3 1:37 gd 44 117   77¾ 75½ 54¾ 55½   Velasquez J^9 Aw29000 85-21 Curium, Watch For Dawn, Equinol 9
17Jan86-8Aqu  1⅛     [•]:48 1:12^3 1:52^1ft  24 115   31½ 32½ 4^7 410½  Santagata N^7 Aw40000 70-22 King'sSwn,StrongSttemnt,Shdowfx 8
   Sep 29 Bel tr.t 5f ft 1:01 h      ●Sep 10 Bel 3f ft :35 h      Sep 5 Bel tr.t 5f ft 1:02^4 h
```

A. When entered in sprints, the colt is best eliminated (37)
B. The horse is best from 7F to 1 1/16M
C. The horse is not well-suited to turf routes
D. The horse does not seem particularly comfortable or well-spotted at any specific distance

476. *Roomie* should be eliminated on distance in races of 7F or less.

A. True (37)
B. False

```
Roomie                         Ch. c. 4, by Naskra—Elopement, by Gallant Romeo
                               Br.—Green R L (Ky)                        1986 12 1 4 2    $28,908
Own.—Sommer Viola       117    Tr.—Martin Frank          $35,000         1985 14 1 1 1    $19,940
                               Lifetime  33 2 5 3  $49,928               Turf  9 0 1 1    $7,420
22Oct86-4Aqu  1 3/16 :48 1:11^3 1:56^4ft     6 117    52½ 4^6 4^9 37¼   Davis R G^6   35000   71-16 Harry L., Our Triumph, Roomie 7
12Oct86-2Bel  1⅛     :46^2 1:11^1 1:50 ft    2 112^7  2½ 2^hd 2^1 2^3   Ortiz E Jr^5  c25000  74-13 Our Triumph, Roomie, Stop Light 8
2Oct86-1Bel   1 1/16 :48^1 1:12^2 1:43 ft    4¾ 112^5 2^hd 3^1 2½ 1^nk  Brown T L^6   25000   87-09 Roomie,AccountReceivble,HotDebt 7
2Sep86-7Pim   1 1/16 :46^3 1:12 1:46 sy      *3 117   5^7 4^5 3^4 23¼   Delgado A^9   Aw13700 71-21 Taras Bulba, Roomie, Space Out 9
22Aug86-7Pim  1 1/16 :47^1 1:12^4 1:46 gd    6½ 117   7^11 7^8 4^6 2¾   Delgado A^2   Aw13700 73-23 VirgininRebel,Roomie,DeckeledEdg 7
2Aug86-4Pim   1 1/16 [T]:48^3 1:13 1:44^4fm  7¼ 117   85½ 78½ 7^11 7^15 Delgado A^4   Aw13700 64-20 Mdow'sDr.Brtt,ChspkBch,Volgogrd 8
13Jly86-3Pha  1 1/16 :47^3 1:12^2 1:45 m     *2½ 118  43½ 3^4 3^2 3^5   Black A S^3   Aw12000 74-21 Royal Rickie, King Size, Roomie 6
20Jun86-5Bel  1¼     [T]:47^4 1:36^4 2:01^3fm 32 117  2½ 8^8 10^10 1012¼ Santagata N^9 Aw25000 74-14 Southjet,SilverVoice,StgeWhisper 12
   Sep 20 Pim 3f ft :38^3 b
```

477. Its record suggests that *Blake's Dancer* performs best as a

```
Blake's Dancer                 Gr. f. 3, by Your Dancer—Most Fortunate, by More Megaton
                               Br.—Loveless M (Cal)                      1986 16 3 5 2    $31,926
  GRABLE T C            114    Tr.—Brinson Ross          $25,000         1985  1 M 1 0    $1,073
Own.—Loveless M                Lifetime  17 3 6 2  $32,999               Turf  1 0 0 0    $1,170
15Oct86-6BM   6f     :22^1 :45^2 1:10^2ft    3¾ 114   7^11 6^11 4^4 31¼ Grable T C^6  [F] 25000  86-17 OneDrum,NturlBlonde,Blke'sDncer 7
3Oct86-9BM    1 1/16 :47 1:11^4 1:44^1ft     2¾ 114   45½ 3^4 3^nk 32½  Grable T C^6  [F] 25000  68-21 Saillnte,SpecilReserve,Blke'sDncer 7
12Sep86-10Bmf 6f     :22^1 :45^3 1:12 ft     18 113   109¾ 98¾ 51½ 11½  Grable T C^2  [F] 16000  79-29 Blke'sDncr,Chris'sGlmor,Forumstr 11
30Jly86-11SR  1 1/16 :45^4 1:10^1 1:41^3ft   5¾ 113   6^15 6^13 6^10 5^9 Mena F^1    [F]Aw13000 87-09 Cue TheSun,Meritarose,Tributeena 6
16Jly86-9Sol  6f     :22 :44^4 1:10 ft       11 114   8^13 7^11 54¾ 43½ Mena F^2      [F] 25000  89-13 OlympicBell,MysteryMaid,IllicitJoy 9
      16Jly86—Veered in; bumped start
26Jun86-8Pln  170    :44^3 1:10^3 1:40 ft    5½ 114   4^7 3^5 2^6 2^8   Mena F^4     [F]Aw15000 86-19 NotSoDistant,Blake'sDancer,Patng 5
19Jun86-6GG   1 1/16 [T]:49^3 1:14^1 1:46^1fm 8 114   53¾ 31½ 31½ 42¼  Lozoya D A^1  [F] 25000  69-22 SelectdPrincss,BluSilk,Sh'sSoBold 8
4Jun86-1GG    1 1/16 :47^4 1:12 1:44^3ft     5½ 114   1^1 1½ 2^2 4^2    Lozoya D A^6  [F] 25000  78-17 Decort,DiscreteAffir,SelectdPrincss 7
      4Jun86—Broke in a tangle
21May86-6GG   1      :47^1 1:12 1:38^4ft     3½ 114   51¾ 42¼ 2^hd 2^1  Lozoya D A^4  [F] 16000  73-17 SelectedPrincess,Blke'sDncr,Profil 8
      21May86—Broke through gate
7May86-7GG    1 1/16 :47^1 1:11^2 1:44^4ft   10 114   33½ 32½ 21½ 2^3  Lamance C^5   [F] 25000  76-20 All Wet, Blake's Dancer, Faye 8
   Oct 24 BM 4f ft :54^4 h     Oct 2 BM 3f ft :38^1 h     Sep 28 BM 5f ft 1:04^4 h     Sep 21 BM 5f ft 1:04^4 h
```

A. late-running sprinter   (37)
B. miler
C. middle distance horse
D. turf router

478. Which conclusion about Vinny's Pride and distance makes the most sense?

Vinny's Pride

					Ro. h. 5, by Tudor Grey—Carrie Diane, by Noble Commander				
Own.—Gloria V A				117	Br.—Gloria V (Ky)		1986	2 0 0 0	
					Tr.—Ferruolo John Jr	$35,000	1985	9 3 1 1	$56,220
					Lifetime 32 8 3 6 $139,530		Turf	2 0 0 0	$780

15Oct86-2Bel	7f :22³ :45⁴ 1:23 gd	3¾ 117	54½ 52½ 76½ 77½	Romero R P⁸	25000	79-20	‡Koffkoff,BigJmTylor,GllopRhythm 9
29Sep86-8Med	6f :22³ :45¹ 1:10¹ft	4½ 116	52½ 64½ 88¾ 710	Murphy D J⁷	32000	81-21	FastCaz,SacredMotion,NationalBid 8
12Oct85-5Bel	7f :22⁴ :46¹ 1:23²ft	4 117	22 22 69 615	Vasquez J¹	75000	70-18	Carjack, Blind Man's Bluff,Poniard 6
5Oct85-1Bel	6½f :22⁴ :46¹ 1:17³sy	3½e 113	54 63 41½ 42½	Santos J A⁴	75000	85-19	Carjack, Stomper, Love That Mac 7
4Apr85-8Aqu	1 :46³ 1:10⁴ 1:36¹ft	3½ 121	1⁴ 11 1½ 2½	Davis R G⁶	Aw30000	84-19	Cooper'sHwk,Vinny'sPride.Spender 7
18Mar85-8Aqu	7f :23³ :47² 1:25⁴ft	4½ 117	31½ 21 13 1nk	Murphy D J⁸	Aw25000	72-38	Vinny'sPride,Bienestar,SpecialCare 9
8Mar85-7Aqu	1¹⁄₁₆[○]:48 1:11³1:44¹ft	3 117	1¹ 11 2hd 1nk	Murphy D J²	75000	89-18	Vinny'sPrd,BluQudrnt,StonyLonsom 7
18Feb85-4Aqu	170[○]:48 1:12³1:43 ft	3¾ 119	1¹ 1½ 2½ 32½	Murphy D J¹	75000	82-28	King'sSwan,NicePirte,Vinny'sPride 8

A. He's versatile at all the regularly run sprint and   (37)
   middle distances
B. He cannot handle six furlongs
C. He's most comfortable on the lead at middle distances
D. He cannot perform as well beyond 1¹⁄₁₆M

479. Under what conditions of eligibility is the notion of being "particularly well-suited to the distance" likely to be most decisive?

A. starter handicap, 4up   (36)
B. Alw, NW4XMC, 3YOs
C. classified allowance, 4up
D. Grade 1 or Grade 2 stakes

480. If a route race bars multiple winners at the distance this season, which horse becomes the strongest contender?

A. the horse with one win at the distance, provided   (36)
   it's the only horse of its kind in the field
B. a horse back from a layoff that had multiple wins
   at the class and distance last season
C. a horse suited to the distance and dropping
   roughly 20 percent in class
D. a consistent sprinter up in class one step and
   stretching out

Answer key: Distance

Minimum Competency Test

431.	D	437.	C
432.	B	438.	A
433.	B	439.	A
434.	B	440.	B
435.	A	441.	B
436.	A	442.	B

Mastery Test

443.	A	453.	C	463.	D	472.	D
444.	A	454.	D	464.	C	473.	D
445.	D	455.	B	465.	B	474.	D
446.	C	456.	C	466.	C	475.	D
447.	A	457.	D	467.	B	476.	B
448.	C	458.	A	468.	A	477.	A
449.	B	459.	B	469.	B	478.	C
450.	B	460.	C	470.	D	479.	C
451.	C	461.	C	471.	A	480.	D
452.	A	462.	B				

CHAPTER 10

Trips and Track Bias

Competencies

38. Recognize the conventional notation of trips and track bias.
39. Interpret trip and bias data.
40. Know the mechanics and visual skills of observing and recognizing the various aspects of trips and biases.
41. Understand the general implications of specific kinds of trouble, position, and mishaps in the running of races.
42. Understand the general implications of specific track biases.
43. Relate trips and biases to other factors of handicapping, especially speed, class, and jockey.
44. Evaluate the probable effects of familiar trips and biases.

	Minimum Competency Test	Mastery Test
Proficiency standards	80%	70%
Number of items	12	50
Passing scores	10	35

Sources of Instruction

- *The Winning Horseplayer*, chapters 2–4, 7, and Appendix 2
- *Betting Thoroughbreds*, chapters 1, 3 & 4
- *Thoroughbred Handicapping: State of the Art*, Chapter 11
- *Fast Track to Thoroughbred Profits*, Chapter 3

Comments

Not prominent in the weaponry of even regular handicappers until recent times, these complementary factors have been anointed as crucial to handicapping success by the new-wave writers who urge practitioners to emphasize data not trapped by the past performances and results charts. These data represent sources of fabulous overlays, the argument holds. And so it is. Also crucial to handicappers is the development and deployment of the unfamiliar skills on which these factors depend—visual skills or observation skills. Not an easy task—either the refinement of the craft itself or the evaluation of its raw material.

Some empirical evidence and a growing body of anecdotal data suggests that certain kinds of trip information are being grossly overvalued by handicappers. Just as plausible is the possibility that track bias remains the most underrated factor of contemporary handicapping.

Definition of Terms

Notation: • Letters and symbols that describe common trips and biases.
• Illustrations
• Slo-1, 3FT, 4B, 4T, 4E, 3S: the horse was one length slow out of the gate, raced 3 wide on the first turn, 4 wide down the backstretch, around the far turn, and entering the stretch, and was 3 wide in the stretch.
• GR+ An extra strong positive rail bias
• BR A negative rail bias
• S+ A strong speed bias
• C A bias that favors closers

TRIPS AND TRACK BIAS: MINIMUM COMPETENCY TEST

481. Which best indicates the presence of a track bias?

A. Frontrunners win the first three races   **(39)**
B. The closers are winning powerfully
C. Favorites are losing repeatedly
D. Outclassed frontrunners are going all the way

482. The easiest bias to detect is

A. a positive speed bias on the rail   **(40)**
B. a negative rail bias
C. a negative outside bias
D. a positive closer bias

483. Slo-2 means

A. A track bias has been slowing the frontrunners by   **(38)**
2 lengths

B. Any negatively biased post position will cost a horse approximately 2 lengths
C. A horse broke roughly 2 lengths slower than the field
D. The rail lane is 2 lengths slower than normal

484. One path equals one length is an acceptable guideline for estimating lengths lost by a horse on the turns.

A. True   **(41)**
B. False

485. The notation for a negative rail bias is

A. BR   **(38)**
B. C+
C. S−
D. R−

486. A negative speed bias is often associated with

A. come-from-behind upsets   **(40)**
B. outside posts
C. bad trips
D. wire-to-wire upsets

487. Speed biases in routes are often suggested by

A. horses spread out like a string of pearls   **(40)**
B. frontrunners losing when they exit outside posts
C. sprinters winning too many route races
D. late-comers bid strongly into the stretch, but "hang"

488. A driving rainstorm is most likely to cause a bias that favors

A. rail horses   **(40)**
B. early speed
C. horses bred to like mud
D. closers

489. The universal track bias is

A. post position #1   **(39)**
B. early speed
C. slop
D. superior class

490. Which is most likely to alter an existing track bias?

  A. rain   **(39)**
  B. a change in the track maintenance
  C. prolonged periods of extreme heat or cold
  D. consecutive days of racing

491. On biased surfaces, which factor of handicapping increases in importance the most?

  A. class   **(43)**
  B. jockey
  C. form
  D. post position

492. A horse running 3 wide on both turns of a middle distance route is losing how many lengths to the horse on the rail?

  A. 2   **(41)**
  B. 3
  C. 4
  D. 6

This is the end of the minimum competency test. Check your answers. If your score falls below standard, please consult the recommended sources of instruction before proceeding to the mastery test.

TRIPS AND TRACK BIAS: MASTERY TEST

493. When horses break from the gate, trip handicappers generally will observe

  A. what happens from inside to outside   **(40)**
  B. stumbles, bumping, and tardy exits
  C. what happens from rear to front
  D. the speed and position of the early pace contestants

494. Which notation suggests the best trip?

  A. 3FT, 4E, 5S   **(38)**
  B. MIHP-T, 4E
  C. Move-B, V-T,E FF
  D. GP-B, Rail T-E-S

495. The best off-track source of track bias information is

A. past performance tables   **(40)**
B. post position studies
C. results charts
D. the running styles of horses that won yesterday

496. Horses encounter the most trouble

A. at the gate   **(40)**
B. on the clubhouse turn
C. on the far turn
D. entering the stretch

497. Which visual skill of trip handicapping is most difficult for practitioners to refine?

A. recording the various actions at the start   **(40)**
B. distinguishing trouble that matters from trouble
   that happens
C. observing paths horses follow at various points
   in the race
D. recognizing the presence of a significant bias

498. Which is the most advantageous position in the late stages of a sprint?

A. on the inside lane of a speed duel   **(41)**
B. outside on a track favoring the closers
C. 1E, Alter, 3S
D. 1E, 2S, GR+

499. One of the most generous mutuels resulting from trip handicapping is

A. a speed horse exiting a "good" race on a C+ track   **(44)**
B. a lone frontrunner on hard turf
C. a classy closer exiting a poor race on an S+ track
D. a pace-pressing type on a GR, S track

500. Which is probably the worst that can happen to a speed horse at the gate?

A. bumped sideways   **(41)**
B. Slo-1, Rush-B, Vise-T
C. bobble
D. Use-G, HH-B

501. Bad-trip information is most useful when

A. it does not appear in the charts or past perfor- **(44)**
   mances
B. the odds next time are higher than normal
C. the horse perseveres and runs well regardless
D. the horses affected finish up the track

502. The most decisive influence of trips on race out-comes is

A. position on the turns   **(39)**
B. gate problems
C. trouble on turns
D. track bias

503. What descriptions in the results charts should be most helpful in alerting handicappers to the presence of a bias?

A. trips of the frontrunners and late-comers   **(40)**
B. positions of the winners at the pre-stretch and
   stretch calls
C. positions on the far turn
D. stretch gains of come-from-behind horses

504. What kind of track bias is most evident from a day's results charts?

A. a negative outside bias   **(40)**
B. a positive rail bias
C. a negative speed bias
D. a positive closer bias

505. What kind of track bias is most evident from the past performance tables?

A. an extra strong good rail   **(40)**
B. a strong closer bias
C. a negative speed bias
D. none

506. Probably the most infrequent track bias is

A. a negative rail bias   **(42)**
B. an outside bias favoring closers
C. a rail bias favoring closers
D. a speed bias outside

507. The most prominent bias in turf racing favors

A. outside speed   (42)
B. inside speed
C. outside posts
D. inside posts

508. What factor is most likely to nullify a positive speed bias on the inside?

A. a weak trainer-jockey connection   (43)
B. a rugged pace duel
C. a closer coming up the rail
D. superior class

509. Which is most impressive on a track that favors speed on the outside?

A. A speed horse goes wire to wire on the inside   (44)
B. A closer wins on the outside
C. A speed horse outside survives a fast pace and
   wins
D. A closer wins along the rail

510. A relatively cheap speed horse lasts until just inside the 1/8th pole on a BR+ surface. Which statement about the horse next time would be most attractive to trip handicappers?

A. It's moving from an outside to an inside post   (44)
B. The horse is wheeled back in five days on a sloppy
   track
C. It's the lone frontrunner while up in class at 10–1
   odds
D. The horse is dropping in class and switching to
   the leading jockey

511. A strong positive speed bias is most likely to help

A. a classy horse on the rail   (42)
B. a speedy favorite breaking from the outside
C. the inside horse in an early pace battle
D. a cheap frontrunner

512. BR, C+ means

A. Closers are winning too many races   (38)
B. Horses have been winning up the rail in the late
   stages

C. When the track surface is "off," closers win

D. A bad rail has been favoring closers strongly

513. What does 5FT, 4 B-T, 5E, 3S mean to a trip handicapper?

A. the horse lost 3 to 5 lengths in a poor trip **(38)**

B. lengths gained and lengths lost at each point of call

C. the horse was wide all the way

D. after stumbling at the start, the horse did not persevere

514. Which horse is likely to rebound most impressively next time?

A. a closer that has been wide all the way **(44)**

B. a frontrunner that stops against a negative rail bias

C. a closer trapped behind a wall of horses on the far turn and entering the stretch

D. a frontrunner that stumbles at the gate

515. A jockey mistake handicappers usually can capitalize on at generous odds next out is

A. taking up on the far turn **(43)**

B. getting caught in a blind switch

C. moving into a hot pace

D. shuffling back on the backstretch

516. Which suggests the easiest kind of trip that probably cannot be duplicated?

A. Stalk **(41)**

B. NP

C. GP

D. Inherit

517. Which is generally worst?

A. Steady **(41)**

B. Check

C. Alter

D. Bobble

518. Which is the most difficult track bias for the disadvantaged horses to overcome?

A. S+   **(42)**
B. BR
C. C+
D. GR

519. Which circumstance is most difficult for superior class
to overcome?

A. stumble-G; rush; V; alter; 3ES   **(42)**
B. move strongly on far turn before taking up while
   entering the stretch
C. an unfavorable track bias
D. a cheap speed horse on a speed-favoring surface

520. The ability of top jockeys is most likely to compen-
sate for

A. a negative speed bias   **(43)**
B. mishaps at the start
C. a bad rail bias
D. trouble on the turns

521. The jockey usually exercises the most control over

A. track bias   **(43)**
B. running position
C. trouble
D. traffic

522. Leading jockeys can be counted upon to do a better job
than their journeymen colleagues in

A. recognizing biases   **(43)**
B. overcoming trouble
C. avoiding trouble
D. exploiting biases

523. Early speed horses are most disadvantaged by

A. a negative rail bias   **(43)**
B. a bias favoring closers
C. an outside post on a positive rail bias
D. a slow start

524. "Wide" on the turf will be generally more disadvantageous than "wide" on the dirt track.

A. True   **(41)**
B. False

525. How can handicappers best recognize a strong track bias?

A. Read the results charts carefully   **(40)**
B. Watch the first few races closely
C. Record the number of frontrunners that have been
   winning recently
D. Recognize how the track surface assisted an oth-
   erwise unpredictable winner or two

526. The most overestimated type of troubled trip is

A. wide on the far turn   **(41)**
B. stumbling at the gate
C. blocked in the upper stretch
D. lugging in or lugging out in the stretch

527. A subtle change of track bias is most likely to be recognized by an expert on

A. speed   **(43)**
B. trips
C. class
D. pace

528. "Wide all the way" is most disadvantageous to

A. early speed   **(43)**
B. the outside posts at middle distances
C. a pace-pressing type
D. closers on the grass

529. A speed handicapper would most likely prefer

A. a 3YO that improved sharply following an easy   **(43)**
   trip
B. an older horse having a competitive figure earned
   following a difficult trip
C. a frontrunner having a competitive figure on an
   even track
D. a closer having a superior figure earned on a bad
   rail bias

530. Speed figures and trip information are best related

   A. numerically, by adding and subtracting points due   **(43)**
     to position on turns and trouble during trips
   B. by interpreting today's figure in the context of the
     preceding figure or two, looking for unusual fig-
     ures that might best be explained by trips
   C. analytically, in a discursive nonrigid manner
   D. by discounting high figures resulting from easy
     trips and enhancing low figures resulting from
     difficult trips

531. A decisive edge in class is most likely to be defeated by a

   A. positive speed bias favoring another horse   **(43)**
   B. troubled trip, combined with an easy trip for an-
     other horse
   C. negative track bias interfering with its running
     style
   D. neither a troubled trip nor a biased track

532. Probably the largest source of future overlays resulting from track bias is

   A. a strong bias that has favored closers on a few   **(44)**
     specific days
   B. a negative rail bias that persists for several days
   C. a persistent positive speed bias
   D. biases that occur regularly due to normal track
     maintenance procedures

533. A positive rail bias means

   A. Speed horses figure to have the best of it   **(39)**
   B. Closers can win a fair share of the races only if
     they finish on the inside
   C. Cheap speed horses on the inside will move up
     dramatically
   D. Outside posts can be eliminated confidently

534. Bumping at the gate is

   A. serious trouble for frontrunners   **(39)**
   B. only serious when it warrants comment in the
     charts or past performance tables
   C. almost impossible for the trip handicapper to in-
     terpret reliably

D. usually nothing more than standard operating procedure

535. Which kind of performance would a speed handi-capper discount the most?

    A. a claiming horse leading to the stretch call against   **(43)**
       a negative rail bias
    B. a significantly improved figure following an easy trip
    C. a low-priced closer running badly from the out-side on a track favoring the outside
    D. an easy frontrunning win on a speed-favoring track

536. Trip handicappers should be most reluctant to excuse

    A. 3YOs that run rank in the early stages of routes   **(39)**
    B. any trouble that attempts to explain a loss in a maiden-claiming race
    C. repeated problems at the gate
    D. 4up that lug in or bear out noticeably in the stretch

537. Which is the most complicating track bias for trip handicappers to exploit?

    A. C+   **(39)**
    B. S
    C. S+
    D. C

538. The most important point of call for observing trips and biases is the

    A. gate   **(40)**
    B. far turn
    C. stretch
    D. clubhouse turn

539. A horse running in the positions 3B, 3T, 4E, 4S should benefit most from a

    A. negative rail bias   **(39)**
    B. even surface and inside post
    C. negative speed bias
    D. positive outside bias

540. Examine the trips below. Which is most likely to improve after running against a negative outside bias?

    A. 4FT, 2B, 3T, 2E, 3S   **(39)**
    B. 2FT, 3B, 4T, 4E, 5S
    C. 3FT, 4B, 5T, 5E, 5S
    D. 5FT, 3B, 3T, 1E, 1S

541. Which is most impressive on a track having a strongly negative rail bias?

    A. a frontrunner leads until inside the 8th pole   **(44)**
    B. a closer wins by three with a final quarter of 24 seconds
    C. a frontrunner completes the half under 45 flat
    D. a horse breaking from the inside post wins

542. A one-path difference on the clubhouse turn amounts to roughly

    A. ½ length   **(39)**
    B. one length
    C. 1½ lengths
    D. 2 lengths

Answer key: Trips and track bias

Minimum Competency Test

481. D	485. A	489. B
482. A	486. A	490. B
483. C	487. A	491. D
484. A	488. B	492. C

Mastery Test

493. C	506. B	519. C	531. A
494. D	507. D	520. D	532. B
495. C	508. C	521. C	533. C
496. C	509. D	522. C	534. D
497. D	510. C	523. B	535. D
498. D	511. D	524. A	536. C
499. A	512. D	525. D	537. D
500. B	513. C	526. A	538. B
501. C	514. B	527. D	539. D
502. D	515. C	528. A	540. C
503. C	516. D	529. B	541. A
504. B	517. B	530. C	542. B
505. D	518. A		

CHAPTER 11

Trainer, Jockey, Weight, and Post Position

Competencies

45. Know the basic facts and probabilities of the jockey, trainer, weight, and post position factors.
46. Comprehend the circumstances under which the jockey, trainer, weight, and post position factors assume an added importance.
47. Identify familiar trainer maneuvers that have been demonstrably effective.
48. Evaluate trainer performance and trainer pattern data effectively.

	Minimum Competency Test	Mastery Test
Proficiency standards	90%	75%
Number of items	16	40
Passing scores	14	30

Sources of Instruction

- *Betting Thoroughbreds*, chapters 5–7, 13 & 14
- *Winning at the Races*, chapters 4, 15, and 23
- *Thoroughbred Handicapping: State of the Art*, chapters 2–4
- *Fast Track to Thoroughbred Profits*, Chapter 5
- *Ainslie's Complete Guide to Thoroughbred Racing*, chapters 11, 14 & 15

Comments

Of these strongly related factors, handicappers would generally agree the trainer reigns supreme. Horses' careers depend upon the talents and idiosyncrasies of their trainers. Handicappers can prosper by accumulating as much information about these individuals as they can lay their hands upon. Performance data which describe general categorical proficiency—of one to three years baseline—separate the wheat from the chaff in numerous situations. Pattern data—of as few as three to five to seven instances—describe training maneuvers encompassing multiple factors and resulting repeatedly in wins at generous odds.

Of jockey, weight, and post position, the conventional wisdom accumulated by folklore, myth, and the vagaries of general unorganized practice has been strongly contradicted by the best probability data we have. Weight especially has been demolished as an independent factor in handicapping. It's nice to distinguish fact from fiction, as best we can at least, in relation to these misunderstood topics.

JOCKEY, TRAINER, WEIGHT, AND POST POSITION: MINIMUM COMPETENCY TEST

543. Contrary to popular belief, picking up weight is a good sign and dropping a few pounds is not.

A. True **(45)**
B. False

544. Top-weighted horses do well enough in all races, but they are significantly more successful in sprints than routes.

A. True **(45)**
B. False

545. Which is the most meaningful assertion about weight?

A. It is not an independent factor in handicapping **(45)**
B. Weight shifts are more significant than added weight
C. The longer the distance, the heavier the weight
D. Weight begins to make a difference above 120 pounds

546. What percentage of jockeys can be expected to recognize and exploit relatively strong track biases?

A. all leading **(45)**
B. a relatively low percent

C. a relatively high percent
D. only a few

547. As a group, the top apprentice jockeys have a probability of winning a fair share of their starts of approximately

A. 0.85   **(45)**
B. 1.00
C. 1.30
D. 1.65

548. Horses sent out by the top ten trainers at the meet generally win significantly more than their fair share of the races, but they also are usually overbet and lose far more money than they should.

A. True   **(45)**
B. False

549. Statistics show clearly that at one-mile tracks the most advantageous post position is

A. 1   **(45)**
B. 2
C. 3 through 5
D. 7 & 8

550. Saving ground is usually most important for jockeys

A. in middle distance races   **(46)**
B. on the far turn
C. on the turf
D. in long sprints

551. In route races at bull rings, post position is not significantly disadvantaged until horses draw farther outside than post

A. 7   **(46)**
B. 8
C. 9
D. 10

552. In what races are a jockey's skills generally most important?

A. maiden   **(46)**
B. claiming

C. classified allowance
D. stakes

553. The leading apprentices do not perform nearly as well in stakes races.

A. True   **(45)**
B. False

554. A leading jockey can be defined as one who

A. ranks among the top ten winners at the meeting   **(46)**
B. wins 20% of his starts
C. wins 15% of his starts
D. rides regularly for a leading stable or trainer

555. Reliable trainer performance data depend upon

A. a one-year baseline   **(48)**
B. data summarizing this season so far and last
C. a three-year baseline
D. as few as thirty races

556. The top ten trainers at a meeting usually dominate their rivals as strongly (statistically) as the top ten jockeys.

A. True   **(45)**
B. False

557. Trainers are generally more important than _____, but less important than _____.

A. trips, form   **(48)**
B. jockey, trips
C. distance, pace
D. breeding, speed

558. Handicappers benefit most if they know the leading trainers' weaknesses and the journeyman trainers' strengths.

A. True   **(48)**
B. False

This is the end of the minimum competency test. Check your answers. If your score falls below standard, consult the recommended sources of instruction before proceeding to the mastery test.

JOCKEY, TRAINER, WEIGHT, AND POST POSITION: MASTERY TEST

559. Statistics indicate horses carrying 120 pounds or more in sprints have a probability of winning of roughly

    A. 0.85   **(45)**
    B. 1.03
    C. 1.42
    D. 1.86

560. Statistics indicate that horses carrying 120 pounds or more in routes have an impact value (probability of winning) of

    A. 0.78   **(45)**
    B. 1.11
    C. 1.80
    D. 2.34

561. Which factor usually determines whether an inside or outside post has an advantage?

    A. the probable early pace   **(46)**
    B. the presence or absence of a speed bias
    C. the distance of the starting gate from the first turn
    D. whether the track surface is wet or dry

562. High-weighted horses of about 124 pounds do best when coming from far behind.

    A. True   **(46)**
    B. False

563. Statistically, the best bets among horses carrying more than 122 pounds occur

    A. in stakes   **(45)**
    B. on the turf
    C. when they figure to get a clear lead
    D. when they won their previous race

564. From a bettor's point of view, which is the most significant conclusion about evaluating trainers?

    A. The top 40 to 60 trainers at a meeting will nor-   **(48)**
          mally win 60 to 75 percent of the races

B. Knowing trainers' weaknesses is generally more important than knowing their strengths
C. The top twenty trainers can be counted upon to dominate the others, regardless of the races they enter
D. Trainer pattern data are far more useful than trainer performance data

565. Which factor is most frequently decisive in handicapping?

A. jockey (46)
B. trainer
C. weight
D. post position

566. One of the best-known effective trainer maneuvers that also throws profits combines a change of jockey and

A. improving form (47)
B. a switch in distance
C. a drop in class
D. weight off

567. Trainers who are experts with the condition book have achieved a deeper understanding of

A. hidden form (47)
B. which horses are eligible to which races
C. changing distances
D. the class demands of the various races

568. A jockey's overall effectiveness is best estimated by

A. earnings per start (46)
B. win percentage in stakes races
C. win percentage during the past two seasons
D. identifying the kinds of races where he wins at 15% or better

569. Speed duels in sprints are more frequently won by horses racing on the outside.

A. True (46)
B. False

570. Why do horses run faster (slightly) when carrying higher weight?

A. the trainer is cracking down while the horse is   **(46)**
   sharp
B. the high-weighted horses usually have a class edge
C. they tend to be older males
D. higher weights are the result of improving form

571. Post position studies indicate the most accurate assertion about position on the turns is

A. The clubhouse turn is less decisive than the far   **(45)**
   turn
B. Each lane farther out from the rail equals one additional length
C. The better horses are advantaged on the outside
D. Come-from-behind horses are not seriously disadvantaged either inside or outside

572. At what distance is post position likely to be most advantageous at mile tracks?

A. 7F   **(46)**
B. 1M
C. 1⅛M
D. 1¼M

573. Linear regression studies of 45,000 6F sprints have revealed that on average horses breaking from post 12 finish behind horses breaking from post 1 by

A. ½ length   **(45)**
B. one length
C. 2 lengths
D. 6 lengths

574. At standard routes (1M to 1⅛M) at one-mile tracks, linear regression studies reveal that on average horses breaking from post 12 will finish behind horses breaking from post 1 by

A. one length   **(45)**
B. 2½ lengths
C. 3½ lengths
D. 6 lengths

575. In one-turn routes, post position studies show that outside posts

A. perform at no significant disadvantage, regardless **(46)**
   of distance
B. do significantly better in mile races
C. do slightly better than post position 1
D. perform better as the distance increases

576. At standard two-turn routes over 1⅛M tracks, the horses breaking from the outside generally will perform

A. slightly better than at one-mile tracks **(46)**
B. twice as badly as at one-mile tracks
C. as expected, except for post 12
D. better if they have a come-from-behind running
   style

577. Trainer pattern data are usually more meaningful to handicappers than trainer performance data.

A. True **(48)**
B. False

578. Trainer performance data are most useful for identifying a leading trainer's

A. strengths **(48)**
B. weaknesses
C. pet jockey
D. return on investment

579. Roughly how many examples are necessary to obtain a reliable insight into an effective trainer pattern?

A. 5 **(48)**
B. 15
C. 30
D. 50

580. Statistics make it unmistakably clear the most successful trainer of 2YOs in the U.S. is

A. Woody Stephens **(45)**
B. Leroy Jolley
C. Lazaro Barrera
D. D. Wayne Lukas

581. A successful trainer maneuver with 3YO maidens is

A. return to sprints after showing speed for 6F in   (47)
   routes
B. blinkers on
C. entering maidens bred for grass against winners
   on the turf
D. a dramatic rise in class following a "big win"

582. Effective trainer maneuvers can be recognized often by paying attention to which of the following related factors?

A. form   (47)
B. class
C. jockey
D. distance

583. Changes of jockey, weight, and post position are usually decisive only

A. when used in a successful trainer maneuver   (46)
B. when combined with other more fundamental
   changes
C. in claiming races
D. when used negatively

584. In what types of races do trainer performance data reveal numerous underlays/overlays commonly misunderstood by the crowd?

A. maiden   (48)
B. allowance
C. stakes
D. turf

585. Trainer performance data indicate that particular strengths and weaknesses are reflected accurately by the general thrust of the data.

A. True   (48)
B. False

586. When evaluating large categories of performance, say sprints and routes, handicappers should expect that effective trainers will win approximately what percentage of their starts?

A. 8%   **(45)**
B. 11%
C. 15%
D. 20%

587. The most significant drug a trainer can administer, as far as handicappers are concerned, is

A. bute   **(45)**
B. a stimulant
C. lasix
D. a depressant

588. The selection of a particular jockey to ride a horse is frequently a window to

A. early pace   **(47)**
B. trainer intentions
C. improved form
D. betting action

589. In which race is the jockey more important than the trainer?

A. the Belmont Stakes   **(46)**
B. a 5-furlong dash for juveniles
C. in the mud
D. the Kentucky Derby

590. The most difficult ride for journeymen jockeys is

A. taking a frontrunner wire to wire   **(46)**
B. pressing the pace, then finishing strongly
C. exiting the outside posts at 1M and 1¹⁄₁₆M at mile tracks
D. coming from last to win with one long late run

591. The horse figures strongly. The trainer has been 0 for 36 for the season. The odds are 13–1. What should handicappers do?

A. take the overlay   **(48)**
B. pass the race
C. bet any other contender that represents an attractive overlay

D. eliminate the horse, but play the race in the cus-
    tomary manner

592. The trainer wins 22% with this kind. Three horses are
closely matched here. The trainer's horse is 8–5, the others 5–
2. What should handicappers do?

A. Bet the trainer's horse   **(48)**
B. Pass the race
C. Bet one of the overlays
D. Bet the trainer's horse to place or show

593. Which is a sensible guideline regarding "A" trainers?

A. bet them with confidence whenever their horses   **(48)**
    figure
B. acceptable with any kind of horse
C. always bet their overlays
D. award extra credit in close situations

594. Which is normally characteristic of a successful trainer
pattern?

A. generous odds   **(47)**
B. unpredictable races
C. familiar jockeys
D. hidden form

595. Which is the most persuasive trainer performance data?

A. 5 for 18 in turf routes   **(48)**
B. 20 for 160 in sprints, ROI of 12%
C. 2 for 35 with first starters last two seasons
D. 6 for 42 with class drops, ROI of 150%

596. The most indicative performance data on younger
trainers is the

A. win percentage overall   **(48)**
B. average odds on winners
C. win percentage with horses claimed
D. win percentage in nonclaiming races

597. Successful trainer patterns frequently can be identified
in the larger categorical performance data.

A. True **(47)**
B. False

598. Which is a fair generalization about the trainer factor?

A. The majority of trainers understand the needs and **(46)** capabilities of horses in a short time
B. Training claiming horses is more difficult than training better horses
C. Training beats breeding
D. A trainer is only as good as the horses he or she gets

Answer key: Jockey, trainer, weight, and post position

Minimum Competency Test

543. A	547. A	551. A	555. C
544. A	548. A	552. D	556. B
545. A	549. A	553. B	557. D
546. D	550. C	554. B	558. A

Mastery Test

559. D	569. B	579. A	589. D
560. B	570. D	580. D	590. D
561. C	571. B	581. C	591. C
562. B	572. B	582. C	592. B
563. C	573. B	583. B	593. C
564. D	574. B	584. A	594. A
565. B	575. A	585. B	595. C
566. C	576. B	586. B	596. A
567. D	577. A	587. C	597. B
568. C	578. B	588. B	598. C

CHAPTER 12

Pedigree, Turf Racing, and Imports

Competencies

49. Know the prepotent and overrated sires for grass, mud, sprint, and route racing.
50. Know the significant statistical relationships between pedigree and performance on the turf.
51. Understand dosage, the dosage index, and the appropriate applications of dosage to the handicapping of familiar racing situations.
52. Relate pedigree to age, conformation, types of races, and other factors of handicapping.
53. Evaluate the relative class and readiness of imports competing under U.S. conditions of eligibility.

	Minimum Competency Test	Mastery Test
Proficiency standards	75%	60%
Number of items	12	45
Passing scores	9	27

Sources of Instruction

- *Thoroughbred Handicapping: State of the Art*, Chapter 5
- *Winning at the Races*, Chapter 22
- "An Analysis of Dosage," *Thoroughbred Record*, Apr. 1984
- *The Handicapper's Condition Book*, chapters 3&4, 11, and Appendix 2

Comments

When I began playing the races, early 1970s, pedigree as a factor in handicapping was practically useless. Beyond crediting the leading speed sires in juvenile dashes, breeding did not apply.

Now the relations between pedigree and performance are better understood, and in two circumstances, at least, far more meaningful. Undeniably, pedigree is predictive of success on the turf. And the provocative research on dosage has pointed handicappers toward greater success whenever the highest grade of thoroughbreds sort themselves out at classic distances.

Handicappers need to know who's who and what's what among mud, grass, sprint, and route sires.

The proliferation of imports from Europe—good horses—and elsewhere has provided handicappers up-to-snuff on that topic with arguably the most generous source of overlays today, and not just on the grass, but more than occasionally on the dirt as well.

Definitions of Terms

- *Prepotent.* The condition characterizing sires that transmit their racing aptitudes to progeny consistently, in relation to sires that do not.

- *Dosage.* The blend of the inherited aptitudes (qualities of speed and endurance) of racehorses.

- *The dosage index.* The ratio of speed to stamina in a horse's immediate four-generation pedigree; expressed numerically, with 1.00 indicating an equal blend of speed and stamina, 2.00 indicating twice as much speed as stamina, and 0.50 indicating twice as much stamina as speed.

PEDIGREE, TURF RACING, AND IMPORTS: MINIMUM COMPETENCY TEST

599. Breeding can be a reliable factor to predict probable winners in the slop and mud.

A. True   (52)
B. False

600. A horse having grass breeding and a record of futility in the slop is likely to run well on the turf.

A. True   **(50)**
B. False

601. ". . . small, cuplike, with a high vertical heel," is a good description of a

A. grass foot   **(52)**
B. poorly conformed yearling's foot
C. mud foot
D. sprinter's front foot

602. Dosage refers to

A. 3YOs preparing for the classics   **(51)**
B. the blend of speed and stamina in a pedigree
C. the amount of brilliance in the sire line
D. the inherited distance potential of racehorses

603. When win consistency and wagering profits are both considered, the leading U.S. turf sire through the 1986 season has been

A. *Northern Dancer*   **(50)**
B. *Hawaii*
C. *T.V. Lark*
D. *Little Current*

604. The *Princequillo* line is famous for

A. mud racing   **(49)**
B. endurance
C. turf racing
D. brilliance

605. A perfect blend of speed and stamina in a horse's pedigree contributes to a dosage index of

A. 1.00   **(51)**
B. 0.50
C. 2.00
D. 4.00

606. The primary factor when evaluating imports under U.S. racing conditions is

A. form   **(53)**
B. trainer

C. class
D. distance

607. Which foreign country offers the highest purses?

A. England (53)
B. France
C. Ireland
D. South Africa

608. Any import exiting a decent performance in an open stakes of Europe has a class advantage in a nonwinners allowance race in the states.

A. True (53)
B. False

609. Grade 1 stakes of Europe can be accepted as the equivalent of the Grade 1 stakes of the U.S.

A. True (53)
B. False

610. An unexceptional Grade 1 horse of South America should be considered acceptable at what U.S. class level?

A. Grade 1 (53)
B. Grade 2
C. Grade 3
D. nonstakes races only

This is the end of the minimum competency test. Check your answers. If your score falls below standard, consult the recommended sources of instruction before proceeding to the mastery test.

PEDIGREE, TURF RACING, AND IMPORTS: MASTERY TEST

611. When win percentage and average win mutuels are combined, the two most effective U.S. grass sires for the past ten years never raced on the turf.

A. True (49)
B. False

612. The most disappointing grass sire of all has been

A. *Forli*   **(49)**
B. *Secretariat*
C. *Vaguely Noble*
D. *Lyphard*

613. This obscure stallion has at times been listed as one of the most productive ten grass sires in the world.

A. *Doodle*   **(49)**
B. *Al Hattab*
C. *Ambernash*
D. *Unconscious*

614. A reputed grass sire whose statistics reveal him as a pretender is

A. *The Minstrel*   **(49)**
B. *Hail To Reason*
C. *Sir Ivor*
D. *One For All*

615. A leading sire with little propensity for producing good grass runners is

A. *In Reality*   **(49)**
B. *Exclusive Native*
C. *Mr. Prospector*
D. *Ack Ack*

616. A sire equally impressive for getting grass runners and mud runners is

A. *Herbager*   **(49)**
B. *Le Fabuleux*
C. *Cinteelo*
D. *Sir Gaylord*

617. A grass horse's feet are best described as

A. having a long, angular slope to the pastern   **(52)**
B. large and dishlike
C. small and cuppy
D. having a flat, vertical heel

618. Which is generally true of 2-year-olds and pedigree?

A. Pedigree supersedes speed in analyzing 2YO   **(52)**
   routes
B. Speed sires have a decisive edge when strongly
   bet
C. Kentucky stallions should be preferred to local
   sires in nonclaiming races
D. The stakes winners of fall will not be the stakes
   winners of spring

619. The preferred dosage index for 2YOs at 5 furlongs is

A. 4.50   **(51)**
B. 5.50
C. 7.50
D. 9.50

620. Approximately what percentage of stakes winners have
a dosage index greater then 4.00?

A. 25%   **(51)**
B. 40%
C. 50%
D. 60%

621. Approximately what percentage of Grade 1 stakes winners at 1¼M or farther have a dosage index greater than 4.00?

A. 2%   **(51)**
B. 5%
C. 10%
D. 20%

622. The dosage guideline figure of 4.00 is best applied to

A. the Kentucky Derby and Belmont Stakes   **(51)**
B. races at 1¼M or farther
C. stakes routes for nonclaiming 3YOs
D. Grade 1 races at classic distances

623. Studies show that grass racing and mud racing do not
mix well.

A. True   **(52)**
B. False

624. For handicappers, the breeding factor is most useful

A. on off-tracks   **(52)**
B. at classic distances
C. on the turf
D. in juvenile races

625. A prepotent sire for slop and mud is

A. *Rock Talk*   **(49)**
B. *Nasrullah*
C. *Damascus*
D. *High Echelon*

626. A prepotent route sire is

A. *In Reality*   **(49)**
B. *Arts and Letters*
C. *Nodouble*
D. *Run The Gauntlet*

627. A prepotent sprint sire is

A. *Full Pocket*   **(49)**
B. *Key To The Mint*
C. *Native Royalty*
D. *Halo*

628. Pedigree studies have revealed the best bets on the grass are

A. older horses that finished 2nd on the turf last out   **(50)**
B. 3YO maidens entered in nonwinners allowance turf routes
C. horses bred for grass which have not yet raced on grass
D. progeny of distance sires at 10–1 or greater at 1⅛M or farther

629. A horse bred for grass has an even better chance of winning on the turf if

A. it is bred for grass top and bottom   **(50)**
B. no other horse in the field is bred for grass
C. no other horse in the field has won on turf
D. it has shipped to the U.S. from Europe

630. The most profits on the grass have descended to handicappers from

A. *Nijinsky II* **(50)**
B. *Stage Door Johnny*
C. *Tom Rolfe*
D. *Hoist The Flag*

631. Besides a turf pedigree, handicappers should insist horses switching to the grass for the first time have

A. trainers that win regularly on the grass **(50)**
B. acceptable dirt form
C. distance breeding too
D. generous odds

632. If a colt has a successful turf sire and the odds are good, how many consecutive losses on the grass should handicappers tolerate?

A. one **(50)**
B. 2
C. 3
D. up to 5

633. A good first effort on turf will probably be even better next out, provided

A. the very next start is also on the turf **(50)**
B. the horse is also bred for grass
C. the odds are below 10–1
D. the class level remains the same or one step higher

634. What kind of 3YO is most likely to win its first start on turf?

A. good form, impressive grass workout last 5 days **(52)**
B. bred for grass, poor dirt form
C. has a grass stride and a router's sire, still a maiden
D. good early speed, big win last out

635. One of the ten leading grass sires is

A. *Exclusive Native* **(49)**
B. *Raise A Native*
C. *Native Dancer*
D. *Native Royalty*

636. The leading sire of "mud" sires is

A. *Graustark*   **(49)**
B. *Herbager*
C. *Bold Ruler*
D. *Grey Dawn*

637. The leading young grass sire in 1987 was

A. *Alydar*   **(49)**
B. *Nijinsky II*
C. *Roberto*
D. *Seattle Slew*

638. Dosage studies of Kentucky Derby starters support the conclusion that

A. No horse having a dosage index above 4.00 is ca-   **(51)**
   pable of winning the Derby
B. Among better 3YOs pedigree usually beats performance
C. A well-balanced pedigree of speed and stamina
   is just as important as past performance
D. As distances increase, stamina becomes propor-
   tionally more important than brilliance

639. A stakes horse having a dosage index of 5.50 is less likely to win

A. against Grade 1 competition   **(51)**
B. when stretching out from sprint to route
C. at 1¼M or farther
D. with a frontrunner's running style

640. Dosage studies force handicappers to conclude that

A. Brilliance is not necessary to win the Kentucky   **(51)**
   Derby
B. Pedigree is just as important as past performance
   in Grade 1 stakes races
C. The truly important sires of the sport contribute
   relatively even influences of speed and stamina
D. Two-year-old stakes winners of spring are not as
   likely to win the 2YO routes of fall

641. *Northern Dancer* has been considered the world's greatest sire for years because

A. He has produced the most stakes winners   **(49)**
B. He is the sire of other highly successful sires
C. His progeny have won the most money
D. His yearlings sell at auction for the highest average dollar amounts

642. A foreign-raced 5YO that has been working regularly but has not raced in seven months has been entered at an unfamiliar distance and is 8–1 on the board.
When should handicappers back the horse regardless?

A. its trainer wins regularly with imports   **(53)**
B. it has a decisive class edge on today's field
C. it has won following similar layoffs in the past
D. it looks sharp in the paddock and post parade and one of the two leading jockeys has been named

643. The most unpredictable imports of all come from

A. Ireland   **(53)**
B. Argentina
C. Australia
D. Germany

644. Regarding imports from South America, only Grade 1 winners and close runners-up are acceptable in U.S. stakes and classified races.

A. True   **(53)**
B. False

645. A fair generalization about European imports is they

A. should not be bet until they demonstrate good   **(53)**
form here
B. often will be entered first out at unsuitable distances
C. cannot be expected to win first out on the dirt
D. often have a class edge under U.S. eligibility conditions

646. Which foreign stakes has probably attracted the best horses?

A. an open stakes of England   **(53)**
B. a Grade 3 stakes of Ireland

C. a Grade 1 stakes of New Zealand
D. a listed stakes of France

647. England cards approximately how many Grade 1 events?

A. 20   (53)
B. 50
C. 80
D. 120

648. Which foreign stakes has probably attracted the best horses?

A. Grade 1, Australia   (53)
B. Grade 2, Italy
C. Grade 3, France
D. Grade 1, Argentina

649. Which is the most sensible guideline for handicappers evaluating imports under U.S. racing conditions?

A. Wait to bet until the imports show positive form   (53)
   under local conditions
B. Prefer imports from stables whose trainers have
   done well with foreign horses in the past
C. Emphasize class and support obvious overlays
   confidently
D. If current form is questionable and either the distance or footing might be uncomfortable, the horses
   are best eliminated

650. A nonwinners twice allowance race at Belmont Park or Santa Anita should be easy pickings for any import that has competed well in which stakes?

A. Grade 2, Ireland   (53)
B. a listed stakes of England
C. Grade 1, Germany
D. all of the above

651. The most definitive event for 2YOs in Europe is

A. William Hill Futurity, England   (53)
B. Moyglare Stud, Ireland
C. Grand Criterium, France
D. Dormello, Italy

652. The most useful information about ungraded foreign stakes races is

A. track class   **(53)**
B. size of the purse
C. names of the winner and close runners-up
D. whether the race is listed on the pages of select international sales catalogs

653. The horse that finishes 4th in the Arc de Triomphe of France or the King George and Queen Elizabeth Diamond Stakes of England is practically a cinch against any kind of ungraded, unlisted stakes competition in the states.

A. True   **(53)**
B. False

654. European imports 4up can be eliminated confidently in their U.S. debuts if they

A. have not raced in more than six months   **(53)**
B. are entered in a graded stakes first out
C. have never been entered in a listed stakes
D. are entered in a dirt race

655. The least impressive imports come here from races in

A. Italy   **(53)**
B. Ireland
C. Canada
D. England

Answer key: Pedigree, turf racing,
and imports

Minimum Competency Test

599. A	603. D	607. B
600. A	604. C	608. B
601. C	605. A	609. A
602. B	606. C	610. D

Mastery Test

611. A	626. D	641. B
612. C	627. A	642. B
613. C	628. C	643. C
614. C	629. A	644. A
615. D	630. B	645. D
616. A	631. D	646. D
617. B	632. B	647. A
618. D	633. A	648. B
619. D	634. B	649. C
620. B	635. A	650. D
621. B	636. B	651. C
622. D	637. C	652. D
623. B	638. C	653. A
624. C	639. C	654. C
625. C	640. D	655. B

CHAPTER 13

Body Language

Competencies

54. Understand the appearance and behavior of the *sharp, ready, dull, frightened, angry,* and *hurting* horses.
55. Know the mechanics of good and poor stride, the conformation of mud and grass feet.
56. Relate body language to common racetrack circumstances, including slop and mud, heat and cold, layoffs, the paddock behavior of grooms and jockeys, the prerace warm-ups, and the starting gate.
57. Interpret equine body language as either a plus or minus in relation to horses' chances.

	Minimum Competency Test	Mastery Test
Proficiency standards	75%	60%
Number of items	12	32
Passing scores	9	20

Sources of Instruction

- *The Body Language of Horses,* chapters 5 & 7
- *The Body Language of the Horse* (video), 55 minutes

Comments

Few handicappers understand horses' body language well enough to use the data as a decisive factor in handicapping. Those who do enjoy the most precious kind of edge: the kind that others do not share.

When my turf club companion Marty Townsend explained how body language had steered him toward a $200 winner, it was not the first time an authentic equine body-language expert had described a killing I could not have participated in regardless.

Nonetheless, most handicappers can comprehend body language well enough to recognize when it might help or hinder the likeliest contention. The tests of the subject here hardly qualify as valid reflections of visual skills that can be demonstrated only at the track. I present them as an integral component of the handicapping curriculum anyhow, anticipating that something elemental might rub off.

An aspect of the body-language review must be stressed. The classical purpose of the paddock and post parade inspection has been to hunt for negative signs. Pre-race detectives wanted to discount paper contenders appearing as overly frightened, sore, sweating, or angry. On this times have changed. Positive signs now are equally vital as negative signs. The unmistakably *sharp* horse has become a prized specimen. At any racetrack it's by backing these impressive-looking athletes that body-language specialists expect to make their major scores. And do.

Definition of Terms

• *Equine body language.* The appearance and behavior profiles of horses preparing to race.

BODY LANGUAGE: MINIMUM COMPETENCY TEST

656. The main purpose of the paddock and post parade inspection is

    A. to identify horses either especially sharp or especially frightened   **(56)**
    B. to look for negative signs
    C. to interpret the body-language profiles of the authentic contenders
    D. to identify positive changes in body language from one race to another

657. The eyes are rolling, whites showing slightly. The head is held high. Ears are flicking about. The tail swishes occasionally. In the post parade the horse moves sideways, head and neck held upward. No washiness is visible. The horse is

    A. ready   **(54)**
    B. sore

C. nervous
D. frightened

658. Most horses enjoy running in the rain.

A. True (54)
B. False

659. The most reliable signs provided by the *sharp* horse include

A. dappled hip, head high, striding out (54)
B. ears pricked forward, gait high, head drooping
C. neck arched, dancing on its toes
D. ears facing rider, rapid stride, gleaming coat

660. A *dull* horse is most apparent from its

A. head (54)
B. eyes
C. coat
D. stride

661. Most races are won by horses that look

A. dull (56)
B. sharp
C. nervous
D. ready

662. A racehorse's ears are a positive sign of sharpness when

A. flat or pinned on the head (54)
B. pricked upright and forward
C. flicking from sound to sound
D. in the airplane position

663. A frightened horse's ears will normally be

A. pinned or in the airplane position (54)
B. straight forward and motionless
C. turned toward the rider
D. flicking about in unsynchronized directions

664. Obvious washiness in the post parade is a negative sign.

A. True (57)
B. False

665. Washiness that intensifies from paddock to walking ring to post parade to post is worst

A. on the neck   **(54)**
B. running down the underbelly
C. at the kidneys
D. on the flanks

666. If a horse feels sore in the post parade, it often

A. clings to the lead pony and moves sideways down   **(56)**
   the track
B. drops the hip on the hurting side and simultaneously droops its head to the opposite side
C. takes a long listless stride, the head and eyes fixed
   forwardly as if trying to move away from its pain
D. leaves the post parade early and begins to work
   out its soreness in a canter

667. *Sharp* horses at long odds should usually be bet.

A. True   **(57)**
B. False

This is the end of the minimum competency test. Check your answers. If your score falls below standard, consult the recommended sources of instruction before proceeding to the mastery test.

BODY LANGUAGE: MASTERY TEST

668. What is the most important fact to understand about horses that are washy in the post parade?

A. Unless the washiness intensifies, it normally   **(57)**
   should be seen as the normal nervousness of an
   athlete preparing to perform
B. The washiness can be part of either a frightened
   or sharp profile, depending upon other body language.
C. Inordinate washiness is significantly more worrisome in routes than in sprints.
D. The most important consideration is whether the
   horse is normally washy or not

669. Dappling is most meaningful

A. following a freshening layoff **(57)**
B. when no other horse has the same bloom
C. when horses already qualify as contenders
D. on the hips of sprinters

670. If the whites of a horse's eyes are clearly visible, it indicates

A. soreness **(54)**
B. nervousness
C. readiness
D. fright

671. In the paddock and walking ring, a reliable sign a horse has become *angry* is

A. head tossing **(54)**
B. fighting the handler
C. eyes rolling
D. tail popping

672. A firm, erect tail is a sign of

A. anger **(54)**
B. nervousness
C. readiness
D. fear

673. A *ready* horse is a picture of quiet confidence.

A. True **(54)**
B. False

674. The most significant change in equine body language is

A. angry to ready **(57)**
B. frightened to dull
C. dull to sharp
D. nervous to ready

675. The kind of foot that frequently becomes most effective in the mud is

A. toed outward, so the legs strike the ground with **(55)**
   a kind of swimming motion
B. round and large, the pasterns angular
C. relatively small and cuppy, and pasterns straight

D. toed inward, the hoofs almost touching one another on impact

676. The most efficient stride is usually

A. deeply curled at the knee   (55)
B. long and fully extended in front
C. short but high and rapid
D. propelled by strong rear legs that hit the ground
at approximately the same time

677. If the strongest contender on paper looks *frightened*,
sore, or *nervous* in the post parade at low but fair odds, what
should handicappers do?

A. bet the second or third choice if offered at gen-   (57)
erous odds
B. expect the horse to run well but lose, and key it
in the two-hole in exactas
C. stick with the horse, but bet less
D. pass the race

678. If noncontenders on paper look particularly *sharp* in
the post parade and the odds are long, the most sensible procedure is

A. pass the race   (57)
B. bet the sharp horse to win, along with the paper
selection, provided both are overlays
C. ignore the sharp horse today, but record its body
language for future reference
D. bet the sharp horse to place or show

679. The most effective stride on the turf

A. skips over the grass lightly   (55)
B. cups the grass firmly and surely
C. is high and straight, moving up and down in short
quick steps
D. is deeply curled at the knees

680. If a groom fights or mishandles an *angry* or *frightened*
horse in the paddock or walking ring, what might handicappers
fairly conclude?

A. The horse is not well-intended today   (57)
B. The tug of war is a minor nuisance to the horse
and not of any real significance

C. The trainer is not dependable on the body-language factor
D. The horse will very probably lose regardless

681. The pre-race warm-ups are especially important to
monitor the behavior of horses that appear

A. angry   (56)
B. dull
C. frightened
D. hurting

682. The *ready*, playful, or eager horse is particularly ap-
pealing

A. after a layoff   (56)
B. in the mud
C. in the cold
D. following a dull performance on a day it looked
   dull

683. An overworked claiming horse often appears

A. underweight, especially in the hindquarters   (56)
B. in long front tendon bandages
C. flabby in the chest
D. deceptively sharp, head erect, eyes moving, but
   the ears will be flat or in the airplane position

684. After the horses have returned to be unsaddled, the
telltale signs that a race has been overexerting or exhausting
include

A. tail erect, turning sideways, head held high   (56)
B. ears pinned, hips dropping, stride slow and short
C. nostrils flaring rapidly, unable to stand still, sweat
   pouring off both flanks, moving in small circles
D. forelegs spread, mouth open, head alternatively
   up and down while gasping for air

685. If during the canter that ends the post parade the jockey
has to stand up and take a tight hold on the reins, the horse is

A. sharp   (56)
B. frightened
C. angry
D. hurting

686. Many horses look dull on paper but sharp on the track. Which guideline is most useful in evaluating these horses' chances?

A. Sharp horses appear so infrequently, they should   **(57)**
   usually be covered in the win pool, even as a second win bet
B. Sharp horses can be counted upon to run better than expected, notably if they look dull on paper
C. A sharp horse can be bet confidently to win, provided it is the only horse of its kind in the field
D. Sharp horses should be bet confidently only when they shape up as contenders during the paper-and-pencil phase of handicapping

687. What does the *sharp* horse normally have that the *ready* horse does not?

A. neck arched   **(54)**
B. ears pricked
C. dappling
D. dancing feet

688. The difference between the tail swishing and the tail popping is the difference between fright and anger.

A. True   **(54)**
B. False

689. How can handicappers best tell whether a horse obviously *frightened* in the paddock and walking ring has settled down and will run its race after all?

A. It walks quietly during the post parade   **(56)**
B. It relaxes and works handily during the warm-ups
C. It enters the gate willingly
D. Its washiness diminishes as the race approaches

690. The body-language expert waits eagerly to see this horse.

A. won an all-out driving finish, looks dull today   **(57)**
B. lost badly when favored, looks sharp today
C. nervous repeatedly, calm today
D. sharp horse, long odds

691. If a relaxed horse becomes agitated as soon as the jockey mounts, the horse is probably

A. frightened, but still capable of winning (56)
B. ready, and deserves extra credit
C. angry, and will lose
D. hurting, and will lose

692. A positive body-language sign in the slop is

A. on its toes and stepping high (56)
B. back feet planted down firmly while walking
C. tail up
D. on the muscle

693. A particularly negative sign following a lengthy lay-off is

A. unusually sharp profile (56)
B. dull coat
C. washiness
D. a large belly

694. The most traumatic experience for a racehorse is

A. bleeding internally (56)
B. dehydration
C. falling down
D. losing by a nose

695. Because of differences in temperament and running styles, fillies of equal speed and ability are most likely to beat males

A. in sprints (56)
B. at middle distances
C. at classic distances
D. on the grass

696. A drugged horse is noticeable from the appearance and behavior of its

A. head (56)
B. eyes
C. ears
D. stride

697. *Sharp* horses are more interesting as authentic long-shots

A. in contentious races   **(57)**
B. at 50–1 or higher
C. if they have been recently claimed
D. in fields devoid of legitimate contenders

698. Approximately what percentage of races at major tracks can handicappers expect will be won by *frightened, angry,* and *hurting* horses as a group?

A. 5%   **(57)**
B. 10%
C. 20%
D. 25%

699. Among closely matched contenders, the best way to evaluate the horses further using body language is

A. Discount the horses showing negative signs   **(57)**
B. Award extra credit to any sharp or ready horse
C. Eliminate any horse that is frightened, angry, or hurting
D. Bet the sharp horse, provided it is the only one of its kind

Answer key: Body language

Minimum Competency Test

656. C	660. C	664. B
657. D	661. A	665. C
658. B	662. B	666. B
659. C	663. D	667. B

Mastery Test

668. B	676. B	684. D	692. B
669. C	677. A	685. A	693. D
670. D	678. B	686. B	694. C
671. D	679. A	687. C	695. C
672. C	680. C	688. A	696. C
673. A	681. D	689. C	697. D
674. C	682. B	690. B	698. B
675. C	683. A	691. C	699. B

CHAPTER 14

Probability, Odds, Pari-Mutuel Wagering, and Money Management Methods

Competencies

58. Know the basic facts of probability and the principles of pari-mutuel wagering and money management.
59. Estimate probabilities from given handicapping situations and convert probabilities to odds.
60. Calculate a handicapper's expectation from given performance data.
61. Identify underlays and overlays.
62. Understand the dynamics, advantages, and disadvantages of the conventional money management methods.
63. Evaluate wagering decisions appropriate to the handicapping probabilities and pari-mutuel odds in familiar racing situations.

	Minimum Competency Test	Mastery Test
Proficiency standards	80%	70%
Number of items	20	51
Passing scores	16	36

Sources of Instruction

- *Thoroughbred Handicapping as an Investment*, chapters 1, 3, 4, 6, 11, 12–13, 15–18, 21–25
- *A Winning Thoroughbred Strategy*, chapters 1–6, 11–12, 14–16

- Dr. Z's Beat the Racetrack, chapters (3–6, 9, 16)
- Betting at the Racetrack, chapters 1–4, 7
- "Optimal Betting," The Best of Thoroughbred Handicapping, #2
- Thoroughbred Handicapping: State of the Art, Chapter 14

Comments

If the customer's knowledge of betting and money management at the races is as desperately low as is routinely cited in the texts, just about everyone can be expected to butcher these competency tests on the first pass-through.

The optimistic view, alternately, is that developing proficiency in betting and managing money at the races is far simpler than handicapping well.

Definition of Terms

- Probability. The ratio of favorable outcomes to total outcomes.

- Expectation. The expected return on the invested dollar, based upon win percentage and average odds on winners.

- The Kelly Criterion. The proposition that a bankroll grows at an optimal rate when a bettor wagers a fixed percentage amount equal to his advantage in the game.

- Underlay. An overestimation of a horse's chances of winning.

- Overlay. An underestimation of a horse's chances of winning.

PROBABILITY, ODDS, PARI-MUTUEL WAGERING, AND MONEY MANAGEMENT METHODS: MINIMUM COMPETENCY TEST

700. An underlay is

A. any odds-on favorite   (61)
B. any horse whose real chances have been under-
estimated
C. any horse whose real chances have been overes-
timated
D. a false favorite

701. The chances of drawing an ace in a standard deck of cards is $\frac{4}{52}$. So the winning chances of any horse in a 12-horse field is $\frac{1}{12}$.

A. True   **(58)**
B. False

702. If a horse has a 20% chance of winning, the proper odds are 4–1.

A. True   **(59)**
B. False

703. A handicapping morning line has the desirable mathematical property that the probabilities should add to 1.

A. True   **(58)**
B. False

704. The ultimate authority of mathematical probability forces us to conclude that the most likely winner of the season is not a good bet if it is not a fair price.

A. True   **(58)**
B. False

705. The probability that any handicapping characteristic, such as "days away" or "finish last out," will win as often as we would expect can be calculated as

A. the percentage of winners that have a certain   **(59)**
   handicapping characteristic in common
B. the number of contenders in a race having the
   characteristic of interest minus one
C. the percentage of winners having a certain characteristic divided by the percentage of starters
   having the same characteristic
D. the percentage of winning favorites having the
   given characteristic

706. The simple formula that tells racetrack handicappers (who keep records) how much they can expect to win or lose for every dollar they bet is

Expectation = Odds to $1 × P(W) − P(L) where:

Odds means average odds on winners
P (W) means the win percentage
P (L) means the loss percentage

A. True   **(60)**
B. False

707. In practical terms, the axiom that no method of money management can convert a negative expectation into profits means

    A. You can't beat the races   **(58)**
    B. The probability that a horse will win is more important than its odds
    C. Money management is more important than handicapping skill
    D. Never bet the underlays

708. If ten horses in a Breeders' Cup field have roughly equal chances to win, the fair-value odds on any would be

    A. 4–1   **(59)**
    B. 9–1
    C. 10–1
    D. 11–1

709. The handicapper who gets 30% winners at average odds of 5–2 for the season is a winner.

    A. True   **(60)**
    B. False

710. In a contentious field featuring five evenly matched horses, which odds line offers a 20% overlay?

    A. 4–1   **(61)**
    B. 5–1
    C. 6–1
    D. 10–1

711. If a horse has roughly the same chance as four other horses, the fair-value odds cannot dip below

    A. 3–1   **(59)**
    B. 4–1
    C. 5–1
    D. 10–1

712. Given no handicapping information, what are the fair-value odds on any random nonfavorite in an 11-horse field?

    A. 9–1   **(59)**
    B. 10–1
    C. 12–1
    D. 14–1

713. Accurate class ratings will usually reveal more overlays in nonclaiming routes.

A. True   **(61)**
B. False

714. Mathematical expectation can be defined as the dollar amount you win on average multiplied by your win percentage *minus* the amount you lose ($2) multiplied by your loss percentage.

A. True   **(60)**
B. False

715. Studies show repeatedly the crowd loses $.09 per dollar bet on their favorites. Anyone who bets $2 on the favorite 1000 consecutive times should therefore lose approximately

A. $90   **(60)**
B. $180
C. $900
D. $9000

716. The worst money management method at the racetrack is

A. hyper-Kelly   **(62)**
B. fixed percentage of capital
C. due-column progressions
D. 1 unit to win, 2 units to place

717. Fixed percentage betting at 5% of capital is too aggressive for most recreational handicappers, even winners.

A. True   **(62)**
B. False

718. Studies show clearly the public estimates the win probabilities better than it estimates place and show probabilities.

A. True   **(58)**
B. False

719. The favorite has a better chance in a small field.

A. True   **(63)**
B. False

This is the end of the minimum competency test. Check your answers. If your score falls below standard, please consult the recommended sources of instruction before proceeding to the mastery test.

PROBABILITY, ODDS, PARI-MUTUEL WAGERING, AND MONEY MANAGEMENT METHODS: MASTERY TEST

720. Which statement reflects the realities of handicapping proficiency and pari-mutuel wagering at the racetrack?

A. You can beat a race, but you can't beat the races   **(58)**
B. You can't beat a race, but you can beat the races
C. You can't beat the races
D. You can beat the races, but not for long

721. The main reason talented handicappers lose money at the races is

A. they bet too many races   **(58)**
B. the increase in exotic wagers
C. the increase in the number of small fields
D. they bet too many underlays

722. An overlay refers to

A. horses that are underbet   **(61)**
B. odds below real chances
C. overbet favorites
D. longshots

723. A 30% handicapper at average odds at 2–1 on winners can expect to

A. lose 10% of his seasonal investment   **(60)**
B. win 2.5% of his bankroll
C. win 15% for the season
D. lose about one-half his bankroll

724. If we can use a handicapping method to estimate the probability that Horse A will win, we can also estimate its fair-value odds by dividing its percentage chance into 100 and subtracting 1.

A. True   **(59)**
B. False

725. A handicapper has a win percentage of 33% with an average mutuel on winners of $7. What is his expected return (net profit) on each dollar invested?

A. $.15   **(60)**
B. $.075
C. $.33
D. unknown

726. In any contentious field, the favorite is an underlay.

A. True   **(61)**
B. False

727. Anybody who gets 40% winners regularly at average odds of 5–2 (2.5 to 1) and makes $200 flat bets on 300 prime selections for the season should win approximately

A. $24,000   **(60)**
B. $48,000
C. $72,000
D. $96,000

728. The best best in the show pool will usually be

A. longshots, provided the favorite figures to run out   **(63)**
B. medium-priced overlays in the win pool
C. favorites that have been overbet to win
D. horses going off from 5–2 to 15–1

729. Low-priced favorites to place are seldom a good bet.

A. True   **(58)**
B. False

730. A handicapper having 35% proficiency with average odds on winners of 5–2 can expect to win roughly how much on every dollar bet?

A. $.15   **(60)**
B. $.25
C. $.45
D. $.55

731. To estimate how much a win bettor can earn for a season, multiply the total amount wagered by the single-race expectation or the gain expected for each wagered dollar.

A. True   **(60)**
B. False

732. Excellent speed figures can identify more overlays among

A. claiming routes   **(61)**
B. nonclaiming sprints
C. stakes horses
D. claiming horses on the rise

733. Which is an underlay?

A. 40% chance to win, odds 5–2   **(61)**
B. 33% chance to win, odds 2–1
C. 50% chance to win, odds 7–5
D. 20% chance to win, odds 3–1

734. Which is the most attractive overlay?

A. 20% chance to win, odds 7–1   **(61)**
B. 15% chance to win, odds 19–1
C. 40% chance to win, odds 9–2
D. 30% chance to win, odds 6–1

735. A handicapper's net on the invested dollar is $.10. If he bets $100,000 in flat bets across the season, he should

A. win $1000   **(60)**
B. lose the track take
C. win $10,000
D. lose $90,000

736. A horse's probability of winning and a bettor's expectation are interchangeable.

A. True   **(58)**
B. False

737. In unfair games (negative expectation), a maximum boldness betting strategy is optimal.

A. True   **(58)**
B. False

738. In favorable games (positive expectation), a minimum boldness betting strategy is optimal.

A. True   **(58)**

B. False

739. The optimal bet is equal to

A. the probability the horse will win   **(58)**

B. 5% of the bankroll

C. the expectation divided by the dollar odds

D. 1% of the bankroll

740. Base bet plus square root of the profits is a low-risk method of determining whether an untested handicapping angle actually works.

A. True   **(62)**

B. False

741. Base bet plus square root of the profits minimizes risk to the small bettor because as profits grow

A. The base bet remains a minimum $2   **(62)**

B. You bet more when winning and less when losing

C. The next bet is always an increasingly smaller percentage of the net gain

D. The method becomes increasingly sensitive to longshots

742. Which percentage of bankroll betting strategy would be too bold for a 30% handicapper who gets 5–2 on winners?

A. 1%   **(62)**

B. 1.5%

C. 2%

D. 3%

743. When implemented properly in a winning situation, which is the only method of money management in risk-benefit games (racing) that never taps out?

A. base bet plus square root of the profits   **(62)**

B. the Kelly Criterion

C. fixed percentage-minimum

D. flat betting

744. Which betting strategy taps out about 20% of the time when betting 5% of capital at normal levels of handicapping proficiency, that is, 30% winners at 5–2 odds.

266 THE ABCS OF THOROUGHBRED HANDICAPPING

A. flat betting (62)
B. unit wagering at the odds
C. base bet plus square root of the profits
D. all of the above

745. Which betting strategy has the property that the growth of bankroll in a winner's game will be optimal?

A. Kelly betting (62)
B. base bet + square root of the profits
C. fixed percentage
D. betting a minimum following a loss and a fixed percentage following a win

746. The main problem in applying Kelly wagering techniques to racetrack money management is

A. minimizing losses during normal losing runs (62)
B. estimating the probabilities accurately
C. the wide variations in money won from season to season using the same performance estimates
D. the length of time it takes to earn significant profits

747. Place overlays are more frequent than show overlays.

A. True (61)
B. False

748. A 35% handicapper getting average odds of 2–1 on winners is a loser.

A. True (60)
B. False

749. At major tracks like Belmont Park or Oaklawn Park, place and show overlays should have an expectation (return on the invested dollar) of at least

A. 1.10 (61)
B. 1.14
C. 1.18
D. 1.25

750. At minor tracks the dollar expectation of place and show overlays should be at least

A. 1.18   **(61)**
B. 1.25
C. 1.40
D. 1.50

751. The silliest wagering pattern at the races is

A. exotic wagering   **(62)**
B. longshots to place or show
C. one unit to win, 2 units to place
D. betting more after a loss

752. The fair-value return on a $5 exacta where both the top and bottom horses are 3–1 is approximately

A. $60   **(59)**
B. $75
C. $100
D. $150

753. Which would be a tenable win-betting strategy for contentious races?

A. Bet any contender at odds of 5–1 or more   **(63)**
B. Dutch the race covering all contenders
C. Bet all the overlays
D. Bet any contender at odds above 10–1

754. Assuming the field contains more than eight horses, a perfectly plausible strategy for developing a handicapper's morning line is to assign 80% of the probabilities to the contenders and 20% to the other horses.

A. True   **(63)**
B. False

755. Nicely priced exacta combinations that figure reasonably well often appear to pay off as underlays because

A. Longshots in exactas are generally overbet   **(59)**
B. The fields are too small
C. The public has underestimated one or both horses in the win pool badly
D. The take on exacta wagers is exorbitantly high

756. A good way to bet strong favorites as exacta keys in a 12-horse field is

A. on top of the 2nd choice only   **(63)**
B. on top of the next 3 choices
C. top wheel the favorite
D. bottom wheel the favorite

757. Which is a good strategy for betting daily doubles?

A. top choice in either half to the field in the other   **(63)**
   half
B. top choice to top choice
C. top three in either half to top two in other half
D. top two in each half to one another

758. The type of exotic wager that offers the best value in relation to the probabilities of winning is the

A. daily double   **(63)**
B. exacta
C. quinella
D. triple

759. If the three contenders in a ten-horse field have a relatively equal chance to win, any is a 20% overlay at odds of

A. 2–1   **(59)**
B. 5–2
C. 3–1
D. 4–1

760. In general, the most unsuccessful exacta wager is the

A. favorite on the bottom   **(63)**
B. a pair of longshots
C. a 3-horse baseball
D. key horse on top only

761. Which usually is true of exacta wagering?

A. The favorite on top of a longshot is often an   **(62)**
   overlay
B. Longshots should be keyed in top wheels only
C. Two medium-priced horses offer the best over-
   lays
D. The key horse should always be boxed

762. Which racetrack skill is the most difficult to perform well?

A. handicapping the horses   **(58)**
B. money management
C. passing contentious or unreliable races
D. betting properly

763. The consensus favorite is a better bet

A. at less than even-money   **(63)**
B. if it has a decisive edge at a fair price
C. when used on the bottom in exactas
D. in sprints than in routes

764. If the top choice in an exacta is 3–1 and the bottom choice is 4–1, what is the probability the combination will click?

A. .06   **(59)**
B. .11
C. .22
D. cannot be determined

765. The fair-value payoff of any exacta is the size of the bet divided by the probability the combination will occur.

A. True   **(61)**
B. False

766. The overlay value of an exacta payoff should approach at least

A. 10%   **(61)**
B. 20%
C. 40%
D. 50%

767. For a consistent winning handicapper, flat betting loses which crucial attribute of effective money management?

A. The tap-out rate is too high during normal losing   **(62)**
     runs
B. Overlays cannot be bet properly
C. The rate of growth of the bankroll can be signifi-
     cantly slower than optimal
D. The size of the bet does not vary in accord with
     the strength of the handicapper's opinions

768. If a handicapper knows he gets 35% winners at average odds of 5–2 and therefore has a 22% expectation on the in-

vested dollar, which money management method has the attributes that it simultaneously will (a) minimize the risk of overbetting, (b) provide the optimum rate of growth of the bankroll, and (c) never tap out?

A. flat betting　　　　　　　　　　　　　　　　　　　**(62)**
B. fixed percentage
C. base bet plus square root of the profits
D. Kelly Criterion

769. The four contenders in a closely matched stakes sprint have earned speed figures that give them an 18%, 16%, 16%, and 15% chance of winning, respectively. Which horses deserve a bet?

A. any that is an attractive overlay　　　　　　　　　　**(61)**
B. the longshot among the four, if any
C. the favorite among the four
D. none

770. A class handicapper rates every horse in an eight-horse field from 10 to 100. The four low-rated horses have a total of 200 class points. The four high-rated horses are:

| Horse A | 82 | Horse C | 80 |
| Horse B | 88 | Horse D | 75 |

What are the minimum odds this handicapper should accept on his top-rated horse?

A. 7–1　　　　　　　　　　　　　　　　　　　　　　**(63)**
B. 3–1
C. 10–1
D. 5–1

Answer key: Probability, odds, pari-mutuel wagering, and money management methods

Minimum Competency Test

700. C	705. C	710. B	715. B
701. B	706. A	711. B	716. C
702. A	707. D	712. D	717. A
703. A	708. B	713. B	718. A
704. A	709. A	714. A	719. B

Mastery Test

720. B	730. B	740. A	750. A	760. C
721. D	731. A	741. C	751. B	761. C
722. A	732. D	742. D	752. C	762. A
723. A	733. D	743. B	753. C	763. B
724. A	734. B	744. D	754. A	764. A
725. A	735. C	745. A	755. C	765. A
726. A	736. B	746. B	756. D	766. B
727. A	737. A	747. B	757. D	767. C
728. C	738. A	748. B	758. B	768. D
729. B	739. C	749. B	759. D	769. A
				770. D

Performance Tests

Performance Test A

APPLIED HANDICAPPING SKILLS

A matched-pair of performance tests assess not only the higher-order thinking skills (analysis, synthesis, and evaluation), but the skills of the trade handicappers must demonstrate every day.

Below are the competencies and performance standards handicappers are expected to meet. The criterion *performance points* refers to the win percentage multiplied by the average odds on winners.

Competencies

64. *Analysis.* Identify horses that figure best on specific handicapping factors, that is, speed, class, pace, early speed, et al.
65. *Synthesis.* From a field of horses or a given number of contenders, select the most probable winner.
66. *Evaluation.* Identify underlays and overlays.

	Test Form	No. of Items	Pass-ing Scores	Win %	Ave. Odds	Perfor-mance Points	Edge (ROI)
	A	60	18	30	3–1	90	.20
	A	60	20	33	5–2	82.5	.15
Performance Standards							
	B	60	18	30	3–1	90	.20
	B	60	20	33	5–2	82.5	.15

Comments

Each test form contains roughly thirty items from the Western tracks and thirty from the Eastern-Central tracks. Each form contains 16–17 items that assess analysis, 17–18 that assess synthesis, and 26–27 that assess evaluation.

Besides a correct answer, each item has a numerical value ranging from 1 to 12. These values correspond to the actual odds on winners or to the probability of getting an item right. By multiplying the percentage of correct answers and the "average odds" on the correct responses, handicappers arrive at a total of *performance points*.

Handicappers earning the points specified by the preceding performance standards—or more—have a strong edge on the game. Handicappers earning 100 points or better can virtually clobber the races. Handicappers earning fewer than 75 points are playing a losing game.

As to procedure, complete Performance Test A first. Answer no more than ten items per session. If your performance on form A falls below standard, review the competency tests before proceeding to Performance Test B. If your performance slackens still, repeat the competency tests and performance tests in cycles until the desired proficiency has been established.

Note. Some past performances are marked. Ignore the markings unless advised otherwise. Use your customary methods to handicap the races provided.

1. Which horse figures to outgun this maiden-claiming field?

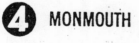

6 FURLONGS. (1.08) MAIDEN CLAIMING. Purse $7,500. Fillies and mares, 3-year-olds and upward. Weight, 3-year-olds, 116 lbs. Older, 122 lbs. Claiming price $25,000 for each $2,500 to $20,000, 2 lbs.

A.   **(65)**

Full Line	Dk. b. or br. f. 3, by Full Out—Classy Line, by Big Spruce		Lifetime	1986 0 M 0 0
Own.—Hidden Lane Stable	$22,500	Br.—Russell C H (Va)	114	0 0 0 0
		Tr.—Forbes John H		

LATEST WORKOUTS ... Jly 27 Mth 5f my 1:02 bg ●Jly 21 Mth 6f fst 1:16½ b   Jly 16 Mth 5f fst 1:02½ b   Jly 11 Mth 5f fst 1:02½ b

B.

Cry A Bit — B. f. 3, by Sir Jinsky—Dom's Dotty Jet, by Jet Stream II — $20,000 — Br.—MAraspin L (NJ) — Tr.—Stokiosa Richard — 1057
Own.—Labue F
Lifetime 2 0 0 0 — 1987 2 M 0 0 — 1986 0 M 0 0

20Jly87- 1Mth gd 6f	:22⅗ :46⅕ 1:12⅘	3+ⒻMd 16000	8 3 73¼ 78½ 79½ 718¾	Nied E7	b	109	53.70	57-26	Polarize 1165 Princess Luisa 1222½ Christines Star 1162	Outrun	9
13Jly87- 9Mth fst 6f	:22⅕ :46 1:13	3+ⒻMd 20000	6 7 1016 1019 1014 1020	Nied E7		109	49.00	55-21	Flying Flash 1182½ Bob's Bet 109½ Wondecor 1144	Outrun	11

LATEST WORKOUTS Jly 28 Mth 4f fst :49⅗ b Jly 18 Mth 3f fst :37 bg Jly 6 Mth 4f fst :49⅕ bg ●Jun 26 Mth 3f fst :36 bg

C.

Wondecor — B. f. 3, by Air Forbes Won—Art Deco, by Alto Ribot — $22,500 — Br.—Greyhound Stable (Ky) — Tr.—Jolin Louis F — 114
Own.—High Five Stable
Lifetime 14 0 7 4 $17,415 — 1987 4 M 2 2 $5,000 — 1986 10 M 5 2 $12,415

13Jly87- 9Mth fst 6f	:22⅕ :46 1:13	3+ⒻMd 18000	3 8 57½ 41½ 31½ 33	Thomas D B	b	114	2.50	72-21	Flying Flash 1182½ Bob's Bet 109½ Wondecor 1144	Steadied	11
18Jun87-10Mth fst 6f	:22⅘ :46 1:11⅘	3+ⒻMd 22000	12 3 31 31 21 25	Heath M J7	b	108	*1.80	76-14	HerMjestyCrrie1155Wondecor1062½DespirNot1153	Best of others	12
29May87- 4Mth fst 6f	:21⅗ :45 1:11⅗	ⒻClm 20000	8 4 45½ 33½ 32½ 32¾	Heath M J5	b	106	67.50	80-12	Piper Over 1152 Camp Follower 110¾ Wondecor 1062½	Evenly	12
22May87- 1GS fst 6f	:22⅘ :46⅕ 1:13⅘	3+ⒻMd 15000	1 2 1½ 1hd 11 2½	Romero J A5	b	109	*1.20	74-24	Hotel El Dorado 114½ Wondecor 1091½ Pockapenny 1142	Gamely	5
3Dec86- 3Med my 6f	:22⅗ :47 1:13⅗	ⒻMd 32000	5 8 31½ 2hd 2hd 53½	Thomas D B	b	117	*1.70	70-21	Sunny Her 1172 Sal's Signal 113½ Bold Moona 116½	Weakened	10
17Nov86-10Med fst 6f	:22⅘ :45⅘ 1:11⅗	ⒻMd 32000	4 3 21½ 21½ 21 23½	Thomas D B	b	118	4.60	81-17	Never an Angel 1183½Wondecor1182MerryMercedes1182½	Gamely	10
30Oct86- 4Med fst 6f	:22⅘ :46⅘ 1:12⅗	ⒻMd Sp Wt	9 1 3½ 42½ 75 78½	Meszaros G	b	117	9.00	71-23	Pamiris 117¾ Darlington County 1172 Lotus Spring 117¾	Tired	9
9Oct86- 1Med fst 6f	:23⅗ :47⅗ 1:12⅗	ⒻMd Sp Wt	1 5 2hd 42½ 48½ 817	Thomas D B	b	117	3.00	62-20	Gracious Belle 1174 Platinum Doll 1172 Top Test 1123	Tired	11
20Sep86- 6Med fst 6f	:22⅘ :45⅗ 1:12⅘	ⒻMd Sp Wt	3 4 2hd 1hd 13½ 2no	Thomas D B	b	117	3.30	78-22	Tuneful Ann 117no Wondecor 117¾ PlatinumDoll1171½	Just failed	11
2Sep86- 6Pha fst 6f	:22⅗ :46⅗ 1:13⅕	ⒻMd Sp Wt	1 2 1hd 1hd 2½ 31	Meszaros G	b	117	3.00	74-16	Perfect Magic 117¾FolieJoyeuse117nkWondecor117hd	Drifted out	7

LATEST WORKOUTS Jly 25 Mth 4f fst :54 b Jly 11 Mth 5f fst 1:05⅗ b Jly 7 Mth 5f fst 1:00⅘ h Jun 17 Mth 3f fst :37⅗ b

D.

Les Pleiades — B. f. 3, by Plugged Nickle—Synclinal, by Vaguely Noble — $25,000 — Br.—Watson T & Free (NY) — Tr.—Hernandez Ramon M — 1097
Own.—Free W
Lifetime 8 0 1 1 $6,510 — 1987 8 M 1 1 $6,510 — 1986 0 M 0 0

2Jly87- 4Mth sly 6f	:22 :45⅗ 1:12⅘	3+ⒻMd 20000	9 9 912 810 612 410	Santagata N	116	12.60	68-17	AlluringProspect1092½DespairNot1164OccsionlDrem1165½	Rallied	10
4Jun87- 2Bel sly 6f	:22⅘ :47 1:13⅗	3+ⒻMd 35000	2 8 67 66 59 611½	Santos J	114	6.20	62-21	Smokmontngold116noNtvPrformr1143½Bsn…1055½	Saved ground	9
20May87- 9Bel gd 6f	:22⅘ :46 1:11	3+ⒻMd 45000	3 9 109½ 87¾ 89 812½	Badamo J J5	104	4.10	73-17	Magical 1131¾ George's M. C. 1134¾ Hear the Rhythm113½	Outrun	12
10May87- 4Bel fst 1	:48⅘ 1:15⅕ 1:41⅘	3+ⒻMd 45000	8 5 1hd 2hd 1hd 36½	Badamo J J5	104	3.30	50-25	No Butter 1133½ Kiss Who 1133 Les Pleiades 1043½	Weakened	10
29Apr87- 2Aqu my 6f	:22⅘ :46⅗ 1:12⅗	3+ⒻMd 45000	8 9 88½ 87 66 44	Badamo J J5	103	3.10	74-21	ProfessorBonnie1122½MatchMadeline111½Decoration106¾	Late bid	10
17Apr87- 6Aqu gd 6f	:22⅘ :47⅕ 1:12⅕	3+ⒻMd 35000	2 13 116½ 66 35½ 25½	Hernandez R	113	4.60	74-23	Dame Lisa 1135½ Les Pleiades 113nk Restless Gem 1072	Rallied	13
1Apr87- 2Aqu fst 7f	:23⅕ :46⅗ 1:25⅕	3+ⒻMd 35000	4 12 87½ 710 69½ 46½	Hernandez R	114	7.80	68-16	[D]Smokiemountingold113noVnillBn1144K.K.'sDrm1152½	Slow start	13
9Mar87- 3Aqu fst 6f [•]	:23⅘ :49 1:14⅘	ⒻMd 35000	4 9 65 66½ 54½ 67	Santos J A	121	*2.50	63-22	TopThisOne1212Mrs.Watters121¾HoustonGold1072½	Lacked room	12

LATEST WORKOUTS Jly 16 Bel tr.t 4f fst :49⅗ b May 31 Bel tr.t 4f fst :50 b

E.

Klassy Gem — Dk. b. or br. f. 3, by Klassy Flight—Carolyns Serenade, by Royal Serenade — $25,000 — Br.—Cataldo J H (Fla) — Tr.—Longo Salvatore J — 116
Own.—Cataldo J H
Lifetime 3 0 0 1 $900 — 1987 1 M 0 0 — 1986 2 M 0 1 $900

14Jly87- 6Mth fst 6f	:22⅘ :46⅕ 1:12⅘	3+ⒻMd Sp Wt	9 4 31 42 67½ 918¾	Edwards J W	b	116	20.40	57-23	Silver Reality 1161 Well Enough Alone 1163 Chervil 1114¾	Tired	10
13Oct86- 7Suf fst 6f	:22 :45⅗ 1:13⅘	ⒻMd Sp Wt	5 3 1hd 2hd 2½ 816¾	Vargas J L		118	*2.70	56-25	Rare Lead 1185 Foolish Saxon 1181 Fashion Queen 118hd	Tired	9
8Sep86- 7Suf fst 6f	:23 :47⅘ 1:14⅗	ⒻMd Sp Wt	3 9 1hd 1½ 1hd 38½	Ritvo T		118	5.40	60-26	Future Bright 1138½Sharpe'sFerry118hdKlassyGem1182	Weakened	9

LATEST WORKOUTS Jly 25 Mth 5f fst 1:01⅗ h Jly 7 Mth 3f fst :37⅘ b Jun 30 Mth 6f fst 1:14⅘ h Jun 23 Mth 5f fst 1:01 hg

F.

Bob's Bet — Ch. f. 3, by Nasty And Bold—Comfort Lass, by Soy Numero Uno — $25,000 — Br.—Nuckols Bros (Ky) — Tr.—Heard Dennis — 116
Own.—Lank G
Lifetime 5 0 2 0 $5,790 — 1987 5 M 2 0 $5,790 — 1986 0 M 0 0

13Jly87- 9Mth fst 6f	:22⅕ :46 1:13	3+ⒻMd c-20000	9 2 33 3nk 1½ 22½	Diaz L F7	109	*1.90	72-21	Flying Flash 1182½ Bob's Bet 109½ Wondecor 1144	Game try	11
3Jly87- 4Mth fst 6f	:22⅘ :45⅗ 1:11⅕	3+ⒻMd Sp Wt	9 1 63¾ 35 47½ 48	Diaz L F7	109	4.60	76-13	Amber Gem 1222 Larkridge 116½ Chervil 1165½	Weakened	10
20Jun87- 1Mth fst 1 1/16	:47⅕ 1:11⅗ 1:43⅕	3+ⒻMd Sp Wt	6 2 3½ 32 38 415	Santagata N	114	5.60	74-13	La Fey Morgan 1146 Heier Hai 1145½ Larkridge 114½	Tired	9
13Jun87- 1Mth fst 6f	:21⅗ :44⅗ 1:11⅘	3+ⒻMd Sp Wt	6 5 67¾ 66½ 53½ 64	Santagata N	115	3.50	77-12	Timely Times 115½ Quaint 115¾ La Fey Morgan 1151	Outrun	8
2Jun87- 5Mth fst 6f	:22⅘ :46 1:12⅕	3+ⒻMd Sp Wt	5 4 3½ 31 1hd 2no	Santagata N	115	*2.20	79-16	Proud Delight 115no Bob's Bet 1152 Like Mink 1155½	Gamely	8

LATEST WORKOUTS May 30 Mth 3f fst :36⅘ bg

2. One of the horses is a class stickout under the conditions and won like it at 3–1. Which is it?

9th Santa Anita

TURF COURSE
1 MILE
SANTA ANITA
Start
Finish

1 MILE. (Turf). (1.35) ALLOWANCE. Purse $35,000. 4–year–olds and upward which are non–winners of $3,000 twice other than maiden, claiming or starter. Weight, 121 lbs. Non–winners of two races other than claiming at one mile or over since February 15 allowed 3 lbs.; of such a race other than maiden or claiming since then, 5 lbs.

A. **(64)**

***Putting** B. c. 4, by Kris—Popaway, by Run the Gantlet
STEVENS G L 116 Br.—OrbitInvstmtLtd&TbInvCoLtd (Fr) 1987 1 0 0 1 $4,500
Own.—Sofro D I Tr.—Canani Julio C 1986 7 2 2 0 $48,984
Lifetime 9 2 2 1 $53,484 Turf 9 2 2 1 $53,484
8Feb87-5SA a6½f (T):21^{1} $:43^{4}$$1{:}14^{4}$fm 4½ 115 6^{5} 5^{3}½ 5^{1}¾ 3^{1}¼ Stevens GL^{10} Aw30000 84-09 Hard Round, Irish Stories,Putting 12
8Feb87—Wide into stretch, lugged in
2Oct86-5SA 1⅛(T):47 1:12 $1{:}49^{4}$fm 4 115 5^{4} 4^{1}¾ 2^{1}½ 2^{1}¼ McCarronCJ^{6} Aw30000 77-22 Kingsbury, Putting, Travet 10
2Oct86—Broke slowly, rank; lugged in
17Aug86◆2Deauville(Fra) a1¼ $2{:}15^{4}$gd 16 128 (T) 6^{1}½ SmniH PxMdmJnCtrie Star Maite, Neferou, Milouin 9
14Jly86◆5StCloud(Fra) a1¼ $2{:}04^{1}$gd 26 123 (T) 9^{16} SmniH PxEgnAdm(Gr2) Un Desperado, Sharrood,Directing 10
23Jun86◆5Lyon(Fra) a1⅜ gd 5¼ 117 (T) 1^{1}½ AsmssnC G P de Lyon Putting, Narghile, Juba Dollar 7
23Jun86—No time taken
9Jun86◆7StCloud(Fra) a1¼ $2{:}10^{3}$gd 6½ 123 (T) 1^{hd} SamniH PxFchr(Mdn) Putting, Metro Express, Barood 10
19May86◆2StCloud(Fra) a1$\frac{5}{16}$ $2{:}15^{1}$gd 3 121 (T) 2¾ Samani H PxClstrte VaguelyDelight,Putting,SahrDncer 14
2May86◆7Laffitte(Fra) a1 $1{:}38^{1}$sf 48 121 (T) 4^{4} Samani H PxTntII Lesotho, Eastbell, Mihaarb 13
12Nov85◆8Laffitte(Fra) a1 $1{:}43^{1}$sf 83 120 (T) 13 PoirirO PxDagor(Mdn) Arctic Blast, Malakim, Barood 20
Apr 16 SA (T) 6f fm $1{:}13^{4}$ h (d) ●Apr 10 SA 7f ft $1{:}26^{2}$ h Apr 5 SA 6f ft $1{:}13^{3}$ h Mar 30 SA 5f ft $1{:}00^{2}$ h

B.

Dad's Quest B. h. 6, by Wing Out—Betty's Beau, by Gun Bow
PATTON D B 111^{5} Br.—Dinges V & Clara (Cal) 1987 5 1 0 1 $18,800
Own.—Dinges Clara Tr.—Dinges Vernon L 1986 7 0 0 0 $3,825
Lifetime 25 2 1 4 $55,605 Turf 7 0 0 0 $2,025
11Apr87-5SA a6½f (T):21^{3} $:44^{2}$$1{:}14^{3}$fm 25 111^{5} 7^{3}¾ 5^{1}½ 7^{5}¼ 8^{5}¼ Patton D B^{3} Aw33000 81-18 DnceDirector,Mrgm,FbulousSound 10
29Mar87-5SA a6½f (T):21^{3} :44 $1{:}15^{1}$fm 35 113^{5} 9^{7}½ 9^{6}¼ 9^{5}¾ 6^{3}½ Patton D B^{11} Aw33000 79-19 Danczone,FbulousSound,SlneCstle 12
1Feb87-3SA 6f $:21^{2}$ $:44^{4}$ 1:11 ft 50 113^{5} 7^{6}½ 7^{2}¾ 3^{2} 1^{no} Patton D B^{4} Aw26000 83-16 Dad's Quest, Athlone,WassIDancer 10
1Feb87—Steadied into drive
15Jan87-3SA 6f $:21^{2}$ $:44^{4}$ 1:11 ft 19 112^{5} 6^{8}½ 5^{7}½ 5^{7} 4^{6} Patton D B^{5} Aw26000 77-25 EightyBelowZero,Athlone,FstRomo 8
3Jan87-1SA 6f $:21^{4}$ $:44^{4}$ $1{:}11^{1}$ft 31 111^{5} 9^{5}¾ 7^{5}¼ 4^{5} 3^{2} Patton D B^{9} [S] 20000 80-16 KidShelleen,JustTheFcts,Dd'sQust 10
3Jan87—Pinched at start; wide final 3/8
19Apr86-2SA 6½f $:21^{3}$ $:44^{2}$ $1{:}17^{2}$ft 15 115 8^{11} 7^{11} 9^{8}¾ 7^{4}¾ Cruz J B 3 20000 78-19 Jacart, Gran Barba, Neutral Player 9
19Apr86—Lugged out 1/2
5Apr86-5SA a6½f (T):21^{3} $:44^{2}$1:15 fm 54 116 8^{4}¼ 6^{3}½ 7^{6}¼ 7^{5}¾ Cruz J B 10 Aw24000 78-17 Tuono, He's A Looker, Muralto 11
5Apr86—Wide stretch
7Mar86-7SA 6½f :22 $:44^{4}$ $1{:}16^{1}$ft 14 112^{5} 10^{6}¾ 10^{8}¾ 9^{11} 10^{13} Black C A 9 Aw28000 76-14 High Hook, Tuono, Muralto 11
23Feb86-2SA a6½f (T):21^{3} $:44^{2}$$1{:}16^{1}$fm 30 113^{5} 5^{2}½ 5^{4} 5^{5}½ 4^{5}½ Aragon V A 10 Aw27000 72-24 Brianchon,DonSanders,ErthToGry 12
23Feb86—Floated out late
6Feb86-7SA 1 $:45^{4}$ $1{:}10^{2}$ $1{:}36^{4}$ft 17 111^{5} 5^{3}¼ 4^{1}½ 5^{2}½ 6^{5}¾ Black C A 1 Aw28000 78-19 Vigor'sPrince,BasicImge,ARightIde 8
6Feb86—Bumped 1/8
Apr 6 SA 5f ft $1{:}00^{1}$ h Mar 24 SA 6f ft 1:11 h Mar 18 SA 5f ft $:59^{2}$ h Mar 14 SA 3f ft $:35^{4}$ h

C.

***Cherry Hill** B. h. 6, by Shirley Heights—Spring In Rome, by Forli
DELAHOUSSAYE E 116 Br.—Fittocks Stud Ltd (Eng) 1985 6 1 3 2 $24,179
Own.—Chllngwth Bnjmn-Dcktt et al Tr.—Sullivan John 1984 4 M 3 0 $7,172
Lifetime 11 1 6 3 $32,287 Turf 11 1 6 3 $32,287
9Nov85◆5Doncaster(Eng) 1½ $2{:}42^{4}$sf 10 137 (T) 2^{3} CarsonW W Hill Nov H Bold Rex, Cherry Hill,Ballydurrow 24
26Oct85◆3Newbury(Eng) 1⅜ 2:25 gd 6 140 (T) 2^{nk} CrsonW Tns Vlly Eggs H Ballydurrow, CherryHill, Fire Bay 10
11Oct85◆3Ascot(Eng) 1¼ $2{:}07^{4}$gd 4½ 126 (T) 1½ EddrP Mecca Bkmkr H CherryHill,RoyalHalo,TheGme'sUp 12
28Sep85◆1Ascot(Eng) 1½ $2{:}29^{4}$fm 7 129 (T) 3^{4}½ Eddery P Red Deer H Salient, Chiefdom, Cherry Hill 8
18May85◆2Newbury(Eng) 1⅜ $2{:}21^{4}$gd 5½ 128 (T) 3^{1} CrsonW Lndn Gld Cp H Estoc, RentOrBuy, CherryHill 14
24Apr85◆4Pontefract(Eng) 1½ $2{:}38^{2}$gd *1 119 (T) 2½ Ives T Fryston ArtEdict, CherryHill, TheClown 18
14Jly84◆7York(Eng) 1½ $2{:}38^{4}$gd *3-5 126 (T) 2^{hd} SbrWR Fountns (Mdn) Bespoke, Cherry Hill, Dealaway 4
23Jun84◆4Ascot(Eng) 1½ $2{:}33^{2}$fm 3½ 121 (T) 24 CarsonW Chrchill Stakes The Miller, Cherry Hill, Dealaway 5
Apr 18 SA (T) 5f fm $1{:}02^{1}$ h (d) Apr 13 SA HC 6f fm $1{:}16^{1}$ h (d) ●Apr 9 SA (T) 5f fm 1:01 h (d) Apr 3 SA (T) 5f fm 1:02 h (d)

D.

'Rinnegato B. c. 4, by Fleet Twist—Pop's Jun, by Czar Alexander
PINCAY L JR 116 Br.—Cacciotti T (Cal) 1987 1 1 0 0 $15,950
Own.—Cacciotti T Tr.—Marti Pedro 1986 7 1 1 3 $24,975
Lifetime 8 2 1 3 $40,925 Turf 1 1 0 0 $15,950
9Apr87-5SA a6½f (T):21^{3} $:43^{4}$$1{:}14^{2}$fm 3¼ 118 1½ 1½ 1^{1}½ 1^{2}¾ Pincay L Jr^{6} Aw29000 87-09 Rinnegato, Recognized, Mondanite 9
9Apr87—Broke in a tangle
20Jly86-8Hol 6f $:22^{1}$ $:45^{4}$ $1{:}11^{1}$ft 3¾ 116 2½ 3½ 2^{1}½ 2^{2} Romero R P 2 Aw22000 86-10 Quick Twist, Rinnegato, Krestige 6
20Jly86—Bumped start
26Jun86-1Hol 6f :22 :45 $1{:}09^{4}$ft 4 116 3^{2} 3^{3}½ 4^{3}¼ 3^{3}¾ Stevens G L^{1} 62500 91-12 J. R. Johnson, Totality, Rinnegato 8
8May86-7Hol 7f :22 $:44^{4}$ $1{:}22^{3}$ft 14 122 2^{1}½ 3^{1}½ 8^{9}½ 9^{10} StevensGL^{9} [S]Aw20000 81-14 IdlQulity,SocityRod,TommyThHwk 9
25Apr86-3Hol 6f $:22^{1}$ $:45^{4}$ $1{:}10^{4}$ft 2¼ 120 2½ 1½ 2^{1} 3^{2} StevensGL^{3} [S]Aw20000 88-16 DevilsBrigade,DonB.Blue,Rinnegato 5
25Apr86—Bumped early drive

9Apr86-6SA 6f :213 :451 1:101ft 3½ 118 11 11½ 11½ 1hd Stevens G L7 [S]Mdn 87-18 Rinnegato,Marvin'sPolicy,MrkChip 8
22Mar86-6SA 6f :214 :451 1:104ft *9-5 117 3nk 31 35½ 46½ Marquez C7 Mdn 77-19 Irish Stories, War Pilot, TrumpUp 12
8Mar86-6SA 6½f :214 :444 1:171sy *7-5 118 33½ 33½ 34 38½ Marquez C8 Mdn 75-19 Raise A Pound,TrumpUp,Rinnegato 9
●Apr 1 SA 5f ft :592 h Mar 24 Hol 7f ft 1:29 h Mar 19 Hol 6f ft 1:153 hg ●Mar 11 Hol 6f ft 1:142 h

E.

***Eliminante**
PEDROZA M A **116**
Own.—Four Four Forty Farms
Ch. g. 6, by Practicante—Elevacion, by Aristophanes
Br.—Haras La Biznaga (Arg)
Tr.—Dorick Robert
Lifetime 23 2 4 6 $61,173
1987 5 1 1 1 $29,300
1986 10 0 1 3 $17,875
Turf 19 2 4 5 $54,248

12Apr87-5SA 1⅛Ⓣ:4631:1121:472fm 13 117 35 41½ 1hd 21 Pedroza MA6 Aw35000 89-15 Havildar, Eliminante, Twice Bold 9
28Mar87-5SA 1⅛Ⓣ:4711:1111:473fm 11 118 42½ 42 21½ 31¼ Pedroza MA8 Aw35000 88-12 Lord Grundy, Starsalot, Eliminante 9
1Mar87-7SA 1⅛Ⓣ:4721:1141:491fm 14 118 1012 98 77 54¾ Ortega L E1 Aw33000 76-18 Aloma's Tobin, Starsalot, Bananas 10
21Feb87-7SA 1⅛Ⓣ:4731:1141:481fm 17 119 99¼ 97¾ 64½ 52¾ Ortega L E2 Aw33000 83-17 NorthrnProvidr,Rosdl,RomnMgstrit 9
21Feb87—Very wide stretch
3Jan87-5SA 1¼Ⓣ:4731:37 2:023fm 8½ 117 43½ 31½ 1½ 11¼ Pedroza MA5 Aw28000 74-24 Eliminnte,RussinLogic,GreyWriter 10
8Nov86-6Hol 1⅛Ⓣ:48 1:12 1:49 fm 5 116 43 42 41¼ 3hd ♦Pedroza MA4 Aw24000 83-11 Parson John, Rodrigue,Eliminante 12
♦8Nov86—Dead heat; Bumped late
22Oct86-5SA 1⅛Ⓣ:4541:1131:483fm 9½ 118 411 42½ 11½ 2hd Pedroza MA4 Aw27000 84-12 Thresh It Out,Eliminante,Noticiero 7
22Oct86—Bumped late
4Oct86-8SA 1 Ⓣ:4631:1011:35 fm 59 113 47½ 66½ 66 67½ PdrzMA6 Cl F W Kr H 94 — Palace Music, ‡Mangaki,Skywalker 6
5Sep86-5Dmr 1⅛Ⓣ:4631:1111:50 fm 15 117 611 65½ 2hd 31 PedrozaMA10 Aw23000 83-16 GoodThoughtWilly,Nurly,Eliminnt 12
27Jly86-5Dmr 1$\frac{1}{16}$Ⓣ:4641:11 1:423fm 19 117 84 72¾ 65 32¼ Pedroza MA9 Aw20000 91-04 Travet, Sly Remark, Eliminante 12
Apr 5 SA 4f ft :493 h Mar 23 SA 5f ft 1:001 h Mar 17 SA 4f ft :491 h

F.

Fabulous Sound
BAZE G **116**
Own.—Silver Star Stable
Ch. c. 4, by Messenger of Song—La Vie, by Le Fabuleux
Br.—Carver Stable (Cal)
Tr.—Bunn Thomas M Jr
Lifetime 12 2 4 2 $43,650
1987 2 0 1 1 $11,550
1986 10 2 3 1 $32,100
Turf 7 1 3 1 $31,800

11Apr87-5SA a6½f Ⓣ:213 :4421:143fm *2 117 41½ 41 31½ 31¾ Pincay L Jr 6 Aw33000 84-18 DnceDirector,Mrgm,FbulousSound 10
29Mar87-5SA a6½f Ⓣ:213 :44 1:151fm 38 116 41 31 41¼ 21½ Cordero AJr 4 Aw33000 81-19 Danczone,FbulousSound,SlneCstle 12
30Oct86-5SA a6½f Ⓣ:214 :4441:151fm 6¾ 116 42 32½ 42½ 54½ Hawley S 5 Aw28000 78-17 Arcadius, Sans Rival, Will Spring 10
30Oct86—Steadied 1/8
18Oct86-8BM 1$\frac{1}{16}$Ⓣ:4721:1221:441fm 37 114 42 42 67 77¼ ♦Hansen R D 6 Ascot H 75-16 FullChrm,PrinceBobbyB.,Spllbound 9
♦18Oct86—Dead heat; Ducked out start
5Sep86-8Dmr 1$\frac{1}{16}$:454 1:102 1:414ft 32 116 21 86 914 — DlhossyE 4 [R]El Cajon — — Tasso, Southern Halo, Bright Tom 9
5Sep86—Eased; Broke slowly
21Aug86-7Dmr 1 Ⓣ:4521:1011:353fm*9-5 117 21 21 11½ 11¼ Pincay L Jr 6 Aw21000 94-06 FbulousSound,TimForSkrto,HotMtl 6
21Aug86—Broke in air
9Aug86-5Dmr 1 Ⓣ:4621:11 1:36 fm 3¾ 116 11 1½ 12 2½ McCrronCJ 10 Aw20000 91-04 BrghtTom,FbulousSond,CtByGlss 10
9Aug86—Veered out start
24Jly86-5Dmr 1 Ⓣ:47 1:1131:361fm 3½ 116 1½ 2hd 2hd 2nk McCarronCJ 5 Aw20000 91-10 KmrdgRod,FbulousSond,Rvl'sBolro 8
24Jly86—Lugged out early
3Jly86-3Hol 1 :45 1:103 1:36 ft *3-5 115 14 13 15 16 McCarron C J 8 M50000 83-16 Fabulous Sound,Palomo,Aeroflame 9
3Jly86—Ducked out leaving chute; lugged out backstretch
22Jun86-2Hol 6f :221 :46 1:103ft 12 115 31½ 31½ 31½ 2no McCarron C J 1 M50000 91-08 HighestScript,FbulousSound,BluIc 10
Mar 22 Hol 7f sy 1:30 h Mar 11 Hol 6f ft 1:153 h Mar 5 Hol 5f ft 1:02 h Feb 27 Hol 5f ft 1:04 h

G.

Allez Allez
SIBILLE R **116**
Own.—Keith H
B. h. 5, by Alleged—Emerald Green, by Sir Ivor
Br.—Eclipse Investments (Ky)
Tr.—Harlow Robert E
Lifetime 19 1 1 0 $18,915
1986 10 0 1 0 $9,700
1985 8 1 0 0 $9,215
Turf 14 1 0 0 $13,565

4Oct86-5SA 1$\frac{1}{16}$:461 1:104 1:423ft 10 1135 54½ 43 79 817½ Black C A 4 Aw27000 70-18 Shahaab,Mr.Media,ThalassinoAsteri 9
13Sep86-10Pom 1$\frac{1}{16}$:451 1:103 1:44 ft 2½ 1135 2½ 21 43½ 510 Black C A 2 Aw27000 81-10 Bugrin,LordAllison,NorthrnProvidr 9
7Sep86-7Dmr 1$\frac{1}{16}$:452 1:094 1:411ft 40 113 76¾ 66 46½ 610¼ OrtgLE 8 [R]Wndy Snds 84-13 Varick, Epidaurus, Coastliner 8
20Aug86-8Dmr 1⅛:454 1:094 1:462ft 71 109 43½ 42 45 710½ Black C A 2 Cabrillo H 87-11 HopefulWord,Epidaurus,Attention 10
20Aug86—Rough start
2Aug86-7Dmr 1 :444 1:101 1:354ft 20 118 76¾ 12½ 11½ 2½ Patterson A 2 Aw20000 88-12 Genuine John, Allez Allez, Sirtaki 8
2Aug86—Lost whip at 1/16
15Jun86-5Hol 1$\frac{1}{16}$Ⓣ:4711:11 1:411fm 14 116 3½ 41¼ 84¼ 76½ Patterson A 2 Aw21000 91 — Shanaar, Well Related, Atreak 12
15Jun86—Bumped start
10May86-7Hol 1⅛Ⓣ:4631:1111:473fm 15 116 78½ 31 107 1111 Stevens GL 12 Aw22800 83-08 Dan Thatch, Will Spring, T. V. Oil 12
20Apr86-5SA a6½f Ⓣ:21 :44 1:151fm 5½ 117 41½ 43½ 1119 — McCarronCJ 2 Aw24000 — — LincolnPark,Stemilion,WsslDncer 11
20Apr86—Eased
9Feb86-5SA 1¼Ⓣ:4731:37 2:022fm 8¼ 116 11½ 1½ 2hd 44 DelhoussyeE 3 Aw32000 71-25 Catane, Lord Grundy,PrimeAssett 10
9Feb86—Lugged in badly through stretch
19Jan86-5SA 1⅛Ⓣ:4641:1131:493fm 8½ 117 52½ 104¾ 55 43½ Pincay L Jr 1 Aw26000 75-18 Nasib, Royal Recourse, Caro'sLad 10
19Jan86—Rank early, steadied intervals backstretch; wide into stretch
Apr 17 SA 5f ft 1:033 h Apr 9 SA 7f ft 1:272 h Apr 3 SA 6f ft 1:141 h Mar 29 SA 6f ft 1:152 h

H.

Roman Magestraite — B. c. 4, by Run the Gantlet—Worrisome Thing, by Cyane
TORO F 3-0 — 116
Br.—Rathbun Mr-Mrs H T (Ky) — 1987 4 0 1 2 $16,975
Tr.—Frankel Robert — 1986 9 2 0 1 $47,125
Own.—Raymond W C — Lifetime 16 2 2 3 $67,850 — Turf 8 1 0 3 $41,575

11Apr87-5SA a6½f Ⓣ:213 :4421:143fm 3½ 116 86¾ 83¼ 65 53¾ Ortega L E7 Aw33000 82-18 DnceDirector,Mrgm.,FbulousSound 10
11Apr87—Wide into, through stretch
21Feb87-7SA 1⅛Ⓣ:4731:1141:481fm 5¾ 116 52¼ 52¾ 52¼ 31 DelhoussyeE6 Aw33000 85-17 NorthrnProvidr,Rosdl,RomnMgstrit 9
8Feb87-7SA 1 1/16:454 1:101 1:431ft 3¾ 114 54½ 53 52½ 23½ Stevens G L8 Aw32000 81-14 GrchWondr,RmnMgstrt,Wtch'nWn 8
1Feb87-7SA 1⅛Ⓣ:4611:1021:481fm 4¾ 115 52½ 21½ 2hd 31¾ Stevens G L8 Aw32000 84-16 DnThtch,PlumCertin,RomnMgstrit 10
27Dec86-5SA 1⅛Ⓣ:4621:1211:492fm 5 114 44½ 2½ 3½ 65½ Stevens G L9 Aw31000 74-20 MisterWonderfulII,Jota,DanThtch 12
12Dec86-8Hol 6f :223 :454 1:101ft 9½ 114 42½ 43 46½ 56½ Solis A6 Aw25000 85-20 Paisano Pete, Danczone, HighHook 6
7Jun86-8Hol 1⅛Ⓣ:4741:1141:47 fm 9¾ 114 54 53½ 74¼ 76½ Soto SB5 Cinema H 90-02 Manila, Vernon Castle,FullOfStars 10
7Jun86—Grade II
11May86-7Hol 1 1/16Ⓣ:4621:1021:414fm 5¾ 116 75¼ 92½ 41¼ 32½ Delahoussaye E2 Sptlt 92-06 Mazzad,Autobot,RomanMgestrite 12
11May86—Checked stretch

3. One horse fits the eligibility conditions perfectly. Which is it?

4th Fairmount

1 1/16 MILES. (1.42⅕) CLAIMING. Purse $3,200. 3-year-olds and upward, registered bred and/or foaled in Illinois, which have not won two races at one mile or over in 1986–87. Weight, 3-year-olds, 113 lbs.; older, 122 lbs. Non-winners of a race at one mile or over since June 15 allowed 3 lbs.; one such race since May 15, 6 lbs. Claiming price $3,000.

A. **(64)**

Victory Woods — Dk. b. or br. g. 5, by Ironwood—Ouija Trick, by Ouija Board
Br.—Sanders Marvin (Ill) — 1987 5 2 0 1 $3,760
Own.—Porter Robert — 119 — Tr.—Hammond Kim — $3,000 — 1986 12 1 2 2 $4,442
Lifetime 33 5 4 6 $19,459

13Jly87-2FP 1 1/16:48 1:141 1:461ft *2¼ 116 22 12 15 15¾ Patin K C 1 Ⓢ 3000 80-25 Victory Woods, Deke, Doc's Fun 8
3Jly87-8FP 6f :222 :454 1:12 ft 8½ 122 87½ 911 98¾ 86 Martinez N C 3 4000 77-21 AstroBreker,BlueProspct,StrokLvl 10
20Jun87-2FP 170:48 1:132 1:441ft 7 116 51¾ 43 32½ 32¼ Rettele J O 2 3000 78-20 Pat'sCt,TeddyBerry,VictoryWoods 10
6Jun87-2FP 6f :23 :471 1:134ft 4 116 85¾ 65 51¾ 11 ♦Guidry M 6 Ⓢ 3000 74-22 VictoryWoods,NoJst,SouthrnMud 10
♦6Jun87—Dead heat
23May87-8FP 6f :223 :461 1:123ft 18 116 97½ 97¾ 78 54 Gall D 8 5000 76-26 PgnJubilee,Jck'sBrndy,ShoutWHey 9
5Nov86-7FP 6f :224 :472 1:143sy *8-5 116 98¾ 88¾ 45½ 3¾ Gall D 5 2500 69-31 GntlSun,WddingCk,VictoryWoods 10
18Oct86-6FP 6f :231 :47 1:13 ft 4 119 95 87 58 25 Brinkley J A 9 2500 73-27 ThreeKisss,VictoryWoods,GntlSun 10
9Oct86-7FP 6f :231 :471 1:133ft 10 119 64¼ 43 412 21¾ Brinkley J A 5 2500 73-31 Mag'sLast,VictoryWoods,Galaking 10
Jun 19 FP 3f ft :37 b

B.

Dalee Delight — B. g. 4, by Island Sultan—Miss North Fork, by Encono
Br.—Virant John & Mary (Ill) — 1987 6 1 1 0 $2,928
Own.—Virant John — 119 — Tr.—Porter Brent — $3,000 — 1986 6 1 1 0 $5,706
Lifetime 12 2 2 0 $8,634

13Jly87-2FP 1 1/16:48 1:141 1:461ft 5½ 119 42¼ 57 616 720¼ Swatman W 4 Ⓢ 3000 60-25 Victory Woods, Deke, Doc's Fun 8
1Jun87-4FP 1 1/16:482 1:134 1:492ft 6 116 2hd 21 1hd 12½ Macias G 2 Ⓢ 5000 64-24 DlDlight,Mr.T.'sbchBum,ThFinlPg 10
6May87-10FP 6f :23 :464 1:131ft 10 116 42 43 44½ 26 Macias G 3 Ⓢ 4000 71-26 Bob'sLeder,DleeDelight,TheFinlPg 10
6Apr87-10FP 6f :223 :47 1:132ft 7½ 117 84¾ 54¾ 55½ 64½ Gammon B 2 Ⓢ 4000 71-21 HoneyOfAFlyer,Boone'sDrm,Znsu 10
28Mar87-6FP 5½f:223 :471 1:06 ft 2¾ 116 3nk 4nk 2hd 65 Gammon B 2 Ⓢ 4000 82-11 Subverse, Tambo Day,RowdyPride 10
13Mar87-10FP 5f :213 :46 :59 ft 5¾ 116 55½ 69¼ 710 77½ Bowlds M A 8 5000 84-11 Symascus, Trade Deficit, KitKerri 10
12Dec86-3Bml 6f :243 :491 1:144ft 2¼ 119 1hd 11 16 115 Ebanks R C7 ⓈM5000 85-18 DleeDelight,CountryBoyBlue,Clibt 10
7Nov86-1Bml 6f :243 :491 1:173ft *6-5 117 77¾ 68 69½ 48¼ Ebanks R C5 ⓈM5000 63-22 StormRunnr,MjorBt,NorthrnIllnos 10
7Nov86—Squeezed back start
Jun 27 FP 5f ft 1:043 b

C.

Exclusive Triple

Own.—Akins Robert **116**

Ch. g. 5, by Exclusive Call—Petite Mary, by Idaho Kid
Br.—Corwin Joel W (Ill) 1987 9 0 1 1 $1,110
Tr.—Essenpreis Edward **$3,000** 1986 20 6 3 0 $14,933
Lifetime 47 9 9 2 $25,677

16Jly87-5EIP	1	:472	1:13	1:401ft	34	121	34½	32½	42½	21	Cahanin K P8		2500	73-15	Dnrt'sDrm,ExclusivTrpl,FntstcGuy	14
29Jun87-4FP	1⅛	:483	1:133	1:524ft	14	122	51¾	5¾	56	78½	Martinez N C10		3000	72-21	Deke,Supportivenss,Qun'sRoylBoy	10
25Jun87-2FP	6f	:23	:471	1:131ft	13	122	73	75	76	78¼	Breaux C H7		3000	64-23	ShoutWHey,Iwnbngnt,TwilightCrr	10
29May87-4FP	1 1/16	:482	1:14	1:48 ft	4¾	116	33	23	23	37½	Rettele J O2	S	3000	63-27	AmbtosOph,D.C.'sBomr,ExclsvTrpl	10
14May87-4FP	6f	:231	:471	1:131ft	13	116	107	107½	54¾	52	Gale M A10		3000	75-23	JohnLrk,ThRghtExt,HstorcJourny	10
24Apr87-2FP	6f	:231	:464	1:123ft	15	122	105¾	87¼	86¼	66¼	Gale M A9	S	3000	74-23	Southern Mud, Poka Dandy, Kal	10
6Apr87-3FP	6f	:23	:464	1:124ft	14	122	104¾	108½	98¼	99¼	Medina N R8		3000	70-21	ContryBoyJff,Exbron,Qn'sRoylBy	10
22Mar87-10FP	5½f	:223	:473	1:081sy	11	116	710	1014	1013	1012½	Jones R V5		3000	63-19	KthysBeu,TeSucer,HoistTheMony	10

22Mar87—Drifted in upper stretch
Jun 24 FP 4f ft :492 b

D.

R. Fleet Prince

Own.—Baird & Adams **116**

B. g. 6, by Prince Astro—R Lov A Bal Tomata, by Ballydonnell
Br.—Hellman Clara J (Ill) 1987 11 1 1 4 $4,774
Tr.—Baird John W **$3,000** 1986 13 3 1 1 $7,204
Lifetime 62 10 10 6 $63,741 Turf 2 0 0 0

15Jly87-4FP	6f	:222	:462	1:123ft	4	116	31	2hd	1½	2no	Macias G 8	3000	80-24	BobYounger,R.FletPrinc,ChillyMc	10
3Jly87-3FP	6f	:224	:461	1:12 ft	5¾	116	2hd	3½	21	32¼	Macias G 8	3000	81-21	Tunedup,SecretProof,R.FleetPrinc	10
10Jun87-6FP	6f	:224	:462	1:122ft	*9-5	119	33½	34	44½	56	Rettele J O 8	3000	75-23	NoProblemPles,HyMr.Cool,WslyH.	10
25May87-3FP	6f	:224	:462	1:122ft	9¼	116	51¼	64¾	57	710¼	Gall D 6	5000	71-22	Retrieved, Intoxicator, Patrick Joe	9
9May87-4FP	6f	:223	:462	1:13 ft	8¾	119	42¼	42½	31	31¼	Rettele J O 5	4000	77-23	SizzleFritz,MyleShoe,R.FleetPrince	8
29Apr87-7FP	6f	:223	:462	1:13 ft	5	116	33	34	33	1no	Rettele J O 6	4000	78-24	R.FleetPrince,ChddisMission,Girrd	10
18Apr87-10FP	6f	:22	:452	1:122ft	5¾	116	55	43½	34	31	Gall D 7	4000	80-19	CtchItBuck,LosMusicos,R.FltPrnc	10
9Apr87-10FP	6f	:221	:454	1:122ft	4½	116	53¼	54½	33½	44½	Gall D 6	4000	76-19	Icynoo, Mr.T.Tamale,CatchItBuck	10

Jun 30 FP 4f m :512 b

E.

Dramatic Action

Own.—Fluegel Fred **122**

Ch. g. 5, by That's a Nice—Dramatically, by Timeless Moment
Br.—Sitzberger Frank (Ill) 1987 6 1 1 1 $1,327
Tr.—Gilbert Harold **$3,000** 1986 13 0 0 1 $950
Lifetime 29 2 3 2 $5,991

Entered 27Jly87- 4 FP

18Jly87-11Ato	170	:484	1:15	1:48 gd	4½	115	812	77½	34	11½	Schaber D D 5	2500	71-27	DrmticAction,LosingBttl.ElctricStr	8
4Jly87-11Ato	170	:474	1:141	1:461ft	9¾	120	76½	77	54½	23	Schaber D D 1	2500	77-16	WesternHope,DrmticAction,SotFire	7
27Jun87-6Ato	170	:48	1:131	1:452ft	22	120	24	33½	35¼	58½	Schaber D D 6	2500	75-16	Chrlmyboy,BbblngBrw,CntrlldGnt	10
20Jun87-11Ato	1 1/16	:49	1:16	1:503gd	74	121	43½	44½	61¾	31½	Knowles J J 2	2500	63-26	B.J.Spa,PcingShdow,DrmticAction	10
13Jun87-11Ato	170	:481	1:142	1:473ft	22	120	63¾	53	72¼	87	Fisher W R8	2500	66-19	LittleRedElf,ShrpSteppr,T.J.'sAfric	9
6Jun87-8Ato	6f	:24	:473	1:143ft	82	122	87½	815	911	87¼	Fisher W R 7	2500	77-23	LuckyR.J.,SirTuffenuff,ChteuWine	10
6Nov86-3FP	6f	:224	:471	1:144m	19	116	1015	1025	1023	1025¼	Sellers S J10	2500	44-32	MissileThrt,CpturdPhrs,BilliCrroll	10
4Oct86-2FP	1 1/16	:483	1:141	1:463m	48	122	96¾	86¼	911	920¼	Vinson J L5	2500	58-17	Radyla, Whipping Boss, Raboone	10

Jun 2 Ato 3f ft :391 b

4. Which horse is best on class?

A. **(64)**

Winter Treasure

PINCAY L JR
Own.—Grossman J M **117**

Ch. f. 4, by Vigors—Minstrel Miss, by Poona II
Br.—Grossman J M (Ky) 1986 12 5 4 0 $137,325
Tr.—Mandella Richard 1985 1 M 0 0
Lifetime 13 5 4 0 $137,325 Turf 1 0 0 0

13Dec86-4Hol	6f	:214	:451	1:101ft	*4-5	121	65¼	63¼	34	21½	Pincay L Jr6	ⒻHcp0	90-09	StridingEsy,WintrTrsur,BoldNSpcil	6
13Dec86—Wide backstretch, through stretch															
31Oct86-8SA	1 1/16	:463	1:112	1:431ft	3¼	118	2½	2hd	21	21¼	VIIPA6	ⒻLnda Vst H	84-16	Mrinn'sGirl,WinterTresur,FinKudos	9
31Oct86—Grade III															
22Oct86-8SA	6½f	:221	:452	1:161ft	3½	117	1hd	11½	12½	1¾	VIIPA3	ⒻCascapdia H	89-23	WinterTresure,HerRoylty,FmilyStyl	5
22Oct86—Lugged out early															
6Sep86-7Dmr	6½f	:22	:45	1:153ft	4¾	117	55½	43	31½	2¾	Pincay LJr2	ⒻAw40000	93-12	HerRoylty,WinterTresure,WildKitty	6
6Sep86—Veered in start															
4Jun86-8Hol	7f	:22	:444	1:222ft	3¼	119	67	67	38	49¼	PincyLJr3	ⒻRailbird	83-18	Melair, Comparability, SilentArrival	7
4Jun86—Grade III; Veered out start															
21May86-8Hol	6f	:222	:454	1:104ft	3¾	117	63¾	51½	11½	15½	PncyLJr4	ⒻDrma Crtc	90-13	WintrTrsur,T.V.Rsidul,ChickOrTwo	9
18Apr86-7SA	6½f	:221	:454	1:171ft	*4-5	120	32½	2hd	11½	1½	Pincay LJr5	ⒻAw28000	84-21	WintrTrsur,MissBnson,ViolinMlody	5
18Apr86—Bumped start															

21Mar86-5SA a6½f Ⓣ:21^3 :44 1:16 fm *2¼ 117 6^{4½} 6^{3½} 6^5 7^{7¼} PcLJr^1 ⒻⓇSwt Diane 72-21 Nature'sWy,TopCorsge,SilentArrivl 9
21Mar86—Checked, altered path early stretch
1Mar86-8SA 1 :46 1:10^2 1:36^{1}ft 3 117 2^{1½} 3^2 4^2 4^{2½} PncLJr^4 ⒻLs Vrgnes 84-16 LifAtThTop,TwilightRdg,AnEmprss 7
1Mar86—Grade III
15Feb86-7SA 6f :21^4 :45^2 1:10^{1}ft *9-5 120 2^{2½} 2½ 1^{3½} 1^{10} McCrrnCJ^7 ⒻAw26000 87-14 WinterTresure,Blcktop,Shezlottldy 7
Dec 27 SA 3f ft :35^3 h Dec 9 Hol 5f ft 1:00 h Dec 4 Hol 6f ft 1:16^2 h Nov 17 Hol 4f ft :50^1 h

B.

Life At The Top
ROMERO R P **124**
Own.—Klein & French Jr

B. f. 4, by Seattle Slew—See You At the Top, by Riva Ridge
Br.—Eaton Farms Inc et al (Ky) 1986 18 6 5 4 $821,349
Tr.—Lukas D Wayne 1985 3 1 1 1 $21,950
Lifetime 21 7 6 5 $843,299 Turf 1 0 0 0

29Nov86-9Med 1⅛:47^3 1:11^3 1:51 ft *6-5 120 1^2 1^{1½} 1^{2½} 1^{hd} RrRP^1 ⒻLong Look H 78-23 LifeAtThTop,SqunSong,CoupDFusil 6
29Nov86—Grade II
16Nov86-8Aqu 1¼:49 1:38^1 2:03^{4}ft 3¼ 118 1^6 1^{1½} 1^{1½} 1^1 RmrRP^1 ⒻLadies H 77-23 LifeAtTheTop,CoupDFusil,StlAKiss 8
16Nov86—Grade I
1Nov86-9SA 1 Ⓣ:46^{3}1:10^{4}1:36^{3}fm 3¼ 120 1½ 7^{2¾}11^{13}11^{12} Day P^4 ⒻMidwick H 82-07 Aberuschka, Duckweed, Sclva 12
1Nov86—Wide 3/8, into stretch
11Oct86-7Kee 1⅛:46 1:10^4 1:48^{1}ft *2½ 119 2^1 2½ 2^1 3^{1½} McCrrCJ^7 ⒻSpinster 94-12 Top Corsage, Endear,LifeAtTheTop 8
11Oct86—Grade I
4Oct86-6Bel 1 :47^2 1:11^1 1:34^{2}ft 2 118 1^{1½} 1^{2½} 1^5 1^4 McCrrCJ^2 ⒻRrePrfme 93-14 Life At The Top, Lotka, Funistrada 6
4Oct86—Grade III
13Sep86-8Pha 1$\frac{1}{16}$:46^3 1:11^1 1:42^{4}ft 7-5 121 2^1 2½ 2^{1½} 2^1 Day P^7 ⒻCotillion H 89-20 ToesKnows,LifeAtTheTop,I'mSwts 8
13Sep86—Grade III
27Aug86-8Bel 1⅛:46^2 1:10^1 1:48^{2}ft 6-5 118 1^{1½} 2^{hd} 1^{hd} 2^{¾} CrdrAJr^4 ⒻGazelle H 84-16 ClssyCthy,LifeAtTheTop,DynmicStr 4
27Aug86—Grade I
9Aug86-8Sar 1¼:47^1 1:37 2:04^{1}ft 3¾ 121 1^5 1^3 1^1 3^{3¼} CrdrAJr^7 ⒻAlabama 76-17 ClssyCthy,VlleyVictory,LifAtThTop 7
9Aug86—Grade I
19Jly86-9Mth 1⅛:46^1 1:10^4 1:49^{3}ft *6-5 121 3^{4½} 3^3 3^{nk} 4^{2¼} SntsJA^2 ⒻMth Oaks 84-13 FighterFox,ToesKnows,DynmicStr 12
19Jly86—Grade I
6Jly86-8Bel 1½:48^1 2:02^4 2:28 ft *8-5 121 1^{1½} 2^{hd} 2^5 2^{11} StsJA^6 ⒻC C A Oaks 69-16 Valley Victory,LifeAtTheTop,Lotka 8
6Jly86—Grade I
Dec 30 SA 4f ft :50^3 b Dec 23 Hol 4f ft :49^1 h

C.

Sari's Heroine
VALENZUELA P A **119**
Own.—Grinstead & Rochelle

Dk. b. or br. f. 4, by Our Hero—Sari's Dream Girl, by Any Time Now
Br.—Murty Fm & Blue DiamndRch (Ky) 1986 12 4 5 0 $204,100
Tr.—Stute Melvin F 1985 9 2 4 0 $97,809
Lifetime 21 6 9 0 $301,909 Turf 2 0 2 0 $27,000

14Dec86-8BM 6f :22^2 :44^3 1:08^{4}ft *6-5 117 2^2 3^2 3^{1½} 2½ CstAL^1 ⒻChlds Hsp H 94-17 Luisant, Sari's Heroine, Witchery 8
8Nov86-8Hol 6f Ⓣ:22 :44^{4}1:09^{1}fm 7¾ 115 3^1 3^{1½} 2½ 2^{1½} VlnlPA^5 ⒻBlu Dlght H 92-11 RngoonRuby,Sri'sHeroine,TxDodge 6
8Nov86—Bumped break; steadied 4 1/2
19Oct86-8BM 6f :21^4 :44^1 1:08^{4}ft 9½ 115 2^2 2^2 2^3 2^4 LmnceC^8 ⒻC H Rsl H 91-17 TkMyPictur,Sri'sHroin,Comprbility 9
27Jun86-8Cby 6½f :22^3 :45^3 1:17^{4}ft *2½ 112 2^{hd} 3^3 9^{14}10^{22½} SolisA^1 ⒻMity Miss H 69-21 MmrsOfD,HstHrFlg,Spnky'sScnds 11
4Jun86-8Hol 7f :22 :44^4 1:22^{2}ft 7½ 122 4^3 4^{4½} 6^{13} 6^{17¼} Solis A^2 ⒻRailbird 75-18 Melair, Comparability, SilentArrival 7
4Jun86—Grade III
27Apr86-8Aqu 6f :22^1 :45^3 1:11 ft *3-2 118 4^{4½} 5^7 6^{5¼} 6^{8¼} Solis A^4 ⒻPrioress 78-20 Rligiosity,FightrFox,TromphDNskr 8
27Apr86—Grade III
4Apr86-8GG 1 :47^2 1:12^2 1:39 ft *2-3 117 1^{2½} 1^2 1^2 1^{2½} Solis A^3 ⒻSorority 73-27 Sr'sHron,ShotgnWddng,Chnng'sAlb 7
5Mar86-8SA a6½f Ⓣ:21^1 :44 1:14^{4}fm 4½ 120 1^1 1^1 1^{2½} 2^{1¾} Solis A^3 ⒻLa Habra 83-15 HiddenLight,Sri'sHeroin,TopCorsg 12
22Feb86-8GG 6f :22^1 :44^4 1:10^{3}gd *1-3 122 2^{hd} 2^{hd} 2^{hd} 2^{1½} Mena F^2 ⒻVallejo 84-13 RightCutious,Sri'sHeroin,ApplRoyl 8
22Feb86—Broke in, bumped
5Feb86-8SA 7f :22^2 :45^1 1:23^{2}ft 2¾ 119 1^{hd} 1^{1½} 1^{1½} 1no Solis A^6 ⒻSta Ynez 83-19 Sri'sHeroine,AnEmprss,LifAtThTop 8
5Feb86—Grade III
●Dec 24 SA 5f ft :58^3 h Dec 11 Hol 4f ft :48^1 h ●Nov 28 Hol 6f ft 1:13 h Nov 22 Hol 4f ft :47^3 h

D.

Top Corsage
SHOEMAKER W **122**
Own.—Dandar Farm

Dk. b. or br. f. 4, by Topsider—Corsage, by Native Royalty
Br.—Elmendorf Farm (Ky) 1986 18 7 4 4 $561,155
Tr.—Fanning Jerry 1985 6 1 0 3 $35,492
Lifetime 24 8 4 7 $596,647 Turf 12 3 4 3 $255,345

23Nov86-8Hol 1⅛Ⓣ:47^{3}1:11^{3}1:48 fm 4¼ 120 2^2 2^{1½} 3^{1½} 6^{5¾} PncLJr^3 ⒻMtrarch Iv 82-13 Auspiciante, Aberuschka, Reloy 12
23Nov86—Grade I; Rank, steadied 7 1/2
2Nov86-8SA 1¼Ⓣ:46^{3}1:35^{4}2:01^{2}fm *3½ 118 1^{1½} 1^{1½} 1½ 2½ StsGL^6 ⒻYlw Rbn Iv 79-20 Bonne Ile, Top Corsage, Carotene 12
2Nov86—Grade I
25Oct86-7Kee 1$\frac{1}{16}$Ⓣ:49 1:16 1:50 yl *7-5 121 3^{2½} 2½ 1^{hd} 3^4 StnsGL^8 ⒻQun Eliz 76-21 Lotka, Minstress, Top Corsage 9
25Oct86—Grade III
11Oct86-7Kee 1⅛:46 1:10^4 1:48^{1}ft 9¾ 119 1^1 1½ 1^1 1^{¾} HwleyS^4 ⒻSpinster 96-12 Top Corsage, Endear,LifeAtTheTop 8
11Oct86—Grade I

21Sep86-10LaD 1⅛ :48 1:12³ 1:50⁴ft *2-5 120 1¹ 1¹½ 1¹½ 1³ StvnsGL⁵ Ⓕ La D Oaks 91-23 TopCorsg,HppyHllwMss,SclBsnss 11
28Aug86-6AP 1⅛ :46¹ 1:10³ 1:49²ft 4 120 1¹½ 1² 1⁵ 1⁹½ StnsGL⁷ Ⓕ Arl Oaks 84-19 TopCorsage,LadyGallant,PnelPul 10
28Aug86—Grade III
20Aug86-6AP 1¹⁄₁₆ Ⓣ:47 1:12²1:44¹fm*4-5 120 3³ 2hd 2hd 1¹¾ HwlyS³ Ⓕ Pucker Up 86-11 TopCorsage,Mrinn'sGirl,Innsbruck 10
20Aug86—Grade III
3Aug86-8Dmr 1 Ⓣ:46 1:11 1:35¹fm 4 115 7³½ 8²½ 3¹½ 4³½ Toro F⁸ La Jla Mi H 92-08 VrnonCstl,TrpolShors,Mrvn'sPlcy 12
3Aug86—Grade III; Fanned 5 wide into stretch
11Jly86-8Hol 1¹⁄₁₆ Ⓣ:45⁴1:10¹1:40⁴fm 2 115 4² 3½ 1²½ 1³½ Toro F⁵ Ⓕ Aw27000 100 — TopCorsg,AffctonAffrmd,PrncssCrl 5
28Jun86-9Cby 1¹⁄₁₆ Ⓣ:46²1:10³1:42²fm *2½ 117 1¹½ 1¹ 1¹½ 3¹½ Black K⁷ Ⓕ Cby Oaks — — PuzzleBook,DustyFare,TopCorsge 12
Dec 30 SA 6f ft 1:14² h Dec 24 SA 4f ft :48³ h Nov 19 SA 6f gd 1:16² h ●Nov 11 SA 3f ft :35 h

E.

Spirit Of Fighter
VELEZ J A JR **117**
Own.—Hurtak & Punches
Dk. b. or br. f. 4, by Gallant Knave—Some One Finer, by Lord Rebeau
Br.—Devries E R (Fla) 1986 10 8 2 0 $206,917
Tr.—Hurtak Daniel 1985 4 3 0 0 $25,250
Lifetime 14 11 2 0 $232,167 Turf 1 0 0 0 $150

13Dec86-9Crc 7f :23¹ :47 1:25²ft *2-3 128 1½ 1¹½ 1hd 1no VlJAJr² Ⓕ PembrkLkH 89-22 Spirit of Fighter, Jose'sBomb,Truly 5
23Nov86-9Crc 6f :22¹ :45³ 1:11⁴ft *1-3 126 1¹ 1¹½ 1½ 1¹¼ FiresE¹ Ⓕ Miss Trop H 92-18 SpiritofFightr,Jos'sBomb,FlurDSoll 6
8Nov86-9Crc 7f :22³ :46 1:24⁴ft *4-5 124 1hd 1hd 1² 1³½ VlJAJr² Ⓕ Lago Mar H 92-16 SpiritofFighter,ThirtyZip,FlurDSolil 6
26Oct86-9Crc 6f :22² :46 1:11³ft *2-3 122 1hd 1hd 1² 1⁴ VlJAJr⁶ Ⓕ Miss DadeH 93-16 SpiritofFightr,FlurDSolil,L'f'sLight 7
15Oct86-9Crc 6f :22 :45³ 1:12¹sy *4-5 120 2½ 2hd 1½ 1¹ VlJAJr⁶ Ⓕ JacarandaH 90-24 SprtofFghtr,FrstPrdcton,GlorsGlry 6
27Sep86-9Crc 7f :22³ :45⁴ 1:24⁴ft *6-5 117 1½ 1¹½ 1² 1½ EspJC² Ⓕ Brns RetrnH 92-15 SpiritofFighter,ThirtyZip,Lif'sLight 7
17Sep86-9Crc 7f :22³ :45⁴ 1:24²ft *4-5 117 5²½ 4⁴ 2¹½ 1½ LestrRN⁶ Ⓕ Beverly H 94-18 SpiritofFightr,KlondikKut,GntlScrn 9
10Sep86-7Crc 6½f :22 :45 1:18³ft *1 113 1½ 1¹ 1⁴ 1³ EspinozJC¹ Ⓕ Aw18300 92-16 SpiritofFighter,DelicteLdy,KingMio 7
31Aug86-5Crc 7f :22³ :45⁴ 1:24¹ft *1 112 1¹ 1¹ 2½ 2¹ Lester R N⁶ Ⓕ Aw18800 94-12 ThirtyZip,SpiritofFighter,DelictLdy 6
20Jan86-9GP 6f :22¹ :45³ 1:11 ft 6¾ 114 5²¾ 2¹½ 2⁴ 2⁵ Vergara O⁵ Ⓕ Old Hat 79-24 Noranc, Spirit of Fighter,Bespeak 15
Dec 28 Crc 4f sy :49 b

F.

Striding Easy
BAZE G **114**
Own.—Scharbauer Dorothy
B. f. 4, by Victory Stride—Lady Meda, by Sir Ribot
Br.—F Turner Jr Estate (Okla) 1986 6 3 1 0 $60,990
Tr.—Van Berg Jack C 1985 3 2 0 0 $8,454
Lifetime 9 5 1 0 $69,444

13Dec86-4Hol 6f :21⁴ :45¹ 1:10¹ft 9½ 113 2hd 1hd 1³½ 1¹½ Baze G¹ Ⓕ HcpO 92-09 StridingEsy,WintrTrsur,Bo'dNSpcil 6
28Nov86-3Hol 7f :22¹ :45¹ 1:23²ft *8-5 117 1hd 1hd 2½ 5²½ Pincay LJr³ Ⓕ Aw28000 84-14 Sign Off, Good Zar, Ambra Ridge 6
28Nov86—Veered out break
2Nov86-5SA 6f :21² :44¹ 1:10²ft 8½ 117 2² 3³ 3² 1¹¾ Day P³ Ⓕ Aw28000 86-10 StridingEsy,LoversNtive,FlyingJuli 9
8Oct86-6SA 6f :22 :45¹ 1:10¹ft *8-5 115 1¹ 2hd 2¹½ 4³¾ ShoemkrW¹ Ⓕ Aw28000 83-20 TomboyBls,Symbolclly,BlconyPss 10
8Oct86—Lugged out backstretch
12Sep86-11Pom 6½f :21⁴ :45 1:17 ft 5 117 1½ 1² 1² 1²¾ MenaF⁶ Ⓕ Ⓡ Las Ninas 95-11 StridingEasy,TropiclHolidy,FirlyOld 9
6Jly86-7Hol 6f :21³ :44⁴ 1:10 ft 5½ 114 1½ 1½ 1¹½ 2hd McCrrnCJ² Ⓕ Aw20000 94-09 DrmAboutYo,StrdngEsy,Bggr'sWllt 8
6Jly86—Lugged out backstretch
23Jun85-11Rui 4f :21³ :47¹sy *8-5 120 1 3nk 5²¾ 5⁴¾ NcdmsJ¹⁰ Norgor Fut 82-13 MyKndLm,J.R.Jhnsn,TrckAmbssdr 10
14Jun85-10Rui 4f :22 :46 ft 8-5 120 2 1¹½ 1² 1¹½ Nicodemus J³ Fut Trl 93-11 StridingEsy,J.R.Johnson,SyRitNow 9
31May85-2Rui 4f :21⁴ :45⁴ft 8 118 1 1¹½ 1² 1⁶½ Rodriguez JM⁵ Ⓕ Mdn 94-06 StrongEsy,BrrrMss,MssPcosConty 10
Nov 21 SA 5f ft 1:01 h Nov 12 SA 4f ft :47¹ h

5. Which horse deserves a plus for its current form?

2 BELMONT

INNER TURF COURSE
1¼ MILES
BELMONT PARK

1 ¼ MILES. (InnerTurf). (1.58⅘) CLAIMING. Purse $24,000. 4-year-olds and upward. Weight, 122 lbs. Non-winners of two races over a mile since July 1 allowed 3 lbs. Of such a race since then 5 lbs. Claiming price $50,000; for each $2,500 to $45,000 2 lbs. (Races when entered to be claimed for $40,000 or less not considered.)

A. **(64)**

Pillar Of Strength
Own.—Brooks R G Jr
B. c. 4, by Roberto—Little Red Robin, by Ribot
$50,000 Br.—Galbreath D M (Ky)
Tr.—DiSanto Glenn B
117
Lifetime 1987 5 1 0 0 $4,819
10 2 2 0 1986 5 1 2 0 $21,580
$26,399 Turf 4 1 1 0 $19,360

5Jly87- 7Rkmfm 1¹⁄₁₆ Ⓣ:48⅗ 1:14 1:48⅕ 3↑ Clm 20000 5 12 12¹⁴ 12¹³ 10⁹½ 9⁷ Shelton R L b 116 6.00 91-05 Solid Grip 115½ Tiger Lake 116no Oxford Star 116¾ Outrun 12
14Jun87- 9FL fst 1¹⁄₁₆ :48 1:12⅖ 1:44⅗ 3↑ Handicap 2 4 5⁷½ 4⁴½ 4⁷ 4⁹ Saul D b 108 6.90 84-12 Dot O' Spice 111² SpruceArrow116⁷CostlyContract114no No rally 5
7Jun87- 8FL sly 1 :47⅗ 1:12⅖ 1:39⅖ 3↑ Alw 7000 1 8 5⁵ 5⁴½ 4³ 5²¾ Saul D b 119 4.50 85-12 LordPenguin113¹ArmoredKnight105ndPoisonPnny116¹ No factor 8
12May87- 7FL fst 1¹⁄₁₆ :48⅕ 1:13⅘ 1:48⅗ 3↑ Alw 6600 4 6 6¹⁵ 6⁷ 5⁴ 1½ Saul D b 116 *2.10 73-25 Pillar Of Strength 116½ Proud Guy 111¹½ Ironfields 111¾ Driving 7
5May87- 9FL fst 6f :22⅘ :46⅖ 1:12 3↑ Alw 6500 2 6 5¹⁰ 6⁸ 5⁶ 5⁵½ Saul D b 116 15.50 84-16 One for Wiff 116½ Iron Empire 109¾ Gold Pace 112²½ No factor 8
24May86- 6Bel gd 1¼ Ⓣ:48⅗ 1:39⅗ 2:04⅘ 3↑ Md Sp Wt 10 8 8⁸½ 1½ 1hd 1nk Maple E b 113 *2.00 70-27 PillarOfStrength113nkTwiceCharming113²½RoylSmuri113⁴ Driving 12
18May86- 3Bel fm 1¼ Ⓣ:49⅕ 1:37⅗ 2:02⅘ 3↑ Md Sp Wt 1 10 9⁷¾ 4⁶ 2⁵ 2⁴¾ Maple E b 113 6.20 75-13 Silver Voice 113⁴¾ Pillar OfStrength113¾ZoningBoard124¹ Rallied 12
8Apr86-10Hia fm *1¹⁄₁₆ Ⓣ 1:44⅘ 3↑ Md Sp Wt 9 9 8¹² 6¹⁰ 6⁴ 4⁴ Cruguet J 112 *1.40 70-23 ⒹTwiceChrming112²TokenOfYouth112ndAshwniKumr113² Rallied 10
21Mar86- 8Hia sly 1⅛ :46⅕ 1:11⅘ 1:52⅕ Md Sp Wt 7 6 6¹⁵ 5⁶ 3⁴ 2² McCauley W H 119 *2.60 69-17 Cox's Best 119² Pillar Of Strength 119½ Dewar'sHall119¾ Gaining 8
29Jan86- 6GP fst 7f :22⅗ :46 1:25⅘ Md Sp Wt 4 12 12¹³ 10¹¹ 9¹⁴ 7¹³½ Bailey J D 122 4.70 61-26 Ravel's Bolero 122³½ Exuberback 117³ Clever Alibi 122¹ Outrun 12
LATEST WORKOUTS ●Jly 28 Sar tr.t 3f fst :36⅗ h Jly 16 Sar Ⓣ 4f fm :53 b (d)

B.

***Trooper Thornton** Gr. c. 4, by Thatching—Dinsero, by Sea Hawk II
Own.—Torsney J C $50,000 Br.—Torsney J (Ire) Tr.—Schulhofer Flint S 117
Lifetime 17 3 0 1 $32,365 | 1987 5 0 0 0 $2,290 | 1986 6 3 0 0 $29,565 | Turf 17 3 0 1 $32,365

13Jly87- 8Bel fm 1 1/16 Ⓣ:46⅘ 1:10⅗ 1:41⅗ 3+Handicap 5 7 55¼ 41¾ 79½ 817¼ Samyn J L 109 20.40 71-19 I Rejoice 110¾ Island Sun 115¾ Explosive Dancer1123½ Poor start 8
16Jun87- 6Mth fm 1 Ⓣ:47⅘ 1:11⅗ 1:36⅖ 3+Alw 25000 2 9 911 86 52¼ 52½ Cruguet J 115 13.60 90-08 MyBigBoy115nkArrivedOnTime1191½FullCourg119½ Off sluggishly 9
4Apr87- 6GP fm 1 1/16 Ⓣ:47⅖ 1:11⅖ 1:41⅖ Alw 19000 5 5 512 56 48½ 47 Cruguet J 117 12.60 86-10 MightyMemory1194½KingsRiverII1171½ArrivedOnTim1191 Outrun 5
13Mar87- 8GP gd *1 Ⓣ 1:40⅘ Alw 19000 4 8 77½ 43½ 47 711 Cruguet J 117 8.50 65-35 Trubulare 1171 New Colony 1222½ Infantry 117no Tired 11
17Feb87- 8Hia fm *1 1/16 Ⓣ 1:43 Alw 21000 7 8 63¼ 51¼ 74¼ 810¼ Cruguet J 116 17.30 73-17 Icy Groom 1161 Kings River II 1162 Trubulare1162¼ Lacked room 10
29Jly86♦4Galway(Ire) sf*1 1/16 1:58⅕ Ⓣ McDonogh Hcp 1214 Manning D 118 9.00 — — Alder Rose 124hd OutAndAbout1181 GrannysBank1251½ Bid, tired 13
20Jly86♦5Leopardst'n(Ire) gd 1⅛ 1:55⅗ Ⓣ GoldenPagesLeopardstownH 1¾ Manning D 109 7.00 — — Trooper Thornton109¾ Acclaimation1183 IrishFolly122½ Bid, drvg 20
11Jun86♦3PhoenixPk(Ire) gd 1⅛ 1:54⅗ Ⓣ June Hcp 11 Craine S 117 7.00 — — TrooperThornton1171 DromondHill1301 Dochs1391 Bid, led, held 19
14May86♦5PhoenixPk(Ire) sf 1 1:59⅕ Ⓣ Friends Of St Vincent Hcp 44 Nolan A J 105 4.00 — — Cariadsion 111½ Dochas 1272½ Stormy Run 1261 Bid, wknd 8
7May86♦1PhoenixPk(Ire) sf 1 1:52 Ⓣ HughesGibbAppr.Hcp 11 Nolan A J 106 *2.50 — — TrooperThornton1061 Touloum1131½ OutAndAbout1222 Bid, drvg 10
LATEST WORKOUTS Jly 5 Bel 4f fst :48 h Jun 30 Bel 4f fst :51⅘ b Jun 25 Bel Ⓣ 4f fm :49⅘ b (d) Jun 13 Bel 4f fst :49 b

C.

***Cornish Gem II** Dk. b. or br. h. 8, by Cornish Prince—Jeanie Duff, by Majestic Prince
Own.—Atrib J $45,000 Br.—Zandona Mrs C A (Eng) Tr.—Pascuma James J Jr 113
Lifetime 55 7 11 9 $155,094 | 1987 6 0 1 1 $11,040 | 1986 14 0 4 2 $39,880 | Turf 49 7 11 9 $153,774

15Jly87- 2Bel gd 1⅜ Ⓣ:49 1:39⅘ 2:19⅗ Clm 45000 3 4 46 55½ 54½ 45¾ Vasquez J 114 7.00 58-34 Cloutier 113nk Classic Move 1175½ I'm NoYankee117hd No threat 7
6Jun87- 5Bel fm 1¼ Ⓣ:47⅕ 1:37⅘ 2:03 Clm 45000 6 3 39½ 1½ 25 25¾ Samyn J L 113 6.20 73-24 Stage Setter1155¾CornishGemII113nkVatzaMatter117hd Game try 9
28May87- 5Bel fm 1 1/16 Ⓣ:46⅖ 1:10⅗ 1:42⅗ Clm 45000 10 7 105¾ 86¼ 64¾ 54 Lovato F Jr 113 10.10 79-16 ⒹPatchy Groundfog 117no City Council II 1171¼Onslow1132 Wide 10
28May87-Placed fourth through disqualification
15May87- 2Bel fm 1¼ Ⓣ:50⅕ 1:40⅕ 2:04 Clm 47500 1 5 64½ 53 54 35 Lovato F Jr 115 6.80 69-29 ClssicMove117noPrinceOfDestiny1175CornishGmII115no Steadied 9
1May87- 6Aqu gd 1⅛ Ⓣ:51⅗ 1:16⅖ 1:55⅖ Clm 50000 5 2 21½ 2½ 31 52 Lovato F Jr 117 9.50 56-41 Stage Setter 113nkClassicMove113nkBarbadianReef1131½ Used up 7
24Apr87- 2Aqu gd 1 1/16 Ⓣ:49⅕ 1:15⅖ 1:48 Clm 70000 4 5 55 88¾ 816 816¾ Lovato F Jr 114 26.10 48-35 AllHandsOnDeck117noVatzaMatter1135BrbdinReef1133 No factor 10
22Dec86- 3Aqu fst 1⅛ ⊡:47⅗ 1:12⅘ 1:52⅕ 3+Clm 50000 5 2 48½ 63¾ 76 910½ Lovato F Jr 117 33.30 70-17 Vinny's Pride 113½ Barbadian Reef 1173½ Askrano 1171½ Tired 11
20Oct86- 3Bel fm 1 Ⓣ:47 1:11 1:35⅘ 3+Alw 40000 4 4 43½ 33½ 35½ 35 Lovato F Jr 115 *1.40e 81-19 My Man John 115nk Silver Surfer1154¾CornishGemII1157¾ Evenly 6
6Oct86- 2Bel gd 1 Ⓣ:48 1:13⅕ 1:40⅖ 3+Clm 50000 7 4 45½ 49 32 21½ Lovato F Jr 117 8.00 61-39 Golden ChampII1151½CornishGemII1171StageSetter108nk Rallied 11
6Sep86- 3Bel gd 1 1/16 Ⓣ:49 1:13⅖ 1:45 3+Clm 75000 1 2 42 73¾ 74¾ 86½ Martens G 112 16.10 69-27 New Terms 112no Majestic Roberto 118hd Braddells 1222¾ Tired 8
LATEST WORKOUTS Jly 23 Aqu Ⓣ 5f gd 1:03 h Jun 25 Aqu Ⓣ 5f gd 1:02⅘ h (d) Jun 18 Aqu Ⓣ 3f fm :38 b (d)

D.

Cloutier B. g. 5, by The Minstrel—Perfect Foil, by Sword Dancer
Own.—Rand R R $50,000 Br.—Carelaine Farm-Vintage Meadow Assoc (Md) Tr.—Klesaris Robert P 119
Lifetime 42 8 8 8 $122,795 | 1987 8 4 1 0 $44,630 | 1986 14 2 2 2 $40,180 | Turf 30 8 6 4 $106,042

15Jly87- 2Bel gd 1⅜ Ⓣ:49 1:39⅘ 2:19⅗ Clm 45000 2 5 58½ 42½ 2½ 1nk Pezua J M 113 3.10 64-34 Cloutier 113nk Classic Move 1175½ I'm No Yankee 117hd Driving 7
17Jun87- 5Bel fm 1⅜ Ⓣ:50⅗ 1:39⅗ 2:17 Clm 35000 7 3 32 21 2½ 1nk Pezua J M 117 *2.30 77-24 Cloutier 117nk King's Prophesy1172½Uncompromise1176¾ Driving 12
6May87-10GP fm *1½ Ⓣ 2:30⅖ Clm 30000 5 2 211 22½ 12 14½ Pezua J M 117 *1.20 92-10 Cloutier 1174½ Padrilario 1173 Soaring Bee 1132 Driving 9
19Apr87- 9GP gd *1½ Ⓣ 2:33⅕ Clm 50000 1 4 419 56 67 67¾ Perret C 113 4.60 70-23 DanceCaller1132DonEdurdo113hdLondonExchnge113nk No factor 10
29Mar87-11GP gd *1 1/16 Ⓣ 1:46⅖ Clm 45000 10 7 78¾ 76¾ 57½ 52½ Romero R P 117 4.20 71-23 Braddells 117no Perplejo 108½ Imperial Palace 1132 Late bid 10
6Mar87-11Hia fm 1½ Ⓣ 2:29⅘ Clm 40000 8 9 87¼ 21½ 23 2hd Perret C 114 5.70 81-09 Dance to the Wire 116hd Cloutier114½Padrilario112no Just missed 10
17Jan87-11Hia fm 1½ Ⓣ 2:30⅘ Clm 32000 8 5 49 32 42½ 1hd Perret C 116 *3.00 76-17 Cloutier 116hd He's Unstoppable 114no PleasureTreat1123 Driving 11
10Jan87- 7Hia gd *1⅜ Ⓣ 1:59⅗ Clm 40000 6 11 119¾ 128½ 109¼ 85¼ Perret C 114 11.10 59-32 London Exchange 116nk Temujin 113½ Masterful 116no Outrun 12
23Nov86- 1Aqu fst 1⅛ :49 1:13⅖ 1:52⅕ 3+Clm 25000 8 9 917 913 914 915 Santos J A 117 11.70 59-23 Mr. Tatt 117¾ Waldman 115hd Arctic Song 1063½ Outrun 9
18Oct86- 4Bel gd 1¼ Ⓣ:50 1:40⅕ 2:05 3+Clm 45000 1 3 39 711 48½ 57½ Santos J A 113 8.70 61-29 Future Fable1131¾HowAboutNow1133¼Translucid1132½ Weakened 11
LATEST WORKOUTS Jly 4 Mth 6f fst 1:15⅘ b Jun 12 Mth 6f fst 1:15⅗ b Jun 4 Mth 5f gd 1:06 b

E.

King's Prophesy B. g. 6, by Gold And Myrrh—Colorcast, by Carry Back
Own.—Springbrook Farm $45,000 Br.—Carter W D (NY) Tr.—Turner William H Jr 113
Lifetime 34 9 5 7 $98,625 | 1987 3 0 1 2 $9,300 | 1986 12 4 1 2 $40,944 | Turf 28 9 5 6 $96,430

17Jun87- 5Bel fm 1⅜ Ⓣ:50⅗ 1:39⅗ 2:17 Clm 35000 5 7 74½ 31 1½ 2nk Cruguet J b 117 3.40 77-24 Cloutier117nkKing'sProphesy1172½Uncompromise1176¾ Sharp try 12
3Jun87- 4Bel gd 1 Ⓣ:47⅖ 1:11⅗ 1:38⅗ Clm 35000 5 10 84¾ 32 34 32¾ Cruguet J b 117 *1.90 69-37 I'm No Yankee 1122½ Askrano 117nkKing'sProphesy1174 Late bid 12
9May87-10Pim fm 1 1/16 Ⓣ:46 1:10⅕ 1:41⅘ Clm 50000 2 7 78¼ 64½ 610 38 Hutton G W b 114 6.20 86-06 CovertOpertion1148ChespekBch114noKing'sProphsy114hd Rallied 10
31Oct86- 8Pha fm 1 1/16 Ⓣ:48⅕ 1:12⅗ 1:44⅘ 3+Clm 32000 4 7 94½ 93½ 76¼ 67 Barrera C b 119 *1.20 71-22 Flight of Time116nkB.A.Captain1163½ANativeYank116nk Wide str. 10
23Oct86- 9Lrl fm 1 Ⓣ:47⅕ 1:12⅘ 1:37⅕ 3+Alw 15500 4 6 31½ 31 31 11¾ Hutton G W b 117 *1.70 84-17 King'sProphesy1171¾DeckeledEdge1151ChespekeBch1131 Driving 8
6Oct86- 6Lrl fm 1⅛ Ⓣ:45⅖ 1:11⅕ 1:50 3+Clm 25000 7 3 33 22 14 15½ Hutton G W b 117 2.10 87-17 King'sProphesy1175½HilToNuset1123½ThinkThunder117hd Driving 9
19Sep86- 6Pim fm 1 1/16 Ⓣ:46⅖ 1:11 1:43 3+Clm 25000 2 5 56 43½ 44½ 24½ Hutton G W b 117 1.60 84-07 GenerlStrike1174½King'sProphesy1171½ⒹC.A.'sBlues1171½ Rallied 6
9Sep86- 7Pim fm 1 1/16 Ⓣ:47 1:11⅖ 1:43⅖ Clm 25000 7 6 67½ 66½ 65 35½ Hutton G W b 114 3.00 80-14 Snowden'sGold1151½GenerlStrike1144King'sProphsy1141½ Rallied 8
29Aug86- 6Bel gd 1 1/16 Ⓣ:49 1:13⅘ 1:46⅕ 3+ⓈAlw 29500 1 1 11 31 43½ 57 Romero R P b 117 *2.10 58-31 Romanizer 117no Root Canal 1172½ Ground Shaker 1142½ Tired 7
21Aug86- 2Sar fm 1⅝ Ⓣ:52⅕ 2:02 2:40⅖ 3+Clm 35000 10 3 2½ 11 35 511 Romero R P b 117 5.30 72-13 Tisa Feast 117¾ Terson 1175½ Bristol Who 1171¾ Weakened 10
LATEST WORKOUTS Jly 28 Bel 4f fst :49 h Jly 21 Bel 5f gd 1:01 h Jly 11 Bel tr.t 5f fst 1:02⅕ b Jun 26 Bel tr.t 4f fst :48⅗ h

F.

Prince Of Destiny Ch. g. 4, by Caucasus—Dream Date, by Rough'n Tumble
$50,000 Br.—Fuller P (Ky) Tr.—Bush Thomas M
117
Own.—Parrish Hill Farm
Lifetime 22 4 3 2 $61,535 | 1987 6 0 2 1 $17,260 | 1986 16 4 1 1 $44,275 | Turf 10 1 2 2 $29,725

Entered 29Jly87- 8 BEL

17Jly87- 8Bel	fm	1⅜	Ⓣ:50 1:38⅗ 2:15⅘	3↑Alw 31000	4	6	6^{5}	$6^{4¾}$	$6^{4¾}$	$7^{3¾}$	Santos J A	b 117	4.50	75-22	Nantahela 108^{1} Hawaiian Palm 117^{hd} Attention 117^{hd}	No factor	7
14Jun87- 7Bel	fm	1 1/16	Ⓣ:45⅘ 1:10 1:41⅘	3↑Alw 31000	3	5	$7^{8¾}$	$5^{7½}$	5^{3}	3^{2}	Vasquez J	b 117	8.30	85-16	G'DayMate117^{nk}SimplyMjestic111^{1¾}PrinceOfDestiny117^{4½}	Rallied	10
29May87- 5Bel	fm	1 1/16	Ⓣ:48⅖ 1:11⅖ 1:41⅗	3↑Alw 31000	2	2	2½	2½	2^{hd}	2^{nk}	Vasquez J	b 119	4.80	88-19	DnceCrdFilled119^{nk}PrincOfDstiny119½MjsticRobrto119^{hd}	Brushed	5
15May87- 2Bel	fm	1¼	Ⓣ:50⅕ 1:40⅕ 2:04	Clm 50000	4	7	$5^{4½}$	2^{hd}	2½	2no	Vasquez J	b 117	*2.40	74-29	ClssicMov117^{no}PrincOfDstiny117^{5}CornishGmII115^{no}	Just missed	9
1May87- 6Aqu	gd	1⅛	Ⓣ:51⅗ 1:16⅖ 1:55⅖	Clm 50000	2	5	5^{4}	6^{4}	$5^{2½}$	$4^{1¾}$	Bailey J D	b 117	5.40	56-41	Stage Setter113^{nk}ClassicMove113^{nk}BarbadianReef113^{1¼}	Steadied	7
15Apr87- 1Aqu	fst	1⅛	:48⅗ 1:12⅖ 1:50	Clm 50000	4	4	$4^{2½}$	$5^{5½}$	6^{12}	$6^{16¾}$	Vasquez J	b 117	29.80	68-19	Mr. Tatt 113^{hd} Road To Ponder 117^{1½} Equal Terms 108^{4¾}	Off slow	7
8Dec86- 8Aqu	fst	1⅝	⊡:13⅗ 2:07⅖ 2:46⅖	3↑Handicap	4	7	7^{17}	7^{12}	6^{22}	6^{23}	Nuesch D	b 105	45.20	57-20	Feeling Gallant 114¾ Jane's Dilemma 115^{4½} Carjack 122½	Outrun	7
28Nov86- 1Aqu	fst	1⅛	:47⅗ 1:12 1:50⅘	3↑Clm 35000	8	6	$6^{5¼}$	$6^{2¼}$	$5^{4¼}$	$5^{5½}$	Migliore R	b 115	7.00	75-18	How About Now 117^{nk} Askrano 117^{nk} Mr. Tatt117^{2½}	Needed rally	8
15Nov86- 3Pha	fst	1 1/16	:46⅖ 1:09⅘ 1:42⅖	3↑Alw 13500	4	6	6^{16}	6^{19}	4^{15}	$4^{12½}$	Wilson R	b 114	6.00	79-14	Mr. JoeLane115^{2½}ClaridgeDrive115^{9}MajesticPeace116^{1}	No factor	6
31Oct86- 7Aqu	fst	1⅛	:48⅗ 1:12⅖ 1:50⅕	3↑Alw 29000	8	8	8^{10}	8^{11}	8^{19}	$7^{24½}$	Migliore R	b 114	17.30	59-20	Pine Belt 117^{1¾} Fly Me Again 117^{1¾} Harry L. 110^{nk}	Outrun	9

LATEST WORKOUTS Jly 28 Bel 3f fst :38 b Jly 15 Bel 4f gd :51⅖ b Jly 11 Bel 6f fst 1:17⅖ b Jly 5 Bel 4f fst :51 b

G.

Unanswered B. c. 4, by Tom Rolfe—What's the Reason, by Hail to Reason
$50,000 Br.—Whitney Mrs J H (Ky) Tr.—Reinacher Robert Jr
117
Own.—Greentree Stable
Lifetime 12 2 4 1 $48,780 | 1987 1 0 0 0 | 1986 8 2 3 0 $41,180 | Turf 2 0 1 0 $5,500

12Jly87- 5Bel	fst	1 1/16	:46⅘ 1:11⅕ 1:43⅘	3↑Alw 28000	7	5	$5^{3½}$	$5^{7¾}$	5^{11}	5^{12}	Romero R P	b 117	16.90	71-25	Conquer 115no Pi Phi Prince 111^{1½} Temperate 117^{3½}	Tired	7
13Sep86- 1Bel	fst	1¼	:48⅘ 1:38⅗ 2:04	3↑Alw 26000	7	5	$5^{4½}$	1½	1^{hd}	2¾	Velasquez J	b 116	3.20	77-11	Fly Me Again 117¾Unanswered116^{hd}ShiningAsset117^{9¼}	Weakened	7
24Aug86- 5Sar	fm	1⅜	Ⓣ:50⅗ 1:39⅕ 2:17⅕	3↑Alw 26000	7	4	4^{6}	$6^{9½}$	6^{10}	5^{8}	Romero R P	117	2.80	74-23	Prince Daniel 112½ Dark Flood 117^{1¾} Seattle Sunrise 112^{3}	Tired	7
9Aug86- 6Sar	fst	1¼	:51 1:39⅘ 2:05⅕	3↑Alw 25000	4	2	2^{1}	3^{nk}	1^{hd}	$1^{1¾}$	Romero R P	113	*1.40	74-17	Unanswered 113^{1¾} Curtin 112^{6½} Maltese Cross 112^{nk}	Driving	5
25Jly86- 8Bel	fm	1¼	Ⓣ:50 1:39⅕ 2:03⅖	3↑Alw 25000	3	8	8^{7}	$8^{8½}$	$5^{7¾}$	$2^{6¼}$	Romero R P	b 111	7.30	71-19	I'mHopeful116^{6¼}Unnswered111^{no}TheLoneRnger106¾	Gained place	8
5Jun86- 1Bel	fst	1 1/16	:47⅕ 1:11⅗ 1:42⅘	Alw 25000	4	6	$7^{7½}$	6^{8}	$4^{9½}$	$4^{10¼}$	Santos J A	b 117	2.60	78-17	BoyishCharm117½LifeGuard117^{7¾}Deadman'sCurve117^{2½}	No factor	7
15May86- 1Bel	fst	1 1/16	:45⅖ 1:09⅖ 1:42⅖	Alw 25000	4	6	$6^{8½}$	6^{7}	$4^{3½}$	$2^{1¼}$	Romero R P	b 117	5.20	89-16	Grand Exchange 117^{1¼} Unanswered 117^{2} Wise Axe117¾	Lost whip	7
11Feb86- 8GP	fst	1 1/16	:48 1:13⅕ 1:48⅖	Alw 16000	4	11	11^{12}	11^{18}	10^{12}	$8^{7½}$	Romero R P	b 119	3.10	51-38	LuckyTiger117^{1}HoldTheWorld117^{nk}LordOfTheNight119^{no}	Outrun	12
29Jan86- 4GP	fst	7f	:22⅗ :46 1:25⅖	Md Sp Wt	7	8	$7^{7½}$	6^{10}	4^{2}	1^{1}	Romero R P	b 122	*2.00	77-26	Unanswered 122^{1} Classic Move 122^{7} Entertain 122½	Driving	12
22Nov85- 6Aqu	sly	1	:47⅗ 1:13 1:39⅘	Md Sp Wt	8	4	$5^{2½}$	5^{4}	$3^{5½}$	$3^{2¼}$	Velasquez J	b 118	*1.10	65-25	Waseca 118^{2} Man Up 118^{nk} Unanswered 118^{4¾}	Rallied	9

LATEST WORKOUTS Jly 6 Bel 5f fst 1:03 b Jun 29 Bel 4f fst :50 bg Jun 22 Bel 5f fst :59⅗ h Jun 15 Bel 5f fst 1:02 b

6. One horse in this field has a decisive advantage on either speed or class. Which is it?

3rd Santa Anita

6 FURLONGS. (1.07⅗) CLAIMING. Purse $15,000. 4-year-olds and upward. Weights, 4-year-olds, 120 lbs.; older, 121 lbs. Non-winners of two races since November 3 allowed 3 lbs.; of a race since then, 5 lbs. Claiming price $16,000; for each $1,000 to $13,000 allowed 1 lb. (Races when entered for $12,500 or less not considered).

A. **(64)**

Polly's Ruler Ch. g. 8, by The Irish Lord—Miss Polly Bee, by Traveling Dust
KAENEL J L 7+ **116** Br.—Jo-Don Farms (Cal) Tr.—Heap Blake **$16,000**
Own.—Brunette Vera C Lifetime 42 11 13 3 $155,122
1986 14 6 3 2 $36,502 | 1984 9 0 2 1 $14,820 | Turf 3 1 0 0 $20,600

21Dec86-1Hol	6f	$:22^{2}$	$:46^{1}$	$1:11^{1}$ft	3	117	1^{1}	1^{hd}	1½	$2^{1¼}$	Kaenel J L^{7}	20000	86-15	SndDigger,Polly'sRuler,Andrew'NM	8
21Dec86—Broke in, bumped															
6Dec86-5Hol	6f	$:21^{4}$	$:45^{2}$	$1:11^{1}$gd	*6-5	119	2½	2^{hd}	$1^{1½}$	$1^{2½}$	Kaenel J L^{4}	Ⓢ 10000	87-16	Polly'sRuler,PhilipNoln,UpThePole	8
6Dec86—Lugged in stretch															
15Nov86-1Hol	6f	$:22^{3}$	:46	$1:10^{4}$ft	2¼	116	1^{1}	$1^{1½}$	$1^{2½}$	1^{4}	Kaenel J L^{1}	Ⓢ 12500	89-14	Polly'sRulr,SolidSpirit,InNturlForm	6
15Nov86—Bumped break, lugged in late															
3Nov86-1SA	6f	$:21^{3}$	$:44^{4}$	1:11 ft	17	116	3^{3}	3^{4}	3^{3}	4½	Kaenel J L^{7}	Ⓢ 12500	82-14	HachalaTachl,Melchip,ShuttleOne	10
3Nov86—Lugged in stretch															
27Sep86-9Tdn	6f	$:22^{2}$	$:46^{1}$	$1:12^{2}$m	*8-5	116	1^{1}	1½	1½	2^{nk}	Placke D^{4}	11500	82-28	NightRover,Polly'sRuler,ThKyoKid	6
14Sep86-8Tdn	6f	$:22^{2}$	$:45^{4}$	$1:11^{4}$ft	*2½	122	$1^{1½}$	$1^{1½}$	$1^{1½}$	1^{1}	Placke D^{7}	8500	85-25	Polly'sRuler,Crossbrek,NightRovr	10
23Aug86-7Tdn	6f	$:21^{4}$	:46	$1:11^{3}$sy	6½	116	2^{4}	2^{4}	2^{6}	$2^{8½}$	Placke D^{1}	11500	77-26	Khamfin, Polly's Ruler, Reedbuck	10
10Aug86-6Tdn	6f	$:21^{4}$	$:45^{4}$	$1:13^{2}$sy	*2¼	119	2½	2^{hd}	1^{hd}	1^{1}	Placke D^{5}	8500	77-26	Polly'sRlr,SprrowHwk,SmrtStrtgy	10
20Jly86-7Tdn	6f	$:22^{1}$	:46	$1:11^{2}$ft	2¾	116	2^{hd}	1½	1^{hd}	3^{4}	Salvaggio M V^{8}	11500	83-26	DncingHre,ThCtCmBck,Polly'sRulr	9
4Jly86-7Tdn	6f	$:21^{4}$	:45	1:12 ft	5¼	116	2^{5}	2^{6}	2^{5}	$3^{2½}$	Salvaggio MV^{12}	11500	81-24	Jcksndnns,ThCtCmBck,Polly'sRlr	12

B.

Economic Growth — Dk. b. or br. g. 5, by The Irish Lord—Adivinanza, by Parrot

CORDOVA D W 3– 113 — Br.—Jawl Bros (BC-C) — 1986 14 4 1 4 $20,851

Tr.—Norris Jerry $13,000 — 1985 13 1 3 2 $6,838

Own.—Poyer & Steinmann — Lifetime 27 5 4 6 $27,689

10Dec86-7Hol 6f :22 :454 1:111ft 20 117 74¼ 63¾ 44 44½ Pedroza M A7 25000 82-20 Rnbow'sCp,EllsBrvstSong,BldTpsdr 8

10Dec86—Wide 3/8; lugged in final 1/8

6Dec86-3Hol 6f :224 :46 1:104gd 7½ 115 21½ 33 45½ 48¼ Kaenel J L4 45000 81-16 Nordicus, Juntura,KingOfCalifornia 4

19Nov86-8Hol 6f :22 :452 1:111ft 52 1115 67½ 65 45 45 Gibson R G3 Aw21000 82-21 IrishStories,Hrper'sRidge,Notoriety 6

19Nov86—Checked 1/2

29Aug86-8EP 6½f :224 :461 1:172ft 6½ 112 2hd 1hd 2hd 2nk Duran R C6 Aw10000 91-19 BrgndyBons,EconomcGrwth,T'sOn 6

24Aug86-7EP 6½f :211 :453 1:173ft 9-5 114 32½ 31 2hd 31¼ Duran R C1 25000 89-21 GoldnPos,SkpNLv,EconomcGrowth 4

2Aug86-7EP 6½f :222 :46 1:174ft *6-5 114 21 2hd 1hd 11½ Duran R C1 15000 89-20 EconmcGrwth,Mr.Knwldgbl,GldnPs 7

21Jly86-7EP 6½f :223 :454 1:172ft 19 114 2hd 1hd 11 12½ Duran R C6 11500 91-19 EcnmcGrwth,CrprtPwr,Mr.Knldgbl 7

12Jly86-6EP 6½f :223 :461 1:191gd 5¼ 111 51¼ 51¼ 21½ 32 Krasner S2 10000 80-22 QnsMssngr,Nrotc,EconomcGrowth 7

21Jun86-5EP 6½f :222 :454 1:182ft 15 110 21 21 12 14 Duran R C3 8000 86-19 EcnmcGrwth,MnnyMstrd,PlcPrtctn 8

7Jun86-9EP 6½f :223 :462 1:19 ft 8½ 114 2hd 1hd 2½ 32 Loseth C3 6500 81-21 Lvntr,SmoothLndng,EconmcGrwth 9

Dec 3 Hol 4f ft :481 h — Nov 15 Hol 6f ft 1:132 h — Nov 9 Hol 5f ft 1:022 h — Nov 4 Hol 4f ft :493 h

C.

Neutral Player — Dk. b. or br. g. 7, by Triple Bend—Elizabeth Play, by Graphic

STEVENS G L 5–N(5) 118 — Br.—Penn O (Ky) — 1986 19 4 2 3 $50,985

Tr.—Murphy Marcus J $16,000 — 1985 10 2 1 2 $23,350

Own.—Dilena & Konis — Lifetime 73 13 10 12 $165,436 — Turf 4 0 0 0 $1,090

13Dec86-1Hol 6f :214 :45 1:102ft 7¾ 116 97½ 76¾ 53½ 1½ Stevens G L6 16000 91-09 Neutral Player, Illuminize, Rodney 10

22Nov86-1Hol 6f :222 :46 1:11 ft *6-5 116 2½ 2hd 11½ 14½ ValenzuelaPA1 c10000 88-13 NeutrlPlyr,Chucklctor,TuscnKnight 5

22Nov86—Lugged in late

9Nov86-4Hol 1 :451 1:104 1:373ft *3¾ 116 11½ 2½ 21½ 44½ ValenzuelaPA11 10000 70-16 Bob'sIntnt,RunningDbonir,Crimuri 11

12Oct86-1SA 6½f :22 :452 1:174ft *3 116 2hd 1hd 41½ 87½ McCarron C J2 16000 73-21 Unagloshi,Menswear,StrOfAmeric 12

12Oct86—Bumped start

20Sep86-10Pom 1 1/16 :454 1:111 1:431ft 4½ 1115 45 45 69 719¼ Black C A8 20000 76-09 Restage, Hatamoto,LyphardChimes 9

17Aug86-7Dmr 1 1/16 :453 1:101 1:432ft 6 1115 2½ 2hd 32 75¼ Black C A8 25000 78-16 BngBngBng,MrkInThSky,OnEdRm 10

27Jly86-9Dmr 1 1/16 :454 1:102 1:422ft *3 118 11½ 1½ 1hd 21¾ McCarron C J2 25000 86-10 MstrCwston,NutrlPlyr,Rvolutionry 10

4Jly86-3Hol 6f :22 :451 1:10 ft 6½ 119 32 34 47 37 Stevens G L4 25000 87-09 FlyngLssons,ToughEnvoy,NutrlPlyr 7

18Jun86-1Hol 1 :452 1:101 1:353ft 9½ 1115 11½ 3nk 42½ 55¾ Black C A1 32000 79-15 PssdThRul,ToughEnvoy,CrystlCort 7

1Jun86-1Hol 1⅛ :453 1:102 1:504ft 2¾ 1145 36½ 35½ 31½ 53 Black C A5 c25000 80-14 BouncngBttons,SrStr,MrkInThSky 6

Dec 30 SA 3f ft :364 h — Dec 9 Hol 4f ft :492 h — Dec 3 Hol 3f ft :373 h — Nov 28 Hol 4f ft :49 h

D.

***Vaigly Oh** — B. h. 5, by Vaigly Great—Final Act, by Decoy Boy

BAZE G 0–0 116 — Br.—Smith E J (Ire) — 1986 2 0 0 0

Tr.—West Ted $16,000 — 1985 2 0 0 0

Own.—Piemonte-Webb-West — Lifetime 10 3 1 0 $14,958 — Turf 7 3 1 0 $14,958

25Jan86-9SA 1⅛ :463 1:112 1:503ft 60 115 87¾ 1111 1124 — Baze G6 25000 — — HurricneHec,DrkSuce,RoosvltRod 11

25Jan86—Eased

15Jan86-3SA 6½f :211 :434 1:152ft 63 115 1014 1015 1014 1010¾ Baze G9 50000 82-14 Coyotero, Zac K., Lord Pancho 10

15Jan86—In distress after finish

29Mar85-8SA a6½f Ⓣ:214 :441 1:141fm 20 118 54 55 77½ 810½ EstrdJJr1 ⓇCWhtnhm 77-12 PntdCnyon,SpctclrLov,RsngChum 9

27Feb85-8SA 6f :214 :443 1:091ft 28 115 76½ 88½ 89 810½ EstradJJr3 ⓇBls Chca 81-17 Prtnsor,ColtFortyFour,RlunchATun 8

27Feb85—Bumped, shuffled back after start

22Sep84 ♦ 4Newbury(Eng) 6f 1:173gd 14 123 Ⓣ 55½ Mercer J MilReef(Gr2) LoclSuitor,Presidium,Bssenthwite 12

23Aug84 ♦ 1York(Eng) 5f :593gd 3¼ 123 Ⓣ 1nk CauthenS Prnc Wales Vaigly Oh, Provideo, Pettingale 5

9Jly84 ♦ 4Windsor(Eng) 5f 1:01 gd 2 129 Ⓣ 11 EdderyP Falmouth Bay VaiglyOh,ShootPool,JollyBusiness 10

2Jly84 ♦ 1Windsor(Eng) 5f 1:013gd *2¼ 126 Ⓣ 12 EddrP Mrbe Arch (Mdn) ViglyOh,Hnry'sVntur,BrghtDomno 16

26May84 ♦ 6Lingfield(Eng) 5f 1:021gd 2¼ 126 Ⓣ 25 CrsonW Elephant (Mdn) Abutaia, VaiglyOh,StableRelations 16

11May84 ♦ 1Lingfield(Eng) 5f 1:012gd 7 126 Ⓣ 55¼ EddryP Tndr King (Mdn) Overtrump, NoRebate, JustJones 11

Dec 26 SA 5f ft 1:012 h — Dec 20 SA 5f ft 1:022 h — Dec 11 SA 4f ft :481 h — Dec 4 SA 3f ft :362 h

E.

Grenoble

ORTEGA L E

Own.—De La Merced R A or A A Jr

116

Ch. g. 7, by Grenfall—Cheri Meri, by Meritorious

Br.—Palmer J F (Cal)

Tr.—Chasteen William W **$16,000**

Lifetime 79 9 13 12 $176,731

1986 19 3 5 0 $40,395

1985 16 1 3 4 $21,415

Turf 2 0 0 0 $3,000

21Dec86-1Hol 6f :22^{2} :46^{1} 1:11^{1}ft 21 119 7$^{4\frac{3}{4}}$ 7$^{5\frac{1}{4}}$ 6$^{5\frac{1}{2}}$ 6$^{10\frac{3}{4}}$ Castanon A L^{4} 20000 76-15 SndDigger,Polly'sRuler,Andrew'NM 8

21Dec86—Wide 3/8 turn

13Dec86-1Hol 6f :21^{4} :45 1:10^{2}ft 9¼ 122 10^{10}10^{12} 9$^{9\frac{1}{4}}$ 9$^{9\frac{3}{4}}$ DelahoussayeE^{3} 16000 81-09 Neutral Player, Illuminize, Rodney 10

13Dec86—Broke slowly, wide in stretch

27Nov86-3Hol 6f :21^{4} :45 1:10^{3}ft 10 122 6^{12} 6^{8} 5^{7} 4^{5} Ortega L E^{2} 16000 85-18 Ells Bravest Song, Jacart, FallFlyer 7

27Nov86—Steadied start

8Nov86-9Hol 6f :22^{2} :45^{4} 1:10^{3}ft 4¼ 119 6$^{4\frac{1}{4}}$ 5^{6} 6^{9} 6$^{12\frac{3}{4}}$ Ortega L E^{6} 25000 77-13 SandDigger,Amarone,Billy'sSpecial 6

8Nov86—Lugged out badly; wide final 3/8

31Oct86-7SA 7f :22^{3} :45^{3} 1:23 ft 9¼ 116 7$^{4\frac{1}{4}}$ 9$^{9\frac{3}{4}}$ 9^{13} 8$^{10\frac{3}{4}}$ Ortega L E^{6} 32000 74-16 GryPinstrip,CoursngEgl,Yukon'sStr 9

18Oct86-5SA 6f :21^{4} :44^{4} 1:11 ft 10 116 8$^{8\frac{1}{2}}$ 5^{8} 3$^{5\frac{1}{2}}$ 1no Ortega L E^{5} 25000 83-20 Grenoble, Bizeboy, Calabonga 9

5Oct86-2SA 6f :21^{3} :44^{3} 1:10^{2}ft 11 115 10$^{5\frac{3}{4}}$ 7^{6} 4$^{3\frac{1}{2}}$ 1$^{1\frac{1}{2}}$ Ortega L E^{1} 20000 86-15 Grenoble, John's Jove, Inquisitive 12

25Sep86-9Pom 6½f :22^{1} :47 1:21^{1}m 3½ 116 5$^{4\frac{1}{2}}$ 5^{7} 3^{4} 2^{nk} Ortega L E^{4} 16000 74-30 DownRnge,Grenobl,DistinctivlyDon 7

F.

Family Fox

SIBILLE R

Own.—B C L Racng St-Boyer-Fox

116

B. g. 8, by Bob Mathias—Family Light, by Limelight

Br.—Stringer J (Ore)

Tr.—Cianci Jon **$16,000**

Lifetime 76 13 11 16 $167,375

1986 13 1 1 1 $19,650

1985 17 3 1 2 $47,175

27Nov86-3Hol 6f :21^{4} :45 1:10^{3}ft 6¼ 117 7^{12} 7^{12} 7^{11} 7^{10} Toro F^{4} 16000 80-18 Ells Bravest Song, Jacart, FallFlyer 7

27Nov86—Lugged out 3/8, wide into stretch

16Nov86-4Hol 7f :22 :44^{3} 1:24^{1}ft 13 117 5^{3} 5$^{5\frac{1}{2}}$ 8$^{6\frac{1}{4}}$ 6$^{6\frac{3}{4}}$ Toro F^{12} 20000 76-18 Pegus, Pialor, Amarone 12

25Oct86-9SA 6f :22 :45^{1} 1:10^{2}ft 17 116 11$^{9\frac{1}{4}}$11$^{9\frac{3}{4}}$11$^{9\frac{1}{4}}$10$^{8\frac{1}{4}}$ Ortega L E^{10} 20000 78-17 StarOfAmerica,Rodney,SndDigger 11

25Oct86—Broke in a tangle; lugged out backstretch

25Apr86-5Hol 1 :45^{4} 1:10^{4} 1:37 ft *8-5 116 5^{3} 5$^{5\frac{1}{2}}$ 5$^{5\frac{1}{2}}$ 4^{8} Ortega L E^{3} 16000 70-16 JohnTheTough,ColdNos,MorsCodII 7

25Apr86—Wide on turn

19Apr86-2SA 6½f :21^{3} :44^{2} 1:17^{2}ft *3 115 8^{11} 9^{12} 8$^{7\frac{3}{4}}$ 4$^{2\frac{1}{2}}$ Stevens G L^{7} 20000 80-19 Jacart, Gran Barba, Neutral Player 9

19Apr86—Bumped hard start; wide, lugged in final 1/8

13Apr86-5SA 7f :22^{1} :45 1:22^{2}ft 13 116 7$^{8\frac{3}{4}}$ 8$^{7\frac{1}{2}}$ 6$^{6\frac{1}{4}}$ 4$^{7\frac{1}{2}}$ Stevens G L^{3} Aw24000 80-15 Danczone, Bizeboy, Lord Pancho 9

13Apr86—Wide into stretch

4Apr86-7SA 6½f :21^{3} :44^{3} 1:16^{3}ft 5½ 116 10$^{8\frac{1}{4}}$ 8^{9} 10$^{7\frac{1}{4}}$ 5$^{6\frac{1}{4}}$ Stevens G L^{12} 25000 81-23 Bizeboy, Le Ricain, Calabonga 12

4Apr86—Fanned wide late

22Feb86-6SA 7f :22^{4} :45^{3} 1:22^{4}ft 2½ 116 8^{5} 4$^{1\frac{1}{2}}$ 2^{hd} 1$^{2\frac{3}{4}}$ Stevens G L^{8} 16000 86-16 FmlyFox,Rchrd'sGotch,DstnctvlyDn 8

9Feb86-2SA 6½f :21^{3} :44^{2} 1:16^{3}ft 10 114 12$^{9\frac{3}{4}}$11$^{9\frac{1}{4}}$ 4$^{5\frac{1}{2}}$ 2^{2} Stevens G L^{12} 14000 85-16 NeutrlPlyer,FmilyFox,SwordPrinc 12

9Feb86—Wide into stretch

Dec 31 SA 4f ft :48^{1} h Dec 18 SA 5f ft 1:00^{2} h Dec 11 SA 4f ft :47^{2} h Nov 25 SA 3f ft :35^{1} h

G.

Sword Prince

DELAHOUSSAYE E

Own.—Dattilo D O

116

Dk. b. or br. g. 5, by Cornish Prince—Sword Fish, by New Policy

Br.—Palisair Place (Ky)

Tr.—Wright Robert **$16,000**

Lifetime 21 2 2 4 $32,900

1986 12 0 0 4 $10,425

1985 6 2 2 0 $22,100

4Jly86-3Hol 6f :22 :45^{1} 1:10 ft 14 111^{5} 7$^{7\frac{3}{4}}$ 7^{1} 6^{11} 7$^{11\frac{3}{4}}$ Black C A^{2} 25000 82-09 FlyngLssons,ToughEnvoy,NutrlPlyr 7

4Jly86—Lugged out, wide

22Jun86-1Hol 6f :22 :45^{1} 1:10 ft 5½ 111^{5} 4^{4} 4$^{3\frac{1}{4}}$ 3$^{3\frac{1}{2}}$ 3$^{3\frac{3}{4}}$ Black C A^{6} 25000 90-08 SndDiggr,FlyingLssons,SwordPrinc 7

22Jun86—Bumped at start

29May86-4Hol 1 :45^{2} 1:10^{4} 1:36^{4}ft 16 111^{5} 1^{hd} 2^{hd} 2$^{1\frac{1}{2}}$ 4$^{3\frac{1}{4}}$ Black C A^{5} 20000 76-18 Whidbey Tea, Mandato,Espontaneo 8

17May86-3Hol 6f :22^{3} :45^{4} 1:11 ft 52 111^{5} 5^{4} 5$^{5\frac{1}{2}}$ 5$^{4\frac{3}{4}}$ 3$^{2\frac{1}{4}}$ Black C A^{9} 20000 87-14 PowerfulEyes,Grenobl,SwordPrinc 11

1May86-7Hol 7f :22^{2} :45^{2} 1:24^{2}ft 19 116 3^{2} 5$^{3\frac{1}{2}}$ 9^{10} 7$^{8\frac{1}{2}}$ Kaenel J L^{9} 20000 73-17 Bold Topsider, Doodlesack,Shantin 9

1May86—Wide on turn

21Apr86-3SA 6f :21^{4} :45 1:10^{3}ft 57 116 11$^{8\frac{3}{4}}$11$^{7\frac{3}{4}}$ 9$^{5\frac{1}{2}}$ 7$^{4\frac{1}{4}}$ Ortega L E^{7} 25000 81-16 Reinbow'sCup,Timlin,BoldTopsidr 12

21Apr86—Jumped fallen horse at 5/16

4Apr86-7SA 6½f :21^{3} :44^{3} 1:16^{3}ft 98 116 5^{5} 6^{6} 8$^{6\frac{3}{4}}$ 9$^{6\frac{3}{4}}$ Kaenel J L^{9} 25000 80-23 Bizeboy, Le Ricain, Calabonga 12

22Mar86-9SA 1$\frac{1}{16}$:45^{4} 1:11^{2} 1:43^{3}ft 20 116 2$^{\frac{1}{2}}$ 4^{3} 8^{19} 9$^{24\frac{1}{2}}$ Ortega L E^{6} 25000 58-19 GoodThoghtWlly,Bronzno,RosvltRd 9

22Mar86—Eased in stretch

9Mar86-2SA 6f :21^{3} :44^{3} 1:10^{2}sy 7 117 11^{10} 8^{12} 8^{10} 8$^{12\frac{1}{4}}$ Stevens G L^{4} c20000 74-19 Ells BravestSong,HarryJr.,Bizeboy 11

9Mar86—Placed seventh through disqualification

20Feb86-5SA 6f :22 :45^{4} 1:11^{1}m 4 117 4$^{1\frac{3}{4}}$ 4^{2} 3^{5} 3$^{7\frac{1}{2}}$ Solis A^{6} 20000 74-27 DoubleDeficit,Clbong,SwordPrince 7

Dec 28 SA 6f ft 1:13^{2} h Dec 23 SA 4f ft :48^{2} h Dec 18 SA 6f ft 1:13^{3} h Dec 13 SA 5f ft 1:01^{4} h

H.

Forbes Reply 2-N
PATTON D B 112⁵
Own.—Haffner M & Michael Ann

Dk. b. or br. c. 4, by Bold Forbes—Soft Reply, by Personality
Br.—Haffner M & Michael Ann (Ky) 1986 3 1 0 0 $6,050
Tr.—Stidham Michael $16,000 1985 1 M 0 0 $1,425
Lifetime 4 1 0 0 $7,475

24Dec86-3Hol 7f :22 :45² 1:24 ft 7 116 3²½ 4⁴ 6⁹½ 6¹²½ Warren R J Jr⁶ 20000 71-20 Pilor,Gordon'sCommnd,PinepplJck 7
24Dec86—Lugged in stretch
30Nov86-4Hol 6f :22¹ :45² 1:10³ft 9¾ 116 7⁶¼ 7⁹½ 7¹¹ 7¹³½ DelhoussyeE⁷ Aw21000 76-16 LansManus,Notoriety,StratfordEst 7
30Nov86—Fanned wide 3/8
12Nov86-6Hol 6f :22² :46² 1:11¹ft *9-5 120 3²½ 2¹½ 1¹ 1⁵½ DelahoussyeE² M32000 87-15 ForbesReply,VariBeau,SpringStreet 6
12Nov86—Lugged in 1/16
10Nov85-6SA 6f :21³ :44³ 1:10¹ft 8 117 5⁵ 4² 5²½ 4⁴ Hernandez R⁷ Mdn 83-14 Electric Blue, Old Bid, David Louis 8
Jan 2 Hol 3f ft :36³ h   Dec 3 Hol 4f ft :49 h   Nov 22 Hol 5f ft 1:00¹ h   Nov 7 Hol 5f ft 1:01¹ hg

I.

Video Sid 3-N
BLACK C A 112
Own.—Harmatuck M S

Ch. g. 4, by Interdicto—Wildcat Fire, by Brush Fire
Br.—Gilbert S M (Fla) 1986 18 2 1 5 $23,495
Tr.—Harmatuck Michael $13,000 Turf 2 0 0 1 $880
Lifetime 18 2 1 5 $23,495

24Dec86-3Hol 7f :22 :45² 1:24 ft 11 114 1¹½ 1½ 3⁵½ 4⁸¾ Black C A¹ 18000 75-20 Pilor,Gordon'sCommnd,PinepplJck 7
6Dec86-6Hol 7f :22¹ :45² 1:24²gd 18 116 2²½ 2²½ 2⁴ 3⁴½ Black C A⁸ 16000 77-16 Noon Sun,PineappleJack,VideoSid 12
6Dec86—Lugged in stretch; returned bleeding from mouth
22Nov86-6Hol 6f :22³ :46 1:11¹ft 25 114 7⁶¾ 5⁶ 4⁵ 3³½ Black C A⁷ 14000 83-13 Manzanero, Pico P., Video Sid 9
22Nov86—Bumped start
6Nov86-2Hol 6f :22⁴ :46⁴ 1:12¹ft 39 116 9⁸½ 8⁵¼ 6⁴½ 5⁴¾ Ortega L E³ 16000 77-17 Toddy Boy, Manzanero, BlackCross 9
6Nov86—Rough start
29Oct86-9SA 1 1/16 :46⁴ 1:11³ 1:44³ft 14 113 6⁴¾ 7⁵¾ 8⁹½ 8¹¹ Solis A⁷ 14000 67-17 BlowTheTrumpts,RySol,EightHost 10
29Oct86—Bumped break; rank 7/8
3Oct86-5SA 6f :22¹ :45² 1:10²ft 50 116 7⁵¾ 9¹⁰ 9¹² 8¹⁴½ Lipham T⁹ 20000 72-17 NtvCptv,Nck'sPrnc,JohnsTomrrw 10
3Oct86—Broke in, bumped

7. If Philadelphia Park is 3 lengths faster than Atlantic City and Monmouth Park is 6 lengths faster than Atlantic City, which horse below gets the top speed figure for its most recent race? Daily track variants for each horse's most recent race are listed to the right of each horse's name.

8 ATLANTIC CITY (6 FURLONGS)

6 FURLONGS. (1.08⅗) CLAIMING. Purse $4,200. Fillies and Mares, 3-year-olds and upward. Weight, 3-year-olds 115 lbs. Older 122 lbs. Non-winners of two races since May 30, allowed 2 lbs. A race since then 4 lbs. A race since May 23, 6 lbs. Claiming Price $4,000.

A. **(64)**

Puff Away FAST 2
Own.—Circle A Stable

Ch. m. 7, by T V Commercial—Smokey's Last, by Henry B Good
$4,000 Br.—Mack E I (NY)
Tr.—Stratton Cindy
109⁷ Lifetime 68 6 15 13 $57,589 1987 12 0 3 1 $4,104 1986 20 2 5 5 $17,585

4Jly87- 4Pha fst 6f :22⅘ :47⅖ 1:14⅗ 3↑ⒻClm 4000 2 4 2½ 2ⁿᵈ 3²½ 6³¼ Lee-Lopez R F b 116 5.50 65-26 MissAckly116ⁿᵒEmphticMov116²OnlyInMyDrms119ⁿᵏ Wide, tired 10
16Jun87- 6Pha fst 6½f :22⅗ :46⅕ 1:20⅘ 3↑ⒻClm 4000 3 5 1ʰᵈ 2¹ 1ʰᵈ 7⁶½ Lee-Lopez R F b 116 *1.40 62-24 Only In My Dreams 116² Quiet Morn 116ⁿᵏ If Only I 116¾ Tired 10
28May87- 4GS fst 6f :22⅕ :45⅘ 1:12⅖ 3↑ⒻClm 4000 5 7 4⁵½ 4⁸ 4⁹ 5¹²½ Lee-Lopez R F b 116 *2.20 67-21 TowerofMischief119¾NativeEmerld119ⁿᵏEmphticMove116¹⁰ Tired 9
14May87- 4GS fst 6f :22⅖ :46⅕ 1:13⅖ 3↑ⒻClm 4000 5 5 3² 2¹½ 2½ 2ⁿᵏ Lee-Lopez R F b 116 3.10 75-23 Mistaken Bid 111ⁿᵏ Puff Away 116ⁿᵒ Blinker Baby 119³ Game try 12
30Apr87-10GS fst 6f :22⅗ :46⅗ 1:13⅕ 3↑ⒻClm 4000 1 2 1¹½ 1³ 1⁵ 2½ Lee-Lopez R F b 116 7.60 75-24 Silverlust 116½ Puff Away 116ⁿᵏ Time For Silver 1091½ Faltered 12
22Apr87- 1GS fst 6f :22⅖ :46⅗ 1:13⅖ ⒻClm 5000 1 6 5²¾ 6⁴¼ 6¹¾ 8⁴½ Lukas M b 116 10.40 70-25 Outduel M. 116² Somebody Fancy 116ⁿᵈ Swallowtail112ⁿᵈ Outrun 8
15Apr87- 2GS fst 6f :22⅖ :46⅕ 1:12⅗ ⒻClm 5000 7 1 6²¾ 5⁶ 4⁷ 5¹⁰¼ Lee-Lopez R F b 116 12.40 69-26 Jetting Lass 116⁵ Outduel M. 116ⁿᵒ Missy'sMink116¹ Raced wide 9
9Mar87- 6Pen fst 6f :22⅖ :46 1:12⅗ ⒻClm 5000 7 2 4³ 4⁶ 5⁷½ 6⁷¼ Baker C J b 116 7.50 74-22 Ocean City Girl 115² Squad Ten 116½ Darla's Pet 116¾ Tired 7
27Feb87-10Pen fst 6f :22⅗ :46⅖ 1:12⅖ ⒻClm 5000 6 3 2¹ 3³ 4⁸ 4⁵¼ Iliescu A b 116 *2.10 77-15 DottieLongleggs115½TrumpetVine116²AmberGall116²¾ Weakened 8
7Feb87- 9Pha fst 6f :22⅗ :47⅖ 1:13⅗ ⒻClm 6000 5 5 5²½ 4³½ 3¹ 3⁵ Black A S b 115 10.10 68-29 All Over Prairie 109⁴ Tootsie Wrapper 117¹ PuffAway115ⁿᵈ Wide 12

B.

Benchy Slow 2
B. m. 5, by On To Glory—Bridal Shower, by Hail to Reason
$4,000 Br.—Harden Norah Linda (Va)
Tr.—Auwarter Edward K
115⁵ Lifetime 34 5 5 4 $22,141 1987 6 1 2 1 $4,274 1986 26 4 3 3 $17,417
Own.—Iuliucci P J

23Jly87- 1Atl fst 5½f :22⅗ :46⅖ 1:07⅕ 3+ ⒻClm 4000 6 1 1hd 22 24 38 Conner M J b 120 2.70 69-22 Hookamadookama 1228HelluvaRaise111noBenchy1201 Drifted out 7
9Jly87- 5Atl sly 6f :22⅕ :46⅘ 1:13⅗ 3+ ⒻClm 5000 2 2 13½ 15 2hd 47 Conner M J b 116 *1.90 67-23 Flip 1164½ Northern Nifty 1202½ Kick And Howl 116no Drifted out 6
1Jly87- 1Atl fst 5½f :22 :46 1:06⅕ 3+ ⒻClm 5000 2 4 12 1hd 22½ 23 Intelisano GPJr b 116 3.20 79-25 Miss Great Above1063Benchy1163ShowingFirst116hd Second best 9
19Jun87- 1Del fst 5f :22 :47 1:00⅗ ⒻClm 4000 1 1 22½ 21 12 11¾ Beimel D W7 b 113 *.90 83-22 Benchy 1131¾ Voguette 1172 Just Anita 117¾ Driving 11
31May87- 5Del fst 6f :22⅕ :46⅕ 1:12⅘ 3+ ⒻClm 3500 6 3 12 13 12 2hd Beimel D W7 b 113 2.80 77-23 Another Move 120hd Benchy 1133 Keoke Coffee 113nk Just failed 11
22May87- 2Del fst 6f :22 :46 1:12⅖ 3+ ⒻClm 3500 2 2 1hd 1hd 3½ 65½ Beimel D W5 b 111 18.40 73-21 Fuzzy Ambition 119½ Robin's Encounter 1161 Fonville 116½ Tired 8
5Dec86- 6Pen fst 6f :22⅗ :47⅕ 1:13⅗ 3+ ⒻClm 3000 7 1 11 2hd 57½ 612½ Leasure W P b 116 11.50 63-31 Our Gitche 1162 J. Scotch 1133½ Fuzzy Ambition 1193 Tired 7
28Nov86- 9Pha fst 6f :22⅖ :46⅕ 1:12⅕ 3+ ⒻClm 4000 8 8 32 44 914 1118¾ Ravelich M b 116 42.20 61-20 Anselma 1165½ Dare Me'sDouble1163½Reception1161½ Tired badly 12
16Nov86- 4Pha fst 6f :22⅗ :46⅕ 1:12 3+ ⒻClm 4000 6 4 3nk 32 47 1011½ Aristone M b 116 39.60 70-16 Emphatic Move 1093½ Disco Quicker 116½ WhoaNellie111hd Tired 12
26Sep86-10Pha fst 6f :22 :45⅘ 1:12⅖ 3+ ⒻClm 5000 8 2 32 34 1118 1117 Bolletino N b 116 32.80 62-23 Stacey'sSpy1102BrimstonePath116noStarryLanding1122½ Stopped 11

C.

Super Kwik Brandi Slow 2
Blk. m. 5, by Resound—Casa Orange, by Polly's Jet
$4,000 Br.—Blake E (Va)
Tr.—Hawthorne Ann
110¹⁰ Lifetime 32 3 2 3 $9,005 1987 8 2 1 2 $5,346 1986 24 1 1 1 $3,659 Turf 1 0 0 0
Own.—Fripp Jerri

23Jly87- 1Atl fst 5½f :22⅗ :46⅖ 1:07⅕ 3+ ⒻClm 4000 7 2 55¾ 48½ 49 49 Pagan N b 120 11.90 68-22 Hookamadookama 1228 Helluva Raise 111no Benchy 1201 Rallied 7
8Jly87- 1Del fst 6f :22⅘ :46⅗ 1:12⅘ ⒻClm 4000 5 3 11½ 12 14 12 Landicini C Jr b 119 7.60 79-22 Super Kwik Brandi 1192 Viramir 1223Lasita'sCrystal113no Driving 7
1Jly87- 1Atl fst 5½f :22 :46 1:06⅕ 3+ ⒻClm 5000 1 6 32½ 46 68½ 78½ Pagan N b 116 23.60 73-25 Miss Great Above 1063 Benchy 1163 Showing First 116hd Tired 9
21Jun87- 1Del fst 6f :22⅘ :46⅗ 1:12⅗ 3+ ⒻClm 5000 7 1 62¾ 42¾ 55 66¾ Pagan N b 119 5.60 71-19 Witchella 1163 Brown Bag 119nk Jaybar's Secret 112½ Tired 7
10Jun87- 3Del fst 6f :23 :47⅖ 1:13⅖ 3+ ⒻClm 5000 6 3 21½ 3½ 2½ 21½ Pagan N b 119 4.00 72-24 Dark Colleen 1171½ SuperKwikBrandi1191½V.R.Swift116no Gamely 9
30May87- 7Del fst 6f :22⅗ :46⅗ 1:12⅗ 3+ ⒻClm 5000 6 1 3½ 2½ 21½ 33½ Pagan N b 119 4.00 75-16 FunAndDms1223MyPrincssOti109½SuprKwikBrnd1193½ Weakened 6
15May87- 6Del my 6f :22⅗ :46⅖ 1:13⅕ 3+ ⒻClm 4000 2 4 42 32 2hd 11½ Pagan N b 116 *3.70 75-26 SuperKwikBrandi1161½Chmelon1111½Pleseletitbeme106nk Driving 10
3May87- 2Del my 6f :22⅘ :46⅗ 1:12⅗ 3+ ⒻClm 5000 4 4 44½ 25 25 35½ Pagan N b 116 12.00 72-18 Jybr'sScrt1115½PrincssVixn104ndSuprKwikBrndi1163½ Best others 9
28Dec86- 5Pen fst 6f :22⅗ :46⅕ 1:11⅗ 3+ ⒻClm 5000 2 8 32 56¾ 713 718¾ Davis M7 b 109 21.60 68-22 Grey Variety 1168 Nineteen Bluff's 1142 I Vahnt 1161½ Tired 12
21Dec86- 5Pen fst 6f :22⅘ :46⅘ 1:13⅕ 3+ ⒻClm 5000 1 10 31½ 34 43½ 43 Davis M7 b 109 55.30 75-19 EmeraldAccount1161RestlessSarah116¾FlightofDrems1191½ Tired 12
LATEST WORKOUTS Jly 18 Atl 4f fst :49 b Jun 29 Atl 3f fst :36⅖ b

D.

Thunder Dust Fast 1
B. m. 5, by Run Dusty Run—Thunderdawn, by Grey Dawn II
$4,000 Br.—Binn M (NY)
Tr.—Bonaventura Paul
111⁵ Lifetime 21 4 1 5 $21,779 1987 10 1 1 2 $6,401 1986 11 3 0 3 $15,378
Own.—Kravetz Ruth

15Jly87- 2Mth fst 6f :22⅘ :46⅖ 1:12⅗ 3+ ⒻClm 5000 2 7 55 46½ 56 78¾ Corbett G W5 b 111 26.10 68-20 ScndlousScrlet116hdHelen'sMelody1163PrfctlyChrming1191 Tired 9
24Jun87- 2Mth fst 6f :22⅗ :46 1:12 3+ ⒻClm 5000 3 6 31 44½ 86¼ 1011¾ McCauley W H b 116 4.30 68-16 SocialGesture109¾ScandalousScarlet1161SilverShm1161¼ Stopped 10
6Jun87- 5FL fst 5½f :22⅖ :47 1:06 3+ ⒻClm 6250 7 4 53 52 31½ 34½ Hulet L b 115 *1.10 82-17 PrmMnstrss1153CountryMdnght1171½ThndrDst115¾ Lacked rally 8
24May87- 1FL fst 5½f :22⅗ :46⅘ 1:06⅖ 3+ ⒻⓈClm 10000 2 4 1hd 1hd 2hd 22½ Hulet L b 115 2.40 81-15 Zyla 1152½ Thunder Dust 115½ Dancin Dorotnea 1153 Weakened 7
8May87- 8FL fst 6f :22⅗ :46⅗ 1:13⅕ 3+ ⒻⓈAlw 10300 4 4 21 21 2hd 62½ McCarthy M J b 116 14.10 80-18 Unhinged Iron 116¾ DustPocket116noFrancophile1161½ Weakened 9
10Apr87- 4GP fst 6f :22 :46⅕ 1:13⅖ ⒻClm 5000 3 2 22½ 22 1½ 31½ Gaffalione S b 117 3.60 70-23 Spirited Girl 117½ MightyOneEye1171ThunderDust1171 Weakened 10
12Mar87- 1GP fst 1¹⁄₁₆ :48 1:13⅗ 1:47⅕ ⒻClm 7500 11 3 43½ 1022 — — Romero R P b 117 4.60 — — Bonnie's Trip 1143½ RealFringe1171½SweeterThanGain1186 Eased 11
27Feb87- 4Hia fst 6f :22 :45⅘ 1:12⅗ ⒻClm 9000 4 4 53¾ 58 911 1013 Romero R P b 112 4.60 64-23 Lawdy LawdyLady1163DustyBritches116noMissFantasy114¾ Tired 12
20Feb87- 2Hia fst 6f :22⅗ :46⅗ 1:12⅘ ⒻClm 5000 4 2 1hd 1hd 11½ 12 Romero R P b 116 6.00 76-27 Thunder Dust 1162 IrishPolitician1161½GoldenGreens120½ Driving 12
10Jan87- 1Hia fst 6f :22⅖ :45⅘ 1:11⅖ ⒻClm 12500 6 7 65½ 67⅓ 89½ 1114½ Fires E 118 18.70 66-16 Sudden Dash 120nk Linda's Jig 1141½ Polly Numeral 1161 Outrun 11
LATEST WORKOUTS Jly 11 Mth 4f fst :49⅗ b Jly 4 Mth 4f fst :49⅘ bg

8. Apply the daily variants to the final times of the races for which they are given. Which horse deserves the best speed figure?

(64)

A.

Bold Batter Up
PINCAY L JR 1–N 116
Own.—A F Hopkins Estate
Ch. h. 6, by Mr Bold Batter—Dress Me Up's Girl, by Aczay
Br.—Hopkins A F (Cal)
Tr.—Sinne Gerald M $20,000
Lifetime 37 4 7 5 $95,400
1987 6 0 2 1 $7,650
1986 4 0 0 0
Turf 2 0 0 0 $1,500

21Mar87-1SA 6f :21³ :44³ 1:10²sy 10 114 96¼ 86 64½ 2nk Douglas R R 4 14000 86-16 ForbesReply,BoldBtterUp,VlDeRoi 12
Fast 3 14Mar87-2SA 6½f :21⁴ :44⁴ 1:16³ft 23 116 42¼ 43½ 21 2hd Douglas R R 6 10000 87-16 Polly'sRuler,BoldBttrUp,VisiblAsst 6
14Mar87—Bumped intervals in stretch
25Feb87-9SA 1¹⁄₁₆ :46⁴ 1:11 1:43⁴m 26 116 22½ 47½ 717 723 Kaenel J L 6 12500 59-22 Shuttle One, Nathan, Navegante 8
16Feb87-9GG 1 :46² 1:10⁴ 1:37 ft 17 116 43 31½ 3nk 33½ Gonzalez R M 5 12500 79-17 OurNordic,BennettPek,BoldBttrUp 7
7Feb87-9SA 1¹⁄₁₆ :46 1:10³ 1:43³ft 25 111⁵ 78½ 99¾ 811 815¼ Cox D W 6 16000 68-14 Fracoza, Restage, Tiffani's Toy 9
1Feb87-7BM 6f :22³ :46 1:10⁴ft 29 115 89¼ 811 813 810 White T C 1 20000 75-25 Cool'nScandlous,AckAck'sJoy,Sptil 8
~~26May86-1Hol~~ 1⅛ :47¹ 1:11³ 1:50 ft 48 116 42½ 44 57½ 67¾ Higuera A R 5 40000 79-17 Item Two, Restage, Bemidgi 7
~~18May86-9Hol~~ T :45 1:10² 1:36 ft 22 116 87¾ 65¼ 87¼ 78¼ Patterson A 12 32000 75-08 KnightSkiing,RightOnRed,Elefnte 12
18May86—Wide final 3/8
21Apr86-7SA 6f :21¹ :44¹ 1:10 ft 7¾ 116 65¼ 56 77 76½ Kaenel J L 6 40000 81-16 Mmmy'sPlsr,EllsBrvstSng,BldNnts 8
21Apr86—Hit gate start
13Apr86-3SA 6½f :21⁴ :44⁴ 1:16⁴ft 22 116 107¼ 117¾ 95¼ 64¼ Ortega L E 12 32000 82-15 Paskanell, Count Geiger, ‡Timlin 12
13Apr86—~~Veered in,~~ bumped at start, 5-wide into stretch
Mar 28 SA 4f ft :48⁴ h

B.

Danchai *
SIBILLE R 118
Own.—Karschamroon T
B. c. 4, by Zante—Rose Honor, by Count of Honor
Br.—Santoro M D (Cal) 1987 4 1 1 0 $13,350
Tr.—Oppegard Victor $20,000 1986 8 1 1 1 $11,175
Lifetime 12 2 2 1 $24,525

Slow 1 22Mar87-9SA 6½f :22 :444 1:17 gd 20 121 4nk 1½ 1½ 2² Sibille R1 Ⓢ 20000 83-23 Bennett Peak, Danchai, Melchip 11
26Feb87-5SA 1⅛ :452 1:102 1:44 ft 13 1125 21½ 1019 1028 — Cox D W7 25000 — — Cold, Exalted Bubble, Julie'sMark 10
26Feb87—Eased
1Feb87-9SA 1⅛ :464 1:112 1:434ft 21 1105 1½ 31½ 1216 1225¾ Cox D W2 32000 56-16 GumFleet,ShowerDecree,Dcontrol 12
1Feb87—Bumped at start
7Jan87-9SA 1 :472 1:12 1:38 m 43 1135 11½ 12½ 13 14½ Cox D W2 25000 78-21 Danchai, Doonsport, ShowerDecree 9
7Jan87—Bumped start
27Nov86-2Hol 6f :222 :462 1:122ft 4½ 120 3nk 11½ 14 13 Ortega L E9 Ⓢ M32000 81-18 Danchai, Vandalero, Perg Jr. 9
27Nov86—Broke in, bumped
20Nov86-4Hol 6f :222 :461 1:11 ft 26 120 63¾ 44 44½ 411 Ortega L E10 Ⓢ M32000 77-16 SaroStr,GetAlongPisno,Kim'sGold 11
20Nov86—Rough start
23Oct86-2SA 6f :214 :452 1:113ft 70 118 73¾ 54½ 46½ 36¼ Ortega L E2 Ⓢ M32000 74-20 ShowerDecree,CavalryClub,Danchi 12
23Oct86—Awarded second purse money; Bumped hard start
29Aug86-3Dmr 7f :222 :461 1:241ft 59 116 32 44½ 819 816 Sibille R9 Ⓢ M32000 68-15 Noon Sun, ZambeziPass,OutCross 11
13Aug86-4Dmr 6f :22 :454 1:111ft 17 116 41½ 31½ 98¾ 910½ Sibille R7 M32000 72-15 NmOfThGm,MgicFddl,LVrn'sKrsm 12
25Jly86-4Dmr 6f :221 :45 1:114ft 69 116 52½ 3nk 3nk 32¾ Sibille R3 Ⓢ M32000 76-18 Honyock, MidnightNotion,Danchai 10
Mar 16 GD tr.t 5f m 1:002 h ●Mar 13 GD tr.t 3f ft :361 h ●Feb 16 GD tr.t 5f ft 1:00 h

C.

Pialor
VALENZUELA P A 120
Own.—Slutzky&WinningWaysStable
B. c. 4, by Zoot Alors—Pia Mater, by Pia Star
Br.—Dollase & Duffel (Cal) 1987 6 2 0 1 $23,200
Tr.—Sadler John W $20,000 1986 14 3 2 2 $26,050
Lifetime 20 5 2 3 $49,250

8Mar87-1SA 6f :211 :442 1:11 gd *8-5 116 31½ 32 31 31¾ Solis A 4 25000 81-15 Roses Are Reb, Paskanell, Pialor 8
8Mar87—Broke in a tangle
Even 27Feb87-5SA 6f :213 :443 1:09 ft *6-5 117 11 1½ 11½ 14½ Solis A 5 Ⓢ c20000 93-16 Pialor, Melchip, Detector 11
14Feb87-2SA 6f :212 :442 1:103sy 6¾ 117 12 14 13½ 12½ Solis A 1 16000 85-17 Pialor, PineappleJack,Polly'sRuler 10
7Feb87-1SA 6f :213 :442 1:102ft 39 116 1½ 1½ 1½ 43 Solis A 8 20000 83-14 ElPrsdntUno,WstBoyII,PtrotGlovs 12
18Jan87-1SA 7f :221 :451 1:243ft 35 115 51½ 64¾ 1216 1219½ Meza R Q12 25000 57-19 Bizeboy, Trento, Superb Moment 12
18Jan87—Lugged in badly
7Jan87-9SA 1 :472 1:12 1:38 m 7½ 118 21½ 44 814 — Meza R Q8 25000 — — Danchai, Doonsport, ShowerDecree 9
7Jan87—Eased; Bumped start, wide 7/8
24Dec86-3Hol 7f :22 :452 1:24 ft *2 115 21½ 2½ 15 15 Castanon A L4 c18000 84-20 Pilor,Gordon'sCommnd,PinepplJck 7
11Dec86-7Hol 7f :222 :46 1:242ft 12 117 1hd 12 1½ 52¼ Castanon A L5 20000 86-21 Fali Flyer, Lord Pancho,ShuttleOne 8
30Dec86-7Hol 6f :221 :452 1:11 ft *3 119 31½ 31½ 31 33½ Castanon A L4 Ⓢ 20000 84-18 GrowlerSndue,ShowerDecree,Pilor 11
16Nov86-4Hol 7f :22 :443 1:241ft 79 117 41½ 43 11½ 22 Castanon A L3 20000 81-18 Pegus, Pialor, Amarone 12
16Nov86—Lugged out late
Mar 27 SA 6f ft 1:142 h Mar 20 SA 4f ft :482 h Feb 23 SA 4f ft :49 h

D.

Ells Bravest Song *
PATTON D B 1095
Own.—Pessin S & S
B. g. 7, by Bravest Roman—Restless Chant, by Restless Wind
Br.—Smith E J (Ky) 1987 4 1 1 0 $11,250
Tr.—Mollica Michael A $18,000 1986 15 5 4 1 $71,300
Lifetime 34 9 9 3 $147,175

Fast 6 19Mar87-1SA 6f :22 :452 1:103ft 4½ 119 11 11½ 11½ 21½ Pedroza M A 10 c12500 83-21 NtiveCptive,EllsBrvestSong,OhDd 11
5Mar87-5SA 6f :213 :443 1:103ft *3 116 1hd 1hd 1hd 1½ DelahoussayeE 1 12500 85-21 EllsBrvestSong,OhDd,TimForSilnc 12
15Feb87-9SA 7f :223 :451 1:241m *2½ 115 1hd 1hd 1hd 67½ Sibille R3 20000 71-17 HurricaneHec,CojakMn,Stemilion 10
18Jan87-1SA 7f :221 :451 1:243ft 7 116 3½ 2hd 3½ 64¾ Sibille R5 25000 72-19 Bizeboy, Trento, Superb Moment 12
18Jan87—Rough start
21Dec86-7Hol 6f :22 :452 1:101ft 5½ 116 2hd 2hd 42 36½ Sibille R 8 32000 86-15 Romaxe, Ondarty, EllsBravestSong 8
10Dec86-7Hol 6f :22 :454 1:111ft 3 117 11½ 11½ 1½ 22 Sibille R 3 25000 85-20 Rnbow'sCp,EllsBrvstSong,BldTpsdr 8
27Nov86-3Hol 6f :214 :45 1:103ft *7-5 117 21½ 21 2½ 12 Sibille R 6 c16000 90-18 Ells Bravest Song, Jacart, FallFlyer 7
12Nov86-7Hol 6f :214 :452 1:103ft 6¾ 117 11 11½ 1½ 2¾ Sibille R 7 16000 89-15 Inqustv,EllsBrvstSong,Rnbow'sCup 8
1Sep86-3Dmr 6f :213 :444 1:10 ft *2½ 118 31½ 32½ 45 78½ Valenzuela P A 4 20000 80-13 Down Range, Calabonga, Coyotero 7
1Sep86—Bumped hard start; lugged in backstretch; bumped again 3/16
22Aug86-1Dmr 6f :214 :45 1:094ft *2-3 122 1hd 2½ 24 54½ Stevens G L 10 c16000 85-14 John's Jove, Double Deficit, Nami 10
Mar 28 SA 4f ft :472 h Feb 7 SA 5f ft 1:011 h

9. None of these horses have yet won on turf. One has an advantage the others cannot match. Find it.

9th Arlington

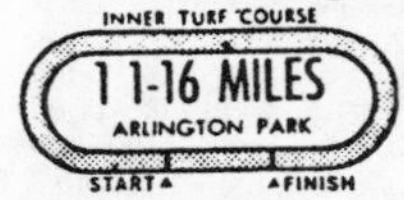

1 1/16 MILES. (InnerTurf). (1.40⅗) ALLOWANCE. Purse $14,000. 3–year–olds which have not won two races. Weight, 121 lbs. Non–winners of $9,600 allowed 3 lbs.; $7,200, 6 lbs.; a race other than claiming, 9 lbs. (Winners preferred.)

Coupled—Petra Forbes and Be My Victim; El Clipper and Timberside; Rakupon and Romeo Tim.

A. **(64)**

Petra Forbes

Own.—Magnificent 8 Stable **118**

Gr. c. 3, by Bold Forbes—Puss in Cahoots, by The Axe II
Br.—Susan Beth Franzheim, II (Ky) 1987 5 1 1 1 $12,480
Tr.—Getz George J 1986 0 M 0 0
Lifetime 5 1 1 1 $12,480

16Jly87-7AP	7f	:22^1	:45^1	1:24^{2}ft	5	115	2^1	2^{3}½	6^{6}¾	8^{20}¾	Diaz J L^3	Aw13000	59-22	RoughSpot,I'mNoPnkr,Hoss'NRydr	8
2Jly87-5AP	6½f	:23	:46	1:17^{2}ft	20	115	1½	2^{hd}	1½	2¾	Diaz J L^8	Aw13000	87-17	AdmBomb,PetrForbes,ClintsPrinc	12
21Jun87-7AP	6f	:22^4	:46^4	1:12^{1}sy	2	113	2^{hd}	3^{1}½	3^5	3^{11}	Diaz J L^3	Aw13000	68-33	Free Hope,J.L.Express,PetraForbes	6
22Mar87-5GP	6f	:22^2	:46	1:12 ft	6¾	122	1½	1^2	1^{1}½	1^1	Baltazar C^{12}	Mdn	79-24	PetrForbs,JustProspctor,LivlyNtiv	12
8Mar87-1GP	6f	:22^1	:45^3	1:12 ft	14	122	5^{2}¾	4^{5}½	4^5	4^7	Baltazar C^9	Mdn	72-25	AChrmngPro,JstProspctor,CrdtLn	11

Jly 26 AP 1 ft 1:47^4 b   Jly 14 AP 4f ft :52^3 b   Jun 30 AP 4f sl :54 b   Jun 19 AP 3f ft :40 b

B.

Up for Bids

Own.—Lucchesi J **112**

Ch. c. 3, by Lobsang—Hearts Are Trumps, by Bold Bidder
Br.—Michael Kostuk (Fla) 1987 8 1 0 1 $4,287
Tr.—Salazar Marco 1986 9 M 2 1 $4,140
Lifetime 17 1 2 2 $8,427

Entered 27Jly87- 9 AP

15Jly87-2AP	7f	:22^1	:47	1:27^{3}sy	33	118	7^{10}	8^{9}¾	8^{11}	8^{16}½	Silva C H^1	18500	47-34	Taravis, Chief Press, Draw Quay	9
14Apr87-8Spt	1	:49	1:15	1:42^{3}sy	11	113	2^{3}½	4^{11}	5^{14}	5^{17}¼	Silva C H^2	Aw21000	50-29	WhitCommndr,FroznDlight,SirWsly	8
7Apr87-7Spt	6½f	:22^3	:46^3	1:19^{4}ft	50	118	7^7	8^{7}¼	9^{7}¼	8^{7}¼	Razo E Jr^2	Aw22200	71-25	Saga, Lt. Mahaffey, Frankie's Pal	9
27Mar87-6Spt	1	:49^2	1:13^4	1:39^{3}ft	8¼	113	3^2	2½	3^3	4^{5}¼	Silva C H^2	Aw20600	77-19	PicnicPower,WillieDon,PlesureSon	6
27Feb87-8Tam	7f	:23^1	:46^3	1:26 ft	80	112	8^{6}¼	9^8	8^{7}¼	7^5	Dominguez CV^7	18500	85-18	GallantFriend,ChiefPlayer,NoSwet	10
4Feb87-8Tam	1 1/16	:47^4	1:14	1:47^{4}ft	9	116	6^{4}¾	5^{2}¾	7^{8}¾	6^{12}½	DePass R^7	c12500	67-19	StealBase,RtionlEyes,ChopperJim	10
21Jan87-5Tam	6f	:23	:47^3	1:14^{3}sy	*3-2	118	5^{4}½	3^{3}½	3^{2}½	1no	DePass R^1	M15000	72-27	UpforBids,FootRce,AmndmntSixtn	9
3Jan87-3Tam	6f	:23	:47	1:13^{4}ft	6	118	7^{3}¾	7^{6}¼	5^5	3^6	DePass R^3	Mdn	70-19	BlzngProspct,BgBlowup,UpforBds	11
10Dec86-4Crc	1 1/16	:49^2	1:15^2	1:50^{1}ft	7¼	120	4^5	6^7	5^{11}	6^{17}½	Hussey C^8	M20000	50-20	Gun Diplomat, Local Air, SirWesley	8
3Dec86-6Crc	1 1/16	:50^1	1:16^4	1:51^{4}ft	*2¾	119	6^{3}¼	4^{3}¼	3^2	2^{1}¼	Hussey C^7	M15000	59-23	HevyLifter,UpforBids,CloverKickr	12

Jly 11 Haw 7f ft 1:29 b   Jly 4 Haw 6f ft 1:20^3 b   Jun 27 Haw 4f ft :52^2 b   Jun 20 Haw 5f ft 1:05^2 b

C.

Burnishing

Own.—Stonewood Farm **115**

Ch. c. 3, by Our Native—Arterial, by Brigadier General
Br.—Campbell Judith L (Mich) 1987 7 1 0 0 $5,796
Tr.—Burns Daniel T 1986 2 M 0 0
Lifetime 9 1 0 0 $5,796

18Jly87-9Det	1 1/16	:47^2	1:14^3	1:46^{4}ft	85	122	16^{16}	15^{17}	14^{16}	8^{10}	Green B $\underline{19}$	[S]Dowling	59-26	PrivtExprss,DncingDvil,Kim'sQuill	19
11Jly87-11Det	170	:48^4	1:14^1	1:46^{3}ft	8½	114	4^{2}½	6^{2}¼	7^{2}¼	4^3	Green B^{10}	[S]Aw11600	61-23	Sacho, LibertyOtto,GourmetCheff	10
17Jun87-7Det	170	:50	1:17	1:50^{1}ft	19	112	5^4	6^{6}¾	6^{8}½	8^{9}¼	Green B $\underline{12}$	Aw7900	37-45	‡ShpInstrctons,Km'sQll,PrdntOffr	12
15May87-5Det	170	:48^3	1:15^3	1:47 ft	33	113	1^1	1^{hd}	1^{hd}	1¾	Green B $\underline{5}$	Mdn	62-30	Burnishing,PrudntOffr,DustyMorgn	8
26Apr87-5Det	6f	:23^2	:48^4	1:16 ft	31	114	10^{10}	9^{9}¼	9^{12}	7^{12}½	Burns M $\underline{2}$	Mdn	47-43	Strikemate,Hagar'sSword,Khroun	12
16Apr87-4Det	5½f	:23^2	:48^2	1:08^{3}ft	30	114	6^9	6^{9}½	6^{7}½	4^{2}¾	Burns M $\underline{11}$	[S]Mdn	69-29	NorthRply,PowrflMnstr,OrphnLdd	12
5Apr87-5Det	5f	:23^3	:49^1	1:02^{3}sy	78	114	6^{5}¾	5^9	5^9	6^{8}¾	Burns M $\underline{8}$	[S]Mdn	65-27	Mt.Wajim,C.W.Seguin,OrphnLddie	11
29Oct86-3Det	6f	:23	:47^2	1:15^{2}ft	85	119	9^{6}½	10^{12}	11^{18}	11^{15}¾	DePass R $\underline{5}$	[S]Mdn	47-32	Teelo, C. W. Seguin, Kharoun	12
8Oct86-3Det	6f	:23	:46^3	1:14^{2}ft	15	119	6^5	9^{13}	9^{13}	8^{12}½	Jones B S $\underline{3}$	[S]Mdn	55-26	TresurKy,WildmnWildr,C.W.Sguin	12

Jly 25 Det 5f gd 1:03 b   Jly 17 Det 3f ft :37 b   Jly 4 Det 5f ft 1:03^3 b   Jun 12 Det 4f ft :52^2 b (d)

D.

I'm No Punker

Own.—Reineman R L Stable Inc **112**

Dk. b. or br. c. 3, by Quadratic—Sweetest Roman, by The Pruner
Br.—Nuckols Bros. (Ky) 1987 5 1 3 0 $13,700
Tr.—Springer Frank R 1986 0 M 0 0
Lifetime 5 1 3 0 $13,700

16Jly87-7AP	7f	:22^1	:45^1	1:24^{2}ft	4	112	8^{8}¼	7^7	4^{2}½	2no	Clark K D^1	Aw13000	80-22	RoughSpot,I'mNoPnkr,Hoss'NRydr	8
25May87-8AP	7f	:22^3	:46^3	1:25^{4}sy	3½	112	6^8	6^{6}½	3^5	2^{6}½	Frazier R L^3	Aw13000	66-29	TheRedRolls,I'mNoPunker,ElClippr	8
18Apr87-8OP	1	:47	1:11^2	1:37^{3}ft	*8-5	113	3^{nk}	2^{hd}	1^{hd}	4^{2}½	Lively J^7	Aw15000	81-13	TwoFlingsADy,BonziBob,EspclIyU.	10
20Mar87-6OP	1 1/16	:47^2	1:12	1:43^{3}ft	9½	113	5^5	4^4	1½	2^{nk}	Lively J^6	Aw14000	83-16	GeneralSilver,I'mNoPunker,Kfiristn	8
25Feb87-3OP	6f	:22^1	:46^3	1:12^{2}ft	13	118	8^{5}¾	7^{5}¾	2½	1^{4}½	Lively J^8	M40000	78-22	I'mNoPunker,BeMyHert,TudorBld	12

Jly 3 AP Ⓣ 5f fm 1:05 b (d)   Jun 29 AP Ⓣ 4f fm :54 b (d)

E.

El Clipper
Own.—Lewis R A **118**

Ch. c. 3, by Naskra—General Partner, by Understanding
Br.—North Ridge Farm (Ky) 1987 9 1 1 4 $18,705
Tr.—Basile Anthony 1986 3 M 2 0 $4,040
Lifetime 12 1 3 4 $22,745 Turf 2 0 1 1 $4,340

10Jly87-9AP	1 1/16 [T]:52 1:173 1:502gd	5¾	114	53	41½	12	2nk	Brumfield D 3	Aw14000	51-49	SaintOxford,ElClipper,NobleBever	10
19Jun87-9AP	1 1/16 [T]:474 1:131 1:452fm	3	118	66¼	33	1hd	33¾	Brumfield D 5	Aw14000	72-24	Base Line, Noble Beaver, ElClipper	9
25May87-8AP	7f :223 :463 1:254sy	5	118	78¼	77½	58	311½	Brumfield D 6	Aw13000	61-29	TheRedRolls,I'mNoPunker,ElClippr	8
15May87-7CD	1 :47 1:132 1:383ft	2¼	118	56½	72½	43½	47	Hawley S 3	Aw17800	69-21	Gone Early, Unleavened, Tomball	7
23Apr87-2Kee	1 1/16 :47 1:112 1:44 ft	3¾	118	43	43½	31½	33½	Day P 6	Aw16900	82-13	Great Contract, Nudge, El Clipper	9
16Apr87-4Kee	6½f :224 :462 1:19 gd	5¼	120	53½	31	11½	12	Hawley S9	Mdn	82-20	ElClipper,TmprncWk,Nicol'sChmp	10
28Feb87-6Hia	7f :23 :454 1:251ft	7¾	121	85½	66¾	56	69	Vasquez J 5	Mdn	68-19	GudlupChut,SlwCtySlw,RoylEqrry	12
10Feb87-5Hia	6f :221 :453 1:112ft	2½	121	77¾	59¼	56½	55¾	Vasquez J3	Mdn	77-27	VisibleForc,CrditLin,Tht'sABlundr	12
11Jan87-3Hia	1⅛ :483 1:132 1:511ft	5	120	66	46	27	312	Penna D2	Mdn	63-19	AviesCopy,TheRelTruth,ElClipper	11
28Dec86-2Crc	7f :222 :464 1:27 gd	*6-5	120	1118	812	45	25½	Lester R N5	Mdn	75-22	HtchetByTwo,ElClippr,RoylEqurry	11

Jly 19 AP 4f ft :514 b Jly 13 AP 5f ft 1:07 b Jun 3 AP 4f sl :513 b

F.

Rakupon
Own.—Kleemann sandi & G W **118**

Ch. c. 3, by As de Copas—Raku, by Bupers
Br.—Bowman Dan-Polk Albert F Jr (Ill) 1987 7 1 0 0 $8,946
Tr.—Giardelli Leonard 1986 4 M 0 1 $1,089
Lifetime 11 1 0 1 $10,035 Turf 2 0 0 0

28Jun87-5AP	1 :46 1:111 1:372ft	63	117	42½	74¾	713	715¾	MrqzCHJr5	[S]Aw15400	58-23	Snny'sInvstmnt,AGdSct,Lt'Whcks	10
19Jun87-9AP	1 1/16 [T]:474 1:131 1:452fm	85	118	816	921	929	931¼	MrquezCHJr8	Aw14000	45-24	Base Line, Noble Beaver, ElClipper	9
8Jun87-5AP	6½f :23 :464 1:184ft	95	112	1017	1022	1016	721	LouvierGP1	[S]Aw14300	60-24	FrtntMmnt,DmtrsSrd,TmprrRsdnt	10
31May87-4AP	6f :223 :462 1:121ft	69	112	97½	710	614	616¾	Patin K C9	[S]Aw14300	62-27	Iwntoski,NorthBergen,ChiefPress	10
8May87-9Spt	1 :484 1:144 1:421ft	10	113	67¾	76¾	41½	75	MlnconKC6	[S]Aw22575	64-23	ChsLprchun,GrryC.,TmporryRsdnt	10
17Apr87-9Spt	1 :503 1:162 1:431ft	15	113	21½	42	31½	1½	Melancon K C1	[S]Mdn	64-30	Rakupon, A Little Salt, Trevian	10
14Mar87-3FG	a1 1/16 (T):492 1:15 1:48 fm	27	1145	86	811	916	819¼	Romero S P8	Mdn	53-22	Carmela's Fella, GayOrbit,Higgins	11
6Nov86-9CD	1 1/16 :491 1:161 1:493m	96	121	33½	89½	1019	1128¼	Gavidia W3	Mdn	32-32	Widdermker,DrienDevil,Timbersid	12
26Oct86-5CD	6f :221 :472 1:151m	48	121	1217	1116	1016	811¾	Moss R3	Mdn	55-29	GaryMorris,MagicWay,Italladdsup	12
30Sep86-6Haw	6f :224 :47 1:122sy	9¾	119	55	59¼	59½	310	Gavidia W5	[S]Mdn	69-19	Hony'sNuggt,SprngHllDncr,Rkupon	5

May 30 AP 3f ft :39 b

G.

Liberty Otto
Own.—WitRA&DEmily&HovnkmpB **115**

Ch. c. 3, by Fools Dance—Bear Cub, by Kentuckian
Br.—Harless Raymond & Karen (Mich) 1987 10 0 2 0 $7,491
Tr.—Waite Dennis L 1986 10 1 0 1 $9,562
Lifetime 20 1 2 1 $17,053

18Jly87-9Det	1 1/16 :472 1:143 1:464ft	13e	122	1213	1113	811	47¼	PllgrnTS13	[S]Dowling	62-26	PrivtExprss,DncingDvil,Kim'sQuill	19
11Jly87-11Det	170 :484 1:141 1:463ft	4	114	96½	74¼	52	2hd	PllgrinoTS5	[S]Aw11600	64-23	Sacho, LibertyOtto,GourmetCheff	10
4Jly87-11Det	1 1/16 :471 1:113 1:454ft	116	114	819	919	723	712½	Pellegrino T S8	Piston	61-26	Complict,BoldMidwy,MrktControl	10
25Jun87-9Det	6f :231 :46 1:132ft	53	114	1116	911	812	56	Pellegrino TS8	Aw7700	67-31	ChngPckts,JmmyCgny,Grg'sHnch	12
17Jun87-7Det	170 :50 1:17 1:501ft	9¼	114	1113	911	1011	78¾	Pellegrino TS4	Aw7900	37-45	‡ShpInstrctons,Km'sQll,PrdntOffr	12
31May87-8Det	170 :482 1:16 1:464ft	16	114	712	66	43½	2nk	Pellegrino TS8	Aw7900	63-33	MyWterloo,LibrtyOtto,JimmyCgny	8
17May87-8Det	170 :474 1:14 1:47 ft	60	114	59¼	47	57½	47¼	Pellegrino TS2	Aw8400	55-34	Proud Double, Eagle Ike, Solo Joe	6
9May87-10Det	6f :224 :463 1:142ft	94e	122	1115	1013	1013	77	PllgrinoTS2	[S]Lansing	61-30	WildFool,Kharoun,SparkesAround	13
1May87-9Det	170 :493 1:164 1:492ft	74	114	711	713	719	722	Pellegrino TS7	Aw8200	28-40	BoldMdwy,JmmyCgny,ClrThWyBob	8
23Apr87-6Det	6f :231 :472 1:151ft	250	114	118¾	1216	1214	1215½	Burns M12	Aw8000	48-44	Sacho,DancingSparks,RoylMrquis	12

H.

Mooney Creek
Own.—Radke R W **112**

Ch. c. 3, by Perrault—Riviere Bleue, by Riverman
Br.—Lerner Paul (Ky) 1987 3 1 0 0 $4,500
Tr.—Hazelton Richard P 1986 0 M 0 0
Lifetime 3 1 0 0 $4,500

23Jly87-3AP	6f :221 :454 1:122ft	6	116	64¾	32	12½	13	MarquezCHJr9	M20000	78-21	MoonyCrk,RoringRivr,Iwnbnownr	12
2Jly87-2AP	6f :223 :441 1:12 ft	5½	1125	3½	32½	33½	76¾	Torres F C7	M20000	73-17	NorfolkIslnd,Unccountble,TxDefrrl	9
21Jun87-3AP	6½f :224 :463 1:202sy	24	116	21	41	1013	1122½	Louviere G P10	Mdn	50-33	FoolishUncl,DydrmBlivr,BstGoods	11

●Jun 17 AP 6f ft 1:14 hg Jun 11 AP 5f ft 1:02 bg Jun 5 AP 5f ft 1:013 b May 30 AP 4f ft :492 b

10. Which horse should benefit most from a fast-slow pace?

A. **(64)**

Kamakhaylyn
PINCAY L JR 116
Own.—Bnstn-Blk-Frmn St et al
Ro. f. 4, by Briar Bend—Kamacross, by Carang
Br.—Vlieland W (Cal) 1987 5 2 0 0 $17,475
Tr.—Bernstein David $16,000 1986 10 2 1 1 $15,606
Lifetime 23 5 1 2 $36,769

18Mar87-1SA 6f :214 :451 1:111ft *3-2 121 2hd 1hd 1½ 1¾ PincayLJr 2 ⒻⓈ c12500 82-17 Kmkhylyn,OhMrie,ImpressiveWind 9
21Feb87-1SA 6½f :213 :444 1:18 ft 14 115 2½ 21 22½ 54¾ Solis A 8 Ⓕ 16000 75-14 Ms.CrokdRd,Mgdln'sMgc,Gld'sGrl 11
12Feb87-1SA 6f :214 :45 1:113ft 5¼ 115 2hd 11½ 12½ 12½ Solis A 7 ⒻⓈ 12500 80-20 Kamakhaylyn, OhMarie,OakPortal 12
28Jan87-3SA 6f :214 :451 1:113ft 44 1105 62¾ 46 79½ 812¼ Cisneros JE 12 Ⓕ 20000 68-21 Jerry'sGoldmine,MarCon,Frenzied 12
28Jan87—Very wide 3/8 turn
19Jan87-3SA 7f :22 :452 1:253ft 5¼ 117 1½ 1hd 12 42¾ VlenzuelPA 11 Ⓕ 16000 69-25 GranEmotion,ArcticLnd,MissDniel 11
24Dec86-1Hol 1 :463 1:122 1:383ft 6 1145 11½ 1½ 34½ 514½ Cisneros J E 3 Ⓕ 16000 55-20 DlghtflTwst,DynmoDrlng,ArFrcBby 7
24Dec86—Bumped start; lugged out stretch
21Nov86-3Hol 1 :453 1:112 1:391ft 10 1105 11½ 12½ 2hd 1hd Cisneros J E 2 Ⓕ 16000 67-20 Kamkhylyn,DelightfulTwist,Mrlene 6
14Nov86-7Hol 6f :22 :454 1:114ft 73 1095 51¾ 31½ 64 104¾ CisnerosJE 2 ⒻⓈ 18000 79-16 CrbbnSongI,GdNwsDll,LckyShwrs 11
2Oct86-3SA 6f :214 :444 1:102ft 54 116 43 44½ 911 1015¼ DelhoussyeE 6 Ⓕ 22500 71-20 SaroGolden,She'sSoBold,L'Athena 12
19Sep86-8Pom 6½f :22 :454 1:171ft 10 114 33½ 36 54 58¾ Stevens S A 4 Ⓕ 25000 85-09 She's SoBold,L'Athena,RochellsGirl 8
19Sep86—Took up 1st turn
Mar 27 SA 4f ft :471 h

B.

Folk's Victory
STEVENS G L 114
Own.—Doss & Keegan
Ch. m. 6, by Folk's Pride—Victory Malii, by Victory Morn
Br.—Hopkins A F (Cal) 1987 4 0 2 0 $5,600
Tr.—Passey Blake $14,000 1986 20 3 3 2 $46,065
Lifetime 49 7 7 4 $73,534 Turf 3 0 0 2 $4,700

14Mar87-1SA 6½f :212 :442 1:191ft 5 116 89 79 56½ 2hd Stevens G L 8 Ⓕ 12500 74-16 PrincessLark,Folk'sVictory,Gaetan 9
26Feb87-1SA 6f :22 :452 1:112ft 5¾ 116 97¾ 98 76½ 64½ DlhoussyE 9 ⒻⓈ 12500 76-22 Oak Portal, Distant Runner,Cuervo 9
16Feb87-1SA 6f :22 :453 1:12 gd 4¼ 1115 84¾ 74¼ 75¼ 63¼ Patton D B 6 Ⓕ 12500 75-21 SprkyGrn,EndlssSrch,GypsyMoon 11
16Feb87—Bumped, jostled start, wide into stretch
16Jan87-1SA 6½f :221 :454 1:181ft 3½ 1115 74½ 74¾ 55¾ 25½ Patton D B 2 Ⓕ c12500 73-18 Ms.CrkdRd,Flk'sVctry,FryGdmthr 12
16Jan87—Lugged out 1/2
12Dec86-5Hol 1 :48 1:132 1:394ft 3 1115 31½ 33 22½ 2½ Patton D B 5 Ⓕ 12500 63-20 MissDnil,Folk'sVctory,FrndlyCrowd 8
12Dec86—Lugged in stretch
27Nov86-1Hol 1 :454 1:12 1:40 ft 15 1115 63¾ 54½ 21½ 2hd Patton D B 6 Ⓕ 16000 63-18 DevlishDzzlr,Folk'sVictory,PrttyStll 8
27Nov86—Wide into stretch, lugged in
14Nov86-4Hol 6f :221 :454 1:111ft 12 119 75¾ 66 57 58¼ Castanon AL 1 Ⓕ 16000 79-16 AceAllegince,FirMissLdr,PulinRvrd 9
24Oct86-9SA 1 1/16 :463 1:124 1:454ft 4 116 75¾ 63¼ 811 816¾ Olivares F 12 Ⓕ c12500 55-20 FrindlyCrowd,BrooksPl,SuprisGift 12
24Oct86—Fanned wide 7/8
13Oct86-9SA 6f :221 :454 1:114ft 5½ 117 54½ 53¼ 43 42¾ Olivares F 6 Ⓕ 13000 76-19 HiddnPst,AncintLdy,Ms.CrookdRod 9
1Oct86-4SA 6½f :221 :452 1:18 ft 12 114 41½ 63½ 62 51¾ Olivares F 1 Ⓕ 18000 78-18 PrettyStall,RedFrenchy,SocietyRiv 9
Feb 12 SA 3f ft :37 h

C.

Oh Marie
PATTON D B 1115
Own.—Rappa Margaret F
B. f. 4, by Quick Dance—Verna Marie, by Bravest Roman
Br.—Benford R M (Cal) 1987 6 1 2 0 $12,950
Tr.—Rappa Frank T $16,000 1986 22 3 0 4 $27,927
Lifetime 28 4 2 4 $40,877

18Mar87-1SA 6f :214 :451 1:111ft 5¼ 1135 74¼ 43½ 32 2¾ Patton D B5 ⒻⓈ 12500 81-17 Kmkhylyn,OhMrie,ImpressiveWind 9
6Mar87-1SA 6f :213 :444 1:111gd 5 116 74 75¾ 76 75¾ Black C A 4 ⒻⓈ 16000 70-21 Oak Portal, Cuervo, Lovely Candy 7
6Mar87—Wide into stretch
21Feb87-1SA 6½f :213 :444 1:18 ft 12 115 95¾ 65½ 67 66¼ Black C A 5 Ⓕ 16000 74-14 Ms.CrokdRd,Mgdln'sMgc,Gld'sGrl 11
21Feb87—Broke slowly; wide into stretch
12Feb87-1SA 6f :214 :45 1:113ft 7¼ 117 95¾ 55 53¾ 22½ BlackCA 10 ⒻⓈ c12500 77-20 Kamakhaylyn, OhMarie,OakPortal 12
12Feb87—Lugged in; bumped 1/2
29Jan87-1SA 6½f :221 :453 1:192ft 7¾ 115 61¾ 44½ 32½ 1½ Black C A 4 ⒻⓈ 12500 73-27 OhMarie,Dimaggio'sPet,AmoDidIt 12
23Jan87-1SA 6f :22 :46 1:13 ft 4 115 95¼ 118¼ 100¾ 77¾ Black C A 12 Ⓕ 12500 65-22 PrncssLrk,PulnRvrd,FryGodmothr 12
23Jan87—Wide into stretch
26Dec86-1SA 6f :214 :45 1:111ft 14 116 97 107¾ 109¼ 109¼ DelhoussyE 11 Ⓕ 16000 73-13 IrishZuni,FullO'Gems,ToBImprssiv 11
26Dec86—Wide final 1/4
4Dec86-3Hol 6f :22 :463 1:121ft 5 116 55 42 34 38 DlhoussyE 2 ⒻⓈ 20000 74-25 I'mTeasableToo,Nicholova,OhMarie 7
29Oct86-2SA 6f :213 :45 1:113ft 3¾ 117 75 66¼ 53¾ 52½ PincayLJr 9 ⒻⓈ c16000 77-17 Brookes Pal, AbOriginal,Testarosa 11
29Oct86—Lugged in late
23Oct86-5SA 6f :214 :45 1:114ft 4 1135 95½ 86¾ 54½ 33 Black C A 9 Ⓕ c12500 76-20 CribbnSongI,Jrry'sGoldmin,OhMri 12

D.

Lucky Showers — B. f. 4, by Forget the Showers—Lucky Lorette, by Olympiad King
PATTON D B — 1135 — Br.—Zemen S E (Cal) — 1987 3 0 0 0
Own.—Breen P E — Tr.—Lewis Craig A — $16,000 — 1986 15 2 3 1 $23,595
Lifetime 18 2 3 1 $23,595 — Turf 1 0 0 0

25Mar87-5SA 6f :214 :451 1:104ft 9 118 42 52½ 74¾ 77 Pedroza M A4 Ⓕ 20000 77-17 LovelyCndy,AmoDidIt,FireMissLdr 8
25Mar87—Bumped start
20Feb87-5SA a6½f Ⓣ:212 :4411:154fm 27 116 2hd 63½ 1012 1018¾ Kaenel J L9 ⒻAw27000 61-19 High Ace, Jam Time, Foufa 10
25Jan87-1SA 6f :22 :453 1:113ft 4¾ 117 1½ 1hd 31½ 912¼ CastanonAL Ⓕ c20000 68-18 Kristin, Fire Miss Leader,Florimel 11
30Dec86-2SA 6f :214 :451 1:112ft 6 116 2½ 2½ 1hd 12 CastanonAL5 Ⓕ 20000 81-18 LuckyShowers,MissDaniel,IrishZuni 8
19Dec86-7Hol 6f :22 :454 1:12 ft 6¼ 115 11 1hd 2hd 23½ CastnonAL5 ⒻⓈ 20000 79-17 DistntRunner,LuckyShowrs,Michcri 9
27Nov86-6Hol 6f :213 :451 1:113ft 23 116 32½ 34½ 89 812½ Sibille R 1 Ⓕ 25000 72-18 GoodNewsDoll,Frenzied,DndyHnnh 9
14Nov86-7Hol 6f :22 :454 1:114ft 46 115 3nk 11½ 11½ 33½ CastnonAL1 ⒻⓈ 20000 80-16 CrbbnSongI,GdNwsDll,LckyShwrs 11
29Oct86-2SA 6f :213 :45 1:113ft 22 115 2½ 2hd 2hd 63½ CastnonAL3 ⒻⓈ 16000 76-17 Brookes Pal, AbOriginal,Testarosa 11
13Oct86-5SA 6f :22 :452 1:111ft 6 116 63¾ 75 68 — DelhoussyeE6 Ⓕ 20000 — — SroGolden,DnceHllHussy,MissDniel 7
13Oct86—Eased
19Sep86-8Pom 6½f :22 :454 1:171ft 3½ 114 2½ 22 32½ 712½ Douglas R R7 Ⓕ 25000 81-09 She's SoBold,L'Athena,RochellsGirl 8
Mar 18 SA 4f ft :472 h — Mar 8 SA 4f gd :474 h — Feb 13 SA 6f ft 1:124 h — Feb 4 SA 5f ft 1:003 h

11. Which maiden is most likely to graduate to the allowance ranks successfully? The track surface has had a C+ bias for three days.

4th Arlington

6 FURLONGS — ARLINGTON PARK

6 FURLONGS. (1.08) ALLOWANCE. Purse $13,000. Fillies. 2-year-olds which have not won two races. Weight, 121 lbs. Non-winners of $9,000 allowed 3 lbs.; $6,600, 6 lbs.; a race other than maiden or claiming, 9 lbs.

Coupled—Madam Q. and House Wine.

A. **(64)**

Madam Q. — B. f. 2, by Raise a Cup—Mistress Q, by Quadrangle
Own.—Calumet Farm — 118 — Br.—Calumet Farm (Ky) — 1987 3 1 1 1 $10,010
Tr.—Foyt A J III
Lifetime 3 1 1 1 $10,010

15Jly87-4AP 5½f :222 :473 1:082sy *1 116 21 12 14 12½ Smith M E 3 ⒻMdn 73-34 Madam Q., Outshine, Sooner's Lass 6
26Jun87-6AP 5½f :222 :464 1:061ft *2-3 117 31½ 23 22½ 32 Day P3 ⒻMdn 82-25 Peach Point, PearlieGold,MadamQ. 8
17Jun87-4AP 5f :224 :463 :592ft *8-5 117 32 2½ 21½ 21½ Day P2 ⒻMdn 87-19 Cushion Cut,MadamQ.,TooTwoReal 5
Jly 25 AP 4f ft :473 h — Jly 8 AP 4f ft :483 h — Jun 8 AP 5f ft 1:022 bg

B.

Countess Di — Ch. f. 2, by Replate—La Contessa, by Blazing Count
Own.—Glen Oak Farm — 118 — Br.—Glen Oak Farm (Ky) — 1987 1 1 0 0 $6,600
Tr.—Fernandez Jose
Lifetime 1 1 0 0 $6,600

12Jun87-3AP 5f :224 :462 :592ft 6 117 31½ 2½ 11½ 16½ Silva C H3 ⒻMdn 89-22 Countess Di, Starwink,OnlyMaisie 11
Jly 23 AP 3f ft :37 b — Jly 17 AP 4f ft :503 b — Jly 10 AP 6f ft 1:16 b — Jly 2 AP 5f ft 1:013 b

C.

Spadiddle — B. f. 2, by Northern Prospect—Pleasure Pal, by Foolish Pleasure
Own.—Bwamazon Farm — 121 — Br.—Scott Savin (Ky) — 1987 2 1 0 0 $11,245
Tr.—Kirk James
Lifetime 2 1 0 0 $11,245

28Jun87-6CD 5½f :222 :462 1:054ft *7-5e 118 32 2½ 11 12½ McDowell M10 ⒻMdn 92-16 Spadiddle,DringDeidre,FlyingRiver 12
21Jun87-6CD 5½f :222 :462 1:062ft 7½ 120 2½ 2hd 2hd 2½ McDowell M9 ⒻMdn 88-17 Punctatum, Spadiddle, Alena Sue 10
21Jun87—Disqualified from purse money
Jly 24 AP 5f ft 1:02 h — Jly 15 CD 6f ft 1:142 h — Jun 16 CD 5f ft 1:023 b — Jun 3 CD 3f m :38 bg

D.

House Wine — B. f. 2, by Conquistador Cielo—Lucinda Lea, by Best Turn
Own.—Calumet Farm — 118 — Br.—Calumet Farm (Ky) — 1987 2 1 0 0 $9,450
Tr.—Foyt A J III
Lifetime 2 1 0 0 $9,450

24Apr87-3Kee 4½f :224 :474 :543ft 4½ 117 6 44 22½ 13 Kaenel J L 6 ⒻMdn 82-18 House Wine, MissSwanky,Mardipen 7
14Apr87-3Kee 4½f :231 :47 :533ft 2½ 117 4 32½ 33½ 43½ Kaenel J L 5 ⒻMdn 83-13 Night Affair, Sarah's Rose, Belgica 8
Jly 30 AP 3f ft :374 b — Jly 23 AP 4f ft :484 b — Jly 13 AP 6f ft 1:171 b — Jly 9 AP 3f ft :371 b

E.

Genuineness
B. f. 2, by Al Nasr—Eloquent, by Exclusive Native
Br.—Harbor View Farm (Ky) 1987 2 1 0 0 $6,600
Own.—Harbor View Farm 118 Tr.—Lukas D Wayne
Lifetime 2 1 0 0 $6,600
15Jly87-1AP 5½f :223 :482 1:091sy 2½ 116 12½ 12½ 15 114 Evans R D7 ⒻMdn 69-34 Gnnnss,RghtCommrcl,NorthrnAllnc 7
1Jly87-1AP 5½f :231 :473 1:054ft 18 117 31½ 42 57 719 Evans R D10 ⒻMdn 67-23 GlwySong,ExclusivFlm,RockNRor 10
Jly 29 AP 4f gd :504 b Jun 14 AP 4f ft :51 b Jun 7 AP 4f ft :51 b

F.

Cushion Cut
Ch. f. 2, by Raise a Man—Julie Prince, by Majestic Prince
Br.—Agnew Dan J (Ky) 1987 3 1 0 0 $7,260
Own.—LukasDWayne&OwensNormn 118 Tr.—Lukas D Wayne
Lifetime 3 1 0 0 $7,260
18Jly87-4AP 6f :221 :46 1:114ft 12 115 2hd 31½ 612 616 Louviere GP2 Aw13000 65-21 Glory Afar, Bob's Debut, Miki Baby 6
17Jun87-4AP 5f :224 :463 :592ft 3½ 117 11½ 1½ 11½ 11½ Smith M E5 ⒻMdn 89-19 Cushion Cut,MadamQ.,TooTwoReal 5
3Jun87-6AP 5f :222 :48 1:011ft 6 117 33½ 23 32½ 412¾ Frazier R L2 ⒻMdn 67-34 She'sFreezing,OnlyMaisie,BbyLiloo 6
Jly 29 AP 4f gd :502 b Jly 3 AP 4f ft :49 b

12. Analyze this maiden route in terms of the probable early pace. Select the likeliest outcome below.

6th Santa Anita

1 1-16 MILES SANTA ANITA START FINISH

1 1/16 MILES. (1.40⅘) MAIDEN. Purse $24,000. 3-year-olds. Weight, 117 lbs.. (Non-starters for a claiming price of $32,000 or less preferred.)

Affstar
Ch. c. 3, by Affirmed—Eastman Star, by Pia Star
TORO F Br.—Fuller P (Ky) 1987 2 M 1 0 $5,775
117 Tr.—Mandella Richard 1986 1 M 0 0 $1,350
Own.—Cooke J K Lifetime 3 0 1 0 $7,125
1Mar87-6SA 6½f :213 :444 1:163ft 5½ 118 21½ 42½ 44 45½ Toro F3 Mdn 81-15 ANewEra,DmscusLd,TeddyBerHug 12
8Feb87-6SA 6f :22 :452 1:101ft 5½ 118 3½ 31 22 24½ Toro F10 Mdn 82-14 Cndi'sGold,Affstr,McKenziePrince 10
1Sep86-6Dmr 6f :22 :444 1:094ft 8¾ 1135 53¼ 46½ 36½ 49¾ Black C A9 Mdn 79-13 SpecilTrick,SwordChrger,ChrlieZe 12
1Sep86—Erratic backstretch; lugged in stretch
Mar 11 SA 5f ft 1:011 h Feb 25 SA 4f gd :513 h (d) Feb 19 SA 4f ft :504 b Feb 6 SA 3f ft :36 b

Five Daddy Five
Dk. b. or br. g. 3, by Nodouble—No No Yvette, by Best Turn
MCHARGUE D G Br.—Calumet Farm (Ky) 1987 2 M 0 1 $2,100
117 Tr.—Mayberry Brian A 1986 0 M 0 0
Own.—Siegel M-Jan-Samantha Lifetime 2 0 0 1 $2,100
22Feb87-6SA 1 1/16 :463 1:12 1:442ft 7 117 1111 87 610 610½ McHargue D G10 Mdn 68-14 Mountncmll,ErnYourStrps,ExtPoll 11
29Jan87-2SA 6½f :22 :453 1:182ft 11 118 1110 76½ 45 31 Baze G8 Mc32000 77-27 Mr.Edlwss,Shcky'sTryst,FvDddyFv
29Jan87—Broke slowly; bumped, altered course 5/16
Mar 11 SA 4f ft :47 hg Mar 3 SA 4f ft :47 h Feb 18 SA 5f ft 1:002 h Jan 26 SA tr.t 4f ft :494 h

Exit Poll
B. c. 3, by Seattle Slew—Exclusive Fir, by Exclusive Native
MCCARRON C J Br.—Forest Acres (Ky) 1987 2 M 1 1 $7,650
117 Tr.—Truman Eddie 1986 0 M 0 0
Own.—Layman G Jr Lifetime 2 0 1 1 $7,650
22Feb87-6SA 1 1/16 :463 1:12 1:442ft *8-5 117 66½ 64½ 45½ 34 Stevens G L6 Mdn 75-14 Mountncmll,ErnYourStrps,ExtPoll 11
22Feb87—Bumped start; lugged out 7/8
31Jan87-6SA 6½f :213 :443 1:163ft 4¼ 118 42½ 32½ 21½ 21¾ Shoemaker W6 Mdn 85-15 Blanco, Exit Poll, Grey Alcha 9
Mar 11 SA 6f ft 1:131 h Feb 18 SA 6f ft 1:142 h Feb 11 SA 5f ft 1:013 h Jan 28 SA 5f ft 1:021 h

Nova Zembla
B. c. 3, by Verbatim—Little Nana, by Lithiot
SHOEMAKER W Br.—Schefler A (Ky) 1987 1 M 0 0
117 Tr.—Fulton John W 1986 0 M 0 0
Own.—Schefler & Cheng Lifetime 1 0 0 0
21Feb87-6SA 6f :211 :44 1:10 ft 14 118 911 1013 89¾ 66¾ Shoemaker W8 Mdn 81-14 McKnzPrnc,CrystlFox,ToghKnght 10
21Feb87—Broke slowly
Feb 13 SA 3f ft :36 h Feb 7 SA 6f ft 1:123 h Feb 1 SA 6f ft 1:141 h

Explicit
Dk. b. or br. c. 3, by Exceller—Cornish Queen, by Cornish Prince
STEINER J J Br.—Appleton A I (Fla) 1987 3 M 0 0 $575
117 Tr.—Tinsley J E Jr 1986 0 M 0 0
Own.—Appleton A I Lifetime 3 0 0 0 $575
22Feb87-6SA 1 1/16 :463 1:12 1:442ft 76 1125 3½ 53½ 1118 1130½ Patton D B4 Mdn 48-14 Mountncmll,ErnYourStrps,ExtPoll 11
22Feb87—Lugged out 3/8
1Feb87-6SA 1 :461 1:113 1:381ft 27 1125 63¾ 66¾ 58¼ 510½ Patton D B3 Mdn 66-16 Famous Forever, Conquer, All Cat 10
25Jan87-6SA 6f :22 :451 1:103ft 51 118 79¾ 79¼ 59 68¼ Ortega L E1 Mdn 77-18 KapaluQuick,ChrtTheStrs,NoMrker 9
25Jan87—Veered in start
Mar 8 SA 4f gd :50 h Mar 1 SA 4f ft :493 h Feb 20 SA 3f ft :351 hg Feb 8 SA 4f ft :50 h

Endorse
PINCAY L JR **117**
Own.—Harbor View Farm
B. c. 3, by Raise a Native—Jevalin, by Dewan
Br.—Kinderhill Corp (NY) **1987 3 M 1 0 $8,520**
Tr.—Lukas D Wayne **1986 5 M 2 0 $10,560**
Lifetime 8 0 3 0 $19,080

8Mar87-4SA 1 1/16 :471 1:121 1:443ft 8¾ 117 56 54½ 56¾ 47¾ Pincay L Jr 10 Mdn 70-15 LocalsOnly,NastyNaskr,TheMedic 10
8Mar87—Poor start; wide into drive
14Jan87-6Aqu 1⅛ ⊡:4941:1411:524ft 5 122 31¼ 42 23½ 24¾ Lovato F Jr 6 Mdn 73-16 Pi Phi Prince,Endorse,Hoistn'Hai! 10
7Jan87-3Aqu 1 1/16 ⊡:4641:1211:472ft 3¼ 122 47½ 46 46½ 42¼ Lovato F Jr 1 Mdn 70-21 MxdEmotns,ChfBlckhwk,MdvlMnd 8
27Dec86-4Aqu 1⅛ ⊡:4731:1311:522ft 3¾ 118 42½ 31½ 23½ 26¾ Romero R P 9 Mdn 73-11 Rolls Aly, Endorse, Bucket Shop 11
14Dec86-6Aqu 1 1/16 ⊡:4831:1311:48 ft 4 118 31½ 811 713 510½ Migliore R 2 Mdn 59-20 Coco'sDouble,Knockon,MdvlMind 11
30Nov86-3Aqu 1 :472 1:124 1:39 ft 13 118 2½ 1hd 1½ 22¾ Migliore R 7 Mdn 68-24 PrisOffice,Endorse,Christophr'sTim 7
14Nov86-6Aqu 6f :214 :454 1:121ft 8½ 118 57¼ 55½ 67½ 69 Romero R P 3 Mdn 71-23 Fort Whoop, Creativity, Sir Bemis 9
1Nov86-2Aqu 6f :222 :462 1:112ft 16 118 3½ 31 44¼ 613¼ McCauley W H 4 Mdn 71-19 Krul, Occum's Razor, Magic Feet 13
Feb 21 Hol 5f ft 1:011 h **Feb 6 Hol 5f ft 1:023 h**

North Of Eden
BLACK C A **117**
Own.—Gentry T
B. c. 3, by Northern Dancer—Garden of Eden, by Exbury
Br.—Gentry T (Ky) **1987 1 M 0 0**
Tr.—Gregson Edwin **1986 0 M 0 0**
Lifetime 1 0 0 0

1Mar87-6SA 6½f :213 :444 1:163ft 56 118 1111 912 712 712 Black C A9 Mdn 75-15 ANewEra,DmscusLd,TeddyBerHug 12
1Mar87—Broke slowly
Mar 9 SA 5f ft 1:00 h **Feb 23 SA 5f ft 1:012 h** **Feb 17 SA 7f ft 1:282 h** **●Feb 8 SA 1 ft 1:414 h**

All Cat
DELAHOUSSAYE E **117**
Own.—Bradley-Chndler-Whittinghm
B. c. 3, by Cougar II—Almira, by Sheet Anchor
Br.—Bradley-Whittinghm-Chndler (Ky) **1987 4 M 0 2 $8,400**
Tr.—Whittingham Charles **1986 1 M 0 0 $1,425**
Lifetime 5 0 0 2 $9,825

18Feb87-8SA 1⅛ :461 1:101 1:484ft 12 115 611 710 612 58¾ Toro F 6 ®Bradbury 76-19 HotAndSmoggy,Barb'sRelic,Reland 7
1Feb87-6SA 1 :461 1:113 1:381ft 4 117 87 56½ 37 35 Black C A 4 Mdn 72-16 Famous Forever, Conquer, All Cat 10
1Feb87—Broke slowly
19Jan87-6SA 1 1/16 :482 1:13 1:454ft 20 117 74 63½ 63¾ 33 Black C A 6 Mdn 69-25 Rupperto, Chatanga, All Cat 8
19Jan87—Off slowly; blocked stretch, wide
3Jan87-6SA 1 1/16 :472 1:113 1:442ft 7½e 117 913 913 712 611¾ Black C A1 Mdn 67-16 SvorFire,NstyNskr,FmousForever 11
7Dec86-5Hol 6f :22 :454 1:112gd 21 118 715 713 69½ 49¼ Black C A6 Mdn 77-18 BoldArchon,FlyingFlgs,Ful'OfFools 7
7Dec86—Wide backstretch
Mar 10 SA 5f ft 1:004 h **Mar 2 SA 5f ft 1:01 h** **Feb 26 SA 5f gd 1:011 h** **Feb 13 SA 5f ft :594 h**

Lord Turk
STEVENS G L **117**
Own.—Saron Stable
Ch. c. 3, by His Majesty—Taba, by Table Play
Br.—Robertson C J (Ky) **1987 2 M 0 0**
Tr.—Jones Gary **1986 0 M 0 0**
Lifetime 2 0 0 0

22Feb87-6SA 1 1/16 :463 1:12 1:442ft 13 117 910 119 914 815¾ Solis A 7 Mdn 63-14 Mountncmll,ErnYourStrps,ExtPoll 11
22Feb87—Bumped start; steadied 3/8, wide into stretch
31Jan87-6SA 6½f :213 :443 1:163ft 5 118 88¾ 810 77 67½ Stevens G L 2 Mdn 79-15 Blanco, Exit Poll, Grey Aloha 9
Mar 11 SA 4f ft :501 h **Mar 7 SA 6f m 1:131 h** **Mar 2 SA 4f ft :51 h** **Feb 18 SA 6f ft 1:14 h**

(64)

A. *Affstar* will go wire to wire from the inside
B. *Exit Poll* will pick up the pieces
C. *Nova Zembia* will get the lead if he breaks smoothly
D. *Endorse* should track the early pace and prove best in the drive

13. Which horse has the best early speed?

8 MONMOUTH 6 FURLONGS MONMOUTH PARK

6 FURLONGS. (1.08) CLAIMING. Purse $14,000. 3-year-olds. Weight, 122 lbs. Non-winners of two races since June 30 allowed 3 lbs.; a race 6 lbs. Claiming price $50,000; for each $2,500 to $40,000 1 lb. (Races where entered for $35,000 or less not considered.)

A. (64)

Mighty Force — Ch. g. 3, by Stalwart—Yoda, by Proudest Roman — $40,000 Br.—Hillbrook Farm (Ky) Tr.—Dowd John — 112 — Lifetime 14 3 1 5 $25.821 — 1987 10 1 1 4 $14,623 — 1986 4 2 0 1 $11,198 — Turf 5 0 0 4 $4,433

Own.—Tombs K & W

20Jly87- 5Mth gd 6f :22⅘ :46 1:12 Clm 35000 3 5 53 42 43¼ 52¾ Madrid A Jr b 116 *.70 77-26 CdllcRnch116½GoldnExplosn1161½Syd sCmmnd116no Lacked rally 6

13Jly87- 3Mth fst 6f :22⅕ :45 1:10⅗ Clm 25000 6 1 2hd 1hd 12 18 Madrid A Jr b 116 5.90 87-21 Mighty Force 1168 Stuvy 1133 Fast Jack 1193 Ridden out 7

19Jun87- 6Mth fm 1⅟₁₆ Ⓣ:4[illegible] 1:13⅕ 1:45⅗ Clm c-20000 9 1 1hd 1hd 63½ 89 Perret C 115 *2.70 68-22 Family Best 117no Michelles Du Nord1111JiveWithFive1151 Tired 12

8Jun87- 8GS fm 1⅟₁₆ Ⓣ:4[illegible] 1:13 1:44⅕ Clm 30000 5 3 42¾ 31 41¾ 32¾ Thornburg B b 114 5.60 84-13 Diplomatic Corps 1122 Family Best115¾MightyForce114nk Evenly 7

26May87- 8GS fm 170 Ⓣ:46[illegible] 1:11⅗ 1:41 Clm 30000 4 3 31½ 2hd 1hd 33 Verge M E 114 5.60 90-06 Bobby's J. S. 1162 Lil Saucy 1161 Mighty Force 1141 Weakened 8

9May87- 4CD fst 6f :21⅗ :45⅗ 1:11⅕ Clm 25000 9 7 75 95¼ 75¼ 65½ Brumfield D 121 4.20 81-14 Sizzling Hell 114nk Salute the Moon 1213 Deal Me Spades 119no 10

28Apr87- 8CD fst 6f :22⅖ :46⅖ 1:10⅖ Alw 17850 4 5 64 64 66 67¾ McDowell M 115 21.90 83-16 Jilsie's Gigalo 1212½ Stalwart Flag 115hd The Corps 1155 6

10Apr87- 2Kee fst 7f :23 :47 1:26⅘ Clm 35000 6 5 32 32 22 22½ Brumfield D 121 *1.90 69-28 Mickey's Lark 1142½ Mighty Force 121nk Deal Me Spades 1132 12

19Mar87-10FG fm *7½f Ⓣ:24⅕ :47⅕ 1:33⅘ Alw 9500 3 1 23 35 39 311½ Bourque K 119 3.50 68-20 Performing Pappy 1194½ Pyrophoric 1197 Mighty Force 119½ 8

11Mar87-10FG fm *5½f Ⓣ:23⅕ :47⅕ 1:07⅗ Clm 30000 8 7 64½ 66½ 77 31¼ Bourque K 113 3.90 81-22 Fast Reputation 113½ Sonny's Affair 113¾ Mighty Force 113nk 9

LATEST WORKOUTS Jly 29 Mth 4f fst :48⅗ h — Jly 6 Mth 5f fst 1:01 h — Jly 1 Mth 6f fst 1:15 h

B.

Lone Quadrant — B. c. 3, by Quadratic—Confalone, by Lorenzaccio — $50,000 Br.—Prince Marian (NY) Tr.—Perkins Ben Jr — 116 — Lifetime 13 2 2 4 $86,121 — 1987 7 0 0 3 $21,393 — 1986 6 2 2 1 $64,728

Own.—Elkcam Sable

5Jly87- 5Bel fst 7f :22⅘ :45⅘ 1:24⅘ 3↑[S]Alw 30000 3 2 21½ 22 813 916¾ Antley C W 111 *3.40 64-24 Proud Guy 1165¾ Edeinash 1132 Core A Apple 116½ Stopped 9

14Jun87- 6Bel fst 6f :22⅕ :46⅕ 1:11⅗ 3↑[S]Alw 30000 4 4 33½ 3nk 2hd 3½ Nuesch D5 104 *2.20 81-20 Lucee's Appeal 114nc Flippant122½LoneQuadrant104nk Weakened 10

2Jun87- 9Mth fst 6f :22⅕ :44⅘ 1:10⅕ Select 2 7 43½ 45 46½ 57 Perret C 114 4.70 82-16 Chrio1121½NeverForgotten114noDeprtingDrm1182½ Saved ground 10

25Apr87- 8Aqu gd 1 :46 1:10⅗ 1:36⅘ [S]Ny Otb Apple 4 3 32 2hd 2½ 32¼ Hernandez R 113 15.90 82-14 Peggy'sDream113nkOmarKhyym1182LoneQuarnt1133¾ Weakened 8

29Mar87- 8Aqu fst 7f :22⅗ :45 1:23⅕ [S]Dewitt Clint 5 1 2½ 1hd 22 36¼ Antley C W b 115 5.00 79-17 OmarKhayyam1144¾HotAmber1141½LoneQuadrnt1153¼ Weakened 6

4Mar87- 8Aqu fst 6f [•]:22⅗ :46⅕ 1:11 [S]Catskill 4 3 21½ 3½ 66 68 Antley C W b 114 4.50 81-16 [D]OmrKhyym1141¾Emorce'sSybling1141¾SwtEnvoy123nk Took up 6

4Mar87-Placed fifth through disqualification

14Feb87- 8GS fst 6f :22 :45⅖ 1:11 Del Valley H 4 4 42¾ 44½ 68 713¾ Wilson R b 114 4.50 73-21 Z. Plasty 1223 Justa Playboy 113¾ Ruler of the Fleet 1141 Tired 7

6Dec86- 8Aqu fst 1⅛ [•]:47⅘ 1:12⅗ 1:54 [S]B F Bongard 5 1 13½ 11½ 2hd 22 Hernandez R b 117 6.80 70-21 SwtEnvoy1122LonQdrnt1173¾TroopCommndr113nk Best of others 9

19Nov86- 6Aqu gd 6f :22⅘ :46⅘ 1:12⅗ [S]Alw 26500 5 1 1hd 12 14 17 Baird E T5 b 117 1.80 78-25 LoneQuadrant1177TroopCommander1172¾TipsyTurvy1173¾ Easily 7

11Nov86- 6Aqu sly 6f :22⅗ :46⅖ 1:12 [S]Md Sp Wt 4 1 1½ 11½ 12½ 16 Baird E T5 b 113 4.60 81-21 Lone Quadrant 1136TerribleTeddy116½OmarKhayyam1162 In hand 10

LATEST WORKOUTS Jly 29 Mth 3f fst :36 b — Jun 27 Mth 4f sly :49⅖ b

C.

Limited Access — Ch. g. 3, by Kris S—Good Routes, by Pass Catcher — $50,000 Br.—Koontz Bina & K (Fla) Tr.—Pierce Joseph H Jr — 116 — Lifetime 18 1 5 4 $29,030 — 1987 14 1 4 4 $25,535 — 1986 4 M 1 0 $3,495 — Turf 1 0 0 0 $125

Own.—Kligman & Pierce Sheila

14Jly87- 5Mth fst 170 :46⅗ 1:11 1:43⅕ 3↑Alw 15000 5 4 45½ 48½ 59 59 McCauley W H b 113 3.30 71-23 Hill Slide 118nk Public Accounter1104HurricaneJohn114nk Outrun 7

27Jun87- 7Mth sly 6f :22⅖ :45⅕ 1:11⅕ 3↑Alw 14000 7 1 54¾ 66½ 55¼ 32¾ Santagata N b 111 4.40 81-16 Raise A Sail 1091 Sal's Shuttle 1131¾ LimitedAccess1111¼ Rallied 8

18Jun87- 8Mth fst 6f :22⅖ :45⅕ 1:10⅕ 3↑Alw 14000 9 8 98¾ 86 64 23½ Madrid A Jr b 111 5.40 85-14 No Points 1143½ Limited Access 1112 Toll Key 116½ 2nd best 9

9Jun87- 8Mth fst 6f :22⅗ :45⅗ 1:10⅖ 3↑Alw 14000 2 5 62¾ 53½ 32½ 21 McCauley W H b 111 4.80 87-19 Cinnamon Red 1091 Limited Access 1112 Le Vroom1162¾ Gamely 7

1Jun87- 8Mth fst 6f :22⅖ :45⅕ 1:10⅘ 3↑Alw 14000 11 10 108½106¼ 45 34¼ McCauley W H b 112 9.90 82-16 Latin Diplomat 1164 Juice 115nk Limited Access 112½ Rallied 11

19Apr87- 5GP fst 6f :21⅘ :45 1:10⅘ 3↑Clm 50000 5 6 611 411 46 32½ Pezua J M b 117 6.50 82-18 Dear Domino 113no Sunny Bend 1172½LimitedAccess1171½ Rallied 6

11Apr87- 8GP fst 1⅟₁₆ :46⅗ 1:11⅗ 1:44⅕ Alw 15000 5 7 713 69 412 619½ Pezua J M b 117 7.70 60-20 RonStevens11914½DrbyJunior122½HogJws117nc Squeezed back st. 8

27Mar87- 6GP fst 7f :22⅘ :45⅘ 1:25 Clm 50000 5 9 910 98¼ 68½ 46 Pezua J M b 117 3.60 73-27 BlckLnvinHwk1131½Mr.Biscuit1174½Don'tKnockIt122no No threat 9

15Mar87- 6GP fst 7f :22⅕ :45⅖ 1:24⅗ Clm 47500 10 1 1016 98 43½ 2hd Pezua J M b 115 15.20 81-23 Don't Knock It117hdLimitedAccess115ncU.S.Aid113nk Just missed 10

8Mar87- 8GP fst 1⅟₁₆ :47⅘ 1:12⅘ 1:47⅕ Alw 15000 7 8 813 810 69½ 511½ Romero R P b 117 12.50 53-25 Avies Copy 1226½ Goa 1223 Mc Forbes 1171½ No threat 8

LATEST WORKOUTS Jly 29 Mth 5f fst 1:00⅘ h — Jly 23 Mth 4f fst :47⅗ h — Jly 7 Mth 5f fst 1:02⅕ b — May 31 Mth 3f fst :40 b

D.

Cadillac Ranch — B. c. 3, by Distinctive Pro—French Cutie, by Vaguely Noble — $45,000 Br.—S-Cuse-Us Stable (Fla) Tr.—Hine Hubert — 114 — Lifetime 10 2 0 2 $19,190 — 1987 10 2 0 2 $19,190 — 1986 0 M 0 0 — Turf 1 0 0 0

Own.—Savin S C

20Jly87- 5Mth gd 6f :22⅗ :46 1:12 Clm 35000 6 1 2½ 2½ 1hd 1½ Gavidia W 116 9.50 80-26 CdillcRnch116½GoldenExplosion1161½Syd'sCommnd116no Driving 6

6Jly87- 8Mth gd 1 Ⓣ:48⅕ 1:39⅗ 3↑Alw 15000 7 4 57 88½ 87 77¾ Hernandez C 110 35.60 69-27 Casa Basso 118¾ Hurricane John 114nc Saxon Way 118¾ Tired 9

26Jun87- 7Mth fst 1⅟₁₆ :47 1:11⅗ 1:45⅖ 3↑Alw 15000 3 2 1hd 53 46 511¼ Hernandez C 109 40.70 67-21 Toll Key 1182 Big Richie 1112½ Silky Cyrus 1182½ Tired 9

1Jun87- 8Mth fst 6f :22⅖ :45⅕ 1:10⅘ 3↑Alw 14000 1 4 31½ 54 711 714¼ Perret C 114 9.50 72-16 Latin Diplomat 1164 Juice 115nk Limited Access 112½ Tired 11

9May87- 7GP fst 6f :22⅖ :45⅘ 1:10⅘ 3↑Alw 15000 5 2 2½ 45½ 59½ 612 Castaneda K 113 10.40 73-19 Sunny Bend 1102 At That Time 1064½ Credit Line 1121 Tired 8

25Apr87- 7GP fst 6f :22⅖ :46 1:12 3↑Md Sp Wt 7 1 31 32 21½ 1nk Perret C 113 *1.60 79-25 CadillacRanch113nkJustaProspector1085½LockedAwy112¾ Driving 9

12Apr87- 7GP fst 6f :21⅘ :45⅗ 1:12 Md Sp Wt 10 1 52¾ 31½ 41¾ 3¾ Perret C 122 4.60 78-23 Dash The Music 122¾ Shaizar 122no Cadillac Ranch 122¾ Rallied 10

28Mar87- 6GP fst 7f :22⅗ :45⅗ 1:25 Md Sp Wt 2 7 2hd 1hd 1hd 36¾ Perret C b 122 4.60 72-21 ValidPursuit1226½ChiefCooper122nkCadillacRnch122hd Weakened 12

14Mar87- 4GP fst 7f :22⅖ :46 1:25⅘ Md Sp Wt 1 6 21 1½ 22½ 67¾ Perret C b 122 2.90 67-18 RunawyCsting1221¼Ddy'sPriscili1152VlidPursuit122nk Weakened 12

15Feb87- 5Hia fst 6f :21⅗ :45 1:11⅖ Md Sp Wt 2 5 64½ 76 79½ 79 Perret C 121 6.20 74-19 DiamondKnight1212JustaProspector1212½FrenchTop121nc Outrun 12

LATEST WORKOUTS Jly 15 Mth 3f my :36 h (d) — Jun 15 Mth 4f fst :49⅘ b — Jun 9 Mth 5f fst 1:00 h

E.

Make Lemonade — B. c. 3, by Temperence Hill—Sculpturesque, by Chompion — $50,000 Br.—Crown Crest Farm (Ky) Tr.—Hauswald Philip — 116 — Lifetime 5 2 0 0 $18,825 — 1987 3 1 0 0 $8,910 — 1986 2 1 0 0 $9,915

Own.—Loblolly Stable

17Jun87- 9Mth fst 1 :46⅗ 1:10⅘ 1:36⅘ 3↑Alw 17000 1 3 41½ 44 47½ 59½ Vigliotti M J 109 4.60 79-16 Hawaiian Buzz 1122 Hybet 1124½ Fact 118no Tired 7

3Jun87- 5Bel fst 7f :23 :46⅕ 1:23⅖ 3↑Alw 27000 1 6 41¾ 52½ 612 612 Romero R P 112 6.20 73-22 Mr. Classic 1172¼ Easton 1171¼ Crivitz 117nk Outrun 7

20Mar87- 8OP fst 6f :21⅘ :45⅘ 1:10⅗ Alw 14000 2 9 34 1hd 2hd 12 Johnson P A 116 2.80 87-16 Make Lemonade 1162 Willing Bid 1161½ Deviser 1151 9

23Oct86- 5Kee fst *7f 1:28⅕ Alw 16300 4 5 4¾ 4¾ 42 43¾ Johnson P A 118 *.90 78 — Saga 118nk Trade Gap 118½ Grantley 1183 6

4Oct86- 2Kee fst *7f 1:27⅖ Md Sp Wt 6 4 51¾ 51½ 12 15¼ Johnson P A 118 3.40e 86-16 Make Lemonade 1185¼ French Magistrate 118¾ Grantley 1182½ 10

4Oct86-Fractional Time Unavailable

LATEST WORKOUTS Jly 7 Mth 4f fst :49⅘ b — Jun 28 Mth 3f my :37⅖ b — ●Jun 15 Bel 6f fst 1:12⅘ h — Jun 10 Bel 4f fst :47⅘ h

F.

Dandy Cut — B. c. 3, by Cutlass—Dandy Current, by Little Current — Lifetime 11 3 1 0 $21,601 — 1986 11 3 1 0 $21,601

$50,000 Br.—Swan T (Fla) — Tr.—Downing Michael W — 116

Own.—Swan T J Jr

11Nov86-10Suf fst 170 :47⅕ 1:12⅕ 1:43⅗ Mles Stndish 8 4 4nk 11 23 711¾ Vargas J L b 117 2.20 70-19 Lacuna 1141½ Blessedly Bold 117no The Mad Doctor 1225 Tired 8

11Nov86-Run in divisions

2Nov86- 9Suf fst 1 :47 1:12 1:38⅘ Alw 12000 2 2 23 21 1½ 15½ Vargas J L b 117 7.10 84-21 Dandy Cut 1175½ Kahili 114½ Lacuna 1141 Drew out 10

17Oct86- 7Med fst 6f :22⅖ :45⅗ 1:11⅗ Clm 28000 7 4 32½ 31½ 21½ 2no Rocco J b 113 7.70 84-19 Laws of the Court 115no Dandy Cut 1135ToughItOut1081 Gamely 9

4Oct86- 8Suf sly 6f :22⅗ :46⅕ 1:13 Cap Cod 1 5 54½ 53½ 57½ 69½ Ritvo T b 117 81.30 66-23 Migrant Man 117½ Kahili 1171¼ Son of a Babe 1131¼ Outrun 8

13Sep86- 3Rkmfst 6f :22⅖ :46⅕ 1:12⅘ Alw 9500 1 1 2½ 22½ 33½ 45¼ Donaghey E C b 122 11.30 75-22 Kahili 1222½ Foxy Ziad 1162¾ Bid's Passage 116hd Weakened 6

6Sep86- 4Rkmfst 6f :22⅖ :46⅗ 1:13⅗ Alw 9000 7 1 3½ 21 12½ 11¼ Donaghey E C b 115 11.10 76-25 Dandy Cut 1151¼ Life Of Sport 1171½ Crimson Mark1133¾ Driving 7

8Aug86- 5Rkmsly 5½f :22 :46⅘ 1:08⅕ Alw 9000 4 1 2½ 2½ 57½ 611 Lapensee M b 117 2.70 68-26 Our River 1151¼ Blessedly Bold 1202 Lucky Flasher 1151 Tired 7

26Jly86- 6Suf fst 5½f :22 :45⅗ 1:05⅕ ⓇKindergrten 12 4 31½ 44¾ 411 514¼ Lapensee M b 117 24.80 83-17 Migrant Man 1177LondonLancer117¾Gwen'sJewel115½ Weakened 12

29Jun86- 7Rkmfst 5f :22⅘ :47⅗ 1:01⅖ Alydar 6 3 1hd 31 44½ 77¾ Lapensee M 116 5.30 69-26 Bid's Passage 1152 Mr. Tactful 116hd Leave It to Tara115no Wide 8

11Jun86- 1Rkmsly 5f :22⅗ :47⅗ 1:01⅖ Md Sp Wt 7 2 12½ 11½ 12½ 12½ Lapensee M 118 6.20 77-27 Dandy Cut 1182½ Life Of Sport 1181¼ JackLandis1183 Ridden out 12

LATEST WORKOUTS Jly 24 Rkm 3f fst :37⅖ h Jly 19 Rkm 6f fst 1:19 b Jly 12 Rkm 6f fst 1:17⅖ b Jly 5 Rkm 6f fst 1:17⅖ hg

G.

Dirty Delbert — Dk. b. or br. g. 3, by No House Call—Country Bee, by Better Bee — Lifetime 17 5 2 0 $40,333 — 1987 10 3 1 0 $29,365 — 1986 7 2 1 0 $10,968 — Turf 1 0 0 0 $750

$40,000 Br.—Thompson Delbert (Fla) — Tr.—Forbes John H — 112

Own.—Shannon P Jr

1Jly87- 3Mth fst 6f :22⅕ :45⅕ 1:10⅘ Clm c-32000 3 2 1hd 11 11½ 1hd Krone J A b 116 *1.20 86-15 Dirty Delbert 116hd Giuseppe 1093 Florida Morn 116nk Lasted 6

18Jun87- 8Mth fst 6f :22⅖ :45⅕ 1:10⅕ 3↑Alw 14000 3 4 31 42½ 22 57 Krone J A b 109 6.60 82-14 No Points 1143½ Limited Access 1112 Toll Key 116½ Weakened 9

2Jun87- 7Mth fst 6f :22⅘ :46 1:10⅗ Clm 25000 2 2 11 12 13½ 17 Krone J A b 116 *1.50 87-16 Dirty Delbert 1167 Tale 116¾ Ten Court 116¾ Handily 9

30Apr87- 6Pim fm 5f Ⓣ:22⅖ :46⅕ :58⅗ Clm 25000 2 1 2hd 11 2hd 4nk Thornburg B b 114 *1.20 93-07 Deflation 114no Plan To Barter114noSpacetoKevin119hd Willingly 9

21Apr87- 9GS fst 6f :22 :45⅖ 1:11⅗ 3↑Alw 10500 5 2 1hd 1½ 3½ 43½ Rocco J b 112 3.50 80-27 Bravo One 1101 Gyrene 116½ Casino Action 1152 Weakened 8

26Mar87- 9GS fst 6f :22⅗ :46 1:11⅘ Alw 10500 1 1 11 1½ 2½ 21 Thornburg B b 116 6.70 82-27 Hold Your Money 1161 DirtyDelbert1167Allemande116hd 2nd best 6

5Mar87- 8GS fst 6f :22⅕ :46⅖ 1:12⅗ Alw 10500 2 5 43½ 53½ 58 513¾ Thornburg B b 116 5.80 65-30 Victartic 1166 Hold Your Money 116nk Inca Inca 1164½ No factor 8

6Feb87- 6Hia fst 6f :22⅕ :45⅖ 1:09⅘ Clm 40000 7 3 21 31 46½ 715¾ Cruguet J b 116 20.30 75-20 Interview 1182½ Bradie Boy 1166½ Mr. Biscuit 116nk Tired 9

21Jan87- 7Hia fst 6f :22⅗ :46⅕ 1:11⅕ Clm 40000 3 1 11 2hd 44¾ 59½ Lester R N b 116 3.20 74-25 Absolute Pitch 116½ True Control 116hd Bradie Boy1168 Faltered 7

4Jan87- 5Crc sly 7f :23⅖ :48⅕ 1:28⅖ Clm 30000 2 4 1hd 11 1½ 1nk Maple E b 116 4.40 74-24 Dirty Delbert 116nk ToIntrepid114nkButler'sRevenge1201½ Lasted 8

LATEST WORKOUTS Jly 29 Mth 3f fst :36⅕ b Jly 21 Mth 5f fst 1:01⅕ h Jly 16 Mth 3f fst :37⅖ b Jun 16 Mth 3f fst :36 b

H.

Royal Performer — Ch. c. 3, by Full Pocket—Sugary Mist, by Nijinsky II — Lifetime 6 1 1 0 $11,730 — 1987 4 0 0 0 $1,730 — 1986 2 1 1 0 $10,000

$50,000 Br.—Nuckols Bros (Ky) — Tr.—Gleaves Philip — 116

Own.—Reineman R L Stable

8Jun87- 7Mth fst 170 :45⅘ 1:10⅖ 1:41⅖ 3↑Alw 15000 7 3 2½ 34 59 615¾ Rocco J b 111 *2.20 74-18 Hybet 1134½ Black Swan 111¾ Public Accounter 1097 Tired 7

1Jun87- 8Mth fst 6f :22⅖ :45⅕ 1:10⅘ 3↑Alw 14000 9 8 93½ 42 33½ 44¾ Rocco J 109 6.10 81-16 Latin Diplomat 1164 Juice 115nk Limited Access 112½ Weakened 11

26Apr87- 9GP fst 1 1/16 :48⅘ 1:13⅖ 1:45⅕ Alw 15000 2 1 31½ 53½ 58 411 Pezua J M 117 5.20 64-27 A Charming Pro 1171½ Billie Osage 1178Sunbury1171½ No mishap 7

4Apr87- 5GP fst 7f :23⅗ :47⅕ 1:24⅘ Alw 14000 10 4 52¼ 74¾ 813 811½ Santos J A 117 4.10 68-23 Charalo 119no Libretto 1173½ A Charming Pro 1221 Tired 11

30Sep86- 6Med fst 6f :22⅖ :45⅕ 1:11 Alw 14000 1 6 42 33 2hd 21 Thomas D B 117 *.50 86-20 VictoryWon1131RoylPerformer1173½Poppy'sLegend1204½ Gamely 6

13Sep86- 1Med fst 6f :22⅘ :46⅖ 1:11⅗ Md Sp Wt 9 7 62½ 31 1hd 12½ Thomas D B 118 6.00 84-20 Royal Performer 1182½ Mohr Silver 1135 Hemi Head118nk Driving 12

LATEST WORKOUTS Jly 27 Mth 4f my :52⅖ b Jly 22 Mth 5f fst 1:06 b Jly 17 Mth 6f fst 1:16 b Jly 13 Mth 5f fst 1:02 b

14. In this hillside turf sprint at 6½F, which horse has the best combination of speed and class?

7th Santa Anita

ABOUT 6 ½ FURLONGS. (Turf). (1.11⅘) MT WILSON STAKES. $48,000 added. Classified fillies and mares. 4-year-olds and upward which are non-winners of a sweepstakes since December 25. Nominations Thursday, March 12 by 11:00 a.m. at $50 each with $100 additional to enter. High weights preferred. Weight, 121 lbs. Non-winners of $18,000 twice since October 1 allowed 3 lbs.; of $22,000 since then, 5 lbs.; of such a race since July 22 or $24,000 in 1986–87, 7 lbs. (Claiming races not considered.) Closed with 13 nominations.

A. (64)

***Rangoon Ruby** — Ch. m. 5, by Sallust—Pretty Crier, by Town Crier

DELAHOUSSAYE E 121 — Br.—Confey Stud Farm Ltd (Ire) — 1987 2 0 1 0 $12,000

Tr.—Drysdale Neil — 1986 8 3 1 2 $100,295

Own.—Kirk Mrs R — Lifetime 20 7 3 2 $137,109 — Turf 14 6 1 0 $98,239

17Jan87-8SA 7f :22² :44⁴ 1:21⁴ft 2 116 69 611 68 64½ DlssE5 ⒻSta Mnca H 86-18 Pine TreeLane,Balladry,HerRoyalty 6

17Jan87—Grade III

1Jan87-8SA 6f :21¹ :44 1:09⁴ft 7 117 810 88¼ 56 2½ DlhssyE5 ⒻLs Flrs H 88-19 PineTreeLne,RngoonRuby,HrRoylty 8

1Jan87—Grade III

8Nov86-8Hol 6f Ⓣ:22 :44⁴1:09¹fm 3½ 116 68¾ 67½ 42¼ 11¼ DlhssE4 ⒻBlu Dlght H 94-11 RngoonRuby,Sri'sHeroine,TxDodge 6

8Nov86—Bumped hard break

24Oct86-8SA a6½f Ⓣ:21¹ :43⁴1:14²fm 2½ 116 56 57½ 43¼ 1½ DlhoussyE1 ⒻAw40000 87-13 RangoonRuby,SpectculrJoke,Luisnt 8

8Oct86-8SA a6½f Ⓣ:21³ :44³1:14⁴fm 6¾ 116 84½ 83¾ 51½ 41¾ DlhssyE4 ⒻAtm Dys H 83-14 Shywing,HerRoyalty,WaterCrystals 9

8Oct86—Wide 3/8 turn; Run in divisions

21Aug86-8Dmr 6½f :21⁴ :44⁴ 1:15³ft 2½ 116 75¼ 55½ 54¼ 31¾ DlhoussyE7 ⒻAw35000 92-17 OurBestTell,DealPrice,RngoonRuby 7

21Aug86—Hopped in air

10Aug86-3Dmr 6½f :21³ :44² 1:14³ft 14 116 57 55½ 34½ 23 DlhssE1 ⒻRch Bndo H 96-08 BoldNSpecial,RngoonRuby,Eloquck 5

10Aug86—Broke slowly

19Jly86-8LA 7f :22¹ :45² 1:22¹ft *1 116 76¾ 52¾ 33 3nk DlhssE7 ⒻChapman H 97-12 LeL'Argnt,LuckyTwist,RngoonRuby 7

19Jly86—Run in divisions

B.

Miss Beverly Hills — Ch. m. 5, by Master Derby—Become a Star, by First Balcony
SOLIS A — 114 — Br.—Mabee Mr-Mrs J C (Ky) — 1987 3 2 0 0 $35,200
Tr.—Velasquez Danny — 1986 19 3 2 7 $89,650
Own.—Greenback Farms — Lifetime 30 7 2 8 $138,065 — Turf 10 2 1 4 $66,600

22Feb87-3SA a6½f Ⓣ:214 :4431:162fm 10 115 76½ 65½ 63½ 1½ Solis A 8 ⒻAw34000 77-22 MissBevrlyHills,Rkindling,Aromcor 9
22Feb87—Wide in stretch
28Jan87-5SA a6½f Ⓣ:212 :4421:16 fm 3½ 117 95¾ 95½ 84¼ 11¼ Pincay L Jr 7 Ⓕ 80000 79-21 MissBeverlyHills,Gossiper,Jiglores 10
28Jan87—Wide into stretch
11Jan87-6SA 7f :223 :451 1:221ft 31 1105 74¾ 88 58½ 611 Patton DB 6 ⒻAw33000 78-21 SldomSnS,TwlghtRdg,OnYrOwnTm 9
21Nov86-8Hol 1 Ⓣ:4811:1221:37 fm 11 116 2½ 2hd 41½ 53¼ Olivares F 3 ⒻAw35000 79-18 FruAltv,Rock'nRollLdr,BlshngRdhd 6
3Nov86-7SA 1 :452 1:101 1:36 ft 28 114 77 910 914 920¼ OlivresF 8 ⒻPrncs Rny 68-14 Infinidad, Fairly Old, Sterrware 9
24Oct86-8SA a6½f Ⓣ:211 :4341:142fm 11 114 33½ 35 65 63½ Olivares F 8 ⒻAw40000 83-13 RangoonRuby,SpectculrJoke,Luisnt 8
23Aug86-8Dmr 1 1/16 :454 1:101 1:412ft 9¼ 111 33 42½ 33 44¾ OlvrsF 4 ⒻChla Vsta H 88-10 Frn'sVlntn,Cnyk'sStr,DntstpThmsc 5
23Aug86—Grade II
8Aug86-7Dmr 1 :454 1:103 1:352ft 7 117 31 1½ 11½ 14 Olivares F 8 ⒻAw23000 91-13 MissBevrlyHills,PollyLFmm,Ptillnt 9
26Jly86-8Dmr 1 1/16 Ⓣ:4741:1131:421fm 52 112 87¼ 78 56 33½ OlrsF 1 Ⓕ[R]Osunitas H 91-05 FlyingGirl,Cnyk'sStr,MssBvrlyHlls 11
26Jly86—Veered out sharply start; Run in divisions
10Jly86-9Hol 1 Ⓣ:4821:1211:36 fm 8½ 112 2hd 1hd 2½ 22½ Olivares F 1 Ⓕ 90000 — — CllAginII,MissBeverlyHills,Jiglores 6
10Jly86—Bumped 3/16
Mar 10 SA 4f ft :504 h   Mar 4 SA 6f ft 1:00 h   Feb 18 SA 4f ft :474 h   Feb 12 SA 4f ft :50 h

C.

An Empress — Ch. f. 4, by Affirmed—Blondy, by Lord Gayle
STEVENS G L — 121 — Br.—Medina Dr I (Ky) — 1987 1 0 0 0
Tr.—Barrera Lazaro S — 1986 18 4 4 5 $340,145
Own.—Harbor View Farm — Lifetime 23 6 5 5 $381,045 — Turf 7 4 2 0 $203,470

24Jan87-8SA 1 1/16 :471 1:114 1:43 ft 7½ 122 55 56½ 611 619 Toro F6 ⒻEl Encino 67-18 SeldomSeenSu,Mirculous,TopCorsg 6
24Jan87—Grade III; Lugged out
21Dec86-8Hol 1 1/16 Ⓣ:4921:1241:413fm 9-5 117 52½ 41¾ 22 21 Toro F3 ⒻDahlia H 85-15 Aberuschka, An Empress, Reloy 7
21Dec86—Grade III
30Nov86-7Hol 1 Ⓣ:4631:1011:342fm *2 118 116¾115 51½ 1½ Toro F8 HcpO 95-12 AnEmprss,Avntno,Cro'sHo'lywood. 12
30Nov86—Wide into stretch
11Nov86-8Hol 1 Ⓣ:4531:1021:351fm*6-5 120 68 53½ 1hd 12 Pincay L Jr1 ⒻHcpO 91-09 AnEmpress,MissAlto,SpcilVictory 10
11Nov86—Wide into stretch; drifted out late
31Oct86-8SA 1 1/16 :463 1:112 1:431ft 4 118 94¾ 52½ 45 45½ StsJA9 ⒻLnda Vst H 79-16 Mrinn'sGirl,WinterTresur,FinKudos 9
31Oct86—Grade III; Rank, lugged out backstretch; wide into, through stretch
27Sep86-7Bel 1 1/16 :461 1:10 1:421sy 4 120 46½ 45 410 49 Stevens G L4 ⒻHcpO 82-17 Coup De Fusil, I'm Sweets,IMeanIt 5
13Sep86-6Bel 1¼[T]:4921:37 2:002fm 7½ 115 1010 86 75¾ 64¼ SntsJA6 ⒻFlwrbwl H 88-09 Dismasted, Scoot, CopeOfFlowers 12
13Sep86—Grade I
18Aug86-8Sar 1 1/16 Ⓣ:47 1:1111:42 fm 4¾ 121 86½ 64½ 32½ 11½ SntosJA1 ⒻNijana 87-09 AnEmpress,Fam,SpringInnocence 11
18Aug86—Grade III
9Aug86-8Sar 1¼ :471 1:37 2:041ft 14 121 47 67 68½ 613½ SntsJA1 ⒻAlabama 65-17 ClssyCthy,VlleyVictory,LifAtThTop 7
9Aug86—Grade I
30Jly86-6Sar 6½f :221 :451 1:16 ft 2 116 78 810 914 914½ Santos J A1 ⒻAw36000 78-13 Clemann'sRose,Verblity,Gene'sLdy 9
Mar 11 SA 5f ft 1:00 h   Mar 4 SA 5f ft :591 h   Feb 26 SA 4f gd :482 h   Jan 20 SA 5f ft :593 h

D.

Aromacor — Dk. b. or br. f. 4, by Bold Ruckus—Tamara, by Up Spirits
OLIVARES F — 118 — Br.—Frostad G C (Ont-C) — 1987 3 0 0 1 $5,100
Tr.—Whittingham Michael — 1986 16 4 5 0 $79,585
Own.—Ventura Stable Inc — Lifetime 29 5 5 2 $100,976 — Turf 9 2 2 1 $53,165

22Feb87-3SA a6½f Ⓣ:214 :4431:162fm 3¼ 118 42½ 41½ 1½ 32¼ Olivares F 4 ⒻAw34000 75-22 MissBevrlyHills,Rkindling,Aromcor 9
22Feb87—Lugged in late
4Feb87-8SA a6½f Ⓣ:222 :4511:15 fm 22 113 42 41½ 63¾ 64 OlivrsF 5 ⒻMonrovia H 80-16 Sari's Heroine, Lichi, Aberuschka 7
4Feb87—Bumped at start, wide into stretch
11Jan87-6SA 7f :223 :451 1:221ft 12 118 42 54 911 917¾ Olivares F 9 ⒻAw33000 71-21 SldomSnS,TwlghtRdg,OnYrOwnTm 9
31Dec86-8SA a6½f Ⓣ:213 :4341:152fm 27 113 76½ 66 33½ 11 Olivares F 5 ⒻAw45000 82-18 Aromacor, Tax Dodge, Sign Off 10
30Nov86-8BM 7½f Ⓣ:23 :4621:293fm 13 113 78 76½ 76½ 78 OlrsF 10 ⒻMs UnvrseH 88-04 Goldenita,TxDodge,AbstrctEnergy 10
1Nov86-9SA 1 Ⓣ:4631:1041:363fm 96 113 103¾ 41½ 98¼ 96¼ OlivrsF 12 ⒻMidwick H 88-07 Aberuschka, Duckweed, Solva 12
1Nov86—Wide 7/8
13Oct86-2WO 7f :233 :464 1:25 sl 5¼ 120 2½ 21 21½ 2½ King R Jr 3 ⒻHcpO 83-22 White Lotus, Aromacor,FoxyAlexis 5
27Sep86-9WO 170 :48 1:13 1:432gd 3¾ 114 54 54½ 59½ 611¾ KRJr 5 ⒻLa Prevoyant 74-20 Cuntlmer,MissTressette,RegncySilk 8
18Sep86-8WO 7f :232 :463 1:25 ft *8-5 115 76 76½ 53½ 52¼ King RJr 3 Ⓕ[S]Aw24000 82-26 MissTressette,DoubleBundles,Relit 8
6Sep86-9WO 1 [T]:4831:1411:40 yl 12 113 94 74 21 21¼ KRJr 8 Ⓕ[S]Ont Colleen 75-23 MssEnchntd,Armcr,DncngOnACld 10
6Sep86—Grade II-C; Steadied; Run in Divisions
Mar 8 SA 5f gd 1:03 h   Mar 2 SA 3f ft :351 h   Feb 12 SA Ⓣ 3f fm :383 h (d)   Jan 29 SA Ⓣ 6f fm 1:154 h (d)

E.

***Wistful Tune** B. f. 4, by Ballad Rock—Nolnocan, by Colum
TORO F 114 Br.—Maher D (Ire) 1987 1 0 0 0 $284
Tr.—Cross Richard J 1986 5 2 1 0 $30,950
Own.—Pearlstein L Lifetime 15 3 2 2 $37,427 Turf 15 3 2 2 $37,427
22Feb87-3SA a6½f ⓣ:214 :4431:162fm 8½ 117 915 910 85½ 53¾ ♦ Pincay L Jr1 ⒻAw34000 73-22 MissBevrlyHills,Rkindling,Aromcor 9
22Feb87—Veered in sharply start; steadied late; ♦Dead heat
19Dec86-8Hol 1⅛ ⓣ:4641:1041:414fm 3½ 115 84¾ 74½ 52½ 1½ Toro F3 ⒻAw26000 85-15 WistfulTun,VvdDncr,ScotchAndDry 8
19Dec86—Lacked room 1/4, knocked off stride 3/16
11Nov86-8Hol 1 ⓣ:4531:1021:351fm 8 115 56½ 31½ 72¾ 77½ Toro F3 ⒻHcp0 83-09 AnEmpress,MissAlto,SpcilVictory 10
11Nov86—Steadied 3/16
14Oct86-7Kee 1⅛ ⓣ:48 1:1341:482gd 9½ 114 46 43½ 44 79½ BrumfldD3 ⒻAw34500 78-18 Mnstrss,LckstGrl,NymphOfThNght 9
4Oct86-8Kee 1⅛ ⓣ:4821:1441:483gd*8-5 114 56 42 21½ 23½ BrumfldD10 ⒻAw23200 83-09 LuckstGrl,WstflTn,SlppnN'Slydng 10
10Sep86-5Dmr 1⅛ ⓣ:4621:1131:43 fm 4¾ 1125 913 32½ 12 12½ Black C A6 ⒻAw23000 91-07 WistfulTune,GoldieHwn,ArtiqueLc 9
10Sep86—Broke very slowly
15Oct85♦3PhoenixPk(Ire) 5f 1:003gd 5 133 ⓣ 2no Roche C Dalsn Nrsry H GossipShop,WistfulTune,Cridsion 12
14Sep85♦3Curragh(Ire) 6f 1:141gd 33 123 ⓣ 87¾ CrrllR ⒻMoyglareStud(Grl) GayleGal,CarhueLady,FlyawyBride 15
10Aug85♦3PhoenixPk(Ire) 6f 1:142yl 50 123 ⓣ 86 Roche C Phoenix(Grl) RoaringRiva,SoDirected,Sherkrine 13
Mar 10 SA 5f ft 1:02 h Mar 4 SA 5f ft 1:014 h Feb 18 SA 5f ft 1:021 h Feb 13 SA 7f ft 1:282 h

F.

***Trudie Domino** B. m. 5, by King of Macedon—Haute Fidelite, by Filiberto
SHOEMAKER W 114 Br.—Bonnefoy G (Fra) 1986 3 2 0 0 $21,279
Tr.—Scott George W 1985 6 3 0 2 $16,122
Own.—Paulson A E Lifetime 12 6 2 2 $42,915 Turf 12 6 2 2 $42,915
29Jun86♦6Longchamp(Fra) a7f 1:211gd 7½ 124 ⓣ 73½ SbrWR Px Prt Maillot(Gr3) NorthrnPrmir,ComrdlnArm,AlFhib 13
4May86♦6Longchamp(Fra) a7f 1:223gd 4½ 118 ⓣ 11 AsssnC Px d Mntrtout TrudieDomino,ComrdinArms,Elisrp 9
30Mar86♦3LaTeste(Fra) a1 : sf 4½ 127 ⓣ 11 DmortrP PxPSchocrn TrudieDomino,LVirgienne,Glyl:mou 9
30Mar86—No time taken
15Aug85♦2Deauville(Fra) a1 1:473sf 10 118 ⓣ 66 Beuley J ⒻPx dLieurey JustInFront,MPetiteCheri,Nitrogn 12
7Jly85♦3LaTeste(Fra) a1 : gd — 118 ⓣ 3hd BeuleyJ PxPDuboscq Laria, Carsac, TrudieDomino 15
7Jly85—No time taken
27May85♦4Tarbes(Fra) a7½f : sf *8-5 128 ⓣ 1nk Beulay J PxLDucruH TrudieDomino, Sisialco, Djouna 7
27May85—No time taken
15Apr85♦2Toulouse(Fra) a7f : gd 3½ 120 ⓣ 11 BeulyJ PxAimry dMleon TrudieDomino,Elegiac,BestRe'urn 13
15Apr85—No time taken
●Mar 10 SLR tr.t 1 ft 1:393 h Mar 2 SLR tr.t 1 ft 1:38 h Feb 23 SLR tr.t 1 ft 1:41 h ●Feb 16 SLR tr.t 6f ft 1:133 h

G.

***Lichi** B. m. 7, by Paderoso—Anchisamira, by Snow Track
BAZE G 118 Br.—Haras Ocoa (Chile) 1987 1 0 1 0 $12,000
Tr.—Jones Gary 1986 11 4 1 1 $104,950
Own.—Preston Farm Lifetime 25 7 3 2 $142,130 Turf 16 5 3 2 $131,845
4Feb87-8SA a6½f ⓣ:222 :4511:15 fm 15 116 31½ 21 22½ 22 Baze G4 ⒻMonrovia H 82-16 Sari's Heroine, Lichi, Aberuschka 7
4Feb87—Bobbled at start
8Oct86-5SA a6½f ⓣ:222 :45 1:143fm 8½ 115 31½ 2½ 2½ 1no Baze G5 ⒻAtm Dys H 86-14 Lichi, Tax Dodge, Outstandingly 7
8Oct86—Run in divisions
6Sep86-7Dmr 6½f :22 :45 1:153ft 10 121 66 64 66 57½ Toro F3 ⒻAw40000 86-12 HerRoylty,WinterTresure,WildKitty 6
26Jly86-5Dmr 1⅛ ⓣ:4741:12 1:423fm 7½ 116 32 52¾ 78 79¾ DlhssyE5 ⒻⓇOsnts H 83-05 Loucoum,Felliniana,SeasonlPickup 8
26Jly86—Run in divisions
4Jly86-5Hol 6f ⓣ:22 :4441:083fm 4½ 116 63½ 53½ 52½ 44½ Toro F1 ⒻHcp0 94 — Aberuschka,Loucoum,BoldNSpecial 7
4Jly86—Altered path early drive
7Jun86-5Hol 6f ⓣ:223 :4521:084fm 4 115 51½ 21 1hd 1no Toro F1 ⒻHcp0 98-02 Lichi, Loucoum, Regal Ties 6
11May86-8Hol 1⅛ ⓣ:4811:1131:48 fm 6½ 115 11 1½ 54 66¼ TrF6 ⒻⓇSmthngryl H 85-06 La Koumia, Sauna, Frau A'tiva 6
18Apr86-8SA a6½f ⓣ:22 :4431:141fm 30 115 52¾ 42½ 42¾ 22½ Toro F4 ⒻⓇMt Wlsn 85-16 Aberuschka, Lichi, Regal Ties 7
6Feb86-8SA a6½f ⓣ:221 :4441:16 fm 3 116 42 32½ 31½ 1¾ DlhoussyE6 ⒻAw34000 79-21 Lichi, Affirming, Wayward Pirate 7
25Jan86-6SA 6f :213 :441 1:083ft 8¾ 116 55½ 65 69½ 510¾ DlhoussyE4 ⒻAw40000 84-11 Circular, Tucked Inside, Boldara 7
Mar 10 SA 6f ft 1:134 h Mar 4 SA 5f ft :594 h Feb 26 SA 4f gd :481 h Feb 18 SA 4f ft :484 h

H.

Firesweeper Dk. b. or br. f. 4, by Drum Fire—Skysweeper, by Ack Ack
PINCAY L JR 116 Br.—Northwest Farms (Wash) 1987 2 0 1 1 $15,750
Tr.—McMeans Bob 1986 12 4 3 2 $109,225
Own.—Northwest Farms Lifetime 21 9 4 3 $266,494
28Feb87-7SA 7f :223 :451 1:224ft 4 120 1½ 11½ 11½ 21½ StevensGL6 ⒻAw45000 84-17 Goldspell,Firesweeper,BalconyPass 7
6Feb87-8SA 6f :213 :434 1:092ft 8 116 1½ 11½ 11 3hd Baze G7 ⒻAw45000 91-15 LeL'Argent,Comprbility,Firesweepr 7
2Nov86-9Lga 1⅛ :47 1:123 1:461m *4-5 123 16 16 24 210½ LosetnC5 ⒻOlympia H 57-31 PopcornPtti,Fireswpr,SongUnsung 5
11Oct86-9Lga 1 :452 1:092 1:354ft *7-5 116 11½ 13 15 12 LosethC8 ⒻAutumn H 90-16 Firesweeper, Classy Cyn,IceStealer 8
7Sep86-9Lga 1⅛ :46 1:101 1:492ft *2½ 116 11 12 12½ 43½ Loseth C5 ⒻAlki H 83-14 Goldnit,SilkChiffon,NorthrnNums 10
17Aug86-9Lga 1⅛ :46 1:094 1:472ft *9-5 118 12½ 13 12½ 1½ Loseth C4 ⒻSacajw H 96-13 Firesweeper,Hrtliftr,Cruisin'TwoSu 6
19Jly86-9Lga 1⅛ :461 1:102 1:413ft 3½ 118 13 1½ 22½ 24½ Baze G7 ⒻSeafair Qn 86-17 TwiceWritten,Firesweeper,Hrtliftr 10
22Jun86-9Lga 1 :451 1:101 1:354ft 8-5 120 15 13 21½ 34 Baze G3 ⒻBtsy Rss H 86-15 Cruisin'TwoSu,Devoner,Firesweepr 8
7Jun86-9Lga 6½f :213 :443 1:164ft *7-5 123 42 3½ 1½ 24½ Baze G8 ⒻDnhe Mm H 80-22 Devoner,Firesweeper,CountrySpice 9
3May86-9Lga 6f :224 :46 1:113ft *6-5 121 11½ 1hd 11½ 12½ Baze G2 ⒻIngnue H 78-22 Fireswepr,MickyJustic,IronLrkMiss 8
●Mar 12 SA ⓣ 3f fm :37 h (d) Mar 8 SA 3f gd :37 h ●Feb 19 SA 7f ft 1:253 h ●Jan 31 SA 6f ft 1:131 h

15. The best combination of speed and class belongs to

③ MONMOUTH 〈6 FURLONGS〉

6 FURLONGS. (1.08) CLAIMING. Purse $6,000. 3-year-olds. Weight, 122 lbs. Non-winners of two races since June 30 allowed 3 lbs.; a race 6 lbs. Claiming price $7,500; for each $250 to $6,500 1 lb. (Races where entered for $5,000 or less not considered.)

A.   (64)

Quirantes   Dk. b. or br. c. 3, by Brooklyn Prince—Speed Zone, by Vitriolic
Own.—Arcieri V A Jr $7,500   Br.—Surless Stables (Fla)   Tr.—Klesaris Robert P   **122**   Lifetime 1987 12 4 2 2 $22,675 / 1986 13 4 2 2 $22,675

B.

Dance A Little   Dk. b. or br. c. 3, by Marshua's Dancer—Little Party, by Sir Gaylord
Own.—Ingram Susan $7,500   Br.—Horst E F Jr (Va)   Tr.—Reese Walter C   **116**   Lifetime 1987 8 1 4 1 $7,985 / 1986 10 1 1 $7,985 2 M 0 0

C.

Saber Clash   B. c. 3, by Foreign Power—Rattling Music, by Rattle Dancer
Own.—Old Glory Stable $6,500   Br.—Johnson & Weist & Wilson (Fla)   Tr.—Tropia Anthony   **112**   Lifetime 1987 10 1 0 3 $7,890 / 1986 13 1 1 3 $1,400 3 M 1 0 $9,290
LATEST WORKOUTS   Jun 1 Mth   4f fst :49   b

D.

Lucky H. J.   Ch. c. 3, by Forward Charger—Perhaps Barbara, by Diplomat Way
Own.—Lucky L Stable $7,500   Br.—Curtin Cheryl A (Fla)   Tr.—Margotta Anthony Jr   **111⁵**   Lifetime 1987 4 0 0 0 $7,950 / 1986 11 1 0 0 $7,950 15 1 0 0 Turf 1 0 0 0
LATEST WORKOUTS   Jly 11 Mth   4f fst :48   h   Jun 11 Mth   5f fst 1:06   b   Jun 6 Mth   4f fst :51½   b

E.

Marcasite   Ch. c. 3, by Explodent—Bessie's Mother, by Olden Times
Own.—Bright View Farm $6,500   Br.—Bright View Farm Inc (NJ)   Tr.—Contessa Gary   **112**   Lifetime 1987 11 1 1 1 $7,237 / 1986 13 1 1 1 $7,237 2 M 0 0 Turf 1 0 0 0
LATEST WORKOUTS   ●Jly 8 Mth   5f sly 1:01¾   h (d)

F.

Harve A Smile B. g. 3, by Infusion—Hansom's Honey, by Hansom Harve
$7,500 Br.—Rodgers W H (Fla) Tr.—Stoklosa Richard
Own.—Alvarez R
109^7 Lifetime 10 1 0 1 $4,260 | 1987 10 1 0 1 $4,260 | 1986 0 M 0 0 | Turf 1 0 0 0

5Jun87- 9Mth gd 1 :47⅘ 1:13⅖ 1:41 Clm 10000 8 7 9^{12} 9^{12} 9^{11} $9^{13½}$ Sousonis S 117 60.90 55-23 Yankee Admiral $113^{1¾}$LouiesPal115^{nk}UniversalForce$115^{3½}$ Outrun 9
21May87- 5GS fst $1\frac{1}{16}$:47⅗ 1:12⅘ 1:46⅗ Clm 12500 5 6 5^9 5^{10} 6^{14} 6^{18} Sousonis S b 119 24.80 57-23 Tocantins 114^3 Rutner Glen 116^8 Mikey C 116^4 Outrun 6
13May87- 6GS fst 1 :47⅗ 1:13⅖ 1:39⅗ Clm 16000 3 8 8^{20} 8^{14} 6^{14} $6^{17½}$ Sousonis S b 113 45.00 59-24 Brooklyn Snimmy 116^4 Al's Answer $116^{4½}$FullLight$113^{½}$ No factor 8
5May87- 1GS my 1 :48 1:14⅕ 1:41⅗ 3+ Md 12500 1 5 $3^{6½}$ 2^2 $2^{1½}$ 1^{nk} Sousonis S b 113 8.00 67-20 Harve A Smile 113^{nk} Blinding Light 121^5 Lush Fyle $121^{3½}$ Driving 7
30Apr87- 7GS fm 1^{70} [T]:47⅗ 1:12⅗ 1:42⅘ 3+ Md Sp Wt 11 9 $10^{9¼}$ 9^{13} $8^{7¼}$ $8^{17¾}$ Sousonis S b 113 110.00 66-16 Saratoga Sun 113^5 Cadent $113^{1¼}$ Royal Decor 123^5 Outrun 12
13Apr87- 3GS fst $1\frac{1}{16}$:47⅖ 1:13⅘ 1:48⅕ 3+ Md Sp Wt 1 10 10^{26} 10^{17} 6^6 $6^{10½}$ Sousonis S b 114 43.70 57-26 Single Turn 123^4 Cadent $114^{3½}$ Lucky Sec 116^{nk} No factor 10
1Apr87- 6GS fst 6f :22⅗ :46⅘ 1:13 Md 15000 4 11 11^{19} 10^{19} 8^{12} $7^{7¾}$ Sousonis S b 122 14.70 69-24 Predictable $115^{1¾}$ Mike's Jewell $120^{3½}$ Elusive Chris 120^{hd} Outrun 12
13Mar87- 1GS fst 6f :23⅕ :47⅘ 1:15 Md 14000 9 2 $7^{4½}$ $8^{8¾}$ $6^{6½}$ $3^{4½}$ Romero J A^7 b 109 65.70 62-32 Pet Tiger 116no Barnet Fair $118^{4½}$ Harve A Smile 109^{nk} Mild rally 9
3Mar87- 2GS fst 6f :23 :47⅘ 1:14 Md 16000 7 6 10^{13} 10^{15} 8^{14} $6^{15¾}$ Romero J A^7 b 111 72.40 56-32 Lil Kell's Brother $118^{3½}$ Barnet Fair$118^{¾}$BeeKnighted118^6 Outrun 10
20Feb87- 7GS fst 6f :23⅖ :47⅕ 1:13 Md 16000 4 7 10^{11} 11^{21} 11^{27} $11^{33½}$ Romero J A^7 111 20.80 43-28 Alpha Buck 116^5 Nastyama 109^4 Metcalf 116^3 Outrun 11
LATEST WORKOUTS Jly 7 Mth 5f fst 1:04 b Jun 30 Mth 4f fst :51⅗ b

G.

The Amber Count Dk. b. or br. g. 3, by Virilify—Chutchki Baby, by Count Amber
$7,500 Br.—Franks John (La) Tr.—Mongeon Kathy
Own.—Rising Sun Stable
111^5 Lifetime 24 1 4 6 $14,107 | 1987 15 1 1 4 $10,330 | 1986 9 M 3 2 $3,777

23Jly87- 2Mth fst 6f :22⅘ :46 1:11⅗ Clm 10000 6 3 3^2 $3^{3½}$ $4^{6½}$ 6^{11} Beccia B K^5 b 111 15.80 71-24 Quirantes 114no Neatests Best $117^{4½}$DanceForAChange107^5 Tired 6
14Jly87- 4Mth fst 1^{70} :48 1:13⅕ 1:45⅘ Clm 10000 5 3 $3^{½}$ 9^{14} 11^{35} — Rocco J b 115 *2.90 — — Phantom Raider $110^{¾}$ Stringbean 115^{nk} TommyClams115^{no} Eased 11
10Jun87- 6Mth fst 6f :22⅘ :46⅗ 1:12⅕ Clm 20000 2 7 7^{13} 7^6 $6^{6¾}$ $6^{16¾}$ McCauley W H b 116 2.90 62-23 JiveWithFive$114^{¾}$SpectaculrComet$116^{2½}$He'sIt115^1 Pinched back 7
2Jun87- 7Mth fst 6f :22⅘ :46 1:10⅗ Clm 20000 3 7 6^3 $6^{3¾}$ 4^4 $4^{8½}$ McCauley W H b 112 4.40 78-16 Dirty Delbert 116^7 Tale $116^{¾}$ Ten Court $116^{¾}$ Rallied 9
15May87- 8GP fst 7f :22⅕ :46 1:24⅘ Clm 18000 6 4 2^6 $2^{1½}$ 1^1 2^{hd} Pezua J M b 113 4.70 80-24 TypicalAnswer112^{hd}TheAmberCount$113^{2½}$TeeTpper$117^{7½}$ Bumped 8
2May87- 5GP fst $1\frac{1}{16}$:47 1:12⅘ 1:47⅖ Clm 17000 9 3 $3^{1½}$ $1^{½}$ $2^{1½}$ $3^{1½}$ Vergara I^5 b 110 8.70 62-23 ExplodingHit$113^{1¼}$LoclGossip117^{nk}TheAmbrCount$110^{½}$ Weakened 11
25Apr87- 2GP fst 7f :22⅗ :45⅗ 1:25⅗ Clm 20000 8 6 7^7 $7^{7¾}$ 5^6 4^3 Vergara I^5 b 110 29.60[D] 73-25 Fast Jack 115^3 Ombo 113no Chieftain's Ridge 117no Bore in 9
25Apr87-Disqualified and placed fifth
1Apr87- 5GP fst $1\frac{1}{16}$:48 1:13⅘ 1:48⅕ Clm 16000 6 2 2^{hd} 1^{hd} $1^{½}$ $5^{3¾}$ Romero R P b 113 3.80 56-25 Fire Animal 117^{hd} Buck A Doe 117^{nk} Hail to the Hour$114^{1½}$ Tired 9
22Mar87- 3GP fst $1\frac{1}{16}$:48⅗ 1:13⅘ 1:47⅕ Clm 15000 9 3 $2^{1½}$ $3^{1½}$ $4^{2¾}$ $4^{2½}$ Romero R P 113 *1.00 62-24 Flying Al 117^2 Kelly's Kris 115no Buck A Doe $117^{½}$ Tired 10
17Mar87-10GP fst $1\frac{1}{16}$:48⅕ 1:13⅘ 1:47⅘ Clm c-10000 3 3 3^4 $2^{1½}$ $1^{1½}$ $1^{7½}$ Pezua J M 117 1.50 64-22 TheAmbrCount$117^{7½}$OutLikLight113^{nk}RlisticGuy$117^{3½}$ Ridden out 12
LATEST WORKOUTS Jun 1 Mth 3f fst :37⅘ b

16. Which horse is the class of the field?

8th Santa Anita

1 ½ MILES. (Turf). (2.23) 25th Running of THE SAN MARINO HANDICAP. $75,000 added. 4-year-olds and upward which have not won *$30,000 other than claiming or starter in 1986-87. By subscription of $50 each to accompany the nomination, $750 additional to start, with $75,000 added, of which $15,000 to second, $11,250 to third, $5,625 to fourth and $1,875 to fifth. Weights, Tuesday, March 10. Starters to be named through the entry box by the closing time of entries. A trophy will be presented to the owner of the winner. *A race worth $30,000 to the winner. Closed Wednesday, March 4, 1987, with 23 nominations.

A. **(64)**

Wild Style Ch. h. 5, by Effervescing—Hempens Pal, by Hempen
OLIVARES F 112 Br.—Kinghaven Farms Ltd (Ont-C) Tr.—Whittingham Michael
Own.—Kinghaven Farms
Lifetime 32 5 4 6 $90,011 | 1987 2 0 0 0 $230 | 1986 14 3 0 4 $56,284 | Turf 13 3 1 3 $55,245

18Jan87-9Hia 1⅛[T] 1:49 fm 9 119 $10^{7¾}$ $11^{5¾}$ 9^7 $8^{6¼}$ DosRmsRA 12 Aw23000 81-14 ArrivedOnTime,Wollston,ThSssmn 12
7Jan87-10Crc 1½[T]:47^4 $2:02^1$ 2:27 gd 98 111 7^{14} $7^{6¾}$ $9^{4¾}$ 6^3 $DsRsRA^5$ Mcknight H 91-18 CremeFriche,FlyingPidgeon,Akbir 10
7Jan87—Grade II
26Dec86-9Crc 1⅛ :49^4 1:15 $1:54^2$sy *9-5 122 2^2 $5^{5½}$ 6^{17} 6^{24} DosRmosRA 2 Aw15000 54-26 Wop Wop, Water Gate, Single Solo 6
14Dec86-9Crc a1⅛[T] $1:45^1$fm 29 115 8^8 $8^{7¼}$ $7^{7¼}$ $8^{3¾}$ BrmfldD 8 Trop Park H 93-08 RacingStr,LyphrdLine,ShowDncer 12
3Dec86-9Crc $1\frac{1}{16}$:48 1:13 $1:46^1$ft 6¼ 113 $6^{9¾}$ 6^{10} 5^{13} $3^{13¾}$ VsquzJ 4 Hurricanes H 74-23 BuckleyBoy,LyphardLine,WildStyle 6
26Oct86-3WO a1⅛[T]:49^3 $1:52^1$ 1:55 gd *9-5 118 $3^{3½}$ $3^{1½}$ $3^{3½}$ $3^{1½}$ Platts R 3 HcpO 57-35 Mac's Reef, Mascot, Wild Style 6
5Oct86-9WO 1½ :50^2 $2:05^2$ $2:32^2$sl 12 115 $7^{4¾}$ 7^{12} 6^{13} $6^{7¼}$ Platts R 8 Niagara H 77-21 GoldenChoice,RoylTrsurr,DoublDn 10
5Oct86—Grade III-C
20Sep86-9WO 1¼[T]:50^3 $1:47^1$ 2:16 sf 8¾ 116 11^{14} $8^{8¼}$ 7^{13} $6^{8½}$ DsRsRA 12 [S]SgrmCpH — — RoylTrsrr,SongofDom,ColNrthrnr 13
20Sep86—Grade III-C
7Sep86-9WO 1¼[T]:49^2 $1:39^2$ $2:05^3$gd 23 115 9^7 $8^{6½}$ $5^{2¼}$ $1^{1½}$ DsRsRA 7 Jc Cup H — — WildStyle,CoolNorthernr,Mr.Bons 11
7Sep86—Grade II-C
11Jly86-9WO a1⅛[T]:47 $1:09^4$ $1:48^4$fm *6-5 119 2^1 $2^{½}$ $4^{3½}$ $3^{3¾}$ Platts R 4 [S]Aw26400 86-11 S. S. Enterprise, Kazbek, WildStyle 6
Mar 9 SA 6f ft $1:14^1$ h ●Mar 2 SA [T] 1 fm $1:42^4$ h (d) Feb 23 SA [T] 7f gd 1:29 h (d) Jan 28 Pay tr.t 5f ft 1:05 b

B.

Keyala — Dk. b. or br. h. 6, by Key to the Kingdom—Alathea, by Lorenzaccio
Br.—de Briones G D (Ky) 1987 3 2 0 1 $42,250
DELAHOUSSAYE E 114 Tr.—Palma Hector O 1986 15 1 2 6 $35,351
Own.—Vicki Beth Stabies Inc Lifetime 42 7 4 10 $137,415 Turf 37 7 4 10 $134,715

31Jan87-5SA 1⅛Ⓣ:4641:1031:472fm 2¾ 119 21 2hd 1hd 1nk DelahoussayeE4 80000 90-09 Keyala, River Of Kings, Sherkin 8
18Jan87-5SA 1¼Ⓣ:4631:36 2:004fm *2¾ 116 22 12 15 17 Valenzuela P A1 80000 83-15 Keyala, Manzotti, Pas De Choix 8
1Jan87-5SA 1⅛Ⓣ:4711:1121:481fm 16 116 73¼ 62¾ 53 32¾ Valenzuela P A9 95000 83-14 Steepbank, River Of Kings, Keyala 9
1Jan87—Wide into stretch
14Dec86-5Hol 1 1/16Ⓣ:4611:10 1:402fm 7½ 113 55½ 53½ 43½ 3¾ Day P7 85000 91-11 Lucky N Green, Emperdori, Keyala 8
16Nov86-9Hol 1 1/16Ⓣ:4631:1031:402fm 4 116 76 73¾ 54 43½ Baze G1 80000 88-07 Steepbank, Jack Tar, Snowcreek 7
15Oct86-5SA 1⅛Ⓣ:47 1:1041:471fm 4 116 95½ 64½ 23 21½ DelahoussayeE5 80000 89-09 River Of Kings, Keyala, Aviator II 10
6Sep86-5Dmr 1⅛Ⓣ:4631:11 1:492fm 5½ 117 1013 85½ 32½ 2nk DelahoussyeE4 c62500 87-09 Aviator II, Keyala, Ono Gummo 10
25Aug86-7Dmr 1 Ⓣ:4611:1021:343fm 13 115 56 76 77 85½ Toro F4 95000 93-01 Tapping Wood, Matafao, Estate 9
25Aug86—Steadied 3/8
6Aug86-7Dmr 1 1/16Ⓣ:48 1:1141:432fm 2¾ 116 62½ 53 43 3hd ‡ Toro F3 80000 89-14 Bozina, Aviator II, Keyala 8
‡ 6Aug86—Dead heat
26Jly86-9Dmr 1 1/16Ⓣ:47 1:1111:42 fm 11 118 109¾105 94¾ 43½ Toro F1 100000 92-05 Bshop'sRngII,PttBonhomm,AvtrII 10
26Jly86—Wide into stretch
Mar 9 SA 6f ft 1:124 h Mar 1 SA 5f ft :591 h Feb 17 SA 5f ft 1:001 h Feb 9 SA 5f ft :592 h

C.

Vilzak — B. c. 4, by Green Dancer—Zippy Do, by Hilarious
Br.—Bedford & Ford (Cal) 1987 3 0 0 1 $6,000
DOUGLAS R R 113 Tr.—Van Berg Jack C 1986 10 2 1 2 $35,806
Own.—Rosenblum H Lifetime 13 2 1 3 $41,806 Turf 11 2 1 2 $35,806

5Mar87-8SA 1⅛ :462 1:104 1:502ft 11 115 45½ 34½ 31½ 31 Douglas R R2 Aw40000 76-21 Mustin Lake, Hills Bid, Vilzak 7
5Mar87—Blocked, altered path 1/8
8Feb87-8SA 1¼ :464 1:343 2:00 ft 77 115 79¼ 712 717 718¾ Toro F8 C H Strb 70-14 Snow Chief, Ferdinand,BroadBrush 8
8Feb87—Grade I
31Jan87-3SA 1⅛Ⓣ:4711:1031:471fm 29 115 68 58 46 65¾ Toro F1 Aw48000 85-09 Over The Ocean, Hermes, Reco 8
31Jan87—Broke out, bumped
16Nov86-6Hol 1¼Ⓣ:4621:1021:464fm 99 122 1012 97½119¼1110½ Meza R Q3 Hol Dby 83-07 ThrillShow,ArDsply,BoldArrngmnt 11
16Nov86—Grade I; Run in divisions; Broke slowly
28Sep86♦3Longchamp(Fra) a1½ 2:412gd 4 124 Ⓣ 12 AsssnC Omnium H Vilzak, Zagliago, RiverSharp 14
14Sep86♦3Longchamp(Fra) a1⅞ 3:214yl 8½ 126 Ⓣ 2nk AsssnC Px d Dngu H Kousudor, Vilzak, Fairolan 19
19Aug86♦6Deauville(Fra) a1 3/16 2:501sf 7 127 Ⓣ 11½ LequuxA Px d St Gtn H Vilzk,ChristinSoldr,Strght'nNrrow 19
3Aug86♦3Deauville(Fra) a1 3/16 2:453gd 15 123 Ⓣ 13 Eddery P Px d Sassy H Pub Royal, Kousudor, RiverSharp 25
17Jly86♦6StCloud(Fra) a1 5/16 2:20 gd*3-5 122 Ⓣ 32½ RnrdD Px d la Brtch(Mdn) Nanuma, Shaiykoun, Vilzak 7
25Jun86♦8Chantilly(Fra) a1⅛ 1:521gd 2¾ 118 Ⓣ 31 RnrdD Px d'Halatte(Mdn) Drister, WaterlooRevenge, Vilzak 11
Feb 27 SA 6f ft 1:142 h Feb 18 SA 1 ft 1:403 h Feb 6 SA 5f ft 1:002 h Jan 30 SA 3f ft :354 hg

D.

Northern Provider — Ch. g. 5, by Staff Writer—New Provider, by New Providence
Br.—McFadden D (Idaho) 1987 4 2 0 1 $37,700
ORTEGA L E 112 Tr.—Lewis Gary 1986 12 0 2 3 $19,640
Own.—Metkovich & Zaharis Lifetime 30 6 5 5 $97,293 Turf 1 1 0 0 $18,150

21Feb87-7SA 1⅛Ⓣ:4731:1141:481fm 43 1105 2hd 3nk 2½ 1hd Patton D B7 Aw33000 86-17 NorthrnProvidr,Rosdl,RomnMgstrit 9
8Feb87-7SA 1 1/16 :454 1:101 1:431ft 18 1095 64¾ 73¾ 42 45½ Patton D B2 Aw32000 79-14 GrcnWondr,RmnMgstrt,Wtch'nWn 8
8Feb87—Brushed rail midstretch
17Jan87-3SA 1 :462 1:111 1:373ft 14 1085 33 42 42½ 31¾ Patton D B1 55000 78-18 Pettrx,SilverHero,NorthernProvidr 8
3Jan87-9SA 1 1/16 :47 1:113 1:433ft 28 116 32½ 2hd 1½ 11½ Simpson B H5 32000 83-16 NorthrnProvdr,Rnbw'sCp,FrgnLgn 10
29Nov86-4Hol 7f :22 :452 1:223ft 24 1115 43 53½ 45 26 Gibson R G6 25000 85-12 Bizeboy,NorthrnProvidr,Yukon'sStr 7
20Nov86-5Hol 1⅛ :464 1:114 1:512ft 47 116 42½ 43 53½ 85¼ Meza R Q7 32000 75-16 Oak TreeII,Bedouin,ValiantGeorge 11
2Nov86-3SA 1 1/16 :461 1:103 1:412ft 15 1085 56½ 57½ 510 513 Patton D B6 35000 81-10 Oricao, Idol, Tough Envoy 6
26Oct86-9SA 1 1/16 :463 1:111 1:434ft 26 1115 56½ 76½ 65¾ 52 Patton D B8 32000 80-16 BngBngBng,TooMchFrT.V.,ItmTw 10
12Oct86-9SA 1 1/16 :463 1:12 1:443ft 38 1095 1hd 1hd 21½ 33½ Patton D B1 28000 74-21 Mmmy'sPlsr,Implsvly,NrthrnPrvdr 12
5Oct86-9SA 1 1/16 :462 1:111 1:424ft 9½ 1115 55½ 72¾ 75¾ 77 Patton D B3 40000 80-15 Tough Envoy, Idol, Tio Nino 10
Mar 9 SA 6f ft 1:163 h Feb 18 SA 4f ft :48 h Feb 4 SA 4f ft :473 h Jan 29 SA 5f ft 1:024 h

E.

***Millero Y Medio *** — B. h. 6, by Mr Long—Maria Blanca, by Blakemere
Br.—Haras Santa Amelia (Chile) 1987 2 1 0 0 $21,575
STEVENS G L 114 Tr.—Anderson Laurie N 1986 8 3 3 0 $17,094
Own.—Jones & Kebow Lifetime 36 11 9 5 $54,972 Turf 9 2 1 1 $5,052

14Feb87-7SA 1½ :492 2:044 2:301sy *1 117 1½ 15 16 18½ Stevens G L 1 80000 85-17 Millero YMedio,Fluctuate,Rampour 6
18Jan87-3SA 1 1/16 :461 1:104 1:441ft 6¾ 116 814 813 69 49 Toro F3 Aw31000 71-19 Oricao,GrecinWonder,ForsytheBoy 8
16Aug86♦6H'podromo(Chile) a1 1:362ft *1 134 1½ Diaz F FrndoMlrBrd(Gr2) Millero y Medio, Judas, Coqueto 7
5Jly86♦8H'podromo(Chile) a1⅜2:183ft 1 134 27½ Diaz F Pdr dRioTlvr(Gr2) Poalco, Millero y Medio,Prontuario 4
11Jun86♦8H'podromo(Chile) a1 1:36 ft — 134 1 Diaz F ClGnzloLrrain Further, information, unavailable 6
31May86♦9H'podromo(Chile) a1⅛ 1:532m — 134 13 Diaz F ClBrndZgrsNvrt MilleroyMedio,PontiusPilte,Snorio 4
31May86—No wagering
26Apr86♦7H'podromo(Chile) a1½ 2:341hy 37 132 21¾ Diaz F G P HpdrChl(Gr1) Poalco, Millero y Medio, Baalbek 12
Mar 9 SA 1 ft 1:413 h Mar 2 SA Ⓣ 7f fm 1:312 h (d) Feb 11 SA 4f ft :47 h Feb 5 SA Ⓣ 1⅛ fm 1:572 h (d)

F.

Rosedale B. c. 4, by Vaguely Noble—Ivory, by Riverman
SHOEMAKER W 117 Br.—Hunt & Bluegrass Farm (Ky) 1987 2 0 1 0 $9,000
Tr.—Whittingham Charles 1986 10 2 7 0 $83,669
Own.—Hunt N B Lifetime 13 2 9 0 $93,558 Turf 13 2 9 0 $93,558
21Feb87-7SA 1⅛Ⓣ:4731:1141:481fm*7-5 117 63¾ 63¼ 41 2hd Pincay L Jr3 Aw33000 86-17 NorthrnProvidr,Rosdl,RomnMgstrit 9
7Feb87-5SA 1⅛Ⓣ:4721:1131:481fm 3¼ 117 98 96¼ 85¾ 44½ Pincay L Jr2 Aw32000 81-13 Santella Mac, Neferou, Starsalot 9
7Feb87—Broke slowly, wide into stretch
9Nov86♦5Rome(Italy) a1¾ 2:583gd 5 121 Ⓣ 33¾ CrsonW Pr Roma(Gr1) Fire of Life, ‡SouthGale, Rosedale 7
9Nov86—Placed second through disqualification
31Oct86♦3Newmarket(Eng) a2 3:412gd 4½ 128 Ⓣ 2½ CarsonW Geo Stubbs Paean, Rosedale, Holy Spark 6
4Oct86♦6Milan(Italy) a1¾ 2:562gd*2-3 128 Ⓣ 21½ MurrayA St Lgr Itlno(Gr2) Commel'Etoile,Rosedle,DucdBustd 6
19Aug86♦4York(Eng) 1¾ 2:58 gd 12 133 Ⓣ 2¾ ThomsnB Melrose H Ostensible, Rosedale, LieInWait 13
21Jly86♦3Ayr(Scot) 1⅞ 3:143gd 5 133 Ⓣ 56 ThsnB Tnnent Trphy H WhitMill,ThPrudntPrinc,SpcilVintg 8
24Jun86♦3Turin(Italy) a1⅝ 2:423gd*1-3 128 Ⓣ 12¾ CrsW Pr Prncp Amdo(Gr2) Rosedale,LoclHerbert,DucdeBusted 7
Mar 10 SA 6f ft 1:153 h Mar 5 SA tr.t 5f ft 1:042 h Feb 18 SA Ⓣ 5f fm 1:021 h (d) Feb 6 SA 3f ft :361 h

G.

***Woolskin** Ch. h. 6, by Wollow—Lady Berry, by Violon d'Ingres
GOMEZ R 108 Br.—Baron Guy de Rothschild (Ire) 1987 1 0 0 0
Tr.—Garry Albert J 1986 4 0 0 0 $750
Own.—Uversa Ltd Inc Lifetime 16 2 1 3 $59,541 Turf 14 2 1 3 $59,541
5Mar87-8SA 1⅛:462 1:104 1:502ft 63 115 716 717 722 726½ Gomez R1 Aw40000 50-21 Mustin Lake, Hills Bid, Vilzak 7
5Mar87—Dwelt
16Nov86-9Hol 1 1/16Ⓣ:4631:1031:402fm 48 116 54 52¾ 77½ 710¾ Simpson B H3 80000 81-07 Steepbank, Jack Tar, Snowcreek 7
5Nov86-9Hol 1 1/16Ⓣ:4711:1121:413fm 63 117 54½ 54¾ 510 515½ Bonilla R4 Aw30000 70-14 Bruiser, River Of Kings, Catane 6
5Nov86—Bumped start
3Oct86-8SA 1⅛Ⓣ:4641:11 1:482fm 60 116 32 54½ 713 717¾ Caraballo R5 Aw35000 67-15 Ifrad, Matafao, Prince Bobby B. 7
3Oct86—Broke slowly; ducked in 3/8
16Sep86-11Pom 6f :214 :442 1:092ft 78 114 109 1021 1021 1027 Caraballo R7 Aprisa H 77-05 BundlOfIron,Mtronomc,ProdstHor 10
16Sep86—Broke slowly
16Jun85♦2Chantilly(Fra) a1½ 2:25 gd 3½ 123 Ⓣ 47½ PggottL La Coupe(Gr3) Romildo, Complice, Darly 5
28Apr85♦5Longchamp(Fra) a1 15/16 3:321gd 4 123 Ⓣ 45 PgttL PxVcmtessVigr(Gr2) Balitou, Yawa, South Gale 10
16Apr85♦5StCloud(Fra) a1 5/16 2:312sf *3-2 121 Ⓣ 34½ Head F Px Altipan Olindo, Tryffoc, Woolskin 12
30Jly84♦5Vichy(Fra) a1½ 2:29 gd*2-5 115 Ⓣ 8 GilbrtA GP de Vchy(Gr3) Nature,Complice,NorthernFashion 13
24Jun84♦4Longchamp(Fra) a1⅞ 3:14 fm 3¾ 123 Ⓣ 2nk DbrcqG G P de Paris(Gr1) At Talaq, Woolskin, Spicey Story 11
Feb 28 Hol 3f ft :381 h Feb 22 Hol 6f ft 1:184 h

H.

Schiller B. g. 5, by Blood Royal—Comet Hill, by Hillary
TORO E 120 Br.—Pulliam C N (Ky) 1987 3 0 1 1 $30,100
Tr.—Pulliam Vivian M 1986 16 0 3 2 $147,350
Own.—Johnson & Pulliam Lifetime 36 3 7 7 $255,250 Turf 20 1 5 4 $213,950
16Feb87-8SA 1½Ⓣ:4612:0142:282gd 16 115 32 3½ 2½ 33¾ SpsnBH4 Sn Lus Ob H 69-27 Louis Le Grand, Zoffany, Schiller 8
16Feb87—Grade II
7Feb87-7SA 1⅛Ⓣ:4521:1011:48 fm 2½ 116 59½ 32 41½ 22½ Simpson BH3 Aw38000 84-13 Bello Horizonte, Schiller, Hills Bid 8
7Feb87—Bumped start; boxed in 1/4
25Jan87-8SA 1¼Ⓣ:4641:36 2:004fm 14 114 54½ 63¼ 74 66½ SpsnBH6 Sn Mrcs H 76-18 Zoffny,LouisLeGrnd,StrwbrryRodII 8
25Jan87—Grade III
24Dec86-8Hol 1¼Ⓣ:4841:3612:00 fm 14 116 52¾ 72¾ 62¼ 21¾ Simpson BH7 600000 S 93-11 Forlitano, Schiller, Skip Out Front 8
7Dec86-8Hol 1½Ⓣ:4742:01 2:254fm 50 126 3nk 89 813 814¼ PdrozMA3 Tf Cp Inv 79-09 Alphabatim, Dahar, Theatrical 8
7Dec86—Grade I
3Nov86-8SA 1¼Ⓣ:47 1:36 2:011fm 25 114 21½ 2hd 2½ 2nk PdrzMA6 C F Burke H 81-19 Louis Le Grand,Schiller,Silveyville 10
3Nov86—Grade I; Bobbled midway
22Oct86-7SA 1⅛Ⓣ:4541:1021:471fm 4¾ 115 75½ 72½ 53 32¼ PedrozaMA10 Aw35000 89-12 Nugget Point, Catane, Schiller 10
22Oct86—Wide into turn
12Oct86-8SA 1½Ⓣ:4642:0032:26 fm 15 126 42 1021 711 611¼ McCrrCJ9 Oak Tree Iv 74-12 Estrapade,Theatrical,UptownSwell 10
12Oct86—Grade I
1Oct86-8SA 1¼Ⓣ:4641:3532:01 fm 8 116 85¼ 83 75½ 85¾ VlnzlPA7 ⓇH P Rsl H 76-18 Glaros, Louis Le Grand, Nadirpour 13
1Oct86—Broke slowly
1Sep86-8Dmr 1⅜Ⓣ:4741:3742:142fm 77 113 52½ 62¾ 41½ 2no PdrzMA1 Dmr Inv H 98-04 Raipillan, Schiller, Shulich 12
1Sep86—Grade II; Veered out, bumped hard start; checked final turn
●Mar 9 SA 6f ft 1:11 h Feb 28 SA 6f ft 1:112 h ●Feb 3 SA 5f ft :593 h Jan 21 SA 5f ft 1:003 h

I.

Bob Back — Dk. b. or br. h. 6, by Roberto—Toter Back, by Carry Back
PINCAY L JR 118 — Br.—Alien J (Ky); Tr.—Scott George W
Own.—Paulson A E — Lifetime 30 5 4 5 $372,333

1987	1	0	1	0	$9,000		
1986	6	0	0	0	$11,928		
Turf	29	5	4	2	$372,333		

5Feb87-8SA	1⅛Ⓣ:4611:1041:48 fm	3¾	117	42½ 31 3½ 2½	Pincay L Jr8	Aw45000	86-13	Forlitano, Bob Back, ‡Aventino	8
25Sep86-8Bel	1 1/16Ⓣ:4631:1031:402fm	4¾	120	69 710 720 727½	Cordero A Jr5	HcpO	66-20	Duluth,FeelingGallnt,IfIHdAHmmer	7
7Sep86-8Bel	1¼[T]:5021:3842:023gd	6	113	83¾ 75 65¾ 77½	SmnJL4	Manhattan H	73-23	Dngr'sHour,PrmrMstr,ExclusvPrtnr	8
7Sep86—Grade I									
23Aug86-7Sar	1 1/16Ⓣ:4611:0931:404fm	18	115	87 87¼ 75¼ 41¾	CrdrAJr2	Bud BrdrsCp	91-08	Dnger'sHour,‡SilverVoice,SlmDriv	10
5Jly86-6Bel	1 1/16:461 1:102 1:422ft	6¼	115	53 58½ 613 616¼	Migliore R4	Aw40000	74-15	Smile, Valiant Lark, Little Missouri	6
21Jun86-5Bel	1 1/16[T]:4721:1021:412fm	*8-5	122	42 42 43 44½	Vasquez J1	HcpO	89-12	JudgeCosta,LateAct,FearlessLeder	5
2Jun86-8Bel	1 Ⓣ:4631:1021:351fm	*1	117	64½ 46½ 78 87½	Vasquez J6	Aw40000	81-11	LightningLep,IsYourPlesure,Duluth	9
21Dec85-8BM	a1⅛Ⓣ 1:47 fm	3½	121	53½ 63 76 64¾	Baze R A7	B M H	108 —	Drumalis, Silveyville, Talakeno	8
21Dec85—Grade II									
2Nov85-6Aqu	1½Ⓣ:48 2:0222:27 fm	3¾e	126	1011 96¾127¾127¼	CordrAJr2	Br Cp Turf	99 —	Pebbles,StrawberryRodII,Mourjne	14
2Nov85—Grade I									
12Oct85-8Bel	1⅜Ⓣ:4831:3722:152fm	5	126	83¾ 54½ 2½ 2nk	CrdrAJr1	Man O War	85-25	Win, Bob Back, Baillamont	8
12Oct85—Grade I; Brushed late									

● Mar 9 SLR tr.t 6f ft 1:11 h Mar 1 SLR tr.t 1¼ ft 2:032 h Feb 21 SLR tr.t 6f ft 1:152 h Feb 16 SLR tr.t 5f ft 1:011 h

J.

***Forlitano** — B. h. 6, by Good Manners—Forlita, by Pardallo
BAZE G 120 — Br.—Haras Ojo de Agua (Arg); Tr.—Whittingham Charles
Own.—Evergreen Thrbrd Farm Inc — Lifetime 19 7 3 1 $178,645

1987	2	1	0	0	$24,750
1986	8	2	2	0	$110,300
Turf	11	3	3	0	$145,371

16Feb87-8SA	1½Ⓣ:4612:0142:282gd	5	116	2hd 2½ 31½ 79¾	Baze G3	Sn Lus Ob H	63-27	Louis Le Grand, Zoffany, Schiller	8
16Feb87—Grade II									
5Feb87-8SA	1⅛Ⓣ:4611:1041:48 fm	*8-5	122	32 42 4¾ 1½	Baze G2	Aw45000	87-13	Forlitano, Bob Back, ‡Aventino	8
5Feb87—Bumped near 1/8									
24Dec86-8Hol	1¼Ⓣ:4841:3612:00 fm	14	114	2hd 2hd 1½ 11¾	Sint-MrtinE6	500000 S	95-11	Forlitano, Schiller, Skip Out Front	8
24Dec86—Drifted in 1/8									
6Dec86-7Hol	1⅛Ⓣ:4811:1111:471fm	4	117	1½ 2hd 1½ 2hd	Baze G3	Aw40000	92-08	Skip Out Front, Forlitano, Formaz	6
27Nov86-7Hol	1 Ⓣ:4641:1021:34 fm	5¼	117	2hd 1hd 1½ 21	Baze G1	Aw40000	96-06	RiverDrummr,Forlitno,TppingWood	7
26Oct86-8SA	1 1/16:463 1:102 1:411ft	22	115	55½ 56 56½ 710½	Toro F7	Goodwd H	84-16	SuperDimond,Epidurus,PrincDonB.	8
26Oct86—Grade III									
1Oct86-7SA	1 1/16:474 1:113 1:422ft	14	119	43½ 53¼ 43 44¾	ShoemkerW4	Aw48000	84-18	Nostalgia'sStar,Vrick,BreMinimum	6
1Oct86—Rough start									
6Sep86-8Dmr	1 1/16Ⓣ:48 1:1131:421fm	8	116	53 73½ 76¾ 66	ShmrW7	ⓇEscnddo H	89-09	Truce Maker, IceHot,TappingWood	7
6Sep86—Wide									
28Jly86-8Dmr	1 1/16Ⓣ:4711:1241:41 fm	4	122	32 42½ 35½ 44¾	ShoemkerW1	Aw40000	96-04	TruceMker,CleverSong,SpctculrJok	7
3Jly86-8Hol	1 1/16Ⓣ:46 1:10 1:401fm	9½	115	22 21 11 11½	ShoemkerW4	Aw40000	103-03	Forlitano, Spectacular Joke, Kalim	6

Mar 10 SA 6f ft 1:124 h Mar 4 SA 5f ft 1:003 h Feb 26 SA 5f gd 1:024 h ● Feb 12 SA Ⓣ 5f fm 1:012 h (d)

K.

***Rampour** — Dk. b. or br. g. 6, by Kashmir II—Rose Ness, by Charlottesville
MEZA R Q 109 — Br.—S A Aga Khan (Fra); Tr.—Palma Hector O
Own.—Longo I S — Lifetime 39 8 5 5 $87,274

1987	3	0	0	1	$8,400
1986	10	1	0	1	$18,650
Turf	37	8	5	4	$81,124

7Mar87-7SA	1¼:473 1:373 2:03 gd	11	113	610 56¾ 56½ 59¼	Olivares F 5	70000	65-19	Truth, Dr. Daly, Kingsbury	6
14Feb87-7SA	1½·492 2:044 2:301sy	5¾	113	43 25 26 39	Olivares F 4	70000	76-17	Miliero YMedio,Fluctuate,Rampour	6
10Jan87-5SA	1⅛Ⓣ:4721:1221:50 gd	26	118	106½104¾104 43¼	Olivares F 2	62500	74-23	Kingsbury,BoardMeeting,AvitorII	10
21Dec86-9Hol	1¼Ⓣ:5021:3812:022fm	11	119	77½ 64¼ 98¼1010½	Olivares F 7	50000	72-15	Kingsbury, Will Spring, PiperJohn	11
12Dec86-9Hol	1⅛Ⓣ:4611:1011:474fm	6½	119	78 74¾ 42 44¼	Olivares F 4	50000	85-13	BordMeting,Mssr,TooMuchForT.V.	9
23Nov86-9Hol	1¼Ⓣ:4811:3642:021fm	8¼	114	913 44½ 41½ 1½	Olivares F 7	57500	84-13	Rampour, Travet, Aviator II	11
9Nov86-9Hol	1⅛Ⓣ:4621:1041:484fm	29	116	1011 97½ 73¼ 32¾	Olivares F 8	50000	81-12	Travet, Will Spring, Rampour	11
15Oct86-5SA	1⅛Ⓣ:47 1:1041:471fm	65	114	85 96¾1014 1017¼	Soto S B 6	75000	74-09	River Of Kings, Keyala, Aviator II	10
15Oct86—Bobbied start									
26May86-6Hol	1¼Ⓣ:49 1:3712:02 fm	30	116	53½ 55 65 78¼	Ortega L E 5	50000	89 —	Crony, Tio Nino, Killyglen	9
13Apr86-9SA	1¼Ⓣ:4531:3512:011fm	4½	116	911 1014 1020 1027¾	Toro F 5	62500	53-17	Penznce,Morry'sChmp,FlyingGene	10

Mar 1 SA 5f ft 1:00 h Feb 7 SA 5f ft 1:014 h Feb 1 SA 5f ft :594 h Jan 25 SA 5f ft 1:032 h

Items 17 through 33 * ask you to select the most probable winner from the past performances given. At times additional information will be provided. Otherwise, only the past performance tables will be provided. Read the conditions carefully. Find the winners.

17.

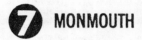

7 MONMOUTH

1⅛ MILES. (Turf). (1.49⅖) ALLOWANCE. Purse $14,000. 3-year-olds and upward which have not won two races. Weight, 3-year-olds 115 lbs.; older, 123 lbs. Non-winners of $9,800 since June 30 allowed 3 lbs.; $6,000 since April 30 5 lbs. (Races where entered for $35,000 or less not considered.)

A.

Proud Harry — Ch. c. 4, by Proud Birdie—Regal Order, by Viceregal
Br.—Marablue Farm (Fla)
Own.—Marablue Farm — Tr.—Schulhofer Randy
113^5

Lifetime 19 1 2 1 $15,780 — 1987 10 1 1 1 $12,700 — 1986 9 M 1 0 $3,080

4Jly87- 3Mth	fst	1⅛	:47	1:11⅕	1:49⅖	3↑Clm 18000	6	8	9^{13}	9^{10}	5^{10}	$4^{10¾}$	McCauley W H	112	15.20	76-10	ParrishPrince111^{6½}StrngeBehvior115^{1½}SportingFree106^{3}	Late bid 9
13Jun87- 2Mth	fst	1$\frac{1}{16}$	:47⅘	1:11⅗	1:43⅗	3↑Clm 12500	3	6	6^{5}	$6^{4¾}$	6^{6}	7^{9}	Murphy D J	115	9.10	78-12	Velvet Time 115^{1} Dirty Birdie 111no Playing Politics 115^{3}	Outrun 7
29May87- 3Mth	fst	170	:48	1:12	1:41⅕	3↑Clm 20000	1	7	$7^{5½}$	$7^{5¾}$	6^{8}	6^{6}	Murphy D J	114	23.50	84-12	Feldspar 115no Classic Impact 115^{2} Hambusher 115^{1¼}	No factor 8
4May87- 9Aqu	sly	1	:46⅘	1:12⅖	1:38⅕	Clm 25000	1	8	$8^{7¼}$	$8^{6½}$	6^{8}	$8^{13¼}$	Cruguet J	119	22.30	62-27	Print Money 115^{1½} Cowboy Up 113^{3} Proud And Tall 112^{nk}	Outrun 9
14Apr87- 2Aqu	fst	1⅛	:49⅖	1:14⅖	1:53⅘	3↑Md 30000	6	11	$10^{7¾}$	$7^{4¾}$	1^{3}	1^{5}	Santos J A	120	*1.20	66-23	ProudHrry120^{5}MrketProphet108^{4}InspctorClousu103^{3}	Ridden out 12
3Apr87- 2Aqu	fst	1	:46⅘	1:12	1:38⅕	3↑Md 30000	11	9	$8^{8½}$	4^{6}	$3^{2½}$	$2^{3¾}$	Santos J A	120	5.20	71-22	Slope Master 112^{3¾} Proud Harry 120^{4} Dawn Revival119^{3}	2nd best 13
15Mar87- 2Aqu	fst	6f	:22⅗	:46⅘	1:13⅕	Md 30000	6	12	13^{17}	12^{10}	$10^{9¾}$	$6^{7¾}$	Brown T	118	10.30	67-24	Greg's Mint122^{2¾}MtAuburnExpress118^{1¼}NativeCoal117^{2¾}	Slow st 13
27Feb87- 9Aqu	fst	1$\frac{1}{16}$	[•]:48⅕	1:13⅗	1:47⅗	Md 30000	10	11	10^{12}	$9^{7¼}$	7^{6}	$6^{6½}$	Brown T L	116	13.50	65-19	Get Me Luce 115¾ I'm No Yankee 118^{nk} St. Andrews 118^{3}	Outrun 11
12Feb87- 2Aqu	fst	1$\frac{1}{16}$	[•]:49⅕	1:15	1:48⅘	Md 30000	8	12	12^{11}	10^{13}	$6^{3¾}$	5^{3}	Brown T	118	7.70	63-23	Sylson 118^{1¼} Celluloid Hero 122¾ Get Me Luce 113½	Outrun 12
2Jan87- 9Aqu	sly	6f	[•]:22⅖	:47	1:13⅗	Md 30000	9	10	9^{12}	9^{11}	$7^{5¼}$	$3^{1¾}$	Brown T L5	113	4.60	74-21	Disguyzor 118^{1½} Money Table 113^{nk} Proud Harry 113^{2}	Belated bid 10

LATEST WORKOUTS Jly 28 Mth 5f fst 1:00⅘ h — Jly 21 Mth 5f fst 1:04⅖ b — Jly 14 Mth 4f fst :51 b — Jun 29 Mth 4f fst :50 b

B.

Meg's Command — Ch. g. 4, by Top Command—Vivacious Meg, by Semi-pro
Br.—Glen Oak Farm (Ky)
Own.—Main Tree Farm — Tr.—Smithwick D Michael
117

Lifetime 14 1 5 0 $13,155 — 1987 7 1 2 0 $6,290 — 1986 2 M 0 0 $130 — Turf 3 1 1 0 $5,600

11Jly87- 1Pen	fm	1½ [T]			2:31⅖	3↑Hcp 5000s	9	4	5^{5}	$7^{3¾}$	$7^{9¼}$	$8^{9½}$	Tillotta N	111	6.00	85-16	Dan Rather 114^{1½} Writer's Son 112^{hd} Tomlin 114^{1¾}	No factor 11
5Jly87- 3Del	fm	1⅛	[T]:48⅖	1:13⅘	1:52⅖	3↑Md Sp Wt	7	5	$6^{5½}$	$10^{6¾}$	4^{3}	1^{nk}	Roe J	122	8.10	82-14	Meg's Command 122^{nk} Pickle Hill 122^{4}ThatCoolCat122^{1½}	Driving 12
27Jun87- 1Pen	fm	5f [T]			:57⅗	3↑Hcp 5000s	10	1	$6^{4¼}$	$7^{4¾}$	3^{3}	2^{nk}	Tillotta N	106	34.70	92-17	Jet Set Johnny 116^{nk} Meg's Command106^{1}PardonMe123½	Rallied 10
24Jun87- 5Del	fst	5f	:22⅗	:47⅕	1:00⅖	3↑Md 5000	11	3	4^{3}	$4^{3½}$	$3^{3½}$	$2^{1¼}$	Roe J	122	9.70	83-19	I'm Positive122^{1½}Meg'sCommand122^{nk}RunningKnife122^{1½}	Rallied 12
10Jun87- 2Del	fst	6f	:22	:46	1:12⅖	Clm 4000	5	3	$4^{4½}$	6^{9}	$6^{7½}$	$5^{7½}$	Fitzgerald J F	116	34.10	71-24	Milingo'sBoy115^{3}DncingCry122^{2}BonieChristopher122^{2}	Weakened 9
30May87-10Pim	gd	6f	:23⅘	:47⅖	1:13⅘	3↑Md 6500	2	2	1^{hd}	$5^{5½}$	11^{19}	$11^{14¼}$	Lloyd J S	122	10.50	62-21	Sipahi 110^{1½} Rainbow Tour 113^{1¼} Pascala 112^{1}	Stopped 12
22May87- 3Del	fst	6f	:22⅕	:46⅖	1:13⅕	3↑Md 12500	2	2	2^{hd}	3^{2}	9^{8}	$9^{14¾}$	Fitzgerald J F	122	4.40	60-21	Talc U Mento 112^{nk} Born to Air 112^{1½} Willi Buck 109^{1½}	Tired 10
8Apr86- 2Kee	fst	6f	:22⅗	:45⅗	1:12⅗	Md Sp Wt	7	3	3^{1}	6^{4}	7^{8}	$7^{13¾}$	Espinoza J C	121	6.20e	66-22	Great View 121^{4} Hurwitz 121^{3} Sonaskra 121¾	11
21Jan86- 7GP	fst	7f	:22⅘	:46⅗	1:26	Md Sp Wt	7	1	$3^{1½}$	4^{nk}	6^{10}	$5^{13½}$	Sellers M S	122	*1.50	60-28	Playing Hard 122^{4} Touchy Avie 122^{1} Rotterdam 122^{3}	Gave way 9
26Nov85- 9CD	sly	6f	:21⅗	:46⅖	1:13	Md Sp Wt	12	2	2^{2}	$2^{2½}$	$5^{5½}$	$5^{5¾}$	Montoya D	121	4.10	74-26	The Flats 121^{2½} At The Start 121no Blandford Park 121^{nk}	12

C.

Turn The Traffic — Dk. b. or br. g. 4, by Traffic Warning—Turn A Lee, by Leematt
Br.—Paxson Mrs H D (Pa)
Own.—Paxson Mrs H D — Tr.—Edens Mary
118

Lifetime 13 1 1 3 $16,055 — 1987 3 0 1 0 $2,850 — 1986 10 1 0 3 $13,205 — Turf 5 0 1 1 $4,910

6Jly87- 8Mth	gd	1	[T]:48⅕		1:39⅗	3↑Alw 15000	1	7	$6^{7½}$	6^{7}	6^{4}	$6^{4¾}$	Edwards J W	118	8.60	72-27	Casa Basso 118¾ Hurricane John 114no Saxon Way 118¾	Outrun 9
6Feb87- 8Hia	fst	1$\frac{1}{16}$	:47⅗	1:11⅗	1:43	Alw 15000	7	7	$8^{5½}$	$7^{9¾}$	7^{12}	$8^{14½}$	Solomone M	119	12.00	72-20	Britton's Mill 116^{3½} Syncopation 116½ Split Rock 116no	Outrun 9
27Jan87- 8Hia	fm	*1$\frac{1}{16}$ [T]			1:55⅗	Alw 15000	4	4	$4^{7½}$	$5^{6¾}$	4^{2}	2^{2}	Edwards J W	119	17.60	82-19	Law Court 116^{2} Turn The Traffic 119¾ Nioro 116¾	Gamely 10
13Nov86- 6Med	fst	1	:48	1:14	1:40	3↑Md Sp Wt	1	8	8^{9}	$4^{3½}$	1^{3}	$1^{5½}$	Edwards J W	118	5.80	75-25	Turn The Traffic 118^{5½}Barefoot'sMiracle113^{nk}Tatupu116^{4}	Driving 9
4Nov86- 4Med	fst	1$\frac{1}{16}$	:48	1:14⅕	1:46⅘	3↑Md Sp Wt	5	7	$6^{7¾}$	$4^{3½}$	4^{4}	$5^{5¼}$	Edwards J W	118	3.60	64-24	Ra 122^{3} Greg's Mint 118^{1} Spiritual Director 118^{1¼}	No response 10
30Oct86- 1Med	sly	1$\frac{1}{16}$	:47	1:12	1:44⅖	3↑Md Sp Wt	1	7	$6^{7½}$	$4^{5½}$	3^{7}	$3^{7½}$	Edwards J W	117	4.60	73-20	Quotidien 122^{6½} Daring 'N Bold 117^{1} TurnTheTraffic117^{11}	Rallied 8
13Sep86- 5Med	fm	1$\frac{1}{16}$	[T]:47⅕	1:11⅗	1:42⅖	3↑Md Sp Wt	7	11	$9^{8¾}$	$6^{7½}$	$5^{7½}$	$3^{6¾}$	Krone J A	116	9.10	81-07	NorweginHill116^{5½}GrustrkinBoy122^{1¼}TurnTheTrffic116^{1½}	Rallied 11
2Sep86- 6Med	fm	1$\frac{1}{16}$	[T]:47⅖	1:11⅘	1:43⅗	3↑Md Sp Wt	1	9	9^{14}	6^{7}	$6^{6¼}$	$4^{5½}$	Krone J A	116	21.80	80-14	Woodcock 122^{2}OctoberStr116^{2½}LmontCrnston116^{1}	Rallied mildly 10
22Aug86-10Mth	fst	1$\frac{1}{16}$	:47⅘	1:13⅕	1:45⅗	3↑Md Sp Wt	8	7	7^{4}	$6^{5¾}$	6^{16}	$6^{18¼}$	Krone J A	115	9.50e	60-18	DaytimeFriend115^{nk}Almarine115^{7}BeyondTheDepth115^{7}	No factor 9
5Aug86-10Mth	fm	1	[T]:49	1:13⅘	1:41⅕	3↑Md Sp Wt	7	6	2^{hd}	1^{hd}	2^{hd}	6^{4}	Terry J	115	7.80	65-27	Nepotism 122^{1¼} Hector's Pup115½StrongCommitment115^{2}	Faded 10

LATEST WORKOUTS Jly 24 Mth 4f fst :49⅗ b — Jly 16 Mth 5f fst 1:02⅖ b — Jly 4 Mth 3f fst :37 b — ●Jun 27 Mth 1 sly 1:41⅗ h

D.

Run Quail Run — Ch. c. 4, by Run Dusty Run—Salem, by Lombard
Br.—Rolling Meadows Farm (Ky)
Own.—O'Mealia Joanne — Tr.—Gorman John
118

Lifetime 14 1 3 0 $20,115 — 1987 8 1 1 0 $13,500 — 1986 6 M 2 0 $6,615 — Turf 1 0 0 0 $150

14Jly87- 5Mth	fst	170	:46⅗	1:11	1:43⅕	3↑Alw 15000	1	7	6^{11}	6^{16}	6^{13}	6^{13}	Imparato J	119	15.60	67-23	Hill Slide 118^{nk} Public Accounter110^{4}HurricaneJohn114^{nk}	Outrun 7
26Jun87- 7Mth	fst	1$\frac{1}{16}$	:47	1:11⅗	1:45⅗	3↑Alw 15000	9	8	8^{8}	6^{8}	$6^{6¾}$	$4^{6¾}$	Imparato J	118	29.80	71-21	Toll Key 113^{2} Big Richie 111^{2¼} Silky Cyrus 118^{2½}	No menace 9
8Jun87- 7Mth	fst	170	:45⅘	1:10⅖	1:41⅗	3↑Alw 15000	2	7	7^{16}	7^{17}	7^{20}	$7^{26¾}$	Terry J	118	7.40	62-18	Hybet 113^{4½} Black Swan 111¾ Public Accounter 109^{7}	Trailed 7
13May87- 8GP	sly	1$\frac{1}{16}$	:49	1:13⅗	1:46⅕	Alw 16000	2	4	4^{5}	$3^{4½}$	2^{3}	$2^{2½}$	Terry J	119	6.70	67-25	Estano 117^{2½} Run Quail Run 119^{4½} Mr Sly Jr. 117^{6}	2nd best 5
6May87- 3GP	fst	1$\frac{1}{16}$	:49	1:12⅗	1:45⅗	3↑Alw 15000	2	6	$5^{5¾}$	5^{18}	4^{16}	$4^{17½}$	Milian J L7	113	7.10	56-22	Sunbury 111^{2} The Red Rolls 112^{6½} Estano 120^{7}	Outrun 6
12Apr87- 9GP	fst	7f	:22	:44⅘	1:23⅕	Alw 14000	8	7	8^{15}	8^{21}	6^{13}	4^{12}	Penna D	122	18.60	76-23	Craftstark 117^{8} New York Swell 122^{2½} BashfulBrave122^{1½}	Outrun 8
17Mar87- 8GP	fm	*1$\frac{1}{16}$ [T]			1:45⅗	Alw 15000	7	8	8^{10}	$8^{8¾}$	$8^{9¾}$	$7^{8½}$	Penna D	122	40.80	70-20	Keycolony 117^{2} Bini 117^{1} Seattlite 117^{hd}	Outrun 11
1Feb87-11Hia	fst	1⅛	:47	1:12⅖	1:52⅕	Md Sp Wt	2	8	7^{13}	$4^{6½}$	$1^{1½}$	1^{2}	Penna D	122	5.90	70-19	Run Quail Run 122^{2} GreatCharmer122^{17}ValD'Lar122^{5½}	Drew clear 12
31Dec86- 3Aqu	fst	6f	[•]:22⅘	:46⅘	1:11⅗	3↑Md Sp Wt	2	6	6^{8}	$6^{7½}$	5^{8}	$5^{7¾}$	Antley C W	120	12.80	79-13	Rexson's Quill 120no Cold Beer 120^{1½} Starry Night 115^{1¼}	No rally 8
22Dec86- 2Aqu	fst	6f	[•]:23⅕	:47⅖	1:13	3↑Md Sp Wt	6	7	6^{4}	$6^{4½}$	$5^{1¾}$	4^{3}	Ward W A	120	6.30[D]	76-17	Tina's Table 117^{1¾}StarryNight115½CollectionAgent120¾	Drifted in 9

22Dec86-Disqualified and placed sixth

LATEST WORKOUTS Jly 29 Mth 4f fst :50 b — Jun 20 Mth 5f fst 1:02 b — Jun 16 Mth 4f fst :50 b — Jun 6 Mth 5f fst 1:04⅖ b

*Note: Items 17–35 address Competency 65.

E.

Saxon Way B. c. 4, by Far North—Julia B, by Herbager
Br.—Jones W L Jr (Ky)
Own.—Top The Marc Stable Tr.—Milne Joan
118 Lifetime 8 1 0 2 $11,290 | 1987 3 0 0 1 $3,000 | 1986 5 1 0 1 $8,290 | Turf 6 1 0 2 $11,290

23Jly87- 7Mth fm 1 1/16 Ⓣ:47⅕ 1:10⅘ 1:43⅖ 3+ Alw 15000 10 8 66½ 79½ 79¾ 58¾ Madrid A Jr 117 7.30 79-09 Chasethebluesaway109¾HurricaneJohn1142RealEse1122 No factor 10
6Jly87- 8Mth gd 1 Ⓣ:48⅕ 1:39⅗ 3+ Alw 15000 5 5 45½ 44 22 3¾ Madrid A Jr 118 5.20 76-27 Casa Basso 118¾ Hurricane John 114no SaxonWay118¾ Weakened 9
8Jun87- 8Mth fm 1 1/16 Ⓣ:47⅘ 1:12 1:43 + 3+ Alw 15000 4 4 42½ 43½ 55 45 Madrid A Jr 118 10.60 81-14 Catch A Cold 1092½ Nantanela1141¼HurricaneJohn1141¼ Even try 8
15Nov86- 5Aqu fst 1 :45⅗ 1:11⅖ 1:37⅗ 3+ Alw 25000 2 7 1010 1212 1218 1224¾ Samyn J L b 115 15.10 53-22 Round The State 108nk Classic Move115hdDalmatian115no Outrun 13
13Oct86- 9Med fm 1 1/16 [T]:46⅗ 1:11⅕ 1:44 3+ Alw 15000 3 2 22 22 45½ 58 Sousonis S 112 5.80 75-17 ValD'Enchere1121¼NorwegianHill1146½Brestplte112nk Weakened 11
16Jun86- 5Mth fm 1 1/16 Ⓣ:47⅖ 1:11⅕ 1:43⅖+ 3+ Alw 14000 2 3 31½ 31½ 42½ 32¾ Walford J 111 2.60 81-19 Base Landing 1182 Able Fat S. 114¾ SaxonWay111nk Needed rally 8
6Jun86- 4GS fm 1 1/16 Ⓣ:47⅕ 1:11⅗ 1:43⅕ 3+ Md Sp Wt 1 1 11½ 12 14 14½ Walford J 114 6.20 93-08 SaxonWy1144½MistyMster116nkPrinceOfDestiny1164½ Drew clear 11
11May86- 3Bel fst 1 :46 1:10⅗ 1:37⅕ Md Sp Wt 3 5 65 55½ 57½ 510¾ Santagata N 122 20.20 65-15 Capo Cane 122¾ Proud World 1221¼ MalteseCross1227½ No factor 7
LATEST WORKOUTS Jly 18 Mth 4f fst :49⅖ b Jly 14 Mth 5f fst 1:03⅗ b Jun 29 Mth 5f fst 1:02 b Jun 20 Mth 5f fst 1:02 b

F.

Hombre de Carrera B. c. 3, by Lyphard's Wish—Decimating Lady, by Mr Clinch
Br.—Marsden James R (Ky)
Own.—Dennehy S C Tr.—Heimer Dennis
112 Lifetime 10 1 2 0 $14,360 | 1987 10 1 2 0 $14,360 | 1986 0 M 0 0 | Turf 4 1 1 0 $11,220

22Jly87- 6Mth fm 1⅛ Ⓣ:50⅘ 1:15⅕ 1:53 + 3+ Md Sp Wt 7 5 63½ 42 11½ 1½ Krone J A 115 *3.10 75-21 Hombre de Carrera 115½ Daufuskie 1152 Beau Nash 1151¾ Driving 9
6Jly87- 6Mth gd 1⅛ Ⓣ:49⅘ 1:15 1:53⅗+ 3+ Md Sp Wt 2 6 53 41½ 2½ 2nk Krone J A 115 15.20 72-27 North Star Light 115nk HombreoeCarrera115hdMasty1123¾ Sharp 10
21Jun87- 6Pha fm 1 70 Ⓣ 47⅗ 1:11⅖ 1:41 3+ Md Sp Wt 3 5 94¼ 87¼ 67½ 611¼ Nied J Jr 113 8.50 81-08 Shamrock Hill 113no Osmunda 1131¾ Free Colony 1133 Stumbled 11
10Jun87- 4GS fm 5f Ⓣ 22⅖ :46⅗ :58⅗ 3+ Md 25000 2 5 63¾ 84¼ 41½ 42½ Wilson R 115 10.90 91-09 Cavu 1151 Morgan's Pleasure 1131 Corneleus 122½ Lacked room 10
9Mar87- 2Lrl fst 6½f :23⅕ :47⅕ 1:18⅗ 3+ Md 18500 4 4 43 77 76½ 710¾ Wiley M C5 107 8.10 77-20 Triple Royalty 112¾ First Double 1222 Avie Gate 1061½ Fell back 8
21Feb87- 4Lrl fst 1 1/16 :50 1:16⅖ 1:50 Md 30000 10 5 33 85¾ 811 99¾ Sellers M S 120 10.40 49-30 ConteDeMontee1201½TrckSpkr115noGoodChristin1202¾ Fell back 10
10Feb87- 2Lrl fst 1 :48 1:14 1:41 Md 30000 4 2 33 77¼ 711 87¾ Chavez S N 120 4.30 59-24 Nijinsky'sSpring120nkConteDeMontee1201½PlnToBrter1162 Tired 8
30Jan87- 6Lrl my 1 1/16 :49⅘ 1:16⅕ 1:49⅗ Md 30000 3 3 31½ 33 33 42½ Chavez S N 120 *2.50 56-29 Copy Text120nkMagicalTune113nkConteDeMontee1202 Weakened 10
16Jan87- 6Lrl fst 1 :48⅕ 1:14⅘ 1:41⅕ Md 30000 11 7 31 2hd 32½ 44½ Chavez S N b 120 4.10 61-32 Liesl'sFling1202½HailToPssion1182SweetBrillince120hd Weakened 11
10Jan87- 3Lrl gd 6f :23⅕ :48 1:14⅘ Md 14500 2 4 43½ 45½ 45 2¾ Wiley M C7 113 *1.80 68-25 SpecilRuler115¾HombredeCrrer1133LstDnceMstr113½ Closed well 11
LATEST WORKOUTS Jun 6 GS 4f fst :50 b

G.

Real Ease B. c. 3, by Alleged—Satilla, by Targowice
Br.—Gallopin Corp (Ky)
Own.—Mastellone B Tr.—Goldberg Alan
112 Lifetime 3 1 0 1 $7,950 | 1987 3 1 0 1 $7,950 | 1986 0 M 0 0 | Turf 2 0 0 1 $1,650

23Jly87- 7Mth fm 1 1/16 Ⓣ:47⅕ 1:10⅘ 1:43⅖ 3+ Alw 15000 6 6 56 37 35 32¾ Santagata N b 112 9.30 85-09 Chasethebluesaway109¾HurricneJohn1142RelEse1122 Closed gap 10
12Jly87- 4Pha fst 1⅛ 1:54⅗ 3+ Md Sp Wt 2 1 11 1hd 1½ 16 Wilson R b 114 5.20 62-22 Real Ease 1146 Quick Tour 1135 Acquiescent 1136 Driving 6
~~6Jly87- 6Mth gd 1⅛ Ⓣ:49⅘ 1:15 1:53⅗+ 3+ Md Sp Wt~~ 8 7 74¾ 64¼ 711 714¾ Santagata N 115 9.00 57-27 North Star Light115nkHombredeCarrera115hdMasty1123½ Outrun 10
LATEST WORKOUTS Jun 8 Mth 5f fst 1:01 hg

H.

Sport Royal B. c. 3, by Secretariat—Linda North, by Northern Dancer
Br.—Taylor E P (Md)
Own.—Gleaves P Tr.—Gleaves Philip
110 Lifetime 6 1 0 1 $9,790 | 1987 6 1 0 1 $9,790 | 1986 0 M 0 0 | Turf 2 1 0 0 $8,100

25Jun87- 9Mth fm 1 1/16 Ⓣ:48 1:12⅖ 1:44 3+ Md Sp Wt 9 7 73¾ 22 1hd 13 Hernandez C 114 2.90 85-12 Sport Royal1143JamieBleu11411CommanderBenji1144 Ridden out 10
8Jun87- 8Mth fm 1 1/16 Ⓣ:47⅘ 1:12 1:43 + 3+ Alw 15000 7 8 810 77½ 76 66 Hernandez C 109 33.60 80-14 Catch A Cold 1092½ Nantahela 1141¼ Hurricane John1141¼ Outrun 8
18Apr87- 3GP fst 1 1/16 :48⅕ 1:13 1:45⅗ Md Sp Wt 4 7 73½ 99 916 1017 Lester R N 122 6.90 57-21 Carborundum 1222½ Tap Writer 1221½ Dusty Boots 1221 Outrun 10
4Apr87- 4GP fst 1 1/16 :47⅖ 1:13 1:47⅗ Md Sp Wt 10 11 1020 812 78¾ 34½ Santos J A 122 6.90 59-23 Derby Junior 1224½ Mollified 122no Sport Royal 1223 Rallied 12
28Mar87- 4GP fst 7f :23 :46⅗ 1:25⅖ Md Sp Wt 1 5 1½ 1½ 22 55¼ Guerra W A 122 5.90 72-21 WngdVctor1223½FlshUncl122noMrktCntrl1221½ Set pace, faltered 12
6Mar87- 4GP fst 6f :22⅖ :46⅕ 1:12⅘ Md Sp Wt 5 10 1010 1113 916 917¾ Guerra W A 122 *2.10 57-25 Im All Snook Up 122no Ron Stevens1224½Bahrain1152½ No factor 11
LATEST WORKOUTS Jly 22 Mth 4f fst :48⅘ b Jly 17 Mth 6f fst 1:16 b ●Jly 12 Mth 5f my 1:05 b Jun 21 Mth 6f fst 1:17⅕ b

I.

Talk Nice Dk. b. or br. c. 4, by Pleasant Colony—Constant Talk, by Cornish Prince
Br.—Evans Robert S (NJ)
Own.—Evans R S Tr.—Thompson J Willard
111 7 Lifetime 11 1 2 3 $19,615 | 1987 3 0 0 1 $1,650 | 1986 8 1 2 2 $17,965 | Turf 1 0 0 0

23Jly87- 8Mth fst 1 :47⅖ 1:12⅕ 1:39⅘ 3+ Alw 15000 2 4 54½ 58½ 57½ 37¾ Heath M J7 111 12.60 66-24 Aly Rat 1145 Public Accounter 1102¾ Talk Nice 1111¼ Rallied 6
9Jly87- 8Mth fst 1 70 :47 1:11⅗ 1:42⅖ 3+ [S]Alw 17500 5 7 86¼ 88¾ 99¾ 911¾ McCauley W H 117 *2.80 72-21 Tavio 117no General Payco 1176½ Jasperado 1132½ Outrun 10
1Jly87- 4Mth fst 6f :22⅕ :45⅕ 1:10⅗ 3+ [S]Alw 17500 8 11 1113 1119½ 1010 1017¾ McCauley W H 116 4.80 69-15 AlltheNumbers1165ChiefResident1161½ClockerHrry114hd Checked 11
14Nov86- 8Med fst 1 :47⅕ 1:12 1:36⅖ 3+ [S]Alw 17500 3 4 31½ 41½ 21 22¼ McCauley W H 118 6.40 91-12 Alioth 1072¼ Talk Nice 118½ Klassy Serenade 1163 Gamely 7
6Nov86- 10Med my 6f :22⅗ :45⅗ 1:10 3+ [S]Alw 17500 1 5 47½ 411 412 310½ McCauley W H 120 3.10 81-20 Will Pay Later 1168½ Duke Will 1142 Talk Nice 1202½ Evenly 5
17Oct86- 6Med fst 6f :23 :46⅗ 1:11⅘ 3+ [S]Md Sp Wt 9 6 61¾ 73¾ 42 1½ McCauley W H 119 8.00 83-19 Talk Nice 119½ King Above 1192 All the Numbers 1192 Driving 12
24Jun86- 5Mth fm 1⅛ Ⓣ:48⅗ 1:13⅘ 1:50⅘+ 3+ Md Sp Wt 10 6 56 72½ 67¾ 612½ Terry J 114 10.00 74-15 CraftyGiboulee1149LikelyKnight114hdDeuvilieLdy118no No factor 11
6Jun86- 1Mth fst 6f :22 :45⅕ 1:11⅕ 3+ [S]Md Sp Wt 6 10 99¼ 85¾ 77½ 66½ Terry J 115 4.90 77-14 Flourescent Gem 115½ Publicizer 115noFiliusStellae1155 Steadied 12
12Apr86- 3GS fst 1 70 :47⅘ 1:14⅖ 1:45⅕ 3+ Md Sp Wt 6 6 55¾ 37 36 34 Vigliotti M J 113 2.10 69-27 [D]Julie's Flag 1141½ Omaha Beach1142½TalkNice1138 lacked a bid 7
24Mar86- 5GS fst 1 :48⅖ 1:14⅗ 1:40⅘ Md Sp Wt 2 1 1½ 1hd 31½ 21½ Vigliotti M J 118 3.20 69-25 Golden Hoofprints 1181½ TalkNice118nkTriandrus1188 Drifted out 9
LATEST WORKOUTS ●Jun 24 Mth 6f fst 1:14 h Jun 18 Mth 5f fst 1:01⅗ h Jun 12 Mth 5f fst 1:02⅘ b Jun 6 Mth 4f fst :51 b

J.

Big Trial Ch. c. 3, by Bailjumper—Cyamome, by Cyane
Br.—Pen-Y-Bryn Farm (Ky)
Own.—McKenney J Tr.—Becker E Wayne
110 Lifetime 13 1 2 1 $26,670 | 1987 10 1 2 1 $25,290 | 1986 3 M 0 0 $1,380 | Turf 4 1 1 0 $19,680

19Jly87- 6Bel fm 1 1/16 [T]:46⅗ 1:11 1:41⅘ Clm 45000 7 4 31½ 3½ 22 25¼ Bailey J D 113 3.00 87-13 River of Sin 1135¼ Big Trial 113¾ Mr. J. V. 1132 Best of others 8
11Jly87- 1Bel fst 1¼ :48⅕ 1:40 2:07⅘ Clm 45000 7 1 16 16 11 35¾ Bailey J D 113 10.20 53-27 Soft Dollars 1131¾ Mr. J. V. 1134 Big Trial 1136 Tired 7
28Jun87- 1Bel fst 1 1/16 :47⅗ 1:12⅖ 1:45⅗ 3+ Alw 27000 6 4 32 57 611 616¼ Bailey J D 111 15.30 58-19 Moonlit Skies 1121¾ Hopzig 1144½ November Beans 1172 Tired 7
13Jun87- 7Bel fm 1 1/16 Ⓣ:46⅕ 1:11 1:43⅕ 3+ Alw 27000 2 4 42 41¾ 42 66¼ Vasquez J b 114 8.60 74-24 Swan Point 1141¼ Rio's Lark 1091¾ Drachma 1112 Lacked room 12
8Jun87- 3Bel fm 1 1/16 Ⓣ:49 1:13 1:44⅘ 3+ Alw 27000 6 5 1½ 12½ 1hd 53¾ Guerra W A b 114 9.10 68-24 Cedar Creek 1091 Carolina North 1091¼ Sol d'Or 119no Weakened 12
21May87- 4Bel gd 1 Ⓣ:47⅗ 1:12 1:39⅗ 3+ Md Sp Wt 5 3 2½ 1hd 15 16 Bailey J D b 113 *2.00 67-34 Big Trial 1136 Grey Basque 1085½ SourceofStrength1135¼ Handily 11
25Mar87- 7GP my 1 1/16 :47⅘ 1:13⅕ 1:47⅗ Md Sp Wt 12 2 2½ 24 33½ 613½ Vasquez J b 122 3.30 49-24 CharlotofWar1225½EstreliaPlateada1221¼TpWriter122½ Weakened 12
7Mar87- 3GP fst 1 1/16 :48⅕ 1:13⅗ 1:47⅗ Md Sp Wt 2 4 34 2hd 21½ 28 Vasquez J 122 *1.50 55-25 L'Minstrel 1228 Big Trial 122½ Beau Nash 12211½ Game try 10
14Feb87- 5Hia fst 7f :22⅗ :45⅕ 1:23⅕ Md Sp Wt 6 11 108¾ 713 917 918½ Vasquez J 121 3.70 68-15 Maceo 12112½ Buy At Home 1211 Born Sunny 121½ Outrun 12
16Jan87- 11Hia fst 7f :23⅕ :46 1:24⅕ Md Sp Wt 7 8 73 63½ 66½ 68 Vasquez J 121 6.50 74-19 Jim Bowie 121¾ Missing Clue 1213½ Snouting 121nk No rally 12
LATEST WORKOUTS Jly 28 Bel 5f fst :59⅗ h Jly 9 Bel 4f sly :49⅖ b Jun 20 Bel 4f fst :47⅖ b Jun 7 Bel 3f fst :36⅖ b

18.

3rd Santa Anita

6 FURLONGS. (1.07⅗) CLAIMING. Purse $22,000. Fillies and mares. 4-year-olds and upward. Weight, 121 lbs. Non-winners of two races since February 15 allowed 3 lbs.; of a race since then, 5 lbs. Claiming price $25,000; if for $22,500 allowed 2 lbs. (Races when entered for $20,000 or less not considered.)

Coupled—Lovely Candy and Universally.

A.

Irish Zuni
PINCAY L JR — 116
Own.—Coelho & Valenti
B. f. 4, by The Irish Lord—Princess Zuni, by Native Royalty
Br.—Valenti & Coelho (Cal) — 1987 2 0 1 0 $3,200
Tr.—McCutcheon James R — $25,000 — 1986 9 2 0 1 $21,725
Lifetime 11 2 1 1 $24,925

8Feb87-1SA 6f :212 :442 1:11 ft 4½ 117 118 99¾ 910 67½ Pincay L Jr 7 Ⓕ 25000 75-14 Florimel,LovelyCandy,LadyHelcha 12
8Feb87—Stumbled at start
16Jan87-9SA 6½f :214 :452 1:173ft 7½ 117 1hd 2hd 1hd 21½ Pincay L Jr 8 Ⓕ 25000 80-18 Bolder Beauty, Irish Zuni,MarCon 12
30Dec86-2SA 6f :214 :451 1:112ft *2½ 117 42 33 33 32¼ Pincay L Jr 5 Ⓕ 20000 79-18 LuckyShowers,MissDaniel,IrishZuni 8
26Dec86-1SA 6f :214 :45 1:111ft 11 117 53 33½ 31½ 11½ Pincay L Jr 8 Ⓕ 16000 82-13 IrishZuni,FullO'Gems,ToBImprssiv 11
19Dec86-7Hol 6f :22 :454 1:12 ft 11 116 72¼ 63¾ 53½ 54½ McHrguDG 4 ⒻⓈ 20000 78-17 DistntRunner,LuckyShowrs,Michcri 9
19Dec86—Lacked room 3/8, lugged in stretch
5Dec86-5Hol 6f :22 :46 1:113ft 15 116 31½ 64½ 86½ 89½ McHargueDG 6 Ⓕ 32000 75-17 SntimntlSong,LdyHlch,Mgdln'sMgc 8
11Oct86-1SA 6f :213 :443 1:101ft 5½ 118 43 45½ 49½ 411¼ Pincay L Jr 7 Ⓕ 32000 76-17 AffordblLuxury,LdyShmn,LomitJwl 7
15Sep86-10Pom 6f :223 :454 1:111ft 18 114 32½ 44 44 55¾ PedrozMA 8 ⒻAw25000 89-08 RdrDwn,Poopydoodle,DuchessZnth 9
26Jly86-2Dmr 6f :222 :46 1:101ft *3-2 117 1½ 1½ 1hd 1½ Pincay L Jr 6 ⒻM50000 87-13 Irish Zuni, For K. B., BolderBeauty 8
16Jly86-1Hol 6f :222 :46 1:104ft 16 114 11 1½ 21 44 Douglas RR 3 ⒻM50000 86-15 Fshionlity,LedingLss,Dncer'sRegrds 7
Mar 30 SA 5f ft 1:012 h Mar 25 SA 4f ft :481 h Mar 20 SA 4f ft :473 h Mar 15 SA 4f ft :514 h

B.

Lovely Candy
VALENZUELA P A — 116
Own.—Daverick Stable & Goldfarb
B. f. 4, by Debonair Roger—Lady of the Mist, by Royal Attack
Br.—Rogers J D (Cal) — 1987 7 2 1 1 $26,125
Tr.—Fanning Jerry — $25,000 — 1986 8 0 0 1 $1,950
Lifetime 20 4 3 2 $52,625

25Mar87-5SA 6f :214 :451 1:104ft *2½ 117 52½ 41¾ 3nk 1½ Pincay L Jr 2 Ⓕ c20000 84-17 LovelyCndy,AmoDidIt,FireMissLdr 8
25Mar87—Off slowly
6Mar87-1SA 6f :213 :444 1:111gd *2 117 64 64½ 64½ 32¼ PincayLJr 2 ⒻⓈ c16000 80-21 Oak Portal, Cuervo, Lovely Candy 7
6Mar87—Jostled start
20Feb87-9SA 1 :452 1:103 1:381ft *3-2 117 17 14 13½ 11¾ Pincay LJr 10 Ⓕ c12500 77-16 LovlyCndy,Dimggio'sPt,SuprisGift 10
14Feb87-1SA 6½f :214 :452 1:174sy 4¾ 117 75 74¾ 89½ 1015½ Pincay L Jr 10 Ⓕ 20000 65-17 MissDaniela,BillyJen,SummerGlow 12
14Feb87—Wide
8Feb87-1SA 6f :212 :442 1:11 ft 62 1085 97½ 67½ 44 21 Cox D W 3 Ⓕ 22500 82-14 Florimel,LovelyCandy,LadyHelcha 12
30Jan87-3SA 6½f :214 :444 1:174ft 187 113 65½ 67 77½ 75 Douglas R R 10 Ⓕ 35000 76-20 Velveteen, Wine Girl, My Tara 12
16Jan87-1SA 6½f :221 :454 1:181ft 4¾ 115 53 63¾ 66¼ 56 StevensGL 10 Ⓕ c12500 73-18 Ms.CrkdRd,Flk'sVctry,FryGdmthr 12
16Jan87—Bumped at 5 1/2
31Dec86-1SA 6f :22 :452 1:113ft *2½ 114 41¾ 45 35 37½ StevensGL 4 ⒻⓈ 12500 72-20 MarCon,Dimggio'sPet,LovelyCndy 10
19Jun86-2Hol 6f :22 :46 1:113ft 4¾ 115 88¼ 96¾ 76 811 McCarron CJ 4 Ⓕ 20000 75-14 SrAndCrfty,AbovThRst,VctorPort 11
19Jun86—Steadied at 5/8
14May86-3Hol 6f :223 :464 1:113ft 6 117 62½ 63¾ 76 68¾ Pincay LJr 5 ⒻⓈ 25000 77-14 AbOrgnl,NorthrnIsl,GlmorosAmbr 12
14May86—Bumped start
Mar 23 SA 3f ft [illegible] h Mar 15 SA 4f ft :472 h Mar 1 SA 4f ft :472 h

C.

Hidden Past
STEVENS G L — 116
Own.—Giuliano-Jackson-Walkeretal
B. m. 5, by Historically—Knowledgeable Lady, by Tree of Knowledge
Br.—Dollase & Hanson (Cal) — 1987 5 1 0 1 $14,850
Tr.—Bernstein David — $25,000 — 1986 15 7 1 1 $49,695
Lifetime 32 9 3 2 $82,745 — Turf 1 0 0 0

18Mar87-7SA 6½f :214 :444 1:17 ft *2½ 118 31 21½ 22½ 32 Stevens G L 8 Ⓕ 25000 83-17 PeggyDee,Ms.CrookdRod,HiddnPst 8
20Feb87-7SA a6½f Ⓣ:214 :441 1:153fm 19 117 42 52½ 75¼ 68¼ Black C A 3 ⒻAw27000 73-19 InConcert,Jerry'sGoldmine,Phylell 10
30Jan87-3SA 6½f :214 :444 1:174ft 3¼ 116 108½ 1010 1214 129¾ Stevens G L 7 Ⓕ 40000 71-20 Velveteen, Wine Girl, My Tara 12
30Jan87—Wide final 3/8
19Jan87-7SA 6½f :214 :444 1:173ft 4¾ 118 32 33 33 12¾ Stevens G L 4 Ⓕ 32000 82-25 HiddenPst,PrimroseKitchns,Vlvtn 10
4Jan87-6SA 6f :22 :452 1:114sy 6 116 86¼ 1112 912 912¾ Stevens G L 6 Ⓕ 40000 66-22 IrishKristin,ThirdMarrige,WineGirl 12
4Jan87—Wide 3/8
14Dec86-1Hol 1 :461 1:112 1:372ft 4½ 116 21½ 34½ 45 68 StevensGL 1 ⒻAw25000 68-18 Mrs.V.,Melva'sPride,Veronic'sQuest 7
16Nov86-2Hol 1 :45 1:104 1:373ft 4 114 34 1½ 14 1nk Stevens G L 6 Ⓕ 30000 75-18 Hidden Past, Vital Score,FleetRain 8
30Oct86-3SA 6f :212 :443 1:112ft 2½ 118 57 68 56½ 2½ Stevens G L 3 Ⓕ c20000 80-18 Walker's Lady,HiddenPast,Frenzied 7
30Oct86—Stumbled break
13Oct86-9SA 6f :221 :454 1:114ft 5 122 43 42¼ 3½ 11¾ Stevens G L 7 Ⓕ c16000 79-19 HiddnPst,AncintLdy,Ms.CrookdRod 9
13Oct86—Bobbled at start
13Sep86-8Lga 6f :22 :453 1:11 m 3¼ 120 58½ 714 720 715 Drexler H 4 Ⓕ 20000 65-32 BarbaricNell,She'sFit,Ms.SatusWay 8
●Mar 26 SA tr.t 3f ft :352 h ●Mar 14 SA tr.t 4f ft :472 h Mar 8 SA 3f gd :352 h Feb 17 SA 4f ft :473 h

D.

***Miss Daniela**
DELAHOUSSAYE E **116**
Own.—Dolan-Kleber-Stachler

B. f. 4, by Dauphin—Reb's Honey, by Reb's Policy
Br.—Achar V (Mex) 1987 7 1 1 2 $23,450
Tr.—Dolan John K $25,000 1986 19 3 2 3 $28,003
Lifetime 32 6 4 5 $55,479

18Mar87-7SA 6½f :214 :444 1:17 ft 7½ 117 75½ 77¼ 56½ 45½ Pincay L Jr 2 Ⓕ 25000 79-17 PeggyDee,Ms.CrookdRod,HiddnPst 8
13Mar87-7SA 6f :213 :45 1:112ft 6¾ 117 85¾ 75½ 54¼ 42 Pincay L Jr 5 Ⓕ 32000 79-21 Florimel, Dancer's Regards, Mush 10
13Mar87—Lugged out backstretch
25Feb87-5SA 1 1/16 :472 1:122 1:451m *2 116 21½ 21½ 22½ 33½ VlenzuelPA 5 Ⓕ c20000 71-22 Text BookLady,Kristin,MissDaniela 8
14Feb87-1SA 6½f :214 :452 1:174sy 4¼ 116 53½ 2hd 14 16½ ValenzuelPA 3 Ⓕ 20000 81-17 MissDaniela,BillyJen,SummerGlow 12
4Feb87-9SA 1 1/16 :464 1:121 1:451ft 6 116 1hd 1hd 1hd 22 ValenzuelPA 4 Ⓕ 20000 73-19 AncientLdy,MissDniel,Sh'sSoBold 10
4Feb87—Broke out, bumped
28Jan87-3SA 6f :214 :451 1:113ft 5¾ 116 106½ 89¼ 58½ 45¾ McHargueDG 7 Ⓕ 20000 74-21 Jerry'sGoldmine,MarCon,Frenzied 12
19Jan87-3SA 7f :22 :452 1:253ft *3½ 116 55 44½ 54½ 31½ McHrgueDG 7 Ⓕ c16000 70-25 GranEmotion,ArcticLnd,MissDniel 11
19Jan87—Wide in stretch
30Dec86-2SA 6f :214 :451 1:112ft 19 116 65¾ 66½ 55½ 22 McHargueDG 4 Ⓕ 20000 79-18 LuckyShowers,MissDaniel,IrishZuni 8
19Dec86-4Hol 1 1/16 :472 1:13 1:46 ft 8 114 1½ 11 1hd 34 CastanonAL 2 Ⓕ c14000 75-17 AncientLady,Julin'sDrem,MissDniel 8
12Dec86-5Hol 1 :48 1:132 1:394ft 5 115 21 12 12½ 1½ Castanon AL 3 Ⓕ 12500 64-20 MissDnil,Folk'sVctory,FrndlyCrowd 8
Apr 1 SA 4f ft :481 h Mar 12 SA 3f ft :361 h Feb 12 SA 4f ft :47 h

E.

Jingle
PEDROZA M A **116**
Own.—Oda H

B. m. 5, by Piaster—Mahdees, by Tentam
Br.—Strauss J (Cal) 1987 4 0 0 0 $2,300
Tr.—Lewis Craig A $25,000 1986 6 1 1 1 $20,700
Lifetime 24 5 4 2 $85,900 Turf 1 0 0 0

13Mar87-7SA 6f :213 :45 1:112ft 4¾ 116 62½ 54½ 87¼ 710¼ Stevens G L 4 Ⓕ 32000 71-21 Florimel, Dancer's Regards, Mush 10
1Mar87-2SA 6f :213 :45 1:103ft 2¾ 116 32½ 33 43½ 67¾ DelhoussyeE 1 Ⓕ 40000 77-15 Agigael, Lacey Linn, Volanda 8
30Jan87-3SA 6½f :214 :444 1:174ft 13 116 2½ 21½ 1hd 42¾ Soto S B 5 Ⓕ 40000 78-20 Velveteen, Wine Girl, My Tara 12
30Jan87—Lugged in stretch
4Jan87-6SA 6f :22 :452 1:114sy 13 116 1½ 1½ 2½ 53½ Soto S B 6 Ⓕ 40000 75-22 IrishKristin,ThirdMarrige,WineGirl 12
6Jun86-1Hol 6f :221 :463 1:112ft 4¾ 114⁵ 55 31¼ 54¾ 711 Black C A 7 Ⓕ 40000 76-15 LuckySilvr,ThirdMrrig,MgnticDncr 8
6Jun86—Bumped hard early stretch; lugged in late
22May86-7Hol 6f :22 :46 1:114ft 2 116 67 76½ 77 711¾ DelhoussyeE 4 Ⓕ 50000 73-15 Bullion, Allez Vite, Dulce Vino 7
16Apr86-7SA 6½f :214 :45 1:172ft *2¼ 116 74 66 32 1½ DelhoussyE 8 Ⓕ c40000 83-24 Jingle, Fighting Marietta, Tamure 12
28Mar86-5SA 6f :214 :444 1:10 ft 6 116 53 33½ 34 24½ DelhoussyeE 1 Ⓕ 40000 83-19 Expect More,Jingle,ThirdMarriage 11
22Jan86-1SA 6f :22 :45 1:104ft 4¼ 116 54½ 58 610 610¾ DelhoussyeE 6 Ⓕ 62500 73-21 ImprssvWnd,FrstPckg,HcklbrryHny 7
22Jan86—Broke through gate
4Jan86-1SA 6f :214 :443 1:091ft 2¾ 116 32 32 23½ 36½ DelhoussyeE 5 Ⓕ 50000 85-13 CountOnLyn,MissRoylMonte,Jingle 6
Feb 12 SA 5f ft :591 h

F.

Universally
CISNEROS J E **111⁵**
Own.—Fanning & Harrison

B. f. 4, by Universal—Westward Wind, by Restless Wind
Br.—Fanning & Harrison (Cal) 1986 9 1 2 2 $17,090
Tr.—Fanning Jerry $25,000 1985 1 M 0 0
Lifetime 10 1 2 2 $17,090

2Oct86-3SA 6f :214 :444 1:102ft 28 116 63¾ 1111 1215 1215¾ Lipham T 12 Ⓕ 25000 70-20 SaroGolden,She'sSoBold,L'Athena 12
19Sep86-8Pom 6½f :22 :454 1:171ft 5½ 114 58 79½ 76 610¾ DominguzRE 6 Ⓕ 25000 83-09 She's SoBold,L'Athena,RochellsGirl 8
16Jly86-9LA 6½f :22 :453 1:17 ft 15 113 55½ 67 613 616 GrridoOL 2 Ⓕ La Palma 76-16 Admat, Fine Kudos, ForeverABlurr 6
9Jly86-3Hol 6f :223 :462 1:112ft 3½e 115 73½ 63¾ 75 75½ Stevens G L 3 Ⓕ 40000 81-18 CoffeeRoll,BeaulahInd,MriSupreme 8
11Jun86-5Hol 6f :223 :46 1:114ft 7½ 115 75¾ 53½ 31½ 2¾ Stevens G L 4 Ⓕ 40000 84-16 MariSupreme,Universlly,CoffeeRoll 9
23May86-1Hol 6f :221 :463 1:122ft 5¾ 118 54½ 41½ 2½ 2nk Toro F 3 Ⓕ 32000 82-23 OkPortl,Universlly,DevelopingGrce 7
23May86—Brushed in drive
9Apr86-3SA 6f :222 :46 1:114ft 4 117 1hd 1hd 1hd 1¾ Lipham T 3 Ⓕ M32000 79-18 Univrslly,Kllny'sHony,Wnsomthng 10
21Mar86-3SA 6f :214 :454 1:114ft *2 117 31½ 2½ 32 32 Lipham T 6 Ⓕ [S] M32000 77-15 Mar Con, NorthernIsle,Universally 10
12Mar86-4SA 6f :222 :462 1:13 sy 7½ 117 54½ 53 33 3½ Lipham T 6 Ⓕ [S] M32000 72-25 CuriousPrincess,Pstreil,Universlly 10
10Jly85-1Hol 5½f :224 :454 1:053ft 13 118 66¾ 610 715 717½ Olivares F 5 Ⓕ [S] Mdn — — VictoriPort,SroGoldn,JoysOfSpring 8
Mar 31 SA 6f ft 1:023 h Mar 23 SA 6f ft 1:162 h Mar 16 SA 6f ft 1:154 h Mar 10 SA 6f ft 1:164 h

G.

Fighting Marietta
OLIVARES F **118**
Own.—McAtee R & Melodie

Dk. b. or br. m. 5, by Cojak—Herb's Judy, by Bald Eagle
Br.—Pegram J H & M E (Cal) 1987 4 1 0 0 $12,125
Tr.—Bernstein David $25,000 1986 13 3 3 1 $49,430
Lifetime 35 7 5 4 $97,155

13Mar87-7SA 6f :213 :45 1:112ft 3¼ 116 2hd 11 2hd 53¼ Olivares F 8 Ⓕ 32000 78-21 Florimel, Dancer's Regards, Mush 10
22Feb87-1SA 6f :213 :444 1:11 ft 13 116 2hd 11 12 12 Olivares F 2 Ⓕ 25000 83-14 FightingMariett,SpurMeOn,TutMi 10
12Feb87-6GG 6f :214 :444 1:11 sy 7¼ 115 21 21 25 613 Lozoya D A 7 Ⓕ 32000 71-24 NtivLothrio,PggyD,Tomorrow'sNws 8
28Jan87-3SA 6f :214 :451 1:119ft 3 116 42 36 47½ 711 Olivares F 8 Ⓕ c20000 69-21 Jerry'sGoldmine,MarCon,Frenzied 12
23Sep86-10Pom 1 1/16 :462 1:111 1:441ft 2½ 116 1hd 1hd 44½ 79¼ Olivares F 7 Ⓕ 25000 81-08 French Star, Bid ForHer,Cabrioleta 8
5Sep86-7Dmr 6f :213 :45 1:102ft 6 114 4¾ 43½ 78½ 712 Olivares F 4 Ⓕ 35000 74-16 Volanda, Lacey Linn, Matchpenny 7
5Sep86—Broke out, bumped
23Aug86-3Dmr 6f :214 :45 1:093ft 3¼ 116 21 32 23 45 Olivares F 3 Ⓕ 40000 85-10 TmmyLu,GingerFlsh,ReputtionMiss 9

11Aug86-5Dmr 1 :452 1:104 1:37 ft 8½ 116 21 21½ 42 65 Olivares F 5 Ⓕ 40000 78-13 WineTster,RdFrnchy,Dlt'sGoldCoin 9
26Jly86-3Dmr 6f :213 :443 1:09 ft *8-5 118 43½ 46 45½ 35½ Olivares F 3 Ⓕ 40000 87-13 ExpectMore,VitlScor,FightingMritt 8
4Jly86-4Hol 6f :214 :451 1:102ft 5½ 119 2½ 2hd 21 63½ Olivares F 7 ⒻAw23000 88-09 RreStrlet,PollysLilRscl,LBellWilson 8
Mar 26 SA 4f ft :471 h Mar 11 SA 4f ft :474 h Mar 2 SA 4f ft :464 h Feb 8 SA 5f ft 1:00 h

H.

Reputation Miss *
SOLIS A 116
Own.—Oakmont Stable Ltd
Ch. m. 7, by Our Hero—Reputation, by Hillary
Br.—Moreno H (Ky) 1987 4 0 1 0 $5,775
Tr.—Arena Joseph $25,000 1986 20 3 2 5 $69,475
Lifetime 76 9 9 13 $221,825 Turf 7 0 0 0 $2,325
6Mar87-9SA 1 :462 1:121 1:38 gd 4 116 76 89½ 89¾ 817 Meza R Q 5 Ⓕ 25000 56-21 BrunedMi,RsonToCounsl,AncintLcy 9
6Mar87—Bumped start
15Feb87-2SA 7f :224 :454 1:26 m 4 116 66¼ 54½ 76 66¾ ValenzuelPA 2 Ⓕ 32000 73-17 Sh'sSoBold,RufflsNBus,ThirdMrrig 8
15Feb87—Wide into stretch
19Jan87-7SA 6½f :214 :444 1:173ft 3½ 118 109¾ 89½ 67½ 44 ValenzuelPA 7 Ⓕ 32000 78-25 HiddenPst,PrimroseKitchns,Vlvtn 10
19Jan87—Broke slowly
9Jan87-3SA 6f :221 :462 1:124sl *1-2 120 58½ 55½ 43½ 23 ValenzuelPA 5 Ⓕ 32000 71-26 Velveteen,ReputationMiss,JmTime 6
10Dec86-9Hol 1 :463 1:113 1:38 ft 5½ 116 67½ 57 32 13½ Solis A 6 Ⓕ 32000 73-20 ReputtionMiss,ArcticLnd,BidForHr 7
10Dec86—Wide into stretch
31Oct86-9SA 1 1/16 :454 1:103 1:434ft 6¾ 116 69½ 58 59 510¼ ValenzuelPA 1 Ⓕ 32000 72-16 Don A Top, VitalScore,FrenchStar 10
17Oct86-5SA 6f :22 :453 1:113ft 10 116 77¼ 74¼ 53 43½ ValenzuelPA 7 Ⓕ 30000 76-21 B. Elite, Spur Me On, Tammy Lu 8
6Oct86-9SA 1 1/16 :461 1:114 1:45 ft 6½ 116 711 76½ 73½ 36¾ ValenzuelPA 5 Ⓕ 32000 69-20 VitlScore,Neumi'sGirl,RputtionMiss 8
5Sep86-9Dmr 1 :46 1:112 1:364ft 5 1095 45 41¾ 44½ 35½ Black C A 4 Ⓕ 35000 78-16 Emacia,BrunedeMai,ReputtionMiss 7
23Aug86-3Dmr 6f :214 :45 1:093ft 15 1115 914 813 79½ 34½ Black C A 9 Ⓕ 40000 85-10 TmmyLu,GingerFish,ReputtionMiss 9
Apr 4 SA 3f ft :362 h Feb 28 SA 5f ft 1:013 h

19. When a single horse outclasses the conditions, the handicapping is virtually complete. Find that horse.

9th Del Mar

1 1/16 MILES. (Turf). (1.40) ALLOWANCE. Purse $23,000. 3-year-olds and upward which are non-winners of $3,000 other than maiden, claiming or starter. Weights, 3-year-olds, 115 lbs.; older, 121 lbs. Non-winners of a race other than claiming at one mile or over since June 15 allowed 3 lbs.

A.

Visible Asset
PATTON D B 1135
Own.—Rancho Rio Hondo
B. g. 5, by Majestic Light—Promised Woman, by Promised Land
Br.—Gentry T (Ky) 1987 12 1 1 4 $22,100
Tr.—Mulhall Richard W 1986 12 3 0 1 $20,235
Lifetime 34 4 1 7 $46,955
28Jun87-5Hol 1 :454 1:11 1:363ft 7 1115 74½ 54 3½ 2hd Patton D B 9 32000 80-12 QulityJet,VisibleAsset,BoldBtterUp 9
28Jun87—Wide 3/8 turn
14Jun87-5Hol 7f :22 :45 1:231ft 16 1115 1014 1012 85 53½ Patton D B 2 32000 84-14 UrbnCowboy,QulityJt,BoldBttrUp 10
14Jun87—Poor start
23May87-1Hol 1 :452 1:103 1:37 ft* 4½ 1105 710 56½ 24 12 Patton D B 6 20000 78-15 VisibleAsset,Detector,BronzeTudor 8
23May87—Broke in a tangle
15May87-6Hol 6½f :213 :441 1:163ft 23 116 1217 1111 89¾ 33¾ DelahoussayeE 4 16000 93-13 LikeShntin,NtiveRelity,VisibleAsst 12
29Apr87-1Hol 6f :221 :452 1:10 ft 8 116 66½ 68 47½ 35½ Baze G 5 12500 87-13 EllsBrvstSong,TscnKnght,VsblAsst 8
12Apr87-1SA 6½f :213 :444 1:17 ft 6¾ 116 77½ 89¼ 911 811¼ DelahoussayeE 9 16000 74-18 FirstBeginning,BlazingZulu,TiHigh 10
12Apr87—Wide final 3/8
3Apr87-1SA 6f :213 :45 1:112ft 16 116 99¾ 97½ 76½ 31¾ DelahoussayeE 8 12500 79-17 Polly'sRuler,StrOfAmric,VisiblAsst 9
3Apr87—Broke in a tangle; wide into stretch
22Mar87-1SA 7f :231 :464 1:262gd 8½ 116 74¼ 73¾ 62¼ 42 Black C A 2 12500 66-23 T. V. Oil, Bruli's Ante, Halo'sSword 8
14Mar87-2SA 6½f :214 :444 1:163ft 38 116 76¾ 78½ 66½ 35½ Black C A 1 10000 81-16 Polly'sRuler,BoldBttrUp,VsiblAsst 9
14Mar87—Steadied 1/8
19Feb87-9SA 1 :463 1:113 1:371ft 16 115 86¼ 76½ 67½ 65¼ Black C A 8 10000 77-13 SwiftMessg,QuickSwp,Cpt'nDoubl 10
Jly 22 Hol 4f ft :473 h Jly 14 Hol 4f ft :48 h Jly 9 Hol 5f ft 1:002 h Jun 22 Hol 3f ft :362 h

B.

Junior Sahib
BAZE G 118
Own.—Green Thumb Farm Stable
B. h. 5, by Sassafras—Miss Arlene, by Honeytex
Br.—Company H F (Fla) 1987 1 0 0 0 $550
Tr.—Ellis Ronald W 1986 5 0 1 0 $6,200
Lifetime 14 1 2 3 $13,883 Turf 11 1 1 3 $7,133
12Jly87-7Hol 6f :214 :441 1:092ft 64 118 67 58 59½ 512 Baze G 5 Aw22000 84-09 MjstcMsson,OlympcPrspct,GrtYnk 7
5Oct86-9SA 1 1/16 :462 1:111 1:424ft 59 116 1½ 2½ 1011 1015¾ Baze G 6 40000 71-15 Tough Envoy, Idol, Tio Nino 10
17Aug86-5Dmr 1 Ⓣ:461 1:103 1:351fm 9 117 73¼ 1013 919 — Toro F 5 Aw20000 — — Rai Den, Coaraze Nay, Lud 10
17Aug86—Eased

5Jly86-9Hol 1⅛Ⓣ:4721:1121:472fm 26 116 32½ 41½ 911 918¼ Stevens G L 8 Aw23000 77-04 Severn Bore, Enviro, Will Spring 10
14Mar86-5SA 1 :461 1:122 1:394sy 13 116 12 11 2½ 2½ Toro F 3 Aw31000 68-30 FbulousPrtndr,JuniorShib,Gnrlzton 8
23Feb86-2SA a6½f Ⓣ:213 :4421:161fm *2½ 117 42 42½ 67½1011 McCarronCJ 9 Aw27000 67-24 Brianchon,DonSanders,ErthToGry 12
21Sep85◆7Milan(Italy) a1 1:382gd 3½ 120 Ⓣ 41 PlanrdiM PrStronaH Wilhemina, Quintero, Filippo 9
31Aug85◆8Milan(Italy) a1 1:361gd 3¾ 105 Ⓣ 45¾ Mulas N PrMntrfnoH Nardil, Video King, Bamboo Cay 5
19Jun85◆5Milan(Italy) a7½f 1:364sf *8-5 123 Ⓣ 1½ JeromM PrValle(Mdn) Junior Sahib, So Young, Kogc 7
1Jun85◆7Milan(Italy) a7f 1:243gd 6¾ 108 Ⓣ 32½ Mulas N PrOzzanoH VampingHex,EgleCrown,JuniorShib 7
Jly 4 SA 5f ft 1:002 h Jun 28 Hol 4f ft :513 h Jun 16 Hol 6f ft 1:124 h Jun 10 Hol 5f ft 1:013 h

C.

Table Glow
STEVENS G L **112**
Own.—Sarkowsky H
B. g. 3, by Never Tabled—Radiant Glow, by Northern Dancer
Br.—Sarkowsky S H (Cal) 1987 5 1 2 1 $17,450
Tr.—Mandella Richard 1986 1 M 0 0
Lifetime 6 1 2 1 $17,450 Turf 2 0 2 0 $9,600

3Jly87-9Hol 1 1/16Ⓣ:4631:1031:414fm 2¾ 114 11½ 11½ 11½ 2nk Stevens G L 9 Aw24000 85-11 BooBoo'sBuckroo,TblGlow,Pondrbl 9
19Jun87-5Hol 1 1/16Ⓣ:46 1:0941:403fm 19 114 1½ 1½ 1½ 2hd Stevens G L 1 Aw24000 91-09 Forlaway,TableGlow,ContactGame 10
12Jun87-6Hol 6f :221 :453 1:112ft 2¾ 115 21 2hd 1hd 11¼ Stevens GL 3 Ⓢ M32000 86-16 TbleGlow,BrothersSteve,L.W.Kidd 11
23May87-4Hol 6f :213 :45 1:111ft *6-5 115 41½ 32½ 65 75½ Stevens G L 6 M40000 81-15 Peppy'sConsul,PolynsinChif,Trlnd 10
13May87-6Hol 6f :213 :443 1:104ft 2¾ 115 22 24 23½ 32¼ Stevens G L 2 M40000 87-15 OlympcProspct,CmnBmbn,TblGlw 11
30Aug86-4Dmr 6f :22 :452 1:102ft 5¼ 118 52¼ 54 710 711¾ Toro F 1 Ⓢ Mdn 74-10 ASignOfLuck,AtTheRitz,NstyNskr 10
30Aug86—Veered in start
Jly 20 Hol 4f ft :48 h Jly 13 Hol 3f ft :371 h Jun 29 Hol 3f ft :37 h Jun 8 Hol 3f ft :394 h

D.

Istoriato
VALENZUELA P A **118**
Own.—Schwartz D
B. c. 4, by Storm Bird—Multiflora, by Beau Max
Br.—King Ranch Inc (Ky) 1987 8 0 1 1 $14,175
Tr.—Lukas D Wayne 1986 6 2 2 0 $11,780
Lifetime 14 2 3 1 $25,955 Turf 10 2 3 1 $22,130

6Jly87-9Hol 1⅛Ⓣ:4611:10 1:474fm 4 115 74 73¾ 76½ 95¾ Stevens G L4 Aw24000 83-11 Star Ribot, First Dibs, Ima Bullet 10
20Jun87-9Hol 1 1/16Ⓣ:4631:1041:412fm 6¼ 117 64 53½ 22¼ 22½ Stevens G L 8 Aw24000 84-13 FvDddyFv,Istorto,BooBoo'sBckroo 9
12Jun87-7Hol 1 1/16Ⓣ:4641:1041:413fm 10 117 53 64 35½ 38¾ Pincay L Jr6 Aw24000 77-14 Danishgar, Top Wing, Istoriato 7
31May87-7Hol 1 :444 1:094 1:362ft 11 115 42 33½ 68½ 612 McCarronCJ8 Aw24000 69-18 Sum Action, Athlone, Mondanite 8
31May87—Wide 3/8 turn
3May87-5Hol 7f :22 :45 1:231ft 15 115 66¾ 65¼ 43 46 Stevens G L4 Aw22000 82-15 Fracoza, Baby Slewy, Mondanite 7
3May87—Bobbled start
19Mar87-5SA 1¼Ⓣ:4631:3532:014fm 6¾ 117 53 86¾ 810 814 ShoemkerW6 Aw31000 64-22 ExotcRvr,WuthrngHghts,RssnLogc 9
18Feb87-5SA 1 :454 1:10 1:363ft 5¾ 117 32 35½ 33½ 43½ Pincay L Jr1 Aw29000 81-19 Alibi Ike, Watch'n Win, Gum Fleet 9
24Jan87-5SA a6½f Ⓣ:213 :44 1:15 fm 5½ 117 44 34 34½ 46¾ Pincay L Jr3 Aw26000 77-17 River Mist, Nurely, Top Wing 12
24Jan87—Bumped start
28Dec86-5SA 1 1/16:462 1:104 1:431ft *2¾ 116 21 46 1019 1022¼ Stevens G L5 Aw28000 63-14 ReEnter,Card'sPlease,InherentKai 16
11Oct86◆3PhoenixPk(Ire) 1 1:371gd 8 122 Ⓣ 28 Roche C Bdrs Cup Prep Teleprompter, Istoriato, Forlaway 5
Jly 1 Hol 4f ft :494 h

E.

L'Empire
TORO F **118**
Own.—Paulson A E
Ch. h. 5, by The Minstrel—Suprina, by Vaguely Noble
Br.—Bedford Farm (Ky) 1987 1 0 0 0
Tr.—Scott George W 1986 7 0 2 1 $12,000
Lifetime 16 1 3 2 $27,155 Turf 16 1 3 2 $27,155

6Jly87-9Hol 1⅛Ⓣ:4611:10 1:474fm *2¾e 115 21 2½ 32½ 72½ Toro F3 Aw24000 86-11 Star Ribot, First Dibs, Ima Bullet 10
17Aug86-9Dmr 1 Ⓣ:46 1:1041:351fm 5¼ 117 11 1hd 21 31¾ ValenzuelPA2 Aw20000 94-05 Sly Remark,WellRelated,L'Empire 10
27Jly86-5Dmr 1 1/16Ⓣ:4641:11 1:423fm 2 117 1½ 1hd 87½ 97¾ Stevens G L2 Aw20000 85-04 Travet, Sly Remark, Elimirante 12
27Jly86—Bore out 7/8
13Jly86-8Hol 1 1/16Ⓣ:4631:1041:413fm 8 116 2hd 2hd 1½ 2½ Stevens G L7 Aw23000 95-03 WillSpring,L'Empire,KimridgeRoad 8
15Jun86-5Hol 1 1/16Ⓣ:4711:11 1:411fm 3½ 116 1hd 1hd 31½ 65½ Stevens G L5 Aw21000 92 — Shanaar, Well Related, Atreak 12
24May86-5Hol 1⅛Ⓣ:4641:11 1:482fm 18 116 17 14 1½ 21½ Solis A2 Aw22000 88-09 Middlesex, L'Empire, Garrion 7
18Apr86-5SA 1¼Ⓣ:4511:36 2:013fm *6-5e 115 2hd 32½ 67¾ 69½ Stevens G L7 Aw26000 69-16 Spice Trade, Garrion, Robersky 8
5Apr86-5SA a6½f Ⓣ:213 :4421:15 fm 6 116 105¼ 96¼ 1010 98¾ McCarronCJ9 Aw24000 75-17 Tuono, He's A Looker, Muralto 11
11Aug85◆5Deauville(Fra) a1¼ 2:142sf *2¼e 121 Ⓣ 914 PccC Px Cte Nrmnde(Gr2) NewBruce,CptiveIslnd,Morespeed 10
1Aug85◆4Deauville(Fra) a1¼ 2:062sf 3½ 123 Ⓣ 22½ PiccioniC Px Vll de Trvll Antheus, L'Empire, River Cafe 11
Jly 23 SLR tr.t 6f ft 1:133 h Jly 16 SLR tr.t 4f ft :50 h Jun 30 SLR tr.t 6f ft 1:123 h Jun 23 SLR tr.t 1 ft 1:391 h

F.

Dhaleem
ORTEGA L E **118**
Own.—Six-S Racing Stable
B. c. 4, by Lyphard—Patia, by Don
Br.—de Chambure-Ouaki Est-Ades (Ky) 1987 9 0 3 1 $20,100
Tr.—Velasquez Danny 1986 3 1 0 0 $3,869
Lifetime 12 1 3 1 $23,969 Turf 10 1 3 1 $23,269

19Jun87-5Hol 1 1/16Ⓣ:46 1:0941:403fm 7½ 117 75½ 74½ 45½ 54¼ Ortega L E 10 Aw24000 87-09 Forlaway,TableGlow,ContactGame 10
19Jun87—Bumped 1/16
6Jun87-11GG 1⅜Ⓣ:4911:3922:18 fm *2 119 31 2hd 1hd 23 Ortega L E 2 Aw16000 72-20 De Soto,Dhaleem,LonesomeDancer 9

16May87-8Hol 1½Ⓣ:4832:0122:263fm 27 113 710117¾1111109¾ Solis A12 Ⓡ Cbllero H 79-12 LordGrndy,GrtCmmnctr,CrcsPrnc 12
2May87-7Hol 1⅛Ⓣ:4841:1241:492fm 3¾ 115 63 42½ 41¾ 31 Meza R Q6 Aw24000 80-13 WuthringHghts,It'sNotMyJob,Dhlm 9
18Apr87-3SA 1⅛Ⓣ:4841:1221:492fm 7¼ 117 64½ 53½ 33 22 Meza R Q7 Aw31000 78-16 Nilambr,Dhleem,WutheringHeights 7
18Apr87—Poor start; wide 3/8 turn
9Apr87-5SA a6½fⓉ:213 :4341:142fm 7 118 89¾ 812 810 75½ Meza R Q8 Aw29000 82-09 Rinnegato, Recognized, Mondanite 9
17Mar87-7SA 1$\frac{1}{16}$:46 1:102 1:423ft 7½ 117 88½ 98¾ 813 818¼ Meza R Q4 Aw31000 70-16 PrinceO'Fire,It'sNotMyJob,Athlone 9
22Feb87-5SA 1¼Ⓣ:4641:36 2:013fm 7½ 115 78½ 42½ 33½ 22¼ Meza R Q2 Aw29000 77-22 Neferou, Dhaleem, Unencumbered 10
22Feb87—Off slowly.
5Feb87-5SA 1$\frac{1}{16}$:462 1:11 1:434ft 35 116 1011 95¾ 86 68½ Meza R Q12 Aw28000 74-22 Centenary, Trump Up, Sun Man 12
5Feb87—Awarded fifth purse money; Off very slowly
18Oct86♦1Newmarket(Eng) 1¼ 2:114gd 12 114 Ⓣ 45½ GlsMA Mace-WrthAprH BenAdhem,Nicoridge,PowerBendr 16
Jly 24 Hol 3f ft :373 h Jly 19 Hol 6f ft 1:152 h Jly 14 Hol 4f ft :493 h Jly 9 Hol 4f ft :492 h

G.

Quietly Bold
MCCARRON C J **112**
Own.—Keller M
Dk. b. or br. c. 3, by Quiet Fling—Cleena, by Canonero II
Br.—Hughes Farm Inc (Ky) 1987 7 0 1 1 $10,108
Tr.—Frankel Robert 1986 8 1 2 3 $62,233
Lifetime 15 1 3 4 $72,341 Turf 6 0 2 1 $46,525

12Jly87-8Bel 1¼Ⓣ:4831:3732:031gd 31 114 56½ 62¾ 66 56¼ Davis RG2 Lexington 72-22 Milesius, Yucca, Rio's Lark 10
12Jly87—Grade II
13Jun87-9Mth 1 :464 1:11 1:372sy 3½ 113 22½ 23 26 410 AntlyCW1 Lng Brnch 76-14 I'mSoBad,MrineCommnd,SrtogSun 6
13Jun87—Grade III
29May87-5Mth 1$\frac{1}{16}$Ⓣ:4731:1121:414fm*6-5 112 45 42½ 33½ 21½ Antley C W6 Aw17000 94-03 Mad Guard, Quietly Bold, De Facto 8
23Apr87-7Aqu 1$\frac{1}{16}$Ⓣ:4841:1411:464gd*9-5 112 53½ 34 56½ 610¼ Migliore R5 Aw27000 61-30 MdnghtCousns,Ptlomt,MstrOfArts 10
25Mar87-7Aqu 1 :461 1:102 1:37 ft 4 117 52½ 63¾ 86 86 Migliore R6 Aw27000 75-27 K.C.'sBstTurn,Brskn,MxdEmotons 10
4Mar87-5Aqu 1$\frac{1}{16}$⊡:4831:1311:45 ft *2½ 117 42 42½ 2½ 3hd Migliore R2 Aw27000 85-16 Girning,K.C.'sBestTurn,QuietlyBold 6
12Feb87-8Aqu 1$\frac{1}{16}$⊡:4721:1241:453gd 6½ 117 54½ 53½ 69½ 513¼ Migliore R1 Whirlaway 69-23 High Brite, Light Prospect,LilFappi 7
29Nov86-8Hol 1$\frac{1}{16}$Ⓣ:4641:1111:414fm 6½ 115 75¼ 62¾ 43½ 33¾ Toro F8 Hst Th Flg 81-10 Persvrd,WildrnssBound,QuitlyBold 9
29Nov86—Grade III; Run in divisions; Boxed far turn
2Nov86-8Aqu 1⅛Ⓣ:48 1:1321:53 gd 17 113 119½ 73 11 2¾ AntleyCW9 Pilgrim 69-28 David's Bird,QuietlyBold,BlueFinn 12
2Nov86—Grade III
20Oct86-6Bel 1$\frac{1}{16}$Ⓣ:4641:1121:443fm 28 115 73½ 43 3½ 4¾ MigliorеR1 To Market 72-19 ButtrfildRod,LightsndMusc,IrshBr 16
Jly 23 Hol 4f ft :47 h Jly 5 Bel 1 ft 1:392 h Jun 28 Bel tr.t 6f m 1:15 h (d) Jun 23 Bel tr.t 6f sy 1:17 b (d)

H.

***Top Ruler**
DELAHOUSSAYE E **118**
Own.—Tong G
B. c. 4, by High Top—Vaguely, by Bold Lad
Br.—Floors Farming (Eng) 1986 6 0 0 0
Tr.—Fulton John W 1985 3 1 0 1 $11,653
Lifetime 9 1 0 1 $11,653 Turf 9 1 0 1 $11,653

21Aug86♦4York(Eng) 1 1:373gd 50 124 Ⓣ 8 RyanW Brdfrd&Bngly H Digger's Rest, Turfah, Truly Rare 14
19Jly86♦4N'wmarket(Eng) 1 1:402gd 25 125 Ⓣ 11 SbrWR Fod Brkrs Trpy H ThenAgin,Pinstripe,SomthingCsul 11
9Jly86♦5Newmarket(Eng) 1¼ 2:05 gd 25 133 Ⓣ 10 AsssC Duke ofCambrdgeH Lastcomer, TwiceBold, Orban 11
31May86♦3Kempton(Eng) 1 1:394gd 20 123 Ⓣ 620 Carson W Heron Faustus, BraveOwen,SitThisOneOut 7
14May86♦4York(Eng) 1$\frac{5}{16}$ 2:113gd 50 126 Ⓣ 610 CrsonW Mca-Dnte(Gr2) Shahrastani, Nomrood, Sirk 7
16Apr86♦3Newmarket(Eng) 7f 1:321gd 8 125 Ⓣ 511 CrsnW Ldbrk Erpn Fre H GreenDesert, Sperry, PilotJet 8
24Oct85♦5Newbury(Eng) a7¼f 1:321gd 7½ 126 Ⓣ 42½ SnbrnWR Hrrs Hill(Gr3) CelticHeir,HollowHand,HelloErnni 12
26Aug85♦4Ripon(Eng) 6f 1:154gd 2¾ 130 Ⓣ 33 Tulk P ChampionTrophy Hallgate, PreciousMetal, TopRuler 7
15Jun85♦1York(Eng) 6f 1:151gd*9-5 126 Ⓣ 12½ PgttL Duches o Knt (Mdn) TopRuler, Respect, Prejudice 10
Jly 23 Hol 7f ft 1:28 h Jly 18 Hol 5f ft 1:02 h Jly 11 Hol 6f ft 1:132 h Jly 4 Hol 5f ft 1:003 h

I.

Darion
SOLIS A **112**
Own.—Glazer Lauren
B. g. 3, by Silent Screen—Uarabeaut, by Dewan
Br.—Winchell V H (Ky) 1987 9 1 2 0 $23,050
Tr.—Lewis Craig A 1986 6 1 2 0 $14,585
Lifetime 15 2 4 0 $37,635 Turf 2 0 0 0 $600

1Jly87-9Hol 1$\frac{1}{16}$:454 1:103 1:432ft 4½ 116 32½ 2½ 1½ 16 Solis A 4 50000 92-13 Darion, P. T. Hustler, El Tremblor 6
6Jun87-5Hol 1$\frac{1}{16}$:473 1:124 1:463ft 5½ 116 2hd 2hd 1½ 23½ Solis A 3 50000 72-17 Patient King, Darion, Some Hitter 6
6Jun87—Came in 1/16
13May87-5Hol 1$\frac{1}{16}$Ⓣ:4731:1131:413fm 9¾ 114 74¾ 85¼ 76 65½ Ortega L E 3 Aw24000 80-13 SuprbKing,FvDddyFv,ErnYourStrps 8
22Apr87-7Hol 1 Ⓣ:4641:1131:363fm 13 114 107½105¼ 65 54¼ Ortega L E 8 Aw24000 80-16 DvidsSmile,Gunburst,TeddyBrHug 10
22Apr87—Lugged out late
27Mar87-5SA 1 :464 1:114 1:374ft 14 116 97¾ 53½ 53 2½ Ortega L E 7 50000 78-23 BooBoo'sBuckroo,Drion,BeucoupJt 9
27Mar87—Poor start
8Mar87-9SA 1$\frac{1}{16}$:464 1:112 1:43 ft 66 114 910 98¾ 812 814 Douglas R R 7 Aw30000 72-15 Barb's Relic, Blanco, Rakaposhi 9
22Feb87-9SA 1 :463 1:112 1:364ft 49 1085 85½ 86 65½ 54½ Patton D B 6 Aw29000 80-14 FlyingFlags,BoldArchon,Ponderble 9
11Feb87-7SA 1$\frac{1}{16}$:46 1:11 1:441ft 23 116 927 922 813 612¾ DelhoussyeE 9 Aw28000 67-17 Rupperto,TlphonCnyon,BoldArchon 9
11Feb87—Off slowly, sluggish early
23Jan87-9SA 1 :461 1:111 1:374ft 14 114 89¼ 89 78 47½ Soto S B 6 50000 72-22 BustYourButtons,Rkposhi,Zt'sPrnc 8
23Jan87—Broke in a tangle
31Dec86-6SA 1$\frac{1}{16}$:47 1:124 1:454ft *9-5 117 32 1½ 14 16½ Cordero A Jr 2 M40000 72-20 Darion, Synergist,SixTwoAndEven 12
Jly 26 Dmr 4f ft :484 h Jly 18 Hol 5f ft 1:004 h Jly 11 Hol 6f ft 1:144 h Jun 28 Hol 3f ft :352 h

20.

5th Santa Anita

1 ¼ MILES. (Turf). (1.57⅘) CLAIMING. Purse $33,000. 4-year-olds and upward. Weights, 4-year-olds, 119 lbs.; older, 121 lbs. Non-winners of two races at one mile and one-eighth or over since November 3 allowed 2 lbs.; of such a race since then, 4 lbs.; of a race at one mile or over since then, 6 lbs. Claiming price $80,000; for each $5,000 to $70,000 allowed 1 lb. (Claiming and starter races for $62,500 or less not considered.)

A.

Keyala — Dk. b. or br. h. 6, by Key to the Kingdom—Alathea, by Lorenzaccio
VALENZUELA P A 115 — Br.—de Briones G D (Ky) — Tr.—Palma Hector O — $80,000
Own.—Vicki Beth Stables Inc — Lifetime 40 5 4 10 $100,565
1987 1 0 0 1 $5,400 / 1986 15 1 2 6 $35,351 / Turf 35 5 4 10 $97,865

1Jan87-5SA 1⅛ Ⓣ:4711:1121:481fm 16 116 7¾ 6¾ 53 3¾ Valenzuela P A9 95000 83-14 Steepbank, River Of Kings, Keyala 9
1Jan87—Wide into stretch
14Dec86-5Hol 1 1/16 Ⓣ:4611:10 1:402fm 7½ 113 55½ 53½ 43½ 3¾ Day P7 85000 91-11 Lucky N Green, Emperdori, Keyala 8
16Nov86-9Hol 1 1/16 Ⓣ:4631:1031:402fm 4 116 76 7¾ 54 4¾ Baze G1 80000 88-07 Steepbank, Jack Tar, Snowcreek 7
15Oct86-5SA 1⅛ Ⓣ:47 1:1041:471fm 4 116 95¼ 64½ 23 21½ DelahoussayeE5 80000 89-09 River Of Kings, Keyala, Aviator II 10
6Sep86-5Dmr 1⅛ Ⓣ:4631:11 1:492fm 5¼ 117 1013 85¼ 32½ 2nk DelahoussayeE4 c62500 87-09 Aviator II, Keyala, Ono Gummo 10
25Aug86-7Dmr 1 Ⓣ:4611:1021:343fm 13 115 56 76 77 85½ Toro F4 95000 93-01 Tapping Wood, Matafao, Estate 9
25Aug86—Steadied 3/8
6Aug86-7Dmr 1 1/16 Ⓣ:48 1:1141:432fm 2¾ 116 62½ 53 43 3hd ♦ Toro F3 80000 89-14 Bozina, Aviator II, Keyala 8
♦ 6Aug86—Dead heat
26Jly86-9Dmr 1 1/16 Ⓣ:47 1:1111:42 fm 11 118 109¼ 105 94¾ 43½ Toro F1 100000 92-05 Bshop'sRngII,PttBonhomm,AvtrII 10
26Jly86—Wide into stretch
21Jun86-9LaD a1 1/16 Ⓣ 1:413fm 22 116 76¼ 4¾ 51¾ 51¼ SimngtonDE4 Aw17000 92-06 TrickyBond,Mimir,Don'tFoolWithM 8
7Jun86-10LaD a7½f Ⓣ 1:29 fm 6½ 116 64¾ 64 43 32¼ SimngtonDE3 Aw16000 92-10 Jamie Joe, Bold Run, Keyala 7
Jan 15 SA 5f ft 1:003 h Jan 9 SA 6f sl 1:013 h Dec 24 SA 5f ft 1:002 h Dec 10 Hol 5f ft 1:014 h

B.

Bouncing Buttons — Ch. g. 6, by Blood Royal—Box of Buttons, by Moolah Bux
KAENEL J L 115 — Br.—Sells D C (Ky) — Tr.—Cofer Riley S — $80,000
Own.—Sells D C — Lifetime 32 8 5 5 $101,530
1986 3 1 0 1 $12,500 / 1985 16 4 4 1 $66,925 / Turf 2 0 0 1 $3,900

26Dec86-9SA 1 1/16 :454 1:102 1:43 ft 7¾ 116 1016 109¼ 56 33½ Kaenel J L7 25000 82-13 Cold,TommyThoms,BoncngBttons 11
1Jun86-1Hol 1⅛ :453 1:102 1:504ft 3¾ 116 611 610 42 1hd Kaenel J L2 25000 83-14 BouncngBttons,SrStr,MrkInThSky 6
18May86-9Hol 1 :45 1:102 1:36 ft 18 116 98¼ 75½ 76¼ 67¼ Kaenel J L11 32000 75-08 KnightSkiing,RightOnRed,Elefnte 12
18May86—Wide final 3/8
22Dec85-9AC 1 1/16 :461 1:102 1:44 ft 3 122 917 614 57 2no EnrzHF10 Ⓡ Cprtv Prs 85-17 HrryJr.,BouncingButtons,CheerOn 11
30Nov85-9Hol 1⅛ :461 1:103 1:483m 3¾ 117 712 69 511 511¾ Kaenel J L6 45000 82-09 AmorousII,VgorosVgors,It'sNvrDll 7
30Nov85—Lost whip at 1/8
11Nov85-5SA 1¼ :464 1:39 2:054gd 5 115 817 2½ 12½ 17 Kaenel J L9 50000 60-26 BouncingButtons,Prngon,CrroPnto 9
26Oct85-9SA 1 1/16 :462 1:12 1:444ft 9¼ 114 813 77 44 11 Kaenel J L8 25000 77-21 BouncingButtons,NoodleRoni,Jovil 8
26Oct85—Wide into stretch
12Oct85-3SA 1⅛ :462 1:11 1:503ft 6¼ 116 616 611 33 21¾ Hernandez R1 22500 74-18 OnEydRomo,BouncngButtons,Muft 7
12Oct85—Veered out sharply, bumped start
20Sep85-12Pomа 1⅛ :463 1:114 1:501ft 8½ 115 118½ 109 1014 813 Castanon A L8 A25000 — — Restage, Faridpour, Mufti 11
14Sep85-10Pom 6½f :22 :453 1:173ft 5¾ 119 912 711 66½ 42¾ Dominguez RE3 25000 — — Delta Trace, Slugfest, Don's Co'op 9
Jan 14 SA 4f ft :501 h Jan 8 SA 6f m 1:024 h Dec 25 SA 3f ft :36 h Dec 20 SA 6f ft 1:151 hg

C.

Pas De Choix — B. h. 5, by Irish River—Star Ship II, by Dicta Drake
ORTEGA L E 113 — Br.—Clovelly Farms (Ky) — Tr.—Canani Julio C — $70,000
Own.—No Choice Stable — Lifetime 28 2 3 0 $46,022
1987 1 0 0 0 / 1986 13 1 1 0 $18,790 / Turf 28 2 3 0 $46,022

10Jan87-5SA 1⅛ Ⓣ:4721:1221:50 gd 17 113 96¼ 94¼ 93½ 65 Ortega L E3 55000 72-23 Kingsbury,BoardMeeting,AvitorII 10
10Jan87—Rough trip
21Dec86-9Hol 1¼ Ⓣ:5021:3812:022fm 6 116 87½ 74¼ 65¼ 54¾ Stevens G L10 50000 78-15 Kingsbury, Will Spring, PiperJohn 11
21Dec86—Wide into stretch
14Dec86-9Hol 1 Ⓣ:4621:1111:362fm 3¾ 116 77¾ 52½ 42¼ 44½ Cordero A Jr4 50000 80-11 LordOfTheWind,Hrdknock'n,Juntur 8
23Nov86-9Hol 1¼ Ⓣ:4811:3642:021fm 8¾ 116 1015 99¼ 85 61½ Stevens G L11 62500 82-13 Rampour, Travet, Aviator II 11
26Aug86 ♦ 4Clairefont'e(Fra a1½ 2:441sf 9 121 Ⓣ 21 MorGW Px Gilm d'Orano Anazid, Pas deChoix, SharpGirl 9
14Aug86 ♦ 5Clairefont'e(Fra a1½ 2:333gd 17 118 Ⓣ 54 MoorGW G P d Clrfntn Persona, ExactlyRight, BlueBelly 9
11Jly86 ♦ 6Evry(Fra) a1 5/16 2:162gd 17 126 Ⓣ 66¾ MoorGW Kmptn Prk ExclusvGm,ChldrnsCornr,FbulosPrl 7
10Jun86 ♦ 4Chantilly(Fra) a1⅛ 1:512gd 20 124 Ⓣ 713 LquuzA Px d'Avly St Lnrd Trotanoy, Idealiste, Tilt 7
24May86 ♦ 5StCloud(Fra) a1 5/16 2:183gd 32 126 Ⓣ 611 Chaille L Px Edellic King Luthier, Grundyssime,InFocus 7
29Mar86 ♦ 4StCloud(Fra) a1 5/16 2:31 gd 9½ 121 Ⓣ 66 Moore GW Px Trnsvl Grundyssime, Moresepeed, Tilt 12
Jan 9 SA 3f sl :38 h Jan 3 SA 5f ft 1:023 h Dec 29 SA 5f ft 1:02 h Dec 28 SA 5f ft 1:02 h

D.

***Straw** B. h. 6, by Thatch—Cooliney Dancer, by Dancer's Image
PINCAY L JR 2-0 115 Br.—O'Malley J F (Ire) 1987 1 0 0 1 $4,500
Tr.—Blincoe Tom $80,000 1986 1 0 0 0 $950
Own.—Carothers G Lifetime 28 7 3 4 $95,873 Turf 15 6 2 2 $73,268
7Jan87-5SA 6½f :22 :444 1:163m 7¾ 116 55 58 47½ 39½ Sibille R1 75000 77-21 RisingChum,AutoCommander,Strw 6
18Jan86-7SA 1⅛Ⓣ:4611:1041:474fm 4½ 115 712 85¾ 67 57¼ Toro F7 115000 81-16 RvrOfKngs,Clnrllr,BoomTownChrl 10
18Jan86—4-wide into drive
15Dec85-6Hol 1 1/16Ⓣ:4711:1111:42 fm*6-5 116 95 74½ 1hd 12 Toro F6 62500 — — Straw, RoyalRecourse,ViceroyLad 12
15Dec85—Wide into stretch
26Oct85-7SA 1¼Ⓣ:48 1:37 2:02 fm*4-5e118 76 63¼ 3½ 2no Toro F6 80000 77-17 Apollo Flight, Straw, Massera 9
26Oct85—Hopped in air
11Oct85-7SA 1⅛Ⓣ:4621:1031:471fm*6-5e120 96¾ 85¾ 45 21¼ Toro F6 100000 90-09 Poly Test, Straw, Palestiglio 10
11Oct85—Disqualified from purse money; Broke slowly
2Sep85-5Dmr 1 Ⓣ:46 1:1031:344fm 14 117 710 65 52½ 1hd Toro F1 80000 98-02 Straw, Caballo, I'll See You 10
2Sep85—Wide stretch
23Jun85-8GG 1¼:47 1:36 2:011ft 5 115 714 712 716 721 CstnedM4 ⓇCtn Inv H 64-13 Grey Missile, Nak Ack,PrinceDonB. 7
23Jun85—Broke in air
8Jun85-8GG 1 1/16:463 1:093 1:41 ft 4 116 810 78¾ 57 35½ CstdM8 ⓇDmg Cl IvH 92-12 Prince Don B., Indian Faker, Straw 8
8Jun85—Hopped in air
25May85-8GG 1 1/16Ⓣ:49 1:1231:44 fm 3 116 912 89½ 67 2¾ CstnedM4 ⓇNoor Iv H 81-18 Position's Best, Straw, Pair OfAces 9
5May85-6GG 1 1/16Ⓣ:48 1:1121:431fm 6 115 58½ 57 22 1nk CastanedaM3 Aw20000 86-15 Straw, Position's Best, Trakady 6
5May85—Bumped start
Dec 31 SA 4f ft :472 h Dec 24 SA 1 ft 1:404 h Dec 12 Hol 6f ft 1:15 h Dec 6 Hol 6f m 1:124 h

E.

Snowcreek B. g. 6, by Dust Commander—Slide Mountain, by Hill Run
TORO F 3-N 115 Br.—Trimble Ann M (Ky) 1987 1 0 0 0
Tr.—Gosden John H M $80,000 1986 8 1 2 3 $49,950
Own.—C-Punch Ranch Lifetime 28 6 6 4 $145,475 Turf 18 4 4 3 $116,125
1Jan87-5SA 1⅛Ⓣ:4711:1121:481fm 11 116 83¾ 94¾ 96¾ 98¼ Toro F1 95000 78-14 Steepbank, River Of Kings, Keyala 9
16Nov86-9Hol 1 1/16Ⓣ:4631:1031:402fm 5 116 64½ 63¼ 44 33¼ Toro F6 80000 88-07 Steepbank, Jack Tar, Snowcreek 7
16Nov86—Broke in a tangle
10May86-9Hol 1⅛Ⓣ:4821:1221:482fm 4½ 119 31½ 31½ 41½ 52½ Lipham T6 80000 87-08 Tapping Wood, Pol AndDic,Pautivo 7
27Apr86-9Hol 1 1/16Ⓣ:4921:1311:43 fm 3½ 116 52 83¼ 72¾ 65 Lipham T2 100000 84-11 Gourami, Emperdori, TappingWood 8
27Apr86—Crowded on turn
12Apr86-5SA 1⅛Ⓣ:4711:1131:473fm 8 115 42 52 21 2½ Lipham T2 Aw35000 88-14 Rich Earth, Snowcreek, Rivlia 8
12Apr86—Extremely wide into stretch
30Mar86-5SA 1⅛Ⓣ:4541:1011:482fm 2½ 116 88 52¼ 3nk 11¼ Toro F10 80000 85-16 Snowcrk,RoylRcors,Bshop'sRngII 12
7Mar86-5SA 1¼Ⓣ:4641:3632:014fm 3½ 116 86 73¼ 22½ 21¼ Toro F8 80000 76-20 RivrOfKings,Snowcrk,Apol'oFlight 12
16Feb86-7SA 1 1/16:46 1:092 1:41 gd 11 115 510 512 412 311½ Toro F6 Aw37000 84-14 SunMaster,CptinVigors,Snowcreek 7
16Feb86—Wide into stretch
17Jan86-5SA 1⅛Ⓣ:4821:1231:49 fm*6-5 116 43½ 75¾ 66¾ 34¾ Toro F8 80000 77-15 Bishop'sRngII,PolAndDc,Snowcrk 10
17Jan86—Steadied 7 1/2
29Dec85-5SA 1⅛Ⓣ:47 1:1041:482fm 8¼ 115 73¾ 63¼ 44 43¼ Toro F4 Aw35000 82-15 LuckyNGrn,CptnVgors,FlotngRsrv 11
●Jan 11 SA 6f ft 1:122 h ●Dec 24 Hol 1 ft 1:403 h ●Dec 19 Hol 7f ft 1:271 h Dec 13 Hol 6f ft 1:14 h

F.

***Marcel** Ch. h. 7, by Carral—Melica, by Maporal
BAZE G 2-N (J) 113 Br.—Haras El Sauce (Chile) 1987 1 0 0 0 $900
Tr.—Jones Gary $70,000 1986 3 1 0 0 $10,450
Own.—Floyd-McGee-Murty Fm etal Lifetime 17 5 2 2 $37,303 Turf 13 5 2 1 $36,043
1Jan87-5SA 1⅛Ⓣ:4711:1121:481fm 20 120 42 51¾ 42 54 Baze G2 100000 82-14 Steepbank, River Of Kings, Keyala 9
27Nov86-7Hol 1 Ⓣ:4641:1021:34 fm 22 116 44½ 41½ 76 66¾ McHrgueDG5 Aw40000 90-06 RiverDrummr,Forlitno,TppingWood 7
31Oct86-3SA 1 1/16:452 1:093 1:421ft 6¾ 116 57½ 611 617 619¼ McHrgueDG6 Aw45000 71-16 ImprtntBsnss,ArcnStndrd,UlttPlsr 6
31Oct86—Lugged out
15Oct86-8BM 1 Ⓣ:46 1:1041:364fm 10 115 53 2hd 11½ 11 Baze R A4 Aw19000 96-04 Marcel,KentuckyLaurel,SafetyBank 6
1Dec84-3Hol 7f :222 :451 1:231ft 22 117 43 44½ 58 510 Murphy D J3 Aw30000 81-03 Somthngwondrfl,StFr,ExplosvPssr 6
22Jan84♦8Valparaiso(Chile a1½ 2:29 fm — 128 Ⓣ 2 Azocar S Cl El Dby(Gr1) Semillero, Marcel, Carro Viejo 11
25Dec83♦9ClubHipico(Chile a1¼ 1:59 fm*2-3 123 Ⓣ 1hd Azocar S Cl Fin deAno Marcel, Randy, Principito 9
6Nov83♦9ClubHipico(Chile a1½ 2:24 fm 17 123 Ⓣ 52¼ AzocrS Cl El Ensayo(Gr1) Lonquimay, Carro Viejo, Medieval 15
16Oct83♦7ClubHipico(Chile a1¼ 2:01 fm 3 121 Ⓣ 13¼ Silva E Cl Johnnie Walker Marcell, Poniak, Lago de Gaton 12
2Oct83♦7ClubHipico(Chile a1¼ 2:003fm 9 123 Ⓣ 98¾ CronP ClNacnlRLyon(Gr1) Lonquimay, Bartolo, Medieval 17
Jan 14 SA 4f ft :481 h Dec 28 SA 5f ft 1:002 h ●Dec 23 Hol 7f ft 1:292 h ●Dec 18 Hol Ⓣ 6f fm 1:124 h (d)

G.

Grey Writer — Dk. b. or br. g. 4, by Full Out—Baby Julie, by Youth
SHOEMAKER W — 113 — Br.—Sturgis J R (Ky) — Tr.—Hutchinson Kathy — $80,000
1987 1 0 0 1 $4,200
1986 13 1 5 3 $34,204
Turf 6 0 1 3 $14,498
Own.—Rey J L–J–Karen Lee — Lifetime 14 1 5 4 $38,404

3Jan87-5SA 1¼ⓣ:4731:37 2:023fm 14 115 1010 74 31½ 31½ Baze G3 Aw28000 73-24 Eliminnte,RussinLogic,GreyWriter 10
3Jan87—Rough start
18Dec86-8Hol 1 1/16 ⓣ:4831:12 1:422fm 3½ 116 32 41½ 41½ 61¾ McHrgueDG3 Aw24000 80-19 SmoothOpertor,Intuitiveness,Stmd 8
18Dec86—Lugged in stretch
30Nov86-9Hol 1⅛ⓣ:4741:1221:483fm 6½ 114 11101052 41½ 3¾ Baze G11 Aw24000 84-12 Illumineux, Padoue, Grey Writer 12
30Nov86—Wide into stretch
15Nov86-7Hol 1 ⓣ:4531:0911:343fm 30 116 915 814 812 36 McHrgueDG9 Aw24000 88-11 Le Belvedere,RiverMist,GreyWriter 9
31Oct86-6SA 6f :212 :443 1:093ft 22 116 11111192 99¾ 610½ Baze G2 50000 79-16 MischievousMtt,Jimed,RosesArRb 11
31Oct86—Lugged in
14Aug86-8Cby 1 1/16 ⓣ:4811:1241:422fm*8-5 113 65½ 21½ 1hd 4nk Razo E Jr6 Aw12300 — — AnothrRundr,Dismissd,LovsEmbrc 11
7Aug86-8Cby 7½f ⓣ:233 :4641:304fm 11 113 911 77 1hd 2hd Razo E Jr5 Aw11800 91-09 Langoldyon,GreyWriter,Felsenthal 12
2Jly86-7Cby 6f :231 :47 1:114ft *4-5 115 22½ 21½ 21½ 23½ Hawley S1 Aw11800 84-16 BnnerPride,GreyWriter,ChiefRlfoot 8
5Jun86-5Cby 6f :23 :464 1:121ft *2 115 62¾ 53¾ 44 22½ Hawley S1 Aw11800 84-20 Harry's S., Grey Writer, Transept 7
23May86-7Cby 1 1/16 :48 1:132 1:481ft 2 118 2hd 2hd 31 45½ Black K3 Aw12300 64-24 On Staff, Quiloy, Novelty 5
Dec 27 SA 5f ft 1:023 h Dec 15 SA 6f ft 1:131 h Nov 25 SA 5f ft 1:013 h

H.

Manzotti — B. c. 4, by Nijinsky II—Shufleur, by Tom Rolfe
SIBILLE R — 113 — Br.—Anne M Stone 1983 Trust (Va) — Tr.—Stidham Michael — $80,000
1986 6 3 0 0 $16,450
Turf 6 3 0 0 $16,450
Own.—Goodman H V — Lifetime 6 3 0 0 $16,450

14Dec86-5Hol 1 1/16 ⓣ:4611:10 1:402fm 45 116 66 75½ 811 812 Olivares F4 100000 80-11 Lucky N Green, Emperdori, Keyala 8
14Dec86—Wide 3/8
30Nov86-10TuP a1 1/16 ⓣ:4911:1331:453fm *1 120 66 65½ 79½ 912¼ Sint-MrtnE10 Scrtrt H 92 — ChuckNLuck,ChiefOfFir,DncTrinr 12
7Jun86-8Hol 1⅛ⓣ:4741:1141:47 fm 24 115 97½ 97 99¾ 910¾ LiphamT2 Cinema H 86-02 Manila, Vernon Castle,FullOfStars 10
7Jun86—Grade II
18May86 ♦5Lyon(Fra) a1⅜ gd 2½ 123 ⓣ 11 Jean D Px dPrc Lomriq Manzotti, Montsoreau,Assurbanipal 5
18May86—No time taken

21. Blinkers on: *Prospectitude* and *Fara's Team.*

4 **BELMONT** — 5½ FURLONGS — BELMONT PARK

5 ½ FURLONGS. (1.03) MAIDEN CLAIMING. Purse $14,000. Fillies. 2-year-olds. Weight, 117 lbs. Claiming Price $50,000; for each $2,500 to $45,000, 2 lbs.

Coupled—Charmin Carmen and Outwit.

A.

Quajenn — B. f. 2, by Clever Trick—Twist Her, by Nativo — $50,000 — Br.—Books & Ricks (Fla) — Tr.—Ribaudo Robert — 117
Lifetime 1 0 1 0 $3,080 — 1987 1 M 1 0 $3,080
Own.—Keller M
15Jun87- 3Bel fst 5f :22⅘ :46⅗ :59⅖ ⒻMd 50000 3 7 64½ 34½ 24 22½ Davis R G 117 4.20 84-19 Do I 1172½ Quajinn 1175½ Noble Viki 1133 Best of others 8
LATEST WORKOUTS Jly 24 Bel 5f fst 1:00⅘ h Jly 19 Bel 5f fst 1:02⅖ h Jly 14 Bel 4f fst :50 b Jly 8 Bel tr.t 4f sly :52 b

B.

Roleplay — B. f. 2, by Rollicking—First Quad, by Quadratic — $45,000 — Br.—Ryehill Farm (Md) — Tr.—Peitz Dan C — 113
Lifetime 1 0 1 0 $2,640 — 1987 1 M 1 0 $2,640
Own.—Ryehill Farm
11Jly87- 3Bel fst 5½f :23 :47⅘ 1:07⅘ ⒻMd 35000 4 2 1hd 11½ 14 21 Bailey J D 117 9.00 77-27 Sherry's Sugar 1131 Roleplay1176PlasticParadise1172½ Weakened 10
LATEST WORKOUTS Jly 26 Bel 3f gd :36⅕ h Jly 21 Bel 3f gd :36⅘ h Jly 5 Bel 4f fst :49⅖ b Jun 14 Bel 5f fst 1:02⅕ h

C.

Final Flash — Ch. f. 2, by Sunny North—Fashion Flash, by Motor Line — $45,000 — Br.—Patrik A. & Johanne D. Everard (Fla) — Tr.—Gregory Edward A Jr — 113
Lifetime 0 0 0 0 — 1987 0 M 0 0
Own.—Everard P A
LATEST WORKOUTS Jly 28 Aqu ⊡ 5f fst 1:02 b Jly 20 Aqu ⊡ 4f fst :48⅘ h Jly 11 Aqu 4f fst :51⅘ b Jly 6 Aqu 4f fst :50⅖ b

D.

Grant Me Serenity — B. f. 2, by Medieval Man—Rustic Gal, by Good Behavin — $45,000 — Br.—Petigrow N (Fla) — Tr.—Campo John P — 113
Lifetime 0 0 0 0 — 1987 0 M 0 0
Own.—Petigrow N
LATEST WORKOUTS Jly 22 Bel 3f fst :35⅘ hg Jly 18 Bel 4f fst :50 bg Jly 11 Bel tr.t 5f fst 1:05 b Jly 4 Bel tr.t 5f fst 1:02⅗ b

E.

Joanie's Native Ch. f. 2, by Joanie's Chief—Exclusive Christy, by Exclusive Native Lifetime 1987 0 M 0 0
Own.—Barberino P $45,000 Br.—Peter Barberino (Ky) 113 0 0 0 0
Tr.—Pascuma Warren J
LATEST WORKOUTS Jly 20 Bel 4f fst :49⅗ bg Jly 14 Bel tr.t 5f fst 1:02 b Jly 6 Bel 5f fst 1:02⅕ hg Jun 22 Bel 5f fst 1:03⅗ h

F.

Prospectitute B. f. 2, by Northern Prospect—Devastating Lady, by The Minstrel Lifetime 1987 1 M 0 0 $130
Own.—Petelain Stable $45,000 Br.—Petelain Stable (Fla) 113 1 0 0 0 $130
Tr.—Byrne Patrick B
30Apr87- 3GP fst 5f :22⅘ :47⅗ 1:00⅕ ⒻMd Sp Wt 9 11 97½ 63½ 64½ 68¾ Pezua J M 119 3.90 76–29 Dark Silver 119^4 Flashy Runner 119½ Action Star 119^{2}¾ Outrun 11
LATEST WORKOUTS Jly 27 Bel 4f fst :47⅗ h Jly 23 Bel 5f fst 1:03⅗ bg Jly 11 Bel 4f fst :49⅖ b Jly 4 Atl 4f fst :51 b

G.

Naskra's Song B. f. 2, by Naskra—Accipiter's Song, by Accipiter Lifetime 1987 0 M 0 0
Own.—Ferruolo J $50,000 Br.—Highclere, Inc. (Ky) 117 0 0 0 0
Tr.—Lenzini John J Jr
LATEST WORKOUTS Jly 27 Aqu ⊡ 4f gd :49⅗ hg(d) Jly 14 Aqu 5f fst 1:02⅖ h Jly 6 Aqu 4f fst :49 bg ●Jun 30 Aqu 4f fst :48 h

H.

Gratis Girl B. f. 2, by Paavo—Sarah For John, by Bravest Roman Lifetime 1987 0 M 0 0
Own.—Oak Lane Stables $45,000 Br.—Levine R (Fla) 113 0 0 0 0
Tr.—Levine Bruce
LATEST WORKOUTS Jly 28 Sar tr.t 5f fst 1:06⅘ bg Jly 21 Sar tr.t 5f fst 1:05⅕ bg Jly 14 Sar tr.t 5f fst 1:04⅕ h Jly 7 Sar tr.t 4f fst :51⅘ b

I.

Charmin Carmen Ch. f. 2, by Summing—Cabinetta, by Cabin Lifetime 1987 4 M 0 0
Own.—Tel-Kay Stable $45,000 Br.—Barrera L (Ky) 106^7 4 0 0 0
Tr.—Barrera Luis
11Jly87- 3Bel fst 5½f :23 :47⅘ 1:07⅖ ⒻMd 35000 6 4 53¼ 43½ 7^{12} 715½ Badamo J J 117 21.80 62–27 Sherry's Sugar 113^1 Roleplay 117^6 Plastic Paradise 117^{2}¼ Tired 10
1Jly87- 3Bel fst 5½f :22⅘ :47⅗ 1:08⅗ ⒻMd 70000 1 3 99 7^{10} 68½ 55½ Badamo J J^5 106 34.60 66–22 Cute Move 115^{1}¼ Flight to Nowhere 113¾ Ap's Piv 113^{hd} Outrun 10
15Jun87- 3Bel fst 5f :22⅘ :46⅗ :59⅖ ⒻMd 47500 2 2 33 79½ 8^{12} 7^{12} Cordero A Jr 115 7.70 75–19 Do I 117^{2}¼ Quajinn 117^{5}½ Noble Viki 113^3 Brief speed 8
17May87- 4Bel fst 5f :22⅗ :46⅖ :59⅗ ⒻMd Sp Wt 2 1 4¾ 63½ 8^{10} 8^{17} Cordero A Jr 117 4.40 70–20 Bubba Dulyah 117no Conium 117^{3}¼ Saucey Duchess 117½ Tired 8
LATEST WORKOUTS Jly 27 Bel 4f fst :48⅕ h Jly 21 Bel tr.t 4f fst :48⅕ h Jun 25 Bel tr.t 4f fst :48⅘ b Jun 9 Bel tr.t 4f fst :50 b

J.

Fara's Team Ch. f. 2, by Tunerup—Specialization, by Princely Native Lifetime 1987 1 M 0 0
Own.—Happy VAlley Farm $50,000 Br.—Happy Valley Farm (Fla) 117 1 0 0 0
Tr.—Dutrow Richard E
15Jly87- 4Bel fst 5½f :22⅕ :46 1:05⅘ ⒻMd Sp Wt 4 3 33 34 67½ 5^{12} Santos J A 117 9.20 74–20 Lost Kitty 117^5 Wet Suit 117^{2}¾ Allie's Castle 117^{2}½ Tired 10
LATEST WORKOUTS Jly 6 Aqu 4f fst :49 b

22. Only two horses fit the conditions. Find one or both. *Banque Privee* is on lasix for the first time.

7th Santa Anita

1 ¼ MILES. (Turf). (1.57⅘) ALLOWANCE. Purse $31,000. Fillies and mares. 4-year-olds and upward, which are non-winners of $3,000 other than maiden, claiming or starter. Weight, 120 lbs. Non-winners of a race other than claiming at one mile and one-eighth since February 1 allowed 3 lbs.

A.

Sundae Service Ch. f. 4, by Run the Gantlet—Sucre Candi, by Candy Spots
ORTEGA L E 117 Br.—Mandysland Farm (Cal) 1987 1 0 0 0 $875
Tr.—Cross Richard J 1986 3 2 0 0 $3,793
Own.—Mandysland Farm Lifetime 4 2 0 0 $4,668 Turf 4 2 0 0 $4,668
22Mar87-7SA 1⅛Ⓣ:47 1:11^{4}1:48^{3}gd 7¾ 116 7^7 73¾ 57½ 511¼ Toro F^2 ⒻAw35000 73-16 TreasureMap,Rivertower,Ofrendada 7
22Mar87—Broke slowly
5Oct86♦6Jarnac(Fra) a1$\frac{3}{16}$: gd*3-5 120 Ⓣ 1^{10} RicardJP Px Albrt Rng SundaeService, LaHeziere, Kasoka 8
5Oct86—No time taken
21Sep86♦4SaintOuen(Fra) a1$\frac{5}{16}$: gd — 115 Ⓣ 4^7 CartierJ Bx Brn d'Argntn Paganelli, Anoushir,RivierePo'aire 12
21Sep86—No time taken
7Sep86♦6Niort(Fra) a1⅜ : sf 9-5 106 Ⓣ 1½ Najeux A Px d St Flrnt SundaeService, Vouvant, RioNoble 3
7Sep86—No time taken
Apr 6 SA 6f ft 1:13 hg Mar 31 SA 4f ft :48^2 h Mar 18 SA Ⓣ 5f fm 1:02^1 h (d) Mar 10 SA 1 ft 1:41^3 h

B.

Keep Dating *
OLIVARES F 117
Own.—Seven Star Stable
Ch. m. 5, by Try Sheep—Keep It Low, by Mandate
Br.—Middle Ranch (Cal) 1987 4 1 0 2 $26,525
Tr.—Velasquez Danny 1986 21 2 2 4 $60,370
Lifetime 46 4 4 8 $113,285 Turf 13 0 2 3 $27,675

21Mar87-6SA 1 1/16 :464 1:113 1:44 sy 4 117 78½ 87½ 77 512½ Solis A4 Ⓕ Aw31000 68-16 Soonermoon,Velveteen,KepHoping 8
21Mar87—Steadied 1st turn
12Mar87-5SA 1 :461 1:114 1:372ft 10 115 96½ 94¾ 65½ 34 Solis A3 Ⓕ 80000 77-19 Jell, Totally Honest, Keep Dating 10
12Mar87—Bobbled start; took up sharply 1/4
28Feb87-5SA 1⅛Ⓣ:4631:1141:502fm 30 114 1hd 2hd 21 34¾ Solis A11 Ⓕ 75000 70-15 Mangez Les, OnPatrol,KeepDating 12
28Feb87—Lugged in early
11Jan87-1SA 1 1/16 :48 1:132 1:462ft 3 117 55½ 32 3½ 1¾ Pincay L Jr4 Ⓕ 50000 69-21 Keep Dating, Jell, Broad Street 6
14Dec86-1Hol 1 :461 1:112 1:372ft 9 116 66 69 78 79½ Olivares F5 Ⓕ Aw25000 66-18 Mrs.V.,Melva'sPride,Veronic'sQuest 7
14Dec86—Wide final 3/8
5Dec86-8Hol 1⅛ :472 1:121 1:503ft 4½ 116 54 42 35 37½ Olivares F3 Ⓕ Aw25000 77-17 CseMoney,Veronic'sQuest,KpDting 6
28Nov86-9Hol 1 1/16 Ⓣ:4621:1041:411fm 8½ 116 47½ 43½ 78½ 79 DelhoussyeE9 Ⓕ 80000 79-11 AffectionAffirmed,Benzin,KindBu 10
28Nov86—Lugged in
17Oct86-7SA 1 1/16 :463 1:112 1:434ft 7½ 116 713 67½ 55½ 44½ Olivares F5 Ⓕ Aw27000 78-21 Annpurn,LCodorniz,Veronic'sQuest 8
17Oct86—Wide backstretch
26Sep86-11Pom 1 1/16 :473 1:134 1:464sl 6 114 711 75¾ 32 33½ OlivaresF5 Ⓕ Ls Mds H 74-29 OurSweetShm,LeL'Argent,KpDting 7
3Sep86-5Dmr 1 1/16 Ⓣ:4741:1231:443fm 3½ 117 31½ 51¾ 33½ 43½ Ortega LE5 Ⓕ Aw23000 79-12 NatalieKnows,Corbella,Ohslewsnn 11
Apr 10 SA 3f ft :364 h Apr 5 SA 6f ft 1:134 h Mar 30 SA 6f ft 1:161 h Mar 7 SA 4f m :504 h

C.

Banque Privee
PINCAY L JR 117
Own.—Clore A
B. f. 4, by Private Account—Le Vague A L'Ame, by Vaguely Noble
Br.—Clore A (Ky) 1987 2 0 0 0 $4,350
Tr.—Frankel Robert 1986 7 1 1 3 $2,852
Lifetime 10 1 1 3 $7,202 Turf 10 1 1 3 $7,202

17Mar87-5SA 1⅛Ⓣ:4731:1231:493fm 4 117 62¾ 62 41¾ 44¾ StevensGL9 Ⓕ Aw31000 74-17 TrolleySong,QueenAlydar,OnPtrol 10
20Feb87-5SA a6½fⓉ:212 :4411:154fm 3 116 74½ 74½ 52½ 42½ StevensGL3 Ⓕ Aw27000 78-19 High Ace, Jam Time, Foufa 10
3Nov86♦1Leicester(Eng) 1¼ 2:093gd 10 115 Ⓣ 38½ Hills R Wysalle Docksider,AsianCup,BanquePrivee 10
17Oct86♦1Catterick(Eng) a1½ 2:412fm 5 115 Ⓣ 2nk Hill P D Crvn Apprntc Crowley, Banque Privee, Shehana 11
17Oct86—Impeded late
6Sep86♦6Kempton(Eng) a1⅜ 2:213gd 11 130 Ⓣ 11 CuthenS Chrtrhouse H TrvlMystry,SlngVh,StrghtThrough 11
26Aug86♦3Ripon(Eng) 1½ 2:54 sf *2¾ 130 Ⓣ 412 Hills R Stv Nsbit H Maladhu,SilentJourney,PrinceStire 7
1Aug86♦5Edinburgh(Scot) 1½ 2:411gd *2 112 Ⓣ 11½ DffldG Stncstle Asset(Mdn) BanquePrivee,MyWillow,MitalaMri 9
1Jly86♦2Folkestone(Eng) 1¼ 2:011fm 8 123 Ⓣ 34 ThomsnB Smeeth Liam, Naatell, Banque Privee 7
14Jun86♦6Bath(Eng) a1¼ 2:104gd 10 123 Ⓣ 34 Hills M Bdmnstr(Mdn) TrvelMystery,Frngnito,BnquePriv 16
21Oct85♦2Leicester(Eng) 7f 1:254fm 10 123 Ⓣ 75½ ThmsnB Ⓕ Hare(Mdn) Dunoof, MirataineVenture,Secuita 20
Apr 6 Hol 6f ft 1:15 h Mar 31 Hol 5f ft 1:011 h ●Mar 25 SA 4f ft :464 h Mar 14 SA 7f ft 1:282 h

D.

***Keep Hoping**
BAZE G 117
Own.—Duffel J A
Ch. f. 4, by Busted—Geoffrey's Sister, by Sparkler
Br.—West R M (Eng) 1987 4 0 1 2 $15,650
Tr.—Robbins Jay M 1986 9 1 1 3 $6,399
Lifetime 14 1 2 5 $22,049 Turf 11 1 1 3 $11,559

21Mar87-6SA 1 1/16 :464 1:113 1:44 sy 9½ 117 65 64¾ 42½ 38½ Toro F3 Ⓕ Aw31000 72-16 Soonermoon,Velveteen,KepHoping 8
27Feb87-7GG 1 :451 1:093 1:353ft 17 118 32 22 23 22½ Maple S5 Ⓕ Aw18000 87-14 FreeToMove,KepHoping,BrginQun 10
8Feb87-8BM 1 1/16 Ⓣ:4831:1341:452gd 20 110 44 64½ 812 814½ MllsJW5 Ⓕ Palo AltoH 61-21 RoylRegtt,BrigdeSpecile,BrownBss 9
10Jan87-8BM a1⅛Ⓣ 1:524gd 15 110 2hd 2½ 11 32 MllsJW2 Ⓕ C D Hrpr H 69-29 RoyalRegtt,WineTster,KeepHoping 6
28Dec86-9BM 1 1/16 :461 1:10 1:412ft 19 115 717 716 411 37 CastnedM2 Ⓕ Aw16000 78-14 CoolScene,FreeToMove,KepHoping 8
28Dec86—Bumped start
5Nov86♦3Edinburgh(Scot) 1⅞ 3:241gd 10 115 Ⓣ 12 CrterG TennentsNov H RfrmPrncss,MssBlcthrn,NmblVtv 16
21Oct86♦6Hamilton(Scot) 1½ 2:452sf 14 111 Ⓣ 2nk Lines R Whirlies H Ivoroski,KeepHoping,FourthTudor 20
6Aug86♦3Ayr(Scot) 1⅝ 2:592gd 6 105 Ⓣ 33½ CrlislN Famous Grouse H Wessex, Shah'sChoice,KeepHoping 9
28Jly86♦3Newcastle(Eng) a1½ 2:424gd *2 128 Ⓣ 34 Miller M Carlsberg H RelttvtyEsy,RhodIslndRd,KpHoping 5
3Jly86♦6Catterick(Eng) a1½ 2:423fm 16 123 Ⓣ 14 Miller M Wakefield H KeepHoping, MadisonGirl, Dallona 6
Apr 8 SA 4f ft :48 h Apr 2 SA 6f ft 1:151 h Mar 16 SA 5f ft 1:004 h Feb 21 GG 5f ft 1:014 h

E.

Corbella
GOMEZ R 117
Own.—Hunter or Kersten
Dk. b. or br. m. 5, by Crow—Blue Rinse, by Cornish Prince
Br.—Pillar Stud Inc (Ky) 1987 5 M 0 2 $5,250
Tr.—Hunter Catherine 1986 9 M 2 0 $12,650
Lifetime 26 0 4 5 $29,464 Turf 19 0 4 3 $20,789

20Mar87-6SA 1 1/16 :453 1:101 1:44 ft 13 116 818 918 918 919½ McHargue D G 2 Mdn 61-17 ArcticDrem,RescuPckgII,Vysotsky 10
6Mar87-6SA 1 1/16 :463 1:113 1:46 gd 11 116 1110 810 37½ 32½ McHrgueDG 10 M50000 68-21 Ahica, Yippyayo, Corbella 11
26Feb87-6SA 1 :473 1:124 1:38 ft 4½ 120 66½ 53 34 36½ McHrguDG3 Ⓕ M50000 71-22 Sweetness, MistyFebruary,Corbella 8
12Feb87-8SA 1⅛Ⓣ:4631:1121:503fm 36 118 1213 1212 1211 1212½ McHrgDG8 Ⓕ Aw28000 62-26 Heln'sMjsty,FlyingFrown,ClvrEdg 12
17Jan87-5SA 1⅛Ⓣ:4531:1111:501fm 51 117 913 95¾ 73¾ 62¾ Black C A8 Ⓕ Aw28000 73-24 QueenAlydr,BelmoneyBy,BonGenre 9
17Jan87—Steadied 3/8
30Dec86-5SA 1⅛Ⓣ:47 1:1121:484fm 56 118 1010 109 88½ 510¾ Black C A4 Ⓕ 80000 72-17 Benzina, Mangez Les, Kinda Beau 10
30Dec86—Off slowly; wide

18Dec86-6Hol 1⅛ Ⓣ:47 1:1131:424fm 10 122 109½ 94½ 43 21¾ Black C A7 ⒻMdn 78-19 LaAffirmed,Corbell,WeddingDncer 10
18Dec86—Wide stretch
30Nov86-5Hol 1⅛ Ⓣ:4741:1131:483fm 133 1095 11111118½12101282¾ Cisneros J E9 Aw24000 76-12 PlumCertin,Rodrigue,Intuitivenss 12
30Nov86—Broke slowly
23Nov86-6Hol 1 Ⓣ:4621:11 1:353fm 45 116 1011107½1119½1113½ Vergara O9 ⒻAw27000 75-13 Cruella, Sporting Ack, Mrs. V. 11
19Oct86-4SA 1 1/16 :472 1:12 1:451ft 14 121 97½ 66¾ 55 46½ Hernandez R5 ⒻMdn 69-18 Goldie Hawn, Bajan Moon,Kinema 10
Apr 2 SA 5f ft 1:033 h Mar 18 SA 3f ft :361 h Feb 19 SA 3f ft :353 h

F.

***Secret Ocean** Dk. b. or br. m. 5, by Most Secret—Ocean Rock, by Rockavon
MCHARGUE D G 117 Br.—Arnold A T (Ire) 1987 2 0 0 0 $725
Own.—Delaney A Tr.—Sullivan John 1986 10 0 0 3 $746
Lifetime 22 2 2 4 $4,544 Turf 21 2 2 4 $4,544
1Apr87-5SA a6½f Ⓣ:214 :4421:15 fm 30 117 67 810 69½ 58½ McHrgDG7 ⒻAw29000 75-14 Jerry'sGoldmine,JmTim,WordHrvst 8
1Apr87—Steadied 1/4
20Feb87-5SA a6½f Ⓣ:212 :4411:154fm 21 117 96 106¾ 84¾ 86½ Sibille R7 ⒻAw27000 73-19 High Ace, Jam Time, Foufa 10
26Nov86-5Aqu 6f :221 :454 1:113sy 39 113 611 612 615 619¾ Davis R G7 Ⓕ 70000 63-19 SkiBunny,PeaceKeeper,MayBeBold 7
16Nov86-6Aqu 1 1/16 Ⓣ:4841:1421:492sf 31 117 35 78½ 915 925½ Davis R G6 ⒻAw26000 32-42 JlousAppl,WthrWtch,SprngInnocnc 9
25Jly86♦6Tipperary(Ire) 1⅛ 1:554gd 6½ 123 Ⓣ 511 MrtnS Rcecrse Bkmkrs H StopThFighting,Kmksi,RosofCrlow 9
19Jly86♦5Leopardst'n(Ire) 7f 1:31 gd *2½ 121 Ⓣ 33½ Roche C Goatstown H HighlyDlightd,Individulist,ScrtOcn 11
9Jly86♦2Naas(Ire) 7f 1:284gd 6 129 Ⓣ 31½ Roche C Clane H HighlyDlghtd,BzrdCologn,ScrtOcn 14
28Jun86♦5Curragh(Ire) a6¼f 1:154gd 20 104 Ⓣ 1316 Hillis R J R Scrry H Ednica, Wolverstar, Rock Alley 19
19Jun86♦5Tipperary(Ire) 7f 1:323fm 6 133 Ⓣ 42½ Roche C Tipperary H Elle VaBon,TwoMinutes,GodsLane 14
17Jun86♦5Dundalk(Ire) a7½f 1:404gd 5 132 Ⓣ 33½ Roche C Crrckmcrss H Eurovision,GlemingTrsur,ScrtOcn 16
Apr 9 SA 4f ft :474 h Mar 30 SA 4f ft :473 h Mar 16 SA 5f ft 1:012 h Mar 10 SA 3f ft :372 h

G.

Belmoney Bay B. f. 4, by Bel Sorel—Vermillionaire, by Quack
PATTON D B 1125 Br.—Mishkin R & Chase (Cal) 1987 3 0 1 1 $9,800
Own.—Mishkin Chase Tr.—Mulhall Richard W 1986 14 1 3 2 $29,275
Lifetime 17 1 4 3 $39,075 Turf 6 0 1 1 $10,900
12Feb87-8SA 1⅛ Ⓣ:4631:1121:503fm *3 117 108¾119¾111010102¾ DlhoussyE7 ⒻAw28000 63-26 Heln'sMjsty,FlyingFrown,ClvrEdg 12
12Feb87—Bumped start
17Jan87-5SA 1⅛ Ⓣ:4531:1111:501fm 7½ 116 611 85½ 63½ 2hd ShoemkrW7 ⒻAw28000 76-24 QueenAlydr,BelmoneyBy,BonGenre 9
17Jan87—Crowded, checked 1/4; wide into stretch
3Jan87-2SA 1⅛ Ⓣ:4641:1111:494fm 36 116 108½106¾ 73¾ 33½ DlhoussyE9 ⒻAw28000 74-24 TobgoDncer,QuenAlydr,BlmonyBy 11
3Jan87—Bumped 1/8
5Dec86-9Hol 1 Ⓣ:4531:1011:35 fm 16 116 812 32½ 78 78¾ Meza R Q3 ⒻAw25000 83-08 Antique Lace, Intently, Queen Joan 9
15Nov86-5Hol 1⅛ Ⓣ:4541:1041:483fm 70 119 1211106½ 95½ 54½ Meza R Q4 ⒻAw24000 80-11 SuperKitten,Arzll,MorningDvotion 12
29Oct86-7SA 1 1/16 :453 1:102 1:433ft 16 117 712 78½ 58½ 57 ShoemkrW3 ⒻAw27000 76-17 RoylAlydr,Veronic'sQuest,AntiquLc 9
3Oct86-7SA 1 1/16 :463 1:113 1:441ft 25 117 77 85½ 67½ 66¾ DlhoussyE2 ⒻAw27000 73-17 FineKudos,SportingAck,SuperKittn 9
19Sep86-11Pom 1 1/16 :461 1:104 1:432ft 32 114 811 713 712 57½ HrdR4 ⒻⓈC T B AMn 87-09 ProperMry,Symboliclly,SilentArrivl 8
7Sep86-2Dmr 1 1/16 :452 1:11 1:44 ft 7 116 814 57 54½ 1¾ DelhoussyeE10 ⒻMdn 80-13 Belmoney Bay, Yacht, Intently 11
7Sep86—Wide into stretch
27Aug86-6Dmr 1 1/16 :452 1:111 1:44 ft *9-5 116 911 79½ 48½ 35 Shoemaker W5 ⒻMdn 75-14 CseMoney,Unconquerd,BlmonyBy 10
27Aug86—Wide 3/8 turn
Apr 5 SA 1 ft 1:414 h Mar 29 SA 6f ft 1:143 h Mar 24 SA 6f ft 1:124 h Mar 19 SA 6f ft 1:14 h

23.

3 BELMONT 7 FURLONGS

7 FURLONGS. (1.20⅗) CLAIMING. Purse $12,500. Fillies and Mares. 4-year-olds and upward. Weight, 122 lbs. Non-winners of two races since July 1, allowed 3 lbs. Of a race since then, 5 lbs. Claiming Price $14,000; for each $1,000 to $12,000, 2 lbs. (Races when entered to be claimed for $10,000 or less not considered.)

A.

Bonnie's Poker * Dk. b. or br. m. 5, by Poker—What a Surprise, by Wise Margin
Own.—Wooton Mary L $13,000 Br.—Garland Mr-Mrs S E (Ky) Tr.—Dutrow Anthony W 1125
Lifetime 58 11 9 10 $153,960 1987 9 3 2 1 $32,140 1986 27 4 4 5 $67,560 Turf 2 0 0 0
10Jly87- 2Bel my 7f :23 :46⅘ 1:25⅘ ⒻClm 14000 7 3 54 31½ 2hd 1½ Santos J A b 117 *2.00 73-28 Bonnie's Poker 117½ Inherently 1121¼ Bold Prima 117nd Driving 8
21Jun87- 1Bel my 6f :22⅗ :45⅖ 1:10⅕ ⒻClm 17500 6 4 2hd 22 25 510½ Santos J A b 119 3.00 78-10 Miss Scandal 1126½ Kissing Booth 1141½ Heather Rose 117¾ Tired 6
11Jun87- 1Bel fst 7f :23 :46⅘ 1:25⅖ ⒻClm 16500 3 2 32 2½ 2½ 1hd Santos J A b 115 *1.80 75-23 Bonnie's Poker115hdMissScandal1125¼SevenRogues117nk Driving 7
31May87- 2Bel fst 6f :22⅕ :45⅖ 1:12 ⒻClm 17500 2 1 25 26 24 52 Santos J A b 117 3.50 78-17 Daddy's Slugger 117hd P. J.'s Blitzen 1171 Glady H 117¾ Tired 8
21May87- 1Bel gd 7f :22⅘ :45⅘ 1:23⅖ ⒻClm 17500 9 1 21 2hd 2½ 21¼ Davis R G b 119 5.40 84-17 FlyingHope1121¼Bonnie'sPoker1194¾LovelyNurs1171 Second best 10
27Apr87- 4Aqu fst 7f :23⅕ :46⅖ 1:25⅖ ⒻClm 22500 8 8 63¾ 76½ 76½ 63¾ Davis R G b 115 10.60 70-29 Daddy's Slugger 115nc Romantic Girl1171½FlyingHope112hd Wide 9
20Apr87- 1Aqu fst 6f :23⅖ :47⅕ 1:12⅕ ⒻClm 17500 6 4 4¾ 2½ 21½ 1hd Davis R G b 117 *1.40 80-22 Bonnie'sPoker117hdMorgan'sRider113hdFlyingHope1126¾ Driving 6
2Apr87- 1Aqu fst 6f :21⅘ :44⅘ 1:11⅖ ⒻClm 17500 8 8 67½ 47 34 24¼ Davis R G b 117 9.70 80-24 SweetRenee1174¼Bonnie'sPoker117nkTmmyDove1141¾ Off slowly 9
23Mar87- 3Aqu fst 7f :23 :46⅘ 1:25⅖ ⒻClm 15500 9 12 88¾ 67 34 34¾ Davis R G b 113 35.10 69-28 Berry's Chapter 1173 Solohi 1131¾ Bonnie's Poker 1133 Mild rally 12
7Nov86- 2Aqu gd 1 :46⅕ 1:11⅘ 1:38 3+ⒻClm 13000 7 7 78¾1114132213281¼ Belmonte J F7 b 108 9.00e 48-21 Dual Role 1171¾ Irish Point 115nc Hidden Fantasy 1178 Outrun 13
LATEST WORKOUTS Jly 21 Aqu ⊡ 4f gd :49 h (d)

B.

***Pretty Colleen** — Own.—Taylor S

Dk. b. or br. m. 6, by Mr Long—Salera, by Sertorius
$14,000 Br.—Haras Santa Amelia (Chile)
Tr.—Violette Richard Jr

117

Lifetime				
8 3 0 0 $6.852				
1987	2	0 0 0		$6,852
1984	6	3 0 0		
Turf	6	3 0 0		$6,852

3Jly87- 2Bel	my	1	:46⅘ 1:12⅖ 1:37⅗	ⒻClm 45000	5 5 715 717 727 729¼	DeCarlo C P	b 113	33.10	46-24 Pasampsi 1177 Wild Women 1131 Iambic Pentameter 1138	Tired	7
20Jun87- 5Bel	fm	1 1/16 Ⓣ	:46⅗ 1:11 1:42⅘	ⒻClm 35000	2 3 33 79 910 812½	DeCarlo C P	b 117	18.90	69-17 Height Of Pleasure 1173¼ Frothy 1172¼ Wild Women 1171	Tired	11
11Nov84 ♦7ClubHipico(Chile	fm*1⅛		1:47⅖	Ⓣ ClasicoPaddockStakes(Gr3)	12	Munoz L	117	5.00	— — Mastuerzo 1232¼ Chunga 117½ Flamenco 1231½		14
11Nov84-Raced in Chile under the name: Nyra											
30Sep84 ♦6ClubHipico(Chile	fm*1 1/16		1:44⅕	Ⓣ ⒻClCuerpoDiplomatico	1hd	Ceron P	112	1.30	— — Nyra 112hd Snaba 1344 Grease 1341		5
2Sep84 ♦6ClubHipico(Chile	fm*1 1/16		1:45	Ⓣ ⒻPolla dePotrancas(Gr1)	6	Ceron P	117	*1.50e	— — Clientela 117½ Arrimate 117½ DHPresura 117		16
19Aug84 ♦9ClubHipico(Chile	sf*1		1:41⅕	Ⓣ ⒻAllowance	1¾	Munoz L	117	*.90	— — Nyra 117¾ Mal Pasar 117½ Cara Al Viento 1171¾		11
28Mar84 ♦2ClubHipico(Chile	fm*6f		1:11	Ⓣ ⒻMaiden Special Weight	1	Ceron P	117	——	— — Further information not available		12
14Mar84 ♦3ClubHipico(Chile	fm*5f		:58⅗	Ⓣ Maiden Special Weight	6	Ceron P	117	——	— — Further information not available		6

LATEST WORKOUTS Jly 15 Bel 3f gd :38 b Jly 12 Bel 4f fst :50⅘ b Jun 29 Bel 6f fst 1:16⅗ b Jun 18 Bel Ⓣ 4f fm :49 b (d)

C.

Strongback — Own.—Muss S

Dk. b. or br. f. 4, by Herculean—Back Out, by Traffic Cop
$12,000 Br.—Rand Adele L (Ky)
Tr.—Hushion Michael

108⁵

Lifetime				
41 4 2 5 $63.820				
1987	15	1 1 2		$20,480
1986	21	3 1 3		$42.620
Turf	5	0 1 0		$4,400

13Jly87- 1Bel	fst	1 1/16	:47⅖ 1:13⅖ 1:47⅕	ⒻClm 12000	5 6 75¼ 22½ 23 22¾	Nuesch D5	108	6.50	63-25 Swept Off 1172¾ Strongback 108½ Zona Rosa 1133	Best of others	9
3Jly87- 1Bel	my	7f	:22⅗ :46⅗ 1:25⅗	ⒻClm 15500	2 7 714 711 47½ 45	Migliore R	113	5.80	69-24 Cross Your Feather 117½BoldPrima1131½ZonaRosa1133	No factor	7
29Jun87- 2Bel	fst	1 1/16	:47⅖ 1:13 1:46⅕	ⒻClm 17500	8 6 66 54½ 48 57½	Nuesch D5	112	10.50	63-25 Berry'sChpter117½HonestNickle1173SimpticZenid1174	No excuse	9
25May87- 2Bel	fst	1 1/16	:47⅖ 1:12⅖ 1:44⅗	ⒻClm 22500	7 8 84¾ 31 35½ 64¼	Badamo J J5	110	16.30	75-16 Nile Flirt 117¾ Charsky 1171¼ Dawn Break 1141¼	Tired	9
20May87- 1Bel	fst	1⅛	:47⅕ 1:12⅖ 1:51⅗	ⒻClm c-17500	3 6 66¼ 64 33 34	Murphy D J	117	3.20	65-17 FaithfulTrveler1103¾MistressDonn110nkStrongbck1174½	Mild gain	7
4May87- 5Aqu	sly	1	:47 1:13⅕ 1:40⅖	ⒻClm 25000	6 5 58½ 38 48 45	Murphy D J	117	5.70	59-27 Nile Flirt 113¾ Far East 1171 Honest Nickle 1173¼	Outrun	6
25Apr87- 1Aqu	my	1⅛	:47 1:12⅘ 1:51⅕	ⒻClm 25000	2 7 69½ 711 58½ 58½	Murphy D J	117	6.10	70-18 FrAndAbove1172NoPlceButWin117nkDoublePurpose1171¾	Outrun	8
14Apr87- 6Aqu	fst	1⅛	:48⅗ 1:13 1:53⅕	3↑ ⒻAlw 27000	3 7 75½ 67½ 57 44¾	Murphy D J	119	20.00	64-23 Darbyvail 1121¾ Swept Off 1142 Card Played 1191	No menace	7
22Mar87- 2Aqu	fst	1	:46⅘ 1:12⅗ 1:38⅘	ⒻClm 30000	4 8 812 912 88½ 711	Murphy D J	114	12.20	61-25 CarlingfordRose1173½LadyBeRegl1175¾FinlStroke113nk	No factor	9
12Mar87- 3Aqu	fst	1⅛	:47⅗ 1:13⅕ 1:53⅕	ⒻClm 25000	7 7 613 611 49 35	Murphy D J	117	10.40	64-30 Montgomery 1124 Bold Prima 1101 Strongback 117nk	Rallied	8

LATEST WORKOUTS Jly 25 Bel tr.t 4f fst :50⅘ b Jly 20 Bel tr.t 4f fst :49⅘ b Jun 25 Bel tr.t 5f fst 1:03 b Jun 20 Bel tr.t 7f fst 1:32 b

D.

Miss Scandal * — Own.—Sabarese T

Ch. f. 4, by Inverness Drive—Lady Corniche, by Cornish Prince
$14,000 Br.—Rutherford M G (Ky)
Tr.—Barrera Oscar S

114⁵

Lifetime				
18 6 1 2 $83.060				
1987	11	4 1 1		$48.320
1986	7	2 0 1		$34,740

16Jly87- 2Bel	fst	6f	:22⅗ :46⅖ 1:12⅕	ⒻClm 17500	6 2 2hd 2hd 1hd 11¼	Belmonte J F5	114	*2.20	79-24 Miss Scandal 1141¼ Private Iron 117no Adda Girl 117hd	Driving	9
21Jun87- 1Bel	my	6f	:22⅗ :45⅖ 1:10⅕	ⒻClm 17500	2 1 1hd 12 15 16½	Belmonte J F5	112	*1.30	89-10 MissScandal1126½KissingBooth1141½HeatherRose117¾	Ridden out	6
11Jun87- 1Bel	fst	7f	:23 :46⅘ 1:25⅖	ⒻClm 17500	7 1 11 1½ 1½ 2hd	Belmonte J F5	112	7.40	75-23 Bonnie'sPoker115hdMissScndl1125¼SevenRogues117nk	Just failed	7
2May87- 1Aqu	fst	6f	:22⅖ :45⅘ 1:11	ⒻClm 35000	1 4 1hd 2hd 53½ 79¼	Antley C W	117	5.20	77-19 KissingBooth1172¾CrlingfordRose1171DmeDeTrefle115½	Stopped	7
27Feb87- 7Aqu	fst	6f ⊡	:21⅘ :45⅕ 1:10⅘	ⒻAlw 27000	9 1 33 42½ 912 914¾	Ortiz E Jr5	112	20.30	75-19 Blum's Majesty 1126¾ Three Hour Lark117hdReactress1171½	Tired	9
13Feb87- 5Aqu	fst	6f ⊡	:22⅕ :46⅕ 1:11⅗	ⒻAlw 27000	6 3 42½ 53½ 57½ 512¼	Antley C W	117	5.80	74-26 TopsInTaps1176¾SkiBunny117noPeacefulAbove119nk	Lacked rally	7
8Feb87- 7Aqu	fst	6f ⊡	:22⅖ :46⅕ 1:11⅕	ⒻAlw 40000	1 7 3½ 1hd 42 56¾	Antley C W	115	2.10e	81-22 What A Flip 115½ Arunji 1102 Likely Gain 115½	Weakened	7
31Jan87- 3Aqu	sly	6f ⊡	:23 :48⅕ 1:14⅗	ⒻClm 47500	1 5 2hd 1hd 12 1½	Antley C W	117	*1.90	71-34 Miss Scandal 117½ Torrid Zone1132¾MotherMaloney1121¾	Driving	6
21Jan87- 2Aqu	sly	6f ⊡	:22⅕ :45⅘ 1:11⅗	ⒻClm 45000	5 2 42½ 31½ 2hd 1nk	Antley C W	115	7.50	86-17 MissScandal115nkPeaceKeeper1171¼MotherMaloney1125¾	Driving	7
14Jan87- 5Aqu	fst	6f ⊡	:22⅖ :45⅖ 1:11⅕	ⒻAlw 27000	4 2 2½ 32½ 31½ 31¼	Belmonte J F5	117	19.10	87-16 Just Gorgeous 112½ Blum's Majesty 112¾MissScandal117½	Evenly	7

LATEST WORKOUTS Jun 3 Bel 3f fst :37 b

E.

Good Contrarian — Own.—Glen Laurel Farms

B. m. 5, by Iron Constitution—Private Sea, by Buck Private
$14,000 Br.—Mangurian Mr-Mrs H T Jr (NY)
Tr.—Zito Nicholas P

117

Lifetime				
44 6 10 5 $70.819				
1987	16	0 2 2		$9,930
1986	15	2 3 3		$24,329
Turf	1	0 0 0		

23Jly87- 1Bel	fst	6f	:22⅕ :46⅗ 1:12⅘	ⒻClm 14000	3 3 45½ 64½ 86 1113¾	Cordero A Jr	b 117	9.60	62-22 Montgomery 117nk Flying Hope 1121½ LatinLook1131	Tired badly	12
16Jly87- 2Bel	fst	6f	:22⅗ :46⅖ 1:12⅕	ⒻClm 17500	3 6 67¼ 78¼ 66½ 65	Munoz R5	b 112	22.80	74-24 Miss Scandal 1141¼ Private Iron 117no Adda Girl 117hd	No factor	9
28Jun87- 9Bel	fst	6f	:22⅘ :47⅖ 1:13⅖	ⒻClm 14000	2 11 76¼ 82½ 43½ 54¼	Nuesch D5	b 112	19.60	69-19 Bold Prima 115½ Inherently 117½ Latin Look 1171¾	Hung	11
18Jun87- 2Bel	fst	7f	:22⅘ :46⅕ 1:25⅖	ⒻClm 14000	8 7 74¾ 45 510 712¾	Pezua J M	b 117	8.20	62-23 Morgan's Raider 1172¾ Timely Raise 1173 Latin Look 1133	Tired	13
8Jun87- 1Bel	fst	6f	:22⅗ :46⅘ 1:12⅕	ⒻClm 14000	8 3 56 55 51½ 64½	Pezua J M	b 117	8.20	74-20 SevenRogues1172½FriscoDelight117¾Morgan'sRaider117nk	Evenly	13
26May87- 9Bel	fst	7f	:23 :46⅖ 1:26	ⒻClm 14000	8 2 42 32¼ 2½ 43½	Pezua J M	b 117	19.10	68-25 SevenRogues1152MistressDonn1121½MsterCution113nk	Weakened	12
16May87- 2Bel	fst	6f	:22⅘ :46⅖ 1:11⅕	ⒻClm 14000	9 3 31 21½ 76½ 1014¼	Antley C W	b 117	18.10	70-18 Royal Tantrum 1173¼Tara'sNative1171½WhyBePractical115½	Tired	14
11Apr87- 2Aqu	fst	1⅛	:47⅘ 1:12⅘ 1:55⅖	ⒻClm 14000	7 3 41¾ 3nk 79¾ 816½	Antley C W	117	6.60	41-23 Rise And Toast 1152¼ Out oftheStorm1143ColorfulMiss1081	Tired	10
2Apr87- 1Aqu	fst	6f	:21⅘ :44⅘ 1:11⅖	ⒻClm 17500	7 4 34 35 45 712½	Maple E	b 117	12.50	71-24 Sweet Renee 1174¼ Bonnie's Poker 117nk TammyDove1141¾	Tired	9
19Mar87- 2Aqu	fst	7f	:23 :46⅘ 1:26⅕	ⒻClm 22500	5 3 31½ 21 46½ 612½	Maple E	b 115	16.40	57-29 Tara's Native 114½ Turnpike Princess 117½ Adda Girl 1175¼	Tired	11

LATEST WORKOUTS Jly 12 Bel 4f fst :49⅗ h Jly 7 Bel 4f fst :50⅗ b

F.

Timely Raise — Own.—Twin Bee Stable

B. f. 4, by Raise A Man—Perquito, by Olden Times
$12,000 Br.—Northwest Farms (Ky)
Tr.—LaBoccetta Frank

113

Lifetime				
48 6 5 8 $86.230				
1987	12	1 1 1		$15.470
1986	22	3 2 5		$50.495
Turf	2	0 0 0		$600

13Jly87- 1Bel	fst	1 1/16	:47⅖ 1:13⅖ 1:47⅕	ⒻClm 14000	2 3 1hd 54 79¼ 716¾	Cruguet J	b 117	13.00	49-25 Swept Off 1172¾ Strongback 108½ Zona Rosa 1133	Stopped	9
3Jly87- 1Bel	my	7f	:22⅗ :46⅗ 1:25⅗	ⒻClm 15500	4 5 56½ 65 714 722¼	Cruguet J	b 113	4.30	52-24 Cross Your Feather 117½ Bold Prima 1131½ ZonaRosa1133	Outrun	7
18Jun87- 2Bel	fst	7f	:22⅘ :46⅕ 1:25⅖	ⒻClm 14000	3 6 64¼ 86¾ 36½ 22¾	Cruguet J	b 117	8.10	72-23 Morgan's Raider 1172¾ Timely Raise 1173 Latin Look1133	Rallied	13
3Jun87- 2Bel	gd	1 1/16	:47 1:12 1:45⅗	ⒻClm 14000	7 1 12 11½ 511 816¾	Badamo J J5	b 112	5.10	57-22 Simpatica Zenaida 1123 Swept Off1171¾BoldPrima1175	Gave way	11
21May87- 1Bel	gd	7f	:22⅘ :45⅘ 1:23⅖	ⒻClm 15500	5 7 43 56½ 57 47	Badamo J J5	108	7.90	78-17 Flying Hope1121¼Bonnie'sPoker1194¾LovelyNurse1171	Early foot	10
11Apr87- 2Aqu	fst	1⅛	:47⅘ 1:12⅘ 1:55⅖	ⒻClm 14000	1 1 2hd 44¼ 46¼ 613½	Santos J A	117	4.30	44-23 Rise And Toast 1152¼ Out oftheStorm1143ColorfulMiss1081	Tired	10
5Apr87- 2Aqu	my	1	:46⅗ 1:12⅘ 1:38⅖	ⒻClm 17500	7 5 75¾ 86½ 87 57¾	Belmonte J F5	b 112	7.00	66-19 Mistress Donna1102¾BoldPrima117nkProHarmony1141¾	No factor	10
17Mar87- 3Aqu	fst	1	:47⅖ 1:13⅕ 1:39⅖	ⒻClm 17500	7 2 1hd 31½ 39 613¼	Badamo J J5	b 114	2.40	56-31 Private Iron 1173½ Kissing Booth 1177ProHarmony1142½	Faltered	12
2Mar87- 1Aqu	gd	1 1/16 ⊡	:47 1:12⅕ 1:45⅕	ⒻClm 22500	7 2 1hd 31 47½ 311½	Badamo J J5	b 110	*2.90	72-15 Holly Hagley1156½FarAndAbove1175TimelyRaise110nk	Evenly late	7
20Feb87- 2Aqu	fst	1 1/16 ⊡	:47⅖ 1:13 1:48⅕	ⒻClm 15500	4 1 14 18 18 14	Badamo J J5	b 108	9.80	69-28 Timely Raise 1084 Berry's Chapter 117nk Wench1172½	Ridden out	12

G.

Latin Look — B. f. 4, by Far Out East--Latin Lassie, by Rixdal — **$12,000** Br.—Kelly T J (Ky) Tr.—Ortiz Paulino O — **113**

Own.—Ginger Lee Stables

Lifetime 28 2 4 4 $47,225 | 1987 15 0 2 3 $13,610 | 1986 11 1 1 1 $19,315

23Jly87- 1Bel fst 6f	:22⅕ :46⅗ 1:12⅘	ⒻClm 12000	2	5	77½	76	42½	31¾	Garcia J A	b 113	15.50	74-22 Montgomery 117nk Flying Hope 1121½ Latin Look 1131	Rallied	12
10Jly87- 2Bel my 7f	:23 :46⅘ 1:25⅘	ⒻClm 14000	8	6	75¼	63¾	57½	69	Pezua J M	b 117	9.00	64-26 Bonnie's Poker 117½ Inherently 1121¼ Bold Prima117nd	No factor	6
26Jun87- 9Bel fst 6f	:22⅘ :47⅖ 1:13⅖	ⒻClm 14000	11	10	96¾	61¼	2½	31	Pezua J M	b 117	8.80	72-19 Bold Prima 115½ Inherently 117½ Latin Look 1171¾	Weakened	11
18Jun87- 2Bel fst 7f	:22⅘ :46⅕ 1:25⅖	ⒻClm 12000	10	9	96¾	97¼	26	35¾	Guerra W A	b 113	8.40	69-23 Morgan's Raider 1172¾ TimelyRaise1173LatinLook1133	Weakened	13
8Jun87- 1Bel fst 6f	:22⅗ :46⅘ 1:12⅕	ⒻClm 12000	12	10	1214	911	85	74¾	Guerra W A	b 113	40.50	74-20 SevenRogues1172½FriscoDlight117¾Moron'sRidr117nk	Raced wide	13
26May87- 9Bel fst 7f	:23 :46⅖ 1:26	ⒻClm 14000	11	6	76½	79	97¾	1015¼	Santagata N	b 117	15.60	57-25 SevenRogues1152MistressDonn1121¼MsterCution113nk	No factor	12
4May87- 3Aqu sly 7f	:22⅗ :46⅖ 1:26⅖	ⒻClm 14000	6	6	611	611	59¼	610¾	Hernandez R	117	3.90	56-27 Tara'sNtive112nkLoylDiplomt106½DolceDolceDolce1176	No factor	7
25Apr87- 9Aqu gd 6f	:22⅗ :46⅖ 1:11⅗	ⒻClm 14000	3	7	54	65½	65¾	47½	McCauley W H	b 117	10.10	77-14 Joyfull Dance 1153½ Oaxaca1171½WhyBePractical1172¼	No excuse	11
19Mar87- 2Aqu fst 7f	:23 :46⅘ 1:26⅕	ⒻClm c-25000	2	8	74¼	88	1116	1119½	Santagata N	b 117	27.50	50-29 Tara's Native 114½ Turnpike Princess 117½ Aoda Girl1175¼	Outrun	11
26Feb87- 2Aqu fst 6f ⊡	:22 :45⅗ 1:11⅗	ⒻClm 35000	6	6	68	76	66¾	712	Santagata N	b 117	15.70	75-16 Torrid Zone 1157 P. J.'s Blitzen 1172¾ Dame DeTrefle110½	Outrun	10

LATEST WORKOUTS Jly 20 Bel tr.t 3f fst :37⅘ b

H.

Lovely Nurse — Ro. m. 6, by Sawbones—Price Fixing, by Time Tested — **$14,000** Br.—Sea Spray Farm (NY) Tr.—Jerkens Steven T — **117**

Own.—Cedar Valley Stable

Lifetime 55 11 7 12 $108,112 | 1987 13 1 1 2 $20,360 | 1986 21 4 4 5 $45,957

26Jly87- 2Bel gd 7f	:23⅕ :46⅖ 1:24	ⒻClm 17500	2	6	3nk	1hd	31½	48	Baird E T	b 117	2.50	74-19 HeatherRose1154¾Inherently1152¼DanzaRustic117hd	Stumbled st.	7
18Jly87- 1Bel fst 7f	:23⅕ :46⅕ 1:25	ⒻClm 22500	2	4	32½	22½	32½	34½	Baird E T	b 115	*.90e	72-20 FigurNvidon1172¼TurnpikPrincss1171¾LovlyNurs1151¼	Weakened	7
11Jly87- 5Pha fst 6f	:22⅗ :46⅗ 1:11⅘ 3+	ⒻClm 22500	2	8	78	74¾	67½	44¼	Baird E T	b 114	6.90	78-21 Black Humor 1162½ Lightling 111nk Bestest Friend 1161½	Rallied	6
21May87- 1Bel gd 7f	:22⅘ :45⅘ 1:23⅖	ⒻClm 16500	1	8	33	33½	34½	36	Migliore R	b 117	3.70	79-17 Flying Hope1121¼Bonnie'sPoker1194½LovelyNurse1171	Weakened	10
9May87- 9Bel fst 6f	:23 :47⅘ 1:13⅗	ⒻClm 17500	6	5	33	22	22½	42	Migliore R	b 119	*1.70	70-29 Tara'sNtive110½Jonnin1131¼FithfulTrveler110nk	Lacked response	7
29Apr87- 1Aqu my 7f	:22⅕ :45⅖ 1:24⅘	ⒻClm 16500	6	2	23	12	11½	11¾	Migliore R	b 115	*1.20	77-21 Lovely Nurse 1151¾ OutoftheStorm1172½MatchSpeed1175	Driving	6
8Apr87- 5Aqu gd 7f	:23⅖ :46⅘ 1:24⅘	ⒻClm 22500	7	6	85	85¾	57	53½	Lovato F Jr	b 115	4.20	73-21 Kissing Booth 115½ Turnpike Princess 117¾AodaGirl117nk	Outrun	8
29Mar87- 5Aqu fst 6f	:21⅗ :44⅘ 1:11⅕	ⒻClm 22500	7	8	1012	911	65	51	Lovato F Jr	b 115	9.70	84-17 Tara's Native 117nk Private Iron 117nk Kissing Booth115½	Rallied	11
4Mar87- 2Aqu fst 6f ⊡	:22⅖ :46 1:11⅘	ⒻClm c-17500	8	6	46	34½	36	44¼	Miceli M	b 117	4.80	81-16 TmmyDov1122¼DnzRstc117¾GoodCntrrn1131¼	Needed closing bid	11
4Mar87-Disqualified from purse money														
27Feb87- 2Aqu fst 6f ⊡	:22⅗ :46⅘ 1:13	ⒻClm 22500	9	12	1212	1115	1012	88¼	Miceli M	b 115	4.70	71-19 SweetRenee1133FlyingHope1101½Tara'sNative112½	Steadied start	12

LATEST WORKOUTS ● Jly 1 Bel tr.t 4f fst :47⅖ h Jun 25 Bel tr.t 5f fst 1:03 b Jun 17 Bel tr.t 4f fst :51 b

I.

Talk About Wings — Dk. b. or br. m. 5, by Advocator—Wings of Night, by Egotistical — **$12,000** Br.—Glen Iris Syndicate (Ky) Tr.—Galluscio Dominick — **113**

Own.—Donnelly Faith R

Lifetime 25 4 3 2 $52,285 | 1986 13 1 1 2 $22,595 | 1985 12 3 2 0 $29,690 | Turf 2 0 0 0

12Sep86- 1Bel fst 1 1/16	:47⅘ 1:13 1:44⅗ 3+	ⒻClm 17500	4	1	43	716	730	737¾	Graell A	b 117	5.90	41-20 Solo Energy 11712¾ Beth's Rose 1091¾Mucchinette112nk	Stopped	7
14Aug86- 1Sar fst 7f	:22⅘ :46 1:23⅗ 3+	ⒻClm 45000	6	6	86½	815	819	722	Graell A	b 113	18.80	63-20 JackieO'Lanterna1134MocoyMonday1132ProHrmony1153	Outrun	8
3Aug86- 9Sar my 7f	:23 :46⅖ 1:25 3+	ⒻClm 35000	5	1	12½	12½	12	12	Graell A	b 117	5.10	77-16 TlkAboutWings1172MissFleming1171½DolcDolcDolc1071½	Driving	7
18Jun86- 5Bel fm 1 1/16 Ⓣ	:47⅗ 1:11⅗ 1:43⅗	ⒻClm 70000	8	1	11½	819	826	832	Graell A	b 113	51.90	51-19 Ayrshire Lass 1174¼ ProudestBabe1083½MarkedLady1132	Stopped	8
28May86- 1Bel fst 7f	:23 :46 1:24⅖	ⒻClm 50000	5	6	76	812	915	919¼	Graell A	b 117	22.10	60-20 SecondStoryGirl1081LadyD.1176½BlackMedlion117nd	Never close	9
7May86- 5Aqu fst 6f	:22⅗ :45⅗ 1:10⅗ 3+	ⒻAlw 27000	1	4	67	611	612	619½	Graell A	b 119	24.70	66-15 Silent Account 1084¼RallyForJustice110ndSherryMary119½	Outrun	6
27Apr86- 5Aqu fst 7f	:23⅕ :46⅘ 1:25 3+	ⒻAlw 27000	3	7	64¾	76½	77	712¼	McCarron G	b 119	7.90	64-20 Kouklamou 119½ Black Medallion 1193¾ Guadery 1074½	Outrun	7
25Mar86- 6Aqu fst 1	:45⅗ 1:10⅖ 1:38⅕	ⒻAlw 29000	6	1	2hd	3½	21	21¾	McCarron G	b 117	33.40	73-26 TarukiStke1171¾TlkAboutWings117nkBethsSong119nd	Held place	9
14Mar86- 5Aqu sly 1⅛	:47⅕ 1:12⅖ 1:52⅗	ⒻAlw 29000	11	2	2½	21	86½	1011¾	McCarron G	b 117	29.70	60-26 Marked Lady 1191 Truly Best 117½ Skyjak 117¾	Tired	11
6Mar86- 8Aqu fst 1 1/16 ⊡	:48 1:13⅗ 1:48⅗	ⒻAlw 40000	9	1	2½	2½	42½	54	McCarron G	b 115	53.40	53-31 Leecoo 1151½ Stay Home 1152 Truly Best 115½	Tired	9

LATEST WORKOUTS Jly 26 Aqu ⊡ 3f my :39 bg(d) Jly 19 Aqu ⊡ 6f fst 1:15 b Jly 13 Aqu 5f fst 1:06⅘ b

J.

Zona Rosa — Ch. f. 4, by Red's copy—Painted Beauty, by Piano Jim — **$14,000** Br.—J E S Stable (Fla) Tr.—Pagano Frank X Jr — **117**

Own.—Barrell L

Lifetime 20 2 2 5 $31,500 | 1987 15 1 1 3 $19,840 | 1986 5 1 1 2 $11,650

13Jly87- 1Bel fst 1 1/16	:47⅖ 1:13⅘ 1:47⅕	ⒻClm 12000	8	7	85¾	78	47	33½	Ortiz E Jr	113	8.80	63-25 Swept Off 1172¾ Strongback 106½ Zona Rosa 1133	Wide	5
3Jly87- 1Bel my 7f	:22⅗ :46⅗ 1:25⅗	ⒻClm 15500	5	6	68	54½	33½	32	Ortiz E Jr	113	18.60	72-24 Cross YourFeather117½BoldPrima1131½ZonaRosa1133	Evenly late	7
18Jun87- 2Bel fst 7f	:22⅘ :46⅕ 1:25⅖	ⒻClm 14000	12	13	1317	1315	715	610	Antley C W	117	23.70	65-23 Morgan's Raider1172¾TimelyRaise1173LatinLook1133	Broke in air	13
3Jun87- 2Bel gd 1 1/16	:47 1:12 1:45⅗	ⒻClm 14000	9	6	56½	69½	712	613	Antley C W	117	11.50	61-22 Simpatica Zenaida 1123 Swept Off 1171¾ Bold Prima 1175	Tired	11
28May87- 9Bel fst 7f	:23 :46⅖ 1:26	ⒻClm 14000	12	10	1013	1119	1216	1119¼	Ortiz E Jr5	112	5.80	55-25 SevenRogues1152MistressDonna1121¼MasterCaution113nk	Outrun	12
17Apr87- 4Aqu gd 1⅛	:48⅘ 1:13⅘ 1:53	ⒻClm 17500	5	6	64½	65	44	35	Ortiz E Jr5	112	10.50	65-23 Mistress Donna 1173¼ Far East 1171¾ Zona Rosa 112nd	Off slowly	7
5Apr87- 2Aqu my 1	:46⅗ 1:12⅗ 1:38⅖	ⒻClm 17500	3	6	52¾	32	43	44¾	Ortiz E Jr5	112	4.30	69-19 MistressDonna1103¾BoldPrima117nkProHarmony1141¾	Weakened	10
29Mar87- 1Aqu fst 1	:45⅘ 1:10⅘ 1:37⅗	ⒻClm 17500	1	1	11½	12	11	21¾	Ortiz E Jr5	112	2.60	76-17 Mistress Donna 1081¾ Zona Rosa 1122 Pro Harmony1143¼	Gamely	7
23Mar87- 3Aqu fst 7f	:23 :46⅘ 1:25⅗	ⒻClm 17500	11	2	77¾	56	57¾	47¾	Ortiz E Jr5	112	4.00	66-28 Berry's Chapter 1173 Soloh. 1131¼ Bonnie's Poker 1133	Mild bid	12
12Mar87- 2Aqu fst 1⅛	:48⅗ 1:14⅖ 1:55⅖	ⒻClm c-14000	9	3	31½	22½	37½	47½	Maple E	119	*1.90	50-30 Out of the Storm 1121 Wench 1125 Princess of Valor 1081½	Wide	9

LATEST WORKOUTS Jly 25 Bel tr.t 5f fst 1:02⅖ b ● Jly 22 Bel 3f fst :35⅕ h Jun 26 Bel 4f fst :49 h Jun 14 Bel tr.t 3f my :37⅕ b

K.

Inherently * — Ch. m. 5, by Princely Native—Frozen Account, by Sham — **$14,000** Br.—Harbor View Farm (Ky) Tr.—Widmer Wayne — **117**

Own.—Toscana John T Jr

Lifetime 36 5 5 8 $89,710 | 1987 7 0 3 0 $9,330 | 1986 9 2 0 2 $24,560 | Turf 2 0 0 0

26Jly87- 2Bel gd 7f	:23⅕ :46⅖ 1:24	ⒻClm 16500	6	1	1nd	2hd	2½	25¾	Venezia M	115	*2.10	76-19 Heather Rose 1155¾ Inherently 1152¼ DanzaRustica117nd	2nd best	7
10Jly87- 2Bel my 7f	:23 :46⅘ 1:25⅘	ⒻClm 14000	4	2	33	42½	32	2½	Nuesch D5	112	2.70	72-26 Bonnie's Poker 117½ Inherently 1121¼ Bold Prima 117hd	Rallied	8
28Jun87- 9Bel fst 6f	:22⅘ :47⅖ 1:13⅖	ⒻClm 14000	9	8	109¾	105½	53¾	2½	Murphy D J	117	6.60	72-19 Bold Prima 115½ Inherently 117½ Latin Look 1171¾	Rallied	11
19Jun87- 1Bel fst 1 1/16	:47 1:12⅖ 1:46	ⒻClm 15500	6	2	32½	32½	45½	57	Pezua J M	113	12.10	65-21 Seven Rogues 1173¾ Swept Off 117nk Honest Nickle 1171	Tired	7
3Jun87- 1Bel fst 6f	:22⅗ :46⅘ 1:12⅕	ⒻClm 14000	5	5	33	22	2½	43½	Nuesch D5	112	20.40	75-20 SevenRogues1172¼FriscoDelight117¾Morgn'sRidr117nk	Weakened	13
26May87- 9Bel fst 7f	:23 :46⅖ 1:26	ⒻClm 14000	10	1	52½	54	76	710¾	Nuesch D5	112	15.50	61-25 Seven Rogues 1152MistressDonna1121½MasterCaution113nk	Tired	12
16May87- 2Bel fst 6f	:22⅘ :46⅖ 1:11⅕	ⒻClm 14000	7	6	2½	53	118¾	1114¾	Terrill R	117	7.30	69-16 Royal Tantrum 1173¼Tara'sNative1171¾WhyBePractical115½	Tired	14
24Jly86- 5Bel fm 1 1/16 Ⓣ	:47 1:11⅕ 1:42⅗ 3+	ⒻAlw 25000	5	2	21	97¾	914	918½	Santagata N	117	20.50	64-16 Rulenska 1173 Legacy of Strength 1173 One For Bess117nk	Tired	10
9Jly86- 5Bel fm 1 Ⓣ	:46⅖ 1:11 1:37⅗ 3+	ⒻAlw 25000	5	2	22½	46	45¼	56	Santagata N	117	18.60	71-21 Bedloe'sLdy1165Roberto'sSocl117ndHighIncSingh117¾	Weakened	8
21Apr86- 5Aqu sly 1	:45⅖ 1:10⅗ 1:37⅗ 3+	ⒻAlw 25000	2	2	26	34½	42	32¾	Santagata N	119	4.00	75-21 ProudestBabe1192½SmallVirtue112nkInherently1192½	Mild lt. resp.	6

L.

Montgomery Ch. f. 4, by Dust Commander—Teton Song, by Tudor Minstrel
$14,000 Br.—Willard Winifred H (Va) **117** Lifetime 21 4 3 0 $54,920 1987 13 3 1 0 $31,600 / 1986 8 1 2 0 $23,320
Own.—Pirozzi J Tr.—Daggett Michael H

23Jly87- 1Bel fst 6f :22⅕ :46⅗ 1:12⅘ ⒻClm 14000 6 6 811 88 53 1nk Davis R G 117 12.60 76-22 Montgomery 117nk Flying Hope 1121½ Latin Look1131 Up in time 12
3Jly87- 1Bel my 7f :22⅗ :46⅗ 1:25⅗ ⒻClm 15500 7 1 21½ 21½ 69 612¾ Belmonte J F5 b 108 6.80 62-24 Cross Your Feather 117½ Bold Prima1131½ZonaRosa1133 Stopped 7
19Jun87- 1Bel fst 1 1/16 :47 1:12⅖ 1:46 ⒻClm 17500 3 1 12 11½ 25 710½ Nuesch D5 b 112 11.10 61-21 Seven Rogues 1173¾ Swept Off 117nk Honest Nickle1171 Used up 7
28May87- 9Bel fst 7f :23 :46⅖ 1:26 ⒻClm c-14000 2 8 31½ 22½ 41 55¾ Cruguet J b 117 5.30 66-25 Seven Rogues 1152MistressDonna1121¼MasterCaution113nk Tired 12
16May87- 3Bel fst 1⅛ :47⅕ 1:12⅕ 1:50⅘ ⒻClm 20000 6 1 13 11 43 611 Ortiz E Jr5 b 108 8.10 52-15 Dawn Break 1124¾ Charsky 1175½ Nile Flirt 117no Stopped 6
8May87- 3Bel fst 1 1/16 :46⅖ 1:12⅕ 1:46⅗ ⒻClm 15500 2 2 2½ 13 1hd 25¼ Ortiz E Jr5 b 108 4.40 64-24 MmCo1155¼Montgomery108nkSevenRogus1132¾ Bumped, drifted 6
30Apr87- 3Aqu fst 1⅛ :46⅘ 1:12⅕ 1:55⅖ ⒻClm 14000 6 1 12½ 11 2hd 52¼ Nuesch D5 b 112 *2.60 56-28 No Such 112½ Pro Harmony 113½ Seven Rogues 112½ Tired 7
25Apr87- 1Aqu my 1⅛ :47 1:12⅘ 1:51⅕ ⒻClm 25000 8 1 11 21 718 828 McCauley W H b 117 5.10 51-16 FrAndAbove1172NoPiceButWin117nkDoublePurpos1171½ Stopped 8
5Apr87- 7Aqu gd 6f :22⅗ :46⅕ 1:10⅘ 3+ⒻAlw 26000 6 3 32 21½ 66½ 613¼ Davis R G b 115 4.30 74-15 Warna Corna 1121 Madam Carol 115no CoralFlight1194¾ Stopped 6
25Mar87- 8Aqu fst 1 :45⅘ 1:10⅖ 1:37⅕ ⒻAlw 27000 4 2 1½ 31½ 718 819¾ Nuesch D5 b 112 2.90 60-27 That's Fine 1172½ May Be Bold 117¾ Sweet Sound 117½ Stopped 8
LATEST WORKOUTS Jly 19 Bel tr.t 4f fst :49⅕ b Jun 16 Bel tr.t 4f fst :49 h ●Jun 9 Bel tr.t 4f fst :48 h

24.

3rd Santa Anita

OUT OF CHUTE / 7 FURLONGS / SANTA ANITA / FINISH

7 FURLONGS. (1.20) ALLOWANCE. Purse $29,000. 4-year-olds and upward which are non-winners of $3,000 other than maiden or claiming. Weight, 120 lbs. Non-winners of a race other than claiming since December 25 allowed 3 lbs.

A.

Decore B. g. 4, by Secretariat—Sight, by Gallant Romeo
COX D W **115**5 Br.—Claiborne Fm & Gamely Corp (Ky) 1987 4 1 1 1 $19,450
Tr.—Proctor Willard L 1986 6 M 5 0 $19,600
Own.—Perry W H (Lessee) Lifetime 10 1 6 1 $39,050 Turf 1 0 1 0 $4,000

13Mar87-6SA 6f :214 :443 1:102ft 2¾ 1135 41½ 33 34 1no Cox D W 12 Mdn 86-21 Decore, Danski, Kebaba 12
27Feb87-6SA 6f :213 :442 1:092ft 4¾ 1145 42½ 31½ 2hd 2hd Cox D W 10 Mdn 91-16 Don's Irish Melody, Decore, Ahica 12
27Feb87—Bumped start
16Feb87-6SA 6½f:221 :451 1:174gd 2½ 119 31 3½ 22½ 32¾ Sibille R 9 Mdn 78-21 Starshield, Pleasant Life, Decore 10
16Feb87—Erratic late
9Jan87-6SA 1 1/16:472 1:124 1:464sl 2½ 1145 2½ 21½ 46½ 614½ Cox D W 7 Mdn 52-26 Jack McCoy, Centenary, Rewana 11
9Jan87—Rough start
14Dec86-3Hol 1⅛Ⓣ:4711:1131:482fm 5½ 1145 32½ 42 2hd 2½ Cox D W 4 Mdn 85-11 Star Ribot, Decore, Padoue 9
14Dec86—Drifted out 7/8; erratic in stretch
12Nov86-4Hol 7f :222 :452 1:232ft *4-5 119 33 31½ 22 22½ Valenzuela P A6 Mdn 85-15 Magic Leader, Decore, Rewana 6
30Oct86-6SA 1 1/16:461 1:112 1:444ft 3 116 21½ 22 31½ 34½ Day P6 Mdn 72-18 Sun Man, ‡Coastal Love, Decore 9
30Oct86—Placed second through disqualification; Rank to place
4Oct86-4SA 6f :214 :452 1:103ft 9½ 118 45 32 33 21½ Lipham T9 Mdn 84-18 Aeroflame, Decore, Park Road 12
4Oct86—Erratic 1/2-1/4
6Sep86-4Dmr 6f :214 :443 1:092ft 62 117 53½ 56¾ 39½ 210 Lipham T6 Mdn 81-12 Salt Dome, Decore, Park Road 11
6Sep86—Wide into stretch
23Aug86-6Dmr 6f :22 :451 1:09 ft 88 116 1217 1214 1223 1219½ Patterson A4 Mdn 73-10 Granito, Danielli, Extranix 12
Mar 28 SA 3f ft :37 h Mar 23 SA 4f ft :493 h Mar 12 SA 3f ft :374 h Feb 26 SA 3f gd :383 h

B.

Hapigrin B. c. 4, by Grentall—Hapiwon, by One for All
MEZA R Q **117** Br.—Malmuth Mr-Mrs M (Cal) 1987 4 1 3 0 $18,950
Tr.—Lerille Arthur J Jr 1986 6 M 1 1 $6,450
Own.—Ayala-Hinds-Hinds Lifetime 10 1 4 1 $25,400

17Mar87-6SA 6½f:22 :452 1:163ft *3-2 118 31½ 21½ 1½ 12 Stevens G L 6 M45000 87-16 Hapigrin,SuperHigh,Predominnce 12
11Feb87-6SA 6½f:22 :453 1:17 ft 4½ 1125 32½ 42 21½ 2hd Patton D B 12 M45000 85-17 Mondanite,Hpigrin,DremsDon'tDie 12
11Feb87—Wide into stretch
23Jan87-6SA 6f :22 :453 1:111ft 3¾ 1125 82½ 63 53½ 24 Patton D B 7 M45000 78-22 Vari Beau, Hapigrin, PrivateEagle 12
23Jan87—Rough trip
10Jan87-4SA 6f :22 :454 1:123gd 7½ 1125 97 74¾ 31 2hd Patton D B 8 M40000 75-20 Ed's Exclusive, Hapigrin,Undenied 11
18Dec86-4Hol 6f :223 :463 1:111ft 4½ 1155 52½ 63½ 54 46¼ Patton D B9 [S]M32000 81-17 GetAlongPaisno,VriBeu,PinoPlyer 11
18Dec86—Wide stretch
22Nov86-2Hol 6f :22 :453 1:11 ft 7½ 1155 118¾ 79 47½ 25 Patton D B7 M32000 83-13 Quardolite, Hapigrin,StormyWorld 12
22Nov86—Lugged in stretch
30Oct86-2SA 6½f:212 :442 1:162ft 16 117 129½ 1011 1119½ 1018¼ Sibille R 10 [S]M32000 70-18 StckyTrggr,SldsByThr,GtAlngPsn 12
30Oct86—Bumped break; lugged out backstretch
28Feb86-4SA 6f :214 :444 1:103ft 14 118 84½ 66½ 55½ 46¾ Sibille R 3 [S]M32000 78-19 LittleMinch,SrosChick,T.C.Sutton 12
28Feb86—Broke slowly, bumped hard start
17Feb86-4SA 6f :213 :451 1:114sy 6½ 118 43 33½ 2½ 34½ Sibille R 2 [S]M32000 75-19 Serious Play,LittleMinch,Hapigrin 11
23Jan86-3SA 6f :22 :453 1:111ft 36 118 54½ 43½ 78 89½ Sibille R 6 M32000 72-18 NturlCourg,NoRightTurn,SrousPly 12
Mar 26 SA 4f ft :493 h Mar 14 SA 4f ft :492 h Mar 9 SA 4f ft :49 h Feb 28 SA 6f ft 1:131 h

C.

Angle Arc

DELAHOUSSAYE E 117

Own.—Asadurian–Asadurian–Winick

Ch. g. 4, by Angle Light—Hurry Countess, by Hurry to Market

Br.—Dickey M (Ky) 1987 4 0 3 0 $16,300

Tr.—Winick Randy 1986 14 2 3 0 $35,550

Lifetime 25 3 7 2 $58,820 Turf 2 0 0 1 $1,650

15Mar87-2SA 6½f :214 :452 1:172ft *3 117 118¼ 109¾ 87¾ 55¾ DelhoussyeE 5 Aw28000 77-20 Don'sIrshMlody,Dvl'sIc,TmFrSkrt 11

15Mar87—Wide final 3/8

28Feb87-9SA 6½f :213 :441 1:163ft 3 116 711 79½ 55 2no DelhoussyeE 4 Aw27000 87-17 Extranix, Angle Arc, Devil's Ice 7

15Feb87-4SA 6½f :213 :443 1:154m 3 116 57½ 57½ 55½ 24 DelahoussayeE 4 50000 87-17 Danczone, Angle Arc, Romaxe 5

25Jan87-2SA 6f :213 :442 1:094ft 6½ 116 611 68 57½ 22½ DelahoussayeE 2 50000 86-18 Ondarty,AngleArc,MischievousMatt 6

25Jan87—Broke slowly, bumped

31Dec86-5SA 6½f :22 :453 1:172ft 6¾ 116 119½ 118¾ 64 21 DelahoussayeE 3 40000 82-20 Watch'n Win, Angle Arc, Idol 12

31Dec86—Broke slowly

27Nov86-5Hol 1 :452 1:103 1:364ft 3¼ 116 65½ 53½ 44½ 44½ Valenzuela P A 5 40000 74-18 Sebucan, Split Winners,BoldDecree 8

27Nov86—Troubled trip

13Nov86-9Hol 1 :453 1:101 1:353ft 2½ 116 21 52½ 45 45¾ DelahoussayeE 7 50000 79-23 MischievousMtt,CojkMn,BoldDecre 9

23Oct86-7SA 1 :45 1:104 1:38 ft 5¼ 116 710 64 72¾ 45¼ DelahoussayeE 2 50000 73-20 BoldDecree,TrojnTrick,Bruli'sAnte 10

23Oct86—Inadvertently struck on head by another rider's whip 1/16

8Oct86-7SA 1 :46 1:104 1:37 ft 11 117 66¾ 75¼ 78 77¼ Pincay L Jr 10 Aw27000 76-20 GrecianWonder,LordAllison,Dnielli 10

8Oct86—Wide 7/8 turn

20Aug86-7Dmr 1 :45 1:093 1:35 ft 2¾ 117 77½ 67¾ 67 616½ Pincay L Jr 4 Aw21000 76-11 Don B. Blue, Lord Allison, Jota 9

20Aug86—Bumped start

Mar 25 SA 6f ft :591 h Mar 10 SA 5f ft 1:00 h ●Feb 25 SA 4f gd :482 h (d) Feb 8 SA 5f ft 1:003 h

D.

Northern Valor

VALENZUELA P A 117

Own.—Ner Joanne H

Ro. c. 4, by Northern Jove—Valarris, by Jerry Crew

Br.—Ner Joanne H (Ky) 1987 1 0 0 0

Tr.—Ner Fabio 1986 8 1 1 2 $19,900

Lifetime 9 1 1 2 $19,900 Turf 1 0 0 0

15Mar87-2SA 6½f :214 :452 1:172ft 95 117 54 66 43 68 Solis A 2 Aw28000 77-20 Don'sIrshMlody,Dvl'sIc,TmFrSkrt 11

17Jly86-6Hol 1 Ⓣ:454 1:101 1:36 fm 8¾ 116 613 611 69½ 67¾ DelahoussayeE 4 62500 — — Dmon'sGme,DoubleQust,CountEric 6

29Jun86-7Hol 7f :212 :442 1:214ft 35 114 75¾ 84¼ 76 710¼ Olivares F 8 Aw19000 85-10 Slyly Gifted, In Toto, Noticiero 8

29Jun86—Wide on turn

8Jun86-6Hol 6f :223 :463 1:111ft *2¼ 116 2½ 1hd 11½ 1no DelahoussayeE 10 Mdn 88-11 NorthrnVlor,Mondnt,MdnghtCcktl 11

25May86-2Hol 6f :224 :463 1:111ft 4½ 116 51¼ 31½ 21½ 21¾ Delahoussaye E 9 Mdn 86-18 SansRival,NorthernValor,Aeroflame 9

25May86—Lugged in stretch

11May86-6Hol 6f :221 :453 1:094ft 6½ 120 52¼ 52¾ 55 48¼ Valenzuela P A 2 Mdn 87-15 Mrvn'sPlcy,PrncOFr,Dn'sIrshMldy 10

27Apr86-6Hol 6f :221 :454 1:102ft 9½ 120 32½ 31 33½ 34¼ Valenzuela P A 8 Mdn 88-15 Rai Den, Devil's Ice, NorthernValor 8

13Apr86-4SA 6½f :22 :451 1:163ft 4½ 118 2hd 21 32 33 Valenzuela P A 4 Mdn 84-15 SmrtLife,Mrtin'sDncer,NorthrnVlor 7

5Apr86-6SA 6f :214 :444 1:102ft 26 118 55½ 47¼ 57 57 Delahoussaye E 1 Mdn 79-20 Jove's Encore, SansRival,Devil'sIce 8

5Apr86—Bobbled, veered in start

Mar 25 Hol 4f ft :482 h Mar 10 Hol 6f ft 1:173 h Mar 4 Hol 3f ft :381 hg Feb 19 Hol 5f ft 1:024 h

E.

Time For Sakarto

STEVENS G L 117

Own.—Timestable

Dk. b. or br. g. 4, by Bold Tropic—Latent Legacy, by Nodouble

Br.—Cardiff Stud Farms (Cal) 1987 2 0 0 1 $4,875

Tr.—Ferraro Stephen 1986 5 1 1 2 $20,000

Lifetime 7 1 1 3 $24,875 Turf 3 0 1 2 $10,650

15Mar87-2SA 6½f :214 :452 1:172ft 13 117 107¼ 98¾ 65¾ 34¾ Stevens G L 1 Aw28000 78-20 Don'sIrshMlody,Dvl'sIc,TmFrSkrt 11

28Feb87-9SA 6½f :213 :441 1:163ft 9½ 116 67 57½ 45 52¾ Stevens G L 3 Aw27000 84-17 Extranix, Angle Arc, Devil's Ice 7

8Oct86-7SA 1 :46 1:104 1:37 ft 5½ 116 88¾ 85¼ 56 65¾ ValenzuelPA 6 Aw27000 77-20 GrecianWonder,LordAllison,Dnielli 10

30Aug86-9Dmr 1 1/16 Ⓣ:47 1:112 1:434fm 3½ 116 99¼ 72¼ 63½ 34½ ValenzuelPA 9 Aw23000 82-11 SansRivl,HilTheBid,TimeForSkrto 12

30Aug86—Wide final 3/8

21Aug86-7Dmr 1 Ⓣ:452 1:101 1:353fm 3½ 116 66 54 42 21¼ ValenzuelPA 2 Aw21000 93-06 FbulousSound,TimForSkrto,HotMtl 6

1Aug86-5Dmr 1 1/16 Ⓣ:47 1:114 1:432fm 5 116 44 63¼ 43½ 34¾ McCarronCJ 3 Aw20000 84-11 Cro'sHollywood,Grgson,TmFrSkrt 10

9Jly86-7Hol 6f :221 :46 1:112ft 6¾ 114 87¼ 77¾ 46½ 1¾ McCarron CJ 10 Ⓢ Mdn 87-18 TmForSkrto,PrncO'Fr,DowdCnyon 11

Mar 24 SA 6f ft 1:133 h Mar 10 SA 5f ft 1:003 h Feb 23 SA 6f ft 1:141 h Feb 18 SA 6f ft 1:14 h

F.

Envious Dancer

MCHARGUE D G 117

Own.—Four D Stable

Ch. h. 5, by Marshua's Dancer—Greeny, by Jean-Pierre

Br.—McMakin & Wainscott (Ky) 1986 2 0 0 0

Tr.—Velasquez Danny 1985 9 2 0 0 $20,150

Lifetime 11 2 0 0 $20,150 Turf 2 0 0 0 $1,325

10Apr86-5SA 1 1/16 :464 1:112 1:434ft 3¾ 118 2hd 25 726 — Pincay L Jr 4 20000 — — MostDetrmind,RightOnRd,WhidbyT 8

10Apr86—Eased

23Mar86-9SA 1 1/16 :462 1:11 1:433ft 16 117 41½ 52¾ 62¾ 86¼ Pincay L Jr 1 40000 77-17 Bdouin,ForignLgion,KnightSkiing 12

28Dec85-5SA 1 :462 1:112 1:362ft 15 116 3nk 3nk 78 711¼ McHrgueDG 7 Aw26000 75-14 VlintGeorge,Mike'sCt,MsterCrofter 9

28Dec85—Fanned wide 7/8

10Nov85-5SA 1⅛ Ⓣ:482 1:124 1:494fm 33 1105 31½ 32 21 54 St Martin E 7 Aw27000 74-18 Ignited, Captain Vigors, Loverue 12

10Nov85—Bumped off stride at 5/16

27Oct85-5SA 1¼Ⓣ:47 1:364 2:023fm 13 1105 45 52½ 64¾ 54¼ St Martin E 6 Aw26000 70-21 Faridpour, North OfLake,Reverent 10
26Aug85-9Dmr 1 1/16:47 1:113 1:434ft 13 116 2½ 2hd 11¼ 11¼ McHargue D G 6 40000 81-17 EnvosDncr,GoodThghtWlly,NtvAct 8
3Aug85-7Dmr 1 1/16:453 1:11 1:421ft 16 112 2½ 41½ 721 830¾ Hawley S 1 Aw19000 58-15 Little Missouri,Stickette,FiscalWin 8
25Jly85-2Dmr 1 1/16:462 1:112 1:432ft 7½ 115 21 1½ 13½ 12½ Hawley S 11 M32000 83-17 EnviousDncer,Tofutti,VlintGeorge 12
17Jly85-1Hol 6f :223 :462 1:104ft 10 115 2hd 2hd 44½ 48½ Sibille R 4 M50000 85-09 Forkintherod,SwordPrinc,Lurl'sTim 8
23Jun85-3Hol 6f :221 :45 1:092ft 54 115 43 49½ 511 59½ Sibille R 3 Mdn 90 — SumExchng,ProfssorRobrts,Absolt 8
Mar 25 SA 5f ft 1:011 h Mar 20 SA 4f ft :481 h Mar 15 SA 1 ft 1:431 h Mar 9 SA 7f ft 1:274 h

25.

2 MONMOUTH

6 FURLONGS
MONMOUTH PARK

6 FURLONGS. (1.08) CLAIMING. Purse $8,000. Fillies. 3-years-old. Weight, 121 lbs. Non-winners of two races since June 30 allowed 3 lbs.; a race 6 lbs. Claiming price $12,500; for each $500 to $10,500 1 lb. (Races where entered for $9,500 or less not considered.)

A.

Accuwoman Dk. b. or br. f. 3, by Akureyri—Lady Beau Away, by Hitting Away
$12,500 Br.—Joselson S I (Pa) 115
Own.—Joselson S I Tr.—Coletti Edward J
Lifetime 2 1 0 0 $3,300 — 1987 2 1 0 0 $3,300 — 1986 0 M 0 0

30Jun87- 6Mth fst 1 :47⅕ 1:12 1:38⅘ ⒻClm 25000 8 6 611 77½ 613 614½ Romero J A5 b 109 5.30 66-13 Smiling Fay 116hd Gentle World 1161½DedhamDancer113½ Outrun 8
11Jun87- 9Mth fst 6f :22⅗ :45⅗ 1:12 3+ⒻMd 10000 8 8 1½ 14 15 19 Romero J A5 b 110 3.70 80-19 Accuwoman 1109 Swoonski 1091¼ Jobeck 1152½ Ridden out 11
LATEST WORKOUTS Jun 26 Mth 4f fst :50⅘ b Jun 20 Mth 4f fst :51 b Jun 5 Mth 6f sly 1:17⅘ b

B.

Jovanka Ro. f. 3, by Homeless—Frank's Rita, by Tropic King II
$12,500 Br.—Brooks Betty (NJ) 115
Own.—Blue Crest Famrs Tr.—Anderson William D
Lifetime 10 4 2 0 $18,775 — 1987 8 3 2 0 $14,575 — 1986 2 1 0 0 $4,200

21Jly87- 2Mth fst 6f :22 :46⅘ 1:14 ⒻClm c-10000 8 1 33½ 43 31½ 2nk Corbett G W5 b 110 *2.10 70-18 Ocali Gal 115nk Jovanka 1103 Silk Jolie 106no Sharp 8
9Jly87- 2Mth fst 6f :22 :45⅗ 1:12⅖ ⒻClm 7500 9 4 2hd 11½ 11½ 1¾ Corbett G W5 b 113 *2.90 78-21 Jovanka 113¾ Daremightythings 113¾ Fast Drive 110nk Driving 10
22Jun87- 3Mth fst 6f :22⅘ :45⅖ 1:12⅗ ⒻClm 7500 7 2 31½ 21 1hd 11 Corbett G W7 b 108 *2.20 77-18 Jovanka 1081 Hostile Takeover 1113½ NovellaCream1081½ Driving 8
3Jun87- 4Mth fst 6f :22⅘ :46⅖ 1:13⅘ ⒻClm 7500 6 4 32 45 3½ 11½ Corbett G W7 b 106 6.00 71-22 Jovanka 1081½ Our Miss Agnes 1151½ Bingo B. 110½ Driving 11
5May87- 7GS my 6f :22⅗ :46⅕ 1:12 3+ⒻⓈClm 6500 9 5 31 21½ 23 23 Moyers L b 112 9.90 79-20 Spray Over 1163 Jovanka 1123 Amger 1162¼ Best of others 10
13Apr87- 2GS fst 6f :22⅗ :46⅘ 1:13⅗ ⒻClm 8000 5 7 74 53½ 813 715 Rocco J b 116 5.20 59-26 Artelia 119½ Flighty Castle 1215½ Legal Lassie 1072 No factor 10
4Apr87- 7GS gd 6f :22⅖ :46 1:12⅖ ⒻClm 11000 4 9 63½ 66¾ 69 69¾ Melendez J D 116 5.20 71-15 Flighty Castle 116¾ Royal Zeus 116¾ Lady Glacier 1166½ Outrun 11
17Mar87- 5GS fst 6f :23 :48 1:14⅘ ⒻAlw 10500 4 1 2hd 68¼ 613 615 Ayarza I 116 11.70 53-31 Anna's Bambi 1161½ Tantaruler 1161¾ Ma Burn 116nk Early foot 6
9Dec86-11Med sly 6f :23⅕ :47 1:12⅖ ⒻMd 16000 9 2 11 — 11 12½ Rocco J 117 3.50 80-19 Jovanka 1172¼ Hop To It 1139¾ Ms. Turbo 117no Fog, driving 9
22Nov86- 6Med fst 6f :22⅘ :47 1:13⅖ ⒻⓈMd Sp Wt 1 12 1011 911 89 811¼ Thornburg B 117 19.10 64-20 Jitters 1171½ Mary's Issue 1174 That's Our Doll 1173 Outrun 12
LATEST WORKOUTS Jly 18 Mth 5f fst 1:02 b ● Jly 8 Mth 3f sly :38⅕ b (d) Jly 4 Mth 5f fst 1:02⅕ b Jun 29 Mth 4f fst :50⅗ b

C.

Princess Jig Ch. f. 3, by Jig Time—Fun Place, by Chateaugay
$15,500 Br.—Big C Farm (Fla) 1105
Own.—Our Aurora Stable Tr.—Seewald Alan
Lifetime 19 3 2 3 $30,385 — 1987 10 1 2 2 $19,715 — 1986 9 2 0 1 $10,670

22Jly87- 5Mth fst 1 :46⅕ 1:12⅕ 1:41⅘ ⒻClm 12500 6 1 18 14 1hd 2hd Corbett G W5 b 109 2.70 66-21 Bingo B. 109hd Princess Jig 109¾ I'm For Deb 116½ FAltered 6
14Jly87- 2Mth fst 6f :22 :45⅖ 1:12⅗ ⒻClm 16000 1 6 1hd 11 2½ 47¼ McCauley W H b 115 3.00e 70-23 Piper Over1103½RaisedProperly1112¼IAin'tLying1151½ Drifted out 9
26Jun87- 5Mth fst 6f :22⅕ :45⅖ 1:11⅘ ⒻClm 20500 8 2 13 12 21 35 Anderson A M7 b 109 3.70 76-21 Flora Bay 115hd Piper Over 1165 Princess Jig 1093 Faltered 8
16Jun87- 7Mth fst 6f :22⅕ :45 1:11⅕ ⒻClm 22500 1 3 2hd 21 42¾ 65¼ McCauley W H b 113 3.60 79-17 Camp Follower 1102½ Parisian Pleasure1131½FloraBay112nk Tired 8
6Jun87- 3Mth fst 6f :23 :46⅖ 1:12⅘ ⒻClm 20000 7 2 2hd 1hd 1hd 31½ Madrid A Jr b 115 2.20 76-17 LonelyProspector1151Nust'sPlsur108½PrincssJig115nk Weakened 8
11Mar87- 7Aqu fst 6f :22 :45⅗ 1:11⅗ ⒻAlw 26000 5 8 53 32½ 37½ 813¾ Santos J A b 116 16.00 69-25 Monogram 1198¾ Miss Natchez 1161 Some Home 1211 Tired 12
2Mar87- 9Aqu gd 6f [•]:22⅘ :45⅗ 1:11⅕ ⒻClm 25000 4 1 1½ 12½ 13½ 14½ Antley C W b 116 4.70 88-15 Princess Jig 1164½ Classi Vogue 1116½ Bird Key 1162 Driving 11
2Feb87- 5Aqu sly 170 [•]:47⅗ 1:13⅗ 1:45⅗ ⒻClm 30000 5 1 11½ 12 23 415¼ Antley C W b 112 6.60 57-24 WltzingMiss11412½ClssyCircl116nkSunny'sDplomt1112½ Weakened 10
10Jan87- 2Aqu gd 6f [•]:23 :46⅕ 1:12⅘ ⒻClm 25000 4 3 11½ 13½ 13½ 2½ Antley C W b 116 3.40 79-10 Speedy Holly 116½ Princess Jig 1165½ Apple Danish1111 Game try 9
3Jan87- 2Aqu sly 6f [•]:22⅗ :46⅕ 1:12⅖ ⒻClm 30000 6 2 2hd 2½ 47½ 612½ Antley C W b 113 10.60 69-16 Degree in Reality 1162¾ Classi Vogue 1112½ Salsera 1115 Tired 9
LATEST WORKOUTS Jly 6 Mth 3f fst :36 bg Jun 2 Mth 4f fst :50⅕ b

D.

Tyson's Bambi B. f. 3, by Real Emperor—Mac's Marauuer, by Miles Tyson
$12,500 Br.—Equinvest Breeding Ltd Partnershp (Md) 115
Own.—Baker D Tr.—Baldwin Alexander D
Lifetime 12 2 5 3 $16,902 — 1987 7 2 2 1 $10,728 — 1986 5 M 3 2 $6,174
Entered 29Jly87- 6 ATL

12Jly87- 7Pim fst 6f :23⅕ :46⅗ 1:13 ⒻClm 11500 6 6 43½ 33 34½ 22 Saumell L 117 17.30 79-20 SharpWings1142Tyson'sBambi117½Georgia'sEmbrace1091 Gamely 9
22Jun87- 2Mth fst 6f :22⅗ :46 1:12⅕ ⒻClm 12500 5 6 73½ 76½ 55 44¼ Daniels E 118 9.30 75-18 Dear Mary 1153 Top This One 115nk Larry's Rose 1151 Mild rally 9
7Jun87- 3Del fst 6f :22⅘ :46 1:11⅖ 3+ⒻClm 11000 7 1 4nk 11 1½ 1nk Lizarzaburu P M 106 17.20 84-19 Tyson's Bambi 106nk Dance for Harry1161½Fionnghal1192 Driving 7
6May87- 8Del fst 6f :22⅖ :46⅖ 1:13⅕ 3+ⒻClm 10000 2 4 41¾ 23½ 25 26½ Lizarzaburu P M 109 4.50 68-33 Raleigh'sCape1196½Tyson'sBambi109noWellPadded116nk Held 2nd 6
25Apr87- 7Del my 6f :22⅘ :47⅕ 1:12⅗ 3+ⒻClm 12500 7 3 42¾ 42½ 35 39½ Lizarzaburu P M 107 8.70 68-25 Miss Arch 1084 Well Padded 1165½ Tyson's Bambi 1072 Rallied 8
29Mar87- 8Tam sly 7f :22⅘ :47⅖ 1:28⅕ ⒻAlw 5300 6 4 33½ 32½ 46½ 614¼ Baxis J 122 6.40 65-26 My Girl Val 10911 Tributex 116nk Cast of Angels 115no Tired 8
8Mar87- 7Tam gd 6f :23⅖ :48 1:15⅖ ⒻMd Sp Wt 1 5 41¾ 41½ 2hd 1½ Baxis J 118 3.80 68-29 Tyson'sBmbi118½PieceOfDeAction111noRollUpthRug1181 Driving 12
24Oct86- 4Pha fst 1 :49⅕ 1:16⅕ 1:43 ⒻMd 12500 4 2 1½ 12 2½ 24 Leasure W P 118 *2.30 55-26 Dustyou 1184 Tyson's Bambi 118nk Prima Star 1163 Drifted in 11
10Oct86- 3Pen fst 6f :22⅖ :46⅕ 1:13 ⒻMd Sp Wt 2 6 57¼ 48 49 35¾ Iliescu A 116 *1.60 73-19 Lunar Times 1165 Proo Roo 116¾ Tyson's Bambi 1162½ Mild rally 8
20Sep86- 3Del fst 5f :22⅗ :46⅖ :58⅘ ⒻMd Sp Wt 4 3 52¼ 34 35 312½ Gilpin V A 118 4.10 79-20 Leslie'sProspct11812AdvncdStt118½Tyson'sBmbi1181 Evenly late 12

E.

Ocali Gal B. f. 3, by Raise A Bid—Sweet Janice, by City Line Lifetime 1987 7 1 1 0 $8,145
$12,500 Br.—Fernung J (Fla) 118 13 2 3 0 1986 6 1 2 0 $10,400
Own.—MacCornack J Tr.—Heimer Dennis $18,545
21Jly87- 2Mth fst 6f :22 :46⅘ 1:14 ⒻClm 10000 6 2 43¾ 22½ 2hd 1nk Krone J A b 115 2.60 70-18 Ocali Gal 115nk Jovanka 110³ Silk Jolie 108nk Driving 8
22Jun87- 2Mth fst 6f :22⅘ :46 1:12⅕ ⒻClm 12500 4 5 4¾ 44 44½ 57¼ McCauley W H b 115 7.10 72-18 Dear Mary 115³ Top This One 115nk Larry'sRose115¹ Lacked a bid 9
29Apr87- 6GS fst 6f :22⅕ :46 1:12 3+ⒻClm 18000 4 2 43 33½ 54½ 511¼ Wilson R b 116 4.70 71-26 Flying Hoofbeats 1095½PeriodPiece114nkSugarNCream114½ Tired 7
16Apr87- 6GS gd 6f :22⅘ :46⅖ 1:12 ⒻClm 45000 7 1 43 45 57½ 58¾ Wilson R b 114 8.90 73-25 StreetWalking1125½SuperAppeling116nkTheAngeimker112¹ Tired 7
17Mar87- 5GS fst 6f :23 :48 1:14⅘ ⒻAlw 10500 2 4 53¾ 55¾ 510 512½ Wilson R b 116 *1.10 55-31 Anna's Bambi 1161½ Tantaruler 1161¾ Ma Burn 116nk no menace 6
1Feb87- 3Pha fst 170 :46⅘ 1:11⅕ 1:41⅕ ⒻAlw 11500 2 1 2hd 34 45 512½ Wilson R b 116 4.00 76-09 SomeKindGood115¹ClutchPerformnc115noSntntiously1155½ Tired 7
14Jan87- 3Pha fst 6f :22 :46⅗ 1:14⅕ ⒻAlw 10500 4 4 66¼ 56 24 26 Vigliotti M J b 114 *1.20 64-33 Spoil Your Dinner 114⁶ Ocali Gal 114⁵ Great Act 120⁸ 2nd best 6
28Dec86- 6Pha fst 6f :22⅖ :46⅗ 1:13⅖ ⒻAlw 10500 5 2 66 66 44½ 21¼ Vigliotti M J b 114 8.50 73-28 First Noel 1141¼OcaliGal114¹BroadwayMiriam114⁴ Closed outside 9
6Sep86- 9Crc fst 7f :23⅗ :48 1:26⅖ ⒻGardenia 1 5 2hd 69 726 729½ Breen R b 113 39.80 54-20 Blues Court 118⁴ Mar Mar 1181½ Jill OfAllTrades112no Early foot 7
24Aug86- 8Crc fst 6f :22⅖ :46 1:13⅕ ⒻⓇDesertVixen 1 8 84 914 915 811 Underwood S b 116 8.70 74-16 MyNichole116noBeauLoveFlowers1161½FoolishAppeal116² Outrun 11
LATEST WORKOUTS ●Jly 13 Mth 3f fst :35⅕ h Jun 15 Mth 4f fst :48 h Jun 8 Mth 3f fst :36⅕ b

F.

Daremightythings B. f. 3, by Baldski—Gold Purse, by Mr Prospector Lifetime 1987 3 1 1 0 $4,600
$12,500 Br.—Hofmann Mr-Mrs P B (Fla) 118 17 1 2 1 1986 14 M 1 1 $3,445
Own.—Marousis Peter Tr.—Harvatt Charles R $8,045
20Jly87- 3Mth gd 1 :47⅖ 1:13⅗ 1:42⅖ ⒻClm c-7500 8 3 3nk 3½ 44 710½ St Leon G b 114 2.80 50-26 Fast Drive 107no Reflective Gal 112hd Dottie McGee 114⁵ Tired 8
9Jly87- 2Mth fst 6f :22 :45⅗ 1:12⅖ ⒻClm 7500 4 8 62¾ 45 43½ 2¾ Anderson A M⁵ b 113 8.00 77-21 Jovanka 113¾ Daremightythings 113¾ Fast Drive 110nk Gaining 10
1Jly87- 9Mth fst 6f :22⅕ :45⅘ 1:12⅘ 3+ⒻMd 10000 7 4 3nk 11 13 14½ Anderson A M⁷ b 109 16.30 76-15 Daremightythings1094½Sipalero1221½LeaveEmHi109nk Ridden out 11
5Dec86- 9Pha fst 6f :23⅖ :48⅕ 1:15 ⒻMd 10000 8 11 63 52¾ 44½ 58½ Ferrer J C b 118 4.90 57-28 EthrlScrt111nkB W Shortck1183½InJon'sEys118nk Wide, lckd rally 12
26Nov86- 4Pha sly 6f :22⅘ :47⅘ 1:14⅘ ⒻMd 12500 11 — — — 69½ 713½ Ferrer J C b 118 10.50 53-26 Jimmy'sDy1183¼AthninFlight1181½ⒹⒽSwtByndBy118 Fog, outrun 12
14Nov86- 5Pha fst 170 :47⅗ 1:14⅕ 1:46⅗ ⒻMd 12500 8 3 3½ 42 54½ 68½ Ferrer J C b 118 *1.90 56-20 Bambi's Sister 1131½ Pique Lady 116½ I'm For Deb 113¹ Tired 12
29Oct86- 2Pha fst 6f :22⅖ :46⅖ 1:13⅕ ⒻMd 16000 3 3 1hd 2hd 21½ 35 Ferrer J C b 118 7.40 70-18 De'sHony1181½SmrtCompny1183½Drmightythings1186½ Weakened 10
2Oct86- 3Pha my 6f :22⅕ :46⅖ 1:13⅖ ⒻMd 18000 5 4 44½ 57½ 713 819¾ Ferrer J C b 116 7.50 54-23 Southern Pass 1181½ Red Sindhi 118nk LeslieTheSnitch118⁶ Tired 8
25Sep86- 1Pha gd 1 :48⅗ 1:14⅗ 1:42⅖ ⒻMd 20000 8 4 32 43 59½ 712¾ Ferrer J C b 118 18.00 49-21 Kostmeplenty1161¼CpitlSpotlight1181½Queen'sCut118nk Steadied 11
28Aug86- 6Pha sly 6f :23 :47⅗ 1:14⅕ ⒻMd 20000 7 2 43¼ 55½ 611 613 Allen K K b 117 20.90 57-25 Flash Once 1173½ Red Sindhi 1151½ Incredible Pro 115² Fell back 9
LATEST WORKOUTS Jun 27 Mth 5f sly 1:01⅖ h Jun 22 Mth 5f fst 1:02 b Jun 16 Mth 4f fst :50 b Jun 10 Mth 4f fst :50⅖ b

G.

Larry's Rose B. f. 3, by Lawrentian—Leebs Irish Rose, by Noble Jay Lifetime 1987 5 1 0 2 $5,525
$12,500 Br.—Hesse Charles J III (NJ) 115 6 1 0 2 1986 1 M 0 0
Own.—Char-Mari Stable Tr.—Gross George F $5,525
23Jly87- 5Mth fst 6f :22⅖ :45⅗ 1:12⅖ ⒻClm 16000 5 2 1½ 11 2hd 35¼ Vigliotti M J 115 11.60 73-24 DarlinDarlene1151¼RaisedProperly113⁴Lrry'sRose115½ Weakened 7
14Jly87- 2Mth fst 6f :22 :45⅖ 1:12⅗ ⒻClm 16000 8 2 51¼ 31 42 68¾ Vigliotti M J 118 13.70 68-23 Piper Over 1103½ Raised Properly 1112¾ I Ain't Lying 1151½ Tired 9
22Jun87- 2Mth fst 6f :22⅘ :46 1:12⅕ ⒻClm 12500 8 3 1½ 11 2hd 33¼ Vigliotti M J 115 5.60 76-18 Dear Mary 115³ Top This One 115nk Larry's Rose 115¹ Weakened 9
10Jun87- 7Mth fst 6f :22⅘ :46⅕ 1:12⅘ 3+ⒻⓈAlw 17500 6 2 1hd 21 53½ 811½ Vigliotti M J 109 29.10 64-23 LittieCutes116nkⒹWltzingEmpress111nkWoodlndMnor114¾ Tired 9
4Jun87- 9Mth fst 6f :22⅘ :45⅗ 1:13 3+ⒻMd 12500 6 3 12½ 15 15 11½ Vigliotti M J 115 6.50 75-19 Larry's Rose 1151½ Houston Gold 108⁵ Jobeck 113¹ Driving 11
29Sep86- 1Med fst 6f :22⅘ :46⅖ 1:12⅘ ⒻMd 20000 3 7 35 26 210 617 Sousonis S 113 27.90 61-21 Lamsa 117¹² Facha 113¹ Fast Drive 117¹ Tired 10
LATEST WORKOUTS Jun 2 Mth 4f fst :50 bg

H.

Dreampuff Ch. f. 3, by Hurok—Fluff Stuff, by Groshawk Lifetime 1986 10 1 1 3 $9,220
$12,500 Br.—Brady J W (Ky) 115 10 1 1 3
Own.—J C J Racing Stable Tr.—DeStefano John M Jr $9,220
24Nov86- 7Med my 6f :22⅘ :46⅖ 1:12⅕ ⒻClm 20000 3 9 913 916 714 713½ Santagata N b 112 26.60 67-27 Leslie The Snitch 111⁷ Porter's Gal 113² Dear Mary 115¹ Outrun 9
12Nov86- 7Med gd 6f :23⅕ :46⅗ 1:11⅘ ⒻClm 18000 7 7 712 713 614 514 Santagata N b 114 10.30 69-21 Fred Moon 118⁸ Bingo B. 1142½ Classy Circle 107½ Outrun 7
1Nov86-11Med fst 6f :22⅘ :46⅘ 1:13⅗ ⒻClm 22000 9 7 98¼ 810 87¾ 76¾ McCauley W H b 115 4.30 67-21 Janie Frisky 1152¼ Orders To Land 113¾ Dear Mary 117no Outrun 10
30Oct86- 8Med sly 1 :48 1:12⅗ 1:38⅘ ⒻAlw 15000 1 8 87¼ 87½ 713 717¼ Terry J b 113 21.90 64-20 Lovelier 120⁶ Spartan Fables 120no WoodlandManor1204½ Outrun 8
24Sep86- 2Med fst 6f :23⅖ :47 1:13⅗ ⒻClm c-22000 6 8 85¼ 75¾ 46 32¼ Terry J b 116 2.30 72-19 Personal Problem 114nk Janie Frisky 114²Dreampuff116nk Rallied 9
13Sep86- 3Pha fst 6f :22⅘ :46⅘ 1:12⅘ ⒻClm 25000 9 8 75¼ 53½ 34 31 Wilson R b 114 6.00 76-20 Dork's Ellen 112½ Nancy's Glory 109½Dreampuff1141¼ Fin. gamely 9
4Sep86- 3Pha fst 1 :48⅘ 1:13⅗ 1:40⅕ ⒻMd 20000 3 3 35 1hd 1½ 1nk Lloyd J S b 117 *2.00 73-20 Dreampuff 117nkQueen'sCut1172¾FancysSweetTreat1156½ Driving 7
29Aug86- 6Pha fst 6f :22⅖ :46⅗ 1:12⅘ ⒻMd 32000 4 5 47 35 37 45½ Ferrer J C b 117 *1.50 71-24 Dundoll 117nk Combative 117⁵ Blow a Kiss 110nk threat 6
20Aug86- 4Pha fst 6f :22⅘ :46⅘ 1:13⅖ ⒻMd 25000 10 9 63¾ 43½ 32 3¾ Ferrer J C b 117 7.50 73-24 Scarlett Miss 117noPetunia'sPrincess115¾Dreampuff1172½ Rallied 11
9Aug86-10Pha fst 6f :23 :47⅘ 1:15⅕ ⒻMd 20000 8 4 76¾ 46½ 32½ 23½ Lloyd J S b 117 3.30 61-26 Momma Kizzie 1173½ Dreampuff 1173½ Dustyou 117hd Rallied 9
LATEST WORKOUTS Jly 17 Mth 6f fst 1:17 bg Jly 10 Mth 5f fst 1:00⅗ h Jly 4 Mth 5f fst 1:04⅕ b ●Jun 27 Mth 4f sly :48 h

26.

2nd Santa Anita

6 FURLONGS. (1.07⅗) CLAIMING. Purse $26,000. 4-year-olds and upward. Weight, 122 lbs. Non-winners of two races since December 25 allowed 3 lbs.; of a race sinne February 1, 5 lbs.; since December 25, 7 lbs. Claiming price $40,000; if for $35,000 allowed 2 lbs. (Races when entered for $32,000 or less not considered.)

A.

Vari Beau 0-0 Ch. c. 4, by Beau's Eagle—Villa V, by Olympiad King
CORDERO A JR Br.—Relatively & Varjun Stables (Cal) 1987 5 1 0 0 $10,750
115 Tr.—Manzi Joseph $35,000 99 1986 11 M 3 2 $13,075
Own.—Dillon & Story Stable Lifetime 16 1 3 2 $23,825
22Mar87-5SA 6½f :21⁴ :45² 1:17⁴gd 33 135 87½ 87 64½ 64¾ Patton D B⁸ Aw29000 76-23 City View, Starshield, MidnightIce 10
4Mar87-5SA 1⅛ :45³ 1:10¹ 1:43²ft 30 117 2½ 2² 98¼ 1114¼ Vlenzuel P A¹⁰ Aw30000 70-16 RidgeReview, Rafel'sDncer, Athlone 12

[illegible]—Bumped hard start
14Feb87-[illegible] 6½f :22 :45^{1} 1:17^{4}sy 22 116 6^{7} 6^{6} 4^{2} 4^{3} Sibille R^{4} Aw26000 78-17 BrilliantLeder,JumpingDoctor,Breu 9
1Feb87-2SA 6½f :21^{3} :44^{1} 1:16^{3}ft 33 117 11$^{9\frac{3}{4}}$11^{11}11^{16}10^{14} Douglas R R^{5} 40000 73-16 Romaxe,LuckyMasadado,Crcksmn 12
1Feb87—Broke slowly
23Jan87-6SA 6f :22 :45^{3} 1:11^{1}ft 5¾ 117 6$^{1\frac{1}{2}}$ 3$^{1\frac{1}{2}}$ 1^{1} 1^{4} Douglas R R^{1} M45000 82-22 Vari Beau, Hapigrin, PrivateEagle 12
23Jan87—Bumped start
21Dec86-6Hol 1$\frac{1}{16}$:47 1:12^{1} 1:45^{4}ft 14 119 7$^{4\frac{1}{4}}$ 4^{3} 3$^{1\frac{1}{2}}$ 6$^{3\frac{1}{2}}$ Vergara O^{7} M32000 76-15 StormyWorld,ZambeziPass,Clpper 12
21Dec86—Steadied, altered path 1/2
18Dec86-4Hol 6f :22^{3} :46^{3} 1:11^{1}ft *3½ 120 6$^{4\frac{3}{4}}$ 5^{3} 2^{3} 2^{5} Vergara O^{1} [S]M32000 82-17 GetAlongPaisno,VriBeu,PinoPlyer 11
10Dec86-2Hol 6f :22^{2} :46^{2} 1:11^{3}ft 16 120 6$^{3\frac{3}{4}}$ 6$^{4\frac{3}{4}}$ 4^{3} 2^{5} Vergara O^{9} [S]M32000 80-20 OutCross,VariBeau,GetAlongPisno 12
22Nov86-2Hol 6f :22 :45^{3} 1:11 ft 5 120 9$^{7\frac{3}{4}}$ 9^{10} 9$^{9\frac{3}{4}}$ 7$^{6\frac{3}{4}}$ Douglas R R^{8} M32000 81-13 Quardolite, Hapigrin,StormyWorld 12
22Nov86—Wide in stretch
12Nov86-6Hol 6f :22^{2} :46^{2} 1:11^{1}ft 5½ 120 5$^{4\frac{1}{2}}$ 4$^{3\frac{1}{2}}$ 3$^{2\frac{1}{2}}$ 2$^{5\frac{1}{2}}$ Douglas R R^{1} M32000 81-15 ForbesReply,VariBeau,SpringStreet 6
Mar 18 SA 5f ft 1:00 h Mar 13 SA 4f ft :49^{1} h Feb 28 SA 5f ft :59^{1} h Feb 23 SA 7f ft 1:27 h

B.

Superb Moment

B. g. 4, by Timeless Moment—Distant Rose, by Distant Day
SIBILLE R 115 Br.—Walden & Benjamin III (Ky) 1987 5 2 1 1 $32,675
Tr.—Harper David B $40,000 1986 7 3 1 1 $33,300
Own.—Select RacingStable(Lessee) Lifetime 12 5 2 2 $65,975
14Mar87-4SA 6½f :21^{4} :44^{2} 1:15^{3}ft 5½ 116 2$^{1\frac{1}{2}}$ 1^{hd} 2^{hd} 2$^{1\frac{3}{4}}$ Sibille R 3 40000 90-16 Crcksmn,SuperbMoment,WstBoyII 8
1Mar87-1SA 6½f :21^{4} :44^{2} 1:16^{2}ft 5 118 4^{4} 3^{2} 2$^{1\frac{1}{2}}$ 1$^{1\frac{1}{2}}$ Sibille R 7 32000 88-15 SprbMomnt,DshonorblGst,Dnsprt 12
21Feb87-2SA 6f :21^{4} :44^{4} 1:09^{4}ft 5¾ 115 6$^{3\frac{1}{2}}$ 6$^{3\frac{1}{2}}$ 5^{4} 5$^{6\frac{1}{2}}$ Sibille R 1 40000 82-14 Crcksmn,LuckyMsddo,ElPrsdntUno 9
24Jan87-2SA 6f :21^{3} :45 1:10^{3}ft 4 115 3$^{1\frac{1}{2}}$ 2$^{1\frac{1}{2}}$ 2$^{1\frac{1}{2}}$ 1$^{1\frac{1}{2}}$ Sibille R 9 32000 85-18 SuperbMoment,Bizeboy,FletAlbrt 10
18Jan87-1SA 7f :22^{1} :45^{1} 1:24^{3}ft 7½ 117 1$^{1\frac{1}{2}}$ 1^{hd} 1$^{1\frac{1}{2}}$ 3$^{1\frac{1}{2}}$ Black C A 6 25000 76-19 Bizeboy, Trento, Superb Moment 12
8Nov86-4Hol 6f :22 :45^{3} 1:10^{4}ft *2 119 3^{1} 2$^{1\frac{1}{2}}$ 1^{3} 1^{3} Sibille R [illegible] c25000 89-13 SprbMmnt,GrdnsCmmnd,FrrBlJns 11
8Nov86—Crowded, steadied near 1/4
5Oct86-3SA 6f :21^{2} :44^{1} 1:10^{2}ft *2½ 116 4$^{1\frac{1}{2}}$ 3$^{1\frac{1}{2}}$ 3^{nk} 1$^{2\frac{1}{2}}$ Sibille R 2 32000 86-15 SprbMomnt,HmngAngl,EghtyBlwZr 9
5Oct86—Broke slowly; bumped at 1/8
15Aug86-3Dmr 6f :21^{4} :45^{2} 1:09^{3}ft 5½ 116 5^{3} 2^{hd} 1$^{1\frac{1}{2}}$ 2$^{2\frac{1}{2}}$ Sibille R 10 40000 87-12 Frcoz,SprbMomnt,Mybrry'sMdnss 12
15Aug86—Wide 3/8 turn
25Jly86-3Dmr 6½f :22^{1} :45^{2} 1:17 ft 2½ 116 1$^{1\frac{1}{2}}$ 1$^{1\frac{1}{2}}$ 3^{nk} 3^{nk} Solis A 6 40000 87-18 TrintyHll,WldPursut,SuprbMomnt 12
29Jun86-7Hol 7f :21^{2} :44^{2} 1:21^{4}ft 23 111 1^{3} 1$^{1\frac{1}{2}}$ 8^{8} 8$^{17\frac{1}{2}}$ Solis A 1 Aw19000 78-10 Slyly Gifted, In Toto, Noticiero 8
Mar 23 SA 4f ft :49^{4} h ●Mar 9 SA 3f ft :35^{1} h Feb 27 SA 3f ft :36^{1} h Feb 17 SA 4f ft :52^{1} h

C.

Doonsport

Dk. b. or br. c. 4, by Matsadoon—Generous Portion, by California Kid
PINCAY L JR 115 Br.—Quality Broodmares (Cal) 1987 5 1 2 2 $24,200
Tr.—Moreno Henry $40,000 1986 11 1 1 2 $19,200
Own.—Finley J L Lifetime 17 3 3 4 $52,200
20Mar87-3SA 6f :21^{2} :44^{3} 1:09^{3}ft 6½ 117 8^{5} 8$^{4\frac{1}{2}}$ 4^{2} 3$^{1\frac{1}{2}}$ Pincay L Jr 2 32000 89-17 ElPrsdntUno,DshonorblGst,Donsprt 9
20Mar87—Steadied into drive
1Mar87-1SA 6½f :21^{4} :44^{2} 1:16^{2}ft *3 117 5$^{4\frac{1}{2}}$ 4$^{3\frac{1}{2}}$ 4$^{2\frac{1}{2}}$ 3$^{1\frac{1}{4}}$ Pincay L Jr 4 32000 87-15 SprbMomnt,DshonorblGst,Dnsprt 12
1Mar87—Rough trip
8Feb87-2SA 6½f :21^{3} :44^{1} 1:15^{3}ft 2¾ 117 7$^{5\frac{3}{4}}$ 8$^{6\frac{1}{2}}$ 4^{8} 2^{4} Pincay L Jr 6 32000 88-14 Bizeboy, Doonsport, MountBidder 11
8Feb87—Broke slowly
21Jan87-5SA 6½f :22^{1} :45^{1} 1:16^{3}ft *6-5 117 3$^{1\frac{1}{2}}$ 1$^{1\frac{1}{2}}$ 1$^{2\frac{1}{2}}$ 1$^{2\frac{1}{2}}$ Pincay L Jr 2 20000 87-19 Doonsport, NativeCaptive,Grenoble 9
7Jan87-9SA 1 :47^{2} 1:12 1:38 m *2½ 118 3^{2} 2$^{2\frac{1}{2}}$ 2^{3} 2$^{4\frac{1}{2}}$ Pincay L Jr 7 25000 73-21 Danchai, Doonsport, ShowerDecree 9
7Jan87—Bumped hard start
27Dec86-2SA 6½f :21^{4} :44^{4} 1:16^{4}ft 7 117 6$^{7\frac{1}{2}}$ 4$^{6\frac{1}{2}}$ 4$^{3\frac{1}{2}}$ 1$^{1\frac{1}{2}}$ Pincay L Jr 6 25000 86-19 Doonsport, BlueIce,ExaltedBubble 10
27Dec86—Broke slowly; wide into stretch
13Dec86-3Hol 7f :22^{2} :45^{2} 1:23^{2}ft 6 117 6$^{4\frac{1}{2}}$ 5$^{4\frac{1}{2}}$ 5$^{4\frac{1}{2}}$ 7^{3} Pincay L Jr 7 [S] 25000 84-09 Gregson,ManyRoads,ShowerDecree 9
13Dec86—Bumped start
13Nov86-9Hol 1 :45^{3} 1:10^{1} 1:35^{3}ft 53 114 8$^{5\frac{1}{2}}$ 6$^{7\frac{1}{2}}$ 6^{12} 6$^{14\frac{1}{2}}$ Solis A 6 45000 70-23 MischievousMtt,CojkMn,BoldDecre 9
23Oct86-7SA 1 :45 1:10^{4} 1:38 ft 4 116 9^{11} 9$^{7\frac{1}{2}}$10$^{5\frac{3}{4}}$10$^{11\frac{3}{4}}$ McHargue D G 1 50000 66-20 BoldDecree,TrojnTrick,Bruli'sAnte 10
23Oct86—Rank 7/8
9Oct86-7SA 6f :21^{3} :44^{3} 1:11^{1}ft 14 116 10$^{9\frac{1}{2}}$10$^{8\frac{1}{2}}$ 7$^{6\frac{3}{4}}$ 7$^{3\frac{1}{2}}$ McHrgue DG 6 Aw25000 78-21 Salt Dome, Incluso,Harper'sRidge 10
Mar 26 SA 4f ft :48^{3} h Mar 13 SA 5f ft 1:03 h Mar 8 SA 5f gd 1:01^{3} h Feb 14 SA tr.t 4f m :53 h

D.

Juntura

Dk. b. or br. g. 7, by Bold Forbes—Joawin, by Donut King
PEDROZA M A 115 Br.—Hancock III & Peters (Ky) 1987 4 0 0 0 $625
Tr.—Harper David B $40,000 1986 15 5 2 3 $89,175
Own.—Tuscany Farms (Lessee) Lifetime 56 8 10 9 $198,775 Turf 9 0 0 2 $12,600
14Mar87-4SA 6½f :21^{4} :44^{2} 1:15^{3}ft 20 116 7$^{5\frac{3}{4}}$ 6$^{6\frac{1}{2}}$ 5$^{7\frac{1}{2}}$ 5$^{7\frac{1}{4}}$ Pedroza M A^{6} 40000 85-16 Crcksmn,SuperbMoment,WstBoyII 8
1Mar87-1SA 6½f :21^{4} :44^{2} 1:16^{2}ft 19 117 11^{11}10^{8} 7$^{6\frac{1}{2}}$ 7^{6} Kaenel J L^{5} 32000 82-15 SprbMomnt,DshonorblGst,Dnsprt 12
21Feb87-9SA 1 :46 1:10^{1} 1:35^{4}ft 8¾ 116 9$^{8\frac{1}{4}}$ 9$^{8\frac{3}{4}}$ 8$^{8\frac{3}{4}}$ 7$^{8\frac{3}{4}}$ Meza R Q^{7} 40000 80-14 MoniBddr,GoodThghtWlly,BldDcr 10
1Feb87-2SA 6½f :21^{3} :44^{1} 1:16^{3}ft 8 116 12^{11}10^{10} 9^{11} 8^{7} Sibille R^{1} 40000 80-16 Romaxe,LuckyMasadado,Crcksmn 12
31Dec86-5SA 6½f :22 :45^{3} 1:17^{2}ft *8-5 116 12^{12} 9$^{7\frac{1}{2}}$ 7$^{4\frac{1}{2}}$ 4$^{2\frac{1}{2}}$ Stevens G L^{1} c40000 81-20 Watch'n Win, Angle Arc, Idol 12
31Dec86—Checked late

14Dec86-9Hol 1 Ⓣ:46 21:11 11:36 2fm 3¼ 116 66½ 63½ 52¾ 33½ Stevens G L6 50000 81-11 LordOfTheWind,Hrdknockin,Juntur 8
14Dec86—Wide 3/8
6Dec86-3Hol 6f :22 4 :46 1:10 4gd 3-2 117 47 45½ 33½ 2½ Stevens G L1 50000 88-16 Nordicus, Juntura,KingOfCalifornia 4
22Nov86-7Hol 7f :22 :45 1 1:22 2ft 3 116 814 79½ 45 21¼ Stevens G L8 50000 91-13 Cracksman, Juntura, Infantryman 8
22Nov86—Wide backstretch
11Nov86-3Hol 6f :22 1 :45 4 1:10 4ft 3¾ 116 62¾ 55 31½ 11½ Stevens G L3 32000 89-20 Juntura, King OfCalifornia,Bizeboy 6
4May86-9Hol 1 :45 3 1:10 3 1:36 2ft 6½ 116 911 68¾ 37½ 38½ Solis A6 50000 72-18 Silver Hero, Ono Gummo, Juntura 9
Mar 23 SA 3f ft :36 3 h Mar 9 SA 3f ft :36 2 h Feb 27 SA 3f ft :37 3 h Feb 18 SA 4f ft :51 1 h

E.

Dishonorable Guest B. g. 4, by Grenfall—Table Flirt, by Round Table
MEZA R Q 4 + Br.—Wygod M J (Ky) 1987 5 0 2 0 $11,675
115 Tr.—Soto Herbert Jr $40,000 1986 3 0 0 1 $2,850
Own.—Konnichiwa Stable & Urrea Lifetime 10 2 2 1 $35,425 Turf 1 0 0 0

20Mar87-3SA 6f :21 2 :44 3 1:09 3ft 7¾ 115 61½ 31½ 21½ 2nk Meza R Q 1 c32000 90-17 ElPrsdntUno,DshonorblGst,Donsprt 9
1Mar87-1SA 6½f :21 4 :44 2 1:16 2ft 8¾ 114 21½ 2½ 1½ 2½ Meza R Q 11 28000 87-15 SprbMomnt,DshonorblGst,Dnsprt 12
1Mar87—Lugged in stretch
8Feb87-2SA 6½f :21 3 :44 1 1:15 3ft 4¾ 115 85¾ 75½ 710 511¼ Meza R Q9 32000 81-14 Bizeboy, Doonsport, MountBidder 11
8Feb87—Rough trip
1Feb87-2SA 6½f :21 3 :44 1 1:16 3ft 5¾ 115 42¼ 43½ 44½ 63½ Meza R Q7 40000 84-16 Romaxe,LuckyMasadado,Crcksmn 12
17Jan87-2SA 6f :21 4 :45 1:10 3ft 5¾ 114 53 54 44½ 45½ Meza R Q6 40000 79-18 Ondarty, Romaxe, Rivets Factor 11
23Nov86-7Hol 6f :22 1 :45 1:09 4ft 4¼ 116 52½ 44½ 42½ 34 Meza R Q4 50000 90-12 BolgerMgic,Vrbotn,DishonorblGust 7
23Nov86—Broke in, bumped; crowded 1/2 to 1/4, wide stretch
27Feb86-8SA a6½f Ⓣ:22 :45 21:16 1fm 6½ 118 42 52 63¾ 64¼ Pincay L Jr9 Aw40000 74-22 RomnMgestrite,MoorgteMn,Delpr 10
27Feb86—Steadied at 3/16
29Jan86-8SA 1⅛:46 2 1:11 1:43 ft 21 117 53¾ 42½ 87¼ 810¾ PincyLJr3 [S]Sta Ctlna 75-15 Ferdinand,VrietyRod,GrndAllegince 8
29Jan86—Fanned wide into stretch
27Dec85-5SA 6½f :22 2 :45 1 1:16 2ft 3¾ 115 2hd 2hd 1hd 11 Meza R Q7 Aw24000 88-16 DishonorblGust,JttingHom,BoldDcr 8
27Dec85—Bumped at start
11Dec85-5Hol 6f :22 1 :46 1 1:11 4ft 5 118 11½ 12 14 12¾ Meza R Q4 M50000 85-19 DshnrblGst,Agg'sLlRdg,MdstKng 10
Mar 11 SA 4f ft :48 1 h Feb 26 SA 5f gd :59 3 h Feb 18 SA 4f ft :48 2 h

F.

Eighty Below Zero Ch. c. 4, by It's Freezing—Alps, by Pavot
MCHARGUE D G 8-N Br.—Stewart D S Jr (Ky) 1987 2 1 0 0 $14,300
117 Tr.—Mayberry Brian A $40,000 1986 11 1 1 3 $19,150
Own.—Siegel M Lifetime 13 2 1 3 $33,450 Turf 2 0 0 0

8Feb87-5SA a6½f Ⓣ:21 1 :43 41:14 4fm 7½ 117 1½ 1hd 31½ 76½ McHrgueDG 2 Aw30000 78-09 Hard Round, Irish Stories,Putting 12
15Jan87-3SA 6f :21 2 :44 1 1:11 ft 9 116 11½ 12 14 13 McHrgueDG 4 Aw26000 83-25 EightyBelowZero,Athlone,FstRomo 8
8Nov86-4Hol 6f :22 :45 3 1:10 4ft 16 116 1½ 1½ 23 46 Pedroza M A 5 25000 83-13 SprbMmnt,GrdnsCmmnd,FrrBlJns 11
8Nov86—Steadied 3/16
26Oct86-1SA 6f :21 3 :45 1:11 ft 11 116 43 53 116¾109¼ Pedroza M A 5 32000 74-16 Sebucan, End Play, Fleet Albert 12
26Oct86—Bumped, steadied entering stretch
5Oct86-3SA 6f :21 2 :44 1 1:10 2ft 12 116 1½ 1½ 1hd 32½ Pedroza M A 3 32000 83-15 SprbMomnt,HmngAngl,EghtyBlwZr 9
5Oct86—Bumped twice 1/8
21Sep86-9Pom 6f :21 4 :45 1:11 1ft 10 114 72¾ 87½ 811 814½ Pedroza M A 5 57500 80-07 TimShr,Hrpr'sRidg,WhipUpThTmpo 8
21Sep86—Wide first turn
8Sep86-3Dmr 6f :21 4 :45 1:09 ft 9½ 116 2hd 3½ 712 911½ Pedroza M A 4 62500 81-14 Notoriety,UrbnCowboy,BolgerMgic 9
24Aug86-7Dmr 6½f :22 :44 4 1:15 3ft 11 114 32½ 35½ 717 721¾ Pedroza MA 1 Aw21000 72-12 Our Lordship,HisRoyalty,Doonsport 8
3Aug86-2Dmr 6f :21 4 :45 1:09 3ft 5½ 119 1½ 13 12 21½ Pedroza M A9 50000 88-10 UrbnCowby,EghtyBlwZr,TmthyDy 10
3Aug86—Broke in, bumped
4Jly86-9Hol 1⅛ Ⓣ:45 41:10 1:41 3fm 35 116 42½ 32 107¾109½ Soto S B 2 Aw23000 86 — Full Charm, Gaelic Knight, Jota 12
Mar 17 SA 5f ft 1:00 3 h Feb 28 SA 6f ft 1:13 1 h

G.

Bizeboy 7-0 Dk. b. or br. h. 5, by Distant Land—Another Lulu, by Majestic Prince
CASTANON A L Br.—Arnold M L (Cal) 1987 5 2 1 0 $28,625
115 Tr.—Shulman Sanford $40,000 1986 15 3 3 4 $53,250
Own.—Charles & ClearValleyStables Lifetime 29 6 4 6 $92,325

20Mar87-3SA 6f :21 2 :44 3 1:09 3ft *1 119 5½ 62 77½ 919½ Stevens G L 9 c32000 70-17 ElPrsdntUno,DshonorblGst,Donsprt 9
20Mar87—Wide
21Feb87-2SA 6f :21 4 :44 4 1:09 4ft *2 116 31½ 41½ 42 45½ Stevens G L 4 40000 84-14 Crcksmn,LuckyMsddo,ElPrsdntUno 5
8Feb87-2SA 6½f :21 3 :44 1 1:15 3ft *2¾ 116 11 11½ 13½ 14 Stevens G L 7 32000 92-14 Bizeboy, Doonsport, MountBidder 11
24Jan87-2SA 6f :21 3 :45 1:10 3ft 4¾ 116 11½ 11½ 11½ 21½ Meza R Q 1 32000 83-18 SuperbMoment,Bizeboy,FletAlbrt 10
18Jan87-1SA 7f :22 1 :45 1 1:24 3ft 4 118 41 31½ 2½ 1½ Cordero A Jr 8 25000 77-19 Bizeboy, Trento, Superb Moment 12
29Nov86-4Hol 7f :22 :45 2 1:22 3ft *6-5 116 11 11 13½ 16 Stevens G L 5 c20000 91-12 Bizeboy,NorthrnProvidr,Yukon'sStr 7
11Nov86-3Hol 6f :22 1 :45 4 1:10 4ft *8-5 117 1hd 2hd 2hd 33 Pincay L Jr 5 32000 86-20 Juntura, King OfCalifornia,Bizeboy 6
18Oct86-5SA 6f :21 4 :44 4 1:11 ft *1 116 1hd 1hd 12½ 2no ValenzuelaPA 8 c25000 83-20 Grenoble, Bizeboy, Calabonga 9
11Oct86-2SA 6f :21 2 :44 3 1:10 2ft 4 118 1hd 12 12½ 32½ Valenzuela P A 8 32000 84-17 Dr. Reality, Gray Pinstripe, Bizeboy 9
11Oct86—Veered in start
10Sep86-3Dmr 6f :22 :45 1:09 3ft *2¾ 121 1½ 2½ 66 610¾ ValenzuelPA 1 Aw24000 79-11 LstMotel,RollANturl,AmzingCourge 6
10Sep86—Broke out, bumped
Mar 16 SA 3f ft :36 3 h Feb 17 SA 4f ft :48 4 h

H.

Mischievous Matt

Dk. b. or br. c. 4, by Run of Luck—Classic Caper, by Pilot John
VALENZUELA P A 4-0 115 — Br.—Waller H E (Wash) — 1987 3 0 0 1 $6,200
Own.—Mevorach & Monroe — Tr.—Stute Melvin F — $40,000 — 1986 15 6 2 1 $67,010
Lifetime 22 6 3 2 $75,510

14Mar87-4SA	6½f	:214	:442	1:153ft	2	116	11½	3½	34	47¼	Valenzuela P A8	40000	85-16	Crcksmn,SuperbMoment,WstBoyII	8
25Jan87-2SA	6f	:213	:442	1:094ft	7	118	43	32½	34	32½	Valenzuela P A3	50000	86-18	Ondarty,AngleArc,MischievousMatt	6
25Jan87—Broke in, bumped															
17Jan87-2SA	6f	:214	:45	1:103ft	4	121	42	22½	23½	55¾	Baze G8	c40000	79-18	Ondarty, Romaxe, Rivets Factor	11
17Jan87—Bumped start															
17Dec86-8Hol	6f	:221	:454	1:111ft	*8-5	114	1hd	2hd	11½	1½	Baze G2	Aw22000	87-22	MschvosMtt,TommyThHwk,Notrty	8
26Nov86-5Hol	1	:454	1:102	1:353ft	*7-5	116	11	11½	2hd	22¼	Valenzuela P A6	62500	83-20	BrightTom,MischivousMtt,InhrntKl	8
13Nov86-9Hol	1	:453	1:101	1:353ft	3½	116	11	11½	13	11¼	Valenzuela P A2	50000	85-23	MischievousMtt,CojkMn,BoldDecre	9
31Oct86-6SA	6f	:212	:443	1:093ft	6½	116	32½	2½	1hd	14	Cordero A Jr8	50000	90-16	MischievousMtt,Jimed,RosesArRb	11
13Oct86-3SA	6f	:22	:453	1:11 ft	*9-5	114	52½	62¼	45½	35	Ortega L E5	c35000	78-19	Wtch'nWin,EndPly,MischievousMtt	6
3Oct86-3SA	6f	:212	:444	1:093ft	3¼	116	22½	21	12	13½	Ortega L E3	20000	90-17	MischievousMatt,PicoP.,TrinityHall	9
11Sep86-10Pom	6½f	:22	:46	1:172ft	11	116	3½	54	78½	88¾	Castanon A L7	25000	84-08	NtvForcst,LnsMnus,RnnngRmpnt	10

Mar 24 SA 5f ft 1:002 h — Mar 8 SA 4f gd :493 h — Feb 27 SA 5f ft :592 h — ●Feb 8 SA 5f ft :581 h

27.

8th Ellis Park

6 FURLONGS. (1.09) CLAIMING. Purse $6,800. Fillies and mares. 3-year-olds and upward. Weight, 3-year-olds, 114 lbs.; older, 121 lbs. Non-winners of a race since June 24 allowed 3 lbs.; a race since May 25, 5 lbs.; a race since March 25, 7 lbs. Claiming price $11,000; if for $10,000 allowed 3 lbs. (Races where entered for $8,250 or less not considered.)

A.

Caramel Flip

Gr. f. 3, by Flip Sal—Caramel Custard, by Accipiter
Br.—Bellefonte, Inc. (Ky) — 1987 8 2 1 0 $14,180
Own.—Akuma Stable — 111 — Tr.—Gothard Marvin L — $11,000 — 1986 10 M 1 0 $4,098
Lifetime 18 2 2 0 $18,278

17Jly87-5EIP	6f	:223	:461	1:122ft	*9-5	118	63¾	86¼	74¾	65¾	Tsuchiya K4	Ⓕ 10000	77-13	HrvstofHvn,GoldBngl,AirFinssWon	8
11Jly87-6EIP	7f	:223	:451	1:233ft	12	105	2½	21½	45	77¼	Tsuchiya K8	Ⓕ 13000	92-14	SuddenlyAmber,Brigatine,IronGold	8
11Jun87-1CD	6f	:214	:46	1:121ft	24	115	42½	53	2½	13	Tsuchiya K2	Ⓕ 7500	82-17	CaramelFlip,SpangledLady,DellJo	12
4May87-7RD	6f	:23	:472	1:134ft	23	119	75	812	713	618	Tsuchiya K8	ⒻAw7980	56-31	ExecutiveIssue,BoldFager,MissFine	8
15Apr87-4Kee	a7f			1:281m	49	117	65	812	817	925¼	TsuchiyaK4	ⒻAw15800	57-17	NickIPltd,ChckthRcord,MyGrtFolly	9
3Apr87-4Kee	7f	:23	:462	1:25 gd	31	115	3½	75	911	914½	TsuchiyaK4	ⒻAw15800	66-20	SmmrPddng,SkThTrth,MyGrtFolly	9
18Feb87-7TP	1	:482	1:151	1:434gd	4¼	121	42	21	1hd	13	Tsuchiya K6	ⒻMdn	56-32	CrmelFlip,GoingClssy,WrTimeBride	8
7Feb87-3TP	6½f	:241	:484	1:21 ft	25	122	75¾	53½	25	211	Tsuchiya K10	ⒻMdn	62-29	BelievItBlovd,CrmlFlip,Tobtthbnd	12

B.

Shirley's Revenge

Gr. f. 4, by Iron Warrior—Prize Blue, by Pia Star
Br.—Pitzer Dr Frank (Ky) — 1987 2 1 0 0 $3,731
Own.—Pitzer F R — 121 — Tr.—Jones Larry — $11,000 — 1986 3 0 0 1 $990
Lifetime 11 2 1 1 $16,622

14Jly87-9EIP	6½f	:222	:46	1:182ft	15	116	32½	34	64	57¼	Foster D E 7	ⒻAw10800	83-18	Becky Cee, Told It All, Late Bid	7
1Jly87-7EIP	6f	:23	:472	1:143sy	2	116	1hd	12	13	14	Foster D E 6	Ⓕ 10000	72-30	Shrly'sRvng,LuckyDplomt,Jlt'sLov	6
19Nov86-9CD	6f	:22	:463	1:12 ft	18	1095	62	75½	98½	916	Doser M E 10	Ⓕ 15000	67-23	Joyful,She'sASleepr,IrishPoliticin	11
9Nov86-5CD	6½f	:23	:473	1:21 gd	15	1095	12	11	31½	43¼	Doser M E 5	Ⓕ 15000	72-27	Sunny Lady, Our LassRosie,Joyful	10
26Oct86-9RD	6f	:214	:452	1:13 m	6½	113	31½	34½	25	35	Foster D E 10	ⒻAw5200	73-29	TmlssAppl,Cnn'sCmmnd,Shrl'sRng	10
15Nov85-4CD	6f	:221	:471	1:141m	16	119	1hd	21	52½	89¼	Miller S E 3	Ⓕ 25000	65-30	AmTndUp,Pon'sPrncss,PrncssGbol	9
7Nov85-6CD	6½f	:222	:461	1:184ft	27	118	32½	98	1011	1015½	Miller S E 9	ⒻAw14275	70-18	BonddMiss,RuffRuffin,SpringButy	11
23Oct85-4Kee	6f	:224	:464	1:134gd	16	115	66½	76½	86¾	810	Miller S E 7	ⒻAw15800	63-25	She's TheMint,Drosera,BondedMiss	9

Jly 25 EIP 5f ft 1:02 b — Jly 8 EIP 5f ft 1:01 b — ●Jun 26 EIP 5f ft 1:003 h

C.

Croyance

B. m. 6, by Nostrum—Credence, by Dark Star
Br.—Nicholson Jessica Bell (Ky) — 1987 7 1 0 3 $7,235
Own.—Booker P & J — 111 — Tr.—Booker John — $10,000 — 1986 8 2 2 1 $9,046
Lifetime 24 5 3 6 $34,144

14Jly87-8EIP	6f	:224	:461	1:113ft	5½	112	2hd	1hd	12	14	Deegan J C 1	Ⓕ 7750	87-18	Croyance,WhtnAce,LuckyDiplomt	11
27Jun87-7EIP	6f	:222	:46	1:112ft	4½	114	45½	45½	43½	45	Deegan J C 2	Ⓕ 8000	83-16	BzrSpirit,AnnieTinsley,DistinctBid	10
11Jun87-3CD	6f	:214	:461	1:121ft	25	114	74½	63½	42½	31¾	Bruin J E 5	Ⓕ 9000	80-17	She'sNative,AnnieTinsley,Croyance	9
2Jun87-3CD	6½f	:223	:464	1:203sy	9½	114	69	65	32½	34¾	Bruin J E 7	Ⓕ 9000	72-23	RaiseTheStage,Vic'sFever,Croynce	7
22May87-3CD	6f	:214	:463	1:12 ft	17	114	86¾	74¾	33½	36½	Bruin J E 5	Ⓕ 9000	76-17	Oh Dears, Our Lass Rosie,Croyance	8
13May87-3CD	6½f	:231	:47	1:174ft	6¾	116	42	54½	69½	617	Bruin J E 7	Ⓕ 10000	74-12	HddnPrsuson,I'mTogh,JmpAnJllytd	7
1May87-4CD	6f	:214	:454	1:112ft	18	116	41	2½	32½	46½	Bruin J E 4	Ⓕ 10000	79-12	She'sNative,I'mTough,RiseTheStge	8
23Dec86-6TP	6½f	:233	:481	1:224ft	9	116	43	41¼	1hd	11½	Bruin J E 6	Ⓕ 8000	64-35	Croyance, MistyPatricia,LadyRolls	10

D.

Pulaski Countess

Own.—Brass Ring Partnership

1047

B. f. 3, by Fluorescent Light—Summer Season, by Nashua
Br.—Brown Mr–Mrs Darrell (Cal)   1987 10 1 2 3 $16,405
Tr.—Mattingly Richard B   **$11,000**   1986   9 2 0 1 $9,366
Lifetime 19 3 2 4 $25,771   Turf 1 0 0 0

4Jly87-7EIP	6f :221 :453 1:11 ft	*7-5 118	711 641 46 38	Troilo W D5	Ⓕ 15000	82-16	AprlFoolM,BoldBrvMry,PlskContss 7
21Jun87-3CD	1 :47 1:13 1:40 ft	*21 117	431 21 12 14	Troilo W D3	Ⓕ 15000	69-17	PlskContss,NwtonsLw,ImpccblLdy 8
10Jun87-6CD	1 :464 1:132 1:393ft	31 112	67 4nk 311 451	Troilo W D5	Ⓕ 23000	65-22	OnlyKidding,ARealHwk,LillyDePeg 8
20May87-5CD	6f :211 :454 1:12 ft	3 117	673 52 42 31	Troilo W D4	Ⓕ 25000	82-18	DD'sStr,ChrmngMssy,PulskCountss 6
5May87-7CD	6f :22 :462 1:114ft	22 112	883 643 761 715	Troilo WD8	ⒻAw15960	69-23	CstleEight,Rich'nQuick,RedBordux 8
10Apr87-6OP	6f :213 :452 1:112ft	*8-5 116	761 551 311 211	Howard D L7	Ⓕ 20000	81-17	Rnnn'Ego,PlskContss,BlckMntnJ. 10
30Mar87-7OP	1 :464 1:12 1:382gd	6 113	56 48 581 519	Howard D L6	Ⓕ 32000	61-22	BettyBeinBad,DelaReef,KeyedtoGo 7

30Mar87—Came in first turn

20Mar87-3OP	6f :22 :454 1:104ft	51 116	753 633 33 38	Howard D L6	Ⓕ 32000	78-16	CoonyDb,BttyBinBd,PulskiCountss 8

Jun 5 CD 4f ft :492 b

E.

Gold Bangle

Own.—Osborne P B

114

B. f. 3, by Lot o' Gold—Wendy Gale, by Assagai
Br.—Isaacs T Mr & Mrs (Ky)   1987 9 2 3 0 $11,245
Tr.—Hack Gary B   **$11,000**   1986   6 1 1 0 $4,412
Lifetime 15 3 4 0 $15,657

17Jly87-5EIP	6f :223 :461 1:122ft	71 116	1hd 1hd 21 22	Girdley J W2	Ⓕ 10000	81-13	HrvstofHvn.GoldBngl,AirFinssWon 8
10Jly87-4RD	51f :222 :453 1:052ft	12 112	31 321 461 56	Neff S 9	ⒻAw8500	82-28	Ray's Praise, Briar Britches,Lisetta 9
17May87-3CD	6f :214 :46 1:122ft	41 116	56 671 681 610	Girdley J W3	Ⓕ 14000	71-18	Early Song Della Jo,ExitStageLeft 6
9May87-5CD	61f :224 :462 1:174ft	40 106	641 661 812 818	Garcia J J8	ⒻAw16500	73-14	Gift Of Glitter, Be Bad, Bellinska 8
27Mar87-6TP	6f :224 :461 1:13 ft	5 1145	211 21 11 111	Girdley J W2	Ⓕ 12500	79-23	GoldBngie,TimeForTosts,MdivlDrm 8
6Mar87-6TP	6f :224 :463 1:14 ft	*8-5 119	54 35 32 22	Cooksey P J1	Ⓕ c7500	72-27	TheLdyEnforcer,GoldBngl,BringUp 7
20Feb87-9TP	61f :232 :48 1:214ft	91 117	561 633 551 413	Sayler B4	ⒻAw11800	56-33	KrenT.,MissCrystlLigh,AntiquDrsdn 7
31Jan87-3TP	6f :23 :474 1:142gd	3 122	46 22 22 211	Sayler B3	Ⓒ 10000	70-22	AntiqueDresden,GoldBangle,Tigrilla 9

F.

Lady Val

Own.—Askew J D

114

B. f. 4, by Quiet Fling—Rose Chapeau, by High Hat
Br.—Smith Mrs Herbert J (Ky)   1987 7 0 0 0 $72
Tr.—Lane Troy   **$11,000**   1986 15 3 3 2 $36,740
Lifetime 31 7 3 2 $57,538

3Jly87-8EIP	6f :223 :46 1:112ft	14 114	46 47 561 662	Miller S E4	Ⓕ 15000	81-13	OnThSxthDy,LghtnngLook,SonrLdy 7
23Jun87-5CD	6f :214 :46 1:123ft	17e 116	121312111011 961	Miller S E5	Ⓕ 15000	74-21	SucyN'Clssy,She'sNtiv,PollyPtuni 12
8Apr87-8OP	6f :221 :46 1:111ft	74 114	96 11731112 991	Holland MA11	Ⓕ 18000	74-20	LimittdLss,PrizHurricn,BoldTiffny 11
31Mar87-7OP	6f :222 :463 1:121ft	21 116	1071 963 851 641	Howard D L3	Ⓕ 16000	74-20	HwiinLdy,TrcieTruestr,ViolentRge 12
10Mar87-8OP	6f :22 :46 1:11 ft	37 116	107 1012 913 9151	Frazier R L9	Ⓕ 25000	69-19	AntSndy,I'mLkThWnd,LovlyAnntt 10
16Feb87-6OP	6f :221 :454 1:11 ft	10 116	79 812 812 6121	Snyder L5	Ⓕ 40000	73-20	LkkrIsQukkr,Trry'sGrl,LttlMssLcky 9
6Feb87-6OP	61f :223 :461 1:033ft	49 1105	833 853 783 6181	Bielby J A7	ⒻAw25000	77-14	MyMris,Littlebitplsur,TylorsPromis 8
13Sep86-9FP	11 :481 1:121 1:44 ft	41e 116	541 58 691 5151	FloresG7	ⒻRosebud	75-15	MissBlueprint,BriffFm,Td'sLstChnc 8

Jun 17 CD 5f ft 1:012 b   Jun 11 CD 5f ft 1:024 b

G.

Our Lass Rosie

Own.—Hesketh & Pieczonka

114

Dk. b. or br. f. 4, by Our Native—Lightfoot Lassie, by Sensitivo
Br.—Petter Stanley D Jr (Ky)   1987 9 0 1 1 $3,100
Tr.—Montgomery William B   **$11,000**   1986 15 4 3 0 $24,489
Lifetime 30 5 5 2 $36,137   Turf 2 0 0 0 $360

2Jun87-3CD	61f :223 :464 1:203sy	2 116	56 55 781 7161	Fletcher R3	Ⓒ c10000	61-23	RaiseTheStage,Vic'sFever,Croynce 7
22May87-3CD	6f :214 :463 1:12 ft	61 116	641 1hd 111 211	Garcia J J7	Ⓕ 10000	81-17	Oh Dears, Our Lass Rosie,Croyance 8
15May87-6CD	61f :231 :47 1:19 ft	91 116	56 43 431 681	McDowell M 5	Ⓕ 15000	76-21	PollyPetunia,MountTiar,TinTopStr 8
25Apr87-6CD	61f :232 :474 1:193ft	31 116	3nk 2hd 411 58	Day P1	Ⓕ 15000	74-18	Dontstponmytos,MyMnky,GssNSss 9
19Mar87-4GP	7f :231 :464 1:253ft	14 113	2hd 31 1015121141	Velez J A Jr 7	Ⓕ 17000	62-23	Lyovrnit,PowdrPrincss,MissyLutk 12
1Mar87-4Hia	7f :23 :454 1:251ft	7 116	31 521 531 771	Pezua J M5	Ⓕ 16000	69-23	IncaGold,Jigtory,Pete'sGrndedme 12
7Feb87-3Hia	7f :224 :463 1:114sy	6 116	11 1hd 1hd 32	Pezua J M8	Ⓕ 16000	79-18	DoublePurpos,Jigtory,OurLssRosi 12
23Jan87-5Hia	7f :234 :472 1:26 ft	51 116	1hd 2hd 781 7101	Fires E 12	Ⓕ 16000	63-28	AwesomeGl,SuddnDsh,Doc'sDlivry 12

Jly 18 EIP 3f ft :36 b   Jly 12 EIP 5f ft 1:023 b   Jun 29 EIP 4f ft :502 b

28.

3rd Santa Anita

6½ FURLONGS. (1.14) ALLOWANCE. Purse $26,000. 3-year-olds. Non-winners of $3,000 other than maiden or claiming. Weight, 119 lbs. Non-winners of a race other than claiming since November 3 allowed 2 lbs.; of such a race since October 1, 4 lbs.

A.

Westerly Wind — B. c. 3, by Inverness Drive—Pet Label, by Petrone
SIBILLE R — **119** — Br.—Jelks J R Sr (Ky) — 1986 5 1 2 1 $20,600
Own.—Jelks J R Sr — Tr.—Wheeler Robert L
Lifetime 5 1 2 1 $20,600

27Dec86-7SA 6f :21^4 :45^1 1:10^{4}ft 2¾ 120 1^{hd} 2^{hd} 2^{hd} 3^{nk} Sibille R^4 Aw26000 84-19 SocilDimond,Cleverege,WstrlyWind 8
27Dec86—Bumped intervals late
3Dec86-8Hol 6f :22 :45^2 1:10^{3}ft 7¾ 120 2^{1½} 3^{1½} 2^{2½} 2^1 Sibille R^3 Aw21000 89-18 SundncSqur,WstrlyWnd,GcldOnGrn 6
3Dec86—Steadied 1/2
16Nov86-3Hol 6f :22^1 :46 1:11^{1}ft 3¾ 118 1^{hd} 1½ 1½ 1^{1¾} Sibille R^6 Mdn 87-18 WstrlyWind,MlibuPrnc,FmousForvr 7
16Nov86—Broke out, bumped
6Nov86-6Hol 6f :22^1 :45^4 1:11^{2}ft 28 118 2^{hd} 1^{hd} 1^1 2^{hd} Sibille R^4 M50000 86-17 ContctGm,WstrlyWind,WsdomDncr 9
7Sep86-6Dmr 6f :22^1 :45^3 1:10^{1}ft 22 117 8^8 10^{15}10^{21}10^{18½} Sibille R^5 Mdn 68-13 Agn'sBolgr,Crbonro,WindwoodLn 11
7Sep86—Broke slowly
●Dec 23 SLR tr.t 5f ft :59^1 h ●Nov 26 SLR tr.t 4f ft :48 h

B.

Cleverege — B. c. 3, by Clever Trick—Cherrywood Clover, by Porterhouse
PATTERSON A — **119** — Br.—Burburry G M & D D Jr (Ky) — 1986 6 1 3 0 $23,570
Own.—Team Esprit — Tr.—Garrison Rudy D
Lifetime 6 1 3 0 $23,570

27Dec86-7SA 6f :21^4 :45^1 1:10^{4}ft 14e 120 2^{hd} 1^{hd} 1^{hd} 2^{nk} Patterson A^5 Aw26000 84-19 SocilDimond,Cleverege,WstrlyWind 8
27Dec86—Bumped intervals late
14Dec86-6Hol 6f :22 :45^3 1:11^{1}ft 10 118 2^1 1^{hd} 1½ 1^{2¼} Patterson A^8 Mdn 87-18 Cleverg,‡RdyToSmok,LovDn'sGtwy 8
18Sep86-11Pom 6½f :21^3 :45 1:17^{2}ft 11 115 2^2 3^{4½} 3^3 4^7 Mena F^6 Beau Brml 86-12 CctusClipper,DoublSong,HighRgrds 6
12Sep86-8Pom 6f :22^3 :46^3 1:12 ft *8-5 113^5 1^{hd} 1^{hd} 1½ 2^{nk} Black C A^6 Mdn 91-11 Lucky Edition,Cleverege,OakWine 10
12Sep86—Bumped late
4Sep86-6Dmr 6f :21^4 :45^1 1:10^{1}ft 2½ 113^5 3^{3½} 3^{1½} 3^{1½} 2^{4½} Black C A^2 M50000 82-14 Supreme Stand, Cleverege, RedGuy 9
11Aug86-6Dmr 6f :22 :45^1 1:10^{2}ft 25 113^5 2^{hd} 2^{1½} 2^4 5^{11½} Black C A^4 M50000 74-13 GoldOnGreen,Darion,LuckyEdition 10
11Aug86—Bumped start, late
Jan 3 SA 6f ft 1:15 h Dec 25 SA 4f ft :49 h Dec 20 Hol 5f ft 1:00^2 h Dec 12 Hol 5f ft 1:01^2 hg

C.

Prince Sassafras — B. c. 3, by Sassafras—Sharp Vision, by Our Native
VALENZUELA P A — **115** — Br.—North Ridge Farm (Ky) — 1986 11 1 3 1 $84,749
Own.—Abtahi-Coelho-Valenti — Tr.—Stute Melvin F — Turf 3 0 2 0 $36,250
Lifetime 11 1 3 1 $84,749

14Dec86-8Hol 1 :44^4 1:09^3 1:36^{1}ft 90 121 2^{1½}10^{9¾}12^{13}12^{16¾} Sibille R^6 Hol Fut 65-18 TempertSil,Alyshb,MstrfulAdvoct 12
14Dec86—Grade I; Lugged out drive
29Nov86-8Hol 1$\frac{1}{16}$Ⓣ:46^{4}1:11^{1}1:41^{4}fm 12 115 2^2 2½ 3^{3½} 5^4 Sibille R^6 Hst Th Flg 81-10 Persvrd,WildrnssBound,QuitlyBold 9
29Nov86—Grade III; Run in divisions; Fanned wide 7/8
15Nov86-8BM 1$\frac{1}{16}$Ⓣ:47 1:12^{3}1:46^{2}fm 3¼ 116 1^{1½} 1½ 1^{hd} 2^3 Sibille R^7 Cal Juv 68-19 WildernessBound,PrinceSassfrs,Wr 8
15Nov86—Grade III; Lost whip late
25Oct86-8BM 1 Ⓣ:46^{4}1:11^{4}1:37^{2}fm*6-5 114 2½ 1½ 2^{hd} 2^3 LamnceC^7 San Mateo 90-03 WildrnssBound,PrncSssfrs,SntnlStr 7
11Oct86-8SA 1$\frac{1}{16}$:46^1 1:11 1:45^{1}ft 42 118 4^{2½} 6^9 6^{12} 6^{10¾} Toro F^2 Norfolk 64-17 Capote, Gulch, Gold On Green 6
11Oct86—Grade I; Checked at 3/8
1Oct86-6SA 1 :46^1 1:11^2 1:37^{4}ft *6-5 117 1^1 1^2 1^{2½} 1^{1¼} Stevens G L^1 Mdn 79-18 PrinceSssfrs,SwordChrger,BScnic 10
1Oct86—Drifted out 1st turn
10Sep86-8Dmr 1 :45^2 1:10^1 1:35^{3}ft 17 114 6^{3¼} 7^{10} 6^{13} 7^{10½} Black CA^3 Dmr Fut 79-11 Qualify, Sacahuista, Brevito 9
10Sep86—Grade I
1Sep86-6AP 1 :44^4 1:11^2 1:37^{1}ft 15 122 1^1 1½ 3^2 4^6 StvnsGL^1 Arl Was Fut 69-22 BtTwic,Conquistros,JzzingAround 11
1Sep86—Grade I
3Aug86-6Dmr 1 :45^3 1:10^4 1:36^{2}ft 7-5 116 1^{hd} 1½ 2^{hd} 2^{2½} Toro F^6 Mdn 83-10 TemperateSil,PrinceSassfrs,BooW. 8
19Jly86-8Hol 6f :22 :45^2 1:11^{3}ft 55 115 7^6 8^8 7^{6½} 4^{2½} Toro F^7 Hol Juv Chp 83-15 CaptainValid,Qulify,JzzingAround 12
19Jly86—Grade II
Jan 3 SA 6f ft 1:14 h ●Dec 27 SA 4f ft :46^3 h Dec 10 Hol 5f ft 1:02^2 h Nov 23 Hol 6f ft 1:12^3 h

D.

The Quipper — Gr. c. 3, by Quip—Priceless Dawn, by Cloudy Dawn
DELAHOUSSAYE E — 115 — Br.—Goldman N & Debra (Cal) — 1986 4 2 0 0 $15,400
Own.—Goldman N & Debra — Tr.—Lewis Craig A
Lifetime 4 2 0 0 $15,400
14Dec86-4Hol 7f :21^{4} :45 1:24^{1}ft 94 115 9$^{6\frac{1}{4}}$ 8$^{2\frac{3}{4}}$ 3$^{1\frac{1}{2}}$ 5$^{2\frac{1}{2}}$ Soto S B^{11} Aw22000 80-18 OrchardSong,Reland,HoustonBrgg 11
20Nov86-3Hol 6f :22 :45^{4} 1:12^{1}ft 4 117 2^{3} 2$^{2\frac{1}{2}}$ 2^{1} 1^{2} Pincay L Jr^{5} 32000 82-16 TheQuipper,Rakaposhi,DoubleSong 8
30Oct86-7SA 6f :21^{4} :45^{1} 1:10^{2}ft 29 116 4$^{1\frac{1}{2}}$ 4$^{2\frac{1}{2}}$ 8$^{9\frac{1}{2}}$ 8$^{15\frac{3}{4}}$ ValenzuelPA^{8} Aw25000 70-18 MstrflAdvoct,HostnBrgg,SprmStnd 8
16Oct86-2SA 6f :22^{1} :45^{4} 1:12^{2}ft 3¾ 118 3^{2} 2^{hd} 1$^{1\frac{1}{2}}$ 1$^{1\frac{3}{4}}$ Pincay L Jr^{4} [S]M32000 76-19 TheQuipper,TakeOne,NeverSmoke 12
Jan 5 SA 6f sy 1:14^{2} h Dec 30 SA 5f ft 1:00^{2} h Dec 24 SA 5f ft 1:01^{3} h Dec 10 Hol 6f ft 1:16 h

E.

Bold Archon — Dk. b. or br. g. 3, by Bold Forbes—Sally Stark, by Graustark
STEVENS G L — 119 — Br.—Jones A U (Ky) — 1986 2 1 0 0 $10,450
Own.—Jones A U — Tr.—Barrera Lazaro S
Lifetime 2 1 0 0 $10,450
30Dec86-8SA 6f :21^{3} :44^{4} 1:10^{2}ft 8½ 114 2^{hd} 2$^{2\frac{1}{2}}$ 5$^{5\frac{1}{2}}$ 6$^{8\frac{3}{4}}$ StevnsGL^{3} San Miguel 77-18 BroadwyPointe,StffRiot,PrtnersBid 8
7Dec86-5Hol 6f :22 :45^{4} 1:11^{2}gd 2¾ 118 1^{hd} 1^{hd} 1$^{1\frac{1}{2}}$ 1$^{\frac{1}{2}}$ Stevens G L^{4} Mdn 86-18 BoldArchon,FlyingFlgs,Ful'OfFools 7
Jan 8 SA 5f m 1:01^{3} h Dec 29 SA 3f ft :35^{3} h Dec 22 Hol 5f ft 1:03^{3} h Dec 16 Hol 3f ft :37^{3} h

F.

Race Book — B. c. 3, by Alleged—Madame Premier, by Raja Baba
PINCAY L JR — 115 — Br.—Warner Marvin L (Ky) — 1986 4 1 1 0 $11,955
Own.—Klein Mr-Mrs E V — Tr.—Lukas D Wayne
Lifetime 4 1 1 0 $11,955
27Dec86-7SA 6f :21^{4} :45^{1} 1:10^{4}ft 4½ 116 3^{nk} 6$^{4\frac{3}{4}}$ 5$^{4\frac{1}{2}}$ 5$^{4\frac{3}{4}}$ Cordero AJr^{3} Aw26000 79-19 SocilDimond,Cleverege,WstrlyWind 8
27Dec86—Broke in, bumped
28Jun86-6CD 5½f :22^{2} :46^{3} 1:05^{3}ft *1 118 2^{hd} 1^{hd} 1$^{\frac{1}{2}}$ 1$^{2\frac{1}{2}}$ Day P^{2} Mdn 93-15 RceBook,TexsProspctor,TrickCrd 12
21Jun86-5CD 5f :22^{3} :46 :58^{4}ft *6-5e 120 2$^{1\frac{1}{2}}$ 2$^{\frac{1}{2}}$ 2$^{1\frac{1}{2}}$ 2^{2} Fires E^{10} Mdn 93-13 Saga, RaceBook,SociallyInformed 10
14Jun86-5CD 5f :22^{3} :46^{1} :58^{4}ft 5 121 1$^{\frac{1}{2}}$ 2^{hd} 2^{1} 5$^{4\frac{1}{4}}$ Davis R G^{1} Mdn 91-15 Erratic, Trick Card, Tea Crackers 8
Jan 2 SA 5f ft 1:03^{3} h Dec 18 SA 7f ft 1:28^{1} h Dec 11 SA 5f ft 1:01 h Dec 4 SA 5f ft 1:01^{4} h

29.

5 ATLANTIC CITY

5 ½ FURLONGS. (1.02⅘) MAIDEN SPECIAL WEIGHT. Purse $7,000. 2-year-olds. Weight, 118 lbs.

Coupled—Run of the Castle and

A.

Torvill — Gr. c. 2, by Icecapade—Greek Victress, by Victoria Park — Lifetime 1987 1 M 0 0
Br.—Juddmonte Farms, Incorporated (Ky) — 1 0 0 0
Own.—Juddmonte Farms — Tr.—Johnson Philip G — 118
18Jly87- 4Mth fst 5½f :23 :47 1:06 Md Sp Wt 9 9 7$^{4\frac{3}{4}}$ 9$^{9\frac{3}{4}}$ 8^{17} 8$^{19\frac{3}{4}}$ Samyn J L 118 10.70 65-21 Plain Foolish 118^{nk} Whirling Ash 118^{8} Harmonious 118¾ Outrun 9
LATEST WORKOUTS ● Jly 26 Fai [·] 4f gd :47⅖ b Jly 17 Fai tr.t 3f fst :36 b Jly 6 Fai tr.t 5f fst 1:03 b Jun 21 Fai tr.t 4f fst :50 b

B.

Run of the Castle — B. c. 2, by Irish Castle—Run Roberta, by Roberto — Lifetime 1987 2 M 1 0 $1,702
Br.—Evans T M (Ky) — 2 0 1 0
Own.—Buckland Farm — Tr.—Pearce Ross R — 118 — $1,702
17Jly87- 3Pen fst 5f :22⅘ :47⅗ 1:00⅖ Md Sp Wt 7 8 10^{6} 10$^{8\frac{3}{4}}$ 7$^{5\frac{3}{4}}$ 4$^{5\frac{3}{4}}$ Sacks E A 116 3.50 76-18 R. K.'s Super Star 116½TorridPace116$^{3\frac{1}{4}}$SirLaunchalot116^{2} Rallied 11
22May87- 1Del fst 5f :23 :48⅕ 1:00⅗ Md Sp Wt 3 2 2nd 2$^{\frac{1}{2}}$ 3$^{\frac{1}{2}}$ 2$^{4\frac{1}{2}}$ Daniels E 118 2.70 78-21 RestlessWords111$^{4\frac{1}{2}}$RunofthCstl118^{nk}Frn'sNodoubt118^{4} Held 2nd 12
LATEST WORKOUTS Jly 28 Del 5f fst 1:04⅘ b Jly 14 Del 5f fst 1:02 b Jly 10 Del 5f fst 1:05⅗ b ● Jly 5 Del 4f fst :48⅕ hg

C.

Up With Your Dukes — Gr. c. 2, by Monteverde—Cool Flower, by Cool Moon — Lifetime 1987 0 M 0 0
Br.—peskoff S D (Ky) — 0 0 0 0
Own.—Limestone Farm — Tr.—Conners Robert F — 118
LATEST WORKOUTS Jly 16 Del 3f fst :37⅘ bg Jly 4 Del 4f fst :49 bg

D.

Kodiak Jack — Dk. b. or br. c. 2, by Restivo—Penthouse Queen, by Forum — Lifetime 1987 3 M 0 1 $896
Br.—Lematta Vivian M (Fla) — 118 — 3 0 0 1
Own.—Lematta Vivian — Tr.—Hill Roberta — $896

20Jly87- 6Atl fst 5f :23 :47⅕ 1:00⅗ Md Sp Wt 1 3 3^2 6^8 7^{11} 7^8 Douthall J D 118 14.30 76-31 Sensational Blaze 118[1] True and Blue 118[hd] Spectrix 118[no] Tired 9
9Jly87- 6Atl sly 5f :22⅘ :47⅖ 1:00⅖ Md Sp Wt 2 2 2^1 1nd 3½ 3$2\frac{1}{2}$ Douthall J D 118 44.40 82-23 Tri Another Jet 118$2\frac{1}{2}$ Spectrix 118[no] KodiakJack118$2\frac{1}{2}$ Weakened 8
2Jly87- 1Atl sly 4½f :22⅘ :48 :54⅘ Md 32000 1 8 8^{10} $8^{9\frac{1}{2}}$ $7^{6\frac{1}{2}}$ Weinberg A[10] 108 4.50 79-14 Wristshot 114[1] Jason Henry 116[nk] Gold Fountain 116½ No factor 10
LATEST WORKOUTS Jly 27 Atl 3f fst :37 bg Jun 18 Atl 4f fst :48 bg Jun 15 Atl 3f fst :39 bg

E.

Spectrix — Ch. c. 2, by On To Glory—Arvent, by Over Arranged — Lifetime 1987 2 M 1 1 $2,170
Br.—Shady Lane Farm (Fla) — 118 — 2 0 1 1
Own.—Mr Eds Stable — Tr.—Pregman John S — $2,170

20Jly87- 6Atl fst 5f :23 :47⅕ 1:00⅗ Md Sp Wt 4 2 2^1 $3^{2\frac{1}{2}}$ 3^3 3^1 Ferrer J C 118 2.00 83-31 Sensational Blaze 118[1]TrueandBlue118[no]Spectrix118[no] Weakened 9
9Jly87- 6Atl sly 5f :22⅘ :47⅖ 1:00⅖ Md Sp Wt 8 4 3^1 2^{hd} 2^{hd} $2^{2\frac{1}{2}}$ Ferrer J C 118 2.60 82-23 Tri Another Jet 118$^{2\frac{1}{2}}$ Spectrix118[hd]KodiakJack118$^{2\frac{1}{2}}$ Drifted out 8
LATEST WORKOUTS Jly 6 Atl 4f fst :49⅘ bg Jly 1 Atl 4f fst :48 h Jun 25 Atl 4f fst :48⅗ hg Jun 17 Atl 4f fst :48⅖ h

F.

True and Blue — B. g. 2, by Hurry Up Blue—A Real Native, by Mr Prospector — Lifetime 1987 1 M 1 0 $1,330
Br.—Petelain Stable (Fla) — 118 — 1 0 1 0
Own.—Petelain Stable — Tr.—Byrne Patrick B — $1,330
Entered 30Jly87- 4 BEL

20Jly87- 6Atl fst 5f :23 :47⅕ 1:00⅗ Md Sp Wt 2 9 4^2 1^1 1^2 2^1 Pagano S R 118 11.00 83-31 Sensational Blaze 118[1] True and Blue 118[hd]Spectrix118[no] Gamely 9
LATEST WORKOUTS Jly 13 Atl 4f fst :50 bg Jly 8 Atl 4f sly :49⅕ b Jun 26 Atl 3f fst :37⅘ b

G.

Blue Ebony — Dk. b. or br. c. 2, by Cassaleria—Princess Doll, by Royal Sting — Lifetime 1987 2 M 0 0 $140
Br.—W. E. Penn (Ky) — 118 — 2 0 0 0
Own.—Clark E S — Tr.—Clark Elmer S Jr — $140

20Jly87- 6Atl fst 5f :23 :47⅕ 1:00⅗ Md Sp Wt 7 8 $6^{4\frac{1}{2}}$ $5^{7\frac{1}{2}}$ $6^{7\frac{1}{2}}$ $6^{5\frac{1}{2}}$ Santos F J 118 19.60 76-31 Sensational Blaze 118[1] True and Blue 118[hd]Spectrix118[no] Outrun 9
9Jly87- 6Atl sly 5f :22⅘ :47⅖ 1:00⅖ Md Sp Wt 7 8 8^{12} [illegible] 7^{10} $6^{10\frac{1}{2}}$ Santos F J 118 15.20 74-23 Tri Another Jet118$^{2\frac{1}{2}}$Spectrix118[hd]KodiakJack118$^{2\frac{1}{2}}$ Broke slowly 8
LATEST WORKOUTS Jly 28 Atl 3f fst :37 bg Jly 17 Atl 3f fst :36⅗ bg ● Jly 6 Atl 5f fst 1:02⅗ bg Jly 4 Atl 3f fst :39⅘ bg

H.

Regal Paradise — B. c. 2, by Regal And Royal—Gold Eyes, by Ortis III — Lifetime 1987 2 M 0 1 $3,665
Br.—Peskoff S D (Fla) — 118 — 2 0 0 1
Own.—M & M Racing Stable — Tr.—Lafayette John B — $3.665

27May87- 9GP fst 5f :23 :47⅗ 1:00⅕ Luther Evans 5 10 $8^{4\frac{1}{2}}$ $5^{5\frac{1}{2}}$ $5^{3\frac{1}{2}}$ 4^{13} Lester R N 112 13.10 72-25 Flashy Runner112$^{8\frac{1}{2}}$FreckleSkates112$^{3\frac{1}{2}}$ZeroCoupon117[1] Late bid 10
22May87- 4GP fst 5f :23 :47⅘ 1:00⅗ Md Sp Wt 8 4 $3^{1\frac{1}{2}}$ 4^2 $5^{3\frac{1}{2}}$ $3^{4\frac{1}{2}}$ Hernandez C 122 5.80 80-24 GayRights122$^{3\frac{1}{2}}$PrinceAllaBreva122$^{\frac{3}{4}}$RegalPardise122$^{1\frac{1}{2}}$ Mild gain 12
LATEST WORKOUTS Jly 29 Atl 4f fst :50 b Jly 16 Atl 4f gd :47⅗ hg Jly 11 Atl 3f fst :38 b

I.

Trick Colony — Dk. b. or br. c. 2, by Pleasant Colony—Cold Trick, by Northern Dancer — Lifetime 1987 0 M 0 0
Br.—T. M. Evans (Ky) — 118 — 0 0 0 0
Own.—Buckland Farm — Tr.—Pearce Ross R
LATEST WORKOUTS Jly 28 Del 5f fst 1:04⅘ b ● Jly 22 Del 5f fst 1:02⅗ bg Jly 14 Del 4f fst :51 b Jly 9 Del 3f fst :36⅘ b

J.

That's a Gleam — B. g. 2, by That's a Nice—Klassy Gleam, by Gleaming — Lifetime 1987 1 M 1 0 $1,120
Br.—Minassian Z (Fla) — 118 — 1 0 1 0
Own.—Minassian Z — Tr.—Minassian Zeke — $1.120

17Jly87- 1Atl fst 5f :22⅗ :47⅘ 1:00⅘ Md 35000 6 3 $5^{4\frac{1}{2}}$ $4^{6\frac{1}{2}}$ 2^3 2^3 Intelisano G P Jr 118 4.40 82-27 HardCopy114[3]That'saGlem118[4]FortunteforSure114½ Second best 7
LATEST WORKOUTS Jly 25 Atl 4f fst :50⅘ b Jly 11 Atl 5f fst 1:02⅗ bg Jun 20 Atl 3f fst :37 bg Jun 13 Atl 4f fst :50 b

30.

9th Santa Anita

1 $\frac{1}{16}$ MILES. (1.40⅕) CLAIMING. Purse $25,000. 4-year-olds and upward. Weights, 4-year-olds, 120 lbs.; older, 121 lbs. Non-winners of two races at one mile or over since November 3 allowed 3 lbs.; of such a race since then, 5 lbs. Claiming price $40,000; if for $35,000 allowed 2 lbs. (Claiming and starter races for $32,000 or less not considered.)

A.

***Le Cid**
SIMPSON B H 118
Own.—Pulliam C N
Ch. h. 8, by Pinhal—Zaipan, by Dusseldorf
Br.—Haras Parana Ltda (Brz)
Tr.—Pulliam Vivian M $40,000
Lifetime 56 9 3 10 $97,361
1986 14 2 0 1 $33,950
1985 17 1 0 1 $25,050
Turf 11 0 0 3 $3,204

31Dec86-7SA 1 :453 1:11 1:364ft 35 116 68½ 66 56½ 58½ Simpson BH3 Aw31000 75-20 Olajuwon,ForsytheBoy,CallTheGurd 7
17Dec86-3Hol 1 1/16 :47 1:122 1:442ft 4½ 116 24 2hd 1hd 1hd Simpson B H6 40000 87-22 LeCid,ForeignLegion,ValintGeorge 6
7Dec86-3Hol 1 :453 1:10 1:354gd 28 116 54½ 46½ 46 48¾ Simpson B H4 62500 75-18 Olajuwon, RisingChum,OncGummo 6
22Nov86-7Hol 7f :22 :451 1:222ft 38 1115 67½ 67 79 78½ Cisneros J E4 50000 84-13 Cracksman, Juntura, Infantryman 8
30Aug86-3Dmr 1 1/16 :451 1:092 1:413ft 6½ 118 67½ 68 67 67½ Pedroza M A6 40000 85-10 ForHimslf,NorthrnProvidr,DnliRidg 8
30Aug86—Bumped start
16Aug86-9Dmr 1 1/16 :452 1:104 1:422ft 10 116 36½ 2hd 1½ 11½ Pedroza M A6 40000 88-13 Le Cid, Jumpoff Joe, Denali Ridge 9
4Aug86-8Dmr 1 1/16 :45 1:101 1:414ft 21 116 78½ 63¾ 53½ 76 Pedroza MA5 Aw23000 85-13 RobertoReason,WarDebt,FullOfStrs 9
11Jun86-8Hol 1 :462 1:103 1:353ft 23 116 55¾ 56 57 57¾ Pedroza MA2 Aw23000 77-16 SouthernHlo,SilverHro,ForsythBoy 5
18May86-4Hol 1 :44 1:084 1:352ft 46 116 59½ 57½ 55½ 32¾ Pedroza M A6 62500 83-08 Stickette, Ells Bravest Sorg, LeCid 7
9May86-7Hol 1 :451 1:102 1:353ft 61 116 63½ 65 57½ 58½ Soto S B2 Aw25000 77-16 Vigor's Prince, Barland, Savio 7
Dec 24 Hol 6f ft 1:151 h Dec 2 Hol 6f ft 1:171 h Nov 16 Hol 5f ft 1:004 h

B.

Au Bon Marche
SIBILLE R 115
Own.—Basso & Liebau
Ch. c. 4, by Broadway Forli—Du Marche, by Montparnasse II
Br.—Whitney T P (Ky)
Tr.—Howard Leigh Ann $40,000
Lifetime 17 2 1 2 $128,510
1986 9 0 1 0 $3,890
1985 8 2 0 2 $124,620
Turf 3 0 1 0 $3,315

27Dec86-5SA 1⅛ Ⓣ:4621:1211:492fm 52 1095 34 41 76 76¾ Patton D B6 Aw31000 73-20 MisterWonderfulII,Jota,DanThtch 12
6Dec86-6BM a1⅛ Ⓣ 1:503gd 13 112 13 2hd 2hd 22 Doocy T T11 Aw17000 80-18 BigDnRyn,AuBonMrch,CptnCondo 11
5Nov86-8Hol 1 :45 1:092 1:352ft 40 115 911 912 912 814¾ Sibille R3 Affrmd H 71-17 Chepskte,PrinceBobbyB.,FullChrm 9
5Nov86—Grade III; Stumbled badly start
13Aug86-5Dmr 1 Ⓣ:4611:1011:35 fm 15 114 53½ 74½ 65½ 65½ Lipham T9 Aw23000 92 — Swallage, Kingsbury, Shanaar 9
4Aug86-8Dmr 1 1/16 :45 1:101 1:414ft 12 112 56¾ 53½ 63¾ 55½ Ortega L E9 Aw23000 86-13 RobertoReason,WarDebt,FullOfStrs 9
21Jly86-8Hol 1¼ :471 1:363 2:033ft 23 114 85½ 89½ 710 611½ OrtegaLE7 Swaps 63-16 Clear Choice, Southern Halo, Jota 9
21Jly86—Grade I
5Jly86-8Hol 1 :443 1:08 1:324ft 272 114 129 1213 815 616½ OrtegLE6 Slvr Scrn H 82-08 Melair, Southern Halo, SnowChief 12
5Jly86—Grade II
21Jun86-3Hol 7f :224 :453 1:221ft 20 112 43 55 66¾ 67½ Ortega L E3 Aw24000 85-09 ‡UltimtePlesure,Pdu,GrndAllegince 6
4Jan86-8Crc 1⅛ :48 1:13 1:542ft 11 119 43½ 64¾ 98 109 VlzJAJr1 Trop Pk Dby 69-13 StrongPrformnc,Dr.DnEys,RlForst 12
4Jan86—Grade II; Steadied
14Dec85-8Aqu 170 ⊡:4721:1321:442ft *1e 119 84½ 63½ 53 44¾ McBethD3 Nashua 73-26 Rj'sRvng,RoylDoulton,BorduxBob 12
14Dec85—Grade III
Dec 15 BM 5f ft 1:013 h

C.

Cojak Man
PATTON D B 1125
Own.—North Ranch Stables
Dk. b. or br. g. 4, by Cojak—Madinus, by Bupers
Br.—Robertson & Miller (Ky)
Tr.—Heaton Bill $40,000
Lifetime 15 5 2 0 $48,549
1986 12 4 2 0 $45,000
1985 3 1 0 0 $3,549

28Dec86-9SA 1 1/16 :47 1:12 1:44 ft *9-5 1155 32½ 32 2½ 2¾ Patton D B7 32000 80-14 Chili Hill, Cojak Man, Brul's Ante 8
18Dec86-3Hol 1 1/16 :463 1:112 1:444ft *2½ 1145 1hd 11½ 12½ 12½ Patton D B2 40000 85-17 Cojak Man, I LoveRacing,Tellapace 7
18Dec86—Lugged out; wide late
10Dec86-3Hol 1 :454 1:104 1:371ft *9-5 1115 52 33 32½ 43½ Patton D B5 50000 74-20 Sebucan, Agitate's Pride, Alibi Ike 7
13Nov86-9Hol 1 :453 1:101 1:353ft 3½ 1115 51½ 21½ 23 21½ Patton D B3 50000 84-23 MischievousMtt,CojkMn,BoldDecre 9
2Nov86-2SA 1 :454 1:104 1:361ft 7½ 1105 31½ 31 1½ 16 Patton D B1 35000 87-10 Cojak Man, Tai High, Chili Hill 10
2Nov86—Steadied 1/4
16Oct86-9SA 1 1/16 :472 1:122 1:44 ft 16 1115 31 1½ 14 16½ Patton D B7 20000 81-19 CojakMan,ResonToStudy,Averted 10
3Oct86-5SA 6f :221 :452 1:102ft 14 1135 65½ 76¾ 66½ 46¾ Patton D B10 20000 79-17 NtvCptv,Nck'sPrnc,JohnsTomrrw 10
3Oct86—Wide into stretch
31Aug86-2Dmr 6f :214 :444 1:084ft 6½ 116 31 58 69 912½ Kaenel J L9 25000 81-12 GrowlrSnd,HndflOfDmnd,Prcntstr 12
23Aug86-1Dmr 6½f :214 :451 1:163ft *2¾ 116 11 12 1½ 1½ Kaenel J L8 20000 89-10 CojkMn,MischievousMtt,CritosLp 8
9Aug86-1Dmr 6f :214 :451 1:103ft 19 116 65½ 64½ 43½ 42½ Kaenel J L1 20000 83-14 Nick'sPrince,GentleReb,Priet'sBeu 9
9Aug86—Bumped start
Jan 7 SA 5f sy 1:032 h (d) Dec 1 SA 5f ft 1:00 h

D.

Danczone
PINCAY L JR 116
Own.—Jhayare Stables
Ch. h. 5, by Vatza—Brooklawn, by Tom Fool
Br.—Bell J G (Ky)
Tr.—Mitchell Mike $40,000
Lifetime 14 4 3 2 $71,650
1986 9 3 2 1 $52,625
1985 5 1 1 1 $19,025
Turf 1 0 0 0

24Dec86-7Hol 6f :22 :452 1:11 ft 2½ 119 64½ 64¾ 42 2½ Stevens G L10 50000 87-20 MsterCrofter,Dnczon,RingOfPlsur 10
24Dec86—Wide stretch
12Dec86-8Hol 6f :223 :454 1:101ft 4 116 21½ 21 22½ 22 Stevens G L5 Aw25000 90-20 Paisano Pete, Danczone, HighHook 6
11Nov86-5Hol 1 :453 1:104 1:362ft *6-5 117 3nk 2hd 66 612 Pincay L Jr3 Aw26000 69-20 DonB.Blue,BoldBrvoII,ForsytheBoy 7
3Nov86-2SA 6½f :213 :441 1:161ft 4½ 117 52½ 41¾ 11½ 12½ Pincay L Jr3 c50000 89-14 Danczone,RivetsFactor,Infantrymn 8
3Nov86—Bumped intervals midstretch, lugged out late

2Jly86-4Hol 7f :22 :443 1:22 ft *8-5 117 52¾ 53½ 34 53¾ Pincay L Jr2 Aw23000 90-09 Ideal Quality, Go Swiftly, Jubilero 6
18Jun86-4Hol 7f :223 :461 1:22 ft 4 117 21 1hd 12½ 13 Pincay L Jr6 62500 94-15 Danczone,Dr.Relity,Mischiefinmind 7
2May86-7Hol 1⅛(T):4741:1041:473fm 23 116 1hd 2½ 22 63½ Kaenel J L8 Aw25000 90-06 Diaghlyphard, Nonno, Kingsbury 10
13Apr86-5SA 7f :221 :45 1:222ft 6 117 44 33 1hd 1¾ Pincay L Jr5 Aw24000 88-15 Danczone, Bizeboy, Lord Pancho 9
13Apr86—Bumped start
16Mar86-7SA 6½f :214 :443 1:162sy 5¾ 117 33 37 37 312½ Pincay L Jr3 Aw2800C 75-24 EllsBrvestSong,DubiTorndo,Dnczon 9
12May85-4Hol 1 :451 1:102 1:353ft 3¼ 120 43 22½ 1½ 11 Pincay L Jr8 Mdn 95-06 Danczone, Baroncello, Starsalot 8
Jan 5 SA 4f sy :482 h Dec 8 Hol 4f gd :481 h Dec 3 Hol 3f ft :362 h Nov 22 Hol 3f ft :35 h

E.

Idol

ORTEGA L E **116**
Own.—Alesia F & Sharon
B. h. 6, by Verbatim—Party Kiss, by Fleet Nasrullah
Br.—Elmendorf Farm (Ky) **1986 8 1 2 2 $30,375**
Tr.—Ippolito Steve $40,000 **1985 10 2 2 1 $31,260**
Lifetime 33 6 7 3 $98,505 **Turf 5 0 0 0 $575**

31Dec86-5SA 6½f :22 :453 1:172ft 9½ 116 106¾ 74¼ 42½ 31 Ortega L E9 40000 82-20 Watch'n Win, Angle Arc, Idol 12
31Dec86—Wide final 3/8
2Nov86-3SA 1 1/16 :461 1:103 1:412ft *8-5 116 45½ 43½ 26 28 Valenzuela P A5 40000 86-10 Oricao, Idol, Tough Envoy 6
5Oct86-9SA 1 1/16 :462 1:111 1:424ft 8 116 87¾ 61¾ 4¾ 2¾ ValenzuelaPA10 40000 86-15 Tough Envoy, Idol, Tio Nino 10
5Oct86—Wide 3/8 turn; lost whip 3/16
7Sep86-9Dmr 1 1/16(T):4711:11 1:423fm 7½ 116 311 310 59 57¾ Valenzuela P A1 50000 85-08 EmperadorAlNorte,Msser,OkTreeII 8
24Aug86-9Dmr 1 1/16 :452 1:093 1:412ft 3¾ 116 613 610 612 45½ Valenzuela P A1 50000 87-12 OnoGummo,TimeForSilenc,Oljuwon 9
24Aug86—Veered out, bumped start; lugged out backstretch, wide into stretch
9Aug86-7Dmr 1 1/16 :453 1:101 1:422ft 9¾ 116 66 52¼ 51¼ 3½ Valenzuela P A7 50000 87-14 Lead On, Impulsively, Idol 11
9Aug86—Wide 3/8 turn
28Jly86-5Dmr 1 1/16 :451 1:094 1:421ft 5 116 45½ 23 11½ 1nk Valenzuela P A6 32000 89-16 Idol, Valiant George,ForeignLegion 8
28Jly86—Wide into stretch
11Jan86-9SA 1 1/16 :46 1:102 1:422ft 5½ 116 32 33 32½ 43½ Ortega L E1 25000 85-11 Son OfRaja,Rajaba,MarkInTheSky 10
23Dec85-9Hol 1⅛ :471 1:12 1:503ft 4½ 118 78¼ 88½ 75¾ 77½ Ortega L E7 30000 76-17 ForeignLegion,MstrNvjo,NoodlRoni 9
7Dec85-9Hol 1 :444 1:093 1:344ft 16 119 88 53 51¾ 2no Castanon A L8 25000 89-12 Noodle Roni, Idol, Foreign Legion 10
7Dec85—Wide into drive
Jan 8 SA 4f m :484 h Dec 27 SA 4f ft :474 h Dec 19 SA 6f ft 1:133 h ●Dec 13 SA 6f ft 1:132 h

F.

Induit

BAZE G **116**
Own.—Carno & Kolbe
B. h. 5, by Briartic—Twice as Pretty, by Twice Worthy
Br.—Schieckedanz G L (Ont-C) **1986 12 0 1 0 $7,970**
Tr.—Carno Louis R $40,000 **1985 11 0 1 0 $9,350**
Lifetime 30 2 2 1 $33,611 **Turf 25 2 2 1 $28,911**

11Nov86-9Hol 1⅛(T):4721:1121:472fm 77 114 46 55¾ 78¼ 811¾ Baze G8 57500 79-09 Aviator II, Auto Commander,Crony 8
10Aug86-9Dmr 1⅜(T):4831:3732:141fm 49 113 33 54 913 917¾ Solis A5 55000 81-01 Sherkin, Travet, Rushad 9
10Aug86—Veered out start
23Jly86-9Dmr 1 1/16(T):4821:1221:431fm 16 113 41¼ 41¾ 41½ 64 Solis A5 55000 86-04 Pettrax, Royal Olympia, Atlantin 8
22Jun86-4GG 1 1/16(T):4711:1121:422fm 6½ 115 42½ 41½ 47 47½ CastanedaM5 Aw18000 82-14 CastlemartinKing,Daniyr,Kingsbury 7
15Jun86-4GG 1 1/16(T):4841:1241:434fm 7¾ 116 53 41¾ 63¾ 64½ Castaneda M5 65000 78-14 PairOfAces,ElMansour,RosaCarnin 6
11May86-6GG 1 1/16(T):4721:1121:432fm 9¾ 114 55½ 44½ 32½ 2½ ♦ Castaneda M4 65000 84-18 Cave Creek, Naturals Grand, Induit 6
♦11May86—Dead heat
21Apr86-9SA 1¼(T):4811:3732:024fm 5¼ 117 53½ 5¾ 84¾ 84¼ Pincay L Jr8 50000 69-20 FbulousMmory,Jl'sMrk,OnoGmmo 11
21Apr86—Rank early
13Apr86-9SA 1¼(T):4531:3512:011fm 64 1095 53 83¼ 75¾ 54¾ Crowder S J9 57500 76-17 Penznce,Morry'sChmp,FlyingGene 10
13Apr86—Fanned wide into stretch
30Mar86-5SA 1⅛(T):4541:1011:482fm 95 116 1215 128 119¼ 108¼ Sibille R6 80000 77-16 Snowcrk,RoylRcors,Bshop'sRngII 12
30Mar86—Wide 7/8 turn
7Mar86-5SA 1¼(T):4641:3632:014fm 82 116 108¼ 104¾ 77½ 78¼ Sibille R9 75000 70-20 RivrOfKings,Snowcrk,Apol'oFlight 12
7Mar86—Steadied at 3/16
Jan 8 SA 3f m :372 h Jan 3 SA 5f ft 1:013 h Dec 30 SA 5f ft 1:02 h Dec 25 SA 3f ft :361 h

G.

Bold Decree

STEVENS G L **115**
Own.—Raymond W C
B. c. 4, by Bold L B—Sweet Kakki Briar, by Etonian
Br.—Jones B C (Ky) **1986 7 2 0 3 $34,125**
Tr.—Frankel Robert $40,000 **1985 5 1 2 1 $13,700**
Lifetime 12 3 2 4 $47,825 **Turf 1 0 0 0**

27Nov86-5Hol 1 :452 1:103 1:364ft *7-5 122 86 43½ 32½ 32½ Stevens G L8 40000 76-18 Sebucan, Split Winners,BoldDecree 8
27Nov86—Broke slowly
13Nov86-9Hol 1 :453 1:101 1:353ft *2½ 119 31 32 34½ 35¾ Stevens G L9 50000 79-23 MischievousMtt,CojkMn,B?ldDecre 9
13Nov86—Fanned wide 1/2; wide into, through stretch
23Oct86-7SA 1 :45 1:104 1:38 ft 6¼ 116 610 74¼ 4¾ 13½ Stevens G L9 50000 78-20 BoldDecree,TrojnTrick,Bruli'sAnte 10
23Oct86—Wide
12Oct86-3SA 1 1/16 :471 1:121 1:444ft *7-5 116 32 2hd 11½ 12 Stevens G L5 40000 77-21 Bold Decree, Convincing,GumFleet 6
12Oct86—Lugged out 7/8
4Oct86-1SA 6½f :214 :45 1:17 ft 4¾ 116 79 77 68 52¼ Stevens G L5 50000 83-18 Inherent Kal, EastTulip,Bruli'sAnte 9
4Oct86—Wide final 3/8
14Sep86-10Pom 6½f :213 :45 1:162ft 5 112 54¼ 59 46½ 34 Ortega L E8 Aw25000 94-08 Tuono, Growler Sandue,BoldDecree 9

11Aug86-7Dmr 6f :213 :443 1:092ft 6¾ 115 66 67 67¼ 45 McCarronCJ5 Aw19000 86-13 RosesArRb,Mr.Mdi,WhipUpThTmpo 7
11Aug86—Bumped start
27Dec85-5SA 6½f :222 :451 1:162ft 8¾ 116 31½ 53¼ 54 31¾ Sibille R1 Aw24000 86-16 DishonorblGust,JttingHom,BoldDcr 8
27Dec85—Wide into stretch
6Oct85-10LaD 1 Ⓣ:4711:1211:381fm 10 113 106¾1212109¾ 710 MlcKC12 MaddenMem 70-19 DustyFare,NewPlymouth,Dr.BeeJy 12
6Oct85—Run in divisions
14Sep85-4LaD 6f :223 :463 1:12 ft *2-3 1155 1hd 12 13 16 Sonnier T J5 Mdn 82-21 BoldDecree,Grenjns,InclindToWin 12
Jan 3 SA 6f ft 1:143 h Dec 28 SA 5f ft 1:004 h Dec 22 SA 5f ft 1:012 h Dec 16 Hol 4f ft :49 h

H.

Alibi Ike
VALENZUELA P A **115**
Own.—Dogwood Stable
B. c. 4, by Alydar—Every Evening, by Roi Dagobert
Br.—Red Oak Farm (Fla) 1986 12 1 1 2 $31,945
Tr.—Russell John W $40,000 Turf 2 0 0 0
Lifetime 12 1 1 2 $31,945

28Dec86-5SA 1 1/16 :462 1:104 1:431ft 11 116 78½1012 918 817¼ ShoemkrW10 Aw28000 68-14 ReEnter,Card'sPlease,InherentKal 10
28Dec86—Lugged out
10Dec86-3Hol 1 :454 1:104 1:371ft 24 116 1½ 2hd 2hd 31½ Solis A4 50000 75-20 Sebucan, Agitate's Pride, Alibi Ike 7
30Nov86-9Hol 1⅛Ⓣ:4741:1221:483fm 21 113 64½ 74¾ 98¼1013¼ ShoemkerW1 Aw24000 72-12 Illumineux, Padoue, Grey Writer 12
2Nov86-9SA 1 :453 1:10 1:351ft 38 116 95¾ 77¼ 58¼ 413 Black C A9 Aw27000 79-10 Midwest King,Danielli,LordAllison 10
2Nov86—Wide final 3/8
23May86-5Bel 1¼Ⓣ:4921:4042:054gd 10 112 2½ 54 10121024¾ Migliore R9 Aw25000 40-35 DeltaDeity,DnceCrdFilled,Gigbyte 12
18May86-6Bel 7f :222 :452 1:222ft 22 117 52½ 52½ 55½ 411 Migliore R2 Aw24000 79-15 Wayar, Johns Treasure, Life Guard 8
6May86-5Aqu 1 :462 1:11 1:361ft 4 117 58 55 46 411¼ Migliore R1 Aw25000 74-21 HaloFire,Concatinate,EveryPlesure 6
6Apr86-7Aqu 1⅛ :472 1:12 1:503m *8-5 119 41½ 43½ 47½ 412 Migliore R3 Aw25000 70-20 PrdeMrshl,SwordRttlr,WimpolMws 8
27Mar86-7Aqu 1 :46 1:111 1:38 ft 3 119 63½ 63¾ 52½ 41½ Santagata N5 Aw25000 74-29 Mr. Classic, GrandExcha[illegible]
13Mar86-6Aqu 1 :471 1:122 1:38 sy *2 122 2½ 2½ 1½ 12¾ Santagata N2 Mdn 76-29 Alibi Ike, Carn[illegible]
Jan 8 Hol 6f ft 1:16 h Dec 24 SA 5f ft 1:02 h Dec 18 Hol 5f ft 1:042 h Nov 26 Hol 6f [illegible]

31.

6th Arlington

6 FURLONGS. (1.08) ALLOWANCE. Purse $14,300 (includes 10% from Illinois Thoroughbred Breeder's Fund). 3-year-olds and upward, Illinois registered, conceived and/or foaled, which have not won two races. Weight, 3-year-olds, 117 lbs.; older, 122 lbs. Non-winners of $9,000 in 1987 allowed 3 lbs.; $6,600 since February 25, 6 lbs.; $4,200 since December 25, 9 lbs. (Races where entered for $20,000 or less not considered in allowances.)

A.

Kilem **113**
Own.—King Farm
B. g. 4, by Tanthem—Kilpedder Lady, by Greek Episode
Br.—King Farm (Ill) 1987 6 0 0 1 $3,819
Tr.—Hoffman Kenneth E 1986 7 1 0 0 $7,366
Lifetime 15 1 0 1 $11,185

20May87-9Spt 1 :483 1:142 1:412ft 21 117 97½1015101810221½ Evans R D8 ⓈAw20790 50-25 AllCorndUp,IllnsMc,TmprryRsdnt 10
8May87-9Spt 1 :484 1:144 1:421ft 27 122 710 87¾ 85¼ 64 Clark K D9 ⓈAw22575 65-23 ChsLprchun,GrryC.,TmporryRsdnt 10
21Apr87-9Spt 6f :233 :474 1:14 ft 30 122 101610121011 812½ King ELJr1 ⓈAw22575 67-29 ColMerchnt,NorthBergn,Frnki'sPl 10
14Apr87-3Spt 6½f :221 :471 1:213sy 29 122 813 79 54½ 32¼ King ELJr4 ⓈAw22050 67-29 ValuedRuler,LeftOnLaramie,Kilem 10
28Mar87-6Spt 1 :484 1:143 1:403ft 51 122 44½ 64½ 67½ 410¾ King ELJr6 ⓈAw23210 66-18 Hrryn'Hoosr,Frnk'sPl,MontryRwrd 9
12Mar87-8Spt 6f :241 :48 1:132ft 46 118 77¼ 812 814 813¾ King ELJr5 ⓈAw22440 69-22 WrgeilhTown,L.M.'sLittlJo,SlowLk 8
20Aug86-5AP 6f :223 :463 1:112ft 86 115 1215121612151218¾ Lindsay R8 ⓈAw14000 66-19 HvngHvHd,Rck'sConsl,WoodnDck 12
15Jly86-9Haw 6f :22 :452 1:11 ft 95 115 88½ 913 917 812 Briggs F R2 ⓈAw15525 74-18 RukenRoyl,Bruce'sBirthdy,DoeNuts 9
1Jly86-9Haw 6f :221 :464 1:123sy 47 115 53¼ 911 912 914½ Briggs F R1 ⓈAw15525 63-20 DcddlyDncn,Brc'sBrthdy,DplmtcB 10
24May86-5Spt 6½f :224 :47 1:191ft 39 115 54½ 74¼ 812 811¾ Briggs F R1 ⓈAw16695 69-15 Mssr.MomntAwy,SHbloIngls,Aqvoc 9

B.

Regal Jeff **108**
Own.—Spleiman J E
Ch. g. 3, by Lord Rebeau—Monarkiss, by Tompion
Br.—Spielman J E (Ill) 1987 1 0 0 0
Tr.—Cunningham Robert T 1986 1 1 0 0 $6,204
Lifetime 2 1 0 0 $6,204

31May87-4AP 6f :223 :462 1:121ft 15 112 87¼ 610 715 821¼ Silva C H8 ⓈAw14300 58-27 Iwntoski,NorthBergen,ChiefPress 10
17Aug86-1Haw 5½f :23 :48 1:074ft 6¼ 119 1½ 11 13 14 Silva C H3 ⓈMdn 73-22 RegalJeff,Palcinto,DependbleDew 12
Jly 10 AP 6f ft 1:182 bg Jly 1 AP 4f ft :491 b Jun 27 AP 4f ft :51 b

C.

Tuff Buster

Own.—BiglowGil&SmthPt&DownsG **113**

B. g. 4, by Island Sultan—Troy's Miss Mille, by Troy Our Boy
Br.—Virant Mary Ann & John (Ill) 1987 2 0 0 0 $858
Tr.—Bigelow Carl 1986 8 1 0 0 $9,142
Lifetime 10 1 0 0 $10,000

8Jly87-5AP	6f	:22	:45^2	1:11^{2}ft	35	120	3^3	3^4	3^4	4$9\frac{1}{4}$	LouvierGE^8	[S]Aw14300	74-20	SssyMr.April,ApcheDncr,TrdDficit	12
17Jun87-7AP	6f	:22^2	:46	1:11 ft	33	116	2$1\frac{1}{2}$	4$1\frac{3}{4}$	6$4\frac{1}{2}$	11$13\frac{1}{4}$	LouvierGE^1	[S]Aw14300	72-19	RlisticTyp,EndZonDncr,ApchDncr	12
7Oct86-9Haw	6f	:22^2	:45^4	1:10^{4}ft	88	117	4$1\frac{1}{2}$	5^3	4$3\frac{1}{4}$	4$8\frac{3}{4}$ †	Briggs F R^6	[S]Aw12705	78-16	Kilovolt,RealisticType,JohnCrmen	10
7Oct86—Broke sharply inside; †Disqualified and placed ninth															
30Sep86-7Haw	6f	:22^1	:45^4	1:11^{2}sy	24	116	2$\frac{1}{2}$	2^4	6^{12}	7$14\frac{3}{4}$	Briggs F R^3	[S]Aw11550	69-19	Aquivoco, Feeling Salty, NuBelleau	7
16Sep86-9Haw	6f	:22^4	:46^3	1:11^{1}ft	27	116	3^1	4$3\frac{1}{2}$	6$4\frac{3}{4}$	6$10\frac{1}{2}$	Briggs F R^1	[S]Aw11550	74-20	Slow Leak, Aquivoco, Feeling Salty	8
31Aug86-5AP	1	:47^2	1:12^4	1:36^{4}ft	14	115	4$2\frac{1}{2}$	5$7\frac{1}{2}$	5^{11}	5$28\frac{1}{2}$	Briggs F R^5	[S]Aw18400	48-18	PapaTricks,BoutDeZan,DremyTune	5
24Aug86-1AP	6f	:23	:47^1	1:13^{3}ft	5	117	5$2\frac{1}{4}$	5$2\frac{1}{4}$	2^{hd}	1$\frac{3}{4}$	Briggs F R^6	[S]Mdn	74-20	Tuff Buster,DaleeDelight,Dependo	11
15Aug86-4Haw	6f	:21^4	:45^3	1:12^{1}ft	22	115	3^5	3^4	4$3\frac{1}{2}$	5$5\frac{3}{4}$	Briggs F R^5	[S]Mdn	74-19	FntsticDsign,InnrFocus,DndyChris	11
27Jun86-9Haw	6f	:22^1	:46^1	1:13^{1}sy	59	115	9$7\frac{3}{4}$	9^{11}	12^{19}	12$20\frac{1}{4}$	Briggs F R^{10}	[S]Mdn	55-21	Powder Pete,St.Rufus,WhiskeyDel	12
20Jun86-5Haw	6f	:22^2	:46	1:12^{2}ft	92	115	10$8\frac{1}{2}$	5$7\frac{1}{2}$	6^{11}	7$12\frac{1}{2}$	Briggs F R^{10}	[S]Mdn	66-25	Hrhm'sImperil,Depndo,CstNoSton	12

●Jly 25 AP 5f ft 1:00^2 h Jly 18 AP 4f ft :49 b Jly 2 AP 4f ft :48^4 b ●Jun 27 AP 4f ft :47^1 h

D.

Trevian

Own.—Sherman E & Denwood D J **113**

B. g. 4, by Terlago—Telzing, by Zingalong
Br.—Springer Frank (Ill) 1987 8 1 1 2 $10,565
Tr.—Humbles Robert L 1986 3 M 1 1 $1,490
Lifetime 11 1 2 3 $12,055

25Jly87-7AP	7f	:23	:46^2	1:24^{4}ft	19	115	4$1\frac{1}{4}$	7^9	6^{10}	5$10\frac{3}{4}$	Silva C H^3	[S]Aw14300	67-22	Endcmnt,BnjmnBckbt,EndZonDncr	9
17Jun87-7AP	6f	:22^2	:46	1:11 ft	20	116	7^6	9^{11}	8$5\frac{3}{4}$	7$9\frac{1}{4}$	Silva C H^5	[S]Aw14300	76-19	RlisticTyp,EndZonDncr,ApchDncr	12
20May87-4Spt	6$\frac{1}{2}$f	:23^1	:47^4	1:19^{4}ft	4$\frac{1}{2}$	122	1$1\frac{1}{2}$	1$1\frac{1}{2}$	1^3	1$2\frac{1}{2}$	Silva C H^7	[S]M20000	78-25	Trevian,CaVaPas,CantankerousBer	9
13May87-5Spt	1	:49^2	1:15^2	1:42^{1}ft	4$\frac{1}{2}$	122	1^1	1$\frac{1}{2}$	1^1	4^4	Silva C H^3	[S]Mdn	65-21	SwiftReflex,MeLnie'sRivr,QuillBid	10
5May87-7Spt	6f	:24	:48^1	1:14^{3}ft	4	122	5^5	3$2\frac{1}{2}$	3$3\frac{1}{2}$	3^2	Silva C H^6	[S]Mdn	75-26	WhatTisIt,CantankerousBer,Trevin	9
17Apr87-9Spt	1	:50^3	1:16^2	1:43^{1}ft	4	117^5	1$1\frac{1}{2}$	2^{hd}	2^{hd}	3^2	Torres F C^4	[S]Mdn	62-30	Rakupon, A Little Salt, Trevian	10
3Apr87-2Spt	6$\frac{1}{2}$f	:22^3	:47^2	1:20^{1}ft	*7-5	122	6^5	6$5\frac{1}{4}$	6^5	6$5\frac{1}{4}$	Desilva A J^4	[S]Mdn	71-23	Overly Glib, Ca VaPas,C.J.'sPrince	10

E.

Mondulick

Own.—Cpm Stables **108**

B. c. 3, by Vencedor—Spirited Florida, by Currock
Br.—Shipp Barry (Ill) 1987 1 0 0 0
Tr.—Tammaro John 1986 4 1 1 1 $39,452
Lifetime 5 1 1 1 $39,452

19Jan87-8Aqu	170[•]	:47	1:13^1	1:43^{3}sy	20	117	9$7\frac{1}{4}$	9^{13}	10^{19}	9$25\frac{1}{2}$	AntlyCW^6	Count Fleet	56-20	Sting'em, Irish Bear, Templar Hill	10
19Jan87—Ducked out															
27Nov86-9CD	1$\frac{1}{16}$	:48^1	1:13^3	1:46^{2}ft	60	113	10^8	8$4\frac{3}{4}$	3$4\frac{1}{2}$	2^4	Kutz D^2	Ky Jky Clb	72-23	Mt.Plesnt,Mondulick,FunnyTunes	11
16Nov86-8Bml	170	:49^1	1:15^3	1:48^{1}ft	11	112	6$7\frac{1}{2}$	5^4	4$5\frac{1}{4}$	4$3\frac{3}{4}$	Bullard BA^4	[S]Cavalier	72-18	Soft Drums, RoyalProctor,Leventi	10
30Oct86-4Bml	6f	:24^1	:48^4	1:16^{2}ft	*3-2	120	4^4	4^2	5$3\frac{1}{2}$	3$2\frac{1}{4}$	Bullard B A^3	Aw6500	75-21	Dmtr'sDncr,PtrBrn'nMry,Mondulck	9
5Oct86-2Haw	6f	:22^2	:46	1:12 ft	3$\frac{1}{4}$	119	5$2\frac{1}{4}$	4$3\frac{1}{2}$	2^{hd}	1^2	Evans R D^9	[S]Mdn	81-18	Mondulick,CatchThisDew,Hg'sGig	12

Jly 26 AP 5f ft 1:03 b Jly 21 AP 5f sy 1:02 b Jly 17 AP 5f ft 1:02 b Jly 9 AP 7f ft 1:28^4 h

F.

Cantankerous Bear

Own.—Medvid Mary **113**

B. c. 4, by Hot Oil—Star o' Dixie, by Dixie Lad
Br.—Cole Jean (Ill) 1987 5 1 1 1 $8,257
Tr.—Thompson Mark L 1986 3 M 0 0
Lifetime 8 1 1 1 $8,257 Turf 1 0 0 0

10Jly87-9AP	1$\frac{1}{16}$[T]	:52	1:17^3	1:50^{2}gd	79	117	1$\frac{1}{2}$	2$\frac{1}{2}$	9^{11}	10^{14}	Briggs F R^6	Aw14000	37-49	SaintOxford,ElClipper,NobleBever	10
17Jun87-7AP	6f	:22^2	:46	1:11 ft	10	116	9$7\frac{3}{4}$	10^{12}	11$7\frac{3}{4}$	10^{11}	LouvierGP^6	[S]Aw14300	74-19	RlisticTyp,EndZonDncr,ApchDncr	12
11Jun87-1AP	6f	:23	:47	1:12^{4}ft	2	123	4^2	3$2\frac{1}{2}$	2^{hd}	1^{hd}	Frazier R L^1	M20000	76-22	CntnkrsBr,RnCptnsBy,ChnLghtnng	8
20May87-4Spt	6$\frac{1}{2}$f	:23^1	:47^4	1:19^{4}ft	*6-5	122	5$3\frac{1}{2}$	4$3\frac{1}{2}$	4$4\frac{1}{2}$	3$3\frac{3}{4}$	Bullard B A^3	[S]M20000	74-25	Trevian,CaVaPas,CantankerousBer	9
5May87-7Spt	6f	:24	:48^1	1:14^{3}ft	5$\frac{3}{4}$	122	6^6	5^4	5$5\frac{1}{2}$	2$1\frac{3}{4}$	Meier R^4	[S]Mdn	75-26	WhatTisIt,CantankerousBer,Trevin	9
20Jun86-5Haw	6f	:22^2	:46	1:12^{2}ft	86	115	4^4	4^6	7^{11}	9$15\frac{1}{4}$	Moran M T^6	[S]Mdn	64-25	Hrhm'sImperil,Depndo,CstNoSton	12
8Jun86-4Haw	6f	:22^4	:47^1	1:12^{2}ft	23	115	8^{10}	8^{14}	9^{17}	10$21\frac{3}{4}$	Briggs F R^5	[S]Mdn	57-26	NoDllince,Hrhm'sImperil,St.Rufus	12
26Apr86-4Spt	6f	:23^2	:47^2	1:12^{2}ft	10	114	8^{17}	8^{18}	8^{17}	7$18\frac{1}{4}$	Richard D^6	[S]Mdn	70-18	PlayAHorn,PowderPete,Mary'sJest	8
26Apr86—Checked first turn															

Jly 18 AP 4f ft :48^1 h Jly 3 AP 4f ft :49^4 b Jun 6 AP 3f ft :36 b May 30 AP 5f ft 1:02^2 b

G.

Chief Press
Own.—R N S Stable & Radke R W **1095**
Dk. b. or br. g. 3, by Hula Chief—No Press, by Nodouble
Br.—Badke R W & Hazelton R P (Ill) 1987 7 1 2 3 $20,346
Tr.—Hazelton Richard P 1986 0 M 0 0
Lifetime 7 1 2 3 $20,346

15Jly87-2AP 7f :221 :47 1:273sy 4 1135 1hd 11 21 24¾ Torres F C3 18500 59-34 Taravis, Chief Press, Draw Quay 9
6Jly87-5AP 6f :221 :46 1:113sy *9-5 118 31½ 32½ 32½ 33¼ Day P6 [S]Aw14300 79-20 Hmmockr,MissouriMountn,ChfPrss 7
31May87-4AP 6f :223 :462 1:121ft 4½ 112 22 2½ 22½ 39½ Fires E3 [S]Aw14300 69-27 Iwntoski,NorthBergen,ChiefPress 10
1Apr87-5Spt 6f :234 :464 1:14 ft 15 1085 33½ 34 33½ 23 Torres F C3 [S]Aw22660 77-24 MyBoyBrett,ChiefPress,VluedRulr 10
23Mar87-5Spt 6½f:221 :462 1:191ft *3½ 113 43½ 35 35½ 46½ Diaz J L6 [S]Aw21230 74-19 GrndmIsTops,MyBoyBrtt,RlstcTyp 10
9Mar87-8Spt 6½f:23 :474 1:201ft *3-2 113 11½ 1½ 21½ 310¾ Diaz J L4 [S]Aw21230 65-29 Bright Brian, Bryan K., Chief Press 8
2Mar87-4Spt 6f :234 :473 1:15 ft *9-5 122 34½ 2hd 1½ 12 Diaz J L7 [S]Mdn 75-20 Chief Press, Dan Swift, Too Bold 10
Jun 20 AP 5f ft 1:02 b Jun 13 AP 3f ft :39 b

32. Emphasize speed and/or pace in this long sprint. *Lay A.C.* is on lasix for the 1st time.

6th Santa Anita

6 ½ FURLONGS. (1.14) CLAIMING. Purse $17,000. 4-year-olds and upward which are non-winners twice since December 25. Weight 121 lbs. Non-winners of a race since February 15 allowed 2 lbs.; of a race since December 25, 4 lbs. Claiming price $16,000; for each $1,000 to $13,000 allowed 1 lb. (Races when entered for $12,500 or less not considered.)

A.

Comets Flare *
PEDROZA M A 5+(5) **117**
Own.—Stewart R D
Dk. b. or br. g. 4, by Impressive—Confectionate, by Reighs Bull
Br.—Monteverdi A F (Cal) 1987 7 1 1 1 $11,500
Tr.—Sanford Thomas $16,000 1986 15 3 1 1 $24,400
Lifetime 26 4 4 3 $45,350

27Mar87-9SA 7f :222 :453 1:242ft 7½ 115 2hd 1½ 13½ 1nk Pedroza M A3 c10000 78-23 CometsFlare,ErnieKing,FamilyFox 12
20Mar87-1SA 6f :22 :451 1:104ft 16 115 52½ 43½ 65½ 78¼ Baze G11 [S] 10000 76-17 Polly's Ruler, Ya Dig,LittleBitIrish 12
20Mar87—Bumped 5/8; lugged in stretch
11Mar87-1SA 6½f:22 :45 1:171ft 9¾ 116 1½ 2hd 1hd 32 Pedroza M A2 10000 82-18 T. V. Oil, Family Fox,CometsFlare 11
18Feb87-1SA 6½f:222 :461 1:18 ft 10 116 21 42½ 910 1012¾ Simpson B H5 10000 67-19 Manzanero, Muralto, With Spirit 11
12Feb87-9SA 6½f:22 :443 1:171ft 12 115 64½ 1014 1013 1014¾ Sibille R8 [S] 10000 69-20 Rodney,DistinctivlyDon,ToddyBoy 10
21Jan87-1SA 6½f:221 :453 1:18 ft 13 115 4¾ 41 74½ 77¾ Sibille R6 12500 72-19 Melchip,M.J.'sDelight,NeutrlPlyer 11
4Jan87-1SA 6½f:214 :45 1:173sy *7-5 117 21½ 21 2hd 2no Sibille R3 c10000 82-22 PckwckLndng,ComtsFlr,SwftMssg 11
19Dec86-5Hol 6f :221 :46 1:113ft *9-5 118 2hd 1hd 11½ 31¾ Stevens G L6 12500 83-17 Air Pirate, St. Alexis, Comets Flare 9
5Dec86-7Hol 1 :45 1:102 1:363ft 5½ 115 1hd 3nk 31½ 78¾ Sibille R1 12500 71-17 Hachi, Son Of Raja,ClassicQuickie 12
19Nov86-6Hol 7f :224 :46 1:241ft 8½ 117 11 11 12 11½ Sibille R8 10000 83-21 Comets Flare,Gulfstreamer,Pulsate 9
●Apr 18 SA 3f ft :35 h Apr 12 SA 3f ft :364 h Apr 6 SA 3f ft :363 h Mar 7 SA 4f m :474 h

B.

Convincing 1-0
DELAHOUSSAYE E **121**
Own.—Banche Mr-Mrs N C
Ch. c. 4, by Believe It—My Sunny Valentine, by Vaguely Noble
Br.—Hancock III & Peters (Ky) 1987 5 1 0 0 $11,725
Tr.—Arena Joseph $16,000 1986 15 2 1 2 $28,490
Lifetime 20 3 1 2 $40,215 Turf 1 0 0 0 $750

12Apr87-9SA 1 1/16:471 1:114 1:44 ft 14 119 1113 1013 1011 711¾ Sibille R2 20000 69-18 Trento, Chagrining, Item Two 12
28Mar87-9SA 1⅛:474 1:124 1:51 ft 5¼ 118 42½ 41½ 55¼ 56¾ Meza R Q3 20000 67-19 PassPassPassed,Trento,MsterNvjo 8
28Mar87—Wide; lugged in stretch
8Mar87-2SA 1½[T]:4742:0432:302gd 18 116 66 74 55 57¼ Sibille R8 Aw30000 56-26 SunMan,RussianLogic,ShadowsFall 9
27Feb87-9SA 1⅛:461 1:11 1:501ft 9¼ 116 812 99¾ 78 1½ DelahoussayeE3 20000 78-16 Convincing,Robrsky,LyphrdChims 10
27Feb87—Broke slowly; wide into stretch
18Feb87-9SA 1 1/16:462 1:112 1:432ft 4¾ 115 68 84¾ 66 66½ Olivares F4 c16000 77-19 Navegante, Robersky, GreyMissile 11
10Dec86-6BM 1 1/16:46 1:103 1:442ft 3½ 114 66 54½ 54¼ 41 Loseth C2 25000 69-21 IvnPhllps,BonVvntDottor,ClWyHlm 7
14Nov86-7BM 1 1/16:464 1:111 1:43 ft 3¾ 114 66½ 64¼ 66½ 65¾ Loseth C2 40000 71-20 Arbitrate,DoctorDakota,GreekNtive 8
31Oct86-5SA 1⅛:461 1:103 1:492ft 22 114 66 63¼ 55½ 44 Pedroza MA5 Aw27000 78-16 Mr. Media, Jota, Rafael's Dancer 9
12Oct86-3SA 1 1/16:471 1:121 1:444ft 3½ 114 54½ 43 34 22 Olivares F2 35000 75-21 Bold Decree, Convincing,GumFleet 6
12Oct86—Pinched at start
27Sep86-9Pom a1⅛:462 1:12 1:503ft 62 114 109 1011 1014 810¼ DouglsRR10 Pom Dby 84-10 LghtnngToch,Rfl'sDncr,BoldBrvII 10
27Sep86—Run in divisions
Mar 25 SA 5f ft :594 h

C.

Lay A. C.
Ch. g. 4, by Come Clean—Noble Glow, by Tumble Wind
CISNEROS J E 109 5 Br.—Trujillo J (Cal) 1987 4 0 0 0
Own.—Trujillo J H Tr.—Carbajal Sal $13,000 1985 5 1 1 1 $23,900
Lifetime 9 1 1 1 $23,900

2Apr87-9SA 1 1/16 :47 1:113 1:442ft 15 115 109½ 1112 912 915½ Gomez R5 12500 63-20 OneEyedRomeo,Bruli'sAnte,Nathn 12
22Mar87-9SA 6½f :22 :444 1:17 gd 55 116 104¾ 107¼ 108½ 910¼ Gomez R5 [S] 20000 75-23 Bennett Peak, Danchai, Melchip 11
1Mar87-1SA 6½f :214 :442 1:162ft 93 1105 32 54 910 1012½ Medero F12 28000 75-15 SprbMomnt,DshonorblGst,Dnsprt 12
21Feb87-2SA 6f :214 :444 1:094ft 45 115 77 77¼ 79 813 Patterson A3 40000 76-14 Crcksmn,LuckyMsddo,ElPrsdntUno 9
21Feb87—Rough start
13Nov85-7Hol 6f :23 :473 1:132gd 3¾ 117 54½ 43 32 22½ DelhoussyeE7 Aw22000 74-26 SmokeyOrbit,LyA.C.,RmblingMonti 7
20ct85-8SA 7f :221 :451 1:233ft 12 115 34½ 77¾ 815 716 McCarron CJ4 Sny Slp 66-17 LouisianSlew,SnowChief,DonB.Blue 8
20ct85—Bumped, jostled at 3 1/2
28Aug85-8Dmr 1 :461 1:111 1:363ft 16 114 43½ 32½ 43 47½ Ortega LE6 Balboa 77-16 Swear, Bright Tom, Smokey Orbit 9
28Aug85—Grade III
31Jly85-8Dmr 6f :223 :463 1:111ft 11 114 73½ 54½ 54½ 33½ Ortega L E8 [S]Grdtn 78-19 BolgerMagic,LittleRedCloud,LyA.C. 9
31Jly85—Pinched back, bumped and steadied at 4 1/2
5Jly85-5Hol 5½f :222 :454 1:044ft 11 118 46 33½ 31½ 13½ Ortega L E11 M50000 — — Lay A. C., Exalted Bubble, Pico P. 12
Apr 11 SA 4f ft :474 h Apr 1 SA 3f ft :354 h Mar 21 SA 3f ft :344 h

D.

Dusty Trader *
Ch. h. 8, by Dusty Canyon—Kudu Glory, by Kudu
SIBILLE R 119 Br.—Qvale K M (Cal) 1987 6 2 0 2 $22,150
Own.—Hale & Hale Jr Tr.—Lewis Gary $16,000 1986 7 2 1 3 $15,715
Lifetime 67 14 14 12 $199,010 Turf 4 0 1 0 $7,865

5Apr87-1SA 7f :221 :444 1:24 ft *3½ 1145 31½ 33 43½ 41½ Gryder A T7 [S] 16000 78-16 Like Shantin, AirPirate,NewStorm 10
19Mar87-1SA 6f :22 :452 1:103ft *2 119 42 53 45 45½ Stevens G L9 c12500 79-21 NtiveCptive,EllsBrvestSong,OlDd 11
4Mar87-1SA 6f :212 :443 1:102ft *1 119 44 44 41 12¾ Stevens G L7 [S] c10000 86-16 Dusty Trader,Bride'sAdvice,YaDig 11
4Mar87—Wide into stretch
25Feb87-1SA 6½f :213 :442 1:171ft *2¾ 120 41 43½ 42½ 32 Solis A3 16000 82-20 Amarone, Tigerillo, Dusty Trader 10
25Feb87—Bumped start; checked, altered course 3/8; wide into stretch
6Feb87-9SA 7f :22 :45 1:232ft 6 116 1hd 11 11½ 11¼ Solis A1 [S] 16000 83-15 Dusty Trader, Grenobie,AguaRusso 8
24Jan87-7BM 6f :222 :451 1:102sy 4 115 31½ 53¼ 64¾ 32½ Lamance C1 c12500 84-24 E. J. Junior, MoveFree,DustyTrader 8
13Dec86-7BM 6f :221 :451 1:102ft *2 114 43½ 44 54 32½ Baze R A6 c16000 84-19 AckAck'sJoy,ShdowWtch,DstyTrdr 9
22Nov86-5BM 6f :23 :461 1:111ft *8-5 114 32½ 32 1½ 11 Lamance C10 c10000 83-24 DustyTrader,DownRange,FireyStr 12
16Nov86-5BM 6f :231 :462 1:102ft 3½ 114 2hd 1hd 2hd 12 Lamance C7 8000 87-21 DustyTrder,StretsmrtNtiv,WhtAStr 8
1Nov86-8BM 6f :224 :462 1:112ft 3¼ 114 42 42½ 43½ 33½ Lamance C1 [S] 8000 78-21 FleetWver,HustleADnce,DustyTrder 8
Apr 1 SA 3f ft :354 h Mar 13 SA 3f ft :362 h

E.

Like Shantin
Dk. b. or br. h. 5, by Exalted Rullah—Career, by Poona II
PATTON D B 116 5 Br.—Christianson C T K (Cal) 1987 3 1 1 0 $11,950
Own.—Christianson & Truman Tr.—Truman Eddie $16,000 1985 3 2 0 1 $21,950
Lifetime 6 3 1 1 $33,900

5Apr87-1SA 7f :221 :444 1:24 ft 4¼ 1085 11 11½ 11½ 11¼ Patton D B 6 [S] 14000 80-16 Like Shantin, AirPirate,NewStorm 10
20Mar87-1SA 6f :22 :451 1:104ft 3½ 115 65½ 76¾ 76 66¼ Cordova D W3 [S] c10000 78-17 Polly's Ruler, Ya Dig,LittleBitIrish 12
4Mar87-2SA 6f :212 :442 1:102ft 6½ 115 3nk 2½ 22½ 22½ Cordova D W6 [S] 10000 83-16 Polly'sRuler,LikShntin,Cody'sChnc 9
18Oct85-2SA 6f :214 :45 1:11 ft 5½ 116 2hd 1hd 1½ 1¾ Kaenel J L2 [S] c16000 83-19 LikShntin,ForgtThPockt,TwoHrts 12
26Jly85-3Dmr 6f :22 :45 1:091ft 7¼ 116 2½ 32 33 36¾ McCrrnCJ7 [S]Aw18000 85-13 MistrGnnro,MostDtrmind,LikShntn 7
26Jly85—Fanned wide at 3/8
20Jun85-2Hol 6f :223 :46 1:11 ft *6-5 115 2hd 35 22 1½ McCarron C J6 [S]Mdn 92-07 LikShntin,RodOfFortun,Cptn'sChnc 9
Apr 16 SA 5f ft 1:043 h Mar 30 SA 5f ft 1:001 h Mar 3 SA 3f ft :373 h Feb 23 SA 5f ft 1:01 h

F.

Shantin *
B. g. 8, by Exalted Rullah—Career, by Poona II
ORTEGA L E 114 Br.—Christianson C T K (Cal) 1987 2 0 1 0 $2,500
Own.—Hold Racing Stable Tr.—Stepp William T $13,000 1986 8 2 0 1 $19,500
Lifetime 48 6 9 9 $113,895

12Apr87-4SA 6½f :214 :452 1:173ft *2½ 117 84¾ 85½ 75¼ 76¼ Pincay L Jr 1 16000 76-18 ErliFirs,GlicMony,Cool'nScndlous 10
1Apr87-1SA 6½f :22 :453 1:18 ft 10 116 74½ 52¼ 22½ 21¾ Simpson B H 5 [S] 10000 78-23 Valcreon, Shantin, Ya Dig 8
1Apr87—Broke through gate; broke slowly
28May86-6Hol 6f :221 :453 1:104ft 15 116 1012 1022 1029 — Kaenel J L1 20000 — — PowrfulEys,FlyingLssons,MhJong 10
28May86—Eased; Very wide 3/8
17May86-3Hol 6f :223 :454 1:11 ft 4 119 119 1012 108¾ 97½ Pedroza M A 4 20000 81-14 PowerfulEyes,Grenobl,SwordPrinc 11
17May86—Bumped break
1May86-7Hol 7f :222 :452 1:242ft 12 119 74¾ 64½ 43 3nk Pedroza M A 4 20000 82-17 Bold Topsider, Doodlesack,Shantin 9
21Apr86-3SA 6f :214 :45 1:103ft 7¾ 116 63½ 75¼ 117 107½ Kaenel J L 11 25000 77-16 Reinbow'sCup,Timlin,BoldTopsidr 12
28Mar86-1SA 6f :213 :45 1:104ft 6½ 116 43 32 21½ 1hd Kaenel J L 5 18000 84-19 Shantin, Conniption Fit, GranBarba 7
20Mar86-2SA 6f :214 :444 1:101ft 11 116 41½ 1½ 1½ 11¾ Kaenel J L 7 [S] 12500 87-19 Shantin,RunningDebonair,IrishCast 9
13Mar86-1SA 6f :214 :454 1:113m 6½ 116 109¼ 810 88 77½ Hernandez R 1 12500 73-30 LckyRoom,PckwckLndng,SprArnd 10
1Mar86-2SA 6½f :221 :451 1:17 ft 9¼ 116 85¼ 99¾ 78¼ 55¾ Hernandez R5 12500 79-16 ForgtTiPockt,Glfstrmr,FrtthPrnc 11
1Mar86—Wide into stretch
Apr 10 SA 3f ft :354 h Mar 30 SA 4f ft :49 h Mar 26 SA 5f ft 1:012 hg Mar 19 SA 6f ft 1:153 h

G.

Numpkins
MCHARGUE D G — 117
Own.—Coscas G G
Ch. g. 4, by Irish Port—Turnover Time, by Hawaii
Br.—O'Neill R J (Cal)
Tr.—Dion Jean Pierre — $16,000
Lifetime 9 2 2 1 $9,020
1987 4 0 0 0
1986 5 2 2 1 $9,020
Turf 1 0 0 1 $700

2Apr87-5SA 6f :213 :444 1:104ft 21 116 31½ 45½ 59½ 69¾ Douglas R R 5 20000 74-20 Pialor, Bold Batter Up,FleetAlbert 10
15Mar87-9SA 1 1/16 :464 1:121 1:444ft 24 114 1hd 32½ 1015 1022½ Douglas R R 10 28000 54-20 RexLke,ShowerDecre,NordicLight 10
28Feb87-3SA 6½f:213 :444 1:171ft 8¼ 117 32 65½ 87½ 89 Castanon A L7 c20000 75-17 ClssicQuck,NghtSwop,Ambuty'sJoy 8
28Feb87—Steadied early
14Feb87-2SA 6f :212 :442 1:103sy 6¼ 115 55 48 59½ 711¼ Olivares F6 c16000 74-17 Pialor, PineappleJack,Polly'sRuler 10
26Dec86-9TuP a7½f ⓣ:253 :491 1:331fm 2¾ 117 1½ 1hd 2hd 32½ Hare K S6 Aw7000 94-03 Chief OfFire,NativeFella,Numpkins 7
10Dec86-10TuP 5½f:232 :483 1:09 sl 2 120 1½ 1½ 2½ 2hd Hare K S1 Aw6500 63-59 Kuhio King, Numpkins,LuckyMagic 5
26Nov86-10TuP 6f :221 :443 1:093ft 4 115 1hd 22 21½ 1no Hare K S3 Aw6800 88-17 Numpkins,GreyRider,NativeForecst 6
9Nov86-8TuP 6f :22 :45 1:101ft 4¼ 111 2½ 2hd 21½ 2½ Guerra V J5 c18000 84-17 Lequori, Numpkins, Native Fella 11
8Oct86-3TuP 6f :214 :443 1:102ft 7½ 118 1hd 1hd 12 15 Guerra V J5 M10000 84-16 Numpkins, EntryDay,SplendidApple 6
Apr 13 SA 5f ft 1:01 h Mar 25 SA 3f ft :342 h Mar 10 SA 6f ft 1:124 h Feb 23 Hol 5f ft 1:024 h

H.

Air Pirate
MEZA R Q — 117
Own.—Fleishman & Levin
B. g. 4, by Pirate's Bounty—Princess Babu, by Our Babu
Br.—Windy Hill TBA (Cal)
Tr.—Soriano Morris — $16,000
Lifetime 20 3 1 2 $52,125
1987 5 0 1 1 $8,575
1986 14 2 0 1 $36,950
Turf 1 0 0 0

5Apr87-1SA 7f :221 :444 1:24 ft 6¼ 115 21 21½ 21½ 21½ Meza R Q 2 Ⓢ 16000 79-16 Like Shantin, AirPirate,NewStorm 10
14Mar87-2SA 6½f:214 :444 1:163ft 2¾ 116 64¾ 66 45½ 45½ DelahoussyeE5 c10000 81-16 Polly'sRuler,BoldBttrUp,VisiblAsst 9
14Mar87—Broke slowly
4Mar87-1SA 6f :212 :443 1:102ft 4 117 1111 910 76½ 45¼ DelhoussyeE4 Ⓢ 10000 81-16 Dusty Trader,Bride'sAdvice,YaDig 11
4Mar87—Bumped start
1Feb87-1SA 6f :22 :451 1:11 ft 4½ 1125 65½ 64¼ 43½ 42¾ Patton D B2 Ⓢ c12500 81-16 Don's Co'op, Rodney, Polly's Ruler 8
1Feb87—Rough start
17Jan87-1SA 6f :22 :454 1:12 ft 15 1105 95¾ 55 41½ 33 Patton D B5 16000 75-18 West Boy II, Unagloshi, AirPirate 12
17Jan87—Bumped start
27Dec86-2SA 6½f:214 :444 1:164ft 8¾ 1095 57 57 54½ 64¼ Patton D B7 22500 82-19 Doonsport, BlueIce,ExaltedBubble 10
19Dec86-5Hol 6f :221 :46 1:113ft 3½ 1105 44½ 44½ 32 1hd Patton D B5 c12500 85-17 Air Pirate, St. Alexis, Comets Flare 9
3Dec86-7Hol 6f :221 :452 1:11 ft 29 1115 116½ 98¼ 65 43¾ Patton D B9 Ⓢ 20000 84-18 GrowlerSndue,ShowerDecree,Pilor 11
3Dec86—Bumped at break
21Nov86-7Hol 7f :22 :45 1:23 ft 6 116 32 42½ 55 — Valenzuela P A6 25000 — — StickyTrigger,NnteTm,PowerLever 8
21Nov86—Eased
19Oct86-5SA 6½f:214 :45 1:171ft 12 113 41¾ 42 87¼ 810¼ Shoemaker W3 40000 74-18 PtriotGlovs,GryPinstrp,Vrttm'sPrd 8
19Oct86—Bumped break
Apr 18 SA 4f ft :472 h Apr 2 SA 4f ft :46 hg Feb 28 Hol 4f ft :514 h ●Feb 23 Hol 3f ft :354 h

I.

Saros Chick
CASTANON A L — 117
Own.—Hidalgo & Quiles
B. c. 4, by Saros—Bic's Chick, by Bicker
Br.—Green Thumb Farm (Cal)
Tr.—Quiles Victor M — $16,000
Lifetime 19 1 2 1 $19,950
1987 4 0 0 0 $1,275
1986 12 1 2 1 $18,425

12Apr87-1SA 6½f:213 :444 1:17 ft 55 116 99¼ 77½ 66 55¾ Pedroza M A 3 16000 79-18 FirstBeginning,BlazingZulu,TiHigh 10
12Apr87—Placed fourth through disqualification; Broke slowly
1Apr87-1SA 6½f:22 :453 1:18 ft 3½ 117 21 31½ 810 712¼ Pincay L Jr 8 Ⓢ c10000 68-23 Valcreon, Shantin, Ya Dig 8
1Apr87—Took up at 1/4
8Mar87-1SA 6f :211 :442 1:11 gd 27 116 87½ 76½ 79½ 610¾ Meza R Q 1 25000 72-15 Roses Are Reb, Paskanell, Pialor 8
27Feb87-5SA 6f :213 :443 1:09 ft 9 116 98¼ 99 914 1018¼ VlenzuelPA6 Ⓢ c20000 75-16 Pialor, Melchip, Detector 11
27Feb87—Bobbled start; wide into stretch
17Jly86-9Hol 7f :224 :463 1:24 ft 3½ 116 66 54 55½ 55¼ DelahoussayeE 7 25000 79-17 PecefulImge,MimiDrem,LeewrdPirt 7
17Jly86—Wide 3/8 turn
11Jly86-3Hol 1 :462 1:112 1:371ft 5 116 21 3nk 42 67½ Shoemaker W 2 40000 69-14 Joab, Inherent Kal, I Love Racing 6
11Jly86—Lugged in stretch
14Jun86-2Hol 6f :22 :452 1:104ft 3¾ 116 75¼ 67 75½ 66½ ValenzuelaPA11 32000 84-14 Time Share, East Tulip, New Doc 12
4Jun86-9Hol 1 :462 1:114 1:37 ft 4 116 41½ 3½ 31½ 44¾ Stevens G L 6 50000 73-18 Gaelic Knight, Joab, Jumbled 7
4Jun86—Hopped in air
15May86-5Hol 1 :453 1:103 1:37 ft 12 116 2½ 1hd 2½ 2¾ Stevens G L 6 40000 77-13 Gaelic Knight, Saros Chick, Joab 9
21Apr86-1SA 1 :461 1:114 1:374ft 10 114 43½ 62¾ 52¾ 44¾ Stevens G L 5 40000 74-16 Joab, Jury Time, Cabriome 10
Mar 27 SA 6f ft 1:124 h Mar 21 SA 4f ft :473 h Mar 16 SA 3f ft :352 h Feb 23 SA 5f ft :532 h

J.

Natural Courage
GRYDER A T 5+ (5) 112⁵
Own.—M B M Enterprises

Ch. g. 4, by L'Natural—Courageous Girl, by Terresto
Br.—Valenti & Coelho (Cal) 1987 5 0 0 0 $425
Tr.—Hageman Walter $16,000 1986 8 2 0 1 $20,700
Lifetime 15 2 0 1 $21,950

21Mar87-1SA 6f :213 :443 1:102sy 35 1115 1hd 1½ 11 52¾ Cox D W1 16000 83-16 ForbesReply,BoldBtterUp,VlDeRoi 12
7Mar87-1SA 6½f :214 :444 1:184gd 20 1115 32 2½ 43 610 Cox D W5 Ⓢ 16000 76-19 Bennett Peak, Don's Tryst,Tigerillo 7
27Feb87-5SA 6f :213 :443 1:09 ft 43 115 63¼ 70½ 812 915¾ Patterson A1 Ⓢ 20000 77-16 Pialor, Melchip, Detector 11
31Jan87-2SA 6f :214 :443 1:093ft 34 115 84¼ 97½ 121512 18¾ Stevens S A2 25000 71-15 Lequori,KidShelleen,TimeToSmok 12
17Jan87-2SA 6f :214 :45 1:103ft 56 114 31 43 1015 — Stevens S A10 40000 — — Ondarty, Romaxe, Rivets Factor 11
17Jan87—Eased
7May86-4Hol 6f :214 :452 1:102ft 11 116 21½ 21½ 1½ 31¾ Pedroza M A5 62500 90-12 Angle Arc,K.Gibran,NaturalCourage 6
17Apr86-7SA 6f :213 :45 1:101ft 11 116 22 42¼ 36½ 612 Stevens G L4 Aw24000 75-22 GrVitting,FullChrm,FollowTheDncr 7
17Apr86—Stumbled at start
30Mar86-7SA 1 :463 1:122 1:393ft 8 116 11½ 1½ 32 58½ Meza R Q2 ⓈAw31000 61-24 Scrapbook, Tourismo, Nick'sPrince 8
30Mar86—Bumped at 1/8
17Mar86-2SA 6f :22 :453 1:123sy 5 117 67½ 55¼ 43½ 42½ Shoemaker W6 c32000 72-27 TrinityHll,GrowlrSndu,BckStrtBlus 7
17Mar86—Broke very slowly
6Mar86-2SA 6f :213 :444 1:101ft 4 118 1hd 11½ 13 13½ ShoemakerW6 Ⓢ 25000 87-15 NaturalCourage,GreyHill,DonThlini 9
Apr 18 SA 3f ft :353 h Apr 12 SA 4f ft :472 h Apr 3 SA 5f ft 1:003 h Mar 30 SA 4f ft :472 h

33.

7th Arlington

1 MILE. (1.32⅘) ALLOWANCE. Purse $16,000. Fillies and mares. 3-year-olds and upward. Illinois registered conceived and/or foaled which have not won $5,700 three times other than maiden, claiming or starter. Weight, 3-year-olds, 116 lbs.; older, 123 lbs. Non-winners of $10,200 since Labory Day allowed 3 lbs.; $7,200 twice since August 18 allowed 6 lbs.; $6,600 twice in 1986-87 allowed 9 lbs. (Maiden, claiming and starter races not considered in allowances.)

A.

Precious Charm
Own.—Evans G Sr & Rice Carol R 123

Dk. b. or br. f. 4, by George Navonod—Dandy Lisa, by Carry Back
Br.—Rice Thomas (Ill) 1987 6 1 1 0 $19,294
Tr.—Bohn Bernard F 1986 11 2 2 2 $31,967
Lifetime 17 3 3 2 $51,261 Turf 1 0 0 0

2Jly87-9AP 1 Ⓣ:4721:13 1:382fm 43 121 812 912 914 911¼ King ELJr 9 ⒻAw17000 73-18 LookWhos'Cmn,Tx'sTts,WllHllDlly 9
22Jun87-8AP 1 :461 1:12 1:382gd 11 118 511 57¾ 46½ 410 King ELJr 2 ⒻAw17000 59-22 PrincessBri,NorthernMidn,DncQun 5
18May87-7Spt 1 :481 1:141 1:414sy 3½ 115 814 610 36 11¼ Meza N 5 ⒻⓈAw21945 71-25 PrciousChrm,ShnnonM.B.,KlinAvnu 8
24Apr87-7Spt 6½f :231 :473 1:211ft 8¾ 116 711 79½ 65 2½ Meza N 7 ⒻⓈAw23835 70-28 RosyRydr,PrciousChrm,Pick'sChick 7
1Apr87-5OP 1 1/16 :472 1:124 1:451ft 7½ 116 711 66½ 66½ 510¾ Johnson P A4 Ⓕ 12500 64-23 KellyAnn,StunchObsession,SlyWhlr 7
11Mar87-4OP 1 1/16 :463 1:113 1:434ft 11 116 827 816 713 719¾ Whited D E 6 Ⓕ 20000 62-18 SilverSugar,LacyDaisy,Dr.Ray'sBby 8
1Oct86-7Haw 6f :224 :463 1:114sy 4¼ 111 67 68½ 54 44½ KngELJr 5 ⒻⓈAw14520 77-21 QukerTyp,RunMissRun,Bold'nPurpl6
17Sep86-5Haw 6f :222 :453 1:102ft 5½ 112 55½ 68 44 34¼ KngELJr 1 ⒻⓈAw13200 85-15 AuntSndy,QukerType,PrciousChrm 6
6Sep86-8Haw 1 1/16 :471 1:123 1:444ft 8¾ 112 814 817 44½ 57 KngELJr 1 ⒻⓈIll Oaks 67-19 ComfortsofHom,WhtPrl,PrttyPlm 10
25Aug86-6AP 7f :222 :452 1:241ft 45 114 1414 1212 810 57 KELJr 9 ⒻⓈColfax Md 74-19 ComfortsfHm,NtvMry,ZngAlngBll 14
Jun 21 AP 3f sy :38 b

B.

Rosy Ryder
Own.—Magnificent 8 Stable 116

B. f. 3, by Red Ryder—Rosalie Mae Wynn, by New Policy
Br.—Santen John D Mr & Mrs (Ill) 1987 5 2 2 0 $39,185
Tr.—Getz George J 1986 2 1 0 0 $4,140
Lifetime 7 3 2 0 $43,325

24May87-8AP 7f :231 :471 1:26 ft 18 110 75 77 56½ 56¾ BrfldD 1 ⒻⓈColfax M 65-27 UniqueType,AirAppeal,CndidType 12
9May87-6Spt 6½f :23 :47 1:194ft 6 113 67¾ 67½ 33 2¾ DesilvAJ 3 ⒻⓈAw24465 77-22 JzzBurger,RosyRyder,InvernessRib 7
24Apr87-7Spt 6½f :231 :473 1:211ft *8-5 111 54½ 32½ 21 1½ Diaz J L 2 ⒻⓈAw23835 71-28 RosyRydr,PrciousChrm,Pick'sChick 7
13Apr87-9Spt 6f :232 :48 1:14 ft 6½ 113 33 21½ 22 23¼ Diaz J L 1 ⒻⓈAw23310 77-23 JazzBurger,RosyRyder,ShnnonM.B. 9
29Mar87-3Spt 6f :24 :474 1:144sy *6-5 113 43 31 1hd 2hd Diaz J L 5 ⒻⓈAw22660 76-19 ‡ProudLine,RosyRyder,Hert'sScrt 10
29Mar87—Bumped by rival several times stretch; Placed first through disqualification
15Oct86-5Bml 6f :24 :484 1:16 ft *8-5 120 11 12 13 12¼ Diaz J L 6 ⒻⓈMdn 79-22 Rosy Ryder, Hech No, Sultan'sMiss 9
6Oct86-6Haw 6f :221 :46 1:122ft *2-3 119 11½ 11 2hd 67½ Gavidia W 3 ⒻⓈMdn 71-18 FrewellAmeli,BlindHope,RocktTyp 10
Jly 30 AP 5f ft 1:02 b Jly 25 AP 6f ft 1:16 b Jly 18 AP 4f ft :494 b Jly 8 AP 6f ft 1:172 b

C.

Cooney Deb — B. f. 3, by Executive Order—Jamie Joy Deb, by Whitesburg
Br.—Craig James C (Ill) — 1987 9 3 3 1 $48,648
Own.—Craig Ent Inc — 116 — Tr.—Fernandez Jose — 1986 7 2 0 1 $9,962
Lifetime 16 5 3 2 $58,610

4Jly87-9FP 6f :221 :451 1:11 ft *6-5 119 22 22 32½ 34¾ BldsMA1 (F)Satin & L 83-20 Candid Type, AirAppeal,CooneyDeb 5
20Jun87-9FP 6f :221 :451 1:104ft 5½ 112 11 12½ 12 11 BldsMA1 (F)[S]P Queen 89-20 Cooney Deb, CandidType,AirAppeal 9
24Apr87-8Spt 6f :24 :481 1:13 ft 5½ 115 11½ 3½ 56½ 511¼ Razo E Jr4 (F)[S]Violet 74-28 UniqueType,JazzBurger,YukonDolly 8
24Apr87—Steadied second turn
13Apr87-8OP 6f :213 :453 1:11 gd 2¼ 116 42 21½ 32 22½ HightowrTW3 Aw16000 82-16 AnythngforLov,ConyDb,ChrystlLrk 6
3Apr87-8OP 6f :222 :462 1:103ft 10 109 1hd 1½ 1hd 21½ HightowrTW8 (F)HcpO 85-17 OnlyaGlnce,CooneyDeb,ReefofGold 8
20Mar87-3OP 6f :22 :454 1:104ft *6-5 114 2hd 2hd 1hd 12 Day P3 (F) 30000 86-16 CoonyDb,BttyBinBd,PulskiCountss 8
12Mar87-5OP 6f :22 :452 1:104ft 3 116 2½ 1hd 1hd 2no HightowrTW8 (F) 25000 86-17 AshlyStwrt,CoonyDb,MrnngPrncss 8
4Mar87-6OP 6f :222 :461 1:111ft 18 112 41¾ 1hd 12 12¾ HightowrTW6 (F) 18000 84-16 Cooney Deb, CoolChris,Sexysense 10
13Feb87-5OP 6f :22 :451 1:103ft 16 111 108 109¾ 1220 1226¾ GonzalezCV 10 (F) 20000 60-15 EbonyJewel,BoldBrvMry,BbyBing 12
14Dec86-8Bml 1 1/16 :47 1:14 1:49 ft 12 119 11 1½ 22½ 812½ Patin K C 8 (F)HcpO 68-14 TimelessJig,RoseThif,SwingOutFr 12
Jly 30 AP 4f ft :504 b Jly 24 AP 5f ft 1:014 b Jly 18 AP 4f ft :504 b Jly 1 AP 4f ft :502 b

D.

Triple Pretty — Dk. b. or br. m. 5, by L'Enjoleur—Century Type, by Levee
Br.—Namen A (Ill) — 1987 7 0 0 0 $2,488
Own.—Bredeson Sharon & Dísko H — 1095 — Tr.—Yanez Moses R — 1986 15 1 1 1 $18,088
Lifetime 34 3 5 1 $52,069 — Turf 9 0 0 0 $2,536

29Jun87-4AP 7f :223 :454 1:244ft 45 114 713 713 718 740¾ SmthME6 (F)[S]Aw17600 37-24 WhataPearl,YukonDolly,NativeMry 7
29Jun87—Bled
14Jun87-7AP 1 [T]:48 1:1241:372fm 87 116 21 22½ 44½ 79¾ Razo E Jr4 (F) 25000 79-08 Kelly'sSuperPt,JtStPg,WllHlloDolly 8
1Jun87-7AP 1 1/16 [T]:4821:12 1:442fm 98 112 67 58 89¾ 814¼ Bullard BA7 (F)Aw17000 67-19 OleBowWower,KpThFithII,BrwCrw 9
24May87-7AP 1 (T):50 1:1541:412gd 76 112 2hd 21½ 66 47 Bullard BA4 (F)Aw17000 61-32 Eva G., Wina Jackpot, LittleSarah 10
9May87-6Spt 6½f :23 :47 1:194ft 53 121 57½ 56½ 56¼ 48¾ RazoEJr6 (F)[S]Aw24465 69-22 JzzBurger,RosyRyder,InvernessRib 7
18Apr87-7Spt 6f :242 :483 1:134ft 3¼e 121 79 79 76¾ 77 PatinKC8 (F)[S]Aw24675 74-21 QkrTyp,SomthngSoRght,InvrnssRb 8
2Apr87-8Spt 6½f :231 :471 1:191ft 92 116 76½ 76½ 710 613 RazoEJr5 (F)[S]Aw25300 68-26 What A Rose, MissAtari,ASlimChic 7
14Nov86-7Bml 6f :241 :482 1:164ft 11 116 710 610 612 58¾ Meza N7 (F)Aw7500 66-32 Love Trip, Marine General, Upkeep 7
7Nov86-8Bml 6f :24 :48 1:142ft 22 116 710 56 46 25½ Meza N3 (F)[S]Aw9200 81-22 DnceingJff,TriplPrtty,HomwyHony 7
26Oct86-8Bml 1 1/16 :481 1:152 1:503sy 9e 111 1011 1014 1020 1024¼ MN10 (F)[S]Hardenbk H 49-21 PrettyPlum,HonyMcDn,SwtOlShri 11
Jly 30 AP 4f ft :502 b Jun 13 AP 3f ft :37 b

E.

Ben's Duchess — Gr. m. 5, by Gallant Romeo—Silverfly, by T V Lark
Br.—Unruh Marilyn M (Ill) — 1987 8 2 2 2 $32,731
Own.—Doubledown Stable Inc — 120 — Tr.—Poulos Ernie T — 1986 6 0 1 1 $5,728
Lifetime 17 3 3 3 $47,807

1Jly87-7AP 6f :23 :473 1:124ft 2 112 22½ 1hd 11½ 11½ Fires E2 (F)[S]Aw16500 76-23 Ben'sDuchess,RullhBess,SideGlnce 6
1Jly87—Drftd out lte trn
20Jun87-6AP 7f :23 :464 1:243ft 8-5 114 52½ 43 35½ 37 Day P6 (F)[S]Aw16500 72-22 TryGuessing,IntrpidMt,Bn'sDuchss 7
6Jun87-2AP 7f :231 :462 1:252ft *1-2 112 2hd 21½ 22 13 Fires E2 (F)[S]Aw14300 75-19 Ben'sDuchess,CaraLrk,OurLittleSis 8
21May87-7Spt 6½f :233 :48 1:203ft 2 121 31½ 31 22½ 24½ PatinKC1 (F)[S]Aw20370 69-26 IntrepidMt,Bn'sDuchss,ChicknPitz 10
4May87-7Spt 6f :241 :49 1:152ft 9 121 84¾ 73 31 2nk PatinKC1 (F)[S]Aw22575 73-26 GoldnJun,Bn'sDuchss,MissAlcinto 10
22Apr87-9Spt 6½f :233 :482 1:214sy *2 121 914 911 88¼ 55½ Meier R4 (F)[S]Aw22575 62-29 SideGlnce,OurLittieSis,Herb'sndSlt 9
11Apr87-3Spt 1 :493 1:151 1:413gd *8-5 121 75½ 65 69½ 511½ KngELJr8 (F)[S]Aw22575 60-21 HrhmsAngl,HrtsScrt,SmthngUnnn 10
11Apr87—Steadied after a half
28Mar87-5Spt 6f :232 :473 1:131ft 3 121 511 611 36½ 37½ KngELJr4 (F)[S]Aw22660 76-18 BlindHope,FrewllAmli,Bn'sDuchss 10
22Sep86-9Haw 6f :221 :454 1:12 ft 7¾ 116 32 43½ 44 53¾ SilvaCH10 (F)[S]Aw11550 77-16 BrightCrissy,BrethingFir,WishGivr 10
8Sep86-6Haw 6f :222 :454 1:121ft ~~*9-5 116~~ 64½ 1011 811 88½ LouvrGP3 (F)[S]Aw11550 71-19 AnswrtVctry,BrghtCrssy,OrLttlSs 10
Jun 3 AP 4f sl :50 b

F.

Temttatenfrustrate — B. m. 5, by Nasty and Bold—Be Victorious, by Stevward
Br.—Schwietert F C (Ill) — 1987 4 0 1 1 $17,169
Own.—Four Horsemen's Ranch — 114 — Tr.—Voelkner Robert G — 1986 6 1 1 1 $20,625
Lifetime 17 3 4 4 $63,849 — Turf 5 0 2 2 $17,926

12Jly87-8AP 1 (T):4721:1211:381gd 2¼e 112 64 21½ 32½ 33½ HIS8 (F)[S]A Peabody H 80-17 SprnInncnc,KllsSprPt,Ttttnfrstrt 13
18Apr87-7Spt 6f :242 :483 1:134ft *2½ 121 31½ 54 56½ 65¾ ClarkKD3 (F)[S]Aw24675 75-21 QkrTyp,SomthngSoRght,InvrnssRb 8
2Apr87-8Spt 6½f :231 :471 1:191ft 5 116 1hd 32 69 716 SpncrSA1 (F)[S]Aw25300 65-26 What A Rose, MissAtari,ASlimChic 7
14Mar87-8Spt 6f :24 :481 1:14 sy 29 112 11½ 11½ 2½ 2nk SpcrSA9 (F)[S]GovLdyH 80-24 WhtARos,Tmtttnfrustrt,HonyMcDn 9
22Nov86-8Bml 170 :49 1:142 1:462sy 32 112 12½ 11½ 22 35½ SpcrSA2 (F)LeFemmeH 79-17 Whtlckygrl,FlrntnFrlc,Tmtttnfrstrt 9
22Nov86—Drifted out drive
26Oct86-8Bml 1 1/16 :481 1:152 1:503sy 9¼ 113 43 47½ 49 713½ BllrdBA1 (F)[S]HrdnbkH 59-21 PrettyPlum,HonyMcDn,SwtOlShri 11
11Oct86-9FP 1 1/16 :471 1:113 1:452ft 13 114 32½ 34½ 913 919¼ RcrdD11 (F)[S]CReevsH 65-24 PrttyPlum,Td'sLstChnc,AcsCourt 11
27Aug86-6AP 1 1/16 (T):4911:1431:482sf 8e 116 32 21 3½ 44 EsRD1 (F)[S]APebodyH 61-39 MgneticType,CrownThLdy,BbyCzr 11
19Aug86-7AP 1 (T):4731:1321:384fm 2½ 117 11 11 1½ 2½ Fires E3 (F)Aw20000 80-26 BbyCzr,Temtttenfrustrt,NtionlTop 10
9Jly86-7Haw 170 :483 1:142 1:44 ft 2½ 119 11½ 11 12½ 15 ClarkKD3 (F)[S]Aw17825 82-20 Tmtttnfrstrt,PrcosChrm,StbbrnIrsh 6
Jun 6 AP 1 ft 1:42 b

G.

Yukon Dolly
Own.—Stella A
1115
Ch. f. 3, by Yukon—Jeterkin, by Ray Jeter
Br.—Stella August M (Ill)
Tr.—Hazelton Richard P
Lifetime 11 3 2 3 $50,830
1987 8 3 1 1 $46,210
1986 3 M 1 2 $4,620
Turf 1 0 0 0

12Jly87-8AP 1 ⓣ:4721:1211:381gd 72 108 74¼108¾1113 1014¼ TrrsFC13 ⒻⓈAPbdyH 70-17 SprnInncnc,KllsSprPt,Ttttnfrstrt 13
29Jun87-4AP 7f :223 :454 1:244ft 4½ 1115 1½ 1½ 1hd 2hd TorrsFC1 ⒻⓈAw17600 78-24 WhataPearl,YukonDolly,NativeMry 7
24May87-8AP 7f :231 :471 1:26 ft 32 115 85 88 913 814½ DiazJL12 ⒻⓈColfax M 57-27 UniqueType,AirAppeal,CndidType 12
24Apr87-8Spt 6f :24 :481 1:13 ft 6 119 32½ 2hd 32 37½ Diaz J L7 ⒻⓈViolet 78-28 UniqueType,JazzBurger,YukonDolly 8
4Apr87-10Spt 6½f :223 :461 1:181ft 6 114 65½ 33½ 44½ 45 Diaz J L4 ⒻRuffian H 81-19 ‡UniqueTyp,CgyExubrnc,P.C.J.Rlxr 9
24Mar87-6Spt 6f :24 :473 1:131ft *2-5 113 1hd 11 15 14½ Diaz J L5 ⒻⓈAw22440 84-21 YukonDolly,StoneHrborSis,GsMony 8
11Mar87-9Spt 6½f :24 :481 1:204ft *4-5 113 11½ 12 12 14½ Diaz J L2 ⒻⓈAw21230 73-24 YukonDolly,GlNmedSu,GrtMrcyB. 10
28Feb87-4Spt 6f :233 :482 1:142ft *6-5 121 21½ 2hd 11½ 16 Diaz J L7 ⒻⓈMdn 78-26 Yukon Dolly, Ru RocGal,BlindHope 9
28Aug86-2AP 6f :224 :471 1:134ft *3-5 120 43 33 34 31¾ Gallitano G1 ⒻⓈMdn 71-19 Ms.MaryM.,BigStreker,YukonDolly 7
13Aug86-9Haw 5½f :233 :46 1:041ft *3-2 119 42 55½ 57½ 311½ Day P4 ⒻMdn 79-17 MnsfildPrk,IrishRdoy,YukonDolly 10
Jly 10 AP ⓣ 3f fm :38 b (d) Jun 19 AP 6f ft 1:17 b Jun 12 AP 6f ft 1:15 b Jun 6 AP 4f ft :50 b

34. Class, form, and speed all count in this advanced non-winners allowance sprint.

3rd Santa Anita

OUT OF CHUTE ▸ 6½ FURLONGS SANTA ANITA • FINISH

6 ½ FURLONGS. (1.14) ALLOWANCE. Purse $33,000. Fillies and mares. 3-year-olds and upward which are non-winners of $3,000 three times other than maiden, claiming, or starter. Weights, 3-year-olds, 119 lbs.; older, 121 lbs. Non-winners of two such races since October 1 allowed 2 lbs.; of such a race of $14,000 since November 3, 4 lbs.; of such a race of $15,000 since October 1, 6 lbs.

A.

Symbolically
VALENZUELA P A
Own.—Harbor View Farm
117
B. f. 3, by Flying Paster—Hail to the Queen, by Native Royalty
Br.—Harbor View Farm (Cal)
Tr.—Barrera Lazaro S
Lifetime 19 3 6 3 $84,250
1986 15 2 3 3 $64,900
1985 4 1 3 0 $19,350
Turf 1 0 0 0 $625

29Nov86-3Hol 7f :222 :451 1:23 ft 13 116 21½ 21 2hd 1hd VlenzulPA5 ⒻAw26000 89-12 Symboliclly,LoversNtiv,FlightAbov 6
29Nov86—Brushed late
19Nov86-7Hol 7f :223 :46 1:23 ft 4½ 114 31 43 46½ 49¾ StevensGL5 ⒻAw24000 79-21 SldomSnS,OnYorOwnTm,Sr'sNwHp 7
19Nov86—Crowded 3/8 turn; bobbled 3/16
2Nov86-5SA 6f :212 :441 1:102ft 14 115 917 914 96¾ 72½ Santos J A7 ⒻAw28000 83-10 StridingEsy,LoversNtive,FlyingJuli 9
26Oct86-5SA 1 1/16 :463 1:111 1:433ft 5½ 114 54 32½ 710 710½ StevensGL8 ⒻAw30000 72-16 Fairly Old, Python, Petillante 9
26Oct86—Wide
15Oct86-3SA 1 :461 1:11 1:373ft 2½ 115 41¾ 31 31 3½ StevensGL5 ⒻAw30000 79-18 ProdiglProtg,FinKudos,Symboliclly 7
15Oct86—Broke slowly
8Oct86-6SA 6f :22 :451 1:101ft 5 114 52¾ 31 33½ 23½ StevensGL7 ⒻAw28000 83-20 TomboyBls,Symbolclly,BlconyPss 10
8Oct86—Broke slowly
28Sep86-10Pom 1 1/16 :463 1:112 1:433ft *6-5 115 11 1hd 2hd 21½ Kaenel J L4 ⒻAmda S 92-09 ProprMry,Symboliclly,TropiclHoldy 6
19Sep86-11Pom 1 1/16 :461 1:104 1:432ft 4 115 41½ 2½ 2hd 2nk VrrO3 ⒻⓈC T B A Mn 94-09 ProperMry,Symboliclly,SilentArrivl 6
1Sep86-9Dmr 1 1/16 ⓣ:4831:1211:43 fm 2½ 114 65½ 55 54 53¾ Baze R A1 ⒻAw25000 87-04 Stall Cloud, Ofrendada, J.D.Canyon 6
1Sep86—Veered in start
24Aug86-3Dmr 1 :452 1:103 1:362ft *4-5 114 42½ 41½ 2hd 41½ Baze R A6 ⒻAw25000 84-12 LaDivertida,GoodZar,PollyLFemme 6
24Aug86—Wide

B.

On Your Own Time
PINCAY L JR
Own.—Oxley J C
119
B. f. 4, by Sharpen Up—Scarlet Rain, by Rainy Lake
Br.—Gaines-McNall-Gordy (Ky)
Tr.—Drysdale Neil
Lifetime 6 3 1 1 $43,950
1986 6 3 1 1 $43,950
Turf 1 0 0 0

11Dec86-8Hol 1 :464 1:114 1:361ft *9-5 117 54 41½ 1½ 13 Pincay LJr4 ⒻAw27000 82-21 OnYourOwnTim,FlightAbov,Python 6
11Dec86—Wide into stretch
19Nov86-7Hol 7f :223 :46 1:23 ft 3½ 117 65½ 55 25 24½ Pincay LJr2 ⒻAw24000 84-21 SldomSnS,OnYorOwnTm,Sr'sNwHp 7
19Nov86—Bobbled break
25Jly86-5Dmr 1 1/16 ⓣ:4841:12 1:431fm 4½ 117 118¼105¼ 97½ 99 Pincay LJr9 ⒻAw23000 81-10 Ocean Wave,Benzina,PassAllHope 11
25Jly86—Broke slowly
29May86-7Hol 7f :213 :451 1:241ft *9-5 122 99¾ 86½ 52½ 1¾ Pincay LJr1 ⒻAw22000 83-18 OnYourOwnTime,GoodZr,OcenWve 9
18May86-2Hol 7f :221 :45 1:224ft 12 123 2hd 1½ 13 14 DelahoussyeE7 ⒻMdn 90-08 OnYourOwnTim,Flood,WordHrvst 10
10Apr86-6SA 6f :213 :451 1:113ft 6½ 120 64¾ 48 44½ 38½ Pincay L Jr2 ⒻMdn 72-21 Temperment,Arzll,OnYourOwnTim 11
10Apr86—Broke slowly
Dec 22 SA 6f ft 1:16 h Dec 17 SA 4f ft :493 h Dec 5 Hol 7f ft 1:29 h Dec 1 Hol 6f ft 1:141 h

C.

Millers Stationery — B. f. 3, by Quadratic—Clamoring, by Elocutionist
PATTON D B — 108⁵ — Br.—Maple Kathyrn M (Ky) — 1986 9 4 0 1 $45,200
Own.—Stidham Kim — Tr.—Stidham Michael — 1985 2 1 1 0 $11,200
Lifetime 11 5 1 1 $56,400

11Dec86-8BM 6f :22³ :45² 1:09⁴ft 4½ 115 2½ 2hd 2hd 12 Maple S4 ⒻAw17000 90-24 MillrsSttonry,Blmondy,DlEmStrght 7
4Aug86-7Dmr 6½f :22 :44⁴ 1:16 ft *6-5 116 1½ 2hd 21½ 75 StevensGL11 ⒻAw21000 87-13 PollysLilRscl,ScrnDoor,Symbolclly 11
17Jly86-4Hol 6f :21⁴ :45¹ 1:10²ft *3-5 118 21 21½ 2½ 13½ ShoemakerW6 Ⓕ 80000 92-17 MillersSttionry,Witchery,Mlv'sPrid 6
25Jun86-7Hol 6f :22 :45¹ 1:10²ft 2¾ 108 2½ 2hd 1½ 13 ShoemkrW5 ⒻAw19000 92-13 MillrsSttionry,ExpctMor,LuckySlvr 7
25Jun86—Lugged in early stretch
14Jun86-7Hol 6f :22¹ :46 1:10³ft 2¾ 114 42 41 44 36½ McCrrCJ10 ⒻAw19000 84-14 RrStrlt,SkipSchoon,MillrsSttionry 11
14Jun86—Wide 3/8 turn
18May86-6Hol 6f :21⁴ :44⁴ 1:08³ft 6½ 114 31 31½ 24 49½ McCrrnCJ2 ⒻAw20000 91-08 Melair, Flying Julia, Argentario 9
30Apr86-5Hol 6f :22 :45⁴ 1:11 ft 5½ 115 41½ 2hd 13½ 13½ Stevens G L6 Ⓕ 50000 89-18 MillrsSttionry,DrmPolicy,Exubrncy 7
10Apr86-7SA 6f :21³ :44⁴ 1:10 ft 26 116 31½ 32½ 67½ 614½ McHrgDG7 ⒻAw24000 73-21 FashionDynasty,Alquizar,Argentrio 8
10Apr86—Lugged out, wide final 3/8
26Mar86-1SA 6f :21² :44² 1:10 ft 9½ 116 43 33 44 56½ McHrgDG5 ⒻAw28000 82-17 Comprblty,FshonDynsty,SDoubyRn 9
26Mar86—Stumbled start
11Aug85-6Dmr 6f :22² :46 1:11¹ft *2¾ 117 1½ 13 15 13 Hawley S5 ⒻMdn 82-11 MillrsSttionry,ArticMoon,LdyExcllr 7
11Aug85—Jostled at start
Dec 24 Hol 3f ft :36⁴ h — Dec 5 Hol 4f ft :48¹ h — Nov 23 Hol 5f ft 1:02² h — Nov 18 Hol 5f ft 1:00⁴ h

D.

Miss O. B. E. — Dk. b. or br. f. 4, by In Reality—Joe's Bee, by King's Bishop
BLACK C A — 115 — Br.—Hughes Farm Inc (Fla) — 1986 3 1 0 1 $19,325
Own.—Royal Lines (Lessee) — Tr.—Gregson Edwin — 1985 4 2 1 1 $31,150
Lifetime 7 3 1 2 $50,475

13Dec86-4Hol 6f :21⁴ :45¹ 1:10¹ft 3 116 41½ 42½ 65½ 57¾ DelhoussyeE5 ⒻHcp0 84-09 StridingEsy,WintrTrsur,BoldNSpcil 6
26Nov86-8Hol 6f :21³ :44⁴ 1:11¹ft 2¾ 115 31½ 33½ 32 3½ DlhoussyE3 ⒻAw35000 86-20 SolmenteUnVez,Witchry,MissO.B.E. 6
26Nov86—Lugged in stretch
31Aug86-7Dmr 6½f :22² :45³ 1:16²ft *7-5 113⁵ 2hd 1hd 11 1½ Black C A6 ⒻAw24000 90-12 Miss O. B. E.,BalconyPass,AllInTune 6
24Nov85-5Hol 7f :22 :45 1:21²ft 5½ 120 2hd 3nk 23 26 DlhoussyE2 ⒻAw22000 91-08 Waterside, Miss O. B. E., Orchestra 6
31Oct85-7SA 6½f :22 :45² 1:16³ft *2-5 118 1½ 2hd 1hd 1½ McCrrnCJ6 ⒻAw25000 87-16 Miss O.B.E.,FireMissLeader,Zythum 7
31Oct85—Bumped at 1/8
13Oct85-2SA 6f :21³ :45² 1:10³ft *2-3 118 1½ 11 17 17½ McCarron C J1 ⒻMdn 85-17 MissO.B.E.,WterfordFlr,NncyNncy 11
11Sep85-6Dmr 6f :22 :45¹ 1:09⁴ft 7 117 2hd 2½ 22½ 32¾ McCarron C J8 ⒻMdn 87-15 SimplySlly,BuffedOrng,MissO.B.E. 12
Dec 23 SA 4f ft :47³ h — Dec 10 SA 3f ft :37 h — Dec 5 SA 4f ft :48¹ h — Nov 22 SA 5f ft :59¹ h

E.

Prodigal Protege * — Dk. b. or br. f. 3, by Pirate's Bounty—Campet, by Contratodes
SHOEMAKER W — 115 — Br.—Mamakos J (Cal) — 1986 14 3 0 0 $56,650
Own.—Lang A — Tr.—Mayer V James — 1985 5 M 0 1 $3,100
Lifetime 19 3 0 1 $59,750 — Turf 4 0 0 0 $1,775

11Nov86-8Hol 1 Ⓣ:45³1:10²1:35¹fm 35 113 43½ 84¾ 94½ 912 ShoemakerW6 ⒻHcp0 79-09 AnEmpress,MissAlto,SpcilVictory 10
15Oct86-3SA 1 :46¹ 1:11 1:37³ft 30 115 2hd 2hd 2hd 1no ShoemkrW3 ⒻAw30000 80-18 ProdiglProtg,FinKudos,Symboliclly 7
4Oct86-7SA 1 :46¹ 1:11⁴ 1:37²ft 70 113 63¼ 73¾ 65½ 66¾ StevensSA3 ⒻAw30000 74-18 Mille Et Une, T.V.Residual,GoodZar 9
4Oct86—Awarded fifth purse money
19Sep86-11Pom 1 1/16 :46¹ 1:10⁴ 1:43²ft 46 114 77 68½ 59 46½ StsSA5 ⒻSC T BAMn 87-09 ProperMry,Symbolclly,SilentArrivl 8
20Aug86-5Dmr 1 1/16 Ⓣ:48 1:11⁴1:43¹fm 11 112 55 64½ 65 55½ ShoemkrW8 ⒻAw21000 85-11 Adalia, Fleet Rain, Ack's Sonata 9
11Aug86-8Dmr 7f :22¹ :45 1:22 ft 77 116 75½ 66 77½ 710½ Sibille R4 ⒻSFlt Trt 85-13 Witchery, RareStarlet,Symbolically 7
2Aug86-8Dmr 1 1/16 Ⓣ:49 1:13¹1:43¹fm 111 115 93¾ 73¾ 56½ 57 SibillR3 ⒻRSn Clmnt 83-10 OurSweetShm,MillEtUn,T.V.Rsidul 10
6Jly86-9Hol 1⅛ :45⁴ 1:10¹ 1:47⁴ft 36 121 49 412 421 431 DlhssE4 ⒻHol Oaks 67-09 HiddenLight,AnEmpress,FmilyStyle 4
6Jly86—Grade I
18Jun86-8Hol 1 :45² 1:10² 1:35⁴ft 12 108 65½ 64 68½ 617½ ShoemkrW2 ⒻAw23000 67-15 Secuenci,StllCloud,MissBevrlyHills 7
18Apr86-8GG 6f :22² :45⁴ 1:11²gd 56 117 77½ 78½ 67½ 54½ LmncC10 ⒻSMiss Cal 77-25 SilentArrivl,LdyMxineD.,Witchery 12
Dec 24 SA 4f ft :47² h — Dec 18 SA 6f ft 1:14³ h — Dec 12 SA 4f ft :48 h — Dec 5 SA 4f ft :48¹ h

F.

Good Zar — Gr. f. 4, by Gran Zar—Good Time, by Real Good Deal
DELAHOUSSAYE E — 117 — Br.—Westerly Stud Farms (Ky) — 1986 13 3 5 2 $87,400
Own.—Jandy Stables — Tr.—Luby Donn — 1985 2 M 1 0 $4,400
Lifetime 15 3 6 2 $91,800

28Nov86-3Hol 7f :22¹ :45¹ 1:23²ft 3½ 119 2hd 2hd 1½ 2½ DlhoussyE2 ⒻAw28000 86-14 Sign Off, Good Zar, Ambra Ridge 6
3Nov86-7SA 1 :45² 1:10¹ 1:36 ft 21 119 2½ 2hd 4¾ 65¾ DlhssyE3 ⒻPrncs Rny 82-14 Infinidad, Fairly Old, Stemware 9
12Oct86-8BM 1 1/16 :47³ 1:12² 1:43³ft 3¾ 114 11½ 1½ 1hd 1¾ Maple S4 ⒻTizna H 74-19 Good Zar, North Sider, Petillante 4
4Oct86-7SA 1 :46¹ 1:11⁴ 1:37²ft 7½ 117 2hd 1hd 1hd 31¼ DlhoussyE8 ⒻAw30000 80-18 Mille Et Une, T.V.Residual,GoodZar 9
4Oct86—Awarded second purse money

14Sep86-11Pom 1 1/16 :464 1:104 1:423ft 11 114 1½ 11 21 37¾ OlrsF1 Ⓕ🅁E B Jhnstn 90-08 Our Best Tell, LeL'Argent,GoodZar 5
24Aug86-3Dmr 1 :452 1:103 1:362ft 6½ 118 2hd 2hd 1hd 2hd DlhoussyE3 ⒻAw25000 86-12 LaDivertida,GoodZar,PollyLFemme 6
8Aug86-7Dmr 1 :454 1:103 1:352ft 4 119 2½ 3½ 33½ 58½ DlhoussyE7 ⒻAw23000 82-13 MissBevrlyHills,PollyLFmm,Ptillnt 9
12Jly86-4Hol 1 :453 1:103 1:361ft 5½ 116 2hd 2hd 1hd 1¾ DlhoussyE6 ⒻAw23000 82-14 Good Zar, SallyRussell,LuckySilver 7
25Jun86-7Hol 6f :22 :451 1:102ft *2¼ 119 68 79¼ 67½ 44½ DlhoussyE4 ⒻAw19000 87-13 MillrsStiony,ExpctMor,LuckySlvr 7
29May86-7Hol 7f :213 :451 1:241ft 9¼ 122 33 31½ 11½ 2¾ DlhoussyE7 ⒻAw22000 82-18 OnYourOwnTime,GoodZr,OcenWve 9
Dec 18 SA 6f ft 1:004 h Dec 11 SA 4f ft :493 h Nov 21 SA 6f ft 1:164 h Nov 12 SA 5f ft 1:014 h

G.

Twilight Ridge B. f. 3, by Cox's Ridge—Waving Sky, by Quibu
Br.—Burrow T E (Fla) 1986 6 0 3 0 $88,500
STEVENS G L 1-0 ? **113** Tr.—Lukas D Wayne 1985 5 3 1 1 $635,638
Own.—Klein Mr-Mrs E V Lifetime 11 3 4 1 $724,138 Turf 1 0 0 0

16Nov86-8BM 1 1/16 :454 1:11 1:432ft *4-5 123 2hd 52¾ 69 615½ CstdM1 ⒻSan Jose H 59-21 NovelSprite,Chnngo'sAlibi,Hertliftr 7
1Nov86-5SA 1¼ :461 1:344 2:011ft *1-2e 119 46 46½ 613 616¾ RmrRP3 ⒻBr Cp Dstff 66-13 Ldy'sScrt,Frn'sVlntin,Outstndingly 8
1Nov86—Grade I; Checked 1st turn
25Oct86-5SA 1⅛Ⓣ:4711:1141:484fm 2¾ 112 3½ 2hd 64 89¾ Meza R Q5 ⒻAw35000 73-17 PerfectMtchII,Rekindling,StllCloud 9
25Oct86—Steadied at 1/8
11Oct86-3SA 1 :46 1:102 1:363ft *1 113 22 21 21½ 24½ StevensGL1 ⒻAw35000 80-17 Wterside,TwilightRidge,AmbrRidge 5
11Oct86—Lugged in, checked at 3/16
23Mar86-8SA 1 1/16 :463 1:112 1:422ft 3-2e 117 21½ 2½ 21 21½ McCrrCJ6 ⒻS A Oaks 87-17 HiddnLight,TwilightRidg,AnEmprss 6
23Mar86—Grade I; Lugged in stretch
1Mar86-8SA 1 :46 1:102 1:361ft *1e 121 43½ 42¼ 21½ 2¾ McCrrCJ7 ⒻLs Vrgnes 86-16 LifAtThTop,TwilightRdg,AnEmprss 7
1Mar86—Grade III; Lugged in, bumped 1/8, again late
1Dec85-8Hol 1 :451 1:102 1:36 gd *2-3 120 63¼ 32 31½ 34¾ PncyLJr8 ⒻHol Strlt 78-16 I'mSplndid,TrimColony,TwilghtRdg 9
1Dec85—Grade I; Lugged in stretch
2Nov85-2Aqu 1 :452 1:104 1:354ft *3-5e 119 52¾ 2hd 12½ 11 VlszJ11 ⒻBr Cp Juv F 87-10 TwilightRidge,FmilyStyle,StlAKiss 12
2Nov85—Grade I
19Oct85-8Pha 6½f :22 :45 1:161ft *2-3 121 2hd 21 33 22½ McNlFA3 ⒻCriticlMis 89-20 Brt'sDrm,TwlghtRdg,TromphDNskr 7
30Jun85-8Bel 5½f :214 :452 1:042ft *2-5 112 21½ 23 21½ 1½ VelsquzJ1 ⒻAstoria 93-19 TwilightRidg,I'mSplndid,Sh'sinTun 8
30Jun85—Grade III
Dec 19 Hol 4f ft :474 h Dec 12 Hol 6f ft 1:004 h Dec 5 Hol 4f ft :484 h

35.

8th Belmont

1 ⅛ MILES. (1.45⅘) HANDICAP. Purse $45,000. 3-year-olds and upward. Weight, Monday, July 27. Declarations by 10:00 A.M., Tuesday, July 28.

A.

Lac Ouimet * B. c. 4, by Pleasant Colony—Northern Sunset, by Northfields
Br.—Payson Virginia Kraft (Ky) 1987 6 2 1 0 $243,303
Own.—Payson Virginia Kraft **122** Tr.—Lundy Richard J 1986 12 4 1 2 $152,040
Lifetime 18 6 2 2 $395,343 Turf 1 0 0 0 $220

4Jly87-8Bel 1¼ :481 1:371 2:03 ft 3¼ 117 12 32 44 44 Maple E5 Suburban H 79-23 Broad Brush,SetStyle,BordeauxBob 5
4Jly87—Grade I
7Jun87-8Bel 1⅛ :47 1:11 1:481ft 3¾ 116 11½ 1½ 12½ 12½ Maple E4 Nassu Cty H 86-22 LcOuimet,FobbyForbes,JohnsTrsur 6
7Jun87—Grade II
16May87-7Pim 1 1/16 :463 1:103 1:432ft 6 118 54 41¾ 52½ 43¼ BrcclVJr9 Bud BrdrsH 84-18 Bgetelle,FobbyForbs,LittlBoldJohn 9
17Apr87-8Aqu 1¼ :463 1:36 2:02 sy 7¾ 114 2½ 11½ 12½ 13¾ Maple E4 Excelsior H 86-22 Lac Ouimet, Alioth, ProudDebonair 9
17Apr87—Grade II
6Apr87-8Aqu 1⅛ :471 1:104 1:484sy *3-2 118 2½ 2½ 23 22½ Maple E2 HcpO 88-20 Alioth,LacOuimet,StrongStatement 5
11Mar87-8GP a1 1/16 Ⓣ 1:513yl 5¼ 117 79 86¼ 58½ 58¼ Guerra W A6 Aw22000 40-51 BrodwyTommy,Wollston,P'cePnthr 9
25Oct86-8Aqu 1⅛ :474 1:114 1:493ft *2 116 21½ 2½ 57 69 Maple E7 Discovery H 78-18 MomentOfHope,GoldAlert,ClrChoic 9
25Oct86—Grade III
27Sep86-9Pha 1⅛ :473 1:111 1:504sy 2¾ 122 66 611 53½ 44¼ BrccilVJr2 Pa Derby 77-17 Broad Brush, Sumptious, Glow 7
27Sep86—Grade II
Jly 27 Bel 5f ft 1:014 b Jly 22 Bel 6f ft 1:13 h Jly 17 Bel 6f ft 1:174 b Jly 1 Bel 5f ft 1:02 b

B.

Summer Tale
B. g. 4, by Nostrum—Warmed Bottom, by Hitting Away
Br.—Buckingham Farm &Freeman (NY) 1987 9 1 0 2 $36,894
Own.—Gold-N-Oats Stable **108** **Tr.—MARTIN GREGORY F** 1986 11 3 2 1 $62,610
Lifetime 20 4 2 3 $99,504 **Turf 2 0 0 1 $3,360**

12Jly87-8FL 1 1/16 :46 1:103 1:433ft 3¾ 115 1212 76 51¾ 33 GrciJ 4 [S]Genese Vly H 95-09 TheSavage,PostTense,SummerTle 12
4Jly87-8Bel 1¼ :481 1:371 2:03 ft 30 107 56 56½ 512 515 GarciJA 3 Suburban H 68-23 Broad Brush,SetStyle,BordeauxBob 5
4Jly87—Grade I
29May87-9Bel 7f :223 :453 1:224ft 25 114 89 66½ 41½ 42¼ Guerra W A 9 80000 86-13 TonkaPss,ScholrsTsk,JmicnGigolo 10
29May87—Squeezed back st.
8Apr87-6Aqu 7f :231 :461 1:232gd 10 1175 63½ 62¾ 41½ 45¼ Ortiz E Jr 3 100000 79-21 FlyMeAgin,DrbyHt,HurdyGurdyMn 7
27Mar87-8Aqu 1 :46 1:093 1:343ft 7 117 54 43 46½ 46½ Hernandez R 7 Aw45000 86-21 Tourd'Or,Tinchn'sPrinc,ScholrsTsk 9
8Mar87-8Aqu 1 1/16 [•]:4811:1241:44 ft 5¾ 111 83¾ 72¾ 52¾ 42¼ VenziM 6 [S]Kings Pt H 88-16 Landing Plot,Mr.Tatt,DoctorInglis 10
8Mar87—Lacked room
20Feb87-8Aqu 1 1/16 [•]:4731:1231:45 ft 10 117 31½ 21½ 2½ 1½ Venezia M 6 Aw31000 85-28 Summer Tale, Reygo, Matafao 8
30Jan87-9Aqu 6f [•]:23 :4641:123sy 21 117 95¾ 73¾ 53½ 33 Hernandez R8 c35000 78-22 Shy Gold, TalcPower,SummerTale 10
Jly 27 Bel 5f ft 1:01 h Jly 21 Bel tr.t 4f ft :50 b ●Jun 19 Bel tr.t 6f ft 1:15 b ●Jun 13 Bel tr.t 5f ft 1:013 h

C.

I Rejoice *
B. g. 4, by Lord Gaylord—Imaglee, by Grey Dawn II
Br.—Isaacs H S (Ky) 1987 2 2 0 0 $54,000
Own.—Brookfield Farms **112** **Tr.—Kelly Edward I** 1986 10 4 3 0 $85,860
Lifetime 12 6 3 0 $139,860 **Turf 5 3 0 0 $57,180**

13Jly87-8Bel 1 1/16 [T]:4621:1031:413fm 2½ 110 1hd 11½ 13 1¾ Davis R G7 HcpO 88-19 IRejoice,IslandSun,ExplosiveDncer 8
4Jly87-7Bel 1 1/16 :471 1:12 1:432ft *6-5 115 11½ 11½ 12½ 17¾ Davis R G4 Aw45000 85-23 I Rejoice, Mugatea, Gallic War 7
1Dec86-8Aqu 6½f :224 :461 1:164ft *1 110 2½ 1hd 1hd 2nk Davis R G3 HcpO 91-25 Landing Plot,IRejoice,CzarNijinsky 6
11Nov86-7Aqu 7f :223 :453 1:23 sy *1 110 2hd 1hd 1½ 2no Davis R G3 HcpO 86-21 MidnightCall,IRejoice,GrandRivulet 6
26Oct86-7Aqu 7f :224 :453 1:222sy *6-5 116 2hd 1hd 12½ 12½ Davis R G4 Aw27000 89-18 I Rejoice, Khozaam, Harry L. 7
19Oct86-6Bel 1 :454 1:10 1:342ft 2 114 21 22 23 23¾ Davis R G6 Aw29000 89-14 Clear Choice, I Rejoice,BalthazarB. 7
26Sep86-8Bel 6f :221 :451 1:092gd 12 113 22 1hd 12 15 Davis R G2 Aw25000 95-15 I Rejoice, Hagley Mill,YankeeAffair 6
27Aug86-7Bel 1 [T]:4711:11 1:36 fm 7 117 52 41 67 910 Guerra W A9 Aw26000 75-18 FrdAstir,Torqumd,ChristinHundrd 10
●Jly 24 Bel 4f ft :47 h Jun 26 Bel 3f ft :372 b ●Jun 18 Bel [T] 7f fm 1:293 h (d) ●Jun 12 Bel 7f ft 1:26 h

D.

Belocolus
B. c. 4, by Big Spruce—Magic, by Buckpasser
Br.—Tartan Farms (Fla) 1987 10 3 2 0 $89,560
Own.—Davis A **112** **Tr.—Moschera Gasper S** 1986 6 1 0 2 $46,752
Lifetime 17 5 2 2 $149,512 **Turf 1 0 0 0**

18Jly87-5Bel 1 1/16 :474 1:12 1:432ft 5¼ 111 11½ 1hd 3nk 11 Bailey J D6 HcpO 85-20 Belocolus, Landing Plot, Carjack 6
8Jly87-1Bel 6f :222 :453 1:111sy 5 122 67½ 66½ 66¼ 67 Bailey J D5 c100000 77-25 Tonka Pass, Zonter, FarawayIsland 6
15Jun87-8Bel 7f :232 :463 1:234ft 7½ 112 3nk 1hd 44 54¼ Bailey J D10 HcpO 79-19 LndingPlot,Mr.Clssic,JmicnGigolo 10
15Jun87—Checked
18May87-8Bel 1 1/16 :451 1:084 1:402ft 6½ 121 21 22½ 35½ 49¾ Bailey J D2 Aw45000 90-15 Tourd'Or,OwnsTroup,Tinchn'sPrinc 6
9May87-8Bel 1 1/16 [T]:49 1:1331:45 gd 5½e110 65 812 821 823½ BileyJD8 Fort Mrcy H 47-33 Glaros, Onyxly, Explosive Dancer 8
9May87—Grade III; Run in Divisions
22Mar87-8Aqu 1 :453 1:103 1:361ft 17 110 65¼ 63½ 57 58½ VenziM2 Westchstr H 76-25 King'sSwn,CutlssRelity,LndingPlot 6
22Mar87—Grade III
18Feb87-8Aqu 1 1/16 [•]:4731:1241:441ft *8-5 115 23 21 1½ 1no Bailey J D2 Aw45000 89-23 Belocolus,RodToPonder,SprkofLov 7
5Feb87-7Aqu 1⅛ [•]:4631:1131:504ft *2-3 117 33 2½ 1½ 11¼ Bailey J D6 Aw28000 88-24 Belocolus, Tull, Curtin 12
Jly 27 Bel 4f ft :464 h ●Jly 15 Bel tr.t 5f ft 1:003 h Jly 5 Bel 4f ft :474 h Jun 29 Bel 4f ft :474 h

E.

Carjack *
B. h. 6, by Cojak—Worlds Of Fun, by Dead Ahead
Br.—Ring Carolyn (Mo) 1987 4 0 1 1 $13,940
Own.—Wimbound Farms **111** **Tr.—Galluscio Dominick** 1986 19 8 1 3 $192,952
Lifetime 65 20 10 10 $441,047 **Turf 3 0 1 0 $2,700**

18Jly87-5Bel 1 1/16 :474 1:12 1:432ft 7¾ 112 52¾ 43½ 42¼ 31 Cruguet J4 HcpO 84-20 Belocolus, Landing Plot, Carjack 6
10Jly87-4Bel 1¼ :49 1:39 2:042gd 3½ 122 32 21½ 22½ 23½ Hernandez R4 100000 72-23 Harry L., Carjack, Sir Cortin 5
24Jun87-1Bel 6½f :231 :463 1:17 ft 7 117 62¼ 64 54½ 47½ Santos J A6 c75000 82-17 Cullendale, Harry L., Shining Asset 7
29May87-9Bel 7f :223 :453 1:224ft 12 116 64½ 78½ 98½ 88 Cruguet J3 85000 80-13 TonkaPss,ScholrsTsk,JmicnGigolo 10
20Dec86-8Aqu 1⅝ [•]:5032:0732:441ft 3½e115 31½ 31½ 52½ 67½ McClWH4 Gllnt Fox H 83-09 BuckleyBoy,FlyMeAgin,FelingGllnt 7
20Dec86—Grade II
8Dec86-8Aqu 1⅝ [•]:1342:0722:462ft 4 122 24 43 44½ 35¼ Cruguet J7 HcpO 75-20 FeelingGallant,Jane'sDilemm,Crjck 7
8Dec86—Lacked room
27Nov86-8Aqu 1 3/16 :492 1:131 1:571gd 3 116 52¼ 43½ 42½ 44¼ CrdrAJr4 Qns Cnty H 72-29 PineBelt,Scrimshaw,CostConscious 6
27Nov86—Grade III
19Nov86-7Aqu 1⅛ :511 1:144 1:521gd *2-3 114 2½ 2hd 1hd 11¼ Cruguet J1 HcpO 74-25 Carjack, Real Courage, Ioskeha 4
Jun 28 Bel 4f ft :502 b Jun 10 Bel 4f ft :49 b

Items 36 through 60 ask you to relate horses' chances to win and the odds provided. They promote the ultimate skill of expert handicapping. All the items assess Competency 66. Odds appear below the response letters.

36. As happens in stakes sprints frequently, five of the six contestants have a reasonable chance on full-dress handicapping.

If bets must be placed, which horse deserves the handicapper's money?

8th Santa Anita

START · 6 FURLONGS · SANTA ANITA · FINISH

6 FURLONGS. (1.07⅗) 35th Running of THE PALOS VERDES HANDICAP. $75,000 added (plus $25,000 Breeders' Cup Premium Awards). All ages. By subscription of $50 each to accompany the nomination and $750 additional to start, with $75,000 added, of which $15,000 to second, $11,250 to third, $5,625 to fourth and $1,875 to fifth. Weights, Monday, December 22. Starters to named through the entry box by the closing time of entries. A trophy will be presented to the owner of the winner. Closed Wednesday, December 17, 1986, with 15 nominations.

A.
3–1

Bolder Than Bold — B. c. 4, by Plum Bold—Fact, by Dancing Moss
BAZE G — 116 — Br.—Bradly-Whttnghm-Chndlr (Ky) — 1986 8 1 5 1 $102,550
Tr.—Whittingham Charles — 1985 5 2 0 1 $39,800
Own.—Bradley-Chndler-Whittinghm — Lifetime 22 4 7 3 $183,782 — Turf 9 0 5 1 $62,250

20Dec86-8Hol 6f Ⓣ:213 :4321:072fm 3¼ 115 42 32½ 31 2¾ Baze G5 Trf Exprs H 102-04 Zany Tactics, BolderThanBold,Faro 5
28Nov86-8Hol 6f :211 :44 1:084ft 4¼ 114 911 911 45 21¾ Baze G10 Ntl Sprt Ch 97-14 BdsdProms,BoldrThnBold,PnTrLn 10
28Nov86—Grade III; Wide into stretch
12Nov86-3Hol 7f :221 :451 1:213ft *9-5 117 55 43½ 11½ 14½ Baze G1 Aw26000 96-15 BoldrThnBold,MyGllntGm,Mtrnmc 6
12Jun86-8Hol 1$\frac{1}{16}$ Ⓣ:4621:1011:401fm 2½ 116 66¾ 63¼ 41½ 32¼ Stevens G L6 Aw25000 101 — Qntllon,WtchForDwn,BoldrThnBold 9
9May86-8Hol 1$\frac{1}{16}$ Ⓣ:4711:1121:403fm 7-5e 115 63½ 52¼ 42 43¾ Stevens G L3 Aw40000 97 — Poly Test, Bleding, Mr. Happy 6
25Apr86-8Hol 1$\frac{1}{16}$ Ⓣ:46 1:0941:401fm 3¼ 117 67½ 63¾ 3nk 22 ShoemkerW2 Aw35000 101 — LittleLook,BolderThnBold,PineBelt 7
25Apr86—Bumped break
28Feb86-8SA a6½f Ⓣ:211 :4321:151fm *9-5 114 97 99¼ 65 2nk Baze G4 Aw35000 83-22 PrismticII,BoldrThnBold,Crcksmn 11
28Feb86—Broke stride, bobbled twice on dirt track
17Jan86-8SA a6½f Ⓣ:221 :45 1:142fm 4e 114 42 31½ 32½ 21¾ Baze G8 Aw45000 85-15 IceHot,BolderThanBold,ForzandoII 8
16Nov85-7Hol 6f :222 :452 1:092ft 29 114 96¼ 83½ 31 11¼ Baze G8 Aw22000 97-14 BolderThanBold,FullHonor,Carload 9
16Nov85—Bumped start
20Mar85-8SA 1⅛ :471 1:12 1:493ft *9-5 118 45½ 43 57 58¼ ShoemkerW4 Ⓡ Brdbry 73-19 Cosmotron,ProtectYourself,Rckonr 6
20Mar85—Veered out start
Dec 26 SA 3f ft :381 h   Dec 16 Hol 5f ft 1:013 h   ●Dec 10 Hol Ⓣ 5f fm 1:003 h (d)   ●Dec 5 Hol 4f ft :461 h

B.
29–1

Sure To Fire — B. h. 5, by Sure Fire—Fluffity Uppity, by Donut King
MEZA R Q — 115 — Br.—Bohm W R & Carole (Cal) — 1986 6 2 0 1 $54,200
Tr.—Luby Donn — 1985 3 1 1 0 $15,800
Own.—Bohm Stable Inc & Neuman — Lifetime 12 4 2 2 $90,850 — Turf 1 0 0 0

28Nov86-8Hol 6f :211 :44 1:084ft 28 120 88¼ 89½ 76½ 78¾ DlhossyE4 Ntl Sprt Ch 90-14 BdsdProms,BoldrThnBold,PnTrLn 10
28Nov86—Grade III
2Nov86-7SA 7f :222 :442 1:212ft 9 116 2½ 2hd 2hd 11½ Valenzuela P A1 Eillo 93-10 Sure To Fire, Rosie's K. T., Estate 5
2Nov86—Broke out, bumped
12Oct86-5SA a6½f Ⓣ:214 :44 1:134fm 6¾ 119 117¼ 119¼ 1011 1115¾ DelhoussyeE5 Aw33000 74-12 PrinceSky,MyGallantGame,Bruiser 12
12Oct86—Very wide into drive
23Sep86-11Pom 6½f :213 :442 1:151ft 2½ 116 44 43½ 41¼ 35½ Olivares F3 Gvnr Cp H 98-08 BundleOfIron,Mtronomic,SurToFir 7
23Sep86—Rank early
31Aug86-3Dmr 6f :22 :45 1:092ft 4½ 118 63¼ 41¾ 2½ 12¾ Baze R A5 Aw24000 91-12 SureToFir,AmzingCourg,RossArRb 7
31Aug86—Wide into stretch
3Aug86-7Dmr 6f :213 :444 1:091ft 3¼ 117 4¾ 62¾ 66 69½ DelhoussyeE2 Aw21000 82-10 Ondarty, High Hook, J. R.Johnson 12
3Aug86—Veered out, bumped start
6Oct85-7SA 6f :213 :442 1:092ft *4-5 121 43½ 43½ 57½ 65½ Hawley S6 Aw28000 85-16 ContryPlsrs,AcSmmons,BoldSmchr 7
2Sep85-7Dmr 6½f :221 :444 1:142ft *3-5 121 31½ 31 22½ 23½ Hawley S2 Aw24000 100-15 SntRosPrince,SureToFir,PrivtJungl 6
9Aug85-7Dmr 6½f :222 :451 1:153ft *6-5 118 22½ 2hd 14 17 Hawley S8 Ⓢ Aw20000 98-15 SureToFire,MostDetrmind,Holmish 8
22Dec84-8BM 6f :22 :442 1:081ft 3½ 115 710 74¾ 52¾ 33¼ Delgadillo C L Stnfrd 95-11 OcenView,LuckyBuccneer,SurToFir 8
22Dec84—Broke in a tangle
Dec 24 SA 4f ft :473 h   Dec 17 SA 5f ft :593 h   Dec 11 SA 4f ft :503 h   Nov 29 Hol 5f ft 1:014 hg

C.

6–1

```
Sun Master                            B. h. 5, by Foolish Pleasure—Sunny Today, by Prince John
  VALENZUELA P A                 117  Br.—Elmendorf Farm (Ky)                      1986 15  4  4  3      $190,113
Own.—Lukas D W                        Tr.—Lukas D Wayne                            1985 15  3  2  3       $70,550
                                     Lifetime   31  7  6  6  $260,663              Turf  3  0  0  0        $2,250
29Nov86-8Aqu  7f  :223  :452 1:214ft   7¼ 126  32  41¼ 42¼ 46¼  RomrRP2  Vosburgh   86-20 King'sSwn,LoveThtMc,CutlssRelity 8
    29Nov86—Grade I
15Nov86-8Aqu  6f  :213  :441 1:084ft   4¼ 117  2½  2hd 2½  35   RomrRP5 Sprtpage H  92-22 BestByTest,King'sSwan,SunMaster 7
    15Nov86—Grade III
 4Nov86-6Aqu  6f  :222  :452 1:09 ft  *1  122  1hd 1½  11½ 14¾  Romero R P1 Aw36000 96-22 SunMster,Rj'sReveng,NwConnction 6
25Oct86-3SA   6f  :213  :442 1:092ft   3¾ 121  41¼ 31½ 3½  1hd  ValenzuelPA4 Aw45000 91-17 SunMaster,Rosie'sK.T.,PartyLeader 5
    25Oct86—Inadvertently struck in head by another rider's whip 1/16
15Oct86-8SA   6f  :212  :434 1:081ft   6e114  33½ 34½ 34  33   StevnsGL4 Anct Tle H 94-18 Groovy, Rosie's K. T., Sun Master  8
15Sep86-8Bel  1 1/16 :461 1:103 1:413ft *1 115 1½ 11½ 1½ 2¾   Skinner K4·     HcpO 93-15 Old Main, Sun Master, ValiantLark  7
 1Sep86-13Rkm 1⅛ :462 1:102 1:50 ft  10  112  11½ 12½ 11  2¾   SnnrK11  Nw Hmsh h  90-16 DoItAginDn,SunMster,‡EntitledTo 14
    1Sep86—Grade III
16Aug86-5Sar  1⅛ :462 1:104 1:493sy   8¾ 113  1½  21½ 25  38½  VlsqzJ4 Bld Reason H 78-22 Romancer, Fuzzy, Sun Master  5
12Jly86-10LA  1⅛ :454 1:102 1:481ft *6-5 122  2hd 2hd 45  511¼ Toro F4   Orng Cty H 84-11 Barland, Bozina, Stickette  7
22Jun86-8Hol  1⅛ :463 1:102 1:473ft  19  115  3½  51¾ 66  68   Toro F8     Bel Air H 91-08 SuperDiamond,Alphbtim,‡Skywlker 8
    22Jun86—Grade III
  Dec 20 Hol 4f ft :48 b        ●Dec 12 Hol 4f ft :461 h
```

D.

3–2

```
Bedside Promise                       Ch. c. 4, by Honest Pleasure—Enchanted Native, by Native Charger
  STEVENS G L                    123  Br.—Farish III & Carter (Ky)                 1986 15  4  5  2      $463,145
Own.—Jawl Brothers                    Tr.—Martin R L                               1985 10  3  2  1      $100,850
                                     Lifetime   29  9  7  3  $578,745              Turf  5  0  1  1       $37,425
28Nov86-8Hol  6f  :211  :44  1:084ft   3½ 122  66  57  33  11¾  StvnsGL1 Ntl Sprt Ch 99-14 BdsdProms,BoldrThnBold,PnTrLn 10
    28Nov86—Grade III; Wide into stretch
 1Nov86-3SA   6f  :211  :433 1:082ft   9  126  75½ 77  55  33   PncyLJr4 Br Cp Sprnt 93-13 Smile,PineTreeLne,BedsidePromise 9
    1Nov86—Grade I; Wide into stretch
15Oct86-8SA   6f  :212  :434 1:081ft  12  118  55  45½ 45½ 43½  PincayLJr8 Anct Tle H 93-18 Groovy, Rosie's K. T., Sun Master  8
    15Oct86—Hopped, bobbled start; wide into stretch
24Aug86-9Lga  1   :444 1:084 1:341ft   6  120  53  42¼ 33½ 2nk  Loseth C4   Lga Mile  98-14 Skywlkr,BdsidPromis,SirMcmillion 7
    24Aug86—Grade II
 3Aug86-9Lga  6½f :213  :441 1:15 ft  *1  119  2½  21  11  1½   Loseth C7      Gov H  94-15 BdsidPromis,SirMcmillion,DustyOk 8
13Jly86-9Lga  1⅛ :46   1:094 1:472ft  2½e119  23½ 2½  11  2½   LosethC10 Brdrs Cp H 95-12 HonorMedl,BedsidePromis,Shrpnl 10
28Jun86-11Pln 6f  :22   :44  1:083ft  *1  123  56  57½ 611 617½ TllKS5 Whtng Mem H  81-11 Cardell,Stan'sBower,MchoComcho 6
26May86-9Lga  6½f :212  :433 1:142ft  10  120  2hd 2hd 12  15½  Loseth C8  Nwst Bdrs 97-22 BedsidePromise,Croso,PolynsinFlyr 8
11May86-4GG   1   :463 1:11  1:363ft *4-5 113  42¼ 42½ 1½  16   Tohill K S1   Aw20000 85-18 BdsdPrms,FrnchsLc,BrghtAndRght 5
    11May86—Steadied 2nd turn
19Apr86-6GG   1 1/16 Ⓣ:463 1:103 1:42 fm 15 112 711 78½ 58½ 59¼ ChpTM2 Brdrs' Cup H 83-09 OceanView,Introspective,Alphbtim 7
    19Apr86—Bumped start
 ●Dec 21 BM 6f m 1:121 h    Dec 13 BM 5f ft :594 h    ●Nov 21 BM 6f ft 1:102 h    ●Nov 14 BM 5f ft :58 h
```

E.

9–1

```
Rocky Marriage                        B. h. 6, by Riva Ridge—Exciting Devorcee, by Candy Spots
  SIBILLE R                      115  Br.—LexingtonThoroughbredSales (Ky)          1986  4  1  0  1       $29,695
Own.—Port & Ramos                     Tr.—Frankel Robert                           1985  8  3  2  1      $138,418
                                     Lifetime   36 11  9  4  $338,257              Turf 11  3  0  1       $45,259
 4Dec86-8Hol  1   :442 1:092 1:362ft   5  115  1hd 13  13  12¾  Sibille R5     Aw40000 81-25 RockyMrrige,Bolton,PolynesinFlyer 6
23Oct86-8SA   a6½f Ⓣ:214 :444 1:142fm 3¾ 116  77  77¼ 77¾ 711½ DelhoussyeE3 Aw45000 75-13 Silvyvill,AllHndsOnDck,FlyngNuggt 7
    23Oct86—Wide into stretch
 2Oct86-8SA   6f  :211  :441 1:094sy   3½ 115  46½ 55½ 53¼ 44¼  Stevens G L5 Aw45000 85-21 Carload,PartyLeader,TkeMyPicture 5
    2Oct86—Veered out start
26Jun86-8Bel  6f  :223  :453 1:092ft *4-5 121  22  21½ 23  33¾  Santos J A4      HcpO 91-17 KyToThFlg,King'sSwn,RockyMrrig  6
 3Oct85-8Bel  6f  :221  :45  1:10 sy *2-5 115  2½  2½  2½  22   Cordero AJr1 Aw36000 90-19 KeyToTheFlg,RockyMrrige,IrishOre 5
 4May85-8Aqu  7f  :214  :44  1:204ft  *1  122  23  21  2½  21¼  Sibille R1   Carter H 96-15 Mt.Livermor,RockyMrrig,CrrDNskr 6
    4May85—Grade II
14Apr85-8Aqu  6f  :222  :45  1:084ft *6-5 119  2hd 1½  14  16¾  CordrAJr4 Bold Ruler 97-22 RockyMrrige,Entropy,MjesticVntur 6
    14Apr85—Grade II
 3Apr85-7Aqu  7f  :224  :444 1:204ft *4-5 121  12  13  16  16¾  Cordero AJr4 Aw36000 97-18 RockyMarriage,I'mSoMerry,Witlist 7
 8Mar85-8SA   7f  :222  :451 1:221ft   2¾e116  1hd 1hd 1½  1½   DelhoussyeE4 Aw40000 89-17 RockyMrrige,Konewh,GeminiDremr 7
11Feb85-8SA   a6½f Ⓣ:204 :43  1:142fm 17 116   106¼ 89¼ 95¾ 83½ DlhoussyE8 Sra Mdr H 83-13 ForzndoII,LuckyBccnr,ChmpgnBd 14
  Dec 25 SA 4f ft :473 h    Dec 19 SA 5f ft 1:004 h    Dec 13 Hol 4f ft :474 h    Dec 3 Hol 3f ft :352 h
```

F.

2–1

Rosie's K. T. Gr. g. 5, by Kfar Tov—Melrose Nugget, by Viking Spirit
PINCAY L JR 5-N 117 Br.—Rous & Millard (Cal) 1986 9 2 5 0 $129,550
Tr.—Sadler John W 1985 6 1 2 2 $46,550
Own.—Millard or Rous Mmes Lifetime 20 6 9 2 $217,200
28Nov86-8Hol 6f :21¹ :44 1:08⁴ft 8½ 120 43½ 45½ 56 57¼ PincyLJr⁹ Ntl Sprt Ch 92-14 BdsdProms,BoldrThnBold,PnTrLn 10
28Nov86—Grade III; Wide into stretch
2Nov86-7SA 7f :22² :44² 1:21²ft *4-5 119 1½ 1hd 1hd 21½ Pincay L Jr³ Eillo 91-10 Sure To Fire, Rosie's K. T., Estate 5
2Nov86—Lugged in stretch; struck by another rider's whip 1/16
25Oct86-3SA 6f :21³ :44² 1:09²ft *3-5 121 2hd 2hd 1hd 2hd DelhoussyeE³ Aw45000 91-17 SunMaster,Rosie'sK.T.,PartyLeader 5
15Oct86-8SA 6f :21² :43⁴ 1:08¹ft 11 117 21½ 23 22½ 22 DlhossyE² Anct Tle H 95-18 Groovy, Rosie's K. T., Sun Master 8
3May86-8Hol 6f :21⁴ :44⁴ 1:10 ft *2-3 116 2hd 2hd 2hd 1hd VlenzulPA² L A H 94-16 Rosie'sK.T.,MneMgic,MuchFinGold 6
3May86—Grade III; Bumped at intervals in stretch
2Apr86-8SA 5½f :21¹ :43³ 1:03 ft *1 119 21½ 22 22½ 22¾ VlenzulPA³ El Cnjo H 93-22 TkeMyPicture,Rosie'sK.T.,FivNorth 5
5Mar86-7SA 6f :21¹ :44 1:09¹ft *2-3 118 1hd 11 13½ 14½ ValenzuelPA² Aw45000 92-13 Rosie'sK.T.,MuchFineGold,PrtyLdr 5
17Feb86-7SA 6f :21² :44² 1:10 sy *4-5 119 22 33 56½ 68 ValenzuelPA² Aw45000 80-19 Bozina,PartyLeader,TeddyNaturally 8
20Jan86-7SA 6f :21³ :43⁴ 1:08²ft 4 118 11½ 11 11 2½ ValenzuelPA⁴ Aw45000 95-16 Halo Folks, Rosie's K. T., Carload 6
6Sep85-7Dmr 6½f :22¹ :44⁴ 1:15²ft 2½ 117 1½ 1hd 2hd 33¼ ValenzuelPA⁶ Aw40000 96-14 FiftySixInRow,DonnrPrty,Ros'sK.T. 6
●Dec 26 SA 3f ft :33³ h Dec 21 Hol 6f ft 1:13⁴ h Dec 14 Hol 3f ft :36² b Nov 23 Hol 5f ft :59 h

37. When middling claiming horses try the turf, handicappers who know what to look for will find overlays that win a surprising number of races. Can you find the kind of overlay I have in mind in the field below?

7 MONMOUTH TURF COURSE 1 1-16 MILES MONMOUTH PARK

1 1/16 MILES. (Turf). (1.41) CLAIMING. Purse $13,000. 3-year-olds. Weight, 122 lbs. Non-winners of three races at one mile or over since June 23 allowed 3 lbs. Two such races 5 lbs. One such race 7 lbs. Claiming Price $32,000; for each $1,000 to $28,000. 1 lb. (Races where entered for $25,000 or less not considered.)

A.

11–1

Dr. Loren B. c. 3, by Gentleman Gene—Chalina Mia, by Dr Fager Lifetime 1987 2 1 0 0 $5,220
$32,000 Br.—Imbesi Joseph (NJ) 115 5 1 0 1 1986 3 M 0 1 $990
Own.—Briardale Stable Tr.—Imbesi Joseph $6,210
Entered 29Jly87-10 MTH
1Jly87- 4Mth fst 6f :22⅕ :45⅕ 1:10⅗ 3+[S]Alw 17500 2 8 62½ 63½ 1110 1118½ Diaz L F⁷ b 106 12.30 68-15 AlltneNumbers116⁵ChiefResident116¹½ClockerHarry114nd Bore in 11
19Jun87- 2Atl fst 7f :22⅘ :45⅗ 1:24⅘ 3+[S]Md Sp Wt 3 5 3½ 1hd 15 16 Conner M J b 114 5.50 78-16 Dr. Loren 114⁶ Explosive Tiger 114⁵Disco'sHomeRun114⁴ Driving 10
24Nov86-10Med my 6f :23 :47⅗ 1:13⅖ [S]Md 20000 3 8 76¾ 611 712 714¼ Edwards J W b 118 *1.70 61-27 Thats Green 118⁷ Judge Hobie 118½ Papa Pio 118³ No factor 12
15Nov86- 6Med fst 6f :23 :46⅖ 1:11⅘ [S]Md Sp Wt 9 11 106¼ 76½ 1012 1014¼ Rocco J b 118 *.90e 69-13 Makin Mischief 118¹ Gatno 118¹ Nobel Bid 118⁸ Outrun 11
23Oct86- 4Med fst 6f :23⅕ :47⅕ 1:12⅘ Md 35000 5 8 98½ 76 64½ 35 Vega A 118 9.00 73-22 Armando 114³ Smoke Chief 114² Dr. Loren 118½ Rallied 10
LATEST WORKOUTS Jly 16 Mth 7f fst 1:30 b Jun 27 Mth 3f sly :37⅖ b Jun 13 Atl 3f fst :35⅗ h Jun 6 Atl 3f fst :37 b

B.

3–1

Tim Moss Dk. b. or br. g. 3, by Fire Dancer—Easteroni, by Negroni Lifetime 1987 8 3 0 1 $20,880
$32,000 Br.—Newchance Farm & Price Properties (Fla) 106⁵ 18 4 0 2 1986 10 1 0 1 $8,465
Own.—Glenspring Farm Tr.—Coletti Edward J $29,345 Turf 4 1 0 1 $9,390
22Jun87- 6Mth fm 1 Ⓣ:48 1:12 1:38⅘ Clm 35000 4 1 1hd 2hd 2hd 3nk Romero J A⁵ b 110 3.70 81-19 Sigmundo 115nk Cavu 113hd Tim Moss 110¾ Held well 10
11Jun87- 7Mth fm 1 1/16 Ⓣ:47⅖ 1:11⅗ 1:45⅕ Clm 25000 2 2 23 22 11 12 Romero J A⁵ b 110 14.60 79-16 Tim Moss 110² Flight in Time 115¹½ Count Ron 106no Driving 9
2Jun87- 6Mth fm 1 1/16 Ⓣ:47⅘ 1:12 1:43⅘+ Clm 30000 3 1 1hd 1hd 42 55¾ Romero J A⁵ b 109 26.80 76-15 WntMothfl115¹½BroklynSnmmy111¾Sgmnd115nk Came over start 9
25Apr87- 2GS my 1 1/16 :48 1:14⅕ 1:47⅘ Alw 11500 4 2 2hd 31 78½ 711½ Romero J A⁵ b 111 5.10 57-18 Who the Heck 116hd Billy Bounce116¾RoyalGoodTime116⁴½ Tired 7
24Mar87- 5GS fst 1 1/16 :48⅖ 1:14⅕ 1:49⅖ Clm 18000 1 1 11 12½ 16 16 Romero J A⁷ b 110 *2.30 61-28 Tim Moss 110⁶ Billy Bounce 112nk Stringbean 115½ Driving 7
4Mar87- 6GS fst 1 1/16 :49 1:15⅕ 1:48⅕ Alw 11500 1 1 12½ 1½ 23 49¾ Romero J A⁷ b 109 11.90 57-30 Break Clean 116⁵¾ Who the Heck 116²½ Keen Marine 116¹½ Tired 7
12Feb87- 5GS fst 170 :46⅘ 1:13⅖ 1:45⅘ Clm 16000 4 2 2hd 1hd 11½ 1hd Romero J A⁷ b 109 4.30 70-22 Tim Moss 109hd Hamby 117½ Nicholas R. 114¹½ Lasted 8
17Jan87- 6Pna fst 1 :47⅕ 1:12⅖ 1:39⅖ Alw 11500 7 7 810 814 717 720¼ Rocco J b 115 26.70 57-25 T. V. Supper 115¹½ Kick Back118¹¼RuleroftheFleet115³ No factor 8
14Dec86- 4Lrl fr 1 :46⅕ 1:12⅕ 1:38⅗ Clm 25000 10 3 31½ 42 52¾ 66 Vigliotti M J b 114 8.10 73-12 Small Victories 108¹½ Ginger Snaps 109¹¾ Prince Rio 115½ Tired 10
25Nov86- 7Pha gd 6f :22⅕ :45⅘ 1:12⅖ Clm 20000 1 4 32 41½ 61¾ 52¼ Allen M⁵ b 112 5.20 77-20 InfirmtvActon117nkHrvrdDrv113¹½RvsRodRunnr115nk Drifted out 8
LATEST WORKOUTS Jly 23 Mth 5f fst 1:02 b Jly 7 Mth 5f fst 1:02⅖ b

C.

9–2

Jive With Five
Own.—Hirsch & Schucker
Dk. b. or br. c. 3, by Giboulee—Paper Bag, by Wolver Hollow
$32,000 Br.—Kentucky Horse Center Inc (Ky)
Tr.—Hirsch Alan
111
Lifetime 18 3 1 7 $30,090
1987 13 2 0 7 $22,740
1986 5 1 1 0 $7,350
Turf 2 0 0 2 $2,585

20Jly87- 7Mtn	gd	170	:46⅗ 1:12⅘ 1:42⅗	Clm 25000	5 4 45¼ 32½ 35 311½	Rocco J	b 115	3.60	71-26	Hoist n' Hail 11710 Exploding Hit111½JiveWithFive1153	Even try	6
30Jun87- 5Mth	fm	1 1/16	Ⓣ:47⅗ 1:11⅘ 1:42⅘	Clm 25000	3 3 42½ 33 35 38	St Leon G	b 115	10.10	83-09	MichellesDuNord1113JungleRg1115JivWithFiv115½	Lacked a rally	9
19Jun87- 6Mth	fm	1 1/16	Ⓣ:49 1:13⅕ 1:45⅗	Clm c-20000	4 6 42½ 51¼ 1½ 31	Rocco J	b 115	4.20	76-22	FmilyBest117hdMichellesDuNord1111JiveWithFive1151	Weakened	12
10Jun87- 6Mth	fst	6f	:22⅘ :46⅗ 1:12⅕	Clm 18000	4 6 66½ 52 3nk 1¾	Rocco J	b 114	10.50	79-23	Jive With Five 114¾ Spectacular Comet 1162½ He's It1151	Driving	7
28May87- 6Pim	fst	1 1/16	:48 1:12⅖ 1:46	Clm 20000	2 3 55 58 69½ 54¼	Sarvis D A5	b 107	7.60	70-23	Prince's Punch 1141¼ Rule The Land109½ChiefOfHearts1141	Tired	6
6May87- 4Pim	fst	1 1/16	:48 1:13⅗ 1:45⅘	Clm 18500	2 4 32 2hd 24 36½	Sarvis D A5	b 109	3.90	69-27	Blue And Bold 1125½ In the Navy 112¾ Jive With Five 1096	Tired	6
7Apr87- 4Pim	my	1 1/16	:47⅗ 1:13⅗ 1:46⅖	Clm 18500	4 7 65½ 42½ 33½ 36½	Sarvis D A5	b 109	2.70	65-25	Sign The Tab 1095 Eleanor Rex1141½JiveWithFive10912	Mild rally	7
1Apr87- 4Pim	fst	1 1/16	:47⅖ 1:12⅘ 1:46⅕	Clm 25000	6 6 77½ 64¼ 65½ 53½	Sarvis D A5	b 109	13.00	69-22	It's a Ginza 119nk Moreno 119no Start Tomorrow 1152¼	Outrun	7
22Mar87- 1Lrl	fst	1	:48 1:13⅘ 1:39⅖	Clm 25000	6 4 48½ 45¼ 55½ 37½	Sarvis D A5	b 109	6.50	68-19	Our Dad Ben 1144¾ Hop Tree 1142½ Jive WithFive109nk	No threat	6
2Mar87- 8Lrl	fst	6½f	:23 :47 1:20⅗	Clm 22500	7 6 67¾ 67½ 57½ 56¾	Sarvis D A5	b 113	9.20	71-32	Mornin' My Lord 1194 E.A.Bishop115½Winforandy1121½	No factor	8

LATEST WORKOUTS Jly 17 Mth 4f fst :48⅖ h Jun 16 Mth 5f fst 1:01⅗ h

D.

15–1

Touchy Decision
Own.—Reineman R L Stable
Dk. b. or br. c. 3, by Forli—Don't Honey Me, by Triple Bend
$32,000 Br.—Nuckols Bros (Ky)
Tr.—Gleaves Philip
113
Lifetime 4 0 0 0 $550
1987 4 M 0 0 $550
1986 0 M 0 0
Turf 2 0 0 0 $420

17Jly87-10Mth	fm	1 1/16	Ⓣ:47⅗ 1:12⅗ 1:45⅕	3↑Md Sp Wt	2 2 21 43½ 918 928½	Rocco J	b 115	5.70	50-20	Flight in Time 1154 Noble Field 1231½ Injun Power 115¾	Tired	11
1Jly87- 5Mth	fm	1 1/16	Ⓣ:49⅖ 1:13⅗ 1:45⅕+	Clm 40000	2 4 78¼ 64¼ 72¼ 54¼	Rocco J	115	38.00	71-20	Sigmundo115nkRingforPeace1152½WhatMouthful117¾	Wide in dr.	8
18Jun87- 6Mth	fst	170	:46⅕ 1:10⅖ 1:42	3↑Md Sp Wt	8 6 712 921 919 920½	Hernandez C	114	23.50	65-14	Stoked 114hd Darn Smart 1144 Nobel Bid 1147½	Outrun	9
2May87- 6GP	fst	7f	:23 :46⅘ 1:24⅗	3↑Md Sp Wt	7 8 117¾109 1022 1026½	Pezua J M	112	9.10	55-23	Joe Gillespie 1135½ Slewdonza 1124½ Foolish Uncle 1125	Outrun	12

LATEST WORKOUTS Jun 26 Mth 5f fst 1:02⅖ b Jun 16 Mth 3f fst :35 b Jun 12 Mth 6f fst 1:14 b Jun 8 Mth 5f fst 1:04 b

E.

15–1

Bold Quacker
Own.—Blue Crest Farms
Ch. c. 3, by Quack—Louisa Jane, by Vertex
$32,000 Br.—Bright View Farm Inc (N.J.)
Tr.—Anderson William D
117
Lifetime 5 1 0 0 $10,620
1987 4 1 0 0 $9,720
1986 1 M 0 0 $900

18Jly87- 6Mth	fst	6f	:22⅘ :46⅕ 1:12⅕	3↑[S]Alw 17500	2 9 107¾119¼ 99¾ 68	Melendez J D	114	31.60	71-21	TakeSanctuary112¾RockLegend1161½LiisonDngereuse1161	Outrun	12
9Jly87- 8Mth	fst	170	:47 1:11⅗ 1:42⅖	3↑[S]Alw 17500	8 2 1hd 2hd 44½ 711	Melendez J D	113	36.10	73-21	Tavio 117nk General Payco 1176½ Jasperado 1132½	Tired	10
1Jly87- 4Mth	fst	6f	:22⅕ :45⅕ 1:10⅗	3↑[S]Alw 17500	10 1 41¾ 87½ 76¼ 79	Melendez J D	114	8.30	78-15	AlltheNumbers1165ChiefResident1161½ClockrHrry114hd	Fell back	11
18Jun87- 4Mth	fst	6f	:22⅗ :45⅘ 1:11⅖	3↑[S]Md Sp Wt	7 5 1½ 1hd 12 1¾	Melendez J D	115	4.30	83-14	BoldQuacker115¾WhipperWave1151¼LordPompadour1221	Driving	10
30Oct86- 5Med	fst	6f	:23⅗ :47⅘ 1:13⅕	[S]Md Sp Wt	6 2 3nk 2hd 1hd 43¾	Melendez J D	118	*2.20	72-23	Belvidere 118nk More Fog 1182½ Smokin Tom 1181	Weakened	8

LATEST WORKOUTS Jun 27 Mth 3f sly :36 b Jun 16 Mth 3f fst :35⅘ b Jun 9 Mth 4f fst :48 h

F.

8–1

Scott's Jet
Own.—Vee Pee Jay Stable
B. c. 3, by Tri Jet—Royal Fancy, by Nashua
$32,000 Br.—Long Island Thoroughbred Breeders (Fla)
Tr.—Ferriola Peter
111
Lifetime 15 1 2 1 $15,295
1987 6 0 0 0 $2,825
1986 9 1 2 1 $12,470
Turf 1 0 0 0

23Apr87- 1Aqu	gd	1⅛	Ⓣ:49 1:14⅖ 1:53⅕	Clm 75000	9 5 43½ 42 56 512¾	Migliore R	b 112	*2.40e	56-30	FoolishPlrt1137½BrvndBright1071¾TurningForHom1132¼	Even try	9
10Apr87- 6Aqu	fst	1	:46⅘ 1:09⅗ 1:36⅖	Clm 45000	8 6 65 56 69½ 69¾	Migliore R	b 113	10.10	74-24	TargetX.1172½SunriseService114nkOleSongn'Dnce1133¼	No factor	9
5Apr87- 4Aqu	my	7f	:23 :46⅖ 1:23⅗	Clm 35000	7 3 43½ 43 43 43	Migliore R	b 117	6.20	80-19	Cayman 115½ Sunrise Service 1172½NationalHeadline117hd	Evenly	9
20Mar87- 7Aqu	fst	1	:46 1:11⅗ 1:38⅕	Clm 75000	3 5 52¾ 64¾ 78 79¾	Santagata N	b 112	6.10	65-27	Trick Card 1121¼ Yet Wave 1163 Dancing Court 1122	Fell back	7
13Mar87- 5Aqu	fst	7f	:22⅘ :46⅕ 1:24⅘	Alw 26000	1 5 34 45 51¼ 42	Santagata N	b 117	35.50	75-29	Coco'sDouble112nkNephrite1171PlesntVrity117¾	Needed response	7
6Feb87- 6Hia	fst	6f	:22⅕ :45⅖ 1:09⅘	Clm c-35000	5 7 710 712 611 511¼	Prado E S	b 112	64.30	86-20	Interview 1182½ Bradie Boy 1166½ Mr. Biscuit 116nk	Outrun	9
24Dec86- 7Crc	gd	1⅛	:50 1:15⅕ 1:55⅗	Alw 12900	5 3 33 44 712 716¾	Collins M S	b 112	11.00	56-26	NoMoreFlowers1156½FabulousDevotion1123C.PoppHll115no	Tired	7
7Dec86- 7Crc	fst	1 1/16	:50 1:15⅖ 1:49⅗	Clm 35000	6 2 21 21 1½ 2no	Collins M S	b 116	12.50	72-20	Go forCommadore118noScott'sJet116¾AlertView1141½	Just failed	7
28Nov86- 4Crc	fst	1 1/16	:48⅘ 1:14⅗ 1:49⅕	Md 25000	10 3 2½ 2½ 11½ 13	Collins M S	b 120	5.00	73-22	Scott's Jet 1203 Swift Trip 120nk Hoist n' Hail 120½	Ridden out	11
12Nov86- 2Crc	fst	1 1/16	:48⅘ 1:14⅗ 1:49⅗	Md Sp Wt	7 8 8⁸½ 712 1013 913½	Collins M S	b 117	12.60	57-22	[D]Plastique 1171 Absolute Pitch 117½ Tiger Rullah 1171½	Outrun	11

LATEST WORKOUTS Jly 28 Aqu [•] 3f fst :36⅗ h Jly 22 Aqu [•] 5f fst 1:03 b Jly 14 Aqu 3f fst :37⅗ b Jun 14 Aqu 3f gd :36⅕ h

38. What should handicappers think of this field's co-favorites?

2nd Santa Anita

START ▾ 6 FURLONGS SANTA ANITA FINISH

6 FURLONGS. (1.07⅗) CLAIMING. Purse $25,000. Fillies and mares. 3-year-olds and upward. Weights, 3-year-olds, 119 lbs.; older, 121 lbs. Non-winners of two races since November 3 allowed 3 lbs.; a race since then, 5 lbs. Claiming price $50,000; if for $45,000 allowed 2 lbs. (Races when entered for $40,000 or less not considered.)

5–1

Fagers Charm

B. m. 5, by Sham—Fagers Charisma, by Dr Fager
Br.—Winchell V H (Ky) 1986 7 0 3 0 $12,980
SIBILLE R 116 Tr.—Taliaferro Charles L $50,000 1985 15 5 4 1 $80,835
Own.—Walter R H Lifetime 37 7 10 1 $109,580 Turf 4 0 0 0 $2,590

17Oct86-8SA a6½f [T]:21 3 :44 2 1:15 2 fm 19 117 43½ 53 76¼ 85 Sibille R2 [F] 80000 77-18 Cherry Maison, Bullion, Witchery 10
3Oct86-8BM 6f :22 2 :45 1:10 3 ft 3 115 32½ 32½ 32 2no CastnedM2 [F]Aw20000 86-21 AbstractEnergy,FagersChrm,Erliest 6
7Sep86-10Bmf 6f :21 3 :44 2 1:10 4 ft 4¼ 115 56½ 45½ 42½ 2nk CastnedM7 [F]Aw22000 85-18 Hylnd'sHiHope,FgrsChrm,NovlSprit 7
21Aug86-9Sac 6f :22 3 :45 1 1:09 3 ft *9-5 114 31 32 2hd 21 CastnedM4 [F]Aw12000 90-18 Hylnd'sHiHope,FgersChrm,Sobrnie 6
2Aug86-9SR 5½f :21 4 :44 4 1:03 2 ft 4¼ 115 85½ 76¼ 67¼ 63¾ CastnedM1 [F]Aw15000 90-11 P.C'sFncy,RivrCityWind,MyDonnB. 8
2Aug86—Wide into stretch
21Jly86-11SR 6f :22 :45 1 1:10 ft 2¼e 115 55¼ 57½ 66 54½ CstdM6 [F][R]E Dstrl H 87-12 SteadyPenny,P.C'sFncy,PetiteShirh 8
21Jly86—Wide 3/8 turn, stretch
4Jly86-8Pln 5½f :22 :45 1:04 ft 2¼e 115 3½ 41 53¾ 45¼ CastnedM4 [F]Aw20000 85-13 PetiteShirah,CanadinJill,MyDonnB. 7
17Nov85-8BM 1 1/16 :47 1:11 1 1:43 ft 6½ 115 1½ 1hd 33 98¼ NcolP1 [F]Woodside H 69-20 MkMAnOffr,DistntDoll,TotlWomn 10
3Nov85-8BM 1 1/16 :46 3 1:10 2 1:42 2 ft 7½ 117 52¼ 63¼ 54 44 HICR7 [F][R]Wtc Wdy H 76-17 Music Queen,TotalWoman,Kyflaca 13
21Oct85-8BM 1 :47 4 1:13 1:39 gd *4-5 115 11½ 1½ 1hd 32 HummlCR6 [F]Aw22000 71-33 RitzyLady,DistantDoll,FagersCharm 7
Dec 27 SA 3f ft :36 2 h Dec 17 SA 5f ft :59 3 h Dec 3 SA 4f ft :48 1 h ●Nov 24 SA 5f ft :59 1 h

4–1

Beaulahland

B. f. 3, by Drum Fire—Phil's Chapeau, by Philately
Br.—CulpepperTb&NrthwstFms (Wash) 1986 11 2 4 1 $40,365
PATTON D B 109 5 Tr.—Dollase Wallace $50,000 1985 9 M 2 5 $20,850
Own.—Dollase-Lucian-McNamee Lifetime 20 2 6 6 $61,215 Turf 2 0 0 1 $4,125

4Dec86-9Hol 1 :45 2 1:10 2 1:36 4 ft *2 108 5 21½ 21½ 31 2¾ Patton D B7 [F] 50000 78-25 LotusDelight,Beaulahland,LdyShmn 7
7Nov86-9Hol 1 :45 1 1:09 4 1:35 2 ft 6½ 108 5 63 53 32 22 Patton D B1 [F] 45000 84-18 Leading Lass, Beaulahland, Mrs. V. 7
9Oct86-1SA 1 :46 2 1:11 4 1:38 2 ft *2¾ 118 98¾ 108¾ 1015 917 McHargueDG8 [F] 40000 59-21 EstrnGlmor,Mlv'sPrd,RbrtsRglGrl 10
9Oct86—Stumbled start
8Sep86-5Dmr 1 [T]:47 1:11 4 1:36 2 fm *2½ 118 75½ 76 52½ 54¾ McHargueDG8 [F] 62500 85-10 Sweetest,DrmticElgnc,DwnOfHop 10
22Aug86-7Dmr 1 [T]:46 3 1:11 1 1:36 1 fm 6¾ 116 2½ 1hd 1hd 32 McHargueDG8 [F] 62500 89-09 WineTaster,Tantalized,Beaulahland 8
26Jly86-7Dmr 1 :45 2 1:11 1:37 1 ft 5¾ 116 22 1½ 11½ 1½ McHrgDG1 [F]Aw20000 82-13 Beulhlnd,Bggr'sWllt,RoylDrby'sLov 8
9Jly86-3Hol 6f :22 3 :46 2 1:11 2 ft 12 116 63 42½ 42 2nk McHargueDG6 [F] 40000 87-18 CoffeeRoll,Beaulahlnd,MriSupreme 8
23Mar86-10TuP 1 :47 1 1:11 4 1:37 2 ft 3-2 118 53½ 43 1hd 13½ StMrtinE6 [F]Lndlce H 82-18 Beaulahland,FrnniePooper,ReilDrin 7
1Mar86-4SA 1 1/16 :45 4 1:10 4 1:44 3 ft 6 117 47 44½ 43 67 Stevens G L4 [F]Mdn 71-16 PuzzleBook,MybAKiss,WddingDncr 9
8Feb86-6SA 1 :46 4 1:11 4 1:38 1 ft 5¾ 117 1½ 1hd 2hd 21¼ Stevens G L9 [F]Mdn 76-19 Miraculous,Beaulahlnd,RunRoylly 10
Dec 21 Hol 5f ft 1:03 h Dec 14 Hol 4f ft :49 1 h ●Dec 1 Hol 4f ft :47 4 h Nov 19 Hol 4f ft :49 4 h

5–1

My Tara

Dk. b. or br. m. 6, by Exceedingly—Shaliah, by Big Burn
Br.—Stock A (NJ) 1986 9 1 2 3 $23,144
STEVENS G L 116 Tr.—Lukas D Wayne $50,000 1985 17 7 2 2 $120,304
Own.—Hatley & Lukas Lifetime 53 15 11 5 $196,516

19Nov86-8CD 7f :23 1 :47 2 1:24 3 ft 7¾ 121 11½ 31 811 823¼ Smith M E4 [F]Aw23550 60-23 Weekend Delight,Marlish,Smartake 8
26Oct86-6CD 6f :22 1 :46 3 1:12 4 m *3e 122 12 1½ 12½ 23 LidbrgDW4 [F]Aw21700 76-29 Umbrella Rig, My Tara, LemhiLove 9
21Oct86-4Kee 6½f :22 2 :45 3 1:17 ft 14 112 11½ 11 11½ 12½ SmithME10 [F]Aw20900 92-12 MyTr,ComingUpRoses,LittleJtSttr 12
26Jly86-10Cby 6f :22 2 :45 1:11 ft 19 118 43¼ 66¾ 64¾ 55¼ Black K7 [F]Eden Praie 87-12 MedievlDecoy,MmorisOfDixi,Avdnc 8
19Jun86-8Cby 6f :22 3 :45 3 1:11 ft *3-2 114 3½ 42½ 42½ 22¾ Allen RDJr5 [F]Aw13800 89-14 SassWithClass,MyTr,BettieBeGood 6
1Jun86-8Cby 6f :23 :46 1 1:13 ft 6½ 117 54½ 56 45½ 33 Black K1 [F]Aw13800 79-24 HoistHrFlg,Toohppyforwords,MyTr 8
17May86-9Cby 6f :23 :46 1 1:12 1 ft 3¾ 117 31½ 33 34 34 Black K2 [F]Aw13800 82-20 MmorsOfDx,Toohppyforwrds,MyTr 6
30Apr86-8Cby 6f :22 2 :45 2 1:11 1 ft *6-5 117 31½ 33½ 44 39 Black K3 [F]Aw13800 82-15 Lil Preppy, Erimo's Lady, My Tara 8
8Apr86-7Kee 6f :22 3 :45 1:11 3 ft 8½ 117 11½ 2½ 43 57¼ Black K1 [F]Aw22600 77-22 WekndDlight,ZnobiEmprss,Prsudbl 7
3Dec85-8Pha 6f :22 4 :46 3 1:11 4 ft *3-2 117 1hd 2hd 2hd 1hd Rocco J5 [F]Aw16000 82-23 My Tara,BestestFriend,ChafingDish 6
Dec 20 Hol 4f ft :49 3 h Dec 13 Hol 4f ft :47 3 h

36–1

Tuta Mia

B. f. 3, by Dimaggio—Dusty Row, by Dusty Canyon
Br.—Valpredo J (Cal) 1986 11 1 0 0 $14,150
VERGARA O 114 Tr.—Aviles Mario $50,000 Turf 2 0 0 0
Own.—Valpredo J Lifetime 11 1 0 0 $14,150

20Dec86-9Hol 1 [T]:45 4 1:10 1 1:35 3 fm 48 115 812 89¾ 812 712½ Vergara O6 [F]Aw24000 76-04 Ohslewsnn,SportingAck,ElevnSirns 8
20Dec86—Bumped break
10Dec86-1Hol 6f :22 :46 1:12 ft 71 110 5 66½ 66½ 66¾ 45 Patton D B6 [F] 50000 78-20 TrumTim,DrmPolcy,AffordblLuxury 8
10Dec86—Bobbled start
28Nov86-5Hol 6f :22 1 :45 2 1:11 1 ft 49 115 73¾ 87½ 79½ 710½ Saint-MrtinE5 [F] 50000 76-14 DuchessZnthe,CrestLdy,BnqutDncr 9
20Jun86-7Hol 1 [T]:45 4 1:10 3 1:35 2 fm 93 112 107¼ 106¼ 97½ 98½ Ortega LE9 [F]Aw21000 — — MediGirl,Jclyn'sChoice,DwnOfHop 10
14Jun86-7Hol 6f :22 1 :46 1:10 3 ft 37 112 5 94¼ 98½ 77½ 99¼ Black C A5 [F]Aw19000 82-14 RrStrlt,SkipSchoon,MillrsSttionry 11
14Jun86—Bumped start
31May86-4Hol 6f :22 3 :45 4 1:11 ft 90 121 63½ 56 46 45¾ Soto S B7 [F]Aw20000 83-16 Argentrio,PromiseMeLuck,CrstLdy 8
31May86—Forced wide 3/8
18May86-6Hol 6f :21 4 :44 4 1:08 3 ft 54 115 5 44 57½ 611 515½ Black C A7 [F]Aw20000 85-08 Melair, Flying Julia, Argentario 9
9May86-4Hol 6f :22 1 :45 3 1:09 4 ft 16 121 65½ 68 59½ 511½ ShoemkrW6 [F]Aw26000 83-16 PollysLlRscl,PrmsMLck,LdyMcClry 6
19Apr86-7SA 1 :46 1 1:11 2 1:39 ft 14 115 67 79¾ 715 614 Solis A2 [F]Aw26000 59-19 SeaDoubyRun,Argentario,OurLutka 8
2Apr86-6SA 6f :21 4 :45 2 1:11 1 ft 4 112 5 21½ 21½ 21 11½ Black C A9 [F][S]Mdn 82-22 TutaMia,Dancer'sRegards,StrwDog 9
Dec 26 SA 4f ft :48 1 h Dec 18 Hol 5f ft 1:01 4 hg Dec 6 Hol 5f m 1:00 4 h Nov 24 Hol 5f ft 1:00 3 h

5–2

Agigael — **PINCAY L JR** — Own.—Shapiro M — **116**

Ch. m. 6, by Agitate—Gaelicwin, by Gaelic Dancer
Br.—Shapiro M (Cal) — 1986 1 0 0 1 $2,850
Tr.—Glauburg Louis — $50,000 — 1985 4 1 1 0 $36,250
Lifetime 26 5 6 3 $129,225 — Turf 14 4 4 2 $103,400

13Nov86-3Hol 6f :222 :454 1:11 ft 6½ 117 42½ 42 22½ 33¼ Pincay L Jr4 Ⓕ 50000 85-23 Duchess Zanthe, TammyLu,Agigael 6
13Nov86—Broke out, bumped
12Oct85-5SA a6½f Ⓣ:213 :44 1:142fm 3½ 116 75¾ 46½ 56 58½ ShoemakerW2 Ⓕ 80000 78-13 RegalTies,LadyMaureen,TableSen 10
20Feb85-8SA a6½f Ⓣ:221 :4421:14 fm 12 116 1½ 12 2hd 42 LozoyaDA3 ⒻMnrva H 87-11 Lina Cavalieri,AirDistingue,Tangent 8
24Jan85-8SA a6½f Ⓣ:212 :4331:141fm 2½ 1145 33½ 32 3nk 2¾ Lozoya D A4 Aw45000 87-12 IrishO'Brien,Agigel,AwesomPromis 6
9Jan85-7SA a6½f Ⓣ:221 :4411:151fm *2½ 1135 31 21 12 11½ Lozoya DA6 ⒻAw40000 83-17 Agigel,SisPlesureFger,ContinntlGirl 8
1Nov84-8SA a6½f Ⓣ:212 :4341:15 fm *3¼ 1115 31½ 21½ 22 1no Lozoya DA9 ⒻAw33000 84-16 Agigael, Early Quest, Fluke 10
2Sep84-7Dmr 1 1/16 Ⓣ:47 1:11 1:423fm 2½ 116 22 22½ 32 65½ McCrrnCJ7 ⒻAw24000 91-05 FncyWings,ClerTlk,ReflectToGlory 9
2Sep84—Bore out 1st turn
17Aug84-8Dmr 1 1/16 Ⓣ:4811:1141:421fm 4½ 117 12 11 12 22 McCrrnCJ1 ⒻAw24000 96-06 Lyprd'sPrincess,Agigl,RflcttoGlory 8
17Aug84—Bore out 1st 3/4
19Jly84-8Hol 1 Ⓣ:47 1:1041:353fm 5½ 118 1hd 12 1hd 32½ PedrozMA3 ⒻAw32000 87-10 ContinntlGirl,Lyphrd'sPrincss,Agigl 7
19Jly84—Steadied while lugging out at 7/8
17May84-7Hol 1 1/16 Ⓣ:4721:12 1:42 fm*8-5 114 11½ 11½ 13 13½ McCrrnCJ1 ⒻAw24000 89-15 Agigael, Colaxe, Olympic Bronze 10
17May84—Lugged out 7/8 turn, down the backstretch
Dec 18 SA 5f ft 1:00 h — Dec 12 SA 1 ft 1:423 h — Dec 4 SA 3f ft :353 h — Nov 29 SA 6f ft 1:14 h

5–2

Cresta Lady — **MEZA R Q** — Own.—Vistas — **114**

B. f. 3, by Cresta Rider—Rare Lady, by Never Bend
Br.—Mabee Mr-Mrs J C (Cal) — 1986 11 2 1 5 $39,655
Tr.—Conaway Larry — $50,000 — 1985 0 M 0 0
Lifetime 11 2 1 5 $39,655

28Nov86-5Hol 6f :221 :452 1:111ft 22 115 2hd 2½ 22 2¾ Meza R Q6 Ⓕ 50000 86-14 DuchessZnthe,CrestLdy,BnqutDncr 9
8Nov86-7Hol 6f :22 :453 1:102ft 39 114 85¼ 99¼ 99¼ 913¾ Meza R Q7 ⒻAw21000 77-13 Andrushka,SuchASplash,BoldDyna 10
8Nov86—Wide final 3/8
26Oct86-3SA 6f :213 :45 1:103ft 27 114 73¾ 64¼ 65¾ 710¼ Doocy T T5 ⒻAw25000 75-16 Sown,HairlessHeiress,Erl'sVlentine 9
12Oct86-2SA 6½f :22 :45 1:164ft 16 114 2½ 2hd 32½ 39½ Doocy T T8 ⒻAw25000 76-21 FlyingJulia,HirlessHeiress,CrestLdy 9
12Oct86—Broke in a tangle
31May86-4Hol 6f :223 :454 1:11 ft 3¾e115 41 32½ 33½ 34¼ VlenzulPA3 ⒻAw20000 85-16 Argentrio,PromiseMeLuck.CrstLdy 8
30Apr86-7GG 6f :214 :441 1:09 ft *7-5 114 2½ 21½ 23 34 Diaz A L5 ⒻAw17000 90-16 OurDerKrissy,AppleRoyle,CrestLdy 8
11Apr86-1SA 6f :22 :45 1:112ft 2¼ 118 12 14 13½ 12¼ Stevens G L6 Ⓕ c50000 81-17 CrestaLady,RufflesNBeus,WineGirl 6
17Mar86-5SA 6½f :22 :46 1:19 sy 5½ 118 22 21 2½ 33¼ Stevens G L4 Ⓕ 50000 72-27 TraumaTime,GrnEmotion,CrestLdy 6
28Feb86-3SA 6f :213 :45 1:11 ft 7 117 1hd 11½ 11½ 12½ Kaenel J L10 ⒻM50000 83-19 CrestaLady,WineGirl,BolderBeuty 10
13Feb86-3SA 6f :213 :443 1:103ft 3¾e118 11½ 1hd 2hd 34½ Kaenel J L9 ⒻM50000 80-14 SeptemberBreeze,WineGirl,GrstLdy 9
13Feb86—Steadied late
Dec 22 SA 4f ft :472 h — ●Dec 14 SA 4f ft :463 h — Dec 8 SA 4f gd :482 h — Nov 20 SA 5f ft 1:002 h

6–1

Trauma Time — **DELAHOUSSAYE E** — Own.—Owen L W — **116**

Ch. f. 3, by Search for Gold—Bonne Enfant, by Deck Hand
Br.—Ballymeehan Farm (Cal) — 1986 17 3 2 3 $53,025
Tr.—Wright Robert — $50,000 — 1985 7 1 2 0 $17,730
Lifetime 24 4 4 3 $70,755 — Turf 1 0 0 0

10Dec86-1Hol 6f :22 :46 1:12 ft 4½ 116 33 34½ 32½ 1nk DelhoussyeE5 Ⓕ 50000 83-20 TrumTim,DrmPolcy,AffordblLuxury 8
10Dec86—Broke in, bumped
7Nov86-9Hol 1 :451 1:094 1:352ft 7½ 115 31 31½ 56 510¼ Kaenel J L2 Ⓕ 50000 76-18 Leading Lass, Beaulahland, Mrs. V. 7
31Oct86-1SA 6f :212 :442 1:11 ft 5¼ 116 64¾ 57½ 45½ 31¾ Kaenel J L6 Ⓕ 40000 81-16 AffordblLuxury,LdyShmn,TrumTim 9
19Oct86-1SA 6½f :212 :443 1:172ft *2¾ 116 23½ 43 67 67 Ortega L E6 Ⓕ 50000 76-18 FlightAbove,DuchessZnth,LdingLss 8
19Oct86—Broke in, bumped
1Oct86-5SA 6f :214 :444 1:102ft 12 114 55½ 55 35 33½ OrtegLE2 ⒻⓈAw25000 83-18 SeriousGal,Luck'sFantsy,TrumTime 7
1Oct86—Bumped start
12Sep86-11Pom 6½f :214 :45 1:17 ft 16 114 55½ 511 610 86½ OrtLE2 ⒻⓇLas Ninas 88-11 StridingEasy,TropiclHolidy,FirlyOld 9
11Aug86-8Dmr 7f :221 :45 1:22 ft 12 114 22 55 57 56 Ortega LE5 ⒻⓈFlt Trt 89-13 Witchery, RareStarlet,Symbolically 7
24Jly86-7Dmr 6f :221 :453 1:10 ft 7 113 41¼ 32 33 2hd OrtegLE4 ⒻⓈAw19000 88-15 TmmyLu,TrumTime,PromiseMLuck 7
10Jly86-9LA 6f :22 :453 1:11 ft 2½ 112 63 51¼ 52½ 52 Ortega LE3 ⒻAw15000 86-17 MissBnson,Nordic'sGirl,Glic'sBond 6
27Jun86-1Hol 6f :223 :461 1:101ft 8½ 114 31 31 22½ 24 OrtegLE6 ⒻⓈAw19000 89-12 SkipSchoon,TrumTim,PromsMLuck 8
Dec 2 SA 3f ft :37 h — Nov 22 SA 4f ft :48 h

A. *Agigael* is an overlay
B. *Cresta Lady* figures to win
C. Both are underlays
D. Both are outclassed in this race

39. Apply what you know about maidens on the grass to select the best conclusion below.

7th Belmont

1 1/16 MILES. (Turf). (1.39⅗) MAIDEN SPECIAL WEIGHT. Purse $24,000. 3-year-olds and upward. Weight, 3-year-olds, 116 lbs. Older, 122 lbs.

6–1

Quiddler
Own.—Delehanty Farm — 116
Dk. b. or br. c. 3, by Raised Socially—Ooloo, by Bold Forbes
Br.—Greely J J (Ky) — 1987 8 M 1 3 $11,420
Tr.—Schmitt William F — 1986 0 M 0 0
Lifetime 8 0 1 3 $11,420

15Jly87-6Bel 7f :231 :464 1:241ft 14 122 52½ 21 25 311½ Romero R P 10 Mdn 69-20 RchsToRchs,AtlsMdnswoon,Qddlr 11
15Jly87—Drifted out
28Jun87-3Bel 7f :222 :452 1:244ft *9-5 114 69 510 39 28 Davis R G 5 M75000 70-19 Naudimar, Quiddler, Aki 8
8Jun87-9Bel 6f :224 :462 1:12 ft 10 114 1013 1011 56 33 Romero R P 6 M75000 77-20 SilkyAppeal,Aeguanimits,Quiddler 12
8May87-2Bel 6f :223 :454 1:11 ft 14 113 910 712 69½ 56 Romero R P7 M75000 79-24 FullColonel,PastFancy,SilkyAppel 11
20Feb87-4Aqu 1⅛ [•]:4921:1441:554ft 3½ 122 23½ 42 52¼ 57½ Martens G7 Mdn 55-28 K.C.'sBestTurn,BucketShop,Goliard 9
11Feb87-4Aqu 1 1/16 [•]:4821:1341:473ft 57 122 32 31½ 2½ 34 Martens G5 Mdn 68-20 Girning, Windy Sails, Quiddler 12
11Feb87—Steadied
28Jan87-5Aqu 6f [•]:224 :4641:121ft 30 122 43½ 54 66½ 57¼ Antley C W12 Mdn 76-18 PttisBoy,Polignc,NorthrnAzimuth 12
14Jan87-4Aqu 6f [•]:222 :4541:121ft 10 122 1111 1114 912 68¾ Santagata N8 M35000 74-16 ClssGift,SlntSnppr,BoxOfChocolts 12
Jun 7 Bel 3f ft :38 b

20–1

Space Code
Own.—Mangurian H T Jr — 116
Ch. g. 3, by Codex—Out in Space, by Royal Orbit
Br.—Mangurian Mr–Mrs H T Jr (Fla) — 1987 4 M 0 0 $990
Tr.—Root Thomas Jr — 1986 0 M 0 0
Lifetime 4 0 0 0 $990

23Jly87-2Bel 1 :471 1:124 1:394ft 12 116 21 2½ 32 45 Thibeau R J 11 M35000 61-22 PrinceofNight,IdlSolution,Snd-Up 12
15Jly87-6Bel 7f :231 :464 1:241ft 63 122 1hd 41½ 811 819½ Thibeau R J 1 Mdn 61-20 RchsToRchs,AtlsMdnswoon,Qddlr 11
6Jun87-1Crc 1 1/16 :491 1:134 1:48 ft 9 114 31 518 835 834 Woodhouse R 6 Mdn 45-15 BlzingBrt,ColonelE.A.,Prrll'sBdBoy 9
31May87-1Crc 6f :22 :461 1:122ft 6 114 66½ 67½ 615 616½ Velez J A Jr 7 Mdn 72-15 Slewdonza,BlazingBart,BonnzCreek 8
Jly 10 Bel tr.t 3f sy :374 b — Jly 5 Bel 3f ft :37 b — Jun 18 Bel 3f ft :371 b

15–1

Superata
Own.—Warfield T — 116
Dk. b. or br. c. 3, by Super Concorde—Krassata, by Nijinsky II
Br.—Moyglare Stud Farm Ltd (Ky) — 1987 9 M 2 0 $8,100
Tr.—Zito Nicholas P — Turf 2 0 0 0
Lifetime 10 0 2 0 $8,100

20Jly87-2Bel 6f :223 :464 1:131m *3-2 116 44½ 37 43¼ 45 Pezua J M 1 M35000 69-15 Hagabee, Fully Satified, De Sade 13
2Jly87-9Bel 6f :222 :461 1:13 sy *2 116 3½ 31½ 24 24¼ Pezua J M 4 M35000 71-27 InheritTheErth,Supert,SpceSttion 10
11Jun87-6Bel 1 1/16 [T]:4611:11 1:433fm 13 114 11½ 12 46½ 914¾ Pezua J M 9 Mdn 63-16 I'mEnthsd,Slvngton,SpctclrSmok 11
5Jun87-9Bel 7f :231 :463 1:242gd 4¼ 114 31½ 21 37 411½ Antley C W 3 M50000 68-19 SintAsph,ComputrCod,SssThMitrd' 9
20May87-4Bel 1 :454 1:103 1:363ft 5 113 11½ 2½ 44½ 67¾ Antley C W 9 M50000 74-17 Dnzide,ComputerCode,StevthJudg 11
8May87-2Bel 6f :223 :454 1:11 ft 5½ 113 67½ 68½ 58 67½ Antley C W9 M75000 77-24 FullColonel,PastFancy,SilkyAppel 11
8May87—Broke slowly
1Apr87-9Aqu 6f :23 :472 1:13 ft *1 112 73¾ 31 2½ 2no Venezia M1 M35000 76-18 SilentSnpper,Suprt,RushingWrrior 11
1Apr87—Slow start
11Feb87-4Aqu 1 1/16 [•]:4821:1341:473ft 7½ 122 52¼ 54½ 914 917¼ Maple E3 Mdn 55-20 Girning, Windy Sails, Quiddler 12
Jly 17 Bel 4f ft :474 h — Jun 29 Bel 4f ft :474 h — Jun 18 Bel 4f ft :48 h — May 30 Bel 4f ft :471 h

20—1

Tanthem Trouble

Own.—Cohn Madeline   **116**

B. c. 3, by Tanthem—Kettle, by Levee Dancer
Br.—Thornton Mr—Mrs C (Ky)   1987 1 M 0 0
Tr.—Smith David   1986 0 M 0 0
Lifetime 1 0 0 0

20Jly87-2Bel   6f :22³ :46⁴ 1:13¹m   29 114   132⁴13¹⁹12¹⁶11¹⁵ Baird E T⁵   M32500 59-15 Hagabee, Fully Satified, Dr Sade 13
20Jly87—Broke slowly
Jly 23 Aqu① 3f gd :39¹ h   ● Jly 18 Aqu 3f gd :36³ h (d)   Jly 5 Aqu 5f ft 1:04 bg   Jun 29 Aqu 4f ft :51³ bg

2—1

Orpheus Island

Own.—Sugar Maple Farm 7—N **116**

Dk. b. or br. c. 3, by Blushing Groom—Euphrosyne, by Judger
Br.—Mirkin Morris J (Ky)   1987 6 M 2 2 $14,340
Tr.—Johnson Philip G   1986 3 M 0 2 $5,280
Lifetime 9 0 2 4 $19,620   Turf 3 0 2 0 $8,820

18Jly87-6Bel   1¹⁄₁₆①:48 1:13¹¹:46⁴gf ³7-5 116   2½ 2¹ 3¹ 41¹¹ Davis R G¹   Mdn 54-35 IrishRue,InAllRespects,Cptln'sEdg 11
24Jun87-4Bel   1¹⁄₄①:48¹¹:37³2:03 fm*8-5 114   1² 12 2½ 2¹½ Davis R G⁹   Mdn 77-21 ComputrCod,OrphsIsland,WsOldOwl 9
11Jun87-4GS   1¹⁄₁₆①:48³1:123¹:44²fm*6-5 114   32½ 3½ 1ʰᵈ 1ⁿᵒ † Wilson R⁵   Mdn 86-16 ‡OrphusIsInd,NickDngr,BrssyDvic 10
†11Jun87—Disqualified and placed second; Came in
14May87-1Bel   7f :22⁴ :45³ 1:23¹ft   3 122   -31½ 21½ 33½ 35½ Samyn J L³   Mdn 80-13 I'mSoBd,SettleKnight,OrphusIsInd 8
30Apr87-6Aqu   7f :22³ :45⁴ 1:25¹ft   4e112   2½ 1ʰᵈ 2½ 33½ Samyn J L¹   Mdn 71-28 CommonwlthClb,Dzng,OrphsIsInd 12
20Apr87-6Aqu   6f :22¹ :46 1:11 ft   9-5e112⁻¹·7⁷ 78½ 813 814½ ˢSamyn J L⁹   Mdn 71-22 Landyap, Divine Providence,Dazing 9
20Apr87—Slow start
18Oct86-5Bel   6f :22⁴ :46 1:11³ft   *2e118   2¹ 1ʰᵈ 2ʰᵈ 3ᵏ Cordero A Jr¹   Mdn 84-17 RomntcTun,OnthCrpt,OrphusIsInd 14
10Oct86-4Bel   7f :22⁴ :46 1:24²ft   42 118   55½ 42½ 32½ 31½ Samyn J L⁹   Mdn 78-17 Gorky, Samerkand, OrpheusIsland 11
10Oct86—Steadied
Jly 24 Bel 4f ft :49⁴ h   ● Jly 19 Bel 5f ft :59² h   Jly 6 Bel 4f ft :47³ h   Jly 1 Bel 3f ft :36 h

3—1

Highly Rated II

Own.—D M Holiday Stable S—N **116**

Gr. c. 3, by Beldale Flutter—Pearl Grey, by Gulf Pearl
Br.—Lord Harrington (Ire)   1987 4 M 1 0 $6,720
Tr.—Cotter Mary M   1986 3 M 2 3 $3,447
Lifetime 11 0 3 3 $10,167   Turf 9 0 2 3 $4,887

18Jly87-6Bel   1 ①:46²1:12 1:37²fm 7½ 116   8¹² 611 22½ 21½ † Migliore R⁴   Mdn 76-20 LordLaser,‡HighlyRatedII,VanMn 12
†18Jly87—Disqualified and placed fourth; Lugged In
4Jly87-4Bel   1¹⁄₁₆:48³ 1:39⁴ 2:06¹ft   11 116   33 43 57½ 27½ Cruguet J¹   Mdn 60-23 Aki, Highly Rated II, Wise Old Owl 6
14May87-3Bel   1¹⁄₁₆①:46³1:113¹:434fm   11 114   33 42½ 85 96½ Murphy D J¹⁰   Mdn 70-22 HsFrquntflyr,Slvington,WnMrchnt 12
23Apr87-6Aqu   6f :22³ :46² 1:11⁴ft   20 114   9¹⁰ 813 713 612½ Murphy D J⁶   M50000 70-24 Sayad'sCommand,PstFncy FirRex 11
27Sep86♠6Curragh(Ire) 1   1:42¹fm 10 122   ① 2⁸ SwnCF   Unidare Nursery H GeraldMac,HighlyRted,AppelToAll 19
11Sep86♠4Tipperary(Ire) 7f   1:40 gd 3 126   ① 64½ GllspD PrefrncProductsPl(Mdn) MidwayRuth, MissGosling,Shrvita 15
18Aug86♠3Roscommon(Ire) 7f   1:41²sf *2½ 126   ① 7¹¹ PrneIID   Goffs Plate(Mdn) Ormus,TrulyFltLrng,GoodTwoShos 14
28Jly86♠2Galway(Ire)1 7f   1:40¹gd*9-5 126   ① 3² PrllD   Athenry Stakes (Mdn) DerbyKelly,GeminiWay,HighlyRted 9
Jly 29 Bel 3f ft :35² h   Jly 1 Bel 4f ft :50 b   ● Jun 27 Bel 7f sy 1:28 h   Jun 15 Bel 5f ft 1:03⁴ h

A. Both maidens having form on the grass are underlays
B. Bred for grass, *Space Code* is a fantastic overlay
C. After a pair of excusable losses when favored on off-tracks, *Superata* figures to improve in its second turf effort and is a definite overlay at 15—1
D. Regardless of odds, no maiden can be supported on the grass until it shows a decent performance over the surface

40. It's January. *Zabaleta* is tons best here, as the odds suggest. What should expert handicappers do?

3rd Santa Anita

6 FURLONGS. (1.07⅗) **ALLOWANCE.** Purse $29,000. 4-year-olds and upward. Non-winners of $3,000 twice other than maiden, claiming or starter. Weight, 4-year-olds, 120 lbs.; older, 121 lbs. Non-winners of two races other than claiming since October 1 allowed 2 lbs.; of such a race of $13,000 since October 1, 4 lbs.

1–1

Zabaleta ·ᴵ⁻ᴺ
STEVENS G L   **116**

B. c. 4, by Shecky Greene—Winver, by Vertex		
Br.—Parr E Q (Ky)	1986 6 2 2 1	$196,450
Tr.—Gosden John H M	1985 0 M 0 0	

Own.—Riordan M D (Lessee)   Lifetime 6 2 2 1 $196,450

3May86-8CD	1¼:451 1:37 2:024ft	16f 126	2¹ 85½12¹⁴12¹⁹¾	McHrDG¹⁵	Ky Derby	63-10	Frdinnd,BoldArrngmnt,BrodBrush 18
3May86—Grade I							
19Apr86-9GS	1⅛:462 1:113 1:51 ft	*6-5 117	1hd 2nd 2nd 2½	McHrDG⁸	GardenStte	73-21	FobbyForbes,Zabalet,MircleWood 18
19Apr86—Ducked out,brshd							
5Apr86-8Aqu	1 :444 1:083 1:343ft	*6-5 121	2¹½ 2³ 23½ 43	McHrDG⁵	Gotham	90-18	Mogambo, ‡Groovy, Tasso 9
5Apr86—Grade II; Placed third through disqualification							
22Mar86-7Aqu	7f :223 :451 1:22 ft	3½ 114	32 3¹ 1hd 14½	McHrDG⁴	Bay Shore	91-25	Zabaleta, Groovy, Belocolus 8
22Mar86—Grade II; Run in Divisions							
26Feb86-8SA	6f :213 :441 1:09 ft	9½ 116	3¹ 3½ 1½ 2½	McHrDG⁶	ⓡBlsaChica	92-16	Ketoh, Zabaleta, Bold And Greene 11
26Feb86—Lugged in badly backstretch; checked off heels early							
9Feb86-6SA	6f :214 :44 1:10 ft	4½ 117	32 2nd 1½ 1hd	McHargue D G¹	Mdn	88-16	Zabalet,AckAckHeir,Intuitiveness 12

Dec 29 SA 5f ft 1:003 h   Dec 24 Hol 5f ft 1:023 h

13–1

Devils Brigade /³
VALENZUELA P A ᴵ⁻ᴼ   **116**   ᴵᴼ/

B. c. 4, by Today 'n Tomorrow—I'm Jazzy, by Tree of Knowledge		
Br.—Moore & Smith (Cal)	1986 7 2 1 1	$31,500
Tr.—Manzi Joseph	Turf 1 0 0 0	

Own.—Husband—Moore—Smith et al   Lifetime 7 2 1 1 $31,500

12Dec86-8Hol	6f :223 :454 1:101ft	5 114	53 56 610 611	ShoemkerW⁴	Aw25000	81-20	Paisano Pete, Danczone, HighHook 6
12Dec86—Crowded at 3 1/2							
30Oct86-5SA	ab1f ①:214 :4441:151fm	3½ 115	53 87½ 95¾ 97¾	ValenzuelPA⁶	Aw28000	75-17	Arcadius, Sans Rival, Will Spring 10
30Oct86—Took up 3 1/2							
25Apr86-3Hol	6f :221 :454 1:104ft	5 120	43 3½ 11 11½	VlenzulPA¹ ⓢAw20000		90-16	DevilsBrigade,DonB.Blue,Rinnegato 5
13Apr86-1SA	1 :461 1:11 1:372ft	4½ 116	87½ 44½ 43½ 42½	ValenzuelPA⁷	Aw26000	78-15	Iron Eyes, AckAckHeir,InherentKal 8
26Mar86-6SA	6f :212 :451 1:11 ft	4½ 117	86½ 74½ 43 12	Valenzuela PA¹ ⓢMdn		83-17	DvilsBrigd,Mrvin'sPolicy,MrkChip 11
16Feb86-1SA	7f :23 :46 1:234ft	2½ 117	45 23½ 22½ 33½	Valenzuela P A⁵	Mdn	78-19	AckAckHir,SprucSkippr,DvilsBrigd 8
8Feb86-3SA	6½f:214 :45 1:173ft	7½ 118	911 88½ 56½ 22¾	Valenzuela PA³ ⓢMdn		79-19	SocietyRod,DvilsBrigd,SpcChllngr 10
8Feb86—Broke slowly, wide into stretch, lugged in							

Dec 30 SA 4f ft :481 h   Dec 25 SA 6f ft 1:132 h   ●Dec 20 SA 4f ft :47 h   Dec 8 Hol 5f od 1:001 h

10–1

High Touch
BAZE G   ᴵ⁻ᴺ   **117**   ᴵᴼ⁷

Dk. b. or br. g. 5, by Rising Market—Libya, by Sir Gaylord		
Br.—Westerly Stud Farms (Cal)	1986 8 1 2 0	$22,650
Tr.—Luby Donn	1985 4 1 0 0	$10,550

Own.—Jandy Stables   Lifetime 12 2 2 0 $33,200   Turf 1 0 0 0

18Oct86-7SA	6f :22 :444 1:092ft	14 117	86¾ 86¾ 45 23½	DelhoussyeE⁸	Aw28000	87-20	Quip Star, High Touch, High Hook 8
8Sep86-7Dmr	1⅛:454 1:10 1:41 ft	8½ 119	21 55 35½ 67½	DelhoussyeE¹	Aw25000	87-14	Ack AckHeir,GoSwiftly,JackNCoke 7
8Sep86—Bumped start; lugged out early							
9Aug86-7Dmr	1⅛:452 1:094 1:424ft	8½ 118	3nk 12½ 13½ 13	DelhoussyeE⁵	Aw20000	86-14	HighTouch,AngleArc,Hrrison'sTurn 7
9Aug86—Lugged in 1/16							
23Jly86-7Dmr	6f :214 :452 1:093ft	6½ 119	73½ 53½ 43½ 52½	StevensGL⁵ ⓢAw19000		88-12	AnothrBloom,Bugrin,FlyingLssons 10
23Jly86—Bumped start							
29Jun86-7Hol	7f :212 :442 1:214ft	3 116	55 42½ 41½ 56½	McHrgueDG²	Aw19000	88-10	Slyly Gifted, In Toto, Noticiero 8
8Jun86-3Hol	6f :22 :453 1:103ft	5½ 117	97½ 97½ 67½ 2¹	Pincay L Jr⁷	Aw18000	90-11	BoldTopsidr,HghTouch,PowrfulEys 9
25May86-7Hol	6f :223 :461 1:104ft	8½ 116	42 42 51½ 73½	Hernandez R²	Aw20000	86-18	Totlity,BoldTopsider,NotTheRegulr 8
25May86—Veered out start							
4May86-7Hol	7f :222 :452 1:24 ft	9 116	3nk 32 44 46	Hernandez R⁵	Aw20000	78-18	Conteal, Lord Pancho,ForsytheBoy 7
4May86—Broke in a tangle							
29Aug85-5Dmr	7½f ①:223 :4541:291fm	32 1075	811 812 79½ 610	Gomez EA¹ ⓢAw23000		83-06	Racey Lace,Bloom'sBeau,Stemilion 8
29Aug85—Rank, lugged out 7/8 turn							
9Aug85-7Dmr	6½f:222 :451 1:153ft	12 113	43 45½ 411 416	Meza R Q⁶ ⓢAw20000		82-15	SureToFire,MostDetrmind,Holmish 8
9Aug85—Lugged in drive							

Dec 31 SA 3f ft :361 h   Dec 24 SA 6f ft 1:134 h   Dec 17 SA 6f ft 1:122 h   Dec 9 SA 5f ft 1:004 h

5—1

High Hook

PINCAY L JR 2—N 117

Own.—Hudson & Summa Stable

B. h. 5, by Exceller—Eehook, by Francis S
Br.—Hudson E J Sr (Ky)
Tr.—Drysdale Neil

				1986	11 1 3 2	$36,560
			109	1985	5 1 2 0	$15,910
Lifetime	16 2 5 2	$52,470		Turf	1 0 0 0	

12Dec86-8Hol	6f :223 :454 1:101ft	4½ 117	32½ 31½ 34 32½	Pincay L Jr¹	Aw25000 89-20	Paisano Pete, Danczone, HighHook 6
30Nov86-4BM	6f :222 :451 1:092ft	3½ 115	52¾ 45 41¼ 2½	Sibille R⁵	Aw18000 91-14	Safety Bank, High Hook,Donnaskra 7
30Oct86-5SA	a6½f ⑦:214 :4441:151fm	7½ 117	74½ 43 53 65¾	SwnburnWR⁸	Aw28000 77-17	Arcadius, Sans Rival, Will Spring 10
18Oct86-7SA	6f :22 :444 1:092ft	3½ 117	62½ 31½ 32½ 34	Pincay L Jr⁷	Aw28000 87-20	Quip Star, High Touch, High Hook 8
15Aug86-7Dmr	7f :221 :45 1:223ft	2½ 117	42 63½ 716 —	Pincay L Jr⁵	Aw21000 —	J. R. Johnson, East Tulip,CoSwiftly 8
15Aug86-Eased; bumped, steadied 3/8
3Aug86-7Dmr	6f :213 :444 1:091ft	15 117	74½ 32 3½ 21½	Pincay L Jr⁹	Aw21000 90-10	Ondarty, High Hook, J. R.Johnson 12
3Aug86-Fanned wide final 3/8
28May86-8Hol	7f :214 :443 1:224ft	*3 119	63¾ 52½ 86¾ 816½	Pincay L Jr⁶	Aw23000 73-15	Air Alert, Go Swiftly, Barland 9
28May86-Wide 3/8 turn
11May86-7Bel	6f :222 :453 1:103ft	3 119	55 62¾ 65 86¼	Maple E⁴	Aw25000 83-15	CalicoJk,FriendlyBlue,BuckleyBoy 10
5Apr86-7Aqu	1 :47 1:112 1:363ft	4 119	41 — — —	Pincay L Jr¹	Aw26000 —	Roy,PathsOfGlory,AlongCameJones 6
5Apr86-Lost rider
22Mar86-3Aqu	7f :243 :49 1:252ft	*7-5 122	1½ 1½ 2½ 2nk	McHrgueDG²	Aw25000 74-25	AmourdeFluv,HighHook,R:tlssSson 6
22Mar86-Bobbled start
Jan 1 SA 3f ft :352 h		Dec 27 SA 5f ft 1:012 b		Dec 22 SA 5f ft 1:014 h		●Dec 17 SA 3f ft :35 h

3—1

Salt Dome 5—N+

DELAHOUSSAYE E 118

Own.—Rutherford M G

Ch. c. 4, by Blushing Groom—Buda Lady, by Crimson Satan
Br.—Rutherford M G (Ky)
Tr.—Brothers Frank L

			1986	3 2 0 0	$23,650
C9			1985	0 M 0 0	
Lifetime	3 2 0 0	$23,650			

5Nov86-8Hol	1 :45 1:092 1:35<ft	6½ 116	86 88½ 812 918½	DlhossyE²	Affrmd H 68-17	Chepskte,PrinceBobbyB.,FullChrm 9
5Nov86-Grade III; Bumped hard start
9Oct86-7SA	6f :213 :443 1:111ft	*2-3 117	2nd 1hd 1hd 11½	DelahoussyeF¹	Aw25000 82-21	Salt Dome, Incluso,Harper'sRidge 10
6Sep86-4Dmr	6f :214 :443 1:092ft	*9-5 117	11¾ 17 110	Delahoussaye E⁹	Mdn 91-12	Salt Dome, Decore, Park Road 11
●Dec 30 SA 5f ft :591 hg		Dec 24 Hol 4f ft :480 h		Dec 15 Hol 4f ft :514 h		Dec 5 Hol 3f ft :372 b

40—1

Smokey Orbit

SIBILLE R 116 1—N

Own.—Kradjian A

Ch. g. 4, by Orbit Dancer—Smokey Rae, by Dodger Blue
Br.—Porter K (Ky)
Tr.—Marikian Charles M

	1986	9 0 2 2	$16,481
	1985	10 2 3 2	$55,125
Lifetime	19 2 5 4	$71,606	Turf	3 0 0 1	$1,573

23Jly86-8Dmr	1 ⑦:4611:1021:341fm	23 114	53½ 911 919 916½	ShmkrW⁴ ℝOceanside 84-04	PrinceBobbyB.,FullChrm,He'sASros 9
23Jly86-Pinched back, took up sharply at 5/16
29Jun86-8Cby	1½:462 1:114 1:513ft	95 114	2hd 3nk 58½ 716½	MrryKC² St Paul Dby 68-17	Cheapskate, Broad Brush, Peripat 12
14Jun86-9Cby	1 :4631:1211:363fm	11 115	43½ 33 33½ 33¾	Allen R D Jr⁸ Aw14300 —	AlsknGmblr,CyprssCrk,SmokyOrbit 9
1Jun86-9Cby	1½:472 1:131 1:471ft	13 115	31½ 1hd 11 22¾	AllnRDJr² Apple Va H 72-24	BlndfordPrk,SmokeyOrbit,FifthStr 7
24May86-8Cby	6½f :223 :453 1:181ft	6-5 115	32 33 33½ 34¾	Hawley S⁵ Aw14300 85-19	Bill 'NHarry,FifthStar,SmokeyOrbit 6
11May86-9Cby	1 :462 1:114 1:38¾gd	*8-5 116	21½ 1hd 21 21¾	Hawley S⁴ Blmngtn H 85-15	Dr.ChoCho,SmokyOrbit,Zd'sSouvnr 5
28Jan86-8SA	a6½f ⑦:214 :4431:151fm	56 116	41 31 46¼ 711½	KenelJL¹ ℝC Whtnhm 72-17	PrincBobbyB.,TommyThHwk,Dlpr 10
12Mar86-8SA	6½f :214 :451 1:172sy	11 114	46 46 54 511	Solis A³ Baldwin 72-25	JettingHome,RoylTresure,ElCorzon 9
29Jan86-8SA	1½:462 1:11 1:43 ft	50 114	42¼ 53 65 79¼	Solis A⁴ ℝS Catalina 77-15	Ferdinand,VrietyRod,GrndAllegince 8
31Dec85-8SA	6f :214 :444 1:103ft	4½ 114	1hd 2hd 2hd 2½	StevensGL¹ Sn Miquel 84-15	DancingPirte,SmokeyOrbit,HyKing 3
31Dec85-Bumped off stride start
Dec 25 SA 4f ft :473 h		Dec 23 SA 4f ft :472 h		Dec 18 SA 6f ft 1:141 h		Dec 12 SA 6f ft 1:132 h

7—1

Northern Policy —N+

SHOEMAKER W 6—N+ 116

Own.—McKay E

Ch. g. 4, by Jacango—Passing Policy, by New Policy
Br.—McKay E & Betty (Wash)
Tr.—Chambers Mike

	1986	13 4 0 2	$23,560
112	1985	0 M 0 0	
Lifetime	13 4 0 2	$23,560		

22Oct86-9Lga	6f :213 :441 1:084ft	*1-2 117	2hd 1hd 11¾ 13¾	DominguzRE⁴ Aw9300 92-20	NorthrnPolicy,JumpingDoctor,Osis 5
17Oct86-9Lga	6½f :214 :441 1:144ft	*6-5 120	1hd 1hd 13 13	Dominguez RE³ 40000 95-18	Northern Policy, Mr. Spade,Zacbee 7
10Oct86-9Lga	6½f :214 :454 1:203m	4½ 112	32½ 32½ 22 73¼	Gibson RG⁶ ℝAw11000 83-43	Mr.Gruff, Worldly Way,HotHomer 10
28Sep86-8Lga	1½:464 1:384½ft	2½ 113	1hd 1hd 112 11½	WrdW² ℝBMrcsPrtH 68-18	Sssy'sHllr,GllntSlor,CrrncyControl 11
9Sep86-9Lga	6f :221 :44 1:151ft	2½ 115	1hd 11 15 13¾	Gibson R G⁵ 20000 53-14	NrthrnPlcy,PickyEmprr,BlzngThng 7
23Aug86-9Lga	6½f :213 :44 1:143ft	3 120	1½ 1½ 2hd 34½	Diaz A L³ 20000 92-15	AgntTodd,PlckyEmpror,NrthrnPlcy 9
7Aug86-9Lga	1 :472 :47 1:141½ft	10 120	21 2hd 21½ 52	Hansen R D⁶ 25000 84-19	GrndHrry,RoylTopper,Whr'sMchis 9
23Jly86-9Lga	1½:471 1:121 1:44m	35 120	41 44½ 47 55	Delgadillo G A⁷ Aw8000 78-16	Hell'sCrossing,DualAccent,Ruffiano 6
12Jly86-9Lga	1½:471 1:123 1:44ft	20 120	12 12 77 711	Hansen R D⁷ Mdn 75-18	NorthrnPolicy,DulAccnt,RcylTopper 7
Dec 25 SA 5f ft :593 h		Dec 22 SA 5f ft 1:012 h		Dec 18 SA 5f ft 1:014 h		Dec 11 SA 5f ft 1:011 h

A. Bet *Zabaleta* to win
B. Back-wheel *Zabaleta* in the exacta
C. Box *Zabaleta* and *Salt Dome* repeatedly in fair-payoff exactas
D. Pass the race

41. Read the conditions carefully. What should be the minimum acceptable odds on *Striding Easy*?

8th Arlington

6 FURLONGS. (1.08) ALLOWANCE. Purse $16,000. Fillies and mares. 3-year-olds and upward which have not won a race since December 25 other than maiden, claiming or starter. Weight, 3-year-olds, 116 lbs.; older, 121 lbs. Non-winners of $10,200 twice in 1986–87 allowed 3 lbs.; $9,600 twice in 1986–87, 6 lbs.; $8,400 since August 18, 9 lbs. (Races where entered for $35,000 or less not considered in allowances.)

12–1

B.'n B.'s Mercedes — Own.—Atkinson H B — **112**
Ch. f. 4, by Dr. Geo Adams—Nearly Almost, by Hempen
Br.—Atkinson H B (Ark) 1987 4 0 0 1 $2,550
Tr.—Smith Jere R 1986 6 2 0 1 $15,335
Lifetime 10 2 0 2 $17,885 Turf 1 0 0 0

15Jly87-7AP 6½f :231 :473 1:202sy 3 115 33 35 514 424¼ Day P5 ⒻAw15000 49-34 CoesseExpress,CopprStr,EsyAnswr 5
17Jun87-8AP 6f :223 :461 1:111ft 11 112 1hd 2hd 31½ 32¾ Day P5 ⒻAw15000 81-19 GiftOfGlittr,GiniDoll,B.'nB.'sMrcds 7
7Apr87-9OP 6f :22 :454 1:11 ft 35 111 3½ 3½ 55¼ 614½ Smith M E5 ⒻAw17000 70-23 TllMSmthng,Z.'sClss,Tohppyfrwrds 7
24Mar87-7OP 6f :222 :46 1:102ft 12 111 1½ 21½ 611 624 Frazier RL2 ⒻAw16000 64-23 Z.'sClass,Preyitagain,PrimroseLane 6
16Jly86-8Haw 6f :203 :45 1:102ft *7-5 114 11 2hd 23 57¾ Day P8 ⒻAw15500 81-12 Copier,CheckTheTime,DncinYvette 8
29Jun86-8Haw a7f Ⓣ:23 :47 1:254fm 9¾ 114 11½ 1hd 41½ 911¾ FirsE9 ⒻGladanhod H — — NoChoice,SharpCrleen,GentleVixen 9
13Jun86-8Haw 6f :221 :463 1:122ft 2 113 12½ 12 12½ 1¾ Fires E4 ⒻAw13500 79-26 B.'nB.'sMercds,Wy'sDrNic,ShrpCrln 8
6Jun86-4Haw 6f :222 :464 1:132gd 6¾ 113 11½ 11 12 12½ Fires E1 ⒻMdn 74-28 B.'nB.'sMrcds,LdyVrnl,ToRsnWhy 11
15Feb86-4OP 6f :22 :471 1:123ft *8-5 114 2hd 2hd 65 812¾ Day P8 ⒻMdn 64-18 LVivt,EspecillyPretty,PocketBustr 11
30Jan86-6FG 6f :214 :464 1:133ft 8 119 14 14 11½ 31½ Perrodin E J1 ⒻMdn 75-22 Trpschor,SpctclrFct,B.'nB.'sMrcds 10
Jly 22 AP 5f ft 1:034 b Jly 13 AP 3f ft :362 b Jly 5 AP 5f gd 1:03 b Jun 30 AP 5f sl 1:02 b

5–1

Cabrini Express — Own.—Gary B J — **116**
B. f. 3, by Cabrini Green—Frozen Expression, by In a Trance
Br.—Gary Bill J (Ky) 1986 8 3 1 2 $72,373
Tr.—Hiles Rick
Lifetime 8 3 1 2 $72,373

22Nov86-8CD 1 1/16 :472 1:124 1:463ft 6¼ 121 31½ 41¼ 53¾ 66½ SolmnM10 ⒻGold Rod 68-23 Stargrass, Zero Minus, Laserette 11
9Nov86-8Pha 1 1/16 :491 1:14 1:481sy 2¾ 121 12 11½ 1hd 22 Wilson R6 ⒻVillager 61-32 FlyingKtun,CbriniExpress,Dr.Myrtl 6
24Oct86-9Med 1 1/16 :47 1:114 1:451ft 4¼ 121 11 3½ 35 67¾ WdsCRJr4 ⒻGardenia 69-21 Collins, Silent Turn, Dr. Myrtle 12
24Oct86—Grade II
5Oct86-8Haw 170 :453 1:11 1:422ft 3¼ 118 13½ 11½ 12 16¼ WodsCRJr4 ⒻDurazna 90-18 CbriniExpress,UniqueTyp,P.C.J.Rlxr 7
20Sep86-9TP 6½f :231 :463 1:21 ft 12 112 31 21 21½ 11 WdsCRJr5 ⒻClipsetta 73-27 CbriniExpress,Pluie'sHoney,Cordi 12
31Aug86-9EIP 6f :223 :452 1:112ft 5¼ 114 64½ 44 35½ 34½ ScHA6 ⒻⓇA M Fisher 83-10 Pluie'sHoney,Cordi,CbriniExpress 12
9Aug86-7EIP 6f :23 :464 1:123ft *6-5 121 11½ 11½ 1½ 12½ Woods C RJr12 ⒻMdn 82-19 CbrnEprss,PrncssfWgs,PrncssNdr 12
13Jly86-5EIP 5f :223 :464 :594m 3½ 119 66½ 53¾ 51¾ 32 Gomez E R7 ⒻMdn 90-22 Redecorated,Cordia,CbriniExpress 10
Jly 26 EIP 4f ft :48 b ● Jly 21 EIP 6f ft 1:122 hg Jly 15 EIP 5f ft 1:004 h Jly 8 EIP 5f ft 1:022 b

6–5

Striding Easy — Own.—Scharbauer Dorothy — **121**
B. f. 4, by Victory Stride—Lady Meda, by Sir Ribot
Br.—F Turner Jr Estate (Okla) 1987 5 0 2 0 $14,350
Tr.—Van Berg Jack C 1986 6 3 1 0 $60,990
Lifetime 14 5 3 0 $83,794

23Jun87-8CD 6f :213 :451 1:103ft 8½ 118 32½ 34 34½ 23½ BssSH3 ⒻFarmington 86-21 LzrShow,StrdngEsy,TnThousndStrs 4
31May87-6Hol 6f :213 :451 1:11 ft 30 115 31 3½ 73¾ 75¼ Baze G8 ⒻAw35000 83-18 Sign Off,Aerturas,MillersStationery 8
1May87-8Hol 6f :214 :451 1:101ft 7 118 3nk 3nk 53½ 79¾ Baze G3 ⒻAw30000 82-13 RreStrlet,MillersSttionery,Secuenci 9
10Feb87-8GG 6f :213 :444 1:081ft 6 115 65½ 54 65¼ 710¾ DocyTT7 ⒻCmlla Urso 87-11 Luisnt,MillersSttionery,NovelSprite 8
18Jan87-8BM 6f :224 :453 1:092ft 7 115 21 2hd 1hd 21¼ DoocyTT5 ⒻSpctclr H 91-26 Luisnt,StridingEsy,MillersSttionery 9
13Dec86-4Hol 6f :214 :451 1:101ft 9¼ 113 2hd 1hd 13½ 11½ Baze G1 ⒻHcp0 92-09 StridingEsy,WintrTrsur,BoldNSpcil 6
28Nov86-3Hol 7f :221 :451 1:232ft *8-5 117 1hd 1hd 2½ 52½ Pincay LJr3 ⒻAw28000 84-14 Sign Off, Good Zar, Ambra Ridge 6
2Nov86-5SA 6f :212 :441 1:102ft 8¼ 117 22 33 32 11¾ Day P3 ⒻAw28000 86-10 StridingEsy,LoversNtive,FlyingJuli 9
8Oct86-6SA 6f :22 :451 1:101ft *8-5 115 11 2hd 21½ 43¾ ShoemkrW1 ⒻAw28000 83-20 TomboyBls,Symbolclly,BlconyPss 10
8Oct86—Lugged out backstretch
12Sep86-11Pom 6½f :214 :45 1:17 ft 5 117 1½ 12 12 12¾ MenaF6 ⒻⓇLas Ninas 95-11 StridingEasy,TropiclHolidy,FirlyOld 9
Jly 3 AP 4f ft :49 b Jun 7 AP 4f ft :48 b

6–1

Shamrock Leader

Own.—Eckrosh J

112

Dk. b. or br. m. 6, by Mr Leader—Floral Princess, by Irish Ruler
Br.—Pinewood Stable (Ky)
Tr.—Eckrosh James E

		1987	2 0 0 1		$2,890
		1986	8 0 0 2		$9,144
Lifetime	25 5 1 6	$82,696	Turf	2 0 0 1	$2,750

28Jun87-6AP	7f :221 :45 1:234ft	3 112	68 69 561 473	Lindsay R6	ⒻAw17000	75-23	DancePleaser,BailFast,RunMrisRun 6
19Jun87-8AP	61f:233 :47 1:174ft	5 112	221 22 321 331	Lindsay R4	ⒻAw19550	82-19	MontnrMss,Lkwhs'Cmn,ShmrckLdr 5
20Jly86-8Haw	61f:221 :45 1:163ft	22 112	75 710 68 693	EnsRD5 ⒻQ Reward H	80-17	Summer Mood, Acquire,BubbleBite 7
15Jun86-7Haw	61f:222 :452 1:163ft	9 115	791 79 46 581	Briggs F R4	Aw20000	82-19	Defrost, The Skeptic, Easy Birdie 8
16May86-8CD	61f:222 :453 1:17 ft	23 115	68 68 531 32	RubbiccoP1 ⒻAw21020	93-16	Sorbet,SpeedyCssini,ShmrockLeder 9
28Apr86-8CD	6f :21 :45 1:104ft	23 118	56 631 623 691	Allen K K5	ⒻAw20200	82-15	PureSunshine,Berevmnt,LittlJtSttr 7
22Mar86-9OP	1 :464 1:114 1:381ft	51 111	883 663 67 67	PttersonG8 ⒻPippin H	74-22	Sf'sButy,Littlbitplsur,BrindyBrindy 5
12Mar86-9OP	6f :214 :45 1:104ft	71 117	891 773 571 46	Maple S2	ⒻAw22000	80-23	Spnkey'sSeconds,Sondor,MissAlic 10
15Feb86-9OP	6f :214 :451 1:101ft	14 114	761 66 65 571	PttrsG11 ⒻA BeautyH	82-18	GrndGlory,HoldMTndr,PrncssMrn 13
8Feb86-6OP	51f:221 :471 1:052ft	6 115	631 621 21 32	PttersonG9 ⒻAw25000	84-19	BrndBrnd,IsIndEmprss,ShmrckLdr 10

Jly 17 AP 4f ft :53 b   Jly 8 AP 4f ft :514 b   Jun 27 AP 3f ft :382 b   Jun 18 AP 3f ft :373 b

30–1

Florentine Frolic ✳

Own.—Hyperion Enterprises Incetal

1105

B. f. 4, by Ginistrelli—Rollicking Lady, by Rollicking
Br.—Hyperion Ent Inc (Ky)
Tr.—Harris Rickey

		1987	8 0 0 0		$2,124
		1986	18 3 4 4		$69,084
Lifetime	31 4 5 4	$79,068	Turf	4 0 1 0	$6,300

23Jly87-8AP	1 ①:4711:12 1:382fm	81 1095	793 66 651 88	Torres F C 8 ⒻⒶAw17000	75-17	DnceQueen,OleBowWower,LisLigh 10
3Jly87-7AP	11/16 ①:4811:1241:444fm	41 112	54 651 53 543	Fires E 2	ⒻAw18000	78-17	Itsagem,Bereavement,Inspiracion II 7
28Jun87-6AP	7f :221 :45 1:234ft	2 112	55 58 613 6213	Evans R D 3 ⒻAw17000	61-23	DancePleaser,BailFast,RunMrisRun 6
7Jun87-8AP	11/16 ①:4721:1121:442fm	49 115	471 511 918 9141	StovrDE1 ⒻBe Faithfl	71-15	SupremeExcellence,MyMafid,Tide 10
15May87-8Spt	1 :484 1:134 1:40 ft	37 115	843 816 821 828	Evans R D1 ⒻAw27400	52-23	MyMfld.FmilyCompct,LLuckyStrik 8
25Apr87-8Spt	1 :483 1:133 1:393ft	85 112	1091 1091 1013 10161	PunKC6 ⒻLady Hal H	66-20	MGlIntDchss,TrmphDNskr,LLcStr 10
11Apr87-4Spt	61f:233 :473 1:194gd	12 119	67 44 311 421	Meier R7	ⒻAw26400	76-21	MyGallntDuchess,PmelPul,MissAtri 7
4Apr87-6Spt	1 :501 1:15 1:40 ft	61 115	42 57 614 626	Evans R D1 ⒻAw25300	54-19	SmrtrByThDy,FmlCmpct,InsprcnII 6
22Nov86-8Bml	170:49 1:142 1:462sy	5 113	541 431 331 25	LrGP3 ⒻLe Femme H	80-17	WhtIckygrl,FlrntnFrlc,TmtItnfrstrt 9
22Nov86—Didn't break alertly						
9Nov86-8Bml	170:484 1:15 1:481ft	51 114	65 66 510 24	Diaz J L2 ⒻDolly Val	72-27	I'mEnchntd,FlorntnFrolc,PrttyPlm 9

Jly 18 AP 5f ft 1:04 b   Jun 20 AP 5f ft 1:02 b

6–1

Hugmeifyouloveme

Own.—Craig Ent Inc

110

B. f. 3, by Star Spangled—Bonny Globe, by Globemaster
Br.—Morgeson Joe A (Ky)
Tr.—Fernandez Jose

	1986	6 3 0 0	$30,190
Lifetime	6 3 0 0	$30,190	

31Aug86-9ElP	6f :223 :452 1:112ft	3 124	33 34 883 810	CdlrRJ9 Ⓕ®AMFisher	78-10	Pluie'sHoney,Cordi,CbriniExpress 12
3Aug86-8Haw	51f:214 :462 1:061ft	41 114	21 2hd 111 111	BrfldD6 ⒻGold Digger	81-19	Hugmeifyouloveme,SeekOut,RelDm 9
13Jly86-8LaD	51f:213 :451 1:054ft	*23 114	851 881 791 641	Frazier R L8	ⒻRebel	82-12	MstrsFrstLdy,CocoM.,Trckyn'Clvr 14
14Jun86-9RD	51f:213 :451 1:041ft	23 116	561 481 451 461	SpusEJJr2 ⒻAmer Bty	87-22	BrnshdBrght,W'rAlrght,MssStlQn 12
6Jun86-4RD	5f :224 :462 :593ft	*2-3 114	14 13 14 14	Sipus E J Jr2 Aw6700	92-26	Hugmfyolovm,SpoldPrfct,LMmCos 6
19May86-3RD	5f :224 :461 :582sl	*3-2 117	121 121 15 110	Sipus E J Jr3 Mc15000	98-23	Hugmeifyouloveme,MndBtty,DltRh 8

Jly 17 AP 4f ft :484 b   Jly 10 AP 5f ft 1:03 b   Jly 2 AP 6f ft 1:16 b   Jun 25 AP 3f ft :37 b

15–1

Medieval Decoy

Own.—Allen Stanley J

121

Dk. b. or br. m. 5, by Medieval Man—Real Decoy, by Duc de Great
Br.—Allen Stanly J (Fla)
Tr.—Wismer Glenn

	1987	1 0 1 0		$2,200
	1986	4 2 0 1		$31,372
Lifetime	10 5 2 1	$55,917		

17Jly87-8Cby	6f :22 :444 1:112ft	*8-5 115	41 311 21 223	AdkinsRM4 ⒻAw11000	86-19	CoffeeRoll,MedivlDcoy,LovlyAnntt 6
26Jly86-10Cby	6f :222 :45 1:11 ft	7 123	33 33 11 12	AllRDJr2 ⒻEden Praie	92-12	MedievlDecoy,MmorisOfDixi,Avdnc 8
26Jun86-8CD	6f :22 :453 1:104ft	31 122	4nk 311 31 321	Allen K K1 ⒻAw19400	88-17	Acquire,Hgley'sRelic,MedievlDecoy 5
25Jan86-9Tam	7f :224 :46 1:252ft	*4-5 124	21 211 211 621	Adkins R M5 ⒻLassie	94-12	IsRoslind,QunAlxndr,FirstPrdicton 12
1Jan86-10Tam	6f :221 :453 1:12 gd	*9-5 124	55 421 11 111	Adkins RM12 ⒻRegret	85-24	MdivlDcoy,Bldski'sHolidy,TriBowl 14
14Dec85-9Tam	51f:223 :46 1:042ft	41 116	24 23 111 17	AdnsRM4 Ⓕ®Ruffian	99-21	Medieval Decoy, MaeveO.,TriBowl 13
5Dec85-9Tam	6f :234 :463 1:123ft	10 114	42 331 11 13	Adkins R M3 Aw4300	82-25	MdivlDcoy,UltimtTumbl,RidnClrion 6
27Jly85-9Cby	51f:214 :45 1:04 ft	16 113	751 1012 814 8141	AdsRM7 ⒻCLindbrgH	— —	NobleScrtry,WoodnStr,FullPromis 10
27Jly85—Run in two divisions, 7th and 9th races						
7Jly85-1Cby	51f:223 :46 1:051ft	31 117	11 12 121 13	Adkins R M4 ⒻMdn	— —	MedievalDecoy,TrdyDncer,AmecJ. 10
20Jun85-5CD	6f :213 :453 1:11 ft	12 114	951 651 321 2hd	Adkins R M8 ⒻMdn	90-17	JovilWitnss,MdvlDcoy,TrustdShot 11

Jly 16 Cby 3f ft :372 h   ●Jly 11 Cby 6f ft 1:131 h   ●Jly 4 Cby 5f ft :593 h   Jun 27 Cby 5f ft 1:012 h

A. 6–5

B. 2–1

C. 5–2

D. 3–1

42. If *Hurricane Hec* is 2–1, *New Storm* is 3–1, and *Rosa Carnina* is 6–1, which horse should be bet?

9th Santa Anita

1⅛ MILES
SANTA ANITA
START FINISH

1⅛ MILES. (1.45⅘) CLAIMING. Purse $18,000. 4-year-olds and upward. Weights, 4-year-olds, 120 lbs.; older, 121 lbs. Non-winners of two races at one mile or over since November 3 allowed 3 lbs.; of such a race since then, 5 lbs. Claiming price $20,000; if for $18,000 allowed 2 lbs. (Claiming and starter races for $16,000 or less not considered).

***Rosa Carnina** — B. g. 6, by Rose Laurel—Miss Trump, by Poleax
SOTO S B — 116 — Br.—Mme Leon de La Bonnelliere (Fra) — 1986 13 1 1 2 $18,575
Tr.—Doumen Christian — $20,000 — 1984 16 3 4 4 $28,336
Own.—Kalish Ada — Lifetime 42 6 9 9 $64,850 — Turf 42 6 9 9 $64,850

21Dec86-9Hol 1¼(T):5021:3812:022fm 29 115 43 52¼ 55 76¼ Vergara O3 45000 77-15 Kingsbury, Will Spring, PiperJohn 11
21Dec86—Steadied, rank early
3Dec86-9Hol 1⅛(T):4731:1121:473fm 21 115 66¾ 65½ 43½ 33½ Vergara O3 45000 86-10 TooMuchForT.V.,Rajhaan,RosCrnin 6
23Nov86-9Hol 1¼(T):4811:3642:021fm 56 116 21 68 1019 1021¼ Vergara O9 57500 63-13 Rampour, Travet, Aviator II 11
11Nov86-9Hol 1⅛(T):4721:1121:472fm 7¾ 116 78 87¾ 88¾ 710¼ DelahoussayeE6 57500 81-09 Aviator II, Auto Commander,Crony 8
11Oct86-7SA 1⅛(T):4631:1031:481fm 47 115 88¼ 811 811 810¼ Soto S B1 Aw45000 76-21 Nasib, Skip Out Front, Pudahuel 8
31Aug86-5Dmr 1⅜(T):4731:38 2:162fm 4 114 49 21½ 2½ 2no Soto S B2 45000 88-12 Rajhaan, Rosa Carnina, Travet 7
6Aug86-7Dmr 1 1/16(T):48 1:1141:432fm 21 116 812 85¼ 65½ 62½ DelahoussayeE8 70000 86-14 Bozina, Aviator II, Keyala 8
6Aug86—Hopped in air
23Jly86-9Dmr 1 1/16(T):4821:1221:431fm 5 116 810 86¾ 63 41 DelahoussayeE8 55000 89-04 Pettrax, Royal Olympia, Ablantin 8
6Jly86-10Hol 1⅛(T):4731:1141:482fm 13 119 66½ 63¼ 22 43 Soto S B5 50000 87-07 TooMuchForT.V.,Rajhn,IronLeder 10
6Jly86—Pinched at start
15Jun86-4GG 1 1/16(T):4841:1241:434fm 29 119 42½ 51¾ 31 31¼ Lamance C2 65000 82-14 PairOfAces,ElMansour,RosaCarnin 6
Dec 14 SA 7f ft 1:254 h — Nov 5 SA 4f ft :484 h

New Storm — B. g. 5, by Petrone—Sands Affair, by Tumble Wind
STEVENS G L — 116 — Br.—McCollum Pattrica (Cal) — 1986 16 2 1 7 $26,105
Tr.—Knight Terry — $20,000 — 1985 22 3 3 1 $27,713
Own.—Italia & Pegram — Lifetime 38 5 4 8 $53,818 — Turf 3 0 0 0 $2,340

13Dec86-9BM 1 1/16:462 1:112 1:431ft 3 113 32 31½ 2½ 21½ Doocy T T7 Aw17000 74-19 CllThGurd,NwStorm,It'sNotMyJob 8
13Dec86—Drifted in late
29Nov86-7BM 1 1/16:454 1:101 1:42 ft 6¾ 113 32 31½ 31½ 31¼ Doocy T T2 Aw16000 81-17 Arbitrte,Petrone'sKismet,NwStorm 9
15Nov86-9BM 1 1/16:461 1:11 1:44 ft 7½ 113 87¾ 53¾ 21 33 Doocy T T7 Aw17000 69-21 Planter, Midnight Ice, New Storm 12
15Nov86—Hopped in air
8Nov86-9BM 1 1/16:47 1:114 1:44 ft *2 114 85¾ 74½ 66 45 Baze R A4 25000 67-25 Wtn'ForBvr,Ptrn'sKsmt,BrnsChrg 9
8Nov86—Broke slowly; ducked out at 1/8
18Oct86-10BM 1 1/16:462 1:11 1:423ft 5 114 21½ 21 15 14 Baze R A5 16000 79-16 New Storm,Frivolissimo,OurNordic 8
24Sep86-9BM 1 :471 1:13 1:393sl 4½ 114 32 32 32 36 Baze R A1 16000 64-31 BigDanRyn,Frivolissimo,NewStorm 7
6Sep86-7Bmf 1 :453 1:10 1:352ft 8½ 115 79½ 58 46½ 37½ Baze R A5 16000 83-18 Sidersell, Big DanRyan,NewStorm 10
6Sep86—Broke in a tangle; lugged out 1st turn
13Aug86-9Dmr 1 1/16:451 1:102 1:431ft 40 116 57 76½ 99½ 910½ Baze R A3 20000 73-15 Revolutionary, Tom, Our Nordic 11
26Jly86-6Aks 170:473 1:112 1:43 ft 14 114 2hd 2hd 2hd 32 Baze R A8 20000 80-23 LiflongAmbition,NtTigr,NwStorm 10
19Jly86-6Aks 1 1/16:481 1:124 1:451ft 4 116 1hd 11 13 3½ Lively J6 18000 76-18 HrdbllBill,CowboyShoes,NewStorm 9
Dec 28 BM 5f ft 1:003 h — ●Dec 10 BM 4f ft :472 h — ●Nov 27 BM 4f ft :463 h

***Estoc** — B. g. 6, by Gay Mecene—Eastern Silk, by Zeddaan
MEZA R Q — 114 — Br.—Bonnefoy & Nicol (Fra) — 1986 6 1 0 0 $19,600
Tr.—Lukas D Wayne — $18,000 — 1985 10 2 1 1 $13,403
Own.—Hatley-Klein-Lukas — Lifetime 25 5 1 2 $41,369 — Turf 24 5 1 2 $41,369

26Dec86-9SA 1 1/16:454 1:102 1:43 ft 36 116 66¼ 65 912 913¾ Stevens S A4 25000 72-13 Cold,TommyThoms,BoncngBttons 11
8Jun86-4Hol 1 1/16(T):4541:0941:404fm 4 116 1112 1112 89 65½ McCarron C J3 50000 94 — Sndy'sEgle,EmprdorAlNor',Rushd 11
26May86-6Hol 1¼(T):49 1:3712:02 fm 6¼ 1115 32 2hd 42 55¼ Black C A1 50000 92 — Crony, Tio Nino, Killyglen 9
25Jan86-5SA 1¼(T):4621:3642:021fm 10 114 21 108¾ 913 916½ McCarron C J6 75000 59-23 PolAndDic,DonnyK.,Morry'sChmp 10
17Jan86-5SA 1⅛(T):4821:1231:49 fm 7½ 116 85¼ 54¼ 46½ 45¼ McCarron C J4 80000 77-15 Bishop'sRngII,PolAndDc,Snowcrk 10
17Jan86—Wide into stretch
5Jan86-5SA 1⅛(T):47 1:1141:512gd 9½ 114 65¼ 63¾ 41½ 11¼ McCarron C J11 57500 70-25 Estoc,RoyalCouncillor,FlyingGene 12
22Dec85-6Hol 1¼(T):5031:3922:04 fm 37 116 1½ 1hd 2½ 31¾ Valenzuela P A9 50000 — — Allowance, Vigorous Vigors,Estoc 12
22Dec85—Lost whip 1/8
13Oct85-4Bel 1¼[T]:5031:40 2:052gd 12 117 99¼ 914 914 912½ Velasquez J7 75000 54-25 Red Brigade, Ski Fleet, Cloutier 9
31Jly85◆5Redcar(Eng) 1⅜ 2:243gd 8-5 133 (T) 24 Lowe J St Jhn Amblnc H InsetLady, Estoc, Wildrush 4
6Jly85◆3Haydock(Eng) 1½ 2:33 gd 20 114 (T) 58 Lowe J Old Nwtn Cp H Clanrallier,RussinNoble,RegISteel 10
Dec 18 SA 7f ft 1:284 h — Dec 9 SA 6f ft 1:162 h — Nov 12 Hol 4f ft :524 h — Nov 4 Hol 3f ft :371 h

One Eyed Romeo — Ch. g. 7, by Romeo—Tahitian Chant, by Distinctive
OLIVARES F — 116 — Br.—Manderly Farm (Ky) — 1986 22 4 4 1 $49,500
Tr.—Shulman Sanford — $20,000 — 1985 23 6 5 2 $77,730
Own.—Lindo-Polyakov-Sunquist — Lifetime 72 12 17 4 $170,282 — Turf 1 0 0 0

17Dec86-5Hol 1 :451 1:104 1:373ft 2¾ 119 21½ 44½ 56 68½ Black C A1 c16000 66-22 Amarone, Gulfstreamer, Oh Dad 7
17Dec86—Lugged out backstretch
4Dec86-5Hol 1⅛:471 1:121 1:521ft 2½ 116 1½ 1½ 12½ 12¾ Black C A2 16000 76-25 OneEyedRomeo,Vinegron,Espontno 5

16Nov86-4Hol 7f :22 :443 1:241ft 9¾ 117 73½ 99¼119¼1114¾ Vergara O9 20000 68-18 Pegus, Pialor, Amarone 12
28Sep86-12Pom 1⅜:471 1:37 2:15 ft 4 113 35½ 21½ 32½ 515¼ Black C A1 H25000 87-09 Mummy'sPlesure,Restge,TulsFlyrII 8
28Sep86—Steadied on turn
19Sep86-10Poma1⅛:453 1:11 1:49 ft *2¼ 1085 1hd 1hd 21 25¾ Black C A5 A25000 96-09 Mmmy'sPlsr,OnEydRomo,DbTrnd 10
1Sep86-7Dmr 1 1/16:46 1:10 1:413ft 4 1115 21½ 21½ 1½ 2nk Black C A5 25000 92-13 Bmdg,OnEydRomo,PlntyConscous 10
17Aug86-7Dmr 1 1/16:453 1:101 1:432ft 7 116 1½ 1hd 11½ 3hd Kaenel J L2 25000 83-16 BngBngBng,MrkInThSky,OnEdRm 10
10Aug86-2Dmr 1 1/16:45 1:093 1:412ft *2½ 1115 52¾ 33½ 46½ 510¾ Black C A9 32000 82-08 ForHimself,Juli'sMrk,ToughEnvoy 10
3Aug86-9Dmr 1 1/16:46 1:101 1:42 ft *8-5 1115 31 2½ 1hd 13 Black C A1 20000 90-10 OnEydRomo,FlthorpMrnr,PsvltRd 12
23Jly86-1Dmr 1 1/16:45 1:094 1:422ft 3¼ 1115 21½ 2½ 1hd 11½ Black C A10 16000 88-12 OnEydRomo,FlthorpMrinr,Susumu 11
Dec 27 SA 5f ft 1:011 h Dec 14 Hol 4f ft :513 h Dec 2 Hol 4f ft :491 h Nov 25 Hol 4f ft :482 h

Lyphard Chimes B. g. 5, by Lyphard—Four Bells, by Quadrangle
PINCAY L JR 3-N 116 Br.—Pillar Stud Inc (Ky) 1986 8 1 0 2 $14,922
Tr.—Lewis Craig A $20,000 1985 7 3 1 1 $11,725
Own.—Pendleton L C Lifetime 16 4 1 3 $26,647 Turf 10 3 1 1 $11,725
26Dec86-9SA 1 1/16:454 1:102 1:43 ft 4 116 56 44½ 89½ 710 Stevens G L8 25000 76-13 Cold,TommyThoms,BoncngBttons 11
20Nov86-5Hol 1⅛:464 1:114 1:512ft 8 116 32½ 21½ 84¾ 97¾ Solis A5 c32000 72-16 Oak TreeII,Bedouin,ValiantGeorge 11
20Nov86—Steadied 1/8
11Oct86-9SA 1 1/16:46 1:112 1:443ft 6½ 116 512 45½ 13 12 Solis A8 20000 78-17 LyphrdChimes,MsterNvjo,GryMissil 8
28Sep86-8Pom 1 1/16:462 1:111 1:434ft 7 116 48½ 46½ 34 31¾ Ortega L E2 20000 90-09 SwiftMessg,MstrNvjo,LyphrdChims 6
20Sep86-10Pom 1 1/16:454 1:111 1:431ft 11 116 611 611 57 39½ Solis A4 20000 85-09 Restage, Hatamoto,LyphardChimes 9
6Sep86-5Dmr 1⅛Ⓣ:463 1:11 1:492fm 21 116 55½ 63½1010 911½ Solis A8 60000 75-09 Aviator II, Keyala, Ono Gummo 10
25Apr86-9Hol 1⅛:472 1:112 1:492ft 16 116 2hd 21 69½ 614¼ Meza R Q5 62500 76-16 CelticVenture,Stickette,VlintGeorg 7
25Apr86—Bumped in stretch
22Mar86-4GG 1 1/16Ⓣ:472 1:112 1:433fm *2¼ 114 811 79¼ 86 74¼ Baze R A2 Aw25000 80-15 Ablantin,ViceroyLd,‡NewAtrction 11
22Mar86—Bumped start
9Oct85♦6York(Eng) 1 5/16 2:172gd 5 133 Ⓣ 613 CauthenS Cleveland H Wantage, Tockala, Santella Boy 11
17Jly85♦3Kempton(Eng) 1¼ 2:032gd 3¼ 118 Ⓣ 12½ CthnS Crawley Warren H LyphrdChimes,Cordonnt,GoodLord 8
Dec 21 Hol 5f ft 1:014 h ●Dec 17 Hol 6f ft 1:144 h ●Dec 11 Hol 6f ft 1:134 h Dec 5 Hol 5f ft 1:001 h

Hurricane Hec X B. h. 6, by Soft Victory—Fly Face, by Haydn
BAZE G 3 116 Br.—Zart A & C C (BC-C) 1986 27 4 1 3 $57,800
Tr.—Haynes Jack B $20,000 1985 16 3 3 1 $23,827
Own.—Cicotti & O'Hara Lifetime 67 17 4 8 $115,407 Turf 5 0 0 0 $1,575
24Dec86-9Hol 1 1/16Ⓣ:464 1:112 1:414fm 8¾ 1095 64½ 62¾ 43½ 52 Patton D B1 22500 83-11 CoursingEagle,Racionl,AncientBlue 9
18Dec86-9Hol 1 :454 1:104 1:364ft 10 114 1hd 44 711 79½ Baze G2 22500 69-17 FallFlyer,BrandImage,Revolutionry 8
23Nov86-2Hol 6f :221 :454 1:11 ft *6-5 117 66¼ 44 42 11¾ Pincay L Jr2 c12500 88-12 HurricaneHec,StrsAtNoon,Melchip 8
23Nov86—Pinched at start
8Nov86-9Hol 6f :222 :454 1:103ft 6½ 115 54 45½ 45½ 43¾ Soto S B2 22500 86-13 SandDigger,Amarone,Billy'sSpecial 6
8Nov86—Broke slowly
31Oct86-7SA 7f :223 :453 1:23 ft 11 114 43 42½ 34½ 56 Soto S B8 28000 79-16 GryPinstrip,CoursngEgl,Yukon'sStr 9
12Oct86-9SA 1 1/16:463 1:12 1:443ft 30 116 79¾ 75¾ 86½ 98½ Soto S B11 32000 69-21 Mmmy'sPlsr,Implsvly,NrthrnPrvdr 12
3Oct86-9SA 1 1/16:454 1:102 1:432ft 9 113 44½ 31 21½ 2¾ Soto S B2 22500 83-17 MrkInThSky,HrrcnHc,ForgtThRng 12
3Oct86—Broke slowly; lugged in, checked drive
13Sep86-11Pom 1 1/16:464 1:111 1:424ft 52 115 66½ 64¾ 912 1014¾ HrnndzR9 P D Shphrd 82-10 Bozn,GovrnmntCrnr,AmrcnStndrd 10
4Sep86-7Dmr 6f :214 :45 1:084ft 11 117 106¼ 97½ 95 46¾ Pincay L Jr5 40000 87-14 TeddyNturlly,ToughEnvoy,Dr.Rlity 10
4Sep86—Fanned wide into stretch
27Aug86-9Dmr 1 Ⓣ:461 1:103 1:352fm 13 113 611 55 64¾ 63¼ Soto S B6 55000 92-05 Auto Commander,RexLake,JackTar 7
27Aug86—Wide into stretch
Dec 16 SA 4f ft :481 h Dec 11 SA 5f ft 1:032 h Nov 5 Hol 5f ft 1:011 h

A. *Rosa Carnina*
B. *New Storm*
C. *Hurricane Hec*
D. None of the above

43. An extra-strong speed bias was operating when this preliminary allowance race was run. Find the best bet at the odds.

9 MONMOUTH 1 MILE 70 YDS MONMOUTH PARK START FINISH

1 MILE 70 YARDS. (1.39⅕) ALLOWANCE. Purse $15,000. 3-year-olds and upward which have not won a race other than maiden, claiming or starter. Weight, 3-year-olds 115 lbs.; older, 123 lbs. Non-winners of $9,800 since June 30 allowed 3 lbs.; $6,000 since June 16 allowed 5 lbs. (Races where entered for $35,000 or less not considered.)

A.
9–2

Bold R. E. B. g. 5, by Buckaroo—Blue Biddy, by Bold Bidder
Own.—O'Keefe J Br.—Nuckols Bros (Ky) Tr.—Sano Merle 118
Lifetime 69 11 11 12 $102,241 | 1987 16 3 2 3 $23,945 | 1986 21 4 2 3 $35,380 | Turf 2 0 0 0 $330

12Jly87- 3Pha fst 170 :46⅖ 1:11⅗ 1:41⅘ 3+ Clm 18000 4 3 2hd 2½ 11 13 Walford J b 116 3.80 86-22 BoldR.E.1163Jck'sGoldrunner11614BigSpruce'sDrem114nk Driving 8
5Jly87- 3Pha yl 1 1/16 (T):49⅖ 1:14⅕ 1:46⅗ Clm 20000 3 5 75½ 55 55½ 54¼ Walford J b 114 26.90 65-31 You're The Top 119nk Granby1122½DedicatedHero116nd No factor 8
23Jun87- 7Pha fst 170 :47⅕ 1:12 1:41⅘ 3+ Clm 18000 4 4 43½ 32 22 24½ Walford J b 116 9.10 81-27 Vicki's Sham 1224½ Bold R. E. 1166½ Five StarRebel1167 2nd best 7
11Jun87- 8GS fst 1 1/16 :47⅘ 1:12⅗ 1:44⅘ 3+ Clm 16000 5 6 54 44½ 22½ 24½ Walford J b 113 8.30 79-23 Vicki's Sham 1194½ Bold R. E.1132JerseyGigolo1143½ Second best 7
1Jun87- 7GS fm 1 1/16 (T):47⅕ 1:11⅗ 1:44⅖ 3+ Clm 17000 8 7 614 1011 1012 1111¼ Walford J b 114 10.80 75-10 Vicki's Sham 114nd Snalom Dancer 1121 Cantonero 112¾ Outrun 12
23May87- 2GS fst 1 1/16 :47 1:12⅕ 1:44⅗ 3+ Clm 11000 8 4 44½ 2½ 13 17½ Walford J b 116 5.10 85-13 Bold R. E. 1167½ Saint Paul 119nk Joyfull Splender 1162 Handily 8
9May87- 5GS fst 6f :22⅖ :46 1:11⅖ 3+ Clm 11000 2 8 54½ 42 3½ 41¾ Ayarza I b 116 9.50 83-22 Obgyn 116¾ Bachelor Boo 116¾ Greenie's Luck 119nk Mild gain 8
28Apr87- 7GS sly 6f :22 :45⅗ 1:11⅕ 3+ Clm c-8500 4 8 75¼ 73¾ 45½ 42¼ Lee-Lopez R F b 116 *1.80 84-21 RambunctiousChief116nkAtlantis1161Rjb'sWillyPop1151 Steadied 10
17Apr87- 7GS my 170 :46⅖ 1:11⅘ 1:42⅗ Clm 8500 8 5 3½ 2hd 2hd 33½ Lee-Lopez R F b 116 3.90 83-19 Eastern Regatta 116nk Zest for Life 1143BoldR.E.1163 Weakened 12
9Apr87- 8GS fst 1 1/16 :48⅕ 1:13⅘ 1:46⅖ Clm 14000 4 3 2hd 31½ 612 921½ Lee-Lopez R F b 116 6.00 54-27 Cheryl's Joke 1163 Red Eye Baby 1167½ CulpepperBill1162½ Tired 10

B.
2–1

Wasichus Ch. c. 3, by Nodouble—Explorare, by Dr Fager
Own.—Tartan Stable Br.—Tartan Farms (Fla) Tr.—Nerud Jan H 103[7]
Lifetime 6 1 0 0 $15,180 | 1987 6 1 0 0 $15,180 | 1986 0 M 0 0 | Turf 2 0 0 0

16Jly87- 7Bel fm 1 1/16 (T):46⅘ 1:11⅗ 1:43⅗ 3+ Alw 27000 2 2 21 22 32½ 53¼ Cruguet J 111 12.60 75-26 TrgetSighted1171GliderPilot117ndAkoochemente117nk Weakened 11
25Jun87- 3Bel fm 1 1/16 (T):46⅕ 1:10 1:42⅕ 3+ Alw 27000 1 4 44½ 64 56½ 57 Cruguet J 111 22.30 78-16 Drachma1142½FrenchChampgne1172¼GlimmerGlen1091¾ Even try 9
10Jun87- 4Bel fst 7f :23 :46⅕ 1:24 3+ Alw 26000 6 6 32½ 42 107¼ 96¾ Cruguet J 110 47.80 75-17 Mean and Crafty 1151¼ Full Colonel 113hd Racer 117no Tired 11
30May87- 6Bel fst 6f :22⅖ :45⅗ 1:10⅕ 3+ Alw 26000 3 9 86½ 77 68 69½ Bailey J D 109 20.20 79-19 FortLigonier1194¾MeanndCrfty108nkPressMyBuzzer112nd Outrun 9
9Mar87- 6Aqu fst 6f [•]:23⅕ :47⅘ 1:13 Md Sp Wt 8 3 1½ 1hd 1hd 12 Venezia M 122 3.70 79-22 Wasichus 1222 Just Two Four One 122½ Briskeen 1226½ Driving 11
21Feb87- 5Aqu fst 6f [•]:22⅘ :47⅕ 1:13 Md Sp Wt 10 6 64½ 54 45½ 48½ Venezia M 122 4.00 70-24 I'm Exuberant 122½ Fast Lead 1226¼ Star Racer 1221¾ Even try 11
LATEST WORKOUTS Jly 29 Bel 4f fst :50 b Jly 11 Bel tr.t 4f fst :48⅖ h Jly 5 Bel 4f fst :49⅕ b Jun 18 Bel 4f fst :48⅕ b

C.
5–1

Bolero's Business Dk. b. or br. g. 5, by Bless Business—Bolero's Maid, by Bolo Bolero
Own.—Four Teyes Stable Br.—Sikorski E (Fla) Tr.—Handy George R 118
Lifetime 33 4 5 2 $41,292 | 1987 6 1 1 1 $8,885 | 1986 12 1 2 0 $12,616 | Turf 1 0 0 0 $231

23Jly87- 6Mth fst 6f :22 :45 1:11⅘ 3+ Clm c-16000 7 4 56 56 53¾ 52 St Leon G 116 *1.40 79-24 Capo Cane116noGeneralNuisance116¾PlayingPolitics116nd Outrun 7
3Jly87- 2Mth fst 6f :22⅕ :45 1:09⅘ 3+ Clm c-12500 6 1 42¼ 31½ 2½ 2nk McCauley W H 116 *1.20 91-13 HomoSoho116nkBolero'sBusinss1163½LittlTuggy1162 Just missed 8
16Jun87-10Mth fst 6f :22⅘ :45⅗ 1:10⅕ 3+ Clm 16000 6 2 41½ 32 32½ 31¾ McCauley W H 116 *1.90 87-17 StraightDncer112noLuckyAppel1161¾Bolero'sBusiness1159 Evenly 8
4Jun87- 2Mth fst 6f :22⅖ :45⅗ 1:10⅘ 3+ Clm 9500 5 1 3½ 2hd 14 15 McCauley W H 115 *1.80 86-19 Bolero's Business 1155 Shabby 1163½ Mr. Mar J. Mar1164 In hand 7
16Feb87- 2Aqu fst 6f [•]:23⅖ :47⅘ 1:13⅗ Clm 14000 7 6 61¼ 52 54 65¾ McCauley W H 117 5.00 71-24 College Cheer 1173¼ HowieofWinloc112nkSweetDevil113nd Evenly 11
31Jan87- 9Aqu sly 1 1/16 [•]:48⅖ 1:14⅘ 1:49⅗ Clm 17500 4 2 1hd 2hd 34 48¾ McCauley W H 117 7.50 53-34 Lucky Belief 1172¼ Fully Reserved 1086 Section Three 117½ Tired 10
31Dec86- 2Aqu fst 1 3/16 [•]:47⅕ 1:12⅖ 1:57⅖ 3+ Clm 20000 6 3 33½ 32½ 57½ 511 Santagata N 113 23.80 80-13 Arctic Song 1152½ Lead The Way 114¾ Our Triumph 1101¼ Tired 9
13Dec86- 3Med fst 1 1/16 :46⅖ 1:11⅗ 1:43⅘ 3+ Clm c-15000 1 7 77 66 69 69¼ Walford J 114 2.30 75-09 Cannon Royal 1172 Massasoit 1103½ Cherry Rum 111nd Outrun 7
28Nov86- 6Med fst 170 :47⅖ 1:12⅗ 1:42⅖ 3+ Clm 20000 6 2 21 2½ 2½ 21 Bielby J A5 109 5.50 83-21 ChiefLouie1131Bolero'sBusinss109¾DirtyBirdi117nd Lost whip str. 6
21Nov86- 3Med fst 6f :23⅖ :47⅖ 1:11⅘ 3+ Clm 14000 4 1 45¼ 43¾ 21½ 2no Bielby J A5 109 9.30 83-19 SuprCount116noBolro'sBsnss109¾EmrgngGrowth1126 Just missed 5
LATEST WORKOUTS Jun 29 Mth 3f fst :37⅗ b

D.
3–1

Silky Beau B. c. 3, by Silky Baby—Agora, by Pantheon
Own.—Zellen L Br.—Schmidt Charles E (Ky) Tr.—Goldberg Alan 110
Lifetime 2 1 1 0 $9,780 | 1986 2 1 1 0 $9,780

15Nov86- 7Pha fst 1 :46⅗ 1:11⅖ 1:36⅘ [R]Nilo Bay 11 8 76 32½ 33 25¾ Lloyd J S 114 16.60 64-14 Harriman 1145¾ Silky Beau114¾RingforPeace1141¾ Slw st., rallied 11
5Nov86- 6Pha sly 170 :48⅗ 1:15⅕ 1:47⅖ Md Sp Wt 4 6 47 2½ 1½ 1nk Lloyd J S 118 4.50 63-28 Silky Beau 118nk Freeze Talks 1196 Kick Back 1184 Driving 6
LATEST WORKOUTS Jly 24 Mth 5f fst 1:01⅕ b Jly 18 Mth 7f fst 1:27⅘ h Jly 13 Mth 5f fst 1:02 b Jly 7 Mth 5f fst 1:03⅗ b

E.
4–1

Eltons Pride Gr. c. 3, by Silver Buck—Classic Queen, by Minnesota Mac
Own.—Cohen Mrs B Br.—Kohr E D (Fla) Tr.—Hine Hubert 110
Lifetime 7 1 0 1 $10,700 | 1987 6 1 0 1 $10,700 | 1986 1 M 0 0 | Turf 1 0 0 0

4Jly87- 2Mth fst 1 :46⅗ 1:11⅕ 1:37⅕ 3+ Alw 15000 1 8 87¼ 86 73¾ 55 Castaneda K b 114 39.10 82-10 Native Aspen 115¾ Freud 112¾ Aly Rat 1143½ Wide late 8
17Jun87- 7Mth fst 1 1/16 :47⅗ 1:11⅗ 1:44⅕ 3+ Alw 14000 8 9 95½ 77¾ 57 57 Castaneda K b 114 22.20 77-16 [DH]WiseEmissary1144[DH]IndinRiver1204MoonlitSkies112no Rallied 9
8Jun87- 8Mth fm 1 1/16 (T):47⅘ 1:12 1:43 + 3+ Alw 15000 6 6 65 88½ 813 89 McCauley W H b 113 19.40 77-14 Catch A Coid 1092½ Nantahela 1141¼ Hurricane John1141¼ Outrun 8
15May87-10GP fst 1 1/16 :48⅘ 1:14 1:46⅕ 3+ Md Sp Wt 5 5 46½ 2hd 2hd 1hd Pezua J M b 112 3.70 70-24 Eltons Pride 112hd Colonel E. A. 1143 Warrens Luck 1121 Driving 8
25Mar87- 7GP my 1 1/16 :47⅘ 1:13⅕ 1:47⅗ Md Sp Wt 2 9 1115 1121 1128 1135 Romero R P b 122 5.40 28-24 Chariot of War 1225½EstrellaPlateada1221½TapWriter122½ Outrun 12
9Feb87- 7Hia fst 1⅛ :49⅖ 1:14⅕ 1:53⅗ Md Sp Wt 2 4 55 65¾ 21½ 33½ Romero R P 120 11.30 59-26 Bally Blue 1202ChariotofWar1201½EltonsPride120¾ Bid. weakened 11
22Aug86- 3Pim sly 6f :24 :47⅘ 1:13⅖ Md Sp Wt 1 3 23 34 46½ 59¾ Byrnes D 120 6.80 69-22 SingHllelujh1202½MinuteNChnge1156¼ScrltGibou120hd Fell back 6
LATEST WORKOUTS Jly 25 Mth 5f fst 1:05 b

F.
5–1

Johnny McCabe — Ch. c. 4, by Fifth Marine—Two on one, by Lord Durham
Own.—Cedar Valle Stable — Br.—Haggard P (Ky) — Tr.—Jerkens Steven T — 118
Lifetime 16 3 1 2 $39,710 — 1987 5 1 0 0 $11,760 — 1986 7 2 0 0 $19,800 — Turf 2 0 0 0

1Jly87- 9Bel fst 7f	:22⅘	:45⅘	1:25⅕	Clm 32500	6	5	1hd	2nd	813	919	Cordero A Jr	b 115	10.90	57-22	Onnagata 115no Saintly Cheif 119nd Wicked Wike 117nk	Stopped	9
20Jun87- 1Bel fst 6f	:22⅘	:45⅘	1:09⅗	Clm 35000	4	3	62¾	32	69½	511¾	Hernandez R	b 117	14.10	80-16	Rexson's Quill1195¾Onnagata115¾SportsMedicine117nk	Weakened	9
30May87- 6Bel fst 6f	:22⅖	:45⅗	1:10⅕ 3+	Alw 26000	4	7	42	44½	78½	913¾	Santos J A	b 119	4.80	76-19	FortLigonier1194¾MeanandCrafty108nkPressMyBuzzer112nd	Tired	9
19Mar87- 5Aqu fst 7f	:23⅗	:46⅖	1:25⅘	Alw 26000	2	8	13	13	11½	43	Santos J A	b 117	*1.00	69-29	Rexson's Quill 117½ Billy Wilbur 117½ Racer 1172	Flattened out	9
4Mar87- 3Aqu fst 6f	[•]:23	:46⅖	1:10⅖	Clm 25000	5	6	2hd	1½	11½	14¾	Santos J A	b 117	14.20	92-16	Johnny McCabe 1174¾ Fugie 117¾ SaltineWarrior113¾	Ridden out	12
6Aug86- 9Sar sf 1	[T]:47⅖	1:12⅖	1:38⅕ 3+	Clm 35000	1	1	21	920	1032	—	Cordero A Jr	b 113	5.20	— —	Terson 117nk Major Event 1172¾ Golden Cnamp II 1173	Eased	10
20Jun86- 9Bel fst 6½f	:22⅗	:45⅖	1:16⅕	Clm 70000	2	3	11½	1hd	76½	811¼	Vasquez J	b 113	12.70	84-10	GoldenOlden1131¾GrandExchange117¾SwitchInTime1133	Used up	11
30May86- 3Bel fm 1 1/16	[T]:47⅘	1:13	1:44	Clm 70000	5	6	62½	52½	53¾	64¾	Santos J A	b 113	4.70	76-13	VivaDancer115¾Concatinte113nkHopingToBeLucky117nk	Steadied	7
2May86- 1Aqu fst 7f	:22⅘	:46⅖	1:25⅗	Clm 50000	5	1	1½	11	11½	11¾	Romero R P	b 117	4.90	73-26	Jonnny McCabe 1171¾ Majestic Dancer 1135Col Yoni119¾	Driving	7
14Apr86- 5Aqu fst 6f	:22⅕	:45⅘	1:12⅖	Clm 50000	1	5	2nd	2hd	64½	85¼	Guerra W A	b 119	11.40	74-24	Dr. Barney 1151 Every Pleasure 117nk Half Past 1171¾	Tired	10

LATEST WORKOUTS Jly 28 Bel 1 fst 1:42⅘ b — Jly 21 Bel tr.t 1 fst 1:44 b — ●Jly 14 Bel tr.t 1 fst 1:42 b — Jly 11 Bel tr.t 4f fst :52 b

G.
7–1

Chimney Sweep — Gr. g. 5, by Bold Forbes—Belle De Nuit, by Warfare
Own.—Glenn Lane — Br.—Hickory Tree Farm (Va) — Tr.—Heard Dennis — 118
Lifetime 32 4 3 5 $51,600 — 1987 8 3 1 1 $17,640 — 1986 11 0 0 3 $5,140 — Turf 13 0 2 1 $15,840

11Jly87- 4Mth fst 1 1/16	:46⅕	1:10⅘	1:44⅖ 3+	Clm c-12500	9	1	1½	12½	12½	11½	Vigliotti M J	b 117	2.80	83-14	Chimney Sweep 1171½Mike'sBoat1154MajesticBurst113no	Driving	9
1Jly87- 2Mth fst 170	:45⅘	1:10⅗	1:41⅕ 3+	Clm 10000	10	1	11½	11	13	1nk	Vigliotti M J	b 115	7.20	90-15	Chimney Sweep115nkDirtyBirdie1152¾NeverSassy1152	Just lasted	10
23Jun87- 4Mth fst 6f	:22⅖	:45⅕	1:10⅖ 3+	Clm 10000	7	8	62½	63½	64½	44	Vigliotti M J	b 116	12.00	84-14	Senor Smoke 1163 Diamond Chip 114nk TigerHiggins116¾	Rallied	10
12Jun87- 2Mth fst 6f	:22⅘	:46	1:11⅗ 3+	Clm c-8000	4	1	2hd	1hd	2hd	22	Krone J A	b 116	*.60	80-20	Sir Kevan 1112 Chimney Sweep 1163TranquilLeader1161	Steadied	7
2Jun87- 4Mth fst 6f	:22⅗	:45⅗	1:10⅗ 3+	Clm 6000	9	3	21	2½	11	15	Krone J A	b 114	5.60	87-16	ChimneySweep1145HiltoOlympus109nkRowdyRoll1171	Ridden out	11
16Feb87- 7Lrl fst 6f	:23⅕	:47⅘	1:13	Clm 6500	1	8	73¾	64	66½	79¾	Nied D	b 114	4.30	68-24	Mirror of Time 1151 Janet's Flash 1122 Ozone 1091	No factor	10
5Feb87- 5Lrl fst 6f	:22⅘	:47⅕	1:13⅕	Clm 8500	5	5	56½	57½	34	32	Nied D	b 114	21.80	75-22	Antiash 114no Strong Support 1092 Chimney Sweep 1142	Rallied	12
3Jan87- 4Lrl fst 7f	:22⅘	:46	1:26⅖	Clm 11500	6	4	77¼	79¼	68¼	810¼	Delgado A	b 114	21.40	66-24	Sauce Bowl 114nk Eighth Edition 1141¾ Antiash 1125	Outrun	8

44. The best bet at the odds is

3rd Santa Anita

1 1/16 MILES. (1.40⅕) CLAIMING. Purse $30,000. 4-year-olds and upward. Weight, 121 lbs Non-winners of two races at one mile or over since February 1 allowed 3 lbs.; of such a race since then, 5 lbs. Claiming price $50,000; if for $45,000 allowed 2 lbs. (Claiming and starter races for $40,000 or less not considered.)

A.
7–5

Poley 3+5
MCCARRON C J — 118
Own.—Bretzfield & Oliver
B. g. 8, by Pia Star—Women's Wear, by Groton
Br.—Oliver & Bretzfield (Ky)
Tr.—Mandella Richard — $50,000
Lifetime 32 8 7 4 $591,675 — 1987 3 1 0 0 $19,350 — 1986 2 0 1 0 $5,625 — Turf 4 1 0 0 $26,200

18Mar87-9SA	1 1/16:47	1:11¹	1:43 ft	4½	116	53½	53½	51¾	11¼	McCarron C J 2	50000	86-17	Poley, Video Kid, Easy Mover	8
16Feb87-9SA	1 1/16:46⁴	1:11	1:43²gd	11	116	21½	2½	41	44¾	Toro F 5	50000	79-21	Olajuwon,PlumbStright,PolAndDic	8
16Feb87—Bumped start, wide 7/8 turn														
4Feb87-3SA	1 1/16:48²	1:12³	1:43²ft	10	116	73¾	73¾	79	59½	Toro F 6	62500	74-19	Silver Hero, Pettrax, It'sNotMyJob	7
4Feb87—Wide into stretch														
24Dec86-7Hol	6f :22	:45²	1:11 ft	7¼	117	86¼	86¾	74¾	43	Shoemaker W 3	50000	85-20	MsterCrofter,Dnczon,RingOfPlsur	10
18Jly86-7Hol	7f :22³	:46	1:23¹ft	4¾	117	33	21	22	2¾	McCarron C J 3	62500	87-14	Savio, Poley, Mischiefinmind	7
21Jly85-11Sol	1 1/16:45³	1:10	1:41³ft	*3-2	117	45½	78	—	—	ChpmnTM5	Val Day H	— —	Pair Of Aces, John's Ruffie, Byron	8
21Jly85—Bled														
30Jun85-3Hol	7f :22	:44³	1:21 ft	4¼	115	54½	54¼	56½	45¼	McCarronCJ4	Aw48000	97-01	Tennessee Rite, Silent Fox, Cardell	6
1Jun85-8Hol	7f :22	:44²	1:20⁴ft	12	115	53	44½	49	46¼	McCrrCJ6	Trpl Bnd H	97-06	FiftySxInRow,Prmrshp,FrnchLgonr	7
24Apr85-8Hol	1 (T):45³	1:09³	1:33³fm	4¼	117	66½	89¾	88¾	813½	McCrronCJ2	Prmre H	81-06	NtvChrmrII,GtoDISI,BthEndsBrnng	8
24Apr85—Checked at 1/4; Run in divisions														
6Apr85-6SA	6f :21²	:44	1:09 ft	4¼	114	87½	811	78	46	McCarronCJ6	Aw45000	87-10	UnbknownsttoM,UsullyRlbl,EsyCsh	9

Apr 16 SA 6f ft :35³ h — Apr 9 SA 3f ft :36³ h — Apr 2 SA 4f ft :48³ h — Mar 12 SA 4f ft :48¹ h

B.

9–2

Grey Gauntlet
DELAHOUSSAYE E **116**
Own.—Bernstein & Giuliano
Ro. g. 5, by Run the Gantlet—Chores, by Grey Dawn II
Br.—Giuliano G & Sons (Ky)
Tr.—Bernstein David **$50,000**
Lifetime 28 2 3 3 $78,075
1987 4 0 2 0 $11,600
1986 6 0 1 0 $6,675
Turf 12 1 0 1 $39,000

24Mar87-8GG 1 Ⓣ:461 1:11 1:371fm 4 116 78¾ 77½ 65 67 CastanedaM6 Aw19000 74-19 Buck Royale, Re Enter,TellFloHello 7
13Mar87-5SA a6½f Ⓣ:22 :442 1:16 fm 5 117 106¾ 94¾ 74¾ 64¼ Toro F3 80000 75-21 Amnothrbrothr,AvitorII,Hydrosttc 10
26Feb87-7SA 7f :223 :444 1:231ft 8 116 88¾ 78¾ 63¼ 21¾ DelahoussayeE1 62500 82-22 J.R.Johnson,GreyGauntlet,AlbertoII 8
15Feb87-5SA 6½f :214 :444 1:162m 18 1095 69½ 56½ 33½ 21½ Patton D B4 70000 86-17 Rising Chum, GreyGauntlet,Pokare 7
15Feb87—Stumbled at start
24May86-9Hol 1 :454 1:111 1:37 ft 6½ 116 78 88½ 812 821¾ Haire D7 16000 56-16 Lithan, One Eyed Romeo, ValDeRoi 8
14Mar86-7SA 1$\frac{1}{16}$:473 1:122 1:453sy *9-5 116 45½ 45½ 48 59¾ McCarron C J 5 40000 63-30 TooMchForT.V.,NtnlEnrgy,HrrcnHc 5
26Feb86-5SA a6½f Ⓣ:214 :443 1:154fm 10 115 104¼ 87¼ 66 66¼ ValenzuelPA7 Aw31000 74-18 Swallage, Go Swiftly, Quality Jet 12
26Feb86—Wide into stretch
16Feb86-5SA 1 :471 1:114 1:382gd 4 117 86½ 85 78½ 613¾ Pincay L Jr7 Aw28000 72-14 RoylRecours,Nordicus,VirginiPrivtr 9
1Feb86-5SA 1 :474 1:13 1:383m 6¼ 116 73¾ 41½ 22 26 DelhoussyeE5 Aw30000 69-24 Full Honor,GreyGauntlet,Ascension 8
1Feb86—Bumped start; wide into stretch
8Jan86-7SA a6½f Ⓣ:211 :434 1:152fm 8 116 1114 1014 107 64¾ DelhoussyeE7 Aw28000 77-17 Odyssus,Amnothrbrothr,Bloom'sB 11
Apr 16 Hol 6f ft 1:011 h Apr 10 Hol 4f ft :482 h Mar 8 Hol 4f ft :492 h Feb 24 Hol 5f ft 1:014 h

C.

7–1

Pettrax
STEVENS S A **116**
Own.—Charlton B W
B. g. 9, by Petrone—Roman Dame, by British Roman
Br.—Charlton B (Cal)
Tr.—Charlton Wayne **$50,000**
Lifetime 69 16 13 4 $519,586
1987 4 1 1 0 $22,500
1986 12 4 2 1 $91,700
Turf 34 6 5 2 $209,325

5Apr87-7SA 1 :454 1:101 1:354ft 4 116 77¼ 87½ 712 615¼ Stevens S A4 50000 74-16 SiberinHro,SilvrHro,SmoothOprtor 8
5Apr87—Lugged out
20Mar87-5SA 1⅛ Ⓣ:461 1:103 1:48 fm 3¾ 118 3½ 63½ 98¼ 920¾ Black C A7 62500 66-15 Dark Accent, Twice Bold, Fothers 10
4Feb87-3SA 1$\frac{1}{16}$:482 1:123 1:432ft 3¾ 120 1½ 1½ 21 21½ Black C A3 62500 82-19 Silver Hero, Pettrax, It'sNotMyJob 7
17Jan87-3SA 1 :462 1:111 1:373ft 6¾ 113 22½ 2hd 1hd 11¼ Black C A6 55000 80-18 Pettrx,SilverHero,NorthernProvidr 8
17Jan87—Bumped start, 1/8
23Aug86-5Dmr 1⅛ Ⓣ:483 1:123 1:49 fm 5¼ 1155 23 22 33½ 2no Black C A4 62500 89-11 Dancebal, Pettrax, Massera 9
23Jly86-9Dmr 1$\frac{1}{16}$ Ⓣ:482 1:122 1:431fm *7-5 116 2hd 3nk 3½ 11 Toro F4 62500 90-04 Pettrax, Royal Olympia, Ablantin 8
29Jun86-9Hol 1$\frac{1}{16}$ Ⓣ:474 1:113 1:413fm 17 116 2½ 2hd 41 52¼ Kaenel J L8 62500 94-02 Caballo,Sndy'sEgle,EveningM'Lord 9
7Jun86-9Hol 1$\frac{1}{16}$ Ⓣ:462 1:101 1:41 fm 15 1125 22 2½ 42½ 52¾ Black C A1 75000 96-02 ‡GoDncer,Bishop'sRingII,PiprJohn 8
25May86-9Hol 1$\frac{1}{16}$ Ⓣ:472 1:104 1:411fm 6½ 1145 1hd 2½ 63½ 57 Black C A6 80000 91-03 Boom Town Charlie,Bozina,Pautivo 7
19Apr86-5SA 1 Ⓣ:464 1:101 1:352fm 8¼ 1155 1hd 21 22½ 1½ Black C A6 80000 — — Pettrax, Kilauea, Mr Chromacopy 11
Mar 30 SA 4f ft :473 b Mar 16 SA 5f ft 1:03 h Mar 8 SA 4f gd :504 h Mar 1 SA 4f ft :474 h

D.

6–1

Double Sheng
STEVENS G L **116**
Own.—4 MSts-Siegel-VHWSts(Lse)
B. c. 4, by Nodouble—Sheng Lue, by Never Bend
Br.—Winchell V H (Ky)
Tr.—Jones Gary **$50,000**
Lifetime 9 1 1 0 $18,350
1987 4 0 0 0
1986 5 1 1 0 $18,350

22Mar87-5SA 6½f :214 :452 1:174gd 12 118 107¾ 76½ 86 76¾ McCarronCJ 7 Aw29000 74-23 City View, Starshield,MidnightIce 10
22Mar87—Wide
4Mar87-5SA 1$\frac{1}{16}$:453 1:101 1:432ft 8¾ 117 32 54½ 62¾ 66½ McHrgueDG 1 Aw30000 77-16 RidgeReview,Rafel'sDncer,Athlone 12
14Feb87-5SA 6½f :22 :451 1:174sy 8½ 116 78½ 77½ 86½ 85½ Solis A 8 Aw26000 75-17 BrilliantLeder,JumpingDoctor,Breu 9
1Feb87-3SA 6f :212 :444 1:11 ft 7¾ 117 97¼ 84¼ 75 63¼ Hawley S 5 Aw26000 80-16 Dad's Quest, Athlone,WasslDancer 10
14May86-7Hol 1 :452 1:104 1:354ft 2¼e 120 65¼ 43 78¾ 713½ Stevens GL 10 Aw22000 70-14 Buckland'sHalo,RaiDen,Hlo'sSword 7
19Apr86-6GG 1⅛ :452 1:094 1:48 ft 19 112 714 712 712 713¼ Toro F5 Cal Dby 80-12 VrnonCstl,ImprosSprt,PrncBbbyB. 10
19Apr86—Grade II
23Mar86-4SA 1$\frac{1}{16}$:463 1:11 1:443ft *6-5 117 31½ 22 3½ 1½ Hawley S2 Mdn 78-17 DoublShng,GoodCommnd,RdgRvw 12
23Feb86-6SA 6f :213 :442 1:092ft *3½ 118 77½ 44½ 32 21¼ Hawley S 4 Mdn 90-11 CrownedJwl,DoublShng,NtivPriss 11
23Feb86—Fanned wide final 3/8
9Feb86-6SA 6f :211 :44 1:10 ft 43 117 1013 99¼ 77½ 42 Hawley S 12 Mdn 86-16 Zabalet,AckAckHeir,Intuitiveness 12
9Feb86—Veered out start, extremely wide into stretch, raced greenly
Apr 15 SA 5f ft 1:002 h Apr 11 SA 4f ft :48 h Mar 18 SA Ⓣ 4f fm :503 h (d) Mar 13 SA 5f ft 1:003 h

E.

10–1

Fracoza — Ch. g. 4, by Messenger of Song—Long Issue, by Long Position
GRYDER A T — 1115 — Br.—Cozza F (Cal) — 1987 6 2 0 0 $23,875
Own.—Ferguson Mrs J K — Tr.—Richardson Thomas F $50,000 — 1986 10 2 1 1 $21,550
Lifetime 16 4 1 1 $45,425

Entered 19Apr87- 9 SA
11Apr87-9SA 1 :46 1:11 1:362ft 6½ 116 21½ 22 34 56¼ Castanon A L 7 c40000 80-16 Bizeboy, Nordicus, Parson John 9
3Apr87-5SA 6½f :22 :453 1:172ft 6½ 116 2hd 1½ 13 14 Castanon A L 11 25000 83-17 Fracoza, Hurricane Hec, Pegus 11
17Mar87-7SA 1 1/16 :46 1:102 1:423ft 11 117 21½ 34 69 714¾ ValenzuelPA 3 Aw31000 73-16 PrinceO'Fire,It'sNotMyJob,Athlone 9
17Mar87—Lugged out.
26Feb87-5SA 1 1/16 :452 1:102 1:44 ft 5 115 11½ 13½ 2hd 45¼ Solis A 8 c25000 76-22 Cold, Exalted Bubble, Julie'sMark 10
7Feb87-9SA 1 1/16 :46 1:103 1:433ft 7½ 115 12½ 12 12½ 12¾ Olivares F 8 16000 83-14 Fracoza, Restage, Tiffani's Toy 9
18Jan87-1SA 7f :221 :451 1:243ft 7 115 95¾ 106¼ 98¼ 98¾ Olivares F 5 25000 68-19 Bizeboy, Trento, Superb Moment 12
18Jan87—Off slowly, wide
29Nov86-1Hol 6f :22 :453 1:104ft 5 117 54 65½ 65½ 67¾ DelahoussayeE 3 32000 81-12 AnotherBloom,Cbriome,GorgSlptHr 7
29Nov86—Broke in, bumped break, wide 3/8, stretch
9Nov86-5Hol 6f :22 :451 1:10 ft 5¾ 116 53¼ 55 68 59¼ Olivares F 8 40000 84-16 Lans Manus, RosesAreReb,Sebucan 8
31Oct86-6SA 6f :212 :443 1:093ft 8¼ 116 63½ 54 45½ 47½ Olivares F 11 50000 82-16 MischievousMtt,Jimed,RosesArRb 11
8Sep86-3Dmr 6f :214 :45 1:09 ft 3¾ 116 54¾ 68¼ 813 79½ Olivares F 5 62500 83-14 Notoriety,UrbnCowboy,BolgerMgic 9
8Sep86—Lugged out badly; took up at 3/16, wide into stretch
Mar 28 SA 5f ft 1:001 h ● Mar 10 SA 4f ft :463 h

F.

5–2

Bizeboy — Dk. b. or br. h. 5, by Distant Land—Another Lulu, by Majestic Prince
BAZE G — 116 — Br.—Arnold M L (Cal) — 1987 7 3 1 0 $44,025
Own.—Charles & ClearValleyStables — Tr.—Shulman Sanford $50,000 — 1986 15 3 3 4 $53,250
Lifetime 31 7 4 6 $107,725

11Apr87-9SA 1 :46 1:11 1:362ft 7 116 11½ 12 14 14½ Baze G 1 40000 86-16 Bizeboy, Nordicus, Parson John 9
29Mar87-2SA 6f :212 :442 1:092ft 11 115 2hd 2hd 42½ 710¾ Castanon A L 7 40000 80-18 Doonsport,SprbMomnt,DshnrblGst 8
29Mar87—Poor start; hit on nose by another rider's whip at 3/16
20Mar87-3SA 6f :212 :443 1:093ft *1 119 5½ 62 77½ 919½ Stevens G L 9 c32000 70-17 ElPrsdntUno,DshonorblGst,Donsprt 9
20Mar87—Wide
21Feb87-2SA 6f :214 :444 1:094ft *2 116 31½ 41½ 42 45¼ Stevens G L 4 40000 84-14 Crcksmn,LuckyMsddo,ElPrsdntUno 9
8Feb87-2SA 6½f :213 :441 1:153ft *2¾ 116 11 11½ 13½ 14 Stevens G L 7 32000 92-14 Bizeboy, Doonsport, MountBidder 11
24Jan87-2SA 6f :213 :45 1:103ft 4¼ 116 11½ 11½ 11½ 21½ Meza R Q 1 32000 83-18 SuperbMoment,Bizeboy,FletAlbrt 10
18Jan87-1SA 7f :221 :451 1:243ft 4 118 41 31½ 2½ 1½ Cordero A Jr 8 25000 77-19 Bizeboy, Trento, Superb Moment 12
29Nov86-4Hol 7f :22 :452 1:223ft *6-5 116 11 11 13½ 16 Stevens G L 4 c25000 91-12 Bizeboy,NorthrnProvidr,Yukon'sStr 7
11Nov86-3Hol 6f :221 :454 1:104ft *8-5 117 1hd 2hd 2hd 33 Pincay L Jr 5 32000 86-20 Juntura, King OfCalifornia,Bizeboy 6
18Oct86-5SA 6f :214 :444 1:11 ft *1 116 1hd 1hd 12½ 2no ValenzuelaPA 8 c25000 83-20 Grenoble, Bizeboy, Calabonga 8
Apr 6 SA 5f ft :594 h Mar 16 SA 3f ft :363 h

45. This is a contentious race for developing 3YOs on the turf. Analyze the race in depth and decide how to play it.

5th Del Mar

1 1/16 MILES. (Turf). (1.40) ALLOWANCE. Purse $23,000. 3–year–olds which are non–winners of $3,000 other than maiden, claiming or starter. Weight, 120 lbs. Non–winners of a race other than claiming at one mile or over since June 1 allowed 3 lbs.

15–1

Grey Aloha — Gr. c. 3, by Grey Dawn II—Miss Mauna Lisa, by Hawaii
OLIVARES F — 117 — Br.—Gentry T (Ky) — 1987 11 1 2 4 $22,125
Own.—Harada & Zamora — Tr.—Wilmot William B — Turf 1 0 0 1 $1,950
Lifetime 11 1 2 4 $22,125

10Jly87-1Hol 1⅛ :46 1:114 1:514ft 3 116 912 63 1½ 18 DelhoussyeE 10 M32000 78-14 GreyAloh,HereDeOne,BoobersTim 12
24Jun87-7GG 1 1/16 Ⓣ :473 1:12 1:441fm *6-5 116 99¼ 97 74¼ 32½ Castaneda M 8 Mdn 78-19 LuckyHroldH.,ChinvtBrdg,GryAloh 10
24Jun87—Bumped, steadied start
5Jun87-2Hol 1 :452 1:101 1:37 ft 3¼ 116 1011 78 77½ 32¼ DelahoussyeE 4 M32000 76-15 Fixation, Very Double, Grey Aloha 12
5Jun87—Bumped start
14May87-6Hol 1 :443 1:09 1:354ft 11 1085 1013 911 711 713¼ North M J 8 M35000 71-13 Billy'sBck,WtchTimGo,MimBound 12
14May87—Bobbled start
6May87-2Hol 1 :462 1:123 1:392ft *1 116 63¾ 43 3nk 2½ DelahoussyeE 1 M32000 65-18 Lomoso, Grey Aloha, Tissar'sBabe 12
22Apr87-2Hol 1 :461 1:12 1:38 ft *2½ 116 44½ 41¾ 41 2¾ DelhoussyeE 11 M32000 72-18 Perg Jr., Grey Aloha, Danceen Kid 12
8Apr87-2SA 6f :214 :451 1:104ft 3¾ 118 1113 813 56½ 32½ Sibille R 6 M32000 81-22 Maricota, Ice Minstrel, GreyAloha 12
8Mar87-4SA 1 1/16 :471 1:121 1:443ft 19 117 67 75¼ 77¼ 912¾ Sibille R 5 Mdn 65-15 LocalsOnly,NastyNaskr,TheMedic 10
22Feb87-6SA 1 1/16 :463 1:12 1:442ft 7¼ 117 76¾ 107½ 710 711¾ Sibille R 1 Mdn 67-14 Mountncmll,ErnYourStrps,ExtPoll 11
31Jan87-6SA 6½f :213 :443 1:163ft 39 118 99¾ 911 65½ 35¾ Sibille R 2 Mdn 81-15 Blanco, Exit Poll, Grey Aloha 9
Jly 22 Hol 5f ft 1:003 h Jly 6 Hol 5f ft 1:011 h Jun 20 Hol 6f ft 1:164 h May 31 Hol 5f ft 1:013 h

20–1

Never Turn Around

BLACK C A **117**
Own.—Klein-Sarkowsky-Wygod

B. c. 3, by Never Tabled—Bulleana, by Reverse
Br.—Klein-Sarkowsky-Wygod (Cal) 1987 2 1 0 0 $6,600
Tr.—Ellis Ronald W 1986 0 M 0 0
Lifetime 2 1 0 0 $6,600

9Jly87-6Hol 1 1/16 :47^1 1:12 1:45 ft *3½ 115 1^1 1^1 1^{1½} 1^{1¾} VlenzulPA^{11} [S]M32000 84-15 NvrTrnArnd,PrprRdr,MmrsOfBrnz 11
10Jun87-6Hol 6f :22^1 :45^4 1:11^{1}ft 2½ 115 4^{2½} 4^{3½} 4^{4½} 6^7 ValenzuelaPA^3 M40000 80-16 NoMonyDown,PolynsinChif,WrAx 10
10Jun87—Bumped start, lugged in
Jly 19 Hol 4f ft :47^4 h Jly 7 Hol 3f ft :37^2 h Jly 1 Hol 6f ft 1:13^4 h Jun 25 Hol 5f ft 1:00^2 h

12–1

Mon Legionnaire

DELAHOUSSAYE E **117**
Own.—Bernheim-Hecht-Karacan

B. c. 3, by Racing Room—Advising Jean, by Noble Jay
Br.—Paine T E & Linda (Cal) 1987 6 1 2 0 $15,725
Tr.—Bunn Thomas M Jr 1986 0 M 0 0
Lifetime 6 1 2 0 $15,725

Entered 29Jly87- 5 DMR

11Jly87-7Hol 1 :45^2 1:10^1 1:36^{2}ft 18 116 5^{1¼} 5^3 5^{1½} 2^{¼} DelahoussayeE 7 62500 80-12 Lrkng'sRoylty,MonLgonnr,CrosLov 7
24Jun87-6Hol 7f :22 :45^1 1:24 ft 4½ 115 4^{2½} 2^{1½} 2^2 1^2 McCarron C J 6 M50000 84-13 MonLgonnr,ExplosvDrm,CrystlFx 12
13Jun87-6Hol 6f :21^4 :45^1 1:09^{3}ft 9¼ 115 4^{3½} 3^2 3^{4½} 4^{7½} Sibille R 2 [S]Mdn 87-11 CabileDeOro,Gslighter,RodOfLuck 11
27May87-4Hol 6f :22^2 :46^3 1:12 ft *6-5 115 3^3 3^1 2^{½} 2^{hd} Sibille R 9 [S]M32000 83-16 BkuBby,MonLegionnire,IrishSmile 12
9Apr87-6SA 6f :22 :45^3 1:10^{1}ft 56 118 3^{nk} 3^1 6^{5½} 6^{7¼} Sibille R^{11} M50000 80-18 Be Scenic,CrystalFox,GoldenBeau 11
27Mar87-6SA 6f :21^4 :45^3 1:11^{3}ft 41 113^5 9^{12}10^{7½} 9^{7¼} 7^{7¾} Patton D B^{11} M50000 72-23 Plum Wishfull,CoolTalker,Guggen 12
● Jun 9 Hol 4f ft :47^2 h Jun 3 Hol 4f ft :48^1 h

5–2

*Jonleat

TORO F **117**
Own.—Watt M

B. g. 3, by Longleat—Swing Gently, by Swing Easy
Br.—Marsh B (Eng) 1987 2 1 1 0 $13,600
Tr.—Pierce Donald 1986 7 1 2 0 $2,932
Lifetime 9 2 3 0 $16,532 **Turf** 8 1 3 0 $7,732

16Jly87-8Hol 1 1/16 Ⓣ:46^{3}1:10^{2}1:41^{2}fm 12 114 5^{4½} 6^{2¾} 4^{1¾} 2^{nk} Stevens G L^8 Aw24000 87-13 Best Solution, Jonleat,PatientKing 9
27Jun87-1Hol 6f :22 :45^3 1:11^{3}ft 64 111^5 2^{hd} 2^{hd} 2^{½} 1^{¾} North M J^7 40000 85-09 Jonleat, Del Volante, Bidders 8
27Jun87—Wide 3/8 turn
25Aug86 ♦3Warwick(Eng) 1 1:45^{3}gd 14 132 Ⓣ 11^{12} CrosslyB Tote Nrsy H SunstBoulvrd,CrmAndGrn,Roumli 15
28Jly86 ♦3Windsor(Eng) 6f 1:14 gd 10 128 Ⓣ 11^{3½} Lucas T Eton Nrsy H Derring Dee, Bioffa, Flair Park 13
7Jun86 ♦4Epsom(Eng) 6f 1:10^{2}gd *4½ 130 Ⓣ 10 EddryP StfInghm Auc JayGee Ell,GreywolfTiger,Bastillia 14
22May86 ♦6Goodwood(Eng) 6f 1:18^{4}sf 4 128 Ⓣ 2^8 Eddery P Hlnkr GulfKing, Jonleat, Tough N Gentle 9
12May86 ♦2Pontefract(Eng) 5f 1:08^{3}sf *6-5 129 Ⓣ 2^{¾} Lucas T Snaith CountTrevisio,Jonlt,Wnslydlwrrior 10
26Apr86 ♦5Leicester(Eng) 5f 1:05^{2}sf *7-5 126 Ⓣ 1^{¾} LucasT Woolsthrp (Mdn) Jonlet,SingingSteven,SilverAncon 10
15Apr86 ♦1Newmarket(Eng) 5f 1:05^{4}gd 3¼ 126 Ⓣ 4^{7½} SnbrWR Stntny (Mdn) MisterMjestic,OnLinr,FrnchTuition 4
Jly 25 Dmr 5f ft 1:02^1 h Jly 11 Hol 6f ft 1:14^3 h Jun 24 Hol 5f ft 1:03^2 h Jun 18 Hol 7f ft 1:29^2 h

7–2

Contact Game

MCCARRON C J **117**
Own.—Hooper F W

Dk. b. or br. c. 3, by Tri Jet—Miami Game, by Crozier
Br.—Hooper F W (Fla) 1987 9 0 3 3 $32,200
Tr.—Russell John W 1986 6 1 0 0 $9,125
Lifetime 15 1 3 3 $41,325 **Turf** 3 0 1 1 $10,200

3Jly87-5Hol 1 1/16 Ⓣ:46^{3}1:10^{3}1:41^{4}fm*8-5 114 5^4 4^{2½} 4^3 4^{4¼} McCarronCJ^7 Aw24000 81-11 BooBoo'sBuckroo,TblGlow,Pondrbl 9
19Jun87-5Hol 1 1/16 Ⓣ:46 1:09^{4}1:40^{3}fm*8-5 109 6^{4½} 5^3 3^4 3^3 ShoemkerW^4 Aw24000 88-09 Forlaway,TableGlow,ContactGame 10
19Jun87—Crowded, bumped start; again into stretch
4Jun87-7Hol 1 1/16 :45^4 1:10^2 1:42^{3}ft *8-5 115 5^{3¼} 4^2 2^1 2^{1½} McCarronCJ^3 Aw24000 94-13 CrystalRun,ContctGme.Ack'sReply 8
13May87-8Hol 1 1/16 Ⓣ:47^{1}1:11^{2}1:41^{2}fm 6 114 2^5 2^{3½} 2^{1½} 2^{hd} McCarronCJ^4 Aw24000 87-13 LgunNtive,ContctGm,Mountincmlii 8
26Apr87-3Hol 6f :21^4 :45^1 1:09^{1}ft 9-5 115 8^{4¾} 4^{3½} 4^{4½} 3^6 McCarronCJ^6 Aw22000 91-09 W. D.Jacks,ANewEra,ContactGame 6
3Apr87-7SA 6f :21^4 :45 1:10 ft 11 116 7^4 5^2 3^{2½} 2^3 Solis A^8 Aw29000 85-17 HonkyTnkDncr,CntctGm,WndwdLn 8
8Mar87-6SA 6f :21^1 :44^2 1:09^{4}ft 9¾ 115 7^{7½} 6^{4½} 4^3 4^{3¼} Solis A^6 Aw28000 86-15 War, Candi's Gold, Laguna Native 8
8Mar87—Checked at break
21Feb87-3SA 6f :22 :45 1:09^{4}ft 9 115 5^{2¼} 4^{1¼} 4^2 3^{4¾} Stevens G L^3 Aw27000 84-14 SimplyMajestic,Blanco.ContctGme 8
21Feb87—Steadied 1/8
6Feb87-3SA 6f :21^1 :43^3 1:08^{4}ft 19 114 6^{6½} 5^6 3^4 4^{4¾} Stevens G L^3 Aw26000 89-15 MountLagun,SweetwterSprings,Wr 7
6Nov86-6Hol 6f :22^1 :45^4 1:11^{2}ft *2½ 118 4^{2½} 3^2 3^1 1^{hd} Solis A^5 M50000 86-17 ContctGm.WstrlyWind,WsdomDncr 9
Jly 24 Hol 6f ft 1:12 h Jly 18 Hol 5f ft 1:01^4 h Jun 28 Hol 6f ft 1:18^2 h ● Jun 13 Hol 5f ft :59^1 h

8–1

Patient King

MEZA R Q **117**
Own.—Chrys C E

Ch. g. 3, by King of Kings—Sigh No More, by Old Mose
Br.—Pascoe III & Wais (Cal) 1987 5 2 0 1 $21,200
Tr.—Robbins Jay M **Turf** 1 0 0 1 $3,600
Lifetime 5 2 0 1 $21,200

16Jly87-8Hol 1 1/16 Ⓣ:46^{3}1:10^{2}1:41^{2}fm 16 114 3^{2½} 3^1 1^{hd} 3^{¾} Meza R Q^6 Aw24000 86-13 Best Solution, Jonleat,PatientKing 9
27Jun87-7Hol 1 1/16 :45^3 1:10^2 1:43 ft 12 109 7^{13} 7^{10} 7^{10} 6^{12¾} ShoemkerW^5 Aw24000 81-09 MagnaPlus,MarkChip,Bigbadndmen 7
6Jun87-5Hol 1 1/16 :47^3 1:12^4 1:46^{3}ft 8¾ 116 6^3 6^{2¼} 3^1 1^{3½} Meza R Q^5 50000 76-17 Patient King, Darion, Some Hitter 6
6Jun87—Blocked into 2nd turn to stretch
28May87-2Hol 1 :45^3 1:11^2 1:37 ft 16 115 3^{1½} 1^{hd} 1^3 1^{8½} Meza R Q^8 [S]M32000 78-16 PtntKng,CrtnlyTogh,IfNotThsWht 11
7May87-2Hol 6f :22^1 :45^4 1:10^{4}ft 17 115 7^{5½} 6^7 7^{10} 6^{14¼} Meza R Q^{11} M32000 75-13 Ack'sRply,ChoosyFrind,SuprJmmy 11
Jly 25 Hol 5f ft 1:02^3 h Jly 10 Hol 6f ft 1:16^3 h Jun 23 Hol 5f ft 1:02^2 h Jun 17 Hol 5f ft 1:02^2 h

4–1

Political Ambition — B. c. 3, by Kirtling—Rose Pink, by Round Table
VALENZUELA P A — 117 — Br.—Jones & Charles (Ky) — 1987 3 1 0 1 $14,525
Tr.—Drysdale Neil — 1986 0 M 0 0
Own.—Clover Racing Stables — Lifetime 3 1 0 1 $14,525

12Jly87-5Hol 1 :45 1:093 1:35 ft *9-5 115 65½ 53¾ 34 33 ValenzuelPA2 Aw24000 85-09 ClticRlity,MrkChip,PoliticlAmbiton 7
12Jly87—Broke slowly
14Jun87-6Hol 7f :222 :452 1:23 ft 5 115 62½ 62½ 1½ 16 Valenzuela P A2 Mdn 89-14 PolitclAmbton,BstOfDnzg,Amrcno 10
29May87-6Hol 6½f :221 :45 1:162ft 31 115 88¼ 78 57½ 58¾ Valenzuela P A6 Mdn 89-16 MajesticMission,Fnticol,Acquired 12
29May87—Broke slowly
Jly 28 Dmr 4f ft :49 h Jly 23 Hol 6f ft 1:133 h Jly 17 Hol 3f ft :36 h Jly 8 Hol 5f ft 1:011 h

15–1

Lucky Harold H. — B. g. 3, by Coulee Man—Kaholo, by Pia Star
BAZE R A — 120 — Br.—Hinch Nan Barich (Cal) — 1987 5 1 0 1 $11,650
Tr.—Johnson K L — Turf 1 1 0 0 $7,150
Own.—Hinch Racing Stable — Lifetime 5 1 0 1 $11,650

17Jly87-11Sol 1 :463 1:102 1:362ft 17 114 32 31 31½ 33½ Judice J C7 Aw14000 88-16 ExclusvPtrot,Dm'Rff,LuckyHroldH. 9
3Jly87-11Pln 1 1/16 :47 1:11 1:43 ft 13 115 55½ 66¾ 64 53½ Maple S2 Pln H 85-15 FairlyAffirmed,EarlySnow,Tm'sWy 6
24Jun87-7GG 1 1/16 Ⓣ:473 1:12 1:441fm 7 116 42 52¾ 1hd 12 Maple S4 Mdn 81-19 LuckyHroldH.,ChinvtBrdg,GryAloh 10
7Jun87-5GG 6f :214 :442 1:10 ft 9½ 116 86¼ 88¾ 89¼ 55½ Maple S3 Mdn 83-10 Dem' Riffa, Litigated, Friend Abe 11
24May87-5GG 6f :214 :443 1:102ft 24 120 85 56½ 56 43 Schrick D L1 Mdn 84-08 GoldRushin',J.D.Commish,SeTwist 10
24May87—Broke slowly
Jly 16 BM 3f ft :364 h Jly 11 BM 5f ft 1:03 h Jly 1 BM 4f ft :49 h ● Jun 22 BM 4f ft :471 h

8–1

***Parc Des Princes** — B. g. 3, by Anfield—French Cooking, by Royal and Regal
STEVENS G L — 120 — Br.—Hampson G W (Eng) — 1987 2 1 0 1 $5,017
Tr.—Vienna Darrell — Turf 2 1 0 1 $5,017
Own.—Forgnone–Klein–Levy et al — Lifetime 2 1 0 1 $5,017
Entered 29Jly87- 8 DMR

22Jun87♦1Pontefract(Eng) 1 1:462gd *4-5 126 Ⓣ 15 DffldG June Mile (Mdn) PrcDesPrinces,Pgitek,EnglishRivr 16
30May87♦3Newmarket(Eng) 1 1:39 gd 33 126 Ⓣ 32¼ AdmsN Hlstn Diat Pils (Mdn) SherShah,Bashayer,PrcDesPrinces 27
Jly 24 Dmr 4f ft :502 h Jly 17 Dmr 4f ft :513 h

11–1

Just Bobby — Ch. c. 3, by Roberto—Hoist Emy's Flag, by Hoist the Flag
SHOEMAKER W — 117 — Br.—Singer C (Ky) — 1987 7 0 0 2 $15,700
Tr.—Proctor Willard L — 1986 3 1 1 0 $14,200
Own.—Singer J — Lifetime 10 1 1 2 $29,900 — Turf 4 0 0 0 $5,800

13Jun87-5Hol 1 :451 1:093 1:343ft 18 1095 98¾ 87¼ 67½ 37¾ Patton D B4 Aw24000 82-11 ErnYorStrps,McKnzPrnc,JstBbby 10
13May87-8Hol 1 1/16 Ⓣ:471 1:112 1:412fm 4¼ 117 89¼ 77½ 56 46¾ Pincay L Jr3 Aw24000 80-13 LgunNtive,ContctGm,Mountincmlli 8
15Apr87-8SA 1⅛ Ⓣ:46 1:11 1:471fm 4 114 87 85¾ 77 57¼ ShmrW10 Ⓡ La Puente 84-11 ThMdic,ChmTm,BustYourButtons 10
15Apr87—Bumped repeatedly; taken up at 1/8
25Mar87-8SA a6½f Ⓣ:212 :434 1:15 fm 17 114 88¾ 89 57½ 56 Cox D W10 Bldwn 78-16 ChmTm,SwttrSprngs,McKnzPrnc 11
12Mar87-8SA a6½f Ⓣ:212 :44 1:16 fm 27 1095 89 76¼ 57½ 54½ Cox D W1 Aw40000 74-21 SwtwtrSprngs,HppyInSpc,ChmTm 10
12Mar87—Broke slowly; wide into, through stretch
30Jan87-7SA 1 :47 1:12 1:372ft 13 1095 85 72¾ 62¼ 42¼ Cox D W6 Aw28000 79-20 The Quipper, Reland, Savor Faire 9
30Jan87—Steadied 9/16
16Jan87-5SA 1 1/16 :464 1:111 1:433ft 3½ 1095 78½ 58 46½ 310 Cox D W9 Aw28000 73-18 Hot AndSmoggy,Reland,JustBobby 9
14Dec86-4Hol 7f :214 :45 1:241ft *8-5 120 107¾ 93¾ 73¾ 84½ ShoemkerW8 Aw22000 78-18 OrchardSong,Reland,HoustonBrgg 11
14Dec86—Wide in stretch
11Oct86-6SA 6½f :214 :444 1:172ft *2¼ 117 79 56½ 42¼ 11¼ Shoemaker W11 Mdn 83-17 JustBobby,Brb'sRlc,ExclusvEnogh 12
11Oct86—Stumbled start
2Aug86-6Dmr 6f :221 :452 1:101ft 2¾ 117 22½ 22½ 22½ 2¾ Shoemaker W6 Mdn 86-12 BiloxiBlues,JustBobby,IceMinstrel 12
Jly 16 SA 5f ft 1:024 h Jly 8 SA 4f ft :49 h Jun 26 SA 3f ft :37 h Jun 12 SA 3f ft :391 h

A. Key *Jonleat* on top of *Grey Aloha*, *Contact Game*, *Parc des Princes*, and *Just Bobby*
B. Bet *Grey Aloha* to win
C. Box *Grey Aloha* and *Just Bobby* and key each on top of *Jonleat* and *Contact Game*
D. Bet *Patient King* to win and key it top and bottom of *Jonleat*, *Contact Game* and *Political Ambition*

46. Read the conditions. Examine the records. Which is the best bet at the odds listed below?

OUT OF CHUTE ▸
6½ FURLONGS
SANTA ANITA
▴FINISH

6 ½ FURLONGS. (1.14) ALLOWANCE. Purse $33,000. Fillies and mares. 4-year-olds and upward which are non-winners of $3,000 twice other than maiden or claiming. Weight, 120 lbs. Non-winners of such a race since February 15 allowed 3 lbs.; of such a race since December 25, 5 lbs.

Alydariel 3–N
DELAHOUSSAYE E — 117 — T23¹
Own.—Hudson E J
Ch. f. 4, by Alydar—Crimson Saint, by Crimson Satan
Br.—Gentry T (Ky) — 1986 2 2 0 0 $22,000
Tr.—Drysdale Neil — 1985 0 M 0 0
Lifetime 2 2 0 0 $22,000
30Dec86-7SA 6f :21³ :45 1:10⁴ft *2½ 118 3½ 2hd 1hd 1½ Pincay L Jr 7 ⒻAw26000 84-18 Alydariel, Bambalor, In Concert 11
13Dec86-4BM 6f :22¹ :45¹ 1:10⁴ft *1 118 5½ 4½ 2² 1no Baze R A 4 ⒻMdn 85-19 Alydariel, Blue Silk, Codex's Bride 10
13Dec86—Off slowly
Mar 29 Hol 4f ft :49⁴ h   Mar 24 Hol 5f ft 1:01² h   Mar 19 Hol 6f ft 1:15⁴ h   Mar 14 Hol 6f ft 1:13⁴ h

'Halo Street 3–N
VALENZUELA P A — 115 — T23¹
Own.—Paulson A E
B. f. 4, by Halo—Street Ballet, by Nijinsky II
Br.—Taylor E P (Md) — 1987 2 0 0 1 $7,575
Tr.—Drysdale Neil — 1986 3 2 0 0 $23,650
Lifetime 5 2 0 1 $31,225
12Mar87-7SA 6f :21⁴ :45 1:09³ft 8½ 115 2½ 3¹ 3² 36½ StevensGL 5 ⒻAw36000 83-19 Rare Starlet, Fairly Old, HaloStreet 6
13Jan87-3SA 6f :21³ :45¹ 1:11¹ft 9 116 5⁵ 5¾ 4½ 4¾ CordroAJr6 ⒻAw29000 78-19 BlconyPss,SeDoubyRun,LuckySilvr 9
13Jan87—Broke slowly
4Jun86-8Hol 7f :22 :44⁴ 1:22²ft 18 114 5³ 5⁶ 7¹⁴ 7¹⁹½ HrnndzR6 ⒻRailbird 73-18 Melair, Comparability, SilentArrival 7
4Jun86—Grade III
24Apr86-5Hol 6f :22² :46 1:10⁴ft 2½ 120 1½ 1½ 1⁴½ 1⁴½ HernndezR3 ⒻAw22000 90-18 Halo Street, Python, Alquizar 5
29Mar86-4SA 6½f :22 :45¹ 1:17³ft 4½ 117 2hd 1½ 1¾ 1nk Stevens G L 3 ⒻMdn 82-20 Halo Street, Clever Edge, Yach 11
Mar 29 SA 4f ft :48¹ h   Mar 24 SA 4f ft :49⁴ h   Mar 18 SA 4f ft :48 h   Mar 10 SA 3f ft :35³ h

Lady Ack 5+
PINCAY L JR — 120 — T23
Own.—Oak Cliff Stable
B. f. 4, by Ack Ack—Assurgent, by Damascus
Br.—Oak Cliff Thoroughbreds Ltd (Ky) — 1987 4 2 1 1 $35,600
Tr.—Gosden John H M — 1986 0 M 0 0
Lifetime 4 2 1 1 $35,600
11Mar87-3SA 6f :21³ :44³ 1:10 ft *4-5 120 1¹ 1½ 1² 1³ Pincay L Jr6 ⒻAw28000 88-18 LdyAck,Jrry'sGoldmin,SuchASplsh 6
11Feb87-5SA 6f :21² :44⁴ 1:10³ft 2½ 119 5½ 4² 4³ 3½ Pincay L Jr6 ⒻAw26000 82-17 BanquetDancer,InConcert,LadyAck 8
16Jan87-6SA 6f :21⁴ :45 1:10 ft *1-2 119 1½ 1½ 1½ 1½ Pincay L Jr3 ⒻMdn 88-18 LadyAck,Tootsiepop,BlueSapphire 10
2Jan87-6SA 6f :21² :44⁴ 1:10 ft 5 119 3½ 2½ 2½ 2¾ Pincay L Jr3 ⒻMdn 84-22 High Ace, LadyAck,ThatFallonGirl 11
2Jan87—Lugged in
●Mar 27 SA 5f ft :59³ h   Mar 2 SA 3f ft :37⁴ b   Feb 23 SA 3f ft :35³ h   ●Feb 1 SA 5f ft :59¹ h

A. *Alydariel* 5–2
B. *Halo Street* 3–1
C. *Lady Ack* 1–1
D. No bet

47. It's July 31. Claiming-race restrictions at minor tracks provide the clues to success. Find the best play at the odds in this Atlantic City dash.

4 ATLANTIC CITY

5 ½ FURLONGS. (1.02⅗) CLAIMING. Purse $4,000. 3-year-olds and upward which have not won a race since January 31. Weight, 3-year-olds, 115 lbs. Older, 122 lbs. Non-winners of two races since December 31, allowed 2 lbs. a race since then 4 lbs. a race since November 30 6 lbs. Claiming Price $4,000.

A.
8–1

Plaza Prince — $4,000 — 116
Own.—Bianchi C R
B. g. 8, by Verbatim—My Concubine, by Forward Pass
Br.—S H & S Thoroughbred Farms (Ky)
Tr.—McCaslin John
Lifetime 109 18 19 11 $149,058 — 1986 19 5 4 1 $18,505 — 1985 20 3 3 0 $11,415 — Turf 12 1 0 3 $6,190
30Oct86- 7Pha fst 1 :47⅕ 1:12⅗ 1:38⅘ 3+Clm 6000 10 5 56½ 10¹⁷ 11²¹ 10¹⁵½ Aristone M b 114 38.50 65-23 Happiness Road 116nk Peaceful Cookie 116nkGretzky116½ Outrun 11
21Sep86- 9Del fm 1½ Ⓣ:48⅗ 2:06⅗ 2:32⅕ 3+Clm 5000 12 2 3½ 12¹⁵ 12³⁴ 12³²½ LizarzaburuPM b 119 *3.60 55-13 Bill Jaffe 109nk Ruling Above 106nk Doggerel 119¹ Tired 12
6Sep86-10Del fst 1⅛ :47⅗ 1:13 1:53⅗ 3+Clm 5000 9 2 1hd 2½ 2⁴ 2⁴½ Greco R A b 122 2.90 64-24 Man of Power 122⁴½ Plaza Prince122¹½Paramedical110¹ 2nd best 9
20Aug86- 7Atl fst 6f :22⅕ :45⅘ 1:11⅖ 3+Clm 8500 5 1 56½ 5¹¹ 5⁹ 56½ Aristone M b 116 4.80 78-21 ColdAsACmbr112¹½ThJck'sOnYo116²½Tmo'sGry114¹½ No threat 6
12Aug86- 1Atl fst 7f :22⅗ :45⅗ 1:24⅗ 3+Clm 6250 5 3 3³ 2⁴ 2½ 1¹ Aristone M b 116 3.10 79-21 Plaza Prince 116¹WarriorInOrbit109¹½KlassyDiamond112⁵ Driving 7
3Aug86-10Del gd 1$\frac{1}{16}$:48 1:13⅕ 1:46⅗ 3+Clm 4500 3 1 1³ 1½ 1hd 1¾ Greco R A b 115 4.00 76-20 Plaza Prince 115¾ Ebony And White 113¹½ Ideal 119¹½ Driving 7
26Jly86- 6Del gd 1$\frac{1}{16}$:47⅘ 1:12⅖ 1:45⅗ 3+Clm 5750 3 3 2hd 35½ 4⁸ 4¹⁵½ Garcia P L b 110 2.70 64-23 [DH]Pemetic 113⁶ [DH]Ideal 116⁶ One For Dom116⁹½ Caused bmping 6
2Jly86- 3Atl sly 1$\frac{1}{16}$:47⅕ 1:12⅕ 1:46⅕ 3+Clm 5000 4 1 2hd 2½ 2¹½ 2²½ Aristone M b 120 *1.50 71-28 Prince Dino 109²½ Plaza Prince 120nk SetAndChat116⁷½ Held 2nd 6
20Jun86- 2Atl gd 1$\frac{1}{16}$:48⅗ 1:13⅗ 1:46⅕ 3+Clm 5000 3 4 2hd 2³ 2³ 2³ Leasure W P b 120 2.90 71-22 Hey Man 116³ Plaza Prince 120nk Yale Key 105²½ Rallied 9
31May86-10Del fst 1½ :50⅕ 2:07 2:32⅘ Clm 4000 2 1 1² 1hd 2hd 2nk Leasure W P b 116 4.60 93-15 SanguineSword116nkPlazaPrince116⁹ReglEscort115½ Just missed 8
LATEST WORKOUTS   Jly 26 Atl 4f fst :49⅗ b   Jly 14 Atl 4f fst :50⅗ b   Jun 25 Atl 1 fst 1:45 b   Jun 17 Atl 7f fst 1:28 b

B.
10–1

Commadore Too — Ch. g. 4, by Commadore C—Little Flakey Too, by Petare — $4,000 — Br.—Cresci Paul (Fla) — Tr.—Maletto Peter — 111 5
Own.—McCall J
Lifetime 29 2 6 0 $16,540 — 1987 7 0 0 0 $540 — 1986 16 2 6 0 $15,790

6Jly87- 2Mth fst 1 1/16 :48 1:12⅖ 1:45⅗ 3+ Clm 6250 1 2 32½ 55½ 68¾ 615¼ Corbett G W7 b 106 21.70 61–14 My Old School 119½ Benign Czar 1062 Simon Le King 1173 Tired 6
27Jun87-10Mth sly 6f :22⅖ :45⅘ 1:11⅖ 3+ Clm 5000 9 2 87½1012 917 921 Terry J b 116 16.80 62–16 GimmeAMarker1097½FleetMirage116nkRunawyEgo1164 No speed 10
9Jun87- 4Mth fst 6f :22⅗ :46 1:11⅗ 3+ Clm 5000 1 7 97½1011 812 713¼ Corbett G W7 b 109 40.30 68–19 RowdyRebel1193¼GimmeAMarker1114Rjb'sWillyPop1092½ Outrun 11
2Jun87- 4Mth fst 6f :22⅗ :45⅗ 1:10⅗ 3+ Clm 6000 2 11 810 710 516 612½ Rujano M b 115 51.40 75–16 ChimneySweep1145HiltoOlympus109nkRowdyRebel1171 No factor 11
15May87- 7GS gd 6f :22⅖ :46⅕ 1:12 3+ Clm 5000 4 9 98¾ 99 78 810 Ferrer J C b 116 18.90 72–23 Rowdy Rebel 1165½ Intheblack 116nk Anvil Man 116½ Outrun 11
1Feb87- 9Pha fst 170 :45⅗ 1:10⅘ 1:41⅗ Clm 6250 1 3 45 45½ 37 511 Colon P b 116 3.80 77–09 Nick's Native Rose 1167½ ValD'Espoir107½ConradWho1112½ Tired 7
15Jan87- 4Pha fst 170 :47⅕ 1:13⅗ 1:45⅘ Clm 6250 6 4 31 1hd 21 44 Colon P b 116 *4.50 62–29 Radar Screen 1152 Conrad Who 110½I.D.Silverine1141½ Weakened 12
13Dec86- 1Med fst 1 :47 1:12⅕ 1:38⅗ Clm 7500 3 7 53¾ 43 22½ 22 Giorgio J M5 b 114 22.80 81–09 Delta Wings 1122 CommadoreToo114¾HastyFellow115no 2nd best 11
18Nov86-10Med sly 6f :23⅗ :47⅖ 1:12⅘ Clm 7500 5 8 93½ 87½ 912 919½ Giorgio J M5 b 113 27.60 59–25 Dactyl Dancer122½RoyalRedAndBlue1165HawaiiFively111¾ Outrun 10
28Oct86- 4Med fst 6f :22⅗ :46⅖ 1:11⅗ Clm 7500 1 9 94½ 95½ 73½ 710½ Giorgio J M5 b 112 17.00 74–19 Gimme A Marker 1162½ Ramblin Ricky 116nk Illuvium1114 Outrun 12
LATEST WORKOUTS Jly 25 Atl 4f fst :48⅕ b ● Jly 15 Mth 3f my :35⅖ hg(d) Jun 25 Mth 3f fst :36⅖ b ● Jun 20 Mth 1 fst 1:41⅗ h

C.
20–1

Ruby Jet — B. g. 4, by Jetmar—Ruby Viener, by Bold Legend — $4,000 — Br.—Cook Judy (NJ) — Tr.—Cook Judy — 108 10
Own.—Allen Win
Lifetime 22 1 0 3 $4,469 — 1987 7 0 0 0 $80 — 1986 14 1 0 3 $4,389

26Jun87- 4Atl fst 6f :22⅗ :46 1:12⅖ 3+ Clm 4000 1 10 88½ 67½ 65½ 54 Strickland L10 b 110 26.30 76–21 Winning Lane 116nk Long Gone John 1161½ Revy 116½ Outrun 11
19Jun87- 4Atl fst 5½f :22⅗ :46⅖ 1:06 3+ Clm 4000 12 10 1015 88½ 67½ 75¾ Strickland L10 b 110 71.40 77–16 Guildee Prince 1112 Snow Gift 116no Fine Gent 116½ Outrun 12
8May87-10GS fst 1 1/16 :48⅘ 1:14⅗ 1:47⅖ 3+ [S]Clm 5000 7 4 43 99½ — — Strickland L10 b 107 80.50 — — Silver Hat 1163½ Boy Thumper109nk SladyDick1114½ Outdistanced 10
2May87- 1Del my 6f :23⅕ :46⅘ 1:11⅘ Clm 4000 7 2 53 46 713 715 Strickland L10 b 112 9.20 67–19 Great Nerve 1154½ Switchblade 1222½ Hat's Off 1191½ Tired 8
23Apr87- 4GS fst 170 :47 1:13⅗ 1:44⅘ 3+ Clm 4000 10 6 59 78½1115 1127¼ Strickland L10 b 109 83.60 46–25 Rattlesnake Rogue 1193½ Val D'Espoir1092½Acclimated1163 Tired 11
16Apr87- 7GS gd 6f :22⅗ :46⅘ 1:12⅘ 3+ [S]Clm 5000 9 11 1117 1114 815 611¾ Strickland L10 b 109 33.80 66–25 Christophr'sTurn116nkEstrnCorridor1163HousOdds1191 No factor 11
11Jan87- 4Pha fst 6½f :23⅕ :47⅗ 1:21⅗ Clm 4000 3 12 1221 1211 910 99¾ Strickland L10 b 108 46.00 55–34 Triple Mad1112½CardiacPack115½[DH]NowWe'veGotHim115 Outrun 12
12Dec86- 4Pen my 5½f :23 :48 1:08⅖ 3+ Md 5000 1 10 911 811 3½ 11 Strickland L10 b 110 3.20 74–27 Ruby Jet 1101 Classic World 120½ Fleet Gusto 1203½ Driving 10
28Nov86- 1Pha fst 6f :22⅘ :46⅖ 1:13⅖ 3+ Md 7000 11 12 109¾ 711 37½ 36½ Strickland L7 b 107 28.20 67–20 HonestDecision1164SunnyHero1152½RubyJt1072½ Didn't brk alrtly 12
14Nov86- 1Pha fst 6f :22⅗ :45⅘ 1:11⅕ 3+ Md 10000 11 2 53½ 54½ 512 1021 Ravelich M b 116 11.80 64–20 Barbolini 1163 Stone Express 1155 Small Bore 1161 Tired 12
LATEST WORKOUTS Jly 28 Atl 3f fst :36⅘ b Jly 18 Atl 5f fst 1:02⅗ b ● Jun 12 Atl 5f fst 1:01 h Jun 6 Atl 4f fst :51 b

D.
3–1

Fragrant Prince — B. g. 9, by Diplomat Way—Fine Fragrance, by Bolinas Boy — $4,000 — Br.—Farnsworth Farm (Fla) — Tr.—Simms Gary P — 116
Own.—Simms G P
Lifetime 64 18 16 6 $128,300 — 1985 8 1 1 1 $6,110 — 1984 1 0 0 0 $50 — Turf 20 8 5 1 $58,785

1Sep85- 8Del fm *1 1/16 Ⓣ 1:44⅕ 3+ Hcp 6500s 9 4 85½ 918 933 932¾ Lynch H D b 117 2.50 72 — The Wiley Fox 1124½ Royal Jove 116nk TorontoJugier1131 Outrun 9
21Jly85- 8Del fm 1⅛ Ⓣ :48⅕ 1:12⅗ 1:50⅘ 3+ Hcp 6500s 6 1 13½ 1hd 1hd 11¾ Winnett B G Jr b 112 2.40 90–20 Fragrant Prince 1121¾ Pen Card 1211 Exact Sam 1188½ Driving 7
14Jly85-10Pen fm 170 Ⓣ 1:41 3+ Clm 8000 12 6 4¾ 2hd 2hd 21 Parrilla R b 115 *3.90 80–13 Papal Order 1151 Fragrant Prince 115noBankOnJohn1152 Gamely 12
27Jun85- 9GS fst 1⅛ :47 1:11⅘ 1:51⅖ 3+ Clm 6000 11 1 1½ 2½ 31½ 35 Terry J b 114 21.70 67–19 Blairway1162GrandOldHerbie1163FragrntPrince114nk Drifted out 12
19Jun85- 9GS fst 1 1/16 :47⅕ 1:12⅗ 1:45⅗ 3+ Clm 6000 11 6 64¾ 32½ 57 67¾ Parrilla R7 b 109 15.30 72–16 Got A Pretty Face 1161 Judge Whaley 1166 St.Gellert120nk Tired 12
28May85- 2Crc fst 6f :22⅗ :45⅘ 1:12⅘ Clm 5000 3 5 64¾ 78¾ 810 84¾ Lynch H D b 112 3.70 82–13 Smokey'sMn112½QuickCosmic1121½ConsumerIndx1121 No factor 9
21May85- 8Crc fst 6½f :22⅗ :46⅕ 1:19⅘ Clm 5000 8 8 78¾ 55½ 51½ 45½ Santos J A b 114 *3.00 80–16 MedievalMovement114¾NiceAndEsy114¾NobleKey1144 No factor 11
9May85- 1Crc fst 6f :22 :46 1:13⅘ Clm 5000 2 9 89¾ 66½ 52½ 53 Madrid S O b 113 4.50 79–13 Gator Glory 112½ Space Jet 114½ Coup d' Audace 1122 Outrun 9
2Jun84- 1Crc 4 9 87¾ 67½ 711 814½ Santos J A b 116 2.80 69 — Ret. lame 8
5Nov83- 2Crc 9 5 2½ 12 12½ 12½ Castaneda K b 116 *1.80 91 — Drew clear 6

E.
30–1

Aggi's Bid * — B. g. 11, by Raise a Bid—Dear Aggi, by Intentionally — $4,000 — Br.—Early Bird Stud (Fla) — Tr.—Bloxham Diane — 116
Own.—Bloxham Diane
Lifetime 132 17 13 20 $101,737 — 1984 12 2 0 0 $6,888 — 1983 15 1 1 2 $5,815 — Turf 3 0 0 0

24Nov84- 6Del fst 170 :47 1:13 1:45⅕ 3+ Clm 3500 7 5 512 79½ 89¾ 822½ Jett R b 113 30.10 45–28 Imperiled 116nk Deb's BestFriend116½BlondieDuck1135 No factor 8
17Nov84- 6Del fst 1 1/16 :48⅕ 1:13⅗ 1:48⅗ 3+ Clm 3500 9 3 54¾ 1118 1129 1136¾ Leasure W P b 113 46.40 28–28 Tullie's Slugger 1152 Impressario 1152 Imperiled 116¾ Tired 11
3Nov84- 6Del fst 1 1/16 :47⅘ 1:13⅗ 1:48⅖ 3+ Clm 3500 6 9 76½ 44½ 65¾ 76¾ Allgood M A b 113 7.10 55–27 Triolic 113nk Imperiled 119no Unconscious Lad 113nk Outrun 11
28Oct84- 6Del fst 6f :22⅗ :45⅘ 1:11⅗ 3+ Clm 5000 5 5 53 78½ 86½ 97½ LizarzaburuPM b 113 36.10 76–16 New Agreement 119nkIrishBalleeer113nkMr.Alhambra1061½ Tired 10
LATEST WORKOUTS Jly 22 Atl 3f gd :37⅖ b Jly 15 Atl 6f sly 1:18⅗ bg Jly 9 Atl 5f gd 1:03⅘ b Jly 2 Atl 4f sly :50⅖ b

F.
5–1

Runaway Ego * — Ch. h. 5, by Escaped—Ego's Delight, by Egotistical — $4,000 — Br.—Shadybrook Farm & Toman (NJ) — Tr.—Fisher John L — 116
Own.—Toman Mrs A J
Lifetime 56 4 7 4 $43,343 — 1987 7 0 0 1 $1,013 — 1986 25 1 4 1 $17,694

25Jly87- 1Mth fst 6f :22⅗ :45⅘ 1:11⅗ 3+ [S]Clm 6000 6 5 53½ 57½ 915 917½ Hannigan L b 114 47.30 65–13 Faraday 1164½ Abuse of Process 120nk TopoftheStar109nk Outrun 9
15Jly87- 4Mth fst 6f :22⅗ :45⅘ 1:13 3+ Clm 5000 1 4 22 44½ 56 910½ Santagata N b 116 17.40 65–20 GoldVictory116hdStandardDeviation1092½WhatACngr1052 Tired 10
4Jly87-11Mth fst 6f :22⅕ :45⅘ 1:11⅕ 3+ [S]Clm 6000 9 2 52½ 54 88½ 88½ Imparato J b 114 28.80 75–10 Same Table 114no Free And Fast 1163 Glacier 1162½ Tired 11
27Jun87-10Mth sly 6f :22⅗ :45⅘ 1:11⅗ 3+ Clm 5000 7 7 55 35 36½ 37½ Imparato J b 116 9.10 75–16 GimmeAMarker1097½FleetMirge116ndRunwyEgo1164 Best of rest 10
12Jun87- 1Mth fst 6f :23 :46⅕ 1:12⅘ 3+ [S]Clm 5000 2 7 63½ 54 67 811 Terry J b 116 3.90 65–20 Just Stanley 111nk House Odds 1161½ Gems ForSale116no Outrun 8
5Jun87- 1Mth sly 5f :23⅕ :47⅗ 1:14⅕ 3+ [S]Clm 5000 7 2 11½ 2½ 3½ 45½ Thomas D B b 116 4.80 63–30 RingerOne1161½TopoftheSt1091½Christophr'sTurn1163 Weakened 9
30May87-10Mth fst 6f :22⅕ :45 1:11⅕ 3+ [S]Clm 6250 10 8 76½ 811 1117 1117¾ Anderson A M7 b 109 11.00 66–14 StrangeBehavior1092½QuitFooling1125ProudChuckie1141½ Outrun 12
1Nov86- 1Med fst 6f :22⅘ :45⅘ 1:11 3+ Clm 5000 6 4 2½ 24 48½ 716 Thomas D B b 116 9.50 71–21 Quick Cosmic 1151½ Tom Smoot 116no HaveTheProof116nk Tired 12
18Oct86-11Med fst 1 1/16 :47⅗ 1:13⅗ 1:46⅗ 3+ [S]Clm 6000 6 1 13 1½ 65½ 815¾ Thomas D B b 113 21.90 54–15 Attaire D'or 1103 Made In Jersey 1054½ Varyking 1174½ Tired 12

48. Examine the records and odds and decide how to play the race. It's Apr. 3.

9th Santa Anita

OUT OF CHUTE ▸
6½ FURLONGS
SANTA ANITA
• FINISH

6 ½ FURLONGS. (1.14) CLAIMING. Purse $31,000. 4-year-olds and upward. Weight, 121 lbs. Non-winners of two races since December 25 allowed 3 lbs.; of a race since then 5 lbs. Claiming price $62,500; for each $2,500 to $55,000 allowed 1 lb. (Races when entered for $50,000 or less not considered.)

10–1

Jetting Home

B. c. 4, by Tri Jet—Mariways, by Maribeau
STEVENS G L 116
Br.—Hooper F W (Fla) 1987 1 0 0 0 $775
Tr.—Richardson Thomas F $62,500 1986 9 2 1 1 $81,250
Own.—Ferguson Mrs J K Lifetime 20 4 4 2 $118,200 Turf 1 0 0 0

19Mar87-7SA 6½f :22 :45 1:161ft 50 1115 73¼ 64½ 56 57 Gryder A T 2 62500 82-21 J.R.Johnson,MyFvortMmnt,QpStr 10
15Aug86-8Dmr 7f :221 :443 1:213ft 32 116 78½ 73¼ 77 69½ McHrgueDG 2 Aw30000 87-12 SouthrnHlo,UltmtPlsur,FlyngNuggt 7
15Aug86—Bumped start
26May86-5Hol 1 :431 1:084 1:354ft 7 115 611 67½ 67½ 53¾ Stevens G L 6 Mehmet 80-17 Tourismo,Arewehvingfunyet,Bolton 6
11May86-7Hol 1$\frac{1}{16}$ ⓣ:4621:1021:414fm 10 116 54¼ 62¼ 114¾ 118½ McHargue D G 8 Sptlt 86-06 Mazaad,Autobot,RomanMgestrite 12
26Apr86-7Hol 7f :222 :453 1:24 ft 4¼ 119 78 75¼ 52¼ 2½ McHargueDG 4 Debonr 83-18 Bolton, JettingHome,SovereignDon 7
6Apr86-5SA 1⅛ :471 1:11 1:483ft 54 122 79½ 712 712 714¼ McHrDG 4 S A Dby 72-15 Snow Chief, Icy Groom, Ferdinand 7
6Apr86—Grade I
12Mar86-8SA 6½f :214 :451 1:172sy 3 116 59½ 57¼ 1hd 13¼ McHrgueDG 1 Baldwin 83-25 JettingHome,RoylTresure,ElCorzon 6
22Feb86-8SA 1 :453 1:102 1:352ft 68 116 55 52½ 44 37 McHrDG4 Sn Rafael 83-16 VarietyRoad,Ferdinnd,JettingHome 9
22Feb86—Grade II; Crowded at 1/4
2Feb86-6SA 1 :49 1:141 1:401m 8½ 118 62¾ 11 12 11 Stevens G L 6 Aw26000 67-28 Jetting Home, Scrapbook,CityView 7
2Feb86—Wide 7/8 turn; bumped 5/8
9Jan86-5SA 6f :213 :442 1:092ft 3 115 913 88½ 79¾ 56¼ Stevens G L 2 Aw24000 85-20 KeenKnight,AnotherBloom,PrssOn 9
Mar 28 SA 4f ft :492 h Mar 11 SA 5f ft 1:003 h Mar 1 SA 5f ft 1:012 h Feb 23 SA 5f ft 1:004 h

5–1

Rising Chum

B. h. 5, by Rising Market—Misty Cachuma, by Montparnasse II
DELAHOUSSAYE E 121
Br.—Westerly Stud Farms (Cal) 1987 4 2 0 0 $35,250
Tr.—Winick Randy $62,500 1986 13 3 5 2 $81,800
Own.—Asadurian–Asadurian–Winick Lifetime 35 10 6 3 $192,880 Turf 11 2 2 1 $53,100

26Feb87-7SA 7f :223 :444 1:231ft *8-5 121 1hd 3nk 3nk 66¾ Pincay L Jr 5 c62500 77-22 J.R.Johnson,GreyGauntlet,AlbertoII 8
26Feb87—Stumbled start
15Feb87-5SA 6½f :214 :444 1:162m *2-5 117 1½ 12 13½ 11½ Pincay L Jr 5 70000 88-17 Rising Chum, GreyGauntlet,Pokare 7
1Feb87-5SA a6½f ⓣ:213 :4421:152fm *8-5 119 3nk 2hd 1hd 43¼ Stevens G L 4 80000 79-16 PrncPcdllo,Amnothrbrothr,PlyTst 10
7Jan87-5SA 6½f :22 :444 1:163m *6-5 117 1hd 12½ 15 16½ Pincay L Jr 6 75000 87-21 RisingChum,AutoCommander,Strw 6
7Dec86-3Hol 1 :453 1:10 1:354gd *1 122 11½ 11½ 1½ 2½ Pincay L Jr 2 62500 83-18 Olajuwon, RisingChum,OnoGummo 6
27Nov86-9Hol 1$\frac{1}{16}$ ⓣ:46 1:0931:404fm *2½ 119 11 11 1hd 1½ Pincay L Jr 5 62500 90-06 RsngChm,AtoCommndr,Hrdknockn 7
27Nov86—Brushed stretch
16Nov86-9Hol 1$\frac{1}{16}$ ⓣ:4631:1031:402fm 3 116 1½ 1hd 32 54¼ Stevens G L 7 80000 88-07 Steepbank, Jack Tar, Snowcreek 7
6Nov86-8Hol 6f :213 :443 1:093ft 3½ 117 32½ 45½ 43½ 34 Stevens G L 4 80000 91-17 QuipStr,MuchFineGold,RisingChum 5
24Oct86-7SA 1$\frac{1}{16}$:46 1:104 1:43 ft 3 115 12 11 12½ 1hd Stevens G L 8 c62500 86-20 Rising Chum,Olajuwon,DarkAccent 8
24Oct86—Stumbled start
30Jly86-7Dmr 7f :214 :442 1:214ft 9 116 45 54¾ 88¼ 89¾ Stevens G L 5 Aw24000 86-11 UltimtePlesure,MneMgic,IdelQulity 8
Apr 1 SA 4f ft :473 h Mar 26 SA 5f ft 1:001 h Mar 17 SA 5f ft :592 h Mar 11 SA 4f ft :481 h

3–1

My Favorite Moment

B. h. 6, by Timeless Moment—My Masindi, by Dragante
VALENZUELA P A 116
Br.—Dinnaken Farm (Ky) 1987 5 0 1 1 $12,275
Tr.—Stute Warren $62,500 1986 4 1 1 1 $31,750
Own.—Connors W L Lifetime 26 8 3 6 $189,915 Turf 2 0 0 0

19Mar87-7SA 6½f :22 :45 1:161ft 3½ 116 1hd 2hd 1hd 22 DelahoussyeE10 62500 87-21 J.R.Johnson,MyFvortMmnt,QpStr 10
19Mar87—Bumped start
13Mar87-5SA a6½f ⓣ:22 :4421:16 fm 4¾ 117 1½ 2hd 51¾ 86¾ Castanon A L2 80000 72-21 Amnothrbrothr,AvitorII,Hydrosttc 10
13Mar87—Bumped, took up 1/8
22Feb87-7SA 6½f :213 :442 1:152ft 21 119 54 42 44 56 Castanon AL8 Aw45000 87-14 GrandAllegiance,Shahmk,TripleSec 8
22Feb87—Fanned wide 3/8
21Jan87-3SA 7f :221 :45 1:232ft 2¾ 116 1hd 1hd 2½ 31¾ Valenzuela P A1 90000 81-19 Emprdor,Mtronomc,MyFvortMmnt 6
21Jan87—Lugged out, bumped at intervals in stretch
9Jan87-8SA 6½f :211 :443 1:18 sl 5¾ 118 36 56½ 710 615½ ValenzuelPA4 Aw45000 64-26 Innmorto,ProudestHour,GminiDrmr 8
9Jan87—Wide into stretch
21Dec86-5Hol 6f :221 :452 1:103ft *1 116 31½ 31½ 31½ 1nk ValenzuelPA2 Aw35000 90-15 MFvrtMmnt,McLndn,AmrcnStndrd 6
21Jun86-5Hol 6f :214 :45 1:092ft 2¼ 116 43 41½ 2½ 21½ DelahoussyeE6 100000 95-09 AmrcnLgn,MyFvrtMmnt,MGllntGm 7
21Jun86—Lost whip start
8Jun86-5Hol 6f :22 :45 1:083ft 3¾ 117 44½ 45½ 37½ 38 DelhoussyeE2 Aw35000 93-11 CsForPs,RgnngCntss,MyFvrtMmnt 6
11Jan86-8SA 7f :214 :434 1:204ft 29 116 66½ 611 616 513 ‡ DlhossyE6 Sn Crls H 83-11 PhonTrick,TmrityPrinc,MyHbitony 6
11Jan86—Grade II; ‡Dead heat
Mar 31 SA 5f ft 1:013 h Mar 26 SA 5f ft 1:022 h Mar 18 SA 3f ft :362 h Mar 12 SA 3f ft :36 h

6–1

```
Quip Star                              B. g. 5, by Quip—Tenino Queen, by Saltville
                                       Br.—Isaacs N (Cal)                       1987  4  0  0  1        $7,200
  PEDROZA M A                 116      Tr.—Lewis Craig A            $62,500     1986 11  3  0  2       $61,100
Own.—Royal T Stable                    Lifetime   28  8  0  5  $121,400         Turf  6  0  0  2       $11,550
19Mar87-7SA   6½f :22  :45  1:161ft   7½ 1115  52½ 42  43  35    Patton D B4    62500 84-21 J.R.Johnson,MyFvortMmnt,QpStr 10
27Feb87-8SA  a6½f Ⓣ:213 :44 1:152fm  26 117   31½ 33½ 811 88¾   Meza R Q8    Aw35000 73-18 LeBelvedere,‡Mr.Media,HardRound 9
29Jan87-8SA  a6½f Ⓣ:212 :44 1:15 fm  10 115   54½ 32  45  45¼   Stevens G L4 Aw34000 79-16 PrincBobbyB.,Mr.Mdi,ThlssnoAstr 10
     29Jan87—Checked, altered course sharply 1/4
16Jan87-7SA   6½f :214 :443 1:162ft   6½ 117   42½ 42½ 67½ 610   Pedroza MA4  Aw33000 78-18 GrandAllegiance,Zabalet,PisnoPete 7
     16Jan87—Lugged out
26Dec86-5SA  a6½f Ⓣ:212 :4411:151fm  8½ 122   64  65  53¾ 52½   Ortega L E5    80000 80-17 Estate, Champion Pilot, Shanaar 12
27Nov86-8Hol  1   :46  1:101 1:35 ft  14 113   1hd 3½  44  410½  PdrMA2 ⓈOn Trust H 78-18 SuperDiamond,Nostalgia'sStr,Bozin 5
     27Nov86—Lugged out late
6Nov86-8Hol   6f  :213 :443 1:093ft   6¾ 117   45  22  11  13½   Pedroza M A3   75000 95-17 QuipStr,MuchFineGold,RisingChum 5
     6Nov86—Lugged out late
18Oct86-7SA   6f  :22  :444 1:092ft   3½ 115   2½  1hd 12  13½   Pedroza MA6  Aw28000 91-20 Quip Star, High Touch, High Hook 8
     18Oct86—Lugged out
8Oct86-3SA    6½f :214 :443 1:16 ft    5 116   52½ 42½ 42½ 33    Pedroza M A6   50000 87-20 Oricao, Teddy Naturally, QuipStar 10
     8Oct86—Pinched start
16Sep86-11Pom 6f  :214 :442 1:092ft   6½ 114   74½ 711 69¼ 65¼   Pedroza MA4 Aprisa H 99-05 BundlOfIron,Mtronomc,ProdstHor 10
     16Sep86—Steadied 7/8
 ●Apr 1 SA 3f ft :342 h        ●Mar 17 SA 4f ft :463 h        Feb 19 SA 4f ft :482 h
```

6–1

```
*Pokare                                Dk. b. or br. g. 6, by Claudio Nicolai—Royal Bird, by King Canary
                                       Br.—Brosnahan G W & Mrs L M (NZ)         1987  4  0  0  1        $6,900
  SHOEMAKER W                 116      Tr.—Longden John E           $62,500     1986 16  3  3  3       $22,336
Own.—Longden J E                       Lifetime   51  9  9  8  $45,963          Turf 49  9  9  7       $41,463
20Mar87-8SA   1 1/16:463 1:103 1:414ft  22 116   61¾ 65¾ 79½ 715   Olivares F4  Aw35000 77-17 JudgeAngelucci,Centenary,October 7
     20Mar87—Crowded start; Wide
8Mar87-5SA   a6½f Ⓣ:211 :4411:153gd    8 117   65½ 66½ 46½ 44¾   Olivares F5  Aw32000 76-26 RivrMist,Intuitvnss,TommyThHwk 10
1Mar87-5SA   a6½f Ⓣ:212 :4421:152fm   8½ 114  107½ 106¾ 66  64¼   Olivares F2    85000 78-18 ChmponPlot,ThlssnoAstr,PnstrpII 11
15Feb87-5SA   6½f :214 :444 1:162m    10 120   56½ 35  23½ 32¾   Olivares F1    80000 85-17 Rising Chum, GreyGauntlet,Pokare 7
22Dec86♦6Southland(NZ) a7f  1:224fm  — 123    Ⓣ 31¼        MtthsT         D B Draught H Reutemann, Connie Lawn, Pokare 10
12Dec86♦9Riccarton(NZ) a6f  1:084fm  — 117    Ⓣ 11½        MtthewsT            Flying H Pokare, CallItQuits,KnightInvader 14
15Nov86♦9Riccarton(NZ) a6f  1:082fm  — 115    Ⓣ 6          MtthsT        Mvmts Stwrts H Orangede,Brenline,CnterburyBelle 18
8Nov86♦8Riccarton(NZ)  a5f   :562fm  — 116    Ⓣ 32½        MtthewsT            Prntpk H Courier Bay, Orangeade, Pokare 15
27Oct86♦9Rangiora(NZ)  a6f  1:104fm  — 119    Ⓣ 2½         MtthsT         Ashly Meats H Dainty Dish, Pokare, Zaheer 13
4Oct86♦9Riccarton(NZ)  a6f  1:122sf  — 121    Ⓣ 5          MtthewsT          Knt Prier H BlckArrow,AegnPrincss,DintyDish 10
 Mar 28 SA 5f ft 1:021 h     ●Mar 18 SA 3f ft :351 h     Feb 28 SA 3f ft :351 h     ●Feb 23 SA HC 5f gd :58 h (d)
```

6–5

```
Cracksman                              Gr. g. 5, by Agitate—Crackl'n Rose, by Traveling Dust
                                       Br.—Jimenez J (Cal)                      1987  3  2  0  1       $30,950
  PINCAY L JR                 116      Tr.—Heaton Bill              $62,500     1986  9  2  0  2       $31,950
Own.—North Ranch Stables               Lifetime   26  8  1  3  $120,175         Turf  3  0  0  1        $5,250
14Mar87-4SA   6½f :214 :442 1:153ft  *8-5 118   42½ 2hd 1hd 11¾   Pincay L Jr2  c40000 92-16 Crcksmn,SuperbMoment,WstBoyII 8
21Feb87-2SA   6f  :214 :444 1:094ft   2¼ 117   42  31  2hd 11    Pincay L Jr5   40000 89-14 Crcksmn,LuckyMsddo,ElPrsdntUno 9
1Feb87-2SA    6½f :213 :441 1:163ft   5¾ 121   52¾ 33  33  3½    Stevens G L10  40000 86-16 Romaxe,LuckyMasadado,Crcksmn 12
24Dec86-7Hol  6f  :22  :452 1:11 ft  *6-5 119   32  32½ 53½ 73¾   Pincay L Jr2   50000 84-20 MsterCrofter,Dnczon,RingOfPlsur 10
     24Dec86—Unwilling to load; lugged in stretch
3Dec86-4Hol   6f  :22  :45  1:094ft   2¼ 117   44½ 43½ 45  33¾   Stevens G L5   80000 90-18 Faro, Debonaire Junior, Cracksman 6
22Nov86-7Hol  7f  :22  :451 1:222ft  *2¾ 116   22½ 21½ 11  11½   Vergara O5     50000 92-13 Cracksman, Juntura, Infantryman 8
     22Nov86—Lugged in late
15Nov86-3Hol  6f  :221 :452 1:10 ft    3 117   1hd 11  11½ 11½   Pincay L Jr1   40000 93-14 Cracksman,RollANturl,PtriotGloves 6
30Jly86-9Dmr  6½f :212 :432 1:144ft   6¾ 116   714 815 816 613½  DelahoussayeE1 50000 84-11 Doria's Delight, Mr. Media,AirAlert 8
     30Jly86—Whipped head at start
18Jly86-7Hol  7f  :223 :46  1:231ft  *7-5 117   66½ 66  56½ 68¼   Stevens G L1   62500 80-14 Savio, Poley, Mischiefinmind 7
     18Jly86—Hopped in air
21Jun86-5Hol  6f  :214 :45  1:092ft   10 116   66½ 76¾ 53½ 55¾   Stevens G L5  100000 91-09 AmrcnLgn,MyFvrtMmnt,MGllntGm 7
     21Jun86—Wide 3/8 turn
 Apr 2 SA 3f ft :352 h      Mar 26 SA 5f ft 1:001 h      Mar 12 Hol 3f ft :37 h      Mar 8 Hol 4f ft :471 h
```

A. Bet *My Favorite Moment* to win

B. Box *Cracksman* and *My Favorite Moment* in fair-payoff exactas

C. Bet *Rising Chum* to win
D. Eliminate *Cracksman* and key *My Favorite Moment* to the others

49. Which statement best informs the decision handicappers might make about this New York 7-furlong sprint?

1 BELMONT

7 FURLONGS. (1.20⅖) CLAIMING. Purse $14,000. Fillies. 3-year-olds. Non-winners of two races since July 1 3 lbs. Of a race since then 5 lbs. Claiming price $17,500 for each $1,000 to $15,500, 2 lbs. Races when entered to be claimed for $14,000 or less not considered.)

7–1

Smokiemountaingold — Dk. b. or br. f. 3, by New Prospect—Smokie Bluffer, by Big Bluffer — $17,500 — Br.—O'Quinn Clayton (Fla) — Tr.—Myer Patrick — 116
Own.—Charstel Stable
Lifetime 8 1 1 0 $11,520 — 1987 8 1 1 0 $11,520 — 1986 0 M 0 0

25Jun87- 9Bel	fst	7f	:23	:47	1:27⅗	ⒻClm 32500	6	2	1½	2hd	1118	1121¾	Graell A	116	23.70	42-25	Red's Bernice 116¾ Tokyo Stutz 112no Protiva 1161	Tired badly 11
15Jun87- 9Bel	fst	7f	:23	:46⅘	1:26⅕	ⒻClm c-25000	4	4	22	21	3½	66½	Cordero A Jr	118	14.40	64-19	TokyoStutz116hdSunny'sDiplomt1162KristhWitch111hd	Weakened 12
4Jun87- 2Bel	sly	6f	:22⅖	:47	1:13⅕	3↑ⒻMd 35000	1	1	12	12½	11½	1no	Cordero A Jr	116	3.70	74-21	Smokiemountingold116noNtivePerformr1143¾Bshkir1055¼	Lasted 8
25May87- 3Bel	fst	6f	:22⅖	:46⅕	1:11⅘	3↑ⒻMd Sp Wt	9	3	43	54	55¼	56¾	Garcia J A	113	27.70	74-16	Toujours Vitesse 1132¼Colombina113¾SunshineAlways1083¾	Tired 10
3May87- 9Aqu	fst	6f	:23⅕	:48	1:14	3↑ⒻMd 35000	1	7	2hd	82¾	89½	818¾	Guerra W A	b 113	*2.60	52-21	GoldenTruckle108¾AllCurrent1133BrshBerndette113½	Brief speed 8
10Apr87- 4Aqu	fst	7f	:23⅕	:46⅖	1:26	3↑ⒻMd 50000	3	5	11	1hd	33	49¾	Santos J A	112	*.70	61-24	Fire Island Dancer 1152 Protiva 1125¾BrightAsAButton1242	Tired 8
1Apr87- 2Aqu	fst	7f	:23⅕	:46⅗	1:25⅕	3↑ⒻMd 35000	10	2	2½	1½	1½	1no	Santos J A	113	3.00Ⓓ	75-18	ⒹSmokiemountingold113noVnillBen1144K.K.'sDrm1152¾	Bore out 13
1Apr87-Disqualified and placed second																		
17Mar87- 4Aqu	fst	6f	:23	:47⅗	1:14	ⒻMd 50000	4	14	41½	32	45½	46¾	Santos J A	121	8.60	64-31	PerCentAnni1122¼BoldRita1211½DiplomticEvening1173	Weakened 14

LATEST WORKOUTS Jly 29 Bel 3f fst :36⅘ b — Jly 23 Bel 5f fst 1:03⅘ b — Jly 16 Bel tr.t 4f fst :49⅗ b — ● Jun 11 Bel tr.t 4f fst :48 h

8–1

Caged — B. f. 3, by Tim the Tiger—Guest, by Sham — $16,500 — Br.—Greely III & Matthew & Tierney (Ky) — Tr.—Dunham Bob G — 114
Own.—Lippman R
Lifetime 18 1 1 0 $13,120 — 1987 10 0 1 0 $7,060 — 1986 8 1 0 0 $6,060

6Jly87- 2Bel	fst	1	:46	1:11⅗	1:40	ⒻClm 15500	7	4	56½	49	49½	410½	Venezia M	b 112	3.80	54-22	Sunny'sDiplomt116noLuckyMrion1124¾YourReflction1165¾	Evenly 8
20Jun87- 9Bel	fst	6f	:22⅗	:47	1:13⅖	ⒻClm 17500	3	6	64	87¾	67	45½	Thibeau R J	b 116	5.90	67-16	Fancy View 1161½ Bird Key 1094 Cheryl's Jig 116no	Wide 8
30May87- 1Bel	fst	6f	:23	:46⅗	1:11⅖	ⒻClm 22500	4	3	3½	55½	66	58¼	Venezia M	b 114	15.20	75-19	Gambler 1161¼ Twenty Degree Bank 1143¼ Sea Escape1091¾	Tired 7
16May87- 4Bel	fst	6f	:23	:47⅕	1:12⅗	ⒻClm 25000	3	5	42	61	64	65	Venezia M	b 116	20.60	72-18	GoldenTruckle1132¼Ensign'sLdy114nkLondonPss1161½	Early foot 10
30Apr87- 5Aqu	fst	6f	:22⅗	:46⅗	1:11⅗	ⒻClm 30000	7	5	73¾	86	814	820	Graell A	b 112	11.10e	63-28	LittleCrisCross1072GiveMeLibrty1141SomKindGood1161¾	Outrun 8
12Mar87- 5Aqu	fst	1⅛	:48⅗	1:14⅗	1:55	ⒻClm 25000	3	2	31½	57	716	822	Venezia M	116	5.90	38-30	Bless Princess 1131 Sunny'sDiplomat1168½AlohaHarriet1161	Tired 9
26Feb87- 3Aqu	fst	6f	⊡:22⅘	:47	1:13⅕	ⒻClm 32500	10	1	75¼	1113	1117	1120	Venezia M	114	11.80	58-23	StelleFilanti110½PrettyScreen1144SomeKindGood1163	Slow start 11
5Feb87- 1Aqu	fst	1 1/16	⊡:48⅗	1:15⅗	1:49⅘	ⒻClm 25000	2	1	11	1½	1hd	2hd	Venezia M	116	4.80	61-24	Perfect From Afar 116hd Caged 116¾ PrettyScreen1091	Sharp try 7
10Jan87- 2Aqu	gd	6f	⊡:23	:46⅕	1:12⅘	ⒻClm 25000	2	6	53½	712	712	811¼	Venezia M	116	5.00	69-10	Speedy Holly 116½ Princess Jig 1165½ AppleDanish1111	No factor 9
1Jan87- 1Aqu	fst	1 1/16	⊡:49	1:15⅘	1:50	ⒻClm 22500	8	4	2hd	1hd	3½	43	Venezia M	114	7.00	57-22	RocketGire1162FncysSwetTrt114¾PrfctFromAfr116nk	Carried out 8

LATEST WORKOUTS ● Jly 16 Aqu 4f fst :47⅖ h — Jun 30 Aqu 3f fst :38⅗ b — ● Jun 9 Aqu 4f fst :48⅘ h

5–2

Fancy View — Ch. f. 3, by Northern View—Linda's Nativeprim, by Native Royalty — $17,500 — Br.—Alchemy & Layman Betty (Ky) — Tr.—Vetter Robert C — 116
Own.—Briar Patch Farm
Lifetime 14 2 0 0 $13,530 — 1987 7 1 0 0 $9,510 — 1986 7 1 0 0 $4,020

20Jly87- 9Bel	my	7f	:23⅕	:46	1:23⅗	ⒻClm 25000	9	12	84¼	55¾	814	1021¾	Doran K	b 116	14.60	62-15	Gentle World1166CountYourSins1163RidgeRoute1142½	Slow start 12
20Jun87- 9Bel	fst	6f	:22⅗	:47	1:13⅖	ⒻClm 17500	5	8	87½	65¼	1hd	11½	Doran K	b 116	9.10	73-16	Fancy View 1161½ Bird Key 1094 Cheryl's Jig 116no	Driving 8
15Jun87- 9Bel	fst	7f	:23	:46⅘	1:26⅕	ⒻClm 20000	8	11	107¾	98¾	53½	53	Doran K	b 112	40.80	68-19	Tokyo Stutz 116hd Sunny'sDiplomat1162KristheWitch111hd	Hung 12
13May87- 2Bel	fst	1 1/16	:47⅗	1:12	1:44⅘	ⒻClm 30000	4	4	53	53	712	713	Cruguet J	112	25.40	65-18	Sunny'sDiplomt1083½PrettyScreen112hdApplDnish1162¾	Dwelt st. 10
30Apr87- 5Aqu	fst	6f	:22⅗	:46⅗	1:11⅗	ⒻClm 35000	8	7	53½	64	58½	611	Cruguet J	116	7.10	72-28	LittleCrisCross1072GiveMeLibrty1141SomKindGood1161¾	Outrun 8
27Mar87- 1Aqu	fst	6f	:22⅗	:46⅘	1:12⅖	ⒻClm 25000	5	13	1313	118	72¾	45	Santos J A	116	29.10	74-21	Raise a Beat 1112 Sea Escape 1112½ Tune Out 114½	Dwelt st. 13
13Jan87- 5Hia	fst	7f	:23	:46⅗	1:26	ⒻClm 18000	7	7	77¾	44½	47	716¼	Espinoza J C	112	8.50	57-22	I'm Audacious 111¾ Cheryl's Jig 1155 Sunny Nany 1194½	Tired 12
25Dec86- 1Crc	fst	7f	:23⅕	:48	1:28⅕	ⒻMd 15000	11	3	64½	42	2hd	15	Molina V H	120	*1.90	75-20	Fancy View 1205 Eskimo Dancer1204DressingTime120nk	Drew off 11
19Nov86- 6Crc	fst	7f	:22⅘	:47	1:27⅖	ⒻMd 30000	3	9	51¾	32½	43½	54½	Molina V H	119	10.30	74-18	LolliLuckLolli117nkHonstLght1193½BurnngSwftly119no	Weakened 10
2Nov86- 1Crc	fst	6f	:22⅕	:46⅘	1:13⅖	ⒻMd 35000	6	9	85¼	44½	32½	58½	Molina V H	116	9.10	75-13	TokiTae1132½SmartOcalFlyer1201ThimblefulofJoy1203	Weakened 9

25–1

Briarcliff — Ch. f. 3, by Bold L B—Sweet Kakki Briar, by Etonian — $15,500 — Br.—Jones Brereton C (KY) — Tr.—Sedlacek Sue — 1057
Own.—Sedlacek Sue
Lifetime 10 0 0 0 $1,320 — 1987 5 M 0 0 — 1986 5 M 0 0 $1,320 — Turf 2 0 0 0

24Jly87- 9Bel	fst	1	:45⅘	1:11⅘	1:40⅕	ⒻClm 15500	7	4	57	811	916	918½	Munoz O R7	b 105	58.00	45-26	Lucky Marion 1121¾ Classy Circle1162½ShareTheWine116¾	Outrun 12
6Jly87- 2Bel	fst	1	:46	1:11⅗	1:40	ⒻClm 15500	3	5	32½	59½	616	619	Garcia J7	b 106	22.90	46-22	Sunny'sDplomt116noLuckyMron1124¾YorRflcton1165¾	Weakened 8
20Jun87- 4Bel	fm	1 1/16	Ⓣ:48⅘	1:12⅗	1:43⅖	ⒻClm 75000	1	3	22	24	718	728½	Samyn J L	b 111	40.80	55-17	Miss Unnameable 1134 Jamara 1113½ Magical 113½	Stopped 7
13Jun87- 2Bel	fm	1⅜	Ⓣ:50	1:40⅗	2:18⅘	ⒻClm 35000	5	4	43	21½	79	714¼	Samyn J L	b 116	29.40	49-24	Perfect From Afar 1161 NewIssueII1162SixthInBed116¾	Fell back 8
28May87- 2Bel	fst	1	:46⅗	1:13⅖	1:41	3↑ⒻMd 30000	10	4	97½	1224	1332	1333¼	Santos J A	b 113	16.40	27-25	Ten Cents A Ride 111½ No No's Sun 1047 Raisin Berry113nk	Tired 14
18Aug86- 6Sar	fst	6f	:22⅖	:46⅖	1:12⅘	ⒻMd Sp Wt	7	5	75	912	916	1022½	Lopez V	b 117	23.40f	53-21	Vicious Queen 1176 Awesome Suzy 1171 Poculation 117nk	Outrun 10
28Jly86- 3Bel	my	5½f	:22⅖	:46⅕	1:05⅗	ⒻMd 45000	4	2	56	56½	79¾	79¾	Lopez V	b 113	17.50	77-14	Victoria Peak 1172¾AftonCooper1131½MostestHostess1131¼	Tired 10
10Jly86- 4Bel	fst	5½f	:23⅕	:46⅘	1:06⅖	ⒻMd 50000	5	5	76	77½	812	813¾	Lopez V	117	7.70	69-23	Evil Elaine 117½ Victoria Peak 1032¾ Reflective Gal 115½	Outrun 9
28Jun86- 6Bel	fst	5½f	:22⅘	:46	1:04⅘	ⒻMd Sp Wt	1	5	710	714	925	929¾	Lopez V	117	5.30e	61-15	NaturalEight1177½SeaBasque1175¼BestofStrangers1172	Fell back 9
25May86- 4Bel	fst	5f	:22	:45⅖	:58⅗	ⒻMd Sp Wt	2	4	67	55½	66	44¼	Lopez V	117	11.40e	90-12	Swingin Nickel 1171½NativePerformer1172JokeBoat117¾	Late bid 8

LATEST WORKOUTS Jun 11 Aqu Ⓣ 3f fm :37⅗ h (d)

5–1

Bird Key B. f. 3, by Jet Diplomacy—Star Island, by Star Envoy
Own.—Lizza Karen $17,500 Br.—Lizza Mrs C (NY) Tr.—O'Connell Richard 1115
Lifetime 16 1 4 4 $25.052 1987 11 0 3 3 $17,520 1986 5 1 1 1 $7,532
20Jly87- 9Bel my 7f :23⅕ :46 1:23⅗ ⒻClm 20000 8 2 74¼ 77¾ 410 612¾ Belmonte J F5 b 107 5.40 71-15 Gentle World 1166 Count Your Sins 1163RidgeRoute1142½ Outrun 12
3Jly87- 9Bel gd 6f :23⅕ :46⅘ 1:12⅕ ⒻClm 20000 1 2 11 2hd 2½ 22¼ Belmonte J F5 b 107 4.10 77-21 London Pass 1162¼ Bird Key 1075 Raisin Berry 116no Held place 9
20Jun87- 9Bel fst 6f :22⅗ :47 1:13⅖ ⒻClm 16500 6 5 52½ 34½ 2hd 21½ Nuesch D5 b 109 3.40 71-16 Fancy View 1161½ Bird Key 1094 Cheryl's Jig 116no Rallied 8
9May87- 1Bel fst 6f :23⅕ :48 1:14⅗ ⒻClm 17500 5 5 54 43½ 32¼ 33 Bailey J D b 116 8.60 64-29 Dame Lisa 1181¼ Twenty Degree Bank 1131¾BirdKey116no Rallied 8
29Apr87- 3Aqu my 6½f :22⅗ :45⅖ 1:18⅗ ⒻClm 17500 6 1 64¾ 55 55 36¼ Lovato F Jr b 116 13.70 76-21 Twenty Degree Bank 1163 Cambler 1163¼ Bird Key 116½ Wide 7
27Mar87- 1Aqu fst 6f :22⅗ :46⅘ 1:12⅖ ⒻClm 25000 4 12 52½ 31 2½ 98½ Lovato F Jr b 116 9.60 70-21 Raise a Beat 1112 Sea Escape 1112½ Tune Out 114½ Stopped 13
14Mar87- 7Aqu fst 6f :22⅖ :46⅘ 1:13⅕ Ⓕ[S]Alw 27000 5 11 108¼ 108½ 117 910¼ Lovato F Jr b 116 24.10 65-28 Peggy's Dream 1162¾ If At First 1112¾ Adanna Dear 111½ Outrun 14
2Mar87- 9Aqu gd 6f ⊡:22⅖ :45⅗ 1:11⅕ ⒻClm 25000 1 10 44 57½ 410 311 Lovato F Jr 116 5.40 77-15 Princess Jig 1164½ Classi Vogue 1116½ Bird Key 1162 Willingly 11
14Feb87- 9Aqu fst 6f ⊡:22⅖ :46⅖ 1:13⅖ ⒻClm 20000 12 1 32 43½ 34 24 Lovato F Jr 113 10.20 73-21 Stelle Filanti 1164 Bird Key 1133¾ Bashkir 111nd Steadied 12
8Feb87- 6Aqu fst 6f ⊡:22⅘ :46⅗ 1:13⅘ Ⓕ[S]Alw 27000 5 4 21 31 21 64 Nuesch D5 b 111 13.30 71-22 FoundaJewel116¾HalleyHallelujah116nk Ms.Jcques1161¾ Bid; tired 9
LATEST WORKOUTS Jly 18 Bel 4f fst :51 b Jun 30 Bel 4f fst :49⅗ b Jun 15 Bel 3f fst :36⅗ h Jun 6 Bel 4f fst :48⅖ h

4–1

Lucky Marion Dk. b. or br. f. 3, by Noble Table—Lucky Nan, by What Luck
Own.—Kleila Gladys T $17,500 Br.—Pribisco Patricia Marant (Fla) Tr.—Tufariello Frank 118
Lifetime 8 2 1 0 $23.140 1987 8 2 1 0 $23,140 1986 0 M 0 0 Turf 1 0 0 0
24Jly87- 9Bel fst 1 :45⅘ 1:11⅘ 1:40⅕ ⒻClm 15500 6 1 12 13 15 11¾ Badamo J J b 112 5.30 64-26 Lucky Marion 1121¾ ClassyCircle1162½ShareTheWine116¾ Driving 12
17Jly87- 4Mth fm 1 1/16 Ⓣ:48 1:12⅖ 1:44⅗ ⒻClm 22500 6 1 2hd 21 1013 1122½ Santagata N b 112 16.30 59-20 PlatinumDoll1141AlluringProspect1144½PaplQueen115nk Stopped 11
6Jly87- 2Bel fst 1 :46 1:11⅗ 1:40 ⒻClm 15500 6 1 11½ 1½ 1½ 2no Badamo J J b 112 5.80 65-22 Sunny'sDiplomt116noLuckyMrion1124¾YourRflction1165¾ Gamely 8
20Jun87- 9Bel fst 6f :22⅗ :47 1:13⅖ ⒻClm 17500 8 2 11 13 44 69¼ Badamo J J5 b 111 *2.40 64-16 Fancy View 1161½ Bird Key 1094 Cheryl's Jig 116no Used up 8
22May87- 2Bel fst 6f :22⅖ :46⅕ 1:11⅘ ⒻClm 35000 2 10 45½ 66½ 815 814¼ Badamo J J5 b 111 6.40 67-20 Some Kinda Good116¾BoldRita1091MorningJo111hd Broke slowly 10
1May87- 5Aqu fst 6f :21⅘ :44⅘ 1:10 ⒻClm 70000 2 1 22½ 310 718 823 Badamo J J5 107 6.30 68-18 Raise a Beat 1076¾ Missile Magic 1112¼ Jessi Jessi 1144¼ Tired 8
8Apr87- 1Aqu my 1 :46⅗ 1:12⅕ 1:38⅘ ⒻAlw 27000 3 2 21½ 59½ 511 412½ Badamo J J5 111 5.10 59-22 Gentle Spirit 116no High Offer 1163½ Graceful Darby 1169 Tired 6
26Mar87- 2Aqu fst 7f :22⅖ :45⅘ 1:25⅗ ⒻMd 50000 9 5 31 1½ 13 17¼ Badamo J J5 116 4.70 73-25 Lucky Marion 1167¼ Bold Rita 1212½MatchMadeline1171½ Driving 11
LATEST WORKOUTS Jly 14 Bel tr.t 4f fst :48⅘ h ●Jun 14 Bel 5f fst 1:00⅘ hg Jun 9 Bel tr.t 4f fst :49⅖ b

A. *Fancy View* is best and a fair bet at 5–2
B. *Bird Key* is the obvious overlay
C. *Lucky Marion* is a good bet at the distance and odds
D. *Smokiemountaingold* can steal the race and represents the most attractive overlay in an otherwise regular race

50. In an open, contentious race, a handicapper finds six prospects.

Which can be bet at the odds?

1st Santa Anita

START
6 FURLONGS
SANTA ANITA

6 FURLONGS. (1.07⅗) CLAIMING. Purse $18,000. 4-year-olds and upward. Weights, 4-year-olds, 121 lbs.; older, 122 lbs. Non-winners of two races since November 3 allowed 3 lbs.; of a race since December 25, 5 lbs.; since November 3, 7 lbs. Claiming price $20,000; if for $18,000 allowed 2 lbs. (Races when entered for $16,000 or less not considered.)

A.
5–1

Blue Ice B. c. 4, by Icecapade—Blue Chip Lu, by Tudor Grey
ORTEGA L E 114 Br.—Fisher Susan B (Ky) 1987 1 0 0 0
Own.—Santopietro G Tr.—Dunn Larry $20,000 1986 11 2 5 1 $28,700
Lifetime 12 2 5 1 $28,700
24Jan87-2SA 6f :21³ :45 1:10³ft 6 113 52¼ 33½ 78½ 812¾ Ortega L E10 28000 72-18 SuperbMoment,Bizeboy,FletAlbrt 10
27Dec86-2SA 6½f :21⁴ :44⁴ 1:16⁴ft 3¼ 116 21½ 21 1½ 21¼ Ortega L E3 25000 85-14 Doonsport, BlueIce,ExaltedBubble 10
27Dec86—Broke slowly
17Dec86-8Hol 6f :22¹ :45⁴ 1:11¹ft 20 114 2hd 3½ 32½ 65¾ Ortega L E5 Aw22000 81-22 MschvosMtt,TommyThHwk,Notrty 8
8Nov86-4Hol 6f :22 :45³ 1:10⁴ft 3¼ 116 2½ 31 46 710¾ Ortega L E10 c25000 78-13 SprbMmnt,GrdnsCmmnd,FrrBlJns 11
29Oct86-3SA 6½f :21³ :44³ 1:16⁴ft 2¾ 118 1½ 12½ 13½ 13 Ortega L E7 c20000 86-17 Blue Ice, Gran Pierre, Dennis D. 9
29Oct86—Bumped start
16Oct86-5SA 6½f :21³ :44⁴ 1:17¹ft *9-5 118 1½ 1hd 2hd 21¾ Ortega L E5 c16000 82-19 Lans Manus, Blue Ice, BlackCross 11
16Oct86—Bobbled at start, lugged out

```
5Oct85-3SA    6f :212 :441 1:102ft    52 118   313 651 76  663   Ortega L E5    32000 79-15 SprbMomnt,HmngAngl,EghtyBlwZr 9
28Aug86-4Dmr  6f :213 :452 1:102ft   *1 117   212 1hd 14  13    Ortega L E10   M32000 86-18 BlueIce,MgicFiddle,MntlBnkRturn 12
13Aug86-2Dmr  6f :214 :452 1:104ft   *2 116   413 31  213 2no   Ortega L E5    M32000 84-15 Brand Image, Blue Ice, Shucinto  12
  13Aug86—Bumped, steadied start; lugged out
18Jly86-1Hol  6f :223 :454 1:104ft   9-5 114   13  2hd 213 213   Ortega L E5    M32000 87-14 Harper'sRidge,BlueIce,BrandImage 8
  18Jly86—Lugged out late
  Jan 17 SA 4f ft :50 h          Dec 10 SA 1ft 1:441 h
```

B.

5—2

Goldy's Commander

STEVENS G L   **115**

Own.—Katayama Nancy & Tracy

B. g. 7, by Bold Dun–Cee—Golden Cammae, by Tarleton Oak
Br.—Moreland R & W (Ind)
Tr.—Shulman Sanford $20,000
Lifetime 42 12 5 3 $117,575

| | 1986 | 4 | 2 | 0 | 1 | $24,250 |
| 1985 | 11 | 4 | 1 | 0 | $46,275 |

```
15May86-1Hol  6f :221 :454 1:101ft   *6-5 119   23  1hd 533 793   Valenzuela P A7  32000 83-13 Timlin, Reinbow's Cup, Ego Buck  7
  15May86—Lugged in stretch
27Apr86-5Hol  6f :223 :46  1:11 ft   *2 117   13  113 14  153   Valenzuela P A6  32000 89-15 Goldy'sCommndr,Don'sDstiny,LRcn 9
15Feb86-5SA   6f :214 :444 1:091ft    3 117   21  3hk 213 39    Solis A4        Aw26000 83-14 GoSwftly,CnnptnFt,Gldy'sCmmndr  8
18Jan86-2SA   61f :213 :44  1:152ft   9 116   113 123 12  13    Solis A4        32000 93-12 Goldy'sCommander,Chevo,Romxe  12
23Dec85-7Hol  6f :22  :452 1:104ft    3 117   1hd 1hd 1hd 1nk   Solis A6        25000 90-17 Goldy'sCommndr,Cprcsnss,KlmPnt  7
8Nov85-5SA    6f :214 :442 1:093ft    23 116   1hd 1hd 2hd 54    Valenzuela P A2  32000 86-13 Andrew'NMe,FiveNorth,Innmorto  10
  8Nov85—Bumped start
9Oct85-6SA    6f :212 :442 1:093ft    43 115   1hd 23  35  6113   Pedroza M A5   40000 78-17 Clbong,Commissionire,LuckyDutch 9
21Jly85-7Hol  6f :222 :46  1:10 ft   9-5 114   2hd 23  213 533   Stevens G L5   45000 93-04 LghngBoy,MgcMmo,LordOfThWnd  8
10Jly85-6Hol  6f :224 :46  1:102ft   *6-5 117   1hd 12  123 113   Stevens G L7   32000 95-07 Goldy'sCommnder,Juntur,DeltTrce  7
24Mar85-1SA   6f :214 :443 1:092ft    5 121   13  123 13  23    Valenzuela P A3  25000 90-12 NorTk,Goldy'sCommndr,IrishS'gtti 6
  Feb 1 SA 5f ft 1:022 h      Jan 24 SA 6f ft 1:01 h      Jan 16 SA 5f ft 1:013 h      Jan 9 Hol 5f ft 1:032 h
```

C.

7—1

Pineapple Jack

CASTANON A L   1—0   **114**

Own.—Gould & Meyers

Ch. g. 4, by Mister Jacket—Ms B's Doll, by Understanding
Br.—Purcell W (Wash)
Tr.—Stute Warren $20,000
Lifetime 16 2 4 3 $15,371

| | 1987 | 3 | 0 | 0 | 1 | $3,825 |
| 1986 | 13 | 2 | 4 | 2 | $11,546 |

```
21Jan87-5SA   6f :221 :451 1:163ft   10 115   643 531 56  443   Castanon A L1  20000 82-19 Doonsport, NativeCaptive,Grenoble 9
  21Jan87—Wide into stretch
10Jan87-2SA   61f :221 :452 1:181gd   35 115   53  33  22  32    Castanon A L1  20000 77-20 BoldTopsidr,Don'sCo'op,PnpplJck  12
  10Jan87—Broke in a tangle
1Jan87-9SA    1 :471 1:12 1:443ft    7 115   1010 993 911 9163   Stevens G L    c16000 62-19 RoosvltRod,ForgotThRng,Espontn 10
24Dec86-3Hol  7f :22  :452 1:24 ft    4 117   793 773 47  353   Pincay L Jr5   18000 79-20 Pilor,Gordon'sCommnd,PineppJck  7
  24Dec86—Wide backside
6Dec86-6Hol   7f :221 :452 1:242gd   19 116   69  69  563 24    Cordero A Jr5  16000 78-16 Noon Sun,PineappleJack,VideoSid 12
  6Dec86—Bumped start
30Nov86-2Hol  7f :222 :454 1:253ft    83 115   2hd 2hd 113 23    Stevens G L2   c10000 75-16 Gulfstremer,PineppleJck,UpThPol 12
22Nov86-6Hol  6f :223 :46  1:11 ft   39 116   893 893 673 563   Baze G4        16000 80-13 Manzanero, Pico P., Video Sid  9
  22Nov86—Broke slowly
29Oct86-3SA   61f :213 :443 1:164ft   19 114   973 912 812 613   Baze G6        18000 73-17 Blue Ice, Gran Pierre, Dennis D.  9
23Oct86-1SA   6f :22  :452 1:113ft    4 118   663 663 64  44    Baze G6        10000 76-20 CeeScoBoy,KarakaLad,Hai'TheEgle 7
  23Oct86—Wide into stretch
28Sep86-7Pla  61f :23  :473 1:122m    61 117   815 811 47  213   Freeman W4     HcpO 67-34 Hydro, Pineapple Jack, Abishai  9
  Feb 6 SA 3f ft :352 h      Jan 28 SA 4f ft :483 h      Jan 18 SA 5f ft 1:022 h
```

D.

39—1

Pialor

SOLIS A   5—N   **116**

Own.—Pignon–Pinner–Pinner

B. c. 4, by Zoot Alors—Pia Mater, by Pia Star
Br.—Dollase & Duffel (Cal)
Tr.—Velasquez Danny $20,000
Lifetime 16 3 2 2 $26,050

| | 1987 | 2 | 0 | 0 | 0 | |
| 1986 | 14 | 3 | 2 | 2 | $26,050 |

```
18Jan87-1SA   7f :221 :451 1:243ft   35 115   513 643 1216 12193   Meza R Q12   25000 57-19 Bizeboy, Trento, Superb Moment  12
  18Jan87—Lugged in badly
7Jan87-9SA    1 :472 1:12 1:38 m     73 118   213 44  814 —     Meza R Q8    25000 — — Danchai, Doonsport, ShowerDecree 9
  7Jan87—Eased; Bumped start, wide 7/8
24Dec86-3Hol  7f :22  :452 1:24 ft   *2 115   213 23  15  15    Castanon A L   c18000 84-20 Pilor,Gordon'sCommnd,PineppJck  7
11Dec86-7Hol  7f :222 :46  1:242ft   12 117   1hd 12  13  523   Castanon A L5  20000 80-21 Fall Flyer, Lord Pancho,ShuttleOne 8
3Dec86-7Hol   6f :221 :452 1:11 ft    3 119   313 313 31  333   Castanon AL4 [S] 20000 84-18 GrowlerSndue,ShowerDecree,Pilor 11
16Nov86-4Hol  7f :22  :443 1:241ft   79 117   413 43  113 22    Castanon A L3  20000 81-18 Pegus, Pialor, Amarone  12
  16Nov86—Lugged out late
```

9Nov86-5Hol 6f :22 :451 1:10 ft 46 117 3½ 44 5¾ 815 Ortega L E1 35000 78-16 Lans Manus, RosesAreReb,Sebucan 8
9Nov86—Broke out, bumped
18Oct86-7AC 6f :222 :442 1:09 ft 4¾ 1115 31 1hd 11½ 11 Delgadillo A2 Aw5000 94-13 Pialor, Quantus, Silver Ticket 9
11Oct86-6AC 6f :222 :45 1:094gd 9-5 114 2hd 21 33½ 36 Delgadillo BD6 Aw5000 84-19 Ramses, Leopold, Pialor 6
14Sep86-10Pom 6½f:213 :45 1:162ft 61 112 66¼ — — — Patterson A2 Aw25000 — — Tuono, Growler Sandue,BoldDecree 9
14Sep86—Pulled up; Lugged out, wide first turn
Jan 31 SA 5f ft 1:002 h Jan 15 SA 4f ft :483 h Jan 2 SA 4f ft :512 b

E.
14–1

El Presidente Uno — B. g. 5, by President—A Honey Belle, by Son Ange
MEZA R Q 117 — Br.—Rolling Meadows Farm (Ky) — 1986 11 1 3 0 $12,787
Own.—Samarzich L J & R — Tr.—Ellis Ronald W $20,000 — 1985 12 1 2 1 $39,855
Lifetime 29 4 6 3 $77,447 — Turf 4 0 0 1 $7,725

28Dec86-9AC 1 1/16 :104 1:352 1:43 ft *9-5 118 21 21 21 21 Lopez A D2 InvH 89-17 Somes Bar, ElPresidenteUno,Cesar 7
14Dec86-9AC 1 :463 1:11 1:37 gd 9-5 114 36½ 2½ 13 11½ Lopez A D4 Aw6000 88-22 El Presidente Uno,SomesBar,Cesar 9
6Dec86-5AC 6f :223 :45 1:102m *1-2 114 3nk 2hd 2hd 2nk Lopez A D3 Aw6000 87-20 InvrnssGol,ElPrsdntUno,MrshllTwn 6
23Nov86-11AC 6f :221 :442 1:09 ft 2¼ 114 1hd 2hd 11½ 21 Lopez A D9 Aw5000 93-12 TmToSmk,ElPrsdntUn,T.H Exprss 10
27Apr86-9AC 1⅛:461 1:103 1:494ft 3 115 2hd 1½ 94¾ 88½ LpzAD7 Ⓡ Rnd Tble H 83-14 Daz Me, T. V. Action, No Pity 12
30Mar86-9AC 1 1/16 :461 1:101 1:422ft *1 122 2½ 21 42 45 EnrHF2 Ⓡ Phar Lap H 88-12 Glance About, Daz Me, T. V. Action 8
20Mar86-8SA a6½f Ⓣ:213 :4421:154gd 32 116 62¾ 52½ 41¾ 53½ St Martin E1 Aw32000 76-20 PaintedCnyon,MyGlintGme,Oromo 12
26Feb86-5SA a6½f Ⓣ:214 :4431:154fm 21 115 2hd 1hd 1hd 44¾ St Martin E8 Aw31000 76-18 Swallage, Go Swiftly, Quality Jet 12
26Feb86—Bumped start
16Feb86-2SA 6½f :22 :444 1:162gd 6¾ 115 3½ 56 815 817¼ Stevens G L7 40000 71-14 GranBarba,Chevo,MrvinCoolbreeze 8
2Feb86-5SA 6½f :222 :46 1:183m 8½ 114 52½ 75¾ 810 713¼ Stevens G L2 75000 64-28 Bozina, Kilauea, Midford 9
Jan 31 SA 5f ft 1:012 h Jan 25 SA 5f ft 1:024 h Jan 19 SA 4f ft :51 h Dec 24 AC 4f gd :50 h

F.
10–1

Don't Fight It — Dk. b. or br. g. 5, by Always Gallant—Destiny's Twist, by Ambehaving
VALENZUELA P A 115 — Br.—Meadowbrook Farms Inc (Fla) — 1987 2 0 0 1 $2,770
Own.—La Croix D — Tr.—La Croix David $20,000 — 1986 14 1 2 2 $17,387
Lifetime 28 7 2 4 $78,278 — Turf 1 0 0 0

22Jan87-5SA 6f :213 :45 1:104ft 8¾ 116 42 31½ 33 44 Baze G8 20000 80-23 LuckyMsddo,Mjesty'sRod,OutCross 9
22Jan87—Wide into stretch
3Jan87-4BM 6f :23 :461 1:11 sy 9½ 115 52½ 42½ 42½ 35½ ‡Tohill K S8 25000 78-23 ThBrgnHntr,AckAck'sJoy,MYAndQ. 9
‡ 3Jan87—Dead heat
30Nov86-7BM 6f :22 :45 1:093ft 4 117 21 2hd 1hd 22 Maple S4 20000 89-14 TouchTim,Don'tFightIt,DtrmindFir 9
30Nov86—Bumped 3/8
15Nov86-6BM 6f :223 :452 1:102ft 5½ 115 87½ 66½ 65½ 74 Maple S5 35000 83-21 RlnchATn,OnLckyStrk,MctoComch 8
26Oct86-2BM 6f :223 :453 1:101ft 15 115 3½ 2hd 12 13 Maple S4 25000 88-20 Don'tFightIt,Andrew'NM,CordovRd 7
4Oct86-7BM 6f :222 :451 1:094ft 21 116 66 86½ 911 910 Maple S2 40000 80-16 Verboten,BuenJefe,RelaunchATune 9
21Sep86-9BM 6f :222 :452 1:093ft 32 115 54½ 53½ 31½ 32½ Maple S8 35000 88-18 BuenJefe,TheAysHvIt,Don'tFightIt 8
21Aug86-8Cby 7½f Ⓣ:234 :4721:302fm 32 1125 64½ 52 4¾ 64¾ Murray K C6 40000 — — Numchuek, Zeppy, Nickel Back 8
26Jly86-9Cby 6½f :223 :452 1:172ft 20 118 43 43½ 43½ 88½ Black K8 Aw13800 85-12 Empror'sCloths,CstlyTrck,ThRyIFrz 9
6Jly86-7Cby 1 :47 1:122 1:384ft 13 119 33 3½ 78 710¾ Black K3 Aw14300 76-15 Katzenjammer,Balaash,PatchofSun 7
Dec 28 BM 5f ft 1:011 h

51. Knowing how to interpret claiming-race eligibility conditions at small tracks can sometimes result in class bonanzas.

Find the best bet at the odds.

7th Fairmount

6 FURLONGS. (1.08⅗) CLAIMING. Purse $4,500. 3-year-olds and upward which have not won a race other than claiming or for a claiming price exceeding $4,000 since May 1, 1987. Weight, 3-year-olds, 115 lbs.; older, 122 lbs. Non-winners of a race since June 15 allowed 3 lbs.; a race since May 15, 6 lbs. Claiming price $5,000. (Races where entered for $3,500 or less not considered in allowances.)

A.

15–1

Cold Decision

Gr. g. 7, by It's Freezing—Fascination Jude, by Decidedly

	Br.—Bright View Farm (NJ)		1987 11 0 1 1	$3,530		
Own.—Baird John W	**116**	Tr.—Baird John W	$5,000	1986 22 4 7 1	$24,338	
		Lifetime 85 6 16 8 $70,291		Turf 3 0 0 0		

13Jly87-9FP	6f	:23^{3}	:47^{1}	1:12^{4}ft	15	116	5^{6}	6^{7}	$5^{5\frac34}$	6^{6}	Rettele J O 2	6500	73-25	Retrieved,CatchItBuck,PagnJubilee	8
26Jun87-9FP	6f	:22^{3}	:45^{4}	1:11^{2}ft	4½	116	$6^{4\frac34}$	6^{11}	4^{10}	4^{7}	Brinkley J A 6	c5000	79-23	Retrieved, Demi Moe,BredForGlory	9
20Jun87-8FP	6f	:22^{2}	:45^{3}	1:11^{2}ft	6¼	116	$5^{4\frac12}$	$5^{8\frac12}$	5^{7}	$5^{7\frac12}$	Brinkley J A9	6500	80-20	RydrRon,PgnJubil,B.J'sCountryBoy	9
5Jun87-9FP	$1\frac{1}{16}$	:47^{4}	1:12^{3}	1:46^{2}ft	11	113	$8^{7\frac12}$	9^{11}	9^{14}	$9^{18\frac14}$	Rettele J O 7	9500	61-23	Rev.Jack,BillyBrd,QuiteCompetitive	9
30May87-9FP	6f	:22^{2}	:45^{4}	1:13 ft	8½	116	$3^{3\frac12}$	$4^{6\frac12}$	$3^{4\frac12}$	$2^{\frac12}$	Brinkley J A 3	8500	77-27	StrkinSmrt,ColdDcision,Holdyourcs	9
18May87-3Spt	6f	:23^{3}	:48^{1}	1:14 sy	5	115	$6^{5\frac12}$	5^{5}	5^{6}	$7^{5\frac12}$	Stover D E 5	c6250	74-25	WhtGust,LittleVicTRe,ActsTooSssy	8
4May87-5Spt	6½f	:22^{4}	:47	1:20^{3}ft	10	115	$7^{6\frac12}$	$6^{4\frac34}$	4^{4}	$3^{\frac12}$	Stover D E 5	6250	73-26	CruzenDud,Jy'sMdow,ColdDcision	10
22Apr87-3Spt	6f	:24^{1}	:47^{4}	1:13^{4}sy	13	114	5^{4}	5^{7}	$6^{5\frac14}$	$5^{5\frac34}$	Clark K D 3	6250	75-29	AppringNightly,CruznDud,WhtGust	8

Jun 16 FP 3f ft :42 b

B.

8–1

Gold Krugerrand *

B. g. 5, by Search for Gold—Drafty Breeze, by Draft Card

	Br.—Freireich & Goodman&Odom (Cal)		1986 17 5 1 1	$13,877		
Own.—Wilgate Thoroughbreds	**116**	Tr.—Beghtol Wilbur C	$5,000	1985 19 3 2 1	$12,562	
		Lifetime 42 9 3 4 $29,364				

14Sep86-2LnN	4½f	:22^{2}		:52^{4}ft	3	117	6	6^{4}	6^{8}	$5^{3\frac12}$	Rashall R D5	2500	88-14	Stomp'N'Smsh,WisChrful,BrodUs	10
9Aug86-5Aks	6f	:22^{4}	:46^{3}	1:15^{1}sy	5	112^{5}	$7^{8\frac34}$	$7^{7\frac14}$	$3^{1\frac12}$	$3^{1\frac12}$	Brown T L3	5000	59-48	HldAllClls,PrncfFrdm,GldKrgrrnd	12
27Jly86-5Aks	6f	:22^{4}	:45^{4}	1:11^{4}ft	8	113^{5}	$4^{4\frac12}$	$6^{2\frac34}$	7^{5}	$7^{5\frac14}$	Brown T L11	5000	73-22	PrncofFrdom,FllSpdAhd,OrPlyboy	12
6Jly86-2Aks	6f	:22^{4}	:46^{1}	1:13^{3}m	6¾	117	$6^{4\frac12}$	$6^{4\frac14}$	$4^{2\frac12}$	1^{1}	Brown T L2	5000	69-36	GoldKrgrrnd,HldAllClls,MksHBddr	11
6Jly86—Drifted out stretch															
13Jun86-5Aks	6f	:21^{3}	:44^{2}	1:10 ft	40	114	3^{2}	$5^{3\frac12}$	11^{14}	$11^{16\frac34}$	Patterson G6	6250	70-16	Savesomegs,KnobbyNote,Truetoo	12
31May86-5Aks	6f	:23^{2}	:47^{1}	1:13^{2}gd	5¼	120	$2^{1\frac12}$	$5^{5\frac12}$	8^{14}	$8^{15\frac14}$	Steinberg PW 10	c5000	55-32	KnobbyNot,Dr.Hrbr,HowAbotTwlv	11
26May86-5Aks	6f	:22^{4}	:45^{4}	1:11^{3}ft	7½	114	7^{6}	$7^{5\frac14}$	7^{4}	$7^{2\frac34}$	Lively J1	6250	76-21	Ballerino, Even Par, Loan Officer	12
17May86-6Aks	6f	:23	:47^{3}	1:15^{2}hy	4¾	115	$1^{\frac12}$	$1^{\frac12}$	1^{5}	$1^{3\frac12}$	Steinberg P W10	5000	60-51	GoldKrgrrnd,Cd'sConty,Strk'sVyg	10

Jly 21 Cka 4f ft :50^{4} b

C.

8–1

Last Hoot

Ro. g. 4, by Zen—Barmissa, by Dunce

	Br.—Hill 'n Dale Farm (Ill)		1987 7 0 2 3	$3,259		
Own.—Nies Ed & Cheryl	**116**	Tr.—Cristel Mark	$5,000	1986 10 3 0 1	$9,493	
		Lifetime 24 4 2 7 $29,718				

13Jly87-9FP	6f	:23^{3}	:47^{1}	1:12^{4}ft	3	116	$6^{6\frac14}$	$5^{6\frac12}$	$7^{8\frac14}$	$8^{7\frac12}$	Sellers S J7	6500	71-25	Retrieved,CatchItBuck,PagnJubilee	8
18Jun87-10FP	6f	:22^{2}	:45^{4}	1:11^{4}gd	2¾	116	$5^{4\frac12}$	$5^{4\frac12}$	$5^{3\frac34}$	$3^{3\frac12}$	Sellers S J6	[S]Aw6090	80-19	Go Star Go, Galaking, Last Hoot	9
29May87-8FP	6f	:22^{4}	:46	1:12^{1}ft	4¾	116	$3^{\frac12}$	$2^{3\frac12}$	2^{4}	$3^{2\frac34}$	Sellers S J2	6500	79-27	Tee Rizzle, Icynoo, Last Hoot	8
20May87-8FP	$1\frac{1}{16}$	:47^{3}	1:12^{3}	1:45^{3}ft	4½	116	$3^{1\frac12}$	2^{1}	$2^{1\frac12}$	$3^{3\frac34}$	Sellers S J1	6500	79-22	Humo Cumash, Magicure,LastHoot	7
13May87-8FP	6f	:22^{2}	:46^{2}	1:12^{3}ft	2	116	5^{6}	$5^{3\frac14}$	4^{1}	$2^{\frac12}$	Sellers S J8	c5000	79-26	Time To Star, Last Hoot,BigDigger	8
2May87-8FP	6f	:22^{3}	:46^{2}	1:12^{4}ft	4½	116	$5^{2\frac14}$	$5^{4\frac34}$	3^{3}	2^{1}	Sellers S J9	5000	78-26	Retrieved, Last Hoot, Los Musicos	9
17Apr87-5FP	6f	:22	:45^{2}	1:11 ft	22	116	$4^{2\frac12}$	$6^{3\frac34}$	$5^{3\frac12}$	$7^{7\frac34}$	Campos M6	[S]Aw7540	80-18	MnoftheHouse,YhPrunr,HurryStn	10
19Sep86-10FP	6f	:22^{3}	:45^{4}	1:10^{4}gd	9¾	115	$5^{1\frac14}$	$5^{2\frac14}$	$3^{3\frac12}$	$3^{4\frac14}$	Gale M A 6	5000	85-19	Torn Sail, Peggin To Win,LastHoot	9

D.

5–2

Girard

Ch. h. 6, by Avatar—Wabash Coed, by Lurullah

	Br.—Polk A F (Ky)		1987 9 3 1 2	$8,070		
Own.—Jacobs Claude	**122**	Tr.—Scott Marvin E	$5,000	1986 13 4 1 0	$15,339	
		Lifetime 32 8 2 5 $32,709				

17Jly87-9FP	6f	:22^{3}	:46	1:12 ft	5	122	$5^{1\frac34}$	2^{hd}	$3^{\frac12}$	$3^{1\frac34}$	Patin K C7	5000	81-24	A Hard Ten, Our Banner, Girard	9
4Jly87-6FP	6f	:22^{2}	:45^{4}	1:11^{3}ft	3¼	119	3^{1}	1^{1}	1^{2}	$1^{\frac34}$	Guidry M8	4000	85-20	Girard,ShoutWaHey,DamonRunyon	8
22Jun87-5FP	6f	:22^{3}	:46^{2}	1:12^{2}ft	6	122	$7^{4\frac14}$	$4^{1\frac14}$	$2^{\frac12}$	1^{1}	Guidry M8	4000	81-23	Girard, Sgt. Di Orio,AwardofMerit	10
4Jun87-10FP	6f	:22^{4}	:46^{3}	1:12^{2}ft	4¼	116	$2^{2\frac12}$	2^{4}	$3^{5\frac12}$	8^{7}	Rettele J O1	5000	74-22	Jack'sBrndy,SizzleFritz,OsgeBully	10
23May87-4FP	6f	:22^{4}	:46^{1}	1:12^{1}ft	*7-5	122	$2^{\frac12}$	$1^{2\frac12}$	$1^{3\frac12}$	1^{7}	Guidry M6	c3000	82-26	Girard, FleetGalloway,ThreeKisses	10
29Apr87-7FP	6f	:22^{3}	:46^{2}	1:13 ft	*2½	116	4^{3}	$2^{1\frac12}$	$2^{2\frac12}$	$3^{1\frac12}$	Cahanin K P5	4000	76-24	R.FleetPrince,ChddisMission,Girrd	10
18Apr87-4FP	6f	:22^{2}	:45^{4}	1:12^{2}ft	*8-5	116	$5^{3\frac12}$	$3^{2\frac12}$	$2^{\frac12}$	2^{nk}	Rettele J O6	c3000	81-19	Ketch Um,Girard,NeatestPleasure	10
3Apr87-10FP	6f	:22^{3}	:45^{4}	1:12^{2}ft	5¾	116	2^{1}	2^{3}	$4^{4\frac12}$	$8^{5\frac12}$	Rettele J O1	5000	75-20	AstroBreaker,TeeRizzle,PleaseFrn	10

E.

4–1

Rio Nite ✻

Dk. b. or br. m. 6, by Aferd—Apple Grabber, by Monitor

Br.—Berndt O C (SD) — 1987 5 2 1 0 $6,814

Own.—Waters Francis **117** Tr.—Burns Richard $5,000 — 1986 7 0 1 1 $2,860

Lifetime 38 12 5 2 $57,505 — Turf 6 1 2 0 $8,290

13Jly87-5FP 1^{70}:47^{3} 1:14 1:45^{1}ft *2¼ 119 21½ 21½ 3^{2} 5^{5} Guidry M^{6} Ⓕ c3000 70-25 Nromo,Lm'sMissLckty,Sndy'sSprt 10

17Jun87-4FP 1$\frac{1}{16}$:47^{1} 1:12^{3} 1:46^{2}ft 2¼ 116 11½ 1½ 11½ 1¾ Guidry M^{7} Ⓕ 4000 79-19 Rio Nite, Kacy Kelly, Justatoy 8

30May87-1AP 6f :22^{3} :46^{4} 1:13^{3}ft *2e 112 1½ 2^{hd} 54½ 79¾ Diaz J L^{2} Ⓕ 5000 62-28 AprlFoolsom,LvThtJzz,FrnchCrckt 12

14May87-1Spt 6½f :24^{3} :48^{4} 1:22^{2}ft *6-5 115 3^{3} 2^{hd} 11½ 1^{2} Diaz J L^{3} Ⓕ 4000 65-28 Rio Nite,RoughPatsy,BrightCrissy 10

6May87-1Spt 6f :24^{1} :47^{4} 1:14^{1}ft *2 115 2½ 2^{hd} 1^{hd} 2^{nk} Meier R^{8} Ⓕ 4000 79-24 April Foolsom,RioNite,RoughPatsy 9

21Oct86-4Bml 6f :23^{4} :48^{1} 1:15^{4}ft *9-5 120 1½ 1^{hd} 21½ 65¾ Diaz J L^{2} Ⓕ 5000 74-18 TrnUpThHt,HrrHnnhHrr,GldnDrms 9

12Oct86-6Bml 6f :23^{4} :48^{3} 1:16^{3}ft *7-5 116 21½ 33½ 4^{9} 4^{12} Diaz J L^{2} Ⓕ 6250 64-23 LayEmAway,ColoradoRose,Jellyben 8

14Sep86-8Beu 1 Ⓣ 1:39^{3}fm*2-3 116 1^{1} 2^{hd} 2^{2} 22½ Feliciano P^{5} Ⓕ 10000 84-14 Twin To Win, Rio Nite, Eleanor B. 9

14Sep86—Fractional times unavailable

F.

3–1

Our Banner

B. g. 4, by True Colors—Isle of Barataria, by Barachois

Br.—Jahr Stables (Ill) — 1987 10 3 2 3 $9,302

Own.—Kister Dr George **122** Tr.—Hammond Jerry $5,000 — 1986 8 0 1 0 $1,114

Lifetime 24 6 3 3 $19,751

17Jly87-9FP 6f :22^{3} :46 1:12 ft 4 122 3½ 1^{hd} 2^{hd} 2^{1} Guidry M 1 5000 82-24 A Hard Ten, Our Banner, Girard 9

24Jun87-10FP 6f :22^{4} :46 1:12^{2}ft *3¼ 119 22½ 21½ 1^{hd} 11½ Guidry M 10 4000 81-23 OurBanner,R.U.RushingMe,TintSo 10

13Jun87-5FP 6f :22^{2} :46^{1} 1:13 ft 9¼ 122 54¼ 33½ 21½ 3½ Medina N R 2 5000 77-24 Intoxicator,LosMusicos,OurBnner 10

1Jun87-7FP 6f :23 :46^{3} 1:12^{4}ft 5¼ 119 2^{hd} 1½ 1^{hd} 2¾ Guidry M 6 4000 78-24 Intoxicator, Our Banner,Exuberon 10

20May87-10FP 6f :22^{4} :46^{1} 1:12^{1}ft 21 119 1^{hd} 12½ 1^{2} 1^{2} Guidry L A 2 4000 82-22 OurBnner,DemiMoe,PegginToWin 10

2May87-2FP 6f :22^{4} :47 1:13^{1}ft 5 119 41¾ 3½ 3^{nk} 34½ Sellers S J 10 c3000 72-26 Astral, Wesley H., Our Banner 10

18Apr87-10FP 6f :22 :45^{2} 1:12^{2}ft 4½ 122 4^{5} 33½ 54¼ 6^{5} Sellers S J 4 4000 76-19 CtchItBuck,LosMusicos,R.FltPrnc 10

9Apr87-6FP 6f :22^{2} :46 1:12 ft 4½ 119 51½ 2^{hd} 2½ 3^{1} Sellers S J 1 3000 82-19 LittleNicky,FayWardlaw,OurBnner 10

G.

30–1

All In Good Tune

B. g. 4, by In Good Tune—Pawnee Gray, by Iron Warrior

Br.—Equine Athletic Conditioning (Ill) — 1987 9 1 0 0 $14,282

Own.—Stede George et al **116** Tr.—Yates Lanny $5,000 — 1986 8 2 0 1 $10,357

Lifetime 24 3 0 1 $25,089

Entered 25Jly87-10 FP

18Jly87-7FP 1$\frac{1}{16}$:48^{1} 1:13^{2} 1:47 ft 14 116 11½ 2^{hd} 6^{7} 612¼ Medina A S 7 4000 64-27 PlanetoCatch,Intoxicator,LipnMgic 7

26Jun87-9FP 6f :22^{3} :45^{4} 1:11^{2}ft 6½ 116 3^{3} 58½ 6^{12} 7^{12} Militello D J 3 5000 74-23 Retrieved, Demi Moe,BredForGlory 9

18Jun87-10FP 6f :22^{2} :45^{4} 1:11^{4}gd 12 119 3^{1} 1^{hd} 3^{nk} 75½ Militello DJ 3 [S]Aw6090 78-19 Go Star Go, Galaking, Last Hoot 9

8Jun87-2AP 6½f :23 :46^{4} 1:20 ft 7 115 1^{hd} 21½ 45½ 611½ Razo E Jr 4 5000 63-24 Anconeus, Mr. Run Run, Teeair 10

31May87-2AP 6f :22^{2} :45^{4} 1:13^{1}ft 17 115 32½ 3^{3} 4^{5} 63¾ Evans R D 10 [S] 7500 70-27 Slow Leak, Dr. Fisher, GreekValue 11

15May87-9Spt 6f :23^{4} :47^{4} 1:13^{1}ft 14 122 7^{9} 109¼ 10^{16} 10^{18} Ebanks R C 2 [S] 25000 66-23 DecidedlyDncin,JermyJt,RoomKys 10

15May87—Checked first turn

30Apr87-9Spt 6½f :23^{2} :47^{4} 1:20^{3}ft *2½ 117 1^{hd} 1^{2} 1^{3} 12¼ Meier R 5 [S]Aw22575 74-25 AllInGoodTn,TmptthTgr,Endcmnt 10

4Apr87-5Spt 6½f :22^{2} :46^{1} 1:18^{4}ft 22 117 1½ 4^{1} 85¾ 812¼ Miller S E 2 [S]Aw21105 71-19 He's A Rake, Rising Zen,SuperF.T. 10

Jun 17 FP 4f ft :51^{2} b

H.

5–1

Dawn's Dusty

Ch. g. 4, by Bob's Dusty—Rozzie Green, by Mr Leader

Br.—Davis Pamela-D & SocolofM (Kan) — 1987 12 0 0 0 $1,913

Own.—Wheeler Jr & Murphy **116** Tr.—Hargrove Gene W $5,000 — 1986 4 2 1 0 $6,480

Lifetime 19 3 2 0 $11,513 — Turf 3 0 0 0 $438

17Jly87-9FP 6f :22^{3} :46 1:12 ft 4½ 116 85¾ 65¼ 53¼ 43½ Gall D^{3} 5000 79-24 A Hard Ten, Our Banner, Girard 9

25Jun87-8FP 6f :22^{1} :46 1:12^{2}ft 4 116 87¼ 55½ 5^{5} 43½ Kurek G^{3} 5000 77-23 Catch ItBuck,OsageBully,ArkyFox 10

3Jun87-9FP 6f :23 :46^{2} 1:11^{2}ft 13 116 65½ 57½ 5^{11} 5^{10} Kurek G^{6} 11500 76-26 HeyLittleMn,BoldZen,RedProspect 6

25May87-9FP 6f :23 :47 1:12^{4}ft 24 116 75¾ 75¼ 64¾ 54¼ Kurek G^{7} 14500 75-22 I'mGrtTwo,ComngOfAg,LghsIrnEgl 8

9May87-6FP 6f :22^{3} :46 1:12^{1}ft 16 116 68½ 7^{9} 6^{13} 4^{5} Gall D^{1} 14500 77-23 I'mGreatTwo,Zentastic,CarolSinghs 7

1May87-6FP 1^{70}:46 1:11^{3} 1:44^{1}ft 23 116 69¼ 6^{11} 6^{10} 6^{7} Sanchez H A^{5} Aw7000 73-25 Foratag, Al Golin's, Here's ToMore 7

22Apr87-9FP 1^{70}:47^{2} 1:13 1:44^{3}ft 7 116 42¾ 5^{3} 57½ 56¾ Sanchez H A^{6} Aw7000 71-26 CulksCrk,Hrsthgry,ThoughtsOfYou 8

30Mar87-5FG a7½f Ⓣ:23^{3} :50^{3}1:36 yl 15 115 1^{1} 1^{hd} 4^{6} 69¾ Leblanc K P^{4} 15000 59-38 Reson'sBoy,StrTopper,BrotherJms 7

Jly 16 FP 3f ft :37^{4} b — Jly 4 FP 4f ft :48^{2} b — Jun 23 FP 3f sy :38^{4} b — Jun 13 FP 4f ft :48^{2} b

52. If *Pettrax* has an early pace advantage and *Olajuwon* a class edge, which horse should be bet at the odds?

A. *It's Not My Job* 10–1
B. *Silver Hero* 7–2
C. *Pettrax* 3–1
D. *Olajuwon* 2–1

3rd Santa Anita

1 1-16 MILES
SANTA ANITA

1 1/16 MILES. (1.40⅕) CLAIMING. Purse $30,000. 4-year-olds and upward. Weights, 4-year-olds, 121 lbs.; older, 122 lbs. Non-winners of two races at one mile or over since December 1 allowed 2 lbs.; of such a race since then, 4 lbs.; of a race any distance since then, 6 lbs. Claiming price $62,500; for each $2,500 to $55,000 allowed 1 lbs. (Claiming and starter races for $50,000 or less not considered.)

It's Not My Job

OLIVARES F **113**
Own.—Clore A

Dk. b. or br. h. 5, by Damascus—Mumkin, by Arts and Letters
Br.—Jason & Knoop Mmes et al (Ky)
Tr.—Doumen Christian **$55,000**
Lifetime 14 1 3 3 $28,630

1987 2 0 0 0 $700
1986 12 1 3 3 $27,930
Turf 7 0 1 1 $7,930

19Jan87-5SA 1¼Ⓣ:4731:3822:041fm 38 117 87¼ 83½ 64¾ 54¾ Sint-MrtnE12 Aw28000 61-29 Intuitiveness, Asian Cup, Neferou 12
19Jan87—Wide into stretch
4Jan87-10TuP 1 1/16:46 1:094 1:412ft 9 114 77½ 77 77¾ 65½ DahlSM10 Mrcpa Fr H 85-12 SonoitBlu,MuiMlody,ChuckNLuck 12
13Dec86-9BM 1 1/16:462 1:112 1:431ft 4½ 114 76¾ 64½ 53½ 32 CampbellBC8 Aw17000 74-19 CllThGurd,NwStorm,It'sNotMyJob 8
23Nov86-9Hol 1¼Ⓣ:4811:3642:021fm 14 116 42 1hd 2hd 82¾ Black C A10 62500 81-13 Rampour, Travet, Aviator II 11
31Oct86-5SA 1⅛:461 1:103 1:492ft 8¼ 120 32 41¾ 67 66¾ Cruz A S6 Aw27000 75-16 Mr. Media, Jota, Rafael's Dancer 9
31Oct86—Broke slowly
11Oct86-5SA 1¼Ⓣ:4711:3642:03 fm 8½ 1145 31½ 42 5¾ 31½ Black C A3 Aw27000 70-21 FortntDncr,‡Rthymno,It'sNtMyJb 11
11Oct86—Inadvertently hit on nose in stretch; Placed second through disqualification
4Oct86-9BM 1 1/16:453 1:101 1:424ft *3-2 117 613 55½ 21 2nk Olivares F6 Aw16000 78-16 Nevr-Rust,It'sNotMyJob,ClvryChrg 9
31Aug86-6Dmr 1 1/16:452 1:102 1:423ft 3½ 122 31½ 42 3½ 1½ Olivares F3 Mdn 87-12 It'sNotMyJob,JckMcCy,Ambssdrl 11
15Aug86-6Dmr 1 1/16:453 1:102 1:423ft 12 122 32 3nk 1hd 3½ Olivares F10 Mdn 86-12 PlumCrtin,TirrDstnt,It'sNotMyJob 11
6Aug86-5Dmr 1⅛Ⓣ:4821:1241:502fm 30 117 64 31½ 32½ 41¾ Olivares F1 Aw20000 80-14 FlyingSnow,Nurely,CashInTheBnk 10
6Aug86—Bobbled 3/16
Jan 31 SA 4f ft :472 h Dec 29 SA 5f ft 1:014 h

Silver Hero

PINCAY L JR **116**
Own.—Asadurian–Asadurian–Winick

Ro. h. 5, by Al Hattab—Tanta Bella, by Blank Check
Br.—Hansen Family Trust (Ky)
Tr.—Winick Randy **$62,500**
Lifetime 27 4 6 1 $99,525

1987 1 0 1 0 $6,000
1986 16 2 3 0 $47,325
Turf 9 1 1 0 $25,700

17Jan87-3SA 1 :462 1:111 1:373ft 5¾ 116 43½ 3½ 2hd 21¼ Cordero A Jr5 62500 79-18 Pettrx,SilverHero,NorthernProvidr 8
17Jan87—Bumped start, 1/8
7Dec86-3Hol 1 :453 1:10 1:354gd 4¼ 116 68½ 612 510 515¼ DelahoussayeE3 62500 69-18 Olajuwon, RisingChum,OnoGummo 6
7Dec86—Wide backstretch
14Nov86-5Hol 1 :443 1:084 1:344ft 2¾ 116 35½ 29 29 29½ DelahoussayeE5 62500 79-16 Oricao, Silver Hero, Rex Lake 6
24Oct86-7SA 1 1/16:46 1:104 1:43 ft *2¾ 116 79½ 77 79¾ 716¼ DelahoussayeE6 62500 70-20 Rising Chum,Olajuwon,DarkAccent 8
24Oct86—Hit gate start; wide into stretch
4Oct86-9SA 1 1/16:472 1:112 1:43 ft 5½ 116 51½ 41¾ 32 21¾ DelahoussayeE5 62500 84-18 GoSwiftly,SilverHro,AutoCommndr 8
4Oct86—Broke slowly
21Sep86-10Pom 1 1/16:461 1:102 1:43 ft 9½ 117 31 41½ 48 516¾ KenelJL5 Ⓡ C B Aflrbh 79-07 Emperdori, Estate, Iron Leader 7
3Sep86-7Dmr 1 1/16Ⓣ:4721:1121:423fm 6¼ 118 76 63½ 63¾ 64 Toro F7 80000 89-12 ExclusivCpd,RivrOfKings,Emprdori 8
3Sep86—Broke slowly
6Aug86-7Dmr 1 1/16Ⓣ:48 1:1141:432fm 9½ 120 76½ 73¾ 54½ 51¼ Pincay L Jr6 80000 88-14 Bozina, Aviator II, Keyala 8
6Aug86—Bumped early
18Jly86-8Hol 1 :453 1:101 1:353ft 5 119 31½ 32 55½ 59¾ McHrgueDG1 Aw30000 75-14 Bolton, Varick, Ascension 6
18Jly86—Checked at start
26Jun86-4Hol 1 :47 1:113 1:354ft 2¾ 117 41½ 42 31 1nk Pincay L Jr3 Aw23000 84-12 SilvrHro,ImpriousSpirit,TrpolShors 6
26Jun86—Bumped start
Jan 31 SA 5f ft :591 h ● Jan 25 SA 5f ft :592 h ● Jan 12 SA 6f ft 1:13 h ● Jan 3 SA 5f ft :593 h

Pettrax

BLACK C A **120**
Own.—Charlton B W

B. g. 9, by Petrone—Roman Dame, by British Roman
Br.—Charlton B (Cal)
Tr.—Charlton Wayne **$62,500**
Lifetime 66 16 12 4 $513,586

1987 1 1 0 0 $16,500
1986 12 4 2 1 $91,700
Turf 33 6 5 2 $209,325

17Jan87-3SA 1 :462 1:111 1:373ft 6¾ 113 22½ 2hd 1hd 11¼ Black C A6 55000 80-18 Pettrx,SilverHero,NorthernProvidr 8
17Jan87—Bumped start, 1/8
23Aug86-5Dmr 1⅛Ⓣ:4831:1231:49 fm 5¼ 1155 23 22 33½ 2no Black C A4 62500 89-11 Dancebel, Pettrax, Massera 9
23Jly86-9Dmr 1 1/16Ⓣ:4821:1221:431fm *7-5 116 2hd 3nk 3½ 11 Toro F4 62500 90-04 Pettrax, Royal Olympia, Ablantin 8
29Jun86-9Hol 1 1/16Ⓣ:4741:1131:413fm 17 116 2½ 2hd 41 52¼ Kaenel J L8 62500 94-02 Caballo,Sndy'sEgle,EveningM'Lord 9
7Jun86-9Hol 1 1/16Ⓣ:4621:1011:41 fm 15 1125 22 2½ 42½ 52¾ Black C A1 75000 96-02 ‡GoDncer,Bishop'sRingII,PiprJohn 8
25May86-9Hol 1 1/16Ⓣ:4721:1041:411fm 6½ 1145 1hd 2½ 63½ 57 Black C A6 80000 91-03 Boom Town Charlie,Bozina,Pautivo 7
19Apr86-5SA 1 Ⓣ:4641:1011:352fm 8¼ 1155 1hd 21 22½ 1½ Black C A6 80000 — — Pettrax, Kilauea, Mr Chromacopy 11
30Mar86-5SA 1⅛Ⓣ:4541:1011:482fm 7 1155 56 62¼ 109¼ 1111¾ Black C A12 80000 73-16 Snowcrk,RoylRcors,Bshop'sRngII 12
8Mar86-7SA 1 1/16:464 1:113 1:44 sy 3 1095 1½ 11 11½ 11½ Black C A1 85000 81-19 Pettrax, Bozina, Honor Medal 7
8Mar86—Lugged out 7/8 turn; drifted out stretch

23Feb86-5SA 1 :454 1:10 1:342ft 7 1085 1½ 2hd 23 23½ Black C A4 85000 92-11 Gourami, Pettrax, Bozina 9
23Feb86—Lugged out backstretch, 3/8 turn
Jan 29 SA 3f ft :38 h Jan 15 SA 3f ft :373 h Jan 9 SA 7f sl 1:293 h Dec 29 SA 7f ft 1:302 h

Olajuwon 96-102-108
STEVENS G L 122
Own.—Sefra D I
Dk. b. or br. g. 5, by Believe It—Nerves of Steel, by Round Table
Br.—Blum P E (Ky) 1986 13 4 2 2 $74,250
Tr.—Canani Julio C $62,500 1985 13 2 2 3 $40,240
Lifetime 32 7 4 6 $133,030 Turf 8 1 0 2 $18,720

31Dec86-7SA 1 :453 1:11 1:364ft 2½ 116 57½ 31 1hd 1½ ValenzuelPA2 Aw31000 84-20 Olajuwon,ForsytheBoy,CallTheGurd 7
31Dec86—Brushed rail 71/2
7Dec86-3Hol 1 :453 1:10 1:354gd 4 114 31½ 21½ 2½ 1½ Stevens G L1 57500 84-18 Olajuwon,,RisingChum,OncGummo 6
5Nov86-7Hol 1⅛ ①:4731:1131:483fm 4 117 811 88½ 79½ 79 Pincay L Jr6 c50000 76-14 Too Much For T. V.,Massera,Tarver 8
5Nov86—Bumped start
24Oct86-7SA 1 1/16 :46 1:104 1:43 ft 3½ 117 69½ 54 32½ 2hd Pincay L Jr2 62500 86-20 Rising Chum,Olajuwon,DarkAccent 8
24Oct86—Lugged in stretch
24Aug86-9Dmr 1 1/16 :452 1:093 1:412ft 4½ 116 917 713 511 35½ DelahoussayeE9 50000 87-12 OnoGummo,TimeForSilenc,Oljuwon 9
9Aug86-7Dmr 1 1/16 :453 1:101 1:422ft 5½ 116 42½ 31½ 31 53¾ Soto S B2 50000 84-14 Lead On, Impulsively, Idol 11
9Aug86—Bumped 1/8
2Aug86-9Dmr 1 1/16 :461 1:103 1:42 ft *4-5 116 43 32 21½ 1½ DelahoussyeE7 c40000 90-12 Olajuwon, Trus T. Danus, Elefante 7
2Aug86—Bumped late
12Jly86-9Hol 1⅛ ①:4641:1021:47 fm *2½ 116 65 55½ 37 36 Valenzuela P A1 50000 91-01 TooMuchForT.V.,Kngsbury,Oljuwon 8
28Jun86-3Hol 1⅛ :452 1:103 1:492ft 5 116 410 45 2hd 2no Valenzuela P A5 62500 90-12 GlacilStrem,Oljuwon,ExclusiveCpde 6
7Jun86-7Hol 1 :453 1:10 1:37 ft *2½ 116 86½ 64½ 64½ 43 DelahoussyeE3 c50000 75-17 Ono Gummo, Menswear, Paskanell 8
Feb 2 SA 4f ft :473 h Jan 27 SA 7f ft 1:283 h Jan 21 SA 4f ft :482 h Jan 15 SA 6f ft 1:14 h

53. The five maidens below were all bred for turf racing. One of them not only won by 15 lengths but was the best bet in the field besides. Find it.

2 BELMONT

1 1/16 MILES. (Turf). (1.39⅗) MAIDEN SPECIAL WEIGHT. Purse $24,000. Fillies and mares. 3-year-olds and upward. Weight, 3-year-olds, 116 lbs., Older, 122 lbs.

A.
7–1

Coupled—Spur Wing and Irish Walk.
Chapel Of Dreams
Own.—Sabarese T M
Ch. f. 3, by Northern Dancer—Terlingua, by Secretariat
Br.—Young W T Storage Inc (Ky)
Tr.—Parisella John
116
Lifetime 1 0 0 0 1986 1 M 0 0
13Nov86- 5Aqu gd 6f :23⅕ :47⅕ 1:12 ⒻMd Sp Wt 7 4 32 65¼ 67½ 711½ Santos J A 117 *2.10 69-20 Fine Timing 1176¾ Starita 117nk Finalmente 117no Weakened 13
LATEST WORKOUTS Jly 16 Bel Ⓣ 6f fm 1:13⅖ h (d) Jly 11 Bel tr.t 4f fst :49 b Jun 25 Bel Ⓣ 6f fm 1:13⅗ h (d) Jun 18 Bel Ⓣ 5f fm 1:00⅘ h (d)

B.
7–2

Dancing Rags
Own.—Hickory Tree Stable
B. f. 3, by Nijinsky II—Glad Rags II, by High Hat
Br.—Hickory Tree Farm (Ky)
Tr.—Stephens Woodford C
116
Lifetime 0 0 0 0 1987 0 M 0 0
1986 0 M 0 0
LATEST WORKOUTS Jly 29 Bel 4f fst :48⅗ h Jly 25 Bel 6f fst 1:13 h Jly 20 Bel 6f fst 1:13⅘ h Jly 16 Bel 4f fst :48⅖ h

C.
9–1

Cherchez Le Cash
Own.—Turnbow C D
Dk. b. or br. f. 3, by Advocator—Rolfina, by Tom Rolfe
Br.—Bonacquisti Robert O (Ky)
Tr.—Sanderson Robert D
116
Lifetime 6 0 0 1 $1,850 1987 6 M 0 1 $1,850
1986 0 M 0 0
11Jun87- 6Bir fst 6f :23⅕ :47⅕ 1:12⅘ 3+ⒻMd Sp Wt 5 4 43 55 57 48¾ Smith L S b 113 23.00 74-19 Duns' Champagne 1224½ DiscoDevil114¾FlyAwayKris1133½ Evenly 9
30May87- 3Bir fst 1 :48 1:13⅕ 1:40⅗ 3+ⒻMd Sp Wt 2 1 12 37 49 414¼ Salvaggio M P b 115 9.50 72-16 Mick's Ms. 1188¾ Disco Devil 1142 Lotsa Pops 1233½ Weakened 5
14May87- 1Bir fst 1 1/16 :48⅘ 1:13⅘ 1:47⅘ 3+ⒻMd Sp Wt 8 5 54½ 46 38½ 313¾ Young S A b 111 24.30 76-13 HoliandDncer1238¾SndBby1044½CherchezLeCsh1112½ Evenly late 10
21Apr87- 4Bir fst 1 :48⅘ 1:14⅖ 1:41⅗ ⒻMd Sp Wt 5 5 54½ 79½ 815 810½ Salvaggio M P b 121 9.30 70-11 Juliet'sDivine121½Ms.HastyLdy1211Fstenyoursetbelt121no Outrun 9
19Mar87- 1Bir fst 6f :22⅕ :46⅕ 1:14⅖ ⒻMd Sp Wt 8 6 98¾ 710 78½ 55¾ Young S A 122 29.90 — — Twirlind1222½ColonelsAvenger117hdRelMowgetter1222 No factor 10
4Jan87- 2Lrl fst 7f :23⅕ :47⅖ 1:25⅘ ⒻMd Sp Wt 6 5 76¾ 77¾ 510 514 Delgado W N5 115 20.50 68-19 AmandaH.120nkD'YouvilleNurse1209¾Willie'sFvorite120no Outrun 7
LATEST WORKOUTS Jly 23 Sar Ⓣ 4f fm :50 h (d) Jly 16 Sar Ⓣ 4f fm :51⅗ b (d) Jun 6 Bir 3f fst :39⅕ b

D.
10–1

Tithing B. f. 3, by Nureyev—Miss Croatoan, by Roanoke Island
Br.—Edelstein–Frand Prtnrshp–Axmar St (Ky) **116** Lifetime 3 0 1 0 $6,440 1987 3 M 1 0 $6,440 1986 0 M 0 0
Own.—Klein La Donna Tr.—Tufariello Frank

16Jly87- 6Bel fst 7f :23⅖ :47⅕ 1:26 3+ ⒻMd Sp Wt 5 2 3½ 41¼ 45 47¼ Venezia M 116 7.90 65-24 Equate 1165 Wakonda 1161 Stocking Feet 1161½ Early foot 8
5Jly87- 6Bel fst 6f :22⅖ :46⅖ 1:12⅘ 3+ ⒻMd Sp Wt 10 11 811 89½ 97¾ 74¼ Badamo J J 116 9.60 72-24 Chilam Balam 116nk Miss Czara 116nk ReallyWelcome1111¾ Wide 12
17May87- 7Bel fst 7f :23 :46 1:23⅕ ⒻMd Sp Wt 2 1 33½ 34½ 27 213½ Badamo J J5 116 25.70 72-20 Top News 12113½ Tithing 1162¼DamascusBelle1216 Best of others 7
LATEST WORKOUTS Jly 23 Bel Ⓣ 5f fm 1:03 b (d) Jly 13 Bel 4f fst :52 b Jly 1 Bel 6f fst 1:16 b Jun 26 Bel 5f fst 1:02⅘ b

E.
5–1

Majeboo Dk. b. or br. f. 3, by His Majesty—Evening Boo Boo, by In Reality
Br.—Kimmel C P (Ky) **116** Lifetime 4 0 0 1 $2,880 1987 3 M 0 1 $2,880 1986 1 M 0 0 Turf 1 0 0 1 $2,880
Own.—Kimmel C P Tr.—Toner James J

29Jun87- 6Bel gd 1 Ⓣ:47⅘ 1:13 1:38⅕ 3+ ⒻMd Sp Wt 12 2 53½ 64 25 310¾ Pezua J M 114 6.90 63-27 Secret Wedding 1228¾ Equate 1142 Majeboo 114¾ Rallied 12
14Jun87- 5Bel fst 6f :22⅕ :46 1:12⅗ 3+ ⒻMd Sp Wt 11 10 1314 117½ 65 63¼ Pezua J M 114 48.00 74-20 Copious114nkVacuousness1151¼GoldOntheRocks114nk No menace 13
16Apr87- 6Aqu fst 6f :23⅕ :47 1:11⅘ ⒻMd Sp Wt 7 1 53½ 815 718 720½ Santos J A 121 29.30 61-22 Cadillacing 12116¾ Drone Qui 121hd Special Weekend1214¼ Outrun 9
11Sep86- 4Bel fst 6f :22⅘ :46⅕ 1:11⅖ ⒻMd Sp Wt 12 11 64½ 79½ 512 614¼ Cordero A Jr 117 9.40 71-21 Valid Line 1176 Rullah Runner 1173¼ Graceful Darby 1172 Outrun 12
LATEST WORKOUTS Jly 27 Bel 4f fst :48⅕ h Jly 20 Bel 6f fst 1:15 b Jly 13 Bel 5f fst 1:03⅘ b Jun 25 Bel Ⓣ 5f fm 1:03 b (d)

54. The overlay that can easily be bet is

9th Santa Anita

1 1/16 MILES. (1.40⅕) CLAIMING. Purse $18,000. Fillies and mares. 4-year-olds and upward. Weights, 120 lbs.; older, 121 lbs. Non-winners of two races at one mile or over since November 3, allowed 3 lbs.; of such a race since then, 5 lbs. Claiming price $20,000; if for $18,000, allowed 2 lbs. (Claiming and starter races for $16,000 or less not considered.)

A.
5–1

Bid For Her Ch. m. 5, by Raise a Bid—Be Hasty, by Flying Lark
Br.—Hinson D L (Fla) 1986 13 2 2 2 $35,085
PEDROZA M A **116** Tr.—Lewis Craig A $20,000 1985 8 1 0 1 $12,375
Own.—Breen & Lewis Lifetime 22 3 2 3 $47,460 Turf 1 0 0 0

27Dec86-9SA 1 1/16 :454 1:111 1:452ft 7 118 22½ 32½ 78 — Pincay L Jr12 Ⓕ 25000 — — DonATop,FrenchStr,Winsomthing 12
27Dec86—Eased
10Dec86-9Hol 1 :463 1:113 1:38 ft 3½ 116 21½ 2½ 2½ 35¾ Pedroza M A7 Ⓕ 32000 67-20 ReputtionMiss,ArcticLnd,BidForHr 7
15Nov86-5Hol 1⅛Ⓣ:4541:1041:483fm 47 116 36 43½ 64 109¼ PedrozMA1 ⒻAw24000 76-11 SuperKitten,Arzll,MorningDvotion 12
15Nov86—Veered out start
31Oct86-9SA 1 1/16 :454 1:103 1:434ft 7½ 116 34 22½ 23½ 48½ Pedroza M A6 Ⓕ 32000 73-16 Don A Top, VitalScore,FrenchStar 10
18Oct86-1SA 1 1/16 :46 1:11 1:454ft 17 116 23½ 21½ 1hd 11¼ Pedroza M A8 Ⓕ 25000 72-20 Bid For Her,DonATop,SocietyRiva 10
4Oct86-3SA 1 :462 1:121 1:39 ft 2½ 118 22½ 11½ 12½ 31½ PedrozaMA3 Ⓕ c20000 71-18 ArcticLand,UniverslMlii,BidForHer 8
23Sep86-10Pom 1 1/16 :462 1:111 1:441ft 15 114 33 31½ 22 22¼ Pedroza M A6 Ⓕ 22500 88-08 French Star, Bid ForHer,Cabrioleta 8
14Sep86-8Pom 6½f :213 :451 1:172ft 23 1145 53¼ 511 67¾ 56¾ Coffman C1 Ⓕ 20000 86-08 SpurMeOn,FrenchStar,PrettyStall 10
4Sep86-5Dmr 1 1/16 :451 1:102 1:431ft 7 116 31 52½ 76¾ 710¼ Lipham T6 Ⓕ 25000 74-14 Ed'sBoldLdy,Neumi'sGirl,SwtWinkl 8
4Sep86—Broke out, bumped
22Aug86-5Dmr 1 1/16 :451 1:103 1:432ft 25 116 32½ 42½ 42 42 Pedroza M A9 Ⓕ 32000 81-14 Emacia, Brune de Mai, VitalScore 12
Jan 1 SA 5f ft 1:034 h Nov 29 Hol 4f ft :494 h

B.
10–1

Neumie's Girl B. m. 5, by Don B—Cuppling, by Dress Up
Br.—Neuman D (Cal) 1986 9 2 3 0 $34,425
SHOEMAKER W **116** Tr.—Jackson Bruce $20,000 1985 15 1 1 2 $23,250
Own.—Stark M Lifetime 29 4 4 2 $69,750 Turf 1 0 0 0

19Dec86-4Hol 1 1/16 :472 1:13 1:46 ft *1 116 32 53 610 816¾ VlenzuelPA3 Ⓕ c16000 62-17 AncientLady,Julin'sDrem,MissDniel 8
21Nov86-9Hol 1⅛ :471 1:12 1:513ft 2¾ 116 31½ 3½ 11 2hd ValenzuelPA7 Ⓕ 20000 79-20 Cbriolet,Neumie'sGirl,Julin'sDrem 10
21Nov86—Lugged in stretch
31Oct86-9SA 1 1/16 :454 1:103 1:434ft 5¼ 118 811 89¾ 69½ 610¼ Pincay L Jr9 Ⓕ 32000 72-16 Don A Top, VitalScore,FrenchStar 10
31Oct86—Wide into stretch
18Oct86-1SA 1 1/16 :46 1:11 1:454ft *1 118 59½ 37½ 34 45½ Pincay L Jr4 Ⓕ c25000 66-20 Bid For Her,DonATop,SocietyRiva 10
8Oct86-9SA 1 1/16 :461 1:114 1:45 ft *9-5 118 58½ 52½ 1½ 2¾ Pincay L Jr3 Ⓕ 32000 75-20 VitlScore,Neumi'sGirl,RputtionMiss 8
8Oct86—Wide into stretch
12Sep86-10Pom 1 1/16 :453 1:112 1:45 ft 12 117 89 76¼ 42½ 11½ HernndezR8 ⒻAw27000 86-11 Neumie'sGirl,Btt'sLdy,UnivrslMlii 10
4Sep86-5Dmr 1 1/16 :451 1:102 1:431ft *3 116 54½ 32 1hd 2½ Stevens G L3 Ⓕ c25000 83-14 Ed'sBoldLdy,Neumi'sGirl,SwtWinkl 8
24Jly86-9Dmr 1 1/16 :454 1:11 1:43 ft *8-5 116 21 1hd 15 19 Stevens G L8 Ⓕ c12500 85-15 Neumie'sGirl,HiddnAngl,DvlishDzzlr 9
10Jly86-3Hol 1 :46 1:114 1:381ft *2¼ 116 2hd 2½ 44½ 610 Stevens G L1 Ⓕ 16000 62-18 ThPntry,SlfSustining,Folk'sVictory 7
12Dec85-2Hol 1 :46 1:111 1:381ft 3½ 115 63¼ 810 812 811¼ Hernandez R9 Ⓕ 16000 61-22 ChrystlEgle,HiddenPst,SwetWinkl 11
Dec 10 Hol 5f ft 1:05 h Nov 11 Hol 5f ft 1:01 h

C.
23–1

Club Dancer — Ro. f. 4, by Lines of Power—Miss Affair, by Fast Hilarious
ARAGON V A — 115 — Br.—Degalia Inc (Ky) — 1986 10 2 1 1 $10,135
Own.—Urquhart J — Tr.—Findlay William A — $20,000 — 1985 2 M 0 0 $180
Lifetime 12 2 1 1 $10,315

27Dec86-9SA 1 1/16 :45 4 1:11 1 1:45 2 ft 83 108 5 10 15 10 12 8 9 6 8 Bielby J A 8 Ⓕ 25000 66-19 DonATop,FrenchStr,Winsomthing 12
30Oct86-9SA 1 1/16 :46 4 1:11 2 1:43 4 ft 17 110 5 12 13 8 8 5 6½ 5 6¼ Black C A 12 Ⓕ 20000 76-18 RufflsNBus,TxtBookLdy,Fool'sHill 12
5Oct86-8Lga 1 1/16 :47 2 1:11 2 1:43 3 ft 5 108 5 8 14 8 12 4 9½ 3 5 Gibson R G 6 Ⓕ 20000 76-17 HrbourPlce,MickiesPride,ClubDncr 8
13Sep86-6Lga 6½f :22 1 :46 1:19 4 m 7½ 107 5 7 15 7 17 6 7½ 2 1½ Gibson R G 5 Ⓕ 25000 68-32 WterStrBby,ClubDncer,SpnishJulie 7
22Aug86-6Lga 1 :46 4 1:12 1 1:37 4 ft 17 110 5 5 4 4 3½ 2 hd 1¾ Gibson R G 5 Ⓕ 16000 80-17 Club Dancer, Fightin Lil, Ivorette 8
6Aug86-2Lga 6f :22 :45 4 1:12 ft 3 118 11 13 9 10 4 6 1 2½ Aragon V A 1 ⒻM12500 76-22 ClubDancer,BellaReva,MissPaulG. 12
18Jly86-4Lga 1 1/16 :47 2 1:12 3 1:46 4 ft *3 118 7 7 9 12 7 12 6 8½ Steiner J J 1 ⒻM16000 56-22 SuprmAllGrl,FlyngKttn,RnnngOdds 9
3Jly86-4Lga 6f :22 :45 2 1:11 ft 12 118 7 8½ 8 7½ 4 7½ 4 4 Steiner J J 3 ⒻM20000 77-20 InKrrCrfty,NkdNymph,ScrmingCt 12
5Jun86-2Lga 6f :21 3 :45 4 1:12 1 ft 6½ 118 9 11 8 7¾ 7 11 4 4½ DomngzRE 9 ⒻM20000 71-21 Makin MyDay,LuckyCache,Chinzia 10
11May86-1Lga 6f :21 3 :44 3 1:09 4 ft 28 118 8 17 8 23 7 18 7 14 DomngzRE 6 ⒻM40000 73-18 MusiclMorig,NturlBlonde,Tbl'sGold 8
Dec 24 SA 4f ft :49 2 h — Dec 19 SA 7f ft 1:30 1 hg — Dec 11 SA 5f ft 1:01 h — Dec 2 SA 6f ft 1:14 3 h

D.
5–2

Arctic Land — B. f. 4, by Bold Forbes—Darling Diane, by His Majesty
STEVENS G L — 117 — Br.—Dominguez J (Ky) — 1986 19 3 2 0 $39,610
Own.—Barrera & Dominguez Jr — Tr.—Barrera Lazaro S — $20,000 — 1985 1 M 0 0
Lifetime 20 3 2 0 $39,610

27Dec86-9SA 1 1/16 :45 4 1:11 1 1:45 2 ft 4½ 117 6 8 7 7½ 4 6 4 5¼ Vergara O 3 Ⓕ 25000 69-19 DonATop,FrenchStr,Winsomthing 12
10Dec86-9Hol 1 :46 3 1:11 3 1:38 ft *2¼ 114 5 5 4 5½ 4 2½ 2 3½ Stevens G L 1 Ⓕ 32000 69-20 ReputtionMiss,ArcticLnd,BidForHr 7
10Dec86—Wide into stretch
26Nov86-6Hol 1 :46 1:11 1 1:37 2 ft 6½ 115 6 2½ 5 2½ 5 5 4 3½ Stevens G L 2 Ⓕ 32000 72-20 RochellsGirl,EsternGlmour,Velvetn 9
12Nov86-9Hol 1⅛ :47 3 1:13 1:51 3 ft 3½ 114 2 hd 1 1 1 3½ 1 3½ Stevens G L 4 Ⓕ 22500 79-15 ArcticLnd,TxtBookLdy,AKissForKt 9
30Oct86-9SA 1 1/16 :46 4 1:11 2 1:43 4 ft *2¼ 120 3 1½ 3 2½ 3 2½ 4 4 Stevens G L 6 Ⓕ 20000 78-18 RufflsNBus,TxtBookLdy,Fool'sHill 12
30Oct86—Broke in a tangle
17Oct86-3SA 1 :45 4 1:11 1:37 4 ft 6½ 115 7 9½ 8 10 7 9 4 8 Stevens G L 1 Ⓕ 25000 71-21 RochelsGirl,LadyHelch,SnowCrem 9
17Oct86—Checked, altered course mid-stretch
4Oct86-3SA 1 :46 2 1:12 1 1:39 ft 8½ 113 6 12 6 5½ 5 4½ 1¾ Stevens G L 5 Ⓕ 20000 73-18 ArcticLand,UniversIMlii,BidForHer 8
4Oct86—Hopped in air
23Sep86-8Pom 6½f :21 2 :45 1:17 3 ft 9½ 115 7 12 5 7 5 5½ 2 2½ Vergara O 1 Ⓕ 16000 90-08 AboveThRst,ArcticLnd,VnillFstDnc 8
4Sep86-9Dmr 1 :45 2 1:11 3 1:37 ft 7½ 115 9 8¼ 9 8¾ 6 8½ 5 9¾ Stevens G L 7 Ⓕ 20000 73-14 EstrnGlmour,ArForcBby,BrooksPl 10
22Aug86-9Dmr 1 1/16 :46 1:11 2 1:44 ft 3½ 116 8 6½ 8 6 6 4½ 6 3¾ Stevens G L 4 Ⓕ 25000 76-14 Nicholova, La Preciosa, Sweetest 9
Jan 5 SA 4f sy :49 3 h — Dec 24 SA 4f ft :48 1 h — Dec 18 Hol 4f ft :48 2 h — Dec 5 Hol 4f ft :49 2 h

E.
9–2

Text Book Lady — Dk. b. or br. f. 4, by Text—With Your Blessing, by Fleet Nasrullah
PINCAY L JR — 115 — Br.—American Investments (Ky) — 1986 15 1 3 1 $20,245
Own.—Brnstn-Blk-Frmn St-Sltn — Tr.—Bernstein David — $20,000 — Turf 1 0 0 0
Lifetime 15 1 3 1 $20,245

11Dec86-1Hol 1 :46 1 1:12 1:37 4 ft 8¾ 110 5 8 5½ 5 3½ 5 4 4 5¼ Patton D B 3 Ⓕ 32000 69-21 Dncer'sRegrds,EsternGlmour,Vlvtn 8
11Dec86—Bumped 1/16
21Nov86-9Hol 1⅛ :47 1 1:12 1:51 3 ft *9-5 114 5 4 5 2¾ 6 7 4 5½ Stevens G L 8 Ⓕ c20000 73-20 Cbriolet,Neumie'sGirl,Julin'sDrem 10
12Nov86-9Hol 1⅛ :47 3 1:13 1:51 3 ft *2¼ 108 5 3 nk 2 1 2 3½ 2 3½ Patton D B 8 Ⓕ 25000 75-15 ArcticLnd,TxtBookLdy,AKissForKt 9
12Nov86—Drifted out 1/16
30Oct86-9SA 1 1/16 :46 4 1:11 2 1:43 4 ft 24 112 5 6 5 5 5 4 3 2½ Patton D B 9 Ⓕ 20000 81-18 RufflsNBus,TxtBookLdy,Fool'sHill 12
13Oct86-7SA 1⅛ Ⓣ :46 1 1:11 1:49 1 fm 155 113 4 3½ 11 7¾ 12 17 12 22 StevnsSA 12 ⒻAw27000 59-19 Darnit, Cruella, Super Kitten 12
12Sep86-10Pom 1 1/16 :45 3 1:11 2 1:45 ft 50 115 9 10 10 12 10 17 8 21 CstnonAL 9 ⒻAw27000 65-11 Neumie'sGirl,Btt'sLdy,UnivrsIMlii 10
21Aug86-6Dmr 1⅛ :46 2 1:11 4 1:50 3 ft 9½ 116 1 1½ 1 1½ 1 4 1 6½ Stevens GL 7 ⒻM32000 77-17 TextBookLady,Getn,OdieCumbers 12
7Aug86-2Dmr 1 1/16 :45 4 1:11 3 1:44 4 ft 33 116 11 12 8 5¼ 7 6½ 4 6½ Olivares F 9 ⒻM32000 69-16 End Cap, Campti, Ice Stepper 12
7Aug86—Broke slowly; crowded, steadied at 3/16
9Jly86-2Hol 1⅛ :46 4 1:13 1:53 2 ft 4 114 3 3 8 5½ 6 12 6 13½ Ortega L E 2 ⒻM32000 56-18 SnowCream,OneForAndre,Shiniest 12
8Jun86-4GG 1 1/16 :46 1:10 2 1:41 2 ft 6½ 115 8 15 10 18 8 23 7 28 Toro F 11 ⒻMdn 68-11 Nomowho,BalletBlanc,GoldenTake 11
Jan 2 SA 5f ft 1:01 h — Dec 27 SA 5f ft 1:00 3 h — Dec 21 SA 5f ft 1:01 1 h — Dec 6 Hol 3f m :35 3 h

F.

11–1

Juliana's Dream — B. m. 7, by Don B—Foxy Juliana, by Gummo

SIMPSON B H — **116** — Br.—Double H J Stable (Cal) — Tr.—Cerin Vladimir — $20,000

1986 14 4 1 1 $47,425

1985 11 3 2 2 $33,225

Own.—Landsburg A — Lifetime 46 8 4 6 $102,475

19Dec86-4Hol	$1\frac{1}{16}$:47^2 1:13 1:46 ft	$2\frac34$	116	$4^{4\frac12}$	$3^{1\frac12}$	2^{hd}	$2^{\frac12}$	Stevens G L^7	Ⓕ 16000	78-17	AncientLady,Julin'sDrem,MissDniel	8
21Nov86-9Hol	$1\frac18$:47^1 1:12 1:51^3ft	5	116	7^{13}	7^{11}	$5^{5\frac12}$	$3^{2\frac34}$	DelhoussyeE^5	Ⓕ 20000	76-20	Cbriolet,Neumie'sGirl,Julin'sDrem	10
6Nov86-5Hol	$1\frac18$:46^4 1:12^2 1:53 ft	*8-5	119	$5^{9\frac12}$	3^6	$1^{1\frac12}$	$1^{1\frac14}$	Stevens G L^1	Ⓕ 12500	72-17	Julin'sDrm,Dlt'sGoldCoin,SuprisGft	8
15Oct86-9SA	$1\frac{1}{16}$:46^3 1:12^4 1:46^2ft	$3\frac34$	116	8^{10}	6^3	$2^{1\frac12}$	$1^{1\frac12}$	Stevens G L^4	Ⓕ 16000	69-18	Julin'sDrm,Mistingutt,DvlishDzzlr	11
3Oct86-1SA	$1\frac{1}{16}$:47^2 1:12^3 1:45^4gd	$3\frac14$	116	6^7	6^6	$6^{5\frac12}$	5^6	Soto S B^3	Ⓕ 12500	66-17	FunnyTumblr,DsrtDw,TrdtonOfHop	8

3Oct86—Checked at 1/8

29Aug86-9Dmr	$1\frac{1}{16}$:45^4 1:11^1 1:44^2ft	5	116	7^{14}	5^{11}	$5^{7\frac12}$	4^5	Soto S B^6	Ⓕ 16000	73-15	ShiveringKiss,DvlishDzzlr,FrnchStr	8
15Aug86-9Dmr	$1\frac{1}{16}$:46 1:11^1 1:43^3ft	11	116	$9^{9\frac34}$	$9^{5\frac34}$	4^7	4^6	HernandezR^{11}	Ⓕ 12500	76-12	Paisana, Hidden Angle, Spending	12

15Aug86—Broke in a tangle

27Jun86-9Hol	$1\frac18$:46^4 1:11^3 1:51^3ft	$4\frac34$	116	7^{12}	6^{15}	8^{18}	—	Hernandez R^2	Ⓕ 12500	— —	Bold Way, French Star,GreenAgain	8

27Jun86—Bled; Threw head at start

5Apr86-3SA	$1\frac{1}{16}$:46^3 1:11^4 1:45^2ft	$5\frac14$	121	7^{15}	8^{16}	9^{18}	$11^{19\frac14}$	Kaenel J L^1	Ⓕ c25000	55-20	SrchForHvn,SnwyWngs,RdFrnchy	11
8Mar86-1SA	$1\frac{1}{16}$:47 1:12^2 1:45^2sy	8	116	7^{14}	7^{12}	7^{11}	$7^{11\frac12}$	Stevens G L^6	Ⓕ 40000	62-19	BrodStreet,‡ErOfTriumph,PressKit	7

Dec 12 SA 5f ft 1:03 h

G.

6–1

Nicholova — B. f. 4, by Numa Pompilius—Aptobe Fleet, by Fleet Nasrullah

KAENEL J L — **115** — Br.—Cannata Mr–Mrs C (Cal) — Tr.—Fulton John W — $20,000

1986 12 3 2 0 $29,825

1985 1 M 0 0 $450

Turf 1 0 0 0

Own.—Cannata Mr–Mrs C — Lifetime 13 3 2 0 $30,275

4Dec86-3Hol	6f :22 :46^3 1:12^1ft	$5\frac12$	116	7^8	5^3	2^3	2^3	Kaenel J L^1	ⒻⓈ 20000	79-25	I'mTeasableToo,Nicholova,OhMarie	7

4Dec86—Steadied 5/8, wide 3/8 turn

17Oct86-3SA	1 :45^4 1:11 1:37^4ft	*$2\frac14$	117	5^5	5^7	8^{12}	$8^{15\frac34}$	Kaenel J L^8	Ⓕ 25000	63-21	RochellsGirl,LadyHelch,SnowCrem	9
10Sep86-5Dmr	$1\frac{1}{16}$Ⓣ:$46^2$1:$11^3$1:43 fm	$8\frac12$	117	2^4	$2^{2\frac12}$	6^9	$6^{10\frac14}$	Kaenel J L^5	ⒻAw23000	81-07	WistfulTune,GoldieHwn,AntiqueLc	9
22Aug86-9Dmr	$1\frac{1}{16}$:46 1:11^2 1:44 ft	$6\frac14$	118	$4^{2\frac12}$	3^1	1^{hd}	$1^{\frac12}$	Kaenel J L^9	Ⓕ 25000	80-14	Nicholova, La Preciosa, Sweetest	9
11Aug86-3Dmr	1 :45^4 1:10^4 1:36^1ft	20	116	3^3	$4^{3\frac12}$	5^{10}	$5^{11\frac12}$	Kaenel J L^2	Ⓕ 32000	75-13	SroGolden,Velveten,CuriousPrincss	8
9Jly86-9Hol	1 :45^3 1:11^2 1:38 ft	11	116	$5^{2\frac14}$	$5^{\frac34}$	$1^{1\frac12}$	1^4	Kaenel J L^1	Ⓕ 25000	73-18	Nicholova, La Preciosa,BrookesPal	9
11Jun86-4Hol	1 :46^3 1:11^3 1:38 ft	3	115	2^{hd}	3^1	4^4	5^7	McCarron CJ^2	Ⓕ 25000	66-16	Pert N Saucy, Saro Golden, Mush	8
21May86-9Hol	7f :22^1 :45^3 1:24^1ft	32	116	$6^{3\frac12}$	$6^{1\frac34}$	$2^{3\frac12}$	2^3	Kaenel J L^1	Ⓕ 25000	80-13	Saro Golden, Nicholova, ReilDarin	10

21May86—Crowded 3/8 turn

4Apr86-1SA	1 :46^4 1:12^1 1:38^3ft	29	116	2^1	$4^{1\frac14}$	5^5	$6^{7\frac14}$	Kaenel J L^2	Ⓕ 40000	68-23	Quick N' Solid, Mush, Velveteen	8

4Apr86—Steadied at 3/16

20Mar86-1SA	$1\frac{1}{16}$:46^4 1:12^2 1:46^3ft	$5\frac12$	117	2^4	2^1	$1^{2\frac12}$	$1^{4\frac12}$	Kaenel JL^8	ⒻⓈM32000	68-19	Nicholova,BelmoneyBay,BayBreeze	9

Dec 29 SA 6f ft 1:16^1 h   Dec 21 Hol 5f ft 1:02^3 h   Nov 23 Hol 5f ft 1:00^1 h   Nov 15 Hol 4f ft :47^2 h

H.

24–1

Decorata — B. f. 4, by Well Decorated—Gazer, by Judger

BAZE G — **115** — Br.—Kem Diane C (Wash) — Tr.—Roberts Craig — $20,000

1986 16 3 0 3 $25,000

1985 2 M 0 0 $900

Turf 1 0 0 0

Own.—K & L Stables — Lifetime 18 3 0 3 $25,900

27Dec86-9SA	$1\frac{1}{16}$:45^4 1:11^1 1:45^2ft	76	114	5^7	$6^{6\frac12}$	6^7	$5^{7\frac12}$	Baze G^6	Ⓕ 25000	66-19	DonATop,FrenchStr,Winsomthing	12
19Dec86-4Hol	$1\frac{1}{16}$:47^2 1:13 1:46 ft	18	114	$2^{\frac12}$	2^1	4^2	$4^{6\frac14}$	Baze G^8	Ⓕ 16000	73-17	AncientLady,Julin'sDrem,MissDniel	8

19Dec86—Wide 7/8 turn

21Sep86-8Lga	$1\frac{1}{16}$:48^2 1:13^1 1:44^1ft	$8\frac34$	115	7^{11}	$7^{9\frac12}$	7^{14}	$7^{11\frac12}$	Wentz M^5	Ⓕ 32000	66-17	Split Tail,MereScintilla,IceHillLady	7
17Aug86-9Lga	$1\frac18$:46 1:09^4 1:47^2ft	25	113	6^{20}	6^{16}	6^{19}	$6^{17\frac12}$	Wentz M^1	ⒻSacajw H	78-13	Firesweeper,Hrtliftr,Cruisin'TwoSu	6
14Aug86-9Lga	$1\frac{1}{16}$:47^2 1:12^1 1:43^2ft	$3\frac12$	115	6^{11}	6^8	$5^{7\frac12}$	4^7	Wentz M^3	ⒻAw9300	75-18	SplitTail,HarbourPlace,MondoTime	6
26Jly86-8Lga	$1\frac{1}{16}$:47 1:11^4 1:45 ft	*$2\frac12$	118	$8^{4\frac34}$	7^5	4^8	$1^{1\frac12}$	Wentz M^8	Ⓕ 25000	74-15	Decorata, Piratical, Long Yardage	8
19Jly86-9Lga	$1\frac{1}{16}$:46^1 1:10^2 1:41^3ft	39	114	9^{13}	8^{14}	7^{16}	7^{15}	WentzM^8	ⒻSeafair Qn	76-17	TwiceWritten,Firesweeper,Hrtliftr	10
2Jly86-9Pln	1^{70}:46^3 1:11 1:42^1ft	$4\frac34$	118	$8^{7\frac34}$	$7^{5\frac14}$	$4^{4\frac12}$	3^{hd}	Lamance C^2	Ⓕ 25000	83-18	She's So Bold, Menaevia, Decorata	8

2Jly86—Lugged in 7 1/2

19Jun86-6GG	$1\frac{1}{16}$Ⓣ:$49^3$1:$14^1$1:46^1fm	$4\frac34$e	117	$7^{5\frac34}$	$7^{7\frac14}$	$7^{7\frac34}$	$7^{7\frac14}$	Lamance C^8	Ⓕ 25000	64-22	SelectdPrincss,BluSilk,Sh'sSoBold	8
4Jun86-1GG	$1\frac{1}{16}$:47^4 1:12 1:44^3ft	13	114	3^1	$2^{\frac12}$	1^2	$1^{1\frac12}$	Lamance C^1	Ⓕ 25000	80-17	Decort,DiscreteAffir,SelectdPrincss	7

Dec 11 SA 3f ft :36^3 h   Dec 2 SA 4f ft :49^2 h   Nov 26 SA 4f ft :49^1 h   Nov 17 SA 6f ft 1:16^1 h

I.
7–1

Ancient Lady
OLIVARES F
Own.—Neich Cynthia
116
Ch. m. 6, by Nostalgia—Lady Maxwell, by Crowned Prince
Br.—Mabee Mr–Mrs J C (Cal) 1986 10 2 1 1 $23,850
Tr.—Velasquez Danny $20,000 1985 6 2 0 0 $28,225
Lifetime 26 8 3 3 $96,225 Turf 1 0 0 0

19Dec86-4Hol 1 1/16 :472 1:13 1:46 ft 5½ 116 55 42½ 31 1½ Olivares F6 Ⓕ 16000 79-17 AncientLady,Julin'sDrem,MissDniel 8
19Nov86-1Hol 1 :461 1:12 1:391ft 6½ 117 611 66½ 45 1¾ Pincay L Jr4 Ⓕ c12500 67-21 Ancient Lady, Faye, Lisaanne 8
12Nov86-9Hol 1⅛ :473 1:13 1:513ft 8½ 116 66¼ 75¼ 811 811 Kaenel J L6 Ⓕ 25000 68-15 ArcticLnd,TxtBookLdy,AKissForKt 9
12Nov86—Wide into stretch
13Oct86-9SA 6f :221 :454 1:114ft 53 116 89½ 87¼ 55 21¾ Hawley S2 Ⓕ 16000 77-19 HiddnPst,AncintLdy,Ms.CrookdRod 9
13Oct86—Broke slowly
23Aug86-6Cby 6f :222 :454 1:114ft 29 111 915 911 99¾ 712 Montoya D8 Ⓕ 22500 76-13 Vivi's Tab, Soshonean,Erimo'sLady 9
10Jly86-9Cby 1 :473 1:121 1:383ft 6½ 114 615 612 512 522¾ Moyers L2 Ⓕ 25000 65-11 WoodfordBelle,IndinHthr,MriofEss 6
16Apr86-9SA 1 1/16 :462 1:111 1:453ft 3 116 619 611 59½ 32¾ HernandezR6 Ⓕ c20000 70-24 LuckySilver,AKissForKti,AncintLdy 8
5Apr86-3SA 1 1/16 :463 1:114 1:452ft 11 115 613 510 44½ 44 Hernandez R6 Ⓕ 25000 70-20 SrchForHvn,SnwyWngs,RdFrnchy 11

55. The Grade 1 American Derby for 3YOs was won in 1987 by an Illinois-bred. Handicappers who understand these top-grade events would have preferred an overlay that ran well, but lost by a small margin. Which 3YO was it?

9th Arlington

1 ¼ MILES. (1.59⅗) 76th Running AMERICAN DERBY ALLOWANCE STAKES (Grade I). $150,000 Added. 3-year-olds. By subscription of $150 each, which should accompany the nomination, $750 to pass the entry box, an additional $750 to start, with $150,000 added, of which 60% of all monies to the owner of the winner, 20% to second, 11% to third, 6% to fourth and 3% to fifth. Weight, 123 lbs. Non-winners of $50,000 three times over one mile allowed 3 lbs.; $50,000 twice at one mile or over in 1987, 5 lbs.; $50,000 or $25,000 twice at one mile or over in 1987, 8 lbs.; $30,000 at one mile or over, 11 lbs. The American Derby will be limited to fourteen starters. Should more than fourteen pass the entry box, the starters will be determined at that time with preference given to winners of graded stakes, next preference, to those that have accumulated the highest earnings in races of one mile or over. As many as four colts may be placed on the also eligible list. Starters to be named through the entry box by the usual time of closing. A trophy to the owner of the winner. (Closed with 25 nominations.)

A.
15–1

Best Solution
Own.—Siegel-Bauer-Estrin et al
112
B. c. 3, by Riverman—Starushka, by Sham
Br.—Moyglare Stud Farm, Ltd. (Ky) 1987 5 1 1 2 $17,087
Tr.—Cross Richard J 1986 2 1 0 0 $2,331
Lifetime 7 2 1 2 $19,418 Turf 7 2 1 2 $19,418

16Jly87-8Hol 1 1/16 Ⓣ:463 1:102 1:412fm 2 115 77 73¾ 73¾ 1nk Toro F9 Aw24000 87-13 Best Solution, Jonleat,PatientKing 9
9May87♦5Leopardst'n(Ire) 1⅛ 1:534gd 4½ 121 Ⓣ 2nk KnMJ CastleKnitwearHcp Brevet,BestSolution,HedofThHous 10
18Apr87♦7PhoenixPk(Ire) 1⅛ 1:591yl 2½ 126 Ⓣ 35 KinnMJ Harp Lager Plate Golden Isle, Orembo, Best Solution 8
28Mar87♦2Leopardst'n(Ire) 1⅛ 1:534sf *2½ 131 Ⓣ 3½ KinnMJ Coolmine Plate HeiressGren,AnothrErl,BstSolution 9
17Mar87♦3Leopardstn'(Ire) 7f 1:322gd *4-5 128 Ⓣ 47 KMJ BurmahCastrolTrophy IslndReef,Isn'thGorgous,OnthTurf 11
14Sep86♦4Curragh(Ire) 7f 1:253gd 8 126 Ⓣ 55¾ PrnllD National Stakes (Gr I) Lockton, Babakaram,RockChanteur 9
30Aug86♦7Curragh(Ire) 7f 1:31 gd 7 126 Ⓣ 1¾ PrnllD MerrionPlate (Mdn) BestSolution,ShrpAction,HzelBoy 14
Jly 12 Hol 6f ft 1:123 h ● Jly 7 Hol 1 ft 1:412 h Jly 1 Hol 7f ft 1:27 h Jun 25 Hol 6f ft 1:141 h

B.
3–1

Avies Copy
Own.—Badgett T B
118
Dk. b. or br. c. 3, by Lord Avie—Display Copy, by Iron Ruler
Br.—Badgett T Brown (Ky) 1987 12 3 2 2 $420,856
Tr.—Kassen David C 1986 3 M 0 0 $1,510
Lifetime 15 3 2 2 $422,366

11Jly87-9AP 1⅛ :454 1:093 1:493ft 5¾ 120 37½ 37½ 35 32½ SolomonM 7 Classic 80-25 Lost Code, Gem Master, AviesCopy 7
11Jly87—Grade I
6Jun87-8Bel 1½ :492 2:03 2:281ft 31 126 12 58 616 725¼ SolomnM 2 Belmont 54-15 Bet Twice, Cryptoclearance, Gulch 9
6Jun87—Grade I
25May87-10GS 1¼ :472 1:371 2:032ft 4¼ 126 13 12 14 1½ SolmnM 1 Jersey Dby 87-24 AviesCopy,ProudestDuke,TmplrHill 9
25May87—Grade II
16May87-9Pim 1 3/16 :471 1:113 1:554ft 24 126 98¾ 96¾ 67 56¼ SolmnM 8 Preakness 82-18 Alysheba,BetTwice,Cryptoclearnce 9
16May87—Grade I

2May87-8CD 1¼:46² 1:36⁴ 2:03²ft 25f 126 10 7½ 4 2½ 3 2½ 3 3 SolmnM 16 Ky Derby 77-20 Alysheba, Bet Twice, Avies Copy 17
2May87—Grade I
23Apr87-7Kee 1⅛:46⁴ 1:10² 1:48²ft 8¾ 121 4 2¼ 3 2½ 5 6 5 9 BrumfildD 5 B Grass 86-13 ‡Alysheba, War, Leo Castelli 5
23Apr87—Grade I
4Apr87-10GP 1⅛:47² 1:11⁴ 1:49³ft 100 118 1 4 1 ½ 2 hd 4 2 CruguetJ 5 Fla Derby 82-23 Cryptoclernc,NoMorFlowrs,Tlinum 9
4Apr87—Grade I
15Mar87-8GP 1 1/16:48 1:13 1:45²ft *3-2 122 3 1½ 2 hd 3 3 2 4 Brumfield D 6 Aw16000 70-23 ProudestDuke,AvisCopy,FunnyTuns 8
8Mar87-8GP 1 1/16:47⁴ 1:12⁴ 1:47¹ft *1 122 2½ 1½ 1 2½ 1 6½ Brumfield D 4 Aw15000 65-25 Avies Copy, Goa, Mc Forbes 8
28Feb87-11Hia 1⅛:46⁴ 1:11 1:50 ft 52f 118 8 9½ 9 6¾ 10 11 10 10¼ VasquezJ7 Flamingo 71-19 Talinum,Cryptoclearnce,LeoCstelli 14
28Feb87—Grade I
Jly 30 AP 3f ft :36 b ●Jly 26 AP 5f ft 1:00 h

C.
5–2

Gem Master ✻ 118
Own.—Calumet Farm
B. c. 3, by Green Dancer—Baby Diamonds, by Habitat
Br.—KinderhillCorp.GeneralPrtner (Ky) 1987 3 1 1 1 $86,855
Tr.—Foyt A J III 1986 7 2 1 1 $88,805
Lifetime 10 3 2 2 $175,660 Turf 1 0 1 0 $3,000

11Jly87-9AP 1⅛:45⁴ 1:09³ 1:49³ft 4 120 4 8½ 4 7½ 2 5 2 2½ Day P 4 Classic 80-25 Lost Code, Gem Master, AviesCopy 7
11Jly87—Grade I
20Jun87-8AP 1 :45¹ 1:10² 1:36³sy 7 120 3 2½ 3 3 1 hd 1 6½ Day P 1 Sheridn 78-22 Gem Master,Madoon,TheRedRolls 10
20Jun87—Grade II
10Jun87-8AP 7f :23 :46 1:24¹ft 7½ 123 7 2½ 5 3 4 3½ 3 3¾ Day P 2 Aw25000 77-22 TheRedRolls,WinDustyWin,GmMstr 8
10Oct86-7Kee 1 1/16:47³ 1:12² 1:45¹ft 11 121 10 5¼ 7 3¾ 9 6¾ 8 6¾ ThibeuRJ 7 Brds Fut 73-16 Orono, Alysheba, Pledge Card 10
10Oct86—Grade II; Carried well wide first turn
27Sep86-8Haw 1 1/16:47 1:11⁴ 1:45 ft 4 112 6 4½ 6 6 2 2½ 1 hd Thibeau R J 1 Haw Juv 73-17 GemMaster,JamesOscar,TwoBgger 9
1Sep86-3AP 1 Ⓣ:47¹ 1:13 1:39¹fm *7-5 117 8 7½ 2 1 2 2 2 1¼ Day P 7 Aw15000 79-19 DoinO.K.,GemMaster,FrenchRussin 8
22Aug86-9AP 1 :46² 1:11¹ 1:36⁴ft 5 120 4 1¾ 2½ 1 hd 1 hd Hawley S10 Mdn 77-14 GemMster,Alyshb,Contrctor'sTun 10
8Aug86-5Cby 6f :22³ :46¹ 1:13¹ft *6-5 117 3 nk 2 hd 2½ 4 1 Smith M E1 Mdn 80-16 SunshineSpkr,RdOn'sTtr,PointClr 12
11Jly86-5Cby 5f :22¹ :46 :58⁴m 6 117 6 7 5 8½ 4 5 3 4 Hawley S5 Mdn 91-14 Sawasee, Sony Blum, Gem Master 8
27Jun86-5Cby 5f :22³ :46⁴ 1:00¹ft 6½ 117 6 10 6 8½ 5 6 4 5½ Hawley S10 Mdn 83-21 Staff Riot, Sawasee, Mostly Sport 10
Jly 30 AP 3f ft :37² b ●Jly 23 AP 5f ft 1:00 b ●Jly 4 AP 5f ft :58³ h Jun 8 AP 3f ft :37 b

D.
5–1

Fortunate Moment 118
Own.—Pinkley Jerry R
Ch. c. 3, by For the Moment—Restless Cat, by Restless Wind
Br.—Pinkley Jerry R (Ill) 1987 5 5 0 0 $92,430
Tr.—Vanier Harvey L 1986 0 M 0 0
Lifetime 5 5 0 0 $92,430

26Jly87-8AP 1⅛:47¹ 1:12 1:50²ft *1-5 118 2½ 2 hd 1½ 1 1 Day P5 Ⓢ J D Hertz 79-28 FortuntMomnt,Iwntosk,MnofthHos 6
16Jly87-8AP 1 :46² 1:11¹ 1:36¹ft *4-5 107 1 1 1½ 1 hd 1 1½ Day P3 Aw17000 80-22 FortunteMomnt,ThRoylFrz,IrishFrz 6
3Jly87-8AP 1 :45² 1:10¹ 1:35 ft *3-2 112 2 1½ 2 2 1 2 1 4 Day P7 Ⓢ Springfield 86-21 FortntMomnt,Iwntosk,ColMrchnt 11
8Jun87-5AP 6½f :23 :46⁴ 1:18⁴ft *2-5 112 1 1 1 1 1 1 1 5 Day P5 Ⓢ Aw14300 81-24 FrtntMmnt,DmtrsSrd,TmprrRsdnt 10
27May87-2AP 6f :22⁴ :47¹ 1:12¹ft *4-5 115 1 1½ 1 1½ 1 4 1 9 Day P1 Ⓢ Mdn 79-21 FrtntMmnt,Snn'sInvstmnt,CntlRd 12
Jly 23 AP 5f ft 1:01³ b Jly 15 AP 3f sy :36¹ b Jly 10 AP 4f ft :47⁴ b Jun 27 AP 1 ft 1:38¹ b

E.
10–1

Fast Forward 118
Own.—Klein E V
B. c. 3, by Pleasant Colony—Just One More Time, by Raise a Native
Br.—Spendthrift Farm (Ky) 1987 12 4 3 0 $222,658
Tr.—Lukas D Wayne 1986 7 1 0 1 $18,880
Lifetime 19 5 3 1 $241,538

11Jly87-9AP 1⅛:45⁴ 1:09³ 1:49³ft 10 120 2 1½ 2 2½ 4 5½ 4 5½ Fires E 5 Classic 77-25 Lost Code, Gem Master, AviesCopy 7
11Jly87—Grade I
20Jun87-8AP 1 :45¹ 1:10² 1:36³sy *4-5 123 6 4½ 5 7½ 4 5 4 7½ FrazierRL 3 Sheridn 70-22 Gem Master,Madoon,TheRedRolls 10
20Jun87—Grade II
6Jun87-9CD 1⅛:47⁴ 1:12¹ 1:50 ft *1-3 120 2½ 1 2½ 1 5 1 6 Frazier R L 1 Jnd Cup 92-13 FastFoward,Unlevened,GretnGreen 5
25May87-10GS 1¼:47² 1:37¹ 2:03²ft 9¼ 126 4 3½ 3 3½ 6 12 8 17 BaileyJD 7 Jersey Dby 70-24 AviesCopy,ProudestDuke,TmplrHill 9
25May87—Grade II
2May87-7CD 1 1/16:47 1:11² 1:43¹ft *4-5e 115 1 1 1 hd 1 1½ 1 5 Day P 4 T Spires 92-09 FstForwrd,SoonrShowrs,Hombuildr 5
18Apr87-9OP 1⅛:46⁴ 1:10⁴ 1:47³ft 2½e 118 6 5 5 2¼ 4 3½ 4 6¾ FrzierRL 6 Aks Dby 89-13 DmonsBgon,Loknfrthbgn,Y'rNBrgn 6
18Apr87—Grade I
11Apr87-8Bir 1⅛:47¹ 1:11² 1:51³ft 2¼ 122 3 2¾ 3 4½ 3 5 4 7¼ Romero R P 1 Ala Dby — — LostCode,Homebuilder,PhntomJt 12
28Mar87-9OP 1 1/16:46 1:10 1:41²ft 4¼ 114 1 2½ 1 1 2½ 2 4 Frazier R L 1 Rebel 90-15 DmonsBgon,FstForwrd,Yo'rNoBrgn 6
17Mar87-9OP 1 1/16:46⁴ 1:11² 1:43¹sy 9-5 115 2 hd 1 hd 1 2 1 12 Day P 3 Aw25000 85-17 FastForward,SavedbyZero,RapidRy 6
27Feb87-8OP 1 :46² 1:11³ 1:38¹sy *6-5 122 2 1½ 1 1 1 4 1 3¾ Snyder L 1 Aw14000 81-23 FastForwrd,GretnGreen,DrienDevil 8
Jly 29 AP 5f gd 1:00⁴ h Jly 8 AP 5f ft 1:00² h ●Jly 1 AP 6f ft 1:14⁴ b Jun 16 AP 3f ft :36¹ b

F.
10–1

K. C.'s Best Turn
Own.—Baker Farm **115**
Gr. c. 3, by Best Turn—Ky Cut Up, by Hatchet Man
Br.—Lundy J T–Whiteley F Y Jr (Ky) 1987 11 3 4 0 $118,334
Tr.—Bailie Sally A 1986 0 M 0 0
Lifetime 11 3 4 0 $118,334

3Jly87-8Bel 1⅛ :47 1:10³ 1:48²gd 12 119 6¹¹ 6¹⁵ 5¹⁶ 4²¹ Davis R G2 Dwyer 64-21 Gone West, PledgeCard,PolishNavy 6
3Jly87—Grade I
19Jun87-6Bel 1$\frac{1}{16}$:46² 1:11 1:42³ft 2¼ 111 6¹² 56 21½ 2nk Davis R G2 Aw31000 89-21 BldSmmt,KC'sBstTrn,EmbrcsSblng 6
6Jun87-4Bel 1⅛ :45³ 1:10¹ 1:49³ft 21 115 10¹⁵109½ 42½ 11½ Davis R G9 Colin 79-15 K.C.'sBstTurn,PldgCrd,OmrKhyym 11
24May87-8Bel 1⅛ :46⁴ 1:10² 1:48 ft 33 114 95¼ 94¾ 79½ 610¼ Bailey JD9 Peter Pan 77-16 LeoCastelli,GoneWest,ShwklitWon 9
24May87—Grade II
1May87-8Aqu 1 :47⁴ 1:11⁴ 1:37 ft *8-5 112 73¾ 72¾ 41¾ 2nk Bailey J D3 Aw28000 81-18 EqulTrms,K.C.'sBstTurn,RondThStt 7
1May87—Blocked for 6f
18Apr87-8Aqu 1⅛ :47 1:11³ 1:49 m 14 126 8¹⁴ 6¹⁵ 7¹⁷ 616½ RmrRP2 Wood Mem 73-15 Gulch, Gone West, Shawklit Won 8
18Apr87—Grade I
25Mar87-7Aqu 1 :46¹ 1:10² 1:37 ft 3 119 74½ 53½ 41½ 11 Santos J A10 Aw27000 81-27 K.C.'sBstTurn,Brskn,MxdEmotons 10
4Mar87-5Aqu 1$\frac{1}{16}$ [•]:48³1:13¹1:45 ft 4 117⁵ 67¼ 66 51½ 2no Baird E T4 Aw27000 85-16 Girning,K.C.'sBestTurn,QuietlyBold 6
20Feb87-4Aqu 1⅛ [•]:49²1:14⁴1:55⁴ft *2-3 117⁵ 8¹¹ 77½ 1hd 12½ Baird E T6 Mdn 63-28 K.C.'sBestTurn,BucketShop,Goliard 9
20Feb87—Checked,driving
1Feb87-6Aqu 1⅛ [•]:49⁴1:15²1:54⁴gd 4½ 117⁵ 67½ 58½ 21½ 21 Baird E T1 Mdn 67-26 Hostn'Hl,K.C.'sBstTrn,FrnchCnnctr 8
Jly 1 Bel 4f ft :49² b Jun 26 Bel 6f ft 1:15⁴ b Jun 14 Bel 5f ft 1:03³ b Jun 3 Bel 6f gd 1:18¹ b

56. Decide which horse is best at the odds.

4th Santa Anita

1 MILE (SANTA ANITA)

1 MILE. (1.33⅗) MAIDEN. Purse $23,000. Fillies. 3-year-olds. Weight, 117 lbs. (Non-starters for a claiming price of $32,000 or less preferred.)

A.
3–1

You Make Me Happy
BLACK C A
Own.—Gentry T **117**
B. f. 3, by Summing—Happy Guess, by Happy Kidan
Br.—Gentry T (Ky) 1987 2 M 1 1 $7,350
Tr.—Fanning Jerry 1986 6 M 0 2 $8,085
Lifetime 8 0 1 3 $15,435

17Jan87-6SA 6f :21⁴ :45¹ 1:11 ft 25 117 76½ 55½ 44½ 22½ Black C A9 ⒻMdn 80-18 TimelyReserve,YouMkMHppy,Foli 12
17Jan87—Broke slowly
3Jan87-4SA 6f :21⁴ :45² 1:10²ft 7½ 117 55½ 55 36 37½ Black C A5 ⒻMdn 78-16 JoyThTrp,HllSwtThng,YMkMHppy 10
25Oct86-4SA 6f :21² :44³ 1:12¹ft 18 112⁵ 66½ 68½ 46½ 31½ Black C A6 ⒻMdn 76-17 Infringe, Folia,YouMakeMeHappy 12
15Oct86-6SA 1$\frac{1}{16}$:47 1:11³ 1:44⁴ft 31 117 45 45½ 5¹⁰ 617½ Lipham T8 ⒻMdn 60-18 MssEndcott,VctorousGrl,Ros'sCntn 9
15Oct86—Bobbled start
24Sep86-11Pomа1⅛ :48¹ 1:15¹ 1:58¹sy 5½ 113 22 25 5¹⁰ 517¾ Solis A2 ⒻBlk Swn 38-32 QuickMssngr,ShrpMovinKris,Alfitz 8
17Sep86-8Pom 1$\frac{1}{16}$:46² 1:12 1:46¹ft *3-2 116 2hd 33 31 35¼ Solis A6 ⒻMdn 75-13 ThnksToJ.P.,VrMrKr,YoMkMHppy 10
17Sep86—Bumped at 1/16
1Sep86-4Dmr 1 :46³ 1:11⁴ 1:37²ft 3½ 116 1½ 3nk 33½ 48½ McHargue DG2 ⒻMdn 73-13 TipASou,Rose'sCntin,AlwysAWomn 9
1Sep86—Bumped hard start
17Aug86-4Dmr 6f :22 :45² 1:10³ft 5½ 117 99½109½ 9¹⁰ 8¹² McHargue DG3 ⒻMdn 73-16 RnsomdCptiv,Silk'sLdy,SuprCook 10
17Aug86—Bumped start
Jan 24 SA 4f ft :48² h Jan 1 SA 4f ft :49² h Dec 26 SA 6f ft 1:13² h Dec 20 SA 5f ft 1:00¹ h

B.
70–1

Time For Hart
BAZE G
Own.—Timestable **117**
B. f. 3, by Verbatim—Time for a Hrt, by Delta Judge
Br.—Timestable (Ky) 1987 1 M 0 0
Tr.—Ferraro Stephen 1986 5 M 0 2 $4,800
Lifetime 6 0 0 2 $4,800

8Jan87-2SA 6f :22 :46 1:13 m 5½ 118 98¾ 98 67 67 ShoemkerW3 ⒻM50000 66-30 Unassailable, ‡Alice Cee,Reiterate 10
21Nov86-4Hol 6f :22¹ :45⁴ 1:11³ft 17 118 76¾ 87 57 37 Baze G4 ⒻM50000 78-20 SlctASong,SpctclrMomnt,TmFrHrt 8
26Oct86-6SA 1 :45³ 1:11 1:38³ft 19 117 56¾ 7¹⁶ 7¹⁷ 719¾ Toro F2 ⒻMdn 55-16 Rose'sCantin,Midee,KeepOnFlying 10
12Oct86-4SA 6f :21³ :45 1:11³ft 17 117 10¹²10¹⁵10¹³1014¾ Toro F7 ⒻMdn 66-21 Sclding,CleverWife,YoursAnytime 11
12Oct86—Steadied start
8Sep86-8Dmr 6f :22 :45¹ 1:09³ft 28 116 98½ 9¹² 9²³ 8¹⁷ KenlJL6 ⒻⓇCoronado 73-14 EvilEline,PerchnceToDrem,KeyBid 9
8Sep86—Wide 3/8 turn
31Aug86-4Dmr 6f :22¹ :45³ 1:11¹ft 13 117 79½ 6¹¹ 38½ 35½ Kaenel J L8 ⒻMdn 76-12 Senora, Folia, Time For Hart 11
31Aug86—Veered out start; wide 3/8 turn
Jan 26 SA 6f ft 1:16³ h Jan 19 SA 5f ft 1:03² h Jan 5 SA 4f sy :51² h Dec 29 SA 1 ft 1:41⁴ h

C.
2–1

Northern Days
MEZA R Q 3-0   **117**
Own.—Paulson A

Dk. b. or br. f. 3, by Magesterial—Let Me In, by Clem
Br.—Spendthrift Farm (Ky)   1987 1 M 0 1 $3,150
Tr.—Gosden John H M   1986 0 M 0 0
Lifetime 1 0 0 1 $3,150

11Jan87-4SA   6f :214 :452 1:111ft   10 117   73¾ 76½ 65   36¼   Valenzuela PA1 ⓕMdn 75-21 SummrSonds,TxsWld,NorthrnDys 12
● Jan 22 SA 7f ft 1:264 h   Dec 24 Hol 4f ft :494 h   ● Dec 20 Hol 6f ft 1:13 h   Dec 15 Hol 6f ft 1:144 h

D.
23–1

Ridgelite 4-0
DELAHOUSSAYE E   **117**
Own.—Stevens S E

Gr. f. 3, by Cox's Ridge—Split the Tab, by Al Hattab
Br.—Dinnaken Farm (Ky)   1987 2 M 0 0 $525
Tr.—Lukas D Wayne   1986 0 M 0 0
Lifetime 2 0 0 0 $525

18Jan87-4SA   1⅛ :49 1:141 1:461ft   20 117   31 42   78¾ 715½   Meza R Q1   ⓕMdn 54-19 Cee's Vigor, Satin Slew, Develop   8
18Jan87—Broke out bumped
3Jan87-4SA   6f :214 :452 1:102ft   35 117   811 89   511 513¼   Romero R P3   ⓕMdn 72-16 JoyThTrp,HllSwtThng,YMkMHppy 10
Jan 28 Hol 3f ft :36 h   Jan 14 Hol 4f ft :501 h   Dec 28 SA 5f ft 1:03 h   Dec 17 Hol 5f ft 1:021 h

E.
50–1

Silver On Grey
PATTON D B 0-0   **1125**
Own.—Haverhals J A

Gr. f. 3, by Silver Buck—Sandspur, by Al Hattab
Br.—Saddle Home Farm (Ky)   1987 1 M 0 0
Tr.—McAnally Ronald   1986 0 M 0 0
Lifetime 1 0 0 0

17Jan87-6SA   6f :214 :451 1:11 ft   175 1125   87¼ 109¾ 89¼   68¼   Patton D B11   ⓕMdn 74-18 TimelyReserve,YouMkMHppy,Foli 12
Jan 26 SA 4f ft :49 h   Jan 10 SA 5f gd 1:061 hg   Jan 5 Hol 4f gd :502 h   ● Dec 15 GD tr.t 6f ft 1:152 hg

F.
2–1

Pink Slipper
SHOEMAKER W 0-0   **117**
Own.—Keck H B

B. f. 3, by Nijinsky II—Ancient Art, by Tell
Br.—Keck H B (Ky)   1987 1 M 0 0
Tr.—Whittingham Charles   1986 1 M 0 0 $475
Lifetime 2 0 0 0 $475

11Jan87-4SA   6f :214 :452 1:11ft   10 117   1191 1810 107½   78¼   Shoemaker W9 ⓕMdn 74-21 SummrSonds,TxsWld,Nort'hrnDys 12
11Jan87—Broke slowly
20Dec86-6Hol   7f :221 :454 1:24 ft   5½ 118   712 79   69¾ 513¼   Shoemaker W7 ⓕMdn 70-15 Chic Shirine, Hilo Baba, Cee'sVigor 8
20Dec86—Broke very slowly; erratic
● Jan 28 SA 4f ft :463 h   Jan 23 SA 1f ft 1:403 h   Jan 18 SA 3f ft :354 h   Jan 8 SA 5f m 1:031 h

G.
5–1

Fiesta Gal
STEVENS G L   **117**
Own.—Klein Mr Mrs E V

B. f. 3, by Alleged—Proud Pattie, by Noble Commander
Br.—Bedford Farm Inc (Ky)   1987 0 M 0 0
Tr.—Lukas D Wayne   1986 0 M 0 0
Lifetime 0 0 0 0

Jan 27 Hol 5f ft 1:01 h   Jan 22 Hol 5f ft 1:003 h   Jan 6 Hol 4f gd :481 h   Dec 29 SA 6f ft 1:133 h

H.
7–1

Meteor Miner
TORO F 0-N   **117**
Own.—Buckland Farm

B. f. 3, by Mr Prospector—Northern Meteor, by Northern Dancer
Br.—Evans T M (Ky)   1987 1 M 0 0
Tr.—Speckert Christopher   1986 2 M 1 0 $3,085
Lifetime 3 0 1 0 $3,085

8Jan87-7SA   1 :473 1:132 1:413m   16 115   66 69½ 67½ 610¾   Toro F6   ⓕAw30000 49-30 Alyaffirm, Infringe, French Etoile 7
8Jan87—Broke slowly
20Nov86-4BM   1⅛ :474 1:121 1:43ft   *6-5 117   612 54½ 45¼ 26   Aragon V A4   ⓕMdn 67-22 MsshghAndmghty,MtorMnr,BrbrSu 8
20Nov86—Bumped start
26Oct86-6SA   1 :453 1:11 1:383ft   8¼ 117   917 1020 614 511¾   Shoemaker W9   ⓕMdn 63-16 Rose'sCantin,Midee,KeepOnFlying 10
26Oct86—Broke slowly; wide
Jan 27 SA 4f ft :522 h   Jan 18 SA 5f ft :372 h   Jan 1 SA 4f ft :483 h   Dec 27 SA 6f ft 1:142 h

57. Knowledge of the probability data on this kind of non-winners allowance race *plus* of the types of horses most likely to score in nonclaiming races at small tracks combines to direct handicappers to a solid winner at a solid price.

Which horse fits the race like a glove and offers nice odds to boot?

ATLANTIC CITY

ABOUT 1 MILE 40 YARDS. (Turf). (1.42½) ALLOWANCE. Purse $8,200. 3-year-olds and upwards, which have not won two races other than Maiden, Claiming or Starter. Weight, 3-year-olds 114 lbs. Older 122 lbs. Non-winners of a race other than Maiden or Claiming at one mile or over since May 30, allowed 3 lbs. Such a race since April 30, 6 lbs.

Coupled—Alert View and Padrilario.

A.
20—1

Comchen Ch. g. 6, by Dirham—Miss Pickering, by Battlefield

Own.—White Margaret   Br.—White Margaret R (Va)   Tr.—Fout P Douglas   116   Lifetime 1987 3 0 0 0 $8,196   1986 5 0 0 1 $830 $22,269   Turf 7 1 0 1

B.
12—1

At First Blush Ch. g. 4, by Terete—Modesty, by Princely Native

Own.—Walsh Ann L   Br.—Seldin Millard (Ky)   Tr.—Walsh James J Jr   116   Lifetime 1987 1 0 0 0 $30   1986 4 2 1 0 $11,000 $11,080   Turf 1 0 0 0 $80

C.
3—1

Alert View B. c. 3, by Northern View—Look Alert, by Prince Alert

Own.—Thocke G   Br.—Alchemy (Ky)   Tr.—Pregman John S Jr   116   Lifetime 1987 8 1 1 1 $12,990   1984 4 4 1 3 3 $23,775 $36,765   Turf 4 0 0 1 $1,150

D.
8—1

Special Agent Ro. h. 6, by Alias Smith—Special Report, by Mongo

Own.—Petelain Stable   Br.—Howe P M (Ky)   Tr.—Byrne Patrick B   116   Lifetime 1987 5 0 0 1 $1,250   1986 10 2 2 1 $28,935 $65,085   Turf 26 3 3 3 $61,005

14Dec86- 7Crc fm *1⅛ Ⓣ 1:47⅘ 3↑Clm 50000 8 9 99 84¾ 76½ 51 Vasquez J b 116 13.40 65–08 DHMoveOverKris114½DHCrovero112½WestMaui112½ In insight str 11
14Nov86- 5Aqu fst 1⅛ :48⅘ 1:12⅗ 1:51 3↑Clm 75000 2 4 48 48 410 425¾ Murphy D J b 113 14.30 54–23 Carjack 122¾ Waitlist 120no Fly Me Again 11225 Unprepared st. 4
20Oct86- 9Bel fm 1 Ⓣ:46⅗ 1:11⅗ 1:36⅗ 3↑Alw 25000 7 10 107½ 66 64 65½ Migliore R b 117 18.30 77–19 Dwno'TheDnc115½ChristinHundrd114nkTorqumd117hd Lacked rally 11
3Oct86- 7Bel gd 1 1/16 Ⓣ:46⅕ 1:11⅕ 1:44⅗ 3↑Alw 26000 7 8 78½ 57 513 626¾ Migliore R b 117 14.90 46–27 Icy Groom 1141½ ChristianaHundred1147½Ioskeha1194¾ No factor 8
19Sep86- 2Bel fm 1 1/16 Ⓣ:48 1:12 1:42⅘ 3↑Clm 45000 1 7 64½ 53 2½ 15 Migliore R b 113 3.10 87–15 SpecialAgent1135DomintingDooley1171½Chimichng1131 Drew off 8
LATEST WORKOUTS Jly 25 Atl 7f fst 1:27⅘ h Jly 21 Atl 3f fst :37⅘ b ● Jly 17 Atl 6f fst 1:16⅘ b Jly 7 Atl 3f fst :36 h

E.
6–1

Mr. Sims Ch. c. 4, by What A Pleasure—Very Lucky, by Stevward
Own.—Minassian Z Br.—Caporella Thomasina (Fla) Tr.—Minassian Zeke 116
Lifetime 25 5 6 2 $54,275 1987 4 0 1 0 $3,535 1986 14 4 3 1 $36,450 Turf 3 0 1 0 $2,555

17Jly87- 9Atl fm 5½f Ⓣ:22 :45⅘ 1:04⅕ 3↑Alw 8000 1 7 72¾ 76 63¾ 63 Pagano S R 116 4.70 89–14 AnotherMember122½MedievalBnker116½FlyingRice116½ No factor 7
27Jun87- 8Pha fst 6f :22⅕ :45⅘ 1:10⅘ 3↑Alw 11500 2 3 33½ 53¾ 46½ 411¾ Thornburg B 116 1.60 75–22 Margerine11611Re DemBones116½SilverStrMedl114nk Weakened 6
17Jun87- 8Pha fst 6f :22⅕ :45⅕ 1:10⅗ 3↑Clm 45000 4 2 22 21½ 41½ 22½ Thornburg B 114 11.50 86–25 Margerine 1162½ Mr. Sims 114hd T. V. Outake 116nk Gamely 8
20May87- 6GP fst 7f :22⅘ :45⅘ 1:23 3↑Alw 16500 3 6 1hd 2hd 516 524 Lester R N 120 6.70 65–20 Quotidien 120no True Prophecy 1204 Homo Adonis1202 Gave way 6
28Aug86- 5Mth sly 1 1/16 :47⅕ 1:12⅕ 1:46⅘ Clm 40000 3 3 31½ 1½ 11½ 11½ Jimenez I J 115 *1.40 73–26 Mr. Sims 1151½ Clear TheRunway1152MajesticDancer112¾ Driving 6
13Aug86- 5Pha fst 6f :22⅘ :45⅗ 1:11 3↑Alw 11000 6 2 3½ 2hd 12 11½ Thornburg B 113 *.70 86–25 Mr. Sims 1131½ Suicide Six 112nk Eskimo Point 1161 Driving 6
30Jly86- 3Mth fst 6f :22⅘ :45⅕ 1:10⅗ Clm 35000 1 2 1hd 1hd 12½ 14 Antley C W 116 *.80 87–15 Mr. Sims 1164 Two Steppin 1162 Kompus 1073½ Handily 6
23Jly86- 8Mth fst 6f :22⅕ :44⅘ 1:10⅕ 3↑Alw 13000 3 5 2hd 1hd 21 55½ Antley C W 112 3.90 84–15 F-Cnnc110nkNorthOfRichmond1152½LyphrdsRidg1143½ Weakened 8
23Jun86- 5Mth fst 6f :22⅘ :46⅕ 1:12⅕ Clm 32000 2 4 2hd 11 13½ 15½ Antley C W 116 *1.20 79–25 Mr. Sims 1165½ Hoist Yer Britches 1121½ExtraIce114½ Ridden out 7
11Jun86- 6Mth fm 1 Ⓣ:46⅗ 1:10⅗ 1:37⅕ Clm 35000 4 2 1hd 11 1hd 22½ Antley C W 116 *2.50 86–10 Biddy 1072½ Mr. Sims 1162 North King 1141½ Game try 10
LATEST WORKOUTS Jly 14 Atl 4f fst :49 b Jun 25 Atl 4f fst :49 b Jun 13 Atl 5f fst 1:01 h Jun 6 Atl 3f fst :37 b

F.
5–1

Spin On Dk. b. or br. h. 6, by Spin Off—Selari's Fancy, by Selari
Own.—Butner T Br.—Butner Joan L (NJ) Tr.—Vosters Lee H 116
Lifetime 26 2 1 5 $38,879 1987 1 0 0 0 $375 1986 12 0 0 3 $10,594 Turf 9 1 1 1 $18,035

10Jly87- 9Atl gd 5½f :21⅘ :45 1:04⅗ 3↑Clm 25000 3 6 55 611 513 410½ Chavez S N b 116 10.60 80–21 Im A Sapsucker 1123 National Bid 1117½ Skipton Landing 112hd 7
24Nov86- 8Med my 1 :47⅗ 1:11⅘ 1:38⅕ 3↑ⓈAlw 21200 6 1 2hd 23 23½ 46¼ Verge M E 116 17.50 78–27 Alioth 1112½ Drewster 112¾ Ernie's Sugar Bowl 1163 Weakened 7
5Nov86- 9Med sly 1 1/16 :47⅗ 1:12⅘ 1:45⅕ 3↑Alw 17000 4 3 55 59½ 519 628 Edwards J W 117 9.20 49–27 Publicizer 1183 Hasty Game 1178 Gallant Helio 1133 Thru early 6
18Oct86-10Med fm 1 1/16 Ⓣ:46⅖ 1:11⅖ 1:43⅘ 3↑ⓈJky Hollow H 4 2 1hd 41 42½ 57¾ Edwards J W 115 61.80 75–16 Hi Ideal 1201 American Diabolo 1152½ La Pawn 116¾ Weakened 9
8Oct86- 7Med fst 1 70 :46⅗ 1:12⅕ 1:42⅘ 3↑ⓈAlw 20000 2 2 22 21 36½ 69¾ Edwards J W 116 5.40 72–23 Noodle Pudding 1115 Drewster 1131 Happy Hoot 1161½ Tired 7
25Sep86- 6Med fm 1 Ⓣ:46⅗ 1:11 1:36 Alw 17000 1 1 1hd 1hd 11 3¾ Edwards J W 117 26.20 97–09 Captain Arthur 113¾MakeADecision111noSpinOn1175½ Drifted out 8
19Sep86-10Med fm 1 1/16 Ⓣ:46 1:10⅘ 1:42⅗ 3↑Clm 35000 6 3 34 43 89 812½ Edwards J W b 116 9.50 76–11 Times Ahead 1091 Remanded II 1121½ Padrilario 1193 Tired 9
5Sep86- 5Med sly 6f :21⅘ :44⅖ 1:10⅕ 3↑ⓈAlw 20000 6 2 47½ 49 49 45¾ Antley C W 116 6.40 85–21 ProsperFger1163½Kryzzchezkke114nkCommunityHill1142 Steadied 7
11Aug86- 7Mth fst 6f :22⅘ :46⅕ 1:11⅕ 3↑ⓈAlw 18700 3 4 22½ 32 55½ 412 Melendez J D b 116 *1.40 72–21 Bob K. 1122 Bold Julius 1116 Run Jolie Run 1124 Tired 7
1Aug86- 9Mth fst 1 :47⅕ 1:11⅘ 1:37⅖ 3↑ⓈAlw 17500 5 2 1hd 2½ 48¼ 621¼ Verge M E 116 7.60 65–20 OwnsTroup113noErni'sSugrBowl11610RockinRodny116no Stopped 7
LATEST WORKOUTS ● Jly 26 Del 4f fst :48 b Jly 21 Del 7f fst 1:28⅘ b Jly 5 Del 4f fst :49 b Jun 27 Del 4f fst :51⅕ b

G.
8–1

Bold Nombre B. g. 5, by Anticipating—No No Baby, by Renombre
Own.—Bebert & Joly Br.—Wirth-Nardom Patricia (NJ) Tr.—Bebert Rudolph 116
Lifetime 48 2 3 7 $19,105 1987 10 0 1 2 $4,012 1986 22 2 2 3 $10,533 Turf 12 0 2 2 $6,378

11Jly87-10Atl sly 1⅛ :48⅕ 1:13⅖ 1:54⅕ 3↑Clm 18000 2 3 32 55 45½ 49½ Hannigan L 112 12.40 52–26 HectorJ.116noGoldenCherokee1167½ElSacramento1122 Weakened 7
27Jun87- 1Pna my 1¼ :49 1:40⅗ 2:07⅖ 3↑Alw 8500s 6 6 56½ 620 628 — Fiorentino C T 116 5.90 — — Raise A Hawk1191¼MorningJoseph1224DanRather1162½ Distanced 6
20Jun87- 6Atl fm 1 40 Ⓣ:47 1:11⅕ 1:39⅘ 3↑Clm 18000 4 6 52¾ 4¾ 31½ 32 Hannigan L 112 5.70 92–08 Padrilario 116noDancer'sFunnyface1092BoldNombre1122 Checked 8
13Jun87- 7GS fm 1⅛ Ⓣ:49⅕ 1:13⅖ 1:48⅖ 3↑Alw 8500s 10 5 43½ 42 34½ 36½ Hannigan L 114 20.80 — — Critofer 1146 WelcomeHomeSon114nkBoldNombre1142½ Steadied 12
7Jun87- 8Pen fm 1 1/16 Ⓣ 1:42⅖ 3↑Clm 20000 3 8 86 52½ 3nk 52¼ Hannigan L 115 12.00 76–12 Misty Master 1161¼ Interplay 112nk HomecomingGame115¾ Tired 9
27May87- 9GS fm 1 Ⓣ:47⅗ 1:12⅕ 1:37⅘ 3↑ⓈAlw 15625 3 7 63¾ 76¼ 67 65¾ Hannigan L 116 43.80 80–09 T. S. Evans116nkGusBuster107hdInquisitivePrince116no No factor 8
16May87-10GS fm *1⅛ Ⓣ:46⅘ 1:10⅗ 1:47⅘ 3↑Alw 8500s 4 11 1221 1116 1115 913¾ Hannigan L 114 30.80 77–05 Double No 1141½ Welcome Home Son 1126 In Traffic1142 Outrun 12
10May87- 3Pen fm 1 1/16 Ⓣ 1:43 Clm 18000 3 4 44½ 41¼ 4¾ 23½ Hannigan L 115 16.60 71–15 Wilisum 1153½ Bold Nombre 1151½ Madeline Sweetie1111½ Rallied 8
2May87-10GS gd 1 1/16 :47⅗ 1:13 1:45⅗ 3↑Alw 11500 5 10 1112 1119 1128 1151 Lopez C C 116 55.60 29–16 MorningJosephn1163TenCentHostge1102Dvil'sVoodoo1083 Outrun 11
27Apr87- 8GS fm 5f Ⓣ:22⅕ :46⅕ :59⅕ 3↑Alw 8500s 10 10 1016 1019 1017 1011¼ Stackhouse GC 114 84.20 80–09 AnotherMember1121½SaintMchree114hdKissySerende1141 Outrun 11
LATEST WORKOUTS Jly 19 Mth 1 fst 1:48 b

H.
4–1

Strategy Talk Ch. h. 5, by High Steel—Good Routes, by Pass Catcher
Own.—Cerulean Farm Br.—Koontz Bina & K (Fla) Tr.—Steen H Kirk Jr 116
Lifetime 47 3 7 7 $53,771 1987 4 1 0 1 $5,359 1986 14 0 1 3 $7,392 Turf 12 1 1 3 $17,522

8Jly87- 9Atl gd 1 1/16 :47⅗ 1:12⅕ 1:44⅕ 3↑Alw 8200 1 5 54¾ 35½ 33½ 36 Conner M J 116 4.40 78–25 Wordy 1123 Eskimo Point 1173 Strategy Talk 1164 Even try 5
27Jun87- 8Atl fst 1⅛ :48 1:12⅗ 1:53 3↑Clm 16000 2 4 48½ 44½ 32½ 1½ Conner M J 116 *2.60 68–18 StrategyTlk116½ReflectNeutrlity1141CollectionAgent1147 Driving 8
25Jan87- 5Hia fst 7f :22⅘ :45 1:24⅖ Clm 20000 2 11 1216 1113 86¼ 43 Gonzalez M A 116 24.80 78–22 Secret War 116no Accipitate 116½ Fugie 1202½ Wide 12
9Jan87- 4Hia fst 7f :23 :45⅗ 1:23⅖ Clm 20000 2 10 1111 1111 109½ 74¾ Pezua J M 116 68.60 81–20 Texola Joe 116no Katzenjammer1161ItsHardtoBelive116hd Outrun 12
29Aug86- 5Atl fm 1 1/16 Ⓣ:47⅗ 1:12⅗ 1:44⅖ 3↑Clm 18000 5 2 1½ 12 32½ 35 Intelisano G P Jr 112 15.90 79–17 Dissonance 1142 Cantonero 1163 Strategy Talk 1122½ Weakened 6
13Aug86- 8Atl fm 1 Ⓣ:47 1:11⅕ 1:36⅕ 3↑Clm 20000 3 4 58½ 58½ 610 67¼ Conner M J 112 23.70 83–13 Marine 1132 Double Ship 1161½ Classic Bend 105nk Outrun 7
2Aug86- 8Atl sly 1 1/16 :46⅖ 1:12 1:46⅖ 3↑Alw 9000 4 5 314 411 58 56½ Conner M J 116 5.20 67–26 Arrived On Time 1152½LustyGrosty1112GreatReef1161½ No threat 7
12Jly86- 8Atl fm *1 1/16 Ⓣ:48⅖ 1:12⅘ 1:47 3↑Alw 9000 3 5 46½ 48½ 56½ 33½ Bielby J A7 109 9.50 78–17 Times Ahead 122no Great Reef 1163½ Strategy Talk 109hd Rallied 9
30Jun86- 8Atl fm 5½f Ⓣ:22⅕ :45⅖ 1:04 3↑Alw 8500 9 2 86½ 67½ 810 76¾ Bielby J A7 109 3.50 86–11 Double Ship 116¾ Emerging Diplomat 104hd Rivelin 109½ Outrun 10
20Jun86- 7Atl gd 1 1/16 :47 1:12⅘ 1:46 3↑Alw 9000 7 3 43½ 510 32 21 Terry J b 116 2.70 74–22 Lyrichord 1221 Strategy Talk 1163¾ Sly Buck 1166½ Rallied 8
LATEST WORKOUTS ● Jly 28 Atl 4f fst :49 b Jly 6 Atl 3f fst :37⅗ b Jun 25 Atl 4f fst :49 b Jun 17 Atl 5f fst 1:02⅗ b

I.
9–2

Pleasant Virginian — B. g. 3, by Pleasant Colony—What a Squaw, by What a Pleasure
Br.—Evans T M (Va)
Own.—Buckland Farm — Tr.—Pearce Ross R — 108
Lifetime 6 2 0 1 $13,175 — 1987 6 2 0 1 $13,175 — 1986 0 M 0 0 — Turf 2 0 0 1 $2,615

5Jly87- 9Pha fst 1$\frac{1}{16}$:49⅘ 1:14⅗ 1:46⅕ Ⓡ The Laurel 1 2 2½ 5^{4}½ 6^{13} 6^{16}¾ Terry J b 116 1.90 56-27 Baramore 116^{3}½ Silver Star Medal 116^{4}½ Baybuck 116^{5} Tired 6
14Jun87- 9Rkmfm 1$\frac{1}{16}$ Ⓣ:48⅖ 1:13⅕ 1:46⅗ Prospector 8 3 3^{1}½ 2^{1}½ 2^{5} 3^{8}¾ Terry J b 111 6.20 97 — Sn'stheSnoow120^{7}¾SyBev'sFirst114^{1}PlsntVirginin111^{3} Weakened 11
18May87- 9GS fm 1 Ⓣ:47⅘ 1:12 1:35⅘ 3+ Alw 12500 3 8 9^{7}¾ 9^{4}½ 5^{8} 5^{11}¾ Alligood M A b 109 4.60 84-04 Morewoods 110^{4}½ T. S. Evans 111^{4}½ Tisa Feast 116^{2}½ Outrun 10
16Apr87-10GS gd 1⅛ :46⅘ 1:11⅖ 1:49⅘ Garden St 4 5 7^{5}½ 7^{7}¾ 9^{15} 9^{18} Winnett B G Jr b 115 15.50 62-18 Mister S. M. 115^{nc} Templar Hill 124^{3}½ Harriman 124^{2} Tired 9
18Apr87-Grade III
25Mar87- 8GS fst 1$\frac{1}{16}$:48⅕ 1:14 1:48 Alw 11500 4 1 1½ 1^{1}½ 1^{5} 1^{8} Winnett B G Jr b 116 *2.20 68-26 PleasantVirginian116^{8}WhotheHeck116^{hd}Baybuck122^{4} Ridden out 7
7Mar87- 1Pen fst 6f :22⅖ :46 1:12⅕ Md Sp Wt 8 4 4^{1}½ 1^{1} 1^{3} 1^{5}¾ Appleby D L Jr b 118 4.30 83-20 Pleasant Virginian118^{5}¾TalcSmoke118^{2}FiercelyLoyal118^{1} Handily 9
LATEST WORKOUTS Jly 26 Del 5f fst 1:01⅖ b ● Jly 21 Del 4f fst :47⅘ h Jun 30 Del 1 fst 1:46⅘ b Jun 25 Del Ⓣ 7f fm 1:39 b (d)

J.
3–1

Padrilario — Dk. b. or br. g. 6, by Soy Numero Uno—Shotsilk, by Jaipur
Br.—Branch G C (Fla)
Own.—Barrick J J — Tr.—Pregman John Jr — 116
Lifetime 58 4 8 11 $57,315 — 1987 11 1 1 2 $10,610 — 1986 16 2 3 4 $24,385 — Turf 35 4 5 7 $46,913

16Jly87- 7Mth fm 1$\frac{1}{16}$ Ⓣ:47⅘ 1:12⅖ 1:44⅘ 3+ Alw 17000 9 10 9^{12} 9^{6}½ 8^{8}½ 8^{8}¾ Ferrer J C b 118 13.50 72-19 Deity Dash 118½ Gallant James 118^{1}½ Nino Bibbia 118^{1}¾ Outrun 10
20Jun87- 6Atl fm 1^{40} Ⓣ:47 1:11⅕ 1:39⅖ 3+ Clm 20000 2 7 6^{2}½ 3½ 2½ 1no Ferrer J C b 116 *1.20 94-08 Padrilario 116no Dancer's Funnyface109^{2}BoldNombre112^{2} Driving 8
13Jun87- 3Mth fm 1⅛ Ⓣ:48⅘ 1:12⅖ 1:50⅕+ 3+ Clm 25000 8 6 6^{10} 7^{11} 3^{8} 3^{8}½ Antley C W b 115 3.30 81-08 ⒹFirst Double 115^{nk} Cantonero 111^{8} Padrilario 115^{2} Steadied 8
6Jun87- 8GS yl *2 Ⓣ 3:29 3+ Handicap 3 1 2^{5} 6^{8} 7^{21} 7^{30}½ Ferrer J C b 117 4.80 — — Break Clean 110½ Dads Reward 109no Polar Parallel116^{2} Stopped 7
6May87-10GP fm *1½ Ⓣ 2:30⅖ Clm 30000 2 1 1^{11} 1^{2}½ 2^{2} 2^{4}½ Lester R N b 117 5.60 87-10 Cloutier 117^{4}½ Padrilario 117^{3} Soaring Bee 113^{2} Second best 9
23Apr87- 9GP fm *1$\frac{1}{16}$ Ⓣ 1:45 Alw 16000 4 1 1^{2} 1½ 7^{10} 8^{13}½ Castaneda K b 117 21.30 67-23 Crafty Giboulee 117^{3}½ Happy Gypsey 117^{1}Seattlite122^{no} Stopped 10
11Apr87- 7GP fm 1$\frac{1}{16}$ Ⓣ:47⅕ 1:11⅖ 1:42⅕ Alw 16000 4 3 3^{2}½ 2^{3} 3^{4} 7^{7}½ Lester R N b 117 24.60 82-07 FlourescentGem117^{2}½Heaven'sGte117¾Keycolony122^{nk} Weakened 12
29Mar87-11GP gd *1$\frac{1}{16}$ Ⓣ 1:46⅖ Clm 45000 2 8 8^{9}¾ 10^{10} 8^{11} 7^{7} Cruguet J b 117 5.80 67-23 Braddells 117no Perplejo 108½ Imperial Palace 113^{2} No factor 10
6Mar87-11Hia fm 1½ Ⓣ 2:29⅘ Clm 40000 5 1 1^{2}½ 1^{1}½ 1^{3} 3½ Lester R N b 112 29.70 80-09 Dance to the Wire 116^{hd} Cloutier 114½ Padrilario 112no Bore out 10
28Feb87- 4Hia fm 1⅛ Ⓣ 1:49⅗ Clm 45000 2 2 6^{3}¾ 8^{4}½ 6^{3}½ 7^{6}¾ Romero R P b 116 20.50 77-15 GoldenCnampII114^{2}½LondonExchange120½FeuD'enfer112^{hd} Tired 12

58. Analyze this exacta race in depth. What's the most sensible way to play it?

9th Santa Anita

1 1-16 MILES
SANTA ANITA

1$\frac{1}{16}$ MILES. (1.40⅕) CLAIMING. Purse $23,000. 4-year-olds and upward. Weights, 4-year-olds, 120 lbs.; older, 121 lbs. Non-winners of two races at one mile or over since December 1 allowed 3 lbs.; of such a race since then, 5 lbs. Claiming price $32,000; for each $2,000 to $28,000 allowed 1 lbs. (Claiming and starter races for $25,000 or less not considered.)

A.
11–1

Shower Decree — B. g. 4, by Forget the Showers—Anybody's Policy, by New Policy
PATTON D B 110^{5} — Br.—Coop-Webb-West (Cal) — 1987 2 0 0 2 $6,000
Own.—The Hat Ranch — Tr.—Stute Melvin F — $32,000 — 1986 6 1 1 1 $12,630
Lifetime 9 1 2 3 $21,630

17Jan87-9SA 1$\frac{1}{16}$:46^{2} 1:11^{2} 1:43^{4}ft 27 110^{5} 5^{7}½ 5^{4} 5^{3} 3^{1}½ Patton D B^{7} 32000 80-18 PiperJohn,ForHimself,ShowerDcr 12
7Jan87-9SA 1 :47^{2} 1:12 1:38 m 3½ 118 5^{3}½ 5^{4}¼ 4^{6}½ 3^{8}½ Stevens G L^{3} c25000 69-21 Danchai, Doonsport, ShowerDecree 9
7Jan87—Rough start
27Dec86-4SA 1$\frac{1}{16}$:47^{1} 1:11^{4} 1:45^{1}ft *2¾ 116 1½ 1^{1} 1^{hd} 1^{1} † Stevens G L^{8} c20000 75-19 ‡ShowrDcr,DckAndHugh,MnyRods 10
27Dec86—Veered out 1/4, drifted in nearing stretch; †Disqualified and placed seventh
13Dec86-3Hol 7f :22^{2} :45^{2} 1:23^{2}ft *2½ 117 3^{1}½ 3^{2}½ 3^{2} 3^{1}½ Stevens G L^{3} Ⓢ 22500 85-09 Gregson,ManyRoads,ShowerDecree 9
3Dec86-7Hol 6f :22^{1} :45^{2} 1:11 ft 3 119 7^{4}½ 6^{6}¾ 4^{3} 2^{3}½ Stevens G L^{1} Ⓢ 20000 84-18 GrowlerSndue,ShowerDecree,Pilor 11
2Nov86-2SA 1 :45^{4} 1:10^{4} 1:36^{1}ft 21 117 9^{7}¼ 9^{12} 9^{14} 9^{23}¼ Baze G^{3} 40000 64-10 Cojak Man, Tai High, Chili Hill 10
2Nov86—Bumped at 7/8
23Oct86-2SA 6f :21^{4} :45^{2} 1:11^{3}ft 3¾ 118 1^{1}½ 1^{2}½ 1^{5} 1^{6} Stevens G L^{3} ⓈM32000 80-20 ShowerDecree,CavalryClub,Danchi 12
23Oct86—Broke in, bumped
20Sep86-6Pom 6½f :21^{4} :45^{1} 1:17^{1}ft 3½ 116 2^{hd} 2^{hd} 2^{1} 6^{13}¾ Sibille R^{8} Mdn 80-09 Throw Home, ParkRoad,SnowTime 9
17Jly85-6Hol 6f :22^{2} :46^{2} 1:12 ft 13 118 3^{3}½ 3^{4}½ 3^{4} 2^{2}½ Estrada J Jr^{9} M50000 84-09 LordAllison,ShowerDcr,Jtt'ngHom 11
Jan 25 SA 4f ft :47^{3} h Jan 14 SA 4f ft :46^{4} h Dec 21 SA 5f ft 1:00^{4} h Dec 11 SA 4f ft :48^{1} h

B.
21–1

Danchai — B. c. 4, by Zante—Rose Honor, by Count of Honor
COX D W 110^{5} — Br.—Santoro M D (Cal) — 1987 1 1 0 0 $9,350
Own.—Karschamroon T — Tr.—Oppegard Victor — $32,000 — 1986 8 1 1 1 $11,175
Lifetime 9 2 1 1 $20,525

7Jan87-9SA 1 :47^{2} 1:12 1:38 m 43 113^{5} 1^{1}½ 1^{2}½ 1^{3} 1^{4}½ Cox D W^{2} 25000 78-21 Danchai, Doonsport, ShowerDecree 9
7Jan87—Bumped start
27Nov86-2Hol 6f :22^{2} :46^{2} 1:12^{2}ft 4⅓ 120 3^{nk} 1^{1}⅓ 1^{4} 1^{3} Ortega L E^{9} ⓈM32000 81-18 Danchai, Vandalero, Perq Jr. 9

```
27Nov86—Broke in, bumped
20Nov86-4Hol   6f :22² :46¹ 1:11 ft   26 120   63¾ 44   44½ 4¹¹   Ortega L E¹⁰ ⒮M32000 77-16 SaroStr,GetAlongPisno,Kim'sGold 11
  20Nov86—Rough start
23Oct86-2SA   6f :21⁴ :45² 1:13ft   70 118   73¾ 54¼ 46½ 36¼   Ortega L E²  ⒮M32000 74-20 ShowerDecree,CavalryClub,Danchi 12
  23Oct86—Awarded second purse money; Bumped hard start
29Aug86-3Dmr  7f :22² :46¹ 1:24¹ft  59 116   32  44¼ 8¹⁹ 8¹⁶   Sibille R⁹   ⒮M32000 68-15 Noon Sun, ZambeziPass,OutCross 11
13Aug86-4Dmr  6f :22  :46¹ 1:11¹ft  17 116   4¹¹ 3¹¹ 98¾ 9¹⁰¼  Sibille R⁷      M32000 72-15 NmOfThGm,MgicFddl,LVrn'sKrsm 12
25Jly86-4Dmr  6f :22¹ :45 1:11⁴ft   69 116   52¼ 3ⁿᵏ 3ⁿᵏ 32¾   Sibille R³      M32000 76-18 Honyock, MidnightNotion,Danchai 10
15May86-6Hol  6f :22² :46² 1:13³ft  95 115   4¾ 65  9¹²¹⁰18¼   Ortega L E¹²    M32000 68-13 H'sAllWondUp,DwnToBt,MgcFddl 12
25Apr86-6Hol  6f :22¹ :46² 1:13 ft  13 115   87¼ 88¾ 7¹⁴10¹⁵¾  Ortega L E⁴     M32000 63-16 MisterStride,StylishRod,DwnToBt 12
  25Apr86—Raced greenly
Jan 28 GD tr.t 5f ft 1:00 h   ● Dec 30 GD tr.t 3f ft :36 h   ● Dec 24 GD tr.t 5f ft 1:00 h   Dec 13 GD tr.t 1f ft :41¹ h
```

C.

17–1

```
Tommy Thoms                          Ch. h. 5, by Tom Rolfe—Princess East, by Prince John
TORO F                               Br.—Elmendorf Farm (Ky)          1987 1 0 0 0        $575
                              116    Tr.—Cross Richard J   $32,000    1986 7 1 2 1     $21,350
Own.—Rickerd-Sherman-Stephens        Lifetime 15 3 2 1    $40,525    Turf 2 0 0 0
17Jan87-9SA   1¹⁄₁₆:46² 1:11² 1:43⁴ft   9¾ 116   6⁹ 65 42½ 51½  Ortega L E⁸   32000 80-18 PiperJohn,ForHimself,ShowerDcr 12
  17Jan87—Bumped late
26Dec86-9SA   1¹⁄₁₆:45⁴ 1:10² 1:43 ft   4¾ 116   2hd 1½ 11½ 2³  Ortega L E²   25000 83-13 Cold,TommyThoms,BoncngBttons 11
18Dec86-8Hol  1¹⁄₁₆①:48³1:12 1:42²fm   21 116   52¾ 74½ 89½ 8¹³½ Kaenel J L²  Aw24000 69-19 SmoothOpertor,Intuitiveness,Stmd 8
  18Dec86—Wide 5/16
29Nov86-7Hol  1  :45⁴ 1:10⁴ 1:36¹ft   *3¾ 116   11  1hd 2½ 31½  Ortega L E³  c20000 80-12 Rnbow'sCp,LordPnch,TmmryThms 10
16Nov86-4Hol  7f :22  :44³ 1:24¹ft    34 117   94½ 65¾ 53½ 43¾  Sibille R¹¹   20000 79-18 Pegus, Pialor, Amarone 12
  16Nov86—Wide down backstretch, through stretch
12Feb86-5SA   1¹⁄₁₆:46³ 1:10⁴ 1:49³ft  *3½ 116   2¹ 2½ 1½ 1¾   Hawley S⁸    c18000 81-16 TommyThoms,Nvgnt,Lyon'sShdw 11
1Feb86-9SA    1¹⁄₁₆:48  1:13¹ 1:46³m   11 116   3½ 2hd 1hd 2¾  Hawley S⁹     18000 67-24 Bedouin, Tommy Thoms, Bemidgi 9
  1Feb86—Bobbled at start; wide 1st turn
19Jan86-9SA   1¹⁄₁₆:46² 1:10⁴ 1:42⁴ft  25 115   65¾ 74½ 9¹⁰ 9¹¹½ Meza R Q⁹   32000 75-12 ForgotThRng,RoosvltRod,Imblsvl 9
  19Jan86—Steadied start
29Dec85-5SA   1  :46¹ 1:11 1:37 ft    23 114   54¾ 5½ 11 1no  Hawley S³      22500 83-12 TommyThoms,BoldInititv,Rformult 8
  29Dec85—Lugged in late
24Jly85-2Dmr  1¹⁄₁₆:46¹ 1:10⁴ 1:43¹ft  16 115   75¼ 47½ 7¹² 8¹³¾ Toro F⁶     28000 70-14 OlimpicBingo,GllntMick,GetMeEvn 8
  24Jly85—Wide into stretch
Jan 13 SA 5f ft 1:01¹ h   Jan 8 Hol 6f ft 1:18 h   Dec 14 Hol 6f ft 1:15 h   Dec 9 Hol 4f ft :52 h
```

D.

17–1

```
Gum Fleet                            B. c. 4, by Gummo—Woman Driver, by Traffic Judge
DELAHOUSSAYE E                       Br.—Ross A (Cal)                 1987 1 0 0 0
                              115    Tr.—Luby Donn   $32,000         1986 10 1 3 1     $19,675
Own.—Ross A                          Lifetime 14 1 3 1    $19,675
17Jan87-9SA   1¹⁄₁₆:46² 1:11² 1:43⁴ft  14 116   8¹¹ 99¾ 76 6²  Delahoussaye E⁶ 32000 80-18 PiperJohn,ForHimself,ShowerDcr 12
28Dec86-9SA   1¹⁄₁₆:47  1:12 1:44 ft   6½ 116   44½ 42 53½ 45¼  Delahoussaye E⁵ 32000 76-14 Chili Hill, Cojak Man, Bruli's Ante 8
  28Dec86—Broke slowly
7Dec86-6Hol   1¹⁄₁₆:45⁴ 1:12¹ 1:51⁴gd  81 116   1hd 2½ 3ⁿᵏ 22¾  Delahoussaye E³ 32000 75-18 VlintGeorge,GumFleet,For'gnLgion 9
2Nov86-2SA    1  :45⁴ 1:10⁴ 1:36¹ft   13 115   10⁸¼10¹³10¹⁵10²⁴½ Black C A⁸   35000 62-10 Cojak Man, Tai High, Chili Hill 10
  2Nov86—Stumbled start
12Oct86-3SA   1¹⁄₁₆:47¹ 1:12¹ 1:44⁴ft  18 111⁵  1hd 1hd 21½ 34½ Black C A¹    40000 72-21 Bold Decree, Convincing,GumFleet 6
15Sep86-6Pom  1¹⁄₁₆:45⁴ 1:11⁴ 1:45³ft  3¾ 114   68½ 55½ 31½ 1hd Olivares F⁹   M32000 83-08 GumFleet,DowdCnyon,ZmbeziPss 10
  15Sep86—Lugged in stretch
29Aug86-2Dmr  1¹⁄₁₆:45⁴ 1:11¹ 1:42²ft  9½ 116   45½ 42½ 25 27½ Olivares F¹¹   M32000 75-15 TierrDistnte,GumFlt,VgulyInnocnt 12
20Aug86-4Dmr  6f :22  :45³ 1:10¹ft    40 116   11⁸ 96¾ 73¾ 23¼ Olivares F²   ⒮M32000 83-11 BonRomeo,GumFleet,SlidesByThr 12
  20Aug86—Broke slowly; crowded, steadied at 3/8
```

E.

23–1

```
Alota Noise                          B. h. 5, by Bold Bidder—Giggling Girl, by Laugh Aloud
MEZA R Q                             Br.—Fisher M (Ky)                1987 1 0 0 0
                              116    Tr.—Gregson Edwin   $32,000     1986 3 1 0 0       $6,600
Own.—Jam Stable & Sears              Lifetime 4 1 0 0    $6,600
15Jan87-3SA   6f :21² :44⁴ 1:11 ft   22 117   8¹² 8¹² 8¹² 7¹¹½ Meza R Q³    Aw26000 71-25 EightyBelowZero,Athlone,FstRomo 8
  15Jan87—Bumped start
14May86-6Hol  1¹⁄₁₆:47  1:12² 1:51³ft  5 121   3¹½ 1½ 14 18½  Meza R Q¹¹   M28000 79-14 AlotNoise,Codx'sRflction,PrivtEgl 12
17Apr86-3SA   1  :47  1:12¹ 1:38³ft  15 113   106¼ 7⁷ 65 6⁷¼ Black C A⁹   M35000 67-22 Oh My Omar, Yippyayo, Pegus 10
  17Apr86—Veered out start, ducked in stretch
17Mar86-1SA   7f :22⁴ :46 1:25 sy   14 120   10⁹ 10¹⁰ 88¾ 6¹⁰¼ Sibille R⁴  M50000 65-27 Sweet Petrone,Members,Yippyayo 11
  17Mar86—Veered in sharply, bumped start
Jan 29 SA 5f ft 1:03³ h   Jan 24 SA 4f ft :49 h   Jan 8 SA 7f m 1:28³ h   Dec 31 SA 6f ft 1:15¹ h
```

F.

6–1

Idol — B. h. 6, by Verbatim—Party Kiss, by Fleet Nasrullah

PEDROZA M A 116 — Br.—Elmendorf Farm (Ky) — 1987 1 0 0 0 $1,875

Own.—Alesia F & Sharon — Tr.—Ippolito Steve $32,000 — 1986 8 1 2 2 $30,375

Lifetime 34 6 7 3 $100,380 — Turf 5 0 0 0 $575

10Jan87-9SA 1 1/16 :48 1:12^{2} 1:44 ft 3¼ 116 5^{4} 6^{4¾} 5^{4½} 4^{7} Ortega L E^{5} 40000 74-20 Danczone, Alibi Ike, Le Cid 7

31Dec86-5SA 6½f :22 :45^{3} 1:17^{2}ft 9½ 116 10^{6¾} 7^{4¼} 4^{2½} 3^{1} Ortega L E^{9} 40000 82-20 Watch'n Win, Angle Arc, Idol 12

31Dec86—Wide final 3/8

2Nov86-3SA 1 1/16 :46^{1} 1:10^{3} 1:41^{2}ft *8-5 116 4^{5½} 4^{3½} 2^{6} 2^{8} Valenzuela P A^{5} 40000 86-10 Oricao, Idol, Tough Envoy 6

5Oct86-9SA 1 1/16 :46^{2} 1:11^{1} 1:42^{4}ft 8 116 8^{7¾} 6^{1¾} 4^{¾} 2^{¾} ValenzuelaPA^{10} 40000 86-15 Tough Envoy, Idol, Tio Nino 10

5Oct86—Wide 3/8 turn; lost whip 3/16

7Sep86-9Dmr 1 1/16 (T):47^{1}1:11 1:42^{3}fm 7½ 116 3^{11} 3^{10} 5^{9} 5^{7¾} Valenzuela P A^{1} 50000 85-08 EmperadorAlNorte,Msser,OkTreeII 8

24Aug86-9Dmr 1 1/16 :45^{2} 1:09^{3} 1:41^{2}ft 3¾ 116 6^{13} 6^{10} 6^{12} 4^{5½} Valenzuela P A^{1} 50000 87-12 OnoGummo,TimeForSilenc,Oljuwon 9

24Aug86—Veered out, bumped start; lugged out backstretch, wide into stretch

9Aug86-7Dmr 1 1/16 :45^{3} 1:10^{1} 1:42^{2}ft 9¾ 116 6^{6} 5^{2¼} 5^{1¼} 3^{½} Valenzuela P A^{7} 50000 87-14 Lead On, Impulsively, Idol 11

9Aug86—Wide 3/8 turn

28Jly86-5Dmr 1 1/16 :45^{1} 1:09^{4} 1:42^{1}ft 5 116 4^{5½} 2^{3} 1^{1½} 1^{nk} Valenzuela P A^{6} 32000 89-16 Idol, Valiant George,ForeignLegion 8

28Jly86—Wide into stretch

11Jan86-9SA 1 1/16 :46 1:10^{2} 1:42^{2}ft 5½ 116 3^{2} 3^{3} 3^{2½} 4^{3½} Ortega L E^{1} 25000 85-11 Son OfRaja,Rajaba,MarkInTheSky 10

23Dec85-9Hol 1⅛ :47^{1} 1:12 1:50^{3}ft 4½ 118 7^{8¼} 8^{8½} 7^{5¾} 7^{7½} Ortega L E^{7} 30000 76-17 ForeignLegion,MstrNvjo,NoodlRoni 9

Jan 26 SA 5f ft 1:00^{3} h — Jan 19 SA 4f ft :50^{2} h — Jan 8 SA 4f m :48^{4} h — Dec 27 SA 4f ft :47^{4} h

G.

10–1

Plumb Straight — B. g. 4, by Plum Bold—Cles, by Charlottesville

BAZE G 115 — Br.—Whiting Mr–Mrs P J (Cal) — 1987 1 0 1 0 $5,600

Own.—Baker & E A Ranches — Tr.—Fulton Jacque $32,000 — 1986 13 1 2 1 $31,100

Lifetime 14 1 3 1 $36,700 — Turf 4 0 1 0 $5,400

4Jan87-7SA 1 1/16 :47^{2} 1:12^{2} 1:47 sy 6¾ 116 6^{4} 4^{4} 4^{1½} 2^{½} Baze G^{2} Aw28000 65-22 BrandImge,PlumbStright,TrumpUp 6

4Jan87—Wide

28Dec86-5SA 1 1/16 :46^{2} 1:10^{4} 1:43^{1}ft 11 118 8^{8¾} 7^{8} 4^{9} 4^{8½} DelhoussyeE^{8} Aw28000 76-14 ReEnter,Card'sPlease,InherentKal 10

30Nov86-5Hol 1⅛ (T):47^{4}1:11^{3}1:48^{3}fm 8 119 5^{4} 8^{5¼} 7^{5} 8^{3¾} Pincay L Jr^{3} Aw24000 81-12 PlumCertin,Rodrigue,Intuitivenss 12

30Nov86—Lugged in down backside

15Nov86-7Hol 1 (T):45^{3}1:09^{1}1:34^{3}fm 11 120 7^{12} 7^{13} 7^{11} 4^{7¾} Baze G^{6} Aw24000 86-11 Le Belvedere,RiverMist,GreyWriter 9

15Nov86—Wide in stretch

18Oct86-4SA 1 1/16 :46 1:10^{4} 1:44^{3}ft 11 117 4^{7} 4^{5} 2^{2½} 1^{½} Delahoussaye E^{3} Mdn 78-20 PlumbStright,VlintCougr,MgicLdr 11

18Oct86—Lugged in drive

5Oct86-4SA 1 1/16 :46^{4} 1:11^{2} 1:44 ft 12 117 4^{2} 2^{½} 2^{1} 5^{3¼} Stevens G L^{2} Mdn 78-15 Midnight Ice, Sun Man, Star Ribot 8

10Sep86-4Dmr 1 :46 1:10^{3} 1:36^{1}ft 9½ 111^{5} 5^{13} 4^{11} 4^{8½} 4^{5¾} Black C A^{2} Mdn 81-11 Extrnx,ThrowHom,Trmn'sCmmndr 9

29Jun86-6Hol 1⅛ (T):46^{4}1:11^{2}1:49 fm 5 114 9^{11} 8^{6¼} 8^{4¼} 6^{4¼} Solis A^{2} Mdn 83-02 Nurely, Temperate, Plum Certain 12

30May86-5Hol 1⅛ (T):48 1:12^{4}1:50 fm 20 115 8^{9¼} 8^{5¾} 6^{1½} 2^{½} Solis A^{9} Mdn 81-13 Jota, PlumbStraight,Lexingtonian 10

17May86-7Hol 1 :45 1:09^{3} 1:35^{1}ft 10 120 5^{5½} 7^{11} 7^{15} 9^{16¾} Meza R Q^{6} Mdn 70-14 Arcadius, PlumCertain,ArtOfDawn 12

Jan 29 SA 5f ft 1:02^{1} h — Jan 24 SA 4f ft :49 h — Dec 26 SA 3f ft :37^{3} h — Dec 21 Hol 6f ft 1:15^{3} h

H.

19–1

Cojak Man — Dk. b. or br. g. 4, by Cojak—Madinus, by Bupers

SHOEMAKER W 117 — Br.—Robertson & Miller (Ky) — 1987 1 0 0 0 $625

Own.—North Ranch Stables — Tr.—Heaton Bill $32,000 — 1986 12 4 2 0 $45,000

Lifetime 16 5 2 0 $49,174

10Jan87-9SA 1 1/16 :48 1:12^{2} 1:44 ft 5½ 112^{5} 4^{4} 5^{4¾} 4^{4½} 5^{8½} Patton D B^{3} 40000 72-20 Danczone, Alibi Ike, Le Cid 7

28Dec86-9SA 1 1/16 :47 1:12 1:44 ft *9-5 115^{5} 3^{2½} 3^{2} 2^{½} 2^{¾} Patton D B^{7} 32000 80-14 Chili Hill, Cojak Man, Bruli's Ante 8

18Dec86-3Hol 1 1/16 :46^{3} 1:11^{2} 1:44^{4}ft *2¼ 114^{5} 1^{hd} 1^{1½} 1^{2½} 1^{4½} Patton D B^{2} 40000 85-17 Cojak Man, I LoveRacing,Teilapace 7

18Dec86—Lugged out; wide late

10Dec86-3Hol 1 :45^{4} 1:10^{4} 1:37^{1}ft *9-5 111^{5} 5^{2} 3^{3} 3^{2½} 4^{3¼} Patton D B^{5} 50000 74-20 Sebucan, Agitate's Pride, Alibi Ike 7

13Nov86-9Hol 1 :45^{3} 1:10^{1} 1:35^{3}ft 3¼ 111^{5} 5^{1¼} 2^{1½} 2^{3} 2^{1¼} Patton D B^{3} 50000 84-23 MischievousMtt,CojkMn,BoldDecre 9

2Nov86-2SA 1 :45^{4} 1:10^{4} 1:36^{1}ft 7½ 110^{5} 3^{1½} 3^{1} 1^{¼} 1^{6} Patton D B^{1} 35000 87-10 Cojak Man, Tai High, Chili Hill 10

2Nov86—Steadied 1/4

16Oct86-9SA 1 1/16 :47^{2} 1:12^{2} 1:44 ft 16 111^{5} 3^{1} 1^{½} 1^{4} 1^{6½} Patton D B^{7} 20000 81-19 CojakMan,ResonToStudy,Averted 10

3Oct86-5SA 6f :22^{1} :45^{2} 1:10^{2}ft 14 113^{5} 6^{5¼} 7^{6¾} 6^{6½} 4^{6¾} Patton D B^{10} 20000 79-17 NtvCptv,Nck'sPrnc,JohnsTomrrw 10

3Oct86—Wide into stretch

31Aug86-2Dmr 6f :21^{4} :44^{4} 1:08^{4}ft 6¼ 116 3^{1} 5^{8} 6^{9} 9^{12½} Kaenel J L^{9} 25000 81-12 GrowlrSnd,HndflOfDmnd,Prcntstr 12

23Aug86-1Dmr 6½f :21^{4} :45^{1} 1:16^{3}ft *2¾ 116 1^{1} 1^{2} 1^{½} 1^{½} Kaenel J L^{8} 20000 89-10 CojkMn,MischievousMtt,CritosLp 8

Jan 7 SA 5f sy 1:03^{2} h (d) — Dec 1 SA 5f ft 1:00 h

I.
9–5

For Himself — Dk. b. or br. g. 6, by Tri Jet—Scatter Plan, by Quadrangle
STEVENS G L 116 — Br.—Glen Hill Farm (Fla) — 1987 1 0 1 0 $4,600
Own.—Sierra Stable — Tr.—Lerille Arthur J Jr $32,000 — 1986 6 3 0 0 $35,750
Lifetime 31 6 5 5 $123,725 — Turf 6 0 2 1 $18,750

17Jan87-9SA 1 1/16 :462 1:112 1:434ft 4¾ 116 33½ 2hd 1hd 21 Meza R Q3 32000 81-18 PiperJohn,ForHimself,ShowerDcr 12
19Oct86-9SA 1 1/16 :463 1:111 1:432ft *7-5 117 11½ 1½ 11 1¾ Stevens G L1 40000 84-18 ForHmslf,Mummy'sPlsr,ToghEnvoy 7
30Aug86-3Dmr 1 1/16 :451 1:092 1:413ft 3 116 1½ 12½ 12 12 Valenzuela P A5 40000 92-10 ForHimslf,NorthrnProvidr,DnliRidg 8
10Aug86-2Dmr 1 1/16 :45 1:093 1:412ft 12 116 11 11½ 12½ 11 Stevens G L1 32000 93-08 ForHimself,Juli'sMrk,ToughEnvoy 10
28Jly86-7Dmr 6½f :214 :451 1:15 ft 26 116 109½ 106½ 78½ 78¾ DelahoussayeE8 32000 88-16 GryPinstripe,MostDtrmind,Bizboy 10
28Jly86—Veered in, bumped start; wide, returned bleeding from mouth
18Jan86-2SA 6½f :213 :44 1:152ft 8¼ 116 54 87¼ 1116 1114¼ McCarron C J10 32000 79-12 Goldy'sCommander,Chevo,Romxe 12
18Jan86—Wide final 3/8
5Jan86-3SA 6½f :22 :45 1:162ft 8¼ 116 62¾ 63 99¼ 99¾ Hernandez R8 40000 78-14 Juntura, Viron, Skookumchuck 10
5Jan86—Veered out, bumped start; returned bleeding from mouth
17Sep85-11Pom 6f :222 :451 1:101ft 40 115 59½ 711 811 68½ Estrada J Jr6 Aprisa H — — Artichoke,MisterGennro,RollANturl 8
17Sep85—Bore out, bumped
15Aug85-5Dmr 6½f :221 :451 1:16 ft 9 115 1hd 11 21 21¼ Pedroza M A4 50000 95-15 GoodFinish,ForHimself,PlesntPowr 7
4Aug85-9Dmr 1 1/16 :453 1:10 1:43 ft 17 116 11 11 3½ 52½ Pedroza M A3 50000 82-17 Easy Mover, Viron, Tom 10
4Aug85—Bumped start
Jan 28 SA 4f ft :472 h — Jan 12 SA 7f ft 1:282 h — Dec 30 SA 7f ft 1:282 h — ●Dec 24 SA 7f ft 1:283 h

J.
38–1

Impulsively — B. g. 7, by Decidedly—Hill Flag, by Hillary
BLACK C A 116 — Br.—Pope Mrs G A Jr (Cal) — 1987 3 1 0 0 $13,275
Own.—Fritz & Lima — Tr.—Carava Jack $32,000 — 1986 22 2 3 7 $59,780
Lifetime 60 9 8 12 $188,060 — Turf 5 0 1 1 $7,200

17Jan87-9SA 1 1/16 :462 1:112 1:434ft 10 116 1013 1011 1111 119¾ Black C A10 32000 72-18 PiperJohn,ForHimself,ShowerDcr 12
17Jan87—Lugged in final 3/8
11Jan87-9SA 1 1/16 :473 1:113 1:443ft 4¼ 117 78 55 33 1½ Pincay L Jr3 25000 78-21 Impulsively, Pegus, Bedouin 9
3Jan87-9SA 1 1/16 :47 1:113 1:433ft 9¾ 116 79 77¼ 55½ 44¼ DelahoussayeE7 32000 79-16 NorthrnProvdr,Rnbw'sCp,FrgnLgn 10
7Dec86-6Hol 1⅛ :472 1:121 1:514gd 6 116 814 812 89¾ 815½ Stevens G L2 32000 62-18 VlintGeorge,GumFleet,ForignLgion 9
7Dec86—Broke slowly
20Nov86-5Hol 1⅛ :464 1:114 1:512ft 7½ 116 913 911 73¾ 52¾ Stevens G L8 32000 77-16 Oak TreeII,Bedouin,ValiantGeorge 11
20Nov86—Steadied 3/16
5Nov86-7Hol 1⅛ Ⓣ:473 1:113 1:483fm 22 116 78¾ 76¾ 56¾ 54¾ Valenzuela P A5 50000 80-14 Too Much For T. V.,Massera,Tarver 8
19Oct86-9SA 1 1/16 :463 1:111 1:432ft 6½ 116 513 68½ 69 68¾ DelahoussayeE4 40000 75-18 ForHmslf,Mummy'sPlsr,ToghEnvoy 7
19Oct86—Wide into stretch
12Oct86-9SA 1 1/16 :463 1:12 1:443ft 5 116 812 86½ 33 2¾ Stevens G L3 c32000 77-21 Mmmy'sPlsr,Implsvly,NrthrnPrvdr 12
5Oct86-9SA 1 1/16 :462 1:111 1:424ft 5½ 116 1013 104½ 64¼ 53½ Stevens G L5 40000 83-15 Tough Envoy, Idol, Tio Nino 10
5Oct86—Broke slowly; wide final 3/8
6Sep86-10Bmf 1 :46 1:10 1:351ft 6½ 115 68½ 55½ 34 34 CastanedaM5 Aw22000 88-18 SomthngGorgous,FolkArt,Implsvly 7
Jan 25 SA 4f ft :483 b — Dec 28 SA 6f ft 1:13 h — Dec 22 SA 5f ft 1:001 h — Dec 15 SA 3f ft :353 h

K.
6–1

Decontrol — Ch. g. 8, by Majestic Light—La Fantastique, by Le Fabuleux
SIBILLE R 116 — Br.—Pinewood Stable (Ky) — 1987 2 1 0 0 $12,075
Own.—Diamant-Harris-Morningstar — Tr.—Stute Warren $32,000 — 1986 2 0 0 0 $2,350
Lifetime 37 10 6 1 $151,850 — Turf 8 2 2 0 $44,550

24Jan87-9SA 1 1/16 :471 1:113 1:434ft 3 116 12 15 13½ 13½ Valenzuela P A9 25000 82-18 Dcontrol,ForgtThRng,DckAndHgh 12
11Jan87-9SA 1 1/16 :473 1:113 1:443ft *2¼ 116 1½ 1hd 2½ 53 Valenzuela P A7 25000 75-21 Impulsively, Pegus, Bedouin 9
11Jan87—Wide 7/8 turn
21Dec86-7Hol 6f :22 :452 1:101ft 25 116 75¼ 64¾ 54 57¼ Castanon A L4 32000 85-15 Romaxe, Ondarty, EllsBravestSong 8
8Jan86-9SA 1 1/16 :464 1:113 1:432ft 5 116 42 41¼ 43 45½ Sibille R2 50000 78-16 VigorousVigors,Swivel,TrusT.Danus 8
14Dec85-1Hol 1 :462 1:113 1:363ft *7-5 116 11 1½ 1½ 1hd Sibille R1 40000 80-14 Decontrol, Juntura, Preprint 6
6Dec85-9Hol 1 :453 1:094 1:351ft 2¼ 116 42 44½ 43 43 Sibille R7 50000 84-17 Menswear, Amarone, Hydrostatic 7
6Dec85—3 wide into drive
11Aug85-9Dmr 1⅛ Ⓣ:502 1:142 1:50 fm *9-5 115 42 31½ 25 45½ Toro F3 62500 82-05 Dunant, Fabuleux Prince,Tyrabellor 9
24Jly85-9Dmr 1 Ⓣ:464 1:113 1:363fm *8-5 116 2hd 1hd 11½ 21 Sibille R3 62500 88-09 Nonno, Decontrol, Super Noble 9
30Jun85-6Hol 1 1/16 Ⓣ:464 1:102 1:411fm 5¼ 116 11½ 1hd 2hd 22¾ Sibille R5 62500 90-09 Sagamore, Decontrol, Viron 12
16Jun85-3Hol 1⅛ :464 1:102 1:481ft 4 116 1hd 11½ 1hd 11¼ Sibille R4 40000 108-02 Decontrol, Golden E., Stickette 6
Jan 22 SA 4f ft :48 h — Jan 17 SA 5f ft 1:011 h — Jan 8 SA 6f m 1:163 h — Jan 2 SA 1 ft 1:431 h

L.
8–1

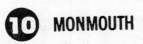

***Cold *** (C15) — PEDROZA M A — 116
Own.—Goudy–Hoogsteen–Kalpakoff
Ch. g. 8, by Arctic Tern—Fort Brune, by Forli
Br.—Lazar H (Eng)
Tr.—Longden Vance J — $32,000
Lifetime 60 12 9 1 $141,000

1987	1	0 0	0	$1,725
1986	13	3 3	0	$42,755
Turf	17	2 3	0	$37,405

17Jan87-9SA 1 1/16 :462 1:112 1:434ft 4¼ 116 912 86¾ 64 41½ Olivares F12 32000 80-18 PiperJohn,ForHimself,ShowerDcr 12
17Jan87—Bumped late
26Dec86-9SA 1 1/16 :454 1:102 1:43 ft 14 114 89¼ 75½ 21½ 13 Olivares F11 22500 86-13 Cold,TommyThoms,BoncngBttons 11
17Aug86-7Dmr* 1 1/16 :453 1:101 1:432ft 25 116 42 31 21½ 42½ Pedroza M A3 25000 80-16 BngBngBng,MrkInThSky,OnEdRm 10
10Aug86-2Dmr 1 1/16 :45 1:093 1:412ft 8¼ 116 87¼ 1013 1025 — Toro F6 32000 — — ForHimself,Juli'sMrk,ToughEnvoy 10
10Aug86—Eased
27Jly86-9Dmr 1 1/16 :454 1:102 1:422ft 11 116 54½ 74 52½ 42¾ Toro F9 25000 85-10 MstrCwston,NutrlPlyr,Rvolutionry 10
27Jly86—Checked, shuffled back 2nd turn
28May86-9Hol 1 :461 1:11 1:363ft 21 116 74¼ 56½ 59 710½ Toro F5 32000 69-15 Knight Skiing, Ego Buck, Elefante 9
18May86-9Hol 1 :45 1:102 1:36 ft 8¼ 116 66¾ 34 66½ 89½ Toro F10 32000 73-08 KnightSkiing,RightOnRed,Elefnte 12
12Apr86-9SA 1 1/16 :46 1:11 1:433ft 11 116 58½ 44 3½ 2hd Toro F3 32000 83-19 Knight Skiing, Cold, Rajaba 9
15Mar86-5SA 1⅛ :46 1:111 1:514m *2½ 118 33 31½ 712 819 Stevens G L7 c20000 51-23 GoodThoughtWilly,Muft,WldPlsur 12
21Feb86-9SA 1 1/16 :464 1:114 1:434gd *2½ 119 67¼ 42 1hd 11¼ Pincay L Jr3 c16000 82-22 Cold,Lighthewayholme,CertainTret 8
Jan 31 SA 3f ft :363 h Jan 25 SA 7f ft 1:302 h Jan 8 SA 6f m 1:194 h ● Dec 20 SA 1 ft 1:401 h

A. Baseball A-C-D and key each on top of I
B. Key I top and bottom with A-C-D-J
C. Box A and C and key each on top of D and I
D. Key A-C-D-J-L on top of I

59. A variety of specialized know-how is required to solve this Monmouth Park turf puzzle. But handicappers who can put the pieces together will discover a very generous winner indeed.

10 MONMOUTH

TURF COURSE
1 MILE
MONMOUTH PARK
Start
Finish

1 MILE. (Turf). (1.35) MAIDEN SPECIAL WEIGHT. Purse $13,500. 3-year-olds and upward. Weight, 3-year-olds, 115 lbs. Older, 123 lbs.

Coupled—Mary Rolfe and Chervil; Manumission and Fairway Double; Fireside Drive and Castle Isle.

A.
3–1

Quick Tour — 115
Own.—Evergreen Farm
Ch. c. 3, by To the Quick—Tour Verte, by Green Dancer
Br.—Evergreen Farm (Ky)
Tr.—Cocks William B
Lifetime 8 0 2 3 $9,765

1987	4	M	1	2	$6,135
1986	4	M	1	1	$3,630
Turf	3	0	1	1	$5,080

12Jly87- 4Pha fst 1⅛ 1:54⅗ 3+ Md Sp Wt 5 2 21 2hd 2½ 26 Thornburg B b 113 2.70 56-22 Real Ease 1146 Quick Tour 1135 Acquiescent 1136 Held place 6
26Jun87- 1Pha fst 1 1/16 :48 1:14⅖ 1:50⅖ 3+ Md Sp Wt 1 5 513 55½ 55½ 34½ Roe J 113 *1.90 47-31 Royal Omerta 113½ Manassas Gap 1224 Quick Tour 113½ Rallied 9
19Jun87- 5Bel fm 1 1/16 Ⓣ:46⅘ 1:12 1:44 3+ Md Sp Wt 7 4 74 44 57½ 59½ Vasquez J 114 3.80 66-19 Hopzig 1141½ Source of Strength 1145½ Picador 1091 No factor 10
7Jun87- 5Bel gd 1 1/16 Ⓣ:47⅘ 1:12⅖ 1:44⅘ 3+ Md Sp Wt 11 2 43½ 21 2½ 34½ Vasquez J 114 21.40 67-23 SwanPoint1142½SourceofStrength1152QuickTour1142¾ Weakened 11
5Nov86- 6Pha sly 170 :48⅗ 1:15⅕ 1:47⅘ Md Sp Wt 5 5 68½ 67½ 69½ 617¼ Thornburg B 118 *1.80 46-28 Silky Beau 118nk Freeze Talks 1196 Kick Back 1184 Bore out 6
15Oct86- 5Med fst 170 :48⅖ 1:13⅘ 1:44⅗ Md Sp Wt 6 4 4¾ 52½ 34½ 33½ Rocco J 118 3.40 70-21 Reland 1182½ Foolish Pirate 1081 Quick Tour 1181 Mild rally 9
23Sep86- 6Pha fm 1 Ⓣ:47⅖ 1:13 1:39⅗ Md Sp Wt 5 6 75½ 41 22½ 2hd Thornburg B 117 2.70 81-19 No Rifling 117hd Quick Tour 1178½ War Spur 1171 Gamely 11
8Sep86- 4Bel fst 5f :22⅗ :45⅗ :57⅕ Md Sp Wt 4 5 58 610 611 513 Vasquez J 118 7.80 85-11 Pledge Card 1184 To the Inch 1186½ Honey Plant 118¾ No factor 7
LATEST WORKOUTS ● Jly 23 Del 4f fst :47⅗ h Jun 1 Del 4f fst :48⅗ bg

B.
10–1

No Bend's Native — 123
Own.—Paxson Mrs H D
Dk. b. or br. g. 4, by No Bend—Native Move, by Restless Native
Br.—Paxson Mrs H D (NY)
Tr.—Edens Mary
Lifetime 10 0 2 0 $6,340

1987	2	M	0	0	
1986	8	M	2	0	$6,340
Turf	5	0	2	0	$5,590

22Jly87- 6Mth fm 1⅛ Ⓣ:50⅘ 1:15⅕ 1:53 + 3+ Md Sp Wt 9 6 52½ 62¾ 813 815¾ Edwards J W b 123 6.30 59-21 Hombre de Carrera 115½ Daufuskie 1152 Beau Nash 1151¾ Tired 9
8Jly87- 3Mth sly 1 1/16 :47⅖ 1:12⅗ 1:46⅘ 3+ Md Sp Wt 2 6 56½ 69½ 615 621 Edwards J W b 123 3.90 50-22 Elite Company 1156GentlemanJohnA.1152InjunPower1152 Outrun 6
23Oct86-10Med fm 1 1/16 Ⓣ:47⅗ 1:12⅘ 1:44⅖ 3+ Md Sp Wt 5 11 106¾ 84¾ 21½ 21 Edwards J W b 117 *3.70 80-14 Chop Slewy 1171NoBend'sNative117noDaring'NBold1175 Held 2nd 12
22Sep86- 4Med fm 1 1/16 Ⓣ:47⅗ 1:12⅖ 1:45⅖ 3+ Md Sp Wt 6 8 87¾ 65½ 1hd 2¾ Edwards J W b 116 13.20 75-22 LamontCranston116¾NoBend'sNative1167SlyandBold116½ Gamely 10
2Sep86- 3Med fm 1 1/16 Ⓣ:48⅗ 1:13 1:43⅘ 3+ Md Sp Wt 7 4 21 2hd 63½ 512¼ Edwards J W b 116 51.40 71-14 Looming Libra 1164 Axe The Kid 1221NativeClown1132½ Faltered 8
22Aug86-10Mth fst 1 1/16 :47⅘ 1:13⅕ 1:45⅖ 3+ Md Sp Wt 3 3 42½ 77¾ 824 834¾ Verge M E b 115 9.50e 43-18 Daytime Friend 115nk Almarine 1157 Beyond TheDepth1157 Tired 9
4Aug86- 6Mth fst 1⅛ :47⅘ 1:12⅕ 1:51⅘ 3+ Md Sp Wt 3 1 21½ 55 717 726 Solomone M b 115 14.20 49-20 Captain Arthur 115no Qui Prince 115¾ Nibron1151¼ Used up early 7
24Jly86- 6Mth fst 170 :47 1:11⅘ 1:42⅘ 3+ Md Sp Wt 12 2 2½ 3½ 54 56¼ Solomone M b 114 48.40e 75-21 Thor'sDancer114nk D SmartLiberl1141½CptnArthur1144 Weakened 12
24Jly86-Placed fourth through disqualification
24Jun86- 5Mth fm 1⅛ Ⓣ:48⅗ 1:13⅘ 1:50⅘+ 3+ Md Sp Wt 9 7 77 62¼ 88¾ 915 Verge M E 114 119.50 71-15 Crafty Giboulee 1149 LikelyKnight114nkDeauvilleLady118no Tired 11
17Jun86- 6Mth fst 6f :23⅖ :47⅕ 1:13 3+ Md Sp Wt 2 10 97½ 1014 1016 1023½ Verge M E 115 14.20e 51-23 Norman's Ryan 1222 Frankinstrelli115nk YankeeAffair122¾ Outrun 10
LATEST WORKOUTS Jly 17 Mth 3f fst :36 b Jly 4 Mth 4f fst :48⅗ h Jun 27 Mth 1 sly 1:43⅗ h Jun 20 Mth 7f fst 1:28 b

C.

6–1

Noble Field — Ch. g. 4, by Sir Ivor—Sack Race, by Cohoes
Br.—Whitney Mrs J H (Ky)
Own.—Greentree Stable — Tr.—Woodington Jamie — 123
Lifetime 14 0 2 2 $13,270 — 1987 5 M 1 1 $5,360 — 1986 9 M 1 1 $7,910 — Turf 9 0 2 2 $12,630

17Jly87-10Mth	fm	1$\frac{1}{16}$	[T]:47⅗ 1:12⅗ 1:45⅕	3↑ Md Sp Wt	4	9	9^{10}	7^{6}	$4^{2\frac{1}{4}}$	2^{4}	Madrid A Jr	123	16.40	75-20 Flight in Time 115^{4} Noble Field 123$^{1\frac{1}{2}}$ Injun Power 115$^{\frac{3}{4}}$	2nd best	11
11Jly87- 3Mtn	fst	1$\frac{1}{16}$	:47⅖ 1:11⅕ 1:43⅕	3↑ Clm 28000	5	6	5^{4}	5^{8}	5^{14}	5^{22}	Hernandez C	111	33.80	67-14 Lovin Breeze 109$^{3\frac{1}{2}}$ Gorli 115^{6} Quick Dip 115$^{4\frac{1}{2}}$	No factor	6
13Jun87- 3Mth	fm	1⅛	[T]:48⅗ 1:12⅖ 1:50⅕ +	3↑ Clm 25000	3	4	4^{6}	$4^{5\frac{1}{2}}$	$4^{8\frac{1}{2}}$	$4^{10\frac{3}{4}}$	Santagata N	115	10.10	79-06 [D]First Double 115^{nk} Cantonero 111^{8} Padrilario 115^{2}	Steadied	8
17Feb87- 5Hia	fst	1⅛	:48 1:12⅗ 1:53	Md Sp Wt	6	10	$9^{8\frac{3}{4}}$	$8^{9\frac{3}{4}}$	6^{10}	$6^{14\frac{1}{2}}$	Brumfield D	122	17.00	51-22 Northern Classic 122$^{1\frac{1}{2}}$ Dr. Peel 122^{1}RoaringRiver122$^{5\frac{1}{2}}$	No factor	11
19Jan87- 6Hia	fm	*1$\frac{1}{16}$	[T] 1:43⅖	Md Sp Wt	10	10	8^{20}	9^{13}	$7^{6\frac{3}{4}}$	3^{8}	Guerra W A	122	7.00	73-16 Skitown 122$^{5\frac{1}{2}}$ Hand Forged 122$^{2\frac{1}{2}}$ Noble Field 122^{hd}	Rallied	12
31Dec86- 5Crc	sly	1⅛	:51⅕ 1:17⅖ 1:57⅗	3↑ Md Sp Wt	4	5	5^{11}	$7^{7\frac{1}{2}}$	7^{9}	$7^{9\frac{1}{4}}$	Guerra W A	120	18.00	52-20 Hl'sSplndr120^{no}ChlcfSir117^{5}Wrthngtnhlls120^{1}	Squeezed back st.	8
17Nov86- 9Aqu	fst	1	:46⅖ 1:11⅖ 1:37⅕	3↑ Md 50000	7	8	$7^{3\frac{1}{2}}$	$8^{5\frac{3}{4}}$	$8^{9\frac{1}{2}}$	8^{13}	Bailey J D	120	13.80	67-20 One's Castle 120$^{6\frac{1}{2}}$ Float Trip 113$^{1\frac{3}{4}}$ Golden Chance 120$^{1\frac{1}{2}}$	Outrun	12
8Oct86- 2Bel	fm	1	[T]:46⅘ 1:12 1:38⅖	3↑ Md Sp Wt	1	6	$5^{3\frac{1}{2}}$	$8^{6\frac{1}{2}}$	$9^{8\frac{3}{4}}$	$11^{11\frac{3}{4}}$	Maple E	119	6.20	61-29 Fleeting Snow 119^{3} I'm No Yankee 119^{2} Send-Up 119^{nk}	Tired	12
1Sep86- 2Bel	fm	1$\frac{1}{16}$	[T]:46⅘ 1:12⅕ 1:42⅘	3↑ Md Sp Wt	11	2	4^{2}	$6^{5\frac{1}{2}}$	6^{8}	$6^{8\frac{3}{4}}$	Romero R P	b 118	6.60	74-18 Strong Adversary 118^{1} Dr. Danzig 122$^{1\frac{1}{2}}$ Master OfArts118^{1}	Tired	12
15Aug86- 1Sar	fm	1⅛	[T]:47⅕ 1:11⅘ 1:50⅖	3↑ Md Sp Wt	12	4	4^{4}	3^{2}	$3^{1\frac{1}{2}}$	$3^{\frac{3}{4}}$	Maple E	117	6.60	74-18 [D]SummerColony117^{hd}SorToTheStrs117$^{\frac{3}{4}}$NobleField117$^{\frac{1}{2}}$	Steadied	12

LATEST WORKOUTS Jly 5 Mth 4f fst :50⅖ b — Jun 29 Mth 3f fst :37 b — Jun 10 Mth 3f fst :37⅕ h

D.

20–1

Babuji — B. c. 3, by Katullus—Ginger Talk, by Ginger Fizz
Br.—Bernstein Phyllis J (NY)
Own.—Chaudry A G — Tr.—Magnier Peter — 108^{7}
Lifetime 3 0 0 0 — 1987 3 M 0 0 — 1986 0 M 0 0

11Jun87- 7Lrl	fst	6f	:23⅕ :47⅗ 1:13	3↑ Md Sp Wt	9	7	$5^{2\frac{1}{4}}$	6^{6}	6^{12}	6^{15}	Roe J	113	12.60	63-25 Nicky's Prince 113$^{2\frac{1}{2}}$ Rebel Ralph 108^{4} Horse Talk 113^{5}	No factor	11
16May87- 2Pim	fst	6f	:23⅗ :47⅗ 1:13	3↑ Md Sp Wt	6	3	1^{hd}	1^{hd}	6^{6}	$10^{10\frac{1}{4}}$	Roe J	114	16.40	71-18 Beth'sBonus112^{no}ExecutiveImage122$^{\frac{1}{2}}$LordsLanding112^{2}	Stopped	11
5May87- 5Pim	gd	6f	:23⅗ :47⅖ 1:13⅖	3↑ Md Sp Wt	3	5	3^{3}	$8^{8\frac{3}{4}}$	9^{12}	$8^{14\frac{1}{2}}$	Lizarzaburu P M	112	5.90	64-25 WinterLight115$^{2\frac{1}{2}}$[D]Nicky'sPrince105$^{\frac{3}{4}}$Brend'sRock105^{2}	Fell back	11

LATEST WORKOUTS Jly 16 Bel 5f fst 1:03 b — Jly 4 Del 1 fst 1:43 h

E.

10–1

Fable Legend — B. c. 3, by Le Fabuleux—Lady of Bagdad, by Bagdad
Br.—Farnsworth Farm & Sainer (Fla)
Own.—Brook D — Tr.—Durso Robert J — 115
Lifetime 0 0 0 0 — 1987 0 M 0 0 — 1986 0 M 0 0

LATEST WORKOUTS Jly 28 Mth 4f fst :48 hg — Jly 11 Mth 5f fst 1:02⅖ b — Jly 7 Mth 4f fst :54 b — Jun 13 Mth 4f fst :48⅘ b

F.

12–1

***Portrait of Power** — Dk. b. or br. c. 4, by Scorpio—Dedham Vale, by Dike
Br.—Corbett M (Ire)
Own.—Dee Pee Stable — Tr.—Jennings Lawrence W — 123
Lifetime 1 0 0 0 — 1985 1 M 0 0 — 1984 0 M 0 0 — Turf 1 0 0 0

8Aug85 ♦ 4LimerickJcn(Ire) sf 7f 1:44⅗ [T] BallsbridgeTallersallsSks 8 Hogan D 120 14.00 — — RommelsChoice120$^{1\frac{1}{2}}$ NosNaGoitne115^{1} RunForEver120$^{\frac{1}{2}}$ Outrun 8

LATEST WORKOUTS ● Jly 24 Mth 6f fst 1:13 hg — Jly 18 Mth 6f fst 1:15 hg — Jly 13 Mth 4f fst :50⅗ bg — Jly 7 Mth 5f fst 1:04 b

G.

7–2

Medieval Mind — B. c. 3, by Medieval Man—Thalamus, by The Minstrel
Br.—Live Oak Stud (Fla)
Own.—Live Oak Plantation — Tr.—Kelly Patrick J — 115
Lifetime 16 0 3 4 $29,740 — 1987 9 M 1 2 $12,480 — 1986 7 M 2 2 $17,260 — Turf 6 0 2 0 $11,560

18Jly87- 6Bel	fm	1	[T]:46⅖ 1:12 1:37⅖	3↑ Md Sp Wt	8	1	1^{6}	1^{6}	$5^{4\frac{1}{2}}$	$8^{10\frac{3}{4}}$	Graell A	b 116	8.00	67-20 Lord Laser 116$^{1\frac{1}{2}}$ [D]Highly Rated II 116$^{4\frac{1}{4}}$ Van Man 116$^{\frac{1}{2}}$	Stopped	12
19Jun87- 2Bel	fst	1	:46⅖ 1:12⅖ 1:39⅗	3↑ Md 50000	5	6	$5^{2\frac{1}{2}}$	$5^{7\frac{1}{2}}$	8^{16}	$8^{16\frac{1}{4}}$	Graell A	b 114	4.10	51-21 You Hop 114^{hd} Aki 114$^{3\frac{1}{2}}$ Wise Old Owl 114$^{1\frac{3}{4}}$	Tired	14
12Jun87- 5Bel	gd	1¼	[T]:47⅗ 1:38⅕ 2:03⅕	3↑ Md Sp Wt	11	1	$1^{2\frac{1}{2}}$	1^{4}	2^{hd}	$4^{5\frac{1}{2}}$	Graell A	b 114	6.30e	72-17 Sahara Dancer 122^{nk} Give Light 114$^{4\frac{1}{2}}$ Osmunda 114$^{\frac{3}{4}}$	Tired	11
7Jun87- 5Bel	gd	1$\frac{1}{16}$	[T]:47⅘ 1:12⅖ 1:44⅘	3↑ Md Sp Wt	8	1	$1^{2\frac{1}{2}}$	1^{1}	4^{4}	6^{13}	Graell A	b 114	11.30	59-23 Swan Point 114$^{2\frac{1}{2}}$ SourceofStrength115^{2}QuickTour114$^{2\frac{3}{4}}$	Used up	11
6May87- 6Bel	my	1$\frac{1}{16}$	:46⅘ 1:12⅕ 1:46	3↑ Md Sp Wt	3	1	1^{1}	$1^{\frac{1}{2}}$	$4^{5\frac{1}{2}}$	$5^{10\frac{3}{4}}$	Graell A	b 113	2.30	61-20 Sir Jove 124$^{\frac{1}{2}}$ Gone Cat 113$^{4\frac{1}{2}}$ Dawn Revival 119$^{4\frac{3}{4}}$	Gave way	7
21Apr87- 3Aqu	fst	1	:45⅕ 1:10⅘ 1:38⅘	Md Sp Wt	6	2	2^{hd}	1^{3}	1^{1}	$3^{2\frac{1}{4}}$	Graell A	b 122	8.60	70-26 Milesius 122^{2} Gone Cat 122^{nk} Medieval Mind 122$^{2\frac{1}{2}}$	Weakened	6
19Mar87- 6Aqu	fst	7f	:23 :46⅗ 1:26⅖	Md Sp Wt	13	2	1^{hd}	2^{hd}	12^{20}	$12^{18\frac{3}{4}}$	Graell A	b 122	*4.00	50-29 Briskeen 122^{2} French Connector 117$^{1\frac{3}{4}}$ Petrinni 122^{nk}	Tired	14
28Feb87- 4Aqu	fst	1$\frac{1}{16}$	[•]:48 1:13⅖ 1:47	Md Sp Wt	10	4	1^{hd}	1^{1}	1^{hd}	$2^{7\frac{3}{4}}$	Graell A	b 122	2.80	67-16 Unleavened 122$^{7\frac{3}{4}}$ Medieval Mind 122$^{1\frac{1}{2}}$ Windy Sails 122^{2}	Wide	10
7Jan87- 3Aqu	fst	1$\frac{1}{16}$	[•]:46⅘ 1:12⅕ 1:47⅖	Md Sp Wt	4	1	1^{6}	$1^{4\frac{1}{2}}$	$1^{1\frac{1}{2}}$	$3^{\frac{3}{4}}$	Graell A	b 122	3.30	72-21 MixedEmotions122^{hd}ChiefBlackhwk122$^{\frac{3}{4}}$MedievlMind122$^{1\frac{3}{4}}$	Tired	8
14Dec86- 6Aqu	fst	1$\frac{1}{16}$	[•]:48⅗ 1:13⅕ 1:48	Md Sp Wt	4	4	$2^{\frac{1}{2}}$	1^{hd}	2^{2}	$3^{5\frac{3}{4}}$	Graell A	118	3.90	64-20 Coco's Double 118^{3} Knockon 118$^{2\frac{3}{4}}$ MedievalMind118^{4}	Weakened	11

LATEST WORKOUTS Jly 27 Bel 3f fst :36⅕ h — Jly 14 Bel 4f fst :47⅗ h — Jly 10 Bel tr.t 3f sly :36⅘ b — ● Jly 4 Bel tr.t 3f fst :36 h

H.

6–1

Mary Rolfe — Ch. f. 3, by Tom Rolfe—Marianna Trench, by Pago Pago
Br.—Mayer Len (Ky)
Own.—Avery N — Tr.—Rieser Steven M — 110
Lifetime 6 0 1 2 $7,250 — 1987 5 M 1 2 $7,250 — 1986 1 M 0 0

10Jly87-10Mth	fst	1$\frac{1}{16}$	:47⅘ 1:13 1:47	3↑[F]Md Sp Wt	2	1	1^{1}	$1^{\frac{1}{2}}$	$2^{\frac{1}{2}}$	3^{3}	Vigliotti M J	115	2.20	67-16 StrdustSurprise115$^{\frac{1}{2}}$GirlofMyDrems115$^{2\frac{1}{2}}$MryRolf115$^{1\frac{3}{4}}$	Weakened	8
11Jun87- 9CD	fst	6f	:21⅘ :45⅘ 1:10⅗	3↑[F]Md Sp Wt	9	2	$6^{2\frac{1}{4}}$	3^{2}	$3^{5\frac{1}{2}}$	$3^{8\frac{1}{2}}$	McDowell M	110	4.20	81-17 Saucy Deb 114$^{2\frac{1}{2}}$ Yvonnes Victory 111^{6} Mary Rolfe 110^{hd}		12
2Jun87- 5CD	sly	6½f	:23 :47⅕ 1:19⅖	3↑[F]Md Sp Wt	9	2	2^{hd}	2^{hd}	2^{3}	4^{11}	McDowell M	111	*2.00	72-23 Cardome 114^{8} Beau Danzig 114no Temptation Love 106^{3}		10
22May87- 9CD	fst	6f	:21⅗ :46 1:11⅕	3↑[F]Md Sp Wt	11	1	$5^{2\frac{1}{2}}$	1^{hd}	$2^{1\frac{1}{2}}$	2^{5}	McDowell M	112	6.50	82-17 Cortufa 112^{5} Mary Rolfe 112^{3} Deliver 112^{1}		11
24Mar87- 4GP	sly	6f	:21⅘ :45⅖ 1:12⅕	[F]Md Sp Wt	3	8	$9^{9\frac{1}{4}}$	10^{20}	10^{17}	$9^{19\frac{1}{2}}$	Penna D	121	5.90	58-23 Great Time 121$^{\frac{1}{2}}$ Niceness 121$^{\frac{1}{2}}$ First Venture 121$^{4\frac{1}{2}}$	Checked	12
2Nov86- 5CD	fst	7f	:23⅗ :47⅕ 1:26⅗	[F]Md Sp Wt	1	3	1^{2}	$1^{\frac{1}{2}}$	3^{1}	$6^{2\frac{3}{4}}$	Johnson P A	121	29.20	70-18 El Barril Sue 121^{hd} Calycanthus 121^{nk} Far Out Chevy 121^{hd}		11

LATEST WORKOUTS Jly 28 Mth 4f fst :48⅘ b — Jly 19 Mth 4f fst :49 b — Jly 4 Mth 6f fst 1:14⅕ h — Jun 21 Mth 5f fst 1:03⅕ b

I.

6–1

```
*Manumission            B. c. 3, by Blakeney—Set Free, by Worden II              Lifetime      1987  3 M 0 1      $1,690
                        Br.—Fonthill Stud (Eng)                                  3 0 0 1       1986  0 M 0 0
  Own.—Straus-Medina Ranch  Tr.—Gleaves Philip                          115      $1,690        Turf  2 0 0 1      $1,560
22Jly87- 6Mth fm 1⅛ Ⓣ:50⅘ 1:15⅕ 1:53 + 3+Md Sp Wt  5 8 87½ 87¼ 67½ 69¾ Rocco J     115  4.20 65-21 Hombre deCarrera115½Daufuskie1152BeauNash1151¾ Forced wide 9
22Apr87- 6GP fm *1 1/16 Ⓣ        1:48   Md Sp Wt     1 3 34½ 35 24 32½  Pezua J M   122 *2.50 63-27 Catch ACold1222½SalineCounty122hdManumission122nc Bid, hung 9
4Apr87- 3GP fst 7f  :23⅗ :47⅘ 1:26⅗      Md Sp Wt     1 7 88 812 710 79  Rivera M A  122 62.20 62-23 Mon Classique 1221 Co Pro 122nk Path 122no  Outrun 9
  LATEST WORKOUTS   Jly 18 Mth 4f fst :50⅘ b   Jly 9 Mth 6f my 1:17⅕ b   Jun 29 Mth 5f fst 1:02⅘ b   Jun 23 Mth 4f fst :51 b
```

J.

8–1

```
Daring 'N Bold          Dk. b. or br. c. 4, by Foolish Pleasure—Lin-D Star, by Graustark   Lifetime   1987  1 M 1 0    $2,600
                        Br.—Lin-Drake Farm (Fla)                                            8 0 4 2    1986  7 M 3 2    $10,730
  Own.—Irwin R D        Tr.—Pierce Joseph H Jr                                      123     $13,330    Turf  2 0 0 1    $1'
   Entered 27Jly87- 3 MTH , finished 3
6Jly87- 3Mth fst 6f   :22⅘ :45⅘ 1:11⅕ 3+Md Sp Wt   5 4 2½ 2hd 2½ 25     Rocco J         b 122 *2.50 79-14 Rightchabee1165Daring'NBold122nkBridgehmpton1221½ Hel'
23Oct86-10Med fm 1 1/16 Ⓣ:47⅗ 1:12⅖ 1:44⅖ 3+Md Sp Wt 1 1 1½ 11 11½ 31   Marquez C HJr b 117 4.20 80-14 Chop Slewy1171NoBend'sNative117noDaring'NBold1175 Gav.
3Oct86- 1Med sly 1 1/16 :47 1:12 1:44⅖ 3+Md Sp Wt  8 1 11 2hd 22 26½    Marquez C HJr b 117 *1.00 74-20 Quotidien 1226½ Daring'NBold1171TurnTheTraffic11711 G
13Sep86- 5Med fm 1 1/16 Ⓣ:47⅕ 1:11⅗ 1:42⅘ 3+Md Sp Wt 4 5 87¾1014 712 710¼ Rocco J       b 116 *.90e 78-07 NorweiginHill1165½GrustrkinBoy1221¼TurnThTrffic1161¼ (
1Sep86- 3Med fst 6f   :22⅖ :45⅗ 1:11⅖ 3+Md Sp Wt   3 5 32½ 33½ 23½ 21¾  Antley C W      b 118 2.10  83-15 Brother Vinnie 1181¾ Daring 'N Bold 1183 Estano 1222
15Aug86- 5Mth fst 6f  :23⅕ :45⅘ 1:11   3+Md Sp Wt   2 3 1hd 2hd 3nk 31½  Day P             117 *1.60 83-17 Solid Man 117¾ Brother Vinnie 117¾ Daring 'N Bold 1172
16Jly86- 6Mth fst 6f  :22⅗ :45⅖ 1:10⅗ 3+Md Sp Wt   8 4 55¼ 46 410 513¾  Antley C W        116 *.70  73-17 NorthOfRichmond116nkLookTomLook11611Nbron1161½
7Jly86- 6Mth fst 6f   :22⅘ :46⅗ 1:11   3+Md Sp Wt   5 2 21 21 2hd 21     Perret C          116 *1.80 84-20 Thundercracker1161Dring'NBold1164Thor'sDncer1165½
  LATEST WORKOUTS   ●Jly 19 Mth 7f fst 1:29 b   Jly 14 Mth 3f fst :36⅖ b   Jly 4 Mth 4f fst :48 b   Jun 19 Mth 5f fst 1:01 h
```

60. The finale on opening day at Santa Anita 1986–87 was a contentious middle distance claiming race. Review the extra information provided and decide the best way to play the race.

Extra information:

1. *Restage* wears front wraps.
2. No strong bias today.
3. *Cold* runs well fresh.
4. Trainers C. Lewis and R. Cross are excellent claiming trainers.

9th Santa Anita

1 1-16 MILES
SANTA ANITA
START FINISH

1 1/16 MILES. (1.40⅕) CLAIMING. Purse $21,000. 3-year-olds and upward. Weights, 3-year-olds, 118 lbs.; older, 121 lbs. Non-winners of two races at one mile or over since October 1 allowed 3 lbs.; of such a race since then, 5 lbs. Claiming price $25,000; if for $22,500 allowed 2 lbs. (Claiming and starter races for $20,000 or less not considered.)

11–1

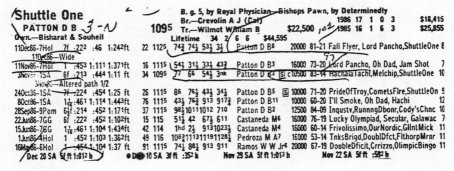

```
Shuttle One                       B. g. 5, by Royal Physician—Bishops Pawn, by Determinedly
                                  Br.—Crevolin A J (Cal)                       1986 17 1 0 3    $18,415
  PATTON D B                1095  Tr.—Wilmot William B             $22,500     1985 16 1 6 3    $25,855
Own.—Bisharat & Souheil           Lifetime  34 2 6 6   $44,595
11Dec86-7Hol  7f :222 :46 1:242ft      22 1125 74¾ 74¼ 53½ 3½    Patton D B8      20000 81-21 Fall Flyer, Lord Pancho,ShuttleOne 8
    11Dec86—Wide
11Nov86-7Hol  1 :453 1:111 1:371ft     16 1115 54½ 31½ 33½ 43¾   Patton D B3      16000 73-20 Lord Pancho, Oh Dad, Jam Shot      7
3Nov86-1SA    6f :213 :444 1:11 ft     34 1095 77 66 54½ 3nk     Patton D B3  Ⓢ c10500 83-14 HachalaTachI,Melchip,ShuttleOne   10
    3Nov86—Altered path 1/2
24Oct86-1SA   7f :224 :454 1:25 ft     26 1115 86 76½ 43½ 34¼    Patton D B5  Ⓢ  10000 71-20 PrideOfTroy,CometsFlre,ShuttleOn  9
8Oct86-1SA    1 1/16 :461 1:114 1:443ft 76 1115 43½ 76¾ 913 917¾ Patton D B11     10000 60-20 I'll Smoke, Oh Dad, Hachi        12
28Sep86-9Pom  6½f :214 :452 1:171ft    37 1115 98½1011 1012 710  Patton D B2      12500 84-09 Inqustv,RunnngDbonr,Cody'sChnc   10
22Jun86-7GG   6f :222 :452 1:102ft     15 115  51¼ 42 67½ 611    Castaneda M6     16000 76-19 Lucky Olympiad, Secular, Galawac  7
15Jun86-7GG   1 1/16 :461 1:104 1:434ft 42 114 1hd 2½ 913 1023½  Castaneda M4     16000 60-14 Frivolissimo,OurNordic,GllntMick 11
1Jun86-4Hol   1 :452 1:103 1:362ft     49 116  108¾1113 1119 1128¼ Pedroza M A7   16000 53-14 TnksBrigd,DoublDfct,FlthorpMrnr  11
16May86-6Hol  1 :454 1:104 1:37 ft     91 1115 74¼ 88¼ 913 911   Ramos W W Jr6    20000 67-19 DoubleDficit,Crrizzo,OlimpicBingo 11
  Dec 20 SA 5f ft 1:012 h   ●Dec 10 SA 3f ft :352 h   Nov 29 SA 5f ft 1:013 h   Nov 22 SA 5f ft :592 h
```

9–2

Tommy Thoms — Ch. c. 4, by Tom Rolfe—Princess East, by Prince John

ORTEGA L E 5-N 116 — Br.—Elmendorf Farm (Ky) — 1986 6 1 1 1 $17,150

Tr.—Cross Richard J $25,000 — 1985 7 2 0 0 $18,600

Own.—Rickerd-Sherman-Stephens — Lifetime 13 3 1 1 $35,750 — Turf 2 0 0 0

18Dec86-8Hol 1 1/16 Ⓣ:4831:12 1:422fm 21 116 52¾ 74¼ 89½ 813¼ Kaenel J L2 Aw24000 69-19 SmoothOpertor,Intuitiveness,Stmd 8

18Dec86—Wide 5/16

29Nov86-7Hol 1 :454 1:104 1:361ft *3¾ 116 11 1hd 2½ 31½ Ortega L E3 c20000 80-12 Rnbow'sCp,LordPnch,TmmyThms 10

16Nov86-4Hol 7f :22 :443 1:241ft 34 117 94½ 65¾ 53¼ 43¾ Sibille R11 20000 79-18 Pegus, Pialor, Amarone 12

16Nov86—Wide down backstretch, through stretch

12Feb86-5SA 1⅛:463 1:104 1:493ft *3½ 115 21 2½ 1½ 1¾ Hawley S6 c18000 81-16 TommyThoms,Nvgnt,Lyon'sShdw 11

1Feb86-9SA 1 1/16:48 1:131 1:463m 11 116 3½ 2hd 1hd 2¾ Hawley S9 18000 67-24 Bedouin, Tommy Thoms, Bemidgi 9

1Feb86—Bobbled at start; wide 1st turn

19Jan86-9SA 1 1/16:462 1:104 1:424ft 25 115 65¾ 74¼ 910 911¾ Meza R Q9 32000 75-12 ForgotThRng,RoosvltRod,Implsvly 8

19Jan86—Steadied start

29Dec85-3SA 1 :461 1:11 1:37 ft 23 114 54¾ 5¾ 11 1no Hawley S3 22500 83-12 TommyThoms,BoldInititv,Rformunt 8

29Dec85—Lugged in late

24Jly85-2Dmr 1 1/16:461 1:104 1:431ft 16 115 75¼ 47½ 712 813¾ Toro F6 28000 70-14 OlimpicBingo,GllntMick,GetMeEvn 8

24Jly85—Wide into stretch

27Jun85-7Hol 1 Ⓣ:4741:1141:361fm 30 114 1011 1014 813 813¾ Shoemaker W3 57500 68-16 Debit, Big Hill To Climb, Ignited 10

14Jun85-5Hol 1⅛:462 1:11 1:512ft 2½ 115 46 32½ 12 13 Hawley S5 M32000 92-06 TommyThoms,Tofutti,Mt.AFortune 8

Dec 14 Hol 6f ft 1:15 h — Dec 9 Hol 4f ft :52 h — Nov 25 SA 4f ft :494 h — Nov 11 SA 5f ft 1:03 h

6–1

***Oak Tree II** — B. h. 6, by Vacilante II—Oak Leaf, by Val de Loir

BAZE G 0-N 118 — Br.—Haras Santa Maria de Araras (Brz) — 1986 12 1 0 4 $26,425

Tr.—Whittingham Charles $25,000 — 1985 3 1 1 0 $727

Own.—Haras Santa Maria de Araras — Lifetime 30 6 5 5 $32,945 — Turf 21 1 3 5 $20,069

7Dec86-6Hol 1⅛:472 1:121 1:514gd 5 119 713 710 53¾ 55½ Baze G6 32000 72-18 VlintGeorge,GumFleet,ForignLgion 9

20Nov86-5Hol 1⅛:464 1:114 1:512ft 23 116 78½ 66½ 3nk 1hd Baze G10 96 32000 80-16 Oak TreeII,Bedouin,ValiantGeorge 11

20Nov86—Wide

5Nov86-7Hol 1⅛Ⓣ:4731:1131:483fm 21 114 57 66½ 68¼ 65½ Baze G2 45000 79-14 Too Much For T. V.,Massera,Tarver 8

7Sep86-9Dmr 1 1/16Ⓣ:4711:11 1:423fm 11 114 514 513 48½ 35 Stevens G L5 45000 88-08 EmperadorAlNorte,Msser,OkTreeII 8

18Jly86-9Hol 1 Ⓣ:4641:1041:353fm *2¾ 116 53½ 4¾ 2½ 3¾ McCarron C J3 40000 — — North Of Lake, Rushad, Oak TreeII 7

6Jly86-10Hol 1⅛Ⓣ:4731:1141:482fm 3 116 76¾ 73¼ 55½ 56 McCarron C J1 50000 84-07 TooMuchForT.V.,Rajhn,IronLeder 10

19Jun86-7Hol 1 1/16Ⓣ:4621:10 1:403fm *2¾ 116 64½ 64¾ 34½ 32¾ McCarron C J2 50000 98 — PlentyConscious,SuperNobl,OkTrII 8

1Jun86-7Hol 1⅛Ⓣ:4731:1211:484fm 6 116 78 73½ 63¾ 64¼ McCarron C J6 62500 84-07 IronLeder,Nonno,SuccessfulBidder 8

17May86-6Hol 1⅛Ⓣ:4741:11 1:48 fm 5½ 1115 74½ 73¾ 42½ 32 Black C A4 62500 90-02 Piper John, TulsaFlyerII,OakTreeII 8

3May86-5Hol 1¼Ⓣ:4711:3542:014fm 23 1095 98½ 94¾ 71½ 43¾ Black C A1 60000 94-03 Julie's Mark, Penzance,PiperJohn 12

Dec 24 SA 3f ft :364 h — Nov 27 Hol 3f ft :381 h — Nov 17 Hol 5f ft 1:032 h — Nov 12 Hol 4f ft :491 h

36–1

***Estoc** 5-0 — B. g. 5, by Gay Mecene—Eastern Silk, by Zeddaan

STEVENS S A 116 — Br.—Bonnefoy & Nicol (Fra) — 1986 5 1 0 0 $19,600

Tr.—Lukas D Wayne $25,000 — 1985 10 2 1 1 $13,403

Own.—Hatley-Klein-Lukas — Lifetime 24 5 1 2 $41,369 — Turf 24 5 1 2 $41,369

8Jun86-4Hol 1 1/16Ⓣ:4541:0941:404fm 4 116 1112 1112 89 65½ McCarron C J3 50000 94 — Sndy'sEgle,EmprdorAlNort,Rushd 11

26May86-7Hol 1¼Ⓣ:49 1:3712:02 fm 6¼ 1115 32 2hd 42 55½ Black C A1 50000 92 — Crony, Tio Nino, Killyglen 9

25Jan86-5SA 1¼Ⓣ:4621:3642:021fm 10 114 21 108¾ 913 916½ McCarron C J6 75000 59-23 PolAndDic,DonnyK.,Morry'sChmp 10

17Jan86-5SA 1⅛Ⓣ:4821:1221:49 fm 7½ 116 85¼ 54¼ 46½ 45¼ McCarron C J4 80000 77-15 Bishop'sRngII,PolAndDc,Snowcrk 10

17Jan86—Wide into stretch

5Jan86-5SA 1⅛Ⓣ:47 1:1141:512gd 9½ 114 65½ 63½ 41½ 11¼ McCarron C J11 57500 70-25 Estoc,RoyalCouncillor,FlyingGene 12

22Dec85-6Hol 1¼Ⓣ:5031:3922:04 fm 37 116 1½ 1hd 2½ 31¾ Valenzuela P A9 50000 — — Allowance, Vigorous Vigors,Estoc 12

22Dec85—Lost whip 1/8

13Oct85-4Bel 1¼🅃:5031:40 2:052gd 12 117 99¼ 914 914 912½ Velasquez J7 75000 54-25 Red Brigade, Ski Fleet, Cloutier 9

31Jly85♦5Redcar(Eng) 1⅜ 2:243gd 8-5 133 Ⓣ 24 Lowe J St Jhn Amblnc H InsetLady, Estoc, Wildrush 4

6Jly85♦3Haydock(Eng) 1½ 2:33 gd 20 114 Ⓣ 58 Lowe J Old Nwtn Cp H Clanrallier,RussinNoble,ReglSteel 10

19Jun85♦6Ascot(Eng) 1½ 2:294gd 14 110 Ⓣ 10 Lowe J Bssbrgh H Clanrallier,LakeValentine,Ledburn 20

Dec 18 SA 7f ft 1:284 h — Dec 9 SA 6f ft 1:162 h — Nov 12 Hol 4f ft :524 h — Nov 4 Hol 3f ft :371 h

99–1

Reserve
SIMPSON B H 0-0 116
Own.—Dolan & Roy
Dk. b. or br. h. 5, by Buckfinder—Irish Mail, by Double Jay
Br.—Keck H B (Ky)
Tr.—Hutchinson Kathy $25,000
Lifetime 27 3 2 5 $48,337
1986 13 2 1 2 $20,162
1985 11 1 0 3 $21,975
Turf 5 0 0 0

16Nov86-1Hol 1 :443 1:103 1:372ft 26 116 79 69½ 610 619½ Baze G7 25000 56-18 Billy's Special, Slugfest, Paskanell 7
16Nov86—Wide
2Nov86-3SA 1 1/16 :461 1:103 1:412ft 28 115 611 613 616 621 Baze G1 40000 73-10 Oricao, Idol, Tough Envoy 6
10Aug86-7Cby 1 :471 1:12 1:392ft 3½ 120 55¾ 55 22½ 22½ Kutz D5 Aw13800 81-17 On Retainer,Reserve,AddisonSteele 6
27Jly86-10Cby 1 :47 1:113 1:373ft 5½ 119 25 43½ 44½ 34¾ Kutz D1 35000 86-15 HollywoodHckett,Joy'sPurpos,Rsrv 5
6Jly86-7Cby 1 :47 1:122 1:384ft 10 1165 43¼ 52¾ 66 63¾ Murray K C6 Aw14300 83-15 Katzenjammer,Balaash,PatchofSun 7
25Jun86-8Cby 1 :462 1:114 1:383ft 23 121 613 612 48½ 47 Hansen R D4 Aw14300 81-16 Siberian Hero, Balaash, Put Away 7
15Jun86-8Cby 1 1/16 Ⓣ:484 1:14 1:44 fm 19 123 106 1010 1017 1029¼ Lidberg D W9 Aw13300 — — IlMrcolo,IronGlov,SmoothSunston 10
18May86-8Cby 1 1/16 :462 1:112 1:454ft 2 121 410 39½ 48½ 311 Smith M E3 Aw13300 71-19 Verbatim'sPride,IronGlove,Reserve 8
9May86-9Cby 1 :474 1:122 1:393ft *2 117 31½ 31½ 1½ 1¾ Smith M E7 Aw12300 83-18 Reserve, Melissa Noel, HeatedFury 7
30Apr86-7Cby 1 :472 1:121 1:383ft 4 115 31 41½ 2hd 12¼ Smith M E 32000 86-15 Reserve, Gunnage, Warmock 6
Dec 22 SA 6f ft 1:15 h   Dec 14 SA 5f ft 1:013 h   Nov 12 SA 4f ft :47 h   Oct 30 SA 4f ft :502 h

19–1

Master Navajo *
SIBILLE R O-N 116
Own.—Tons of Fun Stable &Fought
B. g. 6, by Navajo—Elderflower, by Master Hand
Br.—Lyster & Stiff (Ky)
Tr.—Passey Blake $22,500
Lifetime 49 9 10 6 $153,348
1986 12 1 2 1 $28,645
1985 13 3 4 1 $62,425
Turf 4 0 0 1 $3,190

30Nov86-3Hol 1⅛ :462 1:12 1:514ft 7½ 119 513 58 34 34¼ Stevens S A3 25000 74-16 Tom, Elefante, Master Navajo 6
3Nov86-9SA 1 1/16 :462 1:11 1:43 ft 7 118 814 89 45½ 44¾ Sibille R7 25000 81-14 Bemidgi, Restage, Slugfest 9
19Oct86-11Fno 1⅛ :45 1:101 1:482ft 4 114 614 64½ 32 12½ HmiltonM1 Harvest H 90-13 MstrNvjo,J.R.Johnson,U.LuckyShot 8
11Oct86-9SA 1 1/16 :46 1:112 1:443ft 5¾ 116 717 67½ 23 22 Sibille R7 20000 76-17 LyphrdChimes,MsterNvjo,GryMissil 8
28Sep86-8Pom 1 1/16 :462 1:111 1:434ft 16 116 621 617 69 21½ Cruz J B3 20000 90-09 SwiftMessg,MstrNvjo,LyphrdChims 6
20Sep86-10Pom 1 1/16 :454 1:111 1:431ft 12 116 917 814 89½ 512¾ Cruz J B5 20000 82-05 Restage, Hatamoto,LyphardChimes 9
20Sep86—Wide into stretch
13Aug86-9Dmr 1 1/16 :451 1:102 1:431ft 52 116 1015 96¾ 44½ 53 Cruz J B6 20000 81-15 Revolutionary, Tom, Our Nordic 11
27Jly86-9Dmr 1 1/16 :454 1:102 1:422ft 39 115 107½ 86 74½ 74 Cruz J B3 22500 84-10 MstrCwston,NutrlPlyr,Rvolutionry 10
13Jly86-4Hol 1⅛ :464 1:112 1:504ft 11 116 46½ 44 — — Lipham T3 25000 — — Mark In The Sky, Mufti, Pegus 7
13Jly86—Pulled up
29Jun86-3Hol 1 :453 1:101 1:351ft 19 116 711 78¼ 69 612½ Lipham T4 25000 75-10 Tanks Brigade,Pegus,OlimpicBingo 7

7–1

Bouncing Buttons
KAENEL J L O-N (5) 116
Own.—Sells D C
Ch. g. 5, by Blood Royal—Box of Buttons, by Moolah Bux
Br.—Sells D C (Ky)
Tr.—Cofer Riley S $25,000
Lifetime 31 8 5 4 $98,380
1986 2 1 0 0 $9,350
1985 16 4 4 1 $66,925
Turf 2 0 0 1 $3,900

1Jun86-1Hol 1⅛ :453 1:102 1:504ft 3¾ 116 611 610 42 1hd Kaenel J L2 25000 83-14 BouncngBttons,SrStr,MrkInThSky 6
18May86-9Hol 1 :45 1:102 1:36 ft 18 116 98¼ 75½ 76¾ 67¾ Kaenel J L11 32000 75-08 KnightSkiing,RightOnRed,Elefnte 12
18May86—Wide final 3/8
22Dec85-9AC 1 1/16 :461 1:102 1:44 ft 3 122 917 614 57 2no EnrzHF10 ⓇCprtv Prs 85-17 HrryJr.,BouncingButtons,CheerOn 11
30Nov85-9Hol 1⅛ :461 1:103 1:483m 3¾ 117 712 69 511 511¾ Kaenel J L6 45000 82-09 AmorousII,VgorosVgors,It'sNvrDll 7
30Nov85—Lost whip at 1/8
11Nov85-5SA 1¼ :464 1:39 2:054gd 5 115 817 2½ 12½ 17 Kaenel J L9 50000 60-26 BouncingButtons,Prngon,CrroPnto 9
26Oct85-9SA 1 1/16 :462 1:12 1:444ft 9¼ 114 813 77 44 11 Kaenel J L8 25000 77-21 BouncingButtons,NoodleRoni,Jovil 8
26Oct85—Wide into stretch
12Oct85-3SA 1⅛ :462 1:11 1:503ft 6¼ 116 616 611 33 21¾ Hernandez R1 22500 74-18 OnEydRomo,BouncngButtons,Muft 7
12Oct85—Veered out sharply, bumped start
20Sep85-12Poma 1⅛ :463 1:114 1:501ft 8½ 115 118½ 109 1014 813 Castanon A L8 A25000 — — Restage, Faridpour, Mufti 11
14Sep85-10Pom 6½f :22 :453 1:173ft 5¾ 119 912 711 66½ 42¾ Dominguez RE3 25000 — — Delta Trace, Slugfest, Don's Co'op 9
14Sep85—Bumped start
31Aug85-9Dmr 1 1/16 :461 1:11 1:431ft 2¾ 119 64¾ 31½ 22 21 Pedroza M A6 c20000 83-11 Muft,BouncngButtons,LVrn'sBgMc 9
Dec 20 SA 6f ft 1:151 hg   Dec 15 SA 5f ft 1:014 h   Dec 9 SA 7f ft 1:293 h   Dec 3 SA 6f ft 1:14 hg

4–1

Lyphard Chimes
STEVENS G L 116
Own.—Pendleton L C 3-N+
B. g. 4, by Lyphard—Four Bells, by Quadrangle
Br.—Pillar Stud Inc (Ky)
Tr.—Lewis Craig A $25,000
Lifetime 15 4 1 3 $26,647
1986 7 1 0 2 $14,922
1985 7 3 1 1 $11,725
Turf 10 3 1 1 $11,725

20Nov86-5Hol 1⅛ :464 1:114 1:512ft 8 116 32½ 21½ 84¾ 97¾ Solis A5 c32000 72-16 Oak TreeII,Bedouin,ValiantGeorge 11
20Nov86—Steadied 1/8
11Oct86-9SA 1 1/16 :46 1:112 1:443ft 6½ 116 512 45½ 13 12 Solis A8 20000 78-17 LyphrdChimes,MsterNvjo,GryMissil 8
28Sep86-8Pom 1 1/16 :462 1:111 1:434ft 7 116 48½ 46½ 34 31¾ Ortega L E2 20000 90-09 SwiftMessg,MstrNvjo,LyphrdChims 6
20Sep86-10Pom 1 1/16 :454 1:111 1:431ft 11 116 611 611 57 39½ Solis A4 20000 85-09 Restage, Hatamoto,LyphardChimes 9
6Sep86-5Dmr 1⅛ Ⓣ:463 1:11 1:492fm 21 116 55½ 63½ 1010 911½ Solis A8 60000 75-09 Aviator II, Keyala, Ono Gummo 10

25Apr86-9Hol 1⅛ :472 1:112 1:492ft 16 116 2hd 21 69½ 614¼ Meza R Q5 62500 76-16 CelticVenture,Stickette,VlintGeorg 7
25Apr86—Bumped in stretch
22Mar86-4GG 1 1/16 Ⓣ:4721:1121:433fm *2¼ 114 811 79¼ 86 74¼ Baze R A2 Aw25000 80-15 Ablantin,ViceroyLd,‡NewAtrction 11
22Mar86—Bumped start
9Oct85♦6York(Eng) 1⅝ 2:172gd 5 133 Ⓣ 613 CauthenS Cleveland H Wantage, Tockala, Santella Boy 11
17Jly85♦3Kempton(Eng) 1¼ 2:032gd 3¼ 118 Ⓣ 12½ CthnS Crawley Warren H LyphrdChimes,Cordonnt,GoodLord 8
2Jly85♦4Yarmouth(Eng) 1¼ 2:143gd 4 121 Ⓣ 517 EddrPA Tote Placepot H Dihistan, Sidab, Corridor Key 7
Dec 21 Hol 5f ft 1:014 h ●Dec 17 Hol 6f ft 1:144 h ●Dec 11 Hol 6f ft 1:134 h Dec 5 Hol 5f ft 1:001 h

15–1

Trus T. Danus Dk. b. or br. c. 4, by Mundanus—Am Safe, by Safety Zone
VALENZUELA P A 5-N 116 Br.—Frasson A (Ont-C) 1986 12 0 2 1 $14,310
Tr.—Truman Eddie $25,000 1985 18 4 3 3 $54,177
Own.—Vasquez D & Diana Lifetime 32 5 5 4 $75,807 Turf 4 1 1 0 $12,680
8Nov86-6BM 1 Ⓣ:4711:1211:373fm 28 114 32½ 31½ 64 68 Lozoya D A3 50000 84-08 Diplomat Ruler,IronLeader,Daniyar 7
19Oct86-11Fno 1⅛ :45 1:101 1:482ft 18 114 47 57½ 49 410½ Scott J M2 Harvest H 79-13 MstrNvjo,J.R.Johnson,U.LuckyShot 8
11Oct86-11Fno 1 :442 1:091 1:334ft 6 115 23 21½ 21½ 26 Scott J M2 Aw6000 95-10 TheAysHvIt,TrusT.Dnus,PrinclyPgo 7
28Sep86-12Pom 1⅜ :471 1:37 2:15 ft 26 115 2½ 43½ 712 733¾ Mena F2 H25000 68-09 Mummy'sPlesure,Restge,TulsFlyrII 8
19Sep86-10Pom a1⅛ :453 1:11 1:49 ft 15 113 47 42 511 515 Stevens S A2 A25000 87-09 Mmmy'sPlsr,OnEydRomo,DbTrnd 10
24Aug86-9Dmr 1 1/16 :452 1:093 1:412ft 12 1115 49 46½ 714 711¾ Black C A2 50000 81-12 OnoGummo,TimeForSilenc,Oljuwon 9
24Aug86—Bumped start
9Aug86-7Dmr 1 1/16 :453 1:101 1:422ft 12 116 2½ 2hd 1hd 64½ Toro F8 50000 83-14 Lead On, Impulsively, Idol 11
2Aug86-9Dmr 1 1/16 :461 1:103 1:42 ft 8 116 1½ 1½ 11½ 2½ Toro F1 40000 89-12 Olajuwon, Trus T. Danus, Elefante 7
2Aug86—Drifted out bumped late
4Apr86-7SA 6½f :213 :443 1:163ft 25 116 75½ 109¼ 119¼ 1211 Hawley S2 25000 76-23 Bizeboy, Le Ricain, Calabonga 12
22Mar86-6GG 1 1/16 :472 1:111 1:431ft 17 116 3nk 3½ — — Kaenel J L1 Aw20000 — — Jsn'sDrmmr,BrghtAndRght,BnnttP 8
22Mar86—Eased, Fractious in gate
Dec 3 Hol 4f ft :483 h ●Nov 1 GG 5f ft :593 h

5–2

Restage Dk. b. or br. g. 7, by In Reality—Audit, by Hill Rise
DOMINGUEZ R E 8+ 116 Br.—Glen Hill Farm (Fla) 1986 9 2 3 0 $36,445
Tr.—Spawr William $25,000 1985 11 6 1 0 $111,325
Own.—Alter & Carrillo Lifetime 44 17 7 3 $245,110 Turf 2 0 0 0 $2,625
7Dec86-7BM 1 1/16 :464 1:12 1:461sl 3¾ 114 2hd 2½ 31 41 Dominguez RE8 40000 60-38 EsyMovr,Witin'ForBvr,OrindOrgnl 10
7Dec86—Broke in a tangle
3Nov86-9SA 1 1/16 :462 1:11 1:43 ft 3 114 1½ 12½ 11½ 2no Stevens G L5 22500 86-14 Bemidgi, Restage, Slugfest 9
12Oct86-9SA 1 1/16 :463 1:12 1:443ft 4¾ 116 3nk 3nk 55 66¼ Dominguez RE9 32000 72-21 Mmmy'sPlsr,Implsvly,NrthrnPrvdr 12
12Oct86—Wide into stretch
28Sep86-12Pom 1⅜ :471 1:37 2:15 ft 2 122 1½ 11½ 2½ 22¾ DominguezRE6 H25000 93-09 Mummy'sPlesure,Restge,TulsFlyrII 8
20Sep86-10Pom 1 1/16 :454 1:111 1:431ft *7-5 114 1hd 12 13 15½ Dominguez RE1 18000 95-09 Restage, Hatamoto,LyphardChimes 9
12Jly86-10LA 1⅛ :454 1:102 1:481ft 2¾ 116 1hd 1hd 35 615 Sibille R5 Orng Cty H 80-11 Barland, Bozina, Stickette 7
28Jun86-6Hol 1 :443 1:093 1:362ft 2½ 116 22 21½ 1½ 11½ Sibille R7 40000 81-12 Restage,PassedTheRule,FbulousDd 9
26May86-1Hol 1⅛ :471 1:113 1:50 ft *1 116 11 11 2½ 21¾ Olivares F1 40000 85-17 Item Two, Restage, Bemidgi 7
16May86-9Hol 1⅛ :453 1:11 1:493ft 3½ 116 1½ 13½ 33½ 56¼ Olivares F1 50000 83-19 Bedouin, Vigorous Vigors, Tio Nino 7
16May86—Wide into stretch
16Nov85-9Hol a1⅛ Ⓣ 1:454fm 7 118 1hd 2hd 916 919¼ DominguezRE7 115000 — — Caballo, Steepbank, Cutting Wind 9
16Nov85—Error in placement of starting gate; 3 wide 1st turn
Nov 30 SA 6f ft 1:134 h Nov 23 SA 6f ft 1:134 h Oct 26 SA 6f ft 1:15 h

14–1

***Cold *** Ch. g. 7, by Arctic Tern—Fort Brune, by Forli
OLIVARES F 2-N+ 114 Br.—Lazar H (Eng) 1986 12 2 3 0 $31,205
Tr.—Longden Vance J $22,500 1985 14 4 3 0 $35,290
Own.—Goudy-Hoogsteen-Kalpakoff Lifetime 58 11 9 1 $127,725 Turf 17 2 3 0 $37,405
17Aug86-7Dmr 1 1/16 :453 1:101 1:432ft 25 116 42 31 21½ 42½ Pedroza M A3 25000 80-16 BngBngBng,MrkInThSky,OnEdRm 10
10Aug86-2Dmr 1 1/16 :45 1:093 1:412ft 8¼ 116 87¼ 1013 1025 — Toro F6 32000 — — ForHimself,Juli'sMrk,ToughEnvoy 10
10Aug86—Eased
27Jly86-9Dmr 1 1/16 :454 1:102 1:422ft 11 116 54½ 74 52½ 42¾ Toro F9 25000 85-10 MstrCwston,NutrlPlyr,Rvolutionry 10
27Jly86—Checked, shuffled back 2nd turn
28May86-9Hol 1 :461 1:11 1:363ft 21 116 74¼ 56½ 59 710½ Toro F5 32000 69-15 Knight Skiing, Ego Buck, Elefante 9
18May86-9Hol 1 :45 1:102 1:36 ft 8¼ 116 66¾ 34 66½ 89½ Toro F10 32000 73-08 KnightSkiing,RightOnRed,Elefnte 12
12Apr86-9SA 1 1/16 :46 1:11 1:433ft 11 116 58½ 44 3½ 2hd Toro F3 32000 83-19 Knight Skiing, Cold, Rajaba 9
15Mar86-5SA 1¼ :46 1:111 1:51fm *2½ 118 33 31½ 712 819 Stevens G L7 c20000 51-23 GoodThoughtWilly,Muft,WldPlsur 12
21Feb86-9SA 1 1/16 :464 1:114 1:434gd *2½ 119 67¼ 42 1hd 11½ Pincay L Jr2 c16000 82-22 Cold,Lighthewayholme,CertainTret 8
1Feb86-9BM 1 1/16 :48 1:113 1:44 m *9-5 118 2hd 11½ 21½ 25 Steiner J J2 25000 67-23 Rapid Rogue, Cold, Beau Duncan 6
12Jan86-10BM 1 1/16 :482 1:123 1:445gd *2 115 2hd 11½ 1½ 1hd Steiner J J7 25000 69-24 Cold, Never Rust, Rapid Rogue 8
●Dec 20 SA 1f ft 1:401 h Dec 15 SA 6f ft 1:133 h Dec 11 SA 5f ft 1:001 h ●Dec 6 SA 5f sy 1:002 h

A. Bet *Shuttle One* to win
B. Baseball *Shuttle One, Lyphard Chimes,* and *Cold*
C. Back-wheel *Restage* in the exacta
D. Box *Restage* and *Cold* and key each on top of *Shuttle One* and *Tommy Thoms*

Answer key: Applied handicapping skills

Performance Test A

1. E 5–1	16. F. 7–2	31. E 5–1	46. D 3–1
2. A 3–1	17. H. 9–2	32. J 4–1	47. B 5–1
3. A 4–1	18. G. 5–2	33. C 4–1	48. B 3–1
4. B 1–1	19. G. 7–2	34. C 7–1	49. C 3–1
5. D 6–1	20. A. 2–1	35. A 1–1	50. D &/or E 5–1
6. A 2–1	21. J. 9–2	36. E 4–1	51. G 7–1
7. B 3–1	22. A & C 5–2	37. F 8–1	52. C 3–1
8. C 3–1	23. D 7–2	38. C 3–1	53. A 4–1
9. C 7–1	24. A 2–1	39. A 3–1	54. B 8–1
10. B 3–1	25. C 2–1	40. D 3–1	55. E 5–1
11. D 2–1	26. B or C 7–2	41. D 3–1	56. H 7–1
12. A 3–1	27. B 6–1	42. B 3–1	57. I 9–2
13. G 3–1	28. C 2–1	43. G 7–1	58. A or C 10–1
14. H 6–1	29. F 8–5	44. E 5–1	59. F 12–1
15. E 4–1	30. D 2–1	45. C 5–1	60. D 6–1

Note. To obtain your total performance score, multiply your win percentage by the average odds on your winners. Compare your total to the proficiency standards on page 275.

CHAPTER 16

Performance Test B

Notes

1. Arlington Park races that appear in this test are contested on a track surface having a C bias (favors closers).
2. Monmouth Park races that appear in this test are contested on a track surface having an S+ bias (extra-strong speed bias).
3. Ignore markings that appear on some past performance tables. These cannot be used to analyze the race or specific horses. The author regrets any distractions the markings cause users.
4. For best results, complete no more than ten races a day, making the exercise a six-day test. Review each race in depth, using whatever methods you normally apply.
5. On this form of the test, please do *not* check the correct answers until all 60 items have been completed.

1. The class advantage in this grass field belongs to

9th Del Mar

1 ⅛ MILES. (Turf). (1.46⅗) CLAIMING. Purse $25,000. 3-year-olds and upward. Weights, 3-year-olds, 116 lbs.; older, 122 lbs. Non-winners of two races at one mile or over since June 1 allowed 3 lbs.; of such a race since then, 5 lbs. Claiming price $62,500; for each $2,500 to $55,000 allowed 1 lb. (Claiming and starter races for $50,000 or less not considered).

A.

***Kellsapaul** — Ch. h. 5, by Ahonoera—Lucasta, by High Hat
BAZE R A — **116** — Br.—Berry D (Ire) — Tr.—Vienna Darrell — $55,000
Own.—Murphy W
Lifetime 23 4 2 3 $43,302

1987	7	2 1 2		$34,400
1986	1	0 0 0		$850
Turf	23	4 2 3		$43,302

31Jly87-5Dmr	$1\frac{1}{16}$ Ⓣ	:47^1 1:11^4 1:43 fm	$8\frac{1}{2}$	115	7^6	6^4	5^5	5$6\frac{3}{4}$	Baze R A^3	70000	78-15	Clnrllier,‡He'sASros,CostingCougr	10
19Jun87-8GG	$1\frac{1}{16}$ Ⓣ	:46^4 1:11^2 1:43 fm	*3-5	119	5^4	5$2\frac{3}{4}$	4$2\frac{1}{2}$	$1\frac{3}{4}$	ChapmanTM^4	Aw16000	87-13	Kellsapaul,ArtOfDwn,VrietyExpress	7
4Jun87-8GG	1 Ⓣ	:47 1:11^3 1:37^2 fm	3	119	6$3\frac{3}{4}$	5$2\frac{3}{4}$	$2\frac{1}{2}$	2^2	Baze R A^3	Aw16000	78-20	Rufjan, Kellsapaul, Al Fayez	9
8May87-8GG	1 Ⓣ	:46^4 1:11^2 1:37 fm	*4-5	119	3$3\frac{1}{2}$	3$1\frac{1}{2}$	4$1\frac{1}{4}$	3$2\frac{3}{4}$	ChapmanTM^4	Aw19000	79-18	Sunstorm, ExoticMotion,Kellsapaul	6
26Apr87-6GG	1 Ⓣ	:48^3 1:12^2 1:37^4 fm	*8-5	116	3^2	2$1\frac{1}{2}$	$4\frac{3}{4}$	1$1\frac{1}{2}$	Meza R Q^1	62500	78-25	Kellsapaul,ElMnsour,French'sLuck	7
18Apr87-5SA	1¼ Ⓣ	:48 1:36^3 2:01^1 fm	3	115	$1\frac{1}{2}$	5$2\frac{3}{4}$	4^2	4$3\frac{1}{4}$	Baze G^3	62500	78-16	GretCommunictor,Sherkin,Snowcrk	9
3Apr87-8SA	1⅛ Ⓣ	:45^3 1:09^3 1:46^2 fm	30	107^5	4$2\frac{3}{4}$	4$2\frac{1}{2}$	3^{nk}	3^1	Gryder A T^6	70000	94-09	Palestiglio, Steepbank, Kellsapaul	8
23Feb86-7SA	1⅛ Ⓣ	:47^1 1:12 1:50^4 fm	24	109^5	8$6\frac{1}{2}$	9^7	6^4	5^5	Black C A^3	Aw34000	68-24	Soldat Bleu, Kala Dancer, Solstein	9
10ct85 ♦3Goodwood(Eng)	1	1:40^1 gd	9	125	Ⓣ			7^{12}	CuthenS	RadioVictoryH		Daring, Alqirm, Pearl Blue	13
16Sep85 ♦7Wolverhamp'n(Eng	1	1:40 fm	10	129	Ⓣ			1^{nk}	CauthenS	Bloxwich H		Kellsapaul, Iktiyar, Saucy Singer	17

Jly 28 Dmr 5f ft 1:02^2 h   Jly 22 Dmr 5f ft 1:03 h   Jly 17 Dmr 4f ft :50^1 h   Jun 16 SA 4f ft :52^3 h

B.

***Santo Angelo** — Dk. b. or br. g. 5, by Rose Laurel—Caraimee, by Carvin
SIBILLE R 117 — Br.—Petitpas & Ragobert (Fra) — 1987 2 0 0 0
Tr.—Timphony Vincent $62,500 — 1986 4 0 0 0 $1,200
Own.—Neumann & Timphony — Lifetime 30 4 1 5 $46,146 — Turf 30 4 1 5 $46,145

27Jly87-9Hol 1 1/16 Ⓣ:47 1:102 1:413fm 55 116 56½ 712 715 717¼ Fernandez A L2 62500 68-08 Sherkin, Kingsbury, Aviator II 7
27Jun87-9Hol 1⅛ Ⓣ:474 1:111 1:471fm 52 114 76 76¼ 814 818¾ Fernandez A L7 70000 73-11 Poly Test, Sherkin, Solidified 8
28Aug86-8Dmr 1 1/16 Ⓣ:462 1:102 1:411fm 74 115 611 611 811 812¼ Baze R A5 Aw38000 88-05 Mangaki, Mr. Happy, Quintillion 8
11Apr86-5SA 1⅛ Ⓣ:45 1:091 1:462fm 33 116 59½ 59½ 618 615 DelahoussyeE 7 125000 80-11 Pol And Dic, HonorMedal,PolyTest 7
11Apr86—Broke slowly, eased in stretch
22Mar86-8SA 1¼ Ⓣ:471 1:36 2:012fm 37 115 11½ 43½ 711 712 Vln'PA 2 [R]S Gertrds H 68-20 Val Danseur, Truculent,Willingness 7
13Mar86-8SA 1⅛ Ⓣ:503 1:16 1:553sf 22 116 64½ 77½ 59½ 512 DelhoussyeE 5 Aw48000 37-51 PetitBonhomme,Craelius,WillDncer 7
13Mar86—Took up 7 1/2
11Nov85♦4StCloud(Fra) a1 1:482yl 22 123 Ⓣ 11 BreuxJM PxPrth(Gr3) OverTheOcen,StellGrnd,ClssiclWy 14
8Sep85♦4Longchamp(Fra) a1½ 2:303gd 19 123 Ⓣ 711 GuignrdG Px Niel(Gr3) Mouktar,SintEstephe,PremierRole 10
24Aug85♦4Deauville(Fra) a1¼ 2:183sf 4½ 123 Ⓣ 44 GugnrdG Px Ridgway Alleging, Jemifa, Grundyssime 8
11Aug85♦5Deauville(Fra) a1¼ 2:142sf 8 121 Ⓣ 45 GrdG Px Cte Nrmnde(Gr2) NewBruce,CptiveIslnd,Morespeed 10
Aug 5 Dmr 5f ft 1:011 hg ● Jly 15 SA 7f ft 1:28 h ● Jly 6 SA 1 ft 1:412 h Jun 22 SA 1 ft 1:402 h

C.

***Shadows Fall** — B. c. 4, by Artaius—Headin' Home, by Habitat
PATTERSON A 114 — Br.—GTR Establishment (Ire) — 1987 8 2 1 2 $40,440
Tr.—Greenman Walter $55,000 — 1986 7 1 2 0 $2,057
Own.—Greenman & Trimm — Lifetime 15 3 3 2 $42,497 — Turf 14 3 3 2 $42,497

28Jun87-7GG 1⅞ Ⓣ:493 3:121fm*3-2 116 1015 44 42½ 42¾ Chapman T M9 c25000 — — PairedAndPinted,Lecci,IvnPhillips 12
30May87-10GG 1⅜ Ⓣ:48 1:384 2:172fm*3-2 122 713 53¼ 21½ 23 Baze R A4 50000 75-16 JetAwayBill,ShadowsFll,BuckRoyle 7
17May87-12TuP 1⅞ Ⓣ:25 2:562 3:092fm *1 123 1116 13 16 19 PttrsA2 Hsta La Vs H 118 — ShdowsFll,GueMerson,Overvinsky 12
2May87-6GG 1⅜ Ⓣ:494 1:394 2:182fm 3 115 67¾ 64 33 31¾ Baze R A4 Hcp0 71-26 SalvateTel,PairOfAces,ShadowsFall 6
18Apr87-11GG 1⅜ Ⓣ:48 1:39 2:164fm 5 116 712 54½ 21 11¼ Baze R A4 50000 81-16 ShdowsFll,MinutesAwy,Impulsively 8
27Mar87-7SA 1⅛ :464 1:113 1:50 ft 20 117 67 55¼ 58 610½ Patterson A3 Aw31000 68-23 ArcticDream,It'sNotMyJob,Athlone 7
8Mar87-2SA 1½ Ⓣ:474 2:043 2:302gd 7 116 77 62½ 43 34½ Patterson A2 Aw30000 58-26 SunMan,RussianLogic,ShadowsFall 9
22Feb87-5SA 1¼ Ⓣ:464 1:36 2:013fm 22 115 811 65 56 46 Patterson A8 Aw29000 73-22 Neferou, Dhaleem, Unencumbered 10
11Aug86♦2GowranPark(Ire) 1¼ 2:084gd *2½ 129 Ⓣ 615 SthDV Lwrgrng Apr H LmbrookSlvr,ClsclInflnc,GlorNN'Or 8
17Jly86♦5Killarney(Ire) 1½ 2:52 yl *4-5 125 Ⓣ 11 KinneMJ Kenmre H ShdowsFll,SprngSnowfll,TullyCross 6
Aug 6 Dmr 5f ft 1:013 h

D.

Intuitiveness — Ch. g. 4, by Exclusive Native—Instinctively, by Francis S
SOLIS A 117 — Br.—Harbor View Farm (Ky) — 1987 8 1 1 1 $29,225
Tr.—Barrera Lazaro S $62,500 — 1986 14 1 2 5 $36,350
Own.—Harbor View Farm — Lifetime 25 2 3 7 $68,425 — Turf 10 1 3 1 $38,425

31Jly87-5Dmr 1 1/16 Ⓣ:471 1:114 1:43 fm 17 113 2½ 97 914 918½ Shoemaker W10 70000 66-15 Clnrllier,‡He'sASros,CostingCougr 10
19Apr87-5SA a6½f Ⓣ:212 :434 1:141fm 4 118 52½ 53 64½ 65 Cordero A Jr5 80000 83-11 Pokare, Estate, Lincoln Park 8
11Apr87-5SA a6½f Ⓣ:213 :442 1:143fm 6 116 62¼ 72¾ 55 43½ Castanon AL1 Aw33000 82-18 DnceDirector,Mrgm,FbulousSound 10
11Apr87—Steadied at 1/2
8Mar87-5SA a6½f Ⓣ:211 :441 1:153gd 9¾ 119 44½ 44½ 36 23½ Cordero AJr2 Aw32000 77-26 RivrMist,Intuitvnss,TommyThHwk 10
26Feb87-8SA 1⅛ :461 1:104 1:50 ft 11 117 2hd 2hd 75 812¼ Solis A1 100000 67-22 Manzotti, Poly Test, Dr. Daly 8
8Feb87-5SA a6½f Ⓣ:211 :434 1:144fm 7½ 117 98 64½ 62¼ 52¼ ValenzuelPA3 Aw30000 83-09 Hard Round, Irish Stories,Putting 12
8Feb87—Off slowly, wide
19Jan87-5SA 1¼ Ⓣ:473 1:382 2:041fm 10 116 22 1½ 2hd 1hd ValenzuelPA2 Aw28000 66-29 Intuitiveness, Asian Cup, Neferou 12
10Jan87-7SA 1 :461 1:104 1:371gd 11 116 1½ 2½ 33½ 34¾ Toro F6 Aw28000 77-20 VlintCougr,King'sHed,Intuitiveness 8
28Dec86-5SA 1 1/16 :462 1:104 1:431ft 6½ 116 66 57 69½ 69½ Stevens S A6 Aw28000 75-14 ReEnter,Card'sPlease,InherentKal 10
18Dec86-8Hol 1 1/16 Ⓣ:483 1:12 1:422fm *2¾ 113 1hd 1½ 1hd 2no Stevens S A4 Aw24000 82-19 SmoothOpertor,Intuitiveness,Stmd 8
18Dec86—Lugged in stretch
● Jly 25 Hol 5f ft :592 h Jly 20 Hol 5f ft 1:001 h Jly 14 Hol 5f ft 1:004 h Jly 8 SA 4f ft :473 h

E.

***Millero Y Medio *** — B. h. 6, by Mr Long—Maria Blanca, by Blakemere
STEVENS G L 115 — Br.—Haras Santa Amelia (Chile) — 1987 7 1 0 1 $30,125
Tr.—Anderson Laurie N $57,500 — 1986 8 3 3 0 $17,094
Own.—Jones & Kebow — Lifetime 41 11 9 6 $63,522 — Turf 12 2 1 2 $11,802

28Jun87-7Hol 1½ Ⓣ:47 2:003 2:262fm 19 114 915 75½ 73¼ 31¾ Stevens G L 9 [R]Hcp0 88-11 Circus Prince,Truth,MilleroYMedio 9
28Jun87—Broke slowly
30May87-5Hol 1⅛ :462 1:11 1:50 ft 4½ 116 89¼ 77 45 44¾ Stevens G L 3 50000 82-14 ValiantCougar,ForeignLegion,Poley 9
14May87-5Hol 1⅛ Ⓣ:482 1:123 1:48 fm 5¾ 116 86½ 85¼ 73 63¼ Stevens G L 3 62500 85-08 Rajhaan, Jet Away Bill,DarkAccent 9
18Apr87-7SA 1 1/16 :46 1:104 1:433ft 10 116 78 89 712 710 McHrgueDG 5 Aw35000 73-18 Centenary, Extranix, Prince O' Fire 8
18Apr87—Steadied 5/16
14Mar87-8SA 1½ Ⓣ:474 2:03 2:281fm 11 114 107¼ 96¾ 911 911¾ StnsGL 5 [R]Sn Mrno H 62-22 Rosedale, Forlitano, Bob Back 10
14Feb87-7SA 1½ :492 2:044 2:301sy *1 117 1½ 15 16 18½ Stevens G L 1 80000 85-17 Millero YMedio,Fluctuate,Rampour 6
18Jan87-3SA 1 1/16 :461 1:104 1:441ft 6¾ 116 814 813 69 49 Toro F3 Aw31000 71-19 Oricao,GrecinWonder,ForsytheBoy 8
16Aug86♦6H'podromo(Chile) a1 1:362ft *1 134 1½ Diaz F FrndoMlrBrd(Gr2) Millero y Medio, Judas, Coqueto 7
5Jly86♦8H'podromo(Chile) a1⅜ 2:183ft 1 134 27½ Diaz F Pdr dRioTlvr(Gr2) Poalco, Millero y Medio,Prontuario 4
11Jun86♦8H'podromo(Chile) a1 1:36 ft — 134 1 Diaz F ClGnzloLrrain Further, information, unavailable 6
Jly 27 Dmr 6f ft 1:172 h Jly 15 SA 7f ft 1:30 h ● Jly 8 SA 7f ft 1:274 h Jun 27 SA 4f ft :493 h

F.

Dr. Daly — **B. g. 7, by Quack—Blow Up II, by Abdos**
SIMPSON B H **117** — **Br.—Brdly-Whttnghm-Wyane (Ky)** — **1987 12 0 3 1 $26,395**
Tr.—Gerber Greg D **$62,500** — **1986 9 1 2 1 $31,775**
Own.—Poyer & Steinmann — **Lifetime 53 7 11 4 $260,395** — **Turf 42 6 8 3 $212,720**

27Jun87-10GG 1 Ⓣ:47^{1}1:11^{4}1:37^{1}fm 47 116 6^{4½} 8^{5¾}10^{7½} 9^{7¾} Diaz A L^{12} 40000 73-21 FlkIndsRulr,SonnyBrch,NorthOfLk 12
27Jun87—Steadied 3/8
13Jun87-10GG 1 1/16 Ⓣ:47^{2}1:11^{2}1:43^{3}fm 28 116 7^{2¾} 7^{3½}10^{7} 8^{6} SchvnevldtCP^{11} 40000 78-12 GllntHwk,TellFloHello,NorthOfLk 11
30May87-5Hol 1⅛ :46^{2} 1:11 1:50 ft 9 107^{5} 5^{6} 6^{6} 7^{12} 7^{14¾} Patton D B^{2} 45000 72-14 ValiantCougar,ForeignLegion,Poley 9
15May87-9Hol 1⅛Ⓣ:47 1:10^{2}1:47 fm 17 116 6^{2½} 6^{2¾} 4^{5½} 4^{8½} Stevens G L^{3} 62500 84-12 Sherkin, Shanaar, Snowcreek 7
26Apr87-6GG 1 Ⓣ:48^{3}1:12^{2}1:37^{4}fm 5¾ 116 6^{4¾} 6^{4¾} 6^{4¼} 5^{4} Baze R A^{5} 62500 74-25 Kellsapaul,ElMnsour,French'sLuck 7
9Apr87-8SA 1⅛Ⓣ:45^{3}1:09^{3}1:46^{2}fm 17 116 1^{hd} 2^{1} 7^{3½} 7^{8½} Simpson B H^{7} 80000 86-09 Palestiglio, Steepbank, Kellsapaul 8
20Mar87-5SA 1⅛Ⓣ:46^{1}1:10^{3}1:48 fm 4 116 2½ 3½ 5^{1½} 4^{4¾} Simpson B H^{4} 62500 82-15 Dark Accent, Twice Bold, Fothers 10
7Mar87-7SA 1¼ :47^{3} 1:37^{3} 2:03 gd 7½ 117 3^{1} 1^{hd} 2^{hd} 2^{4} Simpson B H^{4} 80000 70-19 Truth, Dr. Daly, Kingsbury 6
26Feb87-8SA 1⅛ :46^{1} 1:10^{4} 1:50 ft 26 116 3^{2½} 4^{1} 4^{1½} 3^{4} Simpson B H^{4} 100000 75-22 Manzotti, Poly Test, Dr. Daly 8
8Feb87-5BM 7½f Ⓣ:23 :46^{4}1:32^{4}gd*9-5 118 6^{6} 6^{4¼} 3^{1½} 2no Simpson B H^{2} 50000 80-21 Lead On, Dr. Daly, Rommel'sChoice 9
8Feb87—Steadied 3/8
●Aug 5 Dmr 4f ft :47 h — Jly 29 Dmr 5f ft 1:04^{4} h — Jun 24 GG Ⓣ 4f fm :50^{2} h (d)

G.

***Straw** — **B. h. 6, by Thatch—Cooliney Dancer, by Dancer's Image**
BAZE G **116** — **Br.—O'Malley J F (Ire)** — **1987 5 1 0 2 $26,600**
Tr.—Blincoe Tom **$60,000** — **1986 1 0 0 0 $950**
Own.—Carothers G — **Lifetime 32 8 3 5 $117,973** — **Turf 19 7 2 3 $95,368**

31Jly87-5Dmr 1 1/16 Ⓣ:47^{1}1:11^{4}1:43 fm 12 116 8^{6½} 8^{5} 7^{7} 7^{7½} McHargue D G 9 70000 77-15 Clnrllier,‡He'sASros,CostingCougr 10
4Apr87-4SA 1⅛Ⓣ:47^{1}1:10^{3}1:48^{1}fm 4¾ 116 5^{2½} 4^{1¾} 1^{2} 1^{1} McHargue D G 2 62500 86-16 Straw,GreatCommunictor,Rmpour 12
4Feb87-5SA 1⅛Ⓣ:45^{4}1:10^{3}1:48^{3}fm 8 116 6^{8} 6^{5} 5^{3¼} 3^{2¾} McHargue D G 1 62500 81-16 Kingsbury, Dark Accent, Straw 10
4Feb87—Veered out, bumped start, took up approaching 1/8
18Jan87-5SA 1¼Ⓣ:46^{3}1:36 2:00^{4}fm 3 117 1^{2} 2^{2} 6^{9} 6^{17¾} Pincay L Jr 4 80000 65-15 Keyala, Manzotti, Pas De Choix 8
7Jan87-5SA 6½f :22 :44^{4} 1:16^{3}m 7¾ 116 5^{5} 5^{8} 4^{7½} 3^{9½} Sibille R 1 75000 77-21 RisingChum,AutoCommander,Strw 6
18Jan86-7SA 1⅛Ⓣ:46^{1}1:10^{4}1:47^{4}fm 4½ 115 7^{12} 8^{5¾} 6^{7} 5^{7¼} Toro F 7 115000 81-16 RvrOfKngs,Clnrllr,BoomTownChrl 10
18Jan86—4-wide into drive
15Dec85-6Hol 1 1/16 Ⓣ:47^{1}1:11^{1}1:42 fm*6-5 116 9^{5} 7^{4½} 1^{hd} 1^{2} Toro F 6 62500 — — Straw, RoyalRecourse,ViceroyLad 12
15Dec85—Wide into stretch
26Oct85-7SA 1¼Ⓣ:48 1:37 2:02 fm*4-5e 118 7^{6} 6^{3½} 3½ 2no Toro F 6 80000 77-17 Apollo Flight, Straw, Massera 9
26Oct85—Hopped in air
11Oct85-7SA 1⅛Ⓣ:46^{2}1:10^{3}1:47^{1}fm*6-5e 120 9^{6¾} 8^{5¾} 4^{5} 2^{1¼} Toro F 6 100000 90-09 Poly Test, Straw, Palestiglio 10
11Oct85—Disqualified from purse money; Broke slowly
2Sep85-5Dmr 1 Ⓣ:46 1:10^{3}1:34^{4}fm 14 117 7^{10} 6^{5} 5^{2½} 1^{hd} Toro F 1 80000 98-02 Straw, Caballo, I'll See You 10
2Sep85—Wide stretch
Jly 27 Dmr 5f ft 1:02 h — Jly 22 Dmr 1 ft 1:42^{3} h — Jly 8 Cby 7f ft 1:27^{3} h — Jun 28 Cby 7f ft 1:30^{2} h

H.

***Tracing II** — **B. h. 5, by Artaius—Two Rook, by Mill Reef**
WINICK D **114** — **Br.—Snailwell Stud Co (Eng)** — **1987 5 0 0 0 $2,575**
Tr.—Cofer Riley S **$55,000** — **1986 3 0 0 0**
Own.—Pujara M — **Lifetime 17 3 1 1 $12,666** — **Turf 16 3 1 1 $12,666**

1May87-5Hol 1 1/16 Ⓣ:45^{3}1:10 1:41 fm 23 116 6^{7½} 6^{4} 5^{4½} 4^{6¾} Meza R Q^{1} 50000 82-15 Sherkin,SuccessfulBiddr,Amrpour 10
4Apr87-4SA 1⅛Ⓣ:47^{1}1:10^{3}1:48^{1}fm 42 113 11^{10}11^{7½}10^{9¾} 9^{7} Meza R Q^{8} 55000 79-16 Straw,GreatCommunictor,Rmpour 12
4Apr87—Stumbled start
14Feb87-7SA 1½ :49^{2} 2:04^{4} 2:30^{1}sy 6 117 2½ 4^{9½} 5^{21} — McHargue D G^{6} 80000 — — Millero YMedio,Fluctuate,Rampour 6
14Feb87—Eased
1Feb87-7SA 1⅛Ⓣ:46^{1}1:10^{2}1:48^{1}fm 9¼ 116 2½ 4^{1¾} 9^{11}10^{14¾} McHrgueDG^{7} Aw32000 71-16 DnThtch,PlumCertin,RomnMgstrit 10
11Jan87-7SA 1¼Ⓣ:47^{4}1:36^{4}2:02^{2}fm 15 116 5^{5} 7^{2¾} 4^{1½} 5^{2½} ValenzuelPA^{4} Aw31000 72-25 Swink, Dan Thatch, Sly Remark 10
11Jan87—Rank early
26Dec86-5SA a6½f Ⓣ:21^{2} :44^{1}1:15^{1}fm 37 119 12^{11}12^{14}10^{11} 8^{8¼} DelahoussayeE^{1} 80000 75-17 Estate, Champion Pilot, Shanaar 12
26Dec86—Wide into drive
14Jun86♦3Sandown(Eng) 1¼ 2:04^{4}fm 12 130 Ⓣ 9^{27} Waldron P Slvr Gvl H Kalkour, AlYabir, Forchard 11
6Jun86♦4Epsom(Eng) 1½ 2:36^{1}gd 16 127 Ⓣ 10 WldronP Nrthrn Dncr H StateiyForm, Positive, Herradura 10
14Oct85♦3Sandown(Eng) 1¼ 2:10^{3}gd 5 133 Ⓣ 1^{3} Mercer J Coombe H Tracing, KilimanjaroBob, Arnhall 9
30Oct85♦6Newmarket(Eng) 1¼ 2:06^{3}gd 10 119 Ⓣ 2¾ WaldronP Exning H HenrytheLion,Tracing,RitualMusic 14
Jly 26 Dmr 5f ft 1:02^{2} h — Jly 20 SA 6f ft 1:16 h — Jun 19 SA 6f ft 1:14^{4} hg

I.

Georgia River
Ch. c. 4, by Irish River—Prize Spot, by Little Current
TORO F — Br.—Glen Hill Farm (Fla) — 1987 3 0 1 0 $10,925
117 — Tr.—Scott George W — $62,500 — 1986 5 1 2 0 $7,937
Own.—Paulson A E — Lifetime 9 1 3 1 $19,495 — Turf 8 1 3 1 $17,695
25May87-4Hol 1⅛:46 1:11 1:503ft 3 115 68 56½ 49 414 Stevens G L4 Aw24000 70-15 Billy's Back, Baby Slewy,AllezAllez 7
17Apr87-5SA 1⅛Ⓣ:4541:1021:472fm*4-5 117 53 62¾ 44 43¾ Pincay L Jr8 Aw31000 86-14 MidnightIce,ThreshItOut,HloHtch 10
17Apr87—Broke slowly; wide 3/8 turn, lugged in stretch
15Mar87-5SA 1¼Ⓣ:4731:3812:033gd *2¼ 117 42 31 21 2hd Pincay L Jr10 Aw34000 69-24 Plum Certain,GeorgiaRiver,Travet 10
15Mar87—Broke slowly
4Oct86♦3Newmarket(Eng) 1 1/16 1:454gd 33 117 Ⓣ 2728 DuffldG Cmbrdgshr H Dallas, PowerBender, Kabiyla 31
20Sep86♦1Newbury(Eng) 1 1:393gd 3½ 120 Ⓣ 2no Eddery PA Arlington LandofIvory, GeorgiaRiver, Haber 6
20Jun86♦5Ascot(Eng) 1 1:38 fm 8 118 Ⓣ 16 AsmussnC Britannia H Dallas,Navarzato,MisterWonderful 24
9Jun86♦1Goodwood(Eng) 7f 1:28 gd 3½ 121 Ⓣ 23 SbrWR BBC Radio Kent NativeOak, GeorgiaRiver, GlideBy 9
13May86♦5Nottingham(Eng) 1 5/8 1:474gd 3½ 126 Ⓣ 11 Hills R Sneinton GeorgiaRiver, Picea,AlBanshaama 15
24Aug85♦5Newmarket(Eng) 6f 1:144gd 3½ 126 Ⓣ 3nk LxA Mdwch Cmptr(Mdn) Tanaos, Top Guest, Georgia River 15
Aug 3 SLR tr.t 6f ft 1:132 h ● Jly 27 SLR tr.t 6f ft 1:132 h Jly 20 SLR tr.t 6f ft 1:14 h ● Jly 13 SLR tr.t 3f ft :35 h

2. The five juvenile fillies below arrived at the opening day Grade 2 sprint stakes at Saratoga from four different racetracks. How should handicappers analyze the race to get the best line on the youngsters' relative abilities?

8th Saratoga

6 FURLONGS. (1.08) 70th Running THE SCHUYLERVILLE (Grade II). Purse $75,000 Added (Plus $25,000 Breeders' Cup Premium Awards). Fillies. 2-year-olds. By subscription of $150 each, which should accompany the nomination; $1,200 to pass the entry box, with $75,000 added. The added money and all fees to be divided 60% to the winner, 22% to second, 12% to third and 6% to fourth. Weight, 119 lbs. Winners of two Sweepstakes, 2 lbs. additional. Non-winners of a Sweepstakes, allowed 3 lbs. Of a race other than maiden or claiming, 5 lbs. Maidens, 7 lbs. Starters to be named at the closing time of entries. Trophies will be presented to the winning owner, triner or jockey. Closed Wednesday, July 22, 1987 with 35 nominations.

Level
Ch. f. 2, by Topsider—Gauri, by Sir Ivor
Br.—CliborneFrm&TheGmelyCorp (Ky) — 1987 1 1 0 0 $13,800
Own.—Claiborne Farm — 114 — Tr.—Stephens Woodford C
Lifetime 1 1 0 0 $13,800
6Jly87-5Bel 5f :221 :461 :593ft 6¼ 117 2½ 1hd 11½ 1½ Bailey J D7 ⒻMdn 86-22 Level,Allie'sCstle,ToweringSuccess 8
Aug 1 Bel 5f ft 1:01 h Jly 28 Bel 6f ft 1:16 b Jly 24 Bel 4f ft :473 h Jly 20 Bel 5f ft 1:022 b

Tight Slacks
B. f. 2, by Relaunch—Adjacency, by Pretense
Br.—Glen Hill Farm (Fla) — 1987 2 1 1 0 $10,250
Own.—Millman L R — 114 — Tr.—Wheeler Robert E
Lifetime 2 1 1 0 $10,250
25Jun87-4Lrl 5f :222 :46 :584ft *6-5 1145 12 12 12 11½ DesormeuxKJ1 ⒻMdn 91-13 Tight Slacks, EvilAngel,‡MissJ.L.G. 9
9Jun87-1Lrl 5f :214 :461 :594ft *2 1145 1hd 2hd 2hd 2¾ DesormeuxKJ1 ⒻMdn 85-24 La De Da, TightSlacks,MiamiWives 8
● Jly 28 Lrl 4f ft :473 hg Jly 26 Lrl 4f ft :52 b Jly 11 Lrl 4f ft :503 b Jun 17 Lrl 4f ft :50 b

Joe's Tammie
Dk. b. or br. f. 2, by Zoning—Funny Tammy, by Tentam
Br.—Connelly & Imperio (NY) — 1987 3 2 0 1 $62,460
Own.—Melch D S — 119 — Tr.—Vienna Darrell
Lifetime 3 2 0 1 $62,460
15Jly87-8Bel 5½f :222 :464 1:053ft 18 112 73¾ 72¾ 11½ 13¾ BlmntJF4 ⒻAstoria 87-20 Joe'sTammie,WingDance,Justsyno 13
15Jly87—Grade III
28Jun87-4Bel 5½f :23 :464 1:06 ft 6¾ 1125 42½ 3nk 12 12¾ Belmonte J F5 ⒻMdn 85-19 Jo'sTmmi,HvnlyHlo,ConnctingLink 9
8Jun87-4Bel 5f :223 :463 :592ft 12 1125 55 44½ 32½ 33 Belmonte J F1 ⒻMdn 84-20 FlshPrncer,StunchFlme,Joe'sTmmi 8
8Jun87—Steadied
Jly 25 Bel 4f ft :483 h Jun 24 Bel 5f ft 1:03 b Jun 17 Bel 4f ft :491 h Jun 6 Bel 5f ft 1:03 b

Classy Bonnie
B. f. 2, by Borzoi—Starting Rose, by Starting Now
Br.—Cohen B I (Ky) — 1987 2 1 1 0 $10,400
Own.—Cohen B I — 114 — Tr.—Hauswald Phil
Lifetime 2 1 1 0 $10,400
24Jly87-4Mth 5½f :22 :453 1:044ft *8-5 117 1hd 1½ 15 16 Vigliotti M J2 ⒻMdn 91-16 ClssyBonnie,Christin'sMgic,Krovc 12
6Jly87-9Mth 5f :22 :452 :58 ft 11 117 54 54 33½ 23½ Vigliotti M J2 ⒻMdn 90-14 Hushi, Classy Bonnie,MyCaravann 11
Aug 3 Mth 3f ft :362 b Jly 23 Mth 3f ft :373 b Jly 17 Mth 4f ft :482 h Jly 4 Mth 4f ft :49 b

Over All
Ch. f. 2, by Mr Prospector—Full Tigress, by El Tigre Grande
Br.—Singer C (Ky) — 1987 4 2 1 0 $89,280
Own.—Klein E V — 119 — Tr.—Lukas D Wayne
Lifetime 4 2 1 0 $89,280
25Jly87-8Hol 6f :213 :443 1:10 ft 7½ 117 1hd 1½ 11½ 44½ StvnsGL1 Hol Juv Chp 88-16 MiPreferido,MixedPlsur,PurduKing 8
25Jly87—Grade II
11Jly87-8Hol 6f :212 :443 1:103ft *2e116 32½ 32½ 21½ 12½ StnsGL7 ⒻLandaluce 90-12 OvrAll,BluJnBby,Tomorrow'sChild 12
11Jly87—Grade III
20Jun87-7CD 6f :21 :451 1:113gd 2¾ 118 1½ 11 1hd 22 StvnsGL6 ⒻDebutante 83-15 BoldLdyAnne,OverAll,Penny'sGrowl 7
20Jun87—Run in divisions
6Jun87-4Hol 5½f :214 :454 1:053ft 3¾ 116 11 11 13 13 Stevens G L5 ⒻMdn 86-17 Over All, Stanstar, Slide Jet 8
Jly 20 Hol 4f ft :494 b Jly 3 Hol 5f ft :594 h Jun 14 Hol 5f ft 1:002 h

A. pace ratings
B. class ratings
C. early speed
D. speed figures

3. Using the underlined races as pace lines, find the horse having the highest pace rating.

1st Saratoga

6 FURLONGS. (1.08) CLAIMING. Purse $21,000. 3-year-olds and upward. Weight, 3-year-olds, 117 lbs. Older, 122 lbs. Non-winners of two races since July 15 allowed 3 lbs. Of a race since then, 5 lbs. Claiming price $50,000; for each $2,500 to $45,000, 2 lbs. (Races when entered to be claimed for $40,00 or less not considered.)

Coupled—Green Shekel and John Muir; Passing Thunder and Shine Diulus; Count On Romeo and Aswan High.

A.

Quick Departure
Own.—Ferruolo J A **117**
Dk. b. or br. g. 4, by Baldski—Cutalong, by The Axe II
Br.—FrnswrthFm-RbnsG-WldmrFm (Fl) 1987 7 0 1 1 $10,800
Tr.—Lenzini John J Jr **$50,000** 1986 4 1 1 1 $36,606
Lifetime 12 2 2 2 $60,606 Turf 2 0 0 0

5Jly87-4Bel 1 1/16 [T]:47^3 1:10^4 1:42^1 gd 13 117 2^1 3^2½ 7^16 8^27¾ Romero R P7 Aw28000 62-17 Seattlite,HawiinEye,Conventioneer 8
18Jun87-7Bel 1 (T):45^1 1:10 1:35 fm 29 117 7^13 6^6 7^12 7^9 Romero R P 8 Aw28000 81-10 Easton, Seattlite, Nudge 12
18Jun87—Dwelt start
13May87-7Bel 7f :22^2 :45^1 1:23 ft 6¾ 119 5^2¼ 1½ 8^11 8^14¼ Cordero AJr 3 Aw27000 73-18 CrownthLdr,PldgCrd,BoldSummit 11
13May87—Slow start
3May87-1Aqu 6f :22^4 :45^3 1:10^3 ft *2¼ 119 1½ 1^1½ 1½ 2^nk Romero R P 7 Aw27000 88-21 ExclusvGm,QuckDprtur,BoldSmmt 8
23Apr87-5Aqu 7f :22^2 :45^2 1:23^4 ft 7¾ 119 1^hd 1^2 2½ 3^4½ Romero R P 8 Aw27000 77-24 FbulousFlight,Curtin,QuickDeprtur 8
13Apr87-4Aqu 6f :22^1 :45^4 1:10^3 m 4¼ 119 3^2 3^3½ 2^5 4^8 Romero R P 2 Aw27000 80-26 Pentelicus, Wayar, Proud And Tall 6
13Apr87—Lugged in
23Mar87-7Aqu 6f :23 :46^2 1:10^4 ft 7-5 117 4¾ 3^nk 4^3 5^9¼ Cordero AJr 6 Aw27000 78-28 Dr. Koch, Fugie, Upper Star 8
19Apr86-7Aqu 6f :22^2 :45^1 1:09^4 ft 2¾ 117 4^2 2^1½ 2½ 2^nk Pincay L Jr 4 Flip Sal 92-18 SuprDlght,QuckDprtr,NmroUnoPss 7
●Jly 28 Aqu [•] 5f ft 1:00^3 h ●Jly 1 Aqu 4f ft :47^2 hg Jun 11 Aqu (T) 5f fm 1:02^4 h (d)

B.

Giuseppe
Own.—Tartan Stable **112**
B. c. 3, by Fappiano—Magnificence, by Graustark
Br.—Tartan Farms (Fla) 1987 6 0 1 0 $2,600
Tr.—Nerud Jan H **$50,000** 1986 4 2 0 1 $32,040
Lifetime 10 2 1 1 $34,640 Turf 1 0 0 0

26Jly87-6Bel 6f :22^2 :45 1:09^1 gd 15 113 7^9 7^9 7^13 7^14 Migliore R 2 Aw27000 80-19 Fugie, Fort Ligonier, Quick Call 7
1Jly87-3Mth 6f :22^1 :45^1 1:10^4 ft 2½ 109^7 6^2¼ 4^1½ 3^1½ 2^hd Garcia J 1 32000 86-15 DirtyDelbert,Giuseppe,FloridaMorn 6
18Jun87-7Bel 1 (T):45^1 1:10 1:35 fm 20 112 4^11 11^19 12^29 12^28¼ Bailey J D 12 Aw28000 62-10 Easton, Seattlite, Nudge 12
3Jun87-5Bel 7f :23 :46^1 1:23^2 ft 13 110 7^5¾ 7^5¼ 5^6 5^5 Davis R G 2 Aw27000 80-22 Mr. Classic, Easton, Crivitz 7
13May87-7Bel 7f :22^2 :45^1 1:23 ft 13 110 1^1½ 2½ 9^13 9^14¼ Davis R G 1 Aw27000 73-18 CrownthLdr,PldgCrd,BoldSummit 11
13Apr87-4Aqu 6f :22^1 :45^4 1:10^3 m *1-2e 110 4^3½ 5^7 6^17 6^18½ Davis R G 6 Aw27000 69-26 Pentelicus, Wayar, Proud And Tall 6
29Nov86-6Aqu 1 :46^4 1:12^1 1:37^3 ft *8-5 117 5^2¾ 3½ 1^3½ 1^10½ Cordero AJr 3 Aw27000 78-20 Giuseppe,Superceded,SonnyVrbtim 6
1Aug86-8Sar 6f :22^2 :45^2 1:10 ft 38 117 7^6¼ 8^11 9^9¼ 7^11 Davis R G3 Sar Spec'l 79-17 Gulch, Jazzing Around, Java Gold 10
1Aug86—Grade II; Steadied
Aug 6 Sar 4f ft :50^1 b Jly 17 Bel tr.t 4f ft :50^3 b Jun 16 Bel tr.t 4f ft :50^2 b Jun 11 Bel tr.t 4f ft :48^2 b

C.

Green Shekel *
Own.—Barrera O S **108^5**
Dk. b. or br. g. 5, by New Prospect—Sheckyrila, by Shecky Greene
Br.—Herzberg John (Fla) 1987 11 2 2 3 $34,725
Tr.—Barrera Oscar S **$45,000** 1986 13 2 2 4 $99,435
Lifetime 45 13 9 9 $276,604

22Jly87-9Bel 6f :22^1 :45^4 1:11 ft 4 119 1½ 3^2½ 6^6 9^6¾ Davis R G 3 c25000 78-17 TisRoyal,BigMcCoy,FlyingSkipper 11
11Jly87-2Bel 6f :22^3 :46^2 1:12^1 ft 6 113 1^1½ 1^1½ 1^1 3^2½ Davis R G 4 30000 76-27 Over the Wall, Semaj, GreenShekel 8
2Jly87-2Bel 6f :22^1 :45^4 1:12 sy *2 117 1^1½ 1^2 1^3 1^3 Romero R P 6 25000 80-27 GreenShkl,PlcidWtrs,SportsMdicin 6
18Jun87-7Mth 6f :22^1 :44^4 1:09^2 ft 9½ 112 1½ 3^nk 3^2½ 3^5 Krone J A 6 28000 88-14 KingOfBrdlwood,ScrnTrnd,GrnShkl 9
11Jun87-5Bel 6f :23 :46^3 1:11^4 ft *3-2 117 3^1½ 4^3 4^5½ 5^6 Pezua J M 7 25000 75-23 BigMcCoy,Vinny'sPrd,I'mSuprDupr 7
31May87-1Bel 6f :22^2 :46 1:10^2 ft 3½ 112^5 1½ 2^hd 4^3 5^8¾ Badamo J J 1 35000 79-17 Fugie, Bienestar, Flunky Home 6
1Apr87-4Aqu 6f :22^1 :45^1 1:09^2 ft 8¼ 108^5 1^1½ 1^2 1^2 2^nk Ortiz E Jr 2 45000 94-18 FbulousFlight,GrenShkl,OrBonBon 6
22Mar87-1Aqu 6f :23^1 :46^2 1:11^1 ft 6 108^5 1^hd 1^hd 3^3 5^3¾ Ortiz E Jr 2 45000 81-25 FlunkyHome,SportsMdicin,TlcPowr 7

D.

Truth Be Told ✻

Own.—Riccio J 1085

B. g. 5, by In Reality—Amalie, by Bold and Brave
Br.—Carrion Jaime S (Fla) 1987 15 2 2 0 $33,580
Tr.—Ferriola Peter $45,000 1986 2 0 0 0
Lifetime 38 5 6 3 $108,660 Turf 1 0 0 0

```
12Jly87-6Bel  1 1/16:461 1:104 1:442ft  4¼ 1125 21 21½ 46 69¾  Nuesch D 2  Aw31000 70-25 TheWtcher,MtthewsKeep,Mr.Clssic 6
28Jun87-6Bel  7f :23  :461 1:233ft  4¼ 1125 2½ 1½ 11½ 2¾  Nuesch D 2  Aw29000 83-19 FbulousFlight,TruthBTold,ThWtchr 8
21Jun87-9Bel  7f :223 :453 1:222m  *3 1125 12 12 17 110  Nuesch D 8  25000 90-10 TruthBeTold,Temperte,WickdWik 11
10Jun87-1Bel  6½f:224 :453 1:154ft  11 117  97½ 69 37½ 26¾  Maple E2  c17500 89-17 Onnagata, Truth Be Told, IrishIrish 9
1Jun87-1Bel   7f :231 :461 1:234ft  10 117  42 52½ 64 75¾  Maple E2  25000 77-20 SntlyChf,Rxson'sQll,CorncobsRylty 7
23May87-9Bel  6f :22  :452 1:094ft  15 117  78½ 78 68½ 47½  Maple E8  25000 83-13 Fugie, Saintly Cheif,Craig'sPower 11
11May87-9Bel  6f :222 :46  1:11 ft  30 1125 65 88¾ 913 1211  Badamo J J2  35000 74-22 Semaj,ShineDiulus,SaltineWarrior 12
1May87-4Aqu   7f :224 :451 1:233ft  16 1125 64 65½ 53 52¾  Badamo J J3  35000 80-18 Vinny'sPride,SltineWrrior,GoRenor 9
```

E.

Sidi Bou Said ✻

Own.—Kelley Mrs W A 117

B. h. 7, by Ack Ack—Fabulous View, by Le Fabuleux
Br.—Hancock III & Peters (Ky) 1987 6 1 0 1 $17,100
Tr.—Kelley Walter A $50,000 1986 23 6 2 7 $143,676
Lifetime 54 13 6 12 $243,296 Turf 3 0 1 0 $3,600

```
17Jly87-4Bel  7f :234 :462 1:234ft  4¼ 1085 45½ 44 33½ 34½  Nuesch D5  70000 78-20 Don Sanders, Harry L.,SidiBouSaid 6
6Jly87-9Bel   7f :23  :453 1:24 ft  9¾ 117  66 67 51½ 11½  Antley C W8  50000 82-22 Sidi Bou Said, Harry L., John Muir 8
24Jun87-1Bel  6½f:231 :463 1:17 ft  5¾ 113  41½ 42½ 43 610¼  Antley C W3  70000 80-17 Cullendale, Harry L., Shining Asset 7
7Jun87-1Bel   6f :222 :46  1:111ft  20 113  612 69 67½ 48  Brown T L3  70000 76-22 OneBonBon,Zonter,PassingThunder 7
16Jan87-5Aqu  170[•]:48 1:122 1:412ft  8½ 113  54 65¾ 65½ 68¾  Lovato F Jr4  70000 84-18 GoldnImmgrnt,Vnny'sPrd,HnrdCnsl 8
4Jan87-7Aqu   6f [•]:222 :461 1:103ft  7½ 1085  43 55½ 65¾ 64¼  Nuesch D10  70000 86-21 PrisVenture,MjesticEmpir,CoolJo 10
21Nov86-3Aqu  7f :224 :46  1:233gd  3 112  2hd 2hd 34½ 410  Davis R G4  75000 73-22 Sgittrn,PssngThundr,UpPopsAwnnr 5
10Nov86-9Aqu  6f :214 :451 1:094gd  7½ 117  910 89¾ 64¾ 46½  Martens G1  75000 86-18 Sagittarian, Whoop Up, Bienestar 9
   Aug 7 Sar 3f ft :362 h   Jly 29 Bel 4f ft :492 h   Jly 24 Bel 4f ft :504 b   Jly 13 Bel 3f ft :38 b
```

F.

John Muir

Own.—Gagliano S 115

Dk. b. or br. h. 5, by Soy Numero Uno—Wilderness, by Herbager
Br.—Woodside Stud Inc (Ky) 1987 9 1 2 3 $37,700
Tr.—Barrera Oscar S $47,500 1986 11 1 0 4 $23,580
Lifetime 20 2 2 7 $61,280 Turf 1 0 0 0

```
1Aug87-5Bel   1  :454 1:111 1:37 ft  6¾ 117  515 34½ 22½ 24½  Pezua J M3  Aw28000 75-27 StckedPck,JohnMuir,Gnome'sPlsur 6
26Jly87-6Bel  6f :222 :45 1:091gd  11 117  69 68½ 57 57¼  Antley C W4  Aw27000 86-19 Fugie, Fort Ligonier, Quick Call 7
20Jly87-3Bel  1 1/16:454 1:094 1:421m  *2½ 117  68½ 58 38 35½  Samyn J L2  c35000 85-15 Bienestar, Onnagata, John Muir 7
6Jly87-9Bel   7f :23  :453 1:24 ft  9 113  77 89½ 3½ 31¼  Samyn J L1  45000 81-22 Sidi Bou Said, Harry L., John Muir 8
18Jun87-1Bel  1 1/16:482 1:123 1:431ft  5¼ 113  65½ 65 44¼ 44  Samyn J L4  45000 82-23 Harry L., The Savage, Mr. Tatt 7
10Jun87-3Bel  7f :231 :462 1:241ft  11 117  109½1011 55½ 21½  Samyn J L1  35000 79-17 Rxson'sQuill,JohnMuir,GrndRivult 10
1Mar87-5Aqu   1 1/16[•]:48 1:134 1:464sy *6-5 117  58 63½ 32 1nk  Samyn J L3  Aw27000 76-20 JohnMuir,FrenchExprss,Lord'sWish 6
18Feb87-7Aqu  6f [•]:231 :47 1:114ft  4 117  87¼ 86¼ 65½ 46¼  Skinner K2  Aw26000 79-23 UpperStar,Racer,CaptainWimborne 8
   Jly 16 Bel 5f ft 1:032 b   Jun 29 Bel 5f ft 1:012 h
```

G.

The Rogers Four

Own.—Sabarese T M 117

Ch. h. 5, by L'Natural—Marta's Policy, by New Policy
Br.—Franklin & Stein & VassaloJr (Cal) 1987 6 1 0 0 $32,016
Tr.—Parisella John $50,000 1986 3 0 0 0 $1,875
Lifetime 19 6 0 1 $231,141

```
6Mar87-6Aqu   6f [•]:23 :461 1:094ft  6¾ 120  53 53½ 58½ 513½  Hernandez R2  95000 81-17 AswanHigh,ParisVenture,TonkaPss 5
16Feb87-8Aqu  6f [•]:224 :461 1:10 ft  16 108  45 56 59½ 413½  MrCHJr4 Sp'rt Plte H 80-24 ComicBlush,PrisVentur,CutlssRlity 5
1Feb87-8Aqu   6f [•]:222 :453 1:104gd  9½ 117  42 46 412 418¾  Antley C W2 Coaltown 71-26 BestByTest,Rj'sRevng,ComicBlush 5
15Jan87-8Aqu  6f [•]:221 :452 1:102ft  15 116  54½ 42 2hd 11  Antley C W2  HcpO 92-19 ThRogrsFor,Rxsn'sBshp,MjstcEmpr 5
10Jan87-8Aqu  6f [•]:221 :45 1:092gd  24 113  74¾ 75¾ 78 712¾  AntlyCW4 Paumonk H 84-10 BstByTst,ScrtProspctor,GrnKnight 7
3Jan87-8Aqu   1 1/16[•]:464 1:104 1:414m  36 113  22 54 717 817¾  AntlCW7 Aqueduct H 83-16 King'sSwn,Rj'sRvng,CostConscious 8
   3Jan87—Grade III
3May86-8Hol   6f :214 :444 1:10 ft  14 112  47 47½ 58½ 510½  Olivares F6  L A H 83-16 Rosie'sK.T.,MneMgic,MuchFinGold 6
   3May86—Grade III
31Mar86-8Aqu  6f :224 :46 1:093ft  8½ 113  72¾ 62¾ 65 611¾  Santagata N5  HcpO 81-20 LoveThatMac,IrishOre,GreenShekel 7
   ●Aug 1 Sar tr.t 6f ft 1:163 h   Jly 7 Bel tr.t 5f ft 1:02 b   Jun 25 Bel 4f ft :483 h
```

H.

Passing Thunder

Own.—Davis A 117

Ch. h. 5, by Valdez—Happy Summer, by Summer Tan
Br.—Galbreath J W (Ky) 1987 8 1 0 1 $19,200
Tr.—Moschera Gasper S $50,000 1986 27 3 7 3 $95,920
Lifetime 51 6 8 6 $149,920 Turf 1 0 0 0

```
19Jun87-4Bel  6f :222 :454 1:102ft  5½e112  85½ 86¾ 811 812¾  Santos J A6  75000 75-21 Zonter, Crivitz, Bravo Fox 8
```

7Jun87-1Bel 6f :222 :46 1:111ft 10 114 57 54 33½ 35½ Antley C W 4 70000 78-22 OneBonBon,Zonter,PassingThunder 7
14Mar87-6Aqu 6f :224 :461 1:101ft 15 117 73 64¼ 47½ 511 Graell A 4 Aw29000 79-28 PolarEscpde,Reygo,AmourdeFleuve 8
4Mar87-7Aqu 6f [•]:22 :4541:10 ft 23 117 77 77¼ 69 612¾ Graell A 10 Aw29000 81-16 BestDefense,AmourdFluv,Wndrkin 10
11Feb87-5Aqu 6f [•]:222 :4621:111ft 8¾ 119 79 78¼ 69 610¾ McCuleyWH 4 Aw29000 77-20 SwitchInTime,LordWindm-,SltSickl 7
14Jan87-7Aqu 6f [•]:213 :4421:093ft 3½e 112 810 711 69½ 68¼ McCauley W H 8 75000 88-16 PrisVntur,ShinDulus,LordOfThNght 8
8Jan87-8Aqu 6f [•]:23 :47 1:12 ft 3¼ 117 65½ 54 3½ 11 McCuleyWH 5 Aw27000 84-24 PssingThunder,Hberdshr,RollingBy 6
4Jan87-7Aqu 6f [•]:222 :4611:103ft 3½ 119 65 66 55½ 87¼ McCauley W H 5 75000 84-21 PrisVenture,MjesticEmpir,CoolJo 10
Aug 3 Bel 3f ft :37 h   Jly 22 Bel tr.t 3f ft :36 h   Jly 4 Bel tr.t 3f ft :363 h   Jun 29 Bel tr.t 4f ft :52 b

I.

Secretary General

Dk. b. or br. h. 5, by Foolish Pleasure—Sippican, by Stage Door Johnny
Br.—Ryan E Barry (Ky) 1986 3 0 0 1 $1,875
Own.—Allen H 117 Tr.—Russello Anthony $50,000 1985 5 1 0 2 $15,172
Lifetime 11 2 1 3 $32,247

6Jly86-8Crc 6f :22 :45 1:104ft 9½ 116 88 812 912 913¼ St Leon G2 Aw12500 84-14 AmrricoDoubl,I'mForShl,B-ndRviw 9
26Jun86-9Crc 7f :23 :46 1:251sy *8-5 117 2hd 1hd 33 510¼ St Leon G4 Aw12500 80-17 Buckley Boy, Pedantry, John Law 7
12Jun86-9Crc 6½f :23 :471 1:204ft *2 117 58¾ 56½ 54½ 36½ St Leon G2 Aw13900 74-20 BeausBid,Pedantry,SecretryGenerl 6
8May85-8Bel 1 :46 1:111 1:363ft 41 126 64¾ 810 1119 1225½ GuerrWA6 Withers 56-18 El Basco, Another Reef, Concert 12
8May85—Grade II
18Feb85-10GP 1 1/16 :463 1:111 1:433ft 40 112 21½ 2hd 2hd 1124¼ CrugutJ12 Ftn Youth 59-22 PrdTrth,Stphn'sOdyssy,DltAgnDn 14
18Feb85—Grade II
4Feb85-8GP 1 1/16 :463 1:113 1:442ft 3 117 41½ 2hd 21 37¼ Santos J A7 Aw16000 72-18 ProdTrth,CrownngHnrs,ScrtryGnrl 10
19Jan85-6GP 7f :222 :453 1:242ft *2-5 117 2hd 1½ 12 12 Cruguet J5 Aw14000 82-15 ScrtryGnrl,SittinOnHold,FlyrEscp 10
8Jan85-9GP 6f :212 :443 1:102ft *9-5 112 55½ 41¾ 45½ 31½ CrugutJ6 Spect'lr Bid 85-16 CherokeeFst,Vindloo,SecretryGnrl 11
Aug 6 Sar 4f ft :50 bg   Jly 31 Sar 7f ft 1:272 h   ●Jly 26 Sar 5f ft 1:012 h   Jly 21 Sar tr.t 5f ft 1:022 b

J.

Shine Diulus *

B. g. 5, by Christopher R—Bonnie Maggie, by St Bonaventure
Br.—Rooney A J (Md) 1987 10 2 4 0 $57,400
Own.—Davis A 113 Tr.—Moschera Gasper S $45,000 1986 9 4 1 0 $32,625
Lifetime 31 11 6 1 $121,545

16Jly87-5Bel 6f :223 :453 1:104ft 2¾ 113 11 1hd 21½ 44¾ Bailey J D 2 45000 81-24 BigCod,CountOnRomeo,OrBonBon 7
19Jun87-4Bel 6f :222 :454 1:102ft 5¼e 112 11½ 2hd 21½ 43¾ Bailey J D3 75000 84-21 Zonter, Crivitz, Bravo Fox 8
4Jun87-1Bel 6f :22 :453 1:113sy *2½ 113 14 12 12 1no Bailey J D 11 45000 82-21 ShineDiulus,WhtIntensity,Sgittrin 11
11May87-9Bel 6f :222 :46 1:11 ft 8¼ 117 11 1½ 12 2hd Bailey J D 1 35000 85-22 Semaj,ShineDiulus,SaltineWarrior 12
2Mar87-5Aqu 6f [•]:214 :45 1:11 gd *4-5 117 21 33 21½ 57¾ Graell A 2 50000 81-15 Talc Power,GreenShekel,Mr.Meeka 5
14Feb87-7Aqu 6f [•]:221 :46 1:111ft *3 115 11½ 11 3½ 43¾ Graell A 6 Aw40000 84-21 WhtAnEntrnc,CoolJo,RoylDoulton 11
2Feb87-8Aqu 6f [•]:214 :4521:102sy *2 1145 1½ 1½ 22 26 Baird E T 6 Aw33000 86-24 MjesticEmpir,ShinDiulus,AswnHigh 7
21Jan87-8Aqu 6f [•]:214 :45 1:104sy *2 117 11 11½ 14 13¼ Davis R G 6 Aw29000 90-17 ShineDiulus,FrwyIslnd,HyNowHrry 8
Aug 3 Bel 5f ft 1:01 h   Jly 31 Bel 4f ft :502 h   Jly 27 Bel 4f ft :484 h   Jly 12 Bel tr.t 4f ft :50 b

K.

Scottish Monk

Dk. b. or br. g. 4, by Duns Scotus—Loose Wire, by Ruritania
Br.—DriverKthrin&KornrMr-MrsJ (NY) 1987 4 2 1 0 $11,560
Own.—Cirricione Linda 115 Tr.—Czadzeck Mary $45,000 1986 2 1 0 1 $4,810
Lifetime 6 3 1 1 $16,370

2Aug87-9FL 6f :214 :441 1:092ft 5 114 4nk 57 611 612 Hulet L2 [S]Williamson 90-10 SirSmokem,PostTens,MovingndGm 8
19Jly87-6FL 6f :222 :454 1:104ft *2-3 122 11 11½ 12½ 14 Hulet L5 [S]Aw10600 95-10 ScottshMonk,WntGoNorth,BrrstrJy 9
5Jly87-7FL 5½f :22 :453 1:041ft *1-3 116 11 12½ 13 19 Hulet L2 Aw6500 95-11 ScottshMonk,CrgOfCrl,AmrcnFlght 7
15May87-7FL 6f :223 :461 1:113gd *1 116 43 22½ 23 24 Hulet L9 Aw6500 87-17 LordPnguin,ScottishMonk,GoldPc 11
22Jun86-7FL 1 1/16 :473 1:133 1:481ft *2-3 113 11½ 11½ 21 34 O'Brien E J9 Aw5500 71-21 Tony'sHlo,OnforWiff,ScottishMonk 9
22Jun86—Drifted out
11Jun86-6FL 5½f :223 :462 1:043ft 3 113 11½ 13 16 114 O'Brien E J4 [S]Mdn 93-20 ScottshMonk,OnfrWff,AmrcnAngl 12
●Jun 28 FL 6f ft 1:114 h   ●Jun 24 FL 4f ft :482 h

L.

Count On Romeo

B. g. 4, by Romeo—Katy's Countess, by Pago Pago
Br.—Fox Mrs J P (Pa) 1987 12 2 3 2 $51,961
Own.—Cedar Valle Stable 113 Tr.—Jerkens Steven T $45,000 1986 23 6 5 1 $60,430
Lifetime 43 10 9 5 $129,611 Turf 3 0 0 0

29Jly87-1Bel 7f :231 :454 1:23 ft 4½ 113 2½ 21 22½ 25 Pezua J M 3 45000 82-23 Crvtz,ContOnRomo,KngOfBrdlwod 8
16Jly87-5Bel 6f :223 :453 1:104ft 5¼ 113 64 34 32 21¾ Pezua J M 6 45000 84-24 BigCod,CountOnRomeo,OrBonBon 7
5Jly87-9Bel 7f :23 :453 1:24 ft 6½ 117 1hd 2hd 4¾ 63½ Romero R P 3 50000 78-22 Sidi Bou Said, Harry L., John Muir 8
25Jun87-6Bel 6f :222 :46 1:112ft 5¾ 117 43 1½ 11 31¾ Romero R P 8 50000 81-25 WhtIntnsty,Rxson'sQll,CortOnRm 10
14Jun87-2Bel 7f :223 :453 1:232ft 9¾ 117 1hd 2hd 21½ 43¾ Romero R P 7 50000 81-20 HurdyGurdyMn,WhtIntnsty,HrryL. 13
14May87-2Bel 6f :23 :461 1:10 ft 5¾ 117 43 32 41½ 51¼ Byrnes D 2 c50000 89-13 Tis Royal,Dale'sFolly,FlunkyHome 10
25Apr87-8Pim 6f :232 :463 1:104gd 4e 1175 43 44 54¾ 54¾ Sarvis D A 3 Aw25000 87-20 WillardScott,DoverRidge,BeaQulity 7
4Apr87-6GS 6f :213 :442 1:10 gd 3 115 74 74¾ 51¼ 2nk Byrnes D 1 HcpO 92-15 Dnny'sKys,CountOnRomo,SprDlght 9
4Apr87—Drifted out
Jly 14 Bel 4f ft :51 b   Jly 4 Bel tr.t 3f ft :35 b   Jun 11 Bel 5f ft 1:001 h

M.

Aswan High — Ch. h. 5, by Upper Nile—Laraka, by Impressive

Br.—Worswick R J (Ky) — 1987 8 3 0 1 $61,860

Own.—Cedar Valley Stable — 117 — Tr.—Jerkens Steven T — $50,000 — 1986 18 4 6 0 $99,320

Lifetime 44 9 9 3 $194,880

29May87-9Bel 7f :223 :453 1:224ft 9¼ 118 21 2½ 52 54¾ Migliore R7 90000 83-13 TonkaPss,ScholrsTsk,JmicnGigolo 10

13May87-8Bel 6f :221 :454 1:10 ft *2 112 1½ 1hd 2hd 42½ Migliore R2 Hcp0 87-18 OmrKhyym,PrisVentur,JmicnGigolo 7

16Apr87-7Aqu 6f :222 :453 1:094m 4¾ 121 11 11 11½ 14½ Migliore R4 Aw40000 92-15 Aswan High, Paris Venture,Ioskeha 7

6Mar87-6Aqu 6f ⊡:23 :4611:094ft 2¾ 116 1½ 11 11 13¼ Antley C W5 85000 95-17 AswanHigh,ParisVenture,TonkaPss 5

2Feb87-8Aqu 6f ⊡:214 :4521:102sy 4¾ 117 35½ 32½ 33½ 36¼ Antley C W1 Aw33000 86-24 MjesticEmpir,ShinDiulus,AswnHigh 7

21Jan87-5Aqu 6f ⊡:222 :4541:101sy *2½ 117 11½ 11½ 13 15¼ Antley C W1 c50000 93-17 AswnHigh,FlyingSkipper,Dl'sFolly 11

14Jan87-7Aqu 6f ⊡:213 :4421:093ft 4¼ 1075 32½ 22 32½ 54½ Nuesch D2 75000 91-16 PrisVntur,ShinDulus,LordOfThNght 8

4Jan87-7Aqu 6f ⊡:222 :4611:103ft 7½ 117 53 44 43½ 42½ Murphy D J4 75000 88-21 PrisVenture,MjesticEmpir,CoolJo 10

●Aug 3 Bel 4f ft :464 h — Jly 30 Bel 6f ft 1:164 b — Jly 24 Bel tr.t 4f ft :49 b — Jly 5 Bel 5f ft 1:012 h

4. Which horse below gets a form defect?

9th Del Mar

1 1/16 MILES. (1.40) CLAIMING. Purse $14,000. 3-year-olds and upward. Weights, 3-year-olds, 116 lbs.; older, 122 lbs. Non-winners of two races at one mile or over since June 1 allowed 2 lbs.; of such a race since then, 4 lbs.; since April 20, 6 lbs. Claiming price $16,000; if for $14,000, allowed 2 lbs. (Claiming and starter races for $12,500 or less not considered.)

A.

Tommy Thoms — Ch. g. 5, by Tom Rolfe—Princess East, by Prince John

SANTOS J — Br.—Elmendorf Farm (Ky) — 1987 8 1 2 0 $20,550

1115 — Tr.—Lage Armando — $16,000 — 1986 7 1 2 1 $21,350

Own.—AndesInternationalStb&Lage — Lifetime 22 4 4 1 $60,500 — Turf 2 0 0 0

20Jun87-7GG 1 :452 1:10 1:354ft *6-5 116 11 2hd 79½ 813¾ Castaneda M 8 16000 75-12 Nordic Light, Stabilized, Finalized 10

20Jun87—Stumbled start

6Jun87-7GG 1 :453 1:092 1:351ft 4¼ 119 31 31½ 88 87¼ Warren R J Jr 10 25000 85-07 BrginStndrd,FirlyOmen,IvnPhillips 10

6Jun87—Bobbled start

17May87-7GG 1 :453 1:093 1:35 ft 3½ 119 11 1½ 2½ 23 Warren R J Jr 8 25000 90-11 AckLikeM,TommyThoms,FirlyOmn 8

2May87-9GG 1 1/16 :462 1:094 1:424ft 6½ 114 2hd 1½ 11 21½ Warren R J Jr 3 30000 87-13 Impulsively,TommyThoms,CrtinTrt 7

5Apr87-9SA 1 1/16 :461 1:111 1:432ft 6¼ 116 88½ 76¼ 31½ 1hd DelahoussayeE 8 25000 84-16 TommyThoms,RexLke,ILoveRcing 11

5Apr87—Bumped 3/16

27Feb87-9SA 1⅛ :461 1:11 1:501ft *3 115 55½ 42½ 34 63½ Toro F 9 c20000 74-16 Convincing,Robrsky,LyphrdChims 10

1Feb87-9SA 1 1/16 :464 1:112 1:434ft 13 116 75 83¾ 42¼ 54¼ Toro F 3 32000 78-16 GumFleet,ShowerDecree,Dcontrol 12

1Feb87—Roughed at start

17Jan87-9SA 1 1/16 :462 1:112 1:434ft 9¾ 116 69 65 42½ 51½ Ortega L E 8 32000 80-18 PiperJohn,ForHimself,ShowerDcr 12

17Jan87—Bumped late

26Dec86-9SA 1 1/16 :454 1:102 1:43 ft 4¾ 116 2hd 1½ 11½ 23 Ortega L E 2 25000 83-13 Cold,TommyThoms,BoncngBttons 11

18Dec86-8Hol 1 1/16 Ⓣ:4831:12 1:422fm 21 116 52¾ 74¼ 89½ 813¼ Kaenel J L 2 Aw24000 69-19 SmoothOpertor,Intuitiveness,Stmd 8

18Dec86—Wide 5/16

●Jly 27 Dmr 4f ft :472 h — Jly 14 Hol 6f ft 1:141 h — Jly 8 Hol 4f ft :492 h — ●Jun 17 GG 5f ft :592 h

B.

Rain Shelter — B. g. 5, by Shelter Half—Suebee, by Rainy Lake

OLIVARES F — Br.—Fourbros Stable (Md) — 1987 8 0 3 0 $11,325

116 — Tr.—Velasquez Danny — $16,000 — 1986 10 0 2 1 $12,017

Own.—Gentry & Weaver — Lifetime 35 4 9 3 $98,145 — Turf 1 0 0 0

12Jly87-4Hol 6½f :221 :451 1:16 ft 8 116 53¼ 53 53¼ 45 Olivares F 10 16000 95-09 MightyBuck,BlzeFlme,Bruli'sAnte 11

12Jly87—Wide into stretch

24Jun87-9Hol 1 :45 1:10 1:363ft 4 115 2hd 1½ 11 21¼ ValenzuelPA 10 c10000 79-13 Rvolutionry,RnShltr,RunnngDbonr 12

3Jun87-2Hol 7f :221 :451 1:234ft 7½ 116 2hd 31 22 23½ Valenzuela P A 8 12500 81-13 FriscoDnnis,RinShltr,TuscnKnight 12

2May87-3Hol 1 3/16 :481 1:13 1:58 ft *7-5 116 13 1½ 22 22¾ Valenzuela P A 1 10000 — — GllntMinded,RinSheltr,WhitShowrs 7

15Apr87-3SA 1 1/16 :464 1:114 1:451ft 8 1105 1½ 1½ 2hd 42¼ Cisneros J E 4 16000 73-21 NewStorm,Bruli'sAnte,Halo'sSword 5

15Apr87—Bumped at 3/16

1Apr87-9SA 1 1/16 :462 1:114 1:45 ft 16 115 21 32 43½ 45¾ Pedroza M A 3 16000 70-23 Chagrining,Camilla'sBoy,Navegante 7

1Apr87—Bumped 5/16

17Mar87-2SA 1 1/16 :463 1:112 1:434ft 34 117 11 2hd 41½ 58¼ Simpson B H 2 14000 74-16 Trento, Chagrining,Bigbadandmean 8

4Mar87-9SA 1 1/16 :463 1:112 1:441ft 9 116 74¾ 74¼ 57 614¾ DelahoussayeE 7 16000 65-16 Idol, Oak Tree II, Cojak Man 8

4Mar87—Off slowly, bumped

5Nov86-3Hol 1 :452 1:111 1:372ft 3½ 116 31 1½ 32 57 Valenzuela P A2 20000 69-17 Calabonga, Pegus, Vinegarone 7

17Oct86-9SA 1 1/16 :47 1:122 1:453ft 7¼ 117 41½ 1hd 1hd 2½ Meza R Q 7 16000 72-21 Espontneo,RinShelter,JupiterTogee 9

17Oct86—Wide 7/8 turn

Aug 1 Dmr 5f ft :594 h — Jly 27 Dmr 5f ft 1:002 h — Jly 21 Hol 4f ft :52 h — Jly 8 Hol 4f ft :501 h

C.

***Navegante**
MAGALLON P 111 5
Own.—Casella Judy K

Ch. h. 9, by Tantoul—Saima, by Penny Post
Br.—Haras Dadinco (Chile)
Tr.—Casella Judy K **$16,000**
Lifetime 66 8 18 14 $128,967

1987 15 2 4 5 $44,625
1986 14 1 2 2 $21,175
Turf 3 0 1 0 $8,925

24Jly87-9Hol 1 :451 1:102 1:362ft 6¾ 116 22 22 43 44¼ Valenzuela P A 8 16000 77-17 Rvolutionry,MnyGlcirs,BronzTudor 9
28Jun87-2Hol 1 1/16 :462 1:111 1:431ft 8¾ 116 44½ 34 26 414¼ Meza R Q 5 20000 79-12 Vulnrbility,PlumbStrignt,GlicKnght 8
14Jun87-9Hol 1 :453 1:10 1:36 ft 9½ 116 65 34½ 24½ 24½ Valenzuela P A 5 16000 78-14 PaversDream,Navegnte,SeAndSew 12
25May87-2Hol 1 :451 1:11 1:381ft 5½ 116 77 54½ 52 4¾ Meza R Q 1 c12500 71-15 JonO.,SeaAndSew,BusinessSchool 11
9May87-1Hol 1⅛ :48 1:122 1:504ft 3 1115 31 21 32½ 33½ Patton D B 8 16000 79-10 OneEyedRomeo,EverBrillint,Nvgnt 8
23Apr87-9Hol 1 1/16 :462 1:112 1:43 ft 5 1115 21½ 1hd 2½ 2½ Patton D B 5 16000 93-09 New Storm, Navegante,Bruli'sAnte 8
15Apr87-9SA 1 1/16 :47 1:12 1:45 ft 4¾ 1145 63¼ 63¼ 53¾ 33 Patton D B 1 16000 73-21 Tio Nino, Mr. Director, Navegante 8
1Apr87-9SA 1 1/16 :462 1:114 1:45 ft 3 119 54 52½ 33½ 35½ Valenzuela P A 2 16000 70-23 Chagrining,Camilla'sBoy,Navegante7
19Mar87-9SA 1 1/16 :461 1:113 1:444ft 4 121 22 21 22 2nk ValenzuelaPA 7 c12500 77-21 TioNino,Navegnte,TimeForSilence 12
11Mar87-9SA 1⅛ :461 1:11 1:511ft 3¼ 118 43½ 22 12½ 1no Valenzuela P A 6 12500 73-18 Navegante, Idol, Stormy World 9
Jly 18 Hol 4f ft :50 h   Jun 9 Hol 4f ft :511 h

D.

Don's Tryst
STEVENS G L 116
Own.—Leinen Gail E

Ch. g. 4, by Don B—Bert's Tryst, by Bert Kerr
Br.—Coelho & Valenti (Cal)
Tr.—Haynes Jack B **$16,000**
Lifetime 14 3 3 0 $28,950

1987 8 2 3 0 $22,425
1986 6 1 0 0 $6,525

12Jly87-1Hol 1 1/16 :474 1:12 1:433ft *2 116 1½ 1hd 12 1¾ Olivares F 2 12500 91-09 Don'sTryst,BoldSintPt,ExotcArbtor 7
2Jly87-5Hol 6f :221 :452 1:103ft 5 116 11 11 1½ 21¼ Olivares F 7 12500 89-15 Shantin, Don's Tryst, Ayaabi 11
20Jun87-1Hol 6f :214 :451 1:103ft 6¼ 115 11 1½ 2½ 21¼ Olivares F 9 10000 89-11 SrEdgrAlln,Dn'sTryst,DmndCttrII 11
23May87-2Hol 6½f :222 :453 1:164ft 5½ 116 2hd 32½ 58 713 Olivares F 3 12500 83-15 Ells Bravest Song, L.A.Fire,Shantin 9
17Apr87-9SA 6½f :22 :452 1:181ft 3¼ 119 11 11 11½ 75¾ McCarron C J 5 c12500 73-24 Ambly'sJoy,MnyRods,DstnctvlyDn 11
17Apr87—Bumped start; bumped, steadied 3/8
21Mar87-1SA 6f :213 :443 1:102sy *2½ 116 62½ 3½ 53 64¼ McCarron C J 12 16000 82-16 ForbesReply,BoldBtterUp,VlDeRoi 12
21Mar87—Hopped in air
7Mar87-1SA 6½f :214 :444 1:164gd 2¾ 116 11½ 1½ 11½ 22 ♦ Solis A 2 Ⓢ 16000 84-19 Bennett Peak, Don's Tryst,Tigerillo 7
♦ 7Mar87—Dead heat
20Feb87-1SA 6f :213 :45 1:11 ft 5¼ 115 12½ 11½ 11½ 1¾ Solis A 8 Ⓢ 12500 83-16 Don's Tryst, Saro Star, NanteTam 11
20Feb87—Veered in start
23Sep86-5Pom 6f :221 :454 1:113ft 5½ 115 1hd 2hd 55½ 924½ Kaenel J L 5 8000 68-08 Cindrhoof,Pintin'Rinbows,FrstOvrll 9
23Sep86—Broke in air
18Sep86-5Pom 6½f :214 :452 1:182ft 3 118 1hd 22 21 87¾ Sibille R 3 10000 80-12 LodTheWgon,WtrJckt,StrngMusic 10
Aug 1 Dmr 5f ft 1:004 h   Jly 26 Dmr 5f ft 1:004 h   Jun 13 SA 6f ft 1:13 h   ● Jun 6 SA 4f ft :46 h

E.

Aguila
BAZE G 116
Own.—Granja Vista Del Rio Stable

Dk. b. or br. g. 7, by Golden Eagle II—Crimson Flame, by Stage Door Johnny
Br.—Granja Vista Del Rio (Cal)
Tr.—West C R **$16,000**
Lifetime 40 5 3 11 $242,072

1985 7 0 2 1 $22,950
1984 7 1 0 1 $28,250
Turf 19 2 1 3 $71,650

14Sep85-11Pom 1 1/16 :46 1:114 1:44 ft 11 115 1110 99 56¼ 21½ EstrdJJr 10 P D Shprd 95 — ApolloFlight,Agul,MyFvortMomnt 11
26Aug85-8Dmr 1 1/16 Ⓣ:483 1:121 1:422fm 9 114 77½ 76½ 67 41¾ Hawley S 6 90000 94-04 I'll SeeYou,Snowcreek,SharpSinger 7
26Aug85—Wide into stretch
17Aug85-5Dmr 1 1/16 Ⓣ:48 1:114 1:42 fm 4 117 713 712 78 57¼ Valenzuela P A 7 80000 91-03 BoomTownChrli,Pnznc,RoylRcours 7
17Aug85—Crowded late
3Aug85-5Dmr 1⅛ Ⓣ:474 1:12 1:484fm 15 118 68½ 75¼ 52¾ 2hd Valenzuela P A 3 80000 94-06 Nonno, Aguila, Apollo Flight 8
14Jly85-7Hol 1⅛ Ⓣ:47 1:103 1:481fm 3¾ 117 44 32 1½ 51½ Meza R Q 9 62500 87-10 Tea Taster, Bengeo, Viceroy Lad 9
14Jly85—Bumped late
5Jly85-9Hol 1 1/16 Ⓣ:462 1:111 1:414fm 4½ 114 66½ 42 32½ 32¾ Meza R Q 5 75000 87-09 I'll See You, Apollo Flight, Aguila 6
9Jun85-7Hol 1 1/16 Ⓣ:472 1:112 1:414fm 23 116 87¼ 87 87¾ 85¾ Pedroza M A 2 80000 84-11 Donny K., Kilauea, Shuttle Jet 8
25May84-9Hol 1 1/16 Ⓣ:47 1:104 1:41 fm 19 114 76½ 77 77 710¼ Meza R Q 5 125000 84-04 Champagne Bid, Dare You II,Valais 7
16May84-8Hol 1 Ⓣ:482 1:12 1:354fm 7¾ 115 84¼ 97¼ 87¼ 86¾ Olivares F 1 175000 82-08 Acquisition, Match Winner, Garibi 9
10May84-8Hol 1⅛ Ⓣ:48 1:11 1:463fm 28 117 32½ 43½ 611 55¼ Olivares F 2 Aw40000 91-03 Sharp Soinger, All SystemsGo,Naar 8
Aug 2 Dmr 4f ft :484 h   Jly 28 Dmr 6f ft 1:151 h   Jly 22 SA 6f ft 1:15 hg   Jly 18 SA 6f ft 1:152 h

5. Which horses in this nonwinners allowance turf event outclass the conditions?

Additional information:

- The Royal Whip stakes of Ireland offers an $11,000 purse to 3up.
- The Extel Stakes of England offers $33,000 to 3up.
- All other foreign stakes are unlisted.

3rd Santa Anita

1⅛ MILES. (Turf). (1.45⅗) ALLOWANCE. Purse $31,000. 4-year-olds and upward which are non-winners of $3,000 other than maiden, claiming or starter. Weight, 120 lbs. Non-winners of a race other than claiming at one mile or over since February 15 allowed 3 lbs.

A.

Wuthering Heights — B. c. 4, by Lyphard—Behissa, by O'Grady
PINCAY L JR 3+ — 117 — Br.—duPont Scott Marion (Ky) — 1987 1 0 1 0 $6,200
Tr.—Cross Richard J — 1986 3 0 2 1 $10,247
Own.—Malibu Valley Farms — Lifetime 7 1 3 1 $23,114 99/ — Turf 7 1 3 1 $23,114

Entered 17Apr87- 5 SA
19Mar87-5SA 1¼Ⓣ:463 1:353 2:014fm 3¾ 117 42½ 2½ 21½ 21¼ McCarronCJ3 Aw31000 77-22 ExotcRvr,WuthrngHghts,RssnLogc 9
19Mar87—Bumped hard 5/8
12Jly86♦4Curragh(Ire) 1½ 2:411sf 12 131 Ⓣ 2hd Roche C 11k3vl Ryl Whip(Gr3) Dubian, WutheringHeights,Diristan 5
14May86♦3PhoenixPk(Ire) 1¼ : sf 7 121 Ⓣ 36½ HoganR Crock Advrtsng PcificDrift,Rodin,WutheringHights 5
14May86—No time taken
19Apr86♦7PhoenixPk(Ire) 1⅛ 2:091sf *3-2 126 Ⓣ 2¾ Roche C Mr D Plt BnkStp,WuthringHights,LuxuryImg 8
12Oct85♦3Curragh(Ire) 1 1:464yl 8 126 Ⓣ 44½ Roche C Beresfrd (Gr2) FlashofSteel,Eve'sError,DncingZet 8
29Sep85♦3Curragh(Ire) 1 1:434yl 16 122 Ⓣ 41¾ Moses K Frns Fut(Gr3) Woodman,HungryGiant,MdmJohn 10
24Aug85♦7PhoenixPk(Ire) 7f 1:273sf 8 126 Ⓣ 11 RochC RhnGrpPlt(Mdn) WuthrngHghts,Cbntly,Hlo'sSword 17
Apr 15 SA 3f ft :36 h — Apr 10 SA 7f ft 1:282 h — Mar 30 SA 3f ft :371 h — Mar 12 SA Ⓣ 1 fm 1:442 h (d)

B.

Ima Bullet — B. c. 4, by Ack Ack—Salem He, by Salem
CASTANON A L 6+ — 117 — Br.—Johnson-Brokken-Jones (Ky) — 1987 3 0 0 0 $2,325
Tr.—Stute Gary — 1986 11 2 3 2 $36,100
Own.—Abtahi & McGaughy — Lifetime 15 2 3 2 $38,800 — Turf 3 0 0 0 $2,875

3Apr87-8SA 1⅛Ⓣ:473 1:122 1:493fm 17 117 22½ 1hd 31 43¼ Castanon AL 4 Aw31000 76-21 Nurely, De Soto, Surprise Call 7
3Apr87—Steadied 1/8
15Mar87-2SA 6½f :214 :452 1:172ft 18 117 84¼ 78½ 1012 1017¾ ValenzuelPA 9 Aw28000 65-20 Don'sIrshMlody,Dvl'sIc,TmFrSkrt 11
28Feb87-9SA 6½f :213 :441 1:163ft 15 116 34 45½ 66 66¾ Castanon AL2 Aw27000 80-17 Extranix, Angle Arc, Devil's Ice 7
4Jun86-4Hol 7f :223 :46 1:234ft 13 116 31½ 31½ 3½ 31¾ Castanon A L 5 80000 83-18 Hy King, Partez Delight, ImaBullet 6
23May86-6Hol 1⅛Ⓣ:474 1:121 1:491fm 21 116 52¼ 41 52¼ 57¾ CastnonAL 11 Aw22000 78-14 FullOfStars,CostingCougr,Jyenezy 12
11May86-7Hol 1 1/16Ⓣ:462 1:102 1:414fm 45 115 1hd 2hd 52¼ 77 Castanon A L 1 Sptlt 88-06 Mazaad,Autobot,RomanMgestrite 12
24Apr86-3Hol 6f :224 :463 1:111ft 9½ 117 2½ 3½ 1½ 1½ Castanon A L 2 50000 88-18 Ima Bullet, K. Gibran, Clever Coin 5
24Apr86—Broke in a tangle, bumped break
12Apr86-1SA 6½f :213 :443 1:172ft 5½ 116 56 56½ 31½ 31¼ Castanon A L 6 50000 82-19 Clever Coin, ManyRoads,ImaBullet 8
12Apr86—Bobbled at start
6Apr86-9SA 6½f :211 :441 1:163ft 10 116 57½ 55 52¾ 44 Castanon A L 1 62500 83-15 Keen Knight, K. Gibran, GranPierre 8
6Apr86—Bumped at 3/4
16Mar86-3SA 6f :22 :451 1:11 sy *6-5 118 2hd 11 14½ 111½ Pincay L Jr 8 M32000 83-24 ImBullet,MimiDrem,NineStrAdmirl 9
Apr 17 SA 3f ft :372 h — Apr 10 SA 5f ft 1:004 h — Mar 27 SA 7f ft 1:301 h — Mar 21 SA 7f ft 1:29 h

C.

Russian Logic — B. c. 4, by Nijinsky II—Feminine Logic, by Bold Reasoning
BAZE G 0-N — 117 — Br.—Frankel J (Ky) — 1987 5 0 2 1 $18,350
Tr.—Otteson Kimberly — 1986 6 1 4 0 $9,777
Own.—Krdjian-McClure-Milch et al — Lifetime 11 1 6 1 $28,127 — Turf 11 1 6 1 $28,127

19Mar87-5SA 1¼Ⓣ:463 1:353 2:014fm 5 117 86 73¼ 43 31¼ Baze G8 Aw31000 77-22 ExotcRvr,WuthrngHghts,RssnLogc 9
8Mar87-2SA 1½Ⓣ:474 2:043 2:302gd *2¾ 116 97¾ 31 21½ 24 Baze G4 Aw30000 55-26 SunMan,RussianLogic,ShadowsFall 9
8Mar87—Very poor start
13Feb87-5SA 1⅛Ⓣ:472 1:133 1:523gd 4½ 117 1216 116¼ 67½ 46½ DelhoussyeE3 Aw28000 57-36 Bananas, Noticiero, Star Ribot 12
13Feb87—Very wide stretch
19Jan87-5SA 1¼Ⓣ:473 1:382 2:041fm *8-5 115 99¼ 93¾ 96¾ 107 Cordero AJr 5 Aw28000 59-29 Intuitiveness, Asian Cup, Neferou 12
19Jan87—Wide 3/8 turn
3Jan87-5SA 1¼Ⓣ:473 1:37 2:023fm *1 116 76 52½ 44 21½ DelhoussyeE7 Aw28000 73-24 Eliminnte,RussinLogic,GreyWriter 10
3Jan87—Bumped, steadied 1/8
16Nov86-6Hol 1⅛Ⓣ:462 1:102 1:464fm 11 122 912 108 107¾ 108¾ StvnsGL10 Hol Dby 85-07 ThrillShow,ArDsply,BoldArrngmnt 11
16Nov86—Grade I; Run in divisions; Broke slowly
3Nov86-5SA 1⅛Ⓣ:462 1:11 1:491fm *3 114 119¾ 105¾ 44 21¾ Stevens GL11 Aw30000 79-19 Hrms,RussinLogic,Cro'sHollywood 12
3Nov86—Wide 3/8 turn, into stretch
26Jly86♦7Lingfield(Eng) 2 3:31 gd*1-3 126 Ⓣ 17 EdderyP Sunset (Mdn) RussianLogic,FlamingDncer,Mricm 8
28Jun86♦7Newmarket(Eng) 1½ 2:372gd*7-5 112 Ⓣ 28 Hill S Nat FltmnAp (Mdn) Drkom,RussinLogic,WrmWelcome 14
Apr 12 SA tr.t 6f ft 1:163 h — Apr 7 SA tr.t 3f ft :362 h — Mar 5 SA tr.t 4f ft :494 h — Feb 28 SA tr.t 6f ft 1:161 h

D.

***Nilambar**
TORO F 117
Own.—Bollinger & Millhouse
Dk. b. or br. c. 4, by Shergar—Noureen, by Astec
Br.—H H Aga Khan (Ire)
Tr.—Vienna Darrell
Lifetime 9 2 2 2 $7,681
1986 7 2 1 2 $5,986
1985 2 M 1 0 $1,695
Turf 9 2 2 2 $7,681

11Aug86 ♦5Windsor(Eng) a1¼ 2:093gd *1-2 135 Ⓣ 35 Cauthen S Skyport Boon Point, Prince Orac, Nilambar 9
17Aug86 ♦3Goodwood(Eng) 1¼ 2:062fm 8 117 Ⓣ 45½ ThomsonB Extel H Chinoiserie,SwetMovr,ClstilStorm 13
21Jly86 ♦6Windsor(Eng) a1¼ 2:08 gd *1-5 132 Ⓣ 112 Cauthen S July Nilambar, Benarosa, ShajarAdDurr 6
14Jly86 ♦6Windsor(Eng) a1¼ 2:052gd 5½ 118 Ⓣ 11 Cauthen S Southlea Nilambar,Chinoiserie,GalacticHero 13
5Jly86 ♦2Nottingham(Eng) 150 1:433fm *1 126 Ⓣ 32½ SbrWR Ntnghm Ev Pst BrightAsNight, Waajib, Nilambar 8
16Jun86 ♦5Windsor(Eng) a1¼ 2:034gd 3 123 Ⓣ 22 CuthenS Bourne End Esdale, Nilambar, Arrow of Light 10
31May86 ♦1Newmarket(Eng) 1 1:382gd 7 126 Ⓣ 68½ CthnS HlstnDiatPls(Mdn) Farajullah, WalkOnAir,Flashdance 29
31May86—Lacked room
9Oct85 ♦4York(Eng) 1 1:45 gd 2½ 126 Ⓣ 22 Cauthen S York NorthVerdict,Nilambar,Miltescens 10
7Sep85 ♦3Kempton(Eng) 7f 1:251gd 5 123 Ⓣ 813 Mercer J Chrtsy Lck Shahaab, GalacticHero, Fanaan 20
Apr 12 SA Ⓣ 6f fm 1:133 h (d) Apr 6 SA Ⓣ 6f fm 1:152 h (d) Mar 31 SA tr.t 6f ft 1:162 h Mar 16 SA 4f ft :492 h

E.

De Soto
SIBILLE R 117
Own.—Oak Cliff Stable
Dk. b. or br. h. 5, by Riverman—Kankam, by Minera II
Br.—Oak Cliff Thoroughbreds Ltd (Ky)
Tr.—Gosden John H M
Lifetime 9 0 4 1 $20,405
1987 1 M 1 0 $6,200
1986 5 M 2 0 $7,506
Turf 9 0 4 1 $20,405

Entered 17Apr87- 5 SA
3Apr87-8SA 1⅛Ⓣ:473 1:122 1:493fm *8-5 117 64½ 62¼ 44 21¼ Pincay L Jr 1 Aw31000 78-21 Nurely, De Soto, Surprise Call 7
3Apr87—Off slowly
25Sep86 ♦7MLaffitte(Fra) a1⅛ 1:55 yl 4½ 118 Ⓣ 44½ Lee C Px Carteret BlueTip, Pylades, Donato 9
11Jly86 ♦6Evry(Fra) a1 5/16 2:162gd 3½ 120 Ⓣ 56 Lee C Kmptn Prk ExclusvGm,ChldrnsCornr,FbulosPrl 7
3Jly86 ♦6Evry(Fra) a1¼ 2:034gd *9-5 124 Ⓣ 2hd Lee C PxAthisCars CityFortress,DeSoto,SuddnInstinct 8
18Jun86 ♦7MLaffitte(Fra) a1¼ 2:054gd 5 118 Ⓣ 22 Lee C Px Radjah RoyalCndle,DeSoto,MPetiteCherie 11
10Apr86 ♦3Evry(Fra) a1⅛ 1:54 sf 4½ 120 Ⓣ 310 LequuxA Px d Savigny ChildrenCorner,Temoignge,Abetos 10
1Jly85 ♦7StCloud(Fra) a1 5/16 2:112gd *4-5 121 Ⓣ 31¾ LequuxA Px Negofol Montesano,PinkCarnation,DeSoto 13
16Jun85 ♦4Chantilly(Fra) a1½ 2:34 gd 17 121 Ⓣ 41 CuthenS Px du Lys(Gr3) Iades, Saint Estephe,FrenchSchool 7
19May85 ♦1Longchamp(Fra) a1⅜ 2:253sf 4 123 Ⓣ 21 DbrcG PxdLevenns(Mdn) Antheus, DeSoto, Tilt 6
● Mar 29 Hol 6f ft 1:134 h Mar 23 Hol 7f gd 1:283 h Mar 16 Hol 5f ft 1:011 h Mar 10 Hol 1 ft 1:413 h

F.

***Mashhur**
MCHARGUE D G 117
Own.—Freed R
B. g. 4, by Homing—Salsafy, by Tudor Melody
Br.—Waverton Stud Ltd (Eng)
Tr.—Wilmot William B
Lifetime 13 2 1 1 $7,520
1987 2 0 0 0
1986 5 0 0 0
Turf 12 2 1 1 $7,520

26Feb87-5SA 1 1/16 :452 1:102 1:44 ft 63 115 916 914 912 717¾ Black C A3 25000 63-22 Cold, Exalted Bubble, Julie'sMark 10
13Feb87-5SA 1⅛Ⓣ:472 1:133 1:523gd 76 117 1114 106 1119 1129 Castanon AL7 Aw28000 35-36 Bananas, Noticiero, Star Ribot 12
24Oct86 ♦6Doncaster(Eng) 1 1:422gd 20 133 Ⓣ 53 EddryPA Armthrp H WelshMedley,CndinGuest,BllBnus 17
8Sep86 ♦7Nottingham(Eng) 150 1:411fm 12 133 Ⓣ 12 EdderyPA Sterope H CntryGntlmn,Bckrmn,GvngItAllAy 18
5Jly86 ♦1Nottingham(Eng) 1 1:441fm 4 128 Ⓣ 52¼ HwN Ldbrks Gv Yu Mor H Mileometer, Valrach, RafiaRun 16
31May86 ♦2Newmarket(Eng) 1¼ 2:051gd 8 117 Ⓣ 59½ EddrPA Hlstn Exp Lgr H MoonMadness, Janiski, Andartis 8
7May86 ♦6Chester(Eng) a7½f 1:384gd 8 124 Ⓣ 624 SnbrnWR Roodeye Night Out Perhaps, Knyf, Haber 8
1Oct85 ♦6Nottingham(Eng) 1 1:41 fm 6 133 Ⓣ 11 Mercer J Fostn Nsy H Mashhur, G G Magic,KerryMaySing 8
Apr 11 SA 6f ft 1:143 h Apr 4 SA 5f ft 1:011 h Mar 28 SA 4f ft :492 h Mar 11 SA 5f ft 1:004 h

G.

Dhaleem
R Q MEZA 117
Own.—Six-S Racing Stable
B. c. 4, by Lyphard—Patia, by Don
Br.—de Chambure-Ouaki Est-Ades (Ky)
Tr.—Velasquez Danny
Lifetime 7 1 1 0 $10,369
1987 4 0 1 0 $6,500
1986 3 1 0 0 $3,869
Turf 5 1 1 0 $9,669

Entered 17Apr87- 5 SA
9Apr87-5SA a6½f Ⓣ:213 :434 1:142fm 7 118 89¾ 812 810 75¼ Meza R Q8 Aw29000 82-09 Rinnegato, Recognized, Mondanite 9
17Mar87-7SA 1 1/16 :46 1:102 1:423ft 7½ 117 89½ 98¾ 813 818¼ Meza R Q4 Aw31000 70-16 PrinceO'Fire,It'sNotMyJob,Athlone 9
22Feb87-5SA 1¼Ⓣ:464 1:36 2:013fm 7¼ 115 78½ 42½ 33½ 22½ Meza R Q2 Aw29000 77-22 Neferou, Dhaleem, Unencumbered 10
22Feb87—Off slowly
5Feb87-5SA 1 1/16 :462 1:11 1:434ft 35 116 1011 95¾ 86 68¼ Meza R Q12 Aw28000 74-22 Centenary, Trump Up, Sun Man 12
5Feb87—Awarded fifth purse money; Off very slowly
18Oct86 ♦1Newmarket(Eng) 1¼ 2:114gd 12 114 Ⓣ 45½ GlsMA Mace-WrthAprH BenAdhem,Nicoridge,PowerBendr 16
5Sep86 ♦1Kempton(Eng) 1 1:383gd 3½ 121 Ⓣ 511 SnbrWR GfryHmlynH Nordica, Turfah, Paris Turf 10
11Aug86 ♦4Newcastle(Eng) 1 1:444gd 5 120 Ⓣ 1½ SbrWR Grnhead(Mdn) Dhaleem, Docksider, Rivart 18
Apr 4 SA 6f ft 1:162 h Mar 29 SA 5f ft 1:014 h Mar 11 SA 6f ft 1:15 h Mar 3 SA 6f ft 1:132 h

6. Speed figures or pace ratings can separate the four sprinters below. The eligibility conditions provide a telling clue as well. Which horse figures both ways?

7th Arlington

7 FURLONGS / ARLINGTON PARK / START / FINISH

7 FURLONGS. (1.20⅖) ALLOWANCE. Purse $16,000. 3-year-olds and upward which have not won a race in 1987 other than maiden, claiming or starter. Weight, 3-year-olds, 117 lbs.; older, 121 lbs. Non-winners of $9,600 twice in 1986-87 allowed 3 lbs.; $7,200 since May 23, 6 lbs.; $9,000 since August 18, 9 lbs. (Races where entered for $40,000 or less not considered in allowances.)

A.

Gemini Dreamer — Dk. b. or br. h. 7, by Great Above—Luna Moon, by Cool Moon
Own.—Van Berg J C & McKinnon J **115** Br.—Lasater Farm (Fla) Tr.—Van Berg Jack C
Lifetime 86 10 27 23 $392,085
1987 7 0 0 3 $15,260
1986 16 2 8 2 $56,423
Turf 20 2 3 5 $102,362

18Jun87-8AP	7f	:23	:46^1	1:23^{1}ft	*3-2	112	1½	2^{hd}	2½	31½	Day P 5	Aw18000	84-23	TheRoylFreeze,TunerJr.,GminiDrmr	5
1May87-8GC	6f	:21^4	:44^4	1:09 ft	19	115	43½	46	56½	48	CastanedaM 2	Aw22000	86-18	SntRosPrinc,HghHook,Ed'sExclusv	6
8Apr87-7GG	1$\frac{1}{16}$Ⓣ	:46^3	1:10^4	1:42^{1}fm	29	116	1^{hd}	3½	77½	8^{13}	Maple S 8	Aw24000	78-09	CleverSong,CalvryChrge,PirOfAces	8
19Mar87-8GG	1 Ⓣ	:46^3	1:10^4	1:36 fm	16	115	3^4	3^2	4^2	4^2	SchvnvldtCP 3	Aw24000	85-13	PairOfAces,ShowDncer,PerfecTrvel	6
18Feb87-8GG	6f	:22^2	:45^1	1:10 ft	9¾	117	41¼	3^1	3^3	33½	Maple S 3	Aw22000	85-20	CriJillHjji,DysSurpssed,GminiDrmr	5
17Jan87-6BM	6f	:22^3	:45^4	1:10^{2}ft	3½	115	3^2	41¾	4^5	67½	Maple S 4	Aw20000	79-19	Verboten, CariJillHajji,AllTheBucks	8
9Jan87-8SA	6½f	:21^1	:44^3	1:18 sl	45	114	8^{11}	88½	47½	38¼	Baze G 6	Aw45000	72-26	Innmorto,ProudestHour,GminiDrmr	8
21Dec86-5Hol	6f	:22^1	:45^2	1:10^{3}ft	4¾	115	5^5	54½	5^5	5^7	Stevens G L 6	Aw35000	83-15	MFvrtMmnt,McLndn,AmrcnStndrd	6
28Sep86-9TP	6½f	:23^1	:46	1:17^{1}ft	3	119	31½	2^1	21½	41¼	Smith M E 2	Marfa H	91-18	BroadwayWilly,McShne,InstntRuler	5
28Aug86-7AP	6½f	:22^2	:45^2	1:16^{2}ft	6	118	44½	63¼	4^2	33½	Fires E 2	Aw18000	89-19	Clestog,TheRoylFreeze,GeminiDrmr	7

B.

Shoe Danzig — B. c. 4, by Danzig—Love Jenny, by Tell
Own.—Sub-Par Stable **119** Br.—Jones W L Jr & Farish W S (Ky) Tr.—Mott William I
Lifetime 11 4 2 1 $40,910
1987 6 1 2 1 $17,400
1986 5 3 0 0 $23,510

22Jly87-6AP	6f	:22^3	:45^4	1:10 ft	4½	116	4^2	3^2	2^{hd}	12¼	Smith M E^3	50000	90-18	Shoe Danzig, Calestoga, Tyrantson	6
5Jly87-8AP	6f	:22^4	:46^3	1:11^{1}sy	4¼	116	44½	4^4	2^3	2^6	Smith M E^3	50000	78-23	Calestoga, Shoe Danzig, Tyrantson	6
15Jun87-7AP	6f	:22^4	:46^3	1:11^{3}ft	9¾	115	6^4	66½	6^8	57¾	Frazier R L^8	Aw16000	74-29	Battle Cat, Don Sanders, All Lines	8
23May87-8CD	7f	:23^2	:46^2	1:23^{3}ft	*2¼	114	3^2	1½	1^{hd}	2^{hd}	Hawley S^2	Aw23000	88-18	Varennes,ShoeDanzig,BurglarAlarm	7
12May87-8CD	7f	:22^3	:45^4	1:24^{2}ft	3½	114	53½	32½	22½	72½	Melancon L^{10}	Aw21700	81-19	BidMade,DonSnders,RidgeReview	11
14Apr87-8Kee	6f	:23	:46^1	1:11^{2}ft	2½	112	57½	53¾	44½	35¼	Melancon L^3	Aw19200	80-31	BonjourTristesse,T.V.Brg,ShoDnzig	7
28Apr86-7CD	6f	:21^1	:44^3	1:10^{3}ft	*1-2	115	31½	11½	1^2	1no	Melancon L^5	Aw14800	92-15	ShoeDnzig,BlueDerby,Allison'eMte	8
10Apr86-9OP	6f	:22	:45^1	1:10 ft	2	118	41¼	3^{nk}	1½	13½	Snyder L^4	Aw14000	90-19	ShoeDanzig,He'sCrazy,ExtrControl	7
10Apr86—Four wide															
29Mar86-6OP	1	:46^4	1:11^3	1:38^{1}ft	*8-5	117	4^5	21½	43½	46½	Bailey J D^6	Aw14500	74-16	OurLine,NativeLines,SociallyRotten	9
6Mar86-3FG	6f	:22^2	:46	1:11^{1}ft	*8-5	119	3^3	22½	2^{hd}	1½	Ardoin R^2	Mdn	89-20	Shoe Danzig, Delayer,DoubleQuest	10

Jly 3 AP 4f ft :48 b   Jun 10 AP 4f ft :47^4 b

C.

All Lines — B. c. 4, by Lines of Power—Half Cancealed, by Cyane
Own.—Partee W C **112** Br.—Jones Bereton C (Ky) Tr.—Whiting Lynn
Lifetime 5 3 1 1 $31,288
1987 2 0 1 1 $5,160
1986 3 3 0 0 $26,128

28Jun87-7AP	6½f	:22^4	:45^2	1:17^{2}ft	*2-3	112	12½	1^3	2^{hd}	23½	Day P 4	Aw17000	84-23	BttleCt,AllLines,WhitesburgShdow	6
15Jun87-7AP	6f	:22^4	:46^3	1:11^{3}ft	*3-5	115	2^1	22½	22½	3^{nk}	Day P^5	Aw16000	82-29	Battle Cat, Don Sanders, All Lines	8
3Jun86-8CD	6½f	:22^3	:46^1	1:17 ft	*2-5	118	53¾	42½	2^{hd}	1^3	Day P^6	Aw15620	95-20	All Lines, Trobio, Grub	7
29Apr86-7CD	6f	:21^3	:44^4	1:09^{3}ft	*1	118	2^{hd}	1½	1^2	1^4	Melancon L^8	Aw13500	97-13	All Lines, Grub, Fuzzy Bear	8
29Mar86-2OP	6f	:21^3	:45^1	1:10^{3}ft	8½	122	11½	1½	11½	1^2	Melancon L^{10}	Mdn	87-16	AllLines,BuffloBeu,SomeAreHonst	11

Jly 23 AP 6f ft 1:16 b   Jly 18 AP 4f ft :48^3 b   Jun 25 AP 4f ft :49 b   Jun 11 AP 4f ft :50 b

D.

Calestoga ✻ — B. g. 5, by Relaunch—Vitelle, by Montparnasse II
Own.—N &MBoyceRacingStableetal **119** Br.—Rowan & Lavin (Cal) Tr.—Boyce Neil
Lifetime 25 10 7 2 $209,196
1987 3 1 2 0 $12,600
1986 4 2 1 0 $25,400
Turf 2 0 0 0 $912

22Jly87-6AP	6f	:22^3	:45^4	1:10 ft	*2-5	120	2^{hd}	2½	3^{nk}	22¼	Clark K D^2	50000	88-18	Shoe Danzig, Calestoga, Tyrantson	6
5Jly87-8AP	6f	:22^4	:46^3	1:11^{1}sy	*3-5	116	1^1	1^2	1^3	1^6	Clark K D^2	50000	84-23	Calestoga, Shoe Danzig, Tyrantson	6
12Jun87-6AP	6f	:22^2	:45^2	1:10^{3}ft	*6-5	117	2^{hd}	1^{hd}	2^{hd}	2½	Clark K D^4	27500	86-22	Brandy Cutlass, Calestoga, Sa Got	7
28Aug86-7AP	6½f	:22^2	:45^2	1:16^{2}ft	*4-5	118	1½	11½	11½	13½	Day P^3	Aw18000	93-19	Clestog,TheRoylFreeze,GeminiDrmr	7

21Aug86-5AP 6½f :23 :46^2 1:17^{1}ft *4-5 112 2½ 3^{1½} 3^{1½} 2^{1¼} ShoemkerW^3 Aw19000 88-17 Barbery, Calestoga, BroadwayWilly 6
21Aug86—Altered course midstretch
30Jly86-8Haw 6f :22^2 :45^4 1:10 ft *2-3 114 1^{hd} 1^{hd} 1^1 1^2 Day P^5 Aw17000 91-13 Calestoga, Coffer Dam,AllSincerity 6
13Jly86-6Haw 6½f :22^4 :45^3 1:17 ft *4-5 114 1^{hd} 1^{hd} 4^2 5^{8¼} Louviere GP^1 Aw23000 80-22 BobbyBn,WhtsbrgShdow,AwsomAx 8
3Nov85-7Haw 6½f :22^2 :45^2 1:15^{3}ft *3-5 117 1½ 1^{1½} 1^4 1^{9½} HansenRD^8 Oil Capt H 95-16 Calestoga,GallntLibby,SpnishDevil 10
5Oct85-9Haw 1$\frac{3}{16}$ Ⓣ:48^{1}1:14^{1}2:00^{1}yl 10 120 1½ 3^1 8^{15} 8^{31} Silva C H^3 Haw Dby 40-29 DerbyWish,DyShift,ExplosiveDrling 8
23Sep85-8Haw 1$\frac{1}{16}$:47^2 1:11^3 1:45^{3}sy 5¾ 116 1^1 1^2 1^2 1^4 Brumfield D^4 HcpO 70-30 Calestoga, Magloire, Tajawa 6
Jly 18 AP 6f ft 1:14^3 b ● Jun 30 AP 6f sl 1:12^2 h Jun 24 AP 5f ft 1:00^2 h Jun 7 AP 6f ft 1:14^3 b

7. If the class-distance pars are 45⅕ and 1:17⅖, which horse is a stickout?

2nd Santa Anita

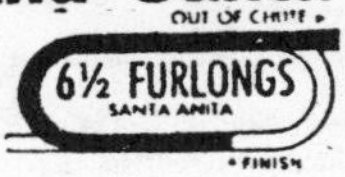

6 ½ FURLONGS. (1.14) CLAIMING. Purse $13,000. 4-year-olds and upward. Weight, 121 lbs. Non-winners of two races since December 25 allowed 3 lbs.; of a race since then, 5 lbs. Claiming price $10,000. (Races when entered for $8,500 or less not considered.)

A.

Visible Asset — **B. g. 5, by Majestic Light—Promised Woman, by Promised Land**
BLACK C A 116 **Br.—Gentry T (Ky)** 1987 3 0 0 0
Tr.—Mulhall Richard W $10,000 1986 12 3 0 1 $20,235
Own.—Rancho Rio Hondo Lifetime 25 3 0 3 $24,855
19Feb87-9SA 1 :46^3 1:11^3 1:37^{1}ft 16 115 8^{6¼} 7^{6½} 6^{7½} 6^{5¼} Black C A^8 10000 77-13 SwiftMessg,QuickSwp,CptinDoubl 10
21Jan87-9SA 1$\frac{1}{16}$:47 1:12^2 1:45 ft 9½ 115 1½ 3^1 10^{15}11^{18½} Black C A^5 10000 57-19 SonOfRaja,InNaturlForm,Booster 11
1Jan87-9SA 1$\frac{1}{16}$:47^1 1:12 1:44^{3}ft 27 116 4^2 10^{11}10^{14}10^{20¾} Black C A^4 16000 57-19 RoosvltRod,ForgotThRng,Espontn 10
16Oct86-1SA 1 :46^1 1:11^3 1:38^{1}ft 9¾ 1115 1^{2½} 1^2 1^{3½} 1^{4½} Black C A^2 10000 77-19 VisibleAsset,BombyBrtndr,BstLdr 10
8Oct86-1SA 1$\frac{1}{16}$:46^1 1:11^4 1:44^{3}ft 5 1115 2½ 1^{hd} 3^{2½} 5^8 Black C A^1 10000 70-20 I'll Smoke, Oh Dad, Hachi 12
22Sep86-13Pom 1$\frac{1}{16}$:46^1 1:11^2 1:44^{3}ft *9-5 1175 3^{2½} 2^{1½} 2^3 3^{1¼} Black C A^7 8500 87-19 ScheerBob,Orn'sBllrd,VisibleAsset 10
13Sep86-9Pom 1$\frac{1}{16}$:46^2 1:11^2 1:44^{3}ft 4 1105 2^{hd} 1^{hd} 1^1 1^{2½} Black C A^6 8500 88-10 VisblAsst,Swpround,ClsscEndvour 10
21Aug86-9Dmr 1⅛ :46 1:10^2 1:50^{3}ft 46 116 1^2 2^{hd} 3^1 6^{5½} Kaenel J L^1 10000 71-17 TheWaliOfSwt,WhidbeyTe,SonOfRj 9
28Jly86-9Dmr 1$\frac{1}{16}$:45^2 1:11^2 1:44^{1}ft 22 1115 1^{hd} 3½ 9^{12}10^{13} Black C A^5 10000 66-16 Police Pursuit, Le Carluret, Hachi 12
11Jly86-9LA 1$\frac{1}{16}$:45^3 1:10^4 1:43^{2}ft 29 1115 4^3 5^{3¾} 6^{10} 6^{16½} Black C A^2 Aw15000 75-14 Arcadius, Dubai Tornado, Fairfax 7
Mar 9 SA 5f ft 1:01^4 h Feb 28 SA 4f ft :47^2 h Feb 6 SA 5f ft :59^2 h Feb 1 SA 4f ft :48 h

B.

Running Debonair — **B. g. 5, by Debonair Roger—My Princess Rose, by Native Royalty**
PEDROZA M A 116 **Br.—Rogers J D (Cal)** 1987 3 0 0 0 $1,225
Tr.—Sena Peter E $10,000 1986 20 2 7 3 $25,070
Own.—Reynolds J H Lifetime 32 3 9 5 $44,070
19Feb87-9SA 1 :46^3 1:11^3 1:37^{1}ft 13 115 2½ 1^{hd} 2^{2½} 5^{4½} Fernandez A L^5 10000 77-13 SwiftMessg,QuickSwp,CptinDoubl 10
12Feb87-9SA 6½f :22 :44^3 1:17^{1}ft 38 116 8^{7½} 7^{11} 6^{7½} 4^{6¼} FernandezAL^3 Ⓢ 10000 78-20 Rodney,DistinctivlyDon,ToddyBoy 10
31Jan87-1SA 6½f :22 :44^4 1:17 ft 8 116 7^{6¼} 7^{9¼} 8^{17} — Fernandez A L^8 12500 — — Dodo's Land, Steamed,MostlyMack 8
31Jan87—Eased
9Nov86-4Hol 1 :45^1 1:10^4 1:37^{3}ft 28 116 3^{3½} 1½ 1^{1½} 2^{1½} Black C A^7 10000 74-16 Rob'sIntnt,RunningDbonir,Crimuri 11
24Oct86-1SA 7f :22^4 :45^4 1:25 ft 4½ 118 4^{2½} 4^3 5^{3½} 5^{5¼} FernandezAL^6 Ⓢ 10000 70-20 PrideOfTroy,CometsFlre,ShuttleOn 9
19Oct86-10AC 6f :22^3 :44^4 1:09 ft 3 1115 4^{4½} 4^{6½} 4^2 1^{nk} Delgadillo A^4 10000 94-13 RunningDbonir,RoundHIIII,Csy'sRy 9
28Sep86-9Pom 6½f :21^4 :45^2 1:17^{1}ft 9¾ 114 6^{4¼} 7^{4¾} 5^{3¾} 2^3 Fernandez A L^3 10500 91-09 Inqustv,RunnngDbonr,Cody'sChnc 10
23Sep86-9Pom 6f :22^1 :45^1 1:10^{4}ft 4¾ 116 6^{4¼} 4^8 5^6 4^{2¼} Castanon A L^2 10000 95-08 Dominant Roni, Melchip, Singlet 10
31Aug86-7AC 6f :21^4 :44 1:08^{2}ft 4¾ 1095 6^{2½} 6^{6¼} 3^3 3^{1¼} Gavica G P^1 10000 96-11 ShrpContrl,HllywdPrty,RnnngDbnr 6
24Aug86-9AC 6f :22^3 :44^2 1:09 ft 7-5 114 4^{1½} 5^{6½} 3^{2½} 2^2 Lopez A D^5 Aw5000 92-14 WingdPrinc,RunningDbonir,Artificr 6
Mar 5 SA tr.t 6f ft 1:15^3 h Feb 28 SA 5f ft 1:01^1 h Feb 7 SA 5f ft 1:00^4 h Jan 24 SA 6f ft 1:15^1 hg

C.

Valentia Island — **B. h. 5, by Sassafras—Flirt 'n' Skirt, by Elevation**
GOMEZ R 116 **Br.—Cashman E C (Fla)** 1986 2 M 0 0
Tr.—Ippolito Steve $10,000 1985 5 M 0 0 $2,700
Own.—Green Thumb Farm Stable Lifetime 7 0 0 0 $2,700
Entered 13Mar87- 6 SA
18Jun86-6Hol 1 :46 1:11^1 1:39 ft 13 120 11^{8¾}10^{9¾}10^{8¼}10^{6¾} Pedroza M A^2 M28000 61-15 SummersHitter,DoctorT.Ar,VllVrdi 12
30May86-2Hol 7f :22^4 :46^2 1:25^{3}ft 28 123 9^{6¼} 7^3 11^{8¾}11^{11¼} Pedroza M A^{11} M32000 65-24 Fletwing,JumpingJklin,NtivForcst 12
7Feb85-4SA 1$\frac{1}{16}$:46^4 1:12^1 1:45^{1}ft 4 118 10^{7½} 9^{7¾} 5^5 4^{5½} DelahoussyeE^8 M32000 69-17 Midnoon,Mt.AFortune,AlrtRspons 11
7Feb85—Drifted out drive
26Jan85-4SA 7f :22^3 :45^2 1:23^{1}ft 8½ 118 4^{3¼} 3^5 5^8 6^{14½} Delahoussaye E^7 Mdn 69-16 Bay Shore Drive,Witan,DinnerTable 7
26Jan85—Bumped at 1/8
20Jan85-6SA 1 :46 1:11 1:37^{1}ft 17 118 — — — — Toro F^2 Mdn — — Forty Share, Bonham, Go Swiftly 7
20Jan85—Lost rider; Stumbled start
13Jan85-6SA 1$\frac{1}{16}$:47^2 1:12^1 1:44^{4}ft 9 118 2^{hd} 3½ 6^{6½} 6^{15} Hawley S^3 Mdn 62-13 Gold Knight, Cosmotron, Dynamite 7
5Jan85-2SA 6f :21^2 :44^1 1:09^{4}ft 58 118 9^{8¼} 7^{9¼} 6^{8¼} 4^{7½} Delahoussaye E^1 Mdn 81-12 Kehi,SumExchnge,TimeOfTheFox 11
Mar 8 SA 4f gd :48^3 h Mar 3 SA 4f ft :48 h Feb 25 SA 6f gd 1:02^4 h (d) Feb 19 SA 6f ft 1:13 h

D.

Polly's Ruler *
PINCAY L JR **121**
Own.—Santa Barbara Stable
Ch. g. 8, by The Irish Lord—Miss Polly Bee, by Travelling Dust
Br.—Jo-Don Farms (Cal) **1987 4 2 0 2 $19,750**
Tr.—Vienna Darrell $10,000 1986 14 6 3 2 $36,502
Lifetime 46 13 13 5 $174,872 Turf 3 1 0 0 $20,600

4Mar87-2SA 6f :21² :44² 1:10²ft 2 119 1hd 1½ 12½ 12¾ Pincay L Jr³ Ⓢ 10000 86-16 Polly'sRuler,LikShntin,Cody'sChnc 9
14Feb87-2SA 6f :21² :44² 1:10³sy *2½ 118 22 24 23½ 35 Pincay L Jr⁶ 16000 80-17 Pialor, PineappleJack,Polly'sRuler 10
14Feb87—Fractious; lugged in
1Feb87-1SA 6f :22 :45¹ 1:11 ft *2½ 121 2½ 3nk 21½ 31¾ Kaenel J L³ Ⓢ c12500 81-16 Don's Co'op, Rodney, Polly's Ruler 8
1Feb87—Bumped start; steadied at 5/8; lugged in
4Jan87-3SA 6f :22 :45¹ 1:10³sy *6-5 116 11 1½ 11½ 1no Kaenel J L¹ 16000 85-22 Polly'sRuler,NeutralPlyer,Grenoble 8
21Dec86-1Hol 6f :22² :46¹ 1:11¹ft 3 117 11 1hd 1½ 21¾ Kaenel J L⁷ 20000 86-15 SndDigger,Polly'sRuler,Andrew'NM 8
21Dec86—Broke in, bumped
6Dec86-5Hol 6f :21⁴ :45² 1:11¹gd *6-5 119 2½ 2hd 11½ 12½ Kaenel J L⁴ Ⓢ 10000 87-16 Polly'sRuler,PhilipNoln,UpThePole 8
6Dec86—Lugged in stretch
15Nov86-1Hol 6f :22³ :46 1:10⁴ft 2½ 119 11 11½ 12½ 14 Kaenel J L¹ Ⓢ 12500 89-14 Polly'sRulr,SolidSpirit,InNturlForm 6
15Nov86—Lugged in late
3Nov86-1SA 6f :21³ :44⁴ 1:11 ft 17 116 33 34 33 4½ Kaenel J L⁷ Ⓢ 12500 82-14 HachalaTachl,Melchip,ShuttleOne 10
3Nov86—Lugged in stretch
27Sep86-9Tdn 6f :22² :46¹ 1:12²m *8-5 116 11 1½ 1½ 2nk Placke D⁴ 11500 82-28 NightRover,Polly'sRuler,ThKyoKid 6
14Sep86-6Tdn 6f :22² :45⁴ 1:11⁴ft *2½ 122 11½ 11½ 11½ 11 Placke D⁷ 8500 85-25 Polly'sRuler,Crossbrek,NightRovr 10

E.

Air Pirate
DELAHOUSSAYE E **116**
Own.—Hutchins & Moulton
B. g. 4, by Pirate's Bounty—Princess Babu, by Our Babu
Br.—Windy Hill TBA (Cal) **1987 3 0 0 1 $4,200**
Tr.—Stidham Michael $10,000 1986 14 2 0 1 $36,950
Lifetime 18 3 0 2 $47,750 Turf 1 0 0 0

4Mar87-1SA 6f :21² :44³ 1:10²ft 4 117 1111 910 76½ 45¼ DelhoussyeE⁴ Ⓢ 10000 81-16 Dusty Trader,Bride'sAdvice,YaDig 11
4Mar87—Bumped start
1Feb87-1SA 6f :22 :45¹ 1:11 ft 4½ 112⁵ 65½ 64¼ 43½ 42¼ Patton D B² Ⓢ c12500 81-16 Don's Co'op, Rodney, Polly's Ruler 8
1Feb87—Rough start
17Jan87-1SA 6f :22 :45⁴ 1:12 ft 15 110⁵ 95¾ 55 41½ 33 Patton D B⁵ 16000 75-18 West Boy II, Unagloshi, AirPirate 12
17Jan87—Bumped start

F.

Baby Duke
MEZA R Q **116**
Own.—Sanders G & Cherie
B. g. 4, by Branford Court—My Lady Envoy, by Envoy
Br.—Specht Mr-Mrs T A (Cal) **1987 1 0 0 0**
Tr.—Mitchell Mike $10,000 1986 10 1 3 0 $13,525
Lifetime 11 1 3 0 $13,525

4Mar87-1SA 6f :21² :44³ 1:10²ft 6½ 117 1hd 1½ 2hd 99 Pincay L Jr⁸ Ⓢ 10000 77-16 Dusty Trader,Bride'sAdvice,YaDig 11
11Jly86-6LA 6½f:22³ :46¹ 1:17³ft *8-5 116 1hd 1hd 3nk 48½ Sibille R⁵ 12500 81-14 ActiveRomn,SummrPlyboy,RivrCod 6
24Jun86-10Pln 6f :22 :46 1:11³ft 4½ 109⁵ 2½ 2hd 2½ 2no Yamamoto T J⁸ 12500 84-11 SoonToEscape,BabyDuke,DonThlini 9
11Jun86-7GG 6f :22¹ :45 1:09³ft 7½ 114 45 32 21½ 45½ Baze R A¹⁰ 16000 85-10 NevrSyDino,SpcilFirwy,Mostccioli 12
30May86-1Hol 7f :22² :45³ 1:26 ft 5½ 116 2½ 22½ 21½ 45½ McCarron C J⁷ 16000 69-24 RidgeFlite,TeeC'sLd,LittlRockHigh 7
30May86—Veered out sharply start; lugged in late
15Apr86-1GG 6f :22² :46¹ 1:12 gd *3-2 114 1hd 2hd 33½ 611½ Diaz A L⁵ 16000 67-25 FlagOfTruce,DrkMence,LittleMhers 7
4Apr86-6GG 6f :22 :45² 1:11⁴ft 2½ 114 2hd 2½ 65½ 611 Diaz A L³ Aw17000 69-27 TrojnTrick,Monty'sPrinc,Cmll'sBoy 7
7Mar86-4GG 6f :22¹ :45² 1:11⁴sy *9-5 114 1hd 2hd 1hd 45½ Diaz A L² Aw16000 77-21 SpdyShnnon,ClpprSkppr,DplmtcRlr 6
21Feb86-6GG 6f :22³ :45³ 1:10⁴m 3½ 114 1½ 1hd 2hd 22 Diaz A L² Aw16000 85-18 The Fitest, Baby Duke, FleetAlbert 6
14Feb86-4GG 6f :22 :45 1:10⁴sy *2½ 118 11 12 14 19 Diaz A L⁵ M16000 85-33 BbyDuke,EsyKindLove,BrndyTruffl 9
Mar 1 SA 4f ft :47¹ hg Feb 24 SA tr.t 5f gd 1:01⁴ h Feb 18 SA 5f ft :59² h Feb 9 SA 5f ft 1:00⁴ h

G.

Bold Batter Up
DOUGLAS R R **116**
Own.—A F Hopkins Estate
Ch. h. 6, by Mr Bold Batter—Dress Me Up's Girl, by Aczay
Br.—Hopkins A F (Cal) **1987 4 0 0 1 $1,650**
Tr.—Sinne Gerald M $10,000 1986 4 0 0 0
Lifetime 35 4 5 5 $89,400 Turf 2 0 0 0 $1,500

25Feb87-9SA 1 1/16 :46⁴ 1:11 1:43⁴m 26 116 22½ 47½ 717 723 Kaenel J L⁶ 12500 59-22 Shuttle One, Nathan, Navegante 8
16Feb87-9GG 1 :46² 1:10⁴ 1:37 ft 17 116 43 31½ 3nk 33½ Gonzalez R M⁵ 12500 79-17 OurNordic,BennettPek,BoldBttrUp 7
7Feb87-9SA 1 1/16 :46 1:10³ 1:43³ft 25 111⁵ 78½ 99¾ 811 815½ Cox D W⁶ 16000 68-14 Fracoza, Restage, Tiffani's Toy 9
1Feb87-7BM 6f :22³ :46 1:10⁴ft 29 115 89½ 811 813 810 White T C¹ 20000 75-25 Cool'nScandlous,AckAck'sJoy,Sptil 8
26May86-1Hol 1⅛ :47¹ 1:11³ 1:50 ft 48 116 42½ 44 57½ 67¾ Higuera A R⁵ 40000 79-17 Item Two, Restage, Bemidgi 7
18May86-9Hol 1 :45 1:10² 1:36 ft 22 116 87¾ 65½ 87½ 78½ Patterson A¹² 32000 75-08 KnightSkiing,RightOnRed,Elefnte 12
18May86—Wide final 3/8
21Apr86-7SA 6f :21¹ :44¹ 1:10 ft 7¾ 116 65½ 56 77 76½ Kaenel J L⁶ 40000 81-16 Mmmy'sPlsr,EllsBrvstSng,BldNnts 8
21Apr86—Hit gate start
13Apr86-3SA 6½f:21⁴ :44⁴ 1:16⁴ft 22 116 107¾ 117¾ 95¼ 64½ Ortega L E¹² 32000 82-15 Paskanell, Count Geiger, ‡Timlin 12
13Apr86—Veered in; bumped at start, 5-wide into stretch
21Apr85-5SA a6½f Ⓣ:21² :43⁴ 1:15 fm 14 114 12¹³ 12¹⁵ 11¹³ 11¹⁰½ Hawley S² 45000 73-14 PttrnMtch,GoldnSovnr,RckDncrII 12
4Apr85-9SA 1 1/16 :46¹ 1:10³ 1:43³ft 6 118 714 714 67¾ 24 DelahoussayeE⁵ 32000 79-15 EsyMover,BoldBtterUp,IrishS'getti 7
4Apr85—Lugged in stretch
Jan 27 SA 4f ft :49¹ h Jan 21 SA 5f ft 1:03³ h

H.

Be Thankful
B. g. 5, by Messenger of Song—Romethee, by Promethee
SIBILLIE R **116** **Br.—Delaney N H (Cal)** **1987 4 0 1 0 $3,750**
Own.—Delaney Jane M **Tr.—Needham Lloyd** **$10,000** **1986 14 1 1 1 $11,975**
Lifetime 33 2 2 4 $30,200

20Feb87-1SA 6f :213 :45 1:11 ft 18 116 85¾ 85½ 76 43¼ Kaenel J L5 Ⓢ 12500 80-16 Don's Tryst, Saro Star, NanteTam 11
20Feb87—Wide final 3/8
1Feb87-1SA 6f :22 :451 1:11 ft 12 116 52½ 53¼ 66½ 66¾ Sibille R7 Ⓢ 12500 77-16 Don's Co'op, Rodney, Polly's Ruler 8
19Jan87-2SA 6f :221 :454 1:121ft 13 116 3nk 42 43 21¾ Kaenel J L8 Ⓢ 10000 75-25 Cody'sChnce,BThnkful,Don'sCo'op 8
19Jan87—Wide final 3/8
2Jan87-1SA 6½f :221 :451 1:174ft 18 116 21½ 45½ 47½ 510 Sibille R9 10000 71-22 GallantChairman,OhDd,WithSpirit 12
20Dec86-7Hol 6f :22 :45 1:103ft 10 117 54½ 58 57 46½ Stevens S A7 10000 83-15 PhilipNoln,GllntChirmn,Dodo'sLnd 9
23Nov86-2Hol 6f :221 :454 1:11 ft 14 116 54¾ 64½ 64 54¼ Sibille R1 12500 84-12 HurricaneHec,StrsAtNoon,Melchip 8
23Nov86—Broke out, bumped; steadied 1/8
3Nov86-1SA 6f :213 :444 1:11 ft 10 116 89½ 78½ 78 84¾ Sibille R6 Ⓢ 12500 78-14 HachalaTachl,Melchip,ShuttleOne 10
3Nov86—Wide final 3/8
12Oct86-1SA 6½f :22 :452 1:174ft 26 116 62 64½ 99 1110¼ Doocy T T11 16000 71-21 Unagloshi,Menswear,StrOfAmeric 12
1Oct86-1SA 6f :214 :45 1:104ft 16 116 42½ 22½ 22½ 33¾ Sibille R12 12500 80-18 Unagloshi, Jacart, Be Thankful 12
8Sep86-2Dmr 6f :214 :454 1:10 ft 8¾ 117 2½ 1½ 2½ 2nk Kaenel J L4 Ⓢ 12500 88-14 StrOfAmeric,BeThnkful,DollrTrppr 7
Feb 14 GD tr.t 5f ft :592 h ●Jan 16 GD tr.t 4f ft :481 h

I.

Parlapiano
Ch. h. 6, by Out of the East—Sister Mel, by Pellinore
Br.—Dante T C (Cal) **1987 1 0 0 0**
ORTEGA L E **116** **Tr.—King Hal** **$10,000** **1986 25 2 6 2 $35,770**
Own.—Hanna B **Lifetime 63 10 12 8 $109,713** **Turf 3 1 1 0 $8,780**

4Mar87-2SA 6f :212 :442 1:102ft 13 115 913 99¼ 99¾ 75¼ Ortega L E 1 Ⓢ 10000 81-16 Polly'sRuler,LikShntin,Cody'sChnc 9
20Dec86-3Hol 1 :453 1:102 1:364ft 3½ 117 56½ 57 36 37¼ Pincay L Jr 2 12500 72-15 Son Of Raja, Melchip, Parlapiano 7
20Dec86—Awarded second purse money
13Dec86-2Hol 7f :22 :451 1:233ft 4¾ 117 98½ 96½ 33 22¾ Pincay L Jr 1 10000 83-09 Cordon, Parlapiano, Ancient Blue 12
13Dec86—Drifted in, bumped 1/16
30Nov86-2Hol 7f :222 :454 1:253ft 4½ 117 108¾108½ 74¾ 52¼ DelahoussayeE 8 10000 74-16 Gulfstremer,PinppleJck,UpThPol 12
30Nov86—Broke in, bumped
3Nov86-1SA 6f :213 :444 1:11 ft 8¾ 116 913 814 89¼ 74¼ Guerra W A 2 Ⓢ 12500 78-14 HachalaTachl,Melchip,ShuttleOne 10
12Oct86-1SA 6½f :22 :452 1:174ft 13 116 116¾1119¼1110109¼ Hawley S 3 16000 71-21 Unagloshi,Menswear,StrOfAmeric 12
12Oct86—Bumped start
1Oct86-9SA 1$\frac{1}{16}$:461 1:11 1:443ft 6 116 58½ 78½ 79 78¾ Ortega L E 4 16000 69-18 PlntyConscous,CptnDoubl,ARghtId 8
16Sep86-8Pom 6½f :22 :45 1:153ft 9½ 116 99¾ 912 811 29 Ortega L E 10 16000 93-05 CoursingEgl,Prlpno,PrcousBmbno 10
15Aug86-1Dmr 6f :22 :451 1:10 ft 9½ 116 67¾ 78¾ 66 43¾ DelahoussayeE 1 20000 84-12 Philosopher,Reinbow'sCup,DeltTrc 7
31Jly86-3Dmr 6f :22 :452 1:094ft 8½ 118 85½ 84¾ 67½ 45½ Ortega L E 8 Ⓢ c16000 83-12 Rodney, Grenoble, Go Go Debonair 8
31Jly86—Bumped hard start; wide final 3/8
Mar 1 SA 5f ft 1:024 h Feb 23 SA 4f ft :522 h Feb 18 SA 5f ft 1:003 h

8. Which horse is most likely to take the early lead?

4 BELMONT 7 FURLONGS BELMONT PARK

7 FURLONGS. (1.20⅘) CLAIMING. Purse $19,000. 4-year-olds and upward. Weight, 122 lbs. Non-winners of two races since July 15 allowed 3 lbs. Of a race since then 5 lbs. Claming price $35,000; for each $2,500 to $30,000, 2 lbs. (Races when entered to be claimed for $25,000 or less not considered.)

A.

Coupled—Harry L. and Green Shekel.

Racer
B. c. 4, by Miswaki—Precious Patty, by Grey Dawn II **Lifetime** **1987 12 0 4 2 $31,120**
$35,000 Br.—Koones R (Ky) **117** **22 1 6 5** **1986 10 1 2 3 $32,100**
Own.—Bobley Susan **Tr.—Hargrave Kenneth** **$63,220** **Turf 1 0 0 0**

22Jly87- 9Bel fst 6f :22⅕ :45⅘ 1:11 Clm c-25000 8 10 1114 1010 76¼ 64½ Bailey J D b 117 12.20 80-17 Tis Royal 117¾ Big McCoy 117¾ Flying Skipper 1153¾ Outrun 11
6Jly87- 9Bel fst 7f :23 :45⅘ 1:24 Clm 50000 2 7 88 79 86¼ 87 Bailey J D b 117 23.10 75-22 Sidi Bou Said 1171¼ Harry L. 117hd John Muir 113hd Outrun 8
18Jun87- 1Bel fst 1$\frac{1}{16}$:48⅖ 1:12⅘ 1:43⅕ Clm 50000 6 6 77½ 78 79½ 611¾ Bailey J D b 117 11.10 74-23 Harry L. 1151 The Savage 117½ Mr. Tatt 1172½ Outrun 7
10Jun87- 4Bel fst 7f :23 :46⅕ 1:24 3+ Alw 26000 5 10 98½ 97¼ 62¾ 31¼ Bailey J D b 117 18.40 81-17 Mean and Crafty 1151¼ Full Colonel 113hd Racer 117nk Fin well 11
10May87- 9Bel fst 6f :23⅕ :47⅖ 1:11⅘ 3+ Alw 26000 9 9 99 86¾ 66 58 Bailey J D b 119 10.70 73-25 Conventioneer 119¾ Heritance 1084½ Legion D'Honour 1101¾ Wide 10
30Apr87- 7Aqu fst 7f :22⅘ :46⅖ 1:24 3+ Alw 26000 7 3 67 65½ 66 64¼ Cordero A Jr b 119 3.10 77-28 Matthews Keep 1131½ Yet Wave 107hd Fort Whoop 1142 Outrun 7
16Apr87- 5Aqu fst 1 :47⅖ 1:12⅖ 1:38 3+ Alw 27000 2 2 21 21½ 21½ 21¾ Cordero A Jr b 119 *1.50 74-22 Military Reaction 1191¾ Racer 1192¾ Diamond Joy 110½ 2nd best 7
10Apr87- 7Aqu fst 7f :23⅕ :45⅖ 1:23⅗ 3+ Alw 26000 5 2 43 33½ 32½ 22 Antley C W b 119 6.40 81-24 Saintly Cherf 1142 Racer 119nk Billy Wilbur 119¾ Gained place 7
19Mar87- 5Aqu fst 7f :23⅖ :46⅖ 1:25⅘ Alw 26000 4 5 78¾ 78½ 45 31 Antley C W b 117 2.80 71-29 Rexson's Quill 117½ Billy Wilbur 117½ Racer 1172 Belated rally 9
8Mar87- 5Aqu fst 170 ⊡ :48⅖ 1:12⅘ 1:42⅘ Alw 27000 2 5 56 34½ 34½ 24½ Antley C W b 117 *1.00 81-16 Keep It Easy 1174½ Racer 117¾ A Mighty Cheer 1224 Rallied wide 6
LATEST WORKOUTS Jun 30 Bel tr.t 3f fst :36 h Jun 6 Bel 4f fst :53 b

B.

Wild Wood * B. g. 4, by Cormorant—Summer Theatre, by Reviewer
Own.—Tufariello F $30,000 Br.—Trojan Star Stable (NY) Tr.—Tufariello Frank 113
Lifetime 4 3 0 0 $107,604 1986 1 0 0 0 $4,164 1985 3 3 0 0 $103,440
5Jan86- 8Aqu fst 1⅟₁₆ [•] :47⅗ 1:12⅘ 1:44⅗ [S]Montauk 2 5 32½ 31½ 44 44½ Venezia M 126 *.60 82-16 Tinchen's Prince 1211½ Bullet Blade 1262FastStep1211 Weakened 7
1Dec85- 8Aqu sly 1⅛ :47 1:11⅘ 1:51⅕ [S]B F Bongard 5 3 32½ 21 1½ 14 Venezia M 119 2.70 79-21 Wild Wood 1194 Tinchen's Prince1152HickoryCreek1174¾ Driving 9
4Nov85- 5Aqu fst 1 :48⅖ 1:13⅗ 1:38⅘ [S]Alw 29000 8 2 31½ 1½ 1½ 12 Venezia M 117 *1.20 72-19 Wild Wood 1172 Hickory Creek 1221 Flag King 1171½ Driving 8
18Oct85- 5Bel fst 7f :22⅗ :46⅘ 1:26⅗ [S]Md Sp Wt 11 1 22½ 1½ 13 17¾ Venezia M 118 *1.50 70-27 WildWood1187¾MjorInvsion1181KepingCompny1181½ Ridden out 13
LATEST WORKOUTS Jly 30 Bel 4f fst :49⅕ b Jly 23 Bel 6f fst 1:17 b ●Jly 17 Bel 5f fst :58⅘ h ●Jly 11 Bel 5f fst 1:00 h

C.

Hoping To Be Lucky Ch. c. 4, by The Irish Lord—Coral Garden, by Windy Sands
Own.—Close L S $35,000 Br.—Ring Connie M (Cal) Tr.—Duncan Susan 117
Lifetime 26 4 1 5 $83,645 1987 8 0 0 0 $3,000 1986 13 3 0 3 $60,320 Turf 6 1 0 1 $21,120
16Jly87- 5Bel fst 6f :22⅗ :45⅗ 1:10⅘ Clm 45000 7 4 42 44½ 44½ 56 Maple E b 113 10.10 80-24 Big Coda 1171¾ CountOnRomeo1132¾OneBonBon113nk Weakened 7
6Jly87- 9Bel fst 7f :23 :45⅗ 1:24 Clm 45000 7 1 2hd 1hd 2hd 53¼ Maple E b 114 12.20 79-22 Sidi Bou Said 1171½ Harry L. 117hd John Muir 113hd Tired 8
25Jun87- 6Bel fst 6f :22⅖ :46 1:11⅖ Clm 47500 5 5 64½ 97 74½ 63 Guerra W A b 115 26.00 80-25 WntIntensity1131¾Rexson'sQuill117hdCountOnRomo117no Outrun 10
28May87- 5Bel fm 1⅟₁₆ [T]:46⅖ 1:10⅗ 1:42⅗ Clm 50000 8 3 63½ 97¾ 914 914¾ Maple E b 117 9.80 66-16 [D]Patchy Groundfog 117no City Council II1171¼Onslow1132 Tired 10
18May87- 5Bel fst 7f :22 :44⅖ 1:22⅘ Clm 72500 3 8 43 43½ 44 44¾ Maple E b 115 20.30 83-15 Tonka Pass 1173 Mr Tatt 108hd One Bon Bon 1131¾ Weakened 8
24Apr87- 2Aqu gd 1⅟₁₆ [T]:49⅕ 1:15⅖ 1:48 Clm 75000 8 7 65 99¾ 1020 922¼ Maple E b 117 6.30 43-35 AllHandsOnDeck117noVatzaMatter1135BarbdinReef1133 No factor 10
14Apr87- 8Aqu fst 7f :23 :45⅗ 1:23⅕ 3+ Alw 29000 6 1 3nk 41¾ 63½ 63½ Maple E b 119 6.70 81-23 TemptSec109nkAmourdeFleuve119¾Getredyfortnshow102nk Tired 8
3Apr87- 7Aqu fst 6f :22⅘ :45⅗ 1:10⅖ Clm 70000 7 4 42½ 43 75½ 43¾ Maple E b 113 31.50 85-22 Grand Rivulet 117no Cool Joe 1142¼ Silver Slate 1171½ No excuse 8
20Aug86- 3Sar fm 1⅟₁₆ [T]:47 1:10⅖ 1:41⅘ Clm 72500 5 4 32 73¾ 99 811¾ Maple E b 115 4.50 76-11 Chesapeake Beach 1191¾ Flash Force 113hd Trubulare1131½ Tired 10
2Aug86- 1Sar fst 6f :22 :45 1:09⅘ 3+ Clm 75000 5 5 69¼ 66 63 45½ Venezia M b 114 12.50 85-10 PassingThunder1174AtomSmasher117noSagittarin1171½ No factor 7
LATEST WORKOUTS Jly 29 Bel 5f fst 1:01⅖ h Jly 16 Bel 4f fst :49⅖ hg Jly 14 Bel 3f fst :38⅘ b Jly 4 Bel 4f fst :50 b

D.

Volt B. g. 4, by Lines Of Power—Case History, by Nearco Blue
Own.—Cline M H $35,000 Br.—Cline M H (Ky) Tr.—Rieser Stanley M 117
Lifetime 29 5 6 3 $67,970 1987 5 1 1 0 $11,425 1986 19 3 5 3 $48,301 Turf 2 0 1 0 $3,000
17Jly87- 9Atl fm 5½f [T]:22 :45⅘ 1:04⅕ 3+ Alw 8000 7 1 51½ 43½ 43½ 41½ Romero J A5 b 111 *.90 90-14 Another Member 122½MedievalBanker116½FlyingRice116½ Evenly 7
27Jun87- 2Mth sly 6f :22⅖ :45⅗ 1:11 3+ Clm 25000 5 2 21 21 21 1½ Krone J A b 116 3.30 85-18 Volt 116½ Big McCoy 1191¾ Prospector Al 1094 Driving 7
18Jun87- 7Mth fst 6f :22⅕ :44⅘ 1:09⅖ 3+ Clm 32000 2 9 78¼ 87¾ 810 810¾ Vigliotti M J b 116 5.20 82-14 KingOfBridlewood1161ScreenTrnd1124GrnShkl1121 Pinched start 9
9Jun87- 6Mth fst 6f :22⅘ :45⅘ 1:10⅘ 3+ Clm 25000 1 1 1hd 1hd 2hd 2hd Vigliotti M J b 116 6.20 86-19 Saltine Warrior 116no Volt 116¾ Lovin Breeze 112no Just missed 7
14Apr87- 3GP fst 6f :22 :45⅕ 1:10 Clm 45000 7 1 51½ 66¼ 69½ 411¼ Fires E b 117 8.60 78-28 O K Amy 1171 What Intensity 115nk Exuberation 11310 No factor 7
26Nov86- 7CD my 6f :21⅘ :45⅗ 1:11⅘ 3+ Alw 18150 1 6 2hd 42½ 62½ 56 Allen K K b 115 2.80 78-23 Bar Tender 111½ Ambersburg 114½ Tis Royal 1142½ 9
16Nov86- 7CD fst 6½f :22⅗ :46⅕ 1:17⅘ 3+ Alw 18150 10 3 63½ 53 44 47½ Meier R b 117 4.60 85-19 Delayer 1114 Ambersburg 113½ Bar Tender 1113 12
30Oct86- 7CD fst 6½f :22⅗ :46 1:17⅘ 3+ Clm 40000 2 4 21½ 2hd 12½ 15 Fires E b 114 5.50 93-22 Volt 1145 Don't Hesitate 117nk Fairly Straight 117nk 11
9Oct86- 8Kee fst 6f :22⅖ :45⅕ 1:10⅕ 3+ Alw 18700 10 1 42 31½ 56½ 611 Johnson P A b 111 3.10 80-15 The Flats 111no Mr Run Run 1112½ Here's To More 1113 10
10Sep86- 3Bel fst 6f :22⅘ :46⅗ 1:11 Clm 62500 8 2 21½ 2½ 4¾ 33½ Santos J A b 115 3.70 83-20 B. C. Sal 117¾ Classic Move 1132¾ Volt 115½ WEakened 8
LATEST WORKOUTS Jly 25 Mth 4f fst :48⅗ h Jly 13 Mth 4f fst :49⅗ b

E.

Rambling Rector B. h. 6, by Blushing Groom—Admiring, by Hail to Reason
Own.—Sommer Viola $35,000 Br.—Mellon Paul (Va) Tr.—Martin Frank 117
Lifetime 54 5 8 5 $139,960 1987 4 0 0 0 1986 24 2 3 3 $60,080 Turf 6 0 0 0 $1,740
16Jly87- 5Bel fst 6f :22⅗ :45⅗ 1:10⅘ Clm 50000 5 7 76½ 711 716 619 Guerra W A b 117 16.00 67-24 Big Coda 1171¾ Count On Romeo 1132¾ One BonBon113nk Outrun 7
24Jun87- 1Bel fst 6½f :23⅕ :46⅗ 1:17 3+ Clm 70000 7 1 2½ 21½ 79 717¼ Garcia J A b 113 7.90 73-17 Cullendale 1173½ Harry L. 1133 Shining Asset 1171 Tired 7
10Jan87- 7Aqu gd 1⅝ [•]:50 2:07⅕ 2:45⅖ Handicap 2 3 32 719 — — Baird E T b 107 3.10 — — Jane's Dilemma 1222¾ Oversea 1107 Future Fable 103½ Eased 7
4Jan87- 7Aqu fst 6f [•]:22⅖ :46⅕ 1:10⅗ Clm c-70000 3 10 96½ 76 86¼ 75 Antley C W 114 *3.10 86-21 Paris Venture 117½ Majestic Empire 1131½CoolJoe117½ No factor 10
20Dec86- 7Aqu fst 6f [•]:22 :45 1:09⅗ 3+ Alw 40000 5 7 811 52½ 32½ 21 Antley C W 115 16.50 95-09 Tonka Pass 1151 Rambling Rector 1153 Isopropyl 1131½ Fin well 9
8Dec86- 8Aqu fst 1⅝ [•]:13⅘ 2:07⅖ 2:46⅖ 3+ Handicap 5 1 14 69 724 731 Davis R G 110 10.20 49-20 Feeling Gallant 114¾ Jane's Dilemma 1154½ Carjack 122½ Stopped 7
27Nov86- 8Aqu gd 1⅟₁₆ :49⅖ 1:13⅕ 1:57⅕ 3+ Qns Cnty H 3 5 21½ 11 63¾ 68¼ Nuesch D b 103 23.10 68-29 Pine Belt 111nk Scrimshaw 1082 Cost Conscious 1112 Tired 6
27Nov86-Grade III
15Nov86- 9Med fst 1⅛ :47⅗ 1:11⅖ 1:48⅗ 3+ Paterson H 6 2 2½ 2hd 42 68 Krone J A b 107 36.00 82-13 Creme Fraiche 1211 Skip Trial 1211¾ Do It Again Dan 1142½ Tired 7
15Nov86-Grade II
1Nov86- 7Aqu fst 1⅛ :47⅘ 1:11⅕ 1:50 3+ Stuyv'snt H 10 7 42¾ 45 1012 1014½ Thibeau R J b 106 25.00 70-19 Little Missouri 116nk Waquoit 1153½ Let's Go Blue 118½ Wide 10
1Nov86-Grade II
28Sep86- 1Bel my 1⅟₁₆ :46⅗ 1:11⅕ 1:42⅗ 3+ Clm c-50000 7 6 66½ 43 42 3½ Bailey J D b 119 *2.80 88-15 Mr.Murtaugh117½BarbadinReef117noRmblingRector1192 Wide str 7
LATEST WORKOUTS Jly 30 Bel 6f fst 1:14 h ●Jly 24 Bel tr.t 4f fst :47 h Jly 10 Bel tr.t 4f sly :48 h Jly 4 Bel tr.t 5f fst 1:00⅖ h

9. The highest pace rating has been earned by

3rd Saratoga

6 FURLONGS. (1.08) CLAIMING. Purse $29,000. 3-year-olds and upward. Weight, 3-year-olds, 117 lbs., Older, 122 lbs. Claiming Price $100,000; for each $5,000 to $75,000, 2 lbs.

Coupled—Quick Departure and Splendid Catch; Aki and Fast Gordy.

A.

Tonka Pass * B. g. 6, by Tonkaton—Pass Anything, by Pass Catcher
Br.—Brinkerhoff E C (Fla) 1987 12 5 1 2 $95,560
Own.—Happy Valley Farm 112 Tr.—Dutrow Richard E $75,000 1986 8 1 3 2 $60,940
Lifetime 39 10 11 5 $232,915 Turf 3 0 1 1 $11,195
13Aug87-1Sar 6½f :22² :45 1:16¹ft 3¾ 117 1½ 3³ 32½ 53¾ Cordero A Jr4 75000 87-14 Crivitz, Dr. Koch, Fabulous Flight 8
27Jly87-5Bel 6½f :22³ :45³ 1:16²ft *1 118 2¹ 31½ 33½ 34½ Cordero A Jr5 90000 88-21 Cullendale, DonSanders,TonkaPass 6
8Jly87-1Bel 6f :22² :45³ 1:11¹sy *6-5 118 3² 2¹ 1½ 11¼ Cordero A Jr6 90000 84-25 Tonka Pass, Zonter, FarawayIsland 6
29Jun87-1Bel 6½f :23 :46² 1:17³ft *1 117 1½ 11½ 1⁴ 1no Cordero A Jr4 75000 87-25 Tonka Pass, Harry L., One Bon Bon 6
15Jun87-8Bel 7f :23² :46³ 1:23⁴ft 3 113 41¾ 41¾ 54½ 43½ Cordero A Jr6 Hcp0 79-19 LndingPlot,Mr.Clssic,JmicnGigolo 10
29May87-9Bel 7f :22³ :45³ 1:22⁴ft *2½ 118 53½ 53½ 1½ 11¼ Pezua J M6 90000 88-13 TonkaPss,ScholrsTsk,JmicnGigolo 10
18May87-5Bel 7f :22 :44² 1:22⁴ft *2 117 3² 31½ 12½ 1³ Antley C W5 75000 88-15 Tonka Pass, Mr. Tatt, One BonBon 8
8May87-1Bel 6½f :22⁴ :45³ 1:16³ft *8-5 117 1² 1³ 1⁴ 1³ Cordero A Jr4 50000 92-24 Tonka Pass, Talc Power,UpperStar 5
Jly 22 Aqu [•] 5f ft 1:01 b ●Jun 26 Aqu 4f ft :47 h

B.

```
Cullendale                                 Dk. b. or br. h. 5, by Sham—Maribold, by Bold And Brave
                                           Br.—Vradelis Elizabeth B (Ky)                    1987  7  2  0  1    $42,123
Own.—Bailey Morris                    122  Tr.—DeStasio Richard T          $100,000         1986 24  2  1 12   $152,532
                                       Lifetime   47  8  4 17  $292,793                     Turf  9  1  0  3    $53,931
 8Aug87-6Sar   6f  :214 :442 1:091ft     8  115  54½ 43½ 42½ 43½   MlrR2 A Phenomenon  90-13 Banker'sJet,RoyalPennnt,SunMster 6
27Jly87-5Bel   6½f :223 :453 1:162ft     8  122  43½ 21½ 1½  11½   Migliore R3   100000 93-21 Cullendale, DonSanders,TonkaPass 6
24Jun87-1Bel   6½f :231 :463 1:17 ft     4½ 117  1½  11½ 12  13½   Migliore R2    75000 90-17 Cullendale, Harry L., Shining Asset 7
17Jun87-1Bel   1  (T):4641:1011:344fm    6½ 1175 56  48  412 618   Nuesch D2     100000 73-24 Hawaiian Eye, Fearless Leader,Alev 7
 3Jun87-8Bel   7f (T):241 :4721:251gd   15  117  84¾ 62¾ 76½10101¼ Nuesch D7     Jaipur 68-37 Raj'sRevenge,Trubulre,GiveATost 11
      3Jun87—Grade III
22May87-8Bel   7f (T):224 :4541:241gd    5¾ 1145 512 59  56½ 36¾   Nuesch D5    Aw40000 76-22 Alev, Senator Brady, Culle1dale 6
      22May87—Off slow
 7Jan87-8Aqu   1 1/16[•]:4741:1111:443ft 21 115  76¾ 73¾ 75¾ 98¾   McCuleyWH7   Aw45000 78-21 Synastry, Grand Rivulet, Khozaam 11
21Dec86-8Aqu   6f [•]:22  :45 1:092ft   17  110  612 67½ 68  67½   NuschD6 Gravesend H 89-14 ComicBlush,King'sSwn,CutlssRlity 6
   Aug 3 Bel 5f ft 1:02 b            Jly 20 Bel tr.t 4f ft :492 b        Jly 13 Bel tr.t 4f ft :50 b
```

C.

```
Aswan High                                 Ch. h. 5, by Upper Nile—Laraka, by Impressive
                                           Br.—Worswick R J (Ky)                            1987  9  3  0  2    $64,380
Own.—Cedar Valley Stable              112  Tr.—Jerkens Steven T            $75,000          1986 18  4  6  0    $99,320
                                       Lifetime   45  9  9  4  $197,400
 8Aug87-1Sar   6f  :214 :45  1:104ft    *2¼ 117  3½  1hd 2½  31¼   Migliore R10   50000 85-13 TruthBTold,SidiBouSid,AswnHigh 10
29May87-9Bel   7f  :223 :453 1:224ft     9¼ 118  21  2½  52  54¾   Migliore R7    90000 83-13 TonkaPss,ScholrsTsk,Jmic1Gigolo 10
13May87-8Bel   6f  :221 :454 1:10 ft    *2  112  1½  1hd 2hd 42½   Migliore R2     HcpO 87-18 OmrKhyym,PrisVentur,JmicnGigolo 7
18Apr87-7Aqu   6f  :222 :453 1:094m      4¾ 121  11  11  11½ 14½   Migliore R4  Aw40000 92-15 Aswan High, Paris Venture,Ioskeha 7
 6Mar87-6Aqu   6f [•]:23  :4611:094ft    2¾ 116  1½  11  11  13¼   Antley C W5    85000 95-17 AswanHigh,ParisVenture,TonkaPss 5
 2Feb87-8Aqu   6f [•]:214 :4521:102sy    4¾ 117  35½ 32½ 33½ 36¼   Antley C W1  Aw33000 86-24 MjesticEmpir,ShinDiulus,AswnHigh 7
21Jan87-5Aqu   6f [•]:222 :4541:101sy   *2½ 117  11½ 11½ 13  15¼   Antley C W1   c50000 93-17 AswnHigh,FlyingSkipper,Dl'sFolly 11
14Jan87-7Aqu   6f [•]:213 :4421:093ft    4½ 1075 32½ 22  32½ 54½   Nuesch D2      75000 91-16 PrisVntur,ShinDulus,LordOfThNght 8
   Aug 16 Sar tr.t 3f ft :374 b      ● Aug 3 Bel 4f ft :464 h     Jly 30 Bel 6f ft 1:164 b     Jly 24 Bel tr.t 4f ft :49 b
```

D.

```
Scholars Task                              B. h. 5, by Naskra—College Bold, by Boldnesian
                                           Br.—Meadowhill (Ky)                              1987 12  2  3  2    $77,310
Own.—Nest Farm Stable                 118  Tr.—Clayton Marjorie            $90,000          1986  9  2  1  1    $42,500
                                       Lifetime   43  7  6  9  $189,155                     Turf  3  0  0  0       $210
13Jun87-7Mth   6f  :223 :452 1:092ft     2½ 117  62¼ 63¾ 87  810¼  Cordero AJr 2 Aw25000 83-12 SunnyFt,ClvrAllmont,RunringBold 9
29May87-9Bel   7f  :223 :453 1:224ft     6½ 120  31½ 42  31½ 21¼  Cordero A Jr 1  95000 87-13 TonkaPss,ScholrsTsk,JmicnGigolo 10
      29May87—Lacked rm. str.
 7May87-8Bel   1 1/16:462 1:112 1:434ft *9-5 119  43  4¾  1½  1hd † Cordero AJr 2 Aw45000 83-21 ‡ScholrsTsk,ComdyTnght,GrndRvlt 6
      † 7May87—Disqualified and placed second; Drftd, bumped
30Apr87-8Aqu   7f  :231 :471 1:241ft     2  119  21  1hd 11  11    Cordero AJr 6 Aw40000 80-28 ScholrsTsk,TemptSc,FbulcusFlight 7
18Apr87-7Aqu   6f  :222 :453 1:094m      3½ 119  54  55  44½ 45    Cordero AJr 3 Aw40000 87-15 Aswan High, Paris Venture,Ioskeha 7
11Apr87-7Aqu   7f  :231 :46  1:23 ft     2¼ 119  22  22  1hd 2no   Cordero AJr 3 Aw40000 86-23 OneBonBon,ScholrsTsk,SovrignDon 6
27Mar87-8Aqu   1   :46  1:093 1:343ft   11  115  42  53½ 36  34½   Cordero AJr 8 Aw45000 88-21 Tourd'Or,Tinchn'sPrinc,ScholrsTsk 9
16Mar87-5Aqu   7f  :231 :47  1:244ft     3¼ 117  41  51¼ 21  1nk   Cordero A Jr 2  75000 77-30 Scholars Task, Cool Joe,SilverSlate 7
   Aug 15 Sar 5f ft 1:02 h           Aug 2 Bel 4f ft :493 b
```

E.

```
Quick Departure                            Dk. b. or br. g. 4, by Baldski—Cutalong, by The Axe II
                                           Br.—FrnswrthFm-RbnsG-WldmrFm (Fl)                1987  7  0  1  1    $10,800
Own.—Ferruolo J A                     112  Tr.—Lenzini John J Jr           $75,000          1986  4  1  1  1    $36,606
                                       Lifetime   12  2  2  2  $60,606                      Turf  2  0  0  0
 5Jly87-4Bel   1 1/16[T]:4731:1041:421gd 13 117  21  32½ 716 827¾  Romero R P7 Aw28000 62-17 Seattlite,HawiinEye,Conventioneer 8
18Jun87-7Bel   1  (T):4511:10 1:35 fm   29  117  713 66  712 79    Romero R P 8 Aw28000 81-10 Easton, Seattlite, Nudge 12
      18Jun87—Dwelt start
13May87-7Bel   7f  :222 :451 1:23 ft     6¾ 119  52¼ 1½  811 814¼  Cordero AJr 3 Aw27000 73-18 CrownthLdr,PldgCrd,BoldSummit 11
      13May87—Slow start
 3May87-1Aqu   6f  :224 :453 1:103ft    *2¼ 119  1½  11½ 1½  2nk   Romero R P 7 Aw27000 88-21 ExclusvGm,QuckDprtur,BoldSmmt 8
23Apr87-5Aqu   7f  :222 :452 1:234ft     7¾ 119  1hd 12  2½  34½   Romero R P 8 Aw27000 77-24 FbulousFlight,Curtin,Quick:Deprtur 8
13Apr87-4Aqu   6f  :221 :454 1:103m      4¼ 119  32  33½ 25  48    Romero R P 2 Aw27000 80-26 Pentelicus, Wayar, Proud And Tall 6
      13Apr87—Lugged in
23Mar87-7Aqu   6f  :23  :462 1:104ft    7-5 117  4¾  3nk 43  59¼   Cordero AJr 6 Aw27000 78-28 Dr. Koch, Fugie, Upper Star 8
19Apr86-7Aqu   6f  :222 :451 1:094ft     2¾ 117  42  21½ 2½  2nk   Pincay L Jr 4  Flip Sal 92-18 SuprDlght,QuckDprtr,NmroUnoPss 7
   Aug 17 Sar 4f ft :50 b            ● Jly 28 Aqu [•] 5f ft 1:003 h      ● Jly 1 Aqu 4f ft :472 hg
```

F.

```
Aki                                   B. c. 3, by Alydar—Dare To Be Bare, by Grey Dawn II
                                      Br.—Cherry ValleyFarmInc&Lickle (Ky)      1987 10 1 1 1      $19,870
Own.—Spielman M                 113   Tr.—Zito Nicholas P           $90,000     Turf  2 0 0 0
                                  Lifetime   10 1 1 1   $19,870
14Aug87-7Sar  1 1/16 (T):48 1:1141:542fm 45 114  42  74½1117 1126¾ Romero RP12 Aw27000 67-08 Irish Rue, True Vigor, Archtekton 12
9Aug87-5Sar   1⅛ :491 1:132 1:511ft  12 114  2hd 67½ 56½ 55½  Day P8       Aw27000 73-18 Pza, Mitral, Silver Candle 8
13Jly87-7Bel  1⅜ [T]:4842:0322:16 fm 21 113  36½ 811 825 828  Romero R P4  Aw28000 49-19 Sure Dad, I'mEnthused,ParisOffice 9
4Jly87-4Bel   1¼ :483 1:394 2:061ft  5½ 116  23  1½  16  17¼  Romero R P2  Mdn 67-23 Aki, Highly Rated II, Wise Old Owl 6
28Jun87-3Bel  7f :222 :452 1:244ft   3¾ 114  46½ 38½ 29  313  Antley C W3  M75000 65-19 Naudimar, Quiddler, Aki 8
19Jun87-2Bel  1 :462 1:122 1:393ft   17 114  21  1hd 13½ 2hd  Santos J A10 M50000 67-21 You Hop, Aki, Wise Old Owl 14
8Jun87-9Bel   6f :224 :462 1:12 ft   27 114  32  33  35½ 66   Antley C W3  M75000 74-20 SilkyAppeal,Aeguanimits,Quiddler 12
4Jun87-4Bel   1 :452 1:104 1:373sy   12 114  44½ 49½ 614 620½ Samyn J L4  Mdn 56-21 ‡Hopzig,WiseEmissary,ThreeThings 6
   Aug 6 Sar 3f ft :36 h        Aug 2 Sar tr.t 4f ft :52 b        Jly 27 Sar 5f ft 1:043 b
```

G.

```
Crivitz                               Ch. c. 4, by Czaravich—Lightning Bug, by Cornish Prince
                                      Br.—Free F W (NY)                         1987 7 2 1 1       $42,020
Own.—Reynolds W L               116   Tr.—Watters Sidney Jr         $85,000     1986 3 2 0 0       $27,600
                                  Lifetime   10 4 1 1   $69,620
13Aug87-1Sar  6½f:222 :45 1:161ft    4¾ 117  31½ 21  11  12   Pezua J M7      75000 91-14 Crivitz, Dr. Koch, Fabulous Flight 8
29Jly87-1Bel  7f :231 :454 1:23 ft  *3¾ 117  1½  11  12½ 15   Santos J A2     50000 87-23 Crvtz,ContOnRomo,KngOfBrdlwod 8
29Jun87-1Bel  6½f:23 :462 1:173ft    3¼ 117  41½ 54  68¼ 48¾  Pezua J M6      75000 78-25 Tonka Pass, Harry L., One Bon Bon 6
19Jun87-4Bel  6f :222 :454 1:102ft   3 112   73¾ 53¾ 32½ 21¾  Pezua J M8      75000 86-21 Zonter, Crivitz, Bravo Fox 8
3Jun87-5Bel   7f :23 :461 1:232ft    2¾ 117  31½ 3½  33½ 33½  Hernandez R7 Aw27000 81-22 Mr. Classic, Easton, Crivitz 7
21May87-6Bel  1 1/16 :46 1:103 1:423ft 6½ 119 32  31½ 43  44   Hernandez R4 Aw28000 85-17 BoldSummit,MtthewsKep,NvrWivr 5
   21May87—Steadied
13May87-7Bel  7f :222 :451 1:23 ft   13 119  85¾ 73¾ 56  44½  Hernandez R7 Aw27000 82-18 CrownthLdr,PldgCrd,BoldSummit 11
   13May87—Broke outside
25Aug86-5Sar  6f :221 :454 1:111ft   2½ 117  42  3½  11  13¾  Martens G7    Aw24000 84-19 Crivitz, Toll Key, Green Kright 7
   ●Aug 21 Sar 3f ft :342 h        Aug 7 Sar 5f ft 1:03 b        Jly 21 Bel 5f gd 1:00 h
```

H.

```
Fast Gordy *                          B. g. 5, by Pas Seul—Queenly Vapors, by Swoon's Son
                                      Br.—Gordonsdale Farm (Va)                 1985 24 6 1 4      $104,441
Own.—Gordonsdale Farm          10710  Tr.—Zito Nicholas P           $100,000    Turf  6 1 1 0      $10,426
                                  Lifetime   24 6 1 4   $104,441
27Nov85-6Aqu  7f :223 :452 1:222gd *6-5 117  1½  13  21  32¾  Davis R G5   Aw27000 86-16 ForCertainDoc,Khozaam,FastGordy 8
23Nov85-5Aqu  1 :452 1:094 1:351m  *8-5 115  13½ 11  12  1hd  Davis R G5   Aw29000 90-14 Fast Gordy, I Enrich, Sky Falcon 6
13Nov85-7Aqu  1 :442 1:083 1:341gd  4 112    12½ 11½ 12½ 12½  Davis R G3     75000 95-11 Fast Gordy, Area Rug, MyManJohn 9
8Nov85-5Aqu   6f :221 :452 1:094ft  8½ 117   21½ 22  24½ 35   Cruguet J6     50000 87-20 GreenShekel,AswanHigh,FstGordy 11
25Oct85-7Aqu  1 :462 1:114 1:372ft  6¾ 113   11  66  714 820¾ Davis R G6     70000 58-28 AccordngToLk,NkdEmpror,SThWy 8
10Oct85-5Med  170:46 1:11 1:414ft  *9-5 117  —   —   —   —    Santos J A3  Aw17000 — — Quckrbow,Domino'sDwn,DoublShip 7
   10Oct85—Lost rider
6Oct85-3Bel   1 1/16 :453 1:11 1:432gd *2¾ 114 11 12  22  45¾  Davis R G6     80000 79-19 Area Rug, Gourami, Cloutier 11
26Sep85-4Bel  1 :45 1:094 1:363m    2 112    14  11½ 12½ 13   Davis R G2     75000 82-17 FstGordy,MyMnJohn,CougrExpress 7
   Aug 15 Sar tr.t 4f ft :51 b        ●Aug 11 Sar tr.t 4f sy :50 b
```

I.

```
Splendid Catch                        B. h. 5, by Nice Catch—Nightly Splendor, by Shining Knight
                                      Br.—King Betty & J A (Fla)                1987 9 1 4 0       $40,850
Own.—Pinkley J                  116   Tr.—Lenzini John J Jr         $85,000     1986 6 1 2 0       $12,625
                                  Lifetime   32 7 10 0   $129,455               Turf 1 0 0 0
13Aug87-1Sar  6½f:222 :45 1:161ft   12 117   42  67  54  43   Velasquez J 1    75000 88-14 Crivitz, Dr. Koch, Fabulous Flight 8
6Jly87-5Mth   6f :214 :442 1:10 ft  4½ 116   77  89  87½ 76½  Santagata N 3 Aw17000 83-14 ScreenTrend,NevrForgottr,Prochil 8
   6Jly87—Stumbled start
21Jun87-9Pha  6½f:223 :453 1:161ft  4½ 116   52½ 54  410 514¼ Nied J Jr 7     Hcp0 78-25 Aeronotic, Super Delight,GraceAve 7
29Apr87-6GP   7f :224 :452 1:224ft *4-5 122  52½ 54½ 64¼ 44¾  Fires E 6     Aw17000 85-21 DubNhoc,SnnyProspctor,TyrntBoss 7
18Apr87-9GP   7f :222 :444 1:222ft  4¾ 117   2hd 1½  1½  22½  Fires E 1     Aw20000 89-21 OnMgcMmnt,SplnddCtch,StBbbV. 12
18Mar87-9GP   7f :222 :444 1:223ft  3¾ 113   51½ 1½  11½ 22½  RmrRP 1 Hallandale H 88-18 Uncle Ho, Splendid Catch,Mugatea 7
7Mar87-9GP    6f :212 :442 1:104ft  11 113   711 79  55½ 2¾   RrRP 6 Sprnt Chmp H 84-25 Dwight D., Splendid Catch,UncleHo 7
31Jan87-9Hia  7f :231 :452 1:233ft  5½ 116   21  24  21  1½   Fires E 10    Aw19500 85-20 SplndidCtch,ChristinHundrd,Shltr 12
   Aug 8 Sar 5f ft :594 h     ●Aug 1 Aqu [·] 5f ft 1:01 h     Jly 25 Aqu [·] 5f m 1:014 h     Jly 16 Pha 5f ft 1:002 h
```

10. How many starters here have "dependable" early speed?

② BELMONT (1 MILE — BELMONT PARK)

1 MILE. (1.33) CLAIMING. Purse $16,000. 3-year-olds. Weight, 122 lbs. Non-winners of two race at a mile or over since July 15 allowed 3 lbs. Of such a race since then 5 lbs. Claiming price $17,500 for each $1,000 to $15,000, 2 lbs. (Races when enterd to be claimed for $14,000 or less not considered.)

Coupled—Cayman, Born to Tempt and Looky Dare.

Logical Stan — Own.—Luckman S M — $16,500 — B. c. 3, by Bold Reason—Anders n' Anders, by Silver Ship — Br.—Luckman S M (NY) — Tr.—Pagano George — 115

Lizette's Boy — Own.—Caronia C A — $15,500 — B. c. 3, by Look Fast—Lizette, by Diplomat Way — Br.—Hughes Stable (Fla) — Tr.—Russo Anthony J — 113

Born to Tempt — Own.—Gagliano S — $15,500 — Ch. g. 3, by Thanks to Tony—Indian Lightning, by Navajo — Br.—Due Process Stable (Fla) — Tr.—Barrera Oscar S — 113

Champagne Penny — Own.—Lake Margaret S — $15,500 — Ro. c. 3, by Last Dance—Reigh Song, by Greek Ship — Br.—Lake Margaret S (Mass) — Tr.—Barbara Robert — 108½

Looky Dare — Own.—Barrera O S — $15,500 — B. c. 3, by Cathy's Reject—Whoppin, by War Trouble — Br.—Penn O (Ky) — Tr.—Barrera Oscar S — 113

Black Swan — Own.—Adler M — $17,500 — B. c. 3, by Quack—Darlin Momma, by Night Invader — Br.—Karlinsky-Ky Horse Ctr-Levin-Pascma (Ky) — Tr.—Martello Gene — 117

Consiere — Own.—Linares E — $17,500 — Dk. b. or br. c. 3, by Batonnier—Vegas Vixen, by T V Lark — Br.—Madden Preston (Ky) — Tr.—Linares Eduardo — 117

Turn On the Speed B. c. 3, by Stop the Music—Reine Ancienne, by Olden Times
Own.—Harry-Hatch Stable $15,500 Br.—Whitney T P (Ky) Tr.—Sciacca Gary 113
Lifetime 21 2 2 5 $37,560 | 1987 13 0 1 2 $10,320 | 1986 8 2 1 3 $27,240

27Jly87- 5Mth fst 6f :22⅘ :45⅗ 1:11⅘ Clm 14000 5 8 88¾ 810 812 813¾ Madrid A Jr b 112 21.80 67-19 Jinsky's Prince 107² Affirmation 110⁵ ScreenMaster119²½ Trailed 8
4Jly87- 9Bel fst 1 :47⅘ 1:13⅘ 1:41 3+Clm 15500 1 3 66 43 78 610¾ Graell A b 113 15.10 49-23 Looky Dare 113nk Pass the Cup 108nk Quietus 110¹½ Tired 9
26Jun87- 1Bel fst 7f :22⅘ :45⅘ 1:25⅕ Clm 30000 1 6 68 713 715 716 Graell A b 113 37.80 60-22 Fatty Boy 117nk Ole Songn'Dance117²½RoyalSlander113hd Outrun 7
24May87- 1Bel fst 1⅛ :48⅖ 1:13 1:51⅘ Clm 20000 9 4 42½ 66½ 816 817¼ Graell A b 113 31.00 51-16 Diamond Joy 117½ Consiere 115no Cedar Creek 117¾ Tired 9
10May87- 3Bel fst 1⅛ :46⅘ 1:15 1:53⅗ Clm 20000 10 2 42 31 56¼ 514 Graell A b 113 36.90 45-25 Hoist n' Hail 112⁶½ Changing Era 117¾ Consiere 117²¾ Tired 11
30Apr87- 1Aqu fst 7f :22⅘ :46⅗ 1:25⅖ Clm 20000 4 4 810 74 76 77¾ Migliore R b 113 17.00 66-28 SovrignJustic117nkBluBiddrLight110²CourtQuill108¹½ Raced wide 8
16Apr87- 2Aqu fst 7f :23⅕ :47⅕ 1:25⅘ Clm 25000 6 2 510 57 69½ 78¾ Migliore R b 117 8.20 63-22 J. C. Recall 117nk Native Guy 117¾ Court Quill 112² Outrun 7
5Apr87- 4Aqu my 7f :23 :46⅖ 1:23⅗ Clm 35000 2 9 97¾ 99¾ 89¼ 79½ Venezia M b 117 19.30 73-19 Cayman115½SunriseService117²½NationalHeadline117hd No factor 9
27Feb87- 1Aqu fst 1⅛ ⊡:49 1:13⅗ 1:52⅘ Clm 45000 6 5 58½ 79 67¾ 614½ Santos J A 113 5.20 64-19 Mixed Emotions 115² Dancing Court 113⁴Mr.J.V.108²½ Dull effort 7
18Feb87- 5Aqu fst 1 3/16 ⊡:48 1:13⅗ 2:00 Clm c-35000 1 3 45½ 43 38 311 Graell A b 117 *1.70 66-23 DimeStoreThief108⁴½ChngingEr119⁶½TurnOnthSpd117³½ No rally 10
LATEST WORKOUTS Jun 19 Bel tr.t 4f fst :49⅖ h

Quietus B. g. 3, by Hold Your Peace—Bashful, by Le Fabuleux
Own.—Gold-N-Oats Stable $17,500 Br.—Tartan Farms (Fla) Tr.—Martin Gregory 117
Lifetime 12 2 1 2 $23,360 | 1987 7 1 1 1 $15,890 | 1986 5 1 0 1 $7,470 | Turf 1 0 0 0 $1,440

24Jly87- 5Bel fst 7f :23⅖ :47⅖ 1:25⅘ Clm 22500 2 6 43½ 21 3½ 1nk Pezua J M b 115 4.50 73-26 Quietus 115nk Keyline Credit 115½ Mixed Emotions 117³½ Driving 8
19Jly87- 6Bel fm 1 1/16 T:46⅗ 1:11 1:41⅘ Clm 45000 4 5 55 54 45½ 48 Munoz R⁷ b 106 26.90 84-13 River of Sin 113⁵¼ Big Trial 113¾ Mr. J. V. 113² No factor 8
4Jly87- 9Bel fst 1 :47⅘ 1:13⅘ 1:41 3+Clm 16500 7 1 2hd 1hd 21 3½ Belmonte J F⁵ b 110 2.80 59-23 Looky Dare 113nk Pass the Cup 108nk Quietus 110¹½ Weakened 9
12Jun87- 9Bel fst 6f :22⅕ :46 1:11⅕ Clm 25000 2 3 79¼ 86¼ 86¼ 88¼ Pezua J M 117 4.50 76-18 Royal Slander 113no Ebony Rig 117⁴ Grotonberg 117²½ Outrun 9
31May87- 9Bel fst 7f :22⅗ :45⅘ 1:25⅗ Clm 25000 11 5 66½ 57 77 87¾ Cordero A Jr b 117 *2.70 66-17 Tell It Honestly 115² H. J.'s Babe 117½ J. C. Recall 115hd Wide 11
13Feb87- 8Hia fst 7f :22⅘ :46 1:24⅕ Clm c-30000 6 1 63 3½ 21½ 24½ Vasquez J b 114 3.90 77-23 Gallant Kelly 116⁴½ Quietus 114¹⁰ Wind's ofDelta116²½ Weakened 8
30Jan87- 5Hia fst 7f :23⅕ :46⅕ 1:24 Clm 50000 8 7 64¼ 97¼ 710 912¼ Vasquez J b 118 27.70 71-20 Tiger Rullah 122½ Armando 114⁴½ Francisco 120¹½ Outrun 11
21Dec86- 8Crc fst 7f :22⅗ :46 1:25⅗ Clm 40000 10 3 35 36 35½ 37¼ Vasquez J b 114 8.90 81-21 Alert View 114⁶½ Captain Albert 114¾ Quietus 114³½ Evenly 10
13Dec86- 7Crc fst 1 1/16 :48 1:14⅖ 1:48⅗ Alw 14100 9 11 1113 1010 911 911¾ Vasquez J b 113 *2.60e 64-22 Bourgeois 117³½ C. Poppa Hall 115no DCaptainAlbert107² Outrun 11
26Nov86- 3Crc fst 7f :23⅕ :46⅘ 1:26⅘ Md 40000 5 1 4¾ 2hd 11 12½ Vasquez J b 120 4.00 82-17 Quietus 120²½ Bee Axe 120⁴ Jet School 120¹ Driving 5
LATEST WORKOUTS Jly 18 Bel tr.t 3f fst :35 h Jly 16 Bel tr.t 5f fst 1:03 b ●Jly 2 Bel tr.t 3f sly :36 h Jun 26 Bel tr.t 4f fst :47⅘ h

Lt. Dunvegan Ch. g. 3, by Silent Screen—Dunvegan Dancer, by Lt Stevens
Own.—Cedar Valle Stable $17,500 Br.—Franks John (La) Tr.—Jerkens Steven T 117
Lifetime 6 2 0 0 $12,900 | 1987 6 2 0 0 $12,900 | 1986 0 M 0 0

24Jly87- 5Mth fst 170 :46⅗ 1:10⅘ 1:42⅕ Clm 12500 1 3 3½ 2hd 1½ 13½ Santagata N 115 7.60 85-16 Lt. Dunvegan115³½FlyingAcross117⁴½RarePirate115hd Going away 7
19Jun87- 2Mth fst 6f :22⅕ :45⅕ 1:10⅘ Clm 16000 2 6 65½ 811 814 711½ Santagata N 116 13.40 74-18 Neatests Best 116¾ Stuvy 116³½ Exploding Hit 116³ Outrun 8
31May87- 9Bel fst 7f :22⅗ :45⅘ 1:25⅗ Clm 25000 2 8 56 1119 1017 1014 Bacamo J J⁵ 112 6.80 60-17 Tell It Honestly 115² H. J.'s Babe 117½ J. C.Recall115hd Fin. early 11
7Mar87- 4Aqu fst 6f ⊡:22⅗ :46 1:10⅗ Clm 50000 3 6 68 68 615 514¾ Lovato F Jr 117 13.40 76-13 Prince Judex 108⁴½ Whoop de Doo 117½ BestThief117³ Lost whip 6
14Feb87- 4Aqu fst 6f ⊡:22⅕ :46⅕ 1:12⅖ Alw 26000 7 4 67¼ 79 711 67½ Lovato F Jr 117 17.40 74-21 Aaron's Concorde 117¾BattleMan122¹SonnyVerbatim112½ Outrun 7
2Feb87- 4Aqu sly 6f ⊡:22⅖ :46⅖ 1:12⅘ Md 45000 2 4 1½ 1hd 1hd 11 Lovato F Jr 118 7.00 80-24 Lt. Dunvegan 118¹ Laughing Gas 122½ Tan Yankee 118¹½ Driving 11
LATEST WORKOUTS Jly 18 Bel 3f fst :36⅖ h Jly 14 Bel 4f fst :48⅗ h Jly 10 Bel 6f sly 1:18⅖ b Jly 5 Bel 5f fst 1:05 b

A. 3
B. 4
C. 5
D. 6

11. The first three races Aug. 9 at Del Mar were taken by the frontrunners. Which indicates the presence of an S+ bias?

A.

1st Del Mar

6 FURLONGS. (1.07⅗) CLAIMING. Purse $15,000. Fillies. 3-year-olds. Weight 121 lbs. Non-winners of two races since June 1 allowed 3 lbs.; of a race since then, 5 lbs. Claiming price $40,000; if for $35,000 allowed 2 lbs. (Races when entered for $32,000 or less not considered)

Folia B. f. 3, by Sunny Clime—Loves Here, by Time Tested
PATTON D B 116⁵ Br.—Hall & King (Fla) Tr.—Mayberry Brian A $40,000
1987 9 3 3 2 $44,725 | 1986 5 M 3 0 $11,600
Own.—Siegel M-Jan-Samantha Lifetime 14 3 6 2 $56,325

11Jly87-5Hol 6f :21⁴ :45¹ 1:11¹ft *6-5 114⁵ 1½ 1² 1³ 1³ Patton D B 7 Ⓕ 40000 87-12 Folia,JaklinAndHide,FallFromGlory 7
20Jun87-6Hol 6f :21³ :45 1:10²ft *8-5e 114⁵ 2½ 2hd 2² 2⁴ Patton D B 9 Ⓕ 40000 87-11 Hoofer's Brew,Folia,MyProperGal 10
4Jun87-5Hol 6f :22 :45² 1:11 ft *7-5 114⁵ 11½ 11½ 12½ 1⁴ Patton D B 6 Ⓕ 40000 88-13 Folia, Dandy Ruth, Clements Creek 7
15Apr87-2SA 6f :21⁴ :45 1:11²ft *9-5 111⁵ 1² 11½ 12½ 12½ Patton D B 1 ⒻM45000 81-21 Folia, Super Wine, Carlota E. 12
15Apr87—Bobbled at start
3Apr87-4SA 6f :21³ :45 1:11⁴ft *9-5 118 13½ 1⁶ 1⁴ 2½ McHrguDG 11 ⒻM50000 78-17 Time For Oats, Folia,Theresa'sJoy 12
3Apr87—Bumped late
18Mar87-4SA 6f :21⁴ :45¹ 1:11 ft *2 118 1² 1¹ 2hd 23½ McHrguDG 11 ⒻM50000 79-17 Lucky Natalie, Folia, Third Down 12
22Feb87-4SA 6f :21³ :44² 1:10 ft 5½ 117 1½ 1½ 21½ 5¹⁰ McHargue DG 1 ⒻMdn 78-14 DontCallMeLdy,PimPoint,ShyLight 8
1Feb87-4SA 6½f :21⁴ :44⁴ 1:17¹ft *3½ 117 1¹ 11½ 11½ 35½ McHargue DG 7 ⒻMdn 78-16 Akron, Jaklin And Hide, Folia 10
1Feb87—Veered in start
17Jan87-6SA 6f :21⁴ :45¹ 1:11 ft 13 117 1¹ 21½ 2² 34¼ McHargue DG 4 ⒻMdn 79-18 TimelyReserve,YouMkMHppy,Foli 12
6Nov86-4Hol 6f :22 :46 1:11⁴ft *8-5 118 1² 11½ 1¹ 22¾ Meza R Q 4 ⒻMdn 81-17 Tri Holly, Folia, Petite Valentine 9
Jly 7 Hol 3f ft :38¹ h

won by ¾ lengths

B.

2nd Del Mar

6 FURLONGS. (1.07⅗) CLAIMING. Purse $16,000. 3-year-olds and upward. Weights, 3-year-olds, 116 lbs.; older, 121 lbs. Non-winners of two races since June 1 allowed 3 lbs.; of a race since then, 5 lbs. Claiming Price $25,000; if for 22,500 allowed 2 lbs. (Races when entered for $20,000 or less not considered)

```
Bride's Advice                      Ch. g. 4, by Advisedly—Joe's Bride, by Traditionalist
 GRYDER A T                         Br.—Hughes Bros Ranch (Cal)              1987 13 4 1 1    $32,200
                             109^5  Tr.—Mascari James E           $22,500    1986  5 1 0 1     $9,400
Own.—Mascari J E                    Lifetime  19 5 1 3  $42,725
27Jly87-4Hol  6f :22   :45^1 1:09^4ft   3 108^5 1^1½ 1^1 1^3 1^5  Gryder A T^1   14000 94-11 Bride'sAdvice,RosesArRb,SndDiggr 6
    27Jly87—Bobbled start
22Jly87-2Hol  6½f:22^1 :45^1 1:17^1ft   6¾ 116  4^1 1^hd 1½ 1^1¼  Castanon A L^6 12500 94-15 Bride'sAdvice,Doodlesck,HighNturl 8
    22Jly87—Wide 3/8 turn
9Jly87-5Hol   6f :22^1 :45^3 1:10^2ft   5¾ 117  6^2¾ 4^3¼ 3^4 3^5¾ Vergara O^6  c10000 85-15 QuickRoundtrp,Wtchng,Brd'sAdvc 12
21Jun87-2Hol  6½f:22^1 :45^2 1:17^3ft   12 111^5 3^1 1^hd 6^2½ 9^9¼ Comber J^7   16000 82-14 Bruli's Ante,Crowning,CutByGlass 10
3Jun87-2Hol   7f :22^1 :45^1 1:23^4ft   4½ 122  3^1 4^3 4^5½ 4^5¾  Solis A^5    c12500 79-13 FriscoDnnis,RinShltr,TuscnKnight 12
22May87-2Hol  6f :22^1 :45^4 1:11^2ft  *2½ 118  4^1½ 1^hd 1^1 1^hd Solis A^6     10000 86-17 Bride'sAdvic,DominntRoni,Amron 12
14May87-1Hol  6f :22   :45^3 1:10 ft    22 115  2^1½ 1½ 1^1 1^1¼   Solis A^9   [S] 10000 93-13 Bride's Advice,Shantin,KingApache 9
7May87-1Hol   6f :22^2 :45^4 1:11^1ft   9½ 115  3^nk 3^3½ 5^8 6^14½ Pedroza M A^1 12500 72-13 PowerfullPul,RmonRod,John'sJove 8
26Apr87-1Hol  6f :22   :45^4 1:11^2ft   22 116  —  —  —  —       Castanon A L^8 16000 — — ToughEnjolur,BlzngZul,Ambty'sJoy 9
    26Apr87—Lost rider
2Apr87-9SA    1 1/16:47 1:11^3 1:44^2ft 5½ 115  4^2½ 9^11 12^29 — Pedroza M A^7 c12500 — — OneEyedRomeo,Bruli'sAnte,Nathn 12
    2Apr87—Eased; Broke very slowly
  Jly 7 SA 3f ft :36^1 h        ● Jun 19 SA 3f ft :33^3 h
```

won by 11 lengths

C.

3rd Del Mar

1 1/16 MILES. (1.40) ALLOWANCE. Purse $25,000. 3-year-olds and upward which are non-winners of $3,000 twice other than maiden, claiming or starter. Weights, 3-year-olds, 116 lbs.; older, 121 lbs. Non-winners of two races other than claiming at one mile or over since June 1 allowed 3 lbs.; of such a race other than maiden or claiming since then, 5 lbs.

```
Native Priss                        Ch. c. 4, by Raise a Native—Priss, by Swoon's Son
 STEVENS G L                        Br.—Jones Mrs J G (Ky)                   1987  2 1 1 0    $16,500
                              116   Tr.—Scott George W                       1986  9 1 1 2    $22,475
Own.—Paulson A E                    Lifetime  11 2 2 2  $38,975              Turf  2 0 1 0     $5,725
22Jly87-8Hol  6½f:22^2 :45^1 1:16^1ft   3 118  1^1½ 1^1½ 1^1 1^¾   Stevens G L 3 Aw22000 99-15 NtivPriss,LittlRdCloud,TmForSkrto 6
    22Jly87—Unwilling to load; broke in, bumped start
28Jun87-6Hol  6f :22   :45^1 1:10^2ft   8¼ 119  2^hd 1^hd 2^hd 2^nk Stevens G L 7 Aw22000 91-12 ANewEr,NtivePriss,BoldAndGreene 7
7Sep86-5Dmr  1 (T):45^4 1:10^2 1:36^1fm 4½ 117  1^1 1^1½ 2½ 4^3   ValenzuelPA 8 Aw23000 88-08 Lud, Sirtaki, Well Related 9
    7Sep86—Broke in, bumped
20Aug86-7Dmr  1 :45 1:09^3 1:35 ft      5¾ 120  1^1½ 2^hd 3^2 5^15¼ McCarronCJ 7 Aw21000 78-11 Don B. Blue, Lord Allison, Jota 9
    20Aug86—Veered in start
2Aug86-2Dmr  1 :45 1:10^2 1:36^1ft    *6-5 116  1^3½ 1^4 1^4 1^2½  Valenzuela P A 6 Mdn 87-12 NativePriss,Temperate,ArtOfDawn 10
    2Aug86—Veered out start
20Jly86-7Hol 1 1/16(T):47^1 1:11 1:42^3fm 6½ 115 1^1½ 1^1½ 1^2½ 2^nk Valenzuela P A 7 Mdn 91-08 Cro'sHollywood,NtvPrss,JckMcCoy 9
6Jly86-6Hol  1 :44^3 1:09^3 1:35^4ft    22 109^5 1½ 2½ 5^5½ 5^8¼   Black C A 6      Mdn 76-09 WarDebt,Extranix,Cro'sHollywood 10
    6Jly86—Veered out, bumped start
11May86-6Hol  6f :22^1 :45^3 1:09^4ft  8¾e 120  3^1½ 6^6¾ 6^7 7^11½ Solis A 9       Mdn 83-15 Mrvn'sPlcy,PrncOFr,Dn'sIrshMldy 10
27Apr86-6Hol  6f :22^1 :45^4 1:10^2ft    2 120  4^5 5^8 5^9½ 5^10½ Pincay L Jr^1    Mdn 81-15 Rai Den, Devil's Ice, NorthernValor 8
23Feb86-6SA   6f :21^3 :44^2 1:09^2ft   5½ 118  2^1½ 3^3½ 2^2 3^5¾  Solis A^8        Mdn 85-11 CrownedJwl,DoublShng,NtivPriss 11
  Aug 3 SLR tr.t 6f ft 1:13^2 h   Jly 16 SLR tr.t 5f ft 1:02^2 h   Jly 9 SLR tr.t 5f ft 1:01 h   ● Jun 25 SLR tr.t 3f ft :33^2 h
```

won by 4 lengths

D. All of the above.

12. Considering only class, how many horses in this field of six are acceptable as contenders under these advanced nonwinners allowance conditions?

8th Arlington

START • **1 MILE. (1.32½) ALLOWANCE. Purse $17,000.** Fillies. 3-year-olds which have not won three races other than maiden or claiming. Weight, 121 lbs. Non-winners of $15,000 in 1987 allowed 3 lbs.; $10,200, 6 lbs.; $7,200 twice, 9 lbs. (Maiden and claiming races not considered in allowances.)

Evil Elaine

Own.—Mathis Don L   **121**

B. f. 3, by Medieval Man—Distinctive Elaine, by Distinctive
Br.—Burnett R C (Fla)   1987   9   1   1   1 $28,236
Tr.—Lukas D Wayne   1986   8   2   1   1 $66,713
Lifetime   17   3   2   2 $94,949   Turf   2   0   0   0

```
9Jly87-8AP   1 ①:47¹¹:122¹:384fm  29 118   2½  21½ 69  616½  Smith M E⑤ⒻAw17000 64-20 MyTurbulentBeu,DicePssr,MissK.B. 8
28Jun87-8AP  1 ①:47⁴¹:121¹¹:38 fm  5½e123  2²  21½ 55½ 710½  Diaz J L 3    ⒻAthenia 75-21 Won'tSheTell,FirstSonnet,ShnNtiv 8
14Jun87-8AP  6f :22  :45 1:104ft   3½e123  42  2²  34  49    Smith M E⁵ ⒻCinderla 77-19 SheenaNtive,DicePsser,FirstSonnet 9
30Apr87-8CD  7f :22² :454 1:234ft  2½e122  32½ 32½ 79  912½  FrzrRL 2 ⒻLa Troienne 74-18 Footy, Sheena Native,OnlyaGlance11
3Apr87-8OP   6f :22² :46² 1:103ft  3½ 122   2hd 2½ 33  79    Day P7       ⒻHcpO 78-17 OnlyaGlnce,CooneyDeb,ReefofGold 8
16Feb87-90P  6f :21⁴ :45¹ 1:093ft  8½ 123   34  33½ 58  517¾  SthME3 ⒻMart Wash 74-20 UptheApalchee,FoxyBer,CthyQuick 6
6Feb87-70P   5½f:22¹ :46¹ 1:042ft  *6-5 121  1hd 2hd 21½ 36¾  Bailey J D⁴ ⒻAw25000 84-14 Foxy Bear, Dr. Myrtle, Evil Elaine 12
30Jan87-6Aqu 6f ⊡:22⁴ :47¹1:14 m  *7-5e116 1½ 1hd 1½  11½   Santos J A⁸ ⒻAw27000 74-22 Evil Elaine, BridalGown,FineTiming 8
1Jan87-8Pha  6f :22¹ :46 1:122ft   *1 121   21½ 21  2²  21½   McNIFA7 ⒻNew Hope 77-31 Ray'sGift,EvilElaine,JillOfAllTrdes 12
6Dec86-8Pha  6½f:21⁴ :44⁴ 1:18¹ft  5½ 121   2¹  31½ 22½ 21½   McNilFA7 ⒻSchuylkill 80-22 Pluie'sHoney,EvilElaine,FoldtheFlg 9
```
Jly 24 AP 5f ft 1:00 h   Jun 8 AP 5f ft 1:01³ b

Harlan Dancer

Own.—Collins T A   **118**

Dk. b. or br. f. 3, by Mari's Book—Lady Harlan, by Terrang
Br.—Collins Thomas A (Ky)   1987   9   3   1   0 $28,925
Tr.—Kendrick Melvin   1986   5   M   0   0 $1,526
Lifetime   14   3   1   0 $30,451   Turf   1   0   0   0

```
28Jun87-8AP   1 ①:47⁴¹:121¹¹:38 fm  59 112   76½ 81⁴ 81⁷ 821½  SrrwsAGJr 7 ⒻAthenia 64-21 Won'tSheTell,FirstSonnet,ShnNtiv 8
14Jun87-8AP   6f :22  :45 1:104ft   101 120  97½ 99½ 91¹ 817½  SrrsAGJr 1    ⒻCinderla 69-19 SheenaNtive,DicePsser,FirstSonnet 9
30May87-4Spt  1 :45⁴ 1:11¹ 1:38 ft   21 112  55½ 611 612 616¾  Lindsay R 1   ⒻArtful 54-28 RoylCielo,OnlyGlnce,LovlyAccount 6
9May87-9OP    1 :49 1:14¹ 1:412ft    16 113  3²  1hd 1hd 11¾   Lindsay R 1 ⒻAw23200 73-22 HrlnDncer,SeekTheTruth,RhondMe 6
31Mar87-9OP   1 :46³ 1:11⁴ 1:381ft   33 1097  45  67½ 711 719  SullivanSD 9 ⒻAw16000 62-20 Monogrm,ExplosiveGirl,Tnthem'sGl 8
   31Mar87—Wide
19Mar87-90P   6f :22¹ :46 1:11 ft    43 1097  54  53½ 44  24    SullivanSD 2 ⒻAw16000 81-22 ShiveringGl,HrlnDncer,ExplosivGirl 8
7Mar87-70P    1 :46³ 1:11² 1:372ft   23 1087  54½ 87¾ 810 814   SullivanSD 2 ⒻAw25000 71-13 Foxy Bear, Dr. Myrtle, A Full Jet 8
11Jan87-9TP   1½:47¹ 1:14 1:50¹gd    4 1117  21½ 13  14  16    Sullivan SD 2 ⒻAw9900 59-26 Harlan Dancer,Quachita,BluePennie 7
1Jan87-6TP    1 :47¹ 1:14 1:414m    5½ 1147  14  15  11  11½   Sullivan S D 2 ⒻMdn 66-24 HarlanDncer,Polcovite,GoingForIt 12
6Dec86-9TP    1 :47² 1:13⁴ 1:403ft   73 114  1113 914 916 930   Lindsay R 12 ⒻGowell 42-25 TimlssJig,Bstofbothworlds,BluPnn 12
```
Jly 26 AP 5f ft 1:03 b   Jly 22 AP 4f ft :51 b   Jly 13 RD 3f gd :33¹ b   Jly 7 AP 3f sy :36 h

---

Silver Witch

Own.—Zimmerman Mary M   **112**

Gr. f. 3, by Vitriolic—Native Silver, by Native Charger
Br.—Zimmerman Mrs Mary M (Ky)   1987   7   1   0   2 $7,300
Tr.—Levitch James M   1986   4   2   1   0 $18,585
Lifetime   11   3   1   2 $25,885   Turf   1   0   0   0

```
9Jly87-8Rkm   1 ①:48²1:14 1:403fm   15 112   1½ 1016 1026 1032½ GonzalezIJr⁸ ⒻAw9000 — — Chrstml,WorthThSm,Shrdn'sSong 10
18Jun87-7Rkm  6f :22  :45¹ 1:11 ft   5 113   1½  2½  2½  33½   GonzalezIJr⁵ ⒻAw9000 85-15 Mm'sDbutnt,WorthThSm,SlvrWtch 7
31May87-9Rkm  6f :21⁴ :45 1:114ft    8-5 112  1hd 2hd 33½ 71²   GonzIzlJr² ⒻRockette 76-20 PrttyProscutor,ForJokrs,LwflJtty 11
25May87-7Rkm  6f :22³ :46 1:114ft    *2 113  11  11½ 12  14½   GonzalezIJr⁴ ⒻAw8500 85-21 Silver Witch, Kim Drouilly,SurfDoll 8
17Jan87-9Tam  6f :22¹ :45⁴ 1:12¹gd  12 116   3½  31½ 57  111¼  DePass R⁵ ⒻHibiscus 76-16 Mar Mar, NaturalEight,UniqueType 9
10Jan87-10Hia 6f :21⁴ :45² 1:094ft   58 111  1hd 2hd 44½ 615   Cruguet J⁴ ⒻJasmine 76-16 Mar Mar, NaturalEight,UniqueType 9
1Jan87-7Crc   6f :23¹ :47³ 1:13 ft   41 115  2hd 2½ 22  34½   Cruguet J² ⒻAw15400 82-22 MySweetReplic,Mrs.Ldr,SilvrWitch 7
13Dec86-6Crc  6f :22³ :46⁴ 1:133ft  *2½ 115  1hd 1² 1½  1no   Cruguet J⁴ ⒻAw11500 83-22 SilvrWitch,Tonk'sBonnyLss,Tr'sBst 9
26Nov86-6CD   6f :21  :45³ 1:131m   *7-5 118  2hd 2½ 3²  65¾   WodsCRJr⁵ ⒻAw16750 71-23 MissStyleQuen,LovlyNdr,Dsigntion 10
12Nov86-6CD   6½f:22⁴ :47² 1:214gd  *3-2 118  11  1½  11  22½   Meier R⁵   ⒻAw15200 68-33 RainGauge,SilverWitch,Designtion 10
```

Island Snow

Own.—Seltzer Edward   **118**

Dk. b. or br. f. 3, by Verbatim—December Sky, by Drone
Br.—Seltzer Edward (Ky)   1987   7   2   0   2 $29,670
Tr.—Trotsek Harry E   1986   8   1   5   2 $24,403
Lifetime   15   3   5   4 $54,073   Turf   2   0   0   1 $2,870

```
25Jun87-9EIP  6f :22² :45² 1:10¹ft   7 121   75½ 87  6⁸ 48½   Foster D E 3 ⒻInangrl 85-16 NickIPltd,Qun'sHighnss,FrskyKttn 10
7Jun87-9CD    1 ①:46¹¹:121¹:39¹fm   29 117  1013 1012 91³ 81³ Bass S H⁶    ⒻRegret — — Jonowo, Lt. Lao, Sum 10
25May87-10RD  1 ①:47¹¹:121¹:384fm  *2½ 118  2³  2²  22½ 33¾   LindsyR² ⒻSpg Bonet 79-13 Lady Lush, Quickner, Island Snow 12
7May87-8Spt   6f :234 :47⁴ 1:133ft  *8-5 115  2²  2hd 13½ 15½  Lindsay R⁴ ⒻAw22700 82-24 IslndSnow,Stembold,BeguilingLook 6
26Feb87-9Spt  6f :234 :48² 1:133sy   7½ 115  55½ 63¾ 45½ 38   Hirdes J⁵    ⒻTulip 74-25 P.C.J.Relaxer,FoldtheFlg,IsIndSnow 8
29Jan87-9FG   6f :22¹ :47 1:13 ft    4½ 119  52½ 67  42½ 11   MrtinezLuis² ⒻAw9000 80-25 IslndSnow,P.C.J.Relxer,TillSunrise 12
9Jan87-8FG    6f :22  :46² 1:122ft   5 119   73½ 65½ 58  43½  PerrodinEJ⁶ ⒻAw9000 79-16 FoxyBear,B.W.Baba,Tanthem'sGal 12
28Dec86-5FG   6f :22¹ :46¹ 1:12 ft  *6-5 119  2hd 3² 33½ 36½  LouviereGE¹ ⒻAw9000 78-22 Fine Dining, B. W.Baba,IslandSnow 9
30Nov86-10FG  6f :23  :49³ 1:18³hy  3½e113 42½ 32½ 3²  21½  LovrGE⁸ ⒻPontalba H 50-51 CthyQuick,IsIndSnow,Prtnr'sCurrss 9
2Nov86-8Bml   6f :23² :47¹ 1:14 ft   6-5 112  43¾ 44½ 59  31¹  Bullard B A⁵  ⒻRaymie 78-15 FlashnDance,CndidType,IsIndSnow 5
```
Jly 19 AP 4f ft :49 b   Jun 16 CD 3f ft :36³ b   • Jun 3 CD 3f m :36 b

```
First Sonnet                                   Dk. b. or br. f. 3, by Mr Leader—Sonneteer, by Soy Numero Uno
                                               Br.—Nuckols Bros (Ky)                      1987  9 1 1 1      $21,512
Own.—R L Reineman Stable Inc          118      Tr.—Vanier Harvey L                        1986  5 2 1 0      $18,595
                                            Lifetime   14 3 2 1   $40,107                 Turf  4 0 1 0       $6,240
18Jly87-8AP   1 1/16(T):4711:12 1:443fm 101 112  12111112 912 811¼  Silva C H13 (F)Mty Isle 73-17 Shot GunBonnie,UniqueType,Sum 13
 9Jly87-8AP   1  (T):4711:1221:384fm*9-5 118  77½ 56½ 42  44    MrqzCHJr5 (F)Aw17000 77-20 MyTurbulentBeu,DicePssr,MissK.B. 8
28Jun87-8AP   1  (T):4741:1211:38 fm  11 118  44½ 45  31  22    MrqzCHJr1 (F)Athenia 83-21 Won'tSheTell,FirstSonnet,ShnNtiv 8
14Jun87-8AP   6f :22   :45  1:104ft   46 120  86¾ 88¾ 45  36½   MrqzCHJr2 (F)Cinderla 79-19 SheenaNtive,DicePsser,FirstSonnet 9
 9Apr87-6Kee  7f :23   :462 1:262ft   3¼ 115  32  3½  1hd 1½    BrumfildD5 (F)Aw18100 74-33 First Sonnet, Jonowo, Rain Gauge 6
19Mar87-9GP  a1  (T)        1:41 fm   27 116  3nk 31  711 912¼  Cruguet J1 (F)Aw22000 63-26 MomsBrthdy,AntqMystq,OrLttlMrg 9
16Feb87-9Hia  6f :223  :452 1:104ft   19 115  4¾  67¼ 66¼ 69    Cruguet J4 (F)Aw17000 77-24 ‡My Pearl, FoldtheFlag,EasterMary 8
27Jan87-9Hia  6f :222  :46  1:104ft   3½ 115  75  66  87¾ 813¾  Cruguet J6 (F)Aw19500 72-22 EllsNoblePeace,LuckyBarMid,Cope 8
18Jan87-6Hia  7f :224  :453 1:241ft   41 115  84¾ 64¼ 52¼ 52½   Cruguet J8 (F)Aw19500 79-19 Swetbrds,FrontFrind's,AdddElgnc 12
26Oct86-8CD   1  :461 1:142 1:423m    27 117  86¾ 95¼ 55½ 69    McKtJ9 (F)Pocahontas 47-29 Bestofbothworlds,Lsertt,Combtiv 12
    Jly 4 AP 4f ft :49 b        Jun 26 AP 3f ft :382 b        Jun 22 AP 4f sy :503 b        Jun 3 AP 5f sl 1:021 b
```

```
Coesse Express                                 B. f. 3, by Dewan—Night Rounds, by Round Table
                                               Br.—Builders Mart Inc (Ky)                 1987  3 3 0 0      $23,400
Own.—Morsches P                       115      Tr.—Bollero Joseph M                       1986  0 M 0 0
                                            Lifetime   3 3 0 0   $23,400
15Jly87-7AP   6½f:231  :473 1:202sy *6-5 115  12½ 12  11  11¼   Fires E 1  (F)Aw15000 73-34 CoesseExpress,CopprStr,EsyAnswr 5
 4Jly87-4AP   7f :224  :462 1:252ft   3¼ 115  1½  11  12  1¾    Fires E 4  (F)Aw13000 75-26 CoesseExpress,NoDoublet,IdleRidg 6
20Jun87-2AP   6½f:23   :464 1:183ft   5½ 116  11½ 12½ 14  12    Fires E 1  (F)Mdn 82-22 CoesseExprss,RstivMiss,SunstRid 12
    Jly 14 AP 3f ft :37 b       Jun 17 AP 4f ft :493 bg       Jun 10 AP 4f ft :514 b        Jun 3 AP 4f sl :492 b
```

A. 2
B. 3
C. 4
D. 5

13. Which horse has a class edge?

A.

```
*Innerspace                                    Ch. c. 4, by Godswalk—Tootens, by Northfields
  CAMPBELL B C                                 Br.—Dillon J (Ire)                         1987  3 1 0 1       $6,960
                                      122      Tr.—Russell John W                         1986 12 1 3 2      $28,144
Own.—Levy Blanche P                         Lifetime   18 2 3 3   $35,104                 Turf 17 2 3 2      $32,104
27Feb87-6GG   .1  :46  1:094 1:35 ft   11 119  55½ 55  44½ 33½   CampbellBC1 Aw20000 89-14 Olajuwon, Easy Mover, Innerspace 7
14Feb87-10TuP 1  (T):4631:1141:38 fm*7-5 112  411 22½ 12  13    Powell J P1  Aw6600 92-08 Innerspace,ExclusivePtriot,VillStr 10
 8Feb87-5SA  a6½f(T):211 :4341:144fm  36 115  108 108¼ 84¾ 64½   Olivares F9 Aw30000 80-09 Hard Round, Irish Stories,Putting 12
27Sep86♦4Evry(Fra)  a5f     :592gd *4½ 119  (T) 42¼  GugnrdG   Px d Pthvrs H King OfAtina, Abitibi, ‡Setagaye 17
     27Sep86—Placed third through disqualification
23Aug86♦3Deauville(Fra) a6f 1:151sf  7¾ 113  (T) 13   GugnrdG    Px d Cgny H WiseBird, Elisharp, Setagaya 17
 9Aug86♦3Deauville(Fra) a5f :59 gd   10 113  (T) 2½   GuignrdG  Px d Blnvlle H CountryCmden,Innerspce,WisBird 15
16Jly86♦4Evry(Fra)  a6½f   1:154gd*4-5 117  (T) 12½  GuignrdG   Px Gldiatr H Innerspace, Trioa, Aukaline 12
24Jun86♦2Chantilly(Fra) a6f 1:152gd   5 108  (T) 42   RmonetC      Px d'Ory H WiseBird,StrangeBird,KingofAtina 15
28May86♦4Evry(Fra)  a6½f   1:182gd *3½ 111  (T) 22   RmntC   Px Vllrs Sr Mrn H Allius, Innerspace, Pirate 21
 9May86♦6MLaffitte(Fra) a6f 1:11 gd  8¾ 106  (T) 2hd  RmontC      Px Du Rey H TenderSpring,Innerspc,KingofAtin 15
  ●Mar 31 GG 7f ft 1:281 h     Mar 24 GG 6f gd 1:173 h      Mar 16 SA 7f ft 1:272 h       Mar 9 SA 6f ft 1:151 h
```

B.

```
Buck Royale                                    B. h. 5, by Buckaroo—Katie L, by Terrang
  SCHACHT R                                    Br.—Blythe Elizabeth (Ky)                  1987  3 1 2 0      $17,850
                                      122      Tr.—Griffiths Riley                        1986  5 1 0 1       $9,345
Own.—Becker–Crispo–Riggio                   Lifetime   11 3 4 1   $36,380                 Turf  1 1 0 0      $10,450
24Mar87-8GG   1  (T):4611:11 1:371fm   9 116  43½ 33½ 2½  12    Schacht R1  Aw19000 81-19 Buck Royale, Re Enter,TellFloHello 7
11Mar87-8GG   1  :461 1:104 1:36 ft   2½ 116  21  21  23  25    Schacht R4  Aw19000 83-23 Ed'sExclusiv,BuckRoyl,AuBonMrch 5
20Feb87-7GG   6f :22   :442 1:09 ft   23 116  31½ 32  33½ 24    Schacht R6  Aw18000 90-18 Chaka,BuckRoyale,BlazingSunshine 6
 2Aug86-7Dmr  1  :444 1:101 1:354ft   12 118  46  87¾ 811 814   Olivares F3 Aw20000 75-12 Genuine John, Allez Allez, Sirtaki 8
     2Aug86—Broke slowly
18Jly86-3Sol  1  :462 1:112 1:36 ft   3¼ 115  1hd 1hd 11  12½   Schacht R2  Aw13000 94-12 BuckRoyl,LondonExprss,BigDnRyn 7
11Jly86-11Sol 1  :464 1:104 1:364ft   9¼ 115  33½ 33½ 31½ 32    Schacht R8  Aw13000 88-15 Fali Plaza, Tell Matt, Buck Royale 9
26Jun86-11Pln 6f :214  :45  1:094ft   9¾ 115  98½ 77½ 510 511¼  CampbellBC9 Aw15000 82-19 DetrmindFir,BobCourtny,John'sJov 9
26Feb86-6GG   1 1/16:464 1:112 1:432ft 3½ 113  2hd 2hd 36  74¾   Castro J7   Aw17000 81-18 Witin'ForBevr,BroomBuck,GtMEvn 8
     26Feb86—Off slowly
12Sep85-10Bmf 1  :453 1:102 1:342ft  *2¾ 1095 32½ 54¾ 48  29    Cisneros J E2 Aw17000 87-25 Sidersell, Buck Royale, GetMeEven 7
31Aug85-7Bmf  1  :461 1:11  1:362ft    6 1085 44  3nk 1½  2½    Cisneros J E2 Aw16000 85-16 Whymemck,BuckRoyle,GetMeEven 6
     31Aug85—Broke in a tangle
  ●Mar 18 GG (T) 3f fm :372 h (d) Mar 7 GG 4f ft :491 h   Feb 28 GG 5f ft 1:002 h       Feb 14 GG 5f gd 1:01 h
```

C.

***Arctic Blast II**
CASTANEDA M 116
Own.—Val d'Or Inc
B. c. 4, by Bellman—Arctic Wave, by Arctic Slave
Br.—British Bloodstock Agency (Fra) 1986 7 1 1 2 $26,387
Tr.—McAnaily Ronald 1985 1 1 0 0 $8,764
Lifetime 8 2 1 2 $35,151 Turf 8 2 1 2 $35,151
14Sep86♦4Longchamp(Fra) a1½ 2:364yl *1-9e 123 Ⓣ 34½ GuignrdG Px Niel(Gr3) Bering, Malakim, ArcticBlast 5
20Aug86♦5Deauvilie(Fra) a1 9/16 2:463yl 10 128 Ⓣ 41½ MorGW Px Mchl Houyvt Alesso, Malakim, Pub Royal 9
4Aug86♦4Clairefont'e(Fra a1⅛ 1:514gd 4 121 Ⓣ 1¾ MossG Px Grrd d Chvgnc ArcticBlast,‡DoubleBed,Adariyoun 13
8Jun86♦4Chantilly (Fra) a1½ 2:24 gd*1-2e 128 Ⓣ 814 LeroyM Px d Jky Clb(Gr1) Bering, Altayan, Bakharoff 13
1Jun86♦2Longchamp(Fra) a1¼ 2:084gd *2½ 128 Ⓣ 3hd MooreGW Px d Tilleuls Eastbell, Ordinance, ArcticBlast 8
20Apr86♦6Longchamp(Fra) a1 3/16 2:332sf 5¾ 128 Ⓣ 66¾ MrGW Px D Guiche(Gr3) BdConduct,HilToRoberto,DoubleBd 8
6Apr86♦2Longchamp(Fra) a1¼ 2:134sf 2¼ 123 Ⓣ 25 MooreGW Px dCrclles PortEtienne,ArcticBlst,LoylDoubl 10
12Nov85♦8MLaffitte(Fra) a1 1:431sf 7 123 Ⓣ 1hd Head F Px Dagor(Mdn) ArcticBlast, Malakim, Barood 20
Apr 2 SA Ⓣ 4f fm :482 h (d) Mar 26 SA Ⓣ 7f fm 1:304 h (d) Mar 20 SA Ⓣ 6f fm 1:152 h (d) Mar 12 SA Ⓣ 6f fm 1:153 h (d)

D.

***Halo Hatch**
JUDICE J C 116
Own.—Finucane Mrs Kathleen
B. g. 4, by Thatch—Novalesa, by Northfields
Br.—Allevamento Alpi Cosie (Ire) 1986 9 1 1 2 $5,373
Tr.—Otteson Kimberly 1985 5 M 2 1 $2,148
Lifetime 14 1 3 3 $7,521 Turf 14 1 3 3 $7,521
20Oct86♦5Chepstow(Eng) 1 1:352gd 8 124 Ⓣ 35 WhtrthS Stk(Clm 42945) EagleDestiny,SwiftsPal,HaloHatch 13
17Sep86♦3Brighton(Eng) 1¼ 2:002fm 10 126 Ⓣ 1018 WhtrtS W & A Gilbey H HawaiinPlm,MrshHrrier,FootPtrol 14
6Sep86♦4Thirsk(Eng) 1 1:40 gd 5 119 Ⓣ 611 Hill R Mail On Sndy H BlueGuitr,BoldSeRover,CrstAction 9
16Aug86♦1Ripon(Eng) 1⅛ 1:544gd 6 129 Ⓣ 21½ Hills R Newby H HonestToil,HloHtch,ChrltonKings 10
5Aug86♦6Brighton(Eng) 1 1:35 gd 10 118 Ⓣ 14 WhtwrthS So Coast HaloHatch,DAningEgle,HutboyLdy 9
26Jly86♦2Warwick(Eng) 1 1:372gd 8 130 Ⓣ 109¾ Clark A Entrtainrs H Admstown,Kindriy,SuprmKngdom 11
12Jly86♦3Salisbury(Eng) 1 1:441gd *4½ 125 Ⓣ 612 WhtwrthS Fair Trial H SwiftsPl,AbsenceofMlice,Trmintor 14
●Mar 29 SA tr.t 6f ft 1:15 h ●Mar 24 SA tr.t 6f ft 1:153 h Mar 19 SA tr.t 6f ft 1:162 h Mar 14 SA 5f ft 1:013 h

14. The six 3YOs below met in a restricted stakes on the grass. Which should be expected to do best on the footing?

A.

***Uptothehilt**
BAZE G 114
Own.—Bollinger & Millhouse
B. c. 3, by Kris—Karine, by Habitat
Br.—Costelloe J P (Ire) 1987 2 1 0 0 $7,437
Tr.—Vienna Darrell 1986 4 1 0 0 $1,520
Lifetime 6 2 0 0 $8,957 Turf 6 2 0 0 $8,957
4May87♦3Doncaster(Eng) 1 1:393gd 8 128 Ⓣ 1nk CrsonW A F Budge H Uptothhilt,KngBlldr,Wnslydlwrror 17
20Apr87♦2Kempton(Eng) 1 1:45 gd 14 133 Ⓣ 11 CarsonW Middlesex H Othet, Mustakbil, DivineCharger 18
31Oct86♦1Newmarket(Eng) 1 1:443gd 12 123 Ⓣ 97½ Reid J Soham House PllrofWsdom,OurAccont,RoylPgnt 15
13Oct86♦1Warwick(Eng) 1 fm 4 126 Ⓣ 1½ CrsonW Brinlow (Mdn) Uptothehilt, Talus, Draw Lots 12
13Oct86—No time taken
16Sep86♦3Lingfield(Eng) a7½f 1:353gd 33 123 Ⓣ 78½ Reid J Cellamn Burr Suhailie, Just A Flutter, Orne 7
2Aug86♦6Newmarket(Eng) 6f 1:134gd 5½ 126 Ⓣ 88 DuffldG Pegasus (Mdn) Mostwelcome, Capewild, GreatAct 12
Jly 22 Dmr 4f ft :504 h Jly 17 Dmr 3f ft :391 h

B.

Captain Valid
BAZE R A 114
Own.—Saron Stable
B. c. 3, by Valid Appeal—Arctic Deb, by Northerly
Br.—Robertson C J (Ky) 1987 3 0 1 0 $5,625
Tr.—Jones Gary 1986 5 2 0 1 $99,534
Lifetime 8 2 1 1 $105,159
20Jun87-7Hol 7f :22 :442 1:224ft 3½ 112 3½ 33 65 57 Solis A 2 Aw25000 83-11 TommyTheHwk,FleetSudn,DonDieg 8
11Jun87-8Hol 6f :22 :451 1:093ft *8-5 114 35 44 56 69¼ McCarronCJ 8 Aw25000 86-18 HonkyTonkDancer,Pilor,ThunderCt 8
24May87-7Hol 6f :214 :45 1:10 ft 3½ 114 32 31½ 2hd 22½ Stevens G L 6 Aw25000 90-13 W.D.Jacks,CaptainValid,ThunderCt 8
27Sep86-8Bel 7f :221 :45 1:224sy 21 122 43 42¼ 611 616 Baze R A 7 Cowdin 72-17 Polish Navy, JavaGold,PhantomJet 8
27Sep86—Grade I
13Sep86-7Bel 7f :23 :454 1:221ft 15 122 55 56 49½ 38¾ Santos JA 3 Futurity 82-11 Gulch,Demon'sBegone,CaptainVlid 7
13Sep86—Grade I
1Sep86-6AP 1 :444 1:112 1:371ft 3¾ 122 21 2½ 44 69¼ McCrrCJ 7 Arl WasFut 66-22 BtTwic,Conquistros,JzzingAround 11
1Sep86—Grade I
19Jly86-8Hol 6f :22 :452 1:113ft 3 117 64½ 65½ 33½ 11½ McCrrCJ 3 Hol JuvChp 86-15 CaptainValid,Qulify,JzzingAround 12
19Jly86—Grade II; Ducked in, steadied early drive
28Jun86-1Hol 5½f :22 :452 1:04 ft *9-5 118 21 2½ 13½ 16 McCarron C J 5 Mdn 94-12 CaptinVlid,AcdemyGrey,BiloxiBlues 7
Jly 24 Hol 7f ft 1:26 h ●Jly 18 Hol 5f ft :584 h Jly 13 Hol 5f ft 1:001 h ●Jly 7 Hol 4f ft :462 h

C.

Sebrof
STEVENS G L **114**
Own.—Jones A U

Dk. b. or br. c. 3, by Bold Forbes—Jamila, by Graustark
Br.—Jones A U (Ky) 1987 2 2 0 0 $22,550
Tr.—Barrera Lazaro S 1986 0 M 0 0
Lifetime 2 2 0 0 $22,550

5Jly87-7Hol 6f :22 :451 1:103ft 4¼ 116 1½ 1hd 1½ 1½ Stevens G L 1 Aw22000 90-11 Sebrof, Penasco, Five Shy 10
21Jun87-6Hol 6f :214 :451 1:104ft *2¼ 115 2½ 2hd 1hd 1no Stevens G L 3 Mdn 89-14 Sebrof, Sedeno, Havewemetyet 12
Jly 20 Hol 5f ft 1:022 h ● Jly 13 Hol 5f ft :583 h Jly 4 Hol 3f ft :353 h Jun 29 Hol 5f ft :594 h

D.

Magna Plus
MEZA R Q **118**
Own.—Hand E J

B. c. 3, by Graustark—Sleep Till Noon, by Ambiorix
Br.—Sturgill Peggy B (Ky) 1987 4 2 1 0 $28,775
Tr.—Gregson Edwin 1986 0 M 0 0
Lifetime 4 2 1 0 $28,775

27Jun87-7Hol 1 1/16 :453 1:102 1:43 ft 6¾ 114 46 44½ 12½ 12 Meza R Q 7 Aw24000 94-09 MagnaPlus,MarkChip,Bigbadndmen 7
7Jun87-4Hol 1 1/16 :47 1:121 1:444ft *3-5 115 42½ 3½ 12½ 19 Meza R Q 4 Mdn 85-17 MagnaPlus,ProudCat,ChinvtBridge 8
24May87-6Hol 1 :452 1:103 1:362ft *4-5 116 42 31½ 21½ 2no Delahoussaye E 1 Mdn 81-13 Don'tsingtheblus,MgnPlus,ProudCt 7
11Apr87-6SA 6f :214 :45 1:113ft 26 118 1215 1111 88½ 52¾ Meza R Q 9 Mdn 77-16 TddyBrHug,HlCommndr,DmscsLd 12
Jly 27 Dmr Ⓣ 4f fm :522 h Jly 22 Hol 5f ft 1:002 h Jly 16 Hol 1 ft 1:393 h Jly 11 Hol 5f ft 1:03 h

E.

Mount Laguna
MCCARRON C J **114**
Own.—Golden Eagle Farm

Ch. c. 3, by Huguenot—Laura's Star, by Key to the Kingdom
Br.—Mabee Mr-Mrs J C (Ky) 1987 7 2 1 1 $51,600
Tr.—Sadler John W 1986 0 M 0 0
Lifetime 7 2 1 1 $51,600

28Mar87-8GG 1 1/16 :45 1:094 1:422ft *4-5 116 2hd 2hd 56 713 CastnedM 7 Gold Rush 78-14 Blanco,RoyalRadar,Bker'sCrossing 10
28Mar87—Stumbled start; ducked in sharply, bumped 3/16
14Mar87-8GG 1 :453 1:113 1:39 m 5 116 11½ 11 24 2½ Castaneda M 5 Lfyette 72-23 Momentus,MountLgun,FlyingFlgs 12
25Feb87-8SA 6f :211 :442 1:103m *3-2 116 21½ 21 2hd 44¼ VlnzlPA 3 Ⓡ Blsa Chca 81-22 SomthingLucky,RdAndBlu,FltingJt 7
25Feb87—Bumped hard 3/16; lugged in stretch
14Feb87-8SA 7f :221 :45 1:234sy 9-5 116 12 11 22½ 35¼ VlnzulPA 6 Sn Vcnte 76-17 StylshWnnr,PrncSssfrs,MountLgun 6
14Feb87—Grade III; Checked at 3/16
6Feb87-3SA 6f :211 :433 1:084ft 6¾ 120 12½ 11½ 11½ 14 ValenzuelPA 6 Aw26000 94-15 MountLagun,SweetwterSprings,Wr 7
24Jan87-3SA 6f :212 :442 1:101ft *3½ 120 21 44 76¼ 89¾ ValenzuelPA 1 Aw26000 77-18 HppyInSpc,SwtwtrSprings,ThQuppr 9
24Jan87—Off slowly
4Jan87-4SA 6f :214 :45 1:104sy *1-2e 118 12 13 12½ 1¾ Valenzuela P A 4 Mdn 84-22 Mount Laguna, Acquired, Conquer 7
4Jan87—Bumped 5 1/2
Jly 24 Hol 7f ft 1:261 h ● Jly 18 Hol 6f ft 1:122 h Jly 12 Hol 5f ft 1:002 h Jly 6 Hol 5f ft 1:034 h

F.

Mon Legionnaire
TORO F **114**
Own.—Bernheim-Hecht-Karacan

B. c. 3, by Racing Room—Advising Jean, by Noble Jay
Br.—Paine T E & Linda (Cal) 1987 6 1 2 0 $15,725
Tr.—Bunn Thomas M Jr 1986 0 M 0 0
Lifetime 6 1 2 0 $15,725

11Jly87-7Hol 1 :452 1:101 1:362ft 18 116 51¼ 53 51¼ 2½ DelahoussayeE 7 62500 80-12 Lrkng'sRoylty,MonLgonnr,CrosLov 7
24Jun87-6Hol 7f :22 :451 1:24 ft 4½ 115 42½ 21½ 22 12 McCarron C J 6 M50000 84-13 MonLgonnr,ExplosvDrm,CrystlFx 12
13Jun87-6Hol 6f :214 :451 1:093ft 9¼ 115 43½ 32 34½ 47½ Sibille R 2 Ⓢ Mdn 87-11 CablloDeOro,Gslighter,RodOfLuck 11
27May87-4Hol 6f :222 :463 1:12 ft *6-5 115 33 31 2½ 2hd Sibille R 9 Ⓢ M32000 83-16 BkuBby,MonLegionnire,IrishSmile 12
9Apr87-6SA 6f :22 :453 1:101ft 56 118 3nk 31 65½ 67¼ Sibille R 11 M50000 80-18 Be Scenic,CrystalFox,GoldenBeau 11
27Mar87-6SA 6f :214 :453 1:113ft 41 1135 912 107½ 97¼ 77¾ Patton D B 11 M50000 72-23 Plum Wishfull,CoolTalker,Guggen 12
● Jun 9 Hol 4f ft :472 h Jun 3 Hol 4f ft :481 h

15. Qualify the entrants on class and form and separate them on pace. Which should win?

2nd Santa Anita

OUT OF CHUTE
6½ FURLONGS
SANTA ANITA
FINISH

6 ½ FURLONGS. (1.14) CLAIMING. Purse $23,000. 4-year-olds and upward. Weights, 4-year-olds, 120 lbs.; older, 121 lbs. Non-winners of two races since November 3 allowed 3 lbs.; of a race since then, 5 lbs. Claiming price $40,000; if for $35,000 allowed 2 lbs. (Races when entered for $32,000 or less not considered.)

A.

Juntura — Dk. b. or br. g. 7, by Bold Forbes—Joawin, by Donut King
SIBILLE R — 116 — Br.—Hancock III & Peters (Ky) — 1986 15 5 2 3 $89,175
Own.—Tuscany Farms (Lessee) — Tr.—Harper David B — $40,000 — 1985 22 1 5 6 $64,925
Lifetime 54 8 10 9 $198,150 — Turf 9 0 0 2 $12,600

31Dec86-5SA 6½f :22 :45³ 1:17²ft *8-5 116 12¹² 97½ 74½ 42½ Stevens G L¹ c40000 81-20 Watch'n Win, Angle Arc, Idol 12
31Dec86—Checked late
14Dec86-9Hol 1 ①:46²1:11¹1:36²fm 3½ 116 66½ 63½ 52¾ 33½ Stevens G L⁶ 50000 81-11 LordOfTheWind,Hrdknock'n,Juntur 8
14Dec86—Wide 3/8
6Dec86-3Hol 6f :22⁴ :46 1:10⁴gd 3-2 117 47 45½ 33½ 2½ Stevens G L¹ 50000 88-16 Nordicus, Juntura,KingOfCalifornia 4
22Nov86-7Hol 7f :22 :45¹ 1:22²ft 3 116 8¹⁴ 79½ 45 21½ Stevens G L⁸ 50000 91-13 Cracksman, Juntura, Infantryman 8
22Nov86—Wide backstretch
11Nov86-3Hol 6f :22¹ :45⁴ 1:10⁴ft 3½ 116 62¾ 55 31½ 11½ Stevens G L³ 32000 89-20 Juntura, King OfCalifornia,Bizeboy 6
4May86-9Hol 1 :45³ 1:10³ 1:36²ft 6½ 116 9¹¹ 68¾ 37½ 38½ Solis A⁶ 50000 72-18 Silver Hero, Ono Gummo, Juntura 9
20Apr86-9SA a6½f ①:21³ :44²1:14⁴fm 11 114 11¹¹119¾109½108½ Stevens G L³ 57500 76-15 Hwkley,RisingChum,French'sLuck 12
9Apr86-1SA 6½f:21⁴ :44⁴ 1:17¹ft 3½ 122 67 65½ 52½ 1½ Stevens G L² 50000 84-18 Juntura, NationalEnergy,Menswear 7
21Mar86-7SA 6f :21² :44 1:09²ft 4½ 121 12¹⁰109¾ 97¾ 74½ Stevens G L¹ 50000 87-15 KingOfCliforni,Cryptrch,Menswer 12
9Mar86-9SA 1$\frac{1}{16}$:47³ 1:12 1:43¹sy 2 119 41½ 43½ 35½ 37½ Valenzuela P A³ 50000 77-19 ForgotThRng,FbulousMmcry,Juntr 4
Jan 27 SA 5f ft 1:00⁴ h — Jan 21 SA 5f ft 1:04 h — Jan 17 SA 5f ft 1:05 h — Jan 11 SA 3f ft :36⁴ h

B.

Roll A Natural — B. g. 7, by L'Natural—Happy Dunce, by Fleet Nasrullah
TORO F — 116 — Br.—Warwick & West (Cal) — 1987 1 0 0 0
Own.—Teichner S & Phyllis — Tr.—Dorfman Leonard — $40,000 — 1986 12 1 2 1 $29,900
Lifetime 55 8 9 2 $138,700 — Turf 4 0 0 1 $4,900

17Jan87-2SA 6f :21⁴ :45 1:10³ft 4½ 116 75¾1011 98½ 77½ DelahoussayeE⁵ 40000 78-18 Ondarty, Romaxe, Rivets Factor 11
17Jan87—Bumped, took up 5/8; wide into stretch
15Nov86-3Hol 6f :22¹ :45² 1:10 ft 3½ 117 2hd 21 21½ 21½ DelahoussayeE⁴ 40000 92-14 Cracksman,RollANturl,PtriotGloves 6
3Nov86-2SA 6½f:21³ :44¹ 1:16¹ft 9 116 67½ 77½ 65½ 64½ Stevens G L⁷ 50000 85-14 Danczone,RivetsFactor,Infantrymn 8
3Nov86—Stumbled start
23Sep86-11Pom 6½f:21³ :44² 1:15¹ft 8½ 116 78½ 711 67½ 67½ Sibille R¹ Gvnr Cp H 97-08 BundleOfIron,Mtronomic,SurToFir 7
23Sep86—Checked at break
10Sep86-3Dmr 6f :22 :45 1:09³ft 2½ 118 6⁸ 66½ 54 2hd DelhoussyeE³ Aw24000 90-11 LstMotel,RollANturl,AmzingCourge 6
10Sep86—Wide final 3/8
27Aug86-5Dmr 6f :21⁴ :45 1:09¹ft 25 116 51½ 62¾ 73 63¾ Sibille R⁵ 50000 88-14 DonnrPrty,TddyNturlly,RivtsFctor 11
27Aug86—Wide in drive
15May86-7Hol 6f :22² :45³ 1:10³ft 16 116 52½ 75½ 74½ 73 DelhoussyeE⁵ Aw23000 88-13 Lincoln Park, Go Swiftly, Conteal 7
15May86—Steadied on backstretch
1May86-5Hol 6f :22³ :46² 1:11 ft 3½ 116 41½ 21½ 31½ 54½ Olivares F² Aw23000 84-17 Mtronomic,OffToRno,Cpriciousnss 6
16Apr86-5SA a6½f ①:22 :44³1:15²fm 16 116 1hd 2hd 21½ 32 DelhoussyeE³ Aw28000 80-17 BlueRazor,Diaghlyphrd,RollANturl 10
29Mar86-3SA 6½f:21⁴ :44⁴ 1:17 ft 5½ 116 61½ 64½ 42½ 11 DelahoussayeE¹⁰ 40000 85-20 RollANturl,CelticVntur,CourgRulr 12
29Mar86—Wide final 1/4
Jan 29 SA 5f ft 1:03³ h — Jan 24 SA 5f ft 1:02⁴ h — ●Jan 16 SA 3f ft :34³ h — Jan 11 SA 5f ft 1:01 h

C.

Tout De Meme — Ch. h. 5, by To the Quick—Anne Campbell, by Never Bend
PATTERSON A — 116 — Br.—Jones B C (Ky) — 1986 3 1 1 0 $10,540
Own.—Lee-Rimrock St-Roy — Tr.—Hutchinson Kathy — $40,000 — 1985 11 2 1 1 $17,416
Lifetime 14 3 2 1 $27,956 — Turf 12 2 1 1 $17,416

26Dec86-5SA a6½f ①:21² :44¹1:15¹fm 29 117 74½ 76 911 1010½ Simpson B H³ 80000 73-17 Estate, Champion Pilot, Shanaar 12
7Jun86-8Cby 1 :46⁴ 1:12³ 1:40 ft *1 121 21 14 1hd 2¾ Black K⁶ Aw14[illegible] 80-26 CheyenneCheree,ToutdeMeme,Blsh 6
22May86-8Cby 6½f:23 :46 1:17²ft 2 118 2hd 11½ 12½ 1½ Black K⁴ Aw12[illegible] 94-21 ToutdeMeme,RoylTroon,VrsityType 6
8Oct85♦3Evry(Fra) a1⅛ 1:51³gd*8-5 129 ① 1³ AsmssnC Px d'Evry H Tout de Meme, Dilling, Polar Maid 9
17Sep85♦2Longchamp(Fra) a1 1:44¹gd 6½ 122 ① 96¾ AsssnC Px d l'Orngere H DonKldoun,LeFbien,SpeedyGrnblr 14
22Jly85♦5StCloud(Fra) a1 1:43 gd 7½ 126 ① 66 PiccioniC Px Motrico NewBruce,SuperLucent,BonnysNic 8
13Jly85♦7MLaffitte(Fra) a1 1:40¹gd 10 134 ① 54¾ AsmssnC Px Rienzo H Kensof, Right Value, Riche Mare 14
6Jun85♦2Chantilly(Fra) a1⅛ 1:56²yl 5½ 123 ① 96¾ AsssnC Px Mrtefntn H Nikalaita, Anka Germania, Kerdan 15
2Apr85♦5StCloud(Fra) a1 1:52³sf 4½ 121 ① 11 AsmssnC Px Jn le Gndc Metal Precieux, Rox,SiberianHero 11
19Nov84♦5StCloud(Fra) a1¼ 2:25 sf 7 121 ① 7¹⁰ AsssnC CrtrmStCld(Gr2) Mouktar, HelloBill, Fitnah 14
Jan 28 SA 3f ft :35² h — Jan 18 SA 6f ft 1:14³ h — Jan 11 SA 6f ft 1:14² h — Dec 18 SA 6f ft 1:14¹ h

D.

Jumbled — Dk. b. or br. c. 4, by Thousandfold—Scramble, by Pronto
MCHARGUE D G — 115 — Br.—Klyza-Rankin-Rankin-Ansui (Ky) — 1986 3 1 0 1 $10,250
Own.—Franklin J L — Tr.—Rowan Mary — $40,000 — 1985 0 M 0 0
Lifetime 3 1 0 1 $10,250

4Jun86-9Hol 1 :46² 1:11⁴ 1:37 ft 21 116 63 51¾ 41½ 34½ Lipham T¹ 50000 74-18 Gaelic Knight, Joab, Jumbled 7
1May86-9Hol 1 :46 1:11³ 1:37³ft 22 116 31½ 43 46 57 Lipham T¹ 50000 68-17 Joab, Cabriome, Many Roads 8
1May86—Broke slowly
16Apr86-3SA 6½f:22 :45¹ 1:18⁴ft 11 118 42½ 44 2hd 1nk Lipham T¹ M32000 76-24 Jumbled,Medieval,NineStarAdmirl 12
●Jan 30 SA 4f ft :46⁴ h — Jan 23 SA 6f ft 1:15² hg — Jan 17 SA 5f ft 1:02⁴ h — Jan 10 SA 5f gd 1:01¹ h

E.

Vari Beau — Ch. c. 4, by Beau's Eagle—Villa V, by Olympiad King

DOUGLAS R R 117 — Br.—Relatively & Varium Stables (Cal) — 1987 1 1 0 0 $8,800

Tr.—Soto Herbert Jr $40,000 — 1986 11 M 3 2 $13,075

Own.—Dillon & Story Stable — Lifetime 12 1 3 2 $21,875

23Jan87-6SA 6f :22 :453 1:111ft 5½ 117 61¼ 31½ 11 14 Douglas R R1 M45000 82-22 Vari Beau, Hapigrin, PrivateEagle 12

23Jan87—Bumped start

21Dec86-6Hol 1 1/16 :47 1:121 1:454ft 14 119 74¼ 43 31½ 63½ Vergara O7 M32000 76-15 StormyWorld,ZambeziPass,Clpper 12

21Dec86—Steadied, altered path 1/2

18Dec86-4Hol 6f :223 :463 1:111ft *3½ 120 64¾ 53 23 25 Vergara O1 [S]M32000 82-17 GetAlongPaisno,VriBeu,PinoPlyer 11

10Dec86-2Hol 6f :222 :462 1:113ft 16 120 63¾ 64¾ 43 25 Vergara O9 [S]M32000 80-20 OutCross,VariBeau,GetAlongPisno 12

22Nov86-2Hol 6f :22 :453 1:11 ft 5 120 97¾ 910 99¾ 76¾ Douglas R R8 M32000 81-13 Quardolite, Hapigrin,StormyWorld 12

F.

Lucky Masadado — Dk. b. or br. g. 5, by Masakado—Let's Get Lucky, by Lucky Mel

PEDROZA M A 114 — Br.—Costello F A (Cal) — 1987 1 1 0 0 $9,350

Tr.—King Hal $35,000 — 1986 13 3 0 3 $18,718

Own.—Hazan B — Lifetime 27 6 4 5 $39,308

22Jan87-5SA 6f :213 :45 1:104ft 5 114 1hd 1½ 11½ 12¾ Stevens G L7 18000 84-23 LuckyMsddo,Mjesty'sRod,OutCross 9

30Dec86-3SA 6f :212 :442 1:112ft 22 116 11 1½ 12½ 1no Cordero A Jr4 12500 81-18 LuckyMasadado,VIDeRoi,Chgrining 7

30Dec86—Broke slowly, erratic in stretch

21Sep86-8Pom 6f :221 :452 1:103ft 54 1145 1hd 21 33 68½ Braswell J M5 12500 89-07 Jacart, Inquisitive, Philip Nolan 10

16Sep86-8Pom 6½f:22 :45 1:153ft 40 119 42½ 32 36 917¾ Douglas R R7 16000 84-05 CoursingEgl,Prlpno,PrcousBmbno 10

16Sep86—Broke slowly

6Sep86-9Bmf 6f :221 :45 1:101ft 25 119 2hd 1hd 63 810½ McGurn C3 25000 78-18 PleasntPower,AirDevil,CooleenJck 10

28Aug86-11Sac 5½f:211 :434 1:023ft 15 120 22 21½ 33 31¾ Tohill K S2 Aw11000 93-13 MchoComcho,Vrbotn,LuckyMsddo 5

17Aug86-9AC 6f :222 :443 1:10 ft *4-5 114 1hd 2hd 11 1nk Enriquez H F3 Aw5000 89-14 LuckyMasaddo,Cinderhoof,Stemed 5

5Aug86-8AC 6f :221 :442 1:082ft 5 1117 3nk 1hd 1½ 33½ Delgadillo A8 Aw6000 93-14 VIDRoi,RunningDbonr,LuckyMsddo 9

27Jly86-9AC 5f :214 :433 :564ft 27 113 31 21 2½ 34 DlgdilloA2 [R]Charro H 95-12 Somes Bar,LoCard,LuckyMasadado 9

16Jly86-6LA 6f :214 :452 1:113ft 26 116 1hd 1nk 2hd 41¾ Kaenel J L5 12500 83-16 Singlet,HachalaTachala,Mr.Rector 10

Jan 30 SA 3f ft :38 h — Jan 20 SA 3f ft :374 h — Jan 14 SA 5f ft 1:01 hg — Jan 8 SA 3f m :381 h

G.

Dishonorable Guest — B. g. 4, by Grenfall—Table Flirt, by Round Table

MEZA R Q 115 — Br.—Wygod M J (Ky) — 1987 1 0 0 0 $1,725

Tr.—Ellis Ronald W $40,000 — 1986 3 0 0 1 $2,850

Own.—Wygod M J — Lifetime 6 2 0 1 $25,475 — Turf 1 0 0 0

17Jan87-2SA 6f :214 :45 1:103ft 5½ 114 53 54 44½ 45½ Meza R Q6 40000 79-18 Ondarty, Romaxe, Rivets Factor 11

23Nov86-7Hol 6f :221 :45 1:094ft 4½ 116 52½ 44½ 42½ 34 Meza R Q4 50000 90-12 BolgerMgic,Vrbotn,DishonorblGust 7

23Nov86—Broke in, bumped; crowded 1/2 to 1/4, wide stretch

27Feb86-8SA a6½f ⓣ:22 :4521:161fm 6½ 118 42 52 63¾ 64¼ Pincay L Jr9 Aw40000 74-22 RomnMgestrite,MoorgteMn,Delpr 10

27Feb86—Bumped, steadied at 3/16

29Jan86-8SA 1 1/16 :462 1:11 1:43 ft 21 117 53¾ 42½ 87½ 810¾ PincyLJr3 [R]Sta Ctlna 75-15 Ferdinand,VrietyRod,GrndAllegince 8

29Jan86—Fanned wide into stretch

27Dec85-5SA 6½f:222 :451 1:162ft 3¾ 115 2hd 2hd 1hd 11 Meza R Q7 Aw24000 88-16 DishonorblGust,JttingHom,BoldDcr 8

27Dec85—Bumped at start

11Dec85-5Hol 6f :221 :461 1:114ft 5 118 11½ 12 14 12¾ Meza R Q4 M50000 85-19 DshnrblGst,Agg'sLlRdg,MdstKng 10

Jan 26 SA 4f ft :501 h — Jan 12 SA 4f ft :484 h — Jan 6 SA 5f gd 1:022 h — Dec 31 SA 5f ft 1:02 h

H.

Costantino — B. c. 4, by Universal—French Dish, by Beau Brummel

BAZE G 115 — Br.—A J B Associates (Cal) — 1986 8 1 1 0 $13,577

Tr.—Barba J Trinidad $40,000 — 1985 2 M 0 0 $850

Own.—A J B Associates — Lifetime 10 1 1 0 $14,427 — Turf 1 0 0 0

8Jun86-10GG 1 1/16 ⓣ:47 1:11 1:424fm 36 114 21 56 816 914 Gonzalez R M7 50000 74-06 YllBrckRd,WkWkWhls,TMchFrT.V. 9

15May86-5Hol 1 :453 1:103 1:37 ft 15 114 54 815 817 821¾ Meza R Q7 35000 56-13 Gaelic Knight, Saros Chick, Joab 9

15May86—Eased through stretch

3May86-9AC 1⅛ :463 1:102 1:50 ft 14 121 11 1½ 32½ 45 FuentesAP6 Clnte Sza 86-15 Menevazzle, Sasebo, Tai High 10

27Mar86-9SA 1 1/16 :462 1:12 1:462ft 2½ 116 1hd 3nk 42 66½ DelahoussayeE3 40000 62-21 Serious Play, Donerley, Manzanero 8

27Mar86—Bumped start

15Mar86-9SA 1 1/16 :463 1:12 1:461m 11 115 64¾ 712 817 — Sibille R7 50000 — — Nick'sPrince,Tourismo,ExltedBubbl 8

15Mar86—Eased; Broke slowly

27Feb86-9SA 1 :461 1:111 1:374ft 9½ 115 1½ 11 11½ 21½ Sibille R4 40000 77-18 Many Roads, Costantino, Joab 8

14Feb86-8SA 1 :454 1:11 1:363ft 24 117 43 1011 1027 — Pincay L Jr8 Aw28000 — — Big Play, Bugarian, ‡Menevazzle 10

14Feb86—Eased; Bobbled start

9Jan86-4SA 1 :47 1:121 1:38 ft 2¾ 117 11 12 13 18 DelhoussyE4 [S]M32000 78-20 Costantino, Tourismo, SarosChick 10

20Dec85-1Hol 7f :222 :452 1:232ft 8 118 31½ 54½ 510 514¾ DelahoussyeE5 [S]Mdn 72-16 GrandAllegiance,CityView,NnteTm 7

20Dec85—Broke in a tangle

5Dec85-6Hol 6f :222 :453 1:10 ft 12 118 53 55¾ 57½ 510¼ Sibille R2 [S]Mdn 84-11 Always Rotten,NanteTam,Jayenezy 8

5Dec85—Pinched at start

Jan 28 Hol 3f ft :361 hg — Jan 23 Hol 7f ft 1:273 h — ● Jan 18 Hol 6f ft 1:144 h — Jan 13 Hol 6f ft 1:15 h

I.

Romaxe — Ch. h. 5, by Galiant Romeo—Sweet Axe, by The Axe II
PATTON D B 1115 — Br.—Lattimore C (Ky) — Tr.—Stidham Michael — $40,000
1987 2 0 2 0 $8,800
1986 4 1 0 1 $13,000
Own.—Blasi-Hutchins-Stidham — Lifetime 18 6 3 3 $57,310 — Turf 1 0 0 0 $660

17Jan87-2SA 6f :214 :45 1:103ft 4¼ 117 86¼ 65½ 34½ 23½ Pincay L Jr2 40000 81-18 Ondarty, Romaxe, Rivets Factor 11
17Jan87—Broke slowly
9Jan87-5SA 6f :222 :461 1:121sl *6-5 120 1½ 2½ 21 2¾ Pincay L Jr4 c32000 76-26 Roses Are Reb,Romaxe,Bruli'sAnte 9
9Jan87—Bumped start
21Dec86-7Hol 6f :22 :452 1:101ft 8 117 1hd 1hd 1½ 11¾ Pincay L Jr5 32000 92-15 Romaxe, Ondarty, EllsBravestSong 8
21Dec86—Lugged out late
11Nov86-3Hol 6f :221 :454 1:104ft 9 116 3nk 44 43 44¼ Meza R Q4 32000 85-20 Juntura, King OfCalifornia Bizeboy 6
11Nov86—Broke in
9Feb86-3SA 6f :214 :443 1:10 ft 5¼ 117 117¾1211 711 812 McHargue DG4 c32000 76-16 National Energy, Conteal, AllWins 12
9Feb86—4-wide into stretch
18Jan86-2SA 6½f :213 :44 1:152ft 15 119 21½ 22½ 34 35¾ McHargue D G1 32000 87-12 Goldy'sCommander,Chevo,Romxe 12
7Dec85-3Haw 6½f :232 :462 1:172ft *2½ 120 11 1hd 4nk 32 Louviere G P3 35000 84-26 WveAsYouGoBy,TheSkeptic,Romxe 6
20Nov85-3Haw 6½f :22 :444 1:18 ft *1 119 21 31½ 4¾ 12¾ Louviere G P1 32500 83-23 Romaxe, Shy Gold, Gumshoes 6
1Nov85-5Haw 6f :214 :452 1:11 sy *6-5 119 54½ 34½ 22½ 1¾ Louviere G P2 25000 86-18 Romaxe, Bank On Jake, Gumshoes 8
16Oct85-9Haw 6f :221 :461 1:114ft 3¾ 119 2hd 2½ 11½ 12¼ Louviere G P6 25000 82-29 Romaxe, BankOnJake,DiscCasting 10
Jan 29 SA 4f ft :481 h — Jan 5 SA tr.t 4f m :483 h — Dec 30 SA 4f ft :481 h — Dec 17 Hol 5f ft 1:002 h

J.

Cracksman — Gr. g. 5, by Agitate—Crackl'n Rose, by Traveling Dust
STEVENS G L 121 — Br.—Jimenez J (Cal) — Tr.—Jimenez James — $40,000
1986 9 2 0 2 $31,950
1985 12 3 0 0 $45,425
Own.—Jimenez J — Lifetime 23 6 1 2 $89,225 — Turf 3 0 0 1 $5,250

24Dec86-7Hol 6f :22 :452 1:11 ft *6-5 119 32 32½ 53½ 73¾ Pincay L Jr2 50000 84-20 MsterCrofter,Dnczon,RingOfPlsur 10
24Dec86—Unwilling to load; lugged in stretch
3Dec86-4Hol 6f :22 :45 1:094ft 2½ 117 44½ 43½ 45 33¾ Stevens G L5 80000 90-18 Faro, Debonaire Junior, Cracksman 6
22Nov86-7Hol 7f :22 :451 1:222ft *2¾ 116 22½ 21½ 11 11¼ Vergara O5 50000 92-13 Cracksman, Juntura, Infantryman 8
22Nov86—Lugged in late
15Nov86-3Hol 6f :221 :452 1:10 ft 3 117 1hd 11 11½ 11½ Pincay L Jr1 40000 93-14 Cracksman,RollANturl,PtriotGloves 6
30Jly86-9Dmr 6½f :212 :432 1:144ft 6¾ 116 714 819 816 613½ DelahoussayeE1 50000 84-11 Doria's Delight, Mr. Media AirAlert 8
30Jly86—Whipped head at start
18Jly86-7Hol 7f :223 :46 1:231ft *7-5 117 66½ 66 56½ 68¼ Stevens G L1 62500 80-14 Savio, Poley, Mischiefinmind 7
18Jly86—Hopped in air
21Jun86-5Hol 6f :214 :45 1:092ft 10 116 66½ 76¾ 53½ 55¾ Stevens G L5 100000 91-09 AmrcnLgn,MyFvrtMmnt,MGllntGm 7
21Jun86—Wide 3/8 turn
6Jun86-8Hol 6f :22 :452 1:094ft 2½ 117 43 44½ 56½ 57½ ValenzuelPA4 Aw24000 87-15 LncolnPrk,MyGllntGm,SpnshMschf 6
6Jun86—Wide final 3/8
28Feb86-8SA a6½f ①:211 :4321:151fm 18 115 2hd 2hd 11½ 31½ VlenzuelPA11 Aw35000 82-22 PrismticII,BoldrThnBold,Crcksmn 11
28Feb86—Lugged in stretch
26Dec85-8SA 7f :223 :45 1:21 ft 19 114 31 31½ 66½ 88½ Solis A7 Malibu 86-13 Banner Bob, Encolure, Carload 9
26Dec85—Grade II
●Jan 30 Hol 3f ft :352 h — Jan 24 Hol 5f ft 1:012 h — Jan 21 Hol 3f ft :38 h — Jan 16 Hol 5f ft 1:004 h

K.

Sebucan — B. c. 4, by Exuberant—Exacting Lady, by Disciplinarian
DELAHOUSSAYE E 120 — Br.—Saiden A (Fla) — Tr.—Barrera Lazaro S — $40,000
1986 9 4 2 1 $42,625
1985 5 M 0 0 $2,125
Own.—Saiden A — Lifetime 14 4 2 1 $44,750

10Dec86-3Hol 1 :454 1:104 1:371ft 4 116 31 1hd 1hd 1hd DelahoussayeE3 50000 77-20 Sebucan, Agitate's Pride, Alibi Ike 7
10Dec86—Broke slowly
27Nov86-5Hol 1 :452 1:103 1:364ft 3½ 116 2½ 1½ 11 11½ DelahoussayeE7 40000 79-18 Sebucan, Split Winners,BoldDecree 8
9Nov86-5Hol 6f :22 :451 1:10 ft *9-5 116 65¾ 66 45½ 35½ DelahoussayeE5 40000 87-16 Lans Manus, RosesAreReb,Sebucan 8
9Nov86—Wide in stretch
26Oct86-1SA 6f :213 :45 1:11 ft 5 116 97 74½ 42½ 1no DelahoussayeE1 32000 83-16 Sebucan, End Play, Fleet Albert 12
26Oct86—Veered out, bumped break; steadied, bumped entering stretch
9Jly86-1Hol 6f :221 :454 1:11 ft 3¾ 116 75½ 53½ 43 41¾ Stevens G L4 50000 87-18 Exubernt'sImge,FleetAlbert,EndPly 7
9Jly86—Bumped start
25Jun86-4Hol 1 :452 1:104 1:371ft 2¾ 116 2½ 2½ 31 64 Stevens G L5 50000 73-13 Trojan Trick, Joab, Inherent Kal 7
5Jun86-2Hol 6f :223 :463 1:11 ft *1 115 31½ 1hd 14 110 Stevens G L6 M32000 89-16 Sbcn,JohnsTomorrow,PlntyOfPlsr. 12
26May86-2Hol 6f :222 :46 1:114ft *2 115 84¾ 53 31½ 2hd Stevens G L2 M32000 85-17 Fracoza, Sebucan, Watch'r Win 12
10May86-2Hol 6f :222 :46 1:11 ft 12 113 65¾ 35 34½ 22 Stevens G L2 M35000 87-12 Cutting Line, Sebucan, T. H. Lark 8
10May86—Impeded at 5/16
12Dec85-3Hol 1 :454 1:114 1:381ft 11 118 21 2hd 54 77½ Pedroza M A9 M40000 64-22 Manzanero,MiamiDrem,Dodo'sLnd 12
●Jan 23 SA 5f ft :583 h — Jan 17 SA 5f ft :592 h — Jan 11 SA 4f ft :493 h — Dec 4 Hol 5f ft :591 h

L.

Roses Are Reb ✻ — **B. g. 4, by Reb's Policy—Personality Rose, by Personality**
SIMPSON B H **115** Br.—Licht R (Cal) 1987 1 1 0 0 $11,550
Tr.—Canani Julio C $40,000 1986 9 3 1 2 $37,950
Own.—Erickson & Thompson Jr Lifetime 10 4 1 2 $49,500

9Jan87-5SA 6f :22^2 :46^1 1:12^{1}sl 4¾ 116 3^1 1½ 1^1 1¾ Simpson B H^8 32000 77-26 Roses Are Reb,Romaxe,Bruli'sAnte 9
9Nov86-5Hol 6f :22 :45^1 1:10 ft 3¼ 116 1^{hd} 2^{hd} 2^{2½} 2^{5½} Stevens G L^3 40000 87-16 Lans Manus, RosesAreReb,Sebucan 8
9Nov86—Veered out, checked start
31Oct86-6SA 6f :21^2 :44^3 1:09^{3}ft 5¾ 114 2^{1½} 3^1 3^{1½} 3^{4½} Stevens G L^3 45000 85-16 MischievousMtt,Jimed,RosesArRb 11
21Sep86-9Pom 6f :21^4 :45 1:11^{1}ft *1 112^5 6^{2¾} 4^3 4^{3½} 5^{4¼} Black C A^3 57500 91-07 TimShr,Hrpr'sRidg,WhipUpThTmpo 8
21Sep86—Bumped at break, wide into lane
11Sep86-11Pom 6½f :22 :45^4 1:16^{4}ft 2¼ 117 1½ 1^{hd} 4^6 4^{10½} Stevens G L^1 Foothill 85-08 J.R.Johnson,ElCorzon,LghtnngToch 8
31Aug86-3Dmr 6f :22 :45 1:09^{2}ft *8-5 111^5 2^{hd} 3^{1½} 4^{1½} 3^{3¾} Black C A^7 Aw24000 87-12 SureToFir,AmzingCourg,RossArRb 7
11Aug86-7Dmr 6f :21^3 :44^3 1:09^{2}ft 5½ 108^5 2^1 2^{1½} 1^{hd} 1¾ Black C A^3 Aw19000 91-13 RosesArRb,Mr.Mdi,WhipUpThTmpo 7
11Aug86—Broke in, bumped
4Aug86-5Dmr 6f :21^4 :45 1:09^{2}ft 12 113^5 2^{hd} 1^{hd} 1^1 1^{1¾} Black C A^6 c32000 91-13 Roses Are Reb,Notoriety,Arbitrate 12
11Jly86-4Hol 6f :22^2 :46^2 1:11^{3}ft 3½ 109^5 5^2 3^{nk} 1^3 1^{3½} Black C A^8 M32000 86-14 RossArRb,BoldBrvoII,‡GntlmnDon 11
7Jun86-4Hol 6f :22^1 :45^4 1:11^{1}ft 6¼ 108^5 5^{3½} 4^{3½} 4^{7½} 4^{10½} Black C A^5 M45000 77-17 Eighty Below Zero, Blue Ice,Felino 8
7Jun86—Broke slowly
Jan 29 SA 4f ft :51^2 h **Jan 23 SA 5f ft 1:00^3 h** **Jan 17 SA 3f ft :35^4 h** **Jan 8 SA 3f m :37^2 h**

16. Understanding form cycles helps dissect this middle distance route for low-priced fillies and mares, but so does knowledge of class and pace. One horse appears to hold the edge on each of the three factors. Which is it?

8 ATLANTIC CITY 1 1-16 MILES ATLANTIC CITY

1 1/16 MILES. (1.41) CLAIMING. Purse $5,400. Fillies and Mares, 3-year-olds and upward. Weight, 3-year-olds 115 lbs. Older 122 lbs. Non-winners of two races at one mile or over since June 3, allowed 2 lbs. One such race 4 lbs. Such a race since May 27, 6 lbs. Claiming Price $6,500 for each $250 to $6,000 2 lbs. (Races where entered for $5,000 or less not considered).

A.

Missy Ed — **Dk. b. or br. m. 7, by Trader Ed—Next Wind, by Next Year**
$6,500 Br.—Mills P D (Pa) **109^7** Lifetime 33 4 5 1 $13,755 1987 3 0 1 0 $878
Own.—Butch A Tr.—Butch Al 1985 5 0 0 0 $216

22Jly87-10Atl fst 6f :22⅘ :47⅖ 1:14 3↑ⒻClm 4000 5 10 10^{6¾} 9^{7½} 8^{2¼} 5^{6½} Gonzalez L^7 109 21.80 65-31 Alan's Gal 116^4 FrenchEpigram111^{1}GoldenMirage116^{hd} No threat 10
9Jly87-2Atl sly 5½f :23⅗ :48 1:08⅖ 3↑ⒻClm 4000 2 5 4^2 4^5 3^{5½} 2^3 Gonzalez L^5 111 50.10 68-23 Hookamaoookama 120^3 Missy Ed111½MyPrincessOti116^{2½} Rallied 9
24Jun87-10Atl fst 6f :22⅖ :47 1:14⅕ 3↑ⒻClm 4000 4 7 2^{hd} 6^{6¾} 10^{12} 10^{15¾} Gonzalez L^5 111 46.30 55-31 Lady Carlton 116^{1¾} Put Her On Ice 116^{nk} Miss Fantasy116^2 Tired 11
6Jly85-2Del fst 1 1/16 :48⅘ 1:13⅗ 1:48⅕ 3↑ⒻClm 3500 4 10 9^{9½} 8^8 8^{14} — Gabriella R 116 8.00 — — Farewell John 109½ Mambold 116½ Where's Kate 116^{5¾} Eased 10
29Jun85-9Del fst 1 1/16 :48⅕ 1:14⅖ 1:49⅕ 3↑ⒻClm 3500 6 2 2½ 1^{1½} 2½ 4^{1¾} Gabriella R 116 44.80 60-27 Sarai Sarah 106^{hd} Where's Kate 116½ Superimposed 116^{1¼} Tired 11
14Jun85-8CT fst 6½f :23⅗ :48 1:22⅘ ⒻClm 3500 3 3 10^{13} 10^{13} 10^{14} 9^{25¼} Shields R E 116 54.10 46-32 Now NowNow114^{1½}Lennie'sRuffian114^3[DH]ImaDancing114 Outrun 10
31May85-8CT fst 7f :24⅖ :49 1:28⅗ ⒻClm 3500 7 6 1^{1½} 1^1 10^{17} 10^{23½} Whitacre G 117 32.10 53-30 Dean's List 114^4 Now Now Now 114^2 Miss Allihil 116^4 Stopped 10
12May85-2CT fst 4½f :22⅕ :46⅘ :53⅗ ⒻClm 3500 3 9 9^{8¼} 9^{11} 7^{6½} Whitacre G 116 47.90 79-14 Pukka Cotton 114^{nk} Whiz First 114^{1½} Know Friends 117^2 Outrun 9
20Oct84-10Del 4 5 9^{13} 10^{18} 10^{20} 10^{18¼} Madrid S O 113 44.80 56 — Outrun 0
8Oct84-4Del 4 4 2^{3½} 6^{8½} 9^{23} 9^{31¾} Stackhouse G C 113 9.60 43 — Stopped 0
LATEST WORKOUTS Jun 13 Atl 3f fst :37 bg

B.

Saru — **B. m. 5, by Overskate—Box Supper, by In Reality**
$6,000 Br.—Lazarus M (NY) **105^7** Lifetime 47 2 3 4 $67,687 1987 7 0 0 0 $268
Own.—Jordan S Tr.—Latrella Mike 1986 13 0 0 0 $219
Turf 11 0 1 2 $16,594

22Jly87-2Atl fst 7f :23⅕ :46⅗ 1:26⅗ 3↑ⒻClm 6500 2 8 8^{5¾} 8^6 5^5 5^{3½} Jimenez C A 116 13.50 65-31 Franchois111^{1½}HertOfSilver111½AmericnFreedom116^{1½} No threat 9
15Jly87-6Atl fm 1⅛ Ⓣ:50 1:15⅕ 1:56⅖ 3↑ⒻClm 7000 11 8 8^{4½} 5^{4¾} 6^{17} 6^{8¾} Chavis S T^5 109 17.10 45-46 All In Free 112^{nk} Annotated 114^2 Special Asset 112no Outrun 12
2Jly87-5Atl sly 6f :22⅖ :45⅗ 1:12⅘ 3↑ⒻClm 6500 3 5 5^{12} 6^{21} 7^{8½} 7^{4½} Chavis S T^5 111 37.90 73-27 Dusty Britches 116½ Franchois 116^1 Debi's Dynasty 111^1 Tired 7
20Jun87-10Atl fm 1 1/16 Ⓣ:47⅗ 1:11⅖ 1:43⅕ 3↑ⒻAlw 8200 6 2 1^{hd} 3^3 6^{16} 6^{16¾} Intelisano G P Jr 116 29.60 73-08 Captivating Appeal 116^2 French Oil 113^{nk} Honest Deb107^{hd} Tired 7
6Apr87-2Aqu sly 6f :22⅕ :45⅗ 1:12⅕ ⒻClm 12000 5 11 11^{16} 11^{17} 11^{10} 8^{9½} DeCarlo C P 113 25.50f 70-20 Jean's Diamond 112½ Oaxaca 112^{nk} Joyfull Dance 115^2 Outrun 12
17Mar87-3Aqu fst 1 :47⅖ 1:13⅕ 1:39⅖ ⒻClm 15500 1 10 9^{13} 10^{11} 11^{18} 11^{19½} Carr D^{10} 103 110.50 49-31 Private Iron 117^{3½} Kissing Booth 117^7 Pro Harmony114^{2½} Outrun 12
9Mar87-2Aqu fst 6f [•]:23⅕ :47⅕ 1:12⅗ ⒻClm 12000 10 10 9^{12} 10^{15} 10^{13} 10^{15} Carr D^{10} 103 51.40 66-22 Boca Grove 117^{3½} Pro Harmony 114^1 Grotona 110^4 Outrun 10
29Oct86-6Pen gd 6f :22⅖ :46 1:13 3↑ⒻAlw 7300 5 5 4^5 5^{9¼} 5^{17} 5^{12¼} Rozell R M 113 7.80 67-24 French Curve 111¾ Miss AlottaRibs113^{1}JustJohnson116^{10} Outrun 5
5Sep86-1Bel fst 6f :23 :46⅘ 1:12 3↑ⒻClm 12000 2 5 5^7 5^{11} 5^{16} 5^{14½} Lee W^{10} 103 16.50 67-18 Sly Iron 117^{6½} My Princess 117^{3¾} Bonnie's Poker117^{1¼} No factor 6
29Aug86-9Bel gd 1 1/16 :47 1:12⅗ 1:45⅘ 3↑ⒻClm 12000 7 1 1^1 5^{3½} 9^{11} 8^{13} Lee W^{10} 103 60.40 60-19 Monongahela Maiden 117^{1¾} Irish Point 115^{1¼}Pambola117^{1¾} Tired 11
LATEST WORKOUTS Jly 13 Atl 4f fst :48⅗ b Jun 9 Atl 3f fst :36⅘ b

C.

Deman Express — B. f. 4, by Exuberant—Miss Yo Deman, by Yo' Deman
$6,500 Br.—Moore Maryann (Fla) Tr.—Sacco William J — 116
Own.—Maryann Moore
Lifetime 18 1 3 2 $14,240 | 1987 4 0 0 1 $660 | 1986 14 1 3 1 $13,580

7Jly87- 4Mth fst 170 :45⅗ 1:11⅗ 1:44 3+ⒻClm 5000 8 1 18 17 12 37 Rivera M A 115 21.60 69-15 La Plus Jolie 1153½ Peaceful Jen 1153½ Deman Express1153 Tired 11
29Jun87- 3Mth fst 6f :22⅕ :45⅕ 1:11⅗ 3+ⒻClm 8000 7 3 51¼ 64 75¾ 611½ Corbett G W7 b 109 39.40 70-19 Irish Goblin 119¾ Fire Diamond 1163¼ Inkie Pinkie 1163 Outrun 7
11Jun87- 2Mth fst 6f :22 :44⅘ 1:11⅖ 3+ⒻClm 12500 6 4 53¼ 57 914 1017¾ McCauley W H b 116 33.50 65-19 Five Star Rose 1192 Bushogin Babe1093StillOurFrisky116no Tired 11
3Jun87- 6Mth fst 6f :22⅗ :46 1:12 3+ⒻClm 16000 9 1 42¾ 75½ 912 918¾ McCauley W H b 116 21.50 62-22 Daisy's Debut 1172 Dear Effie 116no Princess Natalie 1143 Tired 9
29Nov86- 6Med fst 6f :22⅘ :47⅕ 1:12⅗ ⒻClm 20000 1 3 11 31 713 719¾ Krone J A b 115 16.30 60-23 Shaken Bay 1154¾ Irish Mar 113¾ Yes For Real 1183¾ Gave way 7
11Nov86- 7Med sly 6f :22⅗ :46⅕ 1:12 ⒻClm 20000 4 2 2hd 45 613 716 Krone J A b 118 10.20 66-27 Tara's Native 1184 Holly Hagley 1184 Irish Mar 1123 Gave way 7
1Nov86- 8Med fst 6f :22⅖ :46 1:11⅘ ⒻClm 25000 8 5 4nk 31 2½ 69½ Krone J A b 118 28.00 73-21 Saucy Hanne 1152½ Pferdela 107¾ Shaken Bay 1111½ Bid, wknd 8
10Oct86- 8Med fst 6f :22⅖ :45⅖ 1:12 3+ⒻMd Sp Wt 2 2 1hd 12 11½ 11½ Krone J A b 119 10.40 82-20 Deman Express 1191½ Sky Chat 1223 Pincurl 1122 Driving 11
9Sep86- 1Med fst 6f :22⅘ :46⅖ 1:13 3+ⒻMd 28000 9 1 2hd 2½ 32 46½ Krone J A b 114 11.10 70-20 MissRachelToner1185MissFantsy114¾LdysMystery116¾ Weakened 9
25Aug86-10Mth fst 6f :22⅘ :46⅖ 1:12⅖ 3+ⒻMd 20000 6 2 21 2hd 12 43¼ Krone J A b 117 *2.00 75-18 Hapi Cley 107nk Stage Native1151¼RunShanaRun1171¾ Weakened 11
LATEST WORKOUTS ●Jly 29 Mth 4f fst :47⅗ h

D.

Binn N' Bear It — Ro. f. 4, by Upper Nile—Coal Binn, by Wise Exchange
$6,000 Br.—Binn M (Ky) Tr.—Cifarelli Frank — 112
Own.—Binn M
Lifetime 20 1 2 1 $7,903 | 1987 4 0 1 0 $1,263 | 1986 16 1 1 1 $6,640 | Turf 3 0 0 0 $63

25Jly87-10Atl fm *1 40 Ⓣ:47⅘ 1:13⅗ 1:44⅗ 3+ⒻHcp 6500s 5 10 912 611 67½ 66 Parrilla R b 112 45.80 82-13 Fratello's Girl 1121 All In Free115noOurLoveSong1151½ No factor 10
15Jly87- 3Pha fst 1 1/16 :47⅗ 1:12⅘ 1:46 3+ⒻClm 8000 3 7 79 512 713 718½ Alligood M A b 112 10.30 55-19 Hang Around1129½FlyingDaisy1093BewitchingFantasy1191 Outrun 8
10Jun87- 5GS fst 170 :47⅗ 1:14⅘ 1:46⅗ 3+ⒻClm 6500 7 5 55½ 51¼ 2hd 2½ Alligood M A b 116 10.10 65-31 Inca Gold 109½ Binn N' Bear It 1166½ Island Victory116nd Gamely 7
23Mar87- 6GS fst 1 1/16 :48⅕ 1:14 1:47⅘ ⒻClm 8000 2 7 818 826 — — Madrid A Jr b 112 27.90 — — Star Dancing 1197 R. Dazzling Daria 11612 Her Donna 116½ Eased 8
20Nov86- 5Med sly 170 :47⅗ 1:11⅘ 1:46⅖ 3+ⒻClm 10000 4 5 510 815 66½ 69¾ Santagata N b 113 13.20 54-28 Ace Princess 1144 Ivory Lotion 115nk LaPlusJolie1102½ No factor 9
13Nov86-10Med fst 170 :47⅗ 1:13⅘ 1:44⅘ 3+ⒻMd 10000 4 6 43½ 22 2½ 11¼ Santagata N b 118 *1.20 72-25 BinnN'BearIt1181¼CheBellaFemmina1175JerseyFirst1112½ Driving 12
29Oct86- 2Med fst 170 :47 1:14 1:46⅗ 3+ⒻMd 10000 11 9 68½ 54 41½ 2nk Santagata N b 117 3.20 63-21 Sly Wheeler 110nk Binn N' Bear It117¾MyPrincessOti1102 Rallied 12
7Oct86-10Med fst 170 :47⅘ 1:13⅘ 1:46 3+ⒻMd 10000 10 12 109¾ 77½ 56½ 45½ Belmonte J F7 b 110 *2.30 60-23 Run Suerte1071¼LittleLadyJinsky1173½ShamelessToo115¾ Bore in 12
25Sep86- 1Med fst 170 :47⅗ 1:14⅕ 1:46 3+ⒻMd 10000 11 11 98 76¼ 53 42¼ Belmonte J F7 b 111 9.20 64-21 Coral Lace 1131 [D]Brilliant Reason 1161¼ LastCitation118no Wide 11
25Sep86-Placed third through disqualification
18Sep86-10Med fst 1 1/16 :47⅗ 1:13⅕ 1:47⅖ 3+ⒻMd 12500 7 11 88¾ 711 58½ 46 Belmonte J F7 b 109 9.50 60-18 FirstLdyInRed1142½StinSlipprs1112MissFntsy1161½ Rallied mildly 12
LATEST WORKOUTS Jly 9 Bel 5f sly 1:04 hg

E.

Zicks Miss — B. f. 4, by Miteas Well Laff—Rigel Miss, by Drift
$6,500 Br.—Sandy Hill Stable (NJ) Tr.—Dellagatta Perry — 120
Own.—Sandy Hill Stable
Lifetime 21 3 0 3 $15,585 | 1987 7 2 0 1 $10,217 | 1986 14 1 0 2 $5,368 | Turf 3 0 0 0 $220

Entered 30Jly87- 2 ATL , finished 6
15Jly87- 6Atl fm 1⅛ Ⓣ:50 1:15⅕ 1:56⅖ 3+ⒻClm 7500 8 6 53½ 44½ 34 42¼ Parrilla R 118 13.10 52-46 All In Free 112nk Annotated 1142 Special Asset 112no Evenly 12
1Jly87- 3Atl fst 1 1/16 :48⅖ 1:14⅕ 1:48⅕ 3+Ⓕ[S]Clm 6000 1 1 21 1hd 12½ 13½ Parrilla R 120 3.10 64-25 Zicks Miss 1203½ Forbot 111¾ Casino City 1123 Driving 9
24Jun87- 5Atl fst 1⅛ :47⅘ 1:12⅘ 1:54 3+ⒻClm 6500 5 5 54¼ 47 411 413½ Santos F J 116 3.70 49-31 Castle ofGold1074½SpecialAsset1121ColorMeCherry1168 Even try 7
8Jun87- 2GS fst 1 1/16 :49⅖ 1:14⅖ 1:47 3+Ⓕ[S]Clm 5000 6 1 12 13 13 12½ Romero J A5 b 111 8.50 73-21 Zicks Miss 1112½ Stella Dallas 1168 Silverlust 1121 Driving 6
28May87- 1GS fst 1 1/16 :47⅘ 1:13⅘ 1:49⅖ 3+Ⓕ[S]Clm 5000 1 3 47 56 54½ 42 Cantagallo G J 116 4.00 59-21 Forbot 112½ Silverlust 1191¼ Blaze On Blue 106nk Tired 6
18May87- 3GS fst 170 :48⅘ 1:15⅗ 1:47 3+Ⓕ[S]Clm 5000 1 4 34 42 3nk 31 Cantagallo G J 116 8.40 63-27 Forbot 1091 Silverlust 119no Zicks Miss 1166 Held well 6
4May87- 2GS sly 170 :48⅗ 1:14⅗ 1:45⅘ 3+Ⓕ[S]Clm 5000 5 1 2hd 2½ 33½ 410½ Cantagallo G J 116 43.30 59-22 Dusty Girl 1162 Casino City 1116½ Forbot 1102 Tired 7
19Oct86-10Pha fst 1 1/16 :48⅖ 1:13⅕ 1:46⅗ 3+ⒻClm 5000 6 1 54¼ 1016 1020 1026¼ Lopez C C 113 44.00 45-23 Fleeting Love 1195 Silver Snam 116¾ Full Bonnet 1191½ Stopped 10
5Oct86- 4Pha fst 6½f :23⅕ :47⅗ 1:19⅘ 3+ⒻClm 5000 11 2 96¾ 104 811 79¼ Ferrer J C 116 37.30 65-22 Stcey'sSpy1093½StrryLnding116½JcklyntheRipper1162½ No factor 12
21Sep86- 5Del fst 1 1/16 :48 1:13⅗ 1:47⅗ ⒻClm 5000 7 4 46 45 35 38¾ Cole M A 119 7.10 61-29 Hollylady 114¾ Im Designed 1138 Zicks Miss 1193½ Rallied 9

F.

Annie's Gift — B. m. 6, by Pay Tribute—A Gift of Silver, by Mississipian
$6,500 Br.—Honaker & Wells (Ky) Tr.—Harker Terry W — 116
Own.—Harker T W
Lifetime 50 13 4 7 $70,657 | 1987 12 6 0 0 $21,414 | 1986 9 2 1 1 $11,655

24Jly87- 5Atl fst 1 1/16 :48⅕ 1:14⅕ 1:50 3+ⒻClm 6500 5 2 2hd 23½ 417 618½ Conner M J b 116 *.80 36-31 Castle of Gold 1155 Mrs. Rickles 1122 Retton'sGold1158 Stopped 6
29Jun87- 3Mth fst 6f :22⅕ :45⅕ 1:11⅗ 3+ⒻClm 8000 2 7 75¼ 76½ 54¼ 47 Conner M J b 116 11.90 75-19 Irish Goblin 119¾ Fire Diamond 1163¼ Inkie Pinkie 1163 Rallied 7
5Jun87- 8GS fst 1 1/16 :47⅘ 1:13⅘ 1:47⅘ 3+ⒻClm 12000 1 2 2½ 3½ 59½ 615½ Alligood M A b 112 3.70 53-24 Scarlet Glow 1092½ RunForPeace1164½GallantRainbow1125½ Tired 7
26May87- 5GS fst 170 :47⅕ 1:13⅖ 1:45⅖ 3+ⒻClm c-9000 3 1 11 23 612 629½ Aristone M b 114 *1.30 42-23 TlntdBginnr1166½Editor'sDlight1162½OutOfACnnon110hd Stopped 6
12May87- 3GS my 170 :47⅕ 1:13⅗ 1:45⅗ 3+ⒻClm 8500 4 1 11½ 12 1½ 1nk Aristone M b 116 *.70 71-25 Annie's Gift 116nk Gallant Rainbow 1166 Q. Qui 116½ Driving 6
29Apr87- 2GS fst 1 1/16 :47⅕ 1:13 1:49 3+ⒻClm c-6250 3 1 1½ 15 16 16 Rocco J b 114 *.40 63-26 Annie's Gift 1146 Stella Dallas 1091½ Tanmandamas 116½ Easily 6
17Apr87- 5GS my 1 1/16 :48⅕ 1:13⅘ 1:47⅗ ⒻClm 5000 2 1 18 18 110 113 Rocco J b 116 *.70 70-19 Annie's Gift 11613 Precious Fame 1161 Valkyrie 1165 Easily 7
23Mar87- 6GS fst 1 1/16 :48⅕ 1:14 1:47⅘ ⒻClm 8500 3 2 24 49 518 527½ Rocco J b 116 *1.00 41-25 Star Dancing 1197 R. Dazzling Daria 11612 Her Donna 116½ Tired 8
11Feb87- 4Pha fst 1 1/16 :48⅕ 1:13⅕ 1:47⅘ ⒻClm 6250 10 1 15 17 18 116 Rocco J b 116 *3.40 65-32 Annie's Gift 11616 Fancy MissNancy116nkStarDancing1168 Easily 11
4Feb87- 2Pha gd 170 :48 1:14⅕ 1:45⅘ ⒻClm 5000 3 1 14 13 12 15½ Rocco J b 115 *1.70 66-28 Annie's Gift 1155½ Fleeting Love 1088½ Selari's Pride115½ Handily 9
LATEST WORKOUTS Jly 16 Atl 4f gd :48⅕ h ●Jun 25 Atl 4f fst :48⅖ h

G.

Smile Angelina — B. m. 5, by Whitesburg—We All Be Tickled, by Gaylord's Feather
$6,500 Br.—Gridley C (Ky) Tr.—Vansant Edgar L — 116
Own.—Rosenberger G G
Lifetime 42 7 3 13 $73,021 | 1987 4 1 0 1 $3,760 | 1986 11 1 0 4 $15,950 | Turf 10 1 1 4 $17,150

20Jly87- 8Pen fst 6f :22⅖ :46⅖ 1:12⅗ 3+ⒻClm 5000 5 10 107¼ 85¼ 73¾ 1½ Iliescu A b 116 7.90 81-22 Smile Angelina116½LakeTorsion1131MissYorkFederal1162 Driving 11
7Jly87- 2Pim fst 1 1/16 :46⅘ 1:12⅘ 1:45⅘ ⒻClm 10500 8 8 918 915 814 818½ Wright D R b 113 19.10 56-17 Kickoff 10710½ Pride's Choice 115no Tanner's Girl 1141¼ Outrun 9
2Jun87- 2Mth fst 6f :22⅗ :45⅗ 1:10⅘ 3+ⒻClm 10000 2 8 78½ 812 612 311 Rocco J b 116 8.90 75-16 Five StarRose1166BarbaraErin1165SmileAngelina1162½ No threat 9
14May87- 1Pim fst 6f :23⅖ :46⅗ 1:12 ⒻClm 18500 6 6 78¾ 712 717 719½ Reynolds L C b 116 28.70 66-22 No No Nicky 1095½ Chapter Two 1153 Sally's Heroine114½ Trailed 7
10Sep86- 5Pha fm 1 1/16 Ⓣ:47⅕ 1:12 1:44⅗ 3+ⒻClm 25000 9 6 77¾ 52¾ 78¾ 76¾ Thomas D B b 116 7.80 72-16 Dale City 1162½ Lucy Clare 116nd Rich 'n Creamy 114½ Outrun 9
29Aug86- 6Mth fst 1 1/16 :48 1:12⅖ 1:44⅗ 3+ⒻClm 32000 5 4 54½ 42½ 37 39 Antley C W b 115 2.70 73-18 WveringLight1156DoublSmooth1153SmilAnglin115½ Couldn't gain 6
15Aug86- 8Pim fm 1 Ⓣ:47⅕ 1:11⅖ 1:36⅘ 3+ⒻAlw 16000 2 3 49½ 48½ 45 34¾ Miller D A Jr b 119 7.30 90-05 Shaviana 112nk LadyAmalthia1144½SmileAngelina1191¾ No threat 6
2Aug86- 7Pha fst 1 :46⅘ 1:12 1:39⅖ 3+ⒻAlw 14000 8 5 55 67¼ 812 712¾ Vigliotti M J b 116 18.40 64-18 ChicAndSassy1181½UltimateRecusl111¾AmAnEgle118nk No factor 8
9Jun86- 5GS fm 170 Ⓣ:46 1:10⅘ 1:41⅖ 3+ⒻAlw 13500 5 4 47½ 512 68 59½ Black A S b 117 9.60 82-12 Wayette Coghlin117nkHeyMajesty117½Auspicate1175½ Brief speed 6
23May86- 4GS fm 5f Ⓣ:21⅘ :45⅗ :58⅕ 3+ⒻAlw 12500 4 10 1011 1011 97¼ 95¾ Black A S b 116 9.30 90-04 LaughTrack109½TrompheDeNskr1121½RestlessMonk118nk Outrun 11
LATEST WORKOUTS Jun 23 Del 5f fst 1:01 b

H.

American Freedom B. f. 4, by Star Spangled—Sew To Bed, by Mito

$6,500 Br.—Fonzone & McLean (Ky) 116 Lifetime 29 4 6 4 $27,289 1987 17 3 1 3 $16,649 1986 12 1 5 1 $10,640 Turf 1 0 0 0

Own.—Moreton W Tr.—Hawthorne Ann

22Jly87- 2Atl fst 7f :23⅕ :46⅗ 1:26⅗ 3+ⒻClm 6250 5 9 42¼ 31 31 32 Pagan N b 116 *1.90 67-31 Franchois1111½HeartOfSilver111½AmericnFreedom1161½ Fin. well 9

18Jly87- 1Atl fst 6½f :23 :46⅗ 1:19⅖ 3+ⒻClm c-5000 5 3 64¼ 43 52¾ 43 Colon P 120 2.10 86-21 NorthrnNifty1201SunstPrincss1202Dncingforfrinds116hd No rally 7

2Jly87- 5Atl sly 6f :22⅖ :45⅗ 1:12⅘ 3+ⒻClm 6500 6 7 716 721 67½ 52½ Edwards J W 120 2.50 75-27 Dusty Britches 116½ Franchois 1161 Debi'sDynasty1111 No factor 7

25Jun87- 4Mth fm 1 Ⓣ:47⅖ 1:11⅗ 1:38⅕ 3+ⒻAlw 10000s 2 10 1013108½ 78¾ 614 Edwards J W 115 13.40 70-12 Pia's Baby 1153 Scarlet Glow 110½ Lady Ivory 1062 Outrun 10

13Jun87-11Mth sly 6f :22 :45⅖ 1:11⅗ 3+ⒻClm 18000 1 8 715 713 712 712 Edwards J W 117 8.70 70-14 Layovernite 1161¼ Dear Effie 116½ Daisy's Debut 116nk Outrun 8

30May87- 6Mth fst 6f :22⅖ :45⅕ 1:10⅕ 3+ⒻAlw 14000 1 9 98¾ 98¾ 88¼ 89¾ Edwards J W 117 20.30 79-14 Koluctoo's Ruby 109nkNastyAffair1135AdorableAngel1091 Outrun 9

19May87- 6GS sly 6f :22⅕ :46⅖ 1:13⅖ 3+ⒻClm 18000 5 6 614 65¼ 32 11½ Edwards J W 116 8.40 75-25 AmericnFreedom1161½Jy'sPrtyDoll112nkShkyBritchs1162 Driving 6

25Apr87- 3GS my 6f :22⅖ :46⅘ 1:12⅗ 3+ⒻClm 11000 2 8 811 64¾ 34 33¼ Edwards J W 116 3.80 76-18 SisterTrixie116nkHppyApril1113AmericnFreedom1164 Carried out 8

13Apr87- 7GS fst 6f :22⅘ :47 1:13⅕ ⒻClm 8250 1 12 1246109½ 33½ 1½ Edwards J W 115 12.70 76-26 American Freedom 115½ Love Again 113nkLuLu'sGirl1144 Driving 12

1Apr87- 4GS fst 6f :22⅕ :46 1:12⅗ ⒻClm 5000 8 12 1110 88½ 61¾ 12¾ Madrid A Jr 116 8.20 79-24 AmericnFreedom1162¾Hookmdookm116noJettingLss119no Driving 12

Items 17 through 34 ask you to find the most probable winners. If no introductory remarks are provided, evaluate the races by applying your usual and customary handicapping procedures.

17. Two horses in this field are at least slightly more likely to win a Grade 1 event than the others. Find both horses.

8th Santa Anita

1 ¼ MILES. (Turf). (1.57⅖) 39th Running of THE SANTA BARBARA HANDICAP (Grade I). $150,000 added. Fillies and mares. 4-year-olds and upward. By subscription of $100 each to accompany the nomination, $1,500 additional to start, with $150,000 added, of which $30,000 to second, $22,500 to third, $11,250 to fourth and $3,750 to fifth. Weights, Tuesday, March 31. Starters to be named through the entry box by the closing time of entries. A trophy will be presented to the owner of the winner. Closed Wednesday, March 25, 1987 with 16 nominations.

A.

Winter Treasure Ch. f. 4, by Vigors—Minstrel Miss, by Poona II

TORO F 116 Br.—Grossman J M (Ky) 1987 3 0 2 1 $101,250

Tr.—Mandella Richard 1986 12 5 4 0 $137,325

Own.—Grossman J M Lifetime 16 5 6 1 $238,575 Turf 1 0 0 0

1Mar87-8SA 1⅛:454 1:103 1:484ft 34 115 65¾ 62½ 21½ 2hd Toro F2 ⒻS Mg Iv H 85-15 NorthSider,WinterTresur,FruAltiv 12

1Mar87—Grade I

15Feb87-8SA 1⅛:462 1:103 1:493m 3½ 117 34 32½ 22 22½ PncLJr5 ⒻLa Cnda 78-17 FmilyStyle,WinterTresur,Sri'sHroin 6

15Feb87—Grade I

3Jan87-8SA 7f :222 :451 1:223ft 3½ 117 53¼ 31½ 43½ 36 PncLJr2 ⒻLa Brea 81-16 FmilyStyle,Sri'sHeroine,WintrTrsur 6

3Jan87—Grade III; Broke slowly

13Dec86-4Hol 6f :214 :451 1:101ft *4-5 121 65¼ 63¼ 34 21½ Pincay L Jr6 ⒻHcp0 90-09 StridingEsy,WintrTrsur,BoldNSpcil 6

13Dec86—Wide backstretch, through stretch

31Oct86-8SA 1 1/16:463 1:112 1:431ft 3¼ 118 2½ 2hd 21 21¼ VllPA6 ⒻLnda Vst H 84-16 Mrinn'sGirl,WinterTresur,FinKudos 9

31Oct86—Grade III

22Oct86-8SA 6½f:221 :452 1:161ft 3½ 117 1hd 11½ 12½ 1¾ VllPA3 ⒻCascapdia H 89-23 WinterTresure,HerRoylty,FmilyStyl 5

22Oct86—Lugged out early

6Sep86-7Dmr 6½f:22 :45 1:153ft 4¾ 117 55½ 43 31½ 2¾ Pincay LJr2 ⒻAw40000 93-12 HerRoylty,WinterTresure,WildKitty 6

6Sep86—Veered in start

4Jun86-8Hol 7f :22 :444 1:222ft 3¼ 119 67 67 38 49¼ PincyLJr3 ⒻRailbird 83-18 Melair, Comparability, SilentArrival 7

4Jun86—Grade III; Veered out start

21May86-8Hol 6f :222 :454 1:104ft 3¾ 117 63¾ 51¼ 11½ 15½ PncyLJr4 ⒻDrma Crtc 90-13 WintrTrsur,T.V.Rsidul,ChickOrTwo 9

18Apr86-7SA 6½f:221 :454 1:171ft *4-5 120 32½ 2hd 11½ 1½ Pincay LJr5 ⒻAw28000 84-21 WintrTrsur,MissBnson,ViolinMlody 5

18Apr86—Bumped start

Apr 3 SA Ⓣ 4f fm :513 h (d) Mar 28 SA Ⓣ 1 fm 1:394 h (d) Mar 21 SA 6f ft 1:124 h Mar 15 SA 4f ft :482 h

B.

Reloy B. f. 4, by Liley—Rescousse, by Emerson

SHOEMAKER W 120 Br.—Hunt N B (Ky) 1987 3 1 1 0 $100,900

Tr.—Whittingham Charles 1986 10 2 1 4 $135,134

Own.—Hunt N B Lifetime 15 3 3 4 $240,470 Turf 15 3 3 4 $240,470

17Mar87-8SA 1⅛Ⓣ:4811:1141:48 fm 4¾ 116 2½ 11½ 11½ 12 ShrW2 ⒻSta Ana H 87-17 Reloy, Northern Aspen, NorthSider 7

17Mar87—Grade I

4Mar87-7SA 1 Ⓣ:4531:1011:36 fm 4½ 114 911 65¾ 43 2¾ ShmrW8 ⒻⓇB Thtful 94-05 Northern Aspen, Reloy, Benzina 10

19Jan87-8SA 1⅛Ⓣ:4821:1241:501fm 7 118 64 51½ 52¾ 66¼ BazeG2 ⒻSn Grgno H 70-29 Frau Altiva, Auspiciante, Solva 7

19Jan87—Grade II; Wide 3/8 turn

21Dec86-8Hol 1 1/16Ⓣ:4921:1241:413fm 5 118 42 51¾ 32 32¼ StnsGL4 ⒻDahlia H 84-15 Aberuschka, An Empress, Reloy 7

21Dec86—Grade III; Wide backside

```
23Nov86-8Hol  1⅛Ⓣ:4731:1131:48 fm 9¼e120  88½ 97¼ 63¼ 32½  Solis A4  ⒻMtrch Iv  85-13 Auspiciante, Aberuschka, Reloy  12
   23Nov86—Grade I; Wide into stretch
2Nov86-8SA  1¼Ⓣ:4631:3542:012fm 21 118  42 42 87½ 85½  Day P10 ⒻYlw Rbn Iv  74-20 Bonne Ile, Top Corsage, Carotene 12
   2Nov86—Grade I
5Oct86♦5Longchamp(Fra) a1⅛ 1:533fm 7½ 123  Ⓣ 63  SbrWR  ⒻPx de l'Opera(Gr2)  SecretForm, ElleSeule, BlueTip  8
14Sep86♦5Longchamp(Fra) a1½ 2:383yl 10 128  Ⓣ 25  AsssnC  ⒻPx Vermeille(Gr1).  Darara, Reloy, Lacovia  8
17Aug86♦5Deauville(Fra) a1¼  2:052gd 5½ 128  Ⓣ 32¼  AsssC  ⒻPx de Psyche(Gr3)  Darara, Cocotte, Reloy  12
15Jun86♦3Chantilly(Fra) a1 5/16  2:07 gd 4½e128  Ⓣ 79¼  GgnrdG  ⒻPx d Diane(Gr1)  Lacovia, Secret Form, Galunpe  15
   Apr 3 SA 3f ft :352 h   Mar 29 SA 6f ft 1:153 h   Mar 24 SA 3f ft :36 h   Mar 15 SA 3f ft :352 h
```

C.

***Benzina** 1+

```
                                     B. m. 5, by Jaazeiro—Bentinck Hotel, by Red God
                                     Br.—Murray Financial Ltd (Eng)        1987  4 3 0 1   $71,558
DELAHOUSSAYE E              115      Tr.—Vienna Darrell                    1986  3 1 2 0   $27,950
Own.—Trpl Dot Dash St-Vndrvrt        Lifetime 14 7 3 2. $109,016           Turf 14 7 3 2  $109,010
4Mar87-7SA  1 Ⓣ:4531:1011:36 fm 4¼ 118  22½ 2hd 2½ 32¾  DlhssyE2 ⓉⓇB Thtful 92-05 Northern Aspen, Reloy, Benzina 10
11Feb87-3SA  1⅛Ⓣ:4631:1111:504fm*4-5 118  23 23½ 21½ 1hd  DlhoussyE2 ⒻAw48000 73-27 Benzina, Stall Cloud, Cenyak's Star 6
24Jan87-7SA  1⅛Ⓣ:47 1:1131:491fm *2¼ 118  11 1hd 1hd 11¼  DlhossyE11 ⒻAw38000 81-17 Benzina, Rekindling, Mangez Les 11
9Jan87-7SA  1⅛Ⓣ:46 1:1111:493gd 2¼ 116  22 31 31½ 1¾  DlhoussyE8 ⒻAw31000 79-21 Benzina,Obslewsanna,TreasureMp 10
   9Jan87—Checked at intervals 3/8 turn
30Dec86-5SA  1⅛Ⓣ:47 1:1121:484fm*4-5 118  21 11 12½ 11¾  Cordero A Jr3 Ⓕ 80000 83-17 Benzina, Mangez Les, Kinda Beau 10
28Nov86-9Hol  1 1/16Ⓣ:4621:1041:411fm *2 116  37 21½ 22 21½  Cordero A Jr6 Ⓕ 80000 86-11 AffectionAffirmed,Benzin,KindBu 10
25Jly86-5Dmr  1 1/16Ⓣ:4841:12 1:431fm *3¼ 117  94 73 31½ 21½  StevensGL3 ⒻAw23000 88-10 Ocean Wave,Benzina,PassAllHope 11
   25Jly86—Broke slowly
15Oct85♦3Redcar(Eng) a1⅝  2:182fm *2¼ 134  Ⓣ 33  StrkyG  HngngStoneH  Golden Fancy, SeaReppin,Benzina  17
23Sep85♦3Leicester(Eng) 1¼  2:05 fm *3 118  Ⓣ 1½  Clark A  Stag H  Benzina, Bank Parade, Wild Hope  14
14Sep85♦3Chepstow (Eng) 1¼  2:101gd 6 124  Ⓣ 23  McGlonA  Hrseshoe H  Dominion Blue, Benzina,WildHope  16
   Apr 1 SA tr.t 5f ft 1:033 h   Mar 26 SA Ⓣ 6f fm 1:134 h (d)   Mar 20 SA tr.t 4f ft :491 h   Mar 14 SA 4f ft :491 h
```

D.

***Frau Altiva**

```
                                     Dk. b. or br. m. 5, by Frari—Alardeante, by Practicante
                                     Br.—Haras La Biznaga (Arg)            1987  5 1 1 1  $113,700
PINCAY L JR  0-0            117      Tr.—Moreno Henry                      1986  9 1 1 2   $50,225
Own.—Brooks-Brooks Jr-Lawrence       Lifetime 20 5 4 3 $183,944            Turf 13 4 3 2  $133,392
17Mar87-8SA  1⅛Ⓣ:4811:1141:48 fm *2¼ 118  64½ 66 68 57½  PncLJr4 ⒻSta Ana H 79-17 Reloy, Northern Aspen, NorthSider 7
   17Mar87—Grade I
1Mar87-8SA  1⅛ :454 1:103 1:484ft  10 117  1114116¾ 64¼ 31¼  PcLJr9 ⒻS Mg Iv H 84-15 NorthSider,WinterTresur,FruAltiv 12
   1Mar87—Grade I
7Feb87-8SA  1 1/16 :461 1:103 1:423ft  6 118  814 89 66½ 53¾  PcLJr5 ⒻSta Mra H 84-14 Fran'sVlentine,NorthSider,Infinidd 8
   7Feb87—Grade II
19Jan87-8SA  1¼Ⓣ:4821:1241:501fm  9 117  75 73 42½ 11  PcLJr3 ⒻSn Grgno H 76-29 Frau Altiva, Auspiciante, Solva 7
   19Jan87—Grade II
2Jan87-8SA  1⅛Ⓣ:4621:1111:49 fm 5¾ 117  87¾ 74½ 21 21½  Pincay LJr6 ⒻAw48000 81-18 Outstandingly,FrauAltiv,NewBruce 8
   2Jan87—Broke out sharply
17Dec86-7Hol  1¼Ⓣ:4731:3632:011fm*9-5 117  711 52 42½ 22½  Pincay L Jr3 ⒻHcp0 86-13 Domino'sNurse,FruAltiv,SuperKittn 7
   17Dec86—Drifted in, bumped 3/16
21Nov86-8Hol  1 Ⓣ:4811:1221:37 fm 3¼ 117  53½ 31 21 11¼  Pincay LJr 5 ⒻAw35000 82-18 FruAltv,Rock'nRollLdr,BlshngRdhd 6
   21Nov86—Broke in a tangle
11Oct86-3SA  1 :46 1:102 1:363ft  15 115  510 58 56½ 46½  PedrozMA5 ⒻAw35000 78-17 Wterside,TwilightRidge,AmbrRidge 5
18Aug86-7Dmr  1 :452 1:10 1:35 ft  *2¼ 117  710 76 55½ 56  Pincay LJr4 ⒻAw27000 87-14 Stemware, Infinidad, Silent Arrival 7
   18Aug86—Wide into stretch
29Jun86-8Hol  1¼Ⓣ:4641:3411:59 fm 28 112  711 66 56½ 57¾  OrtgLE1 ⒻBv Hlls H 104-02 Estrapade, Treizieme, Sauna 7
   29Jun86—Grade II
   Apr 3 SA 4f ft :483 h   ●Mar 29 SA 1 ft 1:411 h   Mar 23 SA 4f ft :494 h   Mar 15 SA 3f ft :371 h
```

E.

Ivor's Image

```
                                     B. f. 4, by Sir Ivor—Embryo, by Busted
                                     Br.—Impshire Thoroughbreds Ltd (Ky)   1986  6 2 0 1  $262,025
CORDERO A JR  1-N           119      Tr.—Gosden John H M                   1985  6 2 1 1   $25,987
Own.—Fraser S                        Lifetime 12 4 1 2 $288,012            Turf 12 4 1 2  $288,012
1Nov86-6SA  1½Ⓣ:4722:0032:252fm 136 119  64½ 66½ 612 613  SnbrWR7 Br Cp Turf 75-07 Manila, Theatrical, Estrapade 9
   1Nov86—Grade I; Bumped 7/8
19Oct86-3WO  1¼Ⓣ:5221:4632:142yl 6-5 117  54½ 32½ 11½ 11½  SbrWR5 ⒻE P Taylor 35-55 Ivor's Image, Carotene, Blue Tip 10
   19Oct86—Grade II
19Aug86♦5York(Eng) 1½  2:301gd 16 126  Ⓣ 31¼  CuthnS  ⒻYrkshrOaks(Gr1)  Untold, Park Express,Ivor'sImage  11
15Jun86♦3Chantilly(Fra) a1 5/16  2:07 gd 13 128  Ⓣ 42¾  SbrWR  ⒻPx d Diane(Gr1)  Lacovia, Secret Form, Galunpe  15
18May86♦5Milan(Italy) a1⅜  2:173gd *4-5 123  Ⓣ 12  SnbrWR  ⒻOaks d'Italia(Gr1)  Ivor'sImage, Danzica, Crodas  11
7May86♦4Chester(Eng) a1½  2:471gd 5 126  Ⓣ 43¾  SnbrWR  ⒻCheshire Oaks  Salchow, Altiyna, LucayanPrincess  9
20Oct85♦6Milan(Italy) a1  1:394gd 3½ 123  Ⓣ 12  SbrWR  ⒻPrDrmlo(Gr2)  Ivor'sImge,FemmdNuit,BllFrncois  12
5Oct85♦4PhoenixPk(Ire) 7f  1:232gd 6 122  Ⓣ 51¾  Roche C  ⒻPark(Gr3)  GailyGaily, CockneyLass, Acushla  19
13Sep85♦1Goodwood(Eng) 7f  1:291gd *2½ 126  Ⓣ 31½  KmbrlyA  ⒻCarnes Seat  Entrancing, Startino, Ivor's Image  9
21Aug85♦5Yarmouth(Eng) 7f  1:283gd*1-4 123  Ⓣ 1no  KbrlA  ⒻHallQuay(Mdn)  Ivor'sImage,Quicksand,DasaQueen  12
   Apr 2 SA Ⓣ 5f fm 1:031 h (d)   Mar 28 SA Ⓣ 1 fm 1:394 h (d)   Mar 23 SA Ⓣ 1 fm 1:412 h (d)   Mar 18 SA Ⓣ 7f fm 1:282 h (d)
```

F.

An Empress

SOLIS A — 117 — Own.—Harbor View Farm

Ch. f. 4, by Affirmed—Blondy, by Lord Gayle

Br.—Medina Dr I (Ky) — 1987 3 0 2 0 $21,600

Tr.—Barrera Lazaro S — 1986 18 4 4 5 $340,145

Lifetime 25 6 7 5 $402,645 — Turf 9 4 4 0 $225,070

28Mar87-8SA a6½f Ⓣ:213 :44 1:142fm 2½ 119 75½ 63 21½ 2hd StvnsGL3 ⒻLs Cngs H 87-12 Lichi, An Empress, Aromacor 7

28Mar87—Pinched back after start; bumped 1/8

15Mar87-7SA a6½f Ⓣ:221 :4431:151gd 6 121 53½ 66½ 55 21¼ StvnsGL3 Ⓕ[R]Mt Wlsn 82-24 Firesweepr,AnEmprss,TrudiDomino 8

15Mar87—Bumped start

24Jan87-8SA 1 1/16:471 1:114 1:43 ft 7½ 122 55 56½ 611 619 Toro F6 ⒻEl Encno 67-18 SeldomSeenSu,Mirculous,TopCorsg 6

24Jan87—Grade III; Lugged out

21Dec86-8Hol 1 1/16Ⓣ:4921:1241:413fm 9-5 117 52½ 41¾ 22 2¾ Toro F3 ⒻDahlia H 85-15 Aberuschka, An Empress, Reloy 7

21Dec86—Grade III

30Nov86-7Hol 1 Ⓣ:4631:1011:342fm *2 118 116¾115 51¼ 1½ Toro F8 HcpO 95-12 AnEmprss,Avntno,Cro'sHollywood 12

30Nov86—Wide into stretch

11Nov86-8Hol 1 Ⓣ:4531:1021:351fm*6-5 120 68 53¼ 1hd 12 Pincay L Jr1 ⒻHcpO 91-09 AnEmpress,MissAlto,SpcilVictory 10

11Nov86—Wide into stretch

31Oct86-8SA 1 1/16:463 1:112 1:431ft 4 118 94¾ 52½ 45 45½ StsJA9 ⒻLnda Vst H 79-16 Mrinn'sGirl,WinterTresur,FinKudos 9

31Oct86—Grade III; Rank, lugged out backstretch; wide into, through stretch

27Sep86-7Bel 1 1/16:461 1:10 1:421sy 4 120 46½ 45 410 49 Stevens G L4 ⒻHcpO 82-17 Coup De Fusil, I'm Sweets,IMeanIt 5

13Sep86-6Bel 1¼[T]:4921:37 2:002fm 7¼ 115 1010 86 75¾ 64¼ SntsJA6 ⒻFlwrbwl H 88-09 Dismasted, Scoot, CopeOfFlowers 12

13Sep86—Grade I

18Aug86-8Sar 1 1/16Ⓣ:47 1:1111:42 fm 4¾ 121 86½ 64½ 32½ 11¼ SntosJA1 ⒻNijana 87-09 AnEmpress,Fam,SpringInnocence 11

18Aug86—Grade III

Mar 23 SA 5f ft 1:011 h — Mar 11 SA 5f ft 1:00 h — Mar 4 SA 5f ft :591 h — Feb 26 SA 4f gd :482 h

G.

Northern Aspen

STEVENS G L — 119 — Own.—Paulson A E

B. m. 5, by Northern Dancer—Fall Aspen, by Pretense

Br.—Spndthrft Fm–Combs–Kernan (Ky) — 1987 2 1 1 0 $62,1[illegible]

Tr.—Scott George W — 1986 4 0 1 0 $10,166

Lifetime 11 3 2 0 $99,269 — Turf 11 3 2 0 $99,269

17Mar87-8SA 1⅛Ⓣ:4811:1141:48 fm 2½ 119 31½ 21½ 21½ 22 StsGL7 ⒻSta Ana H 85-17 Reloy, Northern Aspen, NorthSider 7

17Mar87—Grade I; Broke slowly

4Mar87-7SA 1 Ⓣ:4531:1011:36 fm 4 114 89½ 32 1½ 1¾ StvnsGL9 Ⓕ[R]B Thtful 95-05 Northern Aspen, Reloy, Benzina 10

26Oct86♦3Longchamp(Fra) a7f 1:231yl 12 134 Ⓣ 34¾ Badel A Px d la Foret(Gr1) Sarab, Risk Me, Whakilyric 16

7Sep86♦4Longchamp(Fra) a1 1:354gd 21 124 Ⓣ 85¾ BadelA Px d Mouln(Gr1) SonicLady, ThrillShow, Lirung 14

27Aug86♦4Deauville(Fra) a1 1:412sf 3 122 Ⓣ 22 LquuxA Px Quincey(Gr3) Apldorn,NrthrnAspn,SplnddMmnt 14

26Apr86♦3Leicester(Eng) 7f 1:31 sf 3¼ 125 Ⓣ 614 Hills R Hlstn Pls Trphy BollinKnight,Shmirekh,HomoSpin 10

18Aug85♦4Deauville(Fra) a1 1:381sf 3½ 118 Ⓣ 105 ‡LquxA PxJcqLeMrois(Gr1) Vin De France, Vertige, RiverMist 11

‡18Aug85—Dead Heat

3Aug85♦4Deauville(Fra) a1 1:40 sf *2¼ 119 Ⓣ 1¾ Head F ⒻPx d'Astrte(Gr2) NorthrnAspn,CpricornBll,GingrLss 11

10Jly85♦3Newmarket(Eng) 1 1:364gd 16 117 Ⓣ 32 LequeuxA ⒻChild(Gr3) Al Bahathri,EverGenial,BellaColora 9

●Mar 28 SLR tr.t 6f ft 1:131 h — ●Mar 13 SLR tr.t 5f ft 1:004 h — Feb 28 SA 6f ft 1:141 h — ●Feb 21 SLR tr.t 6f ft 1:111 h

H.

***Infinidad**

BAZE G — 113 — Own.—Hancock A B III

Dk. b. or br. m. 5, by Mr Long—Infidele, by Trevieres

Br.—Haras Santa Amelia (Chile) — 1987 4 0 0 1 $39,375

Tr.—Whittingham Charles — 1986 9 3 2 1 $124,175

Lifetime 18 7 2 2 $179,066 — Turf 5 2 0 0 $32,407

17Mar87-8SA 1⅛Ⓣ:4811:1141:48 fm 17 114 76 77 78 67½ BlcCA6 ⒻSta Ana H 79-17 Reloy, Northern Aspen, NorthSider 7

17Mar87—Grade I; Checked at start

1Mar87-8SA 1⅛:454 1:103 1:484ft 23 113 1215127¾ 85¼ 41½ BlcCA10 ⒻS Mg Iv H 83-15 NorthSider,WinterTresur,FruAltiv 12

1Mar87—Grade I; Broke through gate; wide into drive

7Feb87-8SA 1 1/16:461 1:103 1:423ft 11 113 710 66½ 55 32¾ Baze G1 ⒻSta Mra H 85-14 Fran'sVlentine,NorthSider,Infinidd 8

7Feb87—Grade II; Wide into stretch

17Jan87-8SA 7f :222 :444 1:214ft 19 114 57 59½ 57½ 53¼ BlcCA4 ⒻS Mnca H 88-18 Pine TreeLane,Balladry,HerRoyalty 6

17Jan87—Grade III

21Dec86-8Hol 1 1/16Ⓣ:4921:1241:413fm 10 114 2½ 2hd 43½ 45¾ BlckCA7 ⒻDahlia H 80-15 Aberuschka, An Empress, Reloy 7

21Dec86—Grade III

6Dec86-8Hol 1⅛:462 1:112 1:50 gd 4¾ 114 67½ 32 22 2½ BlckCA3 ⒻSlvr Bls H 86-16 Family Style, Infinidad, Waterside 7

6Dec86—Grade II; Steadied start

3Nov86-7SA 1 :452 1:101 1:36 ft 6½ 115 87 51¾ 2½ 1¼ BlackCA7 ⒻPrncs Rny 88-14 Infinidad, Fairly Old, Stemware

9Oct86-8SA 1¼:472 1:114 1:491ft 6 114 31½ 31 32½ 34¼ Black C A2 ⒻDulcia H 78-21 Frn'sVlntin,MgnificntLindy,Inf[illegible]

18. Can you find the class standout in this open Saratoga stakes?

7th Saratoga

1 1/16 MILES. (Turf). (1.39⅖) 3rd Running THE DARRYL'S JOY (2nd Division). Purse $75,000 Added. 3-year-olds and upward. By subscription of $150 each, which should accompany the nomination; $300 to pass the entry box, and $300 to start; with $75,000 added. The added money and all fees to be divided 60% to the winner, 22% to second, 12% to third and 6% to fourth. Weights, 3-year-olds, 117 lbs. Older, 122 lbs. Non-winners of a race of $50,000 at a mile or over since May 1, allowed 3 lbs. Of such a race of $35,000 since February 1, 5 lbs. Of such a race of $25,000 since November 1, 7 lbs. (Maiden, claiming, starter and restricted races not considered.) Starters to be named at the closing time of entries. A trophy will be presented to the winning owner. The New York Racing Association reserves the right to transfer this race to the main course. Closed Wednesday, July 22, 1987 with 60 nominations.

Coupled—Lightning Leap and Jack Of Clubs.

A.

I'm A Banker — Dk. b. or br. h. 5, by Truxton King—Bank Officer, by Intentionally
Own.—Davis A — 115 — Br.—Isaacs Harry Z (Ky) — Tr.—Moschera Gasper S
1987 6 0 0 1 $19,746
1986 14 5 4 1 $297,586
Turf 25 7 6 3 $362,192
Lifetime 32 8 7 3 $377,712

11Jly87-8Bel 1⅜[T]:4841:3912:16 yl 14 108 1¹ 1½ 6⁴½ 7¹¹½ Graell A5 Tidal H 65-23 Dance of Life, UptownSwell,Duluth 8
11Jly87—Grade III
25Jun87-8Bel 1¼[T]:4821:36 2:001fm 4½ 113 1² 2¹ 3¹ 3⁴¾ Graell A7 HcpO 88-16 Duluth, Silvino, I'm A Banker 8
13Jun87-8Bel 1⅜[T]:50 1:3812:14 fm 26 110 1¹ 1hd 1hd 5³¾ GraellA4 Bowlng.Gr H 83-24 Theatrical, Akabir, Dance of Life 10
13Jun87—Grade I
5Jun87-7Bel 1 1/16 Ⓣ:4941:14 1:47 sf 2½ 119 1hd 4³ 5⁹½ 5¹⁹½ GraellA2 Blue Lrkspur 41-38 Tlkeno,PrinceDniel,ExplosiveDncer 6
30May87-8Bel 1¼[T]:4811:3622:004fm 20f 111 1½ 1hd 1½ 4³ GraellA1 Red Smith H 87-24 Theatrical, Dance of Life,Equalize 11
30May87—Grade II
15May87-6Bel 1 1/16 Ⓣ:47 1:1141:444fm 3½ 119 1½ 3½ 4⁴½ 4⁷½ Cruguet J5 Aw45000 65-29 Real Courage, Talakeno, Infantry 7
25Oct86-9Lrl 1¼Ⓣ:4611:35 1:592fm 3 112 1¹ 1¹½ 2² 2⁵¾ Graell A4 Turf Cup H 104 — StormOnTheLoose,I'mABnkr,Ronbr 7
25Oct86—Grade III
19Oct86-8Bel 1¼[T]:4911:3832:031fm 20 111 1³ 1² 1¹ 1hd Graell A8 Kelso H 78-23 I'm ABanker,Duluth,PremierMister 9
19Oct86—Grade III
Aug 3 Bel 3f ft :37 b Jly 30 Bel [T] 4f fm :491 b (d) Jly 23 Bel Ⓣ 3f fm :373 b (d)

B.

Lightning Leap — Ch. h. 5, by Nijinsky II—First Feather, by First Landing
Own.—Rokeby Stable — 115 — Br.—Mellon Paul (Va) — Tr.—Miller Mack
1987 1 0 0 0
1986 8 2 1 1 $84,218
Turf 17 5 3 1 $171,934
Lifetime 25 8 5 1 $237,660

15May87-6Bel 1 1/16 Ⓣ:47 1:1141:444fm *2½ 119 2½ 4¹½ 7¹² 7³²¾ Maple E3 Aw45000 39-29 Real Courage, Talakeno, Infantry 7
11Oct86-7Bel 6f Ⓣ:22 :4431:091fm *2 115 3² 2²½ 3⁷ 6¹¹¾ Day P10 Engine One 82-17 Red Wing Dream, Alev, Cullendale 10
13Sep86-5Bel 1 Ⓣ:4621:0931:342fm 3¾ 115 1½ 1¹½ 1⁴ 1¾ Bailey J D2 Cavan 93-09 LghtnngLp,CostConscous,JdgCost 6
30Jly86-7Sar 1 1/16 Ⓣ:47 1:11 1:424fm 3 115 3⁵ 3³½ 6⁶ 6¹⁶½ Bailey JD5 Daryl's Joy 66-21 Mourjane, Island Sun, Little Look 6
5Jly86-7Bel 1 Ⓣ:45 1:0921:344fm 5½ 115 4²½ 3³½ 3³ 3⁴½ RrRP2 Independence 86-16 StyTheCourse,BsktWv,LightningLp 6
21Jun86-9Mth 1 Ⓣ:4631:11 1:354fm*4-5 117 4⁴½ 1½ 1¹ 4¹ BileyJD2 Red Bank H 95-10 Mazatleca, Feeling Gallant, Hildeal 8
21Jun86—Grade III
7Jun86-5Bel 1 1/16 [T]:4741:1241:472sf *8-5 117 4¹¾ 3² 2hd 3nk Bailey J D1 Blue Lark 64-36 Ltnnt'sLrk,‡ExclsvPrtnr,LghtnngLp 6
7Jun86—Placed second through disqualification; Bumped stretch
2Jun86-8Bel 1 Ⓣ:4631:1021:351fm 4 117 1½ 1¹½ 1³ 1²½ Bailey J D2 Aw40000 89-11 LightningLep,IsYourPlesure,Duluth 9
Aug 3 Sar 3f sy :361 b ●Jly 23 Bel 3f ft :35 b ●Jly 16 Bel 6f ft 1:111 h ●Jly 9 Bel 6f sy 1:123 h

C.

Laser Lane — B. c. 4, by The Minstrel—Kris Kris, by Hoist The Flag
Own.—Centennial Farms — 115 — Br.—Oxford StAble (Ky) — Tr.—Jerkens H Allen
1987 2 1 0 0 $22,110
1986 12 4 3 0 $101,843
Turf 8 3 2 0 $90,935
Lifetime 18 5 4 0 $128,793

18Jly87-9Mth 1 1/16 Ⓣ:4641:11 1:413fm 3½ 117 5⁹ 5³½ 5² 4⁴¼ HrnndR6 Oceanport H 93-06 SoverignSong,FlingGllnt,Spllbound 8
18Jly87—Grade III
6Jly87-6Bel 1 Ⓣ:4531:0941:35 fm 5½ 117 3³ 2¹½ 2½ 1²¾ Hernandez R5 Aw31000 90-14 Laser Lane, El Jefe, Easton 7
30Aug86-10Suf a170 Ⓣ 1:432fm*3-2 116 5⁴½ 1¹½ 1¹½ 1½ Vargas JL3 T Writer H 99-05 Laser Lane, Galiant Helio, Curium 10
13Aug86-1Sar 1⅛[T]:4731:1211:492fm *2½ 112 3² 2hd 1²½ 1¹½ Santos J A7 175000 93-14 LaserLne,PrinceDniel,AlbertClipper 8
26Jly86-8Mth 1 1/16 :471 1:11 1:431sy 5½ 114 1hd 3nk 4³½ 4⁸½ Santos J A1 Coastal H 80-15 BrfootMilmn,SlvrComt,BigBuckroo 7
4Jly86-9Mth 1 1/16 Ⓣ:4811:1221:442fm 27 113 1hd 1hd 3³½ 5⁵½ MrCHJr8 Lmplightr H 73-20 OnMgicMomnt,DncofLif,SlvrComt 12
4Jly86—Grade II
21Jun86-8Bel 1 1/16 Ⓣ:46 1:1021:412fm 14 114 2½ 2hd 4²½ 5⁶¾ VelsquezJ5 Hill Prince 82-12 Double Feint, Glow, Jack Of Clubs 7
21Jun86—Grade III
14Jun86-9Mth 1 Ⓣ:4721:12 1:391fm 6½ 112 1¹½ 1¹ 1½ 2hd MordAJr7 LongBranch 79-21 LyphardLine,LaserLne,ABlendOfSix 8
14Jun86—Grade III
●Jly 31 Bel 5f ft :584 h Jly 24 Bel 3f ft :372 b Jly 17 Bel 3f ft :38 b Jly 4 Bel 5f ft 1:003 b

D.

Yankee Affair
B. g. 5, by Northern Fling—My Malchen, by Debbysman
Br.—Derry Meeting Farm (Pa) 1987 4 1 0 1 $30,560
Own.—Jujugen Stable 117 Tr.—Carroll Henry L 1986 13 4 2 3 $76,492
Lifetime 17 5 2 4 $107,052 Turf 2 1 0 1 $29,420

20Jly87-8Bel 1 1/16 [T]:4741:1211:424fm 11 115 43 32 1hd 11 Antley C W1 Aw45000 87-22 YankeeAffair,PrinceDniel,G'DyMte 6
20Jly87—Drifted, driving
11Jly87-5Mth 1 :472 1:111 1:37 ft 3½ 116 2hd 42 52 43¼ Vigliotti M J1 Aw19000 85-14 RoylDoulton,Bowldrom,FlorscntGm 6
20Jun87-6Mth 5f [T]:22 :452 :573fm 15 115 76½ 53 52½ 31¾ Vigliotti M J6 Aw22000 92-12 Lobbit,RedWingDream,YankeeAffir 8
20Jun87—In tight
10May87-7Bel 6f :232 :472 1:103ft 26e 119 42½ 64¼ 712 715¾ Bailey J D2 Aw40000 71-25 LoveThatMac,RoyalPennnt,ElBsco 7
15Nov86-8Pha 1⅛ :46 1:10 1:494ft 3 116 23½ 23 21½ 1nk VglttMJ2 [S]Iroquois H 86-14 Yankee Affair, Ramten,B.A.Captain 8
4Nov86-7Pha 5f :222 :46 :582m 2 118 4¾ 3nk 21½ 33½ Vigliotti M J4 Aw12500 88-23 SouthernCloggr,CoolAsIc,YnkAffir 6
18Oct86-8Pha 7f :221 :45 1:23 ft 3½ 114 43½ 43½ 2½ 11 VlttMJ5 [S]Pa. SprintH 92-17 YnkeeAffir,Donneybrook,NvlCutter 9
6Oct86-8Bel 6f :23 :461 1:101ft *2 117 21 34 58 511½ Bailey J D7 Aw25000 79-24 HagleyMill,Dnotble,PssingThunder 7
Aug 2 Mth 5f ft 1:004 h Jly 7 Mth [T] 7f fm 1:30 b (d) Jly 1 Mth [T] 3f fm :372 b (d) Jun 19 Mth 3f ft :374 b

E.

Talakeno
Dk. b. or br. h. 7, by Vaguely Noble—Katonka, by Minnesota Mac
Br.—Happy Valley Farm (Fla) 1987 4 1 1 0 $48,732
Own.—Happy Valley Farm 119 Tr.—Dutrow Richard E 1986 10 2 1 1 $290,302
Lifetime 45 8 8 4 $669,229 Turf 35 7 5 4 $641,609

11Jly87-8Bel 1⅜ [T]:4841:3912:16 yl 11 117 21 2½ 75½ 69½ Bailey J D2 Tidal H 67-23 Dance of Life, UptownSwell,Duluth 8
11Jly87—Grade III
19Jun87-8Bel 1 [T]:4531:1021:351fm 3½ 122 54 63¾ 44½ 43¾ Cordero A Jr6 Poker 85-19 Double Feint, Onyxly, Island Sun 8
19Jun87—Came out str.
5Jun87-7Bel 1 1/16 [T]:4941:14 1:47 sf *2 119 31½ 12½ 1hd 13½ SntsJA3 Blue Lrkspur 61-38 Tlkeno,PrinceDniel,ExplosiveDncer 6
15May87-6Bel 1 1/16 [T]:47 1:1141:444fm 8 119 42 51¾ 32½ 21¼ Santos J A2 Aw45000 71-29 Real Courage, Talakeno, Infantry 7
7Sep86-8Bel 1¼ [T]:5021:3842:023gd 10 117 62½ 87½ 89¾ 89¾ DvisRG1 Manhattan H 71-23 Dngr'sHour,PrmrMstr,Exc'usvPrtnr 8
7Sep86—Grade I
21Aug86-8Sar 1⅝ [T]:5212:04 2:394fm*3-2 116 33½ 1hd 1hd 1nk CrdrAJr11 Seneca H 86-13 Talakeno, Upper Bend, Akabir 11
21Aug86—Grade III
26Jly86-8Bel 1½ [T]:5212:1242:392sf *3 114 31½ 55½ 39½ 210 CrdrAJr7Swrd Dncr H — — SouthernSultan,Talkeno,TriForSize 8
26Jly86—Grade I
4Jly86-8Hol 1½ [T]:4842:00 2:242fm 38 115 21 1hd 41¾ 66½ VlnzulPA6 Sunset H 113 — Zoffany, Dahar, Flying Pidgeon 8
4Jly86—Grade I
Jly 30 Aqu [T] 1 fm 1:463 b (d) ●Jly 23 Aqu [T] 3f gd :372 h Jly 7 Aqu 5f ft 1:022 b ●Jly 2 Aqu 6f gd 1:17 b

F.

***Mourjane**
Dk. b. or br. h. 7, by Pitskelly—Affaire d'Amour, by Tudor Music
Br.—McKinley W G (Ire) 1987 2 1 0 0 $30,240
Own.—Fernwood Stable 115 Tr.—Skiffington Thomas J 1986 10 3 1 0 $227,106
Lifetime 36 10 6 6 $712,023 Turf 36 10 6 6 $712,023

15Jly87-4Atl 1 3/16 [T]:5121:1611:584sf 6½ 114 55 54 45½ 45½ Perret C1 U Nations H 63-33 Manila, Racing Star, Air Display 5
15Jly87—Grade I
7Jly87-9Mth 1 1/16 [T]:4811:1221:432gd 5½ 114 76½ 75 3½ 11½ Perret C7 Cozzene 88-17 Mourjane, Castelets, Icy Groom 7
19Oct86-8Bel 1¼ [T]:4911:3832:031fm 5 117 811 76½ 610 79½ MigliorеR2 Kelso H 68-23 I'm ABanker,Duluth,PremierMister 9
19Oct86—Grade III
14Sep86-10LaD 1⅜ [T]:5021:40 2:154fm *1 118 1411 124½ 66 75 Santos JA8 La D H 82-11 Gallant Archer, Shulich,Nadirpour 14
14Sep86—Grade III
31Aug86-6AP 1¼ [T]:4641:3712:012fm 6 117 817 56½ 1½ 11¼ SntosJA8 Arlington H 87-11 Mourjane, Will Dancer, CleverSong 9
31Aug86—Grade I
10Aug86-8Sar 1⅛ [T]:4841:1241:504gd*9-5 119 53½ 55¾ 1112 1215½ SntosJA7 B Baruch H 57-25 ExclusivPrtnr,I'mABnkr,CrmFrich 12
10Aug86—Grade II
30Jly86-7Sar 1 1/16 [T]:47 1:11 1:424fm *2½ 119 67½ 65¾ 31½ 11¾ SantosJA2 Daryl's Joy 83-21 Mourjane, Island Sun, Little Look 6
15Apr86-7Kee 1⅛ [T]:4821:1421:543gd 2½ 123 77½ 63½ 44 48½ Samyn J L2 Elkhorn 75-16 Ltnnt'sLrk,LprchnsWsh,MjstcJbot 10
●Aug 3 Fai tr.t 5f ft 1:002 b ●Jly 6 Fai tr.t 3f ft :372 b Jun 26 Fai tr.t 5f ft 1:03 b Jun 15 Fai tr.t 5f ft 1:004 b

G.

Law Court
B. c. 4, by Alleged—Bay Street, by Grundy
Br.—Oceanic Development Co Ltd (Ky) 1987 2 2 0 0 $27,750
Own.—Dogwood Farm 117 Tr.—Tesher Howard M 1986 5 1 0 0 $3,723
Lifetime 8 3 0 0 $31,473 Turf 8 3 0 0 $31,473

11Feb87-9Hia a1½ [T] 2:332fm*9-5 112 913 57 32½ 1no CrdrAJr4 Miami Lakes 67-31 Law Court, After Party,Herradura 12
11Feb87—Steadied, drvng
27Jan87-8Hia a1⅛ [T] 1:552fm*6-5 116 79¾ 46½ 1½ 12 Cordero AJr9 Aw15000 84-19 Law Court, Turn TheTraffic,Nioro 10
17Jun86 ♦2Thirsk(Eng) 1½ 2:36 fm*9-5 133 [T] 1nk CurntR Brick Ponds Hcp Law Court, Regency Square, Vitry 9
12Jun86 ♦5Newbury(Eng) a1⅝ 2:534gd 20 126 [T] 518 WllsT Childrey Stakes(Mdn) White Clover, Shibil, Boon Point 15
31May86 ♦6Newmarket(Eng) a1 11/16 3:141gd 16 126 [T] 49 WllsT MatthewDwsonStks(Mdn) Actinium, Zaajer, Marie Galarte 7
10May86 ♦5Bath(Eng) a1⅞ 2:364gd *2½ 126 [T] 820 CrtR WestLittletonStks(Mdn) JustDavid,Excelbelle,BetterBewre 19
29Apr86 ♦6Bath(Eng) a1⅞ 2:383gd 8 126 [T] 516 CrtR Blathwayt Stakes(Mdn) Golden Heights,Allatum,Bastinado 16
4Oct85 ♦2Newmarket(Eng) 7f 1:263gd 33 126 [T] 19 FrM KalDncerWestleyStk(Mdn) Cromwell Park, Top Guest, Duff 26
Jly 23 Bel [T] 7f fm 1:283 h (d) Jly 16 Bel [T] 5f fm 1:001 h (d) Jly 6 Bel 5f ft 1:01 h Jly 1 Bel 4f ft :51 h

H.

Another Reef *
Ch. h. 5, by Plum Bold—Satin Dancer, by Jig Time
Br.—Ludwig J (NJ) 1987 7 3 0 1 $77,030
Own.—Leachman T K 117 Tr.—Ludwig Jack D 1986 6 1 2 0 $56,536
Lifetime 26 10 4 3 $449,193 Turf 1 0 0 0

18Jly87-5Bel 1 1/16:474 1:12 1:432ft 9-5 122 32½ 3½ 2hd 42 Santos J A 3 HcpO 83-20 Belocolus, Landing Plot, Carjack 6
18Jly87—Off slowly
4Jly87-5Mth 1 :464 1:104 1:353ft *6-5 123 51¾ 31 2½ 1¾ McCarron CJ 3 [S]HcpO 95-10 AnotherRf,OwnsTroup,Bishop'sTim 6
28May87-8Bel 1⅛:452 1:093 1:47 ft 2 118 3½ 2½ 48 414 Cordero A Jr 2 HcpO 78-25 Personal Flag, Landing Plot, Alioth 6
14May87-8Bel 1 :454 1:10 1:342ft 12 116 22½ 11½ 12 12½ Santos J A 2 HcpO 93-13 AnotherReef,SetStyle,CutlassRelity 7
17Apr87-7Aqu 1 :472 1:112 1:362m 6-5 119 53½ 45½ 2½ 1½ Santos J A 4 Aw45000 84-22 AnothrRf,MjsticEmpir,RoylDoulton 5
12Mar87-9GP 7f :231 :463 1:233ft 4 115 31 43 66 34½ Romero R P 6 Aw20000 82-26 Bishop Bob, Mugatea, AnotherReef 8
17Feb87-9Hia 6f :214 :443 1:094ft 4 115 21½ 53¾ 99¼ 914 Santos J A 1 Aw26200 77-22 SwetBobbyV.,WrdOffTroubl,Crushr 9
21Jun86-10Suf 1⅛:471 1:11 1:494ft 18 115 21½ 33½ 1011 1017¾ MigliorеR 1 Mass H 71-12 Skip Trial, Creme Fraiche, ElBasco 11
21Jun86—Grade II
●Jly 30 Bel 5f ft :594 h Jly 14 Bel 4f ft :502 h Jun 29 Bel 5f ft 1:02 h Jun 22 Bel 5f ft 1:013 h

I

Duluth
B. h. 5, by Codex—Graceful Gal, by Key to the Mint
Br.—Genter Frances A Stable (Fla) 1987 8 1 0 3 $82,293
Own.—F A Genter Stable Inc 117 Tr.—Schulhofer Flint S 1986 10 3 2 3 $155,324
Lifetime 30 8 3 7 $369,212 Turf 22 6 2 6 $336,332

26Jly87-10Rkma 1⅛Ⓣ 1:50 fm 3 114 68 53½ 32 31¼ CrugutJ 4 Sweeps H — — Carotene, Damen Hall, Duluth 11
26Jly87—Grade III
11Jly87-8Bel 1⅜[T]:4841:3912:16 yl 8½ 113 37 31½ 2hd 34½ Vasquez J 3 Tidal H 72-23 Dance of Life, UptownSwell,Duluth 8
11Jly87—Grade III
25Jun87-8Bel 1¼[T]:4821:36 2:001fm 14 114 36 33 2½ 13¼ Cruguet J 6 HcpO 93-16 Duluth, Silvino, I'm A Banker 8
25Jun87—Steadied, clear
5Jun87-7Bel 1 1/16Ⓣ:4941:14 1:47 sf 2¾ 119 2hd 22½ 612 625½ CrugtJ 1 Blue Lrkspur 35-38 Tlkeno,PrinceDniel,ExplosiveDncer 6
11Apr87-9GP 1 1/16Ⓣ:47 1:1021:404fm *2½ 112 21 21 65 68 CruguetJ 8 Can Trf H 88-07 Racing Star, Glaros, Salem Drive 9
11Apr87—Grade II; Run in Divisions
21Feb87-10Hia 1½Ⓣ 2:283fm 9½ 114 2hd 21 75¼ 78½ CrugutJ 2 Turf Cup H 78-14 Theatrical,LongMick,CremeFraiche 8
21Feb87—Grade I
31Jan87-10Hia 1 3/16Ⓣ 1:54 fm 13 116 31 1½ 11½ 43¼ CrugutJ 12 B'gnvilla H 84-14 Akabir, ‡Theatrical,FlyingPidgeon 14
31Jan87—Grade II; Rank early; Placed third through disqualification
7Jan87-10Crc 1½Ⓣ:4742:0212:27 gd 3¾ 117 22½ 2hd 2½ 53 CrugutJ 8 Mcknight H 91-18 CremeFriche,FlyingPidgeon,Akbir 10
7Jan87—Grade II
●Aug 3 Sar Ⓣ 4f gd :49 b ●Jly 23 Bel Ⓣ 4f fm :473 h (d) Jly 19 Bel 4f ft :49 b Jly 4 Bel 3f ft :362 h

J.

Jack Of Clubs
B. c. 4, by Sir Ivor—Colony Club, by Tom Rolfe
Br.—Mellon Paul (Va) 1987 2 1 0 0 $18,600
Own.—Rokeby Stables 115 Tr.—Miller Mack 1986 10 3 1 3 $79,240
Lifetime 16 4 2 5 $108,300 Turf 8 2 1 2 $61,480

12Jun87-8Bel 1 1/16Ⓣ:4721:1121:413gd 3½ 122 77½ 55¼ 55 65¼ Romero R P 8 Aw45000 83-17 Silvino, Ioskeha, Conquering Hero 9
20May87-8Bel 1 1/16:48 1:122 1:422gd *6-5 119 21½ 21½ 1hd 11¾ Romero R P 2 Aw31000 90-17 JackOfClubs,Sting'em,PrinceDaniel 4
19Oct86-8Bel 1¼[T]:4911:3832:031fm 16 110 913 88 811 69¼ GuerrWA 4 Kelso H 69-23 I'm ABanker,Duluth,PremierMister 9
19Oct86—Grade III
26Sep86-9Med 1⅜Ⓣ:4911:3942:191yl 5¾ 112 814 84 34½ 37½ BaileyJD 2 Rutgers H 61-30 Pillaster, Southjet, Jack Of Clubs 10
26Sep86—Grade II; Run in Divisions
13Sep86-3Bel 1 1/16[T]:4721:11 1:413fm *2¾ 118 77¼ 64½ 65 1no Bailey J D 1 Aw26000 93-09 JackOfClubs,FarwyIslnd,Torquemd 8
25Aug86-7Sar 1 1/16Ⓣ:47 1:1131:42 fm 2½ 112 86½ 62¾ 2½ 1hd Bailey J D 8 Aw25000 87-15 Jack Of Clubs, Godbey, Loose 12
15Aug86-7Sar 1 1/16Ⓣ:4631:1031:421fm 3¾ 112 54½ 32 22 22¼ Bailey J D 5 Aw25000 84-18 Fred Astaire, Jack OfClubs,Godbey 9
12Jly86-8Bel 1¼[T]:4941:39 2:031yl 6¾ 114 85½ 99 812 711 Bailey JD 4 Lexington 67-22 Manila, Glow, Dance Card Filled 10
12Jly86—Grade II
●Jly 30 Bel 7f ft 1:263 h ●Jly 24 Bel 6f ft 1:13 h Jly 18 Bel 5f ft 1:00 h Jly 13 Bel 4f ft :491 h

K.

Cost Conscious
Dk. b. or br. h. 5, by Believe It—Pennygown, by Herbager
Br.—Phipps O M (Ky) 1987 1 0 0 1 $10,998
Own.—Cohen R B 117 Tr.—Shapoff Stanley R 1986 20 6 5 2 $194,418
Lifetime 27 7 8 4 $238,356 Turf 2 0 1 0 $13,860

3Jan87-8Aqu 1 1/16[•]:4641:1041:414m 3½ 112 43 33½ 35 33½ SmynJL 4 Aqueduct H 97-16 King'sSwn,Rj'sRvng,CostConscious 8
3Jan87—Grade III
22Dec86-8Aqu 1 1/16[•]:4841:1241:441ft *2 116 62 2½ 11 15 Samyn J L 2 HcpO 89-17 CostConscious,RglHumor,MistyMc 8
27Nov86-8Aqu 1 3/16:492 1:131 1:571gd 9¾ 111 42 53½ 32 32¼ CrugutJ 1 Qns Cnty H 74-29 PineBelt,Scrimshaw,CostConscious 6
27Nov86—Grade III
15Nov86-9Med 1⅛:473 1:112 1:483ft 14 112 75 62½ 52 45¼ CrugutJ 7 Paterson H 85-13 CremeFraiche,SkipTril,DoItAginDn 7
15Nov86—Grade II
1Nov86-7Aqu 1⅛:474 1:111 1:50 ft 8½ 110 3nk 21 23 44¼ SamynJL 4 Stuyv'snt H 81-19 LittleMissouri,Wquoit,Let'sGoBlu 10
1Nov86—Grade II
8Oct86-8Bel 1 1/16:462 1:104 1:413ft 5½ 115 31 2hd 16 16 Cruguet J 3 Aw40000 94-19 CostConscious,WikikStr,MrclWood 6
28Sep86-7Bel 7f Ⓣ:231 :47 1:252sf *2¼ 115 58 87½ 712 714½ Samyn J L 8 Sea Bird 63-37 Alev, Braddells, Cullendale 9
13Sep86-5Bel 1 Ⓣ:4621:0931:342fm 8¾ 115 52 43½ 24 2¾ Samyn J L 1 Cavan 92-09 LghtnngLp,CostConscous,JdgCost 6
Jly 30 Bel [T] 7f fm 1:303 b (d) ●Jly 23 Bel 6f ft 1:114 h Jly 18 Bel 5f ft :593 h Jly 14 Bel 4f ft :50 b

19. As regularly happens, of the two likeliest winners here, one will become a conspicuous underlay but the other a juicy overlay. Find the most probable overlay to win.

2nd Saratoga

7 FURLONGS. (1.20⅗) ALLOWANCE. PUrse $26,000. 3-year-olds and upward which have never won a race other than maiden, claiming or starter. Weight, 3-year-olds, 117 lbs. Older, 122 lbs. Non-winners of a race other than claiming since July 15 allowed 3 lbs. Of such a race since July 1, 5 lbs.

A.

Real Account
B. c. 3, by Private Account—Unreality, by In Reality
Br.—Vangeloff Karil (Ky) 1987 4 1 2 0 $24,580
Own.—Pokoik L **1075** **Tr.—DeStasio Richard T** 1986 0 M 0 0
Lifetime 4 1 2 0 $24,580
19Jly87-5Bel 6½f :222 :451 1:162ft 3½ 113 42½ 32 35½ 58¼ Vasquez J7 Aw26000 85-14 Jato d'Agua, Freud, Wild Behavior 9
9Jly87-3Bel 6f :22 :454 1:104m 4½ 1085 55½ 32½ 2½ 21¼ Nuesch D4 Aw26000 85-24 StckedPck,RelAccount,BillyWilbur 7
3Jun87-6Bel 7f :232 :463 1:244ft *1 1175 42 2½ 12 1¾ Nuesch D9 Mdn 78-22 RlAccount,SovrgnInvdr,InAllRspcts 9
23May87-4Bel 6f :221 :451 1:093ft 6¼ 1175 53½ 44 34 22 Nuesch D7 Mdn 90-13 Sl'sShuttle,RelAccount,LivelyNtiv 10
Aug 6 Sar 3f ft :364 b Jly 28 Bel 5f ft :594 h Jly 17 Bel 3f ft :363 b Jly 5 Bel 4f ft :481 h

B.

Homebuilder
Ch. c. 3, by Mr Prospector—Smart Heiress, by Vaguely Noble
Br.—Ryehill Farm (Md) 1987 12 0 3 6 $247,064
Own.—Ryehill Farm **112** **Tr.—Stephens Woodford C** 1986 8 1 1 4 $56,500
Lifetime 20 1 4 10 $303,564 Turf 2 0 0 1 $2,650
27Jun87-10Lrl 1⅛:474 1:12 1:493ft 2½ 114 42 31 2½ 21¼ GrrWA3 Govrn's Cp H 97-16 High Brite,Homebuilder,GreenBook 6
27Jun87—Checked 1st turn
13Jun87-9Tdn 1⅛:462 1:104 1:503ft 7¼ 114 310 39 36 37 GurrWA8 Ohio Derby 77-23 LostCode,ProudestDuke,Hombuildr 9
13Jun87—Grade II
23May87-8Spt 1⅛:46 1:103 1:493ft 5 114 32½ 35 45 42¼ BrumfildD2 Ill Derby 95-16 Lost Code, Blanco, Valid Prospect 7
23May87—Grade III
2May87-7CD 1 1/16:47 1:112 1:431ft 6-5 115 21 2hd 21½ 35 BrmfldD5 Twin Spires 87-09 FstForwrd,SoonrShowrs,Hombuildr 5
11Apr87-8Bir 1⅛:471 1:112 1:513ft 5½ 122 21½ 23 22½ 21¼ BrumfldD10 Ala Derby — — LostCode,Homebuilder,PhntomJt 12
29Mar87-11TP 1 1/16:461 1:103 1:424ft 14 121 63½ 65 45 36½ BrmfldD7 Jim Beam 89-17 J.T.'sPet,FstrThnSound,Hombuildr 12
29Mar87—Grade III; bore in sharply start
14Mar87-10Tam 1 1/16:464 1:112 1:434ft 3½ 116 11 1½ 1hd 21 MapleE1 Tampa Derby 99-11 PhntomJt,Hombuldr,You'rNoBrgn 10
14Mar87—Grade III
22Feb87-8Hia 1 1/16Ⓣ 1:43 fm*6-5 114 68 65 813 1013¼ Maple E9 Aw20400 70-13 Peaceable, Mc Forbes,Superceded 12
Aug 5 Sar 4f ft :48 b Jly 29 Bel 6f ft 1:132 h Jly 25 Bel 5f ft 1:02 b Jly 20 Bel 5f ft 1:04 b

C.

El Atoucha
Dk. b. or br. c. 3, by El Gran Capitan—Surfboard Betty, by Bold Commander
Br.—Hutchison Emily N K (Va) 1987 5 0 2 1 $13,120
Own.—Hutchison Emily Mrs **112** **Tr.—Elder Andrew** 1986 5 1 0 0 $10,528
Lifetime 10 1 2 1 $23,648 Turf 2 0 0 0
29Jly87-7Bel 6f :224 :46 1:111ft 20 111 43½ 41¾ 22½ 21¾ Davis R G1 Aw26000 82-23 PrssMyBuzzr,ElAtouch,BillyWilbur 8
21Jly87-9Pim 5f Ⓣ:222 :46 :583fm 19 111 89¾ 89¼ 88¾ 87½ Pearson D R7 Aw15000 85-07 DiplomaticWay,‡FineWind,ReglAxe 9
20Jun87-6Bel 6f :222 :452 1:10 ft 10 111 76 74½ 67¼ 610¼ Cruguet J8 Aw26000 80-16 Conquer, Quick Call, Big Coda 9
6Jun87-9Bel 6f :222 :454 1:11 ft 42 117 56½ 54½ 51¼ 22¾ Cruguet J4 Aw26000 82-15 Nudge, El Atoucha, Drachma 8
26May87-7Pim 6f :23 :47 1:124m 59 108 23½ 23 21½ 32 Wright D R10 Aw14000 80-21 TkeTheStge,WintrLight,ElAtouch 10
2Nov86-6Lrl 7f :224 :463 1:252gd 4¾ 112 88¼ 67 58 411¾ DlgdoH6 Ⓡ Va Stallion 72-19 Briggs E., Ballet Buff, Laura Jones 8
7Oct86-5Kee a1 1/16Ⓣ 1:482fm 6½ 115 — — — — Brumfield D3 Aw17400 — — GoldnDodgr,MstlySprt,MythclIrsh 10
7Oct86—Lost rider; Frational Time Unavailable
21Sep86-4Del 6f :23 :471 1:124ft 16 118 42¼ 32 2hd 1hd Leasure W P9 Mdn 77-29 ElAtouch,PplEnvoy,SilverChinook 12
Jun 15 Bel 5f ft 1:02 b

D.

Steady Labor
Ch. c. 3, by Exclusive Era—Hardly Working, by Hard Work
Br.—Polk A Jr (Ky) 1987 1 1 0 0 $5,700
Own.—Pinkley J **114** Tr.—Lenzini John J 1986 0 M 0 0
Lifetime 1 1 0 0 $5,700

7Jly87-3Pha 7f :22^2 :45^1 1:23 ft 4$\frac34$ 114 1^1 1$^{1\frac12}$ 1$^{3\frac12}$ 1^9 Nied J Jr^4 Mdn 92-27 SteadyLbor,Pertsemlidis,Augustine 7
●Aug 6 Sar 3f ft :34^2 h Aug 2 Aqu ⊡ 5f ft 1:01^2 h Jly 16 Pha 5f ft 1:01 h Jun 29 Pha 7f ft 1:30 b

E.

Billy Wilbur
Dk. b. or br. c. 4, by Blushing Groom—Admiring, by Hail To Reason
Br.—Mellon Paul (Va) 1987 14 0 1 4 $21,500
Own.—Rory Green Stables **117** Tr.—Sedlacek Michael C 1986 9 1 0 2 $16,320
Lifetime 23 1 1 6 $37,829 Turf 3 0 0 1 $3,240

29Jly87-7Bel 6f :22^4 :46 1:11^{1}ft 10 117 6^8 5$^{3\frac34}$ 4$^{3\frac12}$ 3$^{4\frac14}$ Pezua J M^3 Aw26000 80-23 PrssMyBuzzr,ElAtouch,Bil'yWilbur 8
19Jly87-5Bel 6$\frac12$f :22^2 :45^1 1:16^{2}ft 18 117 5^4 4^5 6^{12} 6$^{10\frac34}$ Davis R G^9 Aw26000 82-14 Jato d'Agua, Freud, Wild Behavior 9
9Jly87-3Bel 6f :22 :45^4 1:10^{4}m 11 117 7^{11} 6^6 5^6 3$^{5\frac34}$ Pezua J M^2 Aw26000 80-24 StckedPck,RelAccount,Bil'yWilbur 7
29Jun87-7Bel 7f :22^4 :46 1:25^{2}ft 20 112^5 8$^{5\frac12}$ 5^5 3^3 6$^{7\frac14}$ Badamo J J^{12} Aw26000 68-25 Life Guard, Quick Call, Temperate 12
13Jun87-7Bel 1$\frac{1}{16}$Ⓣ:46^{1}1:11 1:43^{1}fm 6$\frac14$ 117 7$^{3\frac12}$ 6$^{3\frac34}$ 7^5 10$^{11\frac14}$ Santos J A^6 Aw27000 69-24 Swan Point, Rio's Lark, Drachma 12
27May87-7Bel 1$\frac{1}{16}$Ⓣ:46 1:10^{4}1:42^{4}fm 24 119 6$^{8\frac12}$ 5$^{6\frac12}$ 3$^{3\frac12}$ 3$^{2\frac14}$ Thibeau R J^3 Aw27000 80-19 FoolshPrt,FrnchChmpgn,BllyWlbr 12
30Apr87-7Aqu 7f :22^3 :46^2 1:24 ft 7 114^5 3^3 3^2 3^1 4$^{3\frac12}$ Ortiz E Jr^5 Aw26000 77-28 MatthewsKeep,YetWve,FortWhoop 7
23Apr87-7Aqu 1$\frac{1}{16}$Ⓣ:48^{4}1:14^{1}1:46^{4}gd 5$\frac14$ 119 6^4 6^8 6$^{8\frac12}$ 5$^{9\frac12}$ Antley C W^4 Aw27000 61-30 MdnghtCousns,Ptlomt,MstrOfArts 10
Jun 25 Aqu 3f ft :35^2 h ●Jun 10 Aqu 5f ft :59^4 h

F.

Zajal
B. c. 3, by Seattle Slew—Rainbow Connection, by Halo
Br.—Farish W S & Jones W L Jr (Ky) 1987 2 0 0 0
Own.—Scott P D **112** Tr.—Jolley Leroy 1986 1 1 0 0 $10,536
Lifetime 3 1 0 0 $10,536 Turf 3 1 0 0 $10,536

10May87♦5Longchamp(Fra) a1 1:36^{1}gd 46 128 Ⓣ 13 SbrWR Pouled'EssaiPoulins(Gr1 SovietStr,NobleMinstrl,GloryForvr 14
25Apr87♦3Sandown(Eng) 1¼ 2:07^{1}gd *4-5 119 Ⓣ 7^{12} SbrWR GuardianClassicTril(Gr3) Gulf King, Grand Tour, Bengal Fire 8
20Sep86♦2Ascot(Eng) 6f 1:15^{4}gd 3 126 Ⓣ 1^2 SbrWR ClrenceHouseStks(Mdn) Zajal, Rose Reef, Rockfella 9
Aug 5 Sar 5f ft 1:00^2 bg ●Jly 29 Bel 7f ft 1:26^2 h Jly 13 Bel 5f ft 1:03^3 h Jly 5 Bel 4f ft :50^4 h

G.

***Dis Donc**
B. c. 4, by Gay Mecene—Pacifique, by Traffic
Br.—Schmidt Charles (Fra) 1987 6 1 2 1 $4,4
Own.—Payson Sandra N **117** Tr.—Ruckman Vernon L 1986 3 M 0 0
Lifetime 11 1 2 1 $4,425 Turf 5 0 0 0

31Jly87-5Bel 1$\frac{1}{16}$[T]:47^{3}1:11^{4}1:43^{2}fm 35 117 1^1 1$^{\frac12}$ 7$^{9\frac12}$ 7$^{16\frac12}$ Murphy D J^4 35000 67-13 RightVlue,Stormgrey,Uncompromis
31May87-10CT 1$\frac{1}{16}$:49^2 1:15^1 1:49^{3}ft 3$\frac12$ 117 2^{hd} 2^2 4^9 4^{14} Ho G^6 Aw5300 58-27 Bronson,Lisa'sWhip,Crosstie'sCopy
10May87-6CT 6$\frac12$f :24^2 :48^1 1:21^{1}ft 5 117 4$^{1\frac14}$ 5$^{4\frac12}$ 5^4 2^7 Moreno O^1 Aw5100 72-33 Super K. C. W.,DisDonc,GoldMover
26Apr87-1CT 6$\frac12$f :24 :48^3 1:21^{3}ft *4-5 120 5$^{4\frac12}$ 3^2 2$^{1\frac12}$ 1$^{\frac12}$ Moreno O^7 M16000 77-25 Dis Donc, Lt. Purdy, Slady's Path
12Apr87-1CT 7f :24^2 :49 1:29^{1}ft *3 116 1$^{\frac12}$ 1^{hd} 1$^{1\frac12}$ 2^{nk} Moreno O^4 M15000 74-25 RoaringIndian,DisDonc,FreebyTall
30Mar87-8CT 1$\frac{1}{16}$:48^4 1:14^4 1:50^{1}ft 10 118 2^{hd} 1$^{1\frac12}$ 2^1 3$^{1\frac34}$ Moreno O^5 5000 67-32 GrandVenture,DiscoDougls,DisDonc
24Aug86-2Sar 1$\frac58$Ⓣ:52^{3}2:11 2:42^{4}fm 39 117 9$^{8\frac34}$ 11^{20} 11^{33} 11$^{36\frac12}$ Santos J A^7 Mdn 34-23 PlcInThSn,SmmrClny,ExclsvPrvnc
10Aug86-6Sar 7f :22 :44^4 1:24^{2}ft 19f 117 13^{17} 12^{24} 13^{26} 13^{25} Guerra W A^7 Mdn 55-14 ‡Indian River, Crivitz, Dalmation
Aug 5 Sar 4f ft :48 h ●Jly 27 Sar 3f ft :35^3 h Jly 23 Sar Ⓣ 5f fm 1:03^2 h (d) Jly 16 Sar Ⓣ 4f fm :49^3 h (d)

H.

Creativity
Ch. c. 3, by Alydar—Prismatical, by Distinctive
Br.—Happy Valley Farm (Fla) 1987 4 0 0 0 $3,1
Own.—Happy Valley Farm **112** Tr.—Dutrow Richard E 1986 3 1 1 0 $19,3
Lifetime 7 1 1 0 $22,480

29Jly87-7Bel 6f :22^4 :46 1:11^{1}ft 2$\frac12$ 115 8$^{9\frac12}$ 8$^{6\frac14}$ 6$^{4\frac12}$ 5$^{7\frac12}$ Cordero AJr^4 Aw26000 76-23 PrssMyBuzzr,ElAtouch,BillyWilbur
9Jly87-3Bel 6f :22 :45^4 1:10^{4}m 3$\frac12$ 112 2$^{1\frac12}$ 5^4 4^5 4$^{6\frac14}$ Santos J A^6 Aw26000 80-24 StckedPck,RelAccount,Bil'yWilbur
13May87-4Bel 6f :22^1 :45^2 1:10^{1}ft 4$\frac12$ 117 1$^{1\frac12}$ 1^{hd} 2$^{\frac12}$ 4$^{1\frac12}$ Santos J A^3 Aw26000 87-18 BornToShop,PressMyBuzzer,Nudge
30Mar87-8Aqu 6f :22 :45^1 1:10^{4}ft *6-5 113 2^{hd} 2^{hd} 4$^{5\frac12}$ 8$^{11\frac12}$ Cordero AJr^2 Aw26000 75-25 Prince Judex, Nephrite,AlertPaster
30Mar87—Unruly postparade
24Nov86-6Aqu 6f :21^4 :45^1 1:11^{2}sy *2-3 118 1^1 1^4 1^5 1$^{4\frac12}$ Cordero A Jr^6 Mdn 84-22 Creativity, MisterS.M.,FifthAttack
14Nov86-6Aqu 6f :21^4 :45^4 1:12^{1}ft *4-5e 118 3^{nk} 1$^{\frac12}$ 1$^{\frac12}$ 2$^{\frac12}$ Antley C W^5 Mdn 79-23 Fort Whoop, Creativity, Sir Bemis
27Jun86-5Bel 5$\frac12$f :22^2 :46^3 1:05^{4}ft 3$\frac12$ 118 1^{hd} 2^{hd} 1^{hd} 4^6 Santos J A^6 Mdn 80-17 Wordy, Conquistarose,LockedAway
Aug 6 Sar 3f ft :36 h Jly 28 Aqu ⊡ 3f ft :36^1 h ●Jly 23 Aqu ⊡ 5f ft 1:01 h ●Jly 5 Aqu 5f ft 1:00^2 h

I.

Mixed Emotions

Own.—Vee-Pee-Jay Stable

1075 Dk. b. or br. c. 3, by Northern Prospect—Andrea's Sister, by Wig Out
Br.—Klein LaDonna (Fla)
Tr.—Ferriola Peter

Lifetime 19 2 1 3 $44,190

1987	12	2	1	3	$42,8
1986	7	M	0	0	$1,3

24Jly87-5Bel	7f	:23²	:47²	1:25⁴ft	*2	117	88¾	66	2½	3¾	Cordero A Jr 4	c25000	72-26	Quietus,KeylinCrdit,MixdEmotions
11Jly87-6Bel	1 1/16	:47	1:12³	1:47 ft	4	115	814	66½	36	46	Maple E 3	32500	61-27	NiceCore,LookyDare,NtionlHedline
5Jly87-2Bel	7f	:23³	:46⁴	1:24 ft	5½	113	97¾	810	812	69½	Garcia J A5	45000	72-24	Best Thief, Fatty Boy, Ebony Rig
6Jun87-2Bel	1 1/16	:46²	1:11¹	1:42⁴ft	7½	109	108¾	96¾	810	714½	Pezua J M4	Aw27000	73-15	Landyap, Milesius, Dusty Boots
28May87-3Bel	7f	:23²	:46³	1:24 ft	7¼	115	62¾	77½	55	31¾ ♦	Cordero A Jr1	70000	80-25	IrshChl,Syd'sCommnd,MxdEmotns
♦28May87—Dead heat														
18Apr87-8Aqu	1⅛	:47	1:11³	1:49 m	94	126	46½	316	825	828¾	BilyJD8	Wood Mem	61-15	Gulch, Gone West, Shawkl't Won
18Apr87—Grade I														
4Apr87-6Aqu	1	:45²	1:10¹	1:36⁴sy	3	114	711	813	99¼	810¼	Hernandez R7	Aw27000	72-21	Yucca, Gnome's Pleasure,LeVroon
25Mar87-7Aqu	1	:46¹	1:10²	1:37 ft	20	117	108½	85¼	53	31¾	Hernandez R1	Aw27000	79-27	K.C.'sBstTurn,Brskn,MxdEmotons

Jly 20 Bel 3f ft :37 b Jun 19 Bel 4f ft :48 h

20.

10 ATLANTIC CITY

5½ FURLONGS. (1.02⅗) MAIDEN CLAIMING. Purse $4,000. 3-year-olds and upward. Weight, 3-year-olds 115 lbs. Older 122 lbs. Claiming Price $6,500 for each $250 to $6,000 2 lbs.

A.

Mighty Tower

Own.—D.S.B. Stable

$6,500 Dk. b. or br. g. 3, by North Tower—Taff a Doo, by Holy Land
Br.—Moffett P J (Md)
Tr.—Bostwick Dolly S

1087 Lifetime 1 0 0 0 $195

1987	1	M	0	0	$195
1986	0	M	0	0	

3Jun87- 3Del	fst	6f	:22⅖	:46⅕	1:12⅖	3+Md Sp Wt	3	5	2hd	1½	31	55	Chavez S N	b 112	10.50	74-20	Nino De Oro 122¹ Royal Report 122²BekaaValley112¹½	Weakened 8

LATEST WORKOUTS Jly 16 Del 5f fst 1:02 b Jly 9 Del 4f fst :49⅕ b

B.

Stark Kingdom

Own.—Harker T W

$6,000 B. g. 4, by Little Kingdom—Line o' Silk, by Satin Line
Br.—Hondo Ranch (Ill)
Tr.—Harker Terry W

1135 Lifetime 3 0 0 0 $110

1987	2	M	0	0	$110
1986	1	M	0	0	

9Jly87-10Atl	sly	5½f	:22⅘	:47⅕	1:07⅕	3+Md 6000	7	2	31	89½	1019	1019¾	Olivera M F	118	72.00	57-23	RushingWrrior115¹½NtionlSvge113¹½Fllinlovewithm115⁴	Stopped 10
27Jun87- 6Atl	fst	6f	:22⅕	:45⅕	1:10⅖	3+Md Sp Wt	6	1	45½	625	—	—	Conner M J	122	41.50	— —	Jig Time Ace 114³½ Augustine 114¹½ Frisky Frank 115¹⁴	Eased 6
10Sep86- 1Haw	fst	6f	:22⅘	:46⅗	1:12⅘	3+Md 7500	11	8	99¼	914	1220	1230¾	Essman D W5	111	32.60	46-18	Return Here 111⁶ Draycup 116hd Flying Dart 113¹½	12

LATEST WORKOUTS Jly 4 Atl 4f fst :50⅗ b Jun 20 Atl 3f fst :36 h Jun 13 Atl 3f fst :37⅗ bg

C.

Raise Me Irish

Own.—Meadow Creek FArm

$6,500 Dk. b. or br. g. 3, by Raise a Chief—La Peligrosa, by Irish Castle
Br.—Pedroni Patricia (NJ)
Tr.—Medio Walter

115 Lifetime 11 0 1 0 $1,140

1987	11	M	1	0	$1,140
1986	0	M	0	0	

11Jly87-11Atl	sly	6f	:22⅕	:46⅗	1:14⅖	3+[S]Md 6500	5	4	1hd	22	44	53½	Bolletino N	b 122	5.80	67-26	YuppieSqur111hdDpRunTommy111nkOurFvoritJwl113²	Weakened 11
2Jly87-10Atl	sly	6f	:22⅗	:47⅕	1:14⅖	3+Md 6500	3	7	1hd	21½	49½	58	Bolletino N	b 115	4.00	62-27	Leave a Tip 111½ Chilly Knight 112²½ Lessthenamarker115⁴	Tired 11
5May87- 4GS	my	6f	:22⅕	:46⅖	1:12⅖	3+[S]Md 10000	5	6	23	22½	78	920¾	Alligood M A	b 113	7.10	59-20	V. J.'s Dream 120⁷ Clear And Sunny114nkWiltonCadet111¹½	Wide 10
24Apr87- 4GS	sly	6f	:22⅘	:47⅖	1:13⅗	3+Md 8000	5	1	12	13	11	24½	Alligood M A	b 113	4.50	69-24	Long Drive 115⁴½ Raise Me Irish 113³ Warm Run120nk	Weakened 10
13Apr87-10GS	fst	6f	:22⅗	:47	1:14⅗	Md 9000	7	4	11	12	21½	54½	Alligood M A	b 120	9.40	65-26	MadDogMiller120¹PaythePlyers115²½FleetFootedHrry120nk	Tired 10
1Apr87- 2GS	fst	6f	:22⅘	:47⅕	1:13⅘	3+[S]Md 9000	2	11	42½	31½	34	67¾	Alligood M A	b 112	9.90	65-24	Jasperado 114⁴ Shana Boichik 112½ Perula's Dice 114nk	Tired 12
11Mar87- 4GS	fst	6f	:23	:47⅗	1:15	Md 9000	9	4	31	31½	54½	78¾	Lee-Lopez R F	b 116	19.20	58-28	Foresea 111½ Executive Moment 116⁴ Keep Score 116½	Tired 10
28Feb87- 1GS	fst	6f	:22⅗	:46⅗	1:14	[S]Md 10500	6	6	2½	45½	1016	1016½	Black A S	b 116	6.70	55-26	Castle's Wish 109² Marcasite 118¹ Shana Boichik 116²	Tired 10
10Feb87- 9Pha	fst	6f	:22⅗	:47	1:14	Md 10500	2	5	1hd	2hd	54	66¾	Alligood M A	b 116	35.80	64-27	Mikey C. 118nk Nastyama 110¹ Pride of Entebbe118³½	Weakened 12
31Jan87- 4Pha	fst	6f	:22⅗	:46⅖	1:12	Md 14000	6	10	65¾	57	713	919	Alligood M A	116	38.30	62-21	Royal Good Time 118³ Alpha Buck 118¹½BeeKnighted118hd	Tired 11

LATEST WORKOUTS Jun 30 Atl 3f fst :37⅕ b Jun 23 Atl 3f my :39 b Jun 6 GS 3f fst :37 b

D.

Magnificent Dream

Own.—Millett J

$6,000 Ch. c. 4, by Valdez—Perahim, by Green Dancer
Br.—Bittersweet (Pa)
Tr.—Garey Jack

10810 Lifetime 8 0 0 0 $505

1987	8	M	0	0	$505
1986	0	M	0	0	
Turf	2	0	0	0	$54

23Jly87-10Atl	fst	6f	:23	:46⅗	1:13⅖	3+Md 6000	4	9	925	914	823	717¼	Castaneda K	118	11.70	58-22	Hampton Bays 113³[D]Mingooch115nkOakSummit108⁴	Taken up st 10
23Jly87-Placed sixth through disqualification																		
20Jly87- 7Atl	fm	1⅛	Ⓣ:48⅘	1:12⅘	1:50⅘	3+Clm 6000	3	8	83½	97¾	1015	1015¼	Douthall J D	112	51.20	67-09	Axe The Kid 112¹ Prince Dino 109nk Sea Harrier 116½	Outrun 11
12Jly87-10Del	fm	*2	Ⓣ:49⅗	3:00⅗	3:27⅕	Clm 3500	1	1	12	26	418	724½	Douthall J D	104	40.00	75-07	Kentucky River 110¹¹ Call Louis 117³ PostalPoint117⁴	Very wide 10
23May87- 2Rkm	fst	1 40	:48	1:13⅗	1:42⅘	3+Md 3000	3	7	76½	76½	89	712½	Zoppo B L	b 122	21.40	65-16	Kalphar 110nk Poll Taker 122²½ Caracolejo 115³½	Outrun 10
8May87- 8Suf	fst	6f	:23⅘	:48⅗	1:13⅘	3+Md 3500	2	10	88½	66¾	46½	420¾	Bogochow M A	b 122	5.70	51-33	Finocchio 115¹³ Stop Payment 122⁶¾JustBelieve109¹	Sluggish st. 10
1May87- 8Suf	fst	6f	:23⅖	:48	1:15⅗	3+Md 3500	9	9	89¾	55½	614	717	Bogochow M A	b 122	*1.20	46-37	Free Roberts Jolly 113¹²JauntyJ.O.122⁴Jody'sCandle122nk	Outrun 12
22Apr87- 3Suf	fst	6f	:23⅗	:48⅖	1:15	3+Md 10000	8	9	99½	87¾	78	68½	Bogochow M A	122	3.90	58-30	BlakeTheSnke122¹ShortSelling122¹½LsBrces115⁴	Lost blks. wide 9
20Mar87- 5GP	fst	6f	:22⅗	:46⅖	1:12⅗	Md Sp Wt	10	8	1011	916	915	812	Romero R P	b 122	9.50	64-26	Bashful Brave 122nk Capitalist Tool 122hd WithHope122¹½	Outrun 10

LATEST WORKOUTS Jly 18 Atl 4f fst :49⅕ bg Jly 15 Atl 3f sly :38 b ●Jly 2 Sar Ⓣ 5f fm 1:03⅗ h (d) ●Jun 25 Sar Ⓣ 3f fm :39⅘ b (d)

E.

Smokin Britches B. g. 4, by Bushido—Bakers Chocolate, by Boston Baker
Own.—Fenters D $6,000 Br.—Seth C D (Ky) Tr.—Gianacaci George 118
Lifetime 5 0 0 1 $1,250 | 1986 5 M 0 1 $1,250 | 1985 0 M 0 0

21Oct86- 5Rkmfst 6f :22⅕ :45⅘ 1:14⅕ 3+Md Sp Wt 7 2 2⁴ 2⁷ 4¹¹ 9¹¹½ Coolidge C⁵ 114 16.80 62-29 Clever Choice 119¹½ Weirs Beach 119⁴ Century One 122¹⅞ Tired 10
11Oct86- 5Rkmfst 6f :22⅘ :46⅖ 1:13⅗ 3+Md Sp Wt 3 3 1³ 1⁴ 2³½ 5¹²¾ Coolidge C⁵ 114 18.50 63-28 Foy Gene Jr. 119⁷½WeirsBeach119½BlessMeFather119² Weakened 9
2Oct86- 3Rkmfst 6f :22⅘ :46⅘ 1:13⅘ 3+Md Sp Wt 7 2 1¹ 1¹½ 3½ 3⁶¾ Klein M D 119 8.50 68-24 SupremeLeder122²FoyGenJr.119⁴½SmokinBritchs119¹½ Weakened 8
12Sep86- 5Rkmfst 6f :22⅘ :46⅗ 1:13⅗ 3+Md Sp Wt 6 2 2½ 3² 5⁸ 7¹⁵½ Burns C W 118 4.10 61-28 Kris Jeff 118²½ Bethereintime 122⁴½ Canasty 113¾ Speed for 1/2 8
1Sep86- 3Rkmfst 6f :22⅘ :45⅘ 1:13 3+Md Sp Wt 8 3 2² 2¹½ 3³ 5³¾ Burns C W 118 26.70 75-16 Diamond Dealer 118ⁿᵒ Rotterdam 118²½ Canasty 118¹ Weakened 9
LATEST WORKOUTS Jly 28 Atl 3f fst :35⅗ h

F.

***Kashwhite** Ch. h. 5, by Carwhite—Kashmiri Song, by Kashmir II
Own.—Resk V $6,000 Br.—Watine S R M (Fra) Tr.—Romero Jorge 118
Lifetime 11 0 0 0 $970 | 1985 9 M 0 0 $970 | 1984 2 M 0 0 | Turf 1 0 0 0

16Sep85- 5Crc gd 1⁷⁰ :49⅕ 1:15⅘ 1:47⅘ 3+Md Sp Wt 6 8 8¹⁰ 8¹¹ 8¹⁶ 8¹⁵¾ MacKinze H A 118 56.30 55-21 OhSoSly118ʰᵈShallowDiplomat118ⁿᵏWeakendMrrige118⁶½ Trailed 8
18Jly85- 9Mth fm 1⅟₁₆ Ⓣ:48⅗ 1:13⅕ 1:45⅕+ 3+Md Sp Wt 2 10 6⁵½ 8³½ 6⁵½ 6⁹½ MacKinze H A 115 62.90 — — Gunnage 115²½ Junior Terrace 105² Son of Beauty 123¹½ Blocked 11
10Jly85- 1GS gd 1⅟₁₆ :48 1:13⅘ 1:47⅗ 3+Md 16000 8 9 9⁹½ 7⁹ 6⁴½ 5⁷¾ MacKinze H A 115 5.50 62-17 Vernon Broyles 115²½ Sincere Sir 115⁴ Withstand 115¹½ Outrun 9
28Jun85- 10GS fst 6f :22⅗ :45⅗ 1:11⅗ 3+Md 16000 3 8 10¹⁰ 9¹² 6⁸ 4⁷ MacKinze H A 115 11.10 78-12 TimelyJewell113⁴SpeedyTurk115½SpringingWopper122²½ Mild bid 11
4Jun85- 9GS fst 6f :22⅕ :46 1:12 3+Md 20000 3 12 10¹¹10¹³ 8⁷ 7⁶ Melendez J D 114 8.30 76-15 Gene's Dusty 114ⁿᵏ Bullit 114²½ Rum Cider 114¹ Outrun 12
3Apr85- 9Aqu fst 7f :22⅘ :46 1:24⅗ 3+Md 20000 10 10 10³½ 9⁷½ 8¹² 7⁸¾ Melendez J D 106 76.50 69-18 CrowningChpter122⁴HochmnsFront110ʰᵈJoy'sMony115¹½ Outrun 11
9Mar85- 3Aqu fst 6f ⊡:22⅘ :46⅗ 1:13⅕ Md 25000 4 12 10⁹½11¹⁵ 9²⁰ 8¹¹¾ Melendez J D 122 37.60 66-16 MakeKnots118¹½HochmansFront122²½BeautifulTn120¹½ In traffic 12
22Feb85- 3Key fst 6f :22⅗ :46⅖ 1:12 Md 20000 1 7 6⁸½ 5¹⁴ 5¹² 5¹¹ Melendez J D 118 20.90 70-21 ChiefResident120³SnsitivPrson122¹GoodHrtdJohn117⁶ No factor 7
12Jan85- 3Key fst 1⁷⁰ :46⅘ 1:11⅘ 1:41⅘ Md Sp Wt 4 8 7⁵½ 7⁷ 7⁹ 7¹⁴½ Melendez J H 119 37.90 79-13 Shalom Dancer 119³½ Bro Stache 119³ Perula'sChant119¾ Outrun 9
14Dec84- 4Aqu fst 1⅟₁₆ ⊡:48⅖ 1:14 1:46⅘ Md Sp Wt 9 6 6⁷½ 8¹⁶ 8²⁶ 8³⁰ Melendez J H 118 61.40 48-19 Slewmobile 118⁵ Brink 118½ DHDancin On Pins 118 Outrun 10
LATEST WORKOUTS Jly 21 Mth 4f fst :49⅖ b

G.

Toronto Moon Dk. b. or br. g. 3, by Toronto—Moon Year, by Elysium II
Own.—Mena S $6,000 Br.—Scott J D (Fla) Tr.—Ferreyra Jose 111
Lifetime 5 0 0 0 $305 | 1987 3 M 0 0 $260 | 1986 2 M 0 0 $45 | Turf 1 0 0 0 $220

16Jly87- 10Atl fst 6f :22⅘ :47⅘ 1:14⅗ 3+Md 6000 10 10 11⁹½ 9¹³10²⁰ 8¹¹½ Santiago J M 114 114.50 58-28 Amorville 114² Erath 122³ Page Valley 108¹ Outrun 12
12May87- 1Rkmfst 1⅟₁₆ :49⅗ 1:16⅘ 1:54⅗ 3+Clm 3000 6 7 8¹³ 8¹⁹ 8²⁶ 8⁴⁹½ Amiss D⁵ b 106 11.20 — — Real Sure 116ⁿᵒ Indian Alert 116⁷½ Beach Bully 116⁸½ Outrun 8
14Apr87- 9GP fm *1 Ⓣ 1:38⅘ Alw 22000 6 7 6²½ 8¹⁸ 8³⁰ 8³⁵ Torso M A¹⁰ b 107 108.60 51-17 Bourgeois 115¹ C. Poppa Hall 117¹ First Patriot 117² Outrun 8
24Dec86- 4Crc gd 1⅟₁₆ :50⅘ 1:16⅗ 1:51⅘ Md 15000 1 12 12²⁰12³³12⁴⁶12⁴⁰ Duarte J C b 119 90.70 — — SovereignCrown119½DiplomaticJzz119ⁿᵏRexsonVigil119ⁿᵏ Trailed 12
16Aug86- 2Atl fst 5½f :22⅘ :46⅘ 1:05⅘ Md 12500 4 6 8¹⁵ 9²⁰ 9²³ 9³¹½ Flores F B 119 11.90e 53-12 DistinctNative119ⁿᵏComeOutSwinging115²TheBeaver119³ Outrun 9
LATEST WORKOUTS Jly 24 Atl 4f fst :49⅗ bg Jly 4 Atl 4f fst :49⅖ b ●Jun 28 Atl 4f fst :50 b Jun 20 Atl 4f fst :49⅗ b

H.

Moment Major Ch. c. 3, by Timeless Moment—Ma Plume, by Arts and Letters
Own.—Burch E J $6,500 Br.—Burch J E (Ky) Tr.—Seewald Alan 110⁵
Lifetime 6 0 0 0 $48 | 1987 5 M 0 0 $48 | 1986 1 M 0 0

17Jly87- 2Atl fst 5½f :22⅘ :47 1:07 3+Md 11000 8 1 4²½ 4⁵ 6⁶ 7⁷½ Corbett G W⁵ b 108 3.50 70-27 WhtMeWorry115ʰᵈRechForTheGold115²MichelMercde111² Tired 8
9Jly87- 1Mth fst 6f :22⅘ :45⅘ 1:11⅘ 3+Md 14500 7 4 1½ 2ʰᵈ 5⁵ 8¹³¾ Corbett G W⁵ b 108 39.70 70-21 SpinForTheMoney111³WellSpotted114⁴WhatMeWorry116ʰᵈ Tired 10
10May87- 2Bel fst 6f :23⅕ :46⅕ 1:13⅗ 3+Md 30000 5 4 1ʰᵈ 6³½11¹⁹11²⁴½ Hernandez R b 113 25.50f 48-25 Ebony Rig 114ⁿᵒ Swan Point 113³½ I'm No Yankee115³½ Steadied 11
21Apr87- 9Aqu fst 6f :22⅘ :46⅗ 1:11⅗ 3+Md 30000 5 3 6⁶ 9¹³ 8¹⁷ 6¹⁸½ Vasquez M M 109 34.50 64-26 Be Clever 112¹⁰½ Gray A. 112½ Please Pleasure 108⁴½ Outrun 11
30Jan87- 3Aqu gd 6f ⊡:22⅘ :46⅘ 1:13 Md 35000 11 2 3¹ 10¹¹11²⁹ — Skinner K 122 23.30 — — Kiaora 118²½ Super Scholar 122⁷½ Yucca 122² Eased 11
18Dec86- 4Aqu sly 6f ⊡:22⅘ :47 1:14⅘ Md 35000 10 4 2ʰᵈ 4² 8¹⁴ 8¹⁵½ Skinner K 118 7.00 57-21 GoldnMjsty118¹½SpctclrComt118²½ToTghtBt113½ Tired after half 12
LATEST WORKOUTS Jly 27 Mth 3f my :36 b Jun 30 Mth 3f fst :36⅘ bg Jun 15 Mth 7f fst 1:29 b Jun 4 Mth 5f gd 1:02⅖ b

I.

Papa Giuseppe Gr. g. 6, by Wide Swing—Miss Myrte, by Kanumera
Own.—Cannonball Stable $6,000 Br.—Martino Phyllis (NY) Tr.—Martino Phyllis 108¹⁰
Lifetime 26 0 2 2 $3,316 | 1987 5 M 0 1 $638 | 1986 17 M 2 0 $2,338 | Turf 3 0 0 0

24Jly87- 2Atl fst 6f :22⅘ :46⅗ 1:14 3+Md 6000 6 4 3⁴ 3⁵ 2³ 3³½ Voisin C¹⁰ 108 23.30 68-31 Fallinlovewithme 110³BraveKey122½PapaGiuseppe108³ Weakened 10
16Jly87- 10Atl fst 6f :22⅘ :47⅗ 1:14⅗ 3+Md 6000 12 1 6²½ 5⁴ 6⁷ 6⁷½ Voisin C¹⁰ 108 48.20 62-28 Amorville 114² Erath 122³ Page Valley 108¹ No factor 12
2Jly87- 10Atl sly 6f :22⅘ :47⅕ 1:14⅗ 3+Md 6500 2 9 6⁵½ 6¹¹ 6¹⁵ 7⁹½ Voisin C¹⁰ 112 23.60 60-27 Leave aTip111½ChillyKnight112²½Lessthenamarker115⁴ No factor 11
27Jun87- 6Atl fst 6f :22⅕ :45⅕ 1:10⅗ 3+Md Sp Wt 5 2 6⁵½ 5¹⁹ 5²⁸ 5²⁹ Voisin C¹⁰ 112 29.50 61-18 Jig Time Ace 114¾ Augustine 114¹½ Frisky Frank 115¹⁴ Outrun 6
20Jun87- 5Atl fst 6f :22⅕ :47⅕ 1:13⅘ 3+Md 12000 4 4 7⁶ 9⁹½ 7¹¹ 7¹⁶½ Voisin C¹⁰ b 112 45.30 57-19 Highland King 110⁷½ Hobo Sailor 114²½SugarProspect112¹ Outrun 11
30Dec86- 2Rkmfst 6f :23⅗ :48⅘ 1:16⅘ 3+Md 3000 8 5 4⁴ 4² 2²½ 2⁵ Voisin C⁵ b 117 *1.50 55-35 Rapid Analysis120⁵PapaGiuseppe117½BravePatient120¹ Gained pl 8
26Dec86- 1Rkmfst 6f :24 :50⅖ 1:20⅕ 3+Md 3000 10 4 6²½ 4⁴ 4⁴ 3½ Voisin C⁵ b 117 17.30 42-44 DHunter's Hope 120ʰᵈ Sun Tim 122½ Papa Giuseppe 117½ Sharp 10
26Dec86-Placed second through disqualification
9Dec86- 4Medsly 1⅟₁₆ :47⅘ 1:12⅘ 1:46⅗ 3+Md 10000 3 3 3² 7¹⁸ 9²² 9²⁹ Voisin C¹⁰ b 112 46.70 41-19 Dead Solid Perfect 119½ Mooruk 114²½ V. J.'s Dream112¹⁰½ Tired 9
21Nov86- 1Medfst 6f :23 :47⅕ 1:12⅘ 3+Md 10500 10 1 10⁵½11⁸½ 9¹² 8¹⁷ Voisin C¹⁰ b 108 104.30 63-19 Willdrinksabit 109²½ Doug D. 120³ Sir Kevan 120³ Outrun 12
12Nov86- 4Medgd 6f :23⅕ :47 1:14⅘ 3+Md 10000 4 5 6⁸ 8⁶½ 9⁷½ 9¹³½ Voisin C¹⁰ b 112 78.00 57-21 Tall Drink 115½ Lone Star Charger122²½PleasantLad113²½ Outrun 11
LATEST WORKOUTS ●Jly 13 Atl 3f fst :36⅗ b Jun 13 Atl 5f fst 1:03⅗ bg Jun 8 Atl 5f fst 1:02⅘ b Jun 3 Atl 4f fst :49⅘ b

J.

Stroll On B. g. 3, by Red Wing Bold—Cold Draft, by Mr Brick
Own.—Rowland B A $6,000 Br.—O'Quinn Clayton (Fla) Tr.—Baker James 104⁷
Lifetime 7 0 2 1 $1,860 | 1987 7 M 2 1 $1,860 | 1986 0 M 0 0

17Jly87- 2Atl fst 5½f :22⅘ :47 1:07 3+Md 11000 7 3 7⁶½ 6⁸ 4⁵ 4⁴ Hickson A⁷ b 106 15.70 74-27 WhtMeWorry115ʰᵈRechForTheGold115²MichelMrcd111² Mild bid 8
4Jly87- 5Del fst 6f :22⅕ :46 1:13⅗ Md 5000 9 3 1¹ 1¹ 1½ 6³½ Hickson A⁷ b 111 *2.50 70-17 Gentle Tim 118½ Phone Addict 118ⁿᵏ Page Valley 118¹½ Tired 12
20Jun87- 5Del fst 6f :22⅘ :46⅘ 1:13 Md 5000 10 1 1½ 1¹½ 1³ 2¹½ Hickson A⁷ b 111 3.40 74-25 GiveNoQuarter113¹½StrollOn111²ProsperousLddie118¹ Weakened 12
10Jun87- 6Del fst 6f :22⅘ :57⅘ 1:14 Md 5000 7 2 1ʰᵈ 1½ 2½ 2⁴ Hickson A⁷ b 111 5.20 67-24 For Sham 113⁴ Stroll On 111½ Monarch's Secret 118ʰᵈ 2nd best 9
30May87- 6Del fst 5f :22 :46 :59 3+Md 5000 7 8 8⁶½ 6⁸ 5⁸½ 3⁸ Hickson A⁷ b 105 6.20 83-18 Sur Moolah 116⁶½ Page Valley 112¹½ Stroll On 105½ Rallied 12
23May87- 1Del sly 6f :23⅕ :47⅗ 1:15⅘ Md 5000 9 3 2½ 1⁴ 1⁵ 5² Hickson A⁷ b 111 49.80 61-24 Dr.Urbnd118ⁿᵏEnglishAccent118½Lt'sGtItRock'n111½ Faltered str. 12
15May87- 2Del fst 6f :22⅘ :46⅘ 1:12⅘ Md 5000 2 10 9⁸½10¹⁵10¹⁶10²¹½ Hickson A⁷ b 111 28.10 55-23 Holly Lad 118⁴ Page Valley 118¹¹ Backin Biz 118ⁿᵏ Broke slowly 10

K.

Regal Union — Ch. c. 3, by Raise a Regal—Dewores, by Royal Union
$6,000 Br.—Wilson Dawn A (Fla)
Tr.—Jarvis Louise
111
Lifetime 7 0 0 0 $210 | 1987 6 M 0 0 $160 | 1986 1 M 0 0 $50
Own.—Lynch J

8Jly87-10Atl gd 1 1/16 :47⅘ 1:14 1:49⅕ 3+Md 6000 9 1 12 1hd 55½ 814½ Nunez E O b 110 37.70 44-25 No Doubt A King 1184 Amorville 1141 The Cool Dr. 113½ Tired 11
25Jun87-10Atl fst 6f :22⅗ :46⅗ 1:12⅘ 3+Md 6000 10 5 61½ 77¾ 78½ 713 Conner M J b 110 15.00 65-23 Honest Kick 1108½ Hampton Bays 1131 Sugar Prospect1091 Tired 12
17Jun87-10Mth fst 6f :22⅗ :46 1:12⅗ 3+Md 10000 11 1 74¼ 54½ 75½ 810¾ Corbett G W7 b 108 85.30 66-16 Affirmation 1083½ Lawtown 115no Bonny Charlie 1222½ Outrun 12
2Jun87-10Mth fst 6f :22⅗ :46⅕ 1:12 3+Md 10000 3 7 55½ 911 1019 1018½ Rujano M 115 44.50 61-16 TommyClms1151¾Affirmtion110noNorcliffe'sRuler108nk No threat 11
25Mar87- 7Tam fst 6f :23 :46⅗ 1:13⅖ Md 10500 4 2 1½ 32 47½ 615½ Adkins R M 114 3.90 62-16 Advoruca Kid 1114½DoctorEyeSmith118½OurNiceImage1161 Tired 9
14Mar87- 3Tam fst 6f :22⅘ :46⅖ 1:12⅕ Md Sp Wt 4 1 1hd 2½ 76½ 713 Jawny A 118 38.40 71-11 Greymask 118no Stationary Front 1181GoldPace1184 Spld. to str. 9
21Oct86- 4Crc fst 6f :22⅘ :47⅕ 1:14⅖ Md 15000 10 4 3nk 610 1224 1226¾ O'Farril V L10 108 36.80 52-20 CutEye1182½StrongAsDirt118nkMno'Ice1182½ Raced withoutwhip 12
LATEST WORKOUTS Jun 13 Mth 4f fst :49⅘ bg

21. Grade 1 and Grade 2 sprints are few and unusual and therefore the handicapping is unconventional. It's Jan. 10. Which horse figures best in this 7F event?

8th Santa Anita

7 FURLONGS. (1.20) 49th Running of THE SAN CARLOS HANDICAP (Grade II). $100,000 added (Plus $25,000 Breeders' Cup Premium Awards). 4-year-olds and upward. By subscription of $100 each to accompany the nomination, $100 to pass the entry box and $1,000 additional to start, with $100,000 added, of which $20,000 to second $15,000 to third, $7,500 to fourth and $2,500 to fifth. Weights Tuesday, January 6. Starters to be named through the entry box by the closing time of entries. A trophy will be presented to the owner of the winner. Closed Wednesday, December 31, 1986 with 16 nominations.

Coupled—Epidaurus and Bolder Than Bold.

A.

Super Diamond — B. g. 7, by Pass the Glass—One Chicken Inn, by Gaelic Dancer
PINCAY L JR 125 Br.—Sahm R (Cal)
Tr.—Gregson Edwin
Own.—Sahm R & Ramona
Lifetime 28 12 3 4 $910,283 | 1986 8 5 1 0 $588,200 | 1985 3 1 0 1 $56,050 | Turf 7 1 1 2 $36,850

27Nov86-8Hol 1 :46 1:101 1:35 ft *1-3 126 4¾ 1½ 1½ 1¾ PncLJr5 [S]On Trust H 88-18 SuperDiamond,Nostalgia'sStr,Bozin 5
27Nov86—Wide
26Oct86-8SA 1 1/16 :463 1:102 1:411ft *1 122 21½ 2½ 1hd 12¼ PncyLJr4 Goodwd H 95-16 SuperDimond,Epidurus,PrincDonB. 8
26Oct86—Grade III
20Jly86-9Hol 1¼ :454 1:343 2:002ft 3 118 34½ 32 1hd 11½ PncLJr2 Hol Gd Cp H 90-10 SuperDimond,Alphbtim,Prcisionist 6
20Jly86—Grade I
22Jun86-8Hol 1⅛ :463 1:102 1:473ft *8-5 117 41 41½ 1½ 11¾ PincayLJr1 Bel Air H 99-08 SuperDiamond,Alphbtim,‡Skywlker 8
22Jun86—Grade III
1Jun86-8Hol 1 :441 1:082 1:333ft 17 117 45½ 43½ 21½ 2½ Pincay LJr4 Calfrn 94-14 Precisionist,SuperDimond,Skywlkr 7
1Jun86—Grade I
4May86-4Hol 1 :452 1:101 1:35 ft 3¼ 115 31 41½ 1½ 14 Meza R Q2 Aw45000 88-18 SuperDimond,SunMstr,FlotingRsrv 5
6Apr86-7SA 1 1/16 :461 1:102 1:422ft 3 118 64 42 53¾ 65 Meza R Q4 Aw42000 84-15 Encolure, Koshare, Skywalker 8
6Apr86—Fractious gate; wide into stretch
15Mar86-8SA 6½f :214 :443 1:153m 11 116 32 3½ 21½ 44¼ Meza R Q5 Ptr Grnd H 88-23 Halo Folks,Bozina,AmericanLegion 5
28Jly85-8Dmr 1 1/16 :451 1:091 1:412ft 3 115 45½ 32½ 1hd 1¾ MezaRQ2 Sn Diego H 93-13 SuprDmond,M.DoublM.,FrnchLgonr 7
28Jly85—Grade III
23Jun85-7Hol 1 :441 1:083 1:331ft 8¾ 115 54 45 33 32¾ Meza R Q4 [R]Quack 104 — PrtyLdr,FiftySixInRow,SuprDmond 8
Jan 8 SA 3f m :36 h Jan 3 SA 6f ft 1:141 b ●Dec 29 SA 5f ft :584 h Dec 23 SA 5f ft :592 b

B.

Rocky Marriage — B. h. 7, by Riva Ridge—Exciting Devorcee, by Candy Spots
STEVENS G L 114 Br.—LexingtonThoroughbredSales (Ky)
Tr.—Frankel Robert
Own.—Port & Ramos
Lifetime 37 11 9 5 $349,507 | 1986 5 1 0 2 $40,945 | 1985 8 3 2 1 $138,418 | Turf 11 3 0 1 $45,259

28Dec86-8SA 6f :213 :441 1:082ft 9¾ 115 1hd 1hd 31½ 33¼ Sibille R5 Pls Vrds H 93-14 BdsdProms,BoldrThnBld,RckyMrrg 6
4Dec86-8Hol 1 :442 1:092 1:362ft 5 115 1hd 13 13 12¾ Sibille R5 Aw40000 81-25 RockyMrrige,Bolton,PolynesinFlyer 6
23Oct86-8SA a6½f Ⓣ:214 :444 1:142fm 3¾ 116 77 77¼ 77¾ 711½ DelhoussyeE3 Aw45000 75-13 Silvyvill,AllHndsOnDck,FlyngNuggt 7
23Oct86—Wide into stretch
2Oct86-8SA 6f :211 :441 1:094sy 3½ 115 46½ 55½ 53¼ 44¼ Stevens G L5 Aw45000 85-21 Carload,PartyLeader,TkeMyPicture 5
2Oct86—Veered out start
26Jun86-8Bel 6f :223 :453 1:092ft *4-5 121 22 21½ 23 33¾ Santos J A4 HcpO 91-17 KyToThFlg,King'sSwn,RockyMrrig 6
3Oct85-8Bel 6f :221 :45 1:10 sy *2-5 115 2½ 2½ 2½ 22 Cordero AJr1 Aw36000 90-19 KeyToTheFlg,RockyMrrige,IrishOre 5
4May85-8Aqu 7f :214 :44 1:204ft *1 122 23 21 2½ 21¼ Sibille R1 Carter H 96-15 MtLivermor,RockyMrrig,CrrDNskr 6
4May85—Grade II
14Apr85-8Aqu 6f :222 :45 1:084ft *6-5 119 2hd 1½ 14 16¾ CordrAJr4 Bold Ruler 97-22 RockyMrrige,Entropy,MjesticVntur 6
14Apr85—Grade II
3Apr85-7Aqu 7f :224 :444 1:204ft *4-5 121 12 13 16 16¾ Cordero AJr4 Aw36000 97-18 RockyMarriage,I'mSoMerry,Witlist 7
8Mar85-8SA 7f :222 :451 1:221ft 2¾e 116 1hd 1hd 1½ 1½ DelhoussyeE4 Aw40000 89-17 RockyMrrige,Konewh,GeminiDremr 7
Jan 8 SA 3f m :372 h Dec 25 SA 4f ft :473 h Dec 19 SA 5f ft 1:004 h Dec 13 Hol 4f ft :474 h

C.

Epidaurus
SHOEMAKER W **115**
Own.—Keck H B

Dk. b. or br. h. 5, by Ack Ack—Nas-Mahal, by Nasrullah
Br.—Keck H B (Ky) 1986 9 3 4 1 $210,760
Tr.—Whittingham Charles 1985 8 2 1 1 $37,525
Lifetime 17 5 5 2 $248,285 Turf 2 0 0 0 $800

13Dec86-8Hol 1⅛:461 1:101 1:474ft 2¼ 115 11½ 1hd 2hd 2nk ShmkrW5 Ntv Dvr H 98-09 HopefulWord,Epidurus,Nostlgi'sStr 7
13Dec86—Grade III; Bobbled start
9Nov86-8Hol 1 1/16 Ⓣ:4541:0931:402fm*4-5e116 22½ 22 42 64¼ ShmrW8 V O Unwd H 87-12 Nasib, Will Dancer, Barbery 8
26Oct86-8SA 1 1/16:463 1:102 1:411ft 3-2 116 11½ 1½ 2hd 22¼ ShmrW1 Goodwd H 93-16 SuperDimond,Epidurus,PrincDonB. 8
26Oct86—Grade III
28Sep86-11Poma1⅛:461 1:11 1:483ft *4-5 117 11½ 11 12 15¾ PincayLJr1 Pom Inv H 104-09 Epidaurus, Emperdori, Bozina 7
7Sep86-7Dmr 1 1/16:452 1:094 1:411ft *3-5 113 1hd 1hd 1hd 2nk ShmrW7 Ⓡ Wndy Snds 94-13 Varick, Epidaurus, Coastliner 8
20Aug86-8Dmr 1⅛:454 1:094 1:462ft 3 113 11½ 11 2hd 2¾ ShmkrW10 Cabrillo H 97-11 HopefulWord,Epidaurus,Attention 10
27Jly86-8Dmr 1 1/16:444 1:09 1:404ft 11 113 1½ 3nk 3nk 31¾ ShmkrW8 Sn Dgo H 94-10 Skywalker,Nostalgi'sStr,Epidurus 13
27Jly86—Grade III
2Jly86-8Hol 6f :22 :451 1:092ft *4-5 119 2hd 2hd 2½ 1hd ShoemkerW1 Aw25000 97-09 Epidaurus,ManeMagic,MyGllntGme 6
11Jun86-6Hol 6f :223 :452 1:10 ft *2 116 32 31½ 1½ 11½ ShoemkerW1 Aw21000 94-16 Epidaurus, Totality, Go Swiftly 9
2Oct85-7SA 1 :454 1:101 1:353ft *1 117 1½ 11 1½ 11½ ShoemkerW8 Aw26000 90-17 Epidaurus, Coastliner, ForsytheBoy 9
●Jan 8 SA 3f m :35 h Jan 1 SA 7f ft 1:273 h ●Dec 26 SA 5f ft :582 h ●Dec 20 Hol 3f ft :35 h

D.

Carload *
SIBILLE R **114**
Own.—Glen Hill Farm

Ch. h. 5, by Relaunch—Refresher, by Pretense
Br.—Glen Hill Farm (Fla) 1986 6 1 1 1 $70,320
Tr.—Proctor Willard L 1985 3 1 0 2 $30,400
Lifetime 13 4 2 3 $128,920

28Nov86-8Hol 6f :211 :44 1:084ft 31 116 78 79½ 66½ 47 Sibille R7 Ntl Sprt Ch 92-14 BdsdProms,BoldrThnBold,PnTrLn 10
28Nov86—Grade III
1Nov86-3SA 6f :211 :433 1:082ft 32 126 97¼ 88½ 77¼ 68 ShmkrW6 Br Cp Sprnt 88-13 Smile,PineTreeLne,BedsidePromise 9
1Nov86—Grade I
2Oct86-8SA 6f :211 :441 1:094sy 5½ 115 56¾ 43½ 2hd 11½ McCarronCJ1 Aw45000 89-21 Carload,PartyLeader,TkeMyPicture 5
22Aug86-4AP 6f :214 :44 1:08 ft 3 115 3½ 21½ 23½ 27 Fires E5 I Murphy H 95-14 Taylor'sSpecil,Crlod,ColtFortyFour 5
30Jly86-7Dmr 7f :214 :442 1:214ft *2¼ 116 55 44½ 44 65 ShoemkerW5 Aw24000 91-11 UltimtePlesure,MneMgic,IdelQulity 8
30Jly86—Wide into stretch
20Jan86-7SA 6f :213 :434 1:082ft 4 113 32 32½ 32½ 31¾ ShoemkerW1 Aw45000 94-16 Halo Folks, Rosie's K. T., Carload 6
20Jan86—Erratic in drive
26Dec85-8SA 7f :223 :45 1:21 ft 8¼ 114 2hd 2hd 22½ 33¼ ShomkrW2 Malibu 92-13 Banner Bob, Encolure, Carload 9
26Dec85—Grade II
7Dec85-5Hol 6f :222 :444 1:094ft *4-5 114 3½ 31 1hd 11¼ ShoemkerW7 Aw22000 95-12 Carload, Absolute, Bloom's Beau 7
16Nov85-7Hol 6f :222 :452 1:092ft *9-5 114 2½ 1hd 2hd 34¼ ShoemkerW3 Aw22000 93-14 BolderThanBold,FullHonor,Carload 9
16Nov85—Bumped start
17Oct84-8SA 7f :224 :453 1:234ft *2 117 62¼ 62¼ 52½ 43 ShmkrW5 Snny Slpe 78-18 MtthwTPrkr,PrivtJungl,Dn'sDiblo 11
17Oct84—Grade III; Rough trip
●Jan 9 SA 3f sl :361 b ●Jan 1 SA 6f ft 1:131 h Dec 26 SA 6f ft 1:16 h ●Nov 25 Hol 5f ft :59 h

E.

Sharp Romance
OLIVARES F **110**
Own.—Shkh Mhmmd Al Sabah

Ch. h. 5, by Sharpen Up—Sir Ivor's Favour, by Sir Ivor
Br.—Little W P (Ky) 1987 1 0 0 0 $900
Tr.—Manzi Joseph 1986 15 0 1 2 $9,033
Lifetime 37 2 3 4 $60,449 Turf 34 2 3 4 $59,549

2Jan87-7SA 1 1/16:462 1:11 1:441ft 10 116 11½ 1hd 31 53¼ ValenzuelPA1 Aw36000 77-22 YoungBlde,MustinLk,ThlssinoAstri 6
13Dec86-8Hol 1⅛:461 1:101 1:474ft 138 111 21½ 31½ 79½ 714¼ OlivaresF4 Ntv Dvr H 84-09 HopefulWord,Epidurus,Nostlgi'sStr 7
13Dec86—Grade III
28Nov86-8Hol 6f :211 :44 1:084ft 52 114 1011 1013 99 810¾ ShmkrW3 Ntl Sprt Ch 88-14 BdsdProms,BoldrThnBold,PnTrLn 10
28Nov86—Grade III; Broke slowly
1Nov86-8SA a6½f Ⓣ:212 :4331:134fm 40 116 95 118½ 1010 1014½ AsssnCB7 Morvich H 75-07 RiverDrummer,PrinceSky,PrfcTrvl 11
19Oct86♦6Longchamp(Fra) a5f :554gd 12 137 Ⓣ 43¾ CuthnS Px d Ptit Cvr (Gr3) Parioli, BaiserVole, PremierCuvee 8
5Oct86♦3Longchamp(Fra) a5f :564fm 75 137 Ⓣ 74 Head F Px d l'Abbye(Gr1) Double Schwartz, Parioli, Hallgate 13
27Sep86♦4Ascot(Eng) 6f 1:151gd 50 127 Ⓣ 56 CochrnR Diadem (Gr3) Hallgate, Gwydion, FirmLanding 12
11Sep86♦4Doncaster(Eng) 7f 1:253gd 16 126 Ⓣ 10 CrsonW Kvtn Prk (Gr3) Hadeer, MoonlightLady, Gwydion 12
28Jly86♦4Newcastle(Eng) 7f 1:263gd 20 129 Ⓣ 712 BaxterG Beeswing(Gr3) Hadeer, Hard Round, Tremblant 9
27Jun86♦3Newcastle(Eng) 5f :581fm 10 140 Ⓣ 11 SbrWR Gsfrth Prk Cp H Dublin Lad,Clantime,DurhamPlace 13
Dec 27 SA 7f ft 1:253 h Dec 22 SA 4f ft :482 h Dec 10 Hol 4f ft :481 h Nov 26 Hol 3f ft :354 h

F.

Sir Macamillion
CORDOVA D W **113**
Own.—Wegat & Wegat

Ch. h. 8, by MacArthur Park—Peacock Hill, by Bobby's Legacy
Br.—Cox & Cleary (Cal) 1986 10 3 1 2 $95,850
Tr.—Christin Mark 1985 2 0 0 0
Lifetime 32 10 8 2 $186,575 Turf 5 0 1 0 $4,870

21Dec86-8BM 6f :224 :462 1:121m 4¼ 118 33½ 43 79 811¼ Loseth C3 L Stnfrd H 67-35 BrightAndRight,TripleSec,HolyRscl 8
11Oct86-8BM 7½f Ⓣ:223 :4531:301fm 4¾ 112 21½ 22 63½ 76 HnsnRD7 Mrk's Plc H 87-07 PerfcTrvl,NwAtrction,Position'sBst 9
21Sep86-8BM 6f :221 :444 1:084ft 11 116 3nk 1hd 11½ 14 HnsenRD4 Fall Fstvl H 95-18 SirMcmillion,AmericnLgion,Ondrty 8
6Sep86-9Lga 6f :212 :433 1:074ft *8-5 120 55 44½ 34½ 33 DnRE6 W G Mgnsn H 94-13 Mndtory,BigBdBombr,SirMcmillion 7
24Aug86-9Lga 1 :444 1:084 1:341ft 26 116 41½ 32 44½ 32¼ DmngRE1 Lga Mle H 96-14 Skywlkr,BdsidPromis,SirMcmillion 7

24Aug86—Grade II
3Aug86-9Lga 6½f :213 :441 1:15 ft 9¼ 117 52¼ 52¼ 31½ 2½ Dominguez RE8 Gov H 93-15 BdsidPromis,SirMcmillion,DustyOk 8
13Jly86-11Sol 5½f :213 :443 1:022ft 2½ 117 43½ 43½ 47 56 DmngzRE5 Sol Exp H 93-13 Stn'sBowr,IrishScoundrl,RulrOfFlts 8
13Jly86—Steadied 1/4
12Apr86-8GG 1$\frac{1}{16}$Ⓣ:4621:1111:42 fm 5½ 114 2hd 1hd 77 910½ DnRE7 ⓇTly Pp Iv H 81-09 OcenView,Introspective,DrkAccnt 11
28Feb86-8GG 6f :221 :444 1:084ft *2½ 118 42½ 21 1½ 14 DominguzRE8 Aw22000 95-22 SirMacamillion,Mr.Brilliant,BigEric 9
6Feb86-8GG 6f :23 :454 1:092ft 4 114 42¼ 3½ 2hd 11 DominguzRE4 Aw20000 92-22 Sir Macamillion, Barbex,LordRubic 6
Jan 7 SA 3f sy :391 h (d) Jan 2 BM 7f gd 1:271 h Dec 13 BM 6f ft 1:13 h Dec 7 BM 5f sl 1:022 h

G.

Sun Master — B. h. 6, by Foolish Pleasure—Sunny Today, by Prince John
VALENZUELA P A **115** — Br.—Elmendorf Farm (Ky) — Tr.—Lukas D Wayne
Own.—Lukas D & Lukas J — Lifetime 32 7 6 6 $262,538
1986 16 4 4 3 $191,988
1985 15 3 2 3 $70,550
Turf 3 0 0 0 $2,250

28Dec86-8SA 6f :213 :441 1:082ft 6¼ 117 3½ 53 55½ 58¾ VlnzulPA3 Pls Vrds H 87-14 BdsdProms,BoldrThnBld,RckyMrrg 6
28Dec86—Wide into stretch
29Nov86-8Aqu 7f :223 :452 1:214ft 7¼ 126 32 41½ 42¼ 46½ RomrRP2 Vosburgh 86-20 King'sSwn,LoveThtMc,CutlssRelity 8
29Nov86—Grade I
15Nov86-8Aqu 6f :213 :441 1:084ft 4¼ 117 2½ 2hd 2½ 35 RomrRP5 Sprtpage H 92-22 BestByTest,King'sSwan,SunMaster 7
15Nov86—Grade III
4Nov86-6Aqu 6f :222 :452 1:09 ft *1 122 1hd 1½ 11½ 14¾ Romero R P1 Aw36000 96-22 SunMster,Rj'sReveng,NwConnction 6
25Oct86-3SA 6f :213 :442 1:092ft 3¾ 121 41½ 31½ 3½ 1hd ValenzuelPA4 Aw45000 91-17 SunMaster,Rosie'sK.T.,PartyLeader 5
25Oct86—Inadvertently struck in head by another rider's whip 1/16
15Oct86-8SA 6f :212 :434 1:081ft 6e 114 33½ 34½ 34 33 StevnsGL4 Anct Tle H 94-18 Groovy, Rosie's K. T., Sun Master 8
15Sep86-8Bel 1$\frac{1}{16}$:461 1:103 1:413ft *1 115 1½ 11½ 1½ 2¾ Skinner K4 HcpO 93-15 Old Main, Sun Master, ValiantLark 7
1Sep86-13Rkm 1⅛ :462 1:102 1:50 ft 10 112 11½ 12½ 11 2¾ SnnrK11 Nw Hmsh h 90-16 DoItAginDn,SunMster,‡EntitledTo 14
1Sep86—Grade III
16Aug86-5Sar 1⅛ :462 1:104 1:493sy 8¾ 113 1½ 21½ 25 38½ VlsqzJ4 Bld Reason H 78-22 Romancer, Fuzzy, Sun Master 5
12Jly86-10LA 1⅛ :454 1:102 1:481ft *6-5 122 2hd 2hd 45 511½ Toro F4 Orng Cty H 84-11 Barland, Bozina, Stickette 7
Dec 20 Hol 4f ft :48 b ●Dec 12 Hol 4f ft :461 h

H.

Tough Enjoleur — B. h. 5, by L'Enjoleur—Fathers Pillow, by Father John
CISNEROS J E **100** — Br.—Kentucky Horse Center Inc (Ky) — Tr.—Caceres Alerino
Own.—Greek Stables Inc — Lifetime 21 3 0 0 $28,425
1986 17 2 0 0 $21,275
1985 4 1 0 0 $7,150
Turf 1 0 0 0

27Dec86-5SA 1⅛Ⓣ:4621:1211:492fm 139 117 11½ 31 1225 — Stevens S A8 Aw31000 — — MisterWonderfulII,Jota,DanThtch 12
27Dec86—Eased
30Nov86-3Hol 1⅛ :462 1:12 1:514ft 19 1115 15 11½ 69 611½ Patton D B4 25000 66-16 Tom, Elefante, Master Navajo 6
16Nov86-4Hol 7f :22 :443 1:241ft 125 117 63½ 76¾ 65 87¼ Douglas R R5 20000 76-18 Pegus, Pialor, Amarone 12
16Nov86—Broke in, bumped
5Nov86-3Hol 1 :452 1:111 1:372ft 39 116 1½ 41½ 77¾ 713½ Castanon A L6 20000 62-17 Calabonga, Pegus, Vinegarone 7
25Oct86-9SA 6f :22 :451 1:102ft 45 116 85 74½107¾ 97¾ Castanon A L5 20000 78-17 StarOfAmerica,Rodney,SndDigger 11
25Oct86—Pinched at start; wide 3/8 turn
18Oct86-5SA 6f :214 :444 1:11 ft 45 116 77½ — — — Meza R Q7 25000 — — Grenoble, Bizeboy, Calabonga 9
18Oct86—Pulled up
5Oct86-2SA 6f :213 :443 1:102ft 42 115 85¼ 65½ 66½ 54¾ Pedroza M A5 20000 81-15 Grenoble, John's Jove, Inquisitive 12
20Sep86-9Pom 6½f :214 :45 1:163ft 46 116 1hd 2hd 44½ 512¾ Garrido O L3 25000 84-09 Yukon's Star, Slugfest, Calabonga 8
10Sep86-9Dmr 7f :22 :45 1:214ft 53 116 13 2hd1217 1120½ Garrido O L8 25000 76-11 Paskanell,BrndImge,SwiftMessge 12
24Aug86-7Dmr 6½f :22 :444 1:153ft 92 118 44 67½ 822 822¾ Garrido O L7 Aw21000 71-12 Our Lordship,HisRoyalty,Doonsport 8
24Aug86—Steadied twice
Jan 4 SA tr.t 5f m 1:011 h

I.

Bolder Than Bold — B. h. 5, by Plum Bold—Fact, by Dancing Moss
BAZE G **116** — Br.—Bradly-Whttnghm-Chndlr (Ky) — Tr.—Whittingham Charles
Own.—Bradley-Chndler-Whittinghm — Lifetime 23 4 8 3 $205,532
1986 9 1 6 1 $124,300
1985 5 2 0 1 $39,800
Turf 9 0 5 1 $62,250

28Dec86-8SA 6f :213 :441 1:082ft 3½ 116 53 42 2½ 21 Baze G1 Pls Vrds H 95-14 BdsdProms,BoldrThnBld,RckyMrrg 6
20Dec86-8Hol 6f Ⓣ:213 :4321:072fm 3½ 115 42 32½ 31 2¾ Baze G5 Trf Exprs H 102-04 Zany Tactics, BolderThanBold,Faro 5
28Nov86-8Hol 6f :211 :44 1:084ft 4½ 114 911 911 45 21¾ Baze G10 Ntl Sprt Ch 97-14 BdsdProms,BoldrThnBold,OnTrLn 10
28Nov86—Grade III; Wide into stretch
12Nov86-3Hol 7f :221 :451 1:213ft *9-5 117 55 43½ 11½ 14½ Baze G1 Aw26000 96-15 BoldrThnBold,MyGllntGm,Mtrnmc 6
12Jun86-8Hol 1$\frac{1}{16}$Ⓣ:4621:1011:401fm 2½ 116 66¾ 63¼ 41½ 32¼ Stevens G L6 Aw25000 101 — Qntllon,WtchForDwn,BoldrThnBold 9
9May86-8Hol 1$\frac{1}{16}$Ⓣ:4711:1121:403fm 7-5e 115 63½ 52¼ 42 43¾ Stevens G L3 Aw40000 97 — Poly Test, Bleding, Mr. Happy 6
25Apr86-8Hol 1$\frac{1}{16}$Ⓣ:46 1:0941:401fm 3½ 117 67½ 63¾ 3nk 22 ShoemkerW2 Aw35000 101 — LittleLook,BolderThnBold,PineBelt 7
25Apr86—Bumped break
28Feb86-8SA a6½f Ⓣ:211 :4321:151fm*9-5 114 97 99½ 65 2nk Baze G4 Aw35000 83-22 PrismticII,BoldrThnBold,Crcksmn 11
28Feb86—Broke stride, bobbled twice on dirt track
17Jan86-8SA a6½f Ⓣ:221 :45 1:142fm 4e 114 42 31½ 32½ 21¾ Baze G8 Aw45000 85-15 IceHot,BolderThanBold,ForzandoII 8
16Nov85-7Hol 6f :222 :452 1:092ft 29 114 96½ 83½ 31 11½ Baze G8 Aw22000 97-14 BolderThanBold,FullHonor,Carload 9
16Nov85—Bumped start
Jan 6 SA 5f gd 1:032 h Dec 26 SA 3f ft :381 h Dec 16 Hol 5f ft 1:013 h ●Dec 10 Hol Ⓣ 5f fm 1:003 h (d)

J.

Zany Tactics ✻
KAENEL J L
Own.—Brunette Vera C

Dk. b. or br. g. 6, by Zanthe—Escort's Lady, by Escort
Br.—Forth S & Brenda (Cal)
Tr.—Heap Blake
118
Lifetime 21 10 6 2 $261,766
1986 13 5 3 2 $187,260
1985 8 5 3 0 $74,506
Turf 8 4 1 2 $126,850

20Dec86-8Hol 6f Ⓣ:213 :4321:072fm 3¾ 117 21 21½ 1hd 1¾ KenelJL2 Trf Exprs H 103-04 Zany Tactics, BolderThanBold,Faro 5
29Nov86-6Hol 6f Ⓣ:221 :4431:082fm 11 115 1hd 1hd 11 11½ Hansen R D6 HcpO 98-10 Zany Tactics, Mandatory, Ice Hot 8
29Nov86—Lugged in stretch
16Aug86-10Tdn 1⅛:464 1:111 1:494ft 4½ 113 32½ 22 2½ 1no RivrHJr8 Bud Brd Cup 88-16 ZanyTctics,BigCrown,Forkintherod 9
27Jly86-9Tdn 1 1/16:471 1:121 1:453ft *3¼ 115 32 4¾ 3nk 2½ RiveraHJr4 Buckeye H 80-24 BillyTheBest,ZanyTctics,SecretWr 10
6Jly86-8Haw 6f :214 :444 1:091ft 2 112 3½ 1½ 1½ 1½ Meier R6 Navajo H 95-16 ZanyTactics,RegalSearch,RogueStr 6
8Jun86-9Cby 6½f:222 :452 1:174ft 15 115 2hd 3nk 52½ 53¾ LGrnDL10 Chaucer Cp 88-19 Forkintherod,AggisBst,RoylTroon 11
18May86-5Hol 6f Ⓣ:212 :4341:083fm 13 116 32 2hd 12½ 1½ KenelJL5 Nght Mvr H 99-03 ZanyTactics,RetsinaRun,StrVideo 10
18May86—Bumped start
4May86-6GG 1 Ⓣ:47 1:1221:371fm 2½ 116 1½ 11 21½ 32¼ McHrgueDG1 Aw25000 79-20 DarkAccent,CastleTweed,ZnyTctics 6
19Apr86-8SA a6½f Ⓣ:22 :4411:134fm 5½ 116 21 21½ 21½ 44¼ OrtgLE6 Sn Smeon H 86-10 Estate,WillDancer,ExclusivePartner 8
19Apr86—Grade III; Lugged in final 3/8
26Mar86-5SA a6½f Ⓣ:212 :44 1:143fm 3¼ 115 1½ 1hd 12 3½ Toro F2 Aw42000 85-12 ForzandoII,Fortnightly,ZaryTactics 8
Jan 2 SA 6f ft 1:141 h Dec 13 SA 6f ft 1:143 h Nov 26 SA 6f ft 1:153 h Nov 20 SA 5f ft 1:041 h

22. This race brings together 3up in early August. Handicappers who understand the age factor in relation to eligibility conditions should find a nice horse having a clear edge.

6 BELMONT

INNER TURF COURSE
1 1-16 MILES
BELMONT
FINISH START

1 1/16 MILES. (InnerTurf). (1.40⅘) ALLOWANCE. Purse $28,000. Fillies and mares, 3-year-olds and upward which have never won two races other than Maiden, Claiming or Starter. Weight, 3-year-olds, 116 lbs. Older, 122 lbs. Non-winners of a race other than maiden or claiming at a mile or over since July 1 allowed 3 lbs. Of such a race since June 15 5 lbs.

A.
8–1

Hardeeni
Own.—Phelan Mary

B. f. 3, by Baldski—Hard Jewel, by Hard Work
Br.—Cashman Mary Lou (Fla)
Tr.—Preger Mitchell C
111
Lifetime 3 2 1 0 $34,740
1987 2 1 1 0 $21,540
1986 1 1 0 0 $13,200

6Jun87- 3Bel fst 7f :22⅘ :46 1:23⅘ 3+ⒻAlw 27000 1 3 43½ 45 33 22 Davis R G 111 2.70 81-15 Doubles Partner 1122 Hardeeni 1112 Alyaffirm 1124 2nd best 7
13May87- 6Bel fst 6f :21⅘ :45⅕ 1:11 3+ⒻAlw 26000 3 10 813 811 41¾ 1nc Davis R G 110 6.60 85-18 Hardeeni 110nc Nasty Affair 1133 Joke Boat 103nd Just up 10
18Aug86- 4Sar fst 6f :22⅖ :46⅖ 1:12 ⒻMd Sp Wt 5 3 31½ 2½ 11½ 15 Davis R G 117 8.70 80-21 Hardeeni 1175 Shackled 1122½ Buryyourbelief 1173 Ridden out 10
LATEST WORKOUTS Jly 28 Bel 4f fst :47⅗ h Jly 21 Bel 4f gd :48⅖ b ●Jly 16 Bel Ⓣ 4f fm :47⅖ h (d) Jly 12 Bel 4f fst :50 b

B.
6–1

Purify
Own.—Happy Valley Farm

B. f. 4, by Fappiano—Morning Has Broken, by Prince John
Br.—Happy Valley Farm (Fla)
Tr.—Dutrow Richard E
117
Lifetime 18 2 1 2 $42,570
1987 12 1 1 2 $28,770
1986 6 1 0 0 $13,800
Turf 12 2 1 1 $40,590

17Jly87- 7Bel fm 1 1/16 Ⓣ:46⅖ 1:10⅖ 1:43⅘ 3+ⒻAlw 28000 8 4 2½ 11 12 24 Nuesch D5 b 112 12.90 73-22 Far East 1174 Purify 112nk Rivers Of Mist 117nk Weakened 8
10Jly87- 7Bel sf 1 1/16 Ⓣ:49⅗ 1:14 1:47⅕ 3+ⒻAlw 28000 8 3 21 1hd 57½ 614½ Nuesch D5 b 112 8.30 50-35 Debonairly 1224¾ DreamCreek112ndAntiqueMystique1113 Stopped 8
8Jun87- 8Bel fm 1 1/16 Ⓣ:48⅘ 1:12⅖ 1:43⅘ 3+ⒻAlw 28000 2 2 1hd 1½ 12½ 41½ Nuesch D5 b 117 7.50 80-24 SpctculrBv111ncGloriousClling1171¼VvdImprsson117hd Weakened 7
22May87- 7Bel gd 1 1/16 Ⓣ:49 1:12⅗ 1:44⅗ 3+ⒻAlw 27000 7 2 2½ 2hd 12½ 12¼ Nuesch D5 b 114 25.00 79-22 Purify 1142¼ Nastique 1123 Dr.'s Debutante 1132¼ Driving 8
2May87- 8GP fm 1 1/16 Ⓣ:46⅗ 1:11 1:41⅕ Alw 15000 5 2 21½ 21½ 813 917½ Tejeira J b 114 14.90 76-06 Royal E.J. 1173 Sahara Dancer 117¾ Skitown 122no Stopped 11
8Apr87- 6GP fm *1 Ⓣ 1:38 ⒻAlw 15000 4 2 11½ 2hd 23 34½ Tejeira J b 117 14.80 85-14 Bell Mountain 1223½ Ms. Stolley Night 1171Purify117¾ Weakened 11
27Mar87- 8GP fst 7f :23⅕ :46⅗ 1:25⅕ ⒻAlw 15000 2 7 52½ 34 35½ 315 Tejeira J b 117 19.60 63-27 Tuscadoon 1176½ Northern Missy 1178½ Purify 1171 Evenly 9
15Mar87-11GP fm 1 1/16 Ⓣ:47⅗ 1:12⅗ 1:44⅗ ⒻAlw 15000 3 9 76½ 53½ 67 49¾ Tejeira J b 117 24.30 67-18 Fieldy 1173 Bell Mountain 122nk Tuscadoon 1176½ No threat 12
6Mar87- 9Hia fst 6f :22⅕ :45⅗ 1:12 ⒻAlw 18000 4 5 98½1017 812 813 Cordero A Jr b 116 16.30 67-25 Daddyslittleangel 1161 PeaceandQuiet119noDamality1161½ Outrun 11
22Feb87-11Hia fm 1 1/16 Ⓣ 1:42⅗ ⒻAlw 18000 2 1 11 1hd 67 710¾ Tejeira J b 116 30.60 75-13 Rivers Of Mist 116nk Fieldy 116nk Debonairly 1224½ Gave way 12
LATEST WORKOUTS Jly 6 Aqu 5f fst 1:05 b Jun 6 Aqu 3f fst :37 b

C.
9–2

Moms Birthday
Own.—Austrian N R

Dk. b. or br. f. 3, by Malinowski—One Clover Lane, by Soy Numero Uno
Br.—Austrian N (Pa)
Tr.—Tesher Howard M
111
Lifetime 13 2 4 1 $45,165
1987 9 2 2 1 $37,0..
1986 4 M 2 0 $8,140
Turf 7 1 2 0 $28,145

11Jly87- 6Pim fm 1 1/16 Ⓣ:48⅗ 1:13 1:43⅗ ⒻSummerGust 7 7 78½ 54 41 2¾ Bracciale V Jr 115 4.30 85-12 FortunateFcts113¾MomsBirthdy1152½AngelinCounty1172 Gamely 7
11Jly87-Run in divisions
16Jun87- 9Mth fm 1 Ⓣ:47⅖ 1:11⅖ 1:36⅖ ⒻRevidere 7 9 811 55 22½ 25½ Antley C W 114 16.70 87-08 WithoutFethers1205½MomsBirthdy1143YouthfulBrbi114¾ 2nd best 9
16Jun87-Run in divisions
23May87- 9GP gd *1 1/16 Ⓣ 1:45⅘ ⒻHollywood 8 8 8161016 914 88 Londono O J 116 54.90 69-21 Quake Lake 114no My Girl Val 112½ Easter Mary 121no Outrun 10
29Apr87- 9GP fm *1 1/16 Ⓣ 1:43⅕ ⒻHerecm Bride 1 4 56½ 55 713 710¾ Danjean R 116 8.70 79-12 Sum 1212½ Easter Mary 1131 Dawandeh 1162½ Tired 8
12Apr87-10GP fm 1 Ⓣ:46⅘ 1:11 1:35⅗ ⒻQ'n Hopeful 11 13 13111111 69½ 67 Velez J A Jr 112 7.10e 85-17 Sum 1123 Easter Mary 1142 Quake Lake 1131 No factor 13
19Mar87- 9GP fm *1 Ⓣ 1:41 ⒻAlw 22000 2 8 89¼ 61¼ 2nd 1no Velez J A Jr 114 6.40 75-26 MomsBirthdy114noAntiqueMystique116½OurLittlMrgi1144 Driving 9
1Mar87-10Hia fm 1 1/16 Ⓣ 1:42⅘ ⒻPatricia 9 6 67¼ 56½ 64 65¾ Velez J A Jr 112 27.10 78-14 View of Royalty 111nk Single Blade 1111 Clarity 1111½ Faltered 10
16Feb87- 8Hia fst 1⅛ :47⅘ 1:13⅖ 1:54⅕ ⒻMd Sp Wt 1 2 21 12 1½ 1hd Perret C 119 *.90 60-24 Moms Birthday 119hd Tracing 11913 Current Guest 1191¼ Driving 11
2Jan87- 2Crc fst 1 1/16 :49⅕ 1:15 1:48⅗ ⒻMd Sp Wt 6 5 42½ 3½ 31½ 32 Perret C 119 *1.50 74-18 Visiting Bee 1191 Julie's Ice 1141 Moms Birthday 1193 Weakened 8
8Nov86- 8Aqu sly 1⅛ :48⅘ 1:12⅖ 1:52⅕ ⒻMiss Grillo 2— — — — — 619¾ Murphy D J 114 11.00 54-22 Lovelier 1162½ Nastique 1142 Spectacular Bev 1183½ Fog 8
8Nov86-Grade III
LATEST WORKOUTS Jly 7 Mth Ⓣ 5f fm 1:07 b (d) Jun 30 Mth 5f fst 1:00⅗ h Jun 9 Mth Ⓣ 5f fm 1:03 b (d)

D.
2–1

Tamida — B. m. 5, by Tom Rolfe—Oppsie Daisy, by Dewan
Br.—Kubat & Viking Farms (Ky)
Tr.—Jerkens H Allen
Own.—Centennial Farms
117 — Lifetime 9 2 3 0 $44,661 | 1987 4 0 2 0 $14,155 | 1986 5 2 1 0 $30,506 | Turf 8 2 2 0 $43,961

12Jly87- 7Bel gd 1 1/16 (T):46⅗ 1:11 1:43 3+(F)Alw 45000 6 7 63½ 43½ 32½ 21 Hernandez R 115 3.00 80-22 Mighty Wonder 1221 [DH]Tamida 115 [DH]Loa 1152¾ Rallied 9
12Jly87-Dead heat
5Jly87- 9Suf fm *1 1/16 (T) 1:47⅕ 3+(F)Bud Brds H 4 4 31½ 31 51½ 43¾ Drexler H 112 6.90 92-04 Subjective117nk SmoketheQueen1151½SherryMary1161¾ Weakened 8
27Jun87- 5Pna gd 1 1/16 :49⅕ 1:14⅗ 1:48 3+(F)Alw 13500 3 2 22 2½ 23 34½ Ruane J 116 1.90 59-22 [D]GlenwoodSprings1174½MrsnmllowRichs116noTmid1166 Impeded 5
27Jun87-Placed second through disqualification
13Jun87- 6Mth fm 5f (T):22 :45⅕ :57⅗ 3+(F)Alw 25000 2 8 84 73¾ 74¾ 75½ Santagata N 115 4.20 88-08 Aglasini 1041½ Paris Jewel 1151 Quiet Pansy 117no Sluggish start 8
20Sep86- 5Bel hd 1 1/16 [T]:48 1:11⅕ 1:42⅕ 3+(F)Leixable 2 3 32 42½ 42 42 Davis R G 115 5.60 88-10 Slew's Excelier 115nk Tri Argo 115½ Chinguetti1151¼ Needed rally 6
20Sep86-Run In Divisions
12Sep86- 8Bel fm 7f (T):22⅘ :45⅗ 1:22⅕ 3+(F)Manta 7 5 87¾1011 915 813 Cruguet J 115 3.60e 80-06 Give AToast1131¼TaxDodge1193¾LadyOfLeys1151¼ Without speed 11
12Sep86-Run in Divisions
19Jly86- 6Mth gd 1 1/16 (T):48⅖ 1:13 1:45⅕+ 3+(F)Alw 14000 1 2 32 32 21 12 Marquez C H Jr 122 2.20 75-17 Tamida 1222 Dons Beauty 1121 Charming Tigress114¾ Drew clear 3
4Jly86- 4Bel fm 1 1/16 (T):47 1:12⅖ 1:44⅖ 3+(F)Md Sp Wt 6 3 41¾ 21½ 12 18 Santos J A 122 *.80 74-17 Tamida 1228 Yasmean 116nk Debonairly 1152¾ Lugged in, clear 11
LATEST WORKOUTS Jly 22 Bel 5f fst 1:01⅗ h Jun 24 Bel 4f fst :48⅘ b ● Jun 11 Aqu (T) 3f fm :36 h (d) Jun 6 Bel 5f fst 1:02⅘ bg

E.
20–1

Soaring Princess — B. f. 3, by Sensitive Prince—Soar Aloft, by Avatar
Br.—Babcock Shirley N (Ky)
Tr.—Burch William E
Own.—Babcock Shirley N
111 — Lifetime 9 2 1 1 $83,298 | 1987 4 0 0 1 $3,728 | 1986 5 2 1 0 $79,570 | Turf 1 0 0 0

11Jly87- 8Pim fm 1 1/16 (T):47⅖ 1:11 1:42⅕ (F)SummerGust 5 4 56 56½ 55¾ 55½ Murphy D J 113 29.00 86-12 Spectacular Bev 1192 Ice Devise 113nk Heartleaf 1131¼ Evenly 6
11Jly87-Run in divisions
27Jun87- 7Bel sly 1 1/16 :47⅗ 1:12⅗ 1:45⅖ 3+(F)Alw 31000 2 2 21 22½ 37½ 313½ Samyn J L 110 *1.20 61-29 MightyWonder1174¾GoldGlove119nk¾SoringPrincess110 Weakened 4
6Jun87- 3Bel fst 7f :22⅘ :46 1:23⅘ 3+(F)Alw 27000 5 6 76½ 79 66¾ 58¾ Hernandez R 111 10.30 74-15 Doubles Partner 1122 Hardeeni 1112 Alyaffirm 1124 Outrun 7
11Jan87- 8Aqu gd 170 [•]:46⅗ 1:12 1:42⅗ (F)Busanda 1 3 43 54½ 58 513¼ Migliore R b 112 3.50 74-12 Bold Mate 1163¾ Ready to Rule 112½ Flying Katuna 1212½ Tired 6
14Dec86- 8Aqu fst 1 1/16 [•]:48⅖ 1:12⅘ 1:46⅕ (F)Tempted 8 8 66¾ 55½ 58½ 59½ Migliore R 114 3.60 69-20 Silent Turn 119nkGrecianFlight1195½ChaseTheDream119nk Evenly 11
14Dec86-Grade III
23Nov86- 8Aqu fst 1⅛ :48⅗ 1:13⅗ 1:53⅕ (F)Demoiselle 3 4 42 33 25 26 Migliore R 112 6.00 63-23 Tappiano1216SoaringPrincess112nkGracefulDarby112¾ Held place 7
23Nov86-Grade I
29Oct86- 7Aqu fst 7f :22⅗ :44⅘ 1:22⅕ (F)Alw 24000 6 3 31½ 41¼ 21 11½ Migliore R 116 35.50 90-15 Soaring Princess 1161½ Lost Peace 1215¾ My Pearl 114no Driving 8
17Aug86- 1Sar my 6f :22 :45⅘ 1:10⅗ (F)Alw 24000 5 2 54 36 58½ 717 Cordero A Jr 121 5.30 70-11 Bound 1219 Found a Jewel 116nk Karan Ann 1186 Tired 7
3Aug86- 4Sar sly 6f :22⅕ :45⅘ 1:12 (F)Md Sp Wt 4 1 44 45 2hd 12½ Cordero A Jr 117 5.00 80-16 SoaringPrincess1172½PelicanBay1174¾DotsaPleasure1171 DRiving 9
LATEST WORKOUTS Jly 24 Bel 4f fst :48⅘ b Jun 22 Bel 5f fst 1:01 h Jun 16 Bel 3f fst :36 b Jun 4 Bel 4f sly :52 b

F.
4–1

Dream Creek — Ch. f. 3, by The Minstrel—Rio Rita, by Secretariat
Br.—Galbreath Mr-Mrs J W (Ky)
Tr.—Veitch John M
Own.—Darby Dan Farm
111 — Lifetime 5 2 1 0 $36,160 | 1987 4 1 1 0 $22,360 | 1986 1 1 0 0 $13,800 | Turf 5 2 1 0 $36,160

10Jly87- 7Bel sf 1 1/16 [T]:49⅘ 1:14 1:47⅕ 3+(F)Alw 28000 6 7 76 75½ 46 24¾ Bailey J D 112 4.90 60-35 Debonairly 1224¾ Dream Creek 112hdAntiqueMystique1113 Rallied 8
30May87- 7Bel fm 1 1/16 (T):46⅗ 1:10⅘ 1:43⅖ 3+(F)Alw 31000 6 7 88 812 813 814 Bailey J D 110 3.20 65-24 Improyal 119½ Stated 1192¾ [D]Christmas Cove 114¾ Outrun 8
8May87- 7Bel yl 1 1/16 [T]:48 1:14⅕ 1:48 3+(F)Alw 27000 1 5 59 44½ 11½ 14 Romero R P 113 *1.50 61-47 Dream Creek 1134Consecrated112noMadamCarol1191¼ Drew clear 8
1Mar87-10Hia fm 1 1/16 (T) 1:42⅘ (F)Patricia 7 8 99¾1014 914 913 Fires E 112 5.90 71-14 View of Royalty 111nk SingleBlade1111Clarity1111½ Showed little 10
17Oct86- 3Bel gd 1 1/16 [T]:48⅘ 1:14 1:46⅗ (F)Md Sp Wt 8 7 77½ 64¼ 2½ 16¾ Maple E 117 2.60 68-36 DremCreek1176¾CrownAndSceptr1174¾OvrQulifid117¾ Ridden out 8
LATEST WORKOUTS Jly 24 Bel 4f fst :50 b Jly 5 Bel 5f fst 1:02 b Jun 29 Bel 4f fst :49⅗ b Jun 24 Bel 4f fst :49⅖ b

G.
15–1

Evening Sky — Dk. b. or br. f. 3, by Roberto—Sweeping View, by Reviewer
Br.—Firestone Mr-Mrs B R (Va)
Tr.—Mott William I
Own.—Firestone Mrs B R
111 — Lifetime 6 2 0 0 $28,200 | 1986 6 2 0 0 $28,200 | Turf 2 1 0 0 $15,000

18Oct86- 6Bel gd 1 1/16 (T):47⅕ 1:12 1:45⅖ (F)Bold Princes 7 7 65 33 56 513¼ Migliore R 118 6.70 56-25 Spectacular Bev 1164¾ Latin Lyric 114nk Nastique1164¾ Weakened 11
29Sep86- 7Bel gd 1 1/16 (T):47⅘ 1:12⅗ 1:46⅘ (F)Alw 25000 7 3 41½ 32 3½ 11¾ Migliore R 116 18.70 62-30 Evening Sky1161¾KaranAnn1161RainbowMorning1211 Drew clear 11
12Sep86- 5Bel fst 6½f :23⅖ :47 1:19⅕ (F)Alw 24000 3 3 2½ 31 32 62 Migliore R 116 8.00 77-20 Sweetbreads 121nk Karan Ann 116½ Lovelier 118nk Weakened 6
14Aug86- 8Sar fst 6f :22 :45⅖ 1:11 (F)Adirondack 5 6 57 46 46½ 58½ Migliore R 114 22.80 76-20 Sacahuista 1191 Collins 1144½ Release the Lyd 1162 No excuse 7
14Aug86-Grade II
30Jly86- 8Sar fst 6f :22 :45⅖ 1:10⅗ (F)Schuylrvlle 9 5 43 611 812 815½ Migliore R 114 7.60 71-13 Sacahuista 1143½ Our Little Margie 1141¾ Collins 1144 Wide 9
30Jly86-Grade III
11Jly86- 6Bel fst 5½f :22⅘ :46⅖ 1:05⅗ (F)Md Sp Wt 4 4 1½ 11 12½ 13 Migliore R 117 7.10 87-19 EveningSky1173GoldOntheRocks1171¾DzzlingDffodil1172½ Driving 10
LATEST WORKOUTS Jly 22 Bel 6f fst 1:14⅕ hg Jly 13 Bel 6f fst 1:16⅕ b Jly 7 Bel 5f fst 1:01 h Jun 30 Bel 5f fst 1:01⅘ h

H.
15–1

Riverquill — Ch. f. 4, by Riverman—Quilloquick, by Graustark
Br.—Knott Virginia M (Ky)
Tr.—Cocks William B
Own.—Evergreen Farm — 117 — Lifetime 14 2 1 1 $28,540 — 1987 2 0 0 0 $2,700 — 1986 5 2 1 0 $23,200 — Turf 6 2 1 0 $25,900

17Jly87- 7Bel fm 1 1/16 Ⓣ:46⅖ 1:10⅖ 1:43⅘ 3+ⒻAlw 28000 2 8 87½ 66½ 44½ 44½ Vasquez J 117 11.30 72-22 Far East 1174 Purify 112nk Rivers Of Mist 117nk Rallied 8
19Jun87- 8Mth fm 1 1/16 Ⓣ:48⅘ 1:13 1:45⅕ 3+ⒻAlw 17000 2 5 53 53½ 44½ 47½ McCauley W H 118 5.00 71-22 Grande Couture 1182½ Kitonia 1182½ Socialwan 1183 Faded 11
11Oct86- 6Medfm 1 Ⓣ:47 1:11 1:36 3+ⒻAlw 17000 10 3 21½ 21½ 24 27 Vasquez J 114 *1.20 87-08 Native Mommy1147Riverquill1141RushForGold1122½ Second best 10
18Aug86- 8Sar fm 1 1/16 Ⓣ:47 1:11⅕ 1:42 ⒻNijana 6 5 54 52 76 910½ Vasquez J 114 6.30 76-09 An Empress 1211½ Fama 1161¾ Spring Innocence 1143 Tired 11
18Aug86-Grade III
9Jly86- 7Bel fm 1 Ⓣ:46⅘ 1:11 1:36⅘ 3+ⒻAlw 25000 7 3 44 32 2½ 11¾ Vasquez J 116 18.40 81-21 Riverquill 1161¾ Tres Vrai 1111 Chehana 1171 Driving 8
30Jun86- 4Atl fm 1 Ⓣ:47⅖ 1:12⅗ 1:37⅖ 3+ⒻMd Sp Wt 8 5 54 31½ 31 12 Petersen J L 113 *3.60 84-11 Riverquill 1132 Aquatique 113nd Great Trail 1142½ Ridden out 12
21Jun86- 4Mth fst 6f :23 :45⅗ 1:11⅗ 3+ⒻMd Sp Wt 7 4 86¾ 89½ 89¾ 811¼ Bailey J D b 115 43.60 71-16 East of Gaylord 1152 Tri Tuk 1153 Chapter Two 1152½ Outrun 12
29Dec85- 3Aqu fst 170 ⊡:50⅗ 1:17 1:50 ⒻMd Sp Wt 5 1 2½ 3½ 3½ 68¼ Decarlo C P5 b 112 11.20 42-27 Majestic Pleasure 1102½ Vicuna 110½ Liburn 1172 Tired 7
12Dec85- 3Aqu fst 1 1/16 ⊡:49⅕ 1:15 1:47⅗ ⒻMd Sp Wt 1 3 32 22 45 513½ Wynter N A7 110 25.10 60-19 Patricia J. K. 1176Hafrena1171¾CastleHaven1174 Well up, no rally 7
30Nov85- 4Aqu sly 7f :22⅘ :46⅕ 1:24⅕ ⒻMd Sp Wt 3 8 84¾ 68 711 718 McCarron G 117 40.70 62-22 Ann's Bid 1172½ Patricia J. K. 1173¾ Homewrecker 1176¾ Outrun 10
LATEST WORKOUTS Jun 25 Del Ⓣ 5f fm 1:04 b (d) Jun 11 Del Ⓣ 6f fm 1:19 b Jun 4 Del Ⓣ 6f fm 1:14⅘ h

23. It's February 5, 1987. Which is the best choice?

8th Santa Anita

1 ⅛ MILES. (Turf). (1.45⅖) CLASSIFIED ALLOWANCE. Purse $45,000. 4-year-olds and upward which are non-winners of $22,500 at one mile or over 1986–87. Weights, 4-year-olds, 121 lbs.; older, 122 lbs. Non-winners of two such races of $19,250 since July 1 allowed 3 lbs.; of such a race of $22,000 since October 1 allowed 5 lbs.; of such a race since July 1 or $19,250 in 1986–87, 7 lbs. (Claiming races not considered in eligibility only.)

A.

***Aventino** — Ch. g. 4, by Cure the Blues—Sovereign Dona, by Sovereign Path
TORO F — 121 — Br.—Vischer W (Ire) — 1987 1 0 0 0 $2,500
Tr.—Shulman Sanford — 1986 11 6 1 2 $78,033
Own.—Charles & ClearValleyStables — Lifetime 16 7 1 2 $85,242 — Turf 15 7 1 2 $82,742

4Jan87-8SA 1⅛:481 1:123 1:511sy 5¾ 115 22½ 43½ 54¾ 59½ Baze G1 Sn Gabrl H 63-22 Nostlgi'sStr,InevitbleLdr,Spllbound 5
4Jan87—Grade III
14Dec86-7Hol 1⅛Ⓣ:4721:11 1:472fm 4½ 116 2½ 2½ 2½ 1no Baze G6 HcpO 91-11 Aventino,Bruiser,BoldArrangement 8
30Nov86-7Hol 1 Ⓣ:4631:1011:342fm 37 115 84½ 51¼ 21 2½ Baze G11 HcpO 94-12 AnEmprss,Avntno,Cro'sHollywood 12
30Nov86—Wide through stretch, bumped 3/8
21Aug86♦4York(Eng) 1 1:373gd 10 121 Ⓣ 41½ RuttrC Brdfrd&Bngly H Digger'sRest, Turfah, Truly Rare 14
26Jly86♦6Ascot(Eng) 1 1:423gd*9-5 114 Ⓣ 3¾ Hills M Crckr Blteel H SuperTrip, Advance, Aventino 12
23Jly86♦2Sandown(Eng) 1 1:443fm*1-3 118 Ⓣ 35 Hills M Hrprs & Qn H JoyfulDancer,FreeOnBord,Aventino 5
23Jly86—Slow start
10Jly86♦4Newmarket(Eng) 1 1:374fm 4 110 Ⓣ 14 Hills M Adisn Tols H Aventino, Pinstripe, Chief Pal 15
4Jly86♦4Sandown(Eng) 1 1:414gd*3-2 117 Ⓣ 11½ Hills M Wayfoong H Aventino,GorgeousAlgrnon,Rignbu 9
14Jun86♦6Sandown(Eng) 1 1:401fm*7-5 105 Ⓣ 1nk ThmsML Bakr Lrenz H Aventino,BoldPillager,EveryEffort 11
9Jun86♦5Goodwood(Eng) 1 1:41 gd*2-3 119 Ⓣ 14 EddrP BBCRadioSolntH Aventino, BownOver, Nioro 9
Feb 2 SA Ⓣ 5f fm 1:051 h (d) Dec 10 Hol Ⓣ 4f fm :521 h (d)

B.

***Forlitano** — B. h. 6, by Good Manners—Forlita, by Pardallo
BAZE G — 122 — Br.—Haras Ojo de Agua (Arg) — 1986 8 2 2 0 $110,300
Tr.—Whittingham Charles — 1985 3 0 0 0
Own.—Evergreen Thrbrd Farm Inc — Lifetime 17 6 3 1 $153,895 — Turf 9 2 3 0 $120,621

24Dec86-8Hol 1¼Ⓣ:4841:3612:00 fm 14 114 2hd 2hd 1½ 1¾ Sint-MrtinE6 500000 S 95-11 Forlitano, Schiller, Skip Out Front 8
24Dec86—Drifted in 1/8
6Dec86-7Hol 1⅛Ⓣ:4811:1111:471fm 4 117 1½ 2hd 1½ 2hd Baze G3 Aw40000 92-08 Skip Out Front, Forlitano, Formaz 6
27Nov86-7Hol 1 Ⓣ:4641:1021:34 fm 5¼ 117 2hd 1hd 1½ 21 Baze G1 Aw40000 96-06 RiverDrummr,Forlitno,TppingWood 7
26Oct86-8SA 1 1/16:463 1:102 1:411ft 22 115 55½ 56 56½ 710½ Toro F7 Goodwd H 84-16 SuperDimond,Epidurus,PrincDonB. 8
26Oct86—Grade III
1Oct86-7SA 1 1/16:474 1:113 1:422ft 14 119 43½ 53¼ 43 44¾ ShoemkerW4 Aw48000 84-18 Nostalgia'sStar,Vrick,BreMinimum 6
1Oct86—Rough start
6Sep86-8Dmr 1 1/16Ⓣ:48 1:1131:421fm 8 116 53 73½ 76¾ 66 ShmrW7 [R]Escnddo H 89-09 Truce Maker, IceHot,TappingWood 7
6Sep86—Wide
28Jly86-8Dmr 1 1/16Ⓣ:4711:1241:41 fm 4 122 32 42½ 35½ 44¾ ShoemkerW1 Aw40000 96-04 TruceMker,CleverSong,SpctculrJok 7
3Jly86-8Hol 1 1/16Ⓣ:46 1:10 1:401fm 9¼ 115 22 21 11 11½ ShoemkerW4 Aw40000 103-03 Forlitano, Spectacular Joke, Kalim 6
20Oct85-6Bel 1½:48 2:053 2:322ft 3 119 46½ 815 819 826¼ MacBeth D3 HcpO 32-29 PuttingGren,EsyChoic,NorthrlyNtiv 8
12Oct85-8Bel 1⅜Ⓣ:4831:3722:152fm 39 126 2½ 820 831 845 McBtD3 Man O War 40-25 Win, Bob Back, Baillamont 8
12Oct85—Grade I
Feb 3 SA 3f ft :362 h Jan 29 SA 1 ft 1:402 h Jan 23 SA 7f ft 1:272 h ●Jan 18 SA 6f ft 1:131 h

C.

***Star Video**
VALENZUELA P A **115**
Own.—Balk-Frdmn-King Bros St
B. h. 5, by Hittite Glory—More Reliable, by Morston
Br.—Perry A R (Eng) **1987 1 0 1 0 $6,000**
Tr.—Sadler John W **1986 3 0 0 1 $9,000**
Lifetime 23 8 6 1 $74,967 **Turf 23 8 6 1 $74,967**

14Jan87-5SA a6½f Ⓣ:21^4 :44^{2}1:15^{1}fm 6½ 118 3½ 1^{hd} 11½ 2^{nk} Valenzuela P A^4 80000 83-18 Amnotherbrother,StrVideo,Shrkin 10
16Jly86-8Hol 1 Ⓣ:46^{4}1:10 1:33^{3}fm 7¾ 117 4^1 5^3 68½ 6^{11} Pincay L Jr^6 Aw40000 — — BlueRzor,FlotingReserve,PrinceTru 6
16Jly86—Wide 3/8 turn
6Jun86-7Hol 1 Ⓣ:45^{3}1:09^{1}1:33^{2}fm 11 115 53½ 61¾ 41½ 4^3 ValenzuelPA^6 Aw40000 — — Will Dancer, Poly Test, Al Arz 9
18May86-5Hol 6f Ⓣ:21^2 :43^{4}1:08^{3}fm 6½ 116 85¾ 53¼ 53¼ 32½ Toro F^6 Nght Mvr H 96-03 ZanyTactics,RetsinaRun,StrVideo 10
23Dec85-8Hol 1 1/16 Ⓣ:46^{4}1:11 1:41^{3}fm 7 116 3^2 2^{hd} 2^{hd} 1^{hd} McHrDG^3 ⓇSpnc Bay — — Star Video, Nasib, Grey Gauntlet 9
23Dec85—Bumped start
12Dec85-8Hol 1 1/16 Ⓣ:49^{4}1:13^{4}1:43^{4}fm 11 114 73½ 72½ 96¼ 96¼ Hernandez R^6 Aw42000 — — Tights, French Legionaire,BoldRun 9
12Dec85—Rank, wide into stretch; bumped 1/8
19Jun85♦1Ascot(Eng) 7f 1:27^{3}gd 33 122 Ⓣ 75¾ CochrneR Jersey(Gr3) PennineWlk,MimiCount,Herldiste 19
17May85♦5Newbury(Eng) 6f 1:13^{2}gd 14 121 Ⓣ 7^{12} CochrnR Hue-Wms Abha, Orojoya, Al Zawbaah 7
3May85♦3Newmarket(Eng) 6f 1:12 gd 28 133 Ⓣ 106¾ Raymond B Ely H Inishpour, Bulrush, Coincidental 17
15Apr85♦4Folkestone(Eng) 6f 1:22^{4}sf 6-5 129 Ⓣ 2^6 CochrneR Prvy Cncllr Doulab, Star Video, SpeciallyVague 3
Jan 30 SA 7f ft 1:28^2 h **Jan 25 SA 6f ft 1:13^4 h** **Jan 10 SA 5f gd 1:01^2 h** **Jan 2 SA 7f ft 1:28^1 h**

D.

***Montecito**
STEVENS G L **115**
Own.—Bell S J
Ch. h. 5, by Tap On Wood—Amarena, by Aureole
Br.—Citadel Stb Estblshmnt (Ire) **1986 7 1 0 1 $38,350**
Tr.—McAnally Ronald **1985 9 2 0 2 $30,567**
Lifetime 21 4 1 3 $79,406 **Turf 21 4 1 3 $79,406**

13Nov86-8Hol 1⅛ Ⓣ:47^{3}1:11 1:47^{1}fm 8 116 42½ 41¾ 41 41½ ValenzuelPA^5 Aw40000 90-08 Nugget Point, Lofty, Pudahuel 8
26Oct86-7SA 1⅛ Ⓣ:46^{1}1:11 1:48 fm 2 115 64¾ 42½ 43½ 34½ Toro F^5 Aw45000 82-13 Coaraze Nay, Pudahuel, Montecito 6
26Oct86—Broke slowly
10ct86-8SA 1¼ Ⓣ:46^{4}1:35^{3}2:01 fm *3¼ 117 95¾115¼ 97½ 96¼ McCrrCJ^5 ⓇH P RslH 76-18 Glaros, Louis Le Grand, Nadirpour 13
10ct86—Wide into stretch
1Sep86-8Dmr 1⅜ Ⓣ:47^{4}1:37^{4}2:14^{2}fm 7 115 3^1 52½ 83¼ 51½ Toro F^4 Dmr Inv H 96-04 Raipillan, Schiller, Shulich 12
1Sep86—Grade II; Wide into stretch
31Jly86-7Dmr 1 1/16 Ⓣ:47^{1}1:11^{1}1:41^{2}fm*8-5 115 55½ 53½ 31 1¾ Toro F^5 Aw27000 99-04 Montecito, Nasib, Enviro 7
4Jly86-8Hol 1½ Ⓣ:48^{4}2:00 2:24^{2}fm 29 115 6^4 82¾ 62¼ 53¾ Toro F^7 Sunset H 116 — Zoffany, Dahar, Flying Pidgeon 8
4Jly86—Grade I
12Jun86-8Hol 1 1/16 Ⓣ:46^{2}1:10^{1}1:40^{1}fm *2¼ 116 88¾ 74¾ 84½ 8^5 McCarronCJ^2 Aw25000 98 — QntIlon,WtchForDwn,BoldrThnBold 9
3Nov85♦3Nantes(Fra) a1½ : sf — 124 Ⓣ 56½ PccnC Grnd Px de Nants Baby Turk, SoirdeNoces,Rampour 12
3Nov85—No time taken
20Oct85♦5Longchamp(Fra) a1½ 2:34^{3}gd 16 121 Ⓣ 6^5 AsssnC Px dCnsl d Pris(Gr2) JupiterIslnd,BbyTurk,SintEstephe 11
22Sep85♦5Longchamp a1⅞ 3:21^{2}gd*6-5e 123 Ⓣ 64½ AsssnC Px d Ltuce(Gr3) Khaelan, Sciglio, Green Oasis 6
Jan 29 SA 1 ft 1:41 h **● Jan 22 SA Ⓣ 1 fm 1:44 h (d)** **Jan 16 SA 7f ft 1:30^2 h** **Jan 9 SA 6f sl 1:16^4 h**

E.

Perkin Warbeck
DELAHOUSSAYE E **115**
Own.—Sabarese T M
Dk. b. or br. h. 5, by Vaguely Noble—Pretty Pretender, by Quack
Br.—Firman P H (Ky) **1987 1 0 0 0 $230**
Tr.—Lukas D Wayne **1985 7 6 0 0 $43,227**
Lifetime 8 6 0 0 $43,457 **Turf 8 6 0 0 $43,457**

18Jan87-9Hia 1⅛ Ⓣ 1:49 fm 11 113 2^{hd} 2^{hd} 56½1112¼ Vasquez J^4 Aw23000 75-14 ArrivedOnTime,Wollston,ThSssmn 12
30ct85♦5Newmarket(Eng) 1½ 2:35^{1}gd 2 123 Ⓣ 11½ PiggottL Choke Jade PerkinWarbeck, Lundylux,Kirmann 6
14Sep85♦6Doncaster(Eng) a1¼ 2:11 gd*6-5 133 Ⓣ 1^{nk} PggttL HolstenDiatPilsFinalH PerkinWrbeck,NewTick,SittingBull 3
10Aug85♦3Redcar(Eng) 1¼ 2:06 gd *2 138 Ⓣ 1^{hd} Guest R Andy Capp H PerkinWrbeck,RglDiplomt,KillryBy 8
31Jly85♦4Redcar(Eng) 1⅛ 1:54^{4}gd *1 133 Ⓣ 1^3 Guest R Red Cross H PerkinWarbeck,Joli'sGirl,TryNordn 7
28Jun85♦4Doncaster(Eng) 1 1:39^{2}fm*1-5 131 Ⓣ 1^4 Piggott L Stockil PerkinWarbeck, Khalisiyn, Maftir 9
1Jun85♦1Newmarket(Eng) 1 1:40 gd*8-5 126 Ⓣ 11½ PgttL HolstenDiatPils(Mdn) PerkinWrbeck,Positive,ImperilBid 12
2May85♦1Newmarket(Eng) 1⅛ 1:52^{1}gd 10 119 Ⓣ 42½ Piggott L May Corridor Key, Slaney, Eagling 9
Feb 1 SA 5f ft 1:02^2 h **Jan 14 Hia 7f ft 1:35 b**

F.

Mr. Happy
MEZA R Q **115**
Own.—Red Tree Farm
Ch. h. 5, by Little Current—Maiden Bell, by Nashua
Br.—Red Oak Farm (Fla) **1987 1 0 0 0**
Tr.—McAnally Ronald **1986 8 0 1 2 $30,775**
Lifetime 28 5 2 3 $124,613 **Turf 22 4 2 3 $113,913**

8Jan87-8SA 1⅛ Ⓣ:47^{4}1:12^{2}1:49 gd 28 114 4^4 63¾ 67½ 6^{12} Baze G^6 Aw45000 70-18 Mangaki, Catane, Willingness 6
27Nov86-7Hol 1 Ⓣ:46^{4}1:10^{2}1:34 fm 17 116 6^7 62¾ 54½ 54¾ DelhoussyeE^4 Aw40000 92-06 RiverDrummr,Forlitno,TppingWood 7
11Oct86-7SA 1⅛ Ⓣ:46^{3}1:10^{3}1:48^{1}fm 6¾ 115 2^4 23½ 33½ 43½ ValenzuelPA^5 Aw45000 82-21 Nasib, Skip Out Front, Pudahuel 8
28Aug86-8Dmr 1 1/16 Ⓣ:46^{2}1:10^{2}1:41^{1}fm 7½ 119 36½ 32½ 22½ 24½ McCarronCJ^3 Aw38000 95-05 Mangaki, Mr. Happy, Quintillion 8
22Jun86-5Hol 1 1/16 Ⓣ:47^{2}1:11 1:41 fm 14 115 6^5 53½ 5^2 5^3 McCarronCJ^4 Aw40000 96-02 Poly Test, Floating Reserve, Al Arz 6
23May86-8Hol 1 Ⓣ:47^{1}1:11^{2}1:35 fm 18 115 31½ 2^1 62¾ 53½ ValenzuelPA^2 Aw40000 — — Just In Case, Al Arz, First Norman 7
9May86-8Hol 1 1/16 Ⓣ:47^{1}1:11^{2}1:40^{3}fm 12 117 2^1 21½ 2^1 3^2 ValenzuelPA^4 Aw40000 99 — Poly Test, Bleding, Mr. Happy 6
26Mar86-7SA 1⅛ Ⓣ:46 1:10^{3}1:47^{2}fm 19 114 4^3 51¾ 5^7 4^7 Okabe Y^4 Aw48000 83-12 Semillero, Tights, Prismatic II 7
26Mar86—Very rank to backstretch, crowded 3/8 turn, steadied at 1/4

26Feb86-7SA 1⅛Ⓣ:4731:12 1:484fm 29 115 1½ 1hd 2hd 31 ValenzuelPA3 Aw48000 82-18 Val Danseur, Shulich, Mr. Happy 7
23Dec85-8Hol 1$\frac{1}{16}$Ⓣ:4641:11 1:413fm 24 119 75½ 62¼ 43 42¼ Solis A2 Ⓡ Spnc Bay — — Star Video, Nasib, Grey Gauntlet 9
23Dec85—Rank after start
Feb 3 SA 4f ft :484 h Jan 29 SA 6f ft 1:154 h Jan 23 SA 5f ft 1:031 h Jan 17 SA 4f ft :482 h

G.

***Nugget Point**
CORDOVA D W **122**
Own.—McGee Lena Ruth–JD–VL
B. h. 5, by Nureyev—Artists Proof, by Ribot
Br.—Niarchos S (Ire) **1987 2 0 0 0 $7,500**
Tr.—Norris Jerry **1986 8 4 1 2 $140,405**
Lifetime 16 6 1 2 $171,315 Turf 15 6 1 2 $163,815

22Jan87-8SA 1⅛Ⓣ:4721:1131:49 fm 4¾ 121 21½ 1hd 43 64½ Cordova DW7 Aw45000 77-18 Corridor Key, Catane, Narghile 7
4Jan87-8SA 1⅛:481 1:123 1:511sy 7½ 114 44 54½ 44½ 48½ CrdvDW3 Sn Gabrl H 65-22 Nostlgi'sStr,InevitbleLdr,Spllbound 5
4Jan87—Grade III; Broke slowly
20Dec86-8BM a1⅛Ⓣ 1:503yl 14 113 918 96¾ 45½ 23½ CordvDW5 B M H 78-18 PalaceMusic,NuggetPoint,Barbery 10
20Dec86—Grade II
22Nov86-5Hol 1$\frac{1}{16}$Ⓣ:47 1:1121:421fm *2½ 116 95¼ 83¼ 3½ 1½ Stevens G L1 c110000 83-17 NuggetPoint,PolyTest,RivrOfKings 9
22Nov86—Checked, altered path into stretch
13Nov86-8Hol 1⅛Ⓣ:4731:11 1:471fm 3¾ 117 75¾ 63¼ 1hd 1hd Stevens G L6 Aw40000 92-08 Nugget Point, Lofty, Pudahuel 8
22Oct86-7SA 1⅛Ⓣ:4541:1021:471fm 10 117 910 94½ 32½ 11¼ Stevens G L8 Aw35000 91-12 Nugget Point, Catane, Schiller 10
3Oct86-8SA 1⅛Ⓣ:4641:11 1:482fm 7 120 2½ 2hd 42½ 46½ Stevens G L7 Aw35000 78-15 Ifrad, Matafao, Prince Bobby B. 7
16Aug86-4Sar 1$\frac{1}{16}$Ⓣ:4911:1331:444yl *7-5 119 32 32½ 32 33½ Santos J A4 Aw29000 77-26 GoldMeridin,ReglFlier,NuggetPoint 6
4Aug86-6Sar 1$\frac{3}{16}$Ⓣ:4911:13 1:574gd 2¾ 117 31½ 32 2hd 2hd Santos J A8 Aw26000 77-21 ‡AgnTomorrow,NggtPnt,UpprBnd 11
4Aug86—Placed first through disqualification
19Jly86-4Hol 1$\frac{1}{16}$Ⓣ:4621:1021:41 fm 4¾ 116 54½ 52½ 31½ 32 Soto S B6 Aw28000 97-06 Enviro, Severn Bore, Nugget Point 6
19Jly86—Broke slowly
Feb 1 SA 5f ft 1:023 h Jan 21 SA 3f ft :373 h Dec 31 SA 5f ft :592 h Dec 16 Hol 5f ft 1:002 h

H.

Bob Back
PINCAY L JR **115**
Own.—Paulson A E
Dk. b. or br. h. 6, by Roberto—Toter Back, by Carry Back
Br.—Allen J (Ky) **1986 6 0 0 0 $11,928**
Tr.—Scott George W **1985 10 2 2 2 $275,885**
Lifetime 29 5 3 5 $363,333 Turf 28 5 3 2 $363,333

25Sep86-8Bel 1$\frac{1}{16}$Ⓣ:4631:1031:402fm 4¾ 120 69 710 720 727½ Cordero A Jr5 HcpO 66-20 Duluth,FeelingGallnt,IfIHdAHmmer 7
7Sep86-8Bel 1¼Ⓣ:5021:3842:023gd 6 113 83¾ 75 65¾ 77½ SmnJL4 Manhattan H 73-23 Dngr'sHour,PrmrMstr,ExclusvPrtnr 8
7Sep86—Grade I
23Aug86-7Sar 1$\frac{1}{16}$Ⓣ:4611:0931:404fm 18 115 87 87¼ 75¼ 41¾ CrdrAJr2 Bud BrdrsCp 91-08 Dnger'sHour,‡SilverVoice,SlmDriv 10
5Jly86-6Bel 1$\frac{1}{16}$:461 1:102 1:422ft 6¼ 115 53 58½ 613 616¼ Migliore R4 Aw40000 74-15 Smile, Valiant Lark, Little Missouri 6
21Jun86-5Bel 1$\frac{1}{16}$Ⓣ:4721:1021:412fm*8-5 122 42 42 43 44½ Vasquez J1 HcpO 89-12 JudgeCosta,LateAct,FearlessLeder 5
2Jun86-8Bel 1 Ⓣ:4631:1021:351fm *1 117 64½ 46½ 78 87½ Vasquez J6 Aw40000 81-11 LightningLep,IsYourPlesure,Duluth 9
21Dec85-8BM a1⅛Ⓣ 1:47 fm 3½ 121 53½ 63 76 64¾ Baze R A7 B M H 108 — Drumalis, Silveyville, Talakeno 8
21Dec85—Grade II
2Nov85-6Aqu 1½Ⓣ:48 2:0222:27 fm 3¾e 126 1011 96¾127¾127¼ CordrAJr2 Br Cp Turf 99 — Pebbles,StrawberryRodII,Mourjne 14
2Nov85—Grade I
12Oct85-8Bel 1⅜Ⓣ:4831:3722:152fm 5 126 83¾ 54½ 2½ 2nk CrdrAJr1 Man O War 85-25 Win, Bob Back, Baillamont 8
12Oct85—Grade I; Brushed in dr
8Sep85♦4PhoenixPk(Ire) 1¼ 2:091sf 50 132 Ⓣ 23 RmndB Phx Chmp(Gr1) CommancheRun,BobBack,Dmister 11
Jan 30 SLR tr.t 1 ft 1:38 h Jan 24 SLR tr.t 1 ft 1:433 h ●Jan 17 SLR tr.t 1 ft 1:41 h ●Jan 10 SLR tr.t 6f ft 1:134 h

24. Claiming-race restrictions at small tracks regularly give one horse a decisive advantage, as in the race below. Find that horse.

6th Fairmount

6 FURLONGS. (1.08⅗) CLAIMING. Purse $3,100. Fillies and mares. 3-year-olds and upward which have not won two races since October 31, 1986. Weight, 3-year-olds, 115 lbs.; older, 122 lbs. Non-winners of a race since June 15 allowed 3 lbs.; a race since May 15, 6 lbs. Claiming price $3,000.

A.

Eve Of Eaden **119**
Own.—Rosendohl Kenneth Jr
Ch. f. 4, by Tall and Stately—Cinval, by Winged T
Br.—Allen Carl Jr (Ill.) **1987 8 1 2 0 $3,571**
Tr.—Rosendohl Kenneth Sr $3,000 **1986 3 M 0 0 $200**
Lifetime 11 1 2 0 $3,771

20Jly87-4FP 1$\frac{1}{16}$:474 1:14 1:502ft 25 119 37 35½ 32½ 22 ♦Murray K M5 Ⓕ 3000 57-26 TamaraDawn,EveOfEden,InTrouble 9
♦20Jly87—Dead heat
2Jly87-2FP 170:461 1:122 1:441gd 14 122 915 917 914 816½ Martinez N C9 Ⓕ 3000 63-19 Leatherwood,TamrDwn,MissGlend 10
8Jun87-1FP 1$\frac{1}{16}$:484 1:142 1:50 ft 4¾ 122 2½ 211 1hd 13 Martinez NC6 ⒻM3000 61-27 EvOfEdn,ChcklhLss,MyHlmRmdy 10
18May87-1FP 170:482 1:151 1:474ft 4½ 122 33 33½ 32½ 22½ Swatman W6 ⒻM3000 59-23 DaringDoll,EveOfEaden,NewSpark 10
2May87-3FP 170:482 1:151 1:474ft 27 122 810 87¼ 64 57¼ MartinezNC1 ⒻⓈMdn 55-26 Wjim'sStr,FloPok,CountryLineGirl 10
17Apr87-3FP 6f :223 :464 1:12 ft 46 122 911 99¼ 59 414 MrtinezNC10 ⒻⓈMdn 69-18 GoBoonGo,FloPok,CountryLinGirl 10
30Mar87-5FP 5½f :224 :473 1:07 ft 49 122 76 77 64½ 45 Jones R V1 ⒻⓈMdn 77-12 RavishingLdy,FloPok,ElevenCents 10
14Mar87-3FP 5f :223 :464 :591ft 24 122 98¾ 911109¾ 813½ Jones R V9 ⒻⓈMdn 77-07 MssCornshDock,PlmRmntc,Jl'sFn 10

B.

Mary Kemp

Own.—Duncan William **116**

Dk. b. or br. m. 5, by Text—Tavern Lass, by Disciplinarian
Br.—Bromagen G S (Ky) 1987 1 0 0 0
Tr.—Harmon Thad **$3,000** 1986 7 1 1 0 **$4,000**
Lifetime 24 3 3 2 $10,582

9Jly87-2FP	6f	:232	:48	1:141ft	16	122	42¾	107¼	1014	1019½	Brinkley J A 2	Ⓕ 3000	52-27	Steelman'sBaby,TinyBaby,I'mMry	10
23Jun86-5FP	6f	:23	:47	1:131ft	7	116	2½	1011	—	—	Brinkley J A 2	Ⓕ 2500	— —	LovellyLolly,WickcliffSs,Angi'sWy	10
23Jun86—Bled															
28May86-2Haw	6f	:23	:482	1:154ft	8¾	115	53¼	913	1117	1122	Meier R 1	Ⓕ 3500	40-34	TnnHll,AllForThBst,Punky'sPlymt	12
12May86-3Spt	6f	:23	:471	1:133ft	12	122	45½	59	717	715¾	Razo E Jr 6	Ⓕ 4000	66-16	Coryza,DnceNArizon,BestThoughts	9
12May86—Forced wide first turn															
14Apr86-5Spt	6f	:241	:483	1:16 sy	2¼	122	13	11	11	25½	Razo E Jr 3	Ⓕ 4000	64-25	Joy'sBirthday,MryKemp,NisiQueen	7
4Apr86-1Spt	6f	:233	:48	1:143ft	*2¼	119	11½	12	11½	1½	Razo E Jr 3	Ⓕ 3500	77-18	MaryKemp,AfroGal,NaughtyBlonde	7
14Mar86-6Spt	6f	:24	:481	1:143gd	27	122	13	11½	21	46½	Razo E 6	Ⓕ 5000	70-22	MizExubernt,Tht'sAnAOn,HiPristss	7
6Mar86-9Spt	6½f	:224	:47	1:202ft	19	114	42¼	55½	815	821½	Razo E 6	Ⓕ 3500	53-20	Totaly Brass, Onstage, FigureOnMe	8

Jly 6 FP 5f ft 1:04 b

C.

Roman Market

Own.—Harrington M **119**

Dk. b. or br. m. 6, by Corner the Market—Joeno Roman, by Roman Bout
Br.—Greathouse L A (Colo) 1987 6 1 0 0 $2,555
Tr.—Cristel Mark **$3,000** 1986 13 4 0 1 $10,398
Lifetime 48 10 3 4 $27,473

11Jly87-10FP	6f	:232	:48	1:144ft	13	116	85¼	76¼	77¼	42½	Sellers S J 7	Ⓕ 4000	66-25	SycmoreMiss,RoseNix,ScrltVictory	9
27Jun87-5FP	170	:47	1:13	1:45 ft	8¾	116	51¾	78¾	816	919½	Feliciano P5	Ⓕ 4000	56-18	Justatoy, Tu HastyMeTu,RiverWalk	9
19Jun87-10FP	6f	:222	:46	1:133sy	11	116	77¾	69	69	44¾	Feliciano P 6	Ⓕ 4000	70-23	MissTogo,JeniferJunty,Angie'sWy	10
4Jun87-6FP	6f	:233	:474	1:133ft	4	116	31½	2hd	1½	13	Feliciano P 2	Ⓕ 3000	75-22	RomnMrket,ArknssAmult,HritgBll	10
16May87-5FP	6f	:23	:464	1:131ft	19	116	63¾	54½	76¾	79½	Feliciano P 2	Ⓕ 5000	67-27	AineyJo,Hydn'sDumplin,SunnyRoug	9
25Apr87-8FP	6f	:222	:463	1:131ft	30	116	31½	31½	56	66	Feliciano P 3	Ⓕ 5000	71-24	Madam Foo, Divinely, PatsColleen	10
7Nov86-7FP	6f	:222	:461	1:132m	*2½	119	76¼	68¼	57½	77¼	Gall D 3	Ⓕ 2500	69-28	Alison'sPet,DimondPrdox,VnHven	10
18Oct86-10FP	6f	:223	:462	1:141ft	*7-5	116	54½	44½	32½	1nk	Gall D 7	Ⓕ 2500	72-27	RomnMrkt,LovllyLlly,ShmrcksJwl	10

Jly 28 FP 4f ft :521 b

D.

Brenda B. Quick

Own.—Hayer W T **116**

Dk. b. or br. m. 5, by Oak View—Bee El's Courage, by Jackie's Courage
Br.—Hayer William T (Ill) 1987 6 0 0 1 $1,051
Tr.—Hayer William T **$3,000** 1986 8 0 0 0 $405
Lifetime 33 2 1 4 $11,926

2Jly87-8FP	6f	:224	:462	1:121gd	53	116	810	88½	77½	56¼	SwtmnW3	Ⓕ S Aw6900	76-19	SnTrbt,MssCornshDock,BbbsBstBw	8
19Jun87-4FP	6f	:222	:462	1:132sy	10	116	1013	1012	79¼	58¾	Swatman W7	Ⓕ 3000	67-23	ScrltVctory,Clbrtd'sPg,CrflThghts	10
5Jun87-4FP	6f	:23	:471	1:132ft	5	1115	713	711	78¼	56	Durham M B5	Ⓕ 4000	70-23	SilvrSndls,GoLdyJstr,MissChokFun	7
13May87-5FP	6f	:23	:47	1:124ft	35	116	98¾	811	47	36	Swatman W9	Ⓕ 5000	73-26	TuHstyMTu,Kbot'sLdy,BrndB.Qck	10
23Apr87-3FP	6f	:23	:471	1:131ft	29	116	913	99½	78	66	Martinez N C7	Ⓕ 5000	71-25	Interrogtory,CrLrk,Reigh'sProspct	9
12Apr87-7FP	6f	:223	:463	1:13 ft	14	116	67¼	65	43¼	45½	Jones R V3	Ⓕ 5000	72-23	MdmFoo,PrincessChpeu,BurnedOut	7
6Nov86-7FP	6f	:224	:47	1:14 m	23	116	65	54	66	75½	Murray K M8	Ⓕ 5000	67-32	Our MaryAnn,Interrogatory,KellyD.	8
23Oct86-5FP	6f	:223	:463	1:133gd	21	116	1013	109¼	911	76¾	Militello D J9	Ⓕ 5000	68-29	Hrry'sComet,Gbe'sAxe,Intrrogtory	10

E.

Crazy Maniac

Own.—Lohmann L & C & H **122**

Dk. b. or br. m. 6, by Nasfleet Rullah—Pan Gee, by Never Cede
Br.—Millison Larry (Mo) 1987 7 1 0 1 $2,498
Tr.—Hammond Jerry **$3,000** 1986 16 2 2 2 $7,295
Lifetime 33 6 4 4 $18,559

26Jun87-5FP	6f	:224	:464	1:131ft	9-5	122	1hd	1hd	21	33½	Guidry M1	Ⓕ 3000	73-23	ChddsMsson,SndHllsMss,CrzyMnc	10
18Jun87-4FP	6f	:224	:461	1:123gd	6½	116	2hd	13	13½	12	Guidry M9	Ⓕ 3000	80-19	CrzyMnic,SwetOnM,Pggy'sPrincss	10
18May87-4FP	6f	:223	:463	1:13 ft	4½	116	3nk	3½	44½	44¾	Gall D10	Ⓕ 3000	73-23	CkeChllenged,It'sFun,Annette'sPt	10
2May87-6FP	6f	:224	:471	1:143ft	12	116	31½	4¾	4nk	64¼	Cahanin K P9	Ⓕ 3000	66-26	PddsIrsh,Wht'sLndng,ArknssAmlt	10
10Apr87-5FP	6f	:223	:464	1:14 sy	8	111	41½	62¾	65	76½	Gall D6	3000	66-29	RoylRp,CtchMeSon,SouthernMud	10
27Mar87-7FP	5½f	:22	:454	1:05 ft	8	116	65¾	66¼	57½	68¾	Gall D8	Ⓕ 3000	83-11	DimondPrdox,Jllybn,ArknssAmult	10
15Mar87-6FP	5f	:222	:462	:59 sy	4½	116	74¼	78½	710	511¼	Gammon B8	Ⓕ 3000	81-14	PtsColleen,DimondPrdox,SltyDoll	10
7Nov86-5FP	6f	:223	:461	1:13 m	4	116	1½	12	11½	22	Gall D7	Ⓕ 2500	76-28	AsIWasFree,CrazyManiac,WoodTic	9

Jun 17 FP 3f ft :37 b

F.

Midi Miss
B. m. 6, by Brumidi—Cher Lo, by Cheiron
Br.—Ney Charles E (Ill) 1987 6 0 0 C $345
Own.—Walsh Robert 116 Tr.—Walsh Robert $3,000 1986 17 1 1 2 $7,677
Lifetime 42 3 4 4 $20,349

17Jly87-3FP 1$\frac{1}{16}$:483 1:15 1:482ft 5½ 122 13½ 1½ 55½ 612 Breaux C H 5 Ⓕ 3000 57-24 Sndy'sSpirit,LttlBss,RosLynnBunch 9
9Jly87-2FP 6f :232 :48 1:141ft 3¼ 122 73½ 42½ 33 54 Breaux C H 3 Ⓕ 3000 68-27 Steelman'sBaby,TinyBaby,I'mMry 10
20Jun87-5FP 1$\frac{1}{16}$:464 1:13 1:471ft 13 116 12½ 2hd 44 54 Breaux C H 1 Ⓕ 3000 71-20 AsIWsFr,GBnkItMry,Lm'sMssLckt 10
8Jun87-10FP 6f :23 :464 1:131ft 41 117 104 1011 97¼ 64½ Breaux C H 5 Ⓕ 4000 72-27 Pats Colleen,It'sFun,MightBeNice 10
25May87-2FP 6f :23 :47 1:14 ft 16 116 4¾ 75 86¾ 76½ Macias G 2 Ⓕ 3000 66-22 LightnenIrene,ExFox,ShmrocksJwl 9
7May87-10FP 6f :23 :471 1:133ft 14 116 52¼ 87½ 99½ 910¾ Macias G 3 Ⓕ 4000 64-24 RoseNix,RiverWalk,LightnenIrene 10
20Oct86-7FP 170 :464 1:13 1:444sy 15 116 1hd 21 79 815¾ Gale M A 4 Ⓕ 5000 61-20 BllyndCompny,SwtChslon,GmblnBb 8
20Sep86-6FP 6f :221 :452 1:111ft 13 119 43½ 44½ 66 69¾ Breaux C H 2 Ⓕ 8500 77-16 GrndndLucky,MssSnnFn,GtThIodn 7
Jly 6 FP 4f ft :511 b Jun 1 FP 4f ft :494 b

G.

Wendy's Promise
B. f. 4, by Elegant Prince—Wendy's Robbery, by No Robbery
Br.—Beckett Wendy (Calif) 1987 8 1 0 0 $2,212
Own.—Dill Leonard & Max 116 Tr.—Cullip Larry $3,000 1986 20 2 1 3 $7,712
Lifetime 31 3 1 3 $9,924

20Jun87-5FP 1$\frac{1}{16}$:464 1:13 1:471ft 11 116 611 86¼ 87¾ 87½ Guerra V J 9 Ⓕ 3000 67-20 AsIWsFr,GBnkItMry,Lm'sMssLckt 10
17May87-7TuP 1 :463 1:11 1:374ft 8 1095 1012 109¼ 85¼ 43 Devlin J T6 Ⓕ 3500 77-15 TenWvs,UltimtDbt,Lucky'sLstKiss 10
10May87-4TuP 6f :22 :444 1:102ft 16 114 4¾ 2½ 43½ 55 Guerra V J 6 Ⓕ 4000 79-17 MerryHrt,DuchssBll,Lucky'sLstKiss 7
9Mar87-3TuP 1 :472 1:12 1:383ft 3½ 118 31 45½ 69 614¾ Steinberg PW 5 Ⓕ 4000 61-21 Pompeyana, MaryAlice,TwinHearts 7
16Feb87-6TuP 1 :471 1:114 1:374ft 11 111 31 31 75¾ 67¾ Guerra V J 7 Ⓕ 6500 72-17 AxeTheOdds,BlueOnTop,TwinHerts 7
7Feb87-8TuP 1 :472 1:122 1:381ft 12 1105 2hd 2hd 32 65½ Ortiz M V Jr 1 Ⓕ 10000 72-19 MelissNoel,WhirlinGirl,AxeTheOdds 7
17Jan87-3TuP 1 :471 1:111 1:374ft 4½ 114 2½ 1½ 13 16 Licata F 4 Ⓕ 4000 80-17 Wndy'sProms,SnHostss,Romprnd 10
2Jan87-6TuP 1$\frac{1}{16}$:47 1:121 1:45 ft 7¾ 113 43 42¼ 63½ 68½ Licata F 3 Ⓕ 5000 64-18 Soundslikln,PocktBustr,AxThOdds 11
Jly 24 FP 4f ft :504 b Jly 11 FP 3f m :361 b Jly 3 FP 5f ft 1:023 b

25. Los Alamitos is a bull ring. The length of its stretch is 558 feet. Which is your choice?

10th Los Alamitos

6 FURLONGS. (1.08⅗) 1st Running of THE DON BENITO STAKES. $25,000 added. 3-year-olds and upward which have not won $2,500 twice other than maiden, claiming or starter. By subscription of $50 each to accompany the nomination; $150 to pass the entry box, with $25,000 added, of which $5,000 to second, $3,750 to third, $1,187 to fourth, $625 to fifth. Weights, 3-year-olds 115 lbs.; older, 122 lbs. Non-winners of a race other than maiden or claiming since May 10 allowed 3 lbs. Of such a race since April 10, 6 lbs. Nominations closed Sunday, August 2, 1987.

A.

He's A Dancing Man
B. g. 3, by Bolger—Me Voila, by Gummo
WARREN R J JR Br.—Old English Rancho (Cal) 1987 8 2 4 1 $36,900
115 Tr.—Warren Donald 1986 0 M 0 0
Own.—Johnston–Turner et al Lifetime 8 2 4 1 $36,900

24Jly87-5Hol 6½f :224 :453 1:172ft 2¾ 115 41½ 41¼ 31½ 2¾ Shoemaker W3 60000 92-17 BoldJade,He'sADancingMn,Arnjuez 5
11Jly87-7Hol 1 :452 1:101 1:362ft 4 116 2hd 2hd 3nk 52¼ Shoemaker W4 62500 79-12 Lrkng'sRoylty,MonLgonnr,CrosLov 7
11Jly87—Bumped start
20Jun87-3Hol 1 :451 1:10 1:36 ft *7-5 116 41 2½ 11 22 Valenzuela P A3 62500 81-11 Someshine,H'sADncingMn,CrosLov 6
6Jun87-3Hol 6½f :222 :452 1:18 ft 2½ 117 1hd 2hd 1hd 1½ VlenzulPA3 ⓈAw22000 90-17 H'sADncngMn,Nourshd,Nv-MssT.V. 6
23May87-9GG 6f :211 :434 1:092ft 6¼ 122 75¼ 76 34½ 22 WrrenRJJr7 ⓈAw17000 90-13 DstngshdMk,H'sADncngMn,SchLot 8
31Mar87-7GG 6f :213 :443 1:092ft 10 122 84¼ 54 37 39½ WrrenRJJr6 ⓈAw17000 82-20 Agn'sBlgr,OlmpcL.A.,H'sADncngMn 8
17Mar87-5GG 6f :214 :451 1:11 ft 4¾ 120 21 2½ 1½ 12 Warren R J Jr2 ⓈMdn 84-21 H'sADncngMn,FrndlyFrc,PrncHdn 7
18Feb87-1GG 6f :222 :46 1:112ft 9 118 42½ 21½ 22 2½ Warren R JJr1 M28000 81-20 ThirdStar,He'sADancingMn,ScoreIt 9
18Feb87—Broke slowly
Aug 2 Dmr 4f ft :484 h Jly 20 Hol 3f ft :36 h Jly 7 Hol 5f ft 1:002 h Jly 1 Hol 5f ft 1:002 h

B.

Extranix
Ch. c. 4, by Transworld—Little Evil, by Tompion
BLACK C A Br.—Elmendorf Farm (Ky) 1987 7 1 1 1 $28,375
116 Tr.—Mitchell Mike 1986 8 1 3 1 $24,275
Own.—L 4 Stable–Ustin–Ustin Lifetime 15 2 4 2 $52,650 Turf 3 0 0 0 $2,925

20Jun87-7Hol 7f :22 :442 1:224ft 14 119 41½ 65½ 78½ 712 ValenzuelPA5 Aw25000 78-11 TommyTheHwk,FleetSudn DonDieg 8
11Jun87-8Hol 6f :22 :451 1:093ft 8¼ 116 56 66½ 710 813½ ValenzuelPA2 Aw25000 81-18 HonkyTonkDancer,Pilor,ThunderCt 8
11Jun87—Bumped start

25May87-9Hol 1 1/16 :461 1:104 1:424ft *3 117 43½ 33½ 37½ 311 Pincay L Jr6 Aw27000 84-15 Recognized,EightyBlowZrc,Extrnix 6

25May87—Wide 7/8 turn

15May87-5Hol 1 1/16 Ⓣ:47 1:1041:412fm 4¾ 116 2hd 2hd 64½ 97¼ McHrgueDG7 Aw27000 80-12 Starsalot, Decore, Rodain 10

18Apr87-7SA 1 1/16 :46 1:104 1:433ft 3½ 118 11 1½ 1½ 2¾ Pincay L Jr1 Aw35000 82-18 Centenary, Extranix, Prince O' Fire 8

29Mar87-5SA a6½f Ⓣ:213 :44 1:151fm 3 118 52 51¾ 63¾ 42¼ Pincay L Jr9 Aw33000 81-19 Danczone,FbulousSound,SlneCstle 12

28Feb87-9SA 6½f :213 :441 1:163ft 3¾ 116 44½ 35½ 34 1no Solis A5 Aw27000 87-17 Extranix, Angle Arc, Devil's Ice 7

27Sep86-9Pom a1⅛ :462 1:12 1:503ft 14 116 52½ 63½ 913 913½ Sibille R 8 Pom Dby 80-10 LghtnngToch,Rfl'sDncr,BoldBrvII 10

27Sep86—Run in divisions

10Sep86-4Dmr 1 :46 1:103 1:361ft *9-5 116 14½ 13 13 11¾ Valenzuela P A 1 Mdn 87-11 Extrnx,ThrowHom,Trmn'sCmmndr 9

23Aug86-6Dmr 6f :22 :451 1:09 ft 2½ 116 85¾ 63½ 45½ 34½ Valenzuela P A 7 Mdn 88-10 Granito, Danielli, Extranix 12

Aug 1 Dmr 6f ft 1:121 h   Jly 27 Dmr 5f ft 1:011 h   ●Jly 21 Dmr 5f ft :592 h   Jly 17 Dmr 4f ft :491 h

C.

Coursing Eagle

STEVENS S A **116**

Own.—Woods J

Ch. g. 6, by Golden Eagle II—Mary Corzine, by Restless Wind

Br.—Hawn W R (Cal)

Tr.—Goldberg Lore

Lifetime 48 8 9 7 $108,250

1987 9 0 1 0 $5,900

1986 27 7 6 2 $78,825

Turf 2 1 0 0 $6,000

28Jun87-1Hol 1 1/16 :454 1:111 1:434ft 23 1115 21 53¾ 911 1015½ Gryder A T 1 20000 74-12 Power Forward,Chagrininc,OhDad 10

28Jun87—Bumped start

7Jun87-2Hol 1 :463 1:12 1:374ft 13 116 1½ 1hd 54 611 Mena F 7 20000 63-17 Pautivo,PineappleJack,EverBrillint 8

13May87-2Hol 7f :222 :444 1:232ft 13 116 52¼ 54¼ 67½ 79¾ Baze G 7 Ⓢ 20000 77-15 Detector,MYouAndQ.,FriscoDnnis 11

13May87—Bumped start

25Apr87-7Hol 6½f :22 :443 1:16 ft 30 116 63¼ 97¾ 69½ 510¾ Solis A 5 25000 89-13 Pilor,MischievousMtt,ForbesReply 12

18Apr87-10SA 6½f :22 :45 1:163ft 9¼ 115 31½ 43 43½ 22¾ Baze G 1 20000 84-18 NightSwope,CoursingEagle,SaroStr 8

3Apr87-5SA 6½f :22 :453 1:172ft 13 116 52 74¾ 1011 1014¼ Pedroza M A 7 25000 69-17 Fracoza, Hurricane Hec, Pegus 11

22Mar87-9SA 6½f :22 :444 1:17 gd 10 118 5½ 51½ 64 44 Black C A 6 Ⓢ 20000 81-23 Bennett Peak, Danchai, Melchip 11

15Jan87-7SA a6½f Ⓣ:212 :434 1:154fm 22 115 3½ 34 812 — Black C A 5 Aw29000 — — StrtfordEst,TmmyThHwk,CllThGrd 8

15Jan87—Bled

3Jan87-9SA 1 1/16 :47 1:113 1:433ft 7 116 11½ 3½ 44½ 77¾ Baze G 8 32000 75-16 NorthrnProvdr,Rnbw'sCp,FrgnLgn 10

24Dec86-9Hol 1 1/16 Ⓣ:464 1:112 1:414fm 12 116 1hd 1hd 1hd 12 ‡Black C A 3 25000 85-11 CoursingEagle,Racionl,AncientBlue 9

‡24Dec86—Dead heat

●Jly 29 SA 5f ft :59 h   Jly 18 SA 4f ft :493 h   Jun 19 SA 5f ft 1:001 h

D.

As In Eagles

SIBILLE R **115**

Own.—Berger–Goldman–Goldman

B. g. 3, by Somethingfabulous—Snoozeulose, by Walker's

Br.—Goldman & Coleman (Cal)

Tr.—Stute Warren

Lifetime 4 3 0 0 $26,400

1987 3 3 0 0 $26,400

1986 1 M 0 0

31Jly87-3Dmr 6f :214 :443 1:102ft 3¾ 115 2hd 1hd 1½ 1nk CstnonAL 5 Ⓢ Aw21000 86-17 AsInEagles,FancyOts,IrishRobbery 8

16Jly87-7Hol 6f :214 :443 1:102ft *2¼ 116 11½ 11½ 13½ 13½ Castanon A L 1 40000 91-12 As In Eagles, Robert's Lad,Rosasco 6

3Jly87-1Hol 6f :213 :444 1:103ft 6¼ 116 11½ 12½ 15 13½ Castanon A L 2 M32000 90-09 As In Eagles, Hass TheGlass,Blare 12

4Sep86-6Dmr 6f :214 :451 1:101ft 23 118 913 810 87¼ 69 Douglas R R 1 M50000 78-14 Supreme Stand, Cleverege, RedGuy 9

4Sep86—Broke slowly; green backstretch

Jly 29 Dmr 4f ft :484 h   Jly 24 Hol 4f ft :501 h   Jly 11 Hol 3f ft :364 h   Jun 29 Hol 4f ft :514 h

E.

Step Son

VERGARA O **122**

Own.—Engelauf Mr–Mrs G

B. g. 4, by Rene Dingle—Arizona Jubilee, by Spotted Moon

Br.—Engelauf Mr–Mrs G (Cal)

Tr.—Garcia Victor

Lifetime 3 3 0 0 $7,380

1987 3 3 0 0 $7,380

1986 0 M 0 0

18Jly87-9AC 6f :224 :452 1:101ft 6-5 115 1½ 3nk 1hd 12½ Lopez A D 4 Aw5000 88-17 Step Son, Jockey Up, Threw Home 7

27Jun87-9AC 6f :223 :444 1:092ft 3 115 5½ 53 21½ 13 Lopez A D 7 10000 92-17 Step Son, Windy Plane, Trouble T. 8

14Jun87-3AC 6f :221 :442 1:094ft *7-5 120 1hd 1hd 1hd 12 Lopez A D 4 M6250 90-14 Step Son, Five Circles, Ryandale 9

Aug 3 AC 5f ft 1:013 h   Jly 27 AC 6f ft 1:14 h

F.

Fun He Won

AQUINO C **116**

Own.—Ashley M E

Dk. b. or br. g. 4, by Briar Bend—Right On Gal, by Lotsaluck

Br.—Reed M E (Cal)

Tr.—Sylvia Earle K Jr

Lifetime 2 1 0 0 $4,250

1987 2 1 0 0 $4,250

1986 0 M 0 0

7Jly87-11Pln 6f :214 :45 1:093ft 16 1115 43 54½ 55 55¼ Munoz O R6 Aw16000 89-13 SntinlStr,GoldRushin',ChoosyFrind 6

21Jun87-3GG 6f :214 :444 1:112ft 20 1175 41½ 53 52½ 1¾ Munoz O R4 M20000 82-18 FunHeWon,GoldenQuiver,Ephemrl 12

●Jly 28 GD tr.t 6f ft 1:132 hg   ●Jly 21 GD tr.t 6f ft 1:131 hg   Jun 15 Pln 5f ft 1:022 h   Jun 8 Pln 6f ft 1:131 hg

G.

Flying Lieutenant
Dk. b. or br. c. 3, by Flying Paster—Queenly Command, by Empery
CAPITAINE N M 115
Br.—Cardiff Stud Farm (Cal) 1987 6 0 0 0 $7,375
Tr.—Brothers Frank L 1986 8 2 2 1 $104,975
Own.—Dandar Fms-Caridff StudFm
Lifetime 14 2 2 1 $112,350 Turf 2 0 0 0 $3,500

13Jun87-9LaD 1⁷⁰:481 1:141 1:45 m *2½ 112 32 77 713 728¾ Snyder L8 Aw14500 43-23 EdEdwrdo,AckOneSceneOn,Trplud 8
30Apr87-9LaD 6f :23 :462 1:112ft 3½ 114 77¼ 67½ 59 610¾ Perrodin E J3 Aw14000 74-25 Summer Park,ProperNative,Deviser 8
28Mar87-10FG a1⅛Ⓣ:4721:12 1:53 fm 13 115 89¾ 77½ 916 812½ Perrodin EJ4 Life Dby 56-20 PrformngPppy,BluFnn,TrDplomcy 11
15Mar87-11FG 1⅛:472 1:12 1:51 ft 3½ 123 79½ 79½ 67¾ 611¾ PrrodnEJ8 Lou Dby 77-14 J. T.'sPet,AuthenticHero,Plumcake 8
15Mar87—Grade III
14Feb87-8SA 7f :221 :45 1:234sy 14 122 68½ 67¾ 58 48 Toro F4 Sn Vcnte 73-17 StylshWnnr,PrncSssfrs,MountLgun 6
14Feb87—Grade III; Bobbled, steadied start
11Jan87-8BM 6f :223 :46 1:113gd 5¾ 120 89¾ 88¼ 78 55½ Loseth C1 Dtrmne 75-27 PutEmUp,CondctonChrgr,KnoKptn 8
11Jan87—Off slowly
15Nov86-8BM 1₁₆Ⓣ:47 1:1231:462fm *1e120 811 76½ 67½ 59½ CastnedM5 Cal Juv 61-19 WildernessBound,PrinceSssfrs,Wr 8
15Nov86—Grade III
1Nov86-1SA 1₁₆:454 1:102 1:434ft 32f 122 119¾119 811 913¼ Toro F2 Br Cp Juv 69-13 Capote, Qualify, Alysheba 13
1Nov86—Grade I; Bumped stretch; Bumped entering stretch
25Oct86-8SA 1 :444 1:101 1:383ft 3¾ 116 810 69 46 22 Toro F7 Ⓢ B J Rddr 73-17 ‡PsDGurr,FlyngLtnnt,BrodwyPont 11
25Oct86—Took up 1/16, impeded
Jly 31 SA 6f ft 1:142 h Jly 24 SA 5f ft 1:004 h Jly 18 SA 3f ft :363 h

H.

Cleverege
B. c. 3, by Clever Trick—Cherrywood Clover, by Porterhouse
PATTERSON A 116
Br.—Burburry G M & D D Jr (Ky) 1987 2 0 0 0 $1,950
Tr.—Garrison Rudy D 1986 6 1 3 0 $23,570
Own.—Team Esprit
Lifetime 8 1 3 0 $25,520

24Jan87-3SA 6f :212 :442 1:101ft 10 118 32½ 32½ 45½ 69½ Patterson A6 Aw26000 78-18 HppyInSpc,SwtwtrSprings,ThQuppr 9
10Jan87-3SA 6½f:223 :454 1:172gd 6 119 31½ 32½ 33½ 44½ Patterson A2 Aw26000 79-20 PrinceSssfrs,ThQuippr,WstrlyWind 6
27Dec86-7SA 6f :214 :451 1:104ft 14e120 2hd 1hd 1hd 2nk Patterson A5 Aw26000 84-19 SocilDimond,Cleverege,WstrlyWind 8
27Dec86—Bumped intervals late
14Dec86-6Hol 6f :22 :453 1:111ft 10 118 21 1hd 1½ 12½ Patterson A8 Mdn 87-18 Cleverg,‡RdyToSmok,LovDn'sGtwy 8
18Sep86-11Pom 6½f:213 :45 1:172ft 11 115 22 34½ 33 47 Mena F6 Beau Brml 86-12 CctusClipper,DoublSong,HighRgrds 6
12Sep86-8Pom 6f :223 :463 1:12 ft *8-5 1135 1hd 1hd 1½ 2nk Black C A6 Mdn 91-11 Lucky Edition,Cleverege,OakWine 10
12Sep86—Bumped late
4Sep86-6Dmr 6f :214 :451 1:101ft 2½ 1135 33½ 31½ 31½ 24½ Black C A2 M50000 82-14 Supreme Stand, Cleverege, RedGuy 9
11Aug86-6Dmr 6f :22 :451 1:102ft 25 1135 2hd 21½ 24 511½ Black C A4 M50000 74-13 GoldOnGreen,Darion,LuckyEdition 10
11Aug86—Bumped start, late
Aug 4 SA 5f ft 1:013 h Jly 28 SA 4f ft :484 h Jly 22 SA 5f ft 1:032 h Jly 15 SA 5f ft 1:034 h

I.

Fracoza
Ch. g. 4, by Messenger of Song—Long Issue, by Long Position
MENA F 119
Br.—Cozza F (Cal) 1987 11 4 0 1 $56,675
Tr.—Richardson Thomas F 1986 10 2 1 1 $21,550
Own.—Ferguson Mrs J K
Lifetime 21 6 1 2 $78,225

6Jun87-9Hol 1 :444 1:101 1:371ft 16 116 3½ 85¼ 88 816¼ Stevens G L6 80000 61-17 LstCommnd,AmricnLgon,SoctyRod 8
6Jun87—Bumped hard start
29May87-7Hol 6½f:221 :451 1:164ft 11 119 52¼ 34½ 35½ 34¼ Stevens G L1 80000 92-16 MyFvoriteMomnt,Hydrosttic,Frcoz 6
29May87—Lugged out final 1/2
16May87-7Hol 7f :221 :451 1:222ft 9 1155 52¼ 75½ 711 712¾ Gryder A T3 Aw25000 79-13 Superoyale,Wtch'nWin,SocietyRod 7
16May87—Lugged out; checked 3 1/2
3May87-5Hol 7f :22 :45 1:231ft 6½ 1105 51¾ 4¾ 11 12¾ Gryder A T2 Aw22000 88-15 Fracoza, Baby Slewy, Mondanite 7
20Apr87-3SA 1₁₆:461 1:103 1:441ft 11 1115 2½ 2hd 12 1¾ Gryder A T5 50000 80-17 Fracoza, Poley, Double Sheng 6
11Apr87-9SA 1 :46 1:11 1:362ft 6½ 116 21½ 22 34 56½ Castanon A L7 c40000 80-16 Bizeboy, Nordicus, Parson John 9
3Apr87-5SA 6½f:22 :453 1:172ft 6½ 116 2hd 1½ 13 14 Castanon A L11 25000 83-17 Fracoza, Hurricane Hec, Pegus 11
17Mar87-7SA 1₁₆:46 1:102 1:423ft 11 117 21½ 34 69 714¾ ValenzuelPA3 Aw31000 73-16 PrinceO'Fire,It'sNotMyJob,Athlone 9
17Mar87—Lugged out.
26Feb87-5SA 1₁₆:452 1:102 1:44 ft 5 115 11½ 13½ 2hd 45½ Solis A8 c25000 76-22 Cold, Exalted Bubble, Julie'sMark 10
7Feb87-9SA 1₁₆:46 1:103 1:433ft 7½ 115 12½ 12 12½ 12¾ Olivares F8 16000 83-14 Fracoza, Restage, Tiffani's Toy 9
Aug 4 SA 5f ft 1:004 h Jly 28 SA 5f ft 1:024 h Jly 21 SA 5f ft 1:001 h Jly 15 SA 3f ft :364 h

J.

Lans Manus
Ch. g. 4, by Canadian Gil—Six Pillows, by Golden Eagle II
FERNANDEZ A L 116
Br.—Wood Mrs S (Cal) 1987 5 0 1 0 $6,825
Tr.—Stepp William T 1986 14 4 2 1 $42,125
Own.—Conquest Stb-Lanni-Stepp
Lifetime 23 5 4 1 $59,575 Turf 2 0 0 0

23Apr87-8Hol 6f :212 :443 1:091ft 3 116 2½ 2½ 57 515½ ValenzuelPA5 Aw25000 81-09 Don'sIrshMlody,BoldSmochr,REntr 5
29Mar87-5SA a6½f Ⓣ:213 :44 1:151fm 10 116 1½ 2hd 1hd 73½ Olivares F5 Aw33000 79-13 Danczone,FbulousSound,SlneCstle 12
8Mar87-11TuP 6f :211 :43 1:064ft 11 115 62 97¾ 913 918¼ Maple S6 Phx Gld Cp 84-15 Zany Tactics, Faro, Zabaleta 9
8Mar87—Grade III
20Feb87-8SA 6f :213 :44 1:083ft *8-5 117 21½ 21½ 22 22½ Pincay L Jr3 Aw31000 93-16 NorthernPolicy,LnsMnus,Seniority 7
15Jan87-7SA a6½f Ⓣ:212 :4341:154fm *2 118 1hd 1hd 2½ 77¾ Kaenel J L6 Aw29000 72-20 StrtfordEst,TmmyThHwk,ClfThGrd 8
15Jan87—Bumped hard 3/16

26Dec86-8SA	7f	:22^2	:44^4	1:21^3ft	33	116	1^hd	2^hd	31½	810¼	Kaenel JL^2	Malibu	82-13	Ferdinand, Snow Chief,DonB.Blue	12
26Dec86—Grade II															
30Nov86-4Hol	6f	:22^1	:45^2	1:10^3ft	*4-5	116	1^hd	1½	13½	14½	ValenzuelPA^3	Aw21000	90-16	LansManus,Notoriety,StratfordEst	7
9Nov86-5Hol	6f	:22	:45^1	1:10 ft	6½	116	2^hd	1^hd	12½	15½	Valenzuela P A^7	40000	93-16	Lans Manus, RosesAreReb Sebucan	8
29Oct86-1SA	6½f	:21^4	:44^3	1:17 ft	2½	116	1^hd	1½	1½	12¾	Solis A^6	20000	85-17	LansManus,KeniDncer,PecefulImge	8
16Oct86-5SA	6½f	:21^3	:44^4	1:17^1ft	8½	116	2½	2^hd	1^hd	11¾	Solis A^9	16000	84-19	Lans Manus, Blue Ice, BlackCross	11

Jly 23 Hol 5f ft 1:00^2 h   Jly 17 Hol 5f ft 1:00^1 h   Jly 11 Hol 4f ft :47^1 h   Jly 6 Hol 3f ft :35^4 h

26. The track surface has been biased lately in favor of closers. As bias information often does, that should help handicappers focus their efforts here.

8th Arlington

6 ½ FURLONGS. (1.15) ALLOWANCE. Purse $17,000. Fillies and mares. 3-year-olds and upward which have not won $8,400 three times since August 18 other than maiden, claiming, starter or state-bred. Weight, 3-year-olds, 117 lbs.; older, 122 lbs. Non-winners of $12,000 twice since April 4 allowed 3 lbs.; $9,600 twice in 1987, 6 lbs.; $12,000 in 1986-87, 9 lbs. (Maiden, claiming, starter and state-bred races not considered in allowances.)

Coupled—Am Tuned Up and La Lucky Strike.

A.

Chitter Chatter

Own.—Goodwill Stable   114

Dk. b. or br. f. 3, by Caro—Love to Tell, by Tell
Br.—Jones Warner L Jr (Ky)
Tr.—Winfree Donald
Lifetime 7 3 0 2 $39,956

1987 6 3 0 2 $39,956
1986 1 M 0 0

20Jly87-8AP	1	:45^2	1:10^2	1:35^4ft	*6-5	118	1^1	1^1	2^hd	32¾	Day P^4	ⒻAw17000	79-19	Bstofbothworlds,RoylCl,ChttrChttr	6
5Jly87-10Tdn	6f	:21^2	:45	1:11^2ft	4½	113	45½	5^6	11^15	11^11	WdsCRJr^11	ⒻScrltCH	76-20	Azrbijni,‡NicklePlted,DnceOnOver	13
26Jun87-7CD	6½f	:22^1	:45^3	1:17^2ft	*1-2	121	1^1	1^3	13½	12½	MelnconL^7	ⒻAw21300	93-12	ChitterChtter,I'vGotRhythm,Hiling	8
23May87-9CD	1	:45^2	1:11	1:36^4ft	*3-5	117	43½	2^2	2½	3^4	Day P^6	ⒻEdgewood	81-18	Lt.Lo,BetweentheHdgs,ChittrChttr	7
12May87-7CD	6½f	:22^4	:46^3	1:18 ft	*1-3	121	1^2	1^2	12½	1^6	Day P^5	ⒻAw16500	90-19	ChitterChtter,PolrWind,YMoGucho	8
2May87-1CD	6f	:21^1	:44^2	1:09^1ft	*8-5	111	1^2	1^5	1^5	18½	Day P^11	ⒻMdn	97-09	ChttrChttr,MgcMgcMgc,MbrBgm	12
17Oct86-3Kee	a7f			1:28^2ft	*6-5	118	1^hd	1^1	3^4	713¾	Melancon L^7	ⒻMdn	67-19	Pelican Bay, ScornedLass,Tuneful	12

Jly 18 AP 4f ft :48^4 b   Jun 16 CD 5f ft 1:00 h

B.

Moonbeam McQueen

Own.—Swann John lessee   113

B. f. 4, by Miswaki—Seek a Rainbow, by Bolero
Br.—Carl Bill (Ky)
Tr.—Nafzger Carl A
Lifetime 26 3 4 4 $48,620

1987 10 2 2 1 $29,355
1986 14 1 2 3 $19,265
Turf 3 0 0 0 $554

20Jly87-7AP	6f	:22^2	:45^3	1:10^3ft	3¼	117	5^9	5^7	4^2	2no	Hawley S 2	ⒻAw16000	87-19	HostHrFlg,MoonbmMcQn,RnMrsRn	6
13Jly87-8AP	1 1/16 Ⓣ	:48	1:13	1:45^2gd	*2-5e	115	4^7	54½	53¼	6^9	Hawley S 5	ⒻAw18000	71-26	AutumnGlitter,SpruceLuck,Itsagem	6
26Jun87-8Cby	6½f	:22^1	:44^4	1:17^1ft	6¾	115	77¼	66¾	34½	2^3	WrlVL 6	ⒻMighty M H	92-20	HostHrFlg,MoonbmMcQun,LlPrppy	8
26Apr87-10Cby	1^70	:48^1	1:12^2	1:41^3ft	21	115	31½	3^4	38½	514¾	McKtJ 9	ⒻCty O Minn	78-12	HppyHollowMss,WknTnk,TrnndDnc	9
11Apr87-5Kee	6f	:23^2	:47	1:13^3ft	3¼	115	5^2	5^3	2½	14½	Oldham J 6	ⒻAw18100	74-25	MoonbmMcQn,InOnPc,MssKnwAll	10
7Apr87-5Kee	1 1/16	:49	1:14^1	1:48 m	2½	112	1^1	1^hd	57½	5^12	Hawley S 4	ⒻAw20300	54-31	Mm'sNoonr,DwnsAdvoct,BldWitch	6
21Mar87-5OP	6f	:22	:45^2	1:10^1ft	14	119	42½	2^hd	1^hd	1^4	Hawley S 7	ⒻAw14000	89-15	MoonbmMcQun,Snookr,GiftOfGlttr	8
2Mar87-9OP	6f	:22^2	:45^3	1:10^1ft	27	119	64½	7^8	55½	3^5	Kutz D 1	ⒻAw14000	84-19	Z.'sClass,RitaH.,MoonbemMcQueen	8
21Feb87-7OP	6f	:22	:45^2	1:11 ft	13	116	88¾	9^13	8^11	710¼	Smith M E 1	ⒻAw16000	75-20	StrickenRvng,Trry'sSong,IsbllCnns	9
10Feb87-7OP	6f	:22	:45^4	1:10^3ft	9	119	74¼	63½	45½	45¼	Hawley S 9	ⒻAw14000	82-17	StrickenRevenge,Z.'sClass,Snooker	9

Jun 25 Cby 3f gd :37^3 h (d)   ●Jun 21 Cby 6f ft 1:12^2 hg   Jun 17 Cby 4f gd :49^2 h

C.

Gentle Vixen

Own.—Doubledown Stables Inc   116

Dk. b. or br. f. 4, by Gentle King—Latchstring, by Crewman
Br.—Fox Grove Farm (Fla)
Tr.—Poulos Ernie T
Lifetime 27 5 3 7 $100,996

1987 7 1 1 3 $29,306
1986 15 2 1 3 $52,590
Turf 2 0 0 1 $4,061

8Jun87-8AP	6½f	:23^2	:46^4	1:18^3ft	*2-3	121	3^2	4^3	21½	2¾	Fires E^1	ⒻAw17000	81-24	Itsagem,GentleVixen,SmilingNeatly	7
23May87-2Spt	6½f	:24^2	:48^1	1:18^4gd	4¾	115	2^2	3^1	4^4	4^6	Patin K C^2	ⒻHcp0	77-16	BubblBit,FmlyCompct,Whtluckygrl	6
29Apr87-8Spt	6f	:23^4	:48	1:12^4ft	*7-5	115	5^6	1½	1^3	1^4	Meier R^4	ⒻAw26900	86-24	GentleVixen,HoneyMcDn,PririePrk	6
9Apr87-9Spt	6½f	:22^1	:46^2	1:18^1ft	5	119	56½	64½	4^2	3^2	King ELJr^7	ⒻAw26400	84-22	NoChoice,Tex'sToots,GentleVixen	10
12Mar87-5Spt	6f	:24^1	:48	1:12^3ft	3½	115	4^3	4^5	46½	3^6	Silva C H^4	ⒻAw24200	81-22	BubbleBite,VillaSvoye,GentleVixen	6
28Feb87-3Spt	6f	:23^4	:48^1	1:13^4ft	2¼	115	1^hd	43½	5^6	613½	Silva C H^1	ⒻAw24000	67-26	Pamela Paul, Villa Savoye,TopFolly	6
19Jan87-8Hia	6f	:21^4	:45^1	1:09^3ft	76	116	4^5	3^3	33½	35¼	Pezua J M^4	ⒻAw21000	87-18	TeRoom,MissAlleyCt,GentleVixen	10
26Dec86-7Crc	7f	:22^3	:46^4	1:27 sy	15	116	4^2	41¼	3^3	68½	Velez JAJr^4	ⒻAw17300	72-26	Cascade, Avanti Sassa,MedievalEve	6
12Dec86-7Crc	6f	:22^3	:46	1:12 ft	11	114	55½	3^5	34½	3^6	Velez JAJr^4	ⒻAw16000	85-20	Algenib, Marlish, Gentle Vixen	6
8Nov86-9Crc	7f	:22^3	:46	1:24^4ft	29	112	4^1	63¼	67¼	69½	SthAJr^6	ⒻLago Mar H	82-16	SpiritofFighter,ThirtyZip,FlurDSolil	6

Jly 17 AP 4f ft :48 h   Jly 2 AP 5f ft 1:00 b   Jun 4 AP 6f ft 1:13^3 h

D.

Bail Fast
Own.—Stonewood Farm **116**

Ch. f. 4, by Bailjumper—Lake Chapala, by Grand Central
Br.—Stonewood Farm (Mich) 1987 5 1 2 0 $20,929
Tr.—Burns Daniel T 1986 16 6 4 3 $94,886
Lifetime 21 7 6 3 $115,815

11Jly87-8Det	$1\frac{1}{16}$	$:47^2$	$1:12^2$	$1:47^1$ft	6	114	$1^{1\frac{1}{2}}$	1^2	1^3	2^{nk}	Green B 8	ⒻQun Bee	67-23	One by Bandy,BailFast,Brian'sBluff	9
28Jun87-6AP	7f	$:22^1$	:45	$1:23^4$ft	*8-5	118	$2^{1\frac{1}{2}}$	2^2	2^1	$2^{\frac{3}{4}}$	Clark K D 2	ⒻAw17000	82-23	DancePleaser,BailFast,RunMrisRun	6
13Jun87-10Det	6f	$:22^3$	$:46^2$	1:13 ft	*6-5	119	$4^{3\frac{1}{2}}$	4^4	$4^{3\frac{1}{2}}$	$4^{1\frac{3}{4}}$	GrB 11	Ⓕ[S]Larkspur H	73-34	Robetts, Full Promise, Kashanti	11
16May87-8Det	6f	$:22^4$	:46	$1:11^4$ft	9-5	113	$1^{\frac{1}{2}}$	1^{hd}	1^1	$1^{1\frac{1}{2}}$	Green B 7	ⒻAw10500	81-25	Bail Fast, Aries Sue,ThePrivateOne	8
9May87-7Det	6f	$:22^4$	$:46^1$	$1:12^3$ft	4½	114	2^{hd}	$3^{\frac{1}{2}}$	4^3	$7^{6\frac{1}{4}}$	Green B 3	Aw11500	71-30	WhtAGold,ChristophrMx,JmiFrntrit	7
11Oct86-11Det	6f	$:22^3$	$:45^1$	$1:10^4$ft	6¾	115	5^8	5^5	4^3	$1^{\frac{1}{2}}$	Knight LC 8	ⒻAw11000	86-26	Bail Fast, Kashanti, ThePrivateOne	8
17Sep86-9Det	170	$:46^4$	$1:11^1$	$1:42^3$ft	2¼	113	2^3	2^3	2^3	2^2	DePass R 4	ⒻAw9200	82-21	Flight Out, Bail Fast, BraveWoendi	6
30Aug86-12Det	6f	$:22^3$	$:45^4$	$1:11^2$ft	*1-3	122	3^3	$1^{\frac{1}{2}}$	1^3	$1^{3\frac{1}{2}}$	DPssR 3	Ⓕ[S]Ann Arbor	83-19	BilFst,LuckyVolly,C.W.'sConfusion	9
22Aug86-9Det	6f	$:22^2$	$:45^2$	$1:10^3$ft	*3-5	117	2^1	2^1	2^{hd}	$2^{1\frac{1}{2}}$	DePassR 6	Ⓕ[S]Aw11900	85-21	Bandigee, Bail Fast,SorbiePrincess	6
9Aug86-12Det	$1\frac{1}{16}$	$:48^3$	$1:13^1$	$1:47^3$ft	*3-5	122	3^1	$2^{\frac{1}{2}}$	1^1	1^4	DPssR 8	Ⓕ[S]Mich Oaks	65-27	BailFast,LuckyVolley,CrimsonBand	9

● Jly 25 Det 5f gd 1:02 b Jly 6 Det 5f ft 1:06 b Jun 23 Det 5f ft $1:05^4$ b Jun 10 Det 3f ft $:35^3$ h

E.

Am Tuned Up
Own.—Colony Stable-Levitch J M **111^5**

B. f. 4, by Tunerup—Amberhue, by Ambernash
Br.—Wilson Robert (Fla) 1987 8 1 1 4 $24,210
Tr.—Levitch James M 1986 14 3 3 2 $32,785
Lifetime 35 7 7 9 $84,314

9Jly87-7AP	6½f	:23	:46	$1:17^2$ft	13	118	1^1	4^4	$4^{9\frac{1}{2}}$	$4^{9\frac{1}{2}}$	MrqzCHJr 2	ⒻAw16000	78-21	RunMarisaRun,OnlyaGlnce,BridlUp	7
27Jun87-7AP	6f	:22	$:45^3$	1:12 ft	9¼	112	$6^{3\frac{1}{2}}$	4^8	$3^{6\frac{1}{2}}$	3^7	Evans R D 7	ⒻAw16000	73-21	ShrpCrln,AnythngforLov,AmTndUp	8
20Apr87-8Spt	1	$:48^3$	1:14	$1:40^2$ft	2½	115	1^3	2^2	2^4	3^7	Evans R D 3	ⒻAw23800	71-25	FmilyCompct,AllowMe,AmTundUp	6
9Apr87-9Spt	6½f	$:22^1$	$:46^2$	$1:18^1$ft	*7-5	121	3^3	$3^{2\frac{1}{2}}$	5^4	5^6	Evans RD 10	ⒻAw26400	80-22	NoChoice,Tex'sToots,GentleVixen	10
29Mar87-6Spt	6f	$:23^4$	:48	$1:13^4$sy	*9-5	115	$4^{1\frac{1}{2}}$	$5^{1\frac{3}{4}}$	3^1	1^{hd}	Evans R D 3	ⒻAw21300	81-19	AmTunedUp,LadySargent,TopFolly	7
29Mar87—Wide first turn, steadied awaiting room final turn															
2Mar87-7Hia	6f	$:22^2$	$:45^4$	1:11 ft	2¼	116	$4^{1\frac{1}{4}}$	4^2	2^5	$2^{3\frac{1}{2}}$	Pezua J M 6	Ⓕ c32000	81-23	RunMrisRun,AmTundUp,Doubruby	12
2Feb87-7Hia	6f	$:22^1$	$:45^3$	$1:11^1$ft	3¾	114	$6^{3\frac{1}{4}}$	$4^{5\frac{1}{4}}$	4^5	3^3	Pezua J M 8	Ⓕ 37500	81-20	VleRoyle,FoxcroftVlue,AmTundUp	12
11Jan87-7Hia	6f	$:21^4$	$:45^3$	$1:11^3$ft	9¼	112	$7^{4\frac{1}{4}}$	$6^{5\frac{3}{4}}$	3^4	$3^{\frac{1}{2}}$	Pezua J M 10	Ⓕ 35000	81-19	QuintStr,FoxcroftVlue,AmTundUp	12
14Dec86-5Crc	6½f	$:22^3$	$:46^2$	$1:19^2$ft	*1-2e	115	$4^{3\frac{1}{2}}$	4^2	$3^{2\frac{1}{2}}$	$3^{5\frac{1}{4}}$	Gonzalez MA 3	Ⓕ 30000	82-19	LaLuckyStrike,Pferdel,AmTunedUp	7
4Nov86-7Crc	6½f	$:22^4$	$:46^2$	$1:19^3$ft	3½	114^5	1^{hd}	2^{hd}	$4^{1\frac{3}{4}}$	$5^{2\frac{3}{4}}$	Paynter L A 2	Ⓕ 35000	84-23	Gentley,Tht'sAGoodOne,DeeCChrgr	6

Jly 23 AP 4f ft :48 h Jly 17 AP 4f ft $:48^1$ b Jun 26 AP 3f ft :37 b Jun 23 AP 3f ft $:37^2$ b

F.

Dance Pleaser
Own.—C B Farms **113**

B. f. 4, by Honest Pleasure—Parfait Royale, by Damascus
Br.—Evans Dr A (Ky) 1987 5 2 0 0 $17,760
Tr.—Lukas D Wayne 1986 14 3 1 0 $30,350
Lifetime 22 6 1 1 $54,798

20Jly87-7AP	6f	$:22^2$	$:45^3$	$1:10^3$ft	5¼	123	1^2	$1^{\frac{1}{2}}$	3^1	$4^{3\frac{1}{2}}$	Smith M E 6	ⒻAw16000	83-19	HostHrFlg,MoonbmMcQn,RnMrsRn	6
28Jun87-6AP	7f	$:22^1$	:45	$1:23^4$ft	2½	112	$1^{1\frac{1}{2}}$	1^2	1^1	$1^{\frac{3}{4}}$	Smith M E 1	ⒻAw17000	83-23	DancePleaser,BailFast,RunMrisRun	6
28Jun87—Bled															
6Jun87-4AP	6½f	:23	$:46^2$	$1:18^3$ft	6½	117	1^2	$1^{3\frac{1}{2}}$	1^4	$1^{2\frac{1}{2}}$	Smith M E 2	Ⓕ 25000	82-19	DncePleser,Ithinkshe'sgotit,Upkep	6
15Apr87-7Bir	6f	$:22^1$	$:45^4$	$1:11^3$ft	41	116	$6^{2\frac{1}{4}}$	$8^{7\frac{1}{2}}$	9^{16}	$9^{17\frac{1}{2}}$	Jones B S 6	ⒻAw15000	71-15	NobleSecrtry,Burt'sDrm,FlurDSolil	9
10Mar87-7Bir	6f	$:21^4$	$:45^1$	$1:11^1$ft	32	113	$7^{5\frac{1}{4}}$	$7^{6\frac{3}{4}}$	9^{10}	$9^{10\frac{3}{4}}$	Jones B S 9	ⒻAw16000	— —	WkndDlight,MilliProspct,BrghtBlss	9
15Aug86-8Aks	6f	:22	$:44^4$	$1:10^3$ft	15	117	4^4	5^3	$4^{2\frac{1}{2}}$	$7^{5\frac{3}{4}}$	Maple S 3	ⒻMy Juliet	78-19	Hs'nHm,SndhllDmnd,HppyHllMss	10
24Jly86-8Aks	6f	$:22^2$	:45	1:11 ft	5	122	4^2	$3^{2\frac{1}{2}}$	4^3	$4^{3\frac{1}{4}}$	Maple S 6	ⒻAw16100	79-21	MiniDocN'M,Trcy'sEspor,NrvousBb	6
13Jly86-8Aks	$1\frac{1}{16}$	$:46^4$	$1:12^1$	1:46 ft	7¾	115	1^1	$1^{\frac{1}{2}}$	6^{11}	$6^{14\frac{1}{4}}$	Maple S 11	ⒻAw16100	59-23	BeautyCream,Smartake,Athabasca	11
2Jly86-8Aks	6f	$:22^1$	$:45^1$	$1:11^2$ft	2¾	122	3^1	3^{nk}	2^{hd}	1^{nk}	Maple S 5	ⒻAw16100	80-25	DncePlsr,MiniDocN'M,Trcy'sEspoir	5
13Jun86-7Aks	6f	$:22^1$	:45	1:10 ft	5¾	117	2^{hd}	1^2	1^3	1^6	Maple S 8*	ⒻAw15000	87-16	DncePleser,PlsRply,Mri'sMoonMid	9

Jly 10 AP 5f ft $1:01^3$ b Jun 17 AP 4f ft $:49^2$ b Jun 1 AP 4f ft $:48^4$ b

G.

La Lucky Strike
Own.—Colony Stable &LevitchJMSr **111^5**

B. f. 4, by Strike the Anvil—La Americana, by Free Gallant
Br.—Tamargo Dolores S (Fla) 1987 8 2 0 2 $35,072
Tr.—Levitch James M 1986 13 5 3 2 $38,085
Lifetime 21 7 3 4 $73,157 Turf 1 1 0 0 $8,100

31May87-8AP	6f	$:22^3$	:46	$1:11^1$ft	5½	114	6^8	$6^{7\frac{3}{4}}$	$6^{6\frac{1}{2}}$	$6^{7\frac{1}{4}}$	Fires E 3	ⒻFour Wds	76-27	Double Derby, Gift Of Glitter, Foy	6
15May87-8Spt	1	$:48^4$	$1:13^4$	1:40 ft	*3-2	121	$5^{2\frac{3}{4}}$	$3^{2\frac{1}{2}}$	$3^{2\frac{1}{2}}$	$3^{1\frac{3}{4}}$	King ELJr 2	ⒻAw27400	78-23	MyMfld,FmilyCompct,LLuckyStrik	8
25Apr87-8Spt	1	$:48^3$	$1:13^3$	$1:39^3$ft	21	112	$7^{5\frac{1}{2}}$	$6^{3\frac{1}{2}}$	$4^{2\frac{3}{4}}$	3^2	KELJr 10	ⒻLady Hal H	80-20	MGllntDchss,TrmphDNskr,LLcStr	10
11Mar87-10GP	a1	Ⓣ		$1:45^4$yl	5	117	$4^{2\frac{1}{4}}$	$4^{2\frac{1}{4}}$	$4^{\frac{3}{4}}$	$1^{\frac{1}{2}}$	Gonzalez MA 9	Ⓕ 50000	51-51	LLuckyStrik,AitnnBui,SwtJllyBinn	11
14Feb87-3Hia	7f	$:23^1$	:46	$1:23^3$ft	6¾	116	3^1	$2^{1\frac{1}{2}}$	$1^{\frac{1}{2}}$	1^1	GonzlzMA 5	ⒻAw19500	85-15	LaLuckyStrike,FireBreak,DarkTzrin	8
2Feb87-5Hia	6f	$:22^3$	$:45^4$	$1:10^4$ft	13	116	$5^{4\frac{1}{2}}$	4^4	$3^{\frac{1}{2}}$	$4^{1\frac{3}{4}}$	Molina VH 7	ⒻAw19500	84-20	DoubleAngel,GiniDoll,QuensJustic	11
26Jan87-8Hia	7f	$:23^3$	$:46^2$	$1:23^2$ft	*2¼	112	$4^{3\frac{1}{2}}$	4^5	$4^{5\frac{1}{2}}$	$4^{10\frac{3}{4}}$	Pezua J M 5	Ⓕ 50000	75-24	SilverDor,WiseAndHppy,SkiddooU.	8
8Jan87-5Hia	7f	:23	$:46^1$	$1:24^1$ft	*3	116	$5^{3\frac{1}{4}}$	$4^{2\frac{1}{2}}$	$5^{1\frac{1}{4}}$	$4^{1\frac{3}{4}}$	Pezua J M 5	ⒻAw17000	80-19	BtsyMck,LustrousRson,Innsbruck	10
23Dec86-10Crc	6f	$:22^2$	$:46^2$	$1:12^2$ft	*6-5	117	4^2	1^{hd}	1^3	$1^{2\frac{1}{2}}$	Pezua J M 3	Ⓕ c35000	89-19	LLckyStrk,Ms.HppyHor,MllProspct	9
14Dec86-5Crc	6½f	$:22^3$	$:46^2$	$1:19^2$ft	*1-2e	115	$5^{5\frac{1}{2}}$	3^2	1^{hd}	1^3	Pezua J M 1	Ⓕ 30000	88-19	LaLuckyStrike,Pferdel,AmTunedUp	7

Jly 23 AP 3f ft :37 b Jly 10 AP 6f ft $1:14^1$ h Jly 2 AP 5f ft $1:02^2$ b Jun 27 AP 4f ft $:49^2$ b

H.

Pamela Paul

Own.—Ross R–Robbins S–Joyce J   116

B. f. 4, by Be a Rullah—Brave Tea, by Big Brave
Br.—Hochlerin Harvey (Fla)
Tr.—Vinci Charles J

			1987	6	1 1 1	$24,728
			1986	12	2 1 4	$42,395
	Lifetime	26 6 2 6	$82,653	Turf	4 0 0 1	$2,680

11Apr87-4Spt	6¼f :23³ :47³ 1:19⁴gd	6¼ 121	7⁹ 7⁸ 4² 2¹¼	King E Ljr⁵	ⒻAw26400	76-21 MyGalIntDuchess,PmelPul,MissAtri 7
4Apr87-6Spt	1 :50¹ 1:15 1:40 ft	2½ 115	6⁵ 4⁶ 47½ 4⁸	Clark K D⁶	ⒻAw25300	72-19 SmrtrByThDy,FmlCmpct,InsprcnII 6
29Mar87-8Spt	6f :23¹ :46³ 1:12¹sy	2½ 119	71⁸ 71⁶ 7⁹ 76½	Clark K D⁴	ⒻV Berg M	82-19 BubblBit,WonInCourt,Whtluckygirl 8
28Feb87-3Spt	6f :23⁴ :48¹ 1:13⁴ft	*2 115	65½ 64½ 2² 1¾	Clark K D²	ⒻAw24000	81-26 Pamela Paul, Villa Savoye,TopFolly 6
3Feb87-9Hia	7f :23 :46 1:23⁴ft	4½ 119	8⁸ 89½ 71¹ 71¹½	RomeroRP⁶	ⒻAw23000	72-18 Miss Alley Cat,SilverDora,Cascade 10
19Jan87-10Hia	7f :22⁴ :45³ 1:23⁴ft	3³ 112	75½ 75½ 53½ 3²	FrsE⁸ ⒻⓈCris EvertH		82-18 Jose'sBomb,StutteringSrh,PmelPul 8
21Sep86-10LaD	1½ :48 1:12³ 1:50⁴ft	6⁵ 112⁵	11¹⁵11¹⁶ 9¹³ 8¹⁶	BourquK⁹ ⒻLad Oaks		75-23 TopCorsg,HppyHllwMss,SclBsnss 11
28Aug86-6AP	1½ :46¹ 1:10³ 1:49²ft	6⁸ 112	8¹³ 71¹ 4⁸ 3¹⁰	BairdET⁸ ⒻArl Oaks		74-19 TopCorsage,LadyGallant,PmelPul 10
28Aug86—Grade III						
20Aug86-6AP	1⅟₁₆ ⓉⒹ:47 1:12²1:44¹fm	72 112	109½ 88½ 89½ 812½	BrdET⁷ ⒻPucker Up		73-11 TopCorsage,Mrinn'sGirl,Innsbruck 10
20Aug86—Grade III						
12Aug86-8Haw	a1 Ⓣ:48²1:13¹1:38⁴hd	5 115	57½ 7¹⁰ 41² 5⁹	Fires E²	ⒻAw17000	— — SgEppQun,HonyMcDn,OlBowWowr 8

Jly 24 AP 1 ft 1:40 b   Jly 10 AP 5f ft 1:00³ hg   Jly 3 AP 3f ft :37 b

I.

Juliet's Pet

Own.—Van Berg J C   116

B. m. 7, by Romeo—Nervous Pet, by Nervous Energy
Br.—Burns Patrick (Ky)
Tr.—Van Berg Jack C

			1987	9	2 1 0	$19,615
			1986	18	3 3 2	$46,915
	Lifetime	95 14 15 19	$267,553	Turf	19 1 4 3	$39,133

21Jun87-7CD	6½f :22³ :46 1:17 ft	7 117	4½ 63½ 5⁶ 51³	Miller S E ³	ⒻAw26100	82-17 Prime Union, Rita H., Allez Vite 6
6Jun87-7CD	1 :45⁴ 1:11¹ 1:36⁴ft	11 114	1hd 3¹ 56½ 5¹⁰	Bass S H ¹	ⒻAw29400	75-13 BriefFame,MissBlueprint,Shamritn 6
24May87-9CD	6f :21³ :45⁴ 1:11¹ft	6¼ 118	65½ 76½ 76¾ 5⁷	Bass S H ⁷	ⒻAw23000	80-19 DncngDmscs,SlvrPltdCd,MllPrspct 7
28Mar87-8OP	6f :22 :45³ 1:10²ft	3¼ 113	53½ 8⁵ 81¹ 71²¾	Walker B JJr²	ⒻHcpO	75-15 DoubleDrby,ThrArRinbows,MyMris 9
7Mar87-8OP	1 :45⁴ 1:10¹ 1:35³ft	3³ 117	81¹ 91⁸ 91⁸ 92⁸¼	JohnsnPA ⁹	ⒻAw25000	65-13 Ann'sBid,TylorsPromise,Dvy'sDrem 9
25Feb87-8OP	1⅟₁₆:47 1:12 1:43⁴ft	2½ 117	3² 63½ 79½ 81⁴	Day P ³	ⒻAw22000	68-22 NtiveStn.Dvy'sDrem,DoubleAdvntg 8
6Feb87-9TP	1⅟₁₆:47¹ 1:13 1:46³ft	*1 121	1½ 1² 1² 1½	Neff S ³	ⒻAw12600	77-31 Juliet'sPet,LndoftheBold,MenMurn 6
31Jan87-9TP	6½f :23² :46⁴ 1:18³gd	*1 122	4¹½ 44½ 3⁷ 2⁹	Neff S ⁵	ⒻWish Well	76-22 FantasyLover,Juliet'sPet,Ry'sPrise 9
21Jan87-9TP	6f :22 :46 1:12²ft	*4-5 119	2² 2¹½ 21½ 12½	Neff S ⁵	ⒻAw12850	82-27 Juliet's Pet, MissRedoy,NoonDance 7
31Dec86-9TP	1 :47¹ 1:12⁴ 1:40²m	*7-5 118	1² 12½ 12½ 14	Neff S ⁹	ⒻAw12400	73-30 Juliet'sPet,QueenAlph,MenMureen 9

Jly 22 AP 5f ft 1:01 b   Jly 10 AP 5f ft 1:00¹ h   Jly 3 AP 4f ft :48 h   Jun 18 CD 4f ft :49² b

27. Statistically, which Golden Gate maiden is least likely to win?

2nd Golden Gate

6 FURLONGS. (1.07⅘) MAIDEN. Purse $14,000. 3-year-olds. Weight, 120 lbs.

A.

Game Breaker

DOOCY T T

Own.—Geraldi M & N   120

Ro. g. 3, by Irish Stronghold—Little Laura G, by Catchpenny II
Br.—Geraldi M & N (Cal)
Tr.—Offield Duane

			1987	1 M 0 0		$1,050
			1986	1 M 0 1		$1,680
	Lifetime	2 0 0 1	$2,730			

4Apr87-1GG	6f :22 :44³ 1:10¹ft	9½ 120	3¹ 3¹ 33½ 46½	Doocy T T⁴	Mdn	81-12 ElTrmblor,FrOutPlsur,PrncHodown 7
3Sep86-8Bmf	6f :22⁴ :46¹ 1:12 ft	3-2 118	53½ 31½ 2½ 33½	Baze R A ⁵	ⓈMdn	75-21 DizzieBrgin,J.D.Commish,GmeBrekr 6

Apr 14 GG 4f ft :59¹ h   Mar 27 GG 6f ft 1:14² h   Mar 21 GG 4f m :50⁴ hg(d)   Mar 16 GG 5f ft 1:02¹ h

B.

Ballplayer Matthew

GONZALEZ R M

Own.—Dante–Dante–Dante   120

B. c. 3, by Fort Calgary—Power of Aza, by Wing Out
Br.—Dante T C (Cal)
Tr.—Retherford N J

		1986	0 M 0 0
	Lifetime	0 0 0 0	

Apr 11 GG 5f ft 1:00³ h   Apr 7 GG 5f ft 1:00² hg   Apr 1 GG 6f ft 1:14² h   Mar 25 GG 5f ft 1:02² h

C.

Sea Twist
BAZE E
Own.—Anderson D & Celeste
B. c. 3, by Fleet Twist—Sea I'm Lucky, by Windy Sea
120 Br.—Anderson D & Celeste (Cal) 1986 0 M 0 0
Tr.—Waletzko Lloyd V
Lifetime 0 0 0 0
●Apr 16 Pln 3f ft :35 h   Apr 13 Pln 3f ft :35² hg   Apr 9 Pln 6f ft 1:13¹ h   Apr 2 Pln 5f ft :58² h

D.

Sharp Port
DELAHOUSSAYE E
Own.—Golden Eagle Farm
Ch. c. 3, by Sharpen Up—Port Aransas, by Quack
Br.—Mabee Mr-Mrs J C (Ky) 1987 1 M 1 0 $2,800
120 Tr.—Sadler John W 1986 0 M 0 0
Lifetime 1 0 1 0 $2,800
28Mar87-3GG 6f :21⁴ :44⁴ 1:10 ft *9-5 120 4³ 3³ 3¹ 2¾ Delahoussaye E† Mdn 88-14 FriendlyForce,SharpPort,CrigRonld 8
28Mar87—Off slowly
Apr 12 Hol 6f ft 1:14⁴ h   Mar 23 SA 6f ft 1:16 h   Mar 17 SA 5f ft 1:01³ hg   Mar 9 SA 5f ft 1:00⁴ h

E.

Indian Flash
JUDICE J C
Own.—Lee K C
B. g. 3, by Opachisco—Nurse Lyphard, by Lyphard
Br.—Quality Broodmares Ltd (Ky) 1987 1 M 0 1 $1,650
120 Tr.—Foster Charles C 1986 0 M 0 0
Lifetime 1 0 0 1 $1,650
1Apr87-6GG 6f :22 :45¹ 1:10³ft 3 120 5⁴½ 3¹½ 3²½ 3³¼ Judice J C⁵ M32000 83-18 ExubrntFortun,Dr.Socko,IndinFlsh 11
Apr 17 BM 3f ft :36¹ h   Apr 13 BM 6f ft 1:13⁴ h   ●Mar 30 BM 4f ft :46² h   Mar 24 BM 6f ft 1:13³ hg

F.

Compound
BRINGHURST A
Own.—Summa Stable & Toffel
B. g. 3, by Dance Bid—Casa Do Oir, by Turn-to
Br.—Crook J B (Ky) 1987 1 M 0 0
115⁵ Tr.—Feld Jude T 1986 0 M 0 0
Lifetime 1 0 0 0
5Apr87-2SA 6f :21³ :45 1:11 ft 39 118 12¹⁴12¹²12¹⁵10¹³¾ Patterson A3̲ M32000 69-16 SuperbeKing,Gntout,ChoosyFrind 12
5Apr87—Pinched at start
Apr 13 SA 4f ft :47³ hg   Apr 1 SA 6f ft 1:18² h   Mar 25 SA 4f ft :47¹ hg   Mar 19 SA 5f ft 1:02³ hg

G.

North Swell
LAMBERT J
Own.—Gailyndel Farm
B. g. 3, by Balzac—Star Silhouette, by Dancer's Profile
Br.—Gailyndel Farm (NY) 1987 0 M 0 0
120 Tr.—Adams Elven 1986 0 M 0 0
Lifetime 0 0 0 0
Apr 16 GG 3f ft :36² h   Apr 11 GG Tr.1 5f ft :59² hg   Apr 7 GG 4f ft :48¹ hg   Mar 31 GG 7f ft 1:31³ h

H.

Craig Ronald
DIAZ A L
Own.—Bacharach M L
Ch. c. 3, by Mount Hagen—Sunney Regent, by Vice Regent
Br.—Bacharach Mr-Mrs M L (Cal) 1987 3 M 0 2 $4,410
120 Tr.—Delia William 1986 0 M 0 0
Lifetime 3 0 0 2 $4,410
28Mar87-3GG 6f :21⁴ :44⁴ 1:10 ft 9¾ 120 5⁴½ 5⁴½ 4² 3³¼ Diaz A L5̲ Mdn 86-14 FriendlyForce,SharpPort,CrigRonld 8
17Mar87-5GG 6f :21⁴ :45¹ 1:11 ft 5¼ 120 5³½ 4³½ 4⁴½ 5⁶¼ Gonzalez R M⁶ [S]Mdn 78-21 H'sADncngMn,FrndlyFrc,PrncHdn 7
10Feb87-6GG 6f :21⁴ :44² 1:09⁴ft 9¼ 120 3²½ 3³ 3¹½ 3¹¾ Diaz A L³ [S]Mdn 88-11 PridendRson,FrOutPlsur,CrigRonld 8
Apr 15 GG 4f ft :46⁴ h   Apr 9 GG 7f ft 1:30³ h   Mar 16 GG 3f ft :36 h   Mar 10 GG 6f ft 1:13² h

28.

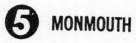

5 MONMOUTH

1 MILE. (1.34⅗) CLAIMING. PUrse $10,000. 3-year-olds and upward. Weight, 3-year-olds, 115 lbs. Older, 122 lbs. Non-winners of three races at one mile or over since June 23 allowed 3 lbs. Two such race, 5 lbs. One such race, 7 lbs. Claiming price $16,000; for each $500 to $14,000, 1 lb. (Races where entered for $12,000 or less not considerd.)

A.

Ambassadorship
Own.—Lagarte Stable
Ch. h. 5, by Our Native—Journey, by What A Pleasure
$14,000 Br.—North Ridge Farm (Ky)
Tr.—Caceres Erickson
111
Lifetime 1987 20 1 1 6 $26,435
44 2 2 10 1986 17 1 0 1 $10,800
$46,075 Turf 6 0 0 0 $140
27Jly87- 1Bel fst 1$\frac{1}{16}$:47⅖ 1:10⅖ 1:45 Clm 13000 1 8 8⁸½ 5⁵½ 5³ 3⁴¼ Velasquez J b 117 6.80 73-21 Sound Proof 117¹¼ Arctic Song 117³ Ambassadorship117¾ Rallied 9
15Jly87- 9Bel fst 7f :23 :46⅗ 1:25⅕ Clm 13000 9 12 12¹⁷11¹⁴ 6⁸ 4⁵¾ Hernandez R b 115 11.50 70-20 Mr. Fife 117⁴¾ Full of Spice 113¾ Cannon Royal 112ⁿᵏ Wide str 12
8Jly87- 9Bel sly 1$\frac{1}{16}$:46⅘ 1:12 1:45⅖ Clm 13000 4 6 6¹¹ 6⁷½ 5⁸½ 3¹¹ Hernandez R b 115 8.40 64-25 Mr. Fife113ⁿᵒConcealedIdentity117¹¹Ambassadorship115¾ Rallied 7
27Jun87- 4Mth sly 1$\frac{1}{16}$:46⅘ 1:11⅖ 1:44⅖ 3+Clm 20000 7 6 7¹⁶ 7¹⁷ 6²¹ 5²¹¼ Rujano M b 114 28.60 62-18 SirPrizeBirthdy1172¾PrrishPrince1115¾ClerThRunwy1122¼ Outrun 7

21Jun87- 9Bel	my	7f	:22⅘ :45⅗ 1:22⅘	Clm 20000	11 8 76 812 816 819	Messina R	b 113	20.50	71-10 Truth Be Told 11210 Temperate 1171 Wicked Wike 117¾	Outrun	11
15Jun87- 1Bel	fst	1	:46⅖ 1:11⅕ 1:36⅗	Clm 20000	7 6 611 68½ 69¾ 414¾	Vasquez M M	b 113	9.90	68-19 Over the Wall 1155½ Golden Chief 117[illegible] Sound Proof1154¾	Outrun	7
23May87- 1Bel	gd	1	Ⓣ:46⅖ 1:11 1:37⅘	Clm 75000	6 9 916 917 918 919¾	Vasquez M M	b 112	24.70	57-25 AllHandsOnDeck118no HawaiianEye116[illegible]essLeder1126	Outrun	9
14May87- 9Bel	fst	7f	:22⅗ :45⅕ 1:23⅗	Clm 20000	9 10 1113 109½ 73¾ 33	Vasquez M M	b 113	11.40	82-13 RusticRomnc1172¾PrintMony119¾Amb[illegible]p1131	Wide; rallied	12
4May87- 9Aqu	sly	1	:46⅘ 1:12⅖ 1:38⅕	Clm 22500	8 9 911 911 911 67½	Badamo J J	b 115	9.00	67-27 Print Money 1151¾ Cowboy Up 1133 Froun And Tall112no	Outrun	9
1May87- 9Aqu	fst	7f	:22⅗ :45⅖ 1:23⅘	Clm 17500	8 11 118¾ 107½ 63½ 21½	Hernandez R	b 119	8.90	80-16 SunnyStar1131½Ambassadorship119¾[illegible]ide115no	Gained place	12

LATEST WORKOUTS Jly 22 Aqu [•] 4f fst :50⅗ b Jly 4 Aqu 5f fst 1:02⅖ h (d) Jun 8 Aqu 5f fst 1:03⅖ b

B.

Klassy Serenade
Own.—Cataldo J H

Dk. b. or br. g. 5, by Klassy Flight—Carolyns Serenade, by Royal Serenade
$16,000 Br.—Cataldo J H (NJ)
Tr.—Serpe Philip M

115

Lifetime							
38 9 2 4	1987	?	0	0	2		$3,440
$70.088	1986	??	8	2	2		$61,263
	Turf	5	0	2	1		$3,990

22Jly87- 7Mth	fst	6f	:21⅘ :45⅕ 1:11⅗	3↑[S]Clm 20000	7 6 67½ 54¾ 65 62½	Edwards J W	b 116	3.30	79-21 Fast Caz 116no SmokinDuck114no NoodlePudding116no	Raced wide	7
15Jly87- 3Mth	fst	1 1/16	:46⅘ 1:12 1:44⅗	3↑ Clm 20000	6 3 34 2½ 41¼ 35¾	Edwards J W	b 115	22.10	77-20 PrrishPrince1171¼MountineerJoe1154KlssySerende1153	Crowded	6
8Jly87- 5Mth	sly	170	1:43⅕	3↑ Clm 25000	5 5 64½ 56½ 514 521	Santagata N	b 115	4.70e	59-22 Prospector Al 108nk NoodlePudding1116½Lumumba115nk	Bore out	7
5Jun87- 8Mth	gd	6f	:22⅗ :46 1:11⅕	3↑[S]Alw 21200	4 6 63½ 64½ 75½ 79¼	Madrid A Jr	b 116	42.30	75-23 MichaelN'Henry116no PrimeTimeGuy1164BornToShop114¾	Outrun	8
25May87- 6GS	fst	6f	:22 :45⅕ 1:11	3↑[S]Handicap	5 3 66½ 79¾ 610 617¾	Edwards J W	b 115	12.30	69-24 Lakeside City 114no Quadall 1121¾ Bob K. 1082½	Outrun	7
6May87- 8GS	fst	1 1/16	:47⅕ 1:11⅘ 1:45⅖	3↑ Clm 45000	1 3 46½ 68 611 620¾	Edwards J W	b 115	2.70e	60-23 Lumumba 1125¼ Million Dollar Boy 115½TwiceTheStar116no	Tired	7
27Apr87- 8GS	fm	5f	Ⓣ:22⅕ :46⅕ :59⅕	3↑ Alw 8500s	9 6 55 43½ 52½ 31½	Vigliotti M J	b 114	2.20	89-09 AnotherMember1121¼SaintMchree114hdKlssySerende1141	Rallied	11
16Apr87- 8GS	gd	6f	:22⅖ :46 1:11⅕	Clm 50000	4 4 41½ 44 45½ 46½	Vigliotti M J	b 116	16.20	79-25 TwiceTheStar116nk DungarvinKing1161¼GrndHorizon's1165	Evenly	7
19Dec86- 1Aqu	my	6f	[•]:22⅘ :46⅗ 1:11⅕	3↑ Clm 45000	4 4 52½ 52¼ 66¾ 610¾	McCauley W H	b 118	7.90	77-20 Don't Hesitate 108hd Harry L. 1173¾ Father Roland 108¾	Tired	6
3Dec86- 9Med	my	6f	:22⅘ :47 1:11⅗	3↑[S]Alw 20000	3 2 22 1hd 12½ 11½	Madrid A Jr	b 122	*1.00	84-21 Klassy Serenade 1221½ Redsom 1153 Seapatrick 115½	Driving	5

LATEST WORKOUTS Jly 7 Mth 3f fst :38 b

C.

Ruler Champ
Own.—Mara T D

B. h. 5, by Iron Ruler—Fabulous Jewel, by Raja Baba
$14,000 Br.—Wold Elaine J (Fla)
Tr.—Solano R

111

Lifetime						
30 5 6 3	1987	9	0	1	0	$6,880
$114.560	1986	8	2	1	2	$50,800

1Jly87- 1Bel	fst	7f	:23⅕ :47 1:24⅕	Clm 17500	7 6 54 74½ 79½ 720	Lovato F Jr	117	9.20	61-22 Askrano 1177 Better Be Single 113nk Attribute 1101¼	Tired badly	8
10Jun87- 3Bel	fst	7f	:23⅕ :46⅖ 1:24⅕	Clm 35000	5 5 31½ 88½ 1018 1020¼	Cordero A Jr	b 117	10.10	61-17 Rexson's Quill 1171½ JohnMuir117hdGrandRivulet1171¼	Brief foot	10
18May87- 5Bel	fst	7f	:22 :44⅖ 1:22⅘	Clm 70000	6 5 54 56½ 818 822	Guerra W A	b 113	27.60	66-15 Tonka Pass 1173 Mr. Tatt 108hd One Bon Bon 1131¾	Fin. early	8
22Apr87- 1Aqu	fst	1⅛	:50 1:14⅘ 1:52⅗	Clm c-25000	5 1 1½ 2hd 1hd 2nk	Cordero A Jr	b 117	*2.20	72-27 Quiet Royalty 117nk RulerChamp117noNijinsky'sRuler1172½	Sharp	8
6Apr87- 3Aqu	sly	1	:45⅗ 1:10⅕ 1:36⅖	Clm 35000	6 3 31½ 33 46½ 49½	Cordero A Jr	b 117	*1.70	75-20 Bienestar 1136 Go Renor 1152¾ Lord's Wish 117½	Weakened	7
26Mar87- 3Aqu	fst	1	:45⅗ 1:09⅘ 1:35⅖	Clm 45000	1 5 42 42½ 32½ 43¾	Cordero A Jr	b 116	5.30	85-25 Revelrout 1141½ Keep It Easy 119nk Dale's Folly 1132	Weakened	9
16Mar87- 5Aqu	fst	7f	:23⅕ :47 1:24⅘	Clm 70000	5 4 2½ 3nk 67 510½	Davis R G	b 113	16.90	66-30 Scholars Task 117nk Cool Joe 1142¾ Silver Slate 1136	Weakened	7
14Feb87- 7Aqu	fst	6f	[•]:22⅕ :46 1:11⅘	Alw 40000	1 6 63½ 74¾ 86¾ 713½	Nuesch D5	b 110	27.00	74-21 What An Entrance 115no Cool Joe 1153RoyalDoulton115¾	Outrun	11
2Feb87- 8Aqu	sly	6f	[•]:21⅘ :45⅖ 1:10⅖	Alw 33000	5 4 710 710 611 614	Ortiz E Jr5	b 112	20.70	78-24 Majestic Empire 1196 Shine Diulus 114nkAswanHigh1173½	Outrun	7
27Apr86- 7Aqu	fst	1	:45⅘ 1:10⅗ 1:36⅘	3↑ Alw 40000	2 1 1½ 1hd 31 53	Guerra W A	b 124	14.50	79-20 Computer'sChoice119nkGrndRivult1192½NoisyWhnHot119no	Tired	6

LATEST WORKOUTS Jly 14 Mth 6f fst 1:18⅘ b Jun 28 Bel tr.t 4f my :48 h (d) Jun 21 Bel tr.t 4f sly :48 h

D.

Flawless Rock
Own.—Filios L A

Dk. b. or br. c. 4, by Blood Royal—Pyridoxine, by What Luck
$16,000 Br.—Filios L A (NJ)
Tr.—Gross George F

115

Lifetime						
9 2 2 0	1987	5	1	1	0	$7,479
$15.719	1986	4	1	1	0	$8,240

15Jly87- 2Mth	fst	1	:46⅘ 1:12 1:39⅘	3↑ Clm 10000	6 6 59 55 31 1nk	Lopez C	115	26.40	74-21 Flawless Rock 115nk My OldSchool1131[D]NeverSassy1151	Driving	9
11Jly87- 4Mth	fst	1 1/16	:46⅕ 1:10⅘ 1:44⅖	3↑ Clm 12500	1 3 44½ 44½ 56½ 59½	Lopez C	115	25.30	73-14 Chimney Sweep 1171½ Mike's Boat 1154MajesticBurst113no	Tired	9
9Jun87- 2Mth	fst	170	:46⅗ 1:11⅘ 1:42⅖	3↑ Clm 6250	7 4 42 3nk 2½ 25	Lopez C	115	3.40	79-19 Rava Ruler 1135 Flawless Rock 115no Oconto 1153	Held place	8
26May87- 8GS	fst	6f	:22⅖ :45⅘ 1:11⅕	3↑[S]Clm 12500	4 3 44 410 413 516	Thomas D B	116	10.00	70-23 MichaelN'Henry1167½ProudCaptin1222Nicky'sInterest1194½	Tired	5
7May87- 9GS	fst	6f	:22⅘ :46⅗ 1:12⅕	3↑[S]Alw 13125	2 5 65½ 68½ 612 515	Thomas D B	116	12.90	66-21 The Buff 1167 All the Numbers 1165 Jasperado 1102	No factor	6
19Aug86- 7Mth	fst	1	:46⅘ 1:11⅗ 1:37⅘	3↑[S]Alw 18700	4 11 85½ 73½ 43½ 23½	Vega A	111	40.00	80-18 Smart Liberal 1153½ Flawless Rock 111½ Almamar 115hd	Gaining	11
7Aug86- 1Mth	fst	170	:47⅖ 1:12⅗ 1:44⅗	3↑[S]Md 12500	1 4 43½ 43½ 21 11½	Vega A	115	5.80	73-20 FlwlessRock1151½Duk'sImprssion1156½Suntun'sLgcy1183	Driving	8
30Jun86- 9Mth	fst	6f	:23⅕ :47⅕ 1:14⅖	3↑ Md 14000	8 10 87½ 812 89¾ 76¾	Rujano M	114	70.60	61-27 Strike Paydirt 115¾ NancyTheGolfer115½PopPopLove115¾	Outrun	10
11Jun86- 4Mth	fst	6f	:23 :46⅗ 1:12⅕	3↑ Md 16000	9 10 99¼ 913 917 816½	Sousonis S5	110	39.60	62-23 Birdie's Comet 1084 Bucktracer120noElectionPreview1152	Outrun	11

LATEST WORKOUTS Jly 7 Mth 4f fst :50 b

E.

Norman's Ryan
Own.—Seltzer N

B. g. 5, by Restless Native—Marian Bender, by Bold Monarch
$16,000 Br.—Seltzer Norman (Md)
Tr.—Gibson Ronald

115

Lifetime						
13 2 0 0	1987	6	1	0	0	$7,515
$15.975	1986	6	1	0	0	$8,460
	Turf	5	0	0	0	$870

15Jly87- 5Mth	fst	6f	:23 :46⅕ 1:11⅗	3↑ Clm 25000	5 7 78¾ 78½ 77¾ 711¾	Rivera M A	b 116	18.90	71-20 Obgyn 119nd Spiderman 116no Community Hall 117no	Trailed	7
6Jun87- 6Mth	fm	1	Ⓣ:46⅘ 1:10⅘ 1:36⅕	3↑ Alw 17000	3 8 814 812 816 821	Thomas D B	b 118	18.10	73-11 Yucca 1128 Allemande 111hd Woodcock 118no	Trailed	8
30May87- 5Mth	fm	1 1/16	Ⓣ:47⅕ 1:11⅖ 1:43⅘+	3↑ Clm 40000	3 1 12 1hd 1½ 44	Thomas D B	b 115	16.10	78-09 Bud Collins 1111 LamontCranston1142½Woodcock115½	Weakened	6
24May87- 7Bel	fst	6f	:22⅕ :44⅘ 1:09⅕	3↑ Alw 27000	2 5 89½ 912 916 815	Garcia J A	b 119	60.40	79-16 Diamond Knight 1101½ Krul 112hd Damascus Drama 1143½	Outrun	9
14May87- 9GS	fst	6f	:22⅖ :45⅘ 1:11⅗	3↑ Alw 11500	4 6 64½ 63½ 65 54½	Thomas D B	b 119	5.00	80-23 RuleroftheFleet1121½PickedClean1161½Seaptrick1161	No menace	7
2Apr87- 8GS	fst	6f	:22⅖ :46⅖ 1:13	Alw 10500	3 6 611 57 32 13½	Thomas D B	117	7.00	77-29 Norman'sRyan1173½Justafull117nkHownowbrowncow117½	Driving	6
18Sep86- 8Med	fm	1	[T]:46⅗ 1:10⅘ 1:36	3↑ Alw 15000	3 5 54½ 810 913 823¾	Rujano M	117	21.80	74-09 Looming Libra 1131 Summer Colony 1131½ Woodcock 1195	Tired	9
8Sep86- 7Bel	fm	1	Ⓣ:46 1:10 1:35⅖	3↑ Alw 25000	9 1 2hd 53½ 68 99½	Santos J A	117	49.10	78-18 Stage Setter 1171½ Blinkers 1131½ Clover King 1174	Tired	12
29Aug86- 4Med	fm	1	[T]:45⅖ 1:10 1:36⅗	3↑ Alw 15000	1 8 1013 923 719 719	Santos J A	117	4.70	76-03 Defarge 1175 Restless Abert 1114 Cold Feet II 117no	Outrun	10
14Jly86- 4Mth	fst	1⅛	:47⅖ 1:11⅘ 1:51⅕	3↑ Alw 14000	9 1 1½ 1½ 31½ 44½	Rujano M	119	6.80	73-23 Bold Screen 113hd Wimpole Mews 1142 OwensTroupe1122½	Tired	9

LATEST WORKOUTS Jly 25 Mth 5f fst 1:03 b Jly 11 Mth 4f fst :52 b

F.

Daytime Friend
Own.—Greenspan & Werner

B. g. 4, by Upper Nile—Pretty Pretender, by Quack
$16,000 Br.—Firman Pamela H (Ky)
Tr.—Maxwell Paul

117

Lifetime						
20 2 6 4	1987	3	1	0	0	$8,600
$39.635	1986	13	1	5	2	$24,615
	Turf	8	0	3	1	$12,535

13Jly87- 6Mth	fst	170	:46⅗ 1:12 1:44⅕	3↑ Clm 16000	2 4 55½ 22 21½ 12½	Rivera M A	b 115	29.10	75-21 Daytime Friend 1152½ Senor Smoke 1154½Participate1111	Driving	8
4Jly87- 3Mth	fst	1⅛	:47 1:11⅕ 1:49⅖	3↑ Clm 20000	4 2 22½ 43 711 717½	Rivera M A	b 115	20.00	69-10 Parrish Prince1116½StrangeBehavior1151½SportingFree1063	Tired	9
16Jun87- 10Mth	fst	6f	:22⅘ :45⅗ 1:10⅕	3↑ Clm 16000	2 6 54 46 411 511¾	Rivera M A	b 116	17.70	77-17 StrightDncer112noLuckyAppel1161½Bolro'sBusinss1169	Weakened	8
3Nov86- 9Med	fm	5f	[T]:22⅗ :45 :58	3↑ Alw 14000	7 7 74 76 88½ 88	Madrid A Jr	b 114	20.90	91-03 Awesome Rebel 106½ Another Ripple 116½ Averno 1071	Outrun	9
25Sep86- 8Med	fm	1 1/16	[T]:47⅕ 1:12 1:44	Clm 50000	4 7 64½ 74¾ 67 59¼	McCauley W H	b 119	6.40	74-09 Tony'sHio116nkNoodlePudding1123EskimoPoint114hd	No menace	8
18Sep86- 8Med	fm	1	[T]:46⅗ 1:10⅘ 1:36	3↑ Alw 15000	7 8 76 78¼ 57 510½	Antley C W	b 113	3.50e	87-09 LoomingLibr1131SummerColony1131½Woodcock1195	No menace	9
9Sep86- 9Med	fm	1 1/16	[T]:46⅗ 1:10⅘ 1:43⅕	3↑ Alw 15000	1 6 75¾ 64½ 41½ 21½	Antley C W	b 113	3.80e	85-12 Captain Arthur 1131½ Daytime Friend 113¾AbieFatS.1122½	Rallied	9
22Aug86- 10Mth	fst	1 1/16	:47⅘ 1:13⅕ 1:45⅖	3↑ Md Sp Wt	1 4 32 2hd 2hd 1nk	Antley C W	b 115	*1.10	78-18 Daytime Friend 115nk Almarine1157BeyondTheDepth1157	Driving	9
5Aug86- 10Mth	fm	1	Ⓣ:49 1:13⅘ 1:41⅕	3↑ Md Sp Wt	3 4 41½ 41½ 62¾ 53¾	Miller B7	b 108	2.30	65-27 Npotism1221¼Hctor'sPup115½StrongCommtmnt1152	No response	10
28Jly86- 5Mth	fst	6f	:22⅘ :45⅘ 1:11⅕	3↑ Md Sp Wt	1 6 68¼ 57¾ 57½ 25½	Miller B7	b 109	4.80	78-17 Look Tom Look 1165½ DaytimeFriend1091Savoy1112	Stumbled st.	6

LATEST WORKOUTS Jly 25 Mth 6f fst 1:15 b Jun 25 Mth 6f fst 1:14⅖ h Jun 10 Mth 6f fst 1:14 hg Jun 3 Mth 6f fst 1:15 b

G.

Law Talk
Own.—Jaranrain J
B. h. 7, by Wardlaw—Tellinoid, by Captain's Gig
$16,000 Br.—Fuentes & Hayman S L (Fla)
Tr.—Tropia Anthony
115
Lifetime 50 9 6 9 $180,593
1987 8 2 1 0 $22,930
1986 16 3 2 2 $51,196
Turf 3 0 0 0

15Jun87- 1Bel fst 1 :46⅖ 1:11⅕ 1:36⅘ Clm 25000 4 1 1hd 2½ 3½ 717¾ Migliore R 117 *1.90 64-19 Over the Wall 1155½ Golden Chief1174SoundProof1154¾ ReL sore 7
7Jun87- 7Bel fst 1⅛ :47⅕ 1:11⅗ 1:42⅘ 3+Alw 45000 6 2 2½ 4½ 714 722¾ Thibeau R J 117 23.20 65-22 Set Style 1172 CutlassReality1177Getreadyfortheshow1092½ Tired 7
29May87- 1Bel fst 1⅛ :47 1:11 1:42⅖ Clm 25000 6 1 1½ 1½ 1hd 21½ Migliore R 117 3.20 89-13 Bar None 1171½ Law Talk 1172½McMichael1171¾ Savaged another 7
22May87- 1Bel fst 1⅛ :46⅘ 1:11⅗ 1:43⅘ Clm 17500 3 2 11 11½ 12 11½ Migliore R 117 *.60 83-20 Law Talk 1171½ Sound Proof 119½ Solo Sporting 1081½ Driving 7
17May87- 9Bel fst 1⅛ :46⅘ 1:11⅕ 1:50⅕ Clm 14000 2 1 14 12½ 14 17¾ Ward W A 117 3.20 76-20 Law Talk 1177¾ RoyalSamurai1082LeadTneWay1143 Bore in, clear 10
13May87- 9Bel fst 7f :22⅘ :46⅕ 1:24 Clm 14000 11 7 75½ 41 31 4¾ Ward W A 117 14.70 81-18 Liberty Rex 110½ Flip For J.K.115hdCannonRoyal117nk Weakened 12
1May87- 9Aqu fst 7f :22⅗ :45⅖ 1:23⅘ Clm 17500 4 4 1hd 11 84½ 911¼ Messina R 117 8.40 71-18 SunnyStar1131½Ambssdorship119½NorthGlde115no Set pace, tired 12
22Apr87- 2Aqu fst 6f :22⅗ :46⅕ 1:12⅛ Clm 17500 5 2 1hd 1hd 2hd 72½ Messina R 117 13.80 77-27 Spectacular Cat 117½ In Law 117nd Royal Rickie 1171 Tired 10
8Nov86- 6Aqu sly 1⅛ :48⅗ 1:11⅗ 1:51 3+Clm 35000 4 — — — — 24½ Messina R 117 5.90 75-22 Frontier Justice 1174½ Law Talk 117hd Revelrout 1171½ Fog 7
3Nov86- 5Aqu fst 7f :22⅘ :45⅕ 1:23 3+Clm 50000 6 6 11½ 11 41½ 78½ Messina R 117 20.70 77-22 Harry L. 1171 Stark Secret 117½ Frontier Justice 1172½ Tired 12
LATEST WORKOUTS ●Jly 29 Aqu ⊡ 5f fst 1:02⅕ b Jly 22 Aqu ⊡ 5f fst 1:00 h Jly 18 Aqu 3f fst :35⅖ h

H.

For Certain Doc
Own.—Chuckalow Stable
Dk. b. or br. h. 5, by Doc Sylvester—For Certain, by In Reality
$16,000 Br.—Parr E Q (Ky)
Tr.—Anderson William D
115
Lifetime 61 5 6 3 $262,785
1987 10 1 0 1 $11,940
1986 17 0 2 0 $14,700
Turf 7 1 0 1 $21,459

17Jly87- 7Mth fst 6f :22⅗ :45⅖ 1:10 3+Clm 40000 6 1 62¾ 79¾ 715 721 Vigliotti M J b 116 36.90 69-19 ScreenTrend1197WintrlimSport115hdClssicImpct1133½ No threat 7
28Jun87- 8Pha fst 6f :22⅕ :45⅗ 1:11⅗ 3+Clm 50000 7 6 712 713 716 715½ Black A S b 116 30.90 67-32 Just Terrific 116no Quadall 112no Sunny Cabin 1072½ Trailed 7
6May87- 8GS fst 1⅛ :47⅕ 1:11⅘ 1:45⅖ 3+Clm 45000 5 7 710 716 718 721½ Romero J A5 b 109 15.50 60-23 Lumumba 1125¼ Million DollarBoy115½TwiceTheStar116no Trailed 7
22Apr87- 8GS fm 1⅛ Ⓣ:47⅗ 1:12⅗ 1:44⅗ Clm 50000 9 3 2½ 42½1021 1031 Romero J A5 b 111 20.50 54-15 L'EtoileDuNord1162Mr.FortyNiner1161½ChespkBch1143½ Stopped 10
4Apr87- 6GS gd 6f :21⅗ :44⅖ 1:10 3+Handicap 2 9 86 89¾ 88¾ 912 Ferrer J C b 112 19.20 80-15 Danny'sKeys117nkCountOnRomeo115hdSuperDelight117nk Outrun 9
23Mar87- 9GS fst 1⅛ :46⅗ 1:12⅕ 1:46⅕ Clm 50000 1 4 36½ 24 3½ 42¼ Vigliotti M J b 116 16.20 75-25 ChiefLouie1121½VictoryAtNewport119½HailToNuset114nk Brushed 8
28Feb87- 6GS fst 6f :22⅕ :45⅗ 1:11⅕ Alw 15000 1 5 44½ 44½ 57¼ 59¾ Vigliotti M J b 114 5.20 76-26 My Rex 117nk Just Terrific 122½ Jay Bar Toughie 1142 Outrun 5
14Feb87- 6GS fst 6f :22⅕ :46 1:11⅘ Alw 15000 4 5 54½ 63¾ 53¾ 35½ Vigliotti M J b 114 2.20 80-21 Lil Tyler 1163 AlaskanGambler1142½ForCertainDoc114nk Steadied 6
4Feb87- 8Pha gd 6f :22⅕ :46 1:11⅗ Alw 15000 2 6 41½ 41¾ 3½ 11½ Vigliotti M J b 114 8.20 83-28 For Certain Doc 1141½ Lil Tyler 1154½ ReliableJeff115hd Drew out 6
10Jan87- 3Aqu gd 6f ⊡:22⅘ :45⅗ 1:10⅕ Clm 45000 7 1 106½ 86½ 87¾107¾ Baird E T5 b 108 12.70 85-10 Tis Royal 1132¼ Sports Medicine 113½ Semaj 1151 Outrun 11
LATEST WORKOUTS Jun 21 Pha 6f fst 1:15⅕ b Jun 9 GS 5f fst 1:00⅗ h Jun 3 GS 4f fst :51⅕ b

29. The track is muddy. It's Jan. 9. Which horse figures to win?

8th Santa Anita

6½ FURLONGS
SANTA ANITA
OUT OF CHUTE
FINISH

6 ½ FURLONGS. (1.14) CLASSIFIED ALLOWANCE. Purse $45,000. 4-year-olds and upward. Non-winners of $19,500 since May 1. Weights, 4-year-olds, 120 lbs.; older, 121 lbs. Non-winners of $16,000 twice since then allowed 3 lbs.; of $18,000 since July 22, 5 lbs.; of such a race since April 21 or $19,250 in 1986-87, 7 lbs. (Claiming races not considered.)

A.

Innamorato
PINCAY L JR
Own.—Duckett & Paniolo Ranch
116
Ch. h. 6, by Blushing Groom—Out Draw, by Speak John
Br.—Elmendorf Farm (Ky)
Tr.—Robbins Jay M
Lifetime 25 5 3 2 $219,398
1986 12 1 2 1 $108,264
1985 7 2 0 1 $104,800
Turf 9 2 1 0 $6,334

2Nov86-7SA 7f :22² :44² 1:21²ft 9-5 114 34½ 33½ 47½ 59¾ Olivares F4 Eillo 83-10 Sure To Fire, Rosie's K. T., Estate 5
2Nov86—Bumped, steadied into stretch
16Oct86-8SA 1 :46 1:10² 1:35³ft 4½ 117 3½ 21½ 23½ 27 Olivares F6 Aw45000 83-19 Hatim, Innamorato, 7
16Oct86—5 Horse Accident
30Aug86-6AP 1 :44³ 1:08¹ 1:34 ft 3¾ 114 56 68¼ 612 615½ HawleyS6 Eqp Mle H 75-15 Smile, Taylor's Special, Red Attack 7
30Aug86—Grade III
17Aug86-8Sar 7f :21⁴ :44¹ 1:21¹m 17 110 55½ 47 46½ 35½ Davis RG8 Forego H 90-11 Groovy, Turkoman, Innamorato 8
17Aug86—Grade II
22Jun86-8Hol 1⅛ :46³ 1:10² 1:47³ft 51 112 2½ 2hd 55 55¼ Olivares F7 Bel Air H 94-08 SuperDiamond,Alphbtim,‡Skywlker 8
22Jun86—Grade III; Wide 7/8 turn
1Jun86-8Hol 1 :44¹ 1:08² 1:33³ft 71 116 56½ 56 56 46¼ Olivares F7 Calfrn 88-14 Precisionist,SuperDimond,Skywlkr 7
1Jun86—Grade I
18May86-8Hol 7f :21¹ :43⁴ 1:21 ft 23 113 58 53½ 3½ 21¾ OlivaresF4 Trpl Bnd H 97-08 Sabona, Innamorato, Michadilla 6
18May86—Brushed midstretch
27Apr86-8Hol 1 :44³ 1:09¹ 1:34⁴ft 8¾ 112 32 43 54½ 57¾ OlivrsF4 M Le Roy H 81-15 Skywalker, Sabona, Al Mamoon 8
27Apr86—Grade II
13Apr86-8SA 1⅛ :45¹ 1:09³ 1:47³ft 12 112 2½ 45½ 418 422¾ HwleyS3 Sn Bnrdno H 68-15 Precisionist, Greinton, Encolure 4
13Apr86—Grade II
28Mar86-7SA 1 :45 1:09³ 1:36¹ft 6¾ 117 16 14½ 14 15 Hawley S2 Aw39000 87-19 Innamorato,Infantryman,Michadilla 6
28Mar86—Bumped start
Jan 6 SA 5f gd 1:01¹ h Dec 26 SA 5f ft :59¹ h Dec 20 SA 4f ft :49³ h Dec 3 SA 7f ft 1:26 h

B.

Tile
SIBILLE R
Own.—Franks John
113
Ch. c. 4, by Honest Plesaure—Kashan, by Damascus
Br.—ClaiborneFm&TheGmelyCorp (Ky)
Tr.—Brothers Frank L
Lifetime 10 4 0 0 $90,244
1986 2 0 0 0 $2,625
1985 8 4 0 0 $87,619

21Dec86-5Hol 6f :22¹ :45² 1:10³ft 5½ 115 1½ 2hd 2hd 41¾ Sibille R3 Aw35000 89-15 MFvrtMmnt,McLndn,AmrcnStndrd 6
12Jan86-10FG 6f :22¹ :47 1:12⁴ft 6¾ 119 97¾ 87½12151110¾ WdsCRJr6 MstrDrbyH 70-35 Doonesbear,Eustoo,NewPlymouth 12

31Dec85-10FG 6f :221 :464 1:132gd *2 121 98¼ 68 69 66½ MIncL9 Sugar Bowl H 71-31 Eustoo,SwinginSway,TimelyAlbert 10

31Dec85—Run in two divisions

28Nov85-9CD 1 1/16 :484 1:141 1:464m 4 122 1hd 1½ 99¾ 913½ MInconL7 Ky Jky Clb 60-27 MustinLke,BchelorBeu,ReglDremr 10

28Nov85—Grade III

9Nov85-8CD 1 :451 1:101 1:371ft *1 122 69 54 21 1hd Day P5 Iroquois 83-23 Tile,BachelorBeau,DncetotheWire 11

29Oct85-8CD 1 :464 1:13 1:391ft *3-5 121 53 2hd 2hd 12 Day P4 Aw18275 73-24 Tile, Doonesbear, Dance totheWire 7

14Aug85-8Sar 6f :214 :45 1:103ft 6 119 33 55½ 66 56½ Day P1 Sanford 80-17 SovereignDon,Roy,CauseForPause 9

14Aug85—Grade II

2Aug85-8Sar 6f :22 :454 1:112ft *4-5 122 84½ 86¼ 811 612 MeInconL5 Sar Spcl 71-17 SovereignDon,HgleyMill,BulletBlde 9

2Aug85—Grade II

28Jun85-8CD 5½f :224 :462 1:042ft 9-5e 115 1½ 11½ 14 16 MInconL3 Bashford M 99-14 Tile, Tug, Sir Grandeur 12

18May85-3CD 4½f :231 :463 :524ft *3-5 118 5 3nk 1hd 11½ Allen K K6 Mdn 93-07 Tile, Stellar Rival, Valiant Champ 7

Jan 6 SA 3f gd :361 h Dec 31 SA 4f ft :491 h ●Dec 18 Hol 4f ft :463 hg Dec 4 Hol 5f ft 1:013 hg

C.

Hilco Scamper B. g. 4, by Knights Choice—Lucky Sport, by Snow Sporting

STEVENS G L **113** Br.—Roche J & Mary (Wash) 1986 1 0 0 0

Own.—Cross-Roche-Wright Tr.—Chambers Mike 1985 6 5 0 0 $229,055

Lifetime 7 5 0 0 $229,055

26Dec86-8SA 7f :222 :444 1:213ft 2½ 120 2hd 1hd 21½ 69 StevnsGL5 Malibu 83-13 Ferdinand, Snow Chief,DonB.Blue 12

26Dec86—Grade II

25Aug85-8Sar 6½f :22 :45 1:182sy *4-5 122 11½ 2hd 23 711¼ StevnsGL5 Hopeful 69-19 PaplPower,Dnny'sKeys,BulletBlde 10

25Aug85—Grade I

10Aug85-9Mth 6f :214 :442 1:104ft *1-2 122 15 17 16 13 StevnsGL6 Sapling 86-13 HilcoScmper,Dnny'sKeys,Mr.Spiffy 9

10Aug85—Grade II; Bumped start

20Jly85-8Hol 6f :214 :444 1:094ft *2-5 120 21½ 1½ 16 17½ StvnsGL5 Hol Jv Chp 98-07 HlcoScmpr,LttlRdCld,Exbrnt'sImg 9

20Jly85—Grade II

30Jun85-5Hol 5½f :212 :433 1:024ft *4-5 117 16 17 16½ 14½ StevensGL1 Dsrt Wine — — HlcoScmpr,LttlRdCloud,SrMhmoud 9

19Jun85-8GG 5½f :212 :443 1:03 ft *2-3 117 11½ 15 18 16 Baze RA6 Tan Kndgtn 96-12 HilcoScamper,Khorseecn,SugrPine 8

18May85-4Lga 5f :221 :444 :564ft *7-5 120 1½ 13 15 115 Baze G2 Mdn 92-18 Hilco Scamper, Hat Rock, Zacbee 8

●Jan 6 SA 4f gd :463 h ●Dec 21 SA 5f ft :582 h ●Dec 16 SA 1 ft 1:41 h ●Dec 11 SA 5f ft :582 h

D.

My Favorite Moment B. h. 6, by Timeless Moment—My Masindi, by Dragante

VALENZUELA P A **118** Br.—Dinnaken Farm (Ky) 1986 4 1 1 1 $31,750

Own.—Conners W L Tr.—Stute Warren 1985 11 4 0 3 $117,250

Lifetime 21 8 2 5 $177,640 Turf 1 0 0 0

21Dec86-5Hol 6f :221 :452 1:103ft *1 116 31½ 31½ 31½ 1nk ValenzuelPA2 Aw35000 90-15 MFvrtMmnt,McLndn,AmrcnStndrd 6

21Jun86-5Hol 6f :214 :45 1:092ft 2½ 116 43 41½ 2½ 21½ DelahoussyeE6 100000 95-09 AmrcnLgn,MyFvrtMmnt,MGllntGm 7

21Jun86—Lost whip start

8Jun86-5Hol 6f :22 :45 1:083ft 3¾ 117 44½ 45½ 37½ 38 DelhoussyeE2 Aw35000 93-11 CsForPs,RgnngCntss,MyFvrtMmnt 6

11Jan86-8SA 7f :214 :434 1:204ft 29 116 66½ 611 616 513 ♦DlhossyE6 Sn Crls H 83-11 PhonTrick,TmrityPrinc,MyHbitony 6

11Jan86—Grade II; ♦Dead heat

29Dec85-8SA 6f :212 :433 1:08 ft 16 116 52¾ 57 59½ 411½ DlhossyE3 Pls Vrds H 86-12 PhoneTrick,FivNorth,DbonirJunior 6

29Dec85—Wide into stretch

13Nov85-8Hol 6f :224 :463 1:112gd 7 118 2hd 43 45½ 59 DlhossyE2 Trf Spnt H 78-26 TmrtyPrnc,FrnchLgonr,DbonrJunor 5

28Oct85-10LA 6f :212 :441 1:083ft 9-5 117 32½ 33½ 2hd 1½ DlhossyE4 Orng Cst H 102-07 MyFvoriteMoment,SilentFox,Mzzo 6

16Oct85-8SA 6f :212 :44 1:091ft 14 117 52¾ 53½ 55½ 52½ DlhssyE1 Anct Title H 89-17 TemerityPrince,DbonirJunior,BidUs 6

14Sep85-11Pom 1 1/16 :46 1:114 1:44 ft *9-5 115 1hd 1½ 2hd 33 HansenRD3 P D Shprd — — ApolloFlight,Agul,MyFvortMomnt 11

1Sep85-7Dmr 1 :45 1:101 1:37 ft 2½ 121 1hd 1hd 1½ 31½ DelhoussyeE5 Aw40000 82-13 JustInCse,TriplSc,MyFvoritMomnt 7

Jan 7 SA 4f sy :494 h (d) Jan 2 SA 6f ft 1:152 h Dec 28 SA 5f ft 1:014 h Dec 18 Hol 5f ft 1:012 h

E.

McLendon B. g. 5, by Washington County—Pocket The Money, by Full Pocket

COX D W **1095** Br.—Steger Mr O L Jr (Ark) 1986 7 2 2 0 $48,582

Own.—Steger Mr-Mrs O L Tr.—Proctor Harry A 1985 13 5 4 2 $51,680

Lifetime 20 7 6 2 $100,262

21Dec86-5Hol 6f :221 :452 1:103ft 10 1105 43 43 42 2nk Cox D W4 Aw35000 90-15 MFvrtMmnt,McLndn,AmrcnStndrd 6

18May86-10LaD 6f :222 :454 1:114m 3½ 120 21½ 31½ 34 55 Tejeira J4 Kgs Court 78-25 AccmplshdLvr,MstrCrftr,Cnd'sByG. 5

4May86-10LaD 5½f :221 :46 1:053ft *2-3 121 55 44 66½ 67½ Snyder L2 Aw17000 80-24 AccomplshdLovr,NghtAbv,LttlSlck 6

4May86—Lost footing start

28Mar86-9OP 6f :22 :45 1:091ft 5¼ 114 2hd 3½ 31½ 86 Snyder L1 Carousel H 88-18 ChrgngFlls,ComSummr,LckyNorth 8

18Mar86-9OP 6f :222 :46 1:104ft *1 111 11 11 13 13 Snyder L2 Aw25000 86-22 McLendon,Pressure,LuckySalvtion 7

1Mar86-9OP 6f :213 :451 1:10 ft 5 112 32 3nk 11 23½ SnyderL9 Ark Trvler H 86-18 Charging Falls,McLendon,Diapason 9

8Feb86-7OP 5½f 1:044ft *8-5 115 32½ 22 1hd 1no Snyder L7 Aw22000 89-19 McLendon,StlRobbing,GminiDrmr 10

17Aug85-9LaD 5½f :22 :454 1:05 ft *4-5 122 1hd 11 12 1½ Snyder L4 Aw16000 95-19 McLendon,ExclusivPond,LittlSlick 7

19Jly85-9LaD 6f :214 :443 1:094ft *4-5 112 21½ 2½ 11½ 11 Snyder L5 Aw13000 93-15 McLendon, Little Slick,NightAbove 6

11Jly85-7LaD 6f :221 :45 1:102ft *7-5 122 1½ 1½ 12½ 1½ Snyder L2 Aw11500 90-15 McLendon,LndingthBid,RturnRqust 9

Jan 1 SA 4f ft :492 h Dec 18 Hol 4f ft :50 h ●Dec 11 SA 4f ft :463 h Dec 5 SA 6f ft 1:14 h

F.

Gemini Dreamer Dk. b. or br. h. 7, by Great Above—Luna Moon, by Cool Moon
BAZE G 114 Br.—Lasater Farm (Fla) 1986 16 2 8 2 $56,423
Own.—Van Berg J C Tr.—Van Berg Jack C 1985 17 1 5 7 $83,301
Lifetime 79 10 27 20 $376,825 Turf 18 2 3 5 $100,562
21Dec86-5Hol 6f :221 :452 1:103ft 4¾ 115 55 54½ 55 57 Stevens G L6 Aw35000 83-15 MFvrtMmnt,McLndn,AmrcnStndrd 6
28Sep86-9TP 6½f :231 :46 1:171ft 3 119 31½ 21 21½ 41¼ Smith M E2 Marfa H 91-18 BroadwayWilly,McShne,InstntRuler 5
28Aug86-7AP 6½f :222 :452 1:162ft 6 118 44½ 63¼ 42 33½ Fires E2 Aw18000 89-19 Clestog,TheRoylFreeze,GeminiDrmr 7
19Aug86-8AP 7f :23 :462 1:234ft 3½ 117 53½ 53½ 42 1nk Day P1 Aw17000 83-18 GeminiDremer,ProudDhbi,ExitFivB. 8
20Jly86-8Aks 6f :224 :453 1:10 ft 2½ 116 54½ 4¾ 3½ 2no Maple S7 Aw16100 87-20 Pressure,GeminiDrmr,LuckySlvtion 7
28Jun86-7CD 7f :224 :444 1:232ft *1 118 43½ 45 24 25 Day P1 HcpO 84-15 BrodwyWlly,GmnDrmr,TrbttoRylty 5
31May86-8CD 6½f :224 :453 1:163ft 4½ 117 52¼ 42½ 41¼ 45 Brumfield D3 HcpO 92-13 Barcelona, McShane, Woodsman 6
23May86-8CD 6f :211 :45 1:101ft *4-5 118 47 44½ 3nk 1hd Day P3 Aw18320 94-19 GeminiDrmr,Woodsmn,DustyProof 7
13May86-8CD 6f :212 :45 1:10 ft 3¼ 115 43 42 3½ 2no Brumfield D4 Aw21020 95-16 Barcelona,GeminiDremer,Woodsmn 6
3May86-9CD 6f :214 :453 1:093ft 9-5 115 41¾ 41½ 2½ 22¼ BraccialeVJr3 Aw17500 95-10 Hbitoni,GeminiDremer,J.R.'sPlesur 5
Dec 15 Hol 5f ft 1:05 h Nov 23 Hol 5f ft 1:031 h

G.

Metronomic B. h. 5, by Crozier—Polly N, by Quibu
STEVENS S A 114 Br.—Hooper F W (Fla) 1986 12 1 3 2 $38,890
Own.—Hooper F W Tr.—Fenstermaker L R 1985 3 0 0 2 $12,300
Lifetime 24 3 5 6 $106,565 Turf 4 0 1 1 $20,200
12Nov86-3Hol 7f :221 :451 1:213ft 8¼ 117 34½ 53½ 43½ 36¼ Stevens G L2 Aw26000 90-15 BoldrThnBold,MyGllntGm,Mtrnmc 6
12Oct86-5SA a6½f ⓣ:214 :44 1:134fm 6 116 65 97¾ 77¼ 610 McHrgueDG7 Aw33000 80-12 PrinceSky,MyGallantGame,Bruiser 12
23Sep86-11Pom 6½f :213 :442 1:151ft 2 116 33 33½ 31 23¼ Solis A6 Gvnr Cp H 101-08 BundleOfIron,Mtronomic,SurToFir 7
16Sep86-11Pom 6f :214 :442 1:092ft 8¾ 115 42½ 57 36 2¾ Solis A2 Aprisa H 103-05 BundlOfIron,Mtronomc,ProdstHor 10
27Aug86-7Dmr 7f :224 :452 1:222ft 9 115 1hd 1hd 3nk 31½ Baze R A1 Aw26000 91-14 Variety Road, Barland, Metronomic 6
13Aug86-3Dmr 6f :213 :443 1:083ft 23 117 45½ 45 35 23½ Baze R A5 Aw24000 91-15 MneMgic,Metronomic,MyGllntGme 6
28Jun86-11Pln 6f :22 :44 1:083ft 13 113 46 47 47 47½ GlRM3 Whtng Mem H 91-11 Cardell,Stan'sBower,MchoComcho 6
28Jun86—Bumped start
21Jun86-5Hol 6f :214 :45 1:092ft 38 116 77 64¾ 64½ 65¾ Sibille R2 100000 91-09 AmrcnLgn,MyFvrtMmnt,MGllntGm 7
1Jun86-9Hol 1 :444 1:092 1:361ft 23 117 58½ 49½ 48½ 53½ McHrgueDG5 Aw32000 78-14 Koshare, Ultimate Pleasure, Jon O. 7
18May86-5Hol 6f ⓣ:212 :434 1:083fm 32 115 43 73½ 73¾ 75¼ VlnzlPA10 Nght Mvr H 94-03 ZanyTactics,RetsinaRun,StrVideo 10
18May86—Bumped off stride 1/16
Jan 6 SA 4f gd :474 h Dec 30 SA 5f ft 1:012 h Dec 18 Hol 5f ft 1:012 h Dec 11 Hol 6f ft 1:15 h

H.

Proudest Hour Dk. b. or br. h. 5, by Proudest Roman—Stage Hour, by Stage Director
DELAHOUSSAYE E 114 Br.—Rogers Red Top &AmrcnData (Ky) 1986 14 1 1 3 $33,225
Own.—Rogers Red Top Farm Tr.—Sullivan John 1985 13 2 3 1 $92,782
Lifetime 34 7 5 4 $204,708 Turf 3 0 0 0
29Nov86-4BM 6f :221 :444 1:09 ft 3½ 113 11½ 1½ 11½ 21½ ShoemkerW3 Aw20000 92-17 BrghtAndRght,ProudstHor,RtsnRn 6
31Oct86-8BM 5½f :222 :453 1:04 ft *2½ 114 32 21 2hd 43¾ Judice J C7 Aw20000 88-21 Holy Rascal,Cardell,TeddyNaturally 9
5Oct86♦3Longchamp(Fra) a5f :564fm 56 137 ⓣ 12 RbnsnP Px d l'Abbye(Gr1) Double Schwartz, Parioli, Hallgate 13
16Sep86-11Pom 6f :214 :442 1:092ft *9-5 116 2hd 2hd 2hd 31¾ Kaenel J L3 Aprisa H 102-05 BundlOfIron,Mtronomc,ProdstHor 10
29Aug86-8Dmr 6f :214 :444 1:091ft 13 115 2hd 1½ 13 31½ Toro F3 Aw38000 90-15 Michdill,FlyingNuggt,ProudstHour 5
16Aug86-8Dmr 6f :212 :441 1:081ft 30 115 1½ 1hd 53 711 Toro F2 Bng Crsby H 86-13 AmericnLegion,BoldBrwly,‡TriplSc 7
16Aug86—Grade III
1Aug86-8Dmr 6½f :213 :441 1:151ft 27 115 1hd 2hd 2hd 52½ Toro F8 Aw35000 93-13 TripleSec,PerfecTrvl,ProtctYourslf 8
26Jun86-8Hol 6f :214 :444 1:092ft 14 116 12 11½ 1hd 34¾ DelhoussyeE2 Aw35000 92-12 AmericnLgion,TriplSc,ProudstHour 6
26Jun86—Bumped start
8Jun86-5Hol 6f :22 :45 1:083ft 9¾ 115 11 22 611 614¾ Solis A3 Aw35000 86-11 CsForPs,RgnngCntss,MyFvrtMmnt 6
8Jun86—Bobbled start
30May86-8GG 5½f :213 :441 1:02 ft 7¾ 114 11 12 13 1½ Judice J C1 Aw22000 101-17 Proudest Hour,Cardell,Stan'sBower 6
Jan 8 SA 3f m :363 b Jan 3 SA 4f ft :484 h Dec 27 SA 4f ft :482 h ●Dec 21 Hol 3f ft :35 h

30.

5 MONMOUTH

1 MILE. (Turf). (1.35) CLAIMING. Purse $13,000. Fillies and mares, 3-year-olds and upward. Weight,3-year-olds, 114 lbs. Older, 122 lbs. Non-winners of three races at one mile or over since June 16 3 lbs. Two Such races, 5 lbs. One such race, 7 lbs. Claiming price $25,000 for each $2,500 to $20,000, 2 lbs. Races where entered for $18,000 or less not considered.

Coupled—Nancy's Basket and First To Go.

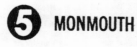

A.

Irish Goblin — B. f. 4, by Tilt Up—Tell She's Irish, by Tell
Own.—Koch R F — $25,000 — Br.—Bach & Kaufman & Tenney (Ky) — Tr.—Araya Rene A — 111
Lifetime 38 7 7 5 $41,365 — 1987 15 4 4 2 $23,500 — 1986 21 3 3 3 $17,865

21Jly87- 4Mtn fst 6f :22⅗ :46⅖ 1:13 3+[F]Clm c-12500 2 5 42¼ 54¼ 43¼ 52¾ Santagata N b 119 *3.10 72-18 Paulie's Pal 116hd Dear Effie 116hd Trafalgar Lass 1162 Even try 11
9Jly87- 3Mtn fst 6f :22 :45⅕ 1:11⅘ 3+[F]Clm c-10000 7 5 41½ 42½ 31 11¼ Santagata N b 119 3.70 81-21 Irish Goblin 1191¼ Bravely Stated 111¾ Inkie Pinkie 1141 Driving 10
29Jun87- 3Mtn fst 6f :22⅕ :45⅕ 1:11⅗ 3+[F]Clm 8000 4 1 61¼ 41 1hd 1¾ Santagata N b 119 2.80 82-19 Irish Goblin 119¾ Fire Diamond 1163½ Inkie Pinkie 1163 Driving 7
20Jun87- 2Mtn fst 1 1/16 :46⅖ 1:11⅖ 1:46⅘ 3+[F]Clm 8000 5 2 21 23½ 21½ 22 Madrid A Jr b 115 6.30 69-13 Major Holbrook 1132 Irish Goblin 115nk LoveAgain115½ Held 2nd 7
4Jun87- 7GS sly 6f :22⅕ :46 1:12⅘ 3+[F]Clm 8500 7 1 33½ 22 21 1½ Madrid A Jr b 116 2.40 76-20 Irish Goblin 116½ Croatia 116hd Terrified Girl 116nk Driving 7
27May87- 6GS fst 6f :22⅖ :45⅘ 1:11 3+[F]Clm 14000 2 7 32 43½ 66¾ 711¾ Moyers L b 116 9.50 75-21 Daisy's Debut 1114 Slave To Fashion 1162¼ Lightling 111nk Tired 8
15May87- 6GS gd 6f :22⅘ :46⅖ 1:11⅗ 3+[F]Clm 11000 5 2 1hd 2nd 4nk 33¾ Edwards J W b 116 7.40 80-23 Perugia 1163½ Look Out Tower 116nk IrishGoblin1161½ Weakened 9
24Apr87- 5GS sly 1 1/16 :48 1:14⅖ 1:48⅕ 3+[F]Clm 11000 1 3 31 1½ 11 23 Madrid A Jr b 116 5.20 64-24 R.DazzlingDaria1163IrishGoblin1162ClareChmpion1125 Weakened 7
13Apr87- 7GS fst 6f :22⅘ :47 1:13⅕ [F]Clm c-8500 4 6 51¾ 98 1012 1115¾ Miceli M b 116 *2.00 60-26 American Freedom 115½ Love Again 113nk Lu Lu's Girl1144 Tired 12
2Apr87- 5GS fst 6f :22⅗ :46⅗ 1:13⅗ [F]Clm c-6500 5 5 32½ 23½ 21½ 13½ Madrid A Jr b 116 *3.50 74-29 Irish Goblin 1163½ Hurry Up Ida 1161 Swallowtail 1052 Driving 10

B.

Jersey Shore — Dk. b. or br. f. 4, by Lord Avie—Sea Royalty, by Native Royalty
Own.—S K S Stable — $25,000 — Br.—spendthrift Farm (Ky) — Tr.—Seewald Alan — 115
Lifetime 22 3 2 3 $38,478 — 1987 3 0 0 0 $1,185 — 1986 13 2 0 3 $24,533 — Turf 8 0 0 3 $9,638

24Jly87- 6Mth fm 1 [T]:48 1:11⅖ 1:37⅘ 3+[F]Clm 25000 9 7 73½ 74¾ 62¼ 42¾ Madrid A Jr b 115 10.70 83-09 Great Trail 1152½ One Judge 111no Pia's Baby 113nk Fin.well 10
16Jun87- 3Mth fst 6f :22⅗ :45⅖ 1:10⅖ 3+[F]Clm 32000 1 6 62½ 63½ 64¼ 59½ Edwards J W b 116 7.80 78-17 JckieO'Lnternn1162¼MissRchelToner1162¼SuperbTim116½ Outrun 6
3Jun87- 7Mth fst 1 :47⅘ 1:12⅕ 1:38 3+[F]Alw 18000 7 4 55 712 718 725½ Edwards J W b 118 18.70 57-22 Syrianette 1183 Sunshine Jill 1187 Chase The Dream 1123½ Tired 7
26Aug86- 5Mth gd 1 [T]:48 1:13⅗ 1:41 [F]Clm 50000 3 5 56½ 54½ 54½ 4¾ McCauley W H b 114 3.50 69-30 Torsion Sez 116½ Dons Beauty 114nk Pete's Trick 112no Rallied 7
5Aug86- 6Mth fm 1 [T]:48⅘ 1:12⅘ 1:39⅗ [F]Clm 50000 7 6 54½ 45½ 54¾ 35½ Rocco J b 114 3.20 71-27 Torsion Sez 1133 Biddy 1162½ Jersey Shore 1142 Bumped start 8
28Jly86- 9Mth fst 1 1/16 :48 1:12⅕ 1:45 3+[F]Alw 16000 5 6 62½ 62 54¾ 42¾ Krone J A b 109 4.20 77-17 In Full View 114¾ Green Boundary1121Lodging1121 Bobbled start 7
18Jly86- 9Mth fm 1 1/16 [T]:48⅖ 1:12⅕ 1:43⅖+ 3+[F]Alw 16000 4 3 44 43½ 41½ 32 Krone J A b 109 7.40 82-15 Miss Double Talk 1191DeltaDaiquiry1171JerseyShore1091¼ Evenly 6
7Jly86- 2Bel fm 1 1/16 [T]:47⅗ 1:12 1:43⅕ [F]Clm 75000 9 4 54 42½ 3½ 45½ Velasquez J b 116 3.50 74-14 Ninja De Oro 112¾ Soft Ruffles 1161¾ CarrieCatte1123 Weakened 11
17Jun86- 9Mth fm 1 [T]:46⅗ 1:11⅖ 1:36⅘ [F]Revidere 5 9 812 78½ 67½ 59 Krone J A b 112 17.10 82-13 Loa 118½ She's A Mystery 1181½ Small Virtue 113nk No factor 9
10May86- 9GS fm 1 1/16 [T]:47⅕ 1:11⅘ 1:44 [F]Princeton H 8 10 85½ 74¾ 52½ 84½ Krone J A b 111 23.90 84-11 Vacherie 112¾ Narrow Escape 113¾ Fragrant Princess116½ Outrun 12
LATEST WORKOUTS ● Jly 20 Mth 4f my :48 h — Jly 6 Mth 1 fst 1:41 b — Jun 27 Mth 1 sly 1:45⅖ b — Jun 13 Mth 3f fst :36⅗ b

C.

Nancy's Basket — B. f. 4, by Fire Dancer—Mon Cherie, by Promise
Own.—Aspen Stable — $25,000 — Br.—Tayloe W Randolph (Fla) — Tr.—Hauswald Jim — 115
Lifetime 27 3 7 5 $34,325 — 1987 6 0 1 1 $4,435 — 1986 13 2 3 4 $20,775 — Turf 6 0 2 2 $8,915

27Jun87- 6Mth sly 1 1/16 :47⅗ 1:12⅗ 1:46⅘ 3+[F]Clm 32000 4 3 32½ 45 512 618¼ McCauley W H b 115 4.40 53-18 Honey's Keys 1153½ One For Bess 11310 Rolfe's Ruby 115no Tired 6
15Jun87- 6Mth fm 1 1/16 [T]:47⅗ 1:12 1:43⅘ 3+[F]Alw 15000 3 2 21 21 33½ 67¼ Hernandez C b 118 4.00 79-11 Kim Kimmie 118¾ Dissembler 1131 Lady Asterisk 1115½ Tired 8
6Jun87- 4Mth fm 1 1/16 [T]:47⅖ 1:12 1:43⅗+ 3+[F]Alw 15000 1 4 41½ 41½ 43 35 Hernandez C b 118 4.10 78-11 Cecina 1125 Midnight Child II 118no Nancy's Basket118hd Rallied 10
20May87- 8GP gd *1 [T] 1:41⅘ [F]Clm 35000 5 3 32 41½ 22½ 24 Valiente D b 113 19.30 67-26 Cougar Best 1134 Nancy's Basket113nkWildWomen117¾ Game try 9
9May87- 10GP yl *1 1/16 [T] 1:45⅖ [F]Clm 30000 6 1 11½ 22 611 923 Pezua J M b 113 5.30 56-20 Recently 113no Calorge 1106 Kelly's Super Pet 1191½ Stopped 10
23Apr87- 8GP fst 7f :22⅖ :45⅗ 1:24⅖ [F]Alw 14000 2 3 63½ 65½ 714 729½ Pezua J M b 117 5.20 52-26 Doodle Do 1174½ Bid Me Adieu 117noMs.StolleyNight122½ Outrun 8
29Oct86- 8Crc fm *1 [T] 1:39⅕ 3+[F]Alw 17900 8 3 21 21½ 21½ 31¼ Lester R N b 112 *1.50 84-15 StutteringSrh1121¼Henriett'sBid117noNncy'sBskt112nk Weakened 8
18Oct86- 8Crc fm 1 [T]:46⅖ 1:11⅕ 1:35⅘ 3+[F]Alw 16900 3 2 21½ 21 1hd 2no Pezua J M b 112 9.50 94-06 Miston114noNancy'sBasket1123½StutteringSarh112no Just missed 12
26Sep86- 3Crc fst 6f :22⅕ :45⅗ 1:12⅗ 3+[F]Clm 20000 1 4 42½ 33 2hd 13½ Pezua J M b 113 6.60 86-15 Nancy'sBasket1133½That'sAGoodOne115hdSuwrd111nk Drew clear 8
6Sep86- 8Crc fst 7f :23⅖ :47⅕ 1:26⅖ 3+[F]Clm 18000 3 6 1hd 1hd 2hd 52¾ Lester R N b 113 3.30 81-20 Getatable 1091 Justice Joker 113½ AnnieBlueeyes1121¼ Weakened 10
LATEST WORKOUTS Jly 28 Mth 5f fst 1:06 b — Jun 26 Mth 3f fst :39 b — Jun 1 Mth 5f fst 1:06⅗ b

D.

Tears — Dk. b. or br. f. 3, by Caro Bambino—Excelencia, by Cougar II
Own.—Bradley & Lundy — $25,000 — Br.—Bradley Mary (Cal) — Tr.—Lundy Richard J — 103
Lifetime 4 0 0 0 — 1987 4 M 0 0 — 1986 0 M 0 0

18Jun87- 10Mth fst 6f :22⅖ :46 1:11⅘ 3+[F]Md 22000 10 8 75¾ 79½ 1016 1122¾ St Leon G b 115 24.80 56-14 Her Majesty Carrie 1155 Wondecor 1082½ DespairNot1153 Outrun 12
2Jun87- 5Mth fst 6f :22⅘ :46 1:12⅕ 3+[F]Md Sp Wt 6 7 811 813 816 716½ St Leon G 115 38.20 62-16 Proud Delight 115no Bob's Bet 1152 Like Mink 1152½ Outrun 8
15May87- 3Bel fst 7f :22⅘ :46⅖ 1:23⅘ 3+[F]Md Sp Wt 1 8 32 53½ 79 719½ Davis R G 113 5.50e 63-09 Bristlin' Belle 1136¾ Early Warning1191¼Strictly1241½ Brief speed 9
16Apr87- 6Aqu fst 6f :23⅕ :47 1:11⅘ [F]Md Sp Wt 6 7 97 916 819 824¾ Bailey J D 121 24.10 58-22 Cadiliacing 1216¾ Drone Qui 121hd Special Weekend1214¼ Outrun 9
LATEST WORKOUTS Jly 25 Mth 3f fst :35⅘ b — Jly 21 Mth 6f fst 1:17 b — Jly 16 Mth 6f fst 1:15⅖ b — Jly 10 Mth 3f fst :35 h

E.

Madam Magoo — Dk. b. or br. f. 4, by Far Out East—Vain, by Native Charger
Own.—Evans R S — $25,000 — Br.—Evans Robert S (NJ) — Tr.—Thompson J Willard — 115
Lifetime 18 4 0 1 $44,568 — 1987 4 1 0 0 $11,700 — 1986 7 1 0 1 $14,028 — Turf 5 0 0 0 $840

16Jly87- 6Mth fm 1 1/16 [T]:47⅖ 1:12 1:44⅘ 3+[F]Clm 30000 8 5 66 89 711 614 Ferrer J C 113 7.80 67-19 Syntonic 1152½ Cuca's Lady 1132 Wild Women 1152½ Outrun 8
1Jly87- 8Mth fst 1 :46⅗ 1:10⅘ 1:37⅖ 3+[F]Alw 18000 7 4 54½ 58 56 54¾ Krone J A 120 4.30 81-15 Relaunch Lass 111½ SocialConduct1143½OhSoBad112nk No factor 8
10Jun87- 5Mth fst 1 :48⅖ 1:13⅖ 1:39 3+[F]Alw 17000 4 3 21 2½ 2½ 1hd Krone J A 118 2.80 76-23 Madam Magoo 118hd Kitonia 11811 That's Fine 1182½ Driving 5
3Jun87- 8Mth fst 6f :22⅘ :45⅗ 1:11⅕ 3+[F]Alw 16000 3 4 73¾ 68½ 55 45¼ Vigliotti M J 116 22.40 79-22 Royal Tri 1094 Novelette 1111 Rebel Runner 116nk Rallied 7
6Sep86- 8Med fst 6f :22⅘ :46⅕ 1:11⅕ 3+[F][S]Alw 20000 2 6 84 77½ 69 48 Krone J A 116 8.20 76-16 HppyHelnB1162½Mom'sOnAndOnly1183MrryTun1132½ No menace 8
19Aug86- 9Mth sf 1 1/16 [T]:48⅖ 1:13⅘ 1:46⅘ [F]L. Silver H· 9 2 22½ 64 910 917¾ Krone J A 111 *59.90 53-29 Spruce Fir 1173 My Mom Ginny 1143 Green Boundary1142½ Tired 10
19Aug86-Grade III
9Aug86- 8Mth fm 1 1/16 [T]:46⅘ 1:11⅗ 1:43⅘+ [F]Am Capable 1 7 85¾ 115½ 83½ 66¾ Krone J A 113 33.10 75-17 Spruce Fir 1132½ Green Boundary 115hdTrueChompion1143½ Wide 11
25Jly86- 8Mth fst 170 :46⅗ 1:11⅕ 1:42⅖ 3+[F][S]Alw 16200 3 4 51¼ 2½ 13 18 Krone J A 108 *1.20 84-16 Madame Magoo 1088 Dancing Annie 1162 SilkBonnet111nk Easily 8
11Jly86- 7Mth fm 1 1/16 [T]:47⅖ 1:11⅖ 1:41⅕+ 3+[F]Alw 14000 1 3 55 68½ 68 44¼ Verge M E 111 27.80 76-13 Air Dancer 1121 Cuca's Lady 1172½ What A Fortune109¾ Late bid 10
20Jun86- 8Mth fst 6f :23⅖ :47 1:12⅗ 3+[F][S]Alw 16200 6 3 52¾ 64½ 53 32¾ Marquez C H Jr 110 2.40 74-24 NoseTweeker112nkShakyShkford1162½MdmeMgoo1102 Mild gain 6
LATEST WORKOUTS ● Jun 24 Mth 6f fst 1:14 h

F.

First To Go — Dk. b. or br. f. 4, by Gentle King—pinner Fair, by Right Combination
Own.—Haywood F — $25,000 — Br.—Rosenthal J (Fla) — Tr.—Hauswald Jim — 115
Lifetime 20 2 2 3 $30,227 — 1987 3 0 0 0 $545 — 1986 14 1 1 2 $18,972 — Turf 3 1 0 0 $8,960

16Jly87- 6Mth fm 1 1/16 [T]:47⅖ 1:12 1:44⅘ 3+[F]Clm 35000 6 2 21 22½ 44½ 59½ Hernandez C b 115 25.70 71-19 Syntonic 1152½ Cuca's Lady 1132 Wild Women 1152½ Tired 8
8Jly87- 7Mth fst 1 1/16 :47 1:12⅗ 1:46⅖ 3+[F]Clm 50000 7 1 2hd 88¾ 823 832¾ Hernandez C b 115 19.30 40-27 Shaken Bay 1154 Cup O'Cake 107½ Double Smooth112¾ Gave way 8
31May87- 8Crc fst 6f :21⅘ :45⅘ 1:13 3+[F]Alw 13900 5 4 34 66¼ 813 812¼ Tejeira J b 119 47.30 74-15 SecondProphcy1122SwinginLow1101½LuckyBrMid1122 No threat 10
27Sep86- 5Crc fm *1 1/16 [T] 1:45 3+[F]Alw 15600 1 1 3nk 33 47 56 Tejeira J b 114 3.60 76-18 Talski 1142 Exuberant Attitude 1161½ Justice Joker 107hd Tired 8
9Jly86- 7Crc fst 7f :22⅗ :46⅖ 1:26⅕ 3+[F]Alw 12500 4 4 1½ 2hd 67¼ 814 Lester R N b 113 3.40 71-17 AnAffirmation1133ExuberantAttitude1162ValeRoyle1111 Stopped 8
19Jun86- 7Crc fst 6½f :22 :45⅖ 1:18⅗ 3+[F]Alw 13900 3 4 3½ 1½ 1hd 24 Lester R N b 114 4.50 88-14 Southern Velvet 1174 First To Go 1143 Weird One 1126¼ Gamely 5

8Jun86-10Crc sly 7f :23⅘ :45 1:26⅘ 3+ Ⓕ Alw 12500 5 7 1½ 2hd 1hd 63 Gonzalez M A b 112 5.10 79-16 PrincessRjhil117noExuberntAttitude1171¼WeirdOn110¾ Weakened 9
21May86- 8Hia sly 1⅛ :47⅘ 1:13⅘ 1:52⅘ ⒻⓈVa Gardens 2 1 1½ 24 411 722 Pennisi F A b 114 4.00 47-29 CougarBest1113HerHonorship1126½RunMarisaRun11410 Gave way 8
10May86- 9Hia fst 1⅛ :46 1:10⅗ 1:50⅗ ⒻPatricia 4 1 18 12½ 44¼ 48½ Sellers M S b 111 7.80 71-16 Opera Diva 1162 True Chompion 1132¾ Judy'sRedShoes1184 Tired 6
26Apr86- 6Hia fm 1 1/16 Ⓣ 1:42⅘ Ⓕ Alw 12800 12 1 1½ 12 13 11¼ Sellers M S b 117 18.00 84-12 First To Go 1171¼ Janjac 117no Danza Rustica 117¾ Driving 12
LATEST WORKOUTS Jly 28 Mth 5f fst 1:00⅗ h Jly 4 Mth 5f fst 1:01⅖ h Jun 29 Mth 5f fst 1:03⅘ b

G.

Play It Hard
Own.—Lane G E
B. f. 4, by Advocator—Play Bold, by Master Bold
$25,000 Br.—Wimborne Farm (Ky)
Tr.—Klesaris Robert P
111
Lifetime 23 7 4 1 $36,580
1987 14 6 2 1 $25,000
1986 9 1 2 0 $11,580
Turf 3 1 1 0 $5,605

19Jly87-10Suf fm *7½f Ⓣ 1:35 3+ Ⓕ Clm 20000 7 5 2½ 2hd 11½ 2¾ Campbell T M b 113 *2.50 87-07 Worth The Sum114¾PlayItHard1132¾KeepDancing1141 Weakened 9
11Jly87-10Suf fm *7½f Ⓣ 1:35⅕ 3+ Ⓕ Clm 7500 7 5 3½ 1hd 16 18½ Campbell T M b 119 *2.60 87-10 Play It Hard 1198½ Ms. Alosa 114nk Splendid Sara 1101 Easily 9
22Jun87- 6Suf fst 170 :47⅖ 1:13⅕ 1:44⅗ 3+ Ⓕ Clm 6500 2 1 1½ 13½ 17 15½ Campbell T M b 117 *1.00 77-23 PlyItHrd1175½Wncturnedmeloose1148KrC'sCopy114½ Ridden out 6
14Jun87- 3Suf fst 6f :23 :47⅖ 1:13⅗ 3+ Ⓕ Clm 5000 2 2 2hd 2hd 12 13½ Campbell T M b 117 3.50 73-24 Play It Hard 1173½ Juvilina 114hd Mom's New Dress 1141 Driving 5
3Jun87- 9Suf fst 170 :47⅗ 1:13 1:44⅘ 3+ Ⓕ Alw 3750s 1 6 56¾ 37 38½ 37½ Pagano S R b 114 3.70 68-21 Antoinette D. 1174 Rocketette 1173½ Play It Hard 1146½ Steadied 7
15May87-10Suf fst 1 :49⅕ 1:15⅗ 1:43⅕ 3+ Ⓕ Clm 3500 1 4 3½ 12½ 13½ 13 Bogochow M A b 119 *.90 60-30 Play It Hard 1193 Nenita 1141¼ Knarys Hawk 11913 Driving 8
8May87-10Suf fst 6f :23⅘ :48⅗ 1:15⅗ 3+ Ⓕ Clm 3500 3 10 31 2hd 13 11¾ Bogochow M A b 119 6.00 63-33 PlyItHrd1191¾LissCommnd116ndSecretEmbrce114½ Drifted. clear 11
26Apr87- 8Suf fst 6f :23⅕ :48⅕ 1:15⅖ 3+ Ⓕ Clm 5000 2 7 66¾ 79 611 79 Bogochow M A b 117 *1.90 55-35 Keep Dancing 114½ All Aces 1094 Enniroc 114no No factor 8
11Apr87- 4Suf fst 1 :48⅖ 1:14⅕ 1:41⅗ Ⓕ Alw 12500 1 3 47½ 511 511 619¼ Bogochow M A b 117 4.60 49-31 Ronliz 1142¾ Oba Kaybee 117hd Little Joy 1178 Brief speed 6
16Mar87- 9Suf fst 6f :23 :49 1:16⅗ Ⓕ Alw 10000 2 7 712 66¾ 1hd 16½ Bogochow M A b 122 *1.00 58-42 PlayItHrd1226½DncingDeverish1222RiverRidgeCreek1192 Handily 7

H.

Flying Flash
Own.—Croll Mrs W A Jr
B. f. 4, by Second Bar—Valaurie, by My Swallow
$25,000 Br.—Bryant Mr–Mrs J C H (Va)
Tr.—Croll Warren A Jr
113
Lifetime 9 1 1 1 $8,005
1987 3 1 1 1 $7,170
1986 6 M 0 0 $835

13Jly87- 9Mth fst 6f :22⅕ :46 1:13 3+ Ⓕ Md 16000 5 5 47 52½ 2½ 12½ Perret C 118 4.70 75-21 Flying Flash 1182½ Bob's Bet 109½ Wondecor 1144 Driving 11
25Jun87- 1Mth fst 6f :22⅕ :45⅖ 1:13 3+ Ⓕ Md 18000 7 2 54½ 59 44½ 2no Perret C 120 6.70 75-17 Majesticant 122no Flying Flash 1201½ Polarize 1151¾ Nosed 10
15Jun87- 9Mth fst 6f :22⅘ :46⅗ 1:12⅖ 3+ Ⓕ Md 16000 10 1 4nk 2hd 11 35½ Perret C 122 42.80 72-16 Supai 1173 Ashley's Pleasure 1152½ Flying Flash 1222½ Weakened 11
3Jly86- 9Mth fst 6f :23⅗ :47⅘ 1:14⅖ 3+ Ⓕ Md 10000 7 9 84½ 87¾ 610 610 Terry J 116 6.80 58-24 Hula'sLegacy1092½FiveStrQueen116½SisterTrixie116nk No menace 11
19Jun86- 1Mth fst 6f :22⅘ :46⅕ 1:12⅖ 3+ Ⓕ Md 16000 10 11 127¼ 99 79½ 614 Terry J 115 *2.50 64-25 Valenciana 1187 Raise A Buckeye 115¾ Its ARobby108½ No factor 12
13Jun86- 4Mth fst 6f :23 :47⅕ 1:14 3+ Ⓕ Md 35000 8 9 95¾ 77 66½ 65½ Antley C W 115 *1.30 64-25 Lisa's Song 115¾ HeartOfSilver1151½AugustBreeze1051½ Steadied 9
10May86- 3Hia sly 7f :23⅗ :46⅘ 1:24⅘ 3+ Ⓕ Md Sp Wt 1 9 86½ 811 716 715¾ Rodriguez F M5 108 7.00 63-20 Lazara 113¾ Following Star 108½ Dancer's Candy 1132 Outrun 9
23Apr86- 7Hia fst 7f :23⅕ :47 1:25⅗ 3+ Ⓕ Md 40000 11 5 54 43 23 43½ Gonzalez M A 113 2.40 72-22 Naskra'sNurse108hdLazr1072½UpperMtecumbe1131 Bid,weakened 11
9Apr86- 6Hia fst 6f :22⅕ :46 1:12⅕ 3+ Ⓕ Md 40000 5 11 86½ 55 65¼ 43½ Gonzalez M A 113 13.60 75-22 Ms. Happy Hour 112no Lazara 1063½ Fleur DeSoleil113hd Late bid 12
LATEST WORKOUTS Jly 28 Mth 4f fst :48 h Jly 19 Mth 5f fst 1:01⅗ h Jly 10 Mth 4f fst :49⅘ b Jly 1 Mth 4f fst :49⅖ b

31.

5th Santa Anita

ABOUT 6 ½ FURLONGS. (Turf). (1.11⅘) CLAIMING. Purse $36,000. Fillies and mares. 4-year-olds and upward. Weight, 122 lbs. Non-winners of two races since December 25 allowed 3 lbs.; of a race since then, 5 lbs. Claiming price $100,000; for each $5,000 to $85,000 allowed 1 lb. (Claiming and starter races for $80,000 or less not considered.)

A.

***Ann Aesthetic**
ORTEGA L E 114
Own.—Youngman Patricia A
Dk. b. or br. f. 4, by Kampala—Injection, by On Your Mark
Br.—Barry R (Ire)
Tr.—West Ted $85,000
Lifetime 8 1 0 0 $2,404
1986 4 0 0 0
1985 4 1 0 0 $2,404
Turf 6 1 0 0 $2,404

30Dec86-7SA 6f :21³ :45 1:10⁴ft 67 116 107¾ 109¾ 89¾ 810 Baze G 10 Ⓕ Aw26000 74-18 Alydariel, Bambalor, In Concert 11
30Dec86—Wide into stretch
13Dec86-6Hol 6f :21³ :45 1:10²ft 76 114 91½ 97¼ 88½ 97½ Baze G 5 Ⓕ Aw22000 83-09 SunlightMiss,QueenMrlen,Bmblor 10
13Dec86—Rough start
30May86 ♦ 4Newmarket(Eng) 6f 1:11 gd 12 120 Ⓣ 54 Eddery P Ⓕ Qnsbury Meteoric, Zalatia, Butsova 11
14May86 ♦ 4Brighton(Eng) 6f 1:11⁴gd 16 128 Ⓣ 65¼ McGlnA Davies&TaleAviv Tussac, Tufuh, Northern Impulse 8
19Jly85 ♦ 5Newbury(Eng) 6f 1:16³gd 20 120 Ⓣ 43½ CauthenS Ⓕ St Cthrn's Northern Eternity,Nashia,Smooch 10
29Jun85 ♦ 1Lingfield(Eng) 6f 1:12³gd 7 123 Ⓣ 11 Ives T Ⓕ Mnfsto(Mdn) AnnAesthetic,Asticour,EstrnHous 16
20May85 ♦ 2Windsor(Eng) 5f 1:02¹gd 12 123 Ⓣ 11 ThomsML Ⓕ Whitehall WelshNote,Alexanjo,Centralspires 15
4May85 ♦ 4Kempton(Eng) 5f 1:00²fm 20 123 Ⓣ 55½ JhnsnE Ⓕ Mntmr(Mdn) DncingFille,SummerhillSpruc,Hotb 7
Mar 9 SA 6f ft 1:02¹ h Feb 13 SA 4f ft :47¹ h Feb 6 SA 5f ft 1:01 h Jan 29 SA 4f ft :49⁴ h

B.

Hairless Heiress
MCHARGUE D G 122
Own.—Siegel M
Dk. b. or br. f. 4, by Baldski—Sheltered, by Roman Sandal
Br.—Brookwood Farm (Md)
Tr.—Mayberry Brian A $100,000
Lifetime 13 4 4 0 $64,375
1987 2 2 0 0 $31,350
1986 11 2 4 0 $33,025
Turf 2 1 0 0 $17,050

21Feb87-5SA a6½f Ⓣ:22 :45 1:16 fm 10 117 1hd 1½ 1½ 1½ McHrgDG8 Ⓕ Aw31000 79-17 HairlessHeiress,Ofrendd,RellyFncy 10
25Jan87-7SA 6f :21² :44⁴ 1:10⁴ft 7¾ 116 41¼ 31 1½ 12 McHrgDG8 Ⓕ Aw26000 84-18 HirlssHirss,DrmPolicy,PrvtSorrow 10
8Nov86-7Hol 6f :22 :45³ 1:10²ft 4 114 32 53½ 64¼ 55½ PedrozMA2 Ⓕ Aw21000 85-13 Andrushka,SuchASplash,BoldDyna 10
26Oct86-3SA 6f :21³ :45 1:10³ft 12 114 1hd 1hd 1hd 21¼ PedrozMA4 Ⓕ Aw25000 84-16 Sown,HairlessHeiress,Erl'sVlentine 9
12Oct86-2SA 6½f :22 :45 1:16⁴ft 4½ 114 1½ 1hd 21½ 26½ PedrozMA5 Ⓕ Aw25000 79-21 FlyingJulia,HirlessHeiress,CrestLdy 9
22Sep86-10Pom 6½f :21² :45 1:17²ft 9¼ 114 2hd 2hd 1hd 21½ PedrozMA5 Ⓕ Aw25000 91-19 RadrDwn,HirlessHeiress,Bett'sLdy 10
8Sep86-5Dmr 1 Ⓣ:47 1:11⁴1:36²fm 9 116 21 2hd 41 98¼ Pedroza M A6 Ⓕ 62500 82-10 Sweetest,DrmticElgnc,DwnOfHop 10
8Sep86—Lugged out 3/8

17Aug86-2Dmr 6f :214 :451 1:101ft 19 116 1hd 111 111 13 Pedroza M A6 ⒻⓈ 40000 87-16 HirlessHeiress,LcyLinn,ForvrABlurr 8
17Aug86—Stumbled start
1Aug86-7Dmr 6f :213 :442 1:092ft 17 116 22 33 37 1010 Solis A3 Ⓕ 50000 81-13 Witchery,DremPolicy,DuchssZnth 10
17Jly86-4Hol 6f :214 :451 1:102ft 15 113 32 341 341 581 Soto S B4 Ⓕ 75000 84-17 MillersSttionry,Witchery,Mlv'sPrjd 6
 Mar 10 SA 4f ft :484 h   Feb 7 SA 5f ft 1:012 h   Jan 17 SA 6f ft 1:164 h

C.

Gossiper 4-N Ⓢ   B. f. 4, by Miswaki—Eavesdrop, by Rock Talk
                                        Br.—Gilster & Cline (Ky)   1987 3 0 1 0 $8,250
BAZE G   114   Tr.—Vienna Darrell $85,000   1986 6 0 0 0 $2,100
Own.—Yong Mrs P L   Lifetime 16 2 2 0 $17,664   Turf 13 2 2 0 $15,564
16Feb87-5SA 61f :221 :451 1:172gd 91 115 42 513 623 65   Baze G 4   Ⓕ 70000 78-21 Jglors,MostPrstgous,Prscll'sCrown 8
28Jan87-5SA a61f Ⓣ:212 :4421 1:16 fm 12 115 631 53 11 211 Baze G3   Ⓕ 80000 78-21 MissBeverlyHills,Gossiper,Jiglores 10
11Jan87-5SA a61f Ⓣ:212 :4421 1:164fm 41 117 11 1hd 2nd 451 ValenzuelPA 2 Ⓕ 80000 70-25 Bullion, Jigalores,MostPrestigious 10
2Nov86-5SA   6f :212 :441 1:102ft 22 115 663 661 861 951 Hawley S 9   ⒻAw28000 81-10 StridingEsy,LoversNtive,FlyingJuli 9
 2Nov86—Wide into stretch
19Oct86-3SA 61f :214 :45 1:173ft 41 1075 12 111 21 441 Black C A 2 ⒻAw28000 78-18 Sign Off, NuclearWinter,Sasha'sJoi 7
 19Oct86—Veered in, bumped 5 1/2
21Jun86♦3Ascot(Eng) 5f   :59 fm 20 118 Ⓣ 9 Ives T SteelPltVctryCupH Orient, TreasureKay, DublinLad 15
14Jun86♦3York(Eng) 6f   1:113gd 16 121 Ⓣ 51 Ives T WilliamHillTrphyH GovernorGeneral,SewHigh,Viltash 12
24May86♦2Haydock(Eng) 6f 1:17 gd 25 118 Ⓣ 541 Ives T StretconSandyLane Bridesmaid, Sperry, Tussac 7
16May86♦5Newbury(Eng) 6f 1:144gd 33 118 Ⓣ 610 WoodsW Hue-Williams GovernorGeneral,NativeOak,Fashd 13
28Sep85♦3Redcar(Eng) 6f   1:123gd 12 128 Ⓣ 591 WoodsW I T M Nsy H Handspring,AfricanRex,HansomLd 13
 Mar 9 SA 5f ft 1:024 h   Mar 3 SA tr.t 4f ft :472 h   Feb 25 SA tr.t 3f gd :36 h   Feb 13 SA 4f ft :482 h

D.

*For Certain U-N   B. m. 5, by Certingo—Goldfoot, by Prince Tenderfoot
                                        Br.—Finegan P (Ire)   1985 7 2 0 0 $7,483
MCCARRON C J   114   Tr.—Vienna Darrell $85,000   1984 5 1 1 0 $3,043
Own.—Bollinger & Milhouse   Lifetime 12 3 1 0 $10,526   Turf 12 3 1 0 $10,526
30Oct85♦2Newmarket(Eng) 6f 1:124gd 12 118 Ⓣ 14 RobnsnP U-N Basnthwit H Coincidental, Bay Presto, Zanata 16
12Sep85♦4Doncaster(Eng) 7f 1:253gd 40 116 Ⓣ 781 RobnsnP Kiveton Prk LuckyRing, Efisio, Soprano 8
5Sep85♦2York(Eng) 6f   1:173gd 11 120 Ⓣ 73 RbnsP U-N Innvatv Mrktng H ValleyMills,Numismtist,CmpsHeth 21
21Aug85♦4Yarmouth(Eng) 6f 1:142gd 11 127 Ⓣ 121 RobnsnP U-N Frank Stone ForCertin,LpofHonour,IndinFlower 6
14Aug85♦3Salisbury(Eng) 6f 1:171sf 14 124 Ⓣ 1hd RmndB Coprs Wesex H ForCertin,IrishCooki,MirclsTkTim 18
24Jly85♦4Yarmouth(Eng) 1   5 130 Ⓣ 521 RobnsnP ⒼApplegateH SecretValentine, Raabihah, Pepeke 5
11Jly85♦5Newmarket(Eng) 7f 1:26 gd 33 112 Ⓣ 74 RbnsnP Bahrin Trphy H Domynga, Adjanada, ChargeAlong 13
 Mar 10 SA 5f ft 1:004 h   Mar 5 SA tr.t 4f ft :48 h   Feb 20 SA tr.t 6f ft 1:151 h ●Feb 10 SA tr.t 6f ft 1:152 h

E.

Rekindling /-   B. f. 4, by Affirmed—Cornish Colleen, by Cornish Prince
                                        Br.—Harbor View Farm (Ky)   1987 3 0 2 0 $17,400
STEVENS G L   117   Tr.—Barrera Lazaro S $100,000   1986 17 3 3 3 $83,765
Own.—Harbor View Farm   Lifetime 20 3 5 3 $101,165   Turf 15 3 4 3 $82,175
6Mar87-8SA   111 :47 1:113 1:431gd 3 115 111 11 24 49 StevensGL 4 ⒻAw40000 74-21 Twilight Ridge, Rea, Jell 6
22Feb87-7SA 11/8Ⓣ:214 :4431 1:62fm 44 114 871 541 53 21 StevensGL 6 ⒻAw34000 76-22 MissBevrlyHills,Rkindling,Aromcor 9
24Jan87-7SA 11/8Ⓣ:111 1:491fm 71 114 21 2nd 2hd 211 StevensGL 2 ⒻAw36000 86-17 Benzina, Rekindling, Mangez Les 11
2Nov86-8Hol 1 :4811 1:1221 1:37 fm 6-5 114 41 1hd 11 421 StevensGL 2 ⒻAw35000 79-18 FruAltv,Rock'nRollLdr,BishngRdhd 6
 2Nov86—Lugged out backstretch
7Nov86-7Hol 11/8Ⓣ:4721 1:1121 :42 fm 41 114 22 21 1hd 323 StevensGL 7 ⒻAw36000 81-16 StlCloud,BlushingRedhd,Rkindling 8
25Oct86-5SA 11/8Ⓣ:4711 1:1141 :484fm 91 1055 11 1hd 111 2nk Black C A 2 ⒻAw35000 83-17 PerfectMtchII,Rekindling,StllCloud 9
 25Oct86—Lugged out early
9Oct86-5SA   a61f Ⓣ:221 :4531 1:153fm 51 1135 411 731 541 55 Black C A 3 ⒻAw33000 76-19 LinpacLeaf,KindaBeau,HelloTexas 12
 9Oct86—Steadied at 3/8
4Sep86-8Dmr 1 :453 1:101 1:421ft 41 115 21 31 411 433 VlnzulPA3 ⒻⒽTry Pns 85-14 MrgrtBooth,T.V.Rsidul,SportngAck 7
24Aug86-8Dmr 11/8Ⓣ:4711:11 1:474fm 17 114 39 45 371 461 BzeRA2 ⒻDmr Oaks 89-04 HiddenLight,Krmr,ShotgunWdding 7
 24Aug86—Grade II; Veered in start
2Aug86-8Dmr 11/8Ⓣ:49 1:1311:431fm 8-5 117 621 833 77 681 PnclJr9 ⒻⒼSn Clmnt 82-10 OurSweetShrm,MillEtUn,T.V.Rsidul 10
 2Aug86—Bumped start; wide
 Mar 2 SA 5f ft :594 ha   ●Feb 17 Hol 5f ft 1:002 h   Feb 8 SA 5f ft :592 h   Jan 31 SA 5f ft 1:011 h

F.

Sweet Drop   B. m. 5, by Sir Jason—Sovereign Way, by Mr Leader
                                        Br.—Degwitz F (Fla)   1987 2 0 0 0 $1,200
DOUGLAS R R /-0   114   Tr.—Azpurua Eduardo Jr $85,000   1986 14 1 0 2 $41,125
Own.—Degwitz F   Lifetime 27 4 1 4 $72,507   Turf 18 3 0 2 $64,205
28Feb87-5SA 11/8Ⓣ:4631:1141:502fm 11 116 653 1211 1083 1010 65 Stevens G L 12 Ⓕ 80000 58-15 Mangez Les, OnPatrol,KeepDating 12
11Feb87-3SA 11/8Ⓣ:4631:1111:504fm 25 114 47 513 519 DouglasRR1 Ⓕ 84000 58-27 Benzina, Stall Cloud, CmpsHeth 8
30Nov86-8BM 73f Ⓣ:23 :4621:293fm 23 114 551 55 421 45 DlsRR5 ⒻMs UnvrseH 91-04 Goldenita,TxDodge,AbstrctEnergy 10
23Nov86-8BM 1 :463 1:11 1:36 ft 13 114 431 471 48 671 Soto S B 4 ⒻWdsde H 80-20 Special Victory,Goldspell,Petillante 8
12Nov86-8Hol 11/8Ⓣ:4821:12 1:413fm 15 115 311 311 341 46 Solis A6 ⒻAw40000 80-14 Solva, Miss Clipper, Duckweed 6
10Oct86-8SA 11/8Ⓣ:4641:1041:481fm 6 114 121 11 32 48 Solis A4 ⒻAw45000 78-14 Bonne Ile, Miss Clipper, StallCloud 6

10Oct86—Bobbled start
10Sep86-7Dmr 1 Ⓣ:4631:1021:352fm 13 115 58 58 54 51½ Solis A1 ⒻAw40000 93-07 Infinidad, Adalia, Regal Ties 7
10Sep86—Broke slowly
14Aug86-8Dmr 1 Ⓣ:4721:1141:351fm 53 115 62¾ 72¾ 53½ 65¾ CstnonAL5 ⒻAw35000 90-04 Auspiciante,RoyalRegatta,Antartic 10
9Jly86-8Hol 1 Ⓣ:4621:1011:342fm 33 115 55 53 54 65¾ Solis A2 ⒻAw40000 — — BlushingAllOver,FolkArt,Cnyk'sStr 8
13Jun86-8Hol 1$\frac{1}{16}$Ⓣ:4621:1021:41 fm 5¼ 117 41½ 43 31 1½ Solis A5 ⒻAw25000 99-01 Sweet Drop, Jigalores, Masha 6
Mar 8 Hol 4f ft :483 hg ●Feb 7 Hol 6f ft 1:132 h Feb 2 Hol 1 ft 1:432 h Jan 25 Hol 7f ft 1:283 h

G.

Fancy Pan
SHOEMAKER W **117**
Own.—Forgnone–Klein–Levy et al

B. f. 4, by Paavo—Fancify, by Diplomat Way
Br.—Fonzone&McLean&VanNagell (Ky) 1987 2 0 0 0
Tr.—Otteson Kimberly $100,000 1986 8 1 0 2 $4,065
Lifetime 15 1 0 3 $6,865 Turf 10 1 0 2 $4,065

17Jan87-5SA 1⅛Ⓣ:4531:1111:501fm*6-5 116 11 12 11 75½ CordroAJr3 ⒻAw28000 70-24 QueenAlydr,BelmoneyBy,BonGenre 9
3Jan87-2SA 1⅛Ⓣ:4641:1111:494fm 8¾ 116 42½ 62¼ 63½ 98¼ Toro F4 ⒻAw28000 70-24 TobgoDncer,QuenAlydr,BlmonyBy 11
3Jan87—Rank early; took up repeatedly final turn
16Oct86♦6Haydock(Eng) 1$\frac{1}{40}$ 1:44 gd 11 126 Ⓣ 815 Lines R Beech H ForwrdRlly,KnightsSecret,LongBy 16
1Oct86♦3Brighton(Eng) 1 fm 6½ 131 Ⓣ 33½ StrkeyG EricSimms H MarshHarrier,FootPatrol,FancyPn 11
1Oct86—No time taken
16Aug86♦1Newbury(Eng) 7f 1:274gd *5½ 107 Ⓣ 16 Lins R Ldbrk Rcng H Pasticcio, EasternHouse, Andika 16
6Aug86♦4Yarmouth(Eng) 7f 1:273gd 7½ 127 Ⓣ 17 Ives T Seacroft H FancyPan,PulhamMills,RareSound 10
30Jly86♦1Doncaster(Eng) 7f 1:272gd 8 112 Ⓣ 44½ Lins R TrnToYrkshire H TheMzll, AirCommnd,KnightSecret 8
9Jun86♦5Leicester(Eng) 7f 1:204fm 25 116 Ⓣ 812 Lines R ⒻOld Dalby FlowerBowl, Riyda, Butsova 17
3Jun86♦7Beverley(Eng) a1$\frac{1}{16}$ 1:452gd 25 111 Ⓣ 311 LinsR Kngs Head(Mdn) Shafy, Coccoluto, FancyPan 13
12Apr86♦1Beverley(Eng) 1¼ 2:12 sf 16 120 Ⓣ 825 LinesR JudiMrdns(Mdn) TopGuest, Bananas, Saronicos 16
Mar 9 SA 6f ft 1:141 h Mar 3 SA tr.t 5f ft 1:032 h Feb 22 SA tr.t 4f ft :503 h Feb 17 SA tr.t 5f ft 1:044 h

H.

***Ocean Wave**
CASTANON A L **114**
Own.—Burke G W

B. m. 5, by Milford—Golden Linnet, by Sing Sing
Br.—Ford H (Eng) 1987 1 0 0 0
Tr.—Lage Armando $85,000 1986 7 2 0 1 $29,075
Lifetime 13 3 0 2 $32,749 Turf 11 3 0 1 $27,874

28Feb87-5SA 1⅛Ⓣ:4631:1141:502fm 15 115 86½ 63½ 1211 1219½ Castanon AL9 Ⓕ 75000 55-15 Mangez Les, OnPatrol,KeepDating 12
9Oct86-5SA a6½f Ⓣ:221 :4531:153fm 28 121 84¼ 52¼ 75¼ 75¼ Soto S B12 ⒻAw33000 76-19 LinpacLeaf,KindaBeau,HelloTexas 12
9Oct86—Wide into stretch
30Aug86-5Dmr 1$\frac{1}{16}$Ⓣ:4631:1121:43 fm 17 122 42 31 41½ 75¼ Soto S B7 ⒻAw28000 86-11 ShortSleeves,PlumTasty,MngezLes 8
7Aug86-8Dmr 1$\frac{1}{16}$Ⓣ:4721:1211:432fm 5¼ 122 53 3nk 3½ 86¼ Soto S B5 ⒻAw27000 83-11 PerfectMatchII,Miranda,PlumTasty 9
7Aug86—Rank down chute; bumped at 3/8
25Jly86-5Dmr 1$\frac{1}{16}$Ⓣ:4841:12 1:431fm 9 121 51¾ 41½ 2hd 11½ Soto S B1 ⒻAw23000 90-10 Ocean Wave,Benzina,PassAllHope 11
20Jun86-9Hol 1 Ⓣ:4531:0931:342fm 23 116 64½ 53 41¾ 1nk Soto S B7 ⒻAw21000 — — Ocean Wave,BonGenre,ArlibraLady 9
12Jun86-9Hol 1 :46 1:104 1:361ft 6¾ 116 32½ 31 44½ 48¾ Ortega LE8 ⒻAw21000 73-20 OurSwtShm,MssRoylMont,St.Mortz 8
29May86-7Hol 7f :213 :451 1:241ft 28 116 64¾ 64¼ 21½ 32¼ Ortega LE9 ⒻAw22000 81-18 OnYourOwnTime,GoodZr,OcenWve 9
30Aug85-7Dmr 1 Ⓣ:4611:1111:36 fm 23 116 65¼ 65½ 31½ 52¼ PedrozMA8 ⒻAw23000 90-10 Gormley, North Mist, Kinda Beau 10
30Aug85—Broke slowly
16Aug85-3Dmr 7½f Ⓣ:23 :4721:301fm 16 116 75 54½ 42 54 PedrozMA2 ⒻAw22000 84-10 Scrabbler, Grey Variety, NorthMist 9
16Aug85—Checked start; lugged in stretch
Feb 18 SA 1 ft 1:46 h Feb 6 SA 7f ft 1:272 h Jan 29 SA Ⓣ 7f fm 1:313 h (d) Jan 16 SA 6f ft 1:15 h

I.

***Ofrendada**
VALENZUELA P A **117**
Own.—Green Thumb Farm Stable

Ch. m. 6, by Ornato—Turca Rubia, by Never
Br.—Haras Zoraida (Arg) 1987 3 0 1 1 $13,400
Tr.—Ippolito Steve $100,000 1986 7 1 3 1 $22,094
Lifetime 32 9 12 4 $58,996 Turf 10 1 5 2 $33,554

21Feb87-5SA a6½f Ⓣ:22 :45 1:16 fm 6½ 116 2hd 2½ 2½ 2½ VlenzulPA9 ⒻAw31000 78-17 HairlessHeiress,Ofrendd,RellyFncy 10
6Feb87-5SA 1⅛Ⓣ:4541:1041:491fm 5¾ 116 34 3nk 1hd 42¾ VlenzulPA8 ⒻAw32000 78-19 SuperKitten,TresureMp,Rivertower 8
23Jan87-8SA 1⅛Ⓣ:4831:1321:502fm 8¼ 116 2hd 1hd 11½ 32 VlenzulPA4 ⒻAw32000 73-25 ScotchAndDry,Rivertower,Ofrendd 7
6Nov86-7Hol 1 Ⓣ:4721:1211:364fm 2½ 116 1½ 1½ 1hd 22¼ VlenzulPA5 ⒻAw26000 81-17 Rock'nRollLeader,Ofrendada,Drnit 12
16Oct86-7SA 1⅛Ⓣ:4641:1121:48 fm 9¼ 115 1½ 1½ 2½ 23 StevensGL6 ⒻAw30000 84-13 Felliniana, Ofrendada, Adalia 8
16Oct86—Bumped at start, lugged in late
4Oct86-7SA 1 :461 1:114 1:372ft 5¼ 117 1hd 2hd 78¾ 715¾ VlenzulPA4 ⒻAw30000 65-18 Mille Et Une, T.V.Residual,GoodZar 9
1Sep86-9Dmr 1$\frac{1}{16}$Ⓣ:4831:1211:43 fm 6½ 117 1½ 1hd 1½ 2hd VlenzulPA5 ⒻAw25000 91-04 Stall Cloud, Ofrendada, J.D.Canyon 6
4Aug86-7Dmr 6½f :22 :444 1:16 ft 19 118 85¼ 108¼ 1112 119½ VlenzulPA1 ⒻAw21000 82-13 PollysLilRscl,ScrnDoor,Symbolclly 11
4Aug86—Crowded, checked at 1/2
2Feb86♦7Hipodromo(Arg) a7f 1:231ft 3 131 12 VldvsJ ⒻCl Asn d Prptrs(Gr3) Ofrendada, Frau Lissette, Gorrita 5
5Jan86♦2LaPlata(Arg) a5f :592ft *1-2 132 34 CceresC Pr Poma Espcl Florida Sun, Oriyera, Ofrendada 5
Mar 13 SA 3f ft :36 h Mar 8 SA 5f gd 1:011 h Mar 2 SA 4f ft :482 h Feb 17 SA 5f ft 1:012 h

J.

Sir's New Hope
DELAHOUSSAYE E **117**
Own.—Malmuth-Malmuth-Mandell

B. m. 5, by Sir Ivor—Hope Renewed, by Never Bend
Br.—Malmuth Mr-Mrs M (Ky) 1987 3 0 0 1 $6,825
Tr.—Cleveland Gene $100,000 1986 10 1 2 1 $31,525
Lifetime 16 2 3 2 $53,625 Turf 6 0 1 1 $13,675

21Feb87-5SA a6½f Ⓣ:22 :45 1:16 fm 14 116 3½ 32 42½ 41½ Sibille R7 ⒻAw31000 77-17 HairlessHeiress,Ofrendd,RellyFncy 10
21Feb87—Bumped start
25Jan87-5SA a6½f Ⓣ:213 :4411:154fm 20 116 3½ 42 44 31 VlenzulPA4 ⒻAw30000 79-18 SunlightMiss,Missen,Sir'sNewHope 9
25Jan87—Drifted out, bumped late
1Jan87-7SA 1 1/16 :461 1:113 1:443ft 11 116 57 64 85½ 811½ Sibille R3 ⒻAw31000 66-19 Annapurna, Python, La Codorniz 9
1Jan87—Wide into stretch
19Dec86-8Hol 1 1/16 Ⓣ:4641:1041:414fm 4 116 42½ 53½ 63½ 56 Sibille R1 ⒻAw26000 79-15 WistfulTun,VvdDncr,ScotchAndDry 8
19Dec86—Altered course, bumped 3/16
4Dec86-7Hol 1⅛ Ⓣ:4731:1141:473fm 27 116 1½ 1hd 21 21 Sibille R5 ⒻAw27000 89-10 Cruell,Sir'sNewHope,Domino'sNurs 8
19Nov86-7Hol 7f :223 :46 1:23 ft 22 116 41½ 31½ 35½ 37½ Sibille R3 ⒻAw24000 82-21 SldomSnS,OnYorOwnTm,Sr'sNwHp 7
2Nov86-5SA 6f :212 :441 1:102ft 47 117 89½ 77 75½ 83½ Sibille R6 ⒻAw28000 83-10 StridingEsy,LoversNtive,FlyingJuli 9
2Nov86—Broke slowly
4Aug86-7Dmr 6½f :22 :444 1:16 ft 28 118 95¾ 75¾ 76¾ 43½ DlhossyE10 ⒻAw21000 89-13 PollysLilRscl,ScrnDoor,Symbolclly 11
4Aug86—Broke slowly
13Jly86-7Hol 7f :222 :452 1:223ft 6½ 116 54½ 66½ 69½ 610 Toro F6 ⒻAw23000 81-15 OurSweetShm,LBellWilson,LDivrtid 8
2Jly86-7Hol 1 1/16 Ⓣ:4731:1111:413fm 12 116 2hd 73¾ 75½ 97½ DlhoussyE3 ⒻAw25000 88-07 Rekindling, T. V. Residual.Kraemer 9
Mar 4 SA 4f ft :494 h Feb 19 SA 3f ft :372 h Feb 12 SA 4f ft :473 h Feb 5 SA 4f ft :474 h

K.

***Fairways Girl**
PINCAY L JR **117**
Own.—Burnison E G

Ch. m. 5, by Young Generation—Sharp Castan, by Sharpen Up
Br.—Vann House Stud (Eng) 1987 2 0 0 0 $1,200
Tr.—Lewis Craig A $100,000 1985 10 1 1 4 $15,873
Lifetime 23 5 2 6 $30,960 Turf 23 5 2 6 $30,960

4Mar87-7SA 1 Ⓣ:4531:1011:36 fm 41 116 12½ 1hd 31 54½ McHrDG7 ⒻⓇBThtful 90-05 Northern Aspen, Reloy, Benzina 10
28Jan87-5SA a6½f Ⓣ:212 :4421:16 fm 5½ 116 1hd 1½ 3½ 64¾ DelhoussyE2 Ⓕ c80000 74-21 MissBeverlyHills,Gossiper,Jiglores 10
5Oct85♦2Haydock(Eng) 6f 1:182gd *3½ 121 Ⓣ 52½ HindlyM Bucklow Hill H Dwn'sDlght,ChplnsClub,LurLormn 11
25Sep85♦3Beverley(Eng) 5f 1:023fm 4 133 Ⓣ 45½ HindlyM RffngraSprint AlZawbaah, Fayruz, YoungPuggy 8
20Sep85♦4Ayr(Scot) 6f 1:18 sf 25 108 Ⓣ 2nk Fry M Ayr Gold Cup H CampsHeath,FirwysGirl,Ameghino 25
12Aug85♦3Newcastle(Eng) 6f 1:152gd 16 115 Ⓣ 1019 HdsnK NrthmbrlndSprntH Orojoya, MelodyPark, Kellytalk 10
2Aug85♦5Thirsk(Eng) 7f 1:274gd *5½ 128 Ⓣ 32½ HndlM Thomas Lord H MountinExprss,BllMrin,FirwysGirl 10
15Jun85♦4York(Eng) 6f 1:13 gd 16 127 Ⓣ 87½ BirxhM Wm Hill Trphy H Si Signor, Orojoya, Sailors Song 12
8Jun85♦4Haydock(Eng) 6f 1:171gd 4 128 Ⓣ 34 HundlyM Sngpr Arlns H Philip, Rosie Dickins, Fairways Girl 9
9May85♦3Chester(Eng) 7f 1:282gd 2¾ 118 Ⓣ 1no BrchM LadbrokeHotelsH FrwysGrl,LpOfHonour,HobornsRos 8
Feb 27 SA 5f ft 1:011 h Feb 19 SA 7f ft 1:271 h Feb 12 SA 5f ft 1:003 h Jan 23 SA 5f ft :592 h

32.

7 **BELMONT**

INNER TURF COURSE
1¼ MILES
BELMONT PARK
START & FINISH

1 ¼ MILES. (InnerTurf). (1.58⅘) ALLOWANCE. Purse $28,000. 3-year-olds and upward which have never won two races other then maiden, claiming or starter. Weight, 3-year-olds, 117 lbs. Older, 122 lbs. Non-winners of a race other than maiden or claiming over a mile since July 15 allowod 5 lbs. Of such a race since July 1, 5 lbs.

A.

***Palace March**
Own.—Firestone B R

B. c. 3, by Cure the Blues—Pride's Palace, by Majestic Prince
Br.—Firestone B R (Ire)
Tr.—Mott William I
112
Lifetime 11 2 2 3 $44,060 — 1987 7 1 2 3 $30,260; 1986 4 1 0 0 $13,800; Turf 4 0 1 2 $13,060

11Jun87- 8Bel fm 1⅜ [T]:48 1:36⅖ 2:13⅗ 3+Alw 28000 7 6 69 45 46½ 37½ Antley C W b 112 3.00 81-16 I'm Hopeful1177SoarToTheStars119½PalaceMarch1123¾ Lost iron 9
25May87- 6Bel fm 1¼ [T]:50⅖ 1:39⅗ 2:03⅖ 3+Alw 28000 5 4 53½ 43 33 3½ Antley C W b 111 2.70 76-15 Foxhall Keene 124no I'm Hopeful 119½ PalaceMarch1113 Fin. well 7
17May87- 6Bel fm 1 1/16 Ⓣ:45⅘ 1:10 1:41⅗ 3+Alw 28000 3 8 87½ 52½ 32½ 22¾ Antley C W b 111 10.10 86-14 Silvino 1192¾ Palace March 111½ Seattlite 1191½ Rallied 12
21Apr87- 7Aqu fst 1⅛ :49⅘ 1:14 1:51⅗ 3+Alw 28000 4 3 32½ 32½ 46¼ 36 Romero R P b 113 5.40 71-26 Conquilot 112no Easton 1196 Palace March 1131¾ Even try 5
27Mar87- 7GP fst 1 1/16 :48⅗ 1:13 1:46⅕ Alw 16000 8 7 62½ 34½ 23 23½ Tejeira J b 117 5.70 66-27 Arab Speaker 1173½ Palace March 117¾ Krul 1191½ Best of others 8
6Mar87- 6Hia fst 1⅛ :48⅕ 1:12⅗ 1:51⅘ Alw 18000 6 5 51½ 43 41¼ 1nd Cordero A Jr b 115 3.70 72-25 Palace March 115nd Bally Blue 121nk Sunshine Bob 1155½ Driving 8
22Feb87- 8Hia fm 1 1/16 Ⓣ 1:43 Alw 20400 10 12 129¾ 1010 913 67½ Day P 114 20.50 75-13 Peaceable 1142½ Mc Forbes 114nd Superceded 1142 No threat 12
8Oct86- 5Bel fst 1 :45⅖ 1:10⅗ 1:36⅗ Alw 25000 6 7 721 616 617 616 Graell A 122 40.90 66-19 Cryptoclearance 1174 King's Galley 1171½ Gone West1172 Outrun 8
27Sep86- 3Bel sly 1 1/16 :46 1:11⅘ 1:45⅘ Md Sp Wt 4 5 57 41½ 12½ 17 Martens G 118 *1.60 73-17 Palace March 1187 Sir Bemis 1182 Be My Victim1183 Ridden out 8
3Sep86- 6Bel fst 7f :22⅕ :45⅕ 1:24⅖ Md Sp Wt 3 10 1012 610 811 65¾ Martens G 118 72.20f 75-15 Showroom 116½ Drachma 1181¼ Petrinni 118¾ Lacked room 13
LATEST WORKOUTS Jly 23 Bel 7f fst 1:28⅗ h Jly 18 Bel 4f fst :49⅖ h Jun 7 Bel 6f fst 1:13⅘ h

B.

Patlomat
Own.—Schwartz B K

Ch. g. 3, by Diplomat Way—Picki Patti, by Minnesota Mac or Gunflint
Br.—Zuiderent Georgette & H (Fla)
Tr.—Alexander Frank A
112
Lifetime 9 2 1 0 $34,090 — 1987 9 2 1 0 $34,090; 1986 0 M 0 0; Turf 6 2 1 0 $33,740

13Jly87- 7Bel fm 1⅜ [T]:48⅘ 2:03⅖ 2:16 3+Alw 28000 2 1 14 1½ 22½ 57 Vasquez J 113 5.40 70-19 Sure Dad 1173¾ I'm Enthused 1161 Paris Office 116¾ Gave way 9
26Jun87- 7Bel fst 1¼ :48⅕ 1:38 2:03⅕ 3+Alw 28000 3 1 1½ 32½ 38 514¾ Vasquez J 115 6.40 67-22 Soar To The Stars 1179 Heritance 1145½Muscovado117nk Used up 7
4Jun87- 7Bel sly 1 1/16 :46⅖ 1:11⅕ 1:43⅖ 3+Alw 28000 2 6 32½ 33½ 27 513 Guerra W A 114 7.60 72-21 Foolish Pirate 11410½ Forbes Way 114ndCoco'sDouble1102¼ Tired 9
18May87- 7Bel fm 1⅜ [T]:50 1:39⅖ 2.17 3+Alw 27000 1 1 12 12 13 14 Guerra W A 110 2.30 72-22 Patlomat 1104 Dance Furlough 119nd Sir Jove 124no Ridden out 8
3May87- 3Aqu gd 1⅛ Ⓣ:50⅖ 1:15⅗ 1:53⅖ 3+Alw 27000 7 2 32½ 42 44 43¾ Guerra W A 110 2.60 65-33 Superceded112nkMsterOfArts1192¾Akoochement119nk Weakened 8
23Apr87- 7Aqu gd 1 1/16 Ⓣ:48⅘ 1:14⅕ 1:46⅘ 3+Alw 27000 3 5 77 45½ 34 21½ Guerra W A 110 6.40 69-30 Midnight Cousins 1191½ Patlomat1102MasterOfArts121nk Gamely 10
22Feb87- 8Hia fm 1 1/16 Ⓣ 1:43 Alw 20400 4 10 88¼ 89½ 1016 810¾ Fires E 120 3.20 72-13 Peaceable 1142½ Mc Forbes 114nd Superceded 1142 No factor 12
20Jan87- 7Hia fm *1⅛ Ⓣ 1:49⅖ Md Sp Wt 6 4 32 21 12 14½ Fires E 120 2.50 84-17 Patlomat 1204½ Foolish Pirate 1202 Deal Me theAces1201 Driving 11
4Jan87- 6Crc sly 6f :22⅘ :47 1:14⅖ Md 40000 4 10 105¼ 811 78¼ 43¾ Fires E 120 9.50 75-24 NativeDignity1201¼KingStutz1202¾HiltheBlue120nd Rallied inside 11
LATEST WORKOUTS Jly 27 Bel 5f fst 1:00⅕ h Jly 7 Bel 5f fst 1:03 b Jun 22 Bel 4f fst :50⅗ b Jun 15 Bel 4f fst :49⅗ b

C.

Race Point Dk. b. or br. g. 4, by Talc—Drylook, by Sky High II
Br.—Mulholland M (NY)
Own.—Offbroadway Stable Tr.—Figueroa Carlos Jr
117 Lifetime 10 2 1 1 $42,450 | 1987 2 0 0 0 $2,700 | 1986 7 2 1 1 $39,750 | Turf 8 2 1 1 $42,450

13Jly87- 8Bel fm 1 1/16 Ⓣ:46⅖ 1:10⅗ 1:41⅗ 3↑Handicap 3 2 32 52¼ 44½ 45 Belmonte J F b 106 37.60 83-19 I Rejoice 110¾ Island Sun 115¾ Explosive Dancer112¾ Weakened 8
18Jun87- 7Bel fm 1 Ⓣ:45⅕ 1:10 1:35 3↑Alw 28000 4 9 1016 98 813 69 Migliore R b 117 30.30 81-10 Easton 1173 Seattlite 1172¾ Nudge 1112 Lacked room 12
24Oct86- 7Aqu fm 1 1/16 Ⓣ:47⅘ 1:12⅖ 1:44⅘ 3↑[S]Alw 29500 4 4 31½ 2hd 42½ 58½ Guerra W A b 119 5.40 72-20 G'DayMate1142¾ExpeditionMoon1141¾RootCanal1173¼ Weakened 8
12Oct86- 1Bel fm 1 Ⓣ:48 1:11⅘ 1:37 3↑[S]Alw 28000 4 1 1½ 1½ 11 12 Santos J A b 119 *1.30 80-15 Race Point1192CatchTheMoon1192¾SummerTale1144¾ Drew clear 7
9Oct86- 7Bel fm 1 1/16 Ⓣ:47⅗ 1:12 1:44⅖ 3↑[S]Alw 29500 1 1 1½ 1hd 1½ 31 Guerra W A b 114 *2.10 73-26 Vatza Matter 114½ ExpeditionMoon114½RacePoint1142 Weakened 12
19Sep86- 4Bel fm 1 Ⓣ:45⅘ 1:10⅕ 1:35⅘ 3↑Md Sp Wt 6 2 21 12 15 12¾ Guerra W A b 118 7.90 86-15 Race Point 1162¾ Catch The Moon 1185½Mr.Fife118hd Ridden out 12
25Aug86- 2Sar fm 1⅛ Ⓣ:47⅖ 1:12 1:50⅖ 3↑[S]Md Sp Wt 7 2 2½ 1hd 2½ 21¾ Santos J A b 117 13.30 73-15 Lyphard'sFeathers1141¾RcePoint1171RuffledGrouse1171¼ Gamely 12
30Jly86- 5Sar fm 1 1/16 [T]:48⅖ 1:13 1:45⅗ 3↑[S]Alw 28000 5 9 86½ 87¾ 66 69½ Guerra W A 111 44.90 68-21 Talc Buster 113nk Rio Belle 1125½ Vatza Matter 1161 Outrun 10
18Jun86- 6Bel fst 6f :22⅘ :46⅕ 1:11⅕ 3↑[S]Md Sp Wt 9 8 109¼1113 913 910 Guerra W A 114 83.60 76-15 Tall Roman 1141¼ Crobosity 1142¾ Mokos 1144¾ Outrun 14
29Nov85- 9Aqu sly 6f :23⅕ :46⅘ 1:11⅗ [S]Md Sp Wt 8 6 88¼1112111510l7¼ Gomez E R 118 44.30 66-22 Nasty And Tough1181Tucker'sCabin1186¼TallRoman1183¾ Outrun 11
LATEST WORKOUTS Jly 2 Aqu 4f gd :53⅕ b Jun 11 Aqu Ⓣ 7f fm 1:32⅗ b (d) Jun 6 Aqu 6f fst 1:16⅖ b

D.

Paris Office Ch. c. 3, by Secretariat—Oui, by Le Fabuleux
Br.—Vanderbilt A G (Md)
Own.—Vanderbilt A G Tr.—Violette Richard A
114 Lifetime 11 2 2 2 $49,900 | 1987 6 1 0 2 $24,420 | 1986 5 1 2 0 $25,480 | Turf 4 0 0 2 $8,220

13Jly87- 7Bel fm 1⅜ [T]:48⅘ 2:03⅘ 2:16 3↑Alw 28000 9 6 611 67 47 34¾ Pezua J M 116 3.50 72-19 Sure Dad 1173¾ I'm Enthused 1161 Paris Office 116¾ Late bid 9
2Jly87- 7Bel sly 1⅛ :49⅘ 1:39⅗ 2:20⅗ 3↑Alw 27000 2 5 54 32½ 1hd 1½ Pezua J M 111 *1.30 77-27 Paris Office 111½ Gone Cat 1122¼ I'm No Yankee 11710 Driving 6
18Jun87- 5Bel fm 1¼ [T]:48⅘ 1:37⅕ 2:01⅘ 3↑Alw 27000 3 9 96¼ 85½ 62¼ 3nk Santos J A 112 *3.60 85-10 I m Enthused 114hd True Vigor 117nk Paris Office 112½ Rallied 12
6Jun87- 9Lrl fm 1 1/16 Ⓣ:46⅖ 1:11⅗ 1:43⅕ [S]H S Finney 4 8 814 87¾ 58 53¼ DeCarlo C P 111 4.70 84-18 Ten Keys 119nk Green Book 1221 Prolinage 1192 Wide 8
23May87- 6Bel gd 1 1/16 [T]:48 1:12⅖ 1:44⅘ 3↑Alw 27000 7 8 811 89½ 64¾ 42¾ Baird E T 108 5.00 74-25 Groomsman 119½ Master Of Arts1192Triumvirate108nk Slow early 8
10May87- 9Bel fst 6f :23⅕ :47⅖ 1:11⅘ 3↑Alw 26000 7 10 109½1012101510l5¾ Vasquez J b 114 20.10 65-25 Conventioneer 119¾ Heritance 1084½LegionD'Honour1101¾ Trailed 10
13Dec86- 8Aqu fst 1 1/16 [•]:47⅕ 1:12⅗ 1:45 Nashua 5 7 719 716 615 617 Samyn J L 114 7.90 68-20 Bold Summit 114nk Drachma 1149½ Perdition's Son 114nk Outrun 8
13Dec86-Grade II
30Nov86- 3Aqu fst 1 :47⅖ 1:12⅘ 1:39 Md Sp Wt 6 6 67¼ 63¼ 41 12¾ Santos J A 118 *1.30 71-24 Paris Office 1162¾ Endorse 118½ Christopher's Time 1182 Driving 7
10Nov86- 6Aqu gd 1 :46 1:11 1:37 Md Sp Wt 7 7 611 67 54 2½ Romero R P 118 *2.40 80-16 Magic Feet 118½ Paris Office 118hd Fast Forward 118hd Fast fin. 8
29Oct86- 4Aqu fst 1 :45⅘ 1:10⅕ 1:36 Md Sp Wt 3 13 107¼ 96¾ 44 25½ Martens G 118 9.40 80-15 Simply Majestic 1185½ ParisOffice118noThurstonHill118nk Rallied 13
LATEST WORKOUTS ●Jly 28 Bel 4f fst :47 h Jly 23 Bel Ⓣ 5f fm 1:03 b (d) Jun 29 Bel 4f fst :49 b Jun 14 Bel 5f fst 1:01 b

E.

Target Sighted B. c. 4, by Sharpen Up—Dangerous Gunner, by Ack Ack
Br.—Johnson Karen & Kathy (Ky)
Own.—Amherst Stable Tr.—Johnson Philip G
114⁵ Lifetime 12 2 3 1 $39,351 | 1987 5 2 0 0 $33,660 | 1986 6 M 2 1 $5,347 | Turf 11 2 3 1 $39,351

16Jly87- 7Bel fm 1 1/16 Ⓣ:46⅘ 1:11⅖ 1:43⅗ 3↑Alw 27000 10 9 96½ 57 43½ 11 Davis R G 117 6.70 78-26 TargetSighted1171GliderPilot117hdAkoochemente117nk Drew out 11
20Jun87- 7Bel fm 1¼ [T]:48⅘ 1:37 2:02⅘ 3↑Alw 27000 3 7 75½ 56 45½ 44 Davis R G 119 *1.60e 78-17 Milesius 1112¼ Romantic Tune 109¾ De Facto 1171 Rallied 10
29May87- 4Bel fm 1⅜ [T]:48⅗ 1:39 2:17⅗ 3↑Md Sp Wt 4 9 813 66 1hd 13¾ Davis R G 124 3.20 69-19 TrgtSgntd1243¾SksOvrVnn1242¾ChrstophrsPppy1134¾ Ridden out 14
14May87- 3Bel fm 1 1/16 Ⓣ:46⅗ 1:11⅗ 1:43⅘ 3↑Md Sp Wt 7 10 97¼ 75¼ 74½ 53¾ Davis R G 124 6.20 73-22 HsFrquntflyr124hdSlvington1131¾WinMrchnt1081 Checked, bmpd 12
14May87-Placed fourth through disqualification
26Apr87- 4Aqu fst 6f :22⅘ :46⅘ 1:11⅗ 3↑Md 70000 4 8 99¼ 913 818 817½ Samyn J L 120 8.80e 65-21 ThunderDrone1131½SilkyAppel1121½DecortedStreker1132½ Outrun 9
19Oct86- 4Bel fm 1 1/16 Ⓣ:48⅕ 1:12⅘ 1:44⅘ 3↑Md Sp Wt 1 7 54 45 45½ 37 Samyn J L 119 *2.10 65-23 Seattlite 119no Imperial Idol 1197 Target Sighted 119nk Rallied 11
1Sep86- 2Bel fm 1 1/16 Ⓣ:46⅘ 1:12⅕ 1:42⅘ 3↑Md Sp Wt 2 9 94¾ 55 43 43¼ Samyn J L 118 10.60 79-18 StrongAdversary1181Dr.Danzig1221¼MasterOfArts1181 Off slowly 12
19Jun86 ♦6Ascot(Eng) fm 1½ 2:29⅘ Ⓣ King George V Hcp 17 Adams N b 111 33.00 — — Moon Madness 1305 Weshaam 1232 Dalgadiyr 1216 No factor 19
30May86 ♦6Hamilton(Scot) sf 1½ 3:02⅘ Ⓣ Pintail Stakes(Mdn) 2¾ Reid J 126 *1.60 — — Sir Brett 121¾ Target Sighted 1261 Nadas 12625 Bid, led 10
31Mar86 ♦6Kempton(Eng) sf 1½ 2:55⅘ Ⓣ Ruthwood Stakes(Mdn) 2nd Ried J 126 7.00 — — Longgnurst126no TrgtSghtd12610 HbbrdsLodg1261½ 2nd thru str 8
LATEST WORKOUTS Jly 30 Bel 5f fst 1:03 b Jly 25 Bel 5f fst 1:02⅘ b Jly 13 Bel 4f fst :49⅘ h Jly 6 Bel 5f fst 1:01⅗ h

F.

Mr. Forty Niner Dk. b. or br. c. 4, by Poison Ivory—Miss Forty Niner, by Mr Prospector
Br.—Aisco Stable (NY)
Own.—Dashner C Tr.—Seefeldt Paul D
119 Lifetime 22 3 4 3 $52,308 | 1987 6 1 2 1 $30,164 | 1986 16 2 2 2 $22,144 | Turf 14 2 4 2 $47,436

15Jly87- 7Bel gd 1 1/16 Ⓣ:47⅘ 1:13⅕ 1:45⅘ 3↑[S]Alw 30500 10 9 86¼ 32½ 2½ 11¾ Cordero A Jr b 117 *2.00 67-34 Mr.FortyNiner1171¾Musial'sMtch1172½PiceInTheSun1172 Driving 11
5Jly87- 7Pen fm 1 1/16 Ⓣ 1:41⅖ 3↑Strohecker 7 8 89¾ 611 512 511¼ Aviles R B b 113 *2.50 72-20 B.A.Cptin1121¾[D]AlongCmeJones110nkGenerlStrik1134¼ No factor 8
18Jun87- 9Lrl fm 1 1/16 Ⓣ:45⅗ 1:09⅖ 1:39⅘ 3↑Clm 65000 6 6 611 610 67½ 31¼ Wiley M C5 b 114 9.40 103 — Rollodka 117¾ Duxun Limited 119½ Mr. Forty Niner 1141¼ Hit rail 6
7Jun87- 9Lrl fm 1⅛ Ⓣ:45⅘ 1:10⅖ 1:47⅗ 3↑Chieftain H 8 9 924 919 713 68¾ Wiley M C b 107 9.90 87-07 Castelets 115½ Tri For Size 1153½ Brilliant Stepper 110nk Outrun 9
15May87- 5Bel fm 1⅜ [T]:48⅕ 1:39⅗ 2:18⅕ 3↑[S]Alw 28500 5 9 911 31 11½ 22¾ Antley C W b 119 *1.30 63-29 Captain Len 1032¾ Mr. Forty Niner1191HandSalute113nk Checked 10
22Apr87- 8GS fm 1 1/16 Ⓣ:47⅖ 1:12⅗ 1:44⅗ Clm 50000 2 10 1012 85¼ 34½ 22 Wilson R b 116 7.70 83-15 L'EtoileDuNord1162Mr.FortyNiner1161½ChespekBch1143½ Rallied 10
15Nov86-10Lrl sf 1 1/16 Ⓣ:49⅘ 1:17⅗ 1:52⅕ 3↑Alw 15000 1 12 1113 811 611 511¾ Delgado A b 114 *3.00 30-48 L'EtoileDuNord114½FirestEmpror1142¼Kycolony1168 Checked st. 12
12Oct86- 7Lrl fm 1 1/16 Ⓣ:46⅘ 1:11⅖ 1:41⅘ 3↑Alw 15000 3 12 1013 912 79¾ 34¼ Delgado A b 113 5.90 90-02 Flying Rice 1171¾ Lordly Manner 1122½Mr.FortyNiner113¾ Rallied 12
3Oct86- 6Lrl fm 1⅛ Ⓣ:46⅖ 1:12⅕ 1:51⅖ Clm 30000 3 7 714 88¼ 42½ 12 Delgado A b 114 10.80 80-18 Mr.FortyNiner1142AnotherShelter115nkYou'reThTop1171½ Driving 9
20Sep86- 7Pim fm 1 1/16 Ⓣ:47 1:10⅗ 1:42 3↑Alw 13700 6 5 63½ 57 49½ 48¾ Hutton G W b 112 6.90 84-07 Loose 1147 Fairest Emperor 114nk Double Bill 1171½ Lacked resp. 9
LATEST WORKOUTS Jun 30 Bow 4f fst :48⅖ h

G.

Core A Apple Dk. b. or br. c. 3, by Duns Scotus—Ruckus, by King's Company
Br.—Edwards James F (NY)
Own.—Friedman H L Tr.—Badgett William Jr
112 Lifetime 12 2 3 2 $52,835 | 1987 11 2 3 2 $52,550 | 1986 1 M 0 0 $285 | Turf 1 0 0 1 $3,780

27Jly87- 2Bel gd 1 1/16 [T]:49 1:13⅕ 1:47⅘ 3↑[S]Alw 31500 7 5 53 54½ 35 36 Garcia J A b 113 4.70 56-27 [DH]Musil'sMtch1176[DH]Finocchio1066CoreAApple1138 Forced out 8
17Jly87- 6Bel fst 1 1/16 :47 1:11⅘ 1:43⅕ 3↑[S]Alw 31500 4 4 32 31½ 26 28½ Garcia J A b 113 3.10 77-20 Criscam 1128½ Core A Apple 1134½ Finocchio 106½ Bobbled st. 6
5Jly87- 5Bel fst 7f :22⅘ :45⅘ 1:24⅖ 3↑[S]Alw 30000 9 7 88 76¼ 57½ 37½ Garcia J A b 116 4.00 72-24 Proud Guy 1165½ Edelnash 1132 CoreAApple116½ P'ssd tired ones 9
22Jun87- 1Bel my 1⅛ :47⅖ 1:11⅗ 1:50⅕ 3↑[S]Alw 30500 3 1 11½ 1½ 16 110 Garcia J A b 109 5.30 76-22 Core A Apple 10910 Campus Cop113¾Roundwood1175 Ridden out 7
11Jun87- 9Bel fst 7f :23⅗ :46⅘ 1:25⅖ 3↑[S]Md Sp Wt 12 1 2½ 2hd 15 16 Garcia J A b 114 8.50 75-23 Core A Apple 1146 EventfulNasnua1144I'mAlbert1142¼ Riddenout 12
23Apr87- 2Aqu fst 1⅛ :49 1:14⅗ 1:54⅖ 3↑Md 35000 9 1 1hd 1½ 21½ 23 Bailey J D 112 6.30 60-24 BnnrCommndr963CorAAppl1126ChrstophrsPppy113¾ Second best 9
6Apr87- 9Aqu sly 1⅛ :47⅖ 1:12⅘ 1:51⅘ 3↑[S]Md Sp Wt 4 8 1211111811123 829½ Antley C W 113 *3.00 46-20 Czar Light 11216 Pinky's Pet 1191¾ Please Comply 1132 Outrun 12
23Mar87- 4Aqu fst 1 :48⅗ 1:15 1:41⅘ Md 35000 4 8 85¼ 67 56 44 Antley C W b 122 3.00 53-28 Heir Forbes 118½ Mystical Empire113½Son'sWish1183 Bumped st. 14
2Mar87- 6Aqu gd 1⅛ [•]:48 1:13 1:53⅕ [S]Md Sp Wt 3 6 66 75¾ 58¾ 58½ Bailey J D 122 23.70 67-15 Captain Len 122nk Duc de Val 122nk Rip 1226 Outrun 12
5Feb87- 6Aqu fst 6f [•]:23 :47⅖ 1:13⅗ [S]Md Sp Wt 11 6 4¾ 43 45½ 66½ Santos J A 122 3.60 69-24 Tribal Instinct 1173½ Angela's Fool122½StrikeAndSpare1171 Tired 12
LATEST WORKOUTS Jly 23 Bel Ⓣ 4f fm :50⅕ b (d) Jly 12 Bel 4f fst :51 b Jly 1 Bel 4f fst :51 b Jun 8 Aqu 4f fst :48⅕ h

H.

I'm Enthused — B. c. 3, by Vigors—Atwinkle, by Hail the Pirates
Own.—Brookfield Farm — Br.—Jonabell Farm (Ky) — Tr.—Kelly Edward I — 112
Lifetime 7 2 1 0 $36,760 — 1987 4 2 1 0 $36,760 — 1986 3 M 0 0 — Turf 4 2 1 0 $36,760

13Jly87- 7Bel fm 1⅜ [T]:48⅘ 2:03⅖ 2:16 3↑Alw 28000 5 4 48½ 33½ 35 23¾ Davis R G b 116 4.20 73-19 Sure Dad 1173¾ I'm Enthused 1161 Paris Office 116¾ Rallied 9
18Jun87- 5Bel fm 1¼ [T]:48⅘ 1:37⅕ 2:01⅘ 3↑Alw 27000 2 8 85¾ 63½ 3nk 1hd Davis R G b 114 7.50 85-10 I'm Enthused 114hd True Vigor 117nk Paris Office 112½ Driving 12
11Jun87- 6Bel fm 1 1/16 Ⓣ:46⅕ 1:11 1:43⅗ 3↑Md Sp Wt 3 8 613 714 22 11½ Davis R G b 114 10.40 76-16 I'mEnthused1141½Salvington1143½SpectacularSmoke1096 Driving 11
31May87- 5Bel fm 1 1/16 Ⓣ:47⅗ 1:11⅗ 1:43⅕ 3↑Md Sp Wt 4 8 87½ 57 65½ 66 Davis R G b 113 24.30 74-20 Sultry Season 1061¼ Don Don 1082¾ Difference 124nd No factor 9
14Dec86- 6Aqu fst 1 1/16 [•]:48⅗ 1:13⅕ 1:48 Md Sp Wt 10 10 1119 1126 1135 1131¼ Hernandez R b 118 49.90 39-20 Coco's Double 1183 Knockon 1182¾ Medieval Mind 1184 Outrun 11
27Nov86- 4Aqu gd 7f :23⅘ :47⅗ 1:25⅘ Md Sp Wt 3 6 21 86¾ 930 936½ Romero R P b 118 3.30e 35-29 Major Beard 1184½ In All Respects 1185 Sir Bemis 118½ Tired 9
23Oct86- 5Aqu fst 7f :22⅘ :46 1:22⅘ Md Sp Wt 9 9 914 1016 1023 1027¼ Romero R P 118 26.40 60-17 Talinum 1185 Bold Summit 116nk Simply Majestic 1162½ Outrun 11
LATEST WORKOUTS Jly 30 Bel [T] 4f fm :49⅗ b (d) Jly 23 Bel Ⓣ 4f fm :50⅖ b (d) Jly 9 Bel 4f sly :54 b Jun 29 Bel 3f fst :37 h

33. When classified restrictions of summer apply to the previous season as well as the current season, handicappers can look first for a particular type of horse that remains eligible. You can find exactly that kind of horse here.

5th Saratoga

1 1/16 MILES. (Turf). (1.39⅖) ALLOWANCE. Purse $45,000. Fillies and mares, 3-year-olds and upward which have never won two races of $18,650 at a mile or over in 1986–87. Weight, 3-year-olds, 117 lbs. Older, 122 lbs. Non-winners of a race of $18,650 at a mile or over since June 1 allowed 3 lbs. Of such a race since April 1, 5 lbs. Of such a race since January 1, 7 lbs.

Coupled—Boom And Bust and Improyal.

A.

Boom And Bust — B. f. 4, by Mr Prospector—Belle Gallante, by Gallant Man
Br.—Evans & Fretheim (Va) — 1987 3 1 0 1 $27,982
Own.—Evans E P — 115 — Tr.—Johnson Philip G — 1986 7 4 1 0 $79,540
Lifetime 10 5 1 1 $107,522 — Turf 1 0 0 0

25Jly87-7Mth 6f :22 :443 1:094ft 3½ 113 88¼ 87¼ 68 36 AtlCW4 ⒻGrecinComd 85-13 GrlPowdr,WllowyMood,BomAndBst 9
25Jly87—Bore out
28Jun87-8Bel 7f :222 :454 1:241ft 4¼ 110 2hd 2½ 612 617¼ DsRG6 ⒻVagrancy H 64-19 NorthSidr,StormndSunshin,Funstrd 6
28Jun87—Grade III
3Jun87-7Bel 7f :223 :444 1:234ft *7-5 117 14 17 16 13¼ Samyn J L3 ⒻAw40000 83-22 BoomAndBust,EtrnlVow,I'mSplndd 6
12Sep86-8Bel 7f Ⓣ:224 :4531:221fm 12 113 22 42½ 815 1015¾ Samyn J L4 ⒻManta 77-08 GiveAToast,TaxDodge,LadyOfLeys 11
12Sep86—Run in Divisions
31Jly86-8Sar 7f :221 :443 1:224ft 5¼ 118 1hd 1½ 43 713¾ SamynJL4 ⒻTest 74-19 StormndSunshn,ClssyCthy,I'mSwts 7
31Jly86—Grade II
5Jly86-1Bel 6f :22 :444 1:094ft *1 114 11½ 14 14 11 Samyn J L3 ⒻRose 93-15 BomAndBst,ScyMssy,DntWrryBtM 6
9Jun86-7Bel 7f :234 :472 1:244ft *1-2 114 52 4nk 11 1½ Samyn J L2 ⒻAw25000 78-17 BoomAndBst,PrvtClrs,GlwngPrspct 5
24May86-1Bel 7f :224 :454 1:221ft *2-5 113 21 1½ 16 110½ Samyn J L3 ⒻAw24000 91-12 BomAndBst,Slly'sHrn,UnlmtdAccnt 6
Jly 23 Bel 4f ft :47 b Jly 18 Bel 7f ft 1:274 b ●Jly 12 Bel 5f ft 1:00 b Jly 7 Bel 4f ft :482 b

B.

***Green Oasis** — B. m. 5, by Green Dancer—La Diffa, by Sir Tor
Br.—S C A de la Perrigne (Fra) — 1987 8 2 2 1 $57,150
Own.—Mandysland Farm — 115 — Tr.—Skiffington Thomas J — 1986 6 1 2 0 $18,610
Lifetime 22 4 4 3 $98,028 — Turf 22 4 4 3 $98,028

22Jly87-6Bel 1½Ⓣ:49 2:0212:271fm 6½ 110 47 31½ 3½ 2¾ Davis R G1 HcpO 87-15 I'm Hopeful, Green Oasis, SureDad 6
13Jun87-9GS 1⅜Ⓣ:5011:39 2:16 fm 5 114 42½ 32 41 45¼ PerrtC4 ⒻVineland H 93-06 CadabraAbra,Santiki,BugEyedBetty 8
13Jun87—Grade III; In close,steadied
14May87-6Bel 1¼[T]:51 1:4022:041fm 2¾ 119 34½ 1½ 13 14 Santos J A2 ⒻAw31000 73-22 GreenOasis,Improyal,CaymanQueen 7
18Apr87-10GP 1½Ⓣ:50 2:0522:312sf 3½e110 811 53¼ 42½ 55½ SnJL11 ⒻOrchid H 61-33 AnkGrmni,SingulrBqust,Ivor'sImg 14
18Apr87—Grade II
4Apr87-9GP 1 1/16Ⓣ:4711:1031:414fm 3¼ 122 817 817 55¾ 36½ StsJA2 Ⓕ[R]Indinsunlit 84-10 AnkaGermni,DesertView,GreenOsis 9
18Mar87-8GP a1 Ⓣ 1:382fm *1 119 75 54½ 32½ 2no Santos J A1 ⒻAw18000 88-18 CertLegis,GreenOsis,MissEnchntd 11
27Feb87-9Hia a1 1/16Ⓣ 1:423fm 3½ 122 611 56 24 44½ Cruguet J5 ⒻAw29000 80-17 Marianna'sGirl,Navarchus,DmeGris 8
16Jan87-7Hia a1⅛Ⓣ 1:504fm*6-5 116 41¾ 2hd 1½ 1nk Perret C8 ⒻAw19000 77-19 Green Oasis, Improyal, Millracer 10
Aug 4 Sar Ⓣ 5f gd 1:003 h ●Jly 17 Fai tr.t 5f ft 1:014 b Jly 11 Fai tr.t 4f ft :473 b Jly 7 Fai tr.t 4f ft :49 b

C.

***Lake Champlain**
Own.—Firestone Mrs B R **115**
B. f. 4, by Kings Lake—Sensibilty, by Hail to Reason
Br.—Firestone Mr-Mrs B R (Ire)
Tr.—Mott William I
Lifetime 18 3 7 3 $141,455
1987 8 1 2 2 $54,172
1986 9 2 4 1 $86,581
Turf 17 3 7 3 $141,455

31Jly87-8Bel 7f ⓣ:23 :45³1:23¹fm*6-5 115 5² 5⁵ 2²½ 2ⁿᵏ RomeroRP1 ⒻAw40000 88-13 RllyForJustice,LkChmplin,Funistrd 8
31Jly87—Slow start
25Jly87-7Bel 1 1/16ⓣ:46⁴1:10²1:42¹fm 2¾ 122 4¹½ 4¹½ 3²½ 3³½ RomeroRP5 ⒻAw45000 81-20 Dismasted, Loa, Lake Champlain 9
8Jly87-8Bel 1 1/16[T]:48¹1:12 1:45²gd *1 122 3ⁿᵏ 1ʰᵈ 1ʰᵈ 3¹ RomeroRP6 ⒻAw45000 73-26 Sorayah, Soliciting,LakeChamplain 6
31May87-8Bel 1¼[T]:49³1:37 2:01 fm 4e113 1¹ 1½ 3ⁿᵏ 4² RrRP2 ⒻNew York H 87-20 AnkGermni,Vidognic,LdKindlyLight 7
31May87—Grade II
20May87-3Bel 1 ⓣ:48²1:13¹1:39¹yl *8-5 119 3² 2¹½ 1²½ 1⁶½ RomeroRP5 ⒻAw31000 69-31 LkeChmplin,Riverbride,UntendedDt 8
10May87-8Bel 1 1/16ⓣ:47 1:12 1:44¹gd 9¾ 114 4³ 6⁴½ 6⁶½ 4⁴½ VsqzJ5 ⒻBeaugay H 70-26 GiveAToast,Videogenic,SmallVirtue 8
10May87—Grade III
24Apr87-7Aqu 1 :46³ 1:11³ 1:37¹m 3¾ 119 5⁶ 7¹⁵ 7²⁷ 7³⁵ Vasquez J7 ⒻAw31000 45-21 Seriously, New Dawn, Pour Me Out 7
7Apr87-8GP a1 1/16ⓣ 1:44⁴fm*3-5 117 3⁵½ 3¹½ 3¹½ 2¹ Perret C8 ⒻAw18000 81-15 ImprdntLov,LkChmpln,FltwodFncy 8
Jun 30 Bel 5f ft 1:03⁴ b Jun 18 Bel 3f ft :36 h

D.

Loa
Own.—Turner Barbara W **115**
B. f. 4, by Hawaii—Tiy, by Nalees Man
Br.—Labrot Barbara (Ky)
Tr.—Turner William H Jr
Lifetime 26 4 5 3 $126,011
1987 9 0 3 1 $37,050
1986 15 4 2 2 $88,961
Turf 13 3 5 0 $99,071

25Jly87-7Bel 1 1/16ⓣ:46⁴1:10²1:42¹fm 4½ 115 1ʰᵈ 1ʰᵈ 1½ 2ⁿᵒ Maple E1 ⒻAw45000 85-20 Dismasted, Loa, Lake Champlain 9
12Jly87-7Bel 1 1/16ⓣ:46³1:11 1:43 gd*9-5 115 4¹¾ 2¹½ 2¹½ 2¹ ‡Maple E8 ⒻAw45000 80-22 Mighty Wonder, Tamida, Loa 9
‡12Jly87—Dead heat
10Jun87-7Bel 1 1/16[T]:48¹1:11⁴1:42⁴fm 5½ 117 4⁶ 3³ 3³½ 2¹¾ Bailey J D5 ⒻAw45000 85-17 Tappiano, Loa, Reel Easy 7
29May87-8Bel 1 1/16ⓣ:46⁴1:10¹1:42 fm 3¾ 119 2¹½ 2³ 3³½ 4⁴½ Samyn J L4 ⒻAw45000 82-19 CertLegis,Soliciting,CourgeousKrn 7
19Mar87-7Aqu 1 :46² 1:11⁴ 1:38¹ft 19 115 2⁵ 2⁵ 4⁵ 4⁶½ Samyn J L8 ⒻAw45000 68-29 BrbicueSuce,MineTonight,LiklyGin 8
27Feb87-8Aqu 1 1/16[•]:47 1:12 1:45 ft 20 105¹⁰ 5¹¹ 5¹³ 5¹¹ 5¹³½ Elias J A4 ⒻAw45000 72-19 Clemanna's Rose,ReelEasy,LadyJin 7
14Feb87-5Aqu 170[•]:46²1:12¹1:44⁴ft 16 107¹⁰ 4⁸½ 4⁷½ 4³½ 3³½ Elias Judy 4 ⒻAw35000 73-21 Lady Jin, Happy Cherokee, Loa 8
15Jan87-7Aqu 170[•]:48²1:13 1:43¹ft 12 122 4³ 5²¾ 5⁵ 5⁵¾ Samyn J L7 Ⓕ 100000 78-19 BthsSong,HppyChrok,VntgChmpgn 7
Aug 3 Bel 6f ft 1:15⁴ b Jly 29 Bel tr.t 5f ft 1:02⁴ b Jly 2 Bel tr.t 4f sy :50⁴ b Jun 26 Bel 5f ft 1:02³ b

E.

Subjective
Own.—Pillar Farms **122**
B. m. 5, by Secretariat—Welsh Garden, by Welsh Saint
Br.—Pillar Stud Inc (Ky)
Tr.—Fisher John R S
Lifetime 26 5 6 4 $134,450
1987 5 2 0 1 $64,920
1986 12 2 6 2 $66,585
Turf 24 5 6 3 $130,955

21Jly87-7Mth 1 1/16ⓣ:48 1:12³1:44 gd 18 117 9⁹ 9⁵¾ 9⁴½ 8⁷½ KrJA10 ⒻEatontownH 77-14 Bailrullah, Princely Proof, Krotz 10
21Jly87—Run in divisions
5Jly87-9Suf a1 1/16ⓣ 1:47¹fm 3¾ 117 7³½ 6¹¾ 3½ 1ⁿᵏ KrnJA1 ⒻBud Brds H 96-04 Subjective,SmoketheQun,ShrryMry 8
6Jun87-6Bel 1 1/16ⓣ:48³1:13²1:45 gd 11 117 5⁷½ 5⁶ 5⁶½ 3⁹ Antley C W2 ⒻTanya 62-29 GracefulDarby,Seriously,Subjective 8
25May87-9GS 1 1/16ⓣ:47²1:11⁴1:43³fm*7-5e114 7⁵¾ 7⁸½ 5²¾ 1² Wilson R5 Ⓕ[R]Iris 90-12 Subjective,GlenwoodSprings,Pechs 8
3May87-7Aqu 1⅛ⓣ:50 1:15²1:53⁴gd 10 119 4⁵ 6³½ 6⁶½ 6⁷¾ Antley CW2 ⒻAw31000 58-33 Popularity,LedKindlyLight Improyl 8
5Dec86-9Med 170 :47² 1:12¹ 1:42²ft 6 113 7⁹ 6⁸ 6⁷ 6⁴¾ AntlCW7 ⒻTigerheart 79-21 GirlPowder,SmllVirtue,BriefRmrks 7
15Nov86-8Lrl 1 :46⁴ 1:11³ 1:35⁴ft 7½ 117 5⁴¾ 3²½ 3⁴ 3⁵½ Antley CW3 Ⓕ[R]Dahlia 87-10 I Mean It, Pot OfAntics,Subjective 7
1Nov86-9Med 1 1/16ⓣ:46¹1:11¹1:42⁴fm 3¾e113 3⁴½ 3² 2ʰᵈ 2ʰᵈ AtlCW5 ⒻDotties Doll 88-15 Kitty Tatch, Subjective, Darbrielle 11
Aug 1 Crc 5f sy 1:02 b Jly 23 Crc 3f ft :39¹ bg Jly 18 Crc 6f ft 1:17¹ b Jly 11 Crc 6f ft 1:18² b

F.

Improyal
Own.—Peace J H **115**
Ch. f. 4, by Riverman—Winsome, by Sir Ivor
Br.—Kinghaven Farms Ltd (Ont-C)
Tr.—Johnson Philip G
Lifetime 19 5 4 2 $109,869
1987 8 2 2 1 $46,178
1986 11 3 2 1 $63,691
Turf 14 5 3 1 $102,788

25Jly87-3Mth 1 ⓣ:46¹1:10²1:36 fm*4-5e115 5⁹ 4¹ 2ʰᵈ 1¹ Antley CW9 ⒻAw19000 95-06 Improyl,LdyoftheNorth,PourMeOut 9
9Jun87-9Mth 1 1/16ⓣ:48⁴1:12⁴1:43²fm*4-5 117 4¹⁰ 4⁸ 4⁶½ 4⁸ DsRG5 ⒻThe VeryOne 76-11 Princely Proof, Duckweed, Pudical 5
9Jun87—Run in divisions
30May87-7Bel 1 1/16ⓣ:46³1:10⁴1:43²fm 4½e119 7⁷½ 7⁵½ 5¹¾ 1½ Davis R G3 ⒻAw31000 79-24 Improyal, Stated, ‡Christmas Cove 8
14May87-6Bel 1¼[T]:51 1:40²2:04¹fm 5½ 119 4⁵ 4¹½ 2³ 2⁴ Samyn J L1 ⒻAw31000 69-22 GreenOasis,Improyal,CaymanQueen 7
3May87-7Aqu 1⅛ⓣ:50 1:15²1:53⁴gd 2e119 3²½ 3¹ 1¹ 3¹ Samyn J L7 ⒻAw31000 65-33 Popularity,LedKindlyLight Improyl 8
2Feb87-8Hia a1 1/16ⓣ 1:42²fm 3 116 2¹ 2ʰᵈ 2½ 7⁵¾ Platts R6 ⒻAw19000 80-21 GoHonyGo,LdKndlyLght,UpptyUp 10
16Jan87-7Hia a1⅛ⓣ 1:50⁴fm 10 119 3¹½ 7⁵½ 4² 2ⁿᵏ Platts R3 ⒻAw19000 77-19 Green Oasis, Improyal, Millracer 10
1Jan87-9Crc 1⅛ :49³ 1:15 1:55 ft 23 114 3²½ 7⁶½ 7⁸½ 6⁶½ PlttsR5 ⒻNew Year H 69-22 FrgrntPrncss,FrstPrdctn,RglPrncss 7
1Jan87—Squeezed back
Jly 19 Bel 6f ft 1:16 b Jly 12 Bel 6f ft 1:15 h Jly 5 Bel 6f ft 1:15 b Jun 29 Bel 6f ft 1:15 h

G.

Spring Innocence
Own.—Triple C Thorostock **115**
B. f. 4, by Sharpen Up—Next Reason, by Hospitality
Br.—Cochonour & Kirkwood (Ill) **1987 8 3 0 0 $65,911**
Tr.—DiMauro Stephen L **1986 10 2 0 3 $54,520**
Lifetime 18 5 0 3 $120,431 **Turf 18 5 0 3 $120,431**

12Jly87-8AP 1 Ⓣ:47^2 1:12^1 1:38^1 gd *2-3 123 95¾ 75¼ 2^2 11½ DP^11 ⒻⓈA PeabodyH 84-17 SprnInncnc,KllsSprPt,Ttttnfrstrt 13
10Jun87-5Bel 1 1/16 Ⓣ:46^2 1:10^2 1:42^2 fm 12 117 7^11 45½ 11½ 1^2 Migliore R^7 ⒻAw31000 84-17 SpringInnocence,AirDncer NewDwn 9
14May87-6Bel 1¼ Ⓣ:51 1:40^2 2:04^1 fm 5¾ 119 6^6 51¾ 3^4 6^7 Migliore R^5 ⒻAw31000 66-22 GreenOasis,Improyal,CaymanQueen 7
3May87-7Aqu 1⅛ Ⓣ:50 1:15^2 1:53^4 gd 12 119 89½ 74¾ 54½ 4^4 Migliore R^1 ⒻAw31000 62-33 Popularity,LedKindlyLight Improyl 8
3May87—Checked, steadied
18Apr87-10GP 1½ Ⓣ:50 2:05^2 2:31^2 sf 181 113 10^14 9^12 11^18 12^16¼ CstdK 10 ⒻOrchid H 51-33 AnkGrmni,SingulrBqust,Ivor'sImg 14
18Apr87—Grade II
4Apr87-9GP 1 1/16 Ⓣ:47^1 1:10^3 1:41^4 fm 9 115 45½ 45½ 45¼ 5^10 StSB 4 ⒻⓇIndiansunlit 81-10 AnkaGermni,DesertView,GreenOsis 9
4Apr87—Checked
28Mar87-9GP a1 1/16 Ⓣ 1:47 gd 5¾ 119 73¼ 3^1 21½ 5^4 Soto S B^10 ⒻAw18000 67-25 Innsbruck,GoHonyGo,StrwWidow 12
11Mar87-6GP a1 1/16 Ⓣ 1:51^2 yl 3 117 41¾ 1hd 1^2 1hd RomeroRP^6 ⒻAw16000 49-51 SpringInnocence,Biddy,CymnQuen 11
Jly 4 Bel tr.t 5f ft 1:04 b **Jun 18 Bel Ⓣ 4f fm :53 b (d)**

H.

Far East
Own.—Davis A **115**
B. f. 4, by Mr Redoy—China Tea, by Round Table
Br.—Forest Retreat Farms Inc (Ky) **1987 12 4 5 0 $81,900**
Tr.—Moschera Gasper S **1986 10 2 0 4 $22,405**
Lifetime 22 6 5 4 $104,305 **Turf 5 4 1 0 $60,660**

Entered 7Aug87- 7 SAR
23Jly87-8Bel 1 1/16 Ⓣ:47^3 1:11^1 1:41^3 fm *2¼ 119 53¾ 1hd 1^2 1^3 Antley CW^7 ⒻAw31000 88-20 FarEast,LaCavtin,AntiqueMystique 8
17Jly87-7Bel 1 1/16 Ⓣ:46^2 1:10^2 1:43^4 fm 3 117 52½ 3^4 2^2 1^4 Cruguet J^1 ⒻAw28000 77-22 Far East, Purify, Rivers Of Mist 8
3Jly87-5Bel 1⅜ :50 1:39^3 2:19^3 m 2¼ 117 4^2 2^4 2^5 2^5 LovatoFJr^4 ⒻAw28000 77-24 Laughing Lady, Far East, Darbyvail 6
14Jun87-4Bel 1 Ⓣ:47^3 1:12 1:36^3 fm *7-5 115 21½ 2^1 1½ 2nk Lovato F Jr^5 Ⓕ c47500 82-16 Alitina, Far East, Syntonic 12
28May87-1Bel 1 1/16 Ⓣ:46^2 1:10^2 1:42^1 fm 9½ 117 4^2 4^2 1½ 1^3 Lovato F Jr^10 Ⓕ 35000 85-16 Far East, LadyDictator,Debonairly 11
16May87-3Bel 1⅛ :47^1 1:12^1 1:50^4 ft *9-5 112^5 33½ 43½ 54½ 510½ Nuesch D^4 Ⓕ 25000 62-18 Dawn Break, Charsky, Nile Flirt 6
4May87-5Aqu 1 :47 1:13^1 1:40^2 sy 2¼ 117 2^2 2^3 2^3 2¾ Lovato F Jr^3 Ⓕ 25000 63-27 Nile Flirt, Far East, Honest Nickle 6
17Apr87-4Aqu 1⅛ :48^4 1:13^4 1:53 gd 2¾ 117 52½ 4^3 2^1 23¼ Lovato F Jr^3 Ⓕ c17500 67-23 Mistress Donna, FarEast,ZonaRosa 7
Aug 3 Bel 4f ft :48^2 h **Jly 15 Bel tr.t 4f ft :49^3 b** **Jly 1 Bel tr.t 4f ft :48 h** **Jun 24 Bel tr.t 4f ft :50 b**

I.

Smoke the Queen
Own.—Bicycle Stable **115**
B. m. 5, by Sir Ivor—Sanctum Sanctorum, by Secretariat
Br.—Hettinger John (NY) **1987 5 0 1 1 $20,620**
Tr.—Hertler John O **1986 15 1 1 6 $68,152**
Lifetime 42 5 4 8 $178,722 **Turf 30 4 4 7 $157,692**

26Jly87-8Bel 1¼ Ⓣ:50^2 1:42 2:07^2 yl 3 115 3^2 52¼ 64¾ 713¾ SnJL^1 ⒻⓈMt Vernon 43-40 LkeCecb,MightyWondr,SwtJllyBinn 9
5Jly87-9Suf a1 1/16 Ⓣ 1:47^1 fm 3¼ 115 41½ 2^1 1½ 2nk SmnJL^3 ⒻBud Brds H 96-04 Subjective,SmoketheQun,ShrryMry 8
18Jun87-8Bel 1 1/16 Ⓣ:47^4 1:11^1 1:41^2 fm 21 111 41¾ 4^2 33½ 3^5 Maple E^3 ⒻHcpO 89-10 Fam,PerfectPoint,SmoketheQueen 7
6Jun87-6Bel 1 1/16 Ⓣ:48^3 1:13^2 1:45 gd 19 117 8^11 79½ 6^12 618½ Davis R G^3 ⒻTanya 52-29 GracefulDarby,Seriously,Subjective 8
25May87-7Bel 7f Ⓣ:23^1 :45^3 1:22^1 fm 20 119 5^5 53½ 57½ 513¼ Maple E^7 ⒻPucker Up 80-15 Small Virtue, SherryMary,Seriously 7
7Dec86-8Aqu 1^70 ⊡:48^2 1:13^1 1:44^4 ft 14 118 4^3 75¾ 99½ 1012¼ Maple E^3 ⒻⓈIroquois 64-18 Anniron,LadyBeRegl,WendyWlker 12
29Nov86-7Aqu 7f :23^1 :46^2 1:24 ft 16 115^7 86½ 74¾ 76¼ 610¼ Nuesch D^7 ⒻAw40000 71-20 ‡Reel Easy,PlasticLady,Robin'sRob 8
31Oct86-8Aqu 1⅛ Ⓣ:49^1 1:14^2 1:52^1 fm 4½ 122 51¾ 82¼ 52¾ 31¼ Maple E^4 ⒻAw40000 73-23 Spruce Luck, Loa, SmoketheQueen 9
31Oct86—Shuffled back
Jly 21 Bel Ⓣ 6f fm 1:12^3 h

34. An interesting race to end this section. The winner romped home handily. Can you find her?

5 ATLANTIC CITY

1 MILE. (Turf). (1.34⅕) CLAIMING. Purse $6,800. Fillies and mares, 3-year-olds and upward. Weights, 3-year-olds, 115 lbs. Older, 122 lbs. Non-winners of two races at one mile or over since June 1, allowed 2 lbs. One such race, 4 lbs. Such a race since May 25, 6 lbs. Claiming price $17,500 for each $1,000 to $15,500, 2 lbs. (Races where entered for $14,000 or less not considered.)

A.

Babe Saportas
Own.—Tagg Taryn
B. m. 5, by Provante—Half Wit, by Dunce
$15,500 Br.—Fantasy Farm (Va)
Tr.—Clark George **112**
Lifetime 15 1 0 2 $7,254 1987 1 0 0 0 1986 7 0 0 1 $1,164

10Jly87- 1Pim fst 1 1/16 :46⅗ 1:12⅖ 1:46⅕ ⒻClm 6500 6 5 34½ 33½ 56½ 56¼ Byrnes D 114 54.20 67-19 Joan's Gold 107^2 Wire Breaker 107nk Brilliant Delight114 3½ Tired 8
23May86- 5Pim fst 1 1/16 :46⅘ 1:13 1:48 ⒻClm 5000 6 8 7^17 6^20 69¼ 59½ Kummer M D^5 112 16.90 54-28 Peck's Love 109^7 NightsAreBetter109no AprilDew114 2½ Stride late 9
5May86- 9Pim fst 1 1/16 :47⅘ 1:13⅖ 1:49 ⒻClm 5000 5 7 6^10 59½ 3^6 45¾ Kummer M D^5 112 30.70 53-26 Jessie Lumbert 114 5½ Ming Rose 109hd Satin Rainbow108nd Tired 10
16Apr86- 2Pim sly 1 1/16 :48 1:13⅗ 1:47⅘ ⒻClm 5000 7 6 68¼ 68¼ 79½ 5^9 Kummer M D^5 111 24.40 56-24 Lady Monica 114 5½ Fast 'N Square 114hd CharmCity119 2½ Outrun 8
19Mar86- 1Pim fst 1 1/16 :48⅖ 1:13⅘ 1:49⅘ ⒻClm 5000 6 8 88¼ 7^15 7^16 722¾ Pino M G b 114 11.90 32-29 Salad Days 114¾ Plenntigood 114^3 Lady Monica 114^4 Outrun 9
7Mar86- 3Pim fst 6f :23⅘ :48 1:14⅕ ⒻClm 5000 8 10 106¼ 10^9 78¼ 77¼ Pino M G b 114 8.70 68-35 Cape Henry 109¾ Creel Ribot 110 3¾ Disc Quick 117¾ Outrun 11
4Feb86- 4Lrl sly 1 :48⅘ 1:15⅘ 1:43⅖ ⒻClm 6500 7 1 21½ 4^6 7^14 613½ Davidson J b 114 5.60 41-31 Gitalong Road 107nk Nun Wiser 109 5¼ Ming Rose 112^1 Tired 7
13Jan86- 2Lrl fst 1 1/16 :48⅕ 1:14 1:48⅕ ⒻClm 6500 3 2 3^2 43½ 22½ 3^4 Davidson J 114 4.40 64-29 Dellis 106^3 U. B. Judge 114^1 Babe Saportas 114¾ Hung 9
30Dec85- 1Lrl fst 1 :46⅕ 1:12 1:39 3↑ⒻClm 11500 3 6 5^11 57¾ 5^9 512¾ Pino M G 114 11.40 64-22 Mini Don 112nk Lady Sher Brooke 117^6 Britt S. 117 5¾ Outrun 7
20Dec85- 1Lrl fst 1 :46⅗ 1:12 1:37⅗ ⒻClm 14500 4 2 22½ 3^4 68½ 710½ Delgado A 114 33.60 73-15 Beth's Eighty Days 114 4½ Imported115no GoldenRollick109nk Tired 8
LATEST WORKOUTS Jly 25 Pim 4f fst :48⅗ h ● Jly 19 Pim 5f fst 1:01⅖ h Jly 2 Pim 5f sly 1:01⅖ hg

B.

Color Me Cherry — B. f. 4, by Cherry Pop—Color Me Pink, by Western Sky II
Own.—Pegasus Racing Stable — $15,500 Br.—Coats T Jr (Fla) Tr.—Fisher Dennis — 1057
Lifetime 48 4 3 9 $31,186 — 1987 15 0 1 1 $4,404 — 1986 19 3 1 7 $20,557 — Turf 16 2 2 1 $14,843

25Jly87-10Atl fm *140 Ⓣ:47⅘ 1:13⅗ 1:44⅗ 3+ⒻHcp 6500s 9 5 67 56 44½ 42½ Nunez E O b 120 *2.70 85-13 Fratello's Girl 1121 All In Free115hdOurLoveSong1151½ Mild rally 10
17Jly87-6Atl fm 1 1/16 Ⓣ:48 1:12⅖ 1:45⅕ 3+ⒻClm 14000 3 6 2½ 11 2hd 2hd Blanco R10 b 106 17.50 80-14 MullOverMe116hdColorMeCherry106nkAqutique1163½ Just missed 12
10Jly87-7Mth fst 1 1/16 :47⅕ 1:11⅘ 1:43⅕ 3+ⒻAlw 12500s 1 5 611 615 625 636 Nunez E O b 115 32.00 53-16 Layovernite 1179½ Scarlet Glow 1179 Time Tuner 1151½ Outrun 6
3Jly87-8Atl fst 5½f :22⅖ :46⅖ 1:06⅕ 3+ⒻClm 11000 3 6 78 711 79½ 75¾ Blanco R10 b 106 21.50 76-32 Five Star Rose 1221½ Bushogin Babe 109nk Aire Pet 1182½ Trailed 7
27Jun87-8Atl fst 1⅛ :48 1:12⅗ 1:53 3+ Clm 16000 6 1 1½ 2hd 47½ 48½ Blanco R10 b 104 9.50 59-18 StrategyTalk116½ReflectNeutrlity1141CollectionAgent1147 Faded 8
24Jun87-5Atl fst 1⅛ :47⅘ 1:12⅘ 1:54 3+ⒻClm 6500 4 2 21 21½ 35 35½ Intelisano GPJr b 116 2.60 57-31 CastleofGold1074½SpecilAsset1121ColorMeCherry1168 Weakened 7
14Jun87-8Del fm 1 Ⓣ:46⅘ 1:11⅕ 1:37 ⒻAlw 9200 1 3 44½ 53½ 4¾ 43 Blanco R10 108 43.10 87-13 Timelessleigh 116no Asticour 1162 Primal Sea 1221 Weakened 8
31May87-7Crc fm 1 1/16 Ⓣ:47⅗ 1:11 1:41⅕ 3+ Alw 12500 2 7 83½ 76¼ 914 916½ Blanco R10 105 65.40 80-08 FbulousDevotion1099PytheFellow112nkThrsiddcoin111½ No threat 11
17May87-8GP gd *1 1/16 Ⓣ 1:47 Clm 35000 10 1 13 43 79 711¾ Blanco R10 102 81.00 59-33 Heaven's Gate 1181 GoldenCherokee113nkActUpon1131 Gave way 10
6May87-10GP fm *1½ Ⓣ 2:30⅖ Clm 25000 1 4 518 613 48½ 49½ Nunez E O b 108 17.90 82-10 Cloutier 1174½ Padrilario 1173 Soaring Bee 1132 Outrun 9
LATEST WORKOUTS Jly 16 Atl 4f gd :52 b ●Jun 11 Atl 4f fst :48⅖ h

C.

Val De Etoile — B. m. 5, by Val De L'Orne—Star of Paducah, by Tudorka
Own.—Famularo Mary J — $17,500 Br.—Petter S D Jr (Ky) Tr.—Famularo Joseph Jr — 106 10
Lifetime 27 3 1 2 $32,413 — 1987 5 0 0 0 $628 — 1986 11 0 0 1 $2,195 — Turf 23 3 1 2 $32,413

17Jly87-6Atl fm 1 1/16 Ⓣ:48 1:12⅖ 1:45⅕ 3+ⒻClm 14000 4 11 104¼ 93½ 54¾ 55¾ Strickland L10 107 8.90 74-14 Mull Over Me116hdColorMeCherry106nkAquatique1163½ No factor 12
1Jly87-9Atl fm *5½f Ⓣ:22⅘ :47⅕ 1:06⅖ 3+ⒻAlw 8000 8 10 1013 1015 1013 810 Strickland L10 106 101.50 71-15 Gold Lake 1224½ Move Over Bud 1072 Sanatatii 112½ Outrun 10
20Jun87-10Atl fm 1 1/16 Ⓣ:47⅗ 1:11⅘ 1:43⅕ 3+ⒻAlw 8200 5 5 65½ 713 731 724¾ Cappacetti G 116 20.80 65-08 Captivating Appeal 1162 French Oil 113nkHonestDeb107hd Outrun 7
9Jun87-9GS gd 1 1/16 Ⓣ:49⅖ 1:13⅗ 1:45⅖ 3+ⒻAlw 12500 2 4 56 67 64¾ 67 Barrera C 116 31.70 74-12 Glenwood Springs 1171½ Shadowfay 116½CupO'Cake1093½ Outrun 7
9Jun87-Placed fifth through disqualification
13May87-8GS fm 1 1/16 Ⓣ:47⅗ 1:12⅖ 1:44 3+ⒻClm 45000 7 4 55½ 88½ 815 827¼ Lee-Lopez R F 112 89.80 61-12 Double Smooth 1153 Native Clown 114nk DH Tagalog 116 Tired 8
30Nov86-6Pha fst 1 :48⅕ 1:14⅕ 1:40⅘ 3+ⒻClm 12500 5 8 811 913 920 927¼ Slaven M 117 99.50 43-27 Ms. Ogynist 1163 Inkie Pinkie 1165½ Taunting Gibe 116nk Tired 10
7Nov86-8Pha gd 1 :47⅗ 1:12⅘ 1:39 3+ⒻAlw 12500 8 9 916 921 929 936 Slaven M 116 89.60 43-20 Pia's Baby 1143 Syl's Pleasure 1133½ Show Music 1134 Trailed 9
24Oct86-5Pha fm 1 1/16 Ⓣ:48⅖ 1:13⅕ 1:45⅖ 3+ⒻClm 18000 5 8 75¾ 86¾ 85¼ 88 Slaven M b 115 91.00 67-19 Marshmallow Riches 1151 Transnative 111½ Go Solo1111¼ Outrun 12
12Oct86-9Pha fm 170 Ⓣ:46⅖ 1:11⅖ 1:41⅗ 3+ⒻClm 10000 2 5 25 96¼ 1116 1120 Dufton E b 117 16.30 69-08 MrshmllowRiches1125BewitchingBee116nkMchOfUlster111¾ Tired 12
17Sep86-9Del fm 1 Ⓣ:47⅘ 1:12⅖ 1:37⅖ 3+ⒻClm 16500 7 5 21½ 85¾ 64¼ 69 Baxis J b 116 9.00 79-14 Primal Sea 1194 Make Happen 112no Bewitching Bee 1171 Tired 11
LATEST WORKOUTS Jun 6 GS 4f fst :50 b

D.

Bud's Jessie — Dk. b. or br. f. 4, by Baldski—Fine Aroma, by Nijinsky II
Own.—Willow Wood Farm — $15,500 Br.—Farnsworth Farm (Fla) Tr.—Thomas George — 112
Lifetime 18 3 0 1 $12,724 — 1987 6 0 0 1 $526 — 1986 8 2 0 0 $9,300 — Turf 1 0 0 0 $64

17Jly87-6Atl fm 1 1/16 Ⓣ:48 1:12⅖ 1:45⅕ 3+ⒻClm 12000 8 1 1½ 21 87 710½ Parrilla R b 112 87.10 69-14 Mull Over Me116hdColorMeCherry106nkAquatique1163½ Gave way 12
9Jly87-2Atl sly 5½f :23⅖ :48 1:08⅖ 3+ⒻClm 4000 4 9 99¾ 911 920 915¾ Weinberg A10 b 108 9.10 55-23 Hookamadookama 1203 Missy Ed111½MyPrincessOti1162½ Outrun 9
14May87-2Bir fst 6f :22 :45⅗ 1:12⅖ ⒻClm 5000 5 3 34 38 32½ 68¾ Luhr R D b 116 4.40 76-13 Clever Emijo 119hd Miss Quip 1164Fame'sFantasy1103¾ Gave way 12
6May87-2Bir fst 6f :22 :46 1:13⅗ ⒻClm 5000 4 8 89½ 76½ 64½ 32 Luhr R D b 116 10.00 78-12 Clever Emijo 116½ Little Miss Suzie1171½Bud'sJessie116nk Rallied 11
26Mar87-4Bir fst 170 :47⅘ 1:15 1:48⅖ ⒻClm 6250 10 3 2hd 32 95½ 107½ Gehri D L b 115 18.30 — — Sabriam 109nk Bewitching Fantasy 1111¾ Revamp 1151 Gave way 11
4Mar87-2Bir fst 6f :22⅗ :46⅕ 1:12⅗ ⒻClm 8000 10 11 1012 109 1012 1021½ Gehri D L b 116 7.70 — — Be Bad 116½ Brilliant Gamble 1191½ Clear Creek Cat119hd Outrun 11
6Nov86-6Pha my 1 :47⅗ 1:13 1:40⅖ ⒻClm 16000 1 5 55½ 69 816 914¾ Ferrer J C b 115 5.10 57-27 Dewanali 1082½ R. DazzlingDaria1153TalentedBeginner114nk Tired 9
19Oct86-4Pha fst 6f :22⅗ :46⅕ 1:12⅕ ⒻClm 16000 2 12 117 108¾ 89½ 76¾ Verge M E b 118 7.50 73-23 Lis'sSong1181½NkedThoughts115½Pmell'sDnce114no Stumbled st. 12
1Oct86-6Pha fst 6f :22⅕ :45⅘ 1:12⅖ ⒻClm 16000 4 5 42 33 21 11 Ferrer J C b 115 7.40 79-21 Bud's Jessie 1151 Rainbow Hammock1083Maggieolus115½ Driving 9
23Aug86-3Mth fst 6f :22⅖ :45 1:11⅖ ⒻClm 20000 2 4 52½ 55½ 57½ 66½ Jimenez I J b 118 27.10 76-12 Parade Of Roses115nkSpeedOutFirst1182HostessBeth115½ Outrun 7
LATEST WORKOUTS Jly 6 Atl 4f fst :48⅘ b Jun 30 Atl 4f fst :50 b

E.

Princess Don Don — Ch. m. 5, by Hawaiian Sound—Corazon, by Olden Times
Own.—Cinemod Stables — $17,500 Br.—Biedenharn & Osborn (Ky) Tr.—Casey James M — 116
Lifetime 43 3 8 9 $67,360 — 1987 9 0 3 2 $13,268 — 1986 15 0 3 4 $17,369 — Turf 14 1 3 4 $15,928

23Jly87-9Atl fm *1 Ⓣ:48⅘ 1:14⅕ 1:41⅗ 3+ⒻClm 20000 10 2 2½ 2hd 1hd 2nk Castaneda K 116 9.90 77-18 His Ex 112nk Princess DonDon116hdHere'sAClassic1162½ Bore out 10
8Jly87-7Mth fst 1 1/16 :47 1:12⅗ 1:46⅖ 3+ⒻClm 50000 6 4 46 75¾ 614 620¾ St Leon G 115 32.70 52-27 Shaken Bay 1154 Cup O'Cake 107½ Double Smooth 112¾ Tired 6
12Jun87-8Mth fm 1 1/16 Ⓣ:48 1:12⅕ 1:43⅖ 3+ⒻAlw 18000 2 3 31 54½ 610 615½ Thomas D B 118 16.90 73-12 Sunshine Jill 118no BurningIssue118½StrawWidow1181¼ Fell back 6
3Jun87-7Mth fst 1 :47⅘ 1:12⅕ 1:38 3+ⒻAlw 18000 2 5 34½ 46 47½ 413½ St Leon G 118 25.40 69-22 Syrianette 1183 Sunshine Jill 1187 Chase The Dream 1123½ Tired 7
17May87-9CD fm 1⅛ Ⓣ:48⅗ 1:13⅕ 1:53 3+ⒻAlw 24300 3 6 55½ 57½ 45 32½ Bruin J E 114 16.20 — — Brief Fame 1142 Princess Br 114½ Princess Don Don 1144 6
8May87-7Bir fst 170 :47⅕ 1:12 1:42⅗ ⒻAlw 11500 5 3 44½ 48 39 49½ O'Donnell E E 116 5.90 94-13 Subtle 'N Sly 1164¾ Twice Regal 1223½GuiltyLass1221½ Weakened 6
17Apr87-7Bir fst 170 :46⅗ 1:12 1:43⅗ ⒻHomewood 2 3 36 49½ 311 212¾ O'Donnell E E 114 5.70 86-13 Lemhi Love 11212¾PrincessDonDon1141¼CristalDust1137 2nd best 5
4Apr87-7Bir fst 170 :47⅘ 1:14⅗ 1:46⅗ ⒻAlw 14000 6 4 54 23 25 21 O'Donnell E E 115 5.00 — — CristlDust1171PrincessDonDon1155½QuitColors1151¼ Second best 7
13Mar87-8Bir fst 170 :46⅗ 1:12⅘ 1:45 ⒻAlw 16000 6 4 57½ 44½ 35 33 O'Donnell E E 115 2.20 — — Distant Doll1152½PrettyTrick121½PrincessDonDon1151¼ Late rally 7
27Dec86-9TP gd 1 1/16 :48 1:14⅖ 1:48⅘ 3+ⒻAlw 11400 7 6 58 56½ 712 813½ Bartram B E b 115 9.20 52-41 Fantasy Lover 1164 Amy Dawn 1181½ Ages 'N Stages 1161½ 9

F.

Franchois — Dk. b. or br. f. 4, by Barachois—Jolly Swinger, by Tumble Turbie
Own.—Kravets Ruth — $15,500 Br.—Arango J A (Fla) Tr.—Bonaventura Paul — 107 5
Lifetime 39 6 3 5 $28,603 — 1987 16 2 1 3 $10,133 — 1986 19 4 2 1 $17,775 — Turf 4 0 0 1 $660

22Jly87-2Atl fst 7f :23⅕ :46⅗ 1:26⅗ 3+ⒻClm 6500 6 6 52½ 11 11 11½ Carter T5 111 4.50 69-31 Franchois 1111½HeartOfSilver111½AmericanFreedom1161½ Driving 9
16Jly87-5Atl fst 6f :22⅗ :47⅕ 1:13⅕ 3+ⒻClm 7500 6 3 56 56 57½ 58 Zoppo B L 113 5.30 68-28 Dusty Britches 114nk Aire Pet 1162½ ExplosiveCandy112nk Evenly 6
2Jly87-5Atl sly 6f :22⅖ :45⅗ 1:12⅘ 3+ⒻClm 6500 5 4 411 312 34½ 2½ Zoppo B L 116 8.80 77-27 Dusty Britches 116½ Franchois 1161 Debi's Dynasty 1111 Rallied 7
25Jun87-8Atl fst 6f :22⅕ :46 1:12 3+ⒻClm 8000 1 6 65½ 57½ 44¼ 44¾ Zoppo B L 114 9.30 77-23 Spray Over 1161½ Weeds Or Roses 116½Swallowtail1103 Mild gain 6
13Jun87-8Rkm fst 6f :22⅖ :46 1:12⅘ 3+ⒻClm 8000 4 7 87¾ 78 55 32½ Delguidice R Jr 114 25.40 77-21 Belmont Hill 113¾ Beautiful Nadine 1131¾ Franchois1144½ Rallied 11
5Jun87-5Rkm my 140 :49⅕ 1:16⅗ 1:48⅗ 3+ⒻAlw 5000s 5 1 3½ 712 718 — Carrasco B 114 14.20 — — Strike Song 1191½ Kathy Keelan 1134¾ Rocky Top 1132½ Eased 7
30May87-8Rkm fm 1⅛ Ⓣ:48⅗ 1:14 1:47⅘ 3+ⒻAlw 8000 7 7 47½ 54 87¾ 813¾ Delguidice R Jr 114 23.00 86 — Strike Song 113¾ PrideofKildare1132½MarthaTucker1134 Bumped 12
21Apr87-4GP fst 7f :22⅘ :46⅖ 1:25⅘ ⒻClm 7500 4 6 62½ 51¾ 712 89 Fires E 117 21.00 66-23 Sweeter Than Gain 1011 Scarlet Fire 115nkMayOlive1173½ Outrun 12
26Mar87-5GP fst 7f :22⅘ :46⅕ 1:26⅖ ⒻClm 7000 5 4 53 43½ 34½ 610 Pezua J M 113 3.80 62-24 SweeterThnGin1143ScrletFire1134½SuperDtnt1171 Lacked fin. bid 12
17Mar87-2GP fst 6f :22⅖ :46 1:12⅕ ⒻClm 7500 4 4 42½ 76¾ 510 39 Gonzalez M A 117 2.60 69-22 Nandy's Jenny 1137 Irish Politician 1172 Franchois117¾ Mild rally 9

G.

Lasar Gal
Ch. f. 4, by Majestic Light—Busy Gal, by Far North
$16,500 Br.—Cox E A Jr (Ky)
Tr.—Dellagatta Perry
104 10
Lifetime 33 3 0 5 $15,368
1987 12 0 0 1 $583
1986 16 3 0 1 $12,365
Turf 1 0 0 0 $63
Own.—Dellagatta P

24Jly87- 7Atl fm *5½f Ⓣ:22⅕ :46⅘ 1:05⅗ 3+ⒻClm 13500 4 10 1012 106 55½ 58 Santiago J M 112 83.30 77-20 Spring 1163½ Palace Treasure 114½ Absurd Bird 1162 No factor 10
16Jly87- 2Atl fst 6f :22⅗ :47⅕ 1:13⅖ 3+ⒻClm 4000 5 7 75½ 57 36½ 311 Parrilla R 116 4.00 64-28 Biddin On A Beauty 1112 TouchofGlory1099LasarGal1163½ Rallied 8
1Jly87- 4Atl fst 6f :22⅖ :46⅘ 1:13⅘ 3+ⒻClm 4000 11 2 62¼ 1112 1211 1220½ Parisi E 118 103.10 52-25 Say It Plain 1162 Alan's Gal 1161½ Heart Of Silver 1152 Outrun 12
24Jun87-10Atl fst 6f :22⅖ :47 1:14⅕ 3+ⒻClm 4000 7 8 83¾ 99 89¼ 915½ Parisi E 118 52.90 55-31 Lady Carlton 1161¾ Put Her On Ice116nk MissFantasy1162 Outrun 11
8May87- 9Del fst 1 1/16 :47⅗ 1:13⅘ 1:48⅗ 3+ⒻClm 3500 7 3 36 916 919 928¾ Strickland L10 110 27.10 36-22 Bonito Wind 120½ Boudoir Girl 1139 Festive Lily 108½ Outrun 9
26Apr87- 6Del fst 5f :22⅘ :48 1:01⅗ 3+ⒻClm 4000 7 5 85¼ 1012 99¾ 910¼ Strickland L10 110 68.20 69-22 Palace Parfait 120nk Mary Jo Rolli1203ClermontNine1201 Outrun 12
16Apr87- 5GS gd 6f :22⅘ :47 1:13⅖ ⒻClm 4000 3 6 65¾ 119 1112 1111¾ Kamada E J 116 35.40 63-25 BlackMedallion1161MaggiePearl1191Hookamdookm1161½ Outrun 11
7Apr87- 7GS my 1 1/16 :48⅕ 1:14⅖ 1:49⅘ ⒻClm 4000 2 1 12½ 1hd 1021 1029¾ Garcia J7 109 14.50 29-28 Apple Franny 1161 Fleeting Love 109nd CieloSereno119½ Stopped 11
31Mar87- 4GS sly 170 :47⅗ 1:14 1:46 ⒻClm 4000 4 1 11½ 21 48½ 811¾ Garcia J O 116 43.60 57-27 Jacklyn the Ripper 116½ All In Free 1164½ MissBayside1166 Tired 12
18Mar87- 2GS fst 6f :22⅖ :46⅗ 1:14⅕ ⒻClm 4000 6 4 31 35½ 59 911¾ Lopez C C 116 24.60 59-25 Time For Silver 1194 OutduelM.1192RainbowHammock109¾ Tired 12
LATEST WORKOUTS Jun 28 Atl 3f fst :36⅖ b Jun 13 Atl 3f fst :36 h

H.

Jersey First
B. f. 4, by Gregorian—Good As Can Be, by Iron Ruler
$15,500 Br.—Due Process Stable (Ky)
Tr.—Thompson Glenn
107 5
Lifetime 16 1 0 2 $4,885
1987 7 1 0 0 $2,790
1986 9 M 0 2 $2,095
Turf 1 0 0 0
Own.—Quiet Winter Farm

24Jly87- 2Mth fst 1 :47⅗ 1:12⅘ 1:40 3+ⒻClm 5000 8 8 73¾ 86¼ 95½ 810¼ Heath M J7 b 108 39.20 63-16 NativeNewJersin1151¼PineTumbly1151½DreToBeGret1103½ Outrun 9
16Jly87- 2Mth fst 170 :47⅗ 1:13⅗ 1:45⅗ 3+ⒻClm 6000 9 5 41½ 43 76½ 76¾ Romero J A5 b 109 34.00 61-23 Starry Moon 1152 Salerno's Baby 110nk Extaby 1081¾ Tired 9
7Jly87- 4Mth fst 170 :45⅖ 1:11⅗ 1:44 3+ⒻClm 5000 3 6 612 411 68½ 510 Bin G S5 b 1104 81.30 66-15 La Plus Jolie1153½PeacefulJen1153½DemanExpress1153 No factor 11
7Jly87-Dead heat
24Jun87- 2Mth fst 6f :22⅗ :46 1:12 3+ⒻClm 5000 6 10 108¾ 99¼ 98¼ 89½ Bin G S7 b 109 48.00 70-16 SocialGesture109¾ScandalousScarlet1161SilverSham1161¼ Outrun 10
30Mar87- 2GS sly 1 1/16 :49⅖ 1:14⅘ 1:48⅖ ⒻClm 5000 2 4 32 48½ 514 622¾ Vigliotti M J b 116 14.00 43-30 Selari's Pride 119½ Dagger Board 11610 Dulce Vita 11210 Tired 6
20Mar87- 2GS fst 170 :48⅗ 1:14⅗ 1:46⅕ ⒻClm 5000 9 6 65 810 713 712¾ Vigliotti M J b 116 17.60 55-29 Dulce Vita 1091 Dagger Board 116¾ Selari's Pride 1192 No factor 11
5Mar87-10GS fst 6f :23 :47⅗ 1:15⅕ ⒻMd 8000 10 8 94¾ 89¾ 51¼ 1no Vigliotti M J b 118 9.30 66-30 Jersey First 118no PrincessMahan118nk Chief'sChassa118nk Driving 12
4Dec86-10Med fst 6f :23 :47 1:14 3+ⒻMd 10500 11 2 87 812 612 49½ Coburn L A7 b 110 4.60 62-23 GurdedLook118½EveryLittleStr1126½ForbiddnLssi1172½ No factor 11
24Nov86- 1Med my 6f :23 :47⅗ 1:14⅖ 3+ⒻMd 10500 6 9 77 811 38½ 38½ Coburn L A7 b 109 5.10 61-27 AmericnFreedom1162½EveryLittlStr1096JrsyFirst1091 No menace 9
13Nov86-10Med fst 170 :47⅗ 1:13⅘ 1:44⅘ 3+ⒻMd 10000 11 5 65½ 58 36½ 36¼ Coburn L A7 b 111 36.00 66-25 BinnN'BearIt1181¼CheBellFemmin1175JerseyFirst1112½ No threat 12
LATEST WORKOUTS Jun 19 Mth 5f fst 1:03⅘ b Jun 13 Mth 4f fst :51⅗ b

35. In overnight handicaps at marathon distances, the highweight regularly goes off an underlay. When that occurs, the best of handicappers can concentrate on finding the most probable overlays. A typical case in point follows. Which horse figures best at the odds?

8th Del Mar

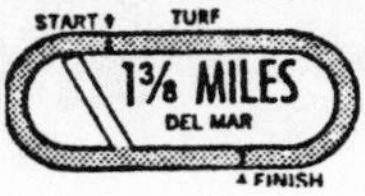

1 ⅜ MILES. (Turf). (2.14) OVERNIGHT HANDICAP. Purse $40,000. 3-year-olds and upward. Nominations close Monday, August 17, by 11:00 a.m., with weights published by 4:00 p.m. Entries by the usual time of closing.

A.

7–2

***Iades**
B. h. 5, by Shirley Heights—Isabella Moretti, by Sir Gaylord
BAZE R A 116
Br.—Razza Dormello Olgiata (Fra)
Tr.—Frankel Robert
Own.—Cranbrook Stables
Lifetime 23 5 4 0 $210,468
1987 6 1 0 0 $85,654
1986 7 1 1 0 $66,153
Turf 22 5 4 0 $210,468

27Jly87-8Hol 1½Ⓣ:4641:5942:25 fm 16 112 54 84¼ 84¼ 63½ Davis RG6 Sunset H 93-08 Swink, Forlitano, Rivlia 10
27Jly87—Grade I; Lugged out 1st turn
11Jly87-8Bel 1⅜[T]:4841:3912:16 yl 17 113 815 85½ 43½ 44½ Davis R G8 Tidal H 72-23 Dance of Life, UptownSwell,Duluth 8
11Jly87—Grade III
29Mar87-11FG a1½Ⓣ:553 2:44 yl 6 112 46 33 1½ 1nk Soto S B4 Gld Cp H 40-60 Iades,RoyalTresurer,FlyingPidgeon 5
8Mar87-7SA 1⅛Ⓣ:4721:1241:493gd 7¼ 114 64½ 62¾ 43½ 54¼ Stevens G L 3 Aw48000 75-26 Rivlia, Chinoiserie, Bello Horizonte 8
16Feb87-8SA 1½Ⓣ:4612:0142:282gd 11 116 66½ 63 64½ 58 Toro F 5 Sn Lus Ob H 65-27 Louis Le Grand, Zoffany, Schiller 8
16Feb87—Grade II
1Feb87-11TuP 1⅛Ⓣ:4631:1121:48 fm 5¼ 117 811 73¾ 85¼ 66¾ Soto S B 7 Tup H 101 — Narghile,SirNaskra,‡SkipOutFront 14
1Feb87—Altered course clubhouse turn; Placed fifth through disqualification
1Nov86-7SA 1¼:46 1:343 2:002ft 193 126 1119 1114 1120 1019 AsssnCB 8 Br Cp Cls 68-13 Skywalker, Turkoman,Precisionist 11
1Nov86—Grade I; Broke slowly
5Oct86♦4Longchamp(Fra) a1½ 2:273fm 99 130 Ⓣ 118¾ LquxA Arc d Trmph(Gr1) Dancing Brave, Bering, Triptych 15
16Aug86♦4Deauville(Fra) a1¼ 2:062gd 3½ 130 Ⓣ 2¾ HedF Px Gontau Biron(Gr3) Over The Ocean, Iades, Baby Turk 10
Aug 15 Dmr 6f ft 1:124 h Aug 10 Dmr Ⓣ 4f fm :494 h (d) Jly 22 Hol 7f ft 1:271 h Jly 7 Hol 7f ft 1:264 h

B.
8–5

***Complice II** B. h. 6, by D'Arras—Kashkawan, by Kashmir II
TORO F 122 Br.—Dufeirelle C (Fra) 1987 2 1 0 1 $57,690
Tr.—Gosden John H M 1986 2 1 0 1 $62,750
Own.—De Moussac P (Lessee) Lifetime 34 7 8 4 $230,290 Turf 34 7 8 4 $230,290

25Jly87-9AP 1½Ⓣ:4922:05 2:302fm 4e 116 510 42 31½ 1½ Toro F8 L Armour H 87-18 ComplcII,AtmnGlttr,ExplosvDrlng 10
25Jly87—Grade II
3Jly87-7Hol 1⅛Ⓣ:4711:11 1:402fm 9-5 115 45 43½ 33 33¼ Toro F3 Aw45000 89-11 Exclusive Partner,Nasib,ComplicelI 6
4May86-8GG 1⅜Ⓣ:4841:3912:162fm 9-5 115 48 42½ 31½ 3½ Baze R A 4 G G H 82-20 Val Danseur, Le Solaret,ComplicelI 5
4May86—Grade II
10Apr86-8SA 1⅛Ⓣ:4511:0921:47 fm 5½ 115 67¼ 65½ 32½ 1½ Toro F3 Aw45000 92-08 Complice II, Fabbiani, Shulich 9
20Oct85♦5Longchamp(Fra) a1½ 2:343gd 5¾ 126 Ⓣ 75¼ DbrqG Px dCnsl d Pris(Gr2) JupiterIslnd,BbyTurk,SintEstephe 11
6Oct85♦4Longchamp(Fra) a1½ 2:292gd 42 130 Ⓣ 14 GibrtA Arc de Trmph(Gr1) ‡Sagace, Rainbow Quest, Kozana 15
8Sep85♦6Longchamp(Fra) a1¼ 2:332gd 21 123 Ⓣ 22½ Gibert A Px Foy(Gr3) Sagace, Complice, Castle Guard 5
29Jly85♦6Vichy(Fra) a1½ 2:302yl *9-5 130 Ⓣ 31¾ GibrtA Gr Px deVichy(Gr3) Lauville, Le Primeur, Complice 9
14Jly85♦5StCloud(Fra) a1 5/16 2:381yl 7½ 128 Ⓣ 2½ Head F PxMrc d Niel(Gr2) Saint Estephe, Complice, Abary 8
16Jun85♦2Chantilly(Fra) a1½ 2:25 gd 8 123 Ⓣ 22½ GibertA La Coupe(Gr3) Romildo, Complice, Darly 5
Aug 17 Dmr Ⓣ 7f fm 1:293 h (d) Aug 10 Dmr Ⓣ 6f fm 1:153 h (d) Aug 3 Dmr Ⓣ 4f fm :494 h Jly 19 Hol 1 ft 1:392 h

C.
6–1

***Millero Y Medio *** B. h. 6, by Mr Long—Maria Blanca, by Blakemere
STEVENS G L 112 Br.—Haras Santa Amelia (Chile) 1987 8 1 1 1 $35,125
Tr.—Anderson Laurie N 1986 8 3 3 0 $17,094
Own.—Jones & Kebow Lifetime 42 11 10 6 $68,522 Turf 13 2 2 2 $16,802

8Aug87-9Dmr 1⅛Ⓣ:48 1:12 1:492fm 3½ 115 79 85¾ 74¼ 21 Stevens G L5 57500 85-13 GeorgiRivr,MillroYMdio,Intuitivnss 9
28Jun87-7Hol 1½Ⓣ:47 2:0032:262fm 19 114 915 75½ 73¼ 31¾ Stevens G L9 ⓇHcp0 88-11 Circus Prince,Truth,MilleroYMedio 9
28Jun87—Broke slowly
30May87-5Hol 1⅛:462 1:11 1:50 ft 4½ 116 89¼ 77 45 44¾ Stevens G L3 50000 82-14 ValiantCougar,ForeignLegion,Poley 9
14May87-5Hol 1⅛Ⓣ:4821:1231:48 fm 5¾ 116 86½ 85¼ 73 63¼ Stevens G L3 62500 85-08 Rajhaan, Jet Away Bill,DarkAccent 9
18Apr87-7SA 1 1/16:46 1:104 1:433ft 10 116 78 89 712 710 McHrgueDG5 Aw35000 73-18 Centenary, Extranix, Prince O' Fire 8
18Apr87—Steadied 5/16
14Mar87-8SA 1½Ⓣ:4742:03 2:281fm 11 114 107¼ 96¾ 911 911¾ StnsGL5 ⓇSn Mrno H 62-22 Rosedale, Forlitano, Bob Back 10
14Feb87-7SA 1½:492 2:044 2:301sy *1 117 1½ 15 16 18½ Stevens G L1 80000 85-17 Millero YMedio,Fluctuate,Rampour 6
18Jan87-3SA 1 1/16:461 1:104 1:441ft 6¾ 116 814 813 69 49 Toro F3 Aw31000 71-19 Oricao,GrecinWonder,ForsytheBoy 8
16Aug86♦6H'podromo(Chile) a1 1:362ft *1 134 1½ Diaz F FrndoMlrBrd(Gr2) Millero y Medio, Judas, Coqueto 7
5Jly86♦8H'podromo(Chile) a1⅜2:183ft 1 134 27½ Diaz F Pdr dRioTlvr(Gr2) Poalco, Millero y Medio,Prontuario 4
Aug 17 Dmr 4f ft :493 h ●Aug 3 Dmr 1 ft 1:41 h Jly 27 Dmr 6f ft 1:172 h Jly 15 SA 7f ft 1:30 h

D.
21–1

Amongst The Stars B. f. 4, by Proctor—Out of This World, by High Top
SOLIS A 110 Br.—Bourbn Intrnatl Syndcte (Ky) 1987 4 1 0 0 $25,875
Tr.—Drysdale Neil 1986 9 3 0 0 $37,802
Own.—Brook-Hancock-Keogh Etal Lifetime 22 6 1 0 $70,243 Turf 22 6 1 0 $70,239

5Aug87-7Dmr 1 Ⓣ:48 1:1131:354fm 18 118 711 711 77¾ 67¼ DlhoussyE2 ⒻAw40000 85-08 AdorableMicol,Aberuschk,Aromcor 7
5Jly87-8Hol 1⅛Ⓣ:45 1:0821:461fm 9 116 816 813 711 67¾ DlhssE3 ⒻBv Hls H 89-03 Auspiciante, Reloy, Festivity 8
5Jly87—Grade II
17Jun87-8Hol 1 1/16Ⓣ:4641:10 1:411fm 5 116 611 69 62¾ 11 DlhoussyE3 ⒻAw45000 88-12 AmongstTheStrs,Fstivity,StllCloud 6
15May87-8Hol 1⅛Ⓣ:4911:13 1:483fm 26 116 63¼ 43 42 52¾ DlhoussyE2 ⒻAw45000 82-12 Santiki,TreasureMap,Helen'sMjesty 7
25Oct86♦4Newbury(Eng) 1½ 2:451sf 66 119 Ⓣ 510 Lowe J St Simon (Gr3) JupiterIslnd,VerdAntique,QueenHln 9
12Oct86♦6Longchamp(Fra) a1 5/16 2:402gd 29 123 Ⓣ 75¾ Lowe J ⒻPx d Roylieu(Gr3) Sharaniya, Kruguy, Luth d'Or 10
14Sep86♦5Hanover(Ger) a1½ 2:42 gd 4½ 128 Ⓣ 43¾ LowJ ⒻDeutschr Stutnprs(Gr3) Prairie Neba, Noretta, Lomela 8
21Aug86♦6York(Eng) 1½ 2:303gd 20 119 Ⓣ 46½ Lowe J ⒻGaltres Startino, Kenanga, Bonshamile 13
13Jly86♦5Krefeld(Ger) a1 7/16 2:283fm 27 121 Ⓣ 1no LoweJ ⒻGobls-Ernrngs(Gr3) AmongstThStrs,PrrNb,EpcrsGrdn 12
11Jun86♦4Newbury(Eng) 1¼ 2:143gd 12 121 Ⓣ 8 Lowe J ⒻBallymcl Std LvendrMist,Bishn,OldDomsdyBook 9
Aug 16 Dmr 6f ft 1:152 h Aug 11 Dmr 3f ft :364 h Aug 1 Dmr 5f ft 1:014 h Jly 21 Hol 6f ft 1:182 h

E.
7–2

Schiller B. g. 5, by Blood Royal—Comet Hill, by Hillary
DELAHOUSSAYE E 118 Br.—Pulliam C N (Ky) 1987 10 1 1 2 $161,650
Tr.—Pulliam Vivian M 1986 16 0 3 2 $147,350
Own.—Johnson & Pulliam Lifetime 43 4 7 8 $386,800 Turf 26 2 5 5 $345,500

27Jly87-8Hol 1½Ⓣ:4641:5942:25 fm 12 114 77 108¼ 107¾ 1011 StevnsGL9 Sunset H 86-08 Swink, Forlitano, Rivlia 10
27Jly87—Grade I; Hopped in air
28Jun87-8Hol 1¼:46 1:343 2:003ft 31 114 1110 1014 1013 915¾ PttnDB3 Hol Gd Cp H 73-12 Ferdinand, Judge Angelucci,Tasso 11
28Jun87—Grade I

14Jun87-8Hol 1½Ⓣ:47 1:5942:241fm 15 116 2½ 2½ 32½ 34½ DlhossyE 5 Hol Inv H 96-03 Rivlia, GreatCommunicator,Schiller 6
14Jun87—Grade I
24May87-8GG 1⅜Ⓣ:4631:3632:141fm 5 116 59¼ 76½ 67 56½ Baze R A 2 G G H 87-12 Rivlia, Air Display, Reco 8
24May87—Grade II
19Apr87-8SA a1¾ Ⓣ:4912:27 2:49 fm 9½ 116 11 31½ 33 43 StvnsGL 3 Sn Jn Iv H 79-11 Rosedale, Wylfa, Rivlia 6
19Apr87—Grade I; Bobbled 5/16; lost whip early drive
4Apr87-8SA 1¼Ⓣ:4641:3532:002fm 5 118 11 1hd 12 1½ StvnsGL 5 Ⓡ St Grtrs H 85-16 Schiller, Wylfa, Forlitano 9
4Apr87—Bumped start
14Mar87-8SA 1½Ⓣ:4742:03 2:281fm 3½ 120 65 84¾ 89¾ 810½ Toro F 8 Ⓡ Sn Mrno H 63-22 Rosedale, Forlitano, Bob Back 10
16Feb87-8SA 1½Ⓣ:4612:0142:282gd 16 115 32 3½ 2½ 33¾ SpsnBH 4 Sn Lus Ob H 69-27 Louis Le Grand, Zoffany, Schiller 8
16Feb87—Grade II
7Feb87-7SA 1⅛Ⓣ:4521:1011:48 fm 2½ 116 59½ 32 41½ 22½ Simpson BH 3 Aw38000 84-13 Bello Horizonte, Schiller, Hills Bid 8
7Feb87—Bumped start; boxed in 1/4
25Jan87-8SA 1¼Ⓣ:4641:36 2:004fm 14 114 54½ 63¼ 74 66½ SpsnBH 6 Sn Mrcs H 76-18 Zoffny,LouisLeGrnd,StrwbrryRodII 8
25Jan87—Grade III
Aug 17 Dmr Ⓣ 5f fm 1:033 h (d) Aug 12 Dmr 6f ft 1:141 h Aug 7 Dmr 6f ft 1:13 h Jly 23 Hol 5f ft 1:002 h

F.
4–1

Circus Prince
PINCAY L JR **117**
Own.—Fleischer & Pennington
B. c. 4, by His Majesty—Joie, by Speak John
Br.—Gailyndel Farms (Cal)
Tr.—Russell John W
Lifetime 18 4 0 1 $104,710
1987 7 1 0 1 $50,500
1986 11 3 0 0 $54,210
Turf 10 3 0 1 $74,900

27Jly87-8Hol 1½Ⓣ:4641:5942:25 fm 11 115 1012 95¼ 73¾ 53¼ Toro F 10 Sunset H 94-08 Swink, Forlitano, Rivlia 10
27Jly87—Grade I
28Jun87-7Hol 1½Ⓣ:47 2:0032:262fm 3 116 710 52 52 1nk McCarron CJ 8 Ⓡ HcpO 90-11 Circus Prince,Truth,MilleroYMedio 9
28Jun87—Blocked early drive
13Jun87-8GG 1½Ⓣ:4832:0312:28 fm 13 115 86¾ 74½ 56½ 45 JudicJC 4 Rllng Grn H 92-12 Forlitano, Lord Grundy, Wylfa 9
13Jun87—Grade III
16May87-8Hol 1½Ⓣ:4832:0122:263fm 45 115 1113 94¾ 85 31¼ CstnAL 11 Ⓡ Cbllero H 88-12 LordGrndy,GrtCmmnctr,CrcsPrnc 12
25Apr87-5Hol 1$\frac{1}{16}$Ⓣ:4711:1131:413fm 12e 116 107 107¾ 85¼ 74 ValenzuelPA 8 Aw30000 82-14 Lord Grundy, Danczone, Havildar 10
1Apr87-8SA 1⅛Ⓣ:4621:1111:474fm 29 116 98 95½ 54 51¼ ValenzuelPA 5 Aw40000 87-14 NorthernProvidr,Attntion,DnThtch 9
11Feb87-8GG 1 :464 1:104 1:361ft 4¾ 116 77½ 79 57 58¼ Judice J C 3 Aw20000 79-21 CertinTret,StudiousOn,SnsitivCopy 7
25Oct86-5BM a1⅛Ⓣ 1:47 fm 3 114 714 44 1hd 14 Judice J C 5 Aw18000 100-03 Circus Prince,Daniyar,FlyingSnow 10
10Oct86-8BM 1$\frac{1}{16}$:474 1:112 1:44 ft 3¼ 114 88 89½ 87 61¾ Judice J C 8 Aw17000 70-18 OrindaOriginl,AirDevil,U.LuckyShot 8
25Sep86-8BM 1$\frac{1}{16}$:482 1:132 1:472sl *8-5 114 58 56½ 57½ 55¼ Judice J C 1 Aw17000 50-35 Fair Go, He's Spirited, Porch Light 5
Aug 18 Dmr 5f ft 1:01 h Aug 13 Dmr 6f ft 1:142 h Aug 6 Dmr Ⓣ 6f fm 1:171 h (d) Jly 21 Hol 7f ft 1:271 h

G.
30–1

Flying Snow
GRYDER A T **107**
Own.—Severinsen D
B. g. 6, by Somethingfabulous—Snow Feathers, by Snow Sporting
Br.—Crook J (Cal)
Tr.—Severinsen Allen
Lifetime 25 4 4 4 $61,750
1987 5 0 1 1 $8,075
1986 8 2 1 2 $29,520
Turf 15 3 3 4 $51,055

12Jly87-10Pln 1$\frac{1}{16}$:472 1:114 1:44 ft 3¾ 116 2½ 42 78½ 811¾ Chapman T M9 25000 72-13 MenCuisine,AppleCk,PirdAndPintd 9
13Jun87-10GG 1$\frac{1}{16}$Ⓣ:4721:1121:433fm 6¼ 114 41½ 42 83 62 Chapman T M4 35000 82-12 GllntHwk,TellFloHello,NorthOfLk 11
23May87-10GG 1$\frac{1}{16}$Ⓣ:4731:1121:432fm 3½ 119 2hd 1½ 31½ 45½ ChapmanTM6 Aw19000 79-20 GallantHawk,MidnightIce,DrbyBoss 8
29Apr87-8GG 1$\frac{1}{16}$Ⓣ:47 1:1111:434fm*8-5 119 42 31½ 21 2no ChapmanTM4 Aw19000 83-17 FlklndsRuler,FlyingSnow,DrbyBoss 9
4Apr87-10GG 1$\frac{1}{16}$Ⓣ 1:43 fm 12 114 35 43½ 23 34½ Schacht R6 45000 82-11 MinutesAwy,SetPoint,FlyingSnow 12
15Nov86-4BM a1⅛Ⓣ 1:49 fm*8-5 114 11 11½ 14 22 Chapman T M 9 65000 88-19 Shayzari,FlyingSnow,RobertoReson 9
25Oct86-5BM a1⅛Ⓣ 1:47 fm*8-5 115 21½ 1hd 3nk 36 ChapmanTM 6 Aw18000 94-03 Circus Prince,Daniyar,FlyingSnow 10
25Oct86—Broke in a tangle
5Oct86-6BM 1⅛Ⓣ:47 1:12 1:493fm 4 115 13 12 13 11 Castaneda M 7 50000 92-08 Flying Snow, Iron Leader, Daniyar 9
6Sep86-5Dmr 1⅛Ⓣ:4631:11 1:492fm 16 116 2½ 2½ 98¾ 1012¼ Shoemaker W 3 55000 75-09 Aviator II, Keyala, Ono Gummo 10
6Aug86-5Dmr 1⅛Ⓣ:4821:1241:502fm 22 117 11 1hd 1½ 1¾ ShoemkerW 6 Aw20000 82-14 FlyingSnow,Nurely,CashInTheBnk 10
Aug 16 Dmr 1 ft 1:42 h Aug 11 Dmr 7f ft 1:282 h Jly 30 GG 6f ft 1:142 h Jly 25 GG 5f ft 1:013 h

36. A trio of 5–2 shots crowd this nonwinners allowance field. Which one is a fair bet? Or is another entrant an even better bet?

9 MONMOUTH 6 FURLONGS MONMOUTH PARK

6 FURLONGS. (1.08) ALLOWANCE. Purse $14,000. 3-year-olds and upward, which have not won a race other than Maiden, Claiming or Starter. Weight, 3-year-olds, 117 lbs., Older, 122 lbs., Non-winners of $9,800 since June 30, allowed 2 lbs., $6,600 since June 23, 4 lbs., $6,000 since June 16, 6 lbs. (Races where entered for $35,000 or less not considered).

A.
5–2

Timpeak — Dk. b. or br. c. 3, by Olden Times—Ute Peak, by Cornish Prince
Own.—Cooke J K — Br.—Deter Jean (Ky) — Tr.—Meyer Jerome C — 115
Lifetime 3 1 2 0 $11,800 — 1987 1 1 0 0 $7,800 — 1986 2 M 2 0 $4,000

27Jly87- 3Mth fst 6f :22⅘ :46 1:11⅕ 3+ Md Sp Wt 4 6 41¼ 2no 11½ 17 Santagata N b 116 4.20 84-19 Timpeak 1167 T. V. Viewer 1163½ Daring 'N Bold122no Ridden out, 6
30Aug86- 2Pha fst 6f :22⅗ :46⅗ 1:12⅕ Md Sp Wt 5 3 41 31½ 21½ 23½ Lloyd J S b 117 *.70 76-16 Quick Cadence 1173½ Timpeak 1171 Dixie Freeze 1172 Rallied 7
19Aug86- 2Pha fst 6f :22⅕ :45⅘ 1:11⅗ Md Sp Wt 3 7 31½ 53 33½ 24½ Ferrer J C b 117 2.80 78-19 Sportin Phil 1174½ Timpeak 1171½ DixieFreeze117nk Lacked room 10
LATEST WORKOUTS Jly 21 Mth 6f fst 1:16⅘ b — Jly 14 Mth 6f fst 1:15 h — Jly 10 Mth 6f fst 1:13⅗ h — Jly 4 Mth 6f fst 1:17⅗ b

B.
5–1

Big Richie — Gr. c. 3, by Wind and Wuthering—Brave and Free, by Warfare
Own.—Sciametta J — Br.—Mitchell F & N (Ky) — Tr.—Sciametta Anthony Jr — 111
Lifetime 13 1 4 1 $26,529 — 1987 4 0 1 0 $3,450 — 1986 9 1 3 1 $23,079 — Turf 1 0 0 1 $4,884

4Jly87- 2Mth fst 1 :46⅗ 1:11⅕ 1:37⅕ 3+ Alw 15000 7 4 52¾ 63½ 63½ 68 Miceli M b 110 7.10 79-10 Native Aspen 115¾ Freud 112¾ Aly Rat 1143½ Tired 8
26Jun87- 7Mth fst 1 1/16 :47 1:11⅗ 1:45⅖ 3+ Alw 15000 6 5 41½ 2½ 2hd 22 Miceli M b 111 3.80 76-21 Toll Key 1182 Big Richie 1112¼ Silky Cyrus 1182½ Couldn't stay 9
16Jun87- 8Mth fst 6f :22⅖ :45⅕ 1:10⅕ 3+ Alw 14000 1 6 63¾ 63½ 75 67¾ Miceli M b 110 12.00 81-14 No Points 1143½ Limited Access 1112 Toll Key 116½ In close 9
8Jun87- 7Mth fst 170 :45⅘ 1:10⅖ 1:41⅖ 3+ Alw 15000 5 5 59 59 69½ 514¾ Miceli M 110 4.30 74-18 Hybet 1134½ Black Swan 111¾ Public Accounter 1097 Outrun 7
27Dec86- 6Pha fst 6f :22⅕ :46⅖ 1:12 Alw 10500 3 9 86¾ 63½ 22 21 Miceli M 114 *1.40 80-21 Kona Way 1141 Big Richie 1143 Ruler of the Fleet 1155 Gamely 12
26Nov86- 5Pha sly 6f :22⅘ :46 1:10⅖ Alw 10500 4 1 3½ 2hd 22 23½ Ferrer J C 114 *1.00 85-26 Be a Ga Tor 1143½ Big Richie 11410 Noble Citation1144 Game try 6
1Nov86- 5Pha fst 1 1/16 :46⅘ 1:11⅗ 1:43⅘ Heritage 5 11 105 71¾ 55 57½ Fiorentino C T 119 28.40 77-09 Phantom Jet 1192½ Relano 1192½ Wordy 1192 Rallied 14
22Oct86- 8Pha fst 1 :47⅖ 1:12⅕ 1:38⅗ Alw 11500 1 3 21½ 21½ 45 49 Fiorentino C T b 114 3.20e 73-22 Well Honored 120nk Heritance 1207½ SilentLeader117½ Weakened 10
11Oct86- 8Pha fm 1 Ⓣ:47⅕ 1:12 1:37⅘ Dragoon 10 4 41½ 2½ 1hd 31½ Fiorentino C T b 114 11.80 87-13 GretLightning1141½NeverForgotten115noBigRichi114no Weakened 11
27Sep86- 3Pha sly 6f :22⅖ :45⅘ 1:11⅘ ⓈSwftprsuit H 2 4 53¾ 3½ 21½ 21 Fiorentino C T b 114 6.90 81-17 FlyingGrnville1141BigRichie114ndNevrForgottn11510 Held second 6
LATEST WORKOUTS Jly 30 Mth 5f fst 1:02 b — Jly 25 Mth 4f fst :48 h — Jly 18 Mth 5f fst 1:02⅘ b — Jun 16 Mth 3f fst :35⅘ bg

C.
5–2

Gambler's Trick — B. h. 5, by Clever Trick—Gambrel, by A Gambler
Own.—Walker W — Br.—Shaw J B (Ky) — Tr.—Perkins Ben W Jr — 116
Lifetime 1 1 0 0 $4,200 — 1987 1 1 0 0 $4,200 — 1986 0 M 0 0

10Jly87- 5Atl gd 5f :22⅕ :46 :59⅕ 3+ Md Sp Wt 2 1 12 13 15 16 Conner M J 122 *1.00 91-21 Gmbler'sTrick1226SquiggyTheGreek1172NorthWrning1151 Easily 6
LATEST WORKOUTS ●Jly 29 Atl 5f fst 1:01 h — Jly 18 Atl 4f fst :49⅕ b — Jly 7 Atl 4f fst :49⅘ bg — Jun 25 Atl 6f fst 1:15⅖ b

D.
5–2

Naskra Native * — B. c. 3, by Star de Naskra—Native Splash, by Raise a Native
Own.—Evans R S — Br.—Evans Robert S (NJ) — Tr.—Thompson J Willard — 111
Lifetime 6 1 1 1 $43,664 — 1987 2 0 0 0 — 1986 4 1 1 1 $43,864

13Jun87- 4Mth fst 6f :22⅕ :44⅗ 1:10⅖ 3+ ⓈAlw 17500 4 7 62¾ 96¾ 108½ 97¾ McCauley W H 112 *2.30 80-12 Credit Line 110½ Take Sanctuary 109nd SuperStated111½ Outrun 11
2Jun87- 9Mth fst 6f :22⅕ :44⅘ 1:10⅕ Select 3 6 64¼ 67 813 711½ McCauley W H 112 *2.80 77-16 Charalo1121½NeverForgotten114ncDepartingDrem1182½ No threat 10
26Aug86- 9Mth fst 6f :22⅕ :45 1:11 ⓈNj Breeders' 5 1 32½ 32½ 35 36¾ Terry J 115 2.40 78-17 SwissNative1156½Codey'sSimulcast114nkNaskraNative1152 Evenly 5
9Aug86- 10Mth fst 6f :22⅗ :45⅘ 1:10⅕ Sapling 3 4 53 58¾ 416 422½ Terry J 122 20.80 66-16 Bet Twice 1222½ Faster Than Sound 1224Homebuilder12216 Tired 5
9Aug86-Grade II
29Jly86- 9Mth sly 5½f :22⅖ :46⅕ 1:05⅕ Tyro 1 6 42 43 25 24 Terry J 116 8.40 85-19 FsterThnSound1224NskrNtive116nkHomebuilder1161 Held second 9
2Jly86- 1Mth sly 5f :22⅘ :46⅗ :59⅕ ⓈMd Sp Wt 1 2 11 1½ 12 11 Terry J 118 2.10 86-24 Naskra Native 1181EasterMary1156MorningPrincess1154½ Driving 8
LATEST WORKOUTS Jly 28 Mth 6f fst 1:13⅗ h — Jly 22 Mth 5f fst 1:02 bg — Jly 16 Mth 5f fst 1:01 b — Jly 10 Mth 4f fst :50⅖ b

E.
12–1

Le Vroom — Ch. g. 4, by Le Fabuleux—Vorhees Pleasure, by What A Pleasure
Own.—Cornman P — Br.—Welcome Farm (Pa) — Tr.—Hirsch Alan — 116
Lifetime 30 3 1 4 $47,780 — 1987 10 0 1 2 $10,880 — 1986 20 3 0 2 $36,900 — Turf 3 0 0 0

15Jly87- 8Mth fst 6f :22⅗ :45⅗ 1:11⅕ 3+ Alw 14000 2 6 64½ 34½ 23 2½ St Leon G 116 8.40 83-20 Sal's Shuttle 110½ Le Vroom 116½ Brother Vinnie 1163½ Rallied 6
6Jly87- 7Mth fst 6f :21⅘ :44⅗ 1:10 3+ Alw 14000 10 1 107 89½ 75½ 44¾ St Leon G 116 12.10 85-14 Lucky Tom Tom 1162½ Brother Vinnie 1161½ Mankaw114¾ Rallied 10
16Jun87- 8Mth fst 6f :22⅖ :45⅕ 1:10⅕ 3+ Alw 14000 5 5 85¾ 74½ 53½ 46 St Leon G 116 17.20 83-14 No Points 1143½ Limited Access 1112 Toll Key 116½ Wide 9
9Jun87- 8Mth fst 6f :22⅗ :45⅗ 1:10⅖ 3+ Alw 14000 3 7 75¾ 76½ 55¾ 33 St Leon G 116 4.60 85-19 Cinnamon Red 1091 Limited Access 1112 Le Vroom 1162¾ Rallied 7
27May87- 7Bel fm 1 1/16 Ⓣ:46 1:10⅘ 1:42⅘ 3+ Alw 27000 11 10 78½ 67 711 714½ Baird E T 119 25.50 67-15 FoolishPirate1121FrenchChampgne1191½BillyWilbur1192½ Outrun 12
30Apr87- 7Aqu fst 7f :22⅗ :46⅖ 1:24 3+ Alw 26000 3 6 44 54 54½ 54 Maple E 119 7.40 77-28 Matthews Keep 1131½ Yet Wave 107no Fort Whoop1142 Fell back 7
4Apr87- 6Aqu sly 1 :45⅗ 1:10⅕ 1:36⅘ 3+ Alw 27000 3 4 57 44½ 43½ 34½ Maple E 119 8.00 77-21 Yucca 1103½ Gnome's Pleasure 1121 Le Vroom 119½ Rallied 9
27Mar87- 7Aqu fst 1 :46⅕ 1:10⅖ 1:36⅕ Alw 27000 2 3 21½ 23 35½ 47¾ Maple E 117 7.30 77-21 GlitteringDwn117nkFullyReserved1126NoQuestion1171½ Gave way 8
28Feb87- 6Aqu fst 6f ⊡:22⅖ :45⅘ 1:11⅕ Alw 26000 3 8 88½ 76¼ 79¼ 79¼ Bailey J D 117 4.10 79-16 Gold Crop 112hd Saintly Cheif 1142¾ Keep It Easy 117½ Outrun 8
18Feb87- 7Aqu fst 6f ⊡:23⅕ :47 1:11⅘ Alw 26000 3 4 54¾ 76¼ 77 57 Antley C W 117 10.40 78-23 Upper Star 1123 Racer 1123¼ Captain Wimborne 117no No threat 8

F.
9–2

Chillanother — Dk. b. or br. c. 3, by Baldski—Cap the Moment, by For the Moment
Own.—East Coast Stable — Br.—Farnsworth Farm & Robins G (Fla) — Tr.—Handy George R — 111
Lifetime 2 1 0 0 $5,100 — 1987 1 1 0 0 $5,100 — 1986 1 M 0 0

22Jly87- 1Mth fst 6f :22⅗ :46⅖ 1:11⅗ 3+ Md 25000 7 1 31 2½ 1hd 14 St Leon G 116 3.50 82-21 Chillanother 1164 Able Cable 1161¼ Bridgehampton 122¾ Handily 9
8Jly86- 6Mth fst 5f :22⅘ :46⅗ :59⅗ Md Sp Wt 7 8 53¼ 75¾ 87¾ 76¾ Santagata N 118 3.20 75-16 Twelfth of Never 118¾ SteakDinner118nkRingforPeace118no Wide 9
LATEST WORKOUTS Jly 30 Mth 4f fst :48 h — Jly 18 Mth 4f fst :50 b — Jly 10 Mth 5f fst 1:01⅖ hg — Jly 4 Mth 4f fst :48⅗ h

37. Which horse figures best at the odds?

9th Santa Anita

6 FURLONGS. (1.07⅗) CLAIMING. Purse $13,000. Fillies and mares. 3-year-olds and upward. Bred in California. Weights, 3-year-olds, 119 lbs.; older, 121 lbs. Non-winners of two races since October 1 allowed 3 lbs.; such a race since then, 5 lbs. Claiming price $12,500; if for $10,500 allowed 2 lbs. (Races when entered for $10,000 or less not considered.)

A.
7–2

Oak Portal — Dk. b. or br. f. 3, by Hyannis Port—Oak Harbor, by Polly's Jet
Br.—Braun Mr-Mrs C A (Cal) — 1986 17 3 3 2 $36,100
OKABE Y 4-N — 116 — Tr.—Shulman Sanford — $12,500 — 1985 4 1 0 0 $7,475
Own.—Caruso-Charles-ClearVlyStbs — Lifetime 21 4 3 2 $43,575

19Dec86-7Hol 6f :22 :45^4 1:12 ft 7¼ 115 6^{2½} 7^{4¼} 7^{4¾} 7^{6½} PedrozMA^6 Ⓕⓢ 20000 76-17 DistntRunner,LuckyShowrs,Michcri 9
19Dec86—Off slowly
10Dec86-6Hol 6f :22 :46 1:12^{4}ft 12 115 5^{1½} 4^{1½} 2^{hd} 1^½ Pedroza M A^7 Ⓕ 16000 79-20 OakPortal,I'mTeasableToo,Mrlene 11
3Dec86-5Hol 1 :46^1 1:11^4 1:37^{4}ft 6¾ 115 1^½ 2^½ 3^{4½} 5^{12} Pedroza M A^2 Ⓕ 16000 62-18 Winsomething,GranEmotion,EndCp 8
20Nov86-7Hol 6f :22 :45^4 1:11^{1}ft 3¼ 115 2^{1½} 3^1 3^{3½} 3^{4½} PedrozMA^3 Ⓕⓢ 16000 82-16 I'mTesbleToo,DistntRunnr,OkPortl 8
14Nov86-7Hol 6f :22 :45^4 1:11^{4}ft 5¾ 115 1^{hd} 7^{3¾} 9^{5¼}11^5 PedrozMA^6 Ⓕⓢ 20000 79-16 CrbbnSongI,GdNwsDll,LckyShwrs 11
2Oct86-3SA 6f :21^4 :44^4 1:10^{2}ft 4 116 1^{hd} 3^{1½} 3^4 5^{6½} Ortega L E^{10} Ⓕ 25000 79-20 SaroGolden,She'sSoBold,L'Athena 12
7Aug86-5Dmr 6f :21^4 :45^2 1:10^{1}ft 5¼ 116 2^{hd} 1^{1½} 2^{hd} 2^{5½} Pedroza M A^6 Ⓕ 32000 81-16 Gayliole, Oak Portal, Procuress 8
21Jly86-8LA 7f :21^4 :45 1:23^{4}ft *2¼ 114 3^{3½} 3^{1½} 5^{7½} 6^{9¾} PedrozMA^5 ⒻAw15000 79-12 HrRoylGrc,ToBImprssv,GrnEmoton 7
22Jun86-4Hol 6f :22^1 :45^4 1:11 ft 9¾ 121 1^1 1^{1½} 1^{1½} 2^{2¼} Pedroza MA^{12} Ⓕ 32000 87-08 MariSupreme,OakPortl,Exuberncy 12
13Jun86-9Hol 1 :46^1 1:11^1 1:36^{3}ft 7 115 2^1 3^{1½} 5^6 5^8 Pedroza M A^3 Ⓕ 40000 72-17 DwnOfHope,Velveteen,RufflesNBus 7
●Dec 27 SA 3f ft :35 hg

B.
47–1

Eagle Reb — Gr. f. 3, by Reb's Policy—Outer Eagle, by Grey Eagle
Br.—Plummer D (Cal) — 1986 4 0 0 0
OLIVARES F 3-0 — 114 — Tr.—Jory Ian — $12,500 — 1985 3 1 0 1 $1,121
Own.—Horne G G — Lifetime 7 1 0 1 $1,121

12Dec86-5Hol 1 :48 1:13^2 1:39^{4}ft 72 113 1^1 2^2 6^{7½} 7^{9¾} Olivares F^7 Ⓕ 12500 54-20 MissDnil,Folk'sVctory,FrndlyCrowd 8
12Dec86—Rough start, broke in tangle
23Nov86-5Hol 6f :22^1 :45^4 1:11^{3}ft 90 114 5^2 9^7 9^{8¾} 9^{14¼} Olivares F^6 Ⓕ 12500 71-12 FullO'Gems,PrettyStall,JacketsSilk 9
12Nov86-5Hol 6f :22^2 :46^3 1:11^{2}ft 78 116 4^2 — — — Kaenel J L^6 Ⓕ 12500 — — Jerry'sGoldmine,FullO'Gms,BillyJn 9
12Nov86—Pulled up
10Oct86-1SA 6f :21^4 :45^2 1:11^{4}ft 40 109^5 7^6 10^{12} 9^{17} 9^{23½} Cisneros J E^4 Ⓕ 12500 55-24 JmTm,Jrry'sGoldmn,FryGodmothr 10
10Oct86—Veered in start
2Sep85-11Wyo 6f :22^3 :47^4 1:14^{1}m 25 122 6^2 5^{2½} 6^{14} 8^{18¾} MfldV^{10} Go Fr Gld Ft — — LuckyMagic,Fazam,PrinceOfMgic 12
24Aug85-8Wyo 6f :22^3 :45^2 1:11^{3}ft 9-5 122 3^1 3^3 3^2 3^3 Hadley S^6 Fut Trl — — Lucky Magic, UpbeatDoll,EagleReb 8
28Jly85-3Wyo 5f :22^3 :46^1 :59^{1}ft *8-5 115 2^{hd} 1^{hd} 2^1 1no Heim K^9 Mdn — — Eagle Reb, Mighty Doll, El Topho 9
Dec 24 Hol 5f ft 1:01^4 h Nov 20 Hol 5f ft 1:02^1 h Nov 12 Hol 3f ft :36^2 h

C.
12–1

I Remember When — Ro. f. 4, by Nostalgia—Basta, by Young Emperor
Br.—Auerbach E (Cal) — 1986 11 M 0 2 $8,125
SOTO S B 0-0 — 114 — Tr.—Lewis Craig A — $10,500 — 1985 3 M 2 0 $5,600
Own.—Royal T Stable — Lifetime 14 0 2 2 $13,725

24Dec86-2Hol 6f :22^4 :46^4 1:12^{3}ft 4¼ 122 6^{2¾} 6^{4¾} 4^6 4^9 Soto S B^2 ⒻM32000 71-20 Betsy'sBest,Surgeon'sChick,Ucello 8
17Dec86-2Hol 6f :22^2 :46^4 1:13^{1}ft 5½ 120 8^9 6^{5½} 4^4 3^2 Soto S B^{10} ⒻⓢM28000 75-22 Chmeleon,ElRyoKid,IRemmbrWhn 11
17Dec86—Wide backstretch, through 3/8
12Dec86-4Hol 6f :22^1 :46^2 1:12^{2}ft 11 120 8^{7½} 6^5 3^{4½} 3^{2¾} Soto S B^8 ⒻM30000 78-20 ApresVlois,SpiritStlr,IRmmbrWhn 12
4Dec86-4Hol 1⅛ :47^4 1:14 1:53^{1}ft 13 120 3^{1½} 2^1 3^{5½} 4^{9½} Soto S B^5 ⒻM28000 62-25 ShdeTheFlme,RightDy,Betsy'sBst 10
19Nov86-2Hol 6f :23 :47^4 1:12^{3}ft 21 115^5 5^2 5^2 7^{4¾} 6^{9½} PattonDB^2 ⒻⓢM28000 70-21 Fransway, Beaulucky, Mrs. Mop 11
11Nov86-6Hol 6f :22 :45^4 1:12^{1}ft 16 115^5 8^{8½} 6^8 5^8 5^{7¾} Patton D B^9 ⒻM28000 74-20 RsonToConsl,PoltGrl,Srgon'sChck 11
6Nov86-3Hol 6f :22^4 :46^4 1:11^{4}ft 20 115^5 6^{3¾} 6^7 5^6 4^{9¼} PattonDB^9 ⒻⓢM28000 75-17 SweetJaspary,Mrs.Mop,FncyHitter 11
6Nov86—Wide final 3/8
22Oct86-2SA 1$\frac{1}{16}$:45^4 1:12^1 1:48^{1}ft 19 119 7^{10} 5^{6½} 6^9 6^{10¾} PedrozaMA^6 ⒻM28000 49-23 Fool's Hill, The Maker, BayBreeze 12
22Oct86—Rank, steadied 7/8
18Oct86-2SA 6f :22 :45^2 1:11^{2}ft 3½ 119 9^{6¼} 6^{8½} 5^{6½} 5^{9½} StevensGL^{10} ⒻM28000 71-20 Hot Skate, Pats Day, Fast Verdict 11
9Oct86-4SA 1$\frac{1}{16}$:47^2 1:13 1:46^{4}ft 4¼ 119 4^{¾} 1^{hd} 3^{1½} 5^{6¼} StevensGL^{10} ⒻM28000 61-21 Campti, Odie Cumbers, Fool's Hill 12

D.

40–1

Love's Luck — B. f. 4, by Run of Luck—Only Love, by Envoy
BRINKERHOFF D — 116 — Br.—Johnson & Griffin (Cal) — 1986 6 1 0 1 $2,034
Own.—C D C Racing Stable Inc — Tr.—Krikorian George — $10,500 — 1985 2 M 0 0 $313
Lifetime 8 1 0 1 $2,347

7Dec86-4AC	6f	:231	:452	1:10 sy	26	114	41¼	66½	413	618½	OntivrosJA2	ⒻAw5500	70-22	VelvetEcho,JolieMdm,GrcisEscrow	8
22Nov86-7AC	6f	:231	:452	1:11 ft	15	118	11	2hd	2hd	1½	Ontiveros JA5	ⒻAlwM	84-13	Love'sLuck,YosemiteRos,AmoDidIt	8
2Nov86-5AC	6f	:222	:45	1:103ft	8¾	1135	21	53	63½	86¾	Delgadillo A3	ⒻMdn	79-12	Qn'sCrrg,PrncssGnvv,CongrssnlGrl	9
19Oct86-6AC	6f	:23	:453	1:112ft	7¼	118	21	21	21	33	Ontiveros JA8	ⒻAlwM	79-13	Cremolt,PrincessGenviv,Lcv'sLuck	9
27Sep86-11AC	6f	:233	:47	1:132gd	9½	118	42	42½	33	46	Ontiveros JA6	ⒻM9000	66-26	BellePrisienne,TiklishLilMiss,Nrvsc	7
27Jan86-2BM	6f	:23	:463	1:12 ft	3¼	1145	74½	68¼	810	77½	Black C A4	ⒻM12500	71-19	InterestDily,GiniBobini,SucySister	11

27Jan86—Bumped start, steadied 3/8

31Oct85-6LA	6½f	:213	:454	1:182ft	5	117	31½	47	57	59¼	EnriquezHF1	ⒻM20000	76-15	Bambinabolger, Bee Elegant,Triene	9
28Oct85-5LA	6f	:221	:46	1:114ft	6	117	43½	45	46	57½	Scott J M5	ⒻM16000	76-07	CheeryTims,MyGoldnBby,ElctricAg	8

28Oct85—Lugged out turns

Dec 29 SLR tr.t 4f ft :492 h   Dec 24 SLR tr.t 3f ft :372 h

E.

3–1

Legal Protection — Ch. f. 4, by Maheras—Wingfield Miss, by Exclusive Native
FERNANDEZ A L — 116 — Br.—McNall B (Cal) — 1986 3 1 1 0 $3,200
Own.—King–King–Landsburg — Tr.—Cerin Vladimir — $12,500 — 1985 10 2 1 1 $19,525
Lifetime 13 3 2 1 $28,725

24May86-3Hol	6f	:223	:462	1:123ft	22	116	117½	107	1213	1212¾	McHargueDG4	Ⓕ 20000	68-16	RdFrnchy,Rogr'sScrtry,MissMufft	12

24May86—Hopped in air

25Apr86-1Hol	6f	:224	:464	1:12 ft	*6-5	116	2hd	2hd	1hd	11	McHrgueDG2	Ⓕ c12500	84-16	LegalProtection,MadAbandon,Jello	6

25Apr86—Bumped in stretch

29Jan86-1SA	6f	:22	:453	1:101ft	4½	117	1½	1hd	21½	25	McHargueDG3	Ⓕ 12500	82-15	Obey, Legal Protection, Jo Be Bold	9

29Jan86—Bumped start

24Dec85-4Hol	6f	:224	:464	1:112ft	8	116	2½	42½	44	45½	McHargueDG8	Ⓕ 16000	81-12	FllForGold,Csild'sChoic,Goldi'sGrl	10
5Dec85-4Hol	6f	:222	:46	1:104ft	*3-2	118	11	1hd	3½	44	Pincay L Jr3	Ⓕ 12500	86-11	TrickyTurn,Goldie'sGirl,FllForGold	9

5Dec85—Bumped at 1/8

F.

5–2

Impressive Wind * — Ch. m. 5, by Impressive—Windy's Luck, by Lucky Mel
PINCAY L JR — 116 — Br.—Allred E C (Cal) — 1986 12 2 1 2 $36,855
Own.—Garelick Stable — Tr.—Kenney Martin — $12,500 — 1985 10 4 3 1 $56,095
Lifetime 30 7 6 3 $105,775 — Turf 1 0 0 0 $390

29Nov86-6TuP	6f	:214	:442	1:09 ft	4¼	1105	1hd	12	2hd	56¼	IammrinoMP4	Ⓕ 12500	85-12	Paul's Date, Crafty Gal, Chillerchat	8
16Nov86-8TuP	6f	:213	:442	1:093ft	4½	115	3nk	42½	88½	89¼	Jones D D7	Ⓕ 20000	79-15	CleverMe,Tributeen,PreciousMrtini	8
22Oct86-9TuP	7½f	Ⓣ:241	:472	1:31 fm	4¼	113	1½	1½	1½	43¼	Jones D D1	Ⓕ 20000	96-01	TwoToPrdise,Siemprvnt,PlyThtTun	7
2Aug86-2Cby	6f	:224	:46	1:113ft	3¼	113	32½	34½	36	312	Johnson P A5	Ⓕ 20000	77-15	Vivi'sTb,PrciousMrtini,ImprssvWnd	6
11Jly86-7Cby	6f	:214	:45	1:121m	3½	114	11	1½	1½	23½	Jones D D2	Ⓕ 20000	82-14	LovelyAnntt,ImprssivWind,Vivi'sTb	5
11Jun86-7Cby	6½f	:23	:47	1:191ft	4¾	114	2hd	2½	57½	516	Jones D D3	Ⓕ 32000	69-23	GlVlentin,ClvrArrngmnt,TrustdShot	7
17May86-10Cby	6f	:223	:454	1:12 ft	18	114	54¾	79½	712	716½	JonsDD1	ⒻHopkins H	70-20	Spnky'sScnds,Crfty'sBng,GrndGlry	7
10May86-9Cby	6f	:223	:452	1:111m	2¼	121	22	22	44	413½	BlackK2	ⒻⓈMakato S	77-12	LilPreppy,HoistHerFlg,SilentSword	5
4May86-8Cby	5½f	:22	:441	1:044ft	2	118	62¾	43¾	44	37¼	Hawley S2	ⒻAw16000	89-17	Spn'sScnds,Thppfrrds,ImprssvWnd	9
2Apr86-1SA	6f	:213	:443	1:104ft	*8-5	121	34	35½	37	510	Pincay L Jr5	Ⓕ c62500	74-22	Layout, Priscilla's Crown, Tamure	6

2Apr86—Lugged out

Dec 14 TuP 4f ft :492 h

G.

24–1

My Mysty Crystal — Ch. f. 3, by Libra Monti—Rullable Myst, by Nasrullah Spy
CASTANON A L — 114 — Br.—Aaron Mrs V C (Cal) — 1986 2 0 0 0
Own.—Eurton W A — Tr.—Eurton Pete — $12,500 — 1985 3 1 0 0 $2,777
Lifetime 5 1 0 0 $2,777

19Dec86-7Hol	6f	:22	:454	1:12 ft	18	115	21	53¼	910	918	Baze G1	ⒻⓈ 20000	65-17	DistntRunner,LuckyShowrs,Michcri	9
4Dec86-3Hol	6f	:22	:463	1:121ft	9¼	115	11½	2½	56½	618	PedrozMA6	ⒻⓈ 20000	64-25	I'mTeasableToo,Nicholova,OhMarie	7
18Sep85-11Pom	6f	:223	:46	1:112ft	23	114	21	32½	917	922	EnrzH8	ⒻBstls & Bws	— —	MissBnson,AplchBld,TropiclHolidy	9

18Sep85—Run in divisions

12Sep85-6Pom	6f	:221	:461	1:121ft	7	114	11	11	22	47	EspndlMA1	ⒻAw18000	— —	Alisage, Miami Lu, Totally Honest	10

12Sep85—Bumped at 1/16

25Aug85-2AC	5f	:221	:454	:574ft	*1	117	11	11	12	15	Espindola MA8	ⒻMdn	94-13	MyMystyCrystl,GreyLdy,NoblSprit	10

Dec 12 Hol 1 ft 1:433 h   Dec 1 Hol 4f ft :481 h   Nov 25 Hol 6f ft 1:14 h   Nov 19 Hol 6f ft 1:144 h

H.
5–1

Our Coquette
B. f. 3, by Blue Eyed Davy—Ginny M, by The Axe II
PATTON D B 3+ 109^5 Br.—Cowden B & Patricia (Cal) 1986 13 0 1 1 $8,060
Tr.—Fanning Jerry $12,500 1985 5 2 0 0 $14,750
Own.—Daverick Stable Lifetime 18 2 1 1 $22,810

18Dec86-1Hol 6f :22^1 :46 1:13 ft 8 110^5 21 1½ 1½ 2^{nk} Patton D B^8 Ⓕ[S] 12500 78-17 SweetJspry,OurCoqutt,AirForcBby 8
10Dec86-6Hol 6f :22 :46 1:12^{4}ft 47 115 8^{5}¼ 7^3 41½ 53 Solis A^1 Ⓕ 16000 76-20 OakPortal,I'mTeasableToo,Mrlene 11
20Nov86-7Hol 6f :22 :45^4 1:11^{1}ft 6 117 53½ 44 46 58½ Pincay L Jr^4 Ⓕ[S] 16000 78-16 I'mTesbleToo,DistntRunnr,OkPortl 8
8Nov86-1Hol 6f :22^3 :46^2 1:12^{1}ft 48 110^5 31½ 33½ 34 34 Patton D B^9 Ⓕ 16000 78-13 Ab Original, Marlene,OurCoquette 11
8Nov86—Wide down backstretch, through stretch
29Oct86-2SA 6f :21^3 :45 1:11^{3}ft 24 110^5 64½ 56 74 94½ VlenzuelFZ^5 Ⓕ[S] 16000 75-17 Brookes Pal, AbOriginal,Testarosa 11
23Sep86-8Pom 6½f :21^2 :45 1:17^{3}ft 6 114 46½ 35 34 47½ Pedroza M A^3 Ⓕ 16000 84-08 AboveThRst,ArcticLnd,VnillFstDnc 8
23Sep86—Fractious in gate
10Sep86-1Dmr 6f :22^1 :46 1:10^{4}ft *3 117 11^{22} 9^{15} 7^{12} 5^9 Pincay L Jr^6 Ⓕ 16000 75-11 MissDniel,MusicIThm,Chip'sSpirit 12
10Sep86—Reared at start
29Aug86-5Dmr 7f :22^3 :45^3 1:24 ft 12 117 1½ 1hd 3nk 57¼ Pincay L Jr^2 Ⓕ 20000 78-15 SrAndCrfty,ArFrcBby,DIEmStrght 11
8Aug86-1Dmr 1$\frac{1}{16}$:45^1 1:11 1:44^{3}ft 8½ 115 43 65½ 710 79¼ Baze R A^6 Ⓕ 20000 68-13 ‡ArcticLnd,Mistinguette,BvrlyDriv 11
31Jly86-1Dmr 6f :21^4 :45^1 1:10 ft 5½ 116 64¼ 55½ 45½ 46 Baze R A^2 Ⓕ 20000 82-12 DistntCommnd,L'Athn,GrySptmbr 11
Dec 5 SA 4f ft :48^2 h Nov 17 SA 4f ft :50^4 h Nov 6 SA 4f ft :49^3 h

I.
5–1

Ab Original
B. f. 3, by Raise an Orphan—Admirably, by Oceanus II
BAZE G 6–N 116 Br.—Anderson E J (Cal) 1986 13 3 3 0 $27,525
Tr.—Glauburg Louis $12,500 1985 1 M 1 0 $2,200
Own.—Anderson E J Lifetime 14 3 4 0 $29,725

10Dec86-6Hol 6f :22 :46 1:12^{4}ft 5½ 118 3½ 2½ 94¾11^{10} Baze G^{11} Ⓕ 16000 69-20 OakPortal,I'mTeasableToo,Mrlene 11
20Nov86-7Hol 6f :22 :45^4 1:11^{1}ft *2½ 113^5 76½ 55 67½ 69¾ Patton D B^5 Ⓕ[S] 16000 77-16 I'mTesbleToo,DistntRunnr,OkPortl 8
20Nov86—Hopped in air
8Nov86-1Hol 6f :22^3 :46^2 1:12^{1}ft *9-5 115 11 11½ 11½ 12½ Pedroza M A^4 Ⓕ 16000 82-13 Ab Original, Marlene,OurCoquette 11
29Oct86-2SA 6f :21^3 :45 1:11^{3}ft 7 115 32½ 31½ 1hd 2½ PedrozMA^{10} Ⓕ[S] 16000 79-17 Brookes Pal, AbOriginal,Testarosa 11
13Oct86-5SA 6f :22 :45^2 1:11^{1}ft 15 114 31 42 711 — Meza R Q^5 Ⓕ 18000 — — SroGolden,DnceHllHussy,MissDniel 7
13Oct86—Eased
10Sep86-2Dmr 6f :22 :45^2 1:10 ft 4½ 117 21 21½ 31½ 6^{11} Pincay L Jr^5 Ⓕ 25000 77-11 GoodNwsTody,LckyShwrs,RchllsGrl 9
10Sep86—Broke out, bumped
20Aug86-2Dmr 6f :22 :45^2 1:10^{3}ft 19 116 41½ 2½ 22 42¾ Douglas R R^2 Ⓕ 25000 82-11 TBImprssv,Sh'sSBld,DstntCmmnd 11
24Jly86-2Dmr 6f :21^4 :45^2 1:10^{3}ft 5½ 111^5 31½ 1hd 31½ 55 Black C A^6 Ⓕ 28000 80-15 LadyShaman,CodedLetters,Gayliole 8
6Jly86-2Hol 6f :22 :45^4 1:11^{2}ft 6½ 110^5 21½ 1hd 2hd 2½ Black C A^2 Ⓕ 25000 86-09 Loveland, Ab Original, Gayliole 11
6Jly86—Lugged out late
22Jun86-4Hol 6f :22^1 :45^4 1:11 ft 7½ 116 41½ 33 89½10^{12}¼ DelhoussyeE^2 Ⓕ 32000 77-08 MariSupreme,OakPortl,Exuberncy 12
22Jun86—Lugged out drive
Dec 27 SA 6f ft 1:17^2 h Dec 20 SA 4f ft :49^4 h Dec 8 Hol 3f gd :37^2 h Nov 29 Hol 3f ft :37^4 h

J.
34–1

Princess Lark
Ch. m. 5, by TV Minstrel—Princess Dumpty, by Dumpty Humpty
COX D W 4–0 109^5 Br.—Jensen Mr–Mrs H W (Cal) 1986 11 1 2 3 $16,325
Tr.—Fresquez Jim $10,500 1985 13 M 3 2 $16,250
Own.—Apostle J L Lifetime 25 1 5 5 $32,575

23Oct86-5SA 6f :21^4 :45 1:11^{4}ft 15 116 43 43 76½ 88 Haddad AM^{12} Ⓕ 12500 71-20 CribbnSongI,Jrry'sGoldmin,OhMri 12
23Oct86—Wide into stretch
31Aug86-1Dmr 6f :22^2 :45^4 1:10^{3}ft 24 118 3½ 31 78 8^{15} BrinkerhoffD^8 Ⓕ 16000 70-12 JazzyLisa,IndinFlower,OrientlChmp 9
31Aug86—Veered in sharply; bumped, steadied start
11Aug86-1Dmr 6f :21^2 :45 1:09^{2}ft 85 118 33½ 31 24 39 BrinkerhoffD^7 Ⓕ 16000 82-13 RdrDwn,QueenDimggio,PrincssLrk 11
2Aug86-5Dmr 6f :21^2 :44^2 1:09^{4}ft 53 120 55½ 67½ 9^{13} 9^{12} BrinkerhoffD^5 Ⓕ 20000 77-12 GingerFish,Nit'sJewl,QunDimggio 12
16Jly86-3LA 6f :22^2 :46^2 1:12^{3}ft 4 122 4nk 1½ 11 1½ Patterson A^6 ⒻM32000 80-16 PrincessLrk,SpiritStelr,NoPrsrvtivs 8
10Jly86-7LA 6f :22^2 :46 1:11^{2}ft *8-5 115^5 53 42½ 32 33¼ Crowder SJ^1 ⒻM28000 83-17 CoddLttrs,Kitty'sWorld,PrncssLrk 10
12Jun86-3Hol 6f :22^4 :47 1:13 ft 3¾ 121 54½ 4¾ 21 41¾ McCrrCJ^{10} Ⓕ[S]M28000 77-20 PhntomMoon,SingAMssg,Go'N'Tll 12
15May86-4Hol 6f :22^4 :46^4 1:12^{1}ft 14 116^5 2hd 11½ 1½ 34 Black C A^7 ⒻM28000 79-13 MyOnlyOn,Winsomthng,PrncssLrk 12
25Apr86-2Hol 6f :22^3 :46^4 1:13^{1}ft 3¼ 116^5 2½ 2½ 21½ 66 Black C A^2 ⒻM28000 72-16 IfNotNwWhn,BvrlyDrv,GrdSchlFnd 9
25Apr86—Bumped hard break
27Mar86-6SA 6f :22 :46 1:11^{4}ft 9½ 113^5 63¾ 44 45½ 27 Gomez E A^8 ⒻM45000 72-21 Ms.DnSchndr,PrncssLrk,PblctyDll 11
27Mar86—Veered out, bumped start; lugged out 3/8
●Dec 26 Hol 4f ft :52 h Dec 14 Hol 6f ft 1:17 h Dec 3 Hol 6f ft :38 h

38. Check the odds here and decide which betting strategy is best. It's Aug. 1.

3rd Arlington

6 FURLONGS. (1.08) MAIDEN. SPECIAL WEIGHT. Purse $11,000. Fillies. 3 and 4-year-olds. Weight, 3-year-olds, 118 lbs.; 4-year-olds, 122 lbs. (Preference to fillies which have not started for less than $20,000.

Coupled—Flood and Dottie Parker.

15–1 **Barony**
B. f. 3, by The Bart—Fermez La Porte, by Arts and Letters
Br.—North Ridge Farm (Ky) 1986 0 M 0 0
Own.—Vanier N A & Morill Mrs F 118 Tr.—Vanier Harvey L
Lifetime 0 0 0 0
Jly 29 AP 4f gd :51 b Jly 24 AP 4f ft :49^2 bg Jly 19 AP 4f ft :53 b Jly 14 AP 4f ft :51^2 b

30–1 **Thank God**
Ch. f. 3, by Golden Act—Native Goddess, by Raise a Native
Br.—Spendthrift Farm (Ky) 1986 0 M 0 0
Own.—Teinowitz Philip 118 Tr.—Getz George J
Lifetime 0 0 0 0
Jly 18 AP 4f ft :51 b Jly 13 AP 5f ft 1:06 b Jly 8 AP 4f ft :53 b

2–1 **Twenty a Day Tim**
B. f. 4, by Recitalist—Driftwood Lane, by Hard Water
Br.—Logue W M (Fla) 1987 2 M 1 0 $2,860
Own.—Logue William M 122 Tr.—Metzler Raymond F 1986 0 M 0 0
Lifetime 2 0 1 0 $2,860
18Jly87-2AP 6f :22^1 :46^1 1:11^{3}ft 8 122 2½ 1^2 1^2 2^2 Smith M E^6 Ⓕ Mdn 80-21 Nckl'sCpck,TwntyDyTm,StrndPlm 12
20Jun87-2AP 6½f :23 :46^4 1:18^{3}ft 13 123 3^{1½} 2^{2½} 3^{5½} 4^{10} SorrowsAGJr^{10} Ⓕ Mdn 72-22 CoesseExprss,RstivMiss,SunstRid 12
Jly 9 AP 5f ft 1:04 b Jly 1 AP 5f ft 1:03 b Jun 11 AP 7f ft 1:27 h Jun 5 AP 5f ft 1:03 b

9–2 **Search Committee**
B. f. 3, by Roberto—Miss Carmie, by T V Lark
Br.—Miss Carmie Partners (Ky) 1986 0 M 0 0
Own.—Pin Oak Farm 118 Tr.—Foyt A J III
Lifetime 0 0 0 0
Jly 30 AP 3f ft :37 b ●Jly 24 AP 6f ft 1:15^3 h Jly 17 AP 6f ft 1:15 h Jly 8 AP 5f ft 1:04 bg

10–1 **Verdigris**
B. f. 3, by Green Forest—Ciao, by Silent Screen
Br.—Mill Ridge Farm Ltd (Ky) 1986 0 M 0 0
Own.—Mill Ridge Farm 118 Tr.—Bell Michael
Lifetime 0 0 0 0
Jly 30 AP 3f ft :37 b Jly 15 CD 5f ft 1:03 b Jly 6 CD 4f gd :49^2 bg Jun 9 CD 4f ft :48^3 h

8–5 **Flood**
Dk. b. or br. f. 4, by Riverman—Hail Maggie, by Hail to Reason
Br.—North Ridge Farm (Ky) 1987 2 M 1 0 $5,225
Own.—Seltzer E A 122 Tr.—Trotsek Harry 1986 1 M 1 0 $3,400
Lifetime 3 0 2 0 $8,625
10May87-6Hol 6f :22 :45^3 1:11^{2}ft *9-5 123 3^1 4^{2½} 2½ 4^1 Stevens G L^5 Ⓕ Mdn 85-17 Enchilada,Camtion,FantasticaLdy 10
25Apr87-4Hol 6f :22 :45^3 1:10^{3}ft 3½ 123 2^{1½} 2½ 2^{2½} 2^5 Stevens G L^2 Ⓕ Mdn 85-13 Raise You, Flood, Ninepaytheline 9
18May86-2Hol 7f :22^1 :45 1:22^{4}ft 19 115 3½ 3^{1½} 2^3 2^4 Toro F^8 Ⓕ Mdn 86-08 OnYourOwnTim,Flood,WordHrvst 10
Jly 10 CD 3f ft :38^3 b Jun 27 CD 6f ft 1:15^3 b Jun 15 CD 4f ft :54^2 b Jun 10 CD 3f gd :35^4 h

12–1 **Pink Perfection**
Ch. f. 3, by Everett's Last—Pink Petals, by Royal Tenny
Br.—Lowrance Everett (Ky) 1986 0 M 0 0
Own.—Lowrance E 118 Tr.—Broussard Joseph E
Lifetime 0 0 0 0
Jly 30 AP 4f ft :53 b Jly 9 AP 5f ft 1:01^2 bg Jly 2 AP 4f ft :48^4 bg ●Jun 27 AP 5f ft 1:00^4 hg

30–1 **Youth and Beauty**
B. f. 3, by Youth—Endora, by Ridan
Br.—McDowell Farm & Starr J L (Ark) 1987 1 M 0 0
Own.—Moore W N 118 Tr.—Clark Pat 1986 0 M 0 0
Lifetime 1 0 0 0
18Jly87-2AP 6f :22^1 :46^1 1:11^{3}ft 19 117 7^{5¾} 5^{3¾} 6^9 7^{10½} Frazier R L^9 Ⓕ Mdn 71-21 Nckl'sCpck,TwntyDyTm,StrndPlm 12
Jly 29 AP 4f gd :49^4 b Jly 12 AP 4f ft :49^2 bg Jly 5 AP 4f gd :51^2 b Jun 10 AP 5f ft 1:02 b

7–1 **Mistress Glendower**
Ch. f. 3, by Roberto—Clever Raise, by Raise a Native
Br.—Farish W S (Ky) 1986 3 M 0 0 $765
Own.—Swann John lessee 118 Tr.—Nafzger Carl
Lifetime 3 0 0 0 $765
30Aug86-5Cby 6f :22^3 :45^3 1:11^{2}ft 33 116 7^{7¼} 7^5 4^{6½} 4^{5¾} Oldham J^7 Ⓕ Mdn 84-08 Abrojo,Lookn'nCookn,EgyptnVrdct 8
17Aug86-5Cby 6f :22^4 :46^1 1:12^{1}ft 20 116 6^{3½} 6^{2¾} 5^{3¾} 5^{6½} Oldham J^5 Ⓕ Mdn 79-14 MyMissBrooks,Abrojo,EgyptnVrdct 8
21Jun86-3Cby 5f :22^3 :46^3 1:00 ft 4¾ 116 5^{2¼} 5^{5¾} 5^6 6^{18} Oldham J^4 Ⓕ Mdn 71-19 RiobyNight,HommdCooki,MidnNm 8
●Jly 29 AP 6f gd 1:15 hg Jly 8 AP 4f ft :49 bg Jun 27 AP 6f ft 1:16 bg Jun 11 AP 5f ft 1:03 bg

A. bet the California shipper *Flood*
B. bet the local favorite *Twenty a Day Tim*
C. crush the *Flood* and *Twenty a Day Tim* quinella
D. no play

39. The outstanding underlay in this maiden field is

6th Santa Anita

START
6 FURLONGS
SANTA ANITA

6 FURLONGS. (1.07⅗) MAIDEN. Purse $21,000. Fillies and mares. 4-year-olds and upward. Weights, 4-year-olds, 119 lbs.; older, 120 lbs. (Non-starters for a claiming price of $32,000 or less in their last three starts preferred.)

A.
23–1

Precise Vision — B. f. 4, by Visualizer—Excellently, by Forli
SHOEMAKER W — 119 — Br.—Hooper F W (Fla) — 1986 2 M 0 0 $1,275
Tr.—Fenstermaker L R — 1985 2 M 2 0 $8,800
Own.—Hooper F W — Lifetime 4 0 2 0 $10,075

10May86-5Hol 6f :223 :461 1:113ft 7¼ 120 64 67½ 610 88½ Shoemaker W4 ⒻMdn 77-12 Elegntly,AnnieV.,Kitty'sEverywher 11
26Apr86-4Hol 6f :221 :462 1:114ft *8-5 122 43 43½ 44½ 48½ McCarron C J2 ⒻMdn 76-18 LdyMcClry,MrgretBooth,AhreCovir 7
26Apr86—Veered out, bumped break
13Jly85-3Hol 6f :222 :461 1:113ft 2¼ 118 11 11½ 11½ 2½ McCarron C J1 ⒻMdn 88-06 Python,PreciseVision,LifeAtThTop 6
29Jun85-1Hol 5f :221 :45 :571ft 7¾ 118 58 37 36 26½ McCarron C J8 ⒻMdn — — Al'sHelen,PreciseVision,QueenSvoy 8
Jan 1 SA 3f ft :383 h Dec 5 Hol 7f ft 1:29 hg Nov 12 Hol 4f ft :481 h Oct 31 SA 3f ft :364 h

B.
92–1

Molinera — Dk. b. or br. f. 4, by Icecapade—Joy's Jewel, by Jacinto
BAZE G — 119 — Br.—Granja Vista Del Rio Sta (Cal) — 1986 3 M 0 0
Tr.—West C R — 1985 0 M 0 0
Own.—Granja Vista del Rio Stable — Lifetime 3 0 0 0

23Oct86-6SA 6f :212 :444 1:10 ft 43 118 42½ 86¼ 1015 1015½ Solis A11 ⒻMdn 72-20 Andrushk,SunlightMiss,DrlingLdy 11
28Aug86-6Dmr 6f :213 :452 1:10 ft 19 116 31 47 815 820 Olivares F8 ⒻMdn 68-18 Luck'sFantasy,Sweetness,SoftlySid 8
28Aug86—Lost whip 5/16
14Aug86-6Dmr 6f :22 :45 1:102ft 17 116 21 45 89 813½ Olivares F10 ⒻMdn 72-17 Queen Marlene, Intently, Take Tip 12
Dec 29 SA 5f ft 1:011 h Dec 17 SA 5f ft 1:01 h Dec 11 SA 5f ft 1:023 h Dec 5 SA 4f ft :493 h

C.
5–1

Lady Ack — B. f. 4, by Ack Ack—Assurgent, by Damascus
PINCAY L JR — 119 — Br.—Oak Cliff Thoroughbreds Ltd (Ky) — 1986 0 M 0 0
Tr.—Gosden John H M — 1985 0 M 0 0
Own.—Oak Cliff Stable — Lifetime 0 0 0 0
●Dec 21 Hol 6f ft 1:121 h Dec 15 Hol 6f ft 1:142 h Dec 10 Hol 3f ft :372 hg Dec 2 Hol 6f ft 1:142 h

D.
74–1

Regal Notion — Dk. b. or br. f. 4, by Regal and Royal—Chiasma, by Chieftain
STEVENS S A — 119 — Br.—Just A Farm (Fla) — 1986 5 M 1 0 $4,975
Tr.—Charlton Wayne — 1985 0 M 0 0
Own.—Charlton B W — Lifetime 5 0 1 0 $4,975

20Nov86-1Hol 6f :221 :46 1:11 ft 15 120 55½ 56½ 57½ 47 Stevens S A6 ⒻMdn 81-16 PrncssOfAck,Tootspp,L'IMssNnsns 8
19Oct86-4SA 1 1/16 :472 1:12 1:451ft 15 118 56 88¼ 811 814½ Kaenel J L2 ⒻMdn 60-18 Goldie Hawn, Bajan Moon,Kinema 10
8Oct86-4SA 1 1/16 :463 1:12 1:452ft 8 117 82¼ 41½ 99¼ 78¼ Kaenel J L5 ⒻMdn 66-20 Royal Alydar,Aspirate,GoldieHawn 11
8Oct86—Wide into stretch
24Aug86-4Dmr 6f :214 :45 1:10 ft 5¼ 116 54½ 66¾ 67 55¼ Kaenel J L10 ⒻMdn 83-12 Serious Gal, Take Tip, Fairly Old 11
4Aug86-2Dmr 6f :22 :452 1:102ft 52 117 33 32 22½ 21¾ Kaenel J L11 ⒻMdn 84-13 Tobins Lady,RegalNotion,Aspirate 12
Dec 27 SA 3f ft :373 h Dec 21 SA 7f ft 1:28 h Dec 13 SA 5f ft 1:013 h Dec 5 SA 4f ft :514 h

E.
6–1

Bajan Moon — B. f. 4, by Majestic Light—Dual Lane, by Olden Times
SIBILLE R — 119 — Br.—Meredith Farm (Ky) — 1986 3 M 2 1 $11,250
Tr.—Frankel Robert — 1985 0 M 0 0
Own.—Moss Mr–Mrs J S — Lifetime 3 0 2 1 $11,250

12Nov86-1Hol 1 :46 1:113 1:383ft *6-5 119 44 33 22½ 33¼ Stevens G L3 ⒻMdn 67-15 QueenJoan,LaAffirmed,BajanMoon 7
12Nov86—Bumped start
19Oct86-4SA 1 1/16 :472 1:12 1:451ft *2¼ 118 1½ 11 2½ 22½ Stevens G L8 ⒻMdn 72-18 Goldie Hawn, Bajan Moon,Kinema 10
4Oct86-2SA 6f :221 :454 1:111ft *2½ 117 56¾ 53½ 34 24 Stevens G L3 ⒻMdn 76-18 Sown, Bajan Moon, Darling Lady 8
Dec 27 SA 5f ft 1:003 h Dec 22 SA 5f ft 1:022 h Dec 16 Hol 5f ft 1:024 h Dec 10 Hol 3f ft :363 h

F.

6—1

Fabulous Trick
BLACK C A   119
Own.—Moss Mr–Mrs J S

Dk. b. or br. f. 4, by Clever Trick—Sailor Frolic, by Cap Size
Br.—Bloodstock Partners (Ky)
Tr.—Frankel Robert

1986   0 M 0 0
1985   0 M 0 0

Lifetime   0 0 0 0

Dec 31 Hol tr.t 4f ft :512 h   ●Dec 19 Hol 5f ft 1:143 h   Dec 13 Hol 4f ft :493 h   Dec 3 AC 7f ft 1:253 h

G.

6—1

Mikiwi
CORDERO A JR   120
Own.—Foster B

B. m. 5, by Eldorado Kid—My Dusty, by Dusty Canyon
Br.—Foster B (Cal)
Tr.—Moerman Gerald C

1986   5 M 2 0 $11,025
1985   4 M 1 2 $8,600

Lifetime   9 0/3 2 $19,625

Date	Dist			Fractions/Time	Cond	Odds	Wt	Calls				Jockey	Class	Speed	Finish
22Nov86–4Hol	6f	:223	:461 1:11	ft	9-5	119	31	621	641	57	Ortega L E4	Mdn	81-13	Brilliant Leader, Rewana, Thaxted 6
23Oct86–6SA	6f	:212	:444 1:10	ft	10	121	851	651	45	441	Cordova D W6	ⒻMdn	83-20	Andrushk,SunlightMiss,DrlingLdy 11
24Jan86–6SA	6f	:221	:454 1:11	ft	21	119	611	521	311	42	Kaenel J L6	ⒻMdn	81-18	LBellWilson,SfriLeder,Tempermnt 12
24Jan86–Checked at 3/8														
15Jan86–6SA	61f	:221	:453 1:17	ft	*8-5	119	411	111	11	21	Kaenel J L4	ⒻMdn	84-14	TimForZimblr,Mikiwi,SlvToFshion 11
2Jan86–6SA	6f	:214	:444 1:093	ft	21	119	21	211	221	231	Kaenel J L1	ⒻMdn	86-16	MostPrstigious,Mikiwi,PublictyDoll 6
27Nov85–6Hol	6f	:223	:463 1:113	ft	41	120	211	32	541	69	Kaenel J L6	ⒻMdn	77-16	Waterford Fair, Devon Diva,Tamil 11
8Nov85–6SA	1		:463 1:104 1:362	ft	81	117	11	2hd	221	351	Kaenel J L4	ⒻMdn	81-13	Petillante, Riverette, Mikiwi 8
24Oct85–6SA	6f	:22	:453 1:112	ft	51	118	42	221	23	23	Kaenel J L6	ⒻM50000	78-20	Lore Of Zorro, Mikiwi, Grenalda 12
24Oct85–Bumped start														
10Oct85–6SA	7f	:223	:452 1:243	ft	50	118	11	1hd	11	341	Kaenel J L12	ⒻM50000	72-18	YurDetermined,DoubleFive,Mikiwi 12

●Dec 28 SA 3f ft :344 h   Dec 14 SA 6f ft 1:13 h   Nov 16 SA 4f ft :484 h   Nov 4 SA 5f ft :594 h

H.

8—1

High Ace
DELAHOUSSAYE E   119
Own.—Delaplane E E

Gr. f. 4, by Relaunch—Community Chest, by Run of Luck
Br.—Lavin & Rowan (Cal)
Tr.—Dunn Larry

1986   1 M 0 1 $2,550
1985   0 M 0 0

Lifetime   1 0 0 1 $2,550

8May86–1Hol 6f :221 :462 1:11 ft 4 120 76 45 341 33 Pincay L Jr7 ⒻⓈMdn 86-14 RareStarlet,DuchessZnthe,HighAce 7
  8May86–Veered out start, wide entering stretch

Dec 28 SA 5f ft 1:004 hg   Dec 22 SA 7f ft 1:272 h   Dec 16 SA 6f ft 1:14 h   Dec 11 SA 6f ft 1:143 h

I.

7—2

That Fallon Girl
STEVENS G L   119
Own.—Hobby Horse Farms

Ch. f. 4, by Valdez—Grace and Savour, by His Majesty
Br.—Forsythe J (Ky)
Tr.—Barrera Lazaro S

1986   3 M 3 0 $10,200
1985   0 M 0 0

Lifetime   3 0/3 0 $10,200

21Jun86–6Hol 7f :222 :453 1:222 ft 8-5 114 31 31 221 25 Stevens G L3 ⒻMdn 87-09 SllyRussll,ThtFllonGrl,Nmtl'NQck 10
7Jun86–6Hol 6f :222 :454 1:11 ft *1 115 421 341 341 221 Stevens G L6 ⒻMdn 87-17 FuriousCee,ThatFallonGirl,HeatUp 10
24May86–6Hol 6f :223 :462 1:11 ft 51 115 521 44 331 22 Stevens G L4 ⒻMdn 87-16 Annie V.,ThatFallonGirl,Sasha'sJoi 12

●Dec 28 SA 5f ft :59 h   Dec 22 Hol 5f ft 1:01 h   ●Dec 16 Hol 4f ft :47 h   Dec 10 Hol 5f ft :352 h

J.

42—1

Sudden Affair
MEZA R Q   119
Own.—Hascol Farms

Dk. b. or br. f. 4, by To the Quick—Summer Affair, by Cornish Prince
Br.—Amvest Corp (Ky)
Tr.—Fanning Jerry

1986   2 M 0 0 $1,425
1985   0 M 0 0

Lifetime   2 0 0 0 $1,425

2Aug86–4Dmr 6f :22 :45 1:10 ft 13 117 871 1221 1211 226 McHargue DG8 ⒻMdn — — Sasha's Joi, Softly Said, Thai Dye 12
  2Aug86–Eased
21Jly86–6Hol 6f :222 :461 1:114 ft *6-5 114 2hd 1hd 1hd 443 Stevens G L7 ⒻMdn 80-16 SpcilStrk,WstrnAdvntur,RsAnAlydr 7

Dec 27 SA 5f ft 1:001 h   Dec 20 SA 6f ft 1:143 hg   Dec 14 SA 6f ft 1:153 h   Dec 8 SA 5f gd 1:011 h

K.

9—5

Wood Elf
VALENZUELA P A   119
Own.—Paulson A E

Dk. b. or br. f. 4, by Syncopate—Swiss Forest, by Dotted Swiss
Br.—Elmendorf Farm (Ky)
Tr.—Whittingham Michael

1986   0 M 0 0
1985   0 M 0 0

Lifetime   0 0 0 0

Dec 30 SA 4f ft :464 h   Dec 24 SA 5f ft :591 h   ●Dec 18 Hol 5f ft :343 hg   Dec 13 Hol 6f ft 1:131 hg

40. Where maiden races are carded on grass, handicappers can spot generous overlays regularly. Find the overlay here.

2nd Saratoga

1 ⅛ MILES. (Turf). (1.45⅘) MAIDEN SPECIAL WEIGHTS. PUrse $27,500. Fillies and Mares, 3-year-old and upward foaled in New York State and approved by the New York State Bred Registry. Weights, 3-year-olds, 117 lbs. Older, 122 lbs.

Coupled—Lady Talc and Pekabo Baby.

A.

4–1

Psychic Fair — Ch. f. 4, by Buckpoint—Genuine Regret, by Sir Wimborne

Br.—Tuttler Mrs W F L (NY) — 1987 7 M 2 1 $11,130

Own.—Nagle K — 1175 — Tr.—Lake Robert P — 1986 4 M 1 1 $1,900

Lifetime 12 0 3 2 $13,030

1Aug87-6Bel 7f :224 :47 1:272ft 7½ 1175 21 22 43¾ 46¼ BelmonteJF 4 ⒻⓈMdn 59-27 EffusivLdy,ShinncockLssi,Ms.Oro 14

2Jly87-4Bel 7f :224 :464 1:284sy *2½ 1175 42 23 23 41 Badamo JJ 11 ⒻⓈMdn 57-27 BalPetitBal,LizasJoy,Hrriet'sLuck 12

27Jun87-9Bel 6f :224 :471 1:13 sy 3 1175 54 33½ 43½ 35¼ Badamo J J 4 ⒻⓈMdn 70-29 MissAnglT.,MyGirlDnn,PsychicFir 11

27Jun87—Steadied

1Jun87-9Bel 6f :223 :464 1:13 ft 9 1175 11 2hd 33½ 47¾ Badamo J J 3 ⒻⓈMdn 67-20 TooBobsRtrn,MtchMdln,LdyIrnsd 10

1Jun87—Slow start

1May87-5Det 6f :232 :48 1:151ft 2¼ 122 31½ 21½ 21½ 2¾ Rydowski S R 6 ⒻMdn 63-40 SesonedBrek,PsychicFir,DncforJuli 9

23Apr87-3Det 6f :234 :482 1:164ft 3¼ 122 41¾ 2hd 2hd 2no Rydowski S R 6 ⒻMdn 56-44 RoyalSuz,PsychicFir,BetYourTricks 8

11Apr87-2Det 5½f :234 :474 1:081ft 8 122 66½ 56 47½ 48 Rydowski S R 5 ⒻMdn 66-32 Swishing, Plashy, Miss Kabylia 8

1Jun86-1Det 6f :231 :471 1:13 ft *6-5 116 54½ 56½ 610 610½ Frazzitta L 5 ⒻMdn 64-24 LadyOfSpring,GoIcyGo,Ou-Fairlwn 6

Jly 28 Aqu ⊡ 3f ft :394 b — Jun 22 Aqu 7f gd 1:302 bg(d) — Jun 9 Aqu 3f ft :384 b

B.

10–1

Fortrix — B. f. 3, by Forlion—Strix, by L'aiglon

Br.—Potter Sylvia & W (NY) — 1987 0 M 0 0

Own.—Potter W — 117 — Tr.—Malen J Lester — 1986 0 M 0 0

Lifetime 0 0 0 0

Jly 22 Bel 5f ft 1:04 bg — Jly 17 Aqu 4f ft :513 b — Jly 14 Aqu 4f ft :501 b — Jun 29 Aqu 4f ft :504 bg

C.

5–1

The Rite Chemistry — Ch. f. 4, by Noholme II—Lady Nephilim, by Binary

Br.—DeLuke D J (NY) — 1987 2 M 0 0 $1,650

Own.—Assunta Louis Farm — 122 — Tr.—Schulhofer Flint S — 1986 1 M 0 1 $2,880

Lifetime 3 0 0 1 $4,530 — Turf 1 0 0 0 $1,650

24Jly87-3Bel 1 1/16 Ⓣ:48 1:122 1:443fm 7½ 122 42½ 63¾ 47 410 Vasquez J2 ⒻⓈMdn 63-23 PrncssDnk,EnrgySqur,DvosDtchss 12

16Jly87-9Bel 6f :224 :472 1:141ft *2¾ 122 52¼ 66 76¼ 76½ Cruguet J8 ⒻⓈMdn 62-24 Forli'sLuck,MtchMdlin,HthrsArrst 12

22Aug86-9Sar 6f :223 :461 1:11 ft 4 117 23½ 25 39½ 317 Martens G11 ⒻⓈMdn 68-17 LPolonise,LibbyDr,ThRitChmistry 11

Aug 3 Sar Ⓣ 4f gd :492 b — Jly 11 Bel 4f ft :482 b — Jly 5 Bel 4f ft :492 b — Jun 30 Bel 4f ft :48 h

D.

15–1

Twoandacut — Dk. b. or br. m. 5, by Singh—Amphoteric, by Sadair

Br.—Sinclari Barbara (NY) — 1987 1 M 0 0

Own.—Disanto G b — 122 — Tr.—Disanto G — 1986 0 M 0 0

Lifetime 1 0 0 0

14Jun87-8Rkm 6f :23 :474 1:144ft 11 1175 87½ 911 917 928 Bryon T S7 ⒻMdn 42-31 MrquiseCut,WckyMrine,NvrRltion 10

Jly 29 Sar tr.t 4f ft :52 b — Jly 16 Sar Ⓣ 6f fm 1:182 b — ●Jun 25 Sar Ⓣ 4f fm :48 h (d) — ●Jun 9 Sar tr.t 3f gd :372 bg

E.

3–1

Harriet's Luck — Ch. f. 3, by What Luck—Hustlin' Harriet, by Rock Talk

Br.—Edwards Mrs J F (NY) — 1987 2 M 0 2 $6,420

Own.—Schatzberg Maureen — 117 — Tr.—Terrill William V — 1986 0 M 0 0

Lifetime 2 0 0 2 $6,420

10Jly87-9Bel 1⅛ :47 1:131 1:554gd 3 116 814 511 37 36¾ Guerra W A9 ⒻⓈMdn 41-23 VioletWho,MyGirlDnn,Hrrit'sLuck 10

2Jly87-4Bel 7f :224 :464 1:284sy 38 116 1216 912 56 3nk Guerra W A8 ⒻⓈMdn 58-27 BalPetitBal,LizasJoy,Hrriet'sLuck 12

2Jly87—Very wide,greenly

Jly 23 Bel 5f ft 1:022 h — Jun 22 Bel 5f ft 1:013 h — Jun 17 Bel 5f ft 1:033 bg — Jun 12 Bel 4f ft :502 b

F.
20–1

Jet South
B. f. 3, by Tri Jet—Courage Please, by Northern Dancer
Br.—Tippett Liz Whitney (NY) 1987 4 M 0 0 $270
Own.—Llangollen Farm **112^{5}** **Tr.—Carroll Del W II** 1986 4 M 0 0
Lifetime 8 0 0 0 $270

10Jly87-9Bel 1⅛ :47 1:13^{1} 1:55^{4}gd 27 111^{5} 1^{hd} 1½ 4^{9} 5^{17½} BelmonteJF 2 Ⓕ[S]Mdn 30-23 VioletWho,MyGirlDnn,Hrrit'sLuck 10
1Jun87-9Bel 6f :22^{3} :46^{4} 1:13 ft 18 114 9^{8½} 9^{10} 8^{14} 8^{14¼} Lovato F Jr 7 Ⓕ[S]Mdn 61-20 TooBobsRtrn,MtchMdln,LdyIrnsd 10
10Mar87-7GP 6f :22^{4} :46^{4} 1:12^{2}ft 50 121 7^{5¼} 5^{8½} 7^{15} 7^{18¼} Gonzalez M A^{6} ⒻMdn 59-28 Novelette, Cindy Rae, Great Time 11
21Feb87-4Hia 6f :22^{1} :45^{3} 1:12^{1}ft 40 120 9^{4½} 11^{11} 11^{23} 11^{25} Maple E^{1} ⒻMdn 54-17 WeeDram,MubarkBegum,Tsm'sStr 12
18Dec86-6Aqu 6f [•]:23^{2} :47^{4} 1:13^{3}sy 12 117 4^{¾} 3^{1½} 2^{3} 5^{9} Maple E^{10} Ⓕ[S]Mdn 67-21 HllyHlllujh,KnDnc,Twlvo'clocktils 12
10Nov86-3Aqu 7f :23^{1} :46^{3} 1:25 gd 15 110^{7} 6^{5} 5^{6½} 4^{5½} 7^{15½} BelmonteJF^{9} Ⓕ[S]Mdn 60-18 Ria'Mae,ChantillyLove,SpringLeaf 12
2Nov86-4Aqu 6f :22^{3} :46^{2} 1:12^{1}ft 24 110^{7} 10^{9} 10^{12} 8^{11} 7^{12½} Belmonte J F^{8} ⒻMdn 67-21 GrecianFlight,SomeHome,Tchaika 12
22Oct86-3Aqu 7f :23 :46^{1} 1:24^{2}ft 18 110^{7} 13^{12} 11^{9½} 10^{11} 9^{11} BelmontJF^{13} Ⓕ[S]Mdn 68-16 MissEmpir,Pggy'sDrm,HllyHlllujh 14
22Oct86—Very wide
●Aug 6 Sar tr.t 5f ft 1:03 b ●Jly 31 Sar tr.t 7f ft 1:31^{3} b Jly 17 Bel 4f ft :50^{3} b Jly 5 Bel tr.t 1 ft 1:44^{3} b

G.
20–1

Buzzy B.
B. f. 3, by Take Your Place—Brazilera, by Proud Clarion
Br.—Fox Crossing FArm (NY) 1987 4 M 0 0
Own.—Gallo A **117** **Tr.—Hargrave Kenneth** Turf 1 0 0 0
Lifetime 4 0 0 0

10Jly87-9Bel 1⅛ :47 1:13^{1} 1:55^{4}gd 15 116 7^{14} 9^{22} 9^{49} 9^{46½} Pezua J M^{5} Ⓕ[S]Mdn — — VioletWho,MyGirlDnn,Hrrit'sLuck 10
17Jun87-7Bel 1$\frac{1}{16}$ [T]:48^{3} 1:14 1:46^{3}fm 17 114 2^{4} 1^{hd} 4^{3½} 5^{9¼} Pezua J M^{3} Ⓕ[S]Mdn 59-24 Table for Four, Tripitaka, TuffSpot 7
17Jun87—Bumped
10Jun87-9Bel 7f :23^{1} :46^{4} 1:26^{3}ft 48 114 12^{13} 12^{20} 12^{27} 12^{28½} Baird E T^{7} Ⓕ[S]Mdn 40-17 ChristyHill,TuffPowdrPuff LzsJoy 12
26Apr87-2Aqu 7f :23^{1} :47^{1} 1:26^{4}ft 38 112 14^{11} 14^{16} 14^{18} 14^{15½} Migliore R 10 ⒻM35000 51-21 RstlssGm,TuffPowdrPff,PlsntStph 14

H.
15–1

Lady Talc
B. f. 3, by Talc—Mardie's Fling, by Barachois
Br.—Pinebourne Farm (N.Y.) 1987 4 M 0 0
Own.—Pinebourne Farm **117** **Tr.—Campo John P** 1986 2 M 0 0
Lifetime 6 0 0 0

15Apr87-9Aqu 7f :23^{1} :46^{4} 1:26^{3}ft 60 114 9^{9} 8^{12} 9^{17} 9^{15¾} Lovato F Jr 5 Ⓕ[S]Mdn 52-19 NtliMkrov,RglContss,ArcticHolidy 11
3Apr87-6Aqu 6f :22^{4} :47 1:13 ft 44 112 11^{9¾} 8^{10} 8^{8½} 8^{8½} Samyn J L 10 Ⓕ[S]Mdn 67-22 VestwrdHo,AmosKeto,MtchMdlin 13
25Feb87-5Aqu 6f [•]:23^{2} :47^{4} 1:14^{1}ft 35 121 9^{9} 9^{5½} 7^{9½} 7^{9¾} Lovato F Jr^{7} Ⓕ[S]Mdn 63-25 AdannaDear,GrabTime,SpringLeaf 11
21Jan87-4Aqu 6f [•]:22^{2} :46^{2} 1:12^{3}sy 17 121 9^{15} 9^{15} 6^{16} 6^{13¾} Lovato F Jr^{6} Ⓕ[S]Mdn 67-17 Ms.Jcques,FrncisMnor,RestlssGm 10
7Nov86-9Aqu 6f :22^{4} :47 1:13^{2}ft 24 117 3^{½} 4^{1¼} 10^{9} 11^{9½} Terry J 4 Ⓕ[S]Mdn 64-21 BookOfJoy,ArctcHldy,Twlv'clcktls 12
6Oct86-5Bel 7f :23^{4} :48 1:27^{2}ft 6¾e 117 3^{½} 3^{2½} 10^{22} 10^{29½} Terry J^{5} Ⓕ[S]Mdn 35-24 LondonPass,MissEmpire,GucciGal 12
Aug 5 Sar Ⓣ 7f fm 1:29^{2} b Jly 27 Bel 5f ft 1:00^{4} hg ●Jly 22 Bel tr.t 3f ft :35^{3} h Jly 16 Bel tr.t 5f ft 1:01 h

I.
8–1

Princess Anastasia
Ch. f. 3, by Russian George—Sea Princess, by My Stifled
Br.—Qui-Will Stable (NY) 1987 1 M 0 0
Own.—Qui-Will Stable **117** **Tr.—Cruguet Denise** Turf 1 0 0 0
Lifetime 1 0 0 0

13Jly87-4Bel 1$\frac{1}{16}$ [T]:48^{2} 1:13 1:45^{2}fm 7¼ 116 2^{1} 6^{4½} 8^{14} 8^{21} Cruguet J^{2} ⒻMdn 53-19 DncingShow,Excllr'sGl,GrmnbyJov 8
Jly 30 Sar 7f ft 1:30 b Jly 9 Sar Tr.Ⓣ 3f fm :37^{2} b (d) Jly 2 Sar Ⓣ 4f fm :51^{2} b (d) Jun 25 Sar Ⓣ 5f fm 1:02^{4} b (d)

J.
20–1

Wood On The Fire
B. f. 3, by Vitriolic—Maria Amalia, by Solo Landing
Br.—Our Seven Stables (NY) 1987 4 M 0 0
Own.—Our Seven Stables **117** **Tr.—Lostritto Joseph A** 1986 0 M 0 0
Lifetime 4 0 0 0

22Apr87-6Aqu 1⅛ :50^{1} 1:15^{4} 1:55^{4}ft 58 109 8^{9½} 8^{16} 8^{30} 8^{38} Thibeau R J 5 ⒻM45000 — — MirculousBst,AwsomSuzy,RisnBrry 8
15Apr87-9Aqu 7f :23^{1} :46^{4} 1:26^{3}ft 87 112 8^{8} 10^{17} 10^{24} 10^{23½} Thibeau R J 9 Ⓕ[S]Mdn 44-19 NtliMkrov,RglContss,ArcticHolidy 11
3Apr87-6Aqu 6f :22^{4} :47 1:13 ft 21f 112 13^{13} 13^{18} 12^{20} 12^{20½} Thibeau R J^{9} Ⓕ[S]Mdn 55-22 VestwrdHo,AmosKeto,MtchMdlin 13
30Mar87-4Aqu 1 :47 1:11^{3} 1:38^{3}ft 21 109 8^{18} 8^{22} 8^{24} 7^{25½} Thibeau R J^{3} ⒻM45000 47-25 Nanno, Shamrock Pass, MissMizzen 8
Aug 6 Sar 4f ft :49^{4} b Jly 29 Bel 3f ft :37 h Jly 20 Bel 6f ft 1:15^{4} b Jly 12 Bel 5f ft 1:02^{4} h

K.
10–1

Lady Ironside
Own.—Albert Diane **122**
Gr. f. 4, by Iron Constitution—Lady Nurse, by Run For Nurse
Br.—Albert Dianne (NY) **1987 11 M 0 4 $15,270**
Tr.—Willis Charles H III **1986 3 M 0 0**
Lifetime 14 0 0 4 $15,270 **Turf 1 0 0 0**

18Jly87-3Bel 1$\frac{1}{16}$Ⓣ:46^{3}1:12 1:43^{3}fm 34 122 2^4 2$^{1\frac{1}{2}}$ 6^7 7^9 Venezia M^1 ⒻMdn 69-20 Strictly, First Shot, Bleach 11
2Jly87-6Bel 7f :22^1 :46 1:26^{4}sy 7 122 6$^{9\frac{1}{2}}$ 6^{14} 5^{13} 5$^{11\frac{1}{2}}$ Venezia M^5 Ⓕ[S]Mdn 56-27 JnRussll,ShnncockLss,DvosDtchss 12
1Jun87-9Bel 6f :22^3 :46^4 1:13 ft 8$\frac{1}{2}$ 122 7^5 5$^{4\frac{1}{2}}$ 4$^{4\frac{1}{2}}$ 3$^{3\frac{3}{4}}$ Samyn J L^8 Ⓕ[S]Mdn 71-20 TooBobsRtrn,MtchMdln,LdyIrnsd 10
1Jun87—Very wide
2May87-6Aqu 7f :23^1 :47^1 1:25^{3}ft 2$\frac{1}{2}$ 124 6$^{3\frac{3}{4}}$ 5^3 3$^{2\frac{1}{2}}$ 3$^{4\frac{1}{4}}$ Samyn J L $\underline{5}$ ⒻMdn 69-19 Rosie'sDncr,ShGonHid,LdyIronsid 11
20Apr87-4Aqu 7f :23^1 :47^1 1:26^{1}ft 11 120 9$^{4\frac{3}{4}}$ 9$^{6\frac{1}{4}}$ 5^6 4^3 Brown T L $\underline{6}$ ⒻM45000 67-22 Protiva, Ume, Decoration 12
27Mar87-4Aqu 7f :22^4 :46 1:26 ft 30 122 7$^{6\frac{1}{4}}$ 6^9 3^8 3$^{1\frac{1}{2}}$ HernndezR $\underline{12}$ Ⓕ[S]Mdn 69-21 BrghtTrbut,MghtyModl,LdyIronsd 13
16Mar87-6Aqu 1$\frac{1}{8}$:48^2 1:15^1 1:57^{3}ft 2 122 4$^{4\frac{1}{2}}$ 4^5 5$^{7\frac{1}{2}}$ 6$^{14\frac{1}{4}}$ HernandezR $\underline{6}$ Ⓕ[S]Mdn 33-30 PonusRidg,MightyModl,Normn'sDr 8
8Mar87-4Aqu 6f [•]:22^3 :46^{3}1:12^{3}ft 6$\frac{1}{2}$ 122 5$^{2\frac{1}{2}}$ 6$^{3\frac{1}{4}}$ 3^4 3$^{3\frac{3}{4}}$ HernandezR $\underline{1}$ Ⓕ[S]Mdn 77-16 NoHoldngBck,Brn'sHony,LdyIronsd 9
8Mar87—Bumped start
Aug 4 Sar Ⓣ 4f gd :49^3 b **Jly 14 Sar tr.t 3f ft :39 b** **Jun 25 Sar Ⓣ 4f fm :48^4 h (d)** **Jun 18 Sar Ⓣ 4f fm :48^2 h (d)**

L.
15–1

Pekabo Baby
Own.—Ogilvie D M **110^7**
Dk. b. or br. f. 3, by J P Brother—Tekabo, by Twice Worthy
Br.—Campo J P & Ogilvie D (NY) **1987 7 M 0 0 $2,880**
Tr.—Campo John P **Turf 1 0 0 0**
Lifetime 7 0 0 0 $2,880

15Jun87-6Bel 1$\frac{1}{16}$Ⓣ:47 1:12^{2}1:44^{3}fm 26 109 8$^{6\frac{3}{4}}$ 10^{13} 10^{24} 10$^{26\frac{1}{4}}$ Thibeau R J $\underline{7}$ [S]Mdn 47-22 Musil'sMtch,Londinium,Pinky'sPt 11
1Jun87-9Bel 6f :22^3 :46^4 1:13 ft 14 114 8$^{6\frac{1}{2}}$ 8$^{7\frac{1}{4}}$ 5$^{8\frac{1}{2}}$ 5$^{7\frac{3}{4}}$ Pezua J M $\underline{6}$ Ⓕ[S]Mdn 67-20 TooBobsRtrn,MtchMdln,LdyIrnsd 10
13May87-5Bel 6f :22^2 :46^2 1:12^{2}ft 28 106^7 10^{30} 9$^{9\frac{1}{4}}$ 6^{12} 6$^{9\frac{3}{4}}$ Carr D $\underline{3}$ Ⓕ[S]Mdn 68-18 Rlity'sKin,LzsJoy,Cormornt'sSong 14
22Apr87-4Aqu 7f :22^3 :45^2 1:24^{2}ft 37 102^{10} 7^6 4^{12} 5^{18} 4$^{16\frac{1}{4}}$ Carr D $\underline{11}$ Ⓕ[S]Mdn 63-27 Joyr'sZus,MightyPrtty,ArctcHoldy 13
3Apr87-5Aqu 6f :22^2 :46^2 1:12 ft 9$\frac{1}{4}$ 112 8$^{9\frac{1}{2}}$ 5$^{8\frac{1}{2}}$ 4^{10} 4^{10} DeCarloCP^{10} Ⓕ[S]Mdn 71-22 LBornqn,DplomtcEvnng,RstlssGm 11
3Apr87—Drifted out
30Mar87-4Aqu 1 :47 1:11^3 1:38^{3}ft 12 111 3$^{2\frac{1}{2}}$ 4$^{7\frac{1}{2}}$ 3^{11} 5^{13} DeCarlo CP^6 ⒻM45000 60-25 Nanno, Shamrock Pass,MissMizzen 8
21Mar87-4Aqu 6$\frac{1}{2}$f :22^4 :47^2 1:19^{2}ft 29e 121 12^{20} 10^{15} 7^{13} 6^{14} Migliore R^6 Ⓕ[S]Mdn 64-28 KyVntur,LBornqun,Twlvo'clocktls 14
Aug 4 Sar Ⓣ 5f gd 1:01^1 b **Jly 16 Bel tr.t 3f ft :38 b** **Jly 7 Bel tr.t 4f ft :51^3 b**

41. Check the odds and decide which conclusion below best summarizes the situation.

1$\frac{1}{16}$ MILES. (1.40$\frac{1}{5}$) CLAIMING. Purse $21,000. 4-year-olds and upward. Weights, 4-year-olds, 120 lbs.; older, 121 lbs. Non-winners of two races at one mile or over since November 3 allowed 3 lbs.; of such a race since then, 5 lbs. Claiming price $25,000; if for $22,500 allowed 2 lbs. (Claiming and starter races for $20,000 or less not considered.)

12–1

Master Navajo ✻
SIBILLE R **116**
Own.—Tons of Fun Stable &Fought
B. g. 7, by Navajo—Elderflower, by Master Hand
Br.—Lyster & Stiff (Ky) **1986 13 1 2 1 $30,220**
Tr.—Passey Blake **$25,000** **1985 13 3 4 1 $62,425**
Lifetime 50 9 10 6 $154,923 **Turf 4 0 0 1 $3,190**

26Dec86-9SA 1$\frac{1}{16}$:45^4 1:10^2 1:43 ft 19 116 11^{17} 11$^{9\frac{3}{4}}$ 6$^{6\frac{1}{2}}$ 4$^{3\frac{3}{4}}$ Sibille R^6 22500 82-13 Cold,TommyThoms,BoncngBttons 11
30Nov86-3Hol 1$\frac{1}{8}$:46^2 1:12 1:51^{4}ft 7$\frac{1}{2}$ 119 5^{13} 5^8 3^4 3$^{4\frac{1}{4}}$ Stevens S A^3 25000 74-16 Tom, Elefante, Master Navajo 6
3Nov86-9SA 1$\frac{1}{16}$:46^2 1:11 1:43 ft 7 118 8^{14} 8^9 4$^{5\frac{1}{2}}$ 4$^{4\frac{3}{4}}$ Sibille R^7 25000 81-14 Bemidgi, Restage, Slugfest 9
19Oct86-11Fno 1$\frac{1}{8}$:45 1:10^1 1:48^{2}ft 4 114 6^{14} 6$^{4\frac{1}{2}}$ 3^2 1$^{2\frac{1}{2}}$ HmiltonM^1 Harvest H 90-13 MstrNvjo,J.R.Johnson,U.LuckyShot 8
11Oct86-9SA 1$\frac{1}{16}$:46 1:11^2 1:44^{3}ft 5$\frac{3}{4}$ 116 7^{17} 6$^{7\frac{1}{2}}$ 2^3 2^2 Sibille R^7 20000 76-17 LyphrdChimes,MsterNvjo,GryMissil 8
28Sep86-8Pom 1$\frac{1}{16}$:46^2 1:11^1 1:43^{4}ft 16 116 6^{21} 6^{17} 6^9 2$^{1\frac{1}{2}}$ Cruz J B^3 20000 90-09 SwiftMessg,MstrNvjo,LyphrdChims 6
20Sep86-10Pom 1$\frac{1}{16}$:45^4 1:11^1 1:43^{1}ft 12 116 9^{17} 8^{14} 8$^{9\frac{1}{2}}$ 5$^{12\frac{3}{4}}$ Cruz J B^5 20000 82-09 Restage, Hatamoto,LyphardChimes 9
20Sep86—Wide into stretch
13Aug86-9Dmr 1$\frac{1}{16}$:45^1 1:10^2 1:43^{1}ft 52 116 10^{15} 9$^{6\frac{3}{4}}$ 4$^{4\frac{1}{2}}$ 5^3 Cruz J B^6 20000 81-15 Revolutionary, Tom, Our Nordic 11
27Jly86-9Dmr 1$\frac{1}{16}$:45^4 1:10^2 1:42^{2}ft 39 115 10$^{7\frac{1}{4}}$ 8^6 7$^{4\frac{1}{2}}$ 7^4 Cruz J B^3 22500 84-10 MstrCwston,NutrlPlyr,Rvolutionry 10
13Jly86-4Hol 1$\frac{1}{8}$:46^4 1:11^2 1:50^{4}ft 11 116 4$^{6\frac{1}{2}}$ 4^4 — — Lipham T^3 25000 — — Mark In The Sky, Mufti, Pegus 7
13Jly86—Pulled up
Dec 19 SA 3f ft :37^3 h **Nov 21 SA 3f ft :36^2 h**

14–1

One Eyed Romeo
BLACK C A **114**
Own.—Lindo-Polyakov-Sundquist
Ch. g. 7, by Romeo—Tahitian Chant, by Distinctive
Br.—Manderly Farm (Ky) **1987 1 0 0 0**
Tr.—Shulman Sanford **$22,500** **1986 22 4 4 1 $49,500**
Lifetime 73 12 17 4 $170,282 **Turf 1 0 0 0**

4Jan87-9SA 1$\frac{1}{8}$:47^3 1:12^2 1:51^{4}sy 4$\frac{1}{4}$ 116 1^{hd} 4^5 7^{32} — Olivares F^4 20000 — — HurricneHec,NewStorm,ShuttleOne 7
4Jan87—Pulled up
17Dec86-5Hol 1 :45^1 1:10^4 1:37^{3}ft 2$\frac{3}{4}$ 119 2$^{1\frac{1}{2}}$ 4$^{4\frac{1}{2}}$ 5^6 6$^{8\frac{1}{2}}$ Black C A^1 c16000 66-22 Amarone, Gulfstreamer, Oh Dad 7
17Dec86—Lugged out backstretch

4Dec86-5Hol 1⅛:471 1:121 1:521ft 2½ 116 1½ 1½ 12½ 12¾ Black C A2 16000 76-25 OneEyedRomeo,Vinegron,Espontno 5
16Nov86-4Hol 7f :22 :443 1:241ft 9¾ 117 73¼ 99¼119¾1114¾ Vergara O9 20000 68-18 Pegus, Pialor, Amarone 12
28Sep86-12Pom 1⅜:471 1:37 2:15 ft 4 113 35½ 21½ 32½ 515¼ Black C A1 H25000 87-09 Mummy'sPlesure,Restge,TulsFlyrII 8
28Sep86—Steadied on turn
19Sep86-10Poma1⅛:453 1:11 1:49 ft *2¼ 1085 1hd 1hd 21 25¾ Black C A5 A25000 96-09 Mmmy'sPlsr,OnEydRomo,DbTrnd 10
1Sep86-7Dmr 1 1/16:46 1:10 1:413ft 4 1115 21½ 21½ 1½ 2nk Black C A5 25000 92-13 Bmdg,OnEydRomo,PlntyConscous 10
17Aug86-7Dmr 1 1/16:453 1:101 1:432ft 7 116 1½ 1hd 11½ 3hd Kaenel J L2 25000 83-16 BngBngBng,MrkInThSky,OnEdRm 10
10Aug86-2Dmr 1 1/16:45 1:093 1:412ft *2½ 1115 52¾ 33½ 46½ 510¾ Black C A9 32000 82-08 ForHimself,Juli'sMrk,ToughEnvoy 10
3Aug86-9Dmr 1 1/16:46 1:101 1:42 ft *8-5 1115 31 2½ 1hd 13 Black C A1 20000 90-10 OnEydRomo,FlthorpMrnr,RsvltRd 12
Dec 27 SA 5f ft 1:011 h Dec 14 Hol 4f ft :513 h Dec 2 Hol 4f ft :491 h Nov 25 Hol 4f ft :482 h

4–1

Impulsively
PINCAY L JR 116
Own.—Fritz & Lima
B. g. 7, by Decidedly—Hill Flag, by Hillary
Br.—Pope Mrs G A Jr (Cal)
Tr.—Carava Jack $25,000
Lifetime 58 8 8 12 $176,510
1987 1 0 0 0 $1,725
1986 22 2 3 7 $59,780
Turf 5 0 1 1 $7,200

3Jan87-9SA 1 1/16:47 1:113 1:433ft 9¾ 116 79 77¼ 55½ 44¼ DelahoussayeE7 32000 79-16 NorthrnProvdr,Rnbw'sCp,FrgnLgn 10
7Dec86-6Hol 1⅛:472 1:121 1:514gd 6 116 814 812 89¾ 815½ Stevens G L2 32000 62-18 VlintGeorge,GumFleet,ForignLgion 9
7Dec86—Broke slowly
20Nov86-5Hol 1⅛:464 1:114 1:512ft 7½ 116 913 911 73¾ 52¾ Stevens G L8 32000 77-16 Oak TreeII,Bedouin,ValiantGeorge 11
20Nov86—Steadied 3/16
5Nov86-7Hol 1⅛Ⓣ:4731:1131:483fm 22 116 78¾ 76¾ 56¾ 54¾ Valenzuela P A5 50000 80-14 Too Much For T. V.,Massera,Tarver 8
19Oct86-9SA 1 1/16:463 1:111 1:432ft 6½ 116 513 68½ 69 68¾ DelahoussayeE4 40000 75-18 ForHmslf,Mummy'sPlsr,ToghEnvoy 7
19Oct86—Wide into stretch
12Oct86-9SA 1 1/16:463 1:12 1:443ft 5 116 812 86½ 33 2¾ Stevens G L3 c32000 77-21 Mmmy'sPlsr,Implsvly,NrthrnPrvdr 12
5Oct86-9SA 1 1/16:462 1:111 1:424ft 5½ 116 1013104½ 64½ 53½ Stevens G L5 40000 83-15 Tough Envoy, Idol, Tio Nino 10
5Oct86—Broke slowly; wide final 3/8
6Sep86-10Bmf 1 :46 1:10 1:351ft 6½ 115 68½ 55½ 34 34 CastanedaM5 Aw22000 88-18 SomthngGorgous,FolkArt,Implsvly 7
24Aug86-9Dmr 1 1/16:452 1:093 1:412ft *2½ 116 817 814 820 813½ McCarron C J8 50000 80-12 OnoGummo,TimeForSilenc,Oljuwon 9
24Aug86—Hopped in air
9Aug86-7Dmr 1 1/16:453 1:101 1:422ft 14 118 1118118½ 84¼ 2½ Stevens G L11 50000 87-14 Lead On, Impulsively, Idol 11
9Aug86—Wide into stretch
Dec 28 SA 6f ft 1:13 h Dec 22 SA 5f ft 1:001 h Dec 15 SA 3f ft :353 h Nov 28 SA 4f ft :47 h

6–1

Gregson
STEVENS G L 115
Own.—Lenvical Stable
B. c. 4, by Somethingfabulous—Rosey Hill, by Hillary
Br.—Pope Mrs G A Jr (Cal)
Tr.—Smith Marion L $25,000
Lifetime 16 3 3 2 $38,950
1986 14 3 3 2 $37,690
1985 2 M 0 0 $1,260
Turf 2 0 1 0 $4,575

27Dec86-4SA 1 1/16:471 1:114 1:451ft 2¾ 116 3½ 43 43 55 Olivares F1 c20000 70-19 ‡ShowrDcr,DckAndHugh,MnyRods 10
27Dec86—Crowded, bumped, steadied 1/4; Placed fourth through disqualification
13Dec86-3Hol 7f :222 :452 1:232ft 3¾ 116 1hd 1½ 11 1no Olivares F4 Ⓢ 25000 87-09 Gregson,ManyRoads,ShowerDecree 9
13Dec86—Broke out, bumped
27Nov86-5Hol 1 :452 1:103 1:364ft 27 116 1½ 2½ 55½ 58½ Olivares F1 40000 70-18 Sebucan, Split Winners,BoldDecree 8
13Nov86-9Hol 1 :453 1:101 1:353ft 28 116 63¾ 77¾ 716 721 Olivares F4 50000 64-23 MischievousMtt,CojkMn,BoldDecre 9
31Oct86-6SA 6f :212 :443 1:093ft 20 1115 109¼109¾1011 911¾ Black C A4 50000 78-16 MischievousMtt,Jimed,RosesArRb 11
31Oct86—Broke out, bumped
1Aug86-5Dmr 1 1/16Ⓣ:47 1:1141:432fm 11 116 74¾ 3½ 2hd 23 Olivares F2 Aw20000 86-11 Cro'sHollywood,Grgson,TmFrSkrt 10
1Aug86—Rank out of chute
13Jly86-8Hol 1 1/16Ⓣ:4631:1041:413fm 20 1035 1hd 1hd 31½ 54¾ Black C A5 Aw23000 91-03 WillSpring,L'Empire,KimridgeRoad 8
29Jun86-2Hol 1⅛:461 1:101 1:494ft *6-5 1115 1hd 12½ 11½ 1hd Black C A4 c25000 88-10 Gregson,FstTrvlinNews,UnivrslDrm 8
15Jun86-1Hol 1⅛:473 1:12 1:502ft 3¾ 1145 12½ 11½ 2½ 21½ Black C A6 32000 83-13 Tai High, Gregson,FastTravlinNews 7
4Jun86-6Hol 1 :453 1:112 1:383ft 18 1145 31½ 41¾ 32 31½ Black C A9 32000 68-18 CuttingLine,MiamiDream,Gregson 10
Jan 8 SA 4f m :503 h Dec 7 Hol 5f m 1:002 h

6–1

Bedouin *
PATTON D B 1115
Own.—Tauber A S
Ro. g. 6, by Al Hattab—Lady in Red, by Prince John
Br.—Elmendorf Farm (Ky)
Tr.—Heaton Bill $25,000
Lifetime 53 9 4 1 $235,119
1987 1 0 0 0 $575
1986 26 6 1 0 $88,075
Turf 12 1 1 0 $29,915

3Jan87-9SA 1 1/16:47 1:113 1:433ft 5½ 1115 68 67 66½ 56 Patton D B3 32000 77-16 NorthrnProvdr,Rnbw'sCp,FrgnLgn 10
3Jan87—Broke slowly
17Dec86-3Hol 1 1/16:47 1:122 1:442ft 4½ 1115 510 57½ 47 45½ Patton D B4 40000 81-22 LeCid,ForeignLegion,ValintGeorge 6
20Nov86-5Hol 1⅛:464 1:114 1:512ft 8¾ 1115 65½ 56½ 1hd 2hd Patton D B3 32000 80-16 Oak TreeII,Bedouin,ValiantGeorge 11
3Nov86-9SA 1 1/16:462 1:11 1:43 ft 7½ 1115 713 78½ 57 54¾ Patton D B9 c25000 81-14 Bemidgi, Restage, Slugfest 9
3Nov86—Bumped break
19Oct86-9SA 1 1/16:463 1:111 1:432ft 12 113 613 58½ 58 58 Hawley S2 35000 76-18 ForHmslf,Mummy'sPlsr,ToghEnvoy 7
12Oct86-9SA 1 1/16:463 1:12 1:443ft 11 116 9121011 98 109¾ Hernandez R5 32000 68-21 Mmmy'sPlsr,Implsvly,NrthrnPrvdr 12
5Oct86-9SA 1 1/16:462 1:111 1:424ft 7½ 116 913 94½ 98½ 98¾ Hernandez R8 40000 78-15 Tough Envoy, Idol, Tio Nino 10
5Oct86—Wide into stretch
24Aug86-9Dmr 1 1/16:452 1:093 1:412ft 12 116 713 915 923 916½ McHargue D G5 50000 77-12 OnoGummo,TimeForSilenc,Oljuwon 9
24Aug86—Wide 7/8 turn; eased late
9Aug86-7Dmr 1 1/16:453 1:101 1:422ft 16 118 914 86½ 95¾ 76 McHargue D G5 50000 82-14 Lead On, Impulsively, Idol 11
9Aug86—Broke very slowly

2Aug86-9Dmr 1 1/16 :461 1:103 1:42 ft 5¼ 118 78¼ 76 67¾ 57½ Hernandez R3 40000 82-12 Diajuwon, Trus T. Danus, Elefante 7
2Aug86—Broke slowly
Dec 30 SA 5f ft :593 h Dec 11 SA 4f ft :511 h Nov 30 SA 5f ft 1:012 h Nov 15 SA 5f ft :593 h

5–2

Decontrol 4FT 393
VALENZUELA P A 116
Own.—Diamant-Harris-Morningstar
Ch. g. 8, by Majestic Light—La Fantastique, by Le Fabuleux
Br.—Pinewood Stable (Ky)
Tr.—Stute Warren $25,000
Lifetime 35 9 6 1 $139,775
1986 2 0 0 0 $2,350
1985 8 3 2 0 $56,650
Turf 8 2 2 0 $44,550

21Dec86-7Hol 6f :22 :452 1:101ft 25 116 75¼ 64¾ 54 57¼ Castanon A L4 32000 85-15 Romaxe, Ondarty, EllsBravestSong 8
8Jan86-9SA 1 1/16 :464 1:113 1:432ft 5 116 42 41¼ 43 45½ Sibille R2 50000 78-16 VigorousVigors,Swivel,TrusT.Danus 8
14Dec85-1Hol 1 :462 1:113 1:363ft *7-5 116 11 1½ 1½ 1hd Sibille R1 40000 80-14 Decontrol, Juntura, Preprint 8
6Dec85-9Hol 1 :453 1:094 1:351ft 2¼ 116 42 44½ 43 43 Sibille R7 50000 84-17 Menswear, Amarone, Hydrostatic 7
6Dec85—3 wide into drive
11Aug85-9Dmr 1⅛ Ⓣ:502 1:142 1:50 fm*9-5 115 42 31½ 25 45½ Toro F3 62500 82-05 Dunant, Fabuleux Prince,Tyrabellor 9
24Jly85-9Dmr 1 Ⓣ:464 1:113 1:363fm*8-5 116 2hd 1hd 11½ 21 Sibille R3 62500 88-09 Nonno, Decontrol, Super Noble 9
30Jun85-6Hol 1 1/16 Ⓣ:464 1:102 1:411fm 5½ 116 11½ 1hd 2hd 22¾ Sibille R5 62500 90-09 Sagamore, Decontrol, Viron 12
16Jun85-3Hol 1⅛ :464 1:102 1:481ft 4 116 1hd 11½ 1hd 11¼ Sibille R4 40000 108-02 Decontrol, Golden E., Stickette 6
17Feb85-7SA 1⅛ Ⓣ:463 1:102 1:481fm 5¾ 118 21 2½ 45½ 77½ ValenzuelPA4 Aw33000 78-14 Champion Pilot, Penzance, Byron 9
3Feb85-9SA 1 1/16 :46 1:102 1:424ft 6 118 33½ 22½ 11½ 11¾ Pedroza M A4 50000 87-12 Decontrol, Right On Red,ItemTwo 10
Jan 8 SA 6f m 1:163 h Jan 2 SA 1 ft 1:431 h Dec 28 SA 1 ft 1:462 h Dec 20 Hol 3f ft :364 h

5–1

***Revolutionary**
MCHARGUE D G 116
Own.—Holt L
Ch. g. 6, by Formidable—Reverente, by Riverman
Br.—Petra Bloodstock Agency (Fra)
Tr.—Holt Lester $25,000
Lifetime 40 5 3 8 $83,640
1986 17 2 1 2 $30,050
1985 3 0 0 1 $2,547
Turf 29 3 2 6 $53,590

18Dec86-9Hol 1 :454 1:104 1:364ft 5½ 116 76¾ 55½ 42½ 3¾ McHargue D G5 25000 78-17 FallFlyer,BrandImage,Revolutionry 8
29Nov86-7Hol 1 :454 1:104 1:361ft 12 116 106¾ 84¾ 64 41½ Solis A9 20000 80-12 Rnbow'sCp,LordPnch,TmmyThms 10
29Nov86—Bumped both sides break, wide backside, stretch
3Nov86-9SA 1 1/16 :462 1:11 1:43 ft 17 116 67 54 67½ 69¾ McHargue D G2 25000 76-14 Bemidgi, Restage, Slugfest 9
3Nov86—Bumped break; lugged out stretch
1Sep86-7Dmr 1 1/16 :46 1:10 1:413ft 24 116 77½ 78½ 1013 1016¼ Fernandez AL1 c25000 76-13 Bmdg,OnEydRomo,PlntyConscous 10
1Sep86—Broke in a tangle
23Aug86-9Dmr 1 1/16 :45 1:103 1:423ft 4½ 116 711 66 69½ 410½ Fernandez A L5 32000 76-10 Bang Bang Bang, Tom, GreyMissile 7
23Aug86—Bumped start
13Aug86-9Dmr 1 1/16 :451 1:102 1:431ft 5 116 69 32½ 1½ 1½ McHrgueDG10 c20000 84-15 Revolutionary, Tom, Our Nordic 11
27Jly86-9Dmr 1 1/16 :454 1:102 1:422ft 5½ 116 84¾ 41½ 31 31¾ McHargue D G1 25000 86-10 MstrCwston,NutrlPlyr,Rvolutionry 10
27Jly86—Wide final 3/8
10Jly86-7Hol 1 :453 1:111 1:364ft 15 116 98¾ 74¾ 4¾ 2hd McHargue D G8 20000 79-18 Lithan,Revolutionry,MsterCwston 10
10Jly86—Bumped start
22Jun86-7Hol 1⅛ Ⓣ:46 1:102 1:471fm 42 1115 32½ 33 1115 — Black C A9 50000 — — Board Meeting, Nonno, Ablantin 11
22Jun86—Eased; Wide 7/8 turn
25May86-10GG 1⅜ Ⓣ:473 1:391 2:164fm 13 114 23 21 31½ 84½ Gonzalez R M6 50000 76-09 Secure II, Hojo, Prairie Breaker 9
Jan 9 SA 3f sl :404 h Dec 30 SA 5f ft 1:022 h Dec 25 SA 4f ft :482 h Dec 13 SA 5f ft 1:003 h

A. *Impulsively* figures to win and the price is fair; bet it
B. *Decontrol* deserves to be favored
C. It's a wide-open race
D. *Revolutionary* is the best bet at the odds
E. *Bedouin* figures, but is overbet

42. Coupled: *Doubles Partner* and *Spectacular Bev*. If there is no bet here, circle the entry. If a bet is found, pick the favorable horse.

8th Saratoga

1 1/16 MILES. (Turf). (1.39⅘) 14th Running THE NIJANA (GRADE III). Purse $75,000 Added. Fillies. 3-year-olds. By subscription of $150 each, which should accompny the nomination; $300 to pass the entry box; $300 to start, with $75,000 added. The added money and all fees to be divided 60% to the winner, 22% to second, 12% tp third and 6% to fourth. 121 lbs. Non-winners of a race of $50,000 at a mile or over since May 1, allwoed 3 lbs., Of such a race since January 1, 5 lbs., Of such a race of $35,000 in 1986–87, 7 lbs. (Maiden, cliaming, starter and restricted races not considered). Starters to be named at the closing time of entries. A trophy will be presented to the winning owner. The New York Racing Association reserves the right to transfer this race to the Main Course. Closed Wednesday, July 29, 1987 with 32 nominations.

Coupled—Doubles Partner and Spectacular Bev; Aglasini and Pour Me Out.

A.

1–2

Doubles Partner B. f. 3, by Damascus—Fabuleux Jane, by Le Fabuleux
Br.—Wilson Ralph C Jr (Md) 1987 7 4 0 0 $102,488
Own.—Oxford Stable 114 Tr.—Hirsch William J Jr 1986 2 1 0 0 $14,520
Lifetime 9 5 0 0 $117,008 Turf 2 2 0 0 $69,988
6Aug87-8Sar 7f :213 :433 1:21 ft 19 118 1212 1212 1214 1116¼ DavisRG14 ⒻTest 81-14 VerySubtle,UptheAplch,SilntTurn 14
6Aug87—Grade II
11Jly87-7Bel 1 1/16 Ⓣ:483 1:121 1:44 yl 2¼ 114 11½ 1½ 11½ 15 RrRP4 ⒻSweet Tooth 76-23 DoublsPrtnr,MysticlLss,GrcfulDrby 6
28Jun87-9Lrl 1 1/16 Ⓣ:464 1:12 1:434fm *1 119 65½ 44 2hd 13½ RrRP3 ⒻⓈPearlNklce 84-15 DoublesPrtner,Ympcl,MissCeeGee 12
6Jun87-3Bel 7f :224 :46 1:234ft *1 112 32½ 32 1hd 12 RomeroRP6 ⒻAw27000 83-15 DoublesPartner,Hardeeni,Alyaffirm 7
6Jun87—Bumped, clear
23May87-8Bel 1 :442 1:091 1:351ft 28 121 32½ 42 86¾ 78½ RomrRP9 ⒻAcorn 80-13 Grecian Flight, Fiesta Gal, Bound 13
23May87—Grade I; Lacked room str
14May87-4Bel 7f :222 :451 1:224ft 2½ 116 21½ 2½ 11½ 12¾ RomeroRP2 ⒻAw26000 88-13 DoublsPrtnr,Pocultion,I'mQuitHigh 8
15Apr87-8GP 7f :223 :453 1:232sy *2½ 116 63½ 54½ 46½ 48 Fires E4 ⒻAw14000 79-25 RoylTr,AdorblAngl,Koluctco'sRby 10
26Oct86-9Aqu 6f :222 :46 1:113sy 7¾ 117 78 55½ 1hd 13½ Cordero A Jr4 ⒻMdn 83-18 DoublsPrtnr,SunstCloud,FinTimng 11
Aug 4 Sar 3f sy :37 b ● Jly 27 Bel 4f ft :46 h Jly 22 Bel 4f ft :50 b Jly 7 Bel 4f ft :493 b

B.

7–2

Graceful Darby B. f. 3, by Darby Creek Road—Graceful Touch, by His Majesty
Br.—Phillips Mr–Mrs J W (Ky) 1987 7 3 0 4 $97,188
Own.—Phillips J W 116 Tr.—Veitch John M 1986 6 1 1 3 $45,508
Lifetime 13 4 1 7 $142,696 Turf 5 3 0 2 $90,708
11Jly87-7Bel 1 1/16 Ⓣ:483 1:121 1:44 yl *4-5 118 54¾ 33½ 35½ 37 BlyJD5 ⒻSweet Tooth 69-23 DoublsPrtnr,MysticlLss,GrcfulDrby 6
27Jun87-8Bel 1⅜ Ⓣ:54 1:46 2:234sf *4-5e 112 44½ 32 32 36¾ BilyJD5 ⒻSheepsh'd H 31-62 StealAKiss,Videogenic,GrcefulDrby 5
27Jun87—Grade II
6Jun87-6Bel 1 1/16 Ⓣ:483 1:132 1:45 gd *6-5 110 67½ 33½ 11 15¼ Bailey J D6 ⒻTanya 71-29 GracefulDarby,Seriously,Subjective 8
21May87-7Bel 1 1/16 Ⓣ:50 1:143 1:464gd *1 111 53 42 11 15¾ Bailey J D5 ⒻAw28000 62-34 GrcfulDrby,LghngLdy,VvdImprsson 6
22Apr87-8Aqu 1 1/16 Ⓣ:48 1:143 1:47 gd 3¾ 112 65½ 53½ 11½ 19 Bailey J D6 ⒻAw28000 70-30 GrcefulDrby,ProudestBbe,RueRlity 9
8Apr87-1Aqu 1 :463 1:121 1:384m 3¾ 116 44 45½ 35½ 33½ Maple E6 ⒻAw27000 68-22 GentleSpirit,HighOffer,GrcefulDrby 6
28Mar87-6Aqu 1 :464 1:113 1:371m 6½ 116 43½ 34½ 35½ 34¼ Maple E7 ⒻAw27000 76-23 HalfSecret,QuePrecios,GrcefulDrby 9
14Dec86-8Aqu 1 1/16 ⊡:482 1:124 1:461ft 11e 112 98 77¼ 69 69½ BilyJD7 ⒻTempted 69-20 SilentTurn,GrcinFlight,ChsThDrm 11
14Dec86—Grade III
● Aug 6 Sar Ⓣ 7f fm 1:25 h ● Jly 30 Bel Ⓣ 5f fm 1:002 h (d) Jly 22 Bel 3f ft :36 b Jly 9 Bel 4f sy :484 b

C.

14–1

Token Gift B. f. 3, by Lyphard—Tokens Only, by Youth
Br.—Schiff J M (Fla) 1987 4 1 0 0 $14,411
Own.—Fox Ridge Farm 114 Tr.—Kelly Thomas J 1986 5 M 1 0 $5,260
Lifetime 9 1 1 0 $19,671 Turf 4 1 1 0 $18,821
13Jun87-9Crc 1 1/16 Ⓣ:454 1:093 1:413fm 3 113 2hd 12 1hd 54¾ LestrRN8 ⒻBegonia H 90 — VwofRoylty,MyGrlVl,ShotGnBonn 10
23May87-9GP a1 1/16 Ⓣ 1:454gd 3½ 112 22 12½ 12 4½ Soto SB4 ⒻHollywood 76-21 QuakeLake,MyGirlVal,EasterMary 10
28Apr87-10GP a1 1/16 Ⓣ 1:44 fm *3-2 121 16 111 118 118½ Lester R N8 ⒻMdn 86-23 TokenGift,GryWingPoint,Ovrnight 10
15Apr87-6GP 1 1/16 :48 1:132 1:463sy *8-5 121 43 43 36½ 49½ Perret C2 ⒻMdn 58-25 Horsafire, Smarted, Blue Thriller 8
13Dec86-4Crc 7f :224 :464 1:263ft 7½ 120 41½ 2hd 44½ 89½ Lester R N7 ⒻMdn 73-22 FortheFirstTim,OrngWv,KnollDriv 12
13Dec86—Steadied early
26Oct86-6Aqu 1 :463 1:131 1:412m *2½ 117 3nk 21 42½ 51¾ Maple E4 ⒻMdn 57-18 AfterThShow,MomsBirthdy,PrisdFr 9
17Sep86-1Bel 1 1/16 Ⓣ:482 1:123 1:44 fm 4½ 117 31½ 21 3½ 25 Maple E3 ⒻMdn 76-17 SpctculrBv,ToknGift,MoststHostss 8
18Aug86-6Sar 6f :222 :462 1:124ft 23f 117 2hd 22½ 610 715¾ Maple E1 ⒻMdn 60-21 ViciousQun,AwsomSuzy,Poccultion 10
Aug 9 Sar 4f ft :484 h Jly 23 Bel Ⓣ 5f fm 1:05 b (d)

D.

11–1

Miss Unnameable B. f. 3, by Great Neck—Chee Sea, by Apalachee
Br.—Fox Ridge Farm (Ky) 1987 11 3 2 0 $64,740
Own.—Tatt Stables 114 Tr.—Widmer Wayne 1986 3 M 1 1 $7,820
Lifetime 14 3 3 1 $72,560 Turf 9 3 3 0 $69,800
1Aug87-3Bel 1 1/16 Ⓣ:453 1:11 1:43 fm *2 112 55 31½ 11 15 Cruguet J 9 ⒻAw27000 81-10 MissUnnmebl,TimForEmrlds,Strit 10
20Jly87-7Bel 1 1/16 Ⓣ:471 1:12 1:433fm *8-5 116 1½ 1hd 3nk 22 Cruguet J 2 ⒻAw27000 76-22 Lepa,MissUnnameble,I'mQuiteHigh 8
20Jly87—Drifted out

5Jly87-7Bel 1 1/16 [T]:4631:1121:44 gd 5 112 1hd 11½ 1½ 42¼ Cruguet J 8 [F]Aw27000 74-17 Wee Small Hours, Twitch, Jamara 12
28Jun87-7Bel 1⅜:49 1:393 2:191ft 3½ 113 22½ 716 737 — Cruguet J 5 [F]Aw27000 — — Debonirly,WinterDove,FrAndAbove 7
28Jun87—Eased
20Jun87-4Bel 1 1/16 [T]:4841:1231:432fm*4-5 113 12 14 15 14 Cruguet J 2 [F] 80000 84-17 Miss Unnameable, Jamara, Magical 7
12Jun87-7Bel 1¼ [T]:49 1:3832:021gd 6¾ 115 12 11½ 11½ 2½ CordroAJr 3 [F]Aw27000 82-17 LoveForAll,MissUnnmebl,MdmCrol 8
12Jun87—Drifted out
27May87-3Bel 1 1/16 [T]:4711:1121:432fm 9½ 1085 12½ 11½ 12 13¾ Belmonte J F 3 [F]Mdn 79-19 MissUnnmebl,Ovrnight,PrlyToWin 12
18May87-4Bel 1¼ [T]:50 1:3912:04 fm 31 1085 1½ 2½ 54 45¾ Belmonte J F3 [F]Mdn 68-22 SurgingCurrent,LoveForAll,Ellabb 11
Jly 15 Bel tr.t 4f ft :51 b

E.
1–2

Spectacular Bev

Gr. f. 3, by Spectacular Bid—Bev Bev, by Nijinsky II
Br.—Wilson Ralph C Jr (Ky) 1987 3 2 0 0 $44,155
Own.—Oxford Stable **114** Tr.—Hirsch William J Jr 1986 5 2 0 2 $62,118
Lifetime 8 4 0 2 $106,273 Turf 6 4 0 0 $93,355

11Jly87-8Pim 1 1/16 [T]:4721:11 1:421fm 9-5 119 78½ 66¾ 32 12 HtrMT3 [F]SummrGust 92-12 SpectacularBev,IceDevise,Heartlef 8
11Jly87—Run in divisions
8Jun87-8Bel 1 1/16 [T]:4841:1221:434fm*6-5 111 45½ 43 43 1hd RomeroRP7 [F]Aw28000 82-24 SpctclrBv,GlorosCllng,VvdImprssn 7
21May87-7Bel 1 1/16 [T]:50 1:1431:464gd 3½ 111 41½ 65 68 46 RomeroRP3 [F]Aw28000 56-34 GrcfulDrby,LghngLdy,VvdImprsson 6
8Nov86-8Aqu 1⅛ :484 1:122 1:521sy 2¼ 118 — — — 34½ RmrRP3 [F]Miss Grillo 69-22 Lovelier, Nastique, SpectacularBev 8
8Nov86—Grade III; Running positions omitted because of weather conditions
18Oct86-6Bel 1 1/16 [T]:4711:12 1:452gd 4½ 116 87½ 53½ 13 14¾ RrRP2 [F]Bold Princes 69-29 SpectacularBev,LtinLyric,Nstique 11
29Sep86-7Bel 1 1/16 [T]:4741:1231:464gd *1 121 76½ 54¾ 54½ 43¾ Samyn J L8 [F]Aw25000 58-30 EvningSky,KrnAnn,RnbowMornng 11
17Sep86-1Bel 1 1/16 [T]:4821:1231:44 fm 2½ 117 77½ 54 2hd 15 Romero R P4 [F]Mdn 81-17 SpctculrBv,ToknGift,MoststHostss 8
27Aug86-3Bel 6f :23 :471 1:113ft 8 117 1217 86½ 48½ 38½ Romero RP3 [F]M75000 75-16 RglPyoff,TooMnySpots,SpctclrBv 12
Aug 11 Sar 3f sy :361 b Aug 6 Sar 5f ft 1:013 h ● Jly 30 Bel [T] 6f fm 1:124 h (d) ● Jly 10 Bel 3f sy :361 h

F.
9–2

Moms Birthday

Dk. b. or br. f. 3, by Malinowski—One Clover Lane, by Soy Numero Uno
Br.—Austrian N (Pa) 1987 10 3 2 1 $53,825
Own.—Austrian N R **114** Tr.—Tesher Howard M 1986 4 M 2 0 $8,140
Lifetime 14 3 4 1 $61,965 Turf 8 2 2 0 $44,945

30Jly87-6Bel 1 1/16 [T]:4741:1121:423fm 4¾ 111 77¾ 55¼ 32 12½ Antley CW3 [F]Aw28000 88-18 Moms Birthday, Tamida, Riverquill 8
11Jly87-6Pim 1 1/16 [T]:4831:13 1:432fm 4½ 115 78½ 54 41 2¾ BrcclVJr7 [F]SmmrGst 85-12 FortntFcts,MomsBrthdy,AnglnCnty 7
11Jly87—Run in divisions
16Jun87-9Mth 1 [T]:4721:1121:362fm 17 114 811 55 22½ 25½ AntleyCW7 [F]Revidere 87-08 WthotFthrs,MomsBrthdy,YthflBrb 9
16Jun87—Run in divisions
23May87-9GP a1 1/16 [T] 1:454gd 55 116 8161016 914 88 LndnOJ8 [F]Hollywood 69-21 QuakeLake,MyGirlVal,EasterMary 10
29Apr87-9GP a1 1/16 [T] 1:431fm 8¾ 116 56½ 55 713 710¾ DnjR1 [F]Herecm Bride 79-12 Sum, Easter Mary, Dawandeh 8
12Apr87-10GP 1 [T]:4641:11 1:353fm 7e112 13111111 69½ 67 VlJAJr11 [F]Q'nHopeful 85-17 Sum, Easter Mary, Quake Lake 13
19Mar87-9GP a1 [T] 1:41 fm 6½ 114 89½ 61½ 2hd 1no Velez JAJr2 [F]Aw22000 75-26 MomsBrthdy,AntqMystq,O'LttlMrg 9
1Mar87-10Hia 1 1/16 [T] 1:424fm 27 112 67¼ 56½ 64 65¾ Velez JAJr9 [F]Patricia 78-14 ViewofRoyalty,SingleBlade,Clarity 10
Aug 7 Sar [T] 4f fm :53 b Jly 7 Mth [T] 5f fm 1:07 b (d) Jun 30 Mth 5f ft 1:003 h

G.
22–1

Pour Me Out

B. f. 3, by Raise a Cup—Safety Razor, by Blade
Br.—BwmzonFrmDivofWhitkrFms (Ky) 1987 6 1 0 3 $28,249
Own.—Montemar Stables **114** Tr.—Johnson Philip G 1986 9 3 0 0 $39,054
Lifetime 15 4 0 3 $67,303 Turf 5 1 0 2 $27,889

25Jly87-3Mth 1 [T]:4611:1021:36 fm*4-5e111 814 74½ 5¾ 33 Pezua J M3 [F]Aw19000 92-06 Improyl,LdyoftheNorth,PourMeOut 9
25Jly87—Bore out
11Jly87-7Bel 1 1/16 [T]:4831:1211:44 yl 5½e114 67½ 56½ 510 514 DsRG1 [F]Sweet Tooth 62-23 DoublsPrtnr,MysticlLss,GrcfulDrby 8
16Jun87-8Mth 1 [T]:4811:1221:37 fm*9-5 120 53 31½ 3nk 33 Davis R G2 [F]Revidere 87-08 Cecina, Easter Mary, Pour Me Out 8
16Jun87—Run in divisions
20May87-6Bel 1 :462 1:11 1:363gd *3-2 110 41½ 31½ 11½ 12¾ Davis R G2 [F]Aw31000 82-17 PourMeOut,ChseThDrm,UnionGold 5
3May87-7Aqu 1⅛ [T]:50 1:1521:534gd 2e110 21 1hd 21 56 Davis R G5 [F]Aw31000 60-33 Popularity,LedKindlyLight,Improyl 8
24Apr87-7Aqu 1 :463 1:113 1:371m 11 110 32 31½ 33 32¾ Davis R G1 [F]Aw31000 77-21 Seriously, New Dawn, Pour Me Out 7
14Dec86-8Aqu 1 1/16 [■]:4821:1241:461ft 11e116 33 65¾ 712 814¾ NschD2 [F]Tempted 64-20 SilentTurn,GrcinFlight,ChsThDrm 11
14Dec86—Grade III
8Nov86-8Aqu 1⅛ :484 1:122 1:521sy 6¾ 118 — — — 48 SmynJL 8 [F]Miss Grillo 66-22 Lovelier, Nastique, SpectacularBev 8
8Nov86—Grade III; Running positions omitted because of weather conditions
Aug 7 Sar tr.t 5f ft 1:032 b Jly 22 Bel 4f ft :483 h Jly 5 Bel 6f ft 1:13 h ● Jun 29 Bel 4f ft :47 h

43. Is there an overlay in this restricted turf stakes? (If not, mark D)

8th Santa Anita

1⅛ MILES. (Turf). (1.45⅘) 7th Running of LA PUENTE STAKES. $60,000 added. 3-year-olds which have never won *$25,000 at one mile or over. (Foals of 1984.) By subscription of $50 each to accompany the nomination, $600 additional to start, with $60,000 added, of which $12,000 to second, $9,000 to third, $4,500 to fourth and $1,500 to fifth. Weight, 120 lbs. (Allowance.) Non-winners of $20,000 at one mile or over or $30,000 any distance allowed 2 lbs.; of $16,000 at one mile or over, 4 lbs.; of such a race of $13,000, 6 lbs. (Maiden and claiming races not considered.) Starters to be named through the entry box by the closing time of entries. A trophy will be presented to the owner of the winner. *A race worth $25,000 to the winner. Closed Wednesday, April 8, 1987, with 17 nominations.

Coupled—All Cat, Ponderable and Mountaincamellia.

A.
6–1

All Cat — B. c. 3, by Cougar II—Almira, by Sheet Anchor
SOLIS A — **114** — Br.—Bradley-Whittinghm-Chndler (Ky) — 1987 5 M 0 3 $12,000
Own.—Bradley-Chndler-Whittinghm — Tr.—Whittingham Charles — 1986 1 M 0 0 $1,425
Lifetime 6 0 0 3 $13,425

15Mar87-6SA 1 1/16 :46^4 1:12^1 1:45^{2}ft 4 117 97¼ 76½ 56½ 33½ Delahoussaye E 8 Mdn 71-20 Affstar, Exit Poll, All Cat 9
15Mar87—Broke slowly; wide into stretch
18Feb87-8SA 1⅛ :46^1 1:10^1 1:48^{4}ft 12 115 6^{11} 7^{10} 6^{12} 58¾ Toro F 6 Ⓡ Brdbry 76-19 HotAndSmoggy,Barb'sRelic,Reland 7
1Feb87-6SA 1 :46^1 1:11^3 1:38^{1}ft 4 117 8^7 56½ 3^7 3^5 Black C A 4 Mdn 72-16 Famous Forever, Conquer, All Cat 10
1Feb87—Broke slowly
19Jan87-6SA 1 1/16 :48^2 1:13 1:45^{4}ft 20 117 7^4 63½ 63¾ 3^3 Black C A 6 Mdn 69-25 Rupperto, Chatanga, All Cat 9
19Jan87—Off slowly; blocked stretch, wide
3Jan87-6SA 1 1/16 :47^2 1:11^3 1:44^{2}ft 7½e 117 9^{13} 9^{13} 7^{12} 611¾ Black C A^1 Mdn 67-16 SvorFire,NstyNskr,FmousForever 11
7Dec86-5Hol 6f :22 :45^4 1:11^{2}gd 21 118 7^{15} 7^{13} 69½ 49¼ Black C A^6 Mdn 77-18 BoldArchon,FlyingFlgs,FullOfFools 7
7Dec86—Wide backstretch
Apr 11 SA 5f ft 1:01^4 h Apr 6 SA 5f ft 1:00^3 h Apr 1 SA 5f ft :59^4 h Mar 27 SA 6f ft 1:14 h

B.
7–1

The Medic — B. c. 3, by Sweet Candy—Mel Has Flipped, by Flip Sal
TORO F — **114** — Br.—Sexton H (Ky) — 1987 7 1 0 2 $21,925
Own.—Giammarino Dr E — Tr.—Jones Gary — 1986 0 M 0 0
Lifetime 7 1 0 2 $21,925

4Apr87-9SA 1 1/16 :45^2 1:10^1 1:43^{2}ft 14 114 78½ 7^7 4^6 32½ Baze G 7 Aw31000 82-17 Jamoke, Laguna Native, The Medic 9
4Apr87—Bumped break, wide 3/8 turn
25Mar87-6SA 1 1/16 :46 1:10^4 1:44 ft 4¼ 118 44½ 3^2 1½ 12¾ McCarronCJ 10 M50000 81-17 TheMedic,Brbr'sChoic,StllitExprss 11
8Mar87-4SA 1 1/16 :47^1 1:12^1 1:44^{3}ft 34 117 9^8 96¼ 66¾ 37¾ Solis A 2 Mdn 70-15 LocalsOnly,NastyNaskr,TheMedic 10
8Mar87—Bumped 3 1/2, 3/8
22Feb87-6SA 1 1/16 :46^3 1:12 1:44^{2}ft 41 117 88¾ 75½ 58½ 55½ Stevens S A 9 Mdn 73-14 Mountncmll,ErnYourStrps,ExtPoll 11
8Feb87-4SA 1 1/16 :46^3 1:12 1:44 ft 32 117 67¼ 42½ 44½ 4^6 Stevens S A 5 Mdn 75-14 NoMrker,NstyNskr,RichesToRiches 8
25Jan87-6SA 6f :22 :45^1 1:10^{3}ft 18 118 43½ 45½ 47½ 57¾ Stevens S A^9 Mdn 77-18 KapaluQuick,ChrtTheStrs,NoMrker 9
25Jan87—Wide into stretch
15Jan87-6SA 6f :22 :45^2 1:11^{4}ft 147 118 11^{10}11^{11} 87½ 52½ Stevens S A^2 M50000 76-25 LuckyBer,TrulyRosie,Rconnoitring 12
15Jan87—Very rough trip
Apr 11 SA 3f ft :37 h Mar 20 SA 5f ft 1:02^3 h Mar 15 SA 4f ft :49^3 h Feb 18 SA 4f ft :48^4 h

C.
5–2

No Marker — Ro. c. 3, by Grey Dawn II—Miss Cevin Levin, by Drone
MCCARRON C J — **118** — Br.—Gowdy B R (Ky) — 1987 5 2 0 1 $32,850
Own.—Gowdy B R — Tr.—Johnson Patricia L — 1986 1 M 0 0
Lifetime 6 2 0 1 $32,850

21Mar87-3SA 1 1/16 :45^4 1:10^1 1:42^{2}sy 6 113^5 1½ 1½ 1^5 1^{10} Cox D W^1 Aw31000 89-16 NoMrker,TelphonCnyon,KpluQuick 8
18Feb87-8SA 1⅛ :46^1 1:10^1 1:48^{4}ft 12 115 32½ 4^4 4^9 6^{10} Solis A^3 Ⓡ Brdbry 75-19 HotAndSmoggy,Barb'sRelic,Reland 7
8Feb87-4SA 1 1/16 :46^3 1:12 1:44 ft 3¾ 117 2^{hd} 1^2 1^4 15½ Valenzuela P A^1 Mdn 81-14 NoMrker,NstyNskr,RichesToRiches 8
25Jan87-6SA 6f :22 :45^1 1:10^{3}ft 9¾ 118 2^{hd} 2^{hd} 32½ 3^5 Meza R Q^7 Mdn 80-18 KapaluQuick,ChrtTheStrs,NoMrker 9
25Jan87—Veered in start
4Jan87-4SA 6f :21^4 :45 1:10^{4}sy 16 118 2^2 2^3 33½ 68¼ Meza R Q^2 Mdn 76-22 Mount Laguna, Acquired, Conquer 7
26Dec86-6SA 6f :21^3 :44^4 1:09^{4}ft 27 117 10^{11}11^{10}11^{11}1114¾ Meza R Q^7 Mdn 74-13 Barb'sRelic,ChartTheStars,Chinati 12
26Dec86—Broke slowly, bumped start; green backstretch
Apr 13 SA Ⓣ 4f fm :51^2 h (d) Apr 6 SA 6f ft 1:14 h Mar 31 SA 4f ft :51^2 h Mar 15 SA 5f ft 1:00 h

D.

9–5

***Chime Time**
PINCAY L JR 120
B. c. 3, by Good Times—Balnespick, by Charlottown
Br.—D Barrott Packaging Ltd (Eng)
Tr.—Sadler John W
Own.—King Bros & MiramarStables
Lifetime 10 5 1 3 $84,645
1987 2 1 0 1 $46,750
1986 8 4 1 2 $37,895
Turf 10 5 1 3 $84,645

25Mar87-8SA a6½f Ⓣ:212 :4341:15 fm *2½ 116 11½ 11½ 12½ 12½ Valenzuela PA1 Bldwn 84-16 ChmTm,SwttrSprngs,McKnzPrnc 11
12Mar87-8SA a6½f Ⓣ:212 :44 1:16 fm*8-5 120 1hd 1hd 2½ 31¾ ValenzuelPA3 Aw40000 77-21 SwtwtrSprngs,HppyInSpc,ChmTm 10
11Oct86♦6York(Eng) 6f 1:114gd 4½ 126 Ⓣ 34 Lucas T Rockingham Mdyan, OnTap, ChimeTime 7
12Sep86♦4Doncaster(Eng) 7f 1:25 gd 11 126 Ⓣ 42½ BrcM L PerierChmpn(Gr2) DontForgtM,DptyGovrnor,WhKnws 9
20Aug86♦4York(Eng) 6f 1:114gd 7 126 Ⓣ 31½ Birch M Gimcrack(Gr2) Wiganthorpe,Mansooj,ChimeTime 11
22Jly86♦2Ayr(Scot) 6f 1:122fm*2-5 129 Ⓣ 11½ Birch M Strathclyde ChimeTime,SinclairLady,TemEffort 5
11Jly86♦1York(Eng) 6f 1:124gd*2-3 128 Ⓣ 16 Birch M Black Duck ChimTim,GlowAgin,PtswoodShootr 4
19Jun86♦5Ascot(Eng) 6f 1:133fm 16 123 Ⓣ 24 Birch M Chesham Minstrella, Chime Time, Luzum 13
6Jun86♦4Haydock(Eng) 6f 1:16 gd 2¾ 123 Ⓣ 1nk Birch M JohnLawlor ChimeTime,ToughNGentl,QulEsprit 7
27May86♦2Redcar(Eng) 6f 1:121fm 12 126 Ⓣ 13 LucasT JohnCross(Mdn) Chime Time, Mubdi, SilverAncona 20
Apr 9 SA Ⓣ 7f fm 1:282 h (d) Apr 4 SA 4f ft :49 h ●Mar 21 SA Ⓣ 5f fm :593 h (d) Mar 9 SA 4f ft :47 hg

E.

9–2

Just Bobby
SHOEMAKER W 114
Ch. c. 3, by Roberto—Hoist Emy's Flag, by Hoist the Flag
Br.—Singer C (Ky)
Tr.—Proctor Willard L
Own.—Singer J
Lifetime 7 1 1 1 $23,000
1987 4 0 0 1 $8,800
1986 3 1 1 0 $14,200
Turf 2 0 0 0 $2,500

25Mar87-8SA a6½f Ⓣ:212 :4341:15 fm 17 114 88¾ 89 57½ 56 Cox D W10 Bldwn 78-16 ChmTm,SwttrSprngs,McKnzPrnc 11
12Mar87-8SA a6½f Ⓣ:212 :44 1:16 fm 27 1095 89 76¼ 57½ 54½ Cox D W1 Aw40000 74-21 SwtwtrSprngs,HppyInSpc,ChmTm 10
12Mar87—Broke slowly; wide into, through stretch
30Jan87-7SA 1 :47 1:12 1:372ft 13 1095 85 72¾ 62¼ 42¼ Cox D W6 Aw28000 79-20 The Quipper, Reland, Savor Faire 9
30Jan87—Steadied 9/16
16Jan87-5SA 1 1/16 :464 1:111 1:433ft 3½ 1095 78½ 58 46½ 310 Cox D W9 Aw28000 73-18 Hot AndSmoggy,Reland,JustBobby 9
14Dec86-4Hol 7f :214 :45 1:241ft *8-5 120 107¾ 93¾ 73¾ 84½ ShoemkerW8 Aw22000 78-18 OrchardSong,Reland,HoustonBrgg 11
14Dec86—Wide in stretch
11Oct86-6SA 6½f :214 :444 1:172ft *2¾ 117 79 56½ 42¼ 11¼ Shoemaker W11 Mdn 83-17 JustBobby,Brb'sRlc,ExclusvEnogh 12
11Oct86—Stumbled start
2Aug86-6Dmr 6f :221 :452 1:101ft 2¾ 117 22½ 22½ 22½ 23 Shoemaker W6 Mdn 86-12 BiloxiBlues,JustBobby,IceMinstrel 12
Apr 14 SA 3f ft :371 h Apr 9 SA 5f ft 1:002 h Apr 3 SA 4f ft :474 h Mar 30 SA 4f ft :502 h

44. How should handicappers play this highly restricted classified allowance race on the grass?

7th Del Mar

1 MILE. (Turf). (1.34⅕) CLASSIFIED ALLOWANCE. Purse $40,000. Fillies and mares. 3-year-olds and upward. Non-winners of $19,500 twice at one mile or over since November 1, 1986. Weights, 3-year-olds, 115 lbs.; older 121 lbs. Non-winners of two such races since October 1, 1986 allowed 3 lbs.; of such a race of $22,000 since April 20, 5 lbs.; of $22,000 any distance since April 20, 7 lbs. (Claiming races not considered.)

15–1

***New Bruce**
PINCAY L JR 114
Ch. m. 5, by Vitiges—New One, by Tyrone
Br.—Knockaney Stud (Ire)
Tr.—Moreno Henry
Own.—Howell C
Lifetime 50 6 7 8 $163,353
1987 3 0 0 1 $7,200
1986 12 1 1 2 $37,154
Turf 50 6 7 8 $163,353

4Mar87-7SA 1 Ⓣ:4531:1011:36 fm 5¾ 117 78½ 1011 913 814 PncyLJr1 Ⓕ[R]B Thtful 81-05 Northern Aspen, Reloy, Benzina 10
19Jan87-8SA 1⅛ Ⓣ:4821:1241:501fm 10 116 42½ 31 74¼ 79¼ VllPA5 ⒻSn Grgno H 67-29 Frau Altiva, Auspiciante, Solva 7
19Jan87—Grade II; Off slowly, rank
2Jan87-8SA 1⅛ Ⓣ:4621:1111:49 fm 7 114 56 63½ 41½ 34¼ ShoemkrW7 ⒻAw48000 78-18 Outstandingly,FrauAltiv,NewBruce 8
2Jan87—Rough start
25Sep86♦5MLaffitte(Fra) a1¼ 2:041yl 5 122 Ⓣ 45½ GrdP La Coup d MLa(Gr3) Antheus, SplendidMoment, Arokar 8
21Sep86♦5Longchamp(Fra) a1¼ 2:082gd 17 122 Ⓣ 41¼ GnrdG Px Prnc d'Orng(Gr3) Fitnah, SaintEstephe, FastTopaze 7
7Sep86♦4Longchamp(Fra) a1 1:354gd 69 124 Ⓣ 97¾ GgnrdG Px d Mouln(Gr1) SonicLady, ThrillShow, Lirung 14
30Aug86♦4Deauville(Fra) a1¼ 2:162sf 7¾ 122 Ⓣ 11½ Badel A Px Ridgway NewBruce, Malakim, SoirdeNoces 12
27Aug86♦4Deauville(Fra) a1 1:412sf 6½ 122 Ⓣ 75¼ BrunuP Px Quincey(Gr3) Apldorn,NrthrnAspn,SplnddMmnt 14
19Aug86♦4Deauville(Fra) a1 1:461sf 4 121 Ⓣ 31 Lequex A Px du Cercle CostaSmerald,Herldiste,NewBruce 11
16Aug86♦4Deauville(Fra) a1¼ 2:062gd 15 120 Ⓣ 107½ BrunP Px Gontau Biron(Gr3) Over The Ocean, Iades, Baby Turk 10
●Jly 27 Dmr 7f ft 1:254 h Jly 21 Hol 3f ft :364 h Jly 15 Hol 4f ft :50 h Jly 13 Hol 5f ft 1:024 h

18–1

Amongst The Stars — **B. f. 4, by Procter—Out of This World, by High Top**

DELAHOUSSAYE E **118** — **Br.—Bourbn Intrnatl Syndcte (Ky)** — **1987 3 1 0 0 $25,875**

Tr.—Drysdale Neil — **1986 9 3 0 0 $37,802**

Own.—Brook-Hancock-Keogh Etal — **Lifetime 21 6 1 0 $70,243** — **Turf 21 6 1 0 $70,239**

5Jly87-8Hol 1⅛Ⓣ:45 1:08^{2}1:46^{1}fm 9 116 8^{16} 8^{13} 7^{11} 6$^{7\frac{3}{4}}$ DlhssE^3 ⒻBv Hls H 89-03 Auspiciante, Reloy, Festivity 8
5Jly87—Grade II
17Jun87-8Hol 1$\frac{1}{16}$Ⓣ:46^{4}1:10 1:41^{1}fm 5 116 6^{11} 6^9 6$^{2\frac{3}{4}}$ 1^1 DlhoussyE^3 ⒻAw45000 88-12 AmongstTheStrs,Fstivity,StllCloud 6
15May87-8Hol 1⅛Ⓣ:49^{1}1:13 1:48^{3}fm 26 116 6$^{3\frac{1}{4}}$ 4^3 4^2 5$^{2\frac{3}{4}}$ DlhoussyE^2 ⒻAw45000 82-12 Santiki,TreasureMap,Helen'sMjesty 7
25Oct86♦4Newbury(Eng) 1½ 2:45^{1}sf 66 119 Ⓣ 5^{10} Lowe J St Simon (Gr3) JupiterIslnd,VerdAntique,QueenHln 9
12Oct86♦6Longchamp(Fra) a1$\frac{7}{16}$ 2:40^{2}gd 29 123 Ⓣ 7$^{5\frac{3}{4}}$ Lowe J ⒻPx d Roylieu(Gr3) Sharaniya, Kruguy, Luth d'Or 10
14Sep86♦5Hanover(Ger) a1½ 2:42 gd 4½ 128 Ⓣ 4$^{3\frac{3}{4}}$ LowJ ⒻDeutschr Stutnprs(Gr3) Prairie Neba, Noretta, Lomela 8
21Aug86♦6York(Eng) 1½ 2:30^{3}gd 20 119 Ⓣ 4$^{6\frac{1}{2}}$ Lowe J ⒻGaltres Startino, Kenanga, Bonshamile 13
13Jly86♦5Krefeld(Ger) a1$\frac{7}{16}$ 2:28^{3}fm 27 121 Ⓣ 1no LoweJ ⒻGobls-Ernrngs(Gr3) AmongstThStrs,PrrNb,EpcrsGrdn 12
11Jun86♦4Newbury(Eng) 1¼ 2:14^{3}gd 12 121 Ⓣ 8 Lowe J ⒻBallymcl Std LvendrMist,Bishn,OldDomsdyBook 9
16May86♦3N'wcastle(Eng) 1¼ 2:12^{2}gd 6 111 Ⓣ 1$^{1\frac{1}{2}}$ Lowe J X Y Z Hcp Amongst The Stars,Forcello,Simsin 9
Aug 1 Dmr 5f ft 1:01^4 h **Jly 21 Hol 6f ft 1:18^2 h** **Jly 16 Hol 4f ft :51^2 h** **Jun 30 Hol 6f ft 1:14^2 h**

23–1

Aromacor — **Dk. b. or br. f. 4, by Bold Ruckus—Tamara, by Up Spirits**

STEVENS G L **118** — **Br.—Frostad G C (Ont-C)** — **1987 11 2 1 2 $99,770**

Tr.—Whittingham Michael — **1986 16 4 5 0 $79,585**

Own.—Ventura Stables Inc — **Lifetime 37 7 6 3 $195,646** — **Turf 17 4 3 2 $147,835**

5Jly87-8Hol 1⅛Ⓣ:45 1:08^{2}1:46^{1}fm 70 112 3^2 4$^{2\frac{1}{2}}$ 5$^{3\frac{1}{2}}$ 4$^{6\frac{3}{4}}$ Solis A^6 ⒻBv Hls H 90-03 Auspiciante, Reloy, Festivity 8
5Jly87—Grade II
13Jun87-9WO 1$\frac{1}{16}$[T]:47^{1}1:11^{2}1:42^{4}fm 2¼ 117 4$^{2\frac{1}{2}}$ 4^2 3$^{1\frac{1}{2}}$ 1^1 SmrDJ^1 Ⓕ[S]Victoriana 90-09 Aromacor,RulingAngel,Cuantalmer 6
3Jun87-8WO 1 [T]:48^{3}1:14 1:40 fm 7-5 117 6^7 6$^{3\frac{1}{2}}$ 4^4 2$^{1\frac{1}{2}}$ King RJr^1 Ⓕ[S]Aw28600 75-11 HanginOnaStar,Aromacor,Cuntlmer 8
8May87-8Hol 1 Ⓣ:47 1:11 1:36 fm 2¾ 116 5^5 3$^{1\frac{1}{2}}$ 1^{hd} 1$^{\frac{3}{4}}$ DlhoussyE^6 ⒻAw30000 87-13 Aromacor,PrincessCariole,HighAce 7
8May87—Drifted out drive
26Apr87-5Hol 1 Ⓣ:47^{3}1:12^{1}1:36^{4}fm 11 116 5$^{3\frac{3}{4}}$ 6$^{2\frac{1}{2}}$ 6$^{3\frac{1}{4}}$ 4$^{2\frac{3}{4}}$ DlhoussyE^6 ⒻAw30000 80-13 Helen's Majesty,Santiki,Rekindling 6
17Apr87-8SA a6½f Ⓣ:21^4 :44^{3}1:15^{3}fm 5¾ 118 5^3 5$^{2\frac{1}{2}}$ 4$^{2\frac{1}{2}}$ 5$^{1\frac{1}{4}}$ OlvrsF^1 Ⓕ[R]Grt Ldy M 80-14 Barbarina,WistfulTune,FairwaysGirl 8
17Apr87—Crowded crossing dirt
28Mar87-8SA a6½f Ⓣ:21^3 :44 1:14^{2}fm 27 112 4$^{2\frac{1}{2}}$ 2½ 1$^{1\frac{1}{2}}$ 3$^{3\frac{1}{2}}$ OlivresF 7 ⒻLs Cngs H 83-12 Lichi, An Empress, Aromacor 7
15Mar87-7SA a6½f Ⓣ:22^1 :44^{3}1:15^{1}gd 15 118 4$^{1\frac{1}{2}}$ 4$^{4\frac{1}{2}}$ 4^5 4$^{3\frac{1}{2}}$ OlivresF 4 Ⓕ[R]Mt Wlsn 79-24 Firesweepr,AnEmprss,TrudiDomino 8
22Feb87-3SA a6½f Ⓣ:21^4 :44^{3}1:16^{2}fm 3¼ 118 4$^{2\frac{1}{2}}$ 4$^{1\frac{1}{2}}$ 1½ 3$^{2\frac{1}{4}}$ Olivares F 4 ⒻAw34000 75-22 MissBevrlyHills,Rkindling,Aromcor 9
22Feb87—Lugged in late
4Feb87-8SA a6½f Ⓣ:22^2 :45^{1}1:15 fm 22 113 4^2 4$^{1\frac{1}{2}}$ 6$^{3\frac{3}{4}}$ 6^4 Olivares F 5 ⒻMnrva H 80-16 Sari's Heroine, Lichi, Aberuschka 7
4Feb87—Bumped at start, wide into stretch
Aug 1 Dmr 5f ft 1:01^1 h **Jly 27 Dmr Ⓣ 7f fm 1:32^3 h** **Jly 23 Dmr 5f ft 1:03 h** **Jly 16 Hol 3f ft :37^4 h**

4–5

***Aberuschka** — **Ch. m. 5, by Thatching—Veruschka, by Lorenzaccio**

VALENZUELA P A **121** — **Br.—Yeomanstown Lodge Stud (Ire)** — **1987 2 1 0 1 $43,200**

Tr.—Frankel Robert — **1986 11 7 2 0 $403,840**

Own.—Moss Mr-Mrs J S — **Lifetime 19 10 3 2 $484,285** — **Turf 18 10 3 2 $478,660**

26Jun87-8Bel 6f Ⓣ:22^2 :45^{2}1:10 gd*4-5 117 5$^{4\frac{1}{2}}$ 5^3 1^{hd} 1½ VllPA^3 ⒻOcean Bound 90-07 Aberuschka,SmallVirtue,SherryMry 8
4Feb87-8SA a6½f Ⓣ:22^2 :45^{1}1:15 fm*3-5 124 7$^{3\frac{3}{4}}$ 6^3 4^3 3$^{2\frac{1}{2}}$ StevnsGL^3 ⒻMnrva H 81-16 Sari's Heroine, Lichi, Aberuschka 7
4Feb87—Steadied at 3/8; at intervals late
21Dec86-8Hol 1$\frac{1}{16}$Ⓣ:49^{2}1:12^{4}1:41^{3}fm*8-5 122 3$^{1\frac{1}{2}}$ 3^{nk} 1^2 1^1 VlnzlPA^6 ⒻDahlia H 86-15 Aberuschka, An Empress, Reloy 7
21Dec86—Grade III
23Nov86-8Hol 1⅛Ⓣ:47^{3}1:13^{1}1:48 fm 11e 123 5^5 5$^{3\frac{1}{4}}$ 1$^{1\frac{1}{2}}$ 2$^{1\frac{1}{2}}$ VlnzlPA^9 ⒻMtrch Iv 86-13 Auspiciante, Aberuschka, Reloy 12
23Nov86—Grade I
1Nov86-9SA 1 Ⓣ:46^{3}1:10^{4}1:36^{3}fm*8-5e 120 3½ 1^{hd} 1$^{2\frac{1}{2}}$ 1^{hd} VlenzulPA^3 ⒻMdwk H 94-07 Aberuschka, Duckweed, Solva 12
7Sep86-8Dmr 1⅛Ⓣ:47^{1}1:11 1:48^{2}fm 3¾ 119 2$^{2\frac{1}{2}}$ 3^1 3^1 4$^{4\frac{1}{4}}$ VlnlPA^6 ⒻRmna H 88-08 Auspiciante, Justicara, Sauna 9
7Sep86—Grade I
9Aug86-8Dmr 1 Ⓣ:46^{1}1:10^{4}1:34^{2}fm 3¼ 118 2^1 2½ 1$^{1\frac{1}{2}}$ 1^{hd} VlnzlPA^6 ⒻPlmr H 100-04 Aberuschka, Sauna,Fran'sValentine 9
9Aug86—Grade II
4Jly86-5Hol 6f Ⓣ:22 :44^{4}1:08^{3}fm*2-3 122 3^2 3$^{1\frac{1}{2}}$ 1½ 1^2 ValenzuelPA^2 ⒻHcp0 99 — Aberuschka,Loucoum,BoldNSpecial 7
19Jun86-8Bel 1$\frac{1}{16}$[T]:48 1:11 1:42 fm 2½ 116 4^2 5$^{1\frac{1}{4}}$ 2½ 1$^{2\frac{1}{2}}$ Migliore R^4 ⒻHcp0 91-18 Aberuschka, Dismasted, Sorayah 6
25May86-9Cby 1 Ⓣ:47 1:11^{3}1:35^{1}fm *2½ 116 5$^{3\frac{1}{4}}$ 4^1 2^{hd} 2$^{1\frac{3}{4}}$ VlnlPA^6 ⒻLady Cby H — — Sauna, Aberuschka, Top Socialite 12
Jly 25 Dmr 6f ft 1:13^1 h **Jly 19 Hol 5f ft 1:01 h** **Jly 13 Hol 6f ft 1:13^1 h** **Jly 6 Hol 4f ft :51^4 h**

5–1

Adorable Micol — Dk. b. or br. f. 4, by Riverman—Turn to Me, by Cyane
TORO F 118 — Br.—Gallagher's Farm Inc (NY) — Tr.—McAnally Ronald
Own.—Gallagher Farm — Lifetime 19 4 2 1 $160,466
1987 7 2 2 0 $122,210
1986 8 1 0 0 $26,203
Turf 19 4 2 1 $160,466

27Jun87-8GG 1 Ⓣ:4711:1121:362fm*1-2 119 78 66¼ 42½ 2no CstdM4 ⒻⓇSt Bl Iv H 85-21 RiverChr,AdorbleMicol,TenderForc 7
6Jun87-8GG 1 Ⓣ:4831:1221:37 fm 3½ 115 75½ 74¼ 41¾ 21 CstdM3 ⒻMiss AmerH 81-20 Solva, Adorable Micol, River Char 7
16May87-8GG 1 1/16 Ⓣ:4741:1131:431fm 15 112 78 74¼ 33 11¼ DiazAL3 ⒻCnts Fgr H 86-20 Adorable Micol, Solva,Nature'sWay 8
16May87—Grade III
15Apr87-5SA a6½f Ⓣ:211 :4331:143fm 4½ 116 65 64½ 33 12¾ Solis A6 ⒻAw33000 86-11 Adorable Micol,HighAce,InConcert 7
15Apr87—Lugged in late
20Mar87-7SA a6½f Ⓣ:213 :44 1:151fm 15 117 89½ 89¾ 87 74¼ McHrgDG2 ⒻAw33000 79-15 Barbarina, Vivid Dancer, InConcert 8
21Feb87-5SA a6½f Ⓣ:22 :45 1:16 fm 7½ 115 54 64 54 84 ShomkrW10 ⒻAw31000 75-17 HairlessHeiress,Ofrendd,RellyFncy 10
25Jan87-5SA a6½f Ⓣ:213 :4411:154fm *2 115 42 32 34 95 ShoemkrW2 ⒻAw30000 75-18 SunlightMiss,Missen,Sir'sNewHope 9
25Jan87—Broke slowly
12Dec86-7Hol 1 1/16 Ⓣ:4711:1111:414fm 3½ 114 89¾ 75¼ 52¼ 42 Solis A3 ⒻHcp0 83-13 Mirculous,SeldomSeenSu,MissAlto 8
1Nov86-9SA 1 Ⓣ:4631:1041:363fm 80 110 61¾ 2hd 22½ 42¼ Hawley S11 ⒻMdwk H 92-07 Aberuschka, Duckweed, Solva 12
1Nov86—Wide 7/8
12Oct86 ♦3Longhamp(Fra) a7f 1:22 gd 17 121 Ⓣ 1013 Boeuf D Px duPin MadeofPerl,CostSmerld,DomVlory 10
Jly 31 Dmr 5f ft 1:013 h ● Jly 25 Hol 5f ft :592 h Jly 19 Hol 5f ft 1:01 h Jly 13 Hol 4f ft :503 h

2–1

Festivity — Gr. f. 4, by Spectacular Bid—Dancing On, by Dancer's Image
MCCARRON C J 121 — Br.—Harbor View Farm (Ky) — Tr.—Barrera Lazaro S
Own.—Harbor View Farm — Lifetime 18 6 3 5 $179,773
1987 4 1 1 1 $57,825
1986 14 5 2 4 $121,948
Turf 12 5 3 2 $158,653

5Jly87-8Hol 1⅛Ⓣ:45 1:0821:461fm 8½ 114 42 32 32 32¼ McCrrCJ2 ⒻBv Hls H 95-03 Auspiciante, Reloy, Festivity 8
5Jly87—Grade II
27Jun87-4Hol 1 1/16 Ⓣ:4631:1031:414fm*4-5 115 43 42 31 1¾ McCrrCJ2 ⒻⓇMatinee 85-11 Festivity, Stall Cloud,WordHarvest 6
17Jun87-8Hol 1 1/16 Ⓣ:4641:10 1:411fm *1 1115 2hd 1hd 1½ 21 Gryder AT5 ⒻAw45000 87-12 AmongstTheStrs,Fstivity,StllCloud 6
17Jun87—Drifted out late
7Jun87-7Hol 1 1/16 Ⓣ:47 1:1041:411fm 9¾e 1055 11½ 1½ 2½ 41¾ Gryder A T2 Aw45000 86-12 Bruiser,RichErth,MisterWondrfulII 8
2Nov86-8SA 1¼Ⓣ:4631:3542:012fm 7½ 118 53½ 95¾109½ 95¾ SntsJA5 ⒻYlw Rbn Iv 74-20 Bonne Ile, Top Corsage, Carotene 12
2Nov86—Grade I
18Oct86-7Bel 1⅜Ⓣ:48 1:38 2:16 gd 2½ 113 96½ 85¼ 34½ 22½ CrgtJ10 ⒻAthenia H 75-29 Dwn'sCurtsey,Festivity,PrfctPoint 10
18Oct86—Grade III
2Oct86-8Bel 1 1/16 Ⓣ:4821:12 1:442gd*4-5 112 64 31½ 12 13¼ Cruguet J3 ⒻAw40000 79-28 Festivity,DesertView,WendyWalker 8
20Sep86-1Bel 1¼Ⓣ:49 1:3712:011hd*2-3 118 52½ 13 14 15½ Cruguet J8 ⒻAw29000 88-10 Festivity, Keep TheFaithII,Guadery 8
6Sep86-6Bel 1 1/16 Ⓣ:4731:1211:444gd 3 118 41¾ 12 13 14½ Cruguet J4 ⒻAw26000 72-27 Festivity,FrgrntPrincess,TllPoppy 11
18Aug86-2Sar 1 3/16 Ⓣ:4811:13 1:551gd 2½ 112 32 32 1hd 13¼ Cruguet J2 ⒻAw25000 90-09 Festivity, Rinaldi, Capability Brown 9
Aug 3 Dmr 4f ft :472 h Jly 28 Dmr 5f ft :594 h Jly 21 Hol 5f ft :594 h Jly 14 Hol 5f ft :594 h

37–1

Down Again — B. f. 3, by Encino—Dawn is Breaking, by Import
GRYDER A T 1035 — Br.—Schibbye & Nebbiolo Place (Ky) — Tr.—Cross Richard J
Own.—Summa Stable & Silverman — Lifetime 8 2 2 0 $33,931
1987 3 0 0 0 $8,625
1986 5 2 2 0 $25,306
Turf 7 2 2 0 $32,806

27Jun87-9Cby 1 1/16 Ⓣ:47 1:11 1:414fm 27 113 97¾105¼ 75¼ 63½ OrtegLE10 ⒻCby Oaks 90-10 Tppino,FutureBright,ViwofRoylty 12
10Jun87-8Hol 1 1/16 :464 1:114 1:44 ft 8½ 112 43 53 57 511¾ OrtLE7 ⒻⓇIts In T Ar 77-16 HelloSweetThing,KeyBid,LdyyNskr 7
10Jun87—Wide 7/8 turn
17May87-8Hol 1 1/16 Ⓣ:4621:1031:411fm 20 113 52 52½ 31½ 42½ OrtLE1 ⒻHnymn H 85-09 PenBlLdy,SomeSenstion,Dvi'sLmb 10
17May87—Grade III
27Sep86 ♦2Curragh(Ire) 5f 1:04 fm 3 127 Ⓣ 2nk Hogan D Goffs GoldenDome,DownAgain,JanMurry 7
7Sep86 ♦2PhoenixPk(Ire) 7f 1:192gd *3½ 126 Ⓣ 3¾ † Eddery P ⒻGfs Slvr Flsh SimpleTaste,Erindale,‡DownAgain 13
† 7Sep86—Disqualified and placed last
23Aug86 ♦5PhoenixPk(Ire) 6f 1:153yl 5 121 Ⓣ 11½ Eddery P ⒻDeb DownAgin,NorthTelstr,SnowFinch 11
19Jly86 ♦3Leopardst'n(Ire) 7f 1:311gd 6 119 Ⓣ 2½ Hogan D Orby SnowFinch,DownAgin,WitTllMondy 8
21Jun86 ♦3Naas(Ire) 6f 1:102fm 8 126 Ⓣ 12 HognD ⒻSubaru(Mdn) DownAgain, NativeSal, Erindale 14
Jly 24 Hol 4f ft :48 hg

A. Key the stickout *Aberuschka* to all the exacta overlays
B. Bet the overlay *Aromacor* to win
C. Box *Festivity* and *Adorable Micol* multiple times
D. Box *Adorable Micol* and *Aromacor* and play each on top of *Aberuschka*

45. Consider the information provided, handicap the race, and decide on the best alternative below.

Horse	Speed Figure	Odds
No Romance	80	7–2
Pirate's Kernel	96	4–5
Suisun Sue	86	6–1

6th Santa Anita

OUT OF CHUTE ▸

6½ FURLONGS
SANTA ANITA
◂ FINISH

6 ½ FURLONGS. (1.14) MAIDEN. Purse $23,000. Fillies. 3-year-olds. Bred in California. Weight 117 lbs. (Non-starters for a claiming price of $32,000 or less preferred.)

No Romance
PINCAY L JR 4 +   117
Own.—Longden E J

B. f. 3, by Kennedy Road—Jungle Tabu, by Jungle Road
Br.—Longden E J (Cal)   1987 1 M 1 0 $4,600
Tr.—Longden Eric J   1986 1 M 0 0 $1,500
Lifetime 2 0 1 0 $6,100

5Apr87-4SA 6½f:222 :461 1:174ft 5½ 117 2½ 21 21½ 2½ Stevens G L³ ⒻMdn 80-16 CreamSauce,NoRomance,PrivteArt 8
  5Apr87—Broke in a tangle
10Oct86-6SA 6f :222 :461 1:112ft 27 117 94¾ 65 45 43½ Meza R Q² ⒻⓈMdn 77-24 FlyingHghr,LyrclPrt,DncAllSummr 11
  10Oct86—Steadied at 5 1/2; took up at 1/2
Apr 11 SA 5f ft 1:00⁴ h   Mar 28 SA 6f ft 1:13⁴ h   Mar 23 SA 6f ft 1:14⁴ hg   Mar 18 SA 6f ft 1:15¹ h

Pockets Of Corn
CISNEROS J E   112⁵
Own.—Narvaez G & Coraleen

Dk. b. or br. f. 3, by Oats and Corn—Fast Pocket, by Full Pocket
Br.—Buccaneer Cruises (Cal)   1986 0 M 0 0
Tr.—Cianci Jon
Lifetime 0 0 0 0

Apr 12 SA 4f ft :47³ h   Apr 6 SA 4f ft :48² h   Apr 1 SA 3f ft :35¹ h   Feb 28 SA 5f ft 1:00⁴ hg

Pirate's Kernel
MEZA R Q   117
Own.—Marden & Wygod

B. f. 3, by Pirate's Bounty—Popcorn Miss, by Old Gratt
Br.—Wygod M J (Cal)   1987 1 M 1 0 $4,600
Tr.—Ellis Ronald W   1986 0 M 0 0
Lifetime 1 0 1 0 $4,600

4Apr87-3SA 6f :212 :441 1:101ft *6-5 117 66¾ 65¾ 27 21½ Stevens G L⁶ ⒻⓈMdn 86-17 MissSprinklt,Pirt'sKrnl,JklinAndHd 8
  4Apr87—Broke slowly
Apr 13 SA 4f ft :46³ h   Mar 29 SA 5f ft :59² hg   Mar 23 SA 5f ft 1:00² h   Mar 26 SA 3f ft :37¹ h

Ninepaytheline
SIBILLE R   117
Own.—Hirmez & Sittu

Ch. f. 3, by Golden Eagle II—Only a Rose, by Groton
Br.—Auerbach E A (Cal)   1987 1 M 0 0 $575
Tr.—Tinsley J E Jr   1986 4 M 1 0 $7,550
Lifetime 5 0 1 0 $8,125

4Apr87-3SA 6f :212 :441 1:101ft 9¾ 117 53¾ 44½ 59 59¾ CastanonAL⁷ ⒻⓈMdn 78-17 MissSprinklt,Pirt'sKrnl,JklinAndHd 8
18Aug86-8Dmr 7f :22 :443 1:223ft 27 115 74½ 87 811 816 BazeRA² ⒻSorrento 76-14 Brave Raj, Breech, Footy 10
  18Aug86—Grade III
9Aug86-6Dmr 6f :221 :453 1:114ft 2½ 117 62¾ 84½ 63½ 54 ShoemkerW⁵ ⒻⓈMdn 75-14 WildManor,Kavalla,HeavyWeather 10
  9Aug86—Bumped start; steadied at 3 1/2, again at 1/8
25Jly86-8Dmr 6f :22 :452 1:11 ft 13 114 53½ 52¾ 53½ 42½ BlackCA² ⒻⓈC T B A 81-18 SrosBrig,JoeyTheTrip,WindyTriplK. 8
  25Jly86—Wide late
11Jly86-6Hol 5½f :222 :454 1:04²ft 15 113⁵ 87½ 88¾ 58¼ 2⁹ Black C A⁸ ⒻMdn 83-14 Schuist,Ninepythlin,AlwysAWomn 11
Apr 15 SA 4f ft :48³ h   Mar 29 SA 5f ft 1:00² h   Mar 23 SA 5f ft 1:02¹ h   Mar 17 SA 6f ft 1:14¹ hg

Rock 'N Roll Girl
HIGUERA A R   117
Own.—Olson Joanne

Ch. f. 3, by Commissioner—Never Say Daisy, by Nentego
Br.—Moseley Marquita (Cal)   1987 1 M 0 0
Tr.—Chasteen William W   1986 0 M 0 0
Lifetime 1 0 0 0

4Apr87-3SA 6f :212 :441 1:101ft 62 117 812 814 818 716¾ Higuera A R² ⒻⓈMdn 70-17 MissSprinklt,Pirt'sKrnl,JklinAndHd8
  4Apr87—Broke slowly; green down backstretch
Mar 20 Hol 3f ft :36³ hg   Mar 14 Hol 5f ft 1:03³ hg   Feb 28 Hol 6f ft 1:16⁴ h   Feb 18 Hol 3f ft :36² hg

Barbie's Best
BRINKERHOFF D   117
Own.—Rock J J

B. f. 3, by Canadian Gil—Sister Barb, by Kentuckian
Br.—Rock J J (Cal)   1987 0 M 0 0
Tr.—Landers Dale   1986 0 M 0 0
Lifetime 0 0 0 0

  Entered 17Apr87- 2 SA
Apr 12 SA 3f ft :37⁴ h   ●Mar 20 AC 6f ft 1:13 h   Mar 12 AC 5f ft 1:00¹ h   Mar 5 AC 4f ft :48 hg

Chica Morena
PATTON D B   112⁵
Own.—Rancho Aguiladoble

B. f. 3, by Dark Encounter—Brown Babe, by Perfect Landing
Br.—Rancho Aguiladoble (Cal)   1987 0 M 0 0
Tr.—Cofer Riley S   1986 0 M 0 0
Lifetime 0 0 0 0

Apr 17 SA 3f ft :35⁴ h   Apr 11 SA 4f ft 1:02¹ h   Mar 26 SA 6f ft 1:14³ hg   Mar 21 SA 6f ft 1:15¹ hg

Súisun Sue — Ch. f. 3, by Commissioner—Perky Freckles, by Nagea

TORO F 7-0 — 117 — Br.—Ridgeley Farm&SuisunStable (Cal) — 1987 2 M 0 1 $3,300

Tr.—Ippolito Steve — 1986 0 M 0 0

Own.—Ridgeley Fm & Suisun St Inc — Lifetime 2 0 0 1 $3,300

4Apr87-3SA 6f :212 :441 1:101ft 2½ 117 2hd 24 716 824¼ ValenzuelPA 2 Ⓕ[S]Mdn 63-17 MissSprinklt,Pirt'sKrnl,JklinAndHd 8

4Apr87—Bumped start

11Mar87-6SA 6f :214 :451 1:103ft 11 117 21 2½ 32 32 Ortega L E 3 Ⓕ[S]Mdn 83-18 PrincessNturl,SlightstPss,SuisunSe 8

11Mar87—Bumped 1/8

Apr 12 SA 4f ft :482 h Mar 30 SA 6f ft 1:172 h Mar 22 SA 5f m 1:004 h Mar 7 SA 4f m :481 h

A. *No Romance*
B. *Pirate's Kernel*
C. *Suisun Sue*
D. None of the above

46. Only a few horses fit the restrictions of this claiming race suitably, and only one has been offered as an overlay. Which horse is it?

4 ATLANTIC CITY — 1 1-16 MILES

1 1/16 MILES. (1.41) CLAIMING. Purse $4,200. 3-year-olds and upward which have not won a race since February 3. Weight, 3-year-olds 115 lbs. Older 122 lbs. Non-winners of two races since January 3, allowed 2 lbs. A race since then 4 lbs. A race since December 3, 6 lbs. Claiming Price $4,000.

A.
30–1

Eliffeur — B. g. 8, by Irish Castle—Bright Word, by Blue Reading — Lifetime 1987 1 0 0 0 $40

$4,000 Br.—Cashman & Hanna Jr (Ky) — 106 10 — 54 6 5 4 — 1986 1 0 0 0

Own.—Shaw R J — Tr.—Shaw Ronald J — $37,222

24Jly87- 4Atl fst 6f :22⅗ :46⅖ 1:12⅘ 3+ Clm 4000 2 12 95½ 88¾ 99½ 88½ Santiago J M10 b 106 62.80 69-31 PoppyPepper1091WonderfulPhntsy1091½Egie'sTouch1111 Outrun 12

20Jun86- 4Atl gd 6f :22⅘ :46⅘ 1:12⅘ 3+ Clm 4000 7 11 97½ 910 1114 1015¾ Keefer M7 b 109 31.50 62-22 TheJoke'sOnYou1161¼A.A.SpecilKind1163½KeenKing1203½ Outrun 11

9Aug85- 4Atl fst 6f :23 :46⅘ 1:12⅕ 3+ Clm 4000 3 8 87 911 917 915¾ Parrilla R b 116 11.90 66-18 Rest 116hd Hilary s Charger 1163 Jollysum's Boy 116no Outrun 9

12Jly85- 5Del fst 6f :22⅗ :46⅕ 1:12⅕ 3+ Clm 3500 7 3 73½ 88¼ 79¾ 711¼ Hagan D P b 116 6.40 69-25 WillrdMountin116¾LetitB'Dunn1123¾He'sNudeToo1165¾ No factor 10

24Nov84- 6Del fst 170 :47 1:13 1:45⅕ 3+ Clm 3500 1 2 23 54½ 53¾ 48¾ Winnett B G Jr b 119 *2.10 62-28 Imperiled 116nk Deb's Best Friend110½BlondieDuck1138 Ret.lame 8

17Nov84- 2Del fst 1 1/16 :48⅕ 1:12⅗ 1:49⅘ 3+ Clm 3500 5 1 14 14½ 14 13½ Winnett B G Jr b 116 *1.00 59-28 Eliffeur 1163½ Lucky Scout 1192 Set And Chat 1162½ Driving 10

11Nov84- 6Del sly 1 1/16 :48 1:14 1:48⅕ 3+ Clm 5000 2 2 32 94¾ 814 911 Morgan M R b 116 7.70 56-31 Uncle Yosh 113nk Rug Raiser 116nk Pukka Luck 1061 Tired 11

2Nov84- 9Key fst 1 1/16 :47⅗ 1:12⅘ 1:47⅕ 3+ Clm 3500 2 1 11 2½ 22 2nk Lee R F b 114 *2.90 68-22 Starve Easy 114nk Eliffeur 1141 Woody Too 1141½ Gamely 12

LATEST WORKOUTS Jly 18 Atl 5f fst 1:02⅖ b Jly 15 Atl 3f sly :36⅗ hg Jly 11 Atl 4f fst :49⅗ b Jly 4 Atl 3f fst :38 b

B.
15–1

Lunade Cancun — B. c. 4, by Advocator—Fun 'n Sun, by Porterhouse — Lifetime 1987 11 0 0 1 $738

$4,000 Br.—Patterson Margaret (Ky) — 116 — 33 2 0 3 — 1986 22 2 0 2 $10,187

Own.—Prettyman Lisa — Tr.—Prettyman Lisa — $10,925 — Turf 1 0 0 0

5Jun87- 6Del my 1 1/16 :48⅕ 1:13⅕ 1:47⅘ Clm 3500 1 6 41½ 45 58½ 69 Reynolds R L b 117 15.50 60-30 Laurel's Leader 1172 Wise Mike 1202½ Believe It Jack1202½ Tired 10

27May87- 1Del fst 1 1/16 :48⅕ 1:13⅘ 1:47⅗ 3+ Clm 3500 2 1 2hd 3nk 2½ 62¾ Ryan J S b 117 31.30 67-28 Wyetown 120no Hoist YourSpirits1201½HandsomePoet120nk Tired 12

22May87- 6Del fst 1 1/16 :48⅕ 1:13⅕ 1:46 3+ Clm 3500 3 3 42 59 512 521 Bin G S5 b 111 15.20 57-21 The Gray Protege 1224½ John U. Fool 1224½ Comedion 1159 Tired 10

8May87- 2Del fst 6f :22⅗ :46⅘ 1:11⅘ Clm 3500 11 2 108 1110 1019 1021½ Brackett S R b 117 10.80 60-22 Work Ethic 1201½ ClubFighter1205½MamaStock'sBoy115½ Outrun 11

25Apr87- 9Del my 1 1/16 :47⅗ 1:14⅖ 1:48⅗ Clm 3500 3 4 42½ 32 38½ 39½ Bin G S5 b 112 26.90 55-25 United Prize 1209 Quobow 113½ Lunade Cancun 1122 Evenly 10

2Apr87- 1GP fst 7f :22⅘ :46⅕ 1:25 Clm 5000 7 2 87¾ 811 814 714 Meade D Jr b 117 109.00 65-24 IceColdGold1172½Super'sLstFight1171LittleAnthony1193½ Outrun 10

26Mar87- 4GP fst 7f :23⅕ :46⅘ 1:26 Clm 5000 9 2 43½ 58 1019 1015¾ Molina V H b 117 137.30 58-24 Fastest Gun 117nk Dancing Major 1171½ Early Royalty1102½ Tired 12

10Mar87- 2GP fst 6f :22⅗ :46⅘ 1:12⅖ Clm 5000 2 10 118¾ 1014 915 915¼ Molina V H b 117 91.40 62-28 Eddie Bubbles 1175 Jungle Zip 1192½ Tribute To Ted 119¾ Outrun 11

22Feb87- 1Hia fst 6f :23⅕ :45⅖ 1:12 Clm 5000 11 3 96¾ 108¾ 1011 87 Molina V H b 116 79.70 73-21 Pure Rascality 120½ Soaring Hawk116noNaroctive116nd No threat 12

25Jan87- 1Hia fst 7f :23⅘ :47 1:25⅘ Clm 5000 1 9 85½ 107¾ 98¾ 96¾ Iliescu A b 116 86.30 67-22 StarTrapper116noEllsGiantStep1221DynamicStrike1091 No factor 11

LATEST WORKOUTS Jly 6 Atl 3f fst :37⅖ b

C.
20–1

Nurse's Melody — Dk. b. or br. c. 4, by Slady Castle—Nurse Kit, by Occupy — Lifetime 1987 5 0 0 0 $222

$4,000 Br.—Tee-N-Jay Farm (NJ) — 116 — 16 1 1 1 — 1986 11 1 1 1 $6,546

Own.—Tee-N-Jay Farms — Tr.—Levine S — $6,768

27Jly87-10Atl fst 1 1/16 :46⅕ 1:11⅖ 1:46⅘ 3+ Clm 4000 2 6 59 413 811 1012½ Bolletino N b 116 16.10 59-20 Pirgar 109hd Reck's Courage 116nk Mongo King 1162½ Tired 12

15Jly87- 8Atl fst 1¼ :49⅖ 1:43 2:10⅘ 3+ Clm 5000 5 7 79½ 79½ 63¾ 87¼ Bolletino N b 116 74.70 48-33 Rollwiththepunches116hdCox'sKing1161½SetAndCht1161½ Outrun 9

9Jly87- 3Atl sly 6½f :23 :46⅗ 1:19 3+ [S]Clm 7500 7 2 53¾ 717 721 726¼ Bolletino N b 116 28.00 64-23 Abuse of Process 116½ Great Bonus 1095½ Glacier 1161 Outrun 7

19Jun87- 7Atl fst 6f :22 :45⅖ 1:11⅗ 3+ [S]Clm 5500 5 6 77¾ 813 76¾ 1032 Intelisano GPJr b 116 80.20 52-16 Abuse of Process 1165GreatBonus1161OurDuke1161½ Broke right 10

20May87- 7Del sly 6f :23 :47⅗ 1:14 3+ Clm 7500 8 6 89½ 911 912 812½ Beimel D W7 b 109 5.50 58-27 Out Again 1094 Holly Lad 115½ Bet Til Dawne 1061 Outrun 10

13Dec86- 1Med fst 1 :47 1:12⅕ 1:38⅖ Clm 7500 10 3 3nk 21 45½ 810 Ortega P Jr7 b 109 58.00 73-09 Delta Wings 1122 Commadore Too 114¾ Hasty Fellow 115nd Tired 11

28Nov86- 4Med fst 6f :23 :46⅗ 1:11⅗ Clm 10000 6 5 31½ 42½ 89½ 914¾ Thomas D B b 116 66.50 69-21 DactylDancer1194½ZonkerHarris1162½RoylRedAndBlue1112½ Tired 10

17Nov86- 2Med fst 6f :22⅗ :45⅘ 1:11⅕ 3+ Clm 10000 5 7 33 34 65¾ 89½ Gomez I b 114 22.20 76-17 Truro 1161½ Mr. Mar J. Mar 1112 Oriental Flyer 116nk Tired 9

31Oct86- 4Med fst 6f :22⅖ :45⅘ 1:11⅘ Clm 10500 10 8 94 87¾ 58½ 59 Corbett G W7 b 105 26.90 74-19 BelieveInSam112¾Nancy'sNaskr1124Birdie'sComet1164 No factor 12

24Oct86- 3Med fst 6f :22⅘ :45⅘ 1:11⅖ 3+ Clm 10500 1 9 94¼ 77 78 75¼ Gomez I b 114 28.40 80-21 Haskins Hope 116½ Jim Would 116½OrientalFlyer112nd Slow start 9

LATEST WORKOUTS Jly 3 Atl 5f my 1:04⅘ b Jun 17 Atl 4f fst :48⅕ h Jun 12 Atl 5f fst 1:01⅘ h

D.

3–1

Neutral Smith
Own.—Salvo D

Gr. g. 6, by Alias Smith—Audene, by Flag Raiser
$4,000 Br.—Hillbrook Farm & Stonereath Farm (Ky)
Tr.—Salvo Thomas J

116

Lifetime	1987	3	0	0	1	$556
60 5 5 8	1986	14	3	1	1	$8,380
$31,468	Turf	5	0	0	0	$1,503

13Jly87- 2Atl	fst	1 1/16	:48⅗ 1:15 1:49	3+Clm 4000	6 8 75½ 41¼ 34 311	Parisi E	b 116	12.40	49-32	Anvil Man 1168½Culater'sGattor1162½NeutralSmith1164½	Mild bid	9
4Jly87- 3Atl	fst	7f	:23⅕ :46⅘ 1:24⅗	3+Hcp 5000s	6 5 76½ 612 619 618	Parisi E	b 111	26.80	61-25	QuitFooling1141RochfordBridge1159GlitteringMount1172½	Outrun	7
26Jun87- 4Atl	fst	6f	:22⅗ :46 1:12⅗	3+Clm 4000	8 11 99 89¾ 78¾ 76½	Parisi E	b 116	49.40	73-21	Winning Lane 116nk Long Gone John 1161¼ Revy 116½	Outrun	11
25Aug86- 3Atl	fst	1 1/16	:48⅘ 1:13⅗ 1:44⅖	3+Clm 5000	3 4 31½ 57¾ 718 719	Aristone M	b 116	44.10	64-18	Hey Man 1221 He Can Fly 1138 Plentyofsense 1168	Tired	7
15Aug86- 7Atl	fst	1 1/16	:47⅖ 1:12⅘ 1:46⅗	3+Clm 5000	4 8 825 824 817 612¼	Aristone M	b 116	25.00	60-21	He Can Fly 116nk Pursuit Jr. 1161 Spirited Song 1164½	Outrun	8
7Aug86- 2Atl	fst	1 1/16	:47⅕ 1:12⅖ 1:46⅗	3+Clm 5000	5 6 69¼ 69 69¾ 67	Drury G E	b 116	12.50	65-22	Staden Frater 120½ He Can Fly 1161 DH LanierPlace113	No factor	8
26Jly86-10Atl	fm	1⅛ Ⓣ	:49⅕ 1:12⅘ 1:50⅗	3+Clm 8000	1 11 1117 1127 1127 1121½	Drury G E	b 112	29.40	61-13	Steve's A'gogo 105½ Take A Mile 1161½ Spruce MeUp1162	Outrun	11
17Jly86- 3Atl	my	1 1/16	:47⅘ 1:13⅗ 1:46⅘	3+Clm 4000	2 4 46½ 41½ 13 16	Drury G E	b 116	4.10	71-22	Neutral Smith 1166 Mustache 1162JigTimeRuler1202½	Ridden out	7
5Jly86- 1Atl	fst	1 1/16	:46⅖ 1:11⅖ 1:44⅗	3+Clm 6000	2 7 614 56½ 46½ 25	Drury G E	b 112	31.70	77-15	Hey Man 1165 Neutral Smith 112½ Ample Power 1121	Drifted out	7
26Jun86- 6Atl	fst	6f	:21 :45⅕ 1:11⅕	3+Clm 8000	6 6 620 623 622 614	Drury G E	b 112	73.50	72-21	Ship Mint 120nk Nepo 1167½ Manulla Gold 1122	Outrun	6

LATEST WORKOUTS Jun 23 Atl 3f my :37⅘ bg Jun 20 Atl 6f fst 1:15 b Jun 13 Atl 5f fst 1:01⅕ h

E.

10–1

Noble Camel
Own.—Tolle F

B. g. 7, by Bold Forbes—Vaguely Deb, by Vaguely Noble
$4,000 Br.—Gatto-Roissard L (Ky)
Tr.—Tolle Floyd M

116

Lifetime	1987	14	0	1	1	$3,920
57 9 8 6	1986	10	3	3	0	$21,737
$68,893	Turf	7	2	0	1	$5,752

29Jly87- 6Pna	fst	1 70	:47⅗ 1:14⅖ 1:45⅘	3+Clm 4000	5 4 411 45 34½ 43	Intelisano G P Jr	116	17.10	63-28	PrinceAviator1162JacksonSummit116hdGrandOldHerbie1161	Wide	11
10Jly87- 8Bir	fst	1 1/16	:48⅕ 1:13⅘ 1:47	3+Clm 3500	2 5 64¼ 65¼ 59½ 513	Arroyave R D	122	3.30	71-17	Devil Gari 1223½ Fire Away 122nk Triple Dip 1221½	Outrun	8
20Jun87- 9Bir	my	1	:49 1:15⅕ 1:42⅗	3+Clm 3500	3 7 69½ 710 47½ 410	Arroyave R D	122	4.00	6[illegible]-29	Guard Proud 117noCutTheCrop122ndDerekAndMe12210	No threat	7
20Jun87-Evening Program												
7May87- 6Bir	sly	1⅛	:48 1:12⅘ 1:53⅗	Clm 5000	12 10 1016 1023 1123 928	Espinoza J C	114	6.10	63-11	Mission In Orbit 1191 All My Dust 1173¾ Pounce 1141	Outrun	12
29Apr87- 2Bir	fst	1 1/16	:48 1:12⅘ 1:46⅗	Clm 5000	5 6 68½ 57¾ 56 42	Espinoza J C	116	2.50	93-08	Yahvkatwairio 116nk Woozley 1091 Beaufouette 122¾	Late bid	10
11Apr87- 2Bir	fst	1 70	:48 1:14⅖ 1:46⅗	Clm 5000	8 9 98 78¼ 55½ 43¼	St Leon G	115	11.40	— —	Transparty 115no Scottie Will 1212¾ Ancient Myth 115½	Rallied	12
3Apr87- 4Bir	fst	1 1/16	:47⅘ 1:13 1:46⅘	Clm 5000	11 5 56 66 94¾ 63	Ketner R	115	15.30	— —	Mission In Orbit 115¾ AnSnucks115nkStarExcelier1211½	No factor	12
3Apr87-Awarded fifth purse money												
19Mar87- 3Bir	fst	1 1/16	:49⅕ 1:14⅗ 1:48⅘	Clm 6250	5 5 53 85¾ 66½ 55½	St Leon G	115	3.40	— —	Holme Play 1151¾ Oconto 1181½ Mission In Orbit 1152	No factor	8
11Mar87- 4Bir	fst	1	:47⅘ 1:12⅘ 1:40	Clm 6250	2 5 53¼ 56½ 53¾ 35¾	Ketner R	115	2.60	— —	Clear TheCourt115½MissionInOrbit1155½NobleCamel1153¾	Rallied	6
3Mar87- 4Bir	fst	1 1/16	:46⅖ 1:13⅕ 1:46⅗	Clm 6250	7 3 3nk 32 22½ 24	Ketner R	115	4.90	— —	Color Me Gone 1154 Noble Camel 1152 HolmePlay115hd	2nd best	8

F.

5–1

Reck's Courage
Own.—Juliano C

Ch. g. 6, by Teddy's Courage—Recreational, by Hilarious
$4,000 Br.—Crocker B & Betty (Fla)
Tr.—Porreca Thomas

116

Lifetime	1987	9	0	1	0	$1,123
45 6 3 3	1986	24	3	2	2	$13,399
$32,980						

27Jly87-10Atl	fst	1 1/16	:46⅕ 1:11⅗ 1:46⅘	3+Clm 4000	7 8 916 613 35 2hd	Landicini C Jr	116	31.60	71-20	Pirgar 109hd Reck's Courage 116nk Mongo King 1162½	Rallied	12
6Jly87- 7Atl	fst	1 1/16	:47⅘ 1:13⅘ 1:48⅖	3+Clm 4000	7 7 77½ 76¼ 89½ 77½	Douthall J D	116	23.50	55-29	Wise Mike 1091 Royal Pharoah 1162 Mongo King 1161½	Outrun	9
26Jun87- 4Atl	fst	6f	:22⅗ :46 1:12⅗	3+Clm 4000	5 8 1012 1012 99¾ 66	Douthall J D	116	44.90	74-21	Winning Lane 116nk Long Gone John 1161¼ Revy 116½	Outrun	11
25May87-11GS	fst	1⅛	:47⅘ 1:12⅘ 1.54	3+Clm 4000	11 3 33 513 1227 1231½	Vigliotti M J	116	33.50	27-24	Devil's Ticket 1163½Lyphard'sBlue1163½CockyRocky116½	Stopped	12
30Apr87- 4GS	fst	1 1/16	:47⅗ 1:13⅖ 1:46⅘	3+Clm 4000	6 9 97¾ 97 88¾ 512	Lukas M	116	69.10	62-24	Roundwood 109no Snakemaker 1163 Arsalan 1167	Outrun	11
10Apr87- 7GS	fst	1	:47⅕ 1:13 1:40⅗	Clm 4000	9 7 57 1012 1019 1025	Lukas M	116	45.10	47-24	Harrah For Pag 1162½ Got My Grey109½Shakemaker1165½	Outrun	12
19Mar87- 7GS	fst	1 70	:47⅖ 1:14⅗ 1:46⅘	Clm 4000	12 6 66½ 56½ 914 1025¼	Lukas M	116	11.90	40-30	Roundwood 109½ For Eternity 116¾ Medieval Master 1167	Tired	12
7Mar87- 4GS	fst	6f	:22⅗ :46⅗ 1:12⅘	Clm 4000	4 10 108¼ 910 79 512	Lukas M	116	8.80	66-31	Alpa Quick 1165 Running Jet 1164½ Slady's Ruller 1162	Wide	11
26Feb87- 7GS	fst	6f	:22⅗ :46⅕ 1:12⅘	Clm 5000	3 10 129¼ 1214 99½ 64¼	Cantagallo G J	116	24.20	74-28	Le Chem De Fer 1163StrideOfJoy116noSuburbanite116no	Late bid	12
16Dec86- 9Pha	fst	1	:47⅘ 1:12⅘ 1:39⅖	3+Clm 5000	2 2 31½ 89½ 1017 1020¼	Lukas M	116	57.50	57-19	Le Roi Roque 1163 Wise Move 1092½ Mr. Walter 1162	Tired	12

LATEST WORKOUTS Jun 20 Atl 3f fst :38 b

G.

8–1

Culater's Gattor *
Own.—Bianchi C

B. g. 7, by Son Excellence—Culateralligator, by Ye
$4,000 Br.—Bianchi C R (Pa)
Tr.—McCaslin John

116

Lifetime	1987	4	0	1	0	$922
45 5 4 3	1986	9	0	2	0	$2,151
$20,322						

20Jly87- 4Atl	fst	1 1/16	:46⅗ 1:12 1:48⅕	3+Clm 4000	8 4 39 513 57½ 56¾	Pagan N	116	6.50	57-31	Metal Hero 116hd Mustache 1163½ Pirgar 1093	Tired	9
13Jly87- 2Atl	fst	1 1/16	:48⅖ 1:15 1:49	3+Clm 4000	9 3 3nk 2hd 24 28½	Pagan N	116	13.60	51-32	Anvil Man 1168½Culater'sGattor1162½NeutralSmith1164½	2nd best	9
6Jly87- 7Atl	fst	1 1/16	:47⅘ 1:13⅘ 1:48⅖	3+Clm 4000	9 2 21 34 64¼ 67½	Pagan N	116	5.40	55-29	Wise Mike 1091 Royal Pharoah 1162 Mongo King 1161½	Tired	9
27Jun87- 2Atl	fst	6f	:22⅗ :46⅕ 1:13⅕	3+Clm 4000	5 4 44 46 52½ 63½	Pagan N	116	*2.40	72-18	TotalBypass116¾Egle'sTouch1161½CtchTheRedeye116nd	No threat	10
30Jun86- 2Atl	fst	1 1/16	:47⅗ 1:12⅗ 1:45⅘	3+Clm 4000	4 2 2hd 23 24 27	Ravelich M	116	6.80	69-23	He Can Fly 1097 Culater's Gattor 1165 Cadson 116no	2nd best	9
21Jun86- 3Atl	fst	6f	:22⅖ :46⅖ 1:12⅘	3+Clm 4000	6 4 66¼ 53½ 43 42½	Leasure W P	116	5.90	75-22	Slam 116nk Jefrod 1161¼ Quadruler 1161	No factor	8
7Jun86- 5Del	fst	6f	:23 :46⅘ 1:12⅕	Clm 3500	3 9 42½ 22 22 22½	Garcia P L	120	6.70	77-19	HatchetMan'sBest1202½Culter'sGttor1201½NeverStop1204	Gamely	12
26May86- 5Del	fst	5f	:22⅖ :46⅕ :58⅖	3+Clm 3500	3 7 62½ 62¾ 56½ 55¾	Cole M A	117	23.30	88-17	Legal Rights 115nk Dig On 1203½ Hilary's Charger 120½	No factor	10
1Mar86- 3Pen	fst	6f	:22⅕ :46⅕ 1:12	Clm 4000	3 7 77¾ 77¾ 711 69¾	Guerra L R	113	20.40	74-22	Special Notice 115nk Rollo 1143½ Elegant Kid 116½	Outrun	7
17Feb86- 6Pen	sly	6f	:22⅘ :46⅘ 1:13⅗	3+ⓈClm 5000	4 8 4nk 33 24 75¼	Guerra L R	113	10.40	71-37	Brooktot 1181 Foolish Fact 1063 Frosty Marsh 119nk	Tired	8

LATEST WORKOUTS Jly 4 Atl 4f fst :50⅖ b Jun 26 Atl 3f fst :36⅕ b Jun 18 Atl 4f fst :48⅗ b Jun 13 Atl 3f fst :36⅕ h

H.

5–1

Shamfastic — Dk. b. or br. g. 5, by Sham—Always Wanted, by Advocator

Own.—Blue Crest Farms — $4,000 — Br.—Floyd & Isaacs (Ky) — Tr.—Anderson William D — 116

Lifetime							
23 3 2 0	1987	4	0	0	0	$964
$29.301	1985	17	2	2	0	$21,017
	Turf	8	1	2	0	$15,355

20Jly87- 4Atl	fst	1$\frac{1}{16}$	:46⅗	1:12	1:48⅕	3↑ Clm 4000	2	2	2^{3}	2^{7}	4^{7}	$4^{6½}$	Melendez J D	b 116	*2.30	57-31	Metal Hero 116^{hd} Mustache 116^{3½} Pirgar 109^{3}	Weakened	9
9Jly87- 8Atl	sly	6f	:22	:45⅗	1:11⅗	3↑ Clm 6000	1	5	4^{4}	5^{8}	$4^{6½}$	4^{8}	Melendez J D	b 114	5.60	76-23	TheHiveFive120^{1}WingedAttrction116^{6½}BrightPrinc116^{½}	No factor	5
30Jun87- 4Mth	fst	6f	:22⅖	:45⅗	1:11⅕	3↑ Clm 6000	10	3	$4^{4½}$	4^{6}	5^{7}	$4^{9½}$	Diaz L^{7}	b 107	6.30	74-13	Rowdy Rebel119^{4}GemsForSale114^{hd}B.G.'sCharger114^{5½}	No factor	10
17Jun87- 4Mth	fst	6f	:22⅕	:45⅗	1:11⅖	3↑ Clm 5000	6	5	$5^{7½}$	5^{7}	$5^{6½}$	6^{9}	Diaz L^{7}	b 109	9.40	74-16	MnJmGrn109^{3½}Rjb'sWllyPop116^{4½}StndrdDvton109^{no}	Lacked rally	10
5Nov85- 4Med	fst	6f	:22⅗	:45⅗	1:11	Clm 10000	1	3	2^{hd}	$5^{3¾}$	8^{11}	$9^{14½}$	Melendez J D	b 116	5.10	73-20	Gosh Oh Glory 116^{1¼} Exuberant Way 116^{¾} Ideal 109no	Tired	10
11Oct85- 2Med	fst	1$\frac{1}{16}$	:46⅘	1:12	1:43⅕	Clm 16000	2	1	1^{1}	$7^{6½}$	7^{10}	$10^{33½}$	Melendez J D	b 115	12.40	53-18	Spirit of Satan 110^{8½}Breastplate113^{¾}BreakDancing117^{½}	Gave way	11
21Sep85- 4Med	fst	6f	:23	:46⅖	1:12⅗	Clm c-12500	7	7	$4^{2½}$	$9^{9¼}$	8^{12}	$8^{10¾}$	Madrid A Jr^{5}	b 114	*1.80	68-23	Neverhadadinner116^{hd}ExuberntWy111^{5}SomeProspect116^{½}	Outrun	12
11Sep85- 1Med	fst	6f	:22⅘	:46⅕	1:11⅗	Clm 10000	1	3	3^{1}	1^{hd}	1^{4}	1^{5}	Madrid A Jr^{5}	b 111	2.60	84-20	Shmfstic111^{5}CrolinKingdom116^{1½}BourbonPlese107^{hd}	Ridden out	8
20Aug85- 5Atl	sly	5½f	:21⅘	:45⅗	1:05	3↑ Clm 20500	1	3	2^{1}	2^{2}	2^{2}	$4^{2¼}$	Walford J	b 109	2.20	87-22	Defier 110^{nk} Sea Horse 116^{1} Cool Sprint 116^{1}	Tired	5
30Jly85-10Mth	gd	1$\frac{1}{16}$	Ⓣ:47	1:11⅗	1:44⅕	Clm 25000	5	2	$1^{½}$	$5^{2¾}$	9^{12}	$9^{22¾}$	Antley C W	b 115	*2.40	61-19	Auction Evader 117^{2} T. Bear Esquire111^{¾}RoaringEagle111^{½}	Tired	11

I.

20–1

Andrashan — Dk. b. or br. g. 5, by Toronto—Make Sense, by Our Dad

Own.—Sager Nancy — $4,000 — Br.—Watson J D (Fla) — Tr.—Sager Stanley W — 116

Lifetime						
44 1 5 4	1987	3	0	0	0	$42
$12,754	1986	22	0	3	3	$5,372
	Turf	1	0	0	0	

27Jly87-10Atl	fst	1$\frac{1}{16}$	:46⅕	1:11⅖	1:46⅘	3↑ Clm 4000	4	3	$3^{8½}$	5^{13}	6^{10}	$6^{8¼}$	Parrilla R	116	70.00	63-20	Pirgar 109no Reck's Courage 116^{nk} Mongo King 116^{2½}	Weakened	12
19Jly87- 6Del	fst	6f	:22⅗	:46⅖	1:12⅖	3↑ Clm 3500	12	4	8^{2}	$8^{6½}$	11^{13}	$11^{9¼}$	LaLande L^{5}	112	99.70	70-20	Silver Turn 110no Wilgrenof's Chase110^{½}Precaster117^{¾}	No factor	12
8Jly87- 6Del	fst	6f	:22⅕	:45⅖	1:11⅗	Clm 3500	8	10	$8^{8¾}$	10^{14}	11^{19}	$11^{15¼}$	Cabrera S	120	50.30	69-22	Briar Ritz 120^{3½} Winter Guise 113^{3½} Silver Turn 113^{1½}	Outrun	12
24Oct86-11Rkm	fst	6f	:22⅖	:46⅖	1:13⅘	3↑ Clm 3000	4	11	11^{13}	10^{14}	8^{11}	$6^{8½}$	Chavis S T^{5}	111	3.80	66-31	Roman River 119^{2½} Bald Reviewer 116^{3¼} DiamondBid122^{1}	Outrun	12
17Oct86- 2Rkm	fst	6f	:22⅕	:46⅘	1:14⅖	3↑ Clm 3000	7	6	$6^{9½}$	7^{8}	$7^{4¼}$	$2^{2½}$	Chavis S T^{5}	111	*2.10	69-29	Big Bet 119^{2½} Andrashan 111^{¾} Bald Reviewer 116^{½}	Fin. well	10
10Oct86-10Rkm	fst	6f	:22⅘	:47⅖	1:14⅕	3↑ Clm 3000	9	12	$8^{6¼}$	$5^{2¾}$	4^{6}	5^{5}	Chavis S T^{5}	111	*2.40	68-28	FloridaFire119^{2¾}JusticeOutFront118^{½}Look'sFaster119^{½}	Slow start	12
3Oct86- 2Rkm	fst	6f	:22⅗	:46⅗	1:13⅖	3↑ Clm 3000	5	10	$8^{6½}$	7^{7}	4^{4}	2^{3}	Heath M^{5}	111	12.00	74-23	Golden Carillon 113^{3} Andrashan 111^{1½} Florida Fire 114^{1¼}	Rallied	12
17Sep86- 5Del	fst	1$\frac{1}{16}$	:48	1:13⅘	1:49⅕	3↑ Clm 5000	4	9	$8^{7¾}$	$9^{8¼}$	9^{22}	8^{15}	Cappacetti G	116	5.00	47-28	Counselor's Kids 106^{1} County Cat 119^{½} Trapper Hill 116^{4}	Outrun	12
10Sep86- 5Del	fst	6f	:22⅘	:46⅘	1:13⅘	3↑ Clm 5000	7	11	$11^{8½}$	10^{7}	5^{5}	$3^{2¼}$	Merida E^{7}	b 109	5.50	70-28	RunForPresident106^{1½}ColletonCounty111^{¾}Andrshn109^{nk}	Mild bid	12
25Aug86- 2Atl	fst	1$\frac{1}{16}$	:47⅘	1:12⅗	1:45⅗	3↑ Clm 4000	3	2	$2^{½}$	$4^{2½}$	5^{6}	$5^{8¾}$	Bin G S^{5}	b 111	64.40	68-18	Rollwiththepunchs109^{¾}SirBrndBoy111^{no}BrvNwDy117^{3}	Weakened	9

LATEST WORKOUTS Jly 5 Pha 4f fst :50 b — Jun 28 Pha 5f fst 1:04⅖ bg — Jun 21 Pha 5f fst 1:03⅗ b — Jun 14 Pha 4f fst :52 b

J.

20–1

Cherokee Reef — B. g. 4, by Cherokee Fellow—Reefing, by Limelight

Own.—McShane Stable — $4,000 — Br.—Onett G L (Fla) — Tr.—Barbierre Carol Ann — 116

Lifetime						
31 1 2 5	1987	16	0	2	3	$2,409
$6,446	1986	15	1	0	2	$4,037

27Jly87-10Atl	fst	1$\frac{1}{16}$	:46⅕	1:11⅖	1:46⅘	3↑ Clm 4000	3	12	10^{17}	8^{19}	7^{11}	$5^{6½}$	Nunez E O	b 116	22.80	65-20	Pirgar 109^{hd} Reck's Courage 116^{nk} Mongo King 116^{2½}	No factor	12
17Jly87- 7Atl	fst	6f	:22⅖	:46⅘	1:13⅕	3↑ Clm 4000	10	12	12^{25}	10^{13}	8^{8}	$6^{7½}$	Nunez E O	b 116	52.00	68-27	Greypont 116^{1} Manulia Gold 109^{1½} Potomac Glow 113^{1}	Outrun	12
8Jly87- 6Del	fst	6f	:22⅕	:45⅖	1:11⅗	Clm 3500	6	5	12^{15}	12^{15}	9^{18}	8^{12}	Petersen J L	b 120	5.10	72-22	Briar Ritz 120^{3½} Winter Guise 113^{3½} Silver Turn 113^{1½}	Outrun	12
23Jun87-10Rkm	sly	6f	:22⅘	:47⅘	1:15⅗	3↑ Clm 3000	10	10	10^{13}	$7^{9½}$	3^{6}	$3^{3¾}$	Nelson D^{5}	b 111	6.20	62-34	Take the Heat 113^{3¼} Apache Devil114^{½}CherokeeReef111^{4½}	Rallied	12
14Jun87- 1Rkm	fst	6f	:23	:48⅖	1:16⅗	3↑ Clm 3000	6	6	$5^{2½}$	$3^{2½}$	$2^{½}$	2no	Nelson D^{5}	b 111	8.30	61-31	Silorsdon'tdnce116^{no}CherokeeReef111^{1¾}TnnStnn119^{2¼}	Just failed	9
6Jun87- 9Rkm	hy	6f	:23⅗	:49⅗	1:17⅖	3↑ Clm 3000	2	4	$9^{7¼}$	8^{5}	$7^{8½}$	9^{8}	Nelson D^{5}	b 111	*1.90	49-49	BrodwyDrmr116^{1¾}Conquror'sTz116^{nk}Scot'sInjnJo116^{hd}	No factor	12
22May87- 9Rkm	fst	6f	:23⅗	:46⅖	1:12⅗	3↑ Clm 3000	6	3	$5^{3¼}$	$5^{4½}$	$5^{1¾}$	$3^{2¾}$	Martin C W	b 116	4.60	78-15	GreatScout113^{nk}Sailorsdon'tdnce111^{2½}CherokeeReef116^{1}	Rallied	10
15May87- 9Rkm	fst	6f	:23⅗	:49	1:18	3↑ Clm 3000	4	9	11^{11}	$10^{8¼}$	6^{5}	$5^{5¾}$	Amiss D^{5}	b 111	8.50	46-42	El Sordo 116^{3¾} Lookout Rock 111^{1} C'est la Guerre 113^{½}	Rallied	11
8May87- 9Rkm	fst	6f	:22⅘	:47⅗	1:16⅘	3↑ Clm 3000	11	8	11^{13}	11^{13}	7^{9}	$3^{1½}$	Ortega r Jr^{5}	b 111	16.20	59-35	Century One 111^{1} War Treaty 112^{nk} Cherokee Reef 111^{½}	Rallied	12
28Mar87- 6Tam	gd	6f	:22⅘	:46⅕	1:12⅘	Clm 7500	5	4	$7^{7¼}$	6^{11}	6^{11}	$7^{13½}$	Werre E	b 120	44.40	67-21	Nash Malone 111^{5} Gallant Idol 119^{1¼} Street Beat 118^{1¼}	Outrun	8

LATEST WORKOUTS Jly 23 Atl 3f fst :38 b — Jly 6 Del 3f fst :37⅘ b

K.

3–1

Jackson Summit — B. c. 4, by Sham—Class Act, by Wajima

Own.—August K — $4,000 — Br.—Isaacs Sidney E (Ky) — Tr.—Manchio Robert S — 116

Lifetime						
31 1 4 3	1987	15	0	1	3	$3,449
$10,793	1986	16	1	3	0	$7,344
	Turf	1	0	0	0	$171

29Jly87- 6Pha	fst	1^{70}	:47⅗	1:14⅖	1:45⅘	3↑ Clm 4000	2	10	7^{17}	$6^{7½}$	4^{5}	2^{2}	Lukas M	b 116	13.60	64-26	PrinceAviator116^{2}JcksonSummit116^{hd}GrndOldHerbie116^{1}	Rallied	11
7Jly87- 9Pha	fst	1$\frac{1}{16}$	:48⅗	1:14⅖	1:48⅗	3↑ Clm 4000	1	5	4^{3}	6^{4}	$6^{5¾}$	5^{3}	Lukas M	b 116	11.50	58-27	Mazorquero Red 119^{½} MetalHero116^{1½}C.B.Alliance119^{1}	No factor	9
30Jun87- 2Pha	fst	1$\frac{1}{16}$	:48	1:13⅗	1:48⅖	3↑ Clm 4000	4	8	5^{7}	$4^{6½}$	4^{5}	$5^{4½}$	Lukas M	b 116	24.70	57-25	NoholmVntr116^{1¾}GoldnHoofprnts112^{2½}MzorqrRd119^{nk}	No factor	8
13Jun87-10GS	fst	6f	:22	:45⅘	1:12⅖	3↑ Clm 4000	8	11	11^{18}	10^{17}	9^{14}	8^{9}	Lukas M	b 116	32.30	71-24	Private Showing 109^{hd} Salsa Jo 116^{3½} Jumpin J. 116^{1½}	Outrun	11
6Jun87- 2Mth	fst	1$\frac{1}{16}$	:48⅘	1:13⅖	1:46	3↑ Clm 5000	2	8	$5^{1¾}$	$6^{4¾}$	7^{11}	7^{19}	Hernandez C	b 115	32.30	56-17	Ginny's Choice 115no Nickie's Mark 115^{5½} In Control 115^{½}	Tired	8
3May87-10Pen	sly	1⅛	:49⅗	1:15⅕	1:55⅗	Clm 5000	9	8	3^{nk}	2^{2}	2^{4}	3^{6}	Hagan D P	b 116	12.20	68-18	Nezami 116^{6} Forever Power119^{hd}JacksonSummit116^{2¼}	Weakened	11
24Apr87- 2Pen	sly	1$\frac{1}{16}$	:48⅗	1:14⅗	1:50	Clm 5000	3	8	$6^{7½}$	$5^{6½}$	5^{5}	4^{4}	Hagan D P	b 116	10.20	52-28	AukeBayBluff122^{1½}ShineOnDewn111^{½}DecemberCourt122^{2}	Outrun	10
12Apr87- 6Pen	fst	1½	:49⅗	2:09⅘	2:36⅗	Clm 5000	1	4	$4^{3¼}$	3^{2}	$4^{4¼}$	4^{9}	Hagan D P	b 116	*1.80	65-20	Kumalo 122^{½} Blazing Ben 122^{5} Happy Gala 105^{3½}	Weakened	7
6Apr87- 4Pen	sly	1^{70}	:47⅕	1:11⅘	1:43⅖	Clm 5000	2	7	4^{8}	3^{9}	5^{16}	6^{23}	Hagan D P	b 116	5.00	60-22	Play Yard 116^{18} Shine On Dewan 111^{nk} Kickin Chicken116^{2}	Tired	9
28Mar87- 5Pen	fst	1⅛	:47⅖	1:12⅗	1:52⅘	Clm 5000	8	7	$5^{9½}$	$4^{1½}$	$4^{4½}$	$3^{6¾}$	Hagan D P	b 116	16.60	81-19	Belleau Wood 116^{3¾} Play Yard 109^{3} JacksonSummit116^{no}	Rallied	11

47. In this maiden-claiming sprint, estimate the fair or acceptable odds on *Crystal Fox*.

6th Santa Anita

6 FURLONGS. (1.07⅗) MAIDEN CLAIMING. Purse $18,000. 3-year-olds. Weight, 118 lbs. Claiming price $50,000; if for $45,000 allowed 2 lbs.

Tissar's Babe
OLIVARES F 2-0 — 116
Own.—Weeden J R
B. c. 3, by In Tissar—Haiku, by Olden Times
Br.—Hawk M & Carolyn (Cal) — 1987 1 M 0 0
Tr.—Fulton Jacque — $45,000 — 1986 3 M 0 0
Lifetime 4 0 0 0

27Mar87-6SA 6f :214 :453 1:113ft 86 116 42 42½ 75½ 1215½ Olivares F 3 M45000 64-23 Plum Wishfull,CoolTalker,Suggen 12
27Mar87—Lost whip 1/4
22Oct86-6SA 6f :212 :443 1:104ft 35 117 44½ 47 816 921 Olivares F 10 [S]Mdn 63-23 L.B.Jklin,SwtwtrSprngs,HlrousFlrt 11
9Oct86-6SA 6f :212 :442 1:102ft 131 117 1116 1115 915 815¼ Olivares F7 [S]Mdn 71-21 BrodwyPoint,HomRunHro,Clvinist 11
30Aug86-4Dmr 6f :22 :452 1:102ft 32 118 63¾ 65½ 1016 1018½ Vergara O6 [S]Mdn 67-10 ASignOfLuck,AtTheRitz,NstyNskr 10
30Aug86—Veered in start
●Apr 3 SA 3f ft :343 h — Mar 23 SA 5f ft 1:011 h — Mar 17 SA 6f ft 1:162 hg — Mar 12 SA 5f ft 1:00 h

Playing For Keeps
DELAHOUSSAYE E U-N — 118
Own.—Hemming Jr & Marino
Ch. c. 3, by Properantes—Playing the Game, by Windy Sea
Br.—Hemming Brothers (Cal) — 1986 0 M 0 0
Tr.—Luby Donn — $50,000
Lifetime 0 0 0 0
Apr 3 SA 6f ft 1:141 hg — Mar 29 SA 6f ft 1:133 h — Mar 23 SA 6f ft 1:142 hg — Mar 16 SA 5f ft 1:004 h

Watch Tim Go
PATTON D B U-N — 113⁵
Own.—Wild Plum Farm
B. c. 3, by Tim The Tiger—Watching Clouds, by Nodouble
Br.—Wild Plum Farm (Colo) — 1987 0 M 0 0
Tr.—Tuck Mary Lou — $50,000 — 1986 0 M 0 0
Lifetime 0 0 0 0
Apr 3 SA 5f ft 1:023 h — Mar 26 SA 5f ft :594 hg — Mar 19 SA 5f ft 1:014 h — Mar 9 SA 6f ft 1:16 h

Be Scenic
SOLIS A 0-0 — 118
Own.—Hooper F W
Ch. c. 3, by If This Be So—Scenic Flight, by Crozier
Br.—Hooper F W (Fla) — 1987 3 M 1 0 $5,500
Tr.—Fenstermaker L R — $50,000 — 1986 7 M 1 3 $13,625
Lifetime 10 0 2 3 $19,125

12Mar87-4SA 6f :214 :444 1:092ft 3¼ 118 108 77 45½ 28 Solis A 9 M50000 83-19 Pewter, BeScenic,PolynesianChief 12
12Mar87—Lugged in; wide into, through stretch
21Feb87-6SA 6f :211 :44 1:10 ft 24 118 810 810 77¾ 53¾ Solis A 1 Mdn 84-14 McKnzPrnc,CrystlFox,ToghKnght 10
21Feb87—Bumped start
8Feb87-6SA 6f :22 :452 1:101ft 27 118 108¾ 87 66½ 48 Solis A 2 Mdn 79-14 Cndi'sGold,Affstr,McKenziePrince 10
8Feb87—Broke slowly, checked 1/2, wide into stretch
26Oct86-4SA 6½f :22 :45 1:162ft 10 117 88¼ 79¾ 75¼ 37½ Day P 7 Mdn 80-16 SludYPesets,MlibuPrince,BeScenic 9
12Oct86-6SA 1 1/16 :47 1:122 1:454ft 6 112⁵ 53 74¾ 1112 1020¾ Black C A 1 Mdn 51-21 FlyingNewsboy,FstDelivry,ChssSt 11
12Oct86—Veered in start
1Oct86-6SA 1 :461 1:112 1:374ft 13 112⁵ 31 22 22½ 34¾ Black C A 2 Mdn 74-18 PrinceSssfrs,SwordChrger,BScnic 10
1Oct86—Checked at 7 1/2
7Sep86-6Dmr 6f :221 :453 1:101ft 7½ 117 32 36 410 59¾ Stevens G L 1 Mdn 77-13 Agn'sBolgr,Crbonro,WindwoodLn 11
24Aug86-6Dmr 6f :223 :461 1:104ft 4 112⁵ 3½ 41½ 46½ 45 Black C A6 Mdn 79-12 ExbrntFlng,BooBoo'sBckro,Prmtng 8
9Aug86-4Dmr 6f :221 :453 1:102ft 18 112⁵ 52 51¾ 32 25 Black C A6 Mdn 81-14 LgunNtiv,BScnic,BooBoo'sBuckroo 8
9Aug86—Lugged in stretch
23Jly86-6Dmr 5½f :22 :45 1:031ft 27 112⁵ 57 56¾ 48½ 310¾ Black C A8 Mdn 84-12 Chisos, Laguna Native, Be Scenic 8
23Jly86—Troubled trip
Apr 4 SA 5f ft 1:014 h — Mar 27 SA 4f ft :484 h — Mar 20 SA 5f ft 1:004 h — Mar 9 SA 6f ft 1:18 h

Polynesian Chief
PINCAY L JR 3-0 — 118
Own.—Lewis-Lewis-Rahe
B. g. 3, by Effervescing—Exotic Sway, by T V Lark
Br.—Speed Farms (Ky) — 1987 6 M 1 3 $10,550
Tr.—Lewis Craig A — $50,000 — 1986 3 M 0 0 $1,275
Lifetime 9 0 1 3 $11,825

12Mar87-4SA 6f :214 :444 1:092ft 3¼ 118 63 44½ 55¾ 38½ Pincay L Jr 11 M50000 82-19 Pewter, BeScenic,PolynesianChief 12
12Mar87—Bobbled start
28Feb87-4SA 6f :214 :443 1:104ft 4½ 118 75½ 66½ 67¼ 33 Pincay L Jr 3 M50000 81-17 VctoryPs,MmrsOfBrnz,PlynsnChf 12
28Feb87—Broke out, bumped; wide into stretch
8Feb87-4SA 1 1/16 :463 1:12 1:44 ft 18 117 1hd 22 817 828½ Delahoussaye E 4 Mdn 52-14 NoMrker,NstyNskr,RichesToRiches 8
8Feb87—Lugged out
28Jan87-4SA 6f :22 :453 1:114ft 6¾ 118 1½ 2½ 21 22½ Pincay L Jr 4 M50000 76-21 Reconnoitring,PolynsinChif,Gntout 9
19Jan87-6SA 1 1/16 :482 1:13 1:454ft 18 117 11 2½ 43 79 Cordero A Jr5 Mdn 63-25 Rupperto, Chatanga, All Cat 9
19Jan87—Lugged out
1Jan87-6SA 6f :214 :452 1:102ft 7 118 77½ 88 57½ 312 Pincay L Jr7 M50000 74-19 HappyInSpce,Wily,PolynesinChief 12
22Jun86-3Hol 5½f :22 :451 1:043ft 33 118 56½ 56 66½ 67 Pedroza M A 5 Mdn 84-06 Qualify, Chisos, Fleet Tito 7
4Jun86-5Hol 5f :221 :46 :581ft 31 118 54¼ 56½ 67 610¾ Pedroza M A6 Mdn 84-18 HonkyTonkDncr,Chsos,BrodwyPnt 10
21May86-5Hol 5f :22 :452 :58 ft 31 118 45½ 44½ 46¼ 46¾ Solis A6 Mdn 89-13 MstrflAdvct,BrdyPnt,HnkTnkDncr 10
Apr 3 SA 4f ft :484 h — Mar 20 SA 4f ft :48 h — Mar 8 SA 4f gd :482 h — Feb 25 SA 3f gd :364 h (d)

Toohip Joey Gotogo
MEZA R Q   118
Own.—Kolbe Barbara T

B. c. 3, by Nantequos—Mrs Usinevetche, by Bold Joey
Br.—RndMdowFm—Vienna—Andrsn (Cal)   1987   0 M 0 0
Tr.—Carno Louis R $50,000   1986   0 M 0 0
Lifetime   0 0 0 0

Apr 3 SA 5f ft 1:02¹ h   Mar 29 SA 6f ft 1:14 hg   Mar 24 SA 5f ft :59⁴ h   Mar 19 SA 5f ft 1:00³ h

---

Memories Of Bronze
STEVENS G L   118
Own.—Ward P

Ch. c. 3, by Nostalgia—Bronze Bobbie, by Tobin Bronze
Br.—Ward P (Cal)   1987   3 M 2 0 $6,575
Tr.—French Neil $50,000   1986   1 M 0 0
Lifetime   4 0 2 0 $6,575

18Mar87-1SA 6½f :22 :44⁴ 1:16³ft 7½ 117 99 710 66½ 58½ Pincay L Jr⁵ [S]Mdn 79-17 PostgmIntrvw,ScndLgnd,GldRshn' 9
28Feb87-4SA 6f :21⁴ :44³ 1:10⁴ft 5½ 118 10¹¹ 99¾ 77½ 22¾ Stevens G L⁹ M50000 81-17 VctoryPs,MmrsOfBrnz,PlynsnChf 12
28Feb87—Stumbled start
4Jan87-2SA 6f :21² :45¹ 1:12 sy 13 118 9¹⁰ 86¾ 42 2½ Stevens G L⁵ M32000 77-22 Cremeri,MmorisOfBronz,FrigidAir 11
31Oct86-4SA 6f :21⁴ :45¹ 1:11⁴ft 9½ 118 9¹³ 9¹⁰ 69 67½ Meza R Q⁵ [S]M32000 72-16 RoyalRadar,NeverSmoke,TakeOne 12
Mar 31 SA 4f ft :49² h   Mar 13 SA 4f ft :48¹ h   Mar 8 SA 4f gd :49² h   Feb 23 SA 6f ft 1:14 hg

---

Inter Alia
ORTEGA L E   116
Own.—Pulliam C N

Ch. g. 3, by Pedrillo—Via Royal, by Blood Royal
Br.—Pulliam C N (Cal)   1987   3 M 0 0 $450
Tr.—Pulliam Vivian M $45,000   1986   1 M 0 0
Lifetime   4 0 0 0 $450

27Mar87-6SA 6f :21⁴ :45³ 1:11³ft 144 116 12¹⁵11⁸½11⁸¾ 55¼ Ortega L E⁴ M45000 75-23 Plum Wishfull,CoolTalker,Guggen 12
27Mar87—Hesitated start
16Jan87-4SA 1¼ :47⁴ 1:13¹ 1:45³ft 54 116 43½ 42 68½ 8¹⁴½ Simpson B H⁵ M35000 59-18 OBatth,TurnBckJohn,Tost`heCjun 12
16Jan87—Broke slowly
1Jan87-6SA 6f :21⁴ :45² 1:10²ft 65 116 11¹²10¹¹ 8¹⁰ 7¹⁶ Simpson B H⁶ M45000 70-19 HappyInSpce,Wily,PolynesinChief 12
1Jan87—Very wide stretch
3Nov86-6SA 1 :47² 1:11³ 1:37¹ft 50 117 89½ 915 923 928 Black C A £ [S]Mdn 54-14 FastDelivery,NstyNskr,HilriousFlirt 9
3Nov86—Broke out, bumped
Apr 4 SA 5f ft 1:00³ h   Mar 20 SA 6f ft 1:14⁴ hg   Mar 14 SA 5f ft 1:00⁴ h   Mar 8 SA 4f gd :48 h

---

Robigus
TORO F   116
Own.—Double K Farms

Dk. b. or br. c. 3, by Agitate—Charge Hilarious, by Fast Hilarious
Br.—Double K Farms (Cal)   1987   0 M 0 0
Tr.—Tinsley J E Jr $45,000   1986   0 M 0 0
Lifetime   0 0 0 0

Apr 3 SA 6f ft 1:14 hg   Mar 28 SA 6f ft 1:14¹ hg   ●Mar 22 SA 5f m :59 h   Mar 16 SA 5f ft 1:00⁴ h

---

Golden Beau
MCHARGUE D G   118
Own.—Golden Eagle Farm

B. c. 3, by Beau's Eagle—Witch Creek, by Our Native
Br.—Mabee Mr—Mrs J C (Cal)   1986   0 M 0 0
Tr.—Sadler John W $50,000
Lifetime   0 0 0 0

Apr 7 SA 3f ft :34¹ h   Apr 1 SA 5f ft 1:01³ hg   Mar 26 SA 6f ft 1:14 hg   Mar 21 SA 6f ft 1:15¹ h

---

Crystal Fox 4 - N (123)
VALENZUELA P A   118
Own.—Elia—Elia—Oak Crest Farm

Dk. b. or br. c. 3, by Raise a Cup—Grey Beard, by Grey Dawn II
Br.—Summerhill & OakCrestFarms (Ky)   1987   3 M 1 0 $5,850
Tr.—Mandella Richard $50,000   1986   1 M 0 1 $1,130
Lifetime   4 0 1 1 $6,980

14Mar87-6SA 6f :21³ :44⁴ 1:09 ft 3 118 43 33½ 47½ 4¹¹½ Valenzuela P A 12 Mdn 82-16 Looknforthbgon,Pnsco,ChstntFrz 12
21Feb87-6SA 6f :21¹ :44 1:10 ft 6½ 118 35½ 36 23½ 22½ Valenzuela P A 5 Mdn 85-14 McKnzPrnc,CrystlFox,ToghKnght 10
21Feb87—Broke slowly
18Jan87-6SA 6½f :22 :45¹ 1:16⁴ft 13 117 2ʰᵈ 2½ 33½ 69½ Valenzuela P A 10 Mdn 77-19 FlyngFlgs,ChrtThStrs,ErnYrStrps 12
23Aug86-4 ga 6f :21⁴ :44⁴ 1:11²ft *6-5 120 65½ 65½ 46½ 3½ Loseth C² Mdn 78-15 Sam's Derby, PutEmUp,CrystalFox 7
Apr 5 SA 5f ft 1:00⁴ h   Mar 31 SA 5f ft 1:03 h   Mar 19 SA 5f ft 1:02³ h   Mar 3 SA 5f ft 1:02² h

---

A. 8–5

B. 5–2

C. 7–2

D. 9–2

48. The stakes below was a companion stakes to Monmouth Park's Grade 1 Haskell Invitational of Aug. 1, 1987. When racetracks program these multistakes cards on big days, the races become contentious and the handicapping unusually difficult. Finding the single solid selection at acceptable odds becomes problematic. But for the best of handicappers a handful of

outstanding overlays with greater than reasonable chances can be counted on to appear. The best bet in the Pukka Princess Stakes was

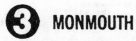

3 MONMOUTH

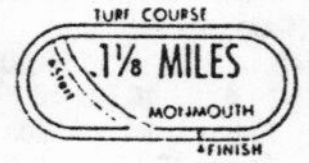

1⅛ MILES. (Turf). (1.49⅖) 4th Running THE PUKKA PRINCESS STAKES (1st Div). Purse $30,000 added. Fillies and mares, 3-year-olds and upward. Free nominations close Tuesday, July 28. $100 supplementary nominations close Thursday, July 30. $300 to pass the entry box, $200 to start with $30,000 added of which 60% of all monies to winner; 20% to second, 11% to third; 6% to fourth and 3% to fifth. Weights, 3-year-olds, 115 lbs.; older, 122 lbs. Non-winners of $30,000 twice in 1987, allowed 3 lbs.; $15,000 twice since April 1, 5 lbs.; $12,500 twice in 1987, 7 lbs.; $12,000 since June 1, 9 lbs. (Maiden, claiming and starter races not considered.) Closed with 73 nominations.

A.
6–1

***Fieldy** — B. f. 4, by Northfields—Gramy, by Tapioca II
Br.—Ribes P (Ire)
Own.—Arriola & Seltzer — Tr.—Skiffington Thomas J — 113
Lifetime 12 3 3 0 $70,830 — 1987 5 2 1 0 $30,230 — 1986 3 0 0 0 — Turf 12 3 3 0 $70,830
Entered 30Jly87- 9 MTH , finished 1

10May87- 9GP gd 1 Ⓣ:47⅕ 1:11⅕ 1:35⅕ 3+Ⓕ Very One H 8 2 2²½ 3² 4²¾ 6⁵½ Perret C 115 *2.60 88-10 First Prediction114noThirtyZip113¹LadyoftheNorth110²½ Faltered 11
16Apr87-10GP sf 1½ Ⓣ:50 2:05⅘ 2:31⅗ 3+Ⓕ Orchid H 7 3 5⁸ 7⁹¾ 10¹⁷ 9¹⁵¾ Pezua J M 116 9.00 51-33 AnkaGermania117noSingularBequest116³Ivor'sImage119hd Outrun 14
18Apr87-Grade II
1Apr87- 8GP gd 1 1/16 Ⓣ:48⅘ 1:13⅗ 1:44⅕ 3+Ⓕ Suwanee H 8 3 4²½ 4³ 3² 1² Perret C 114⁴ 6.80 79-21 DH Fama 114² DH Fieldy 114² Navarchus 114no Driving 8
1Apr87-Grade III; Dead heat; Run in divisions
15Mar87-11GP fm 1 1/16 Ⓣ:47⅗ 1:12⅗ 1:44⅗ Ⓕ Alw 15000 6 6 5⁵ 3¹ 1½ 1³ Vasquez J 117 *1.50 77-18 Fieldy 117³ Bell Mountain 122nk Tuscadoon 117⁶½ Drew clear 12
22Feb87-11Hia fm 1 1/16 Ⓣ 1:42⅗ Ⓕ Alw 18000 3 10 8⁵ 4¹½ 2hd 2nk Cordero A Jr 116 *1.50 86-13 Rivers Of Mist 116nk Fieldy 116nk Debonairly122⁴½ Best of others 12
21Jly86 ♦5StCloud(Fra) gd*1 1:40⅘ Ⓣ Prix Motrico 6⁴½ Guignard G b 122 4.25 — — Shecky Red 128¹ Greenphly 124no Neferou 128nk Prom.wknd 8
14May86 ♦5Longchamp(Fra) gd*1 1:42⅕ Ⓣ Ⓕ Prix de Bagatelle 9⁷¾ Lequeux A 126 6.75 — — Sad Akarad 126nk CArnetSolaire126¾ OnlyStar121hd Well pl.tired 9
13Apr86 ♦4Longchamp(Fra) sf*1 1:52⅗ Ⓣ Ⓕ Prix de la Grotte(Gr3) 9 Eddery P 128 10.00 — — NorthernPremier128hd Beaujolaise128hd Carntion128nk No threat 13
6Oct85 ♦2Longchamp(Fra) gd*1 1:37⅘ Ⓣ Ⓕ PrixMarcelBoussac(Gr1 2nk Lequeux A 121 71.00 — — MidwayLady121nk Fieldy121nk Riverbride121¹½ Prom.game finish 15
3Sep85 ♦6Evry(Fra) gd*1 1:42⅕ Ⓣ Prix Herod 2nk Guignard G 124 2.75 — — Flying Trio 126nk Fieldy 124hd Donacika 124² Game finish 7
LATEST WORKOUTS Jly 28 Bel 4f fst :49⅖ b Jly 23 Bel 6f fst 1:14⅖ b Jly 17 Bel 5f fst 1:01⅕ h Jly 12 Bel 5f fst 1:02⅖ b

B.
10–1

Glorious Calling — B. f. 4, by Nijinsky II—Blue Blood, by Round Table
Br.—Madden Preston (Ky)
Own.—Singer C B — Tr.—Tesher Howard M — 113
Lifetime 14 2 2 1 $29,864 — 1986 5 1 0 1 $5,460 — Turf 14 2 2 1 $29,864

21Jly87- 7Mth gd 1 1/16 Ⓣ:48 1:12⅗ 1:44 3+Ⓕ Eatontown H 9 5 5⁴½ 7³¾ 8⁴ 7⁵ Hernandez C b 111 46.60 80-14 Bairullah 111¹½ Princely Proof 116¹½ Krotz 118¹ Outrun 10
21Jly87-Run in divisions
4Jly87- 9Mth gd 1 1/16 Ⓣ:48⅘ 1:12⅘ 1:45 3+Ⓕ Plesnt Girl 7 8 7⁷ 5⁵ 6²¾ 4⁴¾ Baird E T b 113 6.00 75-20 Krotz 115³ Princess Natalie 113¹½ New Dawn 113no No threat 9
8Jun87- 8Bel fm 1 1/16 [T]:48⅘ 1:12⅖ 1:43⅗ 3+Ⓕ Alw 28000 6 5 7⁷½ 6⁵½ 5⁴ 2nd Davis R G b 117 12.20 82-24 SpctculrBv111noGloriousCling117¹½Vvdimprssion117no Sharp try 7
18Apr87-10GP sf 1½ Ⓣ:50 2:05⅘ 2:31⅗ 3+Ⓕ Orchid H 2 12 13¹⁶ 13¹⁶ 9¹⁵ 7⁹ Molina V H b 109 16.20f 56-33 AnkaGermania117noSingularBequest116³Ivor'sImage119hd Outrun 14
18Apr87-Grade II
8Apr87- 7GP fm *1 Ⓣ 1:38⅘ Ⓕ Alw 15000 2 10 10⁷ 7⁴½ 3³ 1no Pezua J M b 119 3.00 86-14 Glorious Calling 119no Shapely Lines 117² SunnyLiz117¹½ Driving 11
22Feb87-11Hia fm 1 1/16 Ⓣ 1:42⅗ Ⓕ Alw 18000 8 12 12¹⁰ 10⁷ 7⁷½ 5⁶½ Perret C b 119 2.20 80-13 Rivers Of Mist 116nk Fieldy 116nk Debonairly 122⁴½ No threat 12
3Feb87- 8Hia fm *1⅛ Ⓣ 1:50 Ⓕ Alw 15000 3 8 8¹⁷ 8¹¹ 3²½ 2¾ Perret C b 122 5.60 80-21 TopoftnRinbow116¾GloriousCling122nkRhond'sRing116³ Gamely 10
13Jan87- 7Hia fm *1 1/16 Ⓣ 1:45⅗ Ⓕ Alw 17200 5 8 6²½ 5³½ 8⁸¾ 8¹⁰½ Perret C b 122 2.40 59-23 Allegroum 116¹½ Rhonda's Ring 116¹½ Rainy Gal 116no Outrun 9
9Dec86- 3Crc fm *1 1/16 Ⓣ 1:44⅗ 3+Ⓕ Md Sp Wt 8 6 5³½ 3² 1³ 1⁷½ Perret C b 120 *1.60 84-16 GloriousCalling120⁷½MajesticFwe115²Julien'sWy120¾ Ridden out 10
25Sep86- 4Bel fm 1¼ [T]:50⅘ 1:39⅗ 2:04⅗ 3+Ⓕ Md Sp Wt 8 5 4¹½ 1hd 1½ 3² Lovato F Jr b 118 7.00 69-20 Isn't She Nice 118nk Shiitake118¹¾GloriousCalling118³¾ Weakened 10
LATEST WORKOUTS Jly 1 Mth Ⓣ 4f fm :51 b (d) Jun 23 Mth Ⓣ 5f sf 1:07 b (d) Jun 16 Mth 6f fst 1:13 h

C.
8–1

Grande Couture — B. f. 4, by Miswaki—Grande Vogue, by Vaguely Noble
Br.—Wimborne Farm Inc (Ky)
Own.—Wimborne Farms — Tr.—Lundy Richard J — 113
Lifetime 13 3 2 2 $50,767 — 1987 5 1 1 1 $16,787 — 1986 8 2 1 1 $33,980 — Turf 13 3 2 2 $50,767

4Jly87- 9Mth gd 1 1/16 Ⓣ:48⅘ 1:12⅘ 1:45 3+Ⓕ Plesnt Girl 4 7 8⁸ 6⁷ 5¹½ 5⁵ Perret C 114 *2.50 75-20 Krotz 115³ Princess Natalie 113¹½ New Dawn 113nk Blocked 9
19Jun87- 8Mth fm 1 1/16 Ⓣ:48⅗ 1:13 1:45⅕ 3+Ⓕ Alw 17000 4 11 8⁶ 1½ 1¹½ 1²¾ Perret C 118 *1.00 79-22 Grande Couture 118²¾ Kitonia 118²¾ Socialwan 118³ Driving 11
2Jun87- 8Mth fm 1 1/16 Ⓣ:48 1:11⅘ 1:42⅗+ 3+Ⓕ Alw 17000 6 6 5⁵ 2² 2² 2¹½ Perret C 118 2.20 87-15 Allegedum 118¹½GrandeCouture118⁷FeastYourEyes118¹ Game try 8
21May87- 7Bel gd 1 1/16 Ⓣ:50 1:14⅗ 1:46⅘ 3+Ⓕ Alw 26000 1 6 6⁶ 5⁴½ 5⁸ 6¹¹½ Guerra W A 119 3.50 50-34 GracefulDrby1115¾LughingLdy119nkVividImpression119no Outrun 6
6May87- 6GP fm *1 1/16 Ⓣ 1:43⅘ Ⓕ Alw 16000 5 6 6¹³ 5⁴½ 4² 3¾ Velez J A Jr 117 4.00 86-10 Boogie's Joy 117hd Doodie Do 117¾GrandeCouture117² Mild rally 7
14Nov86 ♦5StCloud(Fra) sf*1 1:51⅗ Ⓣ Ⓕ Prix Coronation 8⁶½ Gibert A 128 13.00 — — Sandbank 123¹½ Mineralogie 123½ Mercadah 123nk No threat 13
21Sep86 ♦6Longchamp(Fra) gd*1 1:47 Ⓣ Ⓕ Prix de Liancourt 1hd Gibert A 121 9.10 — — GrandeCouture121hd Mercadd118nk Minerlogie118nk Bid, up late 11
24Aug86 ♦5Deauville(Fra) sf*1 1:49⅗ Ⓣ Ⓕ Prix de laCalonne 6³ Lequeux A 121 4.00 — — RiverDancer 124nk Riverbride 121¹½ Jiflora 128½ Well up, wknd 10
13Jly86 ♦6StCloud(Fra) gd*1 1:42⅕ Ⓣ PrChristian de l'Hermite 3² Asmussen C 120 4.75 — — PersianMews 123¹ GreenMount123¹ GrandeCouture120¾ Fin.well 9
24Jun86 ♦6Chantilly(Fra) gd*1 1:43⅗ Ⓣ Ⓕ Prix des Lilas 4½ Guignard G 123 4.50 — — ScrletFlutter119hd Ticrock119hd Sentimentlit123nk Prom thruout 14
LATEST WORKOUTS Jly 18 Mth 5f fst 1:03⅗ b Jly 11 Mth 3f fst :37⅗ b Jly 1 Mth 5f fst 1:02⅗ b Jun 26 Mth 3f fst :37⅘ b

D.
5–2

***Cecina** — B. f. 3, by Welsh Saint—Hill of Howth, by Sassafras
Br.—Burns M (Ire)
Own.—Lawribru Stable — Tr.—Fisher John R S — 108
Lifetime 10 3 3 0 $48,307 — 1987 5 3 0 0 $37,615 — 1986 5 M 3 0 $10,692 — Turf 10 3 3 0 $48,307

11Jly87- 8Pim fm 1 1/16 Ⓣ:47⅗ 1:11 1:42⅘ Ⓕ SummerGust 2 5 4⁵ 3³½ 4²½ 4³½ Bracciale V Jr 117 *1.30 86-12 Spectacular Bev 119² Ice Devise 113nk Heartleaf113¹½ Weakened 8
11Jly87-Run in divisions
16Jun87- 8Mth fm 1 Ⓣ:48⅕ 1:12⅗ 1:37 Ⓕ Revidere 6 6 6⁵ 6²½ 1hd 1¹ Antley C W 114 3.10 90-08 Cecina 114¹ Easter Mary 114² Pour Me Out 120² Driving 8
16Jun87-Run in divisions
6Jun87- 4Mth fm 1 1/16 Ⓣ:47⅗ 1:12 1:43⅗+ 3+Ⓕ Alw 15000 8 6 5²½ 5¹¾ 1¹½ 1⁵ McCauley W H 112 *2.10 83-11 Cecina 112⁵MidnightChildII118noNancy'sBasket118hd Ridden out 10
22May87- 7Bel gd 1 1/16 [T]:49 1:12⅗ 1:44⅗ 3+Ⓕ Alw 27000 8 3 4² 3² 5³½ 7¹⁰½ Antley C W 110 *1.60 69-22 Purify 114²½ Nastique 112³ Dr.'s Debutante 113²½ Gave way 8

11May87- 2GS 1m 5f [T]:21⅘ :45⅗ :58 3+[F]Md Sp Wt 2 5 45 45 41½ 1½ Wilson R 114 *.30 97-09 Cecina 1141½ Zarlette 107no Advanced State 1141½ Driving 7
25Oct86♦4Leopardst'n(Ire) gd 7f 1:30 [T] Leopardstown Stakes(Gr3) 41½ Roche C 119 14.00 — — Antic Boy 122hd Mulnollande 1221½ Bluebird 126no Fin. well 13
20Sep86♦4Leopardst'n(Ire) fm 1 1:41 [T][F]SilkenGliderStk(Gr3) 21 Kinane M J 116 10.00 — — Inanna 1191 Cecina 1152½ Trek 1191½ Finished well 10
7Sep86♦2PhoenixPk(Ire) gd 7f 1:19⅗ [T][F]GoffsSilverFlashStakes 73½ Craine S 117 16.00 — — Simple Taste 117¾ Erinoale 122no [D]Down Again 126nk Impeded 13
16Aug86♦4Curragh(Ire) gd 7f 1:28⅕ [T] Tyros Stakes 22½ Craine S 117 5.00 — — Tapolite 1242½ Cecina 1171½ DiamondSeal 120¾ Prom thruout 8
29Jly86♦6Galway(Ire) sf*7f 1:36⅘ [T][F]Claregalway Plate(Mdn) 21 Browne M T 126 *1.25 — — Big Break 1261 Cecina 1265 Daybreak Lady 1216 Fin. well 15
LATEST WORKOUTS Jly 7 Fai tr.t 4f fst :48⅗ b ●Jly 2 Fai tr.t 5f fst 1:02 b Jun 2 Fai tr.t 4f fst :47 b

E.

20–1

Pleasant Landing
B. f. 4, by Honest Pleasure—Mystical Landing, by Mystic II
Br.—Valentine Mrs M (Pa)
Tr.—Jennings Lawrence W
Own.—Dee-Pee Stable
113
Lifetime 23 6 2 1 $83,161 | 1987 4 1 0 0 $11,300 | 1986 9 1 1 0 $18,090 | Turf 2 2 0 0 $24,600

4Jly87- 6Mth fst 170 :45⅕ 1:09⅕ 1:40⅕ 3+[F]Alw 25000 6 4 511 39½ 45½ 46 Krone J A 115 16.50 89-10 Natania 115no Girl Powder 1191½ Tricky Squaw 1224½ Lacked rally 8
9Jun87- 5Mth fm 1 [T]:47⅕ 1:11 1:36⅘ 3+[F]Clm 50000 7 4 43½ 21 12 11½ McCauley W H 115 5.40 91-11 Pleasant Landing 1151½ Ida Lewis 115no Fancy Pan 115no Driving 9
28Apr87- 9GP fst 6f :22⅗ :46⅕ 1:11 [F]Alw 20000 4 6 54½ 64¾ 66¾ 56¾ Fires E 115 24.00 77-25 Fleur De Soleil 1172½ Chiteca 1152½ Clever Dream 1151½ No factor 7
13Jan87- 8Pna fst 6½f :23 :47 1:20⅘ [F]Alw 15000 8 6 75½ 811 814 812 Black A S 115 6.70 57-41 Ida Lewis 1151 Madam Joy 1152 Confirmed Affair 117½ No factor 8
28Dec86- 8Lrl fst 6½f :23 :47 1:19⅕ [F]Cameo 6 5 65½ 53 54 43½ Ladner C J Jr 119 55.80 82-24 Azrbijni116½SmrterByTheDy1222½Mrs.Pumphrey113nk Raced wide 6
28Dec86-Run in divisions
13Dec86- 6Lrl fst 6f :22⅗ :46⅗ 1:12 3+[F]Alw 20000 4 7 914 813 811 67½ Ladner C J Jr 115 82.60 76-20 Run Pearl 1203 Breathless Wind 119no Stay Home 1171½ Outrun 9
25Nov86- 9Lrl fst 1 :47⅕ 1:13⅗ 1:39⅕ 3+[F]Alw 20000 3 8 86¾ 86½ 86½ 78¾ Ladner C J Jr 114 38.70 67-23 Lady Loose 1192 Canoodling 1171½ Valid Doge 117nk Outrun 8
14Nov86- 9Lrl fst 1 :46⅕ 1:12 1:37⅘ 3+[F]Alw 19000 6 7 74¾ 63¾ 66¾ 68¾ Saumell L 116 22.80 74-15 CosmicTiger1141½Tattiebogie1221½MeddlinMggie1191½ No factor 7
30Oct86- 8Lrl fst 1 :46⅗ 1:10⅘ 1:36 [F]A Arundel H 8 6 87½ 914 918 824 McCarron G 115 19.30 68-17 Burt's Dream 1143½ NowYourTeapotlin1108½Vacherie1143 Outrun 9
30Oct86-Grade III; Run in Divisions
22Sep86- 8Pim fst 6f :23⅗ :46⅘ 1:12⅗ 3+[F]Alw 18000 2 6 67 67½ 68½ 64½ McCarron G 115 33.00 79-26 Linka 117nk Amerricoinrest 122hd Stay Home 1172½ Trailed 6
LATEST WORKOUTS Jly 28 Mth 5f fst 1:01⅕ h Jly 23 Mth 4f fst :52 b Jly 17 Mth 5f fst 1:02⅘ b Jly 11 Mth 4f fst :47⅘ h

F.

5–1

***Sorayah**
B. m. 5, by Persian Bold—Regal Splendour, by Sovereign Path
Br.—Wachman N H (Ire)
Tr.—Ruhsam Jonathan L
Own.—Donahue Mrs T P
115
Lifetime 28 7 1 3 $129,190 | 1987 3 1 0 0 $34,368 | 1986 11 2 0 1 $50,707 | Turf 27 7 1 3 $129,190

8Jly87- 8Bel gd 1¹⁄₁₆ [T]:48⅕ 1:12 1:45⅗ 3+[F]Alw 45000 4 6 69¾ 54½ 3nk 1hd Davis R G 115 4.50 74-2ꟹ Sorayah 115hd Soliciting 1101 Lake Champlain 1223¾ Driving 6
27Jun87- 8Bel sf 1⅜ [T]:54 1:46 2:23⅘ 3+[F]Sheepsh'd H 2 2 2½ 11 42½ 411¾ Davis R G 111 6.30 26-E2 Steal A Kiss 1113¾ Videogenic 1175 Graceful Darby 1125 Tired 5
27Jun87-Grade II
10Jun87- 7Bel fm 1¹⁄₁₆ [T]:48⅕ 1:11⅘ 1:42⅘ 3+[F]Alw 45000 2 6 69 64½ 55 65 Guerra W A 117 6.30 82-17 Tappiano 1101¾ Loa 117¾ Reel Easy 117nk Wide str. 7
17Jly86- 7Bel fm 1¼ [T]:51⅘ 1:41 2:03⅗ 3+[F]Handicap 3 3 32½ 31 15 15½ Velasquez J 112 1.80 77-21 Sorayah 1125½ Charlotte Amalie 1092¾LuckyTouch110no Drew off 6
28Jun86- 8Bel fm 1⅜ [T]:49⅕ 1:37⅕ 2:14 3+[F]Shepshead H 3 5 86½ 98½ 74½ 55 Velasquez J 112 11.90 82-19 Possible Mate 1243 Tremulous 112nk Dawn's Curtsey 1131¾ Wide 9
28Jun86-Grade II
19Jun86- 8Bel fm 1¹⁄₁₆ [T]:48 1:11 1:42 3+[F]Handicap 3 8 75 4¾ 1½ 33 Vasquez J 113 12.00 88-18 Aberuschka 1162½ Dismasted 116½ Sorayah 1137 Weakened 8
3May86- 9Hia fm 1⅛ [T] 1:47⅗ 3+[F]Blck Heln H 4 5 68½ 79 69 43½ Lester R N 112 18.60 91-17 Shocker T. 1192½ Lake Country 118¾ Dawn's Curtsey114hd Rallied 8
3May86-Grade II
19Apr86-10Hia fm 1¹⁄₁₆ [T] 1:41⅗ 3+[F]Columbina H 5 11 138½ 1310 810 64 Lester R N 113 27.20 86-14 So She Sleeps 115½ Lake Country 119no Bairullah 112½ Mild bid 16
19Apr86-Grade III
5Apr86- 9Hia fm 1¹⁄₁₆ [T] 1:42 3+[F]Hia B Cup H 7 4 47 31½ 33 67½ Velasquez J 115 16.00 81-20 Top Socialite 115½ Duty Dance 1173½ Dawn's Curtsey 1171½ Tired 12
22Mar86- 7Hia sf *1⅛ [T] 1:52⅕ [F]Alw 16000 6 8 99½ 87 47 1nk Velasquez J 115 3.30 70-30 Sorayah 115nk Commended 1172½ Charming Peggy 115nk Driving 11
LATEST WORKOUTS Jun 3 Bel 4f gd :50⅘ b

G.

15–1

With A Twist
B. f. 4, by Fappiano—Classy Twist, by Twist The Axe
Br.—Grace I Br Inc & Newstead Farm (Va)
Tr.—Jerkens H Allen
Own.—Centennial Farm
113
Lifetime 24 3 11 1 $117,490 | 1987 11 1 4 0 $47,870 | 1986 13 2 7 1 $70,420 | Turf 11 1 3 0 $31,080

28Jun87- 8Del fm 1⅛ [T]:47⅘ 1:12 1:43 3+[F]New Castle H 1 8 87½ 84¾ 73¾ 74 Santagata N 118 12.20 85-06 Twixtsiusive 1161½ Air Dancer 113hd Tattiebogle 1141 Outrun 13
10Jun87- 7Bel fm 1¹⁄₁₆ [T]:48⅕ 1:11⅘ 1:42⅘ 3+[F]Alw 45000 4 7 79½ 77½ 67 55 Belmonte J F5 117 5.20 82-17 Tappiano 1101¾ Loa 117¾ Reel Easy 117nk No speed 7
31May87- 4Bel fst 1⅛ :45⅘ 1:10⅗ 1:43⅕ 3+[F]Alw 31000 4 7 712 68 47½ 28½ Belmonte J F5 116 4.80 78-17 Wee Dram 1138½ With A Twist 116hd Pasamosi 1193½ Held place 7
11May87- 8Bel fst 1⅛ :47⅗ 1:11⅘ 1:45⅕ 3+[F]Alw 45000 6 7 76 35½ 31½ 1½ Belmonte J F5 114 4.60 76-22 WithATwist114½Mrs Beeton1192CherokeChill1191 Strong handling 7
29Apr87- 8Aqu gd 1⅛ :48⅕ 1:12⅗ 1:51⅗ 3+[F]Alw 28000 4 5 61¾ 1hd 31 31½ Hernandez R 119 7.60 75-22 Proudest Babe119no[D]GentleSpirit1121½WithATwist1192 Steadied 6
29Apr87-Placed second through disqualification
18Apr87-10GP sf 1½ [T]:50 2:05⅗ 2:31⅗ 3+[F]Orchid H 9 13 1216 1218 1421 1416½ Soto S B 110 16.20f 50-33 AnkaGermania117noSingularBequest1163Ivor'sImage119hd Outrun 14
18Apr87-Grade II

H.

12–1

***Mistress**
Ch. m. 6, by Mr Long—Realidad, by Rigel II
Br.—Haras Santa Amelia (Chile)
Tr.—Sheppard Jonathan E
Own.—Sheppard J E
113
Lifetime 26 5 2 1 $50,852 | 1987 7 0 0 1 $2,500 | 1986 8 0 0 0 $3,114 | Turf 9 0 1 1 $12,344

8Jly87- 8Pha fm 1 [T]:48⅕ 1:12⅘ 1:37 3+[F]Clm 47500 7 5 513 55½ 54 34 Castaneda K 115 2.60e 89-09 Tzarade 1141½ Mamies Greek 1162½ Mistress 115¾ Rallied 7
13Jun87- 9GS fm 1⅜ [T]:50⅕ 1:39 2:16 3+[F]Vineland H 6 5 65 712 76 77¾ Krone J A 107 38.10 90-06 Cadabra Abra 114no Santiki 1133 Bug Eyed Betty 1152 Outrun 8
13Jun87-Grade III
9May87- 9Pim fm 1½ [T]:49⅗ 2:04⅗ 2:28⅗ 3+Dixie H 4 7 713 76½ 67 69 Krone J A 104 74.50 85-06 Akabir 115¾ Little Bold John 117nk Vilzak 1135 No threat 9
9May87-Grade II
18Apr87- 6GS gd 1¹⁄₁₆ :47⅕ 1:12⅘ 1:45 3+[F]Alw 16000 3 7 721 718 717 727½ Fitzgerald J F 115 19.40 55-18 Double Smooth 1154 Wny Jan 1201½ Miss Nata Lu 1152 Trailed 7
7Apr87- 9GS gd 1¹⁄₁₆ :46⅘ 1:12⅗ 1:46⅗ 3+[F]Alw 16000 4 7 721 722 612 412 Fitzgerald J F 115 28.70 64-20 Wny Jan 1152 Pennant Winner 1153½ Miss Nata Lu 1156½ Outrun 7
1Feb87- 5Aqu gd 2¼ [·]:55 3:35⅗ 4:02⅗ Handicap 6 3 410 511 513 519½ Thibe.. R J 108 18.60 27-26 Oversea 1141 Needle Walk 1044½ Beat It Kid 1104 Tired 6
10Jan87- 6Aqu gd 170 [·]:48.. 1:13 1:41⅗ [F]Alw 45000 7 7 714 721 618 620½ Davis R G 115 22.00 70-10 Floating 1155½ Plastic Lady 1153¾ Robin's Rob 115nk Outrun 7
13Dec86- 7Med fst 1¹⁄₁₆ :45⅗ 1:10 1:41⅘ 3+[F]Alw 25000 8 8 821 816 66½ 52½ Krone J A 115 4.40e 92-09 Koluctoo'sRobin1141Aldn'sAmbition115nkChfingDsh1171 Late bid 8
5Dec86- 7Med fst 1¹⁄₁₆ :47 1:12⅗ 1:45⅗ 3+[F]Alw 25000 6 7 715 77 73½ 54 Krone J A 115 15.80e 72-21 Floating 1152½ Brindy Brindy 1101½ Jackie McCleaf115hd Blocked 7
8Nov86- 1Aqu sly 1⅜ :48⅗ 1:38⅘ 2:20 3+[F]Alw 40000 2 7 726 727 721 736 Cordero A Jr 115 6.40 45-22 VintageChmpgne1133CourgeousKren1082BethsS.. 1158½ Trailed 7
LATEST WORKOUTS ●Jly 27 Pha 5f fst 1:00⅘ b Jly 21 Pha 5f fst 1:02⅗ b Jly 7 Pha 4f fst :49⅗ b ●Jun 29 Pha 6f fst 1:16 b

I.
30–1

Native Mommy ✻ — Ch. f. 4, by Qui Native—Swaps Mommy, by Swaps
Br.—Beller S (Ky)
Tr.—Pierce Joseph H Jr
Own.—Irwin Richard D
113
Lifetime 14 5 0 2 $57,950 — 1987 3 0 0 0 $1,500 — 1986 10 5 0 1 $55,450 — Turf 5 2 0 0 $21,960

21Jly87- 7Mth gd 1⅛ Ⓣ:48 1:12⅘ 1:44 3↑ⒻEatontown H 7 2 21 41¾ 109½ 1017¾ McCauley W H 113 21.10 67-14 Bairullah 1111½ Princely Proof 1161½ Krotz 1181 Tired 10
21Jly87-Run in divisions
11Jly87- 8Mth fst 1⅛ :47 1:10⅘ 1:43⅗ 3↑ⒻAlw 25000 1 1 11 11 22½ 48 Hernandez C 115 4.00 80-14 Toscana 1154 Funistrada 1153½ Tattiebogle 115½ Faltered 5
4Jly87- 9Mth gd 1⅛ Ⓣ:48⅘ 1:12⅘ 1:45 3↑ⒻPlesnt Girl 6 2 21 1hd 1hd 66 Hernandez C 113 14.30 74-20 Krotz 1153 Princess Natalie 1131½ New Dawn 113nk Weakened 9
22Nov86- 9Med fst 1⅛ :46⅗ 1:11⅕ 1:45 ⒻHny Bee H 4 2 35 43½ 810 818¼ McCauley W H 116 10.50 60-20 I'm Sweets 121nk Clabber Girl 114no SmarterByTheDay1161 Tired 8
22Nov86-Grade III
6Nov86- 9Med my 1 :47⅕ 1:12 1:37⅕ ⒻHandicap 4 2 2hd 12 12 11¾ McCauley W H 117 *1.40 89-20 Native Mommy 1171¾ Brief Remarks 1178 Vacherie 1189 Driving 5
23Oct86- 5Med fm 1⅛ [T]:47⅗ 1:11⅕ 1:42⅖ 3↑ⒻAlw 18000 4 2 13 13½ 16 18 McCauley W H 114 1.60 91-14 NtivMommy1148TruChompon1141½DoublAdvntg119nk Ridden out 6
11Oct86- 6Med fm 1 Ⓣ:47 1:11 1:36 3↑ⒻAlw 17000 2 1 11½ 11½ 14 17 Romero R P 114 7.60 94-06 Native Mommy 1147 Riverquill1141RushForGold1122½ Ridden out 10
23Sep86- 9Med fst 1⅛ :48 1:12⅗ 1:44⅗ 3↑ⒻAlw 17000 2 5 42½ 22 35½ 412¼ Rocco J 113 *1.60 68-23 True Chompion 1115Quillo'sLove1076Deby'sLight1171½ Weakened 7
12Sep86-10Med fst 1⁷⁰ :47⅗ 1:12⅗ 1:42⅘ 3↑ⒻAlw 15000 2 2 31½ 12 14 16 Rocco J 113 19.90 82-20 Native Mommy 1136 Kitonia 112¾ Shooting Script 1132 Driving 9
25Aug86- 9Mth fst 1 :47 1:12 1:37⅘ 3↑ⒻAlw 16000 1 1 1hd 2hd 2½ 31¾ McCauley W H 113 *2.10 82-16 Mrs Beeton 114no Kitonia 1101¾ Native Mommy 1136 Weakened 8
LATEST WORKOUTS Jly 30 Mth 4f fst :47⅘ h Jly 3 Mth 3f my :37 b (d) Jun 23 Mth 7f fst 1:26 hg

J.
12–1

Kim Kimmie — B. f. 4, by Baldski—Game Gypsy, by Greek Game
Br.—Farnsworth Farm & Sucher M (Fla)
Tr.—Heard Dennis
Own.—Lane G E
113
Lifetime 11 2 4 1 $31,236 — 1987 4 1 1 0 $15,211 — 1986 7 1 3 1 $16,025 — Turf 10 2 3 1 $29,436

21Jly87- 9Mth gd 1⅛ Ⓣ:49⅗ 1:12⅘ 1:43⅘ 3↑ⒻEatontown H 4 1 1½ 1hd 1hd 43½ Krone J A b 109 16.30 82-14 Cadabra Abra 1182½ Treasure Map 115hdSpruceFir1211 Weakened 6
21Jly87-Run in divisions
7Jly87- 7Mth gd 1⅛ Ⓣ:49 1:13⅗ 1:45⅕ 3↑ⒻAlw 17000 8 1 11 11½ 1hd 22¾ Krone J A b 120 2.70 76-17 Biddy 1112¾ Kim Kimmie 1203 Their World 1113 Game try 8
15Jun87- 6Mth fm 1⅛ Ⓣ:47⅗ 1:12 1:43⅘ 3↑ⒻAlw 15000 7 1 11 11 13½ 1¾ Krone J A b 118 *2.10 86-11 Kim Kimmie 118¾ Dissembler 1131 Lady Asterisk 1115½ Driving 8
5Jun87- 3Bel sf 1⅛ [T]:51 1:16 1:47⅘ ⒻClm 70000 4 1 11½ 3½ 33½ 59¼ Krone J A b 113 9.30 54-38 SweetMaryBinn1123ForCertain1174½TopoftheRainbow113hd Tired 6
1Nov86- 9Med fm 1⅛ Ⓣ:46⅕ 1:11⅕ 1:42⅘ 3↑ⒻBetties Doll 6 1 11 21 1119 1124¾ Krone J A b 109 10.60 63-15 Kitty Touch 119hd Subjective 113nk Darbrielle 1131½ Stopped 11
20Sep86- 9Crc fm *1⅛ Ⓣ 1:45⅗ ⒻEgret H 9 4 44 33 42½ 74 Smith A Jr b 112 20.70 90-07 SingularBequest115nkJudy'sRedShoes123nkReglPrincess1142 Tired 12
10Sep86- 5Crc fm *1⅛ Ⓣ 1:46⅘ 3↑ⒻAlw 12500 7 1 12 11½ 2hd 22½ Aviles O B b 116 *1.70 86-11 Cali Doctor Barry1142½KimKimmie1162MatteFinish1121 Game try 9
1Sep86- 5Crc fm *1⅛ Ⓣ 1:45⅗ 3↑Alw 14900 4 2 22 21 43 34¾ Aviles O B b 113 4.60 92-03 Hold That Fool112½KinkysStar1124KimKimmie113nk Saved show 7
9Aug86- 5Crc fm *1 Ⓣ 1:37⅘ 3↑ⒻAlw 14700 1 1 21 22 1½ 2no Aviles O B 117 8.10 92-09 Boogie'sJoy113noKimKimmie1175PeroxidePrincss1122 Just failed 10
31Jly86-10Crc fm 1 Ⓣ:48 1:12⅘ 1:37⅘ 3↑ⒻMd Sp Wt 6 4 31 2hd 1hd 1nk Aviles O B 115 4.60 85-15 Kim Kimmie 115nk Tangy Lady 1151 Frau Beatriz 122no Driving 12
LATEST WORKOUTS Jun 29 Mth 4f fst :50 b

K.
4–1

***Go Honey Go** — B. f. 4, by General Assembly—Go Feather Go, by Go Marching
Br.—Weld Mrs C L (Ire)
Tr.—Hine Hubert
Own.—Sarin S C
113
Lifetime 13 3 4 4 $76,252 — 1987 5 2 1 2 $51,025 — 1986 6 1 1 2 $18,023 — Turf 13 3 4 4 $76,252

5Jly87- 9Crc fm *1⅛ Ⓣ 1:46⅕ 3↑ⒻAspidistra H 2 8 86½ 84½ 44½ 31½ Hernandez C 114 5.30 90-06 Judy's Red Shoes 122¾ Thirty Zip 119¾ Go Honey Go 1141 Rallied 8
28May87- 9GP fm 1⅛ Ⓣ:47 1:11⅘ 1:42 3↑ⒻFlwer Girl H 3 7 712 75½ 31 1nk Hernandez C 111 7.50 90-14 Go HoneyGo111nkLadyoftheNorth1092½She'sContent112¾ Driving 7
3May87- 8GP fm *1⅛ Ⓣ 1:44⅗ ⒻAlw 18000 6 6 56 41 64½ 31½ Fires E 119 1.70 81-13 MssEnchntd117noStrwWdow1121½GoHonyG119hd Rallied outside 7
28Mar87- 9GP gd *1⅛ Ⓣ 1:47 ⒻAlw 18000 3 7 83½ 54 44 23½ Cruguet J 119 *2.30 67-25 Innsbruck 1193½ Go Honey Go 119no Straw Widow 117no Rallied 12
2Feb87- 8Hia fm *1⅛ Ⓣ 1:42⅖ ⒻAlw 19000 2 9 108¾ 99 62½ 1nk Velasquez J 116 14.40 86-21 Go Honey Go 116nk LeadKindlyLight1163½UppityUp119nk Driving 10
21Sep86 ♦6Longchamp(Fra) gd*1 1:47 Ⓣ ⒻPrix de Liancourt 105½ Velasquez J 118 14.00 — — GrandeCouture121hd Mercadd118nk Minerlogie118nk Prom. wknd 11
15Aug86 ♦4Deauville(Fra) gd*1 1:43⅗ Ⓣ ⒻPrix de Lieurey 33½ Badel A 121 3.25 — — Sentimentalite 1282½ Yoko 128¾ Go Honey Go 1212 Fin. well 6
23Jly86 ♦6Evry(Fra) gd*6½f 1:17⅗ Ⓣ Primx Hampton 32½ Badel A 122 9.00 — — Lievre du Sud 116½ Eversince 1222 Go Honey Go 122nk Fin. well 10
26Apr86 ♦5Evry(Fra) sf*1 1:50 Ⓣ ⒻPrix Finlande 56½ Asmussen C 118 4.75 — — FabulousQueen1214 CarnetSolaire123hd Mercadah1212 Bid, wknd 10
2Apr86 ♦7StCloud(Fra) sf*7½f 1:50⅕ Ⓣ Prix Bosalino 1nk Asmussen C 120 *1.00 — — Go Honey Go 120nk Monsieur Lychea 1231½ Rask 123½ Up late 15
LATEST WORKOUTS Jly 28 Mth 5f fst 1:04⅘ b Jun 30 Crc 5f fst 1:03 b

L.
35–1

Scarlet Glow — Ch. m. 5, by Sifounas—Sutter's Dream, by Bupers
Br.—Dance G A (Ky)
Tr.—Lytle William
Own.—Shaw K
113
Lifetime 46 3 7 11 $45,355 — 1987 10 1 3 1 $14,232 — 1986 17 0 4 4 $14,228 — Turf 7 0 2 2 $6,552

23Jly87- 4Mth fm 1⅛ Ⓣ:47⅘ 1:12⅘ 1:50⅘+ 3↑Alw 10000s 4 9 97¼ 96¾ 55 41 Walford J b 113 12.40 87-09 Michelies Du Nord 112¾ Pelt 115nk Gallant James 115no Rallied 9
10Jly87- 7Mth fst 1⅛ :47⅕ 1:11⅘ 1:43⅕ 3↑ⒻAlw 12500s 6 6 510 46½ 29 29¾ Walford J b 117 6.90 79-16 Lavovernite1179¾ScarletGlow1179TimeTuner1151½ Best of others 6
25Jun87- 4Mth fm 1 Ⓣ:47⅗ 1:11⅗ 1:38⅕ 3↑ⒻAlw 10000s 9 9 89¾ 74¾ 33½ 23 Beimel D W7 b 110 4.90 81-12 Fia's Baby 1153 Scarlet Glow 110¾ Lady Ivory 1062 Very wide 10
20Jun87- 1Pha fst 7f :22⅗ :45⅗ 1:24⅗ 3↑ⒻClm 18000 1 8 912 913 57½ 25½ Beimel D W7 b 109 6.20 79-22 Kylena 1165½ Scarlet Glow 109nk Lightling 1111 Gained place 9
5Jun87- 8GS fst 1⅛ :47⅘ 1:13⅗ 1:47⅘ 3↑ⒻClm 14000 4 7 711 63½ 31½ 12½ Beimel D W7 b 109 3.10 69-24 ScarletGlow1092½RunForPeace1164½GlintRinbow1125½ Drew clear 7
30May87- 5GS fm 1⅛ Ⓣ:47⅗ 1:12⅕ 1:44⅗ 3↑ⒻClm 25000 7 10 1010 106½ 98¼ 97 Lee-Lopez R F b 116 13.90 79-05 Snow Leopard 116½ His Ex 112no Dave's Kate 116no No threat 10
21May87- 8GS fst 1⅛ :49⅗ 1:14⅘ 1:46⅗ 3↑ⒻClm 28000 5 4 45½ 56 411 418¾ Santos F J b 112 11.20 57-23 Crolin'sConfti11214MolyLu1141½NordnTnzr1153 Broke sluggishly 5
11Feb87- 9FG fm *1 Ⓣ:47⅗ 1:14 1:40⅗ ⒻClm 17500 9 11 1120 109½ 59 44¼ Woods C R Jr b 117 6.60 72-23 Grassy Meadows 1171 Nathan's Lt.1122½ChampagneDressing1151 12
30Jan87- 9FG fst 1⅛ :49⅗ 1:15⅗ 1:47⅗ ⒻClm 20000 9 8 98 107½ 1010 88¾ Bourque K b 117 9.20 66-17 Sandy Cove 116½ National Top 1171 Ky. Jakie 110nk 10
3Jan87- 5FG fm *1⅛ Ⓣ:48⅕ 1:14⅗ 1:48⅘ ⒻAlw 10000s 9 11 1112 47 23 35 Woods C R Jr b 115 16.60 63-32 Storm Out 1153 Grassy Meadows 1182 Scarlet Glow 115hd 12

49. The best bet is

3rd Santa Anita

1 1-16 MILES
SANTA ANITA

1 1/16 MILES. (1.40⅘) CLAIMING. Purse $26,000. 4-year-olds and upward. Weights, 4-year-olds, 120 lbs.; older, 121 lbs. Non-winners of two races at one mile or over since December 1 allowed 3 lbs.; of such a race since then, 5 lbs. Claiming price $40,000; if for $35,000 allowed 2 lbs. (Claiming and starter races for $32,000 or less not considered).

A.
7–2

Piper John — Dk. b. or br. g. 7, by Kennedy Road—Like John, by Fathers Image
SIBILLE R — 116 — Br.—McColl J B (Ont-C) — Tr.—Passey Blake — $40,000
Own.—Tons Of Fun Stable — Lifetime 63 8 10 13 $239,750
1987 2 1 0 0 $12,650
1986 16 3 4 3 $79,875
Turf 30 4 3 5 $135,815

17Jan87-9SA	1 1/16 :46² 1:11² 1:43⁴ft	*3¾	117	7¹¹	75½	3²	1¹	Pincay L Jr⁵	c32000	82-18	PiperJohn,ForHimself,ShowerDcr	12
10Jan87-5SA	1⅛Ⓣ:47²1:12²1:50 gd	8¾	116	5³	41½	72¾	85½	DelahoussayeE⁶	55000	71-23	Kingsbury,BoardMeeting,AvitorII	10
21Dec86-9Hol	1¼Ⓣ:50²1:38¹2:02²fm	4	117	2¹	2hd	21½	31½	Pincay L Jr⁵	50000	81-15	Kingsbury, Will Spring, PiperJohn	11
13Dec86-9Hol	1 Ⓣ:46³1:10²1:34²fm	9¼	116	4²	2½	2³	44½	Solis A²	62500	90-08	AutoCommander,DrkAccert,Dr.Dly	9
22Nov86-9Hol	1⅛Ⓣ:48 1:12³1:49⁴fm	4¼	117	1hd	2hd	2hd	2¾	Pincay L Jr⁹	50000	78-17	Massera, Piper John, Mount Bidder	9
3Sep86-7Dmr	1 1/16Ⓣ:47²1:11²1:42³fm	8¾	116	3¹	31½	74¾	7⁷	Valenzuela P A⁴	75000	86-12	ExclusivCpd,RivrOfKings,Emprdori	8
10Aug86-5Dmr	1⅜Ⓣ:46³1:36²2:14³fm	4¾	116	21½	2¹	1hd	1no	Valenzuela P A⁸	62500	97-01	Piper John, Pautivo, Promontory	9

10Aug86—Rank early

23Jly86-5Dmr	1 1/16Ⓣ:46²1:13¹1:41³fm	4	118	1hd	2hd	2¹	34½	Stevens G L²	62500	93-04	El Mansour, Massera, Piper John	10
6Jly86-8Hol	1 1/16Ⓣ:47 1:11¹1:41²fm	9¾	116	11½	1hd	21½	43½	Solis A⁴	80000	93-07	Bishop's Ring II, Dr.Daly,GoDancer	8
7Jun86-9Hol	1 1/16Ⓣ:46²1:10¹1:41 fm	8¾	114	1²	1½	2hd	31½	Solis A⁸	75000	97-02	‡GoDncer,Bishop'sRingII,PiprJohn	8

7Jun86—Placed second through disqualification; Impeded late
Jan 4 Hol 6f sy 1:13⁴ h

B.
5–1

Inherent Kal — B. c. 4, by Inherent Star—Kalliste, by Crocation
DELAHOUSSAYE E — 115 — Br.—Svihla A (Cal) — Tr.—Lewis Craig A — $40,000
Own.—Svihla A — Lifetime 23 5 2 5 $74,700
1987 1 0 0 0
1986 19 4 2 5 $68,250
Turf 4 0 0 0 $1,650

30Jan87-5SA	1¼Ⓣ:47 1:36³2:02¹fm	11	116	55½	97¼	10¹⁰	1012¾	DelhoussyeE⁵	Aw28000	63-24	Atreak, ‡Agitate's Pride, Chili Hill	10
28Dec86-5SA	1 1/16 :46² 1:10⁴ 1:43¹ft	11	116	5⁶	2³	2⁵	35¾	ValenzuelPA³	Aw28000	79-14	ReEnter,Card'sPlease,InherentKal	10

28Dec86—Bumped start

10Dec86-3Hol	1 :45⁴ 1:10⁴ 1:37¹ft	2½	116	77½	74¾	5⁴	5⁵	Stevens G L⁶	50000	72-20	Sebucan, Agitate's Pride, Alibi Ike	7
26Nov86-5Hol	1 :45⁴ 1:10² 1:35³ft	5¾	116	87½	68½	57¼	34¼	DelahoussayeE⁵	62500	81-20	BrightTom,MischivousMtt,InhrntKl	8
4Oct86-1SA	6½f :21⁴ :45 1:17 ft	10	118	9¹²	88½	55½	1¾	DelahoussayeE⁶	50000	85-18	Inherent Kal, EastTulip,Brali'sAnte	9
20Sep86-11Pom	1 1/16 :45¹ 1:10³ 1:44 ft	15	114	5¹⁰	4¹³	7¹¹	79¼	HrnndzR³	Ⓡ Derby Trl	82-09	BoldBrvott,Rfl'sDncr,J.R.Johnson	10
30Aug86-9Dmr	1 1/16Ⓣ:47 1:11²1:43⁴fm	7	116	56½	93½	73½	86¼	DelhoussyE¹¹	Aw23000	81-11	SansRivl,HilTheBid,TimeForSkrto	12
8Aug86-3Dmr	1 :46² 1:10⁴ 1:35⁴ft	*8-5	115	3¹	3nk	2hd	2no	DelahoussayeE⁶	62500	89-13	Tahoe Tango,InherentKal,HotMetal	7
25Jly86-7Dmr	1 1/16 :45⁴ 1:10³ 1:43²ft	2½	116	65½	5⁵	32½	1hd	DelahoussayeE³	50000	83-18	InherntKl,Exubrnt'sImg,HloExprss	8
11Jly86-3Hol	1 :46² 1:11² 1:37¹ft	2½	116	67¼	64¾	52½	2hd	DelahoussayeE⁵	40000	77-14	Joab, Inherent Kal, I Love Racing	6

11Jly86—Wide into stretch
Jan 24 SA 6f ft 1:14² h   Jan 20 Hol 6f ft 1:15² h   Jan 13 Hol 5f ft 1:03³ h   Dec 27 SA 3f ft :35¹ h

C.
6–1

Alibi Ike — B. c. 4, by Alydar—Every Evening, by Roi Dagobert
VALENZUELA P A — 115 — Br.—Red Oak Farm (Fla) — Tr.—Russell John W — $40,000
Own.—Dogwood Stable — Lifetime 13 1 2 2 $36,945
1987 1 0 1 0 $5,000
1986 12 1 1 2 $31,945
Turf 2 0 0 0

10Jan87-9SA	1 1/16 :48 1:12² 1:44 ft	15	115	1¹	1hd	2½	2³	Valenzuela P A⁷	40000	78-20	Danczone, Alibi Ike, Le Cid	7
28Dec86-5SA	1 1/16 :46² 1:10⁴ 1:43¹ft	11	116	78½	10¹²	9¹⁸	817¼	ShoemkrW¹⁰	Aw28000	68-14	ReEnter,Card'sPlease,InherentKal	10

28Dec86—Lugged out

10Dec86-3Hol	1 :45⁴ 1:10⁴ 1:37¹ft	24	116	1½	2hd	2hd	31½	Solis A⁴	50000	75-20	Sebucan, Agitate's Pride, Alibi Ike	7
30Nov86-9Hol	1⅛Ⓣ:47⁴1:12²1:48³fm	21	113	64½	74½	98¾	1013¼	ShoemkerW¹	Aw24000	72-12	Illumineux, Padoue, Grey Writer	12
2Nov86-9SA	1 :45³ 1:10 1:35¹ft	38	116	95¾	77¼	58¼	41³	Black C A⁹	Aw27000	79-10	Midwest King,Danielli,LordAllison	10

2Nov86—Wide final 3/8

23May86-5Bel	1¼Ⓣ:49²1:40⁴2:05⁴gd	10	112	2½	5⁴	10¹²	1024¾	Migliore R⁹	Aw25000	40-35	DeltaDeity,DnceCrdFilled,Gigbyte	12
18May86-8Bel	7f :22² :45² 1:22²ft	22	117	52½	52½	55½	41¹	Migliore R²	Aw24000	79-15	Wayar, Johns Treasure, Life Guard	8
6May86-5Aqu	1 :46² 1:11 1:36¹ft	4	117	5⁸	5⁵	4⁶	411¼	Migliore R¹	Aw25000	74-21	HaloFire,Concatinate,EveryPlesure	6
6Apr86-7Aqu	1⅛ :47² 1:12 1:50³m	18-5	119	41½	43½	47½	41²	Migliore R³	Aw25000	70-20	PrdeMrshl,SwordRttlr,WimpolMws	8
27Mar86-7Aqu	1 :46 1:11¹ 1:38 ft	3	119	63½	63¾	52½	41½	Santagata N⁵	Aw25000	74-29	Mr. Classic, GrandExchange,Shear	10

Feb 1 SA 5f ft 1:02¹ h   ● Jan 27 SA 7f ft 1:28² h   ● Jan 20 SA 6f ft 1:13 h   Jan 8 Hol 6f ft 1:16 h

D.
4–5

Too Much For T. V. *
STEVENS G L **118**
Own.—Bronson & Vallone
Dk. b. or br. g. 7, by Zanthe—Small Voice, by Sailor
Br.—Harris Farms Inc (Cal) 1987 1 0 0 0 $2,175
Tr.—Canani Julio C **$40,000** 1986 18 6 2 4 $93,625
Lifetime 61 12 8 13 $199,335 Turf 16 5 1 6 $84,125

15Jan87-7SA a6½f ⓣ:21² :43⁴1:15⁴fm 4½ 116 2hd 2hd 1½ 42½ ValenzuelPA3 Aw29000 77-20 StrtfordEst,TmmyThHwk,CllThGrd 8
15Jan87—Veered out 3/16
24Dec86-5Hol 1 1/16 ⓣ:47²1:11¹1:41²fm*4-5 120 11½ 11½ 1hd 2nk Stevens G L2 45000 87-11 Dr.Dly,TooMchFrT.V.,GdThghtWlly 7
12Dec86-9Hol 1⅛ⓣ:46¹1:10¹1:47⁴fm*8-5 120 2½ 1hd 2½ 32½ Stevens G L9 45000 86-13 BordMeting,Mssr,TooMuchForT.V. 9
3Dec86-9Hol 1⅛ⓣ:47³1:12¹1:47³fm*4-5 117 13 12½ 12½ 13 Stevens G L2 45000 90-10 TooMuchForT.V.,Rajhaan,RosCrnin 6
5Nov86-7Hol 1⅛ⓣ:47³1:13¹1:48³fm*8-5 114 12 11½ 13 1½ Stevens G L3 45000 85-14 Too Much For T. V.,Masse-a,Tarver 8
26Oct86-9SA 1 1/16 :46³ 1:11¹ 1:43⁴ft *8-5 116 1½ 11½ 12½ 2hd Stevens G L2 32000 82-16 BngBngBng,TooMchFrT.V.,ItmTw 10
1Sep86-5Dmr 1 1/16 ⓣ:47¹1:11 1:41²fm 6¼ 118 11½ 1½ 21 34¼ ValenzuelPA8 Aw25000 95-04 Sherkin,DanThtch,TooMuchForT.V. 8
10Aug86-5Dmr 1⅜ⓣ:46³1:36²2:14³fm *2½ 114 11½ 11 2hd 44 Stevens G L3 57500 93-01 Piper John, Pautivo, Promontory 9
12Jly86-9Hol 1⅛ⓣ:46⁴1:10²1:47 fm 3 117 11½ 11½ 13 14 Stevens G L3 45000 97-01 TooMuchForT.V.,Kngsbury,Oljuwon 8
6Jly86-10Hol 1⅛ⓣ:47³1:11⁴1:48²fm 7 114 13 11½ 12 11¼ Stevens G L10 45000 90-07 TooMuchForT.V.,Rajhn,IronLeder 10
Feb 4 SA 5f ft 1:00³ h Jan 29 SA 5f ft 1:01³ h Jan 23 SA 4f ft :49 h Jan 9 SA 4f sl :49⁴ h

E.
6–1

Forgot The Ring *
PATTON D B **109⁵**
Own.—Johnson W R
B. g. 7, by Blushing Groom—Calaba, by Nelcius
Br.—Hunt & Bluegrass Farm (Ky) 1987 3 0 3 0 $10,600
Tr.—Arena Joseph **$35,000** 1986 13 2 1 1 $39,850
Lifetime 56 6 10 8 $145,790 Turf 4 0 0 0 $1,700

24Jan87-9SA 1 1/16 :47¹ 1:11³ 1:43⁴ft *9-5 117 44 36 23½ 23½ Pincay L Jr5 c25000 78-18 Dcontrol,ForgtThRng,DckAndHgh 12
18Jan87-9SA 1 1/16 :46³ 1:11⁴ 1:43³ft 5½ 117 47½ 43 3½ 2no Pincay L Jr11 20000 83-19 Slugfest, Forgot The Ring, Mufti 12
1Jan87-9SA 1 1/16 :47¹ 1:12 1:44³ft 3½ 116 32 1½ 2hd 25 ♦Cordero A Jr6 c16000 73-19 RoosvltRod,ForgotThRng,Espontn 10
♦ 1Jan87—Dead heat
24Dec86-9Hol 1 1/16 ⓣ:46⁴1:11²1:41⁴fm 5 116 31½ 31 32 42 Simpson B H2 25000 83-11 CoursingEagle,Racionl,AncientBlue 9
29Nov86-7Hol 1 :45⁴ 1:10⁴ 1:36¹ft 4½ 116 41½ 31½ 32½ 63½ Pedroza M A10 20000 78-12 Rnbow'sCp,LordPnch,TmmyThms 10
29Nov86—Broke in, bumped
26Oct86-9SA 1 1/16 :46³ 1:11¹ 1:43⁴ft 6¼ 116 2½ 21½ 55½ 87 Ortega L E5 32000 75-16 BngBngBng,TooMchFrT.V.,ItmTw 10
3Oct86-9SA 1 1/16 :45⁴ 1:10² 1:43²ft 16 115 33 2hd 11½ 3¾ Ortega L E3 25000 83-17 MrkInThSky,HrrcnHc,ForgtThRng 12
27Jly86-9Dmr 1 1/16 :45⁴ 1:10² 1:42²ft 7¼ 116 21½ 2½ 41½ 63¾ Pedroza M A5 25000 84-10 MstrCwston,NutrlPlyr,Rvo'utionry 10
13Jly86-4Hol 1⅛ :46⁴ 1:11² 1:50⁴ft 5½ 116 2hd 1hd 32 44½ Pedroza M A4 25000 78-15 Mark In The Sky, Mufti, Pegus 7
13Jly86—Bobbled break
28Jun86-6Hol 1 :44³ 1:09³ 1:36²ft 8¾ 116 33 55 913 — Valenzuela P A2 40000 — — Restage,PassedTheRule,FbulousDd 9
28Jun86—Eased
● Jan 14 SA 5f ft :59² h Dec 14 Hol 5f ft 1:01 h

50. The classified allowance sprint for 3up, now almost extinct, has always been among the handicappers's best friends. The best bet here is

7th Del Mar

6 FURLONGS. (1.07⅘) CLASSIFIED ALLOWANCE. Purse $35,000. 3-year-olds and upward. Non-winners of $18,500 twice since October 1, 1986. Weights, 3-year-olds, 116 lbs.; older, 121 lbs. Non-winners of $22,000 since April 20 allowed 2 lbs.; of $19,250 in 1987, or $16,000 since June 1, 4 lbs.; of $17,000 in 1987, 6 lbs. (Claiming races not considered.)

A.
15–1

My Gallant Game
MCCARRON C J **121**
Own.—Appleton A I
Ch. g. 5, by My Gallant—Maid of Bridlewood, by Raise a Native
Br.—Appleton A I (Fla) 1987 5 1 0 0 $24,175
Tr.—Tinsley J E Jr 1986 16 1 6 3 $70,650
Lifetime 29 4 8 3 $120,550 Turf 7 0 3 0 $21,000

2Aug87-8Dmr 6f :21³ :44² 1:09 ft 28 115 63½ 52 41¾ 54 McCrrCJ5 B Crosby H 89-12 ZnyTctcs,BldrThnBld,MyFvrtMmnt 8
2Aug87—Grade III; Wide into stretch
15Jly87-8Hol 6½f :22³ :45¹ 1:16¹ft 4½ 116 2hd 2hd 11½ 12¾ McCarronCJ5 Aw40000 99-14 MyGllntGm,HighHook,WndwoodLn 6
24Jun87-8Hol 6f :21² :44³ 1:09²ft 23 113⁵ 64¼ 42½ 53½ 54¼ Patton D B7 Aw27000 92-13 HghHook,OrLordshp,HnkyTnkDncr 7
24Jun87—Wide 3/8 turn
14Jan87-5SA a6½f ⓣ:21⁴ :44²1:15¹fm 4 118 73¾ 41¾ 75¼ 76¼ Pincay L Jr6 80000 77-18 Amnotherbrother,StrVideo,Shrkin 10
14Jan87—Off poorly; checked 1/4, wide into stretch

4Jan87-5SA 6½f :213 :441 1:17 sy 2½ 117 54¾ 65¾ 75½ 68¾ Pincay L Jr 5 Aw33000 76-22 Amnotherbrothr,GllntSilor,HillsBid 7
4Jan87—Wide into stretch
29Nov86-6Hol 6f Ⓣ:221 :4431:082fm 19 115 41 32 54 76 Toro F 8 HcpO 92-10 Zany Tactics, Mandatory, Ice Hot 8
12Nov86-3Hol 7f :221 :451 1:213ft 5½ 117 11½ 11 21½ 24½ Toro F 6 Aw26000 91-15 BoldrThnBold,MyGllntGm,Mtrnmc 6
12Oct86-5SA a6½f Ⓣ:214 :44 1:134fm 8½ 117 11½ 11½ 22 24½ Pincay L Jr 12 Aw33000 85-12 PrinceSky,MyGallantGame,Bruiser 12
16Sep86-11Pom 6f :214 :442 1:092ft 5½ 116 53 46 47 53¾ Black C A 5 Aprisa H 100-05 BundlOfIron,Mtronomc,ProdstHor 10
13Aug86-3Dmr 6f :213 :443 1:083ft 6 1125 34 32 23½ 34¾ Black C A 1 Aw24000 90-15 MneMgic,Metronomic,MyGllntGme 6
13Aug86—Erratic backstretch, 3/8 turn
Aug 16 Dmr 6f ft 1:132 h Aug 9 Dmr 4f ft :49 h Jly 29 Dmr 5f ft 1:01 h Jly 22 Hol 4f ft :481 h

B.
14–1

*Petrovich

B. g. 5, by Malinowski—Fizzy, by Gala Performance
Br.—McArdle Mrs D (Ire) 1987 2 0 1 0 $8,000
PEDROZA M A 115 Tr.—Shulman Sanford 1986 9 0 0 4 $11,667
Own.—Charles & ClearValleyStables Lifetime 24 5 5 5 $67,585 Turf 22 5 4 5 $59,585

15Jly87-8Hol 6½f :223 :451 1:161ft *7-5 116 1hd 1hd 21½ 510¾ Pedroza MA2 Aw40000 88-14 MyGllntGm,HighHook,WndwoodLn 6
15Jly87—Stumbled start; lugged out
19Jun87-8Hol 6f :212 :442 1:092ft 20 116 11½ 1½ 11½ 2no Pedroza MA2 Aw35000 96-14 TripleSec,Petrovich,LuckyMasaddo 9
18Oct86♦5Newmarket(Eng) 5f 1:013gd 8 118 Ⓣ 7 Rouse B Bentinck Gwydion, Fayruz, Butsova 10
10Oct86♦5Newmarket(Eng) 5f :584gd 8 117 Ⓣ 33¼ Thomson B Rous Fayruz, StormWarning, Petrovich 7
14Sep86♦5Taby(Sweden) 5½f 1:09 sf *3 134 Ⓣ 76 RosB SARAOpnSpnt(Gr1) SimonSacc, Kellytalk, LeMans 11
23Aug86♦6PhoenixPk 6f 1:15 yl 3 128 Ⓣ 31¾ Craine S Orchrdstwn NorthrnExprss,BrmdClssc,Ptrovch 7
25Jly86♦4Tipperary(Ire) 5f :561gd 7 123 Ⓣ 31 Craine S Tprry Sprnt Ednica, Orojoya, Petrovich 9
5Jly86♦1Sandown(Eng) 5f 1:003gd 12 126 Ⓣ 75½ CarsonW TrflgrHsSpnt Polykratis, Tarib, Treasure Kay 10
20Jun86♦4Ascot(Eng) 5f :591fm 66 129 Ⓣ 13 ThmsnB Kng Stnd(Gr1) LstTycoon,DoublSchwrtz,Gwydion 14
4Jun86♦2Epsom(Eng) 5f :56 gd 7 136 Ⓣ 7 ThomsmB Nghtrdr H Clantime,ImperialJde,BollinEmily 16
Aug 19 Dmr 4f ft :481 h Aug 11 Dmr 6f ft 1:123 h Jly 24 Hol 5f ft 1:01 h Jly 5 Hol 6f ft 1:131 h

C.
6–5

My Favorite Moment

B. h. 6, by Timeless Moment—My Masindi, by Dragante
Br.—Dinnaken Farm (Ky) 1987 9 2 2 2 $54,975
DELAHOUSSAYE E 115 Tr.—Stute Warren 1986 4 1 1 1 $31,750
Own.—Connors W L Lifetime 30 10 4 7 $232,615 Turf 2 0 0 0

2Aug87-8Dmr 6f :213 :442 1:09 ft 8¾ 115 2½ 2hd 2hd 3½ DlhssyE6 B Crosby H 92-12 ZnyTctcs,BldrThnBld,MyFvrtMmnt 8
2Aug87—Grade III; Bumped hard start
29May87-7Hol 6½f :221 :451 1:164ft *2-3 116 21½ 23 22½ 1nk DelahoussayeE5 80000 96-16 MyFvoriteMomnt,Hydrosttic,Frcoz 6
9May87-3Hol 6f :221 :45 1:083ft *9-5 116 21 1hd 1hd 14½ DelahoussayeE1 50000 100-10 MyFvrtMmnt,LckyMsdd,EghtyBlZr 6
3Apr87-9SA 6½f :22 :45 1:163ft 3½ 116 1hd 2hd 2hd 21½ Castanon A L3 62500 85-17 Crcksmn,MyFvortMomnt,JttngHm 6
19Mar87-7SA 6½f :22 :45 1:161ft 3½ 116 1hd 2hd 1hd 22 DelahoussyeE10 62500 87-21 J.R.Johnson,MyFvortMmnt,QpStr 10
19Mar87—Bumped start
13Mar87-5SA a6½f Ⓣ:22 :4421:16 fm 4¾ 117 1½ 2hd 51¾ 86¾ Castanon A L2 80000 72-21 Amnothrbrothr,AvitorII,Hydrosttc 10
13Mar87—Bumped, took up 1/8
22Feb87-7SA 6½f :213 :442 1:152ft 21 119 54 42 44 56 Castanon AL8 Aw45000 87-14 GrandAllegiance,Shahmk,TripleSec 8
22Feb87—Fanned wide 3/8
21Jan87-3SA 7f :221 :45 1:232ft 2¾ 116 1hd 1hd 2½ 31¾ Valenzuela P A1 90000 81-19 Emprdor,Mtronomc,MyFvortMmnt 6
21Jan87—Troubled trip
9Jan87-8SA 6½f :211 :443 1:18 sl 5¾ 118 36 56½ 710 615½ ValenzuelPA4 Aw45000 64-26 Innmorto,ProudestHour,GminiDrmr 8
9Jan87—Wide into stretch
21Dec86-5Hol 6f :221 :452 1:103ft *1 116 31½ 31½ 31½ 1nk ValenzuelPA2 Aw35000 90-15 MFvrtMmnt,McLndn,AmrcnStndrd 6
Aug 20 Dmr 5f ft 1:003 h Aug 15 Dmr 6f ft 1:124 h Aun 10 Dmr 3f ft :364 h Jly 27 Dmr 5f ft :59 h

D.
5–1

High Hook

B. h. 5, by Exceller—Eehook, by Francis S
Br.—Hudson E J Sr (Ky) 1987 10 2 2 4 $59,850
STEVENS G L 115 Tr.—Drysdale Neil 1986 11 1 3 2 $36,560
Own.—Hudson & Summa Stable Lifetime 26 4 7 6 $112,320 Turf 1 0 0 0

10Aug87-8Dmr 6½f :214 :442 1:153ft 5¼ 115 713 711 54½ 32½ Stevens G L1 Aw30000 91-20 Carload, Our Lordship, High Hook 7
15Jly87-8Hol 6½f :223 :451 1:161ft 2 116 55¼ 55 31½ 22¾ Stevens G L4 Aw40000 96-14 MyGllntGm,HighHook,WndwoodLn 6
24Jun87-8Hol 6f :212 :443 1:092ft 10 118 79¼ 76 43 1no Stevens G L1 Aw27000 96-13 HghHook,OrLordshp,HnkyTnkDncr 7
23May87-7Hol 1 :451 1:094 1:351ft 3¼ 116 52 41¾ 33 34½ DelhoussyeE6 Aw30000 82-15 Sperry, Rai Den, High Hook 7
14May87-8Hol 1 :461 1:101 1:35 ft 10 116 66¾ 65¼ 64½ 42½ DelhoussyeE1 Aw45000 85-13 Tasso, Metronomic, Southern Halo 6
1May87-8GG 6f :214 :444 1:09 ft 2¾ 116 66 56½ 43½ 22 Maple S3 Aw22000 92-18 SntRosPrinc,HghHook,Ed'sExclusv 6
8Apr87-8GG 6f :213 :433 1:08 ft 2½ 115 58½ 48½ 34½ 31¼ Baze R A1 Aw22000 98-14 MuiLyphrJ.,BoldSmoochr,HghHook 5
13Mar87-8SA 6½f :213 :441 1:16 ft 9¾ 115 811 810 66½ 31¼ Stevens G L5 Aw36000 89-21 Metronomic,PaisnoPete,HighHook 8
28Jan87-8BM 6f :224 :46 1:104gd *1 115 55 21½ 21 1nk Baze R A5 Aw17000 85-28 High Hook, HotSauceBaby,Jubilero 6
3Jan87-3SA 6f :214 :441 1:094ft 5¼ 117 55 55¾ 43¾ 44½ Pincay L Jr4 Aw29000 85-16 Zabaleta, SaltDome,NorthernPolicy 7
Aug 18 Dmr 4f ft :474 h Aug 7 Dmr 3f ft :39 h Aug 2 Dmr 5f ft :594 h Jly 9 Hol 4f ft :483 b

E.

19–1

Bid Us — Ch. h. 7, by Bold Bidder—Lucky Us, by Nijinsky II
VALENZUELA P A — 115 — Br.—Knott Virginia (Ky) — 1987 6 0 1 2 $26,500
Own.—Lucky Me Stable — Tr.—Manzi Joseph — 1986 6 4 1 0 $141,400
Lifetime 16 5 2 4 $182,025

10Aug87-8Dmr 6½f :21^{4} :44^{2} 1:15^{3}ft 13 117 3^{1} 2^{hd} 3½ 6^{7¾} Pincay L Jr^{7} Aw30000 86-20 Carload, Our Lordship, High Hook 7
30Nov85-8Hol 6f :21^{4} :44^{3} 1:08^{4}m 10 115 6^{7¾} 6^{9} 6^{4¾} 5^{3} DlhssyE^{6} Ntl Spt Chp 97-09 PnchoVill,ChrgingFlls,TemrityPrinc 6
30Nov85—Grade III
16Oct85-8SA 6f :21^{2} :44 1:09^{1}ft 5¾ 115 2^{hd} 1½ 2^{hd} 3^{nk} VlnzlPA^{2} Anct Title H 92-17 TemerityPrince,DbonirJunior,BidUs 6
4Oct85-8SA 6f :21^{2} :44 1:08^{4}ft 3 116 4¾ 3^{2} 2^{1} 3^{1½} DelhoussyeE^{1} Aw45000 92-16 TemerityPrince,TeddyNturlly,BidUs 7
1Sep85-7Dmr 1 :45 1:10^{1} 1:37 ft *2¼ 114 2^{hd} 2^{hd} 2½ 6^{8} McCarronCJ^{6} Aw40000 75-13 JustInCse,TriplSc,MyFvoritMomnt 7
1Sep85—Fanned wide 7/8 turn
8Aug85-8Dmr 6f :21^{4} :44^{4} 1:09^{2}ft 7¾ 115 3^{1} 3^{2} 1^{hd} 2^{hd} Stevens G L^{3} Aw35000 91-19 Triple Sec, Bid Us, Barbed Nale 8
10Aug84-8Dmr 1$\frac{1}{16}$:45 1:09^{2} 1:41^{3}ft *2 119 2½ 2^{hd} 6^{13} — DelhoussyeE^{3} Aw35000 — — Super Diamond, Video Kid, Swivel 6
10Aug84—Pulled up
14Jly84-8Hol 1$\frac{1}{16}$:45^{4} 1:09^{4} 1:41^{3}ft 20 115 1^{2} 1^{1} 1½ 1^{hd} DelhoussyE^{1} Bel Air H 87-15 Bid Us, Retsina Run, Night Mover 10
23Jun84-7Hol 6f :22 :44^{2} 1:09 ft *1 122 1^{hd} 1^{hd} 1^{hd} 1¾ DelhoussyeE^{5} Aw26000 92-18 BidUs,FiftySixInaRow,FastPassage 9
27May84-3Hol 6½f :21^{4} :44^{2} 1:16^{3}ft 2¼ 120 2½ 1½ 1^{1} 1^{1¼} DelhoussyeE^{4} Aw22000 87-18 Bid Us, American Standard,Cordon 7
6May84-7Hol 8-5 115 1 1^{3½} 1^{5½} Delahoussaye E^{5} 92 —
Aug 18 Dmr 4f ft :49^{3} b ●Aug 5 Dmr 4f ft :47 h Jly 31 Dmr 1 ft 1:42^{4} h Jly 26 Dmr 7f ft 1:28^{1} h

F.

13–1

Ultimate Pleasure — B. h. 5, by Foolish Pleasure—Princess Papulee, by Hawaii
PINCAY L JR — 115 — Br.—Ewald J A Jr (Va) — 1986 15 2 3 1 $68,650
Own.—Litman-Miller-Wrtschftr — Tr.—Moreno Henry — 1985 12 2 1 4 $43,775
Lifetime 27 4 4 5 $112,425 — Turf 3 0 0 0 $2,100

26Nov86-7Hol 1 Ⓣ:45^{3}1:09^{2}1:33^{4}fm 11 117 7^{22} 7^{24} 7^{28} — Pincay L Jr 3 Aw33000 — — SkipOutFront,OverTheOcn,LstMotl 7
26Nov86—Eased
31Oct86-3SA 1$\frac{1}{16}$:45^{2} 1:09^{3} 1:42^{1}ft 2½ 117 6^{13} 5^{11} 3^{9½} 3^{6¾} Pincay L Jr 2 Aw45000 83-16 ImprtntBsnss,ArcnStndrd,UlttPlsr 6
16Oct86-8SA 1 :46 1:10^{2} 1:35^{3}ft 7½ 117 7^{7¼} — — — Pincay L Jr 2 Aw45000 — — Hatim, Innamorato, 7
16Oct86—Lost rider; Hit fallen horse
30Aug86-8Dmr 7f :22^{1} :44 1:20^{2}ft 5 117 5^{8} 5^{8½} 5^{7} 4^{4½} PincyLJr 1 P O' Brn H 98-10 BoldBrwly,FirstNormn,AmricnLgon 5
30Aug86—Bumped start
15Aug86-8Dmr 7f :22^{1} :44^{3} 1:21^{3}ft *2 117 6^{5¼} 6^{4¼} 4^{1½} 2no Pincay L Jr 4 Aw30000 97-12 SouthrnHlo,UltmtPlsur,FlyngNuggt 7
15Aug86—Broke slowly; wide into stretch
30Jly86-7Dmr 7f :21^{4} :44^{2} 1:21^{4}ft 5 117 8^{9} 8^{7¼} 5^{4½} 1no Pincay L Jr 3 Aw24000 96-11 UltimtePlesure,MneMgic,IdelQulity 8
30Jly86—5-wide to stretch
18Jly86-8Hol 1 :45^{3} 1:10^{1} 1:35^{3}ft 2½ 117 6^{5½} 6^{5} 4^{4½} 4^{5¼} ValenzuelPA^{3} Aw30000 80-14 Bolton, Varick, Ascension 6
18Jly86—Lugged in stretch
21Jun86-3Hol 7f :22^{4} :45^{3} 1:22^{1}ft 3 117 5^{4} 4^{3} 1^{hd} 1no † Pincay L Jr^{4} Aw24000 93-09 ‡UltimtePlesure,Pdu,GrndAllegince 6
†21Jun86—Disqualified and placed fourth; Steadied 1/8
1Jun86-9Hol 1 :44^{4} 1:09^{2} 1:36^{1}ft 3¼ 117 6^{11} 6^{11} 3^{7} 2^{hd} ValenzuelPA^{1} Aw32000 82-14 Koshare, Ultimate Pleasure, Jon O. 7
8May86-8Hol 1 :46 1:10^{2} 1:34^{4}ft 5½ 119 5^{6½} 4^{3} 4^{1½} 2¾ ValenzuelPA^{4} Aw32000 88-14 Michadilla,UltimatePlesure,Koshre 5
Aug 19 Dmr 4f ft :48^{3} hg Aug 14 Dmr 7f ft 1:29^{3} h Aug 9 Dmr 7f ft 1:30^{2} h Aug 4 Dmr 5f ft 1:01^{2} h

G.

9–5

Olympic Prospect — Ch. g. 3, by Northern Jove—Brilliant Future, by Forli
GRYDER A T — 105^{5} — Br.—Christiana Stables (Ky) — 1987 8 3 1 0 $31,300
Own.—Alsdorf–Opas–Sinatra — Tr.—Sadler John W — 1986 0 M 0 0
Lifetime 8 3 1 0 $31,300

8Aug87-7Dmr 6f :21^{4} :44 1:08 ft 8-5 117 1^{2} 1^{5} 1^{7} 1^{7½} Pincay L Jr 2 Aw21000 98-10 OlympicProspct,LittlRdCloud,Dnski 9
8Aug87—Lost whip 1/16
12Jly87-7Hol 6f :21^{4} :44^{1} 1:09^{2}ft 2¾ 117 1^{1½} 1^{5} 1^{3½} 2^{1¼} Pincay L Jr 7 Aw22000 95-09 MjstcMsson,OlympcPrspct,GrtYnk 7
18Jun87-3Hol 6f :21^{4} :44^{1} 1:09^{4}ft *6-5 119 1^{3½} 1^{6} 1^{7} 1^{4} Pincay L Jr 3 32000 94-11 OlympcPrspct,ShrwdStv,StrdstFlly 7
6Jun87-9GG 6f :21^{1} :43^{2} 1:09^{3}ft 4 119 2^{1} 2^{1½} 7^{5} 7^{9¼} CastanedaM 3 Aw15000 82-07 MagicDoor,SuchaLot,IslandWarrior 7
13May87-6Hol 6f :21^{3} :44^{3} 1:10^{4}ft *1 117 1^{2} 1^{4} 1^{3½} 1^{hd} Pincay L Jr 4 M40000 89-15 OlympcProspct,CmnBmbn,TblGlw 11
13May87—Broke out, bumped
1May87-6Hol 6½f :21^{3} :44^{2} 1:18 ft 2½ 110^{5} 1^{3½} 1^{6} 1^{2½} 4^{5½} Gryder A T 7 M50000 84-13 Nnterre,Peppy'sConsul,MstrThundr 7
27Mar87-6SA 6f :21^{4} :45^{3} 1:11^{3}ft 6 118 6^{3} 6^{4} 8^{7} 9^{9½} Cordova DW^{7} Mc50000 70-23 Plum Wishfull,CoolTalker,Guggen 12
27Mar87—Checked 1/2; crowded into turn
31Jan87-6SA 6½f :21^{3} :44^{3} 1:16^{3}ft 20 118 1^{hd} 1^{hd} 3^{2} 7^{12} Cordova D W^{4} Mdn 75-15 Blanco, Exit Poll, Grey Aloha 9
31Jan87—Lugged in
Aug 18 Dmr 4f ft :48^{2} h Aug 3 Dmr 5f ft 1:01 h Jly 28 Dmr 5f ft 1:00^{2} b Jly 22 Hol 4f ft :50^{3} b

51. Examine the records and odds and pick the best betting strategy below.

8th Santa Anita

1 MILE (SANTA ANITA, START & FINISH)

1 MILE. (1.33⅗) CLASSIFIED ALLOWANCE. Purse $48,000. Fillies and mares. 4-year-olds and upward which are non-winners of $17,000 twice at one mile or over in 1986–87. Weights, 4-year-olds, 120 lbs.; older, 121 lbs. Non-winners of two such races of $16,000 since July 22 allowed 3 lbs.; of such a race of $19,250 since October 1 5 lbs.; of such a race of $18,000 since July 22 or such a race of $22,000 in 1986–87 7 lbs. (Claiming races not considered.)

14–1

Fleet Secretariat
SIBILLE R 116
Own.—Henderson S F
B. m. 6, by Secretariat—Sister Fleet, by Fleet Nasrullah
Br.—Henderson S F (Ky)
Tr.—Taliaferro Charles L
Lifetime 34 6 7 5 $163,435
1987 1 0 0 0
1986 9 3 3 0 $75,130
Turf 7 0 0 3 $17,910

2Jan87-8SA 1⅛Ⓣ:4621:1111:49 fm 33 116 77¾ 85 74¾ 68¾ Baze G2 ⒻAw48000 73-18 Outstandingly,FrauAltiv,NewBruce 8
23Aug86-9EIP 1⅛:461 1:103 1:491ft 3½ 119 58 58½ 35½ 23 MlncL3 ⒻCoca Cola H 91-13 QueenAlexndr,FleetSecretrit,Shrizr 7
9Aug86-9Cby 1$\frac{1}{16}$:473 1:113 1:453ft 4½ 118 613 59½ 24½ 1½ MlncLJ4 ⒻBurnsvle H 83-15 Fleet Secretariat, Rascal Lass,Ante 6
27Jly86-8Cby 7½fⓉ:24 :4721:302gd 5½ 117 1114119 74½ 52½ Hawley S2 ⒻStillwater — — Gerrie Singer, Mr. T.'s Tune,EvaG. 11
21Jun86-8Cby 170:49 1:132 1:442ft *4-5 120 46½ 43 2hd 12 Black K5 ⒻAw14300 79-19 FleetSecretarit,Athbsc,TriplePretty 5
7Jun86-10Cby 1$\frac{1}{16}$:474 1:123 1:462ft 5 117 31½ 31 33½ 23¾ Lidberg D W3 ⒻFargo 75-26 GrndGlory,FleetSecrtrit,Mr.T.'sTun 4
24May86-9Cby 170:482 1:14 1:442ft *3-5 117 67 43 12 18 Black K4 ⒻAw14300 79-19 FltScrtrit,SssWithClss,WvringLight 7
10May86-8Cby 1$\frac{1}{16}$:484 1:134 1:452m 3 117 65 62¾ 1½ 2nk Black K3 ⒻAw14300 84-12 SurburbnSu,FltScrtrit,WvringLight 6
27Apr86-9Cby 170:472 1:113 1:42 sy 4½ 115 77½ 54 55½ 512½ FrndAL8 ⒻCty O Min 78-14 Mr.T.'sTune,Adaptble,SurburbnSue 8
4Apr86-8SA a6½fⓉ:214 :4431:144fm 128 115 84¾ 74¾ 98¼ 97½ Sibille R5 ⒻAw42000 77-16 Aberuschka, Regal Ties, Loucoum 11
Jan 11 SA 6f ft 1:151 h Dec 31 SA 5f ft 1:012 h Dec 26 SA 1 ft 1:413 h Dec 21 SA 7f ft 1:28 h

4–1

Cenyak's Star
TORO F 114
Own.—Dandar Fm & NorthwestFms
Dk. b. or br. m. 5, by Star de Naskra—Miss Cenyak, by Graustark
Br.—Northwest Farms (Ky)
Tr.—Fanning Jerry
Lifetime 21 3 5 1 $110,062
1986 14 2 3 1 $98,150
1985 6 1 1 0 $8,535
Turf 14 2 4 1 $53,887

31Dec86-8SA a6½fⓉ:213 :4341:152fm 3¼ 116 1010 911 99 76½ DlhoussyE1 ⒻAw45000 75-18 Aromacor, Tax Dodge, Sign Off 10
31Dec86—Lugged out late
3Nov86-7SA 1 :452 1:101 1:36 ft 9½ 116 52½ 74¾ 86¾ 79¾ McHrDG2 ⒻPrncs Rny 78-14 Infinidad, Fairly Old, Stemware 9
28Sep86-9Lga 1$\frac{3}{16}$:471 1:124 2:001gd *2-3e120 36½ 31 21½ 45½ StnsGL8 ⒻBle Rbts H 63-32 SilkChiffon,IceSteler,NorthrnNums 8
14Sep86-11Pom 1$\frac{1}{16}$:464 1:104 1:423ft *4-5 115 2½ 32 42½ 47¾ KIJL3 ⒻⓇE B Jhnstn 90-08 Our Best Tell, LeL'Argent,GoodZar 5
23Aug86-8Dmr 1$\frac{1}{16}$:454 1:101 1:412ft 7¾ 116 13 11½ 21 21¾ DlhssE1 ⒻChla Vsta H 91-10 Frn'sVlntn,Cnyk'sStr,DntstpThmsc 5
23Aug86—Grade II
9Aug86-8Dmr 1 Ⓣ:4611:1041:342fm 23 116 11 1½ 33½ 55½ DlhssyE1 ⒻPlmr H 94-04 Aberuschka, Sauna,Fran'sValentine 9
9Aug86—Grade II
26Jly86-8Dmr 1$\frac{1}{16}$Ⓣ:4741:1131:421fm *2¾ 117 12½ 14 12½ 2¾ ToroF7 ⒻⓇOsunitas H 94-05 FlyingGirl,Cnyk'sStr,MssBvrlyHlls 11
26Jly86—Run in divisions
9Jly86-8Hol 1 Ⓣ:4621:1011:342fm 8½ 115 11 11 21 32¼ StevensGL8 ⒻAw40000 — — BlushingAllOver,FolkArt,Cnyk'sStr 8
9Jly86—Lugged out early
15Jun86-8GG 1$\frac{1}{16}$Ⓣ:4721:1121:423fm 3¾ 115 2½ 2½ 98 99¼ Toro F4 ⒻCnts Fqr H 80-14 Sauna, Only, Justicara 9
15Jun86—Grade III; Ducked in start
31May86-8Hol 1 :453 1:101 1:352ft 6½ 114 1½ 21½ 44½ 47 StnsGL1 ⒻHaw H 79-16 DontstopThmusc,TllYou,Frn'sVlntn 6
31May86—Grade II
Jan 18 SA 6f gd 1:134 h Dec 26 SA 5f ft :584 h ●Dec 12 SA 6f ft 1:111 h ●Dec 4 SA 6f ft 1:12 h

11–1

Blushing All Over
WARREN R J JR 116
Own.—Fisher M R
B. m. 5, by Blushing Groom—Victory Kingdom, by Viceregal
Br.—Miller L (Ky)
Tr.—Gregson Edwin
Lifetime 11 5 2 0 $51,410
1986 4 1 0 0 $22,000
1984 7 4 2 0 $29,410
Turf 11 5 2 0 $51,410

1Nov86-9SA 1 Ⓣ:4631:1041:363fm 12 116 2½ 94 1216 1215½ McHrDG10 ⒻMdwckH 78-07 Aberuschka, Duckweed, Solva 12
8Oct86-8SA a6½fⓉ:213 :4431:144fm 8½ 116 73½ 73¼ 4¾ 63 McHrDG1 ⒻAtm DysH 82-14 Shywing,HerRoyalty,WaterCrystals 9
8Oct86—Broke slowly; blocked into drive; Run in divisions
9Aug86-8Dmr 1 Ⓣ:4611:1041:342fm 11 116 53 82¾ 810 811¼ McHrDG7 ⒻPlmr H 89-04 Aberuschka, Sauna,Fran'sValentine 9
9Aug86—Grade II; Bumped start; fanned wide 3/8 turn
9Jly86-8Hol 1 Ⓣ:4621:1011:342fm 5½ 116 45 31½ 11 1¾ McHrgDG6 ⒻAw40000 — — BlushingAllOver,FolkArt,Cnyk'sStr 8
19Sep85♦1MLaffitte(Fra) a1 1:35 gd 8¾ 112 Ⓣ 1no Legrix E de la Tmise H BlshngAllOvr,ClssclWy,ChrmngDk 20
25Aug85♦3Deauville(Fra) a1¼ 2:194sf 4½ 112 Ⓣ 55¼ BnoitG ⒻP FrncsAndreH Lady Day, Thimpu, Gazelia 20
13Aug85♦3Deauville(Fra) a1 1:451sf 5 113 Ⓣ 12 Benoit G ⒻPx d Frncvll H BlushingAllOvr,Piptun,ScrltSlippr 18
24Jly85♦3Compiegne(Fra) a1⅛ 1:481gd 14 106 Ⓣ 13 BnoitG Pc Rob Vlnue H BlushingAllOver, LimitUp, Sharya 11
8Jly85♦6LionAners(Fra) a1¼ : gd — 135 Ⓣ 2¾ Adda P Px de Feneu SpeedyDick,BlushingAllOvr,Thrsit 13
8Jly85—No time taken. Race for Lady and Gentleman riders
Jan 13 SA 3f ft :352 h Jan 8 SA 6f m 1:14 h Jan 1 SA 6f ft 1:132 h Dec 27 Hol tr.t 5f ft 1:041 h

15–1

Ambra Ridge
B. m. 5, by Cox's Ridge—Queen Ambra, by Alhambra
Br.—Hooper F W (Fla) 1987 1 0 0 0 $3,600
STEVENS S A 114 Tr.—Fenstermaker L R 1986 7 1 0 2 $36,250
Own.—Hooper F W Lifetime 24 4 4 6 $138,275 Turf 7 1 1 1 $31,850

2Jan87-8SA 1⅛Ⓣ:4621:1111:49 fm 26 114 13½ 11 31½ 46½ StevensSA8 ⒻAw48000 75-18 Outstandingly,FrauAltiv,NewBruce 8
10Dec86-8Hol 1¹⁄₁₆Ⓣ:4721:11 1:422fm 7¾ 117 2½ 1hd 2hd 1no Solis A2 ⒻAw31000 82-18 AmbraRidge,AffectionAffirmed,Rea 7
28Nov86-3Hol 7f :221 :451 1:232ft 9-5 116 31½ 42 52 31¾ Solis A6 ⒻAw28000 85-14 Sign Off, Good Zar, Ambra Ridge 6
28Nov86—Bumped break, wide through stretch
7Nov86-7Hol 1¹⁄₁₆Ⓣ:4721:1121:42 fm 15 117 12 1½ 3½ 54 Solis A2 ⒻAw30000 80-16 StllCloud,BlushingRedhd,Rkindling 8
11Oct86-3SA 1 :46 1:102 1:363ft 14 115 34 44 34 35¾ Solis A3 ⒻAw35000 79-17 Wterside,TwilightRidge,AmbrRidge 5
11Oct86—Bumped start
15Sep86-11Pom 6½f :213 :45 1:163ft 3½ 114 67½ 610 69 512½ Solis A2 ⒻⓇPio Pico 85-08 BoldVegs,Izbelle'sQuillo,AlwysAHit 8
12Feb86-8SA a6½fⓉ:22 :4431:153fm 9¾ 115 64½ 55 66½ 65 Solis A1 ⒻMnrva H 76-19 WaterCrystals,BaronessDirect,Solv 8
12Feb86—Veered in start
18Jan86-8SA 1¹⁄₁₆:452 1:093 1:414ft 16 114 913 88½ 68½ 46½ Solis A9 ⒻEl Encino 86-12 Lady'sSecret,Shywing,ShrpAscent 10
18Jan86—Grade III
27Dec85-8SA 7f :222 :45 1:222ft 29 114 61¾ 52 32 33½ Solis A3 ⒻLa Brea 84-16 SvnnhSlew,Ldy'sSecret,AmbrRidge 7
27Dec85—Grade III
15Dec85-4Hol 7f :22 :451 1:224ft *8-5 115 32 2hd 12½ 11¾ SolisA5 ⒻⓇStrgt Deal 90-09 Ambra Ridge, In Hopes, Wild Kitty 5
15Dec85—Wide into stretch
Nov 23 Hol 5f ft 1:013 h Nov 16 Hol 5f ft 1:01 h

4–5

Shywing *
Ch. m. 5, by Wing Out—Cheyenne Birdsong, by Restless Wind
Br.—Cardiff Stud Farm (Cal) 1987 1 0 0 0 $4,500
VALENZUELA P A 116 Tr.—Fanning Jerry 1986 14 3 6 2 $267,805
Own.—Crystl Sprng Fm & Hubbard Lifetime 29 7 8 2 $422,930 Turf 9 2 4 1 $135,055

1Jan87-8SA 6f :211 :44 1:094ft 11 119 64¾ 45½ 25 45 VlnzlPA3 ⒻLs Flrs H 84-19 PineTreeLne,RngoonRuby,HrRoylty 8
1Jan87—Grade III
6Dec86-8Hol 1⅛:462 1:112 1:50 gd 2½ 117 44 54½ 614 726¼ PncLJr4 ⒻSlvr Bls H 61-16 Family Style, Infinidad, Waterside 7
6Dec86—Grade II
23Nov86-8Hol 1⅛Ⓣ:4731:1131:48 fm 13 123 12 11½ 43 96¾ ShmrW5 ⒻMtrarch Iv 81-13 Auspiciante, Aberuschka, Reloy 12
23Nov86—Grade I; Lugged out late
1Nov86-5SA 1¼:461 1:344 2:011ft 10 123 57½ 713 719 721¼ PncLJr7 ⒻBr Cp Dstff 62-13 Ldy'sScrt,Frn'sVlntin,Outstndingly 8
1Nov86—Grade I; Wide
19Oct86-8SA 1⅛Ⓣ:46 1:1041:473fm 3¾ 118 21 1hd 2½ 21½ PcLJr2 ⒻLs Plmas H 87-11 Outstandingly, Shywing, Justicara 6
19Oct86—Grade II
8Oct86-8SA a6½fⓉ:213 :4431:144fm *2¾ 120 3½ 3nk 2½ 11¼ PncLJr7 ⒻAtm Dys H 85-14 Shywing,HerRoyalty,WaterCrystals 9
8Oct86—Run in divisions
14Jun86- Hol 1 :452 1:101 1:351ft — 119 3nk 43 32 11 PncLJr2 ⒻⓈValkyr H 87-14 Shywing,Frn'sVlentine,WterCrystls 4
14Jun86—Took up 1/2; No wagering
1Jun86-8GG 7½fⓉ:224 :45 1:293fm*4-5 121 23 2hd 35 22 CstndM6 ⒻMs Amrca 90-16 Solva, Shywing, Spectacular Joke 6
10May86-8Hol 7f :22 :444 1:214ft *8-5 120 41½ 42¾ 3½ 31¾ PcLJr3 ⒻA Gleam H 93-12 Outstandingly, Eloquack, Shywing 5
10May86—Grade III
5Apr86-8GG 1 Ⓣ:4721:1131:361fm*8-5 119 14⅔ 1½ 4¾ 3hd LphT8 ⒻMry Mdlne H 86-08 L'Attrayante, Only, Shywing 10
5Apr86—Drifted out late
Jan 10 SA 5f gd 1:014 h ●Dec 29 SA 5f ft :584 h Dec 21 SA 5f ft :591 h Dec 14 SA 4f ft :472 h

5–2

Waterside
Ch. m. 5, by Topsider—Talk Out, by Tobin Bronze
Br.—Elmendorf Farm (Ky) 1987 1 0 0 0
PINCAY L JR 6-N 118 Tr.—Mandella Richard 1986 6 1 0 2 $44,300
Own.—Cooke J K Lifetime 13 4 2 2 $99,225 Turf 1 0 0 0

1Jan87-8SA 6f :211 :44 1:094ft 13 117 44½ 78 78½ 710½ PncLJr8 ⒻLs Flrs H 78-19 PineTreeLne,RngoonRuby,HrRoylty 8
1Jan87—Grade III; Wide; lugged out
6Dec86-8Hol 1⅛:462 1:112 1:50 gd 8½ 113 11½ 1½ 35½ 310 CrdrAJr5 ⒻSlvr Bls H 77-16 Family Style, Infinidad, Waterside 7
6Dec86—Grade II
3Nov86-7SA 1 :452 1:101 1:36 ft 3½ 117 1½ 1hd 3½ 43¾ PncyLJr4 ⒻPrncs Rny 84-14 Infinidad, Fairly Old, Stemware 9
11Oct86-3SA 1 :46 1:102 1:363ft 2 117 12 11 11½ 14½ Pincay LJr2 ⒻAw35000 85-17 Wterside,TwilightRidge,AmbrRidge 5
30Aug86-5Dmr 1¹⁄₁₆Ⓣ:4631:1121:43 fm*7-5 117 11 1½ 2hd 64¼ Pincay LJr5 ⒻAw28000 87-11 ShortSleeves,PlumTasty,MngezLes 8
30Aug86—Broke stride late
8Aug86-8Dmr 6f :213 :45 1:084ft *3-2 117 21 21 31 42½ Pincay LJr3 ⒻAw24000 91-13 Comprbility,Izbll'sQuillo,SilntArrivl 6
19Jly86-10LA 7f :214 :444 1:23 ft *2-5 121 32½ 33½ 35½ 311 PncLJr1 ⒻChapman H 82-12 ReigningCountess,BoldVegs,Wtrsid 3
19Jly86—Run in divisions
24Nov85-5Hol 7f :22 :45 1:212ft *4-5 120 3nk 1hd 13 16 Pincay LJr6 ⒻAw22000 97-08 Waterside, Miss O. B. E., Orchestra 6
24Nov85—Wide early
3Nov85-8SA 1¹⁄₁₆:45 1:103 1:422ft 3¾ 117 21 2½ 11½ 2hd PcLJr4 ⒻLnda Vsta H 89-15 Savannah Slew,Waterside,Goldspell 8
3Nov85—Grade III
4Oct85-5SA 1¹⁄₁₆:453 1:094 1:422ft *3-5 117 1hd 2hd 12 12½ Pincay LJr4 ⒻAw26000 89-16 Waterside,LuckyRobert,MngezLes 10
●Dec 30 SA 3f ft :333 h Dec 24 SA 5f ft :593 h ●Dec 17 Hol 4f ft :463 h Nov 28 Hol 1 ft 1:404 h

A. Bet *Shywing* as a place or show overlay
B. Bet *Ambra Ridge* to win and box it in an Exacta with *Shywing*
C. Box *Shywing* and *Waterside* in multiple exactas
D. Throw out *Waterside* as an overbet 2nd choice and key *Shywing* on top in exactas to *Fleet Secretariat, Blushing All Over*, and *Ambra Ridge*.

52. Six horses, impressive sprinters, enough public confusion to spread out the betting, the kind of 6F event handicappers at all major tracks confront routinely. By any basic standard, one horse actually figures clearly. Find this solid bet.

3rd Del Mar

6 FURLONGS. (1.07⅗) ALLOWANCE. Purse $26,000. 3-year-olds and upward, non-winners of $3,000 three times other than maiden, claiming or starter. Weights, 3-year-olds, 117 lbs.; older, 122 lbs. Non-winners of two such races since June 1, allowed 2 lbs.; of such a race of $13,000 since July 1, 4 lbs.; since April 20, 6 lbs.

Coupled—Tommy The Hawk and Honky Tonk Dancer.

A.
16–1

Sweetwater Springs B. c. 3, by Tantoul—Mrs Vee Vee, by Ridan
SOLIS A 111 Br.—Goldman & Coleman (Cal) 1987 8 2 3 0 $60,875
Tr.—Stute Warren 1986 4 1 1 0 $17,150
Own.—Berger-Goldman-Goldman Lifetime 12 3 4 0 $78,025 Turf 3 1 1 0 $35,500
24Jun87-8Hol 6f :212 :443 1:092ft 13 114 53¾ 63½ 67 611¾ Castanon AL 4 Aw27000 84-13 HghHook,OrLordshp,HnkyTnkDncr 7
3Jun87-7Hol 6f :22 :45 1:10 ft 4 1075 42½ 42½ 43½ 54¼ Patton D B 4 Aw27000 89-13 SvonTower,LuckyMsddo,PisnoPete 7
10Apr87-8SA a6½f Ⓣ:204 :43 1:142fm 2½ 121 32 2hd 22½ 56 CstnnAL 7 ⓇC Whthm 81-13 TheQuippr,McKnziPrinc,HppyInSpc 7
25Mar87-8SA a6½f Ⓣ:212 :4341:15 fm 3 117 33½ 33½ 22½ 22¼ Castanon A L 3 Bldwn 82-16 ChmTm,SwttrSprngs,McKnzPrnc 11
12Mar87-8SA a6½f Ⓣ:212 :44 1:16 fm 5 118 2hd 2hd 1½ 11¾ Castanon AL 7 Aw40000 79-21 SwtwtrSprngs,HppyInSpc,ChmTm 10
16Feb87-7SA 6f :212 :441 1:104gd 8-5 118 21½ 1½ 11½ 1½ Castanon AL 1 Aw26000 84-21 SwtwtrSprngs,FltngJt,HollywdSrnd6
16Feb87—Bumped stretch
6Feb87-3SA 6f :211 :433 1:084ft 2¾ 118 22½ 21½ 21½ 24 Castanon AL 4 Aw26000 90-15 MountLagun,SweetwterSprings,Wr 7
24Jan87-3SA 6f :212 :442 1:101ft 6¼ 118 42½ 21½ 21½ 22 Castanon AL 9 Aw26000 85-18 HppyInSpc,SwtwtrSprings,ThQuppr9
24Jan87—Lugged in late
14Dec86-4Hol 7f :214 :45 1:241ft 3¾ 120 11 1½ 106¼ 1115¾ ValenzuelPA1 Aw22000 67-18 OrchardSong,Reland,HoustonBrgg 11
23Nov86-1Hol 6f :212 :45 1:103ft 2 118 11 12½ 13 12½ Valenzuela P A 4 Mdn 90-12 SwtwtrSprngs,McKnzPrnc,FllOfFls 6
Aug 13 Dmr 4f ft :471 h Aug 8 Dmr 6f ft 1:15 h Aug 3 Dmr 4f ft :492 h Jly 29 Dmr 6f ft 1:124 h

B.
3–1

Jamoke B. c. 3, by Relaunch—Planning, by Stage Door Johnny
Br.—Glen Hill Farm (Fla) 1987 6 2 0 0 $69,675
SHOEMAKER W 113 Tr.—Proctor Willard L 1986 3 1 0 0 $11,625
Own.—Glen Hill Farm Lifetime 9 3 0 0 $81,300 Turf 1 0 0 0
3Jly87-8Hol 1⅛:46 1:094 1:473ft 18 115 64 53½ 59½ 414¼ Baze G4 Slvr Scrn H 85-09 Candi's Gold, OnTheLine,TheMedic 6
3Jly87—Grade II; Poor start
23May87-8Hol 1$\frac{1}{16}$Ⓣ:4631:1111:43 fm 3 117 65 63¾ 710 614½ ShmkrW6 Wl Rgrs H 64-21 SomethingLucky,TheMedic,Persvrd 9
23May87—Grade III
22Apr87-8Hol 7f :214 :442 1:221ft 3¾ 117 31 31 2hd 11 ShoemkrW5 Debonair 93-18 Jmoke,Persevered,HonkyTonkDncr 7
4Apr87-9SA 1$\frac{1}{16}$:452 1:101 1:432ft 3 114 21 2½ 2hd 1½ ShoemkerW6 Aw31000 84-17 Jamoke, Laguna Native, The Medic 9
22Mar87-2SA 6f :213 :45 1:10 gd 11 1115 43 54¾ 35 24½ † Cox D W5 Aw29000 83-23 Lookinforthbgon,‡Jmok,ClssyVgors 7
22Mar87—Veered in sharply, bumped start; †Disqualified and placed fourth
8Mar87-6SA 6f :211 :442 1:094ft 15 1105 43 41½ 54 55¾ Cox D W8 Aw28000 83-15 War, Candi's Gold, Laguna Native 8
8Mar87—Broke slowly; wide into stretch
30Oct86-7SA 6f :214 :451 1:102ft 7 120 31 52½ 45½ 58¾ Sibille R5 Aw25000 77-18 MstrflAdvoct,HostnBrgg,SprmStnd 8
30Oct86—Rough start
19Oct86-6SA 6f :22 :452 1:11 ft 10 118 1½ 1hd 1hd 13½ Sibille R2 Mdn 83-18 Jamoke,SavorFire,BrigntineDncer 12
3Oct86-6SA 6f :214 :443 1:092ft 3¼ 118 85½ 712 817 823½ McCarron C J8 Mdn 67-17 Cpot,WndwoodLn,BooBoo'sBckro 12
Aug 15 Dmr 3f ft :354 h Aug 9 Dmr 5f ft 1:002 h Aug 2 Dmr 6f ft 1:122 h Jly 25 Dmr 5f ft 1:02 h

C.

10–1

***Thalassino Asteri** B. c. 4, by Formidable—Smooth Siren, by Sea-Bird II

DELAHOUSSAYE E 116 Br.—Hesmonds Stud (Eng) 1987 7 0 1 3 $23,700

Tr.—Palma Hector O 1986 9 2 0 2 $41,150

Own.—LaTre-Rbnstn-VkyBthSt etal Lifetime 19 3 1 5 $68,867 Turf 12 2 1 1 $30,017

2Aug87-3Dmr 6½f :213 :442 1:16 ft 18 116 613 69½ 45 32½ Solis A1 80000 89-12 Brlnd,SlipperySilver,ThlssinoAsteri 6
2Aug87—Wide in stretch

26Mar87-8SA a6½f Ⓣ:213 :4321:151fm 2¾ 117 44 47 34 61½ Pincay L Jr2 Aw37000 81-17 Hydrostatic,SpeedyShannon,RiDen 8
26Mar87—Steadied late

1Mar87-5SA a6½f Ⓣ:212 :4421:152fm 14 117 85¾ 85¼ 33 21¾ Pincay L Jr4 100000 80-18 ChmponPlot,ThlssnoAstr,PnstrpII 11

19Feb87-5SA 1 :46 1:103 1:354ft 11 116 11 2hd 2hd 42 DelhoussyeE1 Aw38000 87-13 Iron Eyes, Hills Bid, Metronomic 8

29Jan67-8SA a6½f Ⓣ:212 :44 1:15 fm 22 116 43 64 55½ 34¾ Baze G9 Aw34000 79-16 PrincBobbyB.,Mr.Mdi,ThlssnoAstr 10

14Jan87-7SA 1⅛Ⓣ:4631:1131:492fm 14 120 11 2hd 51¼ 712 DelhoussyeE1 Aw36000 68-18 MstrWondrflII,Dggr'sRst,BlloHrznt 8

2Jan87-7SA 1$\frac{1}{16}$:462 1:11 1:441ft 3½ 117 21½ 2hd 1½ 3½ DelhoussyeE4 Aw36000 79-22 YoungBlde,MustinLk,ThlssinoAstri 6

7Dec86-7Hol 1 :441 1:093 1:352gd 4½ 115 31 32 32 37½ Stevens G L2 HcpO 78-18 LateRequest,TheFlts,ThlssinoAsteri 7
7Dec86—Lost whip 3/16

28Nov86-7Hol 1 Ⓣ:4631:1041:353fm 3½ 119 11½ 11½ 11½ 1hd DelhoussyeE3 Aw26000 89-11 ThalassinoAsteri,Havildar,PicatrixII 9

11Nov86-5Hol 1 :453 1:104 1:362ft 5 119 51¾ 51¾ 31 41½ Soto S B2 Aw26000 79-20 DonB.Blue,BoldBrvoII,ForsytheBoy 7

Aug 12 Dmr 5f ft :592 h Jly 29 Dmr 4f ft :493 h Jly 22 Hol 6f ft 1:13 h Jly 15 Hol 6f ft 1:14 h

D.

5–2

Honky Tonk Dancer B. c. 3, by Tonkaton—Last Chanz to Danz, by Dynastic

GRYDER A T 1085 Br.—Owens N D (Ky) 1987 4 2 0 2 $42,750

Tr.—Mulhall Richard W 1986 3 1 0 1 $11,900

Own.—Arnold-Clark-Clearman et al Lifetime 7 3 0 3 $54,650

24Jun87-8Hol 6f :212 :443 1:092ft *6-5 1085 43½ 53 32 33½ Gryder A T 2 Aw27000 92-13 HghHook,OrLordshp,HnkyTnkDncr 7

11Jun87-8Hol 6f :22 :451 1:093ft 2¼e 1075 22½ 21 11½ 15 Gryder A T 4 Aw25000 95-18 HonkyTonkDancer,Pilor,ThunderCt 8
11Jun87—Broke in, bumped

22Apr87-8Hol 7f :214 :442 1:221ft *2 117 1½ 1½ 1hd 31 DelhoussyE 3 Debonair 92-18 Jmoke,Persevered,HonkyTonkDncr 7

3Apr87-7SA 6f :214 :45 1:10 ft *7-5 116 31 31 11 13 DelhoussyeE 5 Aw29000 88-17 HonkyTnkDncr,CntctGm,WndwdLn 8

19Jly86-8Hol 6f :22 :452 1:113ft 6½ 117 33 43½ 44 86 DlhssyE8 Hol Juv Chp 80-15 CaptainValid,Qulify,JzzingAround 12
19Jly86—Grade II

4Jun86-5Hol 5f :221 :46 :581ft 4 118 1hd 1hd 11½ 15½ Delahoussaye E8 Mdn 95-18 HonkyTonkDncr,Chsos,BrodwyPnt 10

21May86-5Hol 5f :22 :452 :58 ft 2¾ 118 22½ 2½ 3nk 32¾ Delahoussaye E5 Mdn 93-13 MstrflAdvct,BrdyPnt,HnkTnkDncr 10

Aug 6 Dmr 5f ft :592 h ●Jly 8 Hol 6f ft 1:131 h

E.

3–1

Temptation Time Ch. c. 3, by Olden Times—Mi Quimera, by Good Manners

PINCAY L JR 113 Br.—Preston Fm & Murty Fms (Ky) 1987 6 3 1 0 $41,975

Tr.—Moreno Henry Turf 1 0 0 0

Own.—Wichita Equine Inc Lifetime 6 3 1 0 $41,975

29Jly87-8Dmr 1 Ⓣ:4631:1111:362fm 3½ 117 42 64 65½ 77 PincyLJr 1 ⓇOceanside 82-13 SavonaTower,BeScenic,CelticRelity 8
29Jly87—Rank, steadied early drive; Run in divisions

1Jly87-7Hol 6½f :22 :443 1:161ft 6 117 11½ 11¼ 11 11¾ Pincay L Jr 4 Aw25000 99-13 TempttionTime,Pewtr,Rconnoitring 6

11Jun87-8Hol 6f :22 :451 1:093ft 3½ 117 45½ 34 45 48¼ Pincay L Jr 7 Aw25000 87-18 HonkyTonkDancer,Pilor,ThunderCt 8
11Jun87—Broke in a tangle

29May87-8Hol 6f :214 :451 1:104ft 2¾ 120 1hd 1hd 1½ 11¼ Pincay L Jr 5 Aw22000 89-16 TempttionTime,ANewEr,KingOfBzr 6
29May87—Lugged out stretch

16May87-6Hol 6f :214 :451 1:101ft *1 117 31½ 31 21 11¼ Pincay L Jr 7 Mdn 92-13 TempttionTim,HilCommndr,Fnticol 8
16May87—Lugged out backstretch, 3/8 turn

2May87-4Hol 6f :22 :453 1:103ft 2¾ 115 1½ 1hd 21 22½ Pedroza M A 2 Mdn 87-13 FiveShy,TempttionTim,ChstnutFrz 8
2May87—Bumped start, 1/2; lugged out late

Aug 15 Dmr 3f ft :35 h Aug 10 Dmr 5f ft 1:002 h Aug 5 Dmr 4f ft :473 h Jly 28 Dmr 3f ft :353 h

F.
2–1

Recognized — B. h. 5, by Raise a Native—Responsive, by Reviewer
VALENZUELA P A **118** Br.—Harbor View Farm (Ky) Tr.—Barrera Lazaro S
Own.—Harbor View Farm Lifetime 19 4 5 2 $99,358
1987 10 3 2 0 $63,150
1986 3 0 1 1 $8,160
Turf 3 0 2 0 $11,600

1Aug87-7Dmr 6½f :22 :44^2 1:15^{2}ft 2¼ 116 4^1 2½ 3^1 4^1 ValenzuelPA 2 Aw26000 94-15 BoldSmoochr,DnB.Bl,TmmyThHwk 6
1Aug87—Bobbled start
11Jly87-3Hol 1 :45 1:09 1:34^{3}ft 6½ 117 1^{hd} 2^{hd} 1^1 1^{hd} Valenzuela P A 4 95000 90-12 Rcognizd,Billy'sBck,Amnothrbrothr 7
11Jly87—Bumped start
13Jun87-7Hol 1$\frac{1}{16}$ Ⓣ:46^{4}1:10^{2}1:40^{2}fm 5 122 2½ 2½ 5^5 7^{9½} ValenzuelPA 1 Aw30000 82-08 Castlemartin King, Swink, Kadial 8
13Jun87—Broke out, bumped
25May87-9Hol 1$\frac{1}{16}$:46^1 1:10^4 1:42^{4}ft 4½ 121 2^{1½} 2½ 1^{2½} 1^{3½} ValenzuelPA 4 Aw27000 95-15 Recognized,EightyBlowZro,Extrnix 6
10May87-7Hol 1 :44^4 1:09^3 1:35^{3}ft 2¾ 115 1½ 2½ 1^{hd} 1^{hd} McCarronCJ 5 Aw24000 85-17 Recognized, Danski, Magic Leader 7
16Apr87-5SA a6½f Ⓣ:21^2 :44^{1}1:14^{3}fm *2 117 3^2 2^1 2½ 2^{4½} McCarronCJ 5 Aw29000 81-15 Rufjan, Recognized, T. H. Lark 8
9Apr87-5SA a6½f Ⓣ:21^3 :43^{4}1:14^{2}fm 4¾ 118 3^3 3^{1½} 3^{1½} 2^{2¾} Stevens G L 5 Aw29000 84-09 Rinnegato, Recognized, Mondanite 9
9Apr87—Steadied start
22Mar87-5SA 6½f :21^4 :45^2 1:17^{4}gd 8 118 5^{3½} 4^3 4^{2½} 4^{3¼} Stevens G L^5 Aw29000 78-23 City View, Starshield,MidnightIce 10
15Mar87-2SA 6½f :21^4 :45^2 1:17^{2}ft 4 117 4^3 4^{3½} 5^{5¼} 7^{6¾} Meza R Q^{11} Aw28000 76-20 Don'sIrshMlody,Dvl'sIc,TmFrSkrt 11
15Mar87—Wide 3/8 turn
28Feb87-6SA 6½f :21^4 :44^2 1:15^{2}ft 8 117 7^{6½} 7^{9½} 7^{6¾} 5^{7½} Pincay L Jr^2 Aw27000 86-17 JudgeAngelucci,PrincO'Fir,Strshild 9
Aug 15 Dmr 3f ft :35^3 h Aug 9 Dmr 5f ft :59^1 h ● Jly 26 Dmr 5f ft :59^1 h Jly 19 Hol 5f ft 1:00^4 h

53. The best bet is

6th Santa Anita

OUT OF CHUTE ▸ 6½ FURLONGS SANTA ANITA

6 ½ FURLONGS. (1.14) MAIDEN CLAIMING. Purse $16,000. 4–year–olds and upward. Weights, 4–year–olds, 119 lbs.; older, 120 lbs. Claiming price $50,000; if for $45,000 allowed 2 lbs.

A.
21–1

Dimerio — Ch. g. 4, by Dimaggio—Rowisa, by Windy Sands
SIBILLE R **119** Br.—Tradewinds Farm (Cal) Tr.—Hazelwood Julie K $50,000
Own.—Berliner N & Toni Lifetime 0 0 0 0
1987 0 M 0 0
1986 0 M 0 0
Jan 31 SA 4f ft :47^3 hg ● Jan 26 GD tr. 6f ft 1:13^2 hg Jan 20 SA 6f ft 1:01^2 h Jan 12 SA 4f ft :49^3 h

B.
38–1

Royal Robbie — B. g. 4, by King of Kings—Front Cover, by Frontlash
MCHARGUE D G **119** Br.—Carrasco C & Dorothy L (Cal) Tr.—Buonaiuto John $50,000
Own.—Carrasco-Carrasco-Robinson Lifetime 0 0 0 0
1987 0 M 0 0
1986 0 M 0 0
● Jan 31 Pom 6f ft 1:14 hg Jan 24 SA 6f ft 1:15^2 hg ● Jan 17 Pom 6f ft 1:14^2 h Jan 10 Pom 3f sl :36^2 h

C.
12–1

Detector — Dk. b. or br. g. 5, by Radar Ahead—Crystal Bend, by Triple Bend
VALENZUELA P A **120** Br.—Vail S H (Cal) Tr.—McAnally Ronald $50,000
Own.—Vail S H Lifetime 7 0 0 1 $4,350
1987 1 M 0 0
1986 3 M 0 1 $4,350

22Jan87-6SA 6½f :21^4 :45^1 1:17 ft 52 121 3^2 3^{1½} 4^{5½} 6^{10½} Kaenel J 10 Mdn 74-23 Rufjan, Starshield, Predominance 11
27Dec86-6SA 6f :22 :45^3 1:11 ft 32 1155 7^4 9^{7½} 6^{5¼} 7^{6½} Cox D W^5 Mdn 76-19 General At War,Rufjan,Mondanite 12
19Dec86-1Hol 6f :22 :45^4 1:11 ft 26 1175 4^{1½} 3^{2½} 3^3 3^{6½} Cox D W^6 Mdn 81-17 GretYnkee,Don'sIrishMlody,Dtctor 7
15Feb86-8SA 6½f :22^2 :45 1:15^{2}ft 56 106 4^{1½} 4^{4½} 5^9 5^{11¾} AlvrezA^3 Sra Mdre H 81-14 HaloFolks,PanchoVilla,WiseStrtegy 5
15Feb86—Grade III; Bumped, steadied at 5/8
21Jly85-6Hol 6f :22^3 :45^4 1:09^{4}ft 61 115 7^{5¼} 7^{13} 7^{19} 7^{20½} Olivares F^2 Mdn 77-04 Absolute, Brand Image, Mr. Media 7
20Jun85-2Hol 6f :22^3 :46 1:11 ft 22 115 4^{2¾} 5^{9½} 6^8 7^8 Olivares F^1 Ⓢ Mdn 84-07 LikShntin,RodOfFortun,Cptn'sChnc 9
5Jun85-1Hol 6f :22^1 :45^4 1:09^{1}ft 13 1105 7^{7¾} 8^{17} 8^{18} 8^{24¼} Shaw K^9 Mdn 77-08 Epidaurus,ProfessorRoberts,Enviro 9
Jan 30 SA 4f ft :48 h Jan 19 Hol 4f ft :48^3 h Jan 13 Hol 5f ft 1:04^1 h Jan 8 Hol 5f ft 1:02^2 h

D.

2–1

Sir Drone
DELAHOUSSAYE E — 117
Own.—Yasuda G
Dk. b. or br. c. 4, by Drone—Mademoiselle W, by Chieftain
Br.—King J H & H G (Ky) — 1987 0 M 0 0
Tr.—Palma Hector O — $45,000 — 1986 0 M 0 0
Lifetime 0 0 0 0

Jan 27 SA 6f ft 1:002 h ●Jan 21 SA 4f ft :463 h Jan 15 SA 4f ft :464 h Jan 9 SA 3f sl :373 h

E.

6–1

Dr. Sprocket
SOTO S B — 117
Own.—Austin–Nanayakkara–Zois
B. c. 4, by Circle—Crowded Docket, by Mr Washington
Br.—Turf Bloodstock Ltd II (Va) — 1987 1 M 0 0
Tr.—Gonzalez Sal — $45,000 — 1986 3 M 0 0 $3,325
Lifetime 4 0 0 0 $3,325

22Jan87-6SA	6½f	:214	:451	1:17 ft	20	120	64½	56	57	710¾	Soto S B4	Mdn	74-23	Rufjan, Starshield, Predominance	11
19Dec86-1Hol	6f	:22	:454	1:11 ft	10	120	65	56	57	510¾	Soto S B4	Mdn	77-17	GretYnkee,Don'sIrishMlody,Dtctor	7
22Nov86-4Hol	6f	:223	:461	1:11 ft	14	120	51¼	3nk	31½	44¾	Soto S B6	Mdn	83-13	Brilliant Leader, Rewana, Thaxted	6

22Nov86—Crowded into drive; lugged in stretch

12Nov86-4Hol	7f	:222	:452	1:232ft	11	119	43½	43	47	412¼	Soto S B1	Mdn	75-15	Magic Leader, Decore, Rewana	6

Jan 17 SA 5f ft 1:01 hg Jan 11 SA 1 ft 1:432 h Dec 11 Hol 5f ft 1:011 h Dec 4 Hol 6f ft 1:154 h

F.

27–1

Laughinalltheway
ORTEGA L E — 117
Own.—Moss Mr–Mrs J S
Ch. c. 4, by Foolish Pleasure—Avenare, by Up Spirits
Br.—Rafsky J (Ky) — 1987 2 M 0 0 $1,200
Tr.—Frankel Robert — $45,000 — 1986 1 M 0 0
Lifetime 3 0 0 0 $1,200

25Jan87-4SA	6f	:22	:452	1:111ft	3½	117	98¼	88	69½	611¼	Ortega L E3	M45000	70-18	Inwood Drive, Perg Jr., Sundooner	9

25Jan87—Stumbled start; lugged out

10Jan87-4SA	6f	:22	:454	1:123gd	22	119	1111	116¾	107¼	43¾	Ortega L E7	M50000	71-20	Ed's Exclusive, Hapigrin,Undenied	11
22Jun86-2Hol	6f	:221	:46	1:103ft	11	114	108	1017	914	915¾	Solis A8	M50000	75-08	HighestScript,FbulousSound,BluIc	10

Jan 21 Hol 5f ft 1:003 h ●Dec 31 Hol tr.t 4f ft :51 h Dec 23 Hol 6f ft 1:171 h Dec 17 SA 5f ft :591 h

G.

7–2

Winter Tan
BLACK C A — 119
Own.—Raynes & Wygod
Dk. b. or br. g. 4, by Tobin Bronze—Snow Lily, by Olympiad King
Br.—Wygod M J (Cal) — 1987 1 M 0 0 $1,575
Tr.—Ellis Ronald W — $50,000 — 1986 0 M 0 0
Lifetime 1 0 0 0 $1,575

22Jan87-6SA	6½f	:214	:451	1:17 ft	24	120	1½	2hd	22	48½	Black C A7	Mdn	76-23	Rufjan, Starshield, Predominance	11

Jan 31 SA 4f ft :471 h Jan 18 SA 5f ft 1:02 hg Jan 12 SA 6f ft 1:15 hg Jan 6 SA 5f gd 1:011 h

H.

2–1

Prince O' Fire
BAZE G — 119
Own.—Gonzalez F
Ch. c. 4, by Red Ryder—Thatsyourstory, by Your Alibhai
Br.—Klussman Mr–Mrs W (Cal) — 1986 5 M 3 1 $13,875
Tr.—West Ted — $50,000 — 1985 0 M 0 0
Lifetime 5 0 3 1 $13,875

27Jly86-4Dmr	6f	:22	:452	1:10 ft	2½	117	2hd	1hd	1hd	31	Pincay L Jr2	Mdn	87-10	Lud, Danielli, Prince O' Fire	8
9Jly86-7Hol	6f	:221	:46	1:112ft	*2	114	2hd	12½	13	2¾	Hernandez R11	[S]Mdn	86-18	TmForSkrto,PrncO'Fr,DowdCnyon	11
1Jun86-6Hol	6f	:22	:452	1:104ft	5	115	31½	32	32	43	Hernandez R12	Mdn	87-14	The Great Shark,Blinkers,Norquin	12
23May86-3Hol	6f	:222	:461	1:101ft	2¼	115	21½	21½	24	27	Hernandez R5	[S]Mdn	86-23	BoldBrawley,PrinceOFire,MrkChip	12
11May86-6Hol	6f	:221	:453	1:094ft	28	120	63¼	41¾	31½	22½	Hernandez R5	Mdn	92-15	MrvnSelcy,PrncOFr,Dn'sIrshMldy	10

Jan 29 SA 3f ft :372 h Jan 24 SA 5f ft 1:002 h Jan 18 SA 5f ft 1:014 h Jan 13 SA 4f ft :47 h

I.
22–1

Jose Sent Me — Ch. c. 4, by Super Concorde—She's Armed, by Truxton King
DOUGLAS R R 4-N(5) 119 — Br.—Gentry T (Ky) — 1987 2 M 0 0 $800
Own.—Theisen W — Tr.—Van Berg Jack C $50,000 — 1986 7 M 1 0 $6,150
Lifetime 10 0 1 0 $6,950

23Jan87-6SA 6f :22 :453 1:111ft 5 117 4nk 2hd 21 59 Stevens G L2 M45000 73-22 Vari Beau, Hapigrin, PrivateEagle 12
23Jan87—Broke slowly
10Jan87-4SA 6f :22 :454 1:123gd 7 119 52½ 41¾ 21 56¼ Sibille R4 M50000 69-20 Ed's Exclusive, Hapigrin,Undenied 11
10Jan87—Bumped 5 1/2
12Dec86-6Hol 6f :222 :45 1:121ft 3½ 120 3½ 3½ 22½ 33½ Meza R Q6 M32000 78-20 BornDncing,‡BrotherGen,JosSntM 12
12Dec86—Placed second through disqualification; Impeded at start
13Oct86-6SA 6½f :214 :444 1:172ft 14 117 2hd 31½ 33½ 48½ Kaenel J L6 M50000 74-19 SplitWinnrs,PisnoPt,NightmRobbr 12
6Sep86-4Dmr 6f :214 :443 1:092ft 29 117 31 36½ 411 714¼ Kaenel J L7 Mdn 77-12 Salt Dome, Decore, Park Road 11
10Aug86-4Dmr 6½f :214 :444 1:151ft 40 116 85 1112 1117 1126½ Hernandez R5 Mdn 69-08 OurLordship,Extrnix,NorthernBlzr 11

54. The only potential play in the awful route below was also an underlay. Which horse is it?

7th Los Alamitos

1 1/16 MILES. (1.38⅘) MAIDEN CLAIMING. Purse $7,000. 3-year-olds and upward. Weights, 3-year-olds, 115 lbs.; older, 122 lbs. Claiming price $12,500.

A.
12–1

Native Trimmer — Dk. b. or br. f. 3, by The Pruner—Native Bather, by Native Royalty
SUMMERS N 4-0 113 — Br.—Auerbach E (Cal) — 1987 5 M 3 0 $698
Own.—Tate R G — Tr.—Cassady John $12,500 — 1986 0 M 0 0
Lifetime 5 0 3 0 $698

15Aug87-8LA 1 1/16 :454 1:113 1:45 ft 22 114 913 1016 1023 917½ Furlong K5 [F]M28000 66-14 Corbella, Rio Serena, Big Minute 10
2Aug87-10Pre 7f :233 :481 1:282gd 28 117 63 76½ 811 89¾ Castro J G2 Pre Dby 79-12 BseFltterer,Owhtshow,CrtMeHolme 8
18Jly87-9Pre 7f :242 :484 1:274ft 8 121 32 31½ 25 25 Chance J C3 Dby Trl 87-21 Bwn'sFild,NtivTrimmr,HumblHugh 6
12Jly87-1Pre 7f :242 :491 1:292ft *8-5 119 76¼ 85½ 43½ 21½ Lague L3 [F]Mdn 82-10 Crri'sRvolt,NtivTrimmr,OurOwnStr 8
20Jun87-5Pre 7f :24 :482 1:283ft 7 116 2hd 2hd 12 24 Bazan J2 Mdn 84-11 HumbleHugh,NtivTrimmr,SirPickls 8
●Aug 20 LA 4f ft :492 bg — Jun 28 Pre 3f ft :362 h

B.
5–2

Twentyonegunsalute — B. g. 4, by Color Bearer—Sunshine In, by Fleet Nasrullah
WARREN R J JR 1-N 122 — Br.—Old English Rancho (Cal) — 1987 4 M 1 0 $1,100
Own.—Hayden–Jhnstn–Jhnstn et al — Tr.—Warren Donald $12,500 — 1986 2 M 0 0 $887
Lifetime 7 0 1 0 $1,987

11Aug87-2LA 6f :212 :451 1:11 ft *2 122 44½ 34½ 24 2½ Warren G9 [S]M12500 87-12 Dr.JohnNry,Twntyongnslt,ColAtm 10
17Jun87-5GG 1 1/16 :471 1:113 1:444ft 13 120 1hd 2hd 55 1013¾ Warren RJJr12 M18000 65-15 ClvrEch,CmmndngM,StrmArgmnt 12
10Mar87-6GG 6f :214 :443 1:101ft 7¾ 118 43 44 56½ 69½ Warren R JJr2 M28000 78-18 RglAthorty,Nt'sRbbt,TrndrmsGm 11
10Jan87-4SA 6f :22 :454 1:123gd 20 117 64 85¾ 96¾ 1013¾ Warren R JJr1 M40000 61-20 Ed's Exclusive, Hapigrin,Undenied 11
9Jly86-8LA 6f :221 :462 1:129ft 3½ 1105 77¼ 52¼ 31½ 41 Black C A9 M32000 79-18 VlntGnrton,LghtnngDn,CdDIntrpl 10
3Jan86-3SA 6f :22 :452 1:104ft 9 118 52½ 42 35 57¾ Stevens G L2 M32000 76-17 MschvousMtt,SrousPly,Trcy'sTrn 12
3Jan86—Bumped start
11Dec85-5Hol 6f :221 :461 1:114ft 3 118 45½ 35 612 717½ Pincay L Jr1 M50000 67-19 DshnrblGst,Agg'sLIRdg,MdstKng 10
11Dec85—Bumped at start
Aug 6 LA 3f ft :374 hg — Jly 31 BM 5f ft 1:012 h — Jly 24 BM 6f ft 1:261 h — Jly 17 BM 6f ft 1:15 h

C.
20–1

Sassy Score — Gr. f. 3, by Score Twenty Four—Sassala, by Sassafras
CRUZ J B 0-0 110 — Br.—Zagari S S (Cal) — 1987 3 M 0 0 $450
Own.—Frousiakis G G — Tr.—Frousiakis George $12,500 — 1986 0 M 0 0
Lifetime 3 0 0 0 $450

18Aug87-4LA 6½f :22 :462 1:183ft 19 1105 69½ 719 719 711¾ GilbertCJIII8 [F]M20000 72-14 Kalista,AutumnGle,ReflectiveNtive 9
14Aug87-1LA 6f :213 :451 1:124ft 51 113 920 924 612 410¼ Gilbert C J1 [F]M10500 69-15 FlshingFinsh,Commnc,SongOfElln 10
5Feb87-4SA 1 :471 1:124 1:391ft 56 117 814 815 821 832¾ StevnsSA1 [F][S]M32000 39-22 InhritdDughtr,WingVlvt,MrryTmpr 8
Aug 7 LA 5f ft 1:031 h — Aug 1 SA 5f ft 1:024 h — Jly 28 SA 5f ft 1:032 h — Jly 8 SA 4f ft :491 h

D.

6–1

Imperial Eagle

B. g. 3, by Flying Paster—Invicta, by Kronzeuge

Br.—Ridder B J (Cal) 1987 2 M 0 0

ORTEGA L E 115 Tr.—Hofmans David $12,500 1986 0 M 0 0

Own.—Ridder Thoroughbred Stable Lifetime 2 0 0 0

13Aug87-3Dmr 6f :221 :461 1:114ft 9¾ 1105 75¾ 9101011 913¼ Gryder A T 3 M28000 66-20 Sensitizer, Blare, Raised A Ruler 12

8Jly87-6Hol 6½f :222 :454 1:191ft 20 116 1012108¾ 77½ 68¼ Winick D8 [S]M32000 76-16 RestlessStrnger,RedRumb,ClBred 11

8Jly87—Bumped, pinched back start

Aug 8 Dmr 5f ft 1:004 h Jly 4 Hol 5f ft 1:023 hg Jun 29 Hol 6f ft 1:152 hg Jun 24 Hol 5f ft 1:022 hg

E.

3–2

Miami Bound

B. c. 3, by Tri Jet—Enchanting Susan, by Daryl's Joy

Br.—Hooper F W (Fla) 1987 8 M 2 1 $10,000

PATTON D B 1105 Tr.—Lewis Craig A $12,500 1986 0 M 0 0

Own.—Glazer Lauren Lifetime 8 0 2 1 $10,000

10Aug87-2Dmr 1⅛ :463 1:112 1:503ft 35 116 21½ 42 101011191½ Vergara O 1 M32000 57-20 MmorsOfBronz,WrAx,EmprJmmy 12

5Jun87-2Hol 1 :452 1:101 1:37 ft 4¾ 115 79¼ 66 66½ 66¾ Solis A 2 M32000 71-15 Fixation, Very Double, Grey Aloha 12

23May87-6Hol 1 :453 1:113 1:383ft 7¼ 114 64¼ 73¼ 85¾ 87 Stevens G L 5 M45000 63-15 CmnoBmbno,CrclVwDrv,SprJmmy 10

14May87-6Hol 1 :443 1:09 1:354ft 15 115 89 48½ 48½ 37½ Solis A 1 M40000 76-13 Billy'sBck,WtchTimGo,MimBound 12

30Apr87-6Hol 1 1/16 :47 1:12 1:444ft 8½ 115 53¼ 22 23 26½ Solis A 12 M40000 78-13 ExoticEgle,MimiBound,Splndrific 12

9Apr87-2SA 1 1/16 :464 1:114 1:451ft 3¼ 117 67 46½ 55½ 45½ Solis A6 Mc32000 69-18 HonorFlag,Earthdust,SuperJimmy 12

18Mar87-2SA 1 1/16 :463 1:121 1:461ft 5½ 118 58 46½ 33½ 2no Solis A10 M32000 70-17 TrnBckJohn,MmBond,StlltExprss 12

18Mar87—Bumped start

25Feb87-2SA 6½f :214 :45 1:173ft 16 118 96 67 45½ 47½ Stevens G L2 M32000 74-20 Shcky'sTryst,StndBYrMn,SprJmm 12

F.

10–1

Native Go Step

B. c. 4, by Go Step—Ricky Roy's Pride, by Ricky Roy's Prince

Br.—Langley & Fain Jr (Okla) 1987 3 M 0 0

FERNANDEZ A L 122 Tr.—Williams David E $12,500 1986 0 M 0 0

Own.—Hauser Mary Lifetime 3 0 0 0

13Aug87-2LA 1 1/16 :453 1:121 1:461ft 47 122 1½ 31½ 716 721 Aquino C 2 M12500 57-12 GilddCjun,CloudyTrip,Nwl'sFrstSon 8

31Jly87-4Dmr 6½f :221 :454 1:183ft 105 120 75½ 9121018 1026 Garcia O C 6 M28000 53-17 CostlLove,FirstHolidy,StrCfSvnnh 10

31Jly87—Bumped start

16Jly87-6Hol 6f :222 :454 1:113ft 82 120 96 109¼1214 1214¼ Stevens S A 4 M28000 71-12 NonStop,‡FlyingSonofgun,Vrbllon 12

●Jly 29 SLR tr.t 3f ft :344 hg Jly 23 SLR tr.t 7f ft 1:342 h ●Jly 13 SLR tr.t 4f ft :483 h Jun 27 SLR tr.t 5f ft 1:033 h

G.

8–1

Sailor Bones

Dk. b. or br. g. 3, by Halyard—Chili Spice, by Iron Warrior

Br.—Reynolds W L (Fla) 1987 3 M 0 1 $900

STEVENS S A 115 Tr.—Charlton Wayne $12,500 1986 0 M 0 0

Own.—Charlton B W Lifetime 3 0 0 1 $900

14Aug87-5LA 6f :214 :451 1:111ft 8¼ 115 49½ 46½ 44 37¼ Patterson A 4 M12500 80-15 Stageman, LetMeThru,SailorBones 7

26Jly87-5Hol 6f :221 :452 1:103ft 100 116 108¼ 910 1112 1115¼ Stevens S A 6 M32000 75-12 Cool Talker, Read MyLips,Pastizal 11

16Jly87-2Hol 6f :214 :45 1:102ft 28 116 107 97 78¼ 913½ Stevens S A 7 M32000 77-12 KingOfGrec,ElVquro,DrconicRwrd 12

16Jly87—Pinched at start

Aug 1 SA 5f ft 1:014 h Jly 10 SA 4f ft :471 hg Jly 3 SA 4f ft :474 hg Jun 22 SA 6f ft 1:15 h

H.

7–2

Dad's Command

Ch. g. 4, by Top Command—Bigamia, by Con Brio II

Br.—Noyes J & Murty Farm (Ky) 1987 4 M 0 0 $450

OLDHAM D H 122 Tr.—Lloyd Kim $12,500 1986 2 M 0 0

Own.—Stonegate Farm Inc Lifetime 8 0 0 0 $450 Turf 1 0 0 0

Entered 20Aug87- 4 LA

14Aug87-5LA 6f :214 :451 1:111ft 3-2 122 1hd 1hd 2½ 47½ Oldham D W 1 M12500 79-15 Stageman, LetMeThru,SailorBones 7

11Aug87-8LA 6f :213 :451 1:104ft 6¼ 122 31½ 32 58 612¼ Oldham D W 3 M25000 77-12 Galnish, Pecadillo, Fearless Viking 7

24Jly87-4Hol 1 1/16 [T]:464 1:112 1:433fm 44 122 1113 1113 1126 — Oldham D W4 Mdn — — ‡DefiniteSigns,Frnticol,BstOBunch 11

24Jly87—Eased; Ducked in sharply 7/8

16Jly87-6Hol 6f :222 :454 1:113ft 74 122 41½ 32 31 64¼ Oldham D W1 M32000 81-12 NonStop,‡FlyingSonofgun,Vrbllon 12

16Jly87—Off slowly

6Apr86-6SA 1 1/16 :46 1:11 1:44 ft 51 117 48 819 841 — Lipham T 2 Mdn — — Damon's Game,Serving,IvanPhillips 8

bApr86—Eased
30Mar86-6SA 7f :222 :454 1.234ft 82 117 96½ 96¾111511122½ Kaenel J L 9   Mdn 58-24 El Corazon, Cheapskate, Atreak 12
   30Mar86—Bumped start
26Dec85-4SA 6f :212 :442 1:102ft 72 117 53½ 66½111131113 Kaenel J L 1   Mdn 73-13 Alom'sTobin,CleverHop,RcylTrsur 11
15Dec85-1Hol 6f :222 :461 1:112ft 33 118 62½ 56 78½ 813½ Kaenel J L 7   Mdn 73-09 Bolton,RecentExchnge,RdlMyLips 12
   ● Aug 5 SA 4f ft :474 h   ● Jly 15 SA 3f ft :351 hg   Jly 8 SA 5f ft 1:011 hg   Jun 30 SA 6f ft 1:153 h

I.
4–1
Miltonmiltonmilton

WARREN G   **115**
Own.—Seltzer B E & Florence

Ch. g. 3, by Properantes—Bagger's Delight, by Three Bagger
Br.—Weissman S B (Cal)   1987 9 M 1 2 $4,150
Tr.—Dotson Jim $12,500   1986
Lifetime 9 0 1 2 $4,150

19Aug87-2LA 6½f :213 :454 1:173ft 2½ 1105 46 48 47½ 34 Gilbert C J III 16 M12500 85-12 Ephmrl,PrncSml,Mltnmltonmilton 7
10Aug87-2LA 6f :214 :454 1:11 ft 37 115 56 45½ 35½ 28½ Gilbert C J 1 Ⓢ M32000 80-13 FvPrtnrs,Mltnmltnmltn,C.P.Hrvst 10
16May87-2GG 1⅛:48 1:114 1:51 ft 10 120 2hd 3½ 69½ 713½ Lambert J 4 M16000 64-15 Infinitude,LuckyNeshr,Picho'sBob 10
7May87-1GG 1¼:463 1:121 1:461ft 8 120 811 75½ 42½ 34 Lambert J 12 M12500 68-17 Mbll'sPrnc,SnppRlt,Mltnm'tnmltn 12
31Mar87-6GG 6f :22 :452 1:113ft 26 120 63½ 66½ 56½ 66½ Davidson J R 5 M20000 75-20 Johmere, Indicate, Bewildered 11
7Mar87-6GG 1 :472 1:121 1:384ft 18 120 3½ 45 69 69 Diaz A L 5 M32000 65-16 D.D.TheKid,ExclintLw,KingsRoylty 8
28Feb87-4SA 6f :214 :443 1:104ft 89 118 97½ 89½101410¹³ Jewell J W 10 M50000 71-17 VctoryPs,MmrsOfBrnz,Ply 1snChf 12
13Feb87-4SA 1 :46 1:11 1:364gd 33 117 55½ 59 513 521 Jewell J W 2 Ⓢ M40000 63-20 Auto Focus,KingClyde,PeteNewell 10
28Jan87-6SA 6f :214 :45 1:111ft 80 118 69 811 811 812½ Jewell J W 9 M50000 69-21 Gaelic Bee, Impressive Result, Wily 9
   28Jan87—Lugged in backstretch
   Aug 5 LA 4f ft :493 h

---

55. It's Jan. 17, 1987. The track has been favoring closers strongly for the past ten days. Which horse figures best at the odds in today's opener?

1st Santa Anita

6 FURLONGS. (1.07⅗) CLAIMING. Purse $15,000. 4-year-olds and upward. Weights, 4-year-olds, 120 lbs.; older, 121 lbs. Non-winners of two races since November 3 allowed 3 lbs.; of a race since then, 5 lbs. Claiming price $16,000; if for $14,000 allowed 2 lbs. (Races when entered for $12,500 or less not considered.)

A.
5–1
Unagloshi

MEZA R Q   2–N   **116**
Own.—Shima Dr & Mrs R J

Ch. g. 8, by Exclusive Listing—Future Flame, by Old Pueblo
Br.—Sharp J D (Wash)   1986 20 8 1 2 $54,295
Tr.—Shima Robert J $16,000   1985 9 2 2 1 $14,400
Lifetime 62 17 9 10 $122,865   Turf 4 0 1 0 $3,120

13Dec86-1Hol 6f :214 :45 1:102ft 5 119 64¾ 45½ 43 42 Pincay L Jr 4 c16000 89-09 Neutral Player, Illuminize, Rodney 10
   13Dec86—Lugged out
16Nov86-4Hol 7f :22 :443 1:241ft 5 117 31 31½ 32 77 Pincay L Jr 10 c16000 76-18 Ponus, Pialor, Amarone 12
2Nov86-1SA 6½f :213 :442 1:16 ft *9-5 120 45½ 55½ 56½ 48½ DelahoussayeE 9 c16000 82-10 Rinbow'sCup,WstBoyII,LordPncho 9
   2Nov86—Wide into stretch
12Oct86-1SA 6½f :22 :452 1:174ft 4 116 72 41½ 31 1½ DelahoussayeE 1 16000 81-21 Unagloshi,Menswear,StrOfAmeric 12
10Oct86-1SA 6f :214 :45 1:104ft 4½ 116 10½2 9½0 54½ 1½ DelahoussayeE 9 12500 84-18 Unagloshi, Jacart, Be Thankful 12
   10Oct86—Wide into stretch
7Sep86-1Dmr 6f :221 :452 1:10 ft 8½ 116 66 65½ 74½ 42½ Pedroza M A 4 16000 85-13 CoursingEgl,Qudrupd,Dstn:tvlyDon 8
   7Sep86—Wide into stretch
30Aug86-1Dmr 6f :214 :45 1:092ft 3½ 116 64½ 55½ 35 35½ Baze R A 4 c12500 86-10 ExclusivKing,CoursngEgl,Unglosh 10
4Aug86-1SA 7f :222 :452 1:232ft *2½ 116 31 3½ 1½ 1½ Baze R A 11 c10000 88-13 Unagloshi, Karaka Lad, Jam Shot 12
   4Aug86—Bumped at 3/16
21Jun86-5GG 6f :222 :452 1:103ft 3½ 120 64½ 56 34½ 31½ Hummel C 6 c10000 85-15 HsStormnNormn,PlstcAvn Unglshi 12
8Aug86-7GG 6f :22 :443 1:092ft *2½ 115 34½ 43 55½ 55½ Hummel C R 6 16000 86-11 DeterminedFire,ChdO.,FeltyCould 11
   Jan 11 SA 5f ft 1:012 h   Dec 31 SA 4f ft :484 h   Dec 21 SA 3f ft :362 h   Dec 8 Hol 5f gd 1:013 h

B.

2–1

Just The Facts — Dk. b. or br. h. 5, by Pretense—Er Bear, by Dusty Canyon

KAENEL J L 116 — Br.—Delaneys Stock Farm (Cal) — 1987 1 0 1 0 $3,400

Own.—Saron Stable — Tr.—Jones Gary $16,000 — 1986 2 1 0 0 $15,400

Lifetime 11 3 2 1 $52,175

3Jan87-1SA 6f :214 :444 1:111ft *6-5 116 21 2½ 21½ 22 Kaenel J L10 [S] 20000 80-16 KidShelleen,JustTheFcts,Dd'sQust 10

24Dec86-7Hol 6f :22 :452 1:11 ft 13 116 1hd 2hd 2hd 63¼ Kaenel J L3 45000 85-20 MisterCrofter,Dnczon,RingOfPlsur 10

22Jan86-7SA 6½f :22 :451 1:162ft 4 115 31½ 31 11 13½ Hawley S5 Aw28000 88-21 Just The Facts, Air Alert, Blips 6

22Dec85-5Hol 1 :442 1:092 1:341ft 13 113 1hd 1½ 32½ 510¼ Hawley S6 Aw27000 82-17 Pride Of Ours, Hatim, Ascension 7

16Nov85-7Hol 6f :222 :452 1:092ft 12 114 63¼ 73¼ 75¼ 58½ Hawley S7 Aw22000 88-14 BolderThanBold,FullHonor,Carload 9

16Nov85—Broke out, bumped

12Jan85-8SA 7f :222 :444 1:22 ft — 114 43½ 52¾ 51¾ 62¾ Hawley S6 [S]Cal Bdrs 87-16 ThRogrsFour,NostIgi'sStr,DustyOki 9

12Jan85—No wagering due to power failure

16Dec84-8Hol 1 1/16 :453 1:103 1:432gd 29 121 65¼ 52¼ 1225 1324¾ HawleyS13 Hol Fut'y — — Stphn'sOdyssy,FrstNormn,RghtCn 13

16Dec84—Grade I; Wide 7/8 turn, steadied 1/4

21Nov84-7Hol 1 :461 1:114 1:381gd *8-5 120 1½ 12½ 12½ 1¾ Hawley S6 Aw24000 84-16 JusttheFcts,Dr.Riv,ProtectYourself 7

3Nov84-3SA 6f :22 :451 1:102ft *8-5 118 41½ 1hd 1½ 1½ Hawley S2 [S]Mdn 86-14 JstThFcts,Pckn'Rnbows,RlnchATn 11

3Nov84—Lugged out 3/8

24Oct84-6SA 6f :22 :452 1:104ft 2¾ 117 2hd 2hd 2½ 2½ Hawley S7 [S]Mdn 83-16 Calestoga, Just The Facts, Petrov 10

Dec 19 Hol 6f ft 1:144 hg — Dec 14 Hol 6f ft 1:152 h — Dec 7 Hol 5f m 1:011 hg — Dec 2 Hol 5f ft 1:033 h

C.

6–1

***Amarone** — Dk. b. or br. h. 7, by Realm—Misacre, by St Alphage

PEDROZA M A 118 — Br.—Advani Mrs M (Eng) — 1986 11 2 1 1 $35,900

Own.—Lewis Marjorie — Tr.—Harper David B $16,000 — 1985 13 1 4 0 $36,750

Lifetime 54 8 7 6 $110,654 — Turf 38 6 3 5 $65,129

17Dec86-5Hol 1 :451 1:104 1:373ft *8-5 116 11½ 11 11½ 11¼ Stevens G L6 c16000 75-22 Amarone, Gulfstreamer, Oh Dad 7

17Dec86—Bobbled break

16Nov86-4Hol 7f :22 :443 1:241ft *3-2 117 2½ 21½ 21½ 33¾ Stevens G L8 20000 79-18 Pegus, Pialor, Amarone 12

8Nov86-9Hol 6f :222 :454 1:103ft *9-5 117 11 11½ 2hd 2no Stevens G L5 25000 90-13 SandDigger,Amarone,Billy'sSpecial 6

8Nov86—Broke in a tangle

10Sep86-9Dmr 7f :22 :45 1:214ft 10 1115 23 1hd 61½ 910¼ Black C A2 c25000 86-11 Paskanell,BrndImge,SwiftMessge 12

31May86-5Hol 7f :22 :45 1:232ft 9¼ 116 31 43 98¾ 1014½ Patterson A7 40000 72-16 Rex Lake, Paskanell, Rushad 10

4May86-9Hol 1 :453 1:103 1:362ft *2 116 41¾ 58½ 816 824¼ McCarron C J5 50000 57-18 Silver Hero, Ono Gummo, Juntura 9

4May86—Lugged out drive

20Apr86-9SA a6½f Ⓣ:213 :442 1:144fm 13 118 1½ 1hd 1hd 41½ Pincay L Jr10 62500 83-15 Hwkley,RisingChum,French'sLuck 12

29Mar86-5SA a6½f Ⓣ:211 :44 1:143fm 12 118 21 21 4nk 96 Kaenel J L7 80000 80-15 BmTwnChrl,AmrcnLgn,Sndy'sEgl 11

7Feb86-5SA a6½f Ⓣ:214 :444 1:153fm 8 119 1½ 1½ 1hd 43¼ Kaenel J L1 80000 78-23 Sandy'sEagle,RisingChum,Dedicat 11

2Feb86-5SA 6½f :222 :46 1:183m *3 120 2hd 2hd 22 45½ Pincay L Jr6 80000 71-28 Bozina, Kilauea, Midford 9

Dec 10 Hol 5f ft 1:013 h — Dec 3 Hol 5f ft 1:014 h — Nov 26 Hol 4f ft :47 h

D.

12–1

Video Sid — Ch. g. 4, by Interdicto—Wildcat Fire, by Brush Fire

CASTANON A L 115 — Br.—Gilbert S M (Fla) — 1987 2 0 0 0 $1,125

Own.—Magee & Stute — Tr.—Stute Melvin F $16,000 — 1986 18 2 1 5 $23,495

Lifetime 20 2 1 5 $24,620 — Turf 2 0 0 1 $880

9Jan87-9SA 6f :214 :453 1:124sl 13 115 77½ 56½ 31 77¾ Sibille R5 c12500 66-26 West Boy II, Chagrining, Melchip 11

9Jan87—Steadied 1/16

4Jan87-3SA 6f :22 :451 1:103sy 6 112 42½ 43 44½ 47¼ Black C A8 13000 78-22 Polly'sRuler,NeutralPlyer,Grenobie 8

4Jan87—Lugged in

24Dec86-3Hol 7f :22 :452 1:24 ft 11 114 11½ 1½ 35½ 48¾ Black C A1 18000 75-20 Pilor,Gordon'sCommnd,PirepplJck 7

6Dec86-6Hol 7f :221 :452 1:242gd 18 116 22½ 22½ 24 34½ Black C A8 16000 77-16 Noon Sun,PineappleJack,VideoSid 12

6Dec86—Lugged in stretch; returned bleeding from mouth

22Nov86-6Hol 6f :223 :46 1:111ft 25 114 76¾ 56 45 33½ Black C A7 14000 83-13 Manzanero, Pico P., Video Sid 9

22Nov86—Bumped start

6Nov86-2Hol 6f :224 :464 1:121ft 39 116 98½ 85¼ 64½ 54¾ Ortega L E3 16000 77-17 Toddy Boy, Manzanero, BlackCross 9

6Nov86—Rough start

29Oct86-9SA 1 1/16 :464 1:113 1:443ft 14 113 64¾ 75¾ 89½ 811 Solis A7 14000 67-17 BlowTheTrumpts,RySol,ElgntHost 10

29Oct86—Bumped break; rank 7/8

3Oct86-5SA 6f :221 :452 1:102ft 50 116 75¾ 910 912 814¼ Lipham T9 20000 72-17 NtvCptv,Nck'sPrnc,JohnsTomrrw 10

3Oct86—Broke in, bumped

12Sep86-6Suf 6f :222 :454 1:12 ft 4½ 111 33 56½ 57½ 610¼ Ritvo T1 Aw10500 71-24 SundySuit,CountrySngr,DynmcQust 8

27Aug86-7Mth 6f :221 :454 1:122sy 14 114 43 43½ 2½ 2nk Thomas D B8 22500 78-24 Ripscapade, Video Sid,Exuberation 8

```
  6Apr86—Eased
30Mar86-6SA  7f :222 :454 1.234ft   82 117  96½ 96½111511 22½  Kaenel J L 9    Mdn 58-24 El Corazon, Cheapskate, Atreak  12
  30Mar86—Bumped start
26Dec85-4SA  6f :212 :442 1:102ft   72 117  53½ 66½111311 13   Kaenel J L 1    Mdn 73-13 Alom'sTobin,CleverHop,RcylTrsur  11
15Dec85-1Hol 6f :222 :461 1:112ft   33 118  62½ 56  78½ 813½  Kaenel J L 7    Mdn 73-09 Bolton,RecentExchnge,RdflyLips  12
  ● Aug 5 SA 4f ft :474 h      ● Jly 15 SA 3f ft :351 hg     Jly 8 SA 5f ft 1:011 hg     Jun 30 SA 6f ft 1:153 h
```

I.
4–1

Miltonmiltonmilton
WARREN G **115**
Own.—Seltzer B E & Florence

Ch. g. 3, by Properantes—Bagger's Delight, by Three Bagger
Br.—Weissman S B (Cal)
Tr.—Dotson Jim $12,500

1987	9 M 1 2	$4,150
1986	0 M 0 0	

Lifetime 9 0 1 2 $4,150

```
19Aug87-2LA  6½f:213 :454 1:173ft  2½ 1105  46  48  47½ 34     Gilbert C JIII6  M12500 85-12 Ephmrl,PrncSml,Mltnmltonmlton  7
10Aug87-2LA  6f :214 :454 1:11 ft  37 115   56  45½ 35½ 28½    Gilbert C J1   SM32000 80-13 FvPrtnrs,MltnmltnmltnC.P.Hrvst  10
16May87-2GG  1⅛:48 1:114 1:51 ft   10 120   2ʰᵈ 3½  69½ 713½   Lambert J 4      M16000 64-15 Infinitude,LuckyNeshr,Picho'sBob  10
7May87-1GG   1⅛:463 1:121 1:461ft  8 120    811 75¾ 42½ 34     Lambert J12      M12500 68-17 Mbll'sPrnc,SnppRlt,Mltnm'tnmltn  12
31Mar87-6GG  6f :22 :452 1:113ft   26 120   63½ 66¾ 56½ 66½    Davidson J R5    M20000 75-20 Johmere, Indicate, Bewildered  11
7Mar87-6GG   1 :472 1:121 1:384ft  18 120   3½  45  69  69     Diaz A L 5       M32000 65-16 D.D.TheKid,ExclIntLw,KingsRoylty  8
28Feb87-4SA  6f :214 :443 1:104ft  19 118   97½ 89½1014½1013   Jewell J W 10    M50000 71-17 VctoryPs,MmrsOfBrnz,Ply ₁snChf  12
13Feb87-4SA  1 :46 1:11 1:364gd    33 117   55½ 59  513 521    Jewell J W 2   SM40000 63-20 Auto Focus,KingClyde,PeteNewell  10
28Jan87-6SA  6f :214 :45 1:111ft   80 118   69  811 811 812½   Jewell J W 9     M50000 69-21 Gaelic Bee, Impressive Result, Wily 9
  28Jan87—Lugged in backstretch
  Aug 5 LA 4f ft :493 h
```

55. It's Jan. 17, 1987. The track has been favoring closers strongly for the past ten days. Which horse figures best at the odds in today's opener?

1st Santa Anita

6 FURLONGS. (1.07⅗) CLAIMING. Purse $15,000. 4-year-olds and upward. Weights, 4-year-olds, 120 lbs.; older, 121 lbs. Non-winners of two races since November 3 allowed 3 lbs.; of a race since then, 5 lbs. Claiming price $16,000; if for $14,000 allowed 2 lbs. (Races when entered for $12,500 or less not considered.)

A.
5–1

Unagloshi 2-N
MEZA R Q **116**
Own.—Shima Dr & Mrs R J

Ch. g. 8, by Exclusive Listing—Future Flame, by Old Pueblo
Br.—Sharp J D (Wash)
Tr.—Shima Robert J $16,000

1986	20 8 1 2	$54,295
1985	9 2 2 1	$14,400
Turf	4 0 1 0	$3,120

Lifetime 62 17 9 10 $122,865

```
13Dec86-1Hol 6f :214 :45 1:102ft   5 119   64¾ 45½ 43  42     Pincay L Jr6   c16000 89-09 Neutral Player, Illuminize, Rodney  10
  13Dec86—Lugged out
16Nov86-4Hol 7f :22 :443 1:241ft   5 117   31  31½ 32  77     Pincay L Jr10    26000 76-18 Pegus, Pialor, Amarone  12
2Nov86-1SA   6½f:213 :442 1:16 ft  *9-5 120 45½ 55½ 56½ 48½   DelahoussyeE9  c16000 82-10 Rinbow'sCup,WstBoyII,LordPncho  9
  2Nov86—Wide into stretch                                                          102
12Oct86-1SA  6½f:22 :452 1:174ft   4 116   72  41½ 31  1½      DelahoussayeE1  16000 81-21 Unagloshi,Menswear,StrOfAmeric  12
10Oct86-1SA  6f :22 :45 1:104ft    4½ 116  1012 910 54½ 11½    DelahoussayeE5  12500 84-18 Unagloshi, Jacart, Be Tharkful  12
  10Oct86—Wide into stretch
7Sep86-1Dmr 6f :221 :452 1:10 ft   8½ 116  66  65½ 74½ 42½     Pedroza M A4     16000 85-13 CoursingEgl,Qudrupd,Dstn₋tvlyDon  8
  7Sep86—Wide into stretch
30Aug86-1Dmr 6f :214 :45 1:092ft   3½ 116  64½ 55½ 35  35½     Baze R A4      c12500 86-10 ExclusivKing,CoursngEgl,Unglosh  10
4Aug86-1Dmr 7f :222 :452 1:232ft   *2½ 116 31  3½  1½  1½      Baze R A11     c16000 88-43 Unagloshi, Karaka Lad, Jam Shot  12
  4Aug86—Bumped at 3/16
21Jun86-5GG  6f :222 :452 1:103ft  3½ 120  64½ 56  34½ 31½     Hummel C R6    c10000 85-15 HsStormnNormn,PlstcAvn Unglshi  12
8Jun86-7GG   6f :22 :443 1:092ft   *2½ 115 42½ 43  55½ 55½     Hummel C R5      16000 86-11 DeterminedFire,ChdO₋,FeltyCould  11
  Jan 11 SA 5f ft 1:012 h    Dec 31 SA 4f ft :494 h     Dec 21 SA 3f ft :352 h     Dec 8 Hol 5f gd 1:013 h
```

B.

2–1

Just The Facts — Dk. b. or br. h. 5, by Pretense—Er Bear, by Dusty Canyon
KAENEL J L 7+ 116 — Br.—Delaneys Stock Farm (Cal) 1987 1 0 1 0 $3,400
Own.—Saron Stable — Tr.—Jones Gary $16,000 1986 2 1 0 0 $15,400
Lifetime 11 3 2 1 $52,175

3Jan87-1SA 6f :214 :444 1:111ft *6-5 116 21 2½ 21½ 22 Kaenel J L10 [S] 20000 80-16 KidShelleen,JustTheFcts,Dd'sQust 10
24Dec86-7Hol 6f :22 :452 1:11 ft 13 116 1hd 2hd 2hd 65¾ Kaenel J L5 40000 85-20 MisterCrofter,Dnczon,RingOfPlsur 10
22Jan86-7SA 6½f :22 :451 1:162ft 4 115 31½ 31 11 13½ Hawley S5 Aw28000 88-21 Just The Facts, Air Alert, Blips 6
22Dec85-5Hol 1 :442 1:092 1:341ft 13 113 1hd 1½ 32½ 510½ Hawley S6 Aw27000 82-17 Pride Of Ours, Hatim, Ascension 7
16Nov85-7Hol 6f :222 :452 1:092ft 12 114 63½ 73½ 75½ 58½ Hawley S7 Aw22000 88-14 BolderThanBold,FullHonor,Carload 9
16Nov85—Broke out, bumped
12Jan85-8SA 7f :222 :444 1:22 ft — 114 43½ 52¾ 51¾ 62¾ Hawley S6 [S]Cal Bdrs 87-16 ThRogrsFour,NostIgi'sStr,DustyOki 9
12Jan85—No wagering due to power failure
16Dec84-8Hol 1 1/16 :453 1:103 1:432gd 29 121 65½ 52½1225 1324¾ HawleyS13 Hol Fut'y — — Stphn'sOdyssy,FrstNormn,RghtCn 13
16Dec84—Grade I; Wide 7/8 turn, steadied 1/4
21Nov84-7Hol 1 :461 1:114 1:381gd *8-5 120 1½ 12½ 12½ 1¾ Hawley S6 Aw24000 84-16 JusttheFcts,Dr.Riv,ProtectYourself 7
3Nov84-3SA 6f :22 :451 1:102ft *8-5 118 41½ 1hd 1½ 1½ Hawley S2 [S]Mdn 86-14 JstThFcts,Pckn'Rnbows,RlnchATn 11
3Nov84—Lugged out 3/8
24Oct84-6SA 6f :22 :452 1:104ft 2¾ 117 2hd 2hd 2½ 2½ Hawley S7 [S]Mdn 83-16 Calestoga, Just The Facts, Petrov 10
Dec 19 Hol 6f ft 1:144 hg Dec 14 Hol 6f ft 1:152 h Dec 7 Hol 5f m 1:011 hg Dec 2 Hol 5f ft 1:033 h

C.

6–1

***Amarone** — Dk. b. or br. h. 7, by Realm—Misacre, by St Alphage
PEDROZA M A 5–0 118 — Br.—Advani Mrs M (Eng) 1986 11 2 1 1 $35,900
Own.—Lewis Marjorie — Tr.—Harper David B $16,000 1985 13 1 4 0 $36,750
Lifetime 54 8 7 6 $110,654 Turf 38 6 3 5 $65,129

17Dec86-5Hol 1 :451 1:104 1:373ft *8-5 116 11½ 11 11½ 11½ Stevens G L6 c16000 75-22 Amarone, Gulfstreamer, Oh Dad 7
17Dec86—Bobbled break
16Nov86-4Hol 7f :22 :443 1:241ft *3-2 117 2½ 21½ 21½ 33¾ Stevens G L8 20000 79-18 Pegus, Pialor, Amarone 12
8Nov86-9Hol 6f :222 :454 1:103ft *9-5 117 11 11½ 2hd 2no Stevens G L5 25000 90-13 SandDigger,Amarone,Billy'sSpecial 6
8Nov86—Broke in a tangle
10Sep86-9Dmr 7f :22 :45 1:214ft 10 1115 23 1hd 61½ 910½ Black C A2 c25000 86-11 Paskanell,BrndImge,SwiftMessge 12
31May86-5Hol 7f :22 :45 1:232ft 9½ 116 31 43 98¾1014½ Patterson A7 40000 72-16 Rex Lake, Paskanell, Rushad 10
4May86-9Hol 1 :453 1:103 1:362ft *2 116 41¾ 58½ 816 824½ McCarron C J5 50000 57-18 Silver Hero, Ono Gummo, Juntura 9
4May86—Lugged out drive
20Apr86-9SA a6½f (T):213 :4421:144fm 13 118 1½ 1hd 1hd 41½ Pincay L Jr10 62500 83-15 Hwkley,RisingChum,French'sLuck 12
29Mar86-5SA a6½f (T):211 :44 1:143fm 12 118 21 21 4nk 96 Kaenel J L7 80000 80-15 BmTwnChrl,AmrcnLgn,Sndy'sEgl 11
7Feb86-5SA a6½f (T):214 :4441:153fm 8 119 1½ 1½ 1hd 43½ Kaenel J L1 80000 78-23 Sandy'sEagle,RisingChum,Dedicat 11
2Feb86-5SA 6½f :222 :46 1:183m *3 120 2hd 2hd 22 45½ Pincay L Jr6 80000 71-28 Bozina, Kilauea, Midford 9
Dec 10 Hol 5f ft 1:013 h Dec 3 Hol 5f ft 1:014 h Nov 26 Hol 4f ft :47 h

D.

12–1

Video Sid — Ch. g. 4, by Interdicto—Wildcat Fire, by Brush Fire
CASTANON A L 3-N(5) 115 — Br.—Gilbert S M (Fla) 1987 2 0 0 0 $1,125
Own.—Magee & Stute — Tr.—Stute Melvin F $16,000 1986 18 2 1 5 $23,495
Lifetime 20 2 1 5 $24,620 Turf 2 0 0 1 $880

9Jan87-9SA 6f :214 :453 1:124sl 13 115 77½ 56½ 31 77¾ Sibille R5 c12500 66-26 West Boy II, Chagrining, Melchip 11
9Jan87—Steadied 1/16
4Jan87-3SA 6f :22 :451 1:103sy 6 112 42½ 43 44½ 47½ Black C A8 13000 78-22 Polly'sRuler,NeutralPlyer,Grenobie 8
4Jan87—Lugged in
24Dec86-3Hol 7f :22 :452 1:24 ft 11 114 11½ 1½ 35½ 48¾ Black C A1 18000 75-20 Pilor,Gordon'sCommnd,PirepplJck 7
6Dec86-6Hol 7f :221 :452 1:242gd 18 116 22½ 22½ 24 34½ Black C A8 16000 77-16 Noon Sun,PineappleJack,VideoSid 12
6Dec86—Lugged in stretch; returned bleeding from mouth
22Nov86-6Hol 6f :223 :46 1:111ft 25 114 76¾ 56 45 33½ Black C A7 14000 83-13 Manzanero, Pico P., Video Sid 9
22Nov86—Bumped start
6Nov86-2Hol 6f :224 :464 1:121ft 39 116 98½ 85½ 64½ 54¾ Ortega L E3 16000 77-17 Toddy Boy, Manzanero, BlackCross 9
6Nov86—Rough start
29Oct86-9SA 1 1/16 :464 1:113 1:443ft 14 113 64¾ 75¾ 89½ 811 Solis A7 14000 67-17 BlowTheTrumpts,RySol,ElgntHost 10
29Oct86—Bumped break; rank 7/8
3Oct86-5SA 6f :221 :452 1:102ft 50 116 75¾ 910 912 814½ Lipham T9 20000 72-17 NtvCptv,Nck'sPrnc,JohnsTomrrw 10
3Oct86—Broke in, bumped
12Sep86-6Suf 6f :222 :454 1:12 ft 4½ 111 33 56½ 57½ 610½ Ritvo T1 Aw10500 71-24 SundySuit,CountrySngr,DynmcQust 8
27Aug86-7Mth 6f :221 :454 1:122sy 14 114 43 43½ 2½ 2nk Thomas D B8 22500 78-24 Ripscapade, Video Sid,Exuberation 8

E.
14–1

```
Air Pirate                      B. g. 4, by Pirate's Bounty—Princess Babu, by Our Babu
  PATTON D B               1105 Br.—Windy Hill TBA (Cal)            1986 14 2 0 1   $36,950
Own.—De Palma W                 Tr.—Hill Jay A            $16,000   1985  1 1 0 0    $6,600
                                Lifetime  15 3 0 1  $43,550          Turf 1 0 0 0
27Dec86-2SA   6½f:214 :444 1:164ft   8½ 1095 57 57 54½ 64¼  Patton D B7     22500 82-19 Doonsport, BlueIce,ExaltedBubble
19Dec86-5Hol  6f :221 :46  1:113ft   3¼ 1105 44½ 44½ 32 1hd Patton D B6    c12500 85-17 Air Pirate, St. Alexis, Comets Flare
3Dec86-7Hol   6f :221 :452 1:11 ft   29 1115 116½ 98¼ 65 43¾ Patton D B9  S 20000 84-18 GrowlerSndue,ShowerDecree,Pilor
    3Dec86—Bumped at break
21Nov86-7Hol  7f :22  :45  1:23 ft    6 116  32 42½ 55 —    Valenzuela P A6 25000 — — StickyTrigger,NnteTm,PowerLever
    21Nov86—Eased
19Oct86-5SA   6½f:214 :45  1:171ft   12 113  41¾ 42 87¼ 810¼ Shoemaker W3    40000 74-18 PtriotGlovs,GryPinstrp,Vrttm'sPrd
    19Oct86—Bumped break
4Oct86-1SA    6½f:214 :45  1:17 ft   19 116  69 911 811 74¼  Shoemaker W7    50000 81-18 Inherent Kal, EastTulip,Brali'sAnte
    4Oct86—Lugged in
8Sep86-3Dmr   6f :214 :45  1:09 ft   15 116  68¾ 912 914 811  DelahoussayeE8  62500 82-14 Notoriety,UrbnCowboy,BolgerMgic
31Aug86-3Dmr  6f :22  :45  1:092ft   22 113  42 65¼ 67 79¼    Garrido O L4  Aw24000 82-12 SureToFir,AmzingCourg,RossArRb
15Aug86-7Dmr  7f :221 :45  1:223ft   12 116  72¾ 52¾ 612 614½ DelhoussyeE2 Aw21000 77-12 J. R. Johnson, East Tulip,GoSwiftly
    15Aug86—Crowded, bumped, steadied at 3/8
23Jly86-8Dmr  1 ①:4611:1021:341fm    13 116  63¾ 66 815 813½ DlhssyE7 Ⓡ Oceanside 87-04 PrinceBobbyB.,FullChrm,He'sASros
  Jan 9 Hol 4f ft :48 h       Dec 16 SLR tr.t 4f ft :502 h     ●Nov 29 SLR tr.t 5f ft 1:004 h    Nov 20 SLR tr.t 3f ft :363 h
```

F.
17–1

```
*West Boy II *                  B. h. 7, by Vaciante II—Royal Tom, by Tompion
  BAZE G                    116 Br.—Haras West Point (Brz)           1987  2 1 0 0    $7,150
Own.—Shapiro R                  Tr.—Feld Jude T           $16,000    1986  6 0 1 0    $3,350
                                Lifetime  29 7 5 4  $16,910           Turf 2 0 0 0      $113
9Jan87-9SA    6f :214 :453 1:124sl   17 114  1112 89½ 62¾ 11  Baze G2          10500 74-26 West Boy II, Chagrining, Melchip 11
2Jan87-1SA    6½f:221 :451 1:174ft   3½ 116  87½ 912 812 610  DelahoussayeE6   10000 71-22 GallantChairman,OhDd,WithSpirit 12
    2Jan87—Wide into stretch
17Dec86-5Hol  1  :451 1:104 1:373ft  4½ 116  79¼ 712 79¾ 712½ Ortega L E2     16000 62-22 Amarone, Gulfstreamer, Oh Dad 7
    17Dec86—Wide into stretch
2Nov86-1SA    6½f:213 :442 1:16 ft   12 116  56½ 45¼ 24 21½  Toro F2          16000 88-10 Rinbow'sCup,WstBoyII,LordPncho 9
    2Nov86—Broke slowly
25Oct86-9SA   6f :22  :451 1:102ft   54 1095 98½ 95¾ 65¼ 63¼  Bringhurst A D3 18000 83-17 StarOfAmerica,Rodney,SndDigger 11
17Oct86-1SA   6½f:213 :442 1:171ft   12 115  912 916 711 56¼  Stevens G L8    12500 78-21 Jacart, Up The Pole, Inquisitive 9
27Feb86-7SA   6½f:214 :442 1:153ft   23 113  44 59 69½ 614   Hawley S1        45000 78-18 Juntura, Cryptarch, Knight Skiing 7
2Feb86-1SA    6½f:22  :46  1:181m    25 117  79¾ 78¾ 69½ 613½ McCarronCJ6 Aw24000 65-28 Chevo, Generalization, LordPancho 7
    2Feb86—Wide into stretch
18Sep85♦2CidJardim(Brazil a6½f 1:201ft *9-5 128    1½   Barroso A        Alw WestBoy, Key To Gaiano, Lomage 5
5Sep85♦5CidJardim(Brazil a5½f 1:07 sy   2¼ 128     21½  Barroso A        Alw Leibry, West Boy, Dax Dasher 6
  Dec 29 SA 5f ft 1:011 h      Dec 24 SA 3f ft :36 h      Dec 15 SA 4f ft :494 h      Dec 10 SA 5f ft 1:01 h
```

G.
27–1

```
Premiere                        B. g. 4, by Rare Performer—So What, by Iron Ruler
  MCHARGUE D G              115 Br.—Stevens Herbert K (Ky)           1986  7 2 0 1   $25,065
Own.—Shannon B M                Tr.—Wingfield Robert      $16,000    1985  7 2 2 2   $25,634
                                Lifetime  14 4 2 3  $50,699
27Dec86-2SA   6½f:214 :444 1:164ft   5¾ 116  88½ 712 710 77¼  Cordero A Jr4   25000 79-19 Doonsport, BlueIce,ExaltedBubble 10
16Oct86-3SA   6f :213 :45  1:101ft    4 118  33 45½ 47½ 39½   McHargue D G2   25000 77-19 Pico P., New Doc, Premiere 6
27Sep86-8Pom  6½f:212 :444 1:182ft   6½ 116  713 712 55 2no   Pauline R M2    32000 88-10 ‡Trinity Hall, Premiere, Noon Sun 9
    27Sep86—Bumped intervals stretch; Placed first through disqualification
25Jly86-7Dmr  1 1/16:454 1:103 1:432ft 14 116 75½ 67½ 711 611¼ McHargue D G7  50000 72-18 InherntKl,Exubrnt'sImg,HloExprss 8
10Jly86-5Hol  1  :453 1:104 1:361ft  25 116  66½ 55½ 53 56    McHargue D G6   80000 76-18 AngleArc,TrojanTrick,‡KeenKnight 7
26Jun86-1Hol  6f :22  :45  1:094ft   13 116  75¼ 88¼ 79¼ 79    Shoemaker W2    62500 86-12 J. R. Johnson, Totality, Rirnegato 8
16Apr86-6Kee  6½f:222 :452 1:174gd  *2¼ 115  75¾ 61¾ 2hd 1hd  Woods CRJr4 Aw18100 88-20 Premiere,FlyingTable,Let'sRumble 12
9Nov85-8CD    1  :451 1:101 1:371ft  15 117  1113 97¾ 96½ 77  Woods CRJr7 Iroquois 76-23 Tile,BachelorBeau,DncetotheWire 11
22Oct85-5Kee  a7f             1:284m *7-5 112  31 3½ 13 16    Woods CRJr7 Aw15800 79-26 Premiere, Friendly Blue, FuzzyBear 7
12Oct85-3Kee  7f :233 :471 1:254ft    2 114  2hd 1hd 2hd 21   Woods CRJr1 Aw15800 76-19 Doonesbear, Premiere, Silas Creek 8
  Jan 11 Hol 6f ft 1:154 h      Dec 17 Hol 5f ft 1:012 h      Dec 4 Hol 5f ft :592 h
```

H.

17–1

```
Family Fox                                B. g. 8, by Bob Mathias—Family Light, by Limelight
                                          Br.—Stringer J (Ore)                            1986 13  1  1  1   $19,650
 DELAHOUSSAYE E                     116   Tr.—Cianci Jon                  $16,000         1985 17  3  1  2   $47,175
Own.—B C L Racng St-Boyer-Fox             Lifetime  76 13 11 16  $167,375
27Nov86-3Hol   6f :214  :45  1:103ft   6¼ 117   712 712 711 710   Toro F4        16000 80-18 Ells Bravest Song, Jacart, FallFlyer 7
     27Nov86—Lugged out 3/8, wide into stretch
16Nov86-4Hol   7f :22   :443 1:241ft   13 117   53  55½ 86¼ 66¾   Toro F12       20000 76-18 Pegus, Pialor, Amarone              12
25Oct86-9SA    6f :22   :451 1:102ft   17 116   119¾119¾119¼108¼  Ortega L E10   20000 78-17 StarOfAmerica,Rodney,SndDigger 11
     25Oct86—Broke in a tangle; lugged out backstretch
25Apr86-5Hol   1  :454 1:104 1:37 ft  *8-5 116  53  55½ 55½ 48    Ortega L E3    16000 70-16 JohnTheTough,ColdNos,MorsCodII 7
     25Apr86—Wide on turn
19Apr86-2SA    6½f:213  :442 1:172ft   *3 115   811 912 87¾ 42½   Stevens G L7   20000 80-19 Jacart, Gran Barba, Neutral Player 9
     19Apr86—Rough trip
13Apr86-5SA    7f :221  :45  1:222ft   13 116   78¾ 87½ 66¼ 47½   Stevens G L3 Aw24000 80-15 Danczone, Bizeboy, Lord Pancho  9
     13Apr86—Wide into stretch
```

I.

17–1

```
John's Jove                               Ro. g. 5, by Northern Jove—John's Lass, by Speak John
                                          Br.—Beaconsfield Farm Inc (Ky)                  1986 12  2  1  2   $22,285
 CORDERO A JR                       116   Tr.—Stepp William T             $16,000         1985 15  3  8  3   $37,704
Own.—Campbell-Caraway-Radley              Lifetime  28  5 10  5  $62,329
30Dec86-3SA    6f :212  :442 1:112ft    5 116   36  35½ 36  52¾   Sibille R7     c12500 78-18 LuckyMasadado,VlDeRoi,Chgrining 7
13Dec86-1Hol   6f :214  :45  1:102ft   21 116   44  56½ 87¼ 88    Stevens S A7    16000 83-09 Neutral Player, Illuminize, Rodney 10
6Dec86-2Hol    6f :221  :46  1:114gd *7-5 117   21½ 2½  1hd 11½   Stevens G L7   c10000 84-18 John's Jove, Cordon, Chagrining  8
27Nov86-3Hol   6f :214  :45  1:103ft   2½ 117   34½ 36  35½ 56¾   Stevens G L1    16000 83-18 Ells Bravest Song, Jacart, FallFlyer 7
     27Nov86—Lugged out
5Oct86-2SA     6f :213  :443 1:102ft   6½ 115   1hd 1hd 11½ 21½   ValenzuelaPA10  20000 84-15 Grenoble, John's Jove, Inquisitive 12
13Sep86-8Pom   6½f:221  :453 1:162ft   11 1115  42  69  79  819¾  Black C A5      25000 78-10 Slugfst,Mummy'sPlsur,BoldTopsidr 9
     13Sep86—Bumped, jostled after start, wide stretch
22Aug86-1Dmr   6f :214  :45  1:094ft   8½ 116   2hd 1½  14  12½   ValenzuelaPA5  c16000 89-14 John's Jove, Double Deficit, Nami 10
26Jly86-9SR    6f :214  :442 1:084ft   5¾ 114   65  54¾ 56  57½   Chapman T M3    25000 90-08 PlstcAvnu,SplndourBoy,Don'sDstny 8
13Jly86-3Sol   6f :214  :45  1:094ft   5½ 115   54  31½ 31½ 42    Chapman T M2    25000 92-13 Secular,Psychedelic,‡Gotabetarulek 6
     13Jly86—Placed third through disqualification; Bumped hard start
26Jun86-11Pln  6f :214  :45  1:094ft   19 115   42  31½ 35  38½   Lamance C2    Aw15000 84-19 DetrmindFir,BobCourtny,John'sJov 9
   Jan 15 SA 3f ft :353 h          Nov 25 Hol 3f ft :354 h          Nov 19 Hol 6f ft 1:143 h
```

J.

9–2

```
Philip Nolan                              Dk. b. or br. g. 6, by Pledge Allegiance—In Exile, by Isle of Greece
                                          Br.—Skillstad Phyllis (Cal)                     1987  1  0  0  0    $325
 PINCAY L JR                        116   Tr.—Aguilera Humberto           $16,000         1986  8  4  2  1 $26,930
Own.—Wald-Winner-Winner                   Lifetime  25  9  2  3  $41,966
9Jan87-9SA     6f :214  :453 1:124sl *3-2 116   13½ 14  1hd 56¼   ValenzuelPA10  c12500 68-26 West Boy II, Chagrining, Melchip 11
     9Jan87—Steadied late
20Dec86-7Hol   6f :22   :45  1:103ft *7-5 117   11½ 13  14  15    Olivares F9    c10000 90-15 PhilipNoln,GllntChirmn,Dodo'sLnd 9
     20Dec86—Lugged out
6Dec86-5Hol    6f :214  :452 1:111gd   4½ 117   1½  1hd 21½ 22½   Olivares F5  [S] 10000 84-16 Polly'sRuler,PhilipNoln,UpThePole 8
     6Dec86—Lugged out drive
3Nov86-1SA     6f :213  :444 1:11 ft    6 116   22½ 21½ 23  52    Castanon AL8 [S] 12500 81-14 HachalaTachl,Melchip,ShuttleOne 10
     3Nov86—Steadied late
21Sep86-8Pom   6f :221  :452 1:103ft *7-5 119   41½ 33  23  33¼   Castanon A L2   12500 95-07 Jacart, Inquisitive, Philip Nolan 10
15Sep86-7Pom   6f :224  :453 1:103ft *7-5 116   11  12  13  14¾   Castanon A L3   10000 98-08 PhilipNolan,CeeScoBoy,Eagle'sBek 9
21Jly86-9LA    6½f:213  :442 1:162ft   4¾ 116   12  12  14  12½   Castanon A L8   10000 95-12 PhilipNolan,Luckalot,HachalaTchl 10
11Jly86-8LA    6½f:214  :45  1:163ft   *1 116   12  11½ 1nk 22½   Castanon A L6   10000 91-14 HachalTchl,PhilipNoln,Bob'sIntent 8
7Jly86-6LA     6f :214  :444 1:102ft    4 116   11  11  12  12½   Castanon A L7    5000 91-15 PhilpNoln,UndrcovrEgl,OnBoldMov 9
24Nov85-5AC    6f :224  :452 1:10 ft    3 117   31  54  108 1011  Enriquez H F10   7500 78-15 WingedPrinc,Kjoli,B.K.'sWindyIsl 10
   Dec 30 SA 4f ft :49 h      Dec 15 Hol 4f ft :484 h      Dec 3 Hol 3f ft :36 h      Nov 27 Hol 5f ft 1:00 h
```

K.
41–1

Sum Exchange — B. h. 5, by Somethingfabulous—Best Exchange, by Royal Exchange
STEVENS S A 116 — Br.—Jones R E (Ariz) — Tr.—McIntyre Forrest — $16,000
Own.—Jones R E — Lifetime 11 1 2 2 $29,350
1986 3 0 0 0
1985 8 1 2 2 $29,350
Turf 1 0 0 0 $1,000

31Dec86-5SA 6½f :22 :45³ 1:17²ft 21 116 3nk 63¾ 117 — Meza R Q6 40000 — — Watch'n Win, Angle Arc, Idol 12
31Dec86—Eased
11Aug86-7Dmr 6f :21³ :44³ 1:09²ft 17 118 32 54½ 57 713 Kaenel J L1 Aw19000 78-13 RosesArRb,Mr.Mdi,WhipUpThTmpo 7
11Aug86—Lugged in badly backstretch, 3/8 turn
27Jly86-3Dmr 7f :22¹ :44⁴ 1:21⁴ft 13 118 1½ 2hd 712 716½ Solis A3 Aw19000 79-10 East Tulip, Harrison's Turn, Oricao 7
27Jly86—Veered out start
24Jly85-5Dmr 7½f ①:22 :45 1:29³fm 15 115 14 16 1hd 56 VlnzlPA2 Ⓡ Oceanside 85-09 GryGntlt,BrconsChrg,Jstorfthbys 10
24Jly85—Run in divisions
23Jun85-3Hol 6f :22¹ :45 1:09²ft 3½ 117 1½ 13 13 12½ Pincay L Jr4 Mdn 100 — SumExchng,ProfssorRobrts,Absolt 8
27May85-1Hol 6f :22 :45 1:10 ft 3¾ 115 33 36 35 22 Dominguez R E7 Mdn 95-04 Kleven, Sum Exchange, Carullah 7
5May85-4Hol 6f :22² :45⁴ 1:10¹ft 16 115⁵ 1hd 1½ 3½ 33 Dominguez R E6 Mdn 93-04 Padua, Mr. Media, Sum Exchange 10
2Mar85-6SA 6f :21⁴ :45 1:10³ft 9½ 118 33 34 58½ 610¼ Meza R Q1 Mdn 75-18 PnchoVII,Alln'sPrspct,LckyPrspct 12
2Mar85—Broke in tangle, veered out at gap
9Feb85-6SA 6½f :22¹ :45² 1:17²gd 4 113⁵ 2hd 2hd 1hd 41½ Dominguez RE1 Mdn 82-20 Rich Earth, Equilibre, Reckoner 11
9Feb85—Bore out early
19Jan85-6SA 6f :22¹ :45 1:10²ft 2 113⁵ 2hd 2hd 21 33¾ Dominguez RE3 Mdn 82-16 ColtFortyFr,TmOfThFx,SmExchng 11
Jan 10 GD tr.t 7f gd 1:27¹ h ●Dec 29 GD tr.t 3f ft :36 h Dec 24 GD tr.t 5f ft 1:01⁴ h Dec 18 GD tr.t 6f ft 1:12 h

L.
27–1

Saro Star — B. c. 4, by Saros—Key to the Stars, by Key To The Kingdom
VALENZUELA P A 117 — Br.—Green Thumb Farm (Cal) — Tr.—Manzi Joseph — $16,000
Own.—Green Thumb Farm Stable — Lifetime 9 1 0 1 $9,550
1987 2 0 0 0 $425
1986 4 1 0 1 $7,850

10Jan87-2SA 6½f :22¹ :45² 1:18¹gd 22 117 31 54½ 77 119 Valenzuela P A5 20000 70-20 BoldTopsidr,Don'sCo'op,PnpplJck 12
3Jan87-1SA 6f :21⁴ :44⁴ 1:11¹ft 11 120 63¾ 54½ 55 53½ ValenzuelPA2 Ⓢ 20000 78-16 KidShelleen,JustTheFcts,Dd'sQust 10
20Dec86-1Hol 6f :22² :46² 1:11²ft 3¾ 119 42 5¾ 42½ 34 ValenzuelPA7 Ⓢ 20000 82-15 Nante Tam, Many Roads, Saro Star 7
10Dec86-3Hol 1 :45⁴ 1:10⁴ 1:37¹ft 18 116 2½ 43½ 79 714½ Valenzuela P A2 45000 62-20 Sebucan, Agitate's Pride, Alibi Ike 7
20Nov86-4Hol 6f :22² :46¹ 1:11 ft 6¾ 120 31½ 21½ 1hd 12 VlenzuelPA5 ⓈM32000 88-16 SaroStr,GetAlongPisno,Kim'sGold 11
20Nov86—Lugged in stretch
7Nov86-2Hol 6f :22³ :45⁴ 1:12 ft 7 120 32 33½ 57½ 68¾ VlenzuelPA5 ⓈM32000 74-18 MontnToClrk,Qurdolt,FbulousCon 12
2Sep85-4Dmr 7f :22³ :46¹ 1:24²ft 7½ 116 62½ 64 715 817 Hawley S8 ⓈMdn 69-15 Sobre La Par,CityView,CutByGlass 8
2Sep85—Fanned wide 3/8 turn
4Aug85-5Dmr 1 :46 1:12 1:39 ft 12 116 1½ 45½ 411 411 Hawley S2 Mdn 62-17 DrbyFlr,ClerChoice,StembotCreek 10
20Jly85-1Hol 6f :22³ :46² 1:10⁴ft 10 118 10¹² 8¹⁴ 8¹⁶ 817 Valenzuela PA7 ⓈMdn 76-07 Bolger Magic, Press On, Pico P. 11
20Jly85—Bumped start, wide 3/8 turn
Dec 28 SA 4f ft :48³ h Dec 5 Hol 5f ft 1:01¹ h Nov 29 Hol 4f ft :47⁴ h

56. The proper play here is automatic. Any well-grounded handicapper makes it several dozen times a year.

3rd Del Mar

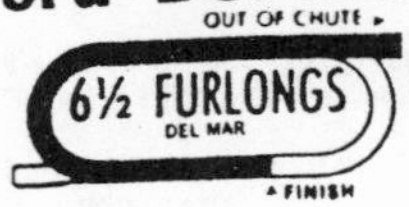
OUT OF CHUTE
6½ FURLONGS
DEL MAR
FINISH

6 ½ FURLONGS. (1.14⅗) ALLOWANCE. Purse $21,000. 3-year-olds and upward bred in California which are non-winners of $3,000 other than maiden or claiming. Weights, 3-year-olds, 116 lbs.; older, 121 lbs. Non-winners of a race other than claiming since June 15, allowed 3 lbs.

A.
6–1

Golden Gauntlet — Ch. c. 3, by Golden Eagle II—Air of Elegance, by Dr Fager
PINCAY L JR 113 — Br.—Mabee Mr-Mrs J C (Cal) — Tr.—Sadler John W
Own.—Golden Eagle Farm — Lifetime 3 2 0 0 $15,375
1987 2 1 0 0 $8,775
1986 1 1 0 0 $6,600

1Mar87-3SA 6½f :22¹ :45 1:16³ft 3½ 114 1hd 1hd 3½ 42¾ Black C A6 ⓈAw27000 84-15 HollywoodSrnd,Rconnoitring,OBtth 6
16Feb87-3SA 6f :21³ :44³ 1:10⁴gd 4½ 118 56 44½ 33½ 12¼ ●Black C A4 32000 84-21 OkWine,GoldenGuntlet,ShrewdStev 7
16Feb87—Broke in a tangle, bumped; checked at 3/16; ●Dead heat
24Dec86-6Hol 6f :22 :45³ 1:11²ft 12 118 31½ 21 21 1no Black C A5 ⓈM32000 86-20 GoldenGauntlet,OBtth,VikingBlue 12
Aug 9 Dmr 5f ft 1:00³ h Aug 3 Dmr 5f ft 1:01² h Jly 28 Dmr 5f ft 1:02² h

B.

18–1

Great Yankee — Ch. g. 4, by Dimaggio—Charge Hilarious, by Fast Hilarious
MEZA R Q — 118 — Br.—Double K Farms (Cal) — 1987 9 4 0 1 $38,050
Tr.—Guiney Irv — 1986 4 1 0 0 $12,200
Own.—Double K Farms — Lifetime 14 5 0 1 $50,600 — Turf 1 0 0 0

27Jly87-9Hol 1 1/16 Ⓣ:47 1:102 1:413fm 9¾ 113 32 32½ 69 610½ Meza R Q3 55000 75-08 Sherkin, Kingsbury, Aviator II 7
12Jly87-7Hol 6f :214 :441 1:092ft 6½ 118 21½ 25 23½ 31½ Meza R Q2 Aw22000 94-09 MjstcMsson,OlympcPrspct,GrtYnk 7
12Jly87—Lugged out final 1/2
4Jly87-7Hol 7f :221 :444 1:221ft *3 114 21 1hd 2hd 1nk Meza R Q6 30000 93-09 GretYnkee,MgicLeder,BoldBtterUp 9
24Jun87-5Hol 6f :22 :45 1:10 ft 6¼ 115 2hd 21 11 12½ Meza R Q1 22500 93-13 GretYnkee,MeYouAndQ.,ShowrDcr 9
24Jun87—Lugged out
13Jun87-2Hol 6f :213 :444 1:101ft 6 114 32 21 1½ 1½ Meza R Q3 18000 92-11 GrtYnk,HighstScrpt,Pppy'sConsul 11
27May87-3Hol 6½f :222 :453 1:171ft 7 115 43½ 34 44 44¾ Sibille R6 22500 89-16 NtiveRelity,ForbsRply,UrbnCowboy 8
21May87-7Hol 6f :221 :454 1:104ft 6 116 41¾ 31½ 3½ 12 Sibille R7 16000 89-12 GrtYnk,KingOfCliforni,PowrfullPul 7
13May87-2Hol 7f :222 :444 1:232ft 15 1095 74¼ 76¾ 77¾ 69 Cisneros J E6 Ⓢ 18000 78-15 Detector,MYouAndQ.,FriscoDnnis 11
13May87—Lugged out 3/8
17Jan87-2SA 6f :214 :45 1:103ft 76 1115 1111 1117 — — Patton D B3 35000 — — Ondarty, Romaxe, Rivets Factor 11
17Jan87—Pulled up; Checked, broke stride 5/8
31Dec86-5SA 6½f :22 :453 1:172ft 9½ 1135 72¾ 107¾ 1011 1011½ Patton D B4 40000 71-20 Watch'n Win, Angle Arc, Idol 12
31Dec86—Broke slowly
Aug 10 Dmr 5f ft 1:002 h — Aug 4 Dmr 5f ft 1:03 h — Jly 22 Hol 5f ft 1:022 h — Jly 2 Hol 4f ft :48 h

C.

4–5

Fancy Oats — Ch. g. 3, by Properantes—Gold Chain, by King's Balcony
SHOEMAKER W — 113 — Br.—Headley & Pegram (Cal) — 1987 2 1 1 0 $16,850
Tr.—Headley Bruce — 1986 0 M 0 0
Own.—Headley & Rancho RioHondo — Lifetime 2 1 1 0 $16,850

31Jly87-3Dmr 6f :214 :443 1:102ft 5¾ 114 79 78 45 2nk ShoemkrW1 ⓈAw21000 86-17 AsInEagles,FancyOts,IrishRobbery 8
5Apr87-6SA 6½f :214 :45 1:171ft 6½ 117 1011 75¼ 32½ 11½ Shoemaker W1 Mdn 84-16 Fancy Oats, Acquired, Social Man 10
5Apr87—Broke slowly; wide 3/8
●Jly 22 Dmr 6f ft 1:134 h — ●Jly 17 Dmr 5f ft 1:001 h — ●Jly 8 SA 5f ft :593 h — ●Jly 1 SA 7f ft 1:271 h

D.

12–1

Tahoe Tango — B. g. 4, by Meneval—Vegas Tango, by Nevada Bin
STEVENS G L — 118 — Br.—Pascoe W T III (Cal) — 1986 3 2 0 0 $16,500
Tr.—Jones Gary — 1985 0 M 0 0
Own.—Schwartz S-Ann-Marcia — Lifetime 3 2 0 0 $16,500

8Oct86-7SA 1 :46 1:104 1:37 ft *3½ 116 43½ 43 67 99¼ Stevens G L 7 Aw27000 74-20 GrecianWonder,LordAllison,Dnielli 10
8Aug86-3Dmr 1 :462 1:104 1:354ft 3¼ 115 1½ 1hd 1hd 1no Stevens G L 2 62500 89-13 Tahoe Tango,InherentKal,HotMetal 7
23Jly86-4Dmr 6½f :224 :453 1:161ft 3 116 2½ 2½ 1hd 11¾ Stevens G L 2 M32000 91-12 TahoeTngo,SirDmon,SlipperySilver 9
23Jly86—Bumped break
Aug 8 Dmr 6f ft 1:134 hg — Aug 3 Dmr 4f ft :483 h — Jly 29 Dmr 4f ft :482 h — Jly 24 Hol 3f ft :364 h

E.

3–1

Irish Robbery — Dk. b. or br. g. 3, by The Irish Lord—Sweet Canary, by No Robbery
SOLIS A — 116 — Br.—Valenti & Coelho (Cal) — 1987 4 1 1 1 $17,400
Tr.—Stute Melvin F — 1986 0 M 0 0
Own.—Coelho-Elliott-Valenti — Lifetime 4 1 1 1 $17,400

31Jly87-3Dmr 6f :214 :443 1:102ft *7-5 117 1hd 2hd 2½ 32¼ Solis A6 ⓈAw21000 84-17 AsInEagles,FancyOts,IrishRobbery 8
18Jly87-7Hol 6½f :22 :443 1:153ft 6¾ 116 11 1½ 11½ 1hd Solis A2 Mdn 102-07 Irish Robbery, Valdad, Dry Ridge 10
18Jly87—Jumped mirror reflection 1/16
6Jly87-6Hol 6f :214 :451 1:10 ft *2½ 116 1½ 2hd 2½ 25½ Solis A2 Mdn 87-14 NicklADnc,IrishRobbry,ExplosvDrm 8
21Jun87-6Hol 6f :214 :451 1:104ft 29 115 4¾ 4nk 43 77¾ Castanon A L12 Mdn 81-14 Sebrof, Sedeno, Havewemetyet 12
21Jun87—Wide 3/8 turn
Jly 24 Hol 5f ft 1:004 h — Jly 13 Hol 5f ft 1:014 h — Jly 3 Hol 5f ft 1:012 h — Jun 28 Hol 6f ft 1:134 h

F.

14–1

Zaney Donut — Dk. b. or br. g. 5, by Zanthe—Donuts to Go, by Donut King
BAZE R A — 121 — Br.—Muller E & Janet (Cal) — 1987 3 1 1 0 $9,725
Tr.—Goodwin Floyd C — 1985 2 M 0 0 $350
Own.—Muller E & Janet H — Lifetime 5 1 1 0 $10,075

31Jly87-3Dmr 6f :214 :443 1:102ft 28 122 33 46 55½ 54 Baze R A8 ⓈAw21000 82-17 AsInEagles,FancyOts,IrishRobbery 8
31Jly87—Lugged in drive

27Jun87-5GG 6f :212 :44 1:094ft *3-2 122 1hd 11 12 12 Hamilton M11 Mdn 90-10 ZnyDonut,GoldnQuivr,J.D.Commsh 12
14Jun87-6GG 1 :454 1:102 1:371ft 6½ 122 1½ 1½ 11 2hd Hamilton M3 Mdn 82-15 Everso,ZneyDonut,NorthernChnce 10
4Dec85-3Hol 1 :462 1:11 1:361ft 43 119 54 66¼ 68¼ 59¾ Walker R2 M50000 72-13 Reserve,Lucklot,Codex'sReflection 7
4Dec85—Bumped at start, lugged out backside and turn
6Nov85-6SA 6f :22 :451 1:11 ft 119 118 119½ 76¼1114 912¾ Walker R7 M50000 70-17 CorrePisno,ErthToGry,BubblyBuc 12
6Nov85—Broke slowly, bumped fallen horse at 1/16, checked
Aug 12 SA 4f ft :49 h Aug 8 SA 1 ft 1:412 h Jly 25 SA 6f ft 1:144 h Jly 17 Sol 3f ft :36 h

57. In this interesting restricted stakes, find the best bet.

8th Santa Anita

1 1/16 MILES. (1.40⅕) 9th Running of THE SANTA LUCIA HANDICAP. $75,000 added. Fillies and mares. 4-year-olds and upward which have not won *$30,000 at one mile or over other than claiming or starter in 1986–87. By subscription of $50 each to accompany the nomination, $750 additional to start, with $75,000 added, of which $15,000 to second, $11,250 to third, $5,625 to fourth and $1,875 to fifth. Weights, Tuesday April 7. Starters to be named through the entry box by the closing time of entries. A trophy will be presented to the owner of the winner. *A race worth $30,000 to the winner. Closed Wednesday, April 1, 1987, with 17 nominations.

A.
11–1

Helen's Majesty — **Ch. f. 4, by His Majesty—Fearless Dame, by Fearless Knight**
Br.—Courtney & Congleton (Ky) — 1987 4 3 1 0 $46,650
BAZE G **115** **Tr.—Luby Donn** — 1985 1 M 0 0
Own.—Robert L Shipp Trust — **Lifetime 5 3 1 0 $46,650** — Turf 2 1 0 0 $15,400

7Mar87-5SA 1 1/16 :474 1:122 1:443gd 5¼ 118 31 2½ 1hd 1no VlenzulPA3 ⒻAw34000 78-19 Helen'sMajesty,Andrushka,Stretley 9
12Feb87-8SA 1⅛Ⓣ:4631:1121:503fm 12 117 42 3nk 1hd 1¾ VlenzulPA6 ⒻAw28000 74-26 Heln'sMjsty,FlyingFrown,ClvrEdg 12
12Feb87—Erratic in stretch
29Jan87-6SA 1 1/16 :481 1:134 1:462ft *2-5e 117 43 2½ 1hd 1¾ Ortega LE8 ⒻMc45000 69-27 Helen'sMjesty,Sweetness,BjnMoon 8
17Jan87-4SA 6f :214 :454 1:121ft 29 117 1012 9½ 45 2¾ Ortega L E8 ⒻM45000 74-18 Li'lMssNonsns,Hln'sMjsty,RvDGzll 12
29Oct85♦2StCloud(Fra) a1 1:461gd 43 123 Ⓣ 16 Legrix E ⒻPx Zriba RiveresduSud,GrndeCouture,Nmp 17
Apr 5 SA 6f ft 1:142 hg Mar 29 SA 4f ft :492 h Mar 24 SA 5f ft 1:002 h Mar 1 SA 6f ft 1:133 h

B.
5–2

Le L'Argent — **Ch. m. 5, by What a Pleasure—Flick Your Bick, by Bicker**
Br.—Benowitz G (Fla) — 1987 3 2 0 0 $52,875
MCHARGUE D G **118** **Tr.—Mandella Richard** — 1986 8 1 3 2 $65,512
Own.—Daley M-R & L Jean — **Lifetime 19 6 5 3 $278,185** — Turf 2 0 0 0 $800

19Feb87-8SA 1 :46 1:102 1:36 ft 3¾ 116 11 2hd 1hd 1¼ DlhoussyE 5 ⒻAw45000 88-13 Le L'Argent, Paradies,Nature'sWay 7
6Feb87-8SA 6f :213 :434 1:092ft 11 116 54 3½ 33 1no DlhoussyE 5 ⒻAw45000 91-15 LeL'Argent,Comprbility,Firesweepr 7
16Jan87-8SA 6f :213 :443 1:094ft 6 116 56½ 55½ 46 44¾ DlhoussyE 6 ⒻAw45000 84-18 Sari's Heroine, Till You, Joni U.Bar 6
26Sep86-11Pom 1 1/16 :473 1:134 1:464sl *8-5 115 66 53½ 21 2hd Solis A 2 ⒻLs Mds.H 77-29 OurSweetShm,LeL'Argent,KpDting 7
26Sep86—Checked into drive
14Sep86-11Pom 1 1/16 :464 1:104 1:423ft 5 114 511 512 32½ 2nk SolsA 2 ⒻⓇE B Jhnstn 98-08 Our Best Tell, LeL'Argent,GoodZar 5
14Sep86—Steadied break
10Aug86-3Dmr 6½f :213 :442 1:143ft 10 117 32½ 42 46½ 48¼ PcLJr 3 ⒻRch Bndo H 91-08 BoldNSpecial,RngoonRuby,Eloquck 5
19Jly86-8LA 7f :221 :452 1:221ft 3-2 119 11½ 11½ 11½ 1nk ♦ PncLJr 2 ⒻChapman H 97-12 LeL'Argnt,LuckyTwist,RngoonRuby 7
♦19Jly86—Dead heat; Run in divisions
29May86-9Hol 1 Ⓣ:4611:1021:35 fm 3 117 2hd 1hd 2hd 54 DlhoussyE 2 ⒻAw32000 — — Antartica, PrincessCariole,Balladry 8
29May86—Bumped start
11May86-8GG 6f :214 :443 1:093ft *4-5 120 67 66½ 36 33 CstndM5 ⒻRchmnd H 88-18 MuiLyphrJ.,ApplngToYou,LL'Argnt 7
26Apr86-8Hol 6f :221 :45 1:093ft 2½ 113 21 32½ 33½ 33½ McCrrCJ5 ⒻSlvrSpnH 92-18 TkeMyPicture,Eloquck,LeL'Argent 5
Apr 8 SA 4f ft :494 b Apr 3 SA 1 ft 1:413 h Mar 28 SA 7f ft 1:283 h Mar 17 SA 6f ft 1:123 h

C.
12–1

Balcony Pass — **Ch. f. 4, by Pass The Glass—Balcony Doll, by First Balcony**
Br.—Qvale K M (Cal) — 1987 4 1 0 1 $28,025
SIBILLE R **113** **Tr.—Headley Bruce** — 1986 3 0 1 1 $9,750
Own.—Qvale K M — **Lifetime 9 3 1 2 $119,975**

28Feb87-7SA 7f :223 :451 1:224ft 24 113 79½ 79¼ 76 33½ Meza R Q3 ⒻAw45000 82-17 Goldspell,Firesweeper,BalconyPass 7
28Feb87—Stumbled start
5Feb87-7SA 1 :453 1:094 1:354ft 4½ 114 714 612 68½ 45¼ StevensGL1 ⒻAw38000 84-22 LoversNtive,Annpurn,TwilightRidg 7
11Jan87-6SA 7f :223 :451 1:221ft 5¼ 118 99¼ 911 79½ 48 Meza R Q5 ⒻAw33000 81-21 SldomSnS,TwlghtRdg,OnY-OwnTm 9
11Jan87—Wide into stretch

1Jan87-3SA 6f :213 :451 1:111ft 6½ 116 89 87¼ 84¾ 1¾ Meza R Q8 ⒻAw29000 82-19 BlconyPss,SeDoubyRun,LuckySilvr 9
26Oct86-5SA 1 1/16 :463 1:111 1:433ft 5½ 112 88 65 55½ 54 Meza R Q7 ⒻAw30000 79-16 Fairly Old, Python, Petillante 9
8Oct86-6SA 6f :22 :451 1:101ft 2 114 75¾ 75¼ 55½ 33¾ McCrrnCJ5 ⒻAw28000 83-20 TomboyBls,Symbolclly,BlconyPss 10
31Aug86-7Dmr 6½f :222 :453 1:162ft 5½ 113 76¼ 76¼ 63¾ 2½ Olivares F5 ⒻAw24000 89-12 Miss O. B.E.,BalconyPass,AllInTune 8
31Aug86—Bobbled start; wide into stretch
28Dec85-8SA 7f :221 :444 1:234ft 10 114 1213 1214 77 1nk MzRQ10 ⒻⓈCal Brdrs 81-14 BlconyPss,Egle'sMusic,SilntArrivl 12
23Oct85-4SA 6f :214 :454 1:12 ft 4¾ 117 1014 911 45½ 11¾ Sibille R11 ⒻⓈM32000 78-25 BlconyPss,WhyNotTll,PllysLlRscl 12
23Oct85—Very wide into stretch
Apr 8 SA 3f ft :353 h Apr 3 SA 6f ft 1:133 h Mar 29 SA 3f ft :353 h Mar 24 SA 3f ft :353 h

D.

25–1

Blushing All Over B. m. 5, by Blushing Groom—Victory Kingdom, by Viceregal
ORTEGA L E 114 Br.—Miller L (Ky) 1987 4 0 1 0 $10,725
Tr.—Frankel Robert 1986 4 1 0 0 $22,000
Own.—Moss J S Lifetime 15 5 3 0 $62,135 Turf 11 5 2 0 $51,410
28Mar87-8Aqu 1 :46 1:103 1:363m 19 108 32½ 45½ 56 63¾ VnziM7 ⒻBd O' Rses 79-23 Ms.Eloise,SpringBeuty,TrickySquw 9
28Mar87—Grade III
19Feb87-8SA 1 :46 1:102 1:36 ft 12 116 74¾ 73½ 51¾ 52¼ StevensGL7 ⒻAw45000 85-13 Le L'Argent, Paradies,Nature'sWay 7
28Jan87-7SA 1 1/16 :47 1:113 1:441ft 2¼ 116 55½ 53¾ 54¼ 67 StevensGL1 ⒻAw45000 73-21 North Sider, Ambra Ridge, SignOff 8
15Jan87-8SA 1 :463 1:111 1:371ft 11 116 53 32 22½ 23 WrrenRJJr3 ⒻAw48000 79-25 Shywing,BlushingAllOvr,AmbrRidg 6
1Nov86-9SA 1 Ⓣ:463 1:104 1:363fm 12 116 2½ 94 1216 1215½ McHrDG10 ⒻMdwk H 78-07 Aberuschka, Duckweed, Solva 12
8Oct86-8SA a6½f Ⓣ:213 :443 1:144fm 8¼ 116 73½ 73¼ 4¾ 63 McHrDG1 ⒻAtm DysH 82-14 Shywing,HerRoyalty,WaterCrystals 9
8Oct86—Broke slowly; blocked into drive; Run in divisions
9Aug86-8Dmr 1 Ⓣ:461 1:104 1:342fm 11 116 53 82¾ 810 811½ McHrDG7 ⒻPlmr H 89-04 Aberuschka, Sauna,Fran'sValentine 9
9Aug86—Grade II; Bumped start; fanned wide 3/8 turn
9Jly86-8Hol 1 Ⓣ:462 1:101 1:342fm 5½ 116 45 31½ 11 1¾ McHrgDG6 ⒻAw40000 — — BlushingAllOver,FolkArt,Cnyk'sStr 8
19Sep85 ♦1MLaffitte(Fra) a1 1:35 gd 8¾ 112 Ⓣ 1no Legrix E de la Tmise H BlshngAllOvr,ClsslWy,ChrmngDk 20
25Aug85 ♦3Deauville(Fra) a1¼ 2:194sf 4¼ 112 Ⓣ 55½ BnoitG ⒻP FrncsAndreH Lady Day, Thimpu, Gazelia 20
Mar 20 Hol 7f ft 1:272 h Mar 14 Hol 6f ft 1:152 h Mar 8 Hol 5f ft 1:001 h Feb 28 SA 5f ft :591 h

E.

31–1

Jell * Ch. m. 6, by Gummo—Interact, by Verbatim
PATTON D B 113 Br.—Elmendorf Farm (Cal) 1987 5 2 1 2 $53,800
Tr.—Borick Robert 1986 6 1 1 1 $31,900
Own.—Four Four Forty Farms Lifetime 45 7 7 10 $190,625 Turf 5 0 0 1 $4,000
12Mar87-5SA 1 :461 1:114 1:372ft 9¾ 1125 85¾ 31½ 21 1no Cox D W6 Ⓕ 75000 81-19 Jell, Totally Honest, Keep Dating 10
6Mar87-8SA 1 1/16 :47 1:113 1:433gd 4½ 1145 54½ 44½ 45 38¼ Cox D W5 ⒻAw40000 75-21 Twilight Ridge, Rea, Jell 6
13Feb87-7SA 1 1/16 :47 1:112 1:442sy 4½ 1115 67 57 31½ 11¼ Patton DB7 ⒻAw32000 79-18 Jell, Private Sorrow,PrincessOfAck 7
25Jan87-3SA 1 :471 1:114 1:373ft 8½ 1115 47 44½ 42 32¼ Cox D W4 ⒻAw32000 78-18 Python, Case Money, Jell 6
11Jan87-1SA 1 1/16 :48 1:132 1:462ft 5 1115 44½ 42½ 41 2¾ Cox D W2 Ⓕ 50000 68-21 Keep Dating, Jell, Broad Street 6
11Jan87—Crowded, altered course 1/16
26Oct86-5SA 1 1/16 :463 1:111 1:433ft 28 1115 911 87¾ 67½ 66 Black C A9 ⒻAw30000 77-16 Fairly Old, Python, Petillante 9
26Oct86—Wide into stretch
31Aug86-7Dmr 6½f :222 :453 1:162ft 29 118 87¾ 87¼ 76¾ 76½ HernndezR4 ⒻAw24000 83-12 Miss O. B.E.,BalconyPass,AllInTune 8
31Aug86—Off slowly, wide
13Mar86-5SA 1 :474 1:134 1:402sy *8-5 1145 55½ 53 33 21¼ Black C A2 Ⓕ 62500 65-30 Emacia, Jell, Blade Of Luck 9
6Mar86-7SA 1 :462 1:11 1:363ft 10 1105 74¼ 62½ 54 32 Black C A3 ⒻAw35000 83-15 Rea, Affection Affirmed, Jell 7
6Mar86—Altered path 1/8
16Feb86-3SA 1 :471 1:124 1:382gd *2¼ 1085 64½ 31 11 12¾ Black C A5 Ⓕ 55000 76-14 Jell, Emacia, Count On Lyn 6
Apr 5 SA 4f ft :491 h Mar 27 SA 5f ft 1:023 h Mar 21 SA 4f ft :502 h Feb 28 SA 5f ft 1:011 h

F.

4–1

Joni U. Bar Dk. b. or br. m. 7, by Nordic Prince—Edes Ilona, by Grey Eagle
OLIVARES F 115 Br.—Cozza F (Cal) 1987 3 0 0 1 $13,500
Tr.—Dorfman Leonard 1986 2 1 0 0 $30,750
Own.—F Cozza Estate Lifetime 26 11 0 4 $204,025 Turf 1 0 0 0
28Feb87-7SA 7f :223 :451 1:224ft 2¾ 116 63½ 64¼ 43½ 43½ Olivares F2 ⒻAw45000 82-17 Goldspell,Firesweeper,BalconyPass 7
6Feb87-8SA 6f :213 :434 1:092ft 2½ 117 75½ 55½ 45 4½ Olivares F3 ⒻAw45000 90-15 LeL'Argent,Compatibility,Firesweepr 7
6Feb87—Very wide stretch
16Jan87-8SA 6f :213 :443 1:094ft 4½ 114 69½ 67½ 68 34 Olivares F1 ⒻAw45000 85-18 Sari's Heroine, Till You, Joni U.Bar 6
16Jan87—Wide into stretch
12Feb86-7SA 1 :453 1:101 1:35 ft 2 117 53 1hd 12 15 Olivares F6 ⒻAw45000 93-16 JoniU.Bar,RascalLss,Overwhelming 6
15Jan86-8SA 7f :221 :44 1:213ft 8½ 120 67½ 68 45½ 43¾ OlvrsF6 ⒻSt Mnca H 88-14 HerRoylty,NorthSider,TkeMyPictur 8
15Jan86—Grade III; Broke slowly
26Oct85-8BM 6f :222 :451 1:091ft 3 119 57 55½ 32½ 11 OlivrsF1 ⒻC H Rssll H 93-16 JoniU.Br,MomntToBuy,BronssDirct 8

7Sep85-3Dmr 7f :222 :452 1:214ft *4-5 115 51¾ 31½ 22½ 11¼ Olivares F2 ⒻAw40000 99-08 Joni U. Bar, Dear Carrie,CouleeBay 7
11Aug85-7Dmr 6½f :22 :451 1:16 ft 3¾ 118 77¼ 68¼ 36 1½ Olivares F6 ⒻAw26000 96-11 JoniU.Bar,SavannhSlew,PtriciJmes 8
1Aug85-7Dmr 6f :221 :45 1:10 ft 8 118 76¼ 55¼ 22½ 12 Olivares F2 ⒻAw20000 88-20 Joni U. Bar, Balladry, Alyanna 7
6Jly85-3Hol 6f :221 :453 1:11 ft 7 116 54½ 45½ 34 32 Olivares F1 ⒻAw30000 90-05 Azorrable,TeaAndScandls,JoniU.Br 6
Apr 10 SA 4f ft :493 h ●Apr 3 SA 7f ft 1:25 h Mar 26 SA 5f ft 1:004 h ●Mar 18 SA 6f ft 1:112 h

G.
5–1

Annapurna B. m. 5, by Raja Baba—Glinka, by Sir Ivor
MEZA R Q 115 Br.—Warner M L (Ohio) Tr.—Gosden John H M
1987 3 1 1 0 $24,650
1986 6 1 1 0 $25,825
Own.—Getty-Phillips-Riordan Lifetime 12 3 3 0 $69,225 Turf 1 0 0 0

5Feb87-7SA 1 :453 1:094 1:354ft 7 119 511 58½ 35 2¾ DlhoussyE2 ⒻAw38000 88-22 LoversNtive,Annpurn,TwilightRidg 7
24Jan87-7SA 1⅛Ⓣ:47 1:1131:491fm 11 118 74¾107 119¾1012½ Meza R Q7 ⒻAw38000 68-17 Benzina, Rekindling, Mangez Les 11
24Jan87—Wide 7/8 turn
1Jan87-7SA 1 1/16 :461 1:113 1:443ft 16 118 67¼ 52½ 1½ 12½ Meza R Q8 ⒻAw31000 78-19 Annapurna, Python, La Codorniz 9
11Dec86-8Hol 1 :464 1:114 1:361ft 8 122 32 31 43 49½ Meza R Q3 ⒻAw27000 72-21 OnYourOwnTim,FlightAbov,Python 6
19Nov86-9Hol 1 :462 1:112 1:371ft 5 122 44 35 36 25 Sibille R6 ⒻAw26000 72-21 Mirculous,Annpurn,DremAboutYou 7
26Oct86-5SA 1 1/16 :463 1:111 1:433ft 5 118 43½ 54 45½ 44 Sibille R1 ⒻAw30000 79-16 Fairly Old, Python, Petillante 9
17Oct86-7SA 1 1/16 :463 1:112 1:434ft 6 116 45½ 43 21½ 12 Sibille R2 ⒻAw27000 82-21 Annpurn,LCodorniz,Veronic'sQuest 8
14Aug86-7Dmr 1 1/16 :454 1:104 1:432ft 7¾ 118 74¼ 64½ 65½ 64 VlenzulPA2 ⒻAw20000 79-17 MargretBooth,Plumpetr,DonATop 10
14Aug86—Bumped start, lugged in stretch
26Jly86-7Dmr 1 :452 1:11 1:371ft 3½ 118 89 77 56 46½ DlhoussyE5 ⒻAw20000 75-13 Beulhlnd,Bggr'sWllt,RoylDrby'sLov 8
26Jun85-1Hol 1 :461 1:114 1:371ft 2½ 115 2hd 3nk 11 13 McCarron C J4 ⒻMdn 87-08 Annpurn,ReigningMlody,FtchNCrry 7
Apr 8 SA 4f ft :491 h Apr 2 SA 1 ft 1:39 h ●Mar 27 SA 7f ft 1:263 h ●Mar 21 SA 7f ft 1:27 h

H.
10–1

Proper Mary Ch. f. 4, by Properantes—My Mary, by Rising Market
WARREN R J JR 115 Br.—Old English Rancho (Cal) Tr.—Warren Donald
1987 1 1 0 0 $25,500
1986 7 3 2 0 $54,175
Own.—Johnston Betty-E W-Judy Lifetime 8 4 2 0 $79,675 Turf 3 1 2 0 $32,700

8Feb87-11TuP 1 1/16Ⓣ:4741:1231:434fm 5 120 42½ 2hd 11½ 1hd WrrRJJr5 ⒻTwlt Tr H 93-07 Proper Mary, FlySoFar,HastyMort 14
28Sep86-10Pom 1 1/16 :463 1:112 1:433ft 2½ 121 21 2hd 1hd 11¼ WrrenRJJr3 ⒻAmda S 93-09 ProprMry,Symboliclly,TropiclHoldy 6
19Sep86-11Pom 1 1/16 :461 1:104 1:432ft 2½ 114 2hd 1½ 1hd 1nk WrrRJJr6 ⒻⓈCTBAM 94-09 ProperMry,Symboliclly,SilentArrivl 8
4Sep86-8Dmr 1 1/16 :453 1:101 1:421ft 13 114 52¾ 64½ 64¼ 54¾ ShmkrW4 ⒻⓇTry Pns 84-14 MrgrtBooth,T.V.Rsidul,SportngAck 7
4Sep86—Lugged out early; steadied at intervals
27Aug86-2Dmr 1 1/16 :454 1:102 1:431ft *4-5 117 21½ 23½ 21½ 12¾ Pincay L Jr9 ⒻMdn 84-14 Proper Mary, Yacht, Dontaskris 9
27Aug86—Lugged in stretch
28Jun86-5Hol 1⅛Ⓣ:4711:1141:49 fm 2½ 114 21 3nk 1½ 2¾ Shoemaker W9 ⒻMdn 86-05 PerfectMtchII,ProperMry,QunJon 12
29May86-6Hol 1 1/16Ⓣ:4641:1131:43 fm 28 117 21 1hd 1½ 2¾ Pincay L Jr 2 ⒻMdn 88-11 JulieWriter,ProperMry,EvningBid 10
29May86—Veered out, bumped start
25Apr86-4Hol 6f :22 :453 1:10 ft 7 120 77¾ 711 714 516½ Pincay L Jr3 ⒻⓈMdn 77-16 Melair,RareStarlet,MrtinDuststorm 7
Apr 8 SA 5f ft 1:00 h ●Apr 2 SA 7f ft 1:263 h Mar 28 SA 5f ft 1:022 h

I.
5–2

Goldspell Gr. m. 5, by Caro—Lucky Spell, by Lucky Mel
PINCAY L JR 117 Br.—Wilder & Burris (Ky) Tr.—Moreno Henry
1987 2 1 0 0 $24,750
1986 4 0 1 0 $11,000
Own.—Burris & Wilder Lifetime 16 5 2 2 $160,135 Turf 3 0 0 0 $6,250

28Feb87-7SA 7f :223 :451 1:224ft 8 117 52½ 52½ 32½ 11½ Pincay LJr7 ⒻAw45000 86-17 Goldspell,Firesweeper,BalconyPass 7
19Feb87-8SA 1 :46 1:102 1:36 ft 3¾ 116 21 1hd 3nk 63 McHrgDG2 ⒻAw45000 85-13 Le L'Argent, Paradies,Nature'sWay 7
13Dec86-8BM a1⅛Ⓣ 1:48 fm 15 113 33 31½ 78 713¾ CpTM2 ⒻCa Jky Cb H 81-05 Solva, Kraemer, Bonne Ile 7
13Dec86—Grade III
23Nov86-8BM 1 :463 1:11 1:36 ft 3¾ 115 33 31½ 21½ 21½ ChpnTM5 ⒻWdsde H 86-20 Special Victory,Goldspell,Petillante 8
1Feb86-8SA 1 1/16 :453 1:12 1:443m 37 114 715 76 611 616½ HrndR7 ⒻSta Mria H 62-24 Love Smitten, Johnica, North Sider 9
1Feb86—Grade II
15Jan86-8SA 7f :221 :44 1:213ft 31 116 89 79½ 57 55¼ HrndR8 ⒻSt Mnca H 87-14 HerRoylty,NorthSider,TkeMyPictur 8
15Jan86—Grade III
3Nov85-8SA 1 1/16 :45 1:103 1:422ft 6 118 55 42½ 32 31¼ HrndR8 ⒻLnda Vsta H 88-15 Savannah Slew,Waterside,Goldspell 8
3Nov85—Grade III
19Oct85-8SA 1⅛Ⓣ:4531:0941:471fm 38 113 54 54½ 34 56½ HrndR6 ⒻLs Plms H 84-12 Estrapade, L'Attrayante, Johnica 11
19Oct85—Grade II
22Sep85-10LaD 1⅛ :48 1:114 1:512ft *8-5 120 2½ 2½ 2½ 2hd HrnndzR2 ⒻLad Oaks 88-20 JustAnythng,Goldspll,CrmsonOrchd 7
6Sep85-8Dmr 1 1/16 :463 1:111 1:412ft 6½ 117 2½ 2hd 13 11¾ Meza RQ2 ⒻⓇTry Pns 93-14 Goldspell, Folk Art, Lucky Roberta 7
Apr 10 SA 3f ft :361 h ●Apr 4 SA 6f ft 1:131 h Mar 30 SA 4f ft :581 h Mar 22 SA 7f m 1:254 h

58. Starter races offer handicappers who know what to look for the passkeys to profits. The winner here keyed the exacta and late double at Atlantic City. Which horse is it?

10 ATLANTIC CITY 1⅛ MILES ATLANTIC CITY

1 ⅛ MILES. (1.46⅗) STARTER HANDICAP. Purse $6,600. 3-year-olds and upward which have started for a claiming price of $5,000 or less since June 1, 1986. Weights Wednesday, July 29. Declarations by 10:00 A.M. Thursday, July 30, 1987. (High Weights on the Scale Preferred.)

A.

8–1

Locranon — Ch. g. 4, by Monteverdi—Crowned Royal, by Raise a Native
Own.—Schwartz Isadora — Br.—Juddmonte Farms (Ky) — Tr.—Damon K Richard — 110
Lifetime 18 3 2 0 $13,477 — 1987 11 2 1 0 $7,611 — 1986 6 1 1 0 $5,866 — Turf 2 0 0 0 $432

24Jly87- 1Atl	fst 1 1/16	:48⅗ 1:14⅕ 1:47⅖	3+ Clm 5000	5 1 11½ 11½ 1hd 2no	Douthall J D	b 116	8.00	68-31	Ⓓ Total Bypass 116no Locranon 116nk Wise Mike 109²	Just missed	6
24Jly87-Placed first through disqualification											
16Jly87- 7Atl	fst 6f	:22⅖ :46⅗ 1:13⅖	3+ Clm 5000	12 1 84¼ 34 21 11½	Douthall J D	b 116	7.60	75-28	Locranon 1161½ Tudor to the Hilt 1143½ Regalito 116½	Driving	12
9Jly87- 4Atl	sly 6f	:22⅘ :46⅘ 1:13	3+ Clm 5000	2 7 74¼ 89 65½ 47	Douthall J D	b 116	4.90	70-23	Deadly Spell 1166½ Eagle's Touch 116hd Revit 116½	Late bid	11
2Jly87- 2Atl	sly 5½f	:22⅕ :46⅖ 1:07	3+ Clm 5000	8 4 66¼ 610 34½ 2½	Douthall J D	b 116	21.80	77-27	Cynic 116½ Locranon 116½ Badge of Silver 1071½	Rallied	8
11May87- 9Pen	fst 1 1/16	:47⅘ 1:12⅘ 1:48	Clm 5000	8 4 42 48 511 59¾	Kamada E J	b 116	14.20	56-21	Fioman 1163¼ Thirty Two Guns 116½ El Fu' 122³	Weakened	9
24Apr87- 2Pen	sly 1 1/16	:48⅗ 1:14⅗ 1:50	Clm 5000	8 3 32½ 79½ 920 1026½	Iliescu A	b 116	7.60	29-28	AukeByBluff1221½ShinOnDwn111½DcmbrCourt122²	Bore in,stop'd	18
6Apr87- 4Pen	sly 170	:47⅕ 1:11⅘ 1:43⅖	Clm 5000	1 2 22 26 215 420¾	Iliescu A	b 116	6.20	63-22	Play Yard11618ShineOnDewan111noKickinChicken116²	Weakened	9
28Mar87- 5Pen	fst 1⅛	:47⅖ 1:12⅗ 1:52⅘	Clm 5000	2 2 22 3½ 33 46¾	Iliescu A	b 116	6.80	81-19	Belleau Wood1163¾PlayYard109³JacksonSummit116hd	Weakened	11
13Mar87- 7Pen	fst 6f	:22 :45⅖ 1:11⅕	Clm 8000	7 1 35½ 66¼ 616 614¼	Colton R E	b 115	17.40	74-21	Babbie On 110² Poutar 116⁵ Press The Six 1123¼	Early foot	7
16Feb87- 6Pen	fst 5½f	:22⅗ :46⅗ 1:05⅕	Clm 10000	6 1 5½ 3nk 65¼ 69	Colton R E	b 115	12.00	81-16	SevenDegrees1162¾HoratiusWay1131¼FastAsTheBreeze109½	Tired	6

LATEST WORKOUTS Jun 27 Atl 3f sly :38 b

B.

5–1

Rochford Bridge — Dk. b. or br. g. 6, by Nielbueh—Pish Posh, by John William
Own.—Flaherty J — Br.—Farnsworth Farm (Fla) — Tr.—Helmetag Robert — 115
Lifetime 94 10 13 16 $83,807 — 1987 18 1 2 2 $7,352 — 1986 32 7 6 5 $39,295 — Turf 1 0 0 1 $682

23Jly87- 8Atl	fst 6f	:22⅗ :46⅖ 1:11⅗	3+ Clm 11000	3 6 65 66½ 66 67¾	Landicini C Jr	b 116	5.50	76-22	Dr. Don H. 1151½ Red Screen 1165½ Made In Jersey 116nk	Trailed	6
15Jly87- 3Atl	fst 1 1/16	:47⅘ 1:13⅖ 1:47⅗	3+ Hcp 5000s	1 3 42 32 23 22½	Landicini C Jr	b 117	5.10	64-33	Regal Art 1112½ RochfordBridge117²SilverJingle113²	Best others	8
4Jly87- 3Atl	fst 7f	:23⅕ :46⅖ 1:24⅗	3+ Hcp 5000s	7 1 21 22 24 21	Landicini C Jr	b 115	1.40	78-25	QutFoolng1141RochfordBrdg115⁹CittrngMount1172½	Second best	7
25Jun87- 7Atl	fm *1 1/16 Ⓣ	:48⅗ 1:13⅗ 1:46⅗	3+ Clm 10000	2 4 42 21 2hd 31½	Landicini C Jr	b 115	9.70	82-16	SpruceMeUp1161½SirLddisPlc114hdRochfordBridg115²	Weakened	10
20Jun87- 2Atl	fst 6½f	:23 :46 1:17⅖	3+ Clm 5000	2 4 41 31½ 12½ 17	Landicini C Jr	b 116	18.60	99-19	RochfordBridge116⁷FredDe'sMight120½AnvilMn116hd	Ridden out	10
8Jun87- 4GS	fst 6f	:22⅕ :45⅖ 1:11⅖	3+ Clm 4000	3 10 108 812 911 913½	Alligood M A	b 116	8.80	71-21	Zango 116² F. Stanton 1193½ Rochares 1161½	Outrun	10
25May87- 4GS	fst 6f	:22⅗ :46⅖ 1:13⅕	3+ Clm 4000	1 8 78¼ 56½ 44 41¼	Alligood M A	b 116	7.50	75-24	NowW'vGotHim116¾OurClownPrinc112noSignifcntly114½	Late bid	10
13May87- 6Del	fst 1 1/16	:48 1:13⅖ 1:46⅖	Clm 4000	5 3 2½ 33 911 913½	Olivera M F	b 120	5.10	62-20	The Gray Protege 1201½ DH Wise Mike 120 DH Tall Tana120¾	Tired	12
1May87-10GS	fst 6f	:22⅖ :45⅘ 1:12⅗	3+ Clm 5000	2 10 117 88 109¾ 73	Ravelich M	b 116	12.90	76-20	F. Stanton 116hd Hornsy 109¹ Damascus Jet 116¾	Outrun	12
27Apr87- 4GS	fst 6f	:22⅗ :46⅗ 1:12⅖	3+ Clm 4000	1 6 72¼ 73¼ 51½ 53½	Ravelich M	b 116	14.20	76-22	SummaryJudgementII116²Greypont116¾BssSinger116½	No factor	11

C.

5–1

Shadowfax — Ch. g. 8, by Eager Native—Monday Prize, by Double Brandy
Own.—Gibellino Z — Br.—C P S Stable (Md) — Tr.—Houghton Ronald B — 111
Lifetime 65 10 7 9 $159.716 — 1987 4 0 2 1 $3,728 — 1986 15 1 2 3 $15,300 — Turf 12 1 1 2 $13,621

18Jly87- 7Pen	fst 1¼	:49⅕ 1:40 2:06	3+ Hcp 5000s	7 7 77¾ 41½ 41¼ 3hd	Hagan D P	b 110	3.20	88-16	DH AlwysAGentlemn123hd DH ClssicSted116hdShdowfx1101¾	Rallied	7
11Jly87- 1Pen	fm 1½ Ⓣ	2:31⅖	3+ Hcp 5000s	1 9 97½ 63¾ 56¾ 54¼	Coie M A	b 112	*4.10	91-16	Dan Rather 1141½ Writer's Son 112hd Tomlin 1141¾	No menace	11
20Jun87- 7Pen	gd 1¼	:46⅗ 1:39 2:05⅕	3+ Hcp 5000s	1 5 53¾ 1½ 11 2nk	Hagan D P	b 110	*1.40	92-18	Tomlin 111nk Shadowfax 110² Czar's Gift 1162½	Just missed	6
15Jun87- 5Pen	fst 6f	:22⅖ :46 1:12⅕	3+ Clm 4500	8 11 125 127½ 83¾ 2½	Hagan D P	b 122	27.90	82-19	Just AIndian119½Shadowfax122hdSilentRunner122no	Broke slowly	12
19Sep86- 7Del	fm 1⅛ Ⓣ	:47⅖ 1:12⅖ 1:50⅗	3+ Clm 9000	4 7 919 87¼ 87¾ 96¾	Jones S R	109	*2.40	84-10	Rightorwrongfrank113nkTicklyBender119nkSteelHert113¹	Outrun	11
25Aug86- 6Atl	fm *1⅛ Ⓣ	:49⅖ 1:14 1:53⅕	3+ Clm 9000	1 9 96¾ 83¼ 51¾ 32½	Peterka G	b 116	6.90	88-09	Bud Collins 1161½ Ginny's Choice 113¹ Shadowfax116½	Very wide	10
16Aug86- 9Pen	sly 1 1/16	:47⅕ 1:12⅗ 1:46⅕	3+ Clm 12500	3 5 512 611 59 45¾	Peterka G	b 117	*1.80	69-20	Verse Effector 1152¾ Arsalan 115² Silver Sceptre 115¹	Outrun	6
26Jly86- 9Atl	fm 1 40 Ⓣ	:46⅘ 1:10⅕ 1:38⅕	3+ Clm 20000	4 8 1010 1113 1115 1113¾	Jones S R	b 120	5.50	— —	Marine 112¹ Case Back 112⁴ Apalachee Warrior 112hd	Outrun	12
17Jly86- 6Atl	my 1 1/16	:47⅕ 1:11⅘ 1:44⅖	3+ Clm 25000	1 4 413 412 33½ 25	Jones B S	b 116	2.70	78-22	Winrebo 108⁵ Shadowfax 116½ Ernie's Sugar Bowl 113⁷	Rallied	4
7Jly86- 7Atl	fst 1 1/16	:46 1:11 1:43⅘	3+ Clm 22500	1 7 714 67½ 21 2¾	Jones S R	b 120	5.60	85-19	Ernie's Sugar Bowl 109¾ Shadowfax 1206½ By A Pro 115¾	Gamely	7

LATEST WORKOUTS Jly 14 Pim 4f fst :49⅗ b

D.

8–5

Hill Slide — B. g. 4, by Temperence Hill—Need No Proof, by Prove It
Own.—J C J Racing Stable — Br.—Davis W R (Fla) — Tr.—DeStefano John M Jr — 124
Lifetime 37 10 2 1 $64.005 — 1987 14 6 1 0 $40,790 — 1986 18 4 1 1 $22,720 — Turf 1 0 0 0 $100

25Jly87- 5Mth	fst 1	:45⅘ 1:10⅕ 1:36⅗	3+ Clm 42500	7 2 44½ 45 46½ 57¾	Madrid A Jr	114	5.50	62-13	Dungarvin King 115⁴ Golden Boy 1152½ Derby Hat 115¾	Tired	7
14Jly87- 5Mth	fst 170	:46⅗ 1:11 1:43⅕	3+ Alw 15000	3 2 2hd 2hd 2hd 1nk	Madrid A Jr	118	4.60	80-23	Hill Slide 118nk PublicAccounter110⁴HurricaneJohn114nk	Driving	7
4Jly87- 2Mth	fst 1	:46⅗ 1:11⅕ 1:37⅕	3+ Alw 15000	4 3 31½ 31 41½ 45	Madrid A Jr	118	5.00	82-10	Native Aspen 115¾ Freud 112¾ Aly Rat 1143½	Bore out, bmpd	8
20Jun87- 3Mth	fst 1 1/16	:46⅖ 1:11⅕ 1:44	3+ Clm 25000	1 4 46½ 31½ 11½ 15	Madrid A Jr	115	7.30	85-13	Hill Slide 115⁵ Classic Impact 1151½ Lumumba 1151¾	Drew clear	7
8Jun87- 2Mth	fst 6f	:22⅘ :46 1:10⅖	3+ Clm 16000	2 4 61¾ 43½ 23½ 24	McCauley W H	116	9.20	84-18	Participate 112⁴ Hill Slide 116³ Homo Soho 114¾	Second best	8
9May87- 8GS	fst 1¾	:48⅘ 3:01⅖	3+ Hcp 5000s	4 1 18 37 415 427	Madrid A Jr	121	*1.30	— —	Morning Joseph 1176½ Arsalan 1127½ Biff Bob 115¹³	Hit rail, rank	8
25Apr87- 5GS	my 1½	:47⅘ 2:05⅗ 2:31⅘	3+ Hcp 5000s	9 2 2½ 15 17 14½	Madrid A Jr	117	4.30	— —	Hill Slide 1174½ Biff Bob 1125½ Mastaba 122²	Ridden out	12
11Apr87- 6GS	fst 1 3/16	:48⅗ 1:13⅘ 2:00	3+ Hcp 5000s	6 3 11 11½ 12 1¾	Madrid A Jr	116	4.90	85-25	Hill Slide 116¾ Jersey Gigolo 1123½ Morning Joseph 1169½	Driving	8
26Mar87- 5GS	fst 1⅛	:48⅕ 1:13⅕ 1:52⅕	3+ Hcp 5000s	2 1 1½ 1½ 12 13½	Madrid A Jr	114	11.00	68-23	Hill Slide 1143½ Jersey Gigolo 1132½ Rava Ruler 113½	Driving	6
14Mar87- 5GS	fst 1¼	:47⅘ 1:41⅗ 2:09⅗	Hcp 5000s	4 5 43½ 54¼ 47 413½	Madrid A Jr	116	3.20	42-29	April Cat 1193½DukeOfWistlewood114⁵RavaRuler114⁵	Needed bid	8

LATEST WORKOUTS Jun 3 Mth 4f fst :48 b

E.

5–2

Regal Art B. g. 3, by Arts and Letters—Somethingregal, by Candy Spots
Br.—Sachs David (Ky)
Own.—Victorian Acres Farm Tr.—Capuano Dale
115 Lifetime 21 6 3 3 $38.880 1987 16 5 3 3 $33,600 1986 5 1 0 0 $5,280 Turf 1 0 0 0

15Jly87- 3Atl fst 1 1/16 :47⅘ 1:13⅗ 1:47⅗ 3+Hcp 5000s 6 1 1hd 1hd 13 12½ Wiley M C b 111 *1.30 67-33 Regal Art 1112½ Rochford Bridge 1172 Silver Jingle 1132 Driving 8
12Jly87- 4Pim fst 1 1/16 :47⅖ 1:12⅘ 1:45⅖ Clm 11500 5 3 31½ 43½ 1hd 2½ Wiley M C5 b 109 *2.70 76-20 Bouvier 114½ Regal Art 109nk Quadrunner 1143 Hung 7
1Jly87- 3Pha fst 1 :48⅖ 1:14 1:41⅗ Clm 12500 5 3 31½ 43¾ 33 22½ Wiley M C5 b 111 *1.80 63-26 Ruther Glen 1092½ Regal Art 111½ Rational Eyes 1094 Gamely 7
22Jun87- 7Lrl fm 1 Ⓣ:46 1:10 1:34⅘ Clm 16500 10 6 63¼ 75¼ 1118 1014¼ Wiley M C5 b 107 14.10 82-05 Watts With You 114½ Lagerfeld 1071½ Wicked Hit 1152 Faded 12
1Jun87- 6Lrl fst 1 :48⅕ 1:13⅗ 1:39⅘ Clm 11500 4 2 31 21½ 22½ 21½ Wiley M C5 b 109 *1.70 71-24 Spouse Equivalent 1141½ RegalArt1091½Eat'UmUp109nk Game try 6
19May87- 1Pim my 1 1/16 :48 1:13⅘ 1:48⅕ Clm 6500 5 3 1hd 16 15 17 Wiley M C5 b 109 2.30 63-29 Regal Art 1097 Every Intent 114no North to Home 1148 Driving 6
15May87- 5Pim fst 1 1/16 :46⅕ 1:11⅘ 1.48 Clm 5000 8 8 312 46¼ 24 1hd Wiley M C5 b 107 *2.50 64-25 ReglArt107hdOwlAndTree114nkRestlssProtg1173 Lost iron, drvng 11
29Apr87- 1Pim fst 1 1/16 :46⅘ 1:12 1:47⅖ Clm 8500 6 5 57½ 57 47 511¼ Wiley M C5 b 114 *2.20 56-22 ScrletGiboulee1072¾UnresonbleKlly1093NorthtoHom112½ No rally 7
23Apr87- 4Pim fst 1 1/16 :48⅕ 1:13 1:45⅕ Clm 11500 2 3 41¾ 41¾ 35 34½ Wiley M C5 b 114 *3.00 73-21 Universal Force 1143 Wicked Hit 1141½ Regal Art 1143 Bore in 6
15Apr87- 8Pim fst 1 1/16 :47⅗ 1:13⅖ 1:46⅗ Clm 14500 9 5 53 77 910 811¾ Hutton G W b 112 *2.80 59-25 Watts With You 1093½ Bouvier 1143 Full Light 1151¼ Outrun 10
LATEST WORKOUTS Jly 26 Bow 3f fst :38⅕ b Jun 9 Bow 5f fst 1:01⅗ h

F.

20–1

Exclusive Vertigo Ch. c. 3, by Exclusive Ribot—Verticism, by Vertex
Br.—Sheats Garland C (Fla)
Own.—Double C Stable Tr.—Shapiro Libby
105 Lifetime 20 2 2 2 $8.482 1987 16 2 2 2 $8.304 1986 4 M 0 0 $178 Turf 1 0 0 0 $180

25Jly87- 8Del fst 1 1/16 :47 1:11⅖ 1:43⅘ 3+Alw 5000s 4 5 520 514 511 517 Lizarzaburu P M 107 31.40 72-10 One For Dom 1221[D]KissMyTan116noReasonToMarch1223 Outrun 5
15Jly87- 3Atl fst 1 1/16 :47⅘ 1:13⅗ 1:47⅗ 3+Hcp 5000s 3 8 814 818 610 610 Intelisano G P Jr 109 11.80 57-33 Regal Art 1112½ Rochford Bridge 1172 Silver Jingle 1132 Outrun 8
25May87- 8GP fm 1 1/16 Ⓣ:48⅕ 1:12⅕ 1:43⅖ 3+Alw 18000 2 8 811 812 79 710¾ Molina V H 109 53.80 72-17 Go Hawk 1092 Royal E.J. 123no Golden Cherokee 113hd Outrun 8
10May87- 4GP fst 1 1/16 :49⅖ 1:15⅕ 1:49⅕ Clm c-9500 3 11 1126 1115 714 611½ Schieman R L7 108 9.60 43-25 Aloha Brother 1171 First Boy 1155½ Crafty Cliff 1171½ No factor 11
30Apr87- 6GP fst 1 1/16 :46⅘ 1:14⅕ 1:49⅕ Clm 7000 9 12 1129 99¾ 23 1no Schieman R L7 108 *2.60 55-29 ExclusVrtgo108noSuprHrry1176½GladImg1134 Forced wide.drvng 12
23Apr87- 1GP fst 7f :23 :47⅕ 1:26⅗ Clm 7000 8 12 1215 1211 96 73 Milian J L10 107 12.60 68-26 Firedan 1171 Who's Wet 117no Security Cap 112hd Outrun 12
15Apr87- 1GP fst 1 1/16 :48 1:14⅗ 1:50 Clm 7500 7 10 1018 99½ 65½ 65 Myres R J Jr 117 5.30 46-36 Poppi's Devil117½WhisperingNative1172JaymeeFlyer110nk Outrun 10
5Apr87- 3GP fst 1 1/16 :48⅘ 1:14⅘ 1:48⅕ Clm 7500 9 9 811 64½ 21½ 22½ Myres R J Jr 117 7.60 57-26 Steve'sMinstrel1132½ExclusiveVertigo1171JymeeFlyr1102½ Rallied 9
29Mar87- 4Tam sly 1 1/16 :48⅖ 1:15⅕ 1:50 Clm 5000 5 10 1024 1021 711 33 Misiewicz L 116 5.50 65-26 Wind God 1161 Lasita's Sword 1072 ExclusiveVertigo1161 Rallied 10
22Mar87- 5Tam fst 1 1/16 :48⅖ 1:14⅖ 1:47⅖ Clm 5000 8 10 1012 66 54 55¾ Gunther S F 116 6.00 77-16 Cherry Bello 112¾ WindGod1161ComeOutSwinging109½ Wide turn 10
LATEST WORKOUTS Jly 10 Atl 5f sly 1:06⅕ b Jly 1 Atl 3f fst :39⅕ b

G.

8–1

Falcon Fifty Dk. b. or br. g. 5, by Tri Jet—Little Niki, by Time Tested
Br.—Burke W J (Fla)
Own.—Tolle F Tr.—Tolle Floyd M
115 Lifetime 49 10 7 4 $43,205 1987 8 2 1 1 $10,252 1986 28 8 4 1 $28,063 Turf 1 0 0 0

11Jly87- 7Pen fst 1 1/16 :47⅕ 1:12⅖ 1:45⅖ 3+Clm 10000 4 6 711 714 714 716½ Aviles R B 119 2.90 62-20 Ten Nobles 1136 Barlow 115¾ Eastern Corridor 1166 Outrun 7
20Jun87- 5Bir sly 1 1/16 :48⅗ 1:14⅕ 1:47⅖ 3+Alw 3500s 3 3 34½ 21½ 12 15 Espinoza J C 116 *1.10 82-16 Falcon Fifty 1165 Delta Dandy 11112¾ Pounce 122nk Ridden out 6
10Jun87- 3Bir fst 1 1/16 :51⅖ 1:16⅖ 1:49⅗ 3+Clm 10000 5 3 33 44 33 2¾ Luhr R D 116 4.70 70-23 J. J. Shufelt 116¾ Falcon Fifty 116hd Trophy Man 1164½ Rallied 6
23May87- 7Pen sly 1¼ :47 1:39⅗ 2:06⅕ 3+Hcp 5000s 5 7 718 66¾ 44½ 38 Colton R E 118 *2.70 79-25 Smooth Rock 1137 Lord De L'Orne 1051 Falcon Fifty118½ Rallied 7
24Mar87- 3Bir fst 170 :46⅗ 1:12 1:44⅖ Clm 10000 6 7 715 69½ 55¼ 43¾ Fox W I Jr 115 *2.00 — — Color Me Gone 115½ The RagMan1152ThreeBangs1151¼ No factor 7
13Mar87- 4Bir fst 1 1/16 :47⅘ 1:13⅕ 1:47⅗ Clm 8000 3 4 414 49½ 33½ 12½ Fox W I Jr 115 2.20 — — Falcon Fifty 1152½ Exasperated 1154½ Rose Blanket 108½ Driving 5
21Feb87- 7Pen fst 1 1/16 :46⅘ 1:12⅖ 1:46⅘ 3+Hcp 4000s 6 6 619 611 55½ 46 Baker C J 126 4.80 66-22 BobbyLondon1141SlytlyRelted1163½Nick'sNtiveRose1181¾ Rallied 6
15Jan87- 7Lrl fst 1⅛ :47⅕ 1:12⅘ 1:54⅕ Clm 11500 9 11 1120 1225 1222 1225¼ Pino M G 114 7.10 50-29 See for Free 114no Paul Daddy 109½ Mr. Wise Guy 1072¼ Outrun 12
13Dec86- 7Pen gd 1⅛ :48⅖ 1:14 1:55 3+Hcp 4000s 6 7 712 68½ 42 2¾ Winnett B G Jr 131 *1.70 76-27 Slytly Related 114¾ Falcon Fifty 1311OlympicScholar1162 Rallied 10
6Dec86- 7Pen fst 1 1/16 :48⅕ 1:13⅖ 1:46⅕ 3+Hcp 4000s 4 8 810 73½ 15 16¾ Winnett B G Jr 124 3.20 75-27 Falcon Fifty 1246¾ Classic Steed1154¾CalicoTomCat113hd Driving 8

59. As happens frequently, the best horse is not so obvious, but the best bet at the odds should be.

5th Santa Anita

ABOUT 6½ FURLONGS. (Turf). (1.11⅘) CLAIMING. Purse $30,000. 4-year-olds and upward. Weights, 4-year-olds, 121 lbs.; older, 122 lbs. Non-winners of two races since October 1 allowed 2 lbs.; of a race since then, 4 lbs. Claiming price $80,000; for each $5,000 to $70,000, allowed 2 lbs. (Races when entered for $62,500 or less not considered.)

A.

6–1

Sherkin B. g. 6, by Vaguely Noble—Kit's Double, by Spring Double
Br.—Givaudan Mrs L (Ky) 1986 10 5 0 1 $73,350
TORO F 116 Tr.—Anderson Laurie N $75,000 1985 1 0 0 0
Own.—Robinson–Roncelli–Sheridan Lifetime 17 7 0 1 $92,428 Turf 17 7 0 1 $92,428

22Oct86-7SA 1⅛Ⓣ:4541:1021:471fm 6½ 1125 88½ 84 42½ 54 Black C A5 Aw35000 87-12 Nugget Point, Catane, Schiller 10
22Oct86—Crowded entering stretch; bumped, steadied 1/8
1Oct86-8SA 1¼Ⓣ:4641:3532:01 fm 6f 116 2hd 31½ 1012 1112½ BlackCA1 [R]H P Rsl H 69-18 Glaros, Louis Le Grand, Nadirpour 13
1Sep86-5Dmr 1 1/16Ⓣ:4711:11 1:412fm*9-5 1135 45½ 42½ 11 12¼ Black C A5 Aw25000 99-04 Sherkin,DanThtch,TooMuchForT.V. 8
10Aug86-9Dmr 1⅜Ⓣ:4831:3732:141fm*7-5 116 11 12 15 17 McCarron C J8 62500 99-01 Sherkin, Travet, Rushad 9
23Jly86-5Dmr 1 1/16Ⓣ:4621:1131:413fm *2½ 1115 3nk 1hd 31 44½ Black C A6 62500 93-04 El Mansour, Massera, Piper John 10

5Jly86-7Hol 1⅛Ⓣ:4721:1131:473fm*6-5 119 3²½ 31 1²½ 1²½ ShoemakerW10 c50000 94-04 Sherkin, Super Noble, Trakady 11
25May86-6Hol 1 Ⓣ:4631:1021:351fm *1 119 5¹½ 4¹½ 1hd 1¹¾ Shoemaker W3 50000 — — Sherkin, Sandy's Eagle, Ablantin 8
17May86-9Hol 1⅛Ⓣ:46 1:0931:473fm 5 114 1¹½ 1hd 1hd 32 Pincay L Jr5 57500 92-02 Evening M'Lord,TeaTaster,Sherkin 8
26Apr86-9Hol 1116Ⓣ:4711:1111:413fm 4 114 13½ 13 13½ 12¾ Shoemaker W2 45000 96-06 Sherkin, Fabulous Memory, Kunto 7
26Apr86—Bumped hard break, steadied
22Mar86-4GG 1116Ⓣ:4721:1121:433fm 29 113 2½ 2hd 52 84½ Lamance C11 Aw25000 80-15 Ablantin,ViceroyLd,‡NewAtrction 11
Jan 10 SA 1 gd 1:441 h Jan 2 SA 7f ft 1:28 h Dec 26 SA 5f ft :594 h Dec 19 SA 5f ft 1:05 h

B.

23–1

*Cutting Wind

Ch. h. 6, by Sharpen Up—Tumble Judy, by Tumble Wind
Br.—Kitone Co Ltd (Ire) 1986 2 0 1 1 $7,940
MCHARGUE D G 116 Tr.—Blincoe Tom $75,000 1985 9 2 2 2 $53,150
Own.—Blincoe & Brown Mmes Lifetime 25 7 4 3 $120,972 Turf 24 7 4 3 $119,397
16Mar86-10TuP 1116Ⓣ:49 1:1311:432fm*7-5 120 74¾ 53 42 22 CastanedaM9 Gvnrs H 93-05 VirgnPrvtr,CuttngWnd,PolkExcus 11
25Jan86-6BM 1116Ⓣ:4741:1221:443fm*4-5 115 78½ 68 35 32 CastanedaM7 Aw22000 83-15 ChlcotonBlz,Poston'sBst,CttngWnd 8
25Jan86—Wide into stretch
28Dec85-6BM 1116Ⓣ:4711:1131:44 fm *8-5 114 510 35½ 1½ 14 CastanedaM2 Aw19000 88-12 Cutting Wind, ‡Dunant, Shayzari 9
8Dec85-9Hol 1116Ⓣ:4741:1211:43 fm 9¾ 114 117¼126½ 95 72¼ Baze R A3 135000 — — ‡Steepbnk,SuperDupont,Plestiglio 12
16Nov85-9Hol a1⅛Ⓣ 1:454fm 7 119 915 84 63¾ 33¼ Solis A9 125000 — — Caballo, Steepbank, Cutting Wind 9
16Nov85—Crowded, steadied early stretch; Error in placement of starting gate
31Oct85-8BM 1116Ⓣ:4631:1021:413fm*3-2 115 55½ 42½ 32½ 21½ CastanedaM3 Aw20000 98 — VicroyLd,CuttingWind,Frnch'sLuck 8
15Aug85-8Dmr 1116Ⓣ:48 1:1111:411fm 3 119 58½ 67 67¾ 55¼ Solis A6 Aw35000 97 — Zoffany, Pol And Dic, Bold Run 6
1Aug85-8Dmr 1116Ⓣ:47 1:11 1:422fm 9 115 610 42½ 1hd 12½ Solis A6 Aw35000 96-09 CuttngWnd,BoldRun,PrncFlormund 6
18Jly85-8Hol 1 Ⓣ:49 1:1211:354fm 20 115 66½ 65½ 52¾ 41¾ Solis A2 Aw45000 82-16 Go Dancer, Bold Run, Ayman 7
3Jly85-8Hol 1⅛Ⓣ:4811:1121:482fm 36 1105 69 67¾ 47 32½ Rohena W5 Aw48000 86-12 Onslow, Pol And Dic, Cutting Wind 6
Dec 31 SA 4f ft :472 h Dec 24 SA 1 ft 1:404 h Dec 12 Hol 7f ft 1:30 h Nov 30 Hol 6f ft 1:134 h

C.

45–1

*Vaigly Oh

B. h. 5, by Vaigly Great—Final Act, by Decoy Boy
Br.—Smith E J (Ire) 1987 2 0 0 0
COX D W 1095 Tr.—West Ted $70,000 1986 2 0 0 0
Own.—Piemonte-Webb-West Lifetime 12 3 1 0 $14,958 Turf 7 3 1 0 $14,958
10Jan87-1SA 6f :222 :461 1:114gd 12e1115 2hd 32 42 66½ Cox D W3 10000 73-20 ValDeRoi,Dodo'sLand,GllntChirmn 10
4Jan87-3SA 6f :22 :451 1:103sy 22 116 31½ 53½ 57 814¼ Baze G4 16000 71-22 Polly'sRuler,NeutralPlyer,Grenoble 8
25Jan86-9SA 1⅛:463 1:112 1:503ft 60 115 87¾1111 1124 — Baze G6 25000 — — HurricneHec,DrkSuce,RoosvltRod 11
25Jan86—Eased
15Jan86-3SA 6½f:211 :434 1:152ft 63 115 1014101510141010¾ Baze G9 50000 82-14 Coyotero, Zac K., Lord Pancho 10
15Jan86—In distress after finish
29Mar85-8SA a6½f Ⓣ:214 :4411:141fm 20 118 54 55 77½ 810½ EstrdJJr1 ⓇCWhtnhm 77-12 PntdCnyon,SpctculrLov,RsngChum 9
27Feb85-8SA 6f :214 :443 1:091ft 28 115 76½ 88½ 89 810½ EstradJJr3 ⓇBls Chca 81-17 Prtnsor,ColtFortyFour,RlunchATun 8
27Feb85—Bumped, shuffled back after start
22Sep84♦4Newbury(Eng) 6f 1:173gd 14 123 Ⓣ 55¼ Mercer J Mil Reef (Gr2) LoclSuitor,Presidium,Bssenthwite 12
23Aug84♦1York(Eng) 5f :593gd 3½ 123 Ⓣ 1nk CauthenS Prnc Wales VaiglyOh, Provideo, Pettingale 5
9Jly84♦4Windsor(Eng) 5f 1:01 gd 2 129 Ⓣ 11 EdderyP Falmouth Bay VaiglyOh,ShootPool,JollyBusiness 10
2Jly84♦1Windsor(Eng) 5f 1:013gd *2¼ 126 Ⓣ 12 EddrP Mrbe Arch(Mdn) ViglyOh,Hnry'sVntur,BrghtDomno 16
26May84♦6Lingfield(Eng) 5f 1:021gd 2½ 126 Ⓣ 25 CrsonW Elephant(Mdn) Abutaia, VaiglyOh,StableRelations 16
Dec 26 SA 5f ft 1:012 h Dec 20 SA 5f ft 1:022 h Dec 11 SA 4f ft :481 h Dec 4 SA 3f ft :362 h

D.

6–1

*Star Video

B. h. 5, by Hittite Glory—More Reliable, by Morston
Br.—Perry A R (Eng) 1986 3 0 0 1 $9,000
VALENZUELA P A 118 Tr.—Sadler John W $80,000 1985 6 1 1 0 $25,501
Own.—Balk-Frdmn-King Bros St Lifetime 22 8 5 1 $68,967 Turf 22 8 5 1 $68,967
16Jly86-8Hol 1 Ⓣ:4641:10 1:333fm 7¾ 117 41 53 68½ 611 Pincay L Jr6 Aw40000 — — BlueRzor,FlotingReserve,PrinceTru 6
16Jly86—Wide 3/8 turn
6Jun86-7Hol 1 Ⓣ:4531:0911:332fm 11 115 53½ 61¾ 41½ 43 ValenzuelPA6 Aw40000 — — Will Dancer, Poly Test, Al Arz 9
18May86-5Hol 6f Ⓣ:212 :4341:083fm 6½ 116 85¾ 53½ 53½ 32½ Toro F6 Nght Mvr H 96-03 ZanyTactics,RetsinaRun,StrVideo 10
23Dec85-8Hol 1116Ⓣ:4641:11 1:413fm 7 116 32 2hd 2hd 1hd McHrDG3 ⓇSpnc Bay — — Star Video, Nasib, Grey Gauntlet 9
23Dec85—Bumped start
12Dec85-8Hol 1116Ⓣ:4941:1341:434fm 11 114 73½ 72½ 96¼ 96¼ Hernandez R6 Aw42000 — — Tights, French Legionaire,BoldRun 9
12Dec85—Rank, wide into stretch; bumped 1/8
19Jun85♦1Ascot(Eng) 7f 1:273gd 33 122 Ⓣ 75¾ CochrneR Jersey(Gr3) PennineWlk,MimiCount,Herld'ste 19
17May85♦5Newbury(Eng) 6f 1:132gd 14 121 Ⓣ 712 CochrnR Hue-Wms Abha, Orojoya, Al Zawbaah 7
3May85♦3Newmarket(Eng) 6f 1:12 gd 20 133 Ⓣ 106¾ Raymond B Ely H Inishpour, Bulrush, Coincidental 17
15Apr85♦4Folkestone(Eng) 6f 1:224sf 6-5 129 Ⓣ 26 CochrneR Prvy Cnclr Doulab, Star Video, SpeciallyVague 3
22Sep84♦4Newbury(Eng) 6f 1:173gd 12 123 Ⓣ 67 Mercer J Mil Reef (Gr2) LoclSuitor,Presidium,Bssenthwite 12
Jan 10 SA 5f gd 1:012 h Jan 2 SA 7f ft 1:281 h Dec 27 SA 5f ft 1:022 h Dec 21 Hol 6f ft 1:141 h

E.

4–1

My Gallant Game — Ch. g. 5, by My Gallant—Maid of Bridlewood, by Raise a Native

PINCAY L JR — 118 — Br.—Appleton A I (Fla) — Tr.—Tinsley J E Jr — $80,000

Own.—Appleton A I

1987	1	0	0	0	
1986	16	1	6	3	$70,650
Turf	6	0	3	0	$21,000
Lifetime	25	3	8	3	$96,375

4Jan87-5SA	6½f	$:21^{3}$	$:44^{1}$	1:17 sy	2½	117	$5^{4\frac{3}{4}}$	$6^{5\frac{3}{4}}$	$7^{5\frac{1}{2}}$	$6^{8\frac{3}{4}}$	Pincay L Jr^{5}	Aw33000	76-22	Amnotherbrothr,GllntSilor,HillsBid	7
4Jan87—Wide into stretch															
29Nov86-6Hol	6f	Ⓣ$:22^{1}$	$:44^{3}$	$1:08^{2}$fm	19	115	4^{1}	3^{2}	5^{4}	7^{6}	Toro F^{8}	HcpO	92-10	Zany Tactics, Mandatory, Ice Hot	8
12Nov86-3Hol	7f	$:22^{1}$	$:45^{1}$	$1:21^{3}$ft	5½	117	$1^{1\frac{1}{2}}$	1^{1}	$2^{1\frac{1}{2}}$	$2^{4\frac{1}{2}}$	Toro F^{6}	Aw26000	91-15	BoldrThnBold,MyGllntGm,Mtrnmc	6
12Oct86-5SA	a6½f	Ⓣ$:21^{4}$	:44	$1:13^{4}$fm	8½	117	$1^{1\frac{1}{2}}$	$1^{1\frac{1}{2}}$	2^{2}	$2^{4\frac{1}{2}}$	Pincay L Jr^{12}	Aw33000	85-12	PrinceSky,MyGallantGame,Bruiser	12
16Sep86-11Pom	6f	$:21^{4}$	$:44^{2}$	$1:09^{2}$ft	5½	116	5^{3}	4^{6}	4^{7}	$5^{3\frac{3}{4}}$	Black C A^{5}	Aprisa H	100-05	BundlOfIron,Mtronomc,ProdstHor	10
13Aug86-3Dmr	6f	$:21^{3}$	$:44^{3}$	$1:08^{3}$ft	6	112^{5}	3^{4}	3^{2}	$2^{3\frac{1}{2}}$	$3^{4\frac{3}{4}}$	Black C A^{1}	Aw24000	90-15	MneMgic,Metronomic,MyGllntGme	6
13Aug86—Erratic backstretch, 3/8 turn															
30Jly86-7Dmr	7f	$:21^{4}$	$:44^{2}$	$1:21^{4}$ft	22	111^{5}	3^{3}	3^{2}	$3^{1\frac{1}{2}}$	$4^{1\frac{1}{2}}$	Black C A^{6}	Aw24000	94-11	UltimtePlesure,MneMgic,IdelQulity	8
2Jly86-8Hol	6f	:22	$:45^{1}$	$1:09^{2}$ft	13	112^{5}	$3^{1\frac{1}{2}}$	$3^{\frac{1}{2}}$	$3^{\frac{1}{2}}$	3^{hd}	Black C A^{2}	Aw25000	97-09	Epidaurus,ManeMagic,MyGllntGme	6
21Jun86-5Hol	6f	$:21^{4}$	:45	$1:09^{2}$ft	13	111^{5}	$5^{3\frac{1}{2}}$	2^{1}	3^{1}	3^{3}	Black C A^{4}	100000	94-09	AmrcnLgn,MyFvrtMmnt,MGllntGm	7
6Jun86-8Hol	6f	:22	$:45^{2}$	$1:09^{4}$ft	*2	112^{5}	1^{2}	1^{hd}	2^{2}	$2^{4\frac{1}{2}}$	Black C A^{5}	Aw24000	90-15	LncolnPrk,MyGllntGm,SpnshMschf	6

Dec 27 SA 6f ft $1:15^{1}$ h   Dec 14 SA 4f ft $:49^{1}$ h

F.

120–1

***Loustros** — Dk. b. or br. h. 5, by Nonoalco—Louzitania, by Sham

ARAGON V A — 114 — Br.—Petra Bloodstock Agency (Eng) — Tr.—Hutchinson Kathy — $70,000

Own.—Lee-Rimrock Stb-Rey

1986	7	1	0	0	$11,917
1985	6	1	1	1	$13,487
Turf	13	3	1	1	$25,739
Lifetime	18	4	1	1	$35,856

14Nov86-5Hol	1	$:44^{3}$	$1:08^{4}$	$1:34^{4}$ft	68	116	5^{8}	6^{15}	5^{20}	5^{25}	Meza R Q^{2}	62500	64-16	Oricao, Silver Hero, Rex Lake	6
14Nov86—Bumped start															
29Oct86-5SA	a6½f	Ⓣ$:21^{2}$	$:43^{4}$	$1:15^{1}$fm	50	115	10^{13}	10^{12}	$10^{9\frac{1}{2}}$	$10^{7\frac{1}{2}}$	Sibille R^{9}	70000	75-17	Stan's Bower, Jack Tar,Steepbank	10
13Jly86-7Cby	6f	$:22^{1}$	:45	1:10 gd	7	121	$6^{7\frac{1}{2}}$	$6^{9\frac{1}{2}}$	$6^{5\frac{1}{2}}$	$6^{6\frac{1}{4}}$	Smith M E^{4}	Aw13800	90-09	Cryptarch, Harry 'N Bill, Caramel	7
20Jun86-8Cby	1	$:47^{1}$	$1:11^{1}$	$1:37^{3}$ft	7½	121	6^{12}	5^{9}	$5^{8\frac{1}{2}}$	$5^{12\frac{1}{4}}$	Black K^{2}	Aw14300	81-22	ExitFiveB.,Machalstva,RoxburyPrk	6
26May86-10Cby	$1\frac{1}{16}$	Ⓣ$:45^{4}$	1:10	$1:40^{2}$fm	11	113	7^{8}	$6^{8\frac{1}{2}}$	4^{8}	$4^{9\frac{1}{4}}$	MoyrsL^{4}	Statesmen H	— —	ReglBrek,Brbery,ChrgingThrough	10
7May86-8Cby	1	$:47^{1}$	$1:11^{4}$	$1:37^{2}$ft	2¾	117	$5^{8\frac{1}{4}}$	$5^{4\frac{1}{2}}$	$5^{2\frac{1}{2}}$	$4^{6\frac{1}{4}}$	Hansen R D^{7}	Aw14300	88-11	Frknthrd,ChrgngThrgh,Vrbtm'sPrd	7
26Apr86-8Cby	6f	$:22^{4}$	$:46^{2}$	$1:11^{3}$ft	7	115	5^{6}	5^{2}	4^{2}	$1^{\frac{1}{2}}$	Hansen R D^{4}	Aw13800	89-14	Loustros, Don't Fight It, Zeppy	6
19Aug85♦6Deauville(Fra)	a1			$1:52^{1}$sf	*3½	127			Ⓣ	$1^{\frac{1}{2}}$	AsssnC	Px d Rouen H		Loustros, Salve, Buis	20
10Aug85♦6Deauville(Fra)	a7f			1:31 sf	11	122			Ⓣ	2^{nk}	AsmssnC	Px d Blry H		Kirk, Loustros, Mount Alpha	18
2Jly85♦4MLafitte(Fra)	$a1\frac{1}{16}$			$1:45^{1}$gd	*3	126			Ⓣ	$9^{5\frac{3}{4}}$	AsmssnC	Px d Cstl H		Le Fabien, Kensof, Tudor Rose	25

Jan 11 SA 5f ft $1:03^{2}$ h   Jan 3 SA 6f ft 1:15 hg   Dec 14 SA 6f ft $1:14^{3}$ h   Dec 3 SA 4f ft $:48^{2}$ h

G.

12–1

Amanotherbrother ✕ — Ch. g. 6, by Amasport—The Merriest, by Nearctic

BAZE G — 116 — Br.—Meadowbrook Farms Inc (Fla) — Tr.—Shulman Sanford — $70,000

Own.—Charles & ClearValleyStables

1987	1	1	0	0	$18,150
1986	16	3	1	2	$68,675
Turf	3	0	1	0	$5,600
Lifetime	52	13	5	9	$208,405

4Jan87-5SA	6½f	$:21^{3}$	$:44^{1}$	1:17 sy	3¾	116	$4^{1\frac{1}{4}}$	$3^{2\frac{1}{2}}$	3^{2}	$1^{\frac{3}{4}}$	Baze G^{3}	Aw33000	85-22	Amnotherbrothr,GllntSilor,HillsBid	7
14Dec86-9Hol	1	Ⓣ$:46^{2}$	$1:11^{1}$	$1:36^{2}$fm	7	119	1^{hd}	$1^{\frac{1}{2}}$	3^{2}	6^{8}	Pedroza M A^{8}	50000	77-11	LordOfTheWind,Hrdknock'n,Juntur	8
6Dec86-9Hol	1	$:46^{1}$	1:11	$1:36^{2}$gd	3	119	$2^{\frac{1}{2}}$	$1^{2\frac{1}{2}}$	1^{3}	1^{1}	Pedroza M A^{6}	50000	81-16	Amanotherbrother,TrumpUp,LedOn	7
22Nov86-7Hol	7f	:22	$:45^{1}$	$1:22^{2}$ft	22	116	$4^{6\frac{1}{2}}$	4^{5}	$3^{4\frac{1}{2}}$	5^{5}	Pedroza M A^{1}	50000	87-13	Cracksman, Juntura, Infantryman	8
8Oct86-3SA	6½f	$:21^{4}$	$:44^{3}$	1:16 ft	15	116	10^{10}	10^{12}	$8^{9\frac{3}{4}}$	$8^{12\frac{1}{2}}$	Shoemaker W^{2}	c50000	77-20	Oricao, Teddy Naturally, QuipStar	10
5Jly86-5Hol	7f	$:22^{1}$	$:44^{4}$	$1:22^{1}$ft	4½	116	$5^{1\frac{3}{4}}$	$4^{1\frac{3}{4}}$	$7^{5\frac{1}{4}}$	$8^{6\frac{3}{4}}$	ValenzuelaPA^{10}	40000	86-08	Rex Lake, Rushad, Paskanell	11
18Jun86-4Hol	7f	$:22^{3}$	$:46^{1}$	1:22 ft	2½	116	—	—	—	—	McCarron C J^{7}	62500	— —	Danczone,Dr.Relity,Mischiefinmind	7
18Jun86—Pulled up															
8Jun86-1Hol	7f	$:22^{3}$	$:45^{3}$	$1:22^{2}$ft	13	116	$3^{\frac{1}{2}}$	2^{hd}	$1^{\frac{1}{2}}$	$3^{1\frac{1}{4}}$	Valenzuela P A^{6}	80000	91-11	AmrcnLgon,RsngChm,Amnthrbrthr	7
18May86-4Hol	1	:44	$1:08^{4}$	$1:35^{2}$ft	*8-5	116	$2^{2\frac{1}{2}}$	2^{3}	$2^{2\frac{1}{2}}$	$5^{4\frac{1}{4}}$	McCarron C J^{7}	62500	82-08	Stickette, Ells Bravest Song, LeCid	7
8May86-8Hol	1	:46	$1:10^{2}$	$1:34^{4}$ft	10	112^{5}	4^{6}	$5^{3\frac{1}{4}}$	5^{5}	$5^{5\frac{1}{4}}$	Black C A^{1}	Aw32000	84-14	Michadilla,UltimatePlesure,Koshre	5

Dec 29 SA 5f ft $1:00^{2}$ h

H.

2–1

***Shanaar** B. h. 5, by Formidable—Princely Maid, by King's Troop
STEVENS G L **118** Br.—Red House Stud (Eng) 1986 9 2 1 2 $38,990
Tr.—Russell John W $80,000 1985 6 1 0 3 $14,913
Own.—Prince Yazid Saud Lifetime 16 3 1 5 $53,903 Turf 16 3 1 5 $53,903
26Dec86-5SA a6½f Ⓣ:212 :4411:151fm 9½ 117 2½ 2½ 1hd 3½ Stevens G L12 80000 82-17 Estate, Champion Pilot, Shanaar 12
23Nov86-6BM a1⅛Ⓣ 1:483fm 3¾ 113 31½ 31 21½ 56 Hansen R D9 Aw19000 86-08 SoldatBleu,DiplomatRuler,JaySwift 9
1Sep86-7AP 1⅛Ⓣ:4721:1241:494fm*6-5 118 24 32 55½ 517 Day P4 Aw18000 71-19 ElMnsour,Progesterone,DerbyWish 8
23Aug86-5AP 1⅛Ⓣ:4821:1311:493fm*1-2 112 1½ 1½ 14 18½ Hawley S4 Aw18000 98-06 Shanaar, Tabuk, Stage Executive 7
13Aug86-5Dmr 1 Ⓣ:4611:1011:35 fm 3½ 119 1½ 1hd 11 32 ShoemkerW3 Aw23000 95 — Swallage, Kingsbury, Shanaar 9
19Jly86-4Hol 1$\frac{1}{16}$Ⓣ:4621:1021:41 fm *2 122 33½ 42 41¾ 44 McCarronCJ5 Aw28000 95-06 Enviro, Severn Bore, Nugget Point 6
27Jun86-8Hol 1⅛Ⓣ:4711:1031:47 fm 2¼ 122 31 53½ 53½ 44¼ ShoemkerW4 Aw23000 93-03 Baroncello, Lord Grundy, Crony 6
15Jun86-5Hol 1$\frac{1}{16}$Ⓣ:4711:11 1:411fm*8-5 116 52 51¾ 1½ 11¼ ShoemkerW7 Aw21000 98 — Shanaar, Well Related, Atreak 12
15Jun86—Ducked out late; returned bleeding from mouth
31May86-9Hol 1$\frac{1}{16}$Ⓣ:4631:1131:422fm 5¼ 116 87½ 82¾ 31 21 ‡Hernandez R6 Aw22000 91-06 Baroncello, Garrion, Shanaar 8
‡31May86—Dead heat; Pinched at start
21Aug85♦5Deauville(Fra) a1 1:492sf 15 119 Ⓣ 55¼ Legrix E Px d Crcl Majuscule,SiberianHero,DancingStr 9
Jan 8 Hol 6f ft 1:16 h Jan 2 SA 6f ft 1:163 h Dec 21 Hol 5f ft 1:014 h Dec 9 Hol 6f ft 1:17 h

I.

36–1

Sans Rival B. c. 4, by Victory Stride—Tudor Owanello, by Ky Colonel
COX D W **1105** Br.—Murty Farm & Mittman (Ky) 1987 1 0 0 0
Tr.—Sherlock Gary $70,000 1986 15 3 3 0 $47,127
Own.—Figgins L R Lifetime 17 3 3 0 $48,402 Turf 7 2 1 0 $28,150
7Jan87-5SA 6½f :22 :444 1:163m 16 117 66½ 611 612 617¾ Baze G2 80000 69-21 RisingChum,AutoCommander,Strw 6
28Dec86-7BM 1$\frac{1}{16}$Ⓣ:48 1:13 1:461gd 15 112 31 12 1hd 11½ Doocy T T1 Aw18000 72-28 SnsRivl,CptinCondo,Robert‥oRson 10
28Nov86-7Hol 1 Ⓣ:4631:1041:353fm 18 117 74¼ 74¾ 710 712¾ McHrgueDG9 Aw26000 76-11 ThalassinoAsteri,Havildar,PicatrixII 9
28Nov86—Wide
14Nov86-9Hol 1$\frac{1}{16}$Ⓣ:4641:1011:411fm 7½ 116 32½ 33½ 69 611¾ McHrgueDG3 Aw26000 76-12 Mr. Media, Picatrix II, Rai Den 7
14Nov66—Wide into backstretch
30Oct86-5SA a6½f Ⓣ:214 :4441:151fm 27 116 86 76 32½ 22½ McHrgueDG2 Aw28000 81-17 Arcadius, Sans Rival, Will Spring 16
2Oct86-5SA 1⅛Ⓣ:47 1:12 1:494fm 54 115 31½ 21½ 35½ 78 Douglas R R9 Aw30000 70-22 Kingsbury, Putting, Travet 10
2Oct86—Veered in start
13Sep86-10Pom 1$\frac{1}{16}$:451 1:103 1:44 ft 15 116 56½ 510 815 819½ Douglas R R3 Aw27000 71-10 Bugrin,LordAllison,NorthrnProvidr 9
30Aug86-9Dmr 1$\frac{1}{16}$Ⓣ:47 1:1121:434fm 75 116 43 4¾ 11 11½ Douglas R R1 Aw23000 87-11 SansRivl,HilTheBid,TimeForSkrto 12
17Aug86-5Dmr 1 Ⓣ:4611:1031:351fm 55 114 21½ 42½ 44½ 67¾ Pedroza MA4 Aw20000 89-05 Rai Den, Coaraze Nay, Lud 10
17Jly86-9LA 6½f :22 :452 1:17 ft *7-5 115 42¼ 64¼ 54½ 44¼ Kaenel J L1 Aw13500 87-11 Time Share,PowerfulEyes,FallFlyer 6
Dec 24 SA 4f ft :464 h Dec 28 SA 6f ft 1:144 h Dec 10 SA 4f ft :474 h Nov 24 SA 4f ft :493 h

J.

3–1

Auto Commander Ch. g. 6, by Dust Commander—Miss Royal Kret, by Royal Note
SHOEMAKER W **114** Br.—T90 Ranch (Ky) 1987 1 0 1 0 $6,000
Tr.—Palma Hector O $70,000 1986 11 4 3 1 $66,775
Own.—RubensteinHM&RJ&LTorreR Lifetime 35 7 9 6 $169,800 Turf 18 4 4 3 $85,725
7Jan87-5SA 6½f :22 :444 1:163m 3 114 44½ 46½ 25 26½ Shoemaker W5 70000 80-21 RisingChum,AutoCommander,Strw 6
26Dec86-5SA a6½f Ⓣ:212 :4411:151fm *2¼ 115 105¾ 96¾ 64¾ 63 Black C A6 70000 80-17 Estate, Champion Pilot, Shanaar 12
26Dec86—Bumped, steadied start
13Dec86-9Hol 1 Ⓣ:4631:1021:342fm 3¾ 116 11½ 1½ 13 13½ Black C A9 62500 95-08 AutoCommander,DrkAccert,Dr.Dly 9
27Nov86-9Hol 1$\frac{1}{16}$Ⓣ:46 1:0931:404fm 2½ 116 43 31 2hd 2½ Black C A7 62500 89-06 RsngChm,AtoCommndr,Hrdknockn 7
27Nov86—Bumped, hit on nose 3/16
11Nov86-9Hol 1⅛Ⓣ:4721:1121:472fm 5¼ 114 11 1hd 1hd 2¾ Black C A2 57500 90-09 Aviator II, Auto Commander,Crony 8
4Oct86-9SA 1$\frac{1}{16}$:472 1:112 1:43 ft 7 117 2½ 1hd 2½ 32¼ Soto S B6 62500 84-18 GoSwiftly,SilverHro,AutoCommndr 8
27Aug86-9Dmr 1 Ⓣ:4611:1031:352fm 3½ 1085 21½ 1hd 1hd 1nk Black C A7 55000 95-05 Auto Commander,RexLake,JackTar 7
17Aug86-3Dmr 6f :22 :45 1:092ft *3-2 115 42 41¼ 53¼ 64 Valenzuela P A7 57500 87-16 Infntrymn,Frnch'sLck,UrbnCowboy 8
17Aug86—Bumped start
30Jly86-4Dmr 6½f :222 :451 1:153ft *3-2 116 31 2hd 12½ 12½ Valenzuela P A7 50000 94-11 AtoCommndr,TddyNtrlly,PtrotGlvs 8
20Jly86-5Hol 6f :223 :454 1:093ft 9-5 116 3½ 1hd 1hd 12 McCarron C J2 c40000 96-10 AutoCommnder,SndDigger,Psknell 5
●Jan 3 SA tr.t 4f ft :483 h Dec 21 Hol 3f ft :361 h Dec 6 Hol 5f m 1:014 h Nov 25 Hol 5f ft :592 h

60. Handicappers surely remember the winner of the all-glamorous million-dollar Travers Stakes (Grade 1) at Saratoga 1987. The question, however, was not which horse was likeliest to win but how should the race have been played?

Additional information:

- Horses having dosage indexes greater than 4.00 include *Gulch*, *Fortunate Moment*, and *Gorky*.
- The Jim Dandy is a Grade 2 stakes for 3YOs.
- The Whitney is a Grade 1 stakes for 3up.
- The Swaps is a Grade 1 stakes for 3YOs.
- The track condition is sloppy.

8th Saratoga

1 ¼ MILES. (2.00) 118th Running THE TRAVERS (Grade I). Purse $1,000,000 added. 3-year-olds. By subscription of $1,500 each which should accompany the nomination; $3,000 to pass the entry box, $7,500 to start, with $1,000,000 added. The added money and all fees to be divided 60% to the winner, 22% to second, 12% to third and 6% to fourth. Weight, 126 lbs. Starters to be named at the closing time of entries. The winner shall have his name inscribed on the Man o' War Cup and a gold plated replica will be presented to the winning owner. Trophies will be presented to the winning owner, trainer and jockey. Closed with 19 nominations Wednesday, August 5, 1987.

Coupled—Gulch and Gorky.

9–1

Polish Navy ✻ **B. c. 3, by Danzig—Navsup, by Tatan**
Br.—Phipps O (Ky) **1987 4 2 1 1 $172,056**
Own.—Phipps O **126** **Tr.—McGaughey Claude III** **1986 5 4 0 0 $364,260**
Lifetime 9 6 1 1 $536,316

9Aug87-8Sar 1⅛ :474 1:113 1:482ft *6-5 117 1½ 11 11½ 12¼ Day P1 Jim Dandy 93-18 PolishNvy,PledgeCrd,Cryptoclernc 7
9Aug87—Grade II
3Jly87-8Bel 1⅛ :47 1:103 1:482gd 2¼ 123 21 22½ 28 313 RomroRP5 Dwyer 72-21 Gone West, PledgeCard,PclishNavy 6
3Jly87—Grade I
26Jun87-3Bel 7f :224 :452 1:231ft *1-9 113 1hd 1½ 13½ 15 Romero R P4 Aw40000 86-22 PolishNavy,ParadeMarshl,Smerknd 4
6Jun87-5Bel 7f :222 :452 1:222ft *2-3 122 21½ 2½ 46½ 28 ♦ RomroRP5 Riva Ridge 82-15 JazzingAround,HighBrite,PolishNvy 7
♦ 6Jun87—Dead heat
1Nov86-1SA 1 1/16 :454 1:102 1:434ft 5¼ 122 76½ 56½ 67½ 711¼ RomrRP6 Br Cp Juv 71-13 Capote, Qualify, Alysheba 13
1Nov86—Grade I
18Oct86-8Bel 1 :474 1:112 1:351ft *2¼ 122 1½ 1½ 1hd 1no RmrRP4 Champagne 89-17 PolishNvy,Demon'sBegone,BetTwic 7
18Oct86—Grade I
27Sep86-8Bel 7f :221 :45 1:224sy *1-2 122 11½ 12 12 11 RomroRP5 Cowdin 88-17 Polish Navy, JavaGold,PhantomJet 8
27Sep86—Grade I
30Aug86-1Bel 6½f :221 :451 1:161ft *1-2 117 1hd 1hd 12 14¼ Romero R P2 Aw24000 94-14 Polish Navy, FirstPatriot,QuickCall 6
Aug 16 Sar tr.t 4f ft :51 b ●Aug 1 Bel 6f ft 1:122 hg Jly 26 Bel 4f gd :51 b Jly 19 Bel 4f ft :47 b

7–1

Cryptoclearance ✻ **Dk. b. or br. c. 3, by Fappiano—Naval Orange, by Hoist the Flag**
Br.—George G Farm Inc (Ky) **1987 10 3 3 2 $699,390**
Own.—Teinowitz P **126** **Tr.—Schulhofer Flint S** **1986 5 2 0 1 $32,400**
Lifetime 15 5 3 3 $731,790

9Aug87-8Sar 1⅛ :474 1:113 1:482ft 9-5 126 53½ 53½ 34 34¾ SntosJA6 Jim Dandy 88-18 PolishNvy,PledgeCrd,Cryptoclernc 7
9Aug87—Grade II
28Jun87-9Cby 1⅛ :47 1:103 1:492ft 7-5 126 812 510 56½ 59¼ PincyLJr4 St Paul Dby 84-10 Lost Code,ProudestDuke,StaffRiot 8
28Jun87—Grade III
6Jun87-8Bel 1½ :492 2:03 2:281ft 4½ 126 69 25 27 214 PincyLJr6 Belmont 65-15 Bet Twice, Cryptoclearance, Gulch 9
6Jun87—Grade I
16May87-9Pim 1 3/16 :471 1:113 1:554ft 2½ 126 87¼ 53¼ 31½ 32 SntosJA9 Preakness 86-18 Alysheba,BetTwice,Cryptoclearnce 9
16May87—Grade I
2May87-8CD 1¼ :462 1:364 2:032ft 6½ 126 1516 74¼ 43½ 43¼ SantosJA1 Ky Derby 77-09 Alysheba, Bet Twice, Avies Copy 17
2May87—Grade I; Lacked room
4Apr87-10GP 1⅛ :472 1:114 1:493ft 2¾ 122 611 72¼ 3½ 1hd SantosJA9 Fla Derby 84-23 Cryptoclernc,NoMorFlowrs,Tlinum 9
4Apr87—Grade I; Bore in, driving
28Feb87-11Hia 1⅛ :464 1:11 1:50 ft *8-5 122 1012 74½ 1hd 2½ SantosJA8 Flamingo 80-19 Talinum,Cryptoclearnce,LeoCstelli 14
28Feb87—Grade I; Rallied wide
7Feb87-10Hia 1⅛ :473 1:114 1:484sy *2 114 46½ 43½ 31½ 11½ SntosJA7 Everglades 87-18 Cryptoclrnc,Momsfurrri,PhntomJt 11
7Feb87—Grade II; Alter course-clr
Aug 17 Sar 5f ft 1:003 b Aug 5 Sar 5f ft :594 b ●Aug 2 Sar 6f ft 1:151 b Jly 27 Bel 5f ft 1:012 b

3–1

Java Gold ✱

B. c. 3, by Key to the Mint—Javamine, by Nijinsky II
Br.—Mellon Paul (Va) 1987 5 4 1 0 $259,020
Own.—Rokeby Stable 126 Tr.—Miller Mack 1986 7 3 1 1 $287,532
Lifetime 12 7 2 1 $546,552

8Aug87-8Sar 1⅛ :46² 1:10² 1:48²ft 2¼ 113 6⁸½ 6⁴ 3³½ 1¾ Day P⁶ Whitney H 93-13 Java Gold, Gulch, Broad Brush
8Aug87—Grade I
10Jly87-8Bel 1 1/16 :48³ 1:12³ 1:43¹gd 1 111 2hd 2hd 1½ 1⁶ Day P¹ Aw45000 86-23 JavaGold,JohnsTreasure,PersonlFlg
29Jun87-8Bel 1 :47² 1:12³ 1:36⁴ft *1-9 109 1¹ 1½ 2hd 2no Day P¹ Aw45000 81-25 Cutlass Reality, Java Gold, ElBasco
18Apr87-5Aqu 6f :22 :45² 1:09²m *1-3 119 4⁵½ 3² 2½ 1³ RomeroRP² Best Turn 94-15 Java Gold, High Brite, Royal Value
4Apr87-7Aqu 6f :22 :45¹ 1:10 sy 6-5 107 3¹ 3²½ 1hd 1⁵¼ Day P¹ Aw29000 91-21 Java Gold, Dr. Koch, Gallic War
22Nov86-8Aqu 1⅛ :47⁴ 1:12¹ 1:49³ft *3-5e114 2² 2hd 1hd 1²¾ Day P¹ Remsen 87-18 Java Gold, Talinum, Drachma
22Nov86—Grade I
18Oct86-8Bel 1 :47⁴ 1:11² 1:35¹ft 3¼ 122 5³½ 5³½ 4⁴ 4³ Day P² Champagne 86-17 PolishNvy,Demon'sBegone,BetTwic
18Oct86—Grade I
27Sep86-8Bel 7f :22¹ :45 1:22⁴sy 8 122 3² 3² 3² 2¹ Bailey JD³ Cowdin 87-17 Polish Navy, JavaGold,PhantomJet
27Sep86—Grade I
●Aug 18 Sar 6f ft 1:11 h Aug 14 Sar 4f ft :48² b ●Aug 6 Sar 4f ft :46³ h ●Jly 31 Bel 1 ft 1:37⁴ h

9–1

Gulch ✱

B. c. 3, by Mr Prospector—Jameela, by Rambunctious
Br.—Brant P M (Ky) 1987 9 3 1 2 $1,027,242
Own.—Brant P M 126 Tr.—Jolley Leroy 1986 7 5 1 0 $437,510
Lifetime 16 8 2 2 $1,464,752

8Aug87-8Sar 1⅛ :46² 1:10² 1:48²ft 3½e117 5⁸ 4²½ 1²½ 2¾ SntosJA¹ Whitney H 92-13 Java Gold, Gulch, Broad Brush 7
8Aug87—Grade I; Drifted out
6Jun87-8Bel 1½ :49² 2:03 2:28¹ft 7¾e126 8¹³ 8¹⁶ 4¹² 3¹⁴ Day P⁹ Belmont 65-15 Bet Twice, Cryptoclearance, Gulch 9
6Jun87—Grade I
25May87-8Bel 1 :44² 1:09¹ 1:34⁴ft 5¾ 110 8¹¹ 6²½ 3nk 1nk Day P⁹ Metropltn H 91-16 Gulch, King's Swan, Broad Brush 9
25May87—Grade I
16May87-9Pim 1 3/16 :47¹ 1:11³ 1:55⁴ft 3½ 126 6⁶¾ 7³¾ 4³½ 4⁵½ CordrAJr⁷ Preakness 82-18 Alysheba,BetTwice,Cryptoclearnce 9
16May87—Grade I
2May87-8CD 1¼ :46² 1:36⁴ 2:03²ft 5e126 16¹⁸ 12⁶¾ 7⁶ 6⁴¼ ShmkrW⁶ Ky Derby 76-09 Alysheba, Bet Twice, Avies Copy 17
2May87—Grade I; Very wide
18Apr87-8Aqu 1⅛ :47 1:11³ 1:49 m 3½ 126 6⁷¾ 4⁴½ 2²½ 1hd SntsJA¹ Wood Mem 90-15 Gulch, Gone West, Shawklit Won 8
18Apr87—Grade I
4Apr87-8Aqu 1 :44² 1:08¹ 1:34³sy 2½ 123 8¹² 6¹² 4⁹½ 3⁹½ VasquezJ⁴ Gotham 83-21 Gone West, Shawklit Won, Gulch 9
4Apr87—Grade II
21Mar87-8Aqu 7f :22² :45³ 1:23¹ft *3-5 123 6³ 5²¾ 2¹½ 1¹ SntosJA³ Bay Shore 85-28 Gulch, High Brite, Shawklit Won 9
21Mar87—Grade II
Aug 20 Sar 3f sy :35⁴ b Aug 15 Sar 6f ft 1:13¹ h ●Aug 5 Sar 5f ft :57² h ●Jly 31 Bel 6f ft 1:12¹ h

21–1

Fortunate Moment

Ch. c. 3, by For The Moment—Restless Cat, by Restless Wind
Br.—Pinkley Jerry R (Ill) 1987 6 6 0 0 $192,780
Own.—Pinkley Jerry R 126 Tr.—Vanier Harvey L 1986 0 M 0 0
Lifetime 6 6 0 0 $192,780

1Aug87-9AP 1¼ :47⁴ 1:37³ 2:03⁴ft 5¼ 118 1½ 1hd 1½ 1½ Fires E⁴ Amer Dby 78-26 FortuntMomnt,FstForwrd,GmMstr 9
1Aug87—Grade I
26Jly87-8AP 1⅛ :47¹ 1:12 1:50²ft *1-5 118 2½ 2hd 1½ 1¹ Day P⁵ [S]J D Hertz 79-28 FortuntMomnt,Iwntosk,MrofthHos 6
16Jly87-8AP 1 :46² 1:11¹ 1:36¹ft *4-5 107 1¹ 1½ 1hd 1¹½ Day P³ Aw17000 80-22 FortunteMomnt,ThRoylFrz,IrishFrz 6
3Jly87-8AP 1 :45² 1:10¹ 1:35 ft *3-2 112 2¹½ 2² 1² 1⁴ Day P⁷ [S]Springfield 86-21 FortntMomnt,Iwntosk,ColMrchnt 11
8Jun87-5AP 6½f :23 :46⁴ 1:18⁴ft *2-5 112 1¹ 1¹ 1¹ 1⁵ Day P⁵ [S]Aw14300 81-24 FrtntMmnt,DmtrsSrd,TmprrRsdnt 10
27May87-2AP 6f :22⁴ :47¹ 1:12¹ft *4-5 115 1¹½ 1¹½ 1⁴ 1⁹ Day P¹ [S]Mdn 79-21 FrtntMmnt,Snn'sInvstmnt,CntlRd 12
Aug 18 Sar 5f ft :58¹ h Aug 8 AP 5f gd 1:02 b Jly 23 AP 5f ft 1:01³ b Jly 15 AP 3f sy :36¹ b

5–2

Alysheba

B. c. 3, by Alydar—Bel Sheba, by Lt Stevens
Br.—Madden Preston (Ky) 1987 7 2 2 1 $1,236,156
Own.—Scharbauer Dorothy&Pamela 126 Tr.—Van Berg Jack C 1986 7 1 4 1 $359,486
Lifetime 14 3 6 2 $1,595,642

1Aug87-9Mth 1⅛ :46³ 1:09³ 1:47 ft 3-2 126 3²½ 2¹ 3²½ 2nk McCrrCJ⁴ Haskell H 99-07 Bet Twice, Alysheba, Lost Code 5
1Aug87—Grade I; In close on turn
6Jun87-8Bel 1½ :49² 2:03 2:28¹ft *4-5 126 4⁷ 4⁷ 3⁹ 4¹⁴¼ McCrrCJ³ Belmont 65-15 Bet Twice, Cryptoclearance, Gulch 9
6Jun87—Grade I; Rough trip
16May87-9Pim 1 3/16 :47¹ 1:11³ 1:55⁴ft *2 126 5⁶½ 4³ 2hd 1½ McCrrCJ⁶ Preakness 88-18 Alysheba,BetTwice,Cryptoclearnce 9
16May87—Grade I
2May87-8CD 1¼ :46² 1:36⁴ 2:03²ft 8½ 126 13¹² 3¹½ 2¹ 1¾ McCrrCJ³ Ky Derby 80-09 Alysheba, Bet Twice, Avies Copy 17
2May87—Grade I; Stumbled mid-str
23Apr87-7Kee 1⅛ :46⁴ 1:10² 1:48²ft *4-5 121 3² 4²½ 2hd 1hd † McCrrCJ⁴ Blue Grass 95-13 ‡Alysheba, War, Leo Castelli 5
23Apr87—Grade I; Ducked out; †Disqualified and placed third
22Mar87-8SA 1 1/16 :46² 1:10⁴ 1:43 gd 3¼ 120 7⁶½ 6³½ 4¾ 2¾ Day P³ S Felipe H 85-23 ChartTheStrs,Alysheb,TemperteSil 8
22Mar87—Grade I; Lugged in str

8Mar87-9SA 1 1/16 :46⁴ 1:11² 1:43 ft *2-3 114 4¾ 45 44 45 Day P 6 Aw30000 81-15 Barb's Relic, Blanco, Rakaposhi 9
14Dec86-8Hol 1 :44⁴ 1:09³ 1:36¹ft 6½e121 4¾ 2½ 2½ 2nk Day P 12 Hol Fut'y 82-18 TempertSil,Alyshb,MstrfulAdvoct 12
14Dec86—Grade I
Aug 20 Sar 4f gd :47 h Aug 14 Sar 1 ft 1:38² h Aug 9 Sar 4f ft :47² b Jly 30 Mth 4f ft :48³ b

5—1
Temperate Sil
Own.—Whittingham C 126
Ro. c. 3, by Temperence Hill—Rukann, by Ruken
Br.—Frankfurt Stables (Ky)
Tr.—Whittingham Charles
1987 5 2 0 1 $432,150
1986 5 3 0 0 $549,625
Lifetime 10 5 0 1 $981,775

26Jly87-9Hol 1¼ :45 1:34² 2:02¹ft *6-5 123 1hd 12½ 13½ 11 ShomkrW4 Swaps 81-12 TemperteSil,Cndi'sGold,PledgeCrd 6
26Jly87—Grade I
3Jly87-8Hol 1⅛ :46 1:09⁴ 1:47³ft *3-5 124 2½ 2hd 47½ 516½ ShmkrW2 Slvr Scrn H 83-09 Candi's Gold, OnTheLine,TheMedic 6
3Jly87—Grade II
4Apr87-5SA 1⅛ :46⁴ 1:10⁴ 1:49 ft ¾ 122 2½ 2½ 12½ 15½ ShmkrW4 S A Derby 84-17 TmprtSl,MstrflAdvoct,SmthngLcky 6
4Apr87—Grade I
22Mar87-8SA 1 1/16 :46² 1:10⁴ 1:43 gd *8-5 122 2½ 2½ 1hd 33½ ShmkrW7 S Felipe H 82-23 ChartTheStrs,Alysheb,TemperteSil 8
22Mar87—Grade I
7Mar87-8SA 1 :45² 1:10 1:35⁴gd 8-5 122 5² 55 49 516¾ ShmkrW7 San Rafael 72-19 MstrflAdct,ChrtThStrs,HtAndSmgg 7
7Mar87—Grade II
14Dec86-8Hol 1 :44⁴ 1:09³ 1:36¹ft 5½ 121 63½ 55 32 1nk ShomkrW3 Hol Fut'y 82-18 TempertSil,Alyshb,MstrfulAdvoct 12
14Dec86—Grade I
10Sep86-8Dmr 1 :45² 1:10¹ 1:35³ft *4-5 117 51¾ 41 56¾ 58½ ShmkrW8 Dmr Fut 81-11 Qualify, Sacahuista, Brevito 9
10Sep86—Grade I
27Aug86-8Dmr 7f :22¹ :45² 1:23 ft *4-5 117 53¾ 32 1hd 12¼ Shoemaker W3 Balboa 90-14 TemperateSil,PolrJet,GoldOnGreen 8
27Aug86—Broke slow
●Aug 18 Sar 5f ft :57¹ h ●Aug 13 Sar 1 ft 1:39³ h ●Aug 7 Dmr 6f ft 1:10¹ h ●Aug 2 Dmr 3f ft :33² h

4—1
Bet Twice
Own.—Cisley Stable&LevyBlancheP 126
B. c. 3, by Sportin' Life—Golden Dust, by Dusty Canyon
Br.—Farish W S & Hudson E J (Ky)
Tr.—Croll Warren A Jr
1987 7 3 3 0 $1,922,642
1986 7 5 0 1 $690,565
Lifetime 14 8 3 1 $2,613,207

1Aug87-9Mth 1⅛ :46³ 1:09³ 1:47 ft *6-5 126 2² 31 1hd 1nk Perret C5 Haskell H 99-07 Bet Twice, Alysheba, Lost Code 5
1Aug87—Grade I
6Jun87-8Bel 1½ :49² 2:03 2:28¹ft 8 126 34 15 17 114 Perret C4 Belmont 79-15 Bet Twice, Cryptoclearance, Gulch 9
6Jun87—Grade I
16May87-9Pim 1 3/16 :47¹ 1:11³ 1:55⁴ft 5 126 32 31½ 1hd 2½ Perret C1 Preakness 87-18 Alysheba,BetTwice,Cryptoclearnce 9
16May87—Grade I
2May87-8CD 1¼ :46² 1:36⁴ 2:03²ft 10 126 65 1hd 11 2¾ PerretC14 Ky Derby 79-09 Alysheba, Bet Twice, Avies Copy 17
2May87—Grade I; Drifted late
4Apr87-10GP 1⅛ :47² 1:11⁴ 1:49³ft *2-3 122 48 42 51¾ 54 Perret C7 Fla Derby 80-23 Cryptoclernc,NoMorFlowrs,Tlinum 9
4Apr87—Grade I; Blockd,lckd room
22Mar87-10GP 1 1/16 :47 1:11⁴ 1:43²ft *1 122 31½ 11½ 12½ 12½ Perret C5 Fountin Yth 84-24 BetTwice,NoMoreFlowers,GoneWst 9
22Mar87—Grade II
28Feb87-9Hia 6f :22² :45¹ 1:10¹ft 3 122 72¾ 53 64¾ 2½ Perret C9 Key West 88-19 Mr.ZippityDoDh,BtTwic,VldProspct 9
1Nov86-1SA 1 1/16 :45⁴ 1:10² 1:43⁴ft 9½ 122 97¾ 66½ 55½ 44¾ PerretC12 Br Cp Juv 77-13 Capote, Qualify, Alysheba 13
1Nov86—Grade I
Aug 21 Sar 3f ft :36⁴ b Aug 17 Sar 5f ft :59 h Aug 11 Mth 1 ft 1:39³ h Aug 7 Mth 4f ft :52 b

9—1
Gorky
Own.—Brant P M 126
B. c. 3, by Key to the Mint—Chelseanna, by Nice Dancer
Br.—Hill 'N' Dale Farms (Ont-C)
Tr.—Jolley Leroy
1987 4 1 1 0 $21,540
1986 3 1 0 0 $14,520
Lifetime 7 2 1 0 $36,060

8Aug87-8Sar 1⅛ :46² 1:10² 1:48²ft 3½e105 2½ 2hd 721 728½ Graell A2 Whitney H 64-13 Java Gold, Gulch, Broad Brush 7
8Aug87—Grade I
16Jly87-8Bel 7f :22³ :46³ 1:24¹ft *3-2 112 32½ 43 22½ 22¼ Santos J A5 Aw27000 78-24 Who Knows, Gorky, Krul 7
6Jun87-5Bel 7f :22² :45² 1:22²ft 8½ 115 64 64 36 59¾ Day P2 Riva Ridge 80-15 JazzingAround,HighBrite,PolishNvy 7
20May87-7Bel 7f :22¹ :45¹ 1:22⁴gd 6¼ 111 31½ 21 1½ 1hd Santos J A3 Aw26000 88-17 Gorky,FondEncounter,King'sGalley 7
18Oct86-8Bel 1 :47⁴ 1:11² 1:35¹ft 22 122 66 69½ 615 617¾ CrdrAJr1 Champagne 71-17 PolishNvy,Demon'sBegone,BetTwic 7
18Oct86—Grade I; Checked
10Oct86-4Bel 7f :22⁴ :46 1:24²ft 10 118 34 32 1½ 1¾ Cordero A Jr5 Mdn 80-17 Gorky, Samerkand, OrpheusIsland 11
15Sep86-4Bel 6f :22³ :46 1:10²ft *2 118 108½ 511 510 414 Santos J A9 Mdn 76-15 Stacked Pack, ItsAcedemic,Yucca 12
15Sep86—Off slowly
●Aug 21 Sar 3f ft :34² h Aug 16 Sar 5f ft 1:01¹ h Aug 5 Sar 5f ft :59¹ h Jly 30 Bel 5f ft 1:03³ b

A. Play *Alysheba* to win
B. Play *Bet Twice* to win
C. Play *Java Gold* to win
D. Key *Alysheba* in exacta boxes with *Java Gold* and *Temperate Sil*

  E. Box *Alysheba, Bet Twice,* and *Java Gold* in exactas
  F. Box *Java Gold* and *Alysheba* and play each on top of *Bet Twice, Temperate Sill, Cryptoclearance,* and *Gulch*
  G. Key *Java Gold* in exacta boxes with *Cryptoclearance* and *Gulch.*

Handicappers who want to compare their scores on Performance Test B with the scores of professionals and other recreational handicappers should record their answers on a separate sheet of paper.

List the number of years you have played the races and mail the completed answer sheet to:

Cynthia Publishing
4455 Los Feliz Blvd.
Suite 1106
Los Angles, Calif. 90027
(include a $20 fee for processing and handling)

Mail your answer sheet now, before checking the answers.
Please print clearly. Include your name and address.

Answer key: Applied handicapping skills

Performance Test B

1. G 9–2	16. C 7–1	31. K 5–1	46. H 5–1
2. D 3–1	17. B & E 5–2	32. H 5–2	47. B 3–1
3. F 6–1	18. F 1–1	33. C 4–1	48. I 12–1
4. A 4–1	19. D 5–1	34. A 11–1	49. C 4–1
5. A,D, & E 5–2	20. A 3–1	35. F 4–1	50. A 8–1
6. D 3–1	21. J 5–2	36. A 3–1	51. D 3–1
7. D 1–1	22. C 9–2	37. I 5–1	52. B 3–1
8. D 5–2	23. B 9–5	38. D 3–1	53. C 8–1
9. B 5–1	24. E 6–1	39. K 9–5	54. E 2–1
10. C 3–1	25. D 7–1	40. F 8–1	55. F or E 7–1
11. B 3–1	26. B 2–1	41. C 3–1	56. E 3–1
12. C 3–1	27. C 3–1	42. B 7–2	57. H 10–1
13. C 3–1	28. G 4–1	43. B 4–1	58. D 1–1
14. D 3–1	29. A 3–1	44. D 3–1	59. G 5–1
15. I 7–1	30. B 2–1	45. D 3–1	60. G 4–1

To obtain a total performance score multiply your win percentage by the average odds on your winners. If your total score falls below the standards on page 275, consult the competency tests and retake Performance Test B. Repeat that cycle until your score on the performance test meets the desired standard.

Quinn, James - High Tech Handicapping in the Information age

Scott, William - Total Victory at the Track

Beyer, A. - My 50,000 years at the Races

Hovdey, J. - Inside Horse Racing

Ainslie - the Compleat Horseplayer

Kennen, Thomas - the Secretariat Factor

Sasuly - Search For the winning Horse

Quirin - Own Thoroughbred Handicapping

Instructional References

Ainslie, Tom. *Ainslie's Complete Guide to Thoroughbred Racing.* Rev. ed. New York: Simon and Schuster, 1986. *1979 edition*

Beyer, Andrew. *Picking Winners.* Boston: Houghton Mifflin Company, 1975.

—*The Winning Horseplayer.* Boston: Houghton Mifflin Company, 1983.

Cramer, Mark. *Fast Track to Thoroughbred Profits.* Secaucus, New Jersey: Lyle Stuart, 1984.

Davidowitz, Steven. *Betting Thoroughbreds.* Rev. ed. New York: E.P. Dutton, 1984.

Davis, Frederick. *Thoroughbred Racing: Percentages and Probabilities.* New York: Millwood Publications, 1974.

Ledbetter, Bonnie (with Ainslie). *The Body Language of Horses.* New York: William Morrow, 1980.

Mahl, Huey. "Money Management." A technical paper, Sports Tyme Handicapping Seminar, Dunes Hotel, Las Vegas, Dec. 12–13, 1979.

Meyer, John. "The T.I.S. Pace Report." *The National Railbird Review,* vol. II, nos. 8 & 9, San Clemente, Ca., 1981.

Mitchell, Dick. *Thoroughbred Handicapping as an Investment.* Los Angeles: Cynthia Publishing, 1986.

—*A Winning Thoroughbred Strategy.* Los Angeles: Cynthia Publishing, 1984.

Quinn, James. *Class of the Field.* New York: William Morrow, 1987.

—*The Handicapper's Condition Book.* Rev. ed. New York: William Morrow, 1986.

Quirin, William L. *Thoroughbred Racing; State of the Art.* New York: William Morrow, 1984.

—*Winning at the Races: Computer Discoveries in Thoroughbred Handicapping.* New York: William Morrow, 1979.

Roman, Steven A. "An Analysis of Dosage." *The Thoroughbred Record*, Apr., 1984.

Sartin, Howard. "Thoroughbred Handicapping; the Dynamics of Incremental Velocity and Energy Distribution." A technical paper, Handicapping Expo '84, Oct. 17–20, 1984. Also, *The Follow-Up*, a newsletter for practitioners of the Sartin Methodology.

Scott, William, L. *How Will Your Horse Run Today?* Baltimore: Amicus Press, 1984.

Selvidge, James. *Hold Your Horses.* Seattle: Jacada Publications, 1974.

Ziemba, William T. (with Hausch). *Beat the Racetrack.* Rev. ed. New York: William Morrow, 1987.

—*Betting at the Racetrack.* Vancouver, B.C.: Dr. Z. Investments, 1985.